THE NOTEBOOKS OF LEONARDO DA VINCI

Compiled and edited

from the original manuscripts

by Jean Paul Richter

In two Volumes

VOLUME II

Dover Publications, Inc., New York

Published in Canada by General Publishing Company, Ltd.,
30 Lesmill Road, Don Mills, Toronto, Ontario.

This Dover edition, first published in 1970, is an unabridged
edition of the work first published in London in 1883 by Sampson
Low, Marston, Searle & Rivington, with the title *The Literary
Works of Leonardo da Vinci*. In the present edition the typo-
graphical errors which have come to our attention, including all
those noted on the Errata pages of the first edition, have been
corrected in the text. The illustrations printed in color in the
original edition are reproduced here in black and white.

Standard Book Number: 486-22573-9
Library of Congress Catalog Card Number: 72-104981

Manufactured in the United States of America
Dover Publications, Inc.
180 Varick Street
New York, N.Y. 10014

CONTENTS OF VOLUME II.

All drawings here reproduced are in pen and ink, unless otherwise stated. The reproductions are of the exact size of the originals, except that Plates LXVI, XCVIII, CVII, CIX, CXI No. 1, CXII, CXIII, CXIV, CXVI, CXVII, CXVIII and CXXII are reduced, and Plate CXIX enlarged. Plate LXV is the frontispiece; Plate LXVI is on p. 134; Plates LXVII—XCVI follow p. 134; Plate XCVII is on p. 312; Plates XCVIII—CXXII follow p. 312.

LIST OF ILLUSTRATIONS IN VOLUME II.

XI.

The notes on Sculpture.

Compared with the mass of manuscript treating of Painting, a very small number of passages bearing on the practice and methods of Sculpture are to be found scattered through the note books; these are here given at the beginning of this section (Nos. 706—709). There is less cause for surprise at finding that the equestrian statue of Francesco Sforza is only incidentally spoken of; for, although Leonardo must have worked at it for a long succession of years, it is not in the nature of the case that it could have given rise to much writing. We may therefore regard it as particularly fortunate that no fewer than thirteen notes in the master's handwriting can be brought together, which seem to throw light on the mysterious history of this famous work. Until now writers on Leonardo were acquainted only with the passages numbered 712, 719, 720, 722 and 723.

In arranging these notes on sculpture I have given the precedence to those which treat of the casting of the monument, not merely because they are the fullest, but more especially with a view to reconstructing the monument, an achievement which really almost lies within our reach by combining and comparing the whole of the materials now brought to light, alike in notes and in sketches.

A good deal of the first two passages, Nos. 710 and 711, which refer to this subject seems obscure and incomprehensible; still, they supplement each other and one contributes in no small degree to the comprehension of the other. A very interesting and instructive commentary on these passages may be found in the fourth chapter of Vasari's

Introduzione della Scultura under the title „Come si fanno i modelli per fare di bronzo le figure grandi e picciole, e come le forme per buttarle; come si armino di ferri, e come si gettino di metallo," &c. *Among the drawings of models of the moulds for casting we find only one which seems to represent the horse in the act of galloping—No.* 713. *All the other designs show the horse as pacing quietly; and as these studies of the horse are accompanied by copious notes as to the method of casting, the question as to the position of the horse in the model finally selected, seems to be decided by preponderating evidence.* "Il cavallo dello Sforza"—*C. Boito remarks very appositely in the Saggio on page* 26, "doveva sembrare fratello al cavallo del Colleoni. E si direbbe che questo fosse figlio del cavallo del Gattamelata, il quale pare figlio di uno dei quattro cavalli che stavano forse sull' Arco di Nerone in Roma" *(now at Venice). The publication of the Saggio also contains the reproduction of a drawing in red chalk, representing a horse walking to the left and supported by a scaffolding, given here on Pl. LXXVI, No.* 1. *It must remain uncertain whether this represents the model as it stood during the preparations for casting it, or whether—as seems to me highly improbable—this sketch shows the model as it was exhibited in* 1493 *on the Piazza del Castello in Milan under a triumphal arch, on the occasion of the marriage of the Emperor Maximilian to Bianca Maria Sforza. The only important point here is to prove that strong evidence seems to show that, of the numerous studies for the equestrian statue, only those which represent the horse pacing agree with the schemes of the final plans.*

The second group of preparatory sketches, representing the horse as galloping, must therefore be considered separately, a distinction which, in recapitulating the history of the origin of the monument seems justified by the note given under No. 720.

Galeazzo Maria Sforza was assassinated in 1476 *before his scheme for erecting a monument to his father Francesco Sforza could be carried into effect. In the following year Lodovico il Moro the young aspirant to the throne was exiled to Pisa, and only returned to Milan in* 1479 *when he was Lord* (Governatore) *of the State of Milan, in* 1480 *after the minister Cecco Simonetta had been murdered. It may have been soon after this that Lodovico il Moro announced a competition for an equestrian statue, and it is tolerably certain that Antonio del Pollajuolo took part in it, from this passage in Vasari's Life of this artist:* "E si trovò, dopo la morte sua, il disegno e modello che a Lodovico Sforza egli aveva fatto per la statua a cavallo di Francesco Sforza, duca di Milano; il quale disegno è nel nostro Libro, in due modi: in uno egli ha sotto Verona; nell'altro, egli tutto armato, e sopra un basamento pieno di battaglie, fa saltare il cavallo addosso a un armato; ma la cagione perchè non mettesse questi disegni in opera, non ho già potuto sapere." *One of Pollajuolo's drawings, as here described, has lately been discovered by Senatore Giovanni Morelli in the Munich Pinacothek. Here the profile of the horseman is a portrait of Francesco Duke of Milan, and under the horse, who is galloping to the left, we see a warrior thrown and lying on the ground; precisely the same idea as we find* in some of Leonardo's designs for the monument, as on Pl. LXVI, LXVII, LXVIII, LXIX and LXXII No. 1; and, as it is impossible to explain this remarkable coincidence by supposing that either artist borrowed it from the other, we can only conclude that in the terms of the competition the subject proposed was the Duke on a horse in full gallop, with a fallen foe under its hoofs.

Leonardo may have been in the competition there and then, but the means for executing the monument do not seem to have been at once forthcoming. It was not perhaps until some years later that Leonardo in a letter to the Duke (No. 719) reminded him of the project for the monument. Then, after he had obeyed a summons to Milan, the plan seems to have been so far modified, perhaps in consequence of a remonstrance on the part of the artist, that a pacing horse was substituted for one galloping, and it may have been at the same time that the colossal dimensions of the statue were first decided on. The designs given on Pl. LXX, LXXI, LXXII, 2 and 3, LXXIII and LXXIV and on pp. 4 and 24, as well as three sketches on Pl. LXIX may be studied with reference to the project in its new form, though it is hardly possible to believe that in either of these we see the design as it was actually carried out. It is probable that in Milan Leonardo worked less on drawings, than in making small models of wax and clay as preparatory to his larger model. Among the drawings enumerated above, one in black chalk, Pl. LXXIII—the upper sketch on the right hand side, reminds us strongly of the antique statue of Marcus Aurelius. If, as it would seem, Leonardo had not until then visited Rome, he might easily have known this statue from drawings by his former master and friend Verrocchio, for Verrocchio had been in Rome for a long time between 1470 and 1480. In 1473 Pope Sixtus IV had this antique equestrian statue restored and placed on a new pedestal in front of the church of San Giovanni in Laterano. Leonardo, although he was painting independently as early as in 1472 is still spoken of as working in Verrocchio's studio in 1477. Two years later the Venetian senate decided on erecting an equestrian statue to Colleoni; and as Verrocchio, to whom the work was entrusted, did not at once move from Florence to Venice—where he died in 1488 before the casting was completed—but on the contrary remained in Florence for some years, perhaps even till 1485, Leonardo probably had the opportunity of seeing all his designs for the equestrian statue at Venice and the red chalk drawing on Pl. LXXIV may be a reminiscence of it.

The pen and ink drawing on Pl. LXXII, No. 3, reminds us of Donatello's statue of Gattamelata at Padua. However it does not appear that Leonardo was ever at Padua before 1499, but we may conclude that he took a special interest in this early bronze statue and the reports he could procure of it, form an incidental remark which is to be found in C. A. 145ª; 432ª, and which will be given in Vol. II under Ricordi or Memoranda.

Among the studies—in the widest sense of the word—made in preparation for this statue we may include the Anatomy of the Horse which Lomazzo and Vasari both mention; the most important parts of this work still exist in the Queen's Library at

Windsor. It was beyond a doubt compiled by Leonardo when at Milan; only a few interesting records to be found among these designs are reproduced in Nos. 716 and 717; but it must be pointed out that out of 40 sheets of studies of the movements of the horse belonging to that treatise, a horse in full gallop occurs but once.

If we may trust the account given by Paulus Jovius—about 1527—Leonardo's horse was represented as "vehementer incitatus et anhelatus". Jovius had probably seen the model exhibited at Milan; but, need we, in fact, infer from this description that the horse was galloping? Compare Vasari's description of the Gattamelata monument at Padua: "Egli [Donatello] vi andò ben volentieri, e fece il cavallo di bronzo, che è in sulla piazza di Sant Antonio, nel quale si dimostra lo sbuffamento ed il fremito del cavallo, ed il grande animo e la fierezza vivacissimamente espressa dall'arte nella figura che lo cavalca".

These descriptions, it seems to me, would only serve to mark the difference between the work of the middle-ages and that of the renaissance.

We learn from a statement of Sabbà da Castiglione that, when Milan was taken by the French in 1499, the model sustained some injury; and this informant, who, however is not invariably trustworthy, adds that Leonardo had devoted fully sixteen years to this work (la forma del cavallo, intorno a cui Leonardo avea sedici anni continui consumati). *This often-quoted passage has given ground for an assumption, which has no other evidence to support it, that Leonardo had lived in Milan ever since 1483. But I believe it is nearer the truth to suppose that this author's statement alludes to the fact that about sixteen years must have past since the competition in which Leonardo had taken part.*

I must in these remarks confine myself strictly to the task in hand and give no more of the history of the Sforza monument than is needed to explain the texts and drawings I have been able to reproduce. In the first place, with regard to the drawings, I may observe that they are all, with the following two exceptions, in the Queen's Library at Windsor Castle; the red chalk drawing on Pl. LXXVI No. 1 is in the MS. C. A. (see No. 712) and the fragmentary pen and ink drawing on page 4 is in the Ambrosian Library. The drawings from Windsor on Pl. LXVI have undergone a trifling reduction from the size of the originals.

There can no longer be the slightest doubt that the well-known engraving of several horsemen (Passavant, Le Peintre-Graveur, Vol. V, p. 181, No. 3) is only a copy after original drawings by Leonardo, executed by some unknown engraver; we have only to compare the engraving with the facsimiles of drawings on Pl. LXV, No. 2, Pl. LXVII, LXVIII and LXIX which, it is quite evident, have served as models for the engraver.

On Pl. LXV No. 1, in the larger sketch to the right hand, only the base is distinctly visible, the figure of the horseman is effaced. Leonardo evidently found it unsatisfactory and therefore rubbed it out.

The base of the monument—the pedestal for the equestrian statue—is repeatedly sketched on a magnificent plan. In the sketch just mentioned it has the character of a shrine or aedicula to contain a sarcophagus. Captives in chains are here represented on the entablature with their backs turned to that portion of the monument which more strictly constitutes the pedestal of the horse. The lower portion of the aedicula is surrounded by columns. In the pen and ink drawing Pl. LXVI—the lower drawing on the right hand side—the sarcophagus is shown between the columns, and above the entablature is a plinth on which the horse stands. But this arrangement perhaps seemed to Leonardo to lack solidity, and in the little sketch on the left hand, below, the sarcophagus is shown as lying under an arched canopy. In this the trophies and the captive warriors are detached from the angles. In the first of these two sketches the place for the trophies is merely indicated by a few strokes; in the third sketch on the left the base is altogether broader, buttresses and pinnacles having been added so as to form three niches. The black chalk drawing on Pl. LXVIII shows a base in which the angles are formed by niches with pilasters. In the little sketch to the extreme left on Pl. LXV, No. 1, the equestrian statue serves to crown a circular temple somewhat resembling Bramante's tempietto of San Pietro in Montorio at Rome, while the sketch above to the right displays an arrangement faintly reminding us of the tomb of the Scaligers in Verona. The base is thus constructed of two platforms or slabs, the upper one considerably smaller than the lower one which is supported on flying buttresses with pinnacles.

On looking over the numerous studies in which the horse is not galloping but merely walking forward, we find only one drawing for the pedestal, and this, to accord with the altered character of the statue, is quieter and simpler in style (Pl. LXXIV). It rises almost vertically from the ground and is exactly as long as the pacing horse. The whole base is here arranged either as an independent baldaquin or else as a projecting canopy over a recess in which the figure of the deceased Duke is seen lying on his sarcophagus; in the latter case it was probably intended as a tomb inside a church. Here, too, it was intended to fill the angles with trophies or captive warriors. Probably only No. 724 in the text refers to the work for the base of the monument.

If we compare the last mentioned sketch with the description of a plan for an equestrian monument to Gian Giacomo Trivulzio (No. 725) it seems by no means impossible that this drawing is a preparatory study for the very monument concerning which the manuscript gives us detailed information. We have no historical record regarding this sketch nor do the archives in the Trivulzio Palace give us any information. The simple monument to the great general in San Nazaro Maggiore in Milan consists merely of a sarcophagus placed in recess high on the wall of an octagonal chapel. The figure of the warrior is lying on the sarcophagus, on which his name is inscribed; a piece of sculpture which is certainly not Leonardo's work. Gian Giacomo Trivulzio died at Chartres in 1518, only five months before Leonardo, and it seems to me highly improbable that this should have been the date of this sketch; under these circumstances it would have been done under the auspices of Francis I, but the Italian general was certainly not in favour with the French monarch at the time. Gian Giacomo Trivulzio was a sworn foe to Ludovico il Moro, whom he strove for years to overthrow. On the 6th September 1499 he marched victorious into Milan at the head of a French army. In a short time, however, he was forced to quit Milan again when Ludovico il Moro bore down upon the city with a force of Swiss troops. On the 15th of April following, after defeating Lodovico at Novara, Trivulzio once more entered Milan as a Conqueror, but his hopes of becoming Governatore *of the place were soon wrecked by intrigue. This victory and triumph, historians tell us, were signalised by acts of vengeance against the dethroned Sforza, and it might have been particularly flattering to him that the casting and construction of the Sforza monument were suspended for the time.*

It must have been at this moment—as it seems to me—that he commissioned the artist to prepare designs for his own monument, which he probably intended should find a place in the Cathedral or in some other church. He, the husband of Marghe-rita di Nicolino Colleoni, would have thought that he had a claim to the same distinc-tion and public homage as his less illustrious connection had received at the hands of the Venetian republic. It was at this very time that Trivulzio had a medal struck with a bust portrait of himself and the following remarkable inscription on the reverse: DEO FAVENTE · 1499 · DICTVS · IO · IA · EXPVLIT · LVDOVICV̄ · SF · (Sfortiam) DVC · (ducem) MLI (Mediolani) · NOĪE (nomine) · REGIS · FRANCORVM · EODEM · ANN · (anno) RED'T (redit) · LVS (Ludovicus) · SVPERATVS ET CAPTVS · EST · AB · EO. *In the Library of the Palazzo Trivulzio there is a MS. of Callimachus Siculus written at the end of the XVth or beginning of the XVIth century. At the beginning of this MS. there is an exquisite illuminated miniature of an equestrian statue with the name of the general on the base; it is however very doubtful whether this has any connection with Leonardo's design.*

Nos. 731—740, which treat of casting bronze, have probably a very indirect bearing on the arrangements made for casting the equestrian statue of Francesco Sforza. Some portions evidently relate to the casting of cannon. Still, in our researches about Leonardo's work on the monument, we may refer to them as giving us some clue to the process of bronze casting at that period.

706.

De statua.

²Se vuoi · fare · vna · figura · di marmo · fa ne · prima vna ³di terra ·, la quale, finita che l' ài, secca e mettila in vna ⁴cassa · che sia · ancora capace ·, dopo la figura tratta ⁵d'esso · loco ·, a ricieuere il marmo · che vuoi scoprir⁶vi dentro la figura · alla · similitudine · di quella · di terra ·; di poi ⁷messa la figura di terra in detta cassa · abbi bacchette ch'ē trino ⁸appū to · per i sua · busi ·, e spingile · dentro · tā to · per ciascuno ⁹buso · che ciascuna bacchetta biā ca · tocca · la figura · in ¹⁰diuersi lochi, e la parte d'esse bacchette, che resta · fori della ¹¹cassa, tigni di nero, e fa il cō trassegno · alla · bacchetta e al ¹²suo · buso · in modo · che a tua · posta · si scō trī; ¹³e trai d'essa · cassa · la figura · di terra · e mettivi il tuo¹⁴pezzo · di marmo, e tā to leua del marmo ·, che tutte le ¹⁵tue · bacchette · si nascondino · sino al loro segnio in detti busi, ¹⁶e per potere questo · meglio fare · fa che tutta · la cassa si po¹⁷ssa · leuare in alto, e'l fondo · d'essa cassa resti sē pre · sotto ¹⁸il marmo ed a questo modo ne potrai · leuare coi ferri ¹⁹con grā facilità.

Of a statue.

If you wish to make a figure in marble, first make one of clay, and when you have finished it, let it dry and place it in a case which should be large enough, after the figure is taken out of it, to receive also the marble, from which you intend to reveal the figure in imitation of the one in clay. After you have put the clay figure into this said case, have little rods which will exactly slip in to the holes in it, and thrust them so far in at each hole that each white rod may touch the figure in different parts of it. And colour the portion of the rod that remains outside black, and mark each rod and each hole with a countersign so that each may fit into its place. Then take the clay figure out of this case and put in your piece of marble, taking off so much of the marble that all your rods may be hidden in the holes as far as their marks; and to be the better able to do this, make the case so that it can be lifted up; but the bottom of it will always remain under the marble and in this way it can be lifted with tools with great ease.

Some practical hints (706—709).

---

706. 1. desstatua. 2. sevolli. 3. tera . . chellai essecha mettila nvna. 4. chassa chessia anchorá [dop atta] "capace". 5. loco . . [chē] schoprir. 7. tera . . chassa . abi bachette. 8. apū to . . esspignile . . tā to [che] per ciasschuno. 9. ciassuna bachetta biā cha tocha. 10. bachette . . ressta. 11. chassa . . effa . . chō trassegnio . . bachetta. 12. sio buso imodo . . atta . . sisschō tri [ettare lasi]. 13. ettrai . . chassa . . tera. 14. pezo . . ettā to . . chettutte. 15. bachette . . naschō dino . . aloro. 16. chettutta . . chassa. 17. chasa ressti. 18. acquesto . . cho. 19. chon.

W. P. 5 *a*]   **707.**

Alcvni àño errato a insegniare alli scultori ²circundare con fili i mēbri · delle loro
figure, ³quasi credendo che essi menbri
sieno d'equale ⁴rotondità, in qualunque
parte da essi fili ⁵circundati sieno.

Some have erred in teaching sculptors to
measure the limbs of their figures with
threads as if they thought that these limbs
were equally round in every part where these
threads were wound about them.

A. 1 *a*]   **708.**

MISURE E CŌPARTITIONE DELLA STATUA.

²Diuidi la testa in 12 gradi, e ciascuno
grado · diuidi in 12 pūti, e ciascuno ³pūto ·
in 12 minvti ·, e i minvti in minimi, e i minimi ī semiminimi.
⁴Grado — punto — minvto — minimo.

MEASUREMENT AND DIVISION OF A STATUE.

Divide the head into 12 degrees, and
each degree divide into 12 points, and each
point into 12 minutes, and the minutes into
minims and the minims into semi minims.
Degree—point—minute—minim.

Ash. I. 19 *b*]   **709.**

¶ Le figure di rilievo che pajono · ī
moto ·, posandole in piè, per ragione deō
cadere jnāzi.

Sculptured figures which appear in motion,
will, in their standing position, actually look
as if they were falling forward.

W. X.]   **710.**

Notes on the casting of the Sforza monument (710—715).

3 Ferri che cingā la forma. ²[Se uolli
fare presti gietti e ³senplici, fagli con vna
cassa ⁴di sabbione di fiume invmidito con
⁵acieto.]

Three braces which bind the mould.
[If you want to make simple casts quickly, make them in a box of river sand wetted with vinegar.]

707. 1. alchuni . . erato ansegniare. 2. chirchundare. 3. menbr. 4. retondita. 5. circhundati.
708. 1. chōpartitione. 2. 12 [parti e] gradi. 3. minvti iminimi e e. 4. grado [minvto] punto.
709. 1. pajano . . chadere.
710. *These passages are written in ink and subsequently crossed through with red chalk.* 3. chon. 4. sabiō . . cho. 6. arai .

709. *figure di rilievo.* Leonardo applies this term
exclusively to wholly detached figures, especially
to those standing free. This note apparently refers
to some particular case, though we have no knowledge of what that may have been. If we suppose
it to refer to the first model of the equestrian statue
of Francesco Sforza (see the introduction to the
notes on Sculpture) this observation may be regarded

as one of his arguments for abandoning the first
scheme of the Sforza Monument, in which the horse
was to be galloping (see page 2). It is also
in favour of this theory that the note is written
in a manuscript volume already completed in 1492.
Leonardo's opinions as to the shortcomings of
plastic works when compared with paintings are
given under No. 655 and 656.

⁶[Quando · tu . avrai · fatto · la ⁷forma · sopra il cauallo e tu ⁸farai la grossezza del metallo ⁹di terra.]

¹⁰Nota · nello allegare · quante · ore · vā · per cētinajo ¹¹[nel gittare ognuno tenga stoppato · il fornello col ¹²suo · infocato]; ¹³[nel dentro di tutta la forma · sia inbeuerato olio ¹⁴di lin seme o di tremētina; e poi sia dato vna mano ¹⁵di poluere di borace e di pece greca con acqua vite, ¹⁶e la forma di fori inpeciata, acciochè stādo sotto ¹⁷terra l'umido non la ...

²⁴[Per maneggiare la forma grāde, fa ne modello della pi²⁵ccola forma; fa una piccola stātia a proportione;] ²⁶[fa le bocche alla forma, mētre ch'è in sul cauallo;] ²⁷¶Tieni le corna · in molle ·, e fondile con cōlla di pesce¶ ²⁸pesa le parti ²⁹della forma, da che quātità ³⁰di metallo ella à a essere occupata, ³¹e tāto ne da al fornello, che ³²a quella parte à a porgere il ³³suo metallo, e questo cognio³⁴scerai a pesare la terra di quella ³⁵parte della forma, dove il fornel³⁶lo colla sua quātità à a rispōde-³⁷re, e questo si fa aciochè 'l ³⁸fornello delle gābe le ēpia, e che ³⁹dalle gābe non abbia a socorrere ⁴⁰alla testa che sarebbe inpossibile] ⁴¹[gitta nel medesimo ⁴²gietto del cauallo ⁴³lo sportello della]

[When you shall have made the mould upon the horse you must make the thickness of the metal in clay.]

Observe in alloying how many hours are wanted for each hundredweight. [In casting each one keep the furnace and its fire well stopped up.] [Let the inside of all the moulds be wetted with linseed oil or oil of turpentine, and then take a handful of powdered borax and Greek pitch with aqua vitae, and pitch the mould over outside so that being under ground the damp may not [damage it?]

[To manage the large mould make a model of the small mould, make a small room in proportion.]

[Make the vents in the mould while it is on the horse.]

Hold the hoofs in the tongs, and cast them with fish glue. Weigh the parts of the mould and the quantity of metal it will take to fill them, and give so much to the furnace that it may afford to each part its amount of metal; and this you may know by weighing the clay of each part of the mould to which the quan᷄ᵗⁱ in the furnace must correspond. And this is done in order that the furnace for the legs when filled may not have to furnish metal from the legs to help out the head, which would be impossible. [Cast at the same casting as the horse the little door]

W. XI.]   711.

FORMA DEL CAVALLO.   THE MOULD FOR THE HORSE.

²Fa il cavallo sopra gambe di ferro ferme e stabili in bo³no fondamēto, poi lo inseva e fa gli la cappa di sopra, ⁴lasciādo ben seccare a suolo a suolo, e questa ingras⁵serai tre dita ·, di poi arma e ferra secondo il biso⁶gno; oltre a di questo cava

Make the horse on legs of iron, strong and well set on a good foundation; then grease it and cover it with a coating, leaving each coat to dry thoroughly layer by layer; and this will thicken it by the breadth of three fingers. Now fix and bind it with

facto. 7. chauallo ettu. 8. grosseza. 10. hore va . . ciētinaro. 11. hognivno . . stopato . . chol. 12. infochato mādiriano ea ū tenpo di stoppi. 13. holio. 14. poi dato. 15. grecha chon acq"a". 16. ella . . chesstādo. 17. lomido nolla \|\|\|\|\|\|\|\|\|\|\|\|\|\| chose. 18. fatte subito chella \|\|\|\|\|\|\|\|\|\|\|\|\|\|\|. 19. il sabione di for \|\|\|\|\|\|\|\|\|\|\|\|\| azzo cioe di. 20. quello da fforme \|\|\|\|\|\|\|\|\|\|\| chon acieto. 21. e ben \|\|\|\|\|\|\|\|\|\|\|. 22. miscia nella forma \|\|\|\|\|\| uno quadrello. 23. pesto . e cienere cō ciara douo e a ceto. 24. manegiare. 25. cholla . . falle una pichola. 26. falle boche. 27. chorna imole effondile chōlla di pesscie. 28. pensa [la forma] le. 30. ella essere ochupata. 31. ettāto. 32. acquella parte a porgiere. 33. ecquesto chogr.io. 34. sscierai . . tera. 35. forne. 36. cholla . . risspōde. 37. ecquesto. 38. gābe ēpinteche *doubtful*. 39. ale . . abiasschorrer. 40. chessa rebe inpossib. 42. chavallo. 43. sportello della. *Here the text breaks off.*

711. 2. ghanbe . . esstabile. 3. sondomēto . . effagli la chappa. 4. scechare assuolo assuclo . . ecquesta. 5. efferra sechondo. 6. chava

710. The importance of the notes included under this number is not diminished by the fact that they have been lightly crossed out with red chalk. Possibly they were the first scheme for some fuller observations which no longer exist; or perhaps they were crossed out when Leonardo found himself obliged to give up the idea of casting the equestrian statue. In the original the first two sketches are above l. 1, and the third below l. 9.

la forma, e poi fa la 7grossezza, e poi riēpi
la forma a mezza a mezza, 8e quella in-
tegra, poi con sua ferri cierchiala e 9cigni
e la ricuoci di dētro dove à a toccare il
brō10zo.

DEL FAR LA FORMA DI PEZZI.

12Segnia sopra il cavallo finito tutti li
pezzi della for13ma, di che tu voi vestire
tal cavallo, e nello interrare 14li taglia in
ogni interratura, acciochè quādo si è fini15sta
la forma che tu la possi cavare e poi ri-
cōmettere 16al primo loco colli sua scōtri
delli cōtrasegni.

17a b quadretto · starà infra la cappa
e'l maschio, cioè 18nel uacuo dove à a
stare il brōzo liquefatto e questi 19tali quadretti di brōzo manterrāno li spati della for-
20ma alla cappa con equal distātia, e per
questo tali 21quadretti sō di grāde inpor-
tantia.

22¶La terra sia mista 23cō rena;
24tollicera, a rēde25re, e pagare la cō-
26sumata.¶

27Secca la 28a suoli. 29Fa la forma
di fori 30di giesso per fugire 31il tēpo
del seccare, 32e la spesa di legnie, e cō
33tal giesso ferma 34li ferri di fori e di
35dentro cō due dita di 36grossezza, fa
terra 37cotta.

38E questa tal forma 39farai in un dì;
vna mez40za navata di giesso 41ti serue.
42Bono.
43Rītasa cō 44colla e terra 45over· chiara
d'ovo 46e mattone e ro47sume.

iron as may be necessary. Moreover take off
the mould and then make the thickness. Then
fill the mould by degrees and make it good
throughout; encircle and bind it with its irons
and bake it inside where it has to touch the bronze.

OF MAKING THE MOULD IN PIECES.

Draw upon the horse, when finished, all
the pieces of the mould with which you wish
to cover the horse, and in laying on the
clay cut it in every piece, so that when the
mould is finished you can take it off, and
then recompose it in its former position with
its joins, by the countersigns.

The square blocks a b will be between
the cover and the core, that is in the hollow
where the melted bronze is to be; and these
square blocks of bronze will support the
intervals between the mould and the cover at
an equal distance, and for this reason these
squares are of great importance.

The clay should be mixed with sand.
Take wax, to return [what is not used]
and to pay for what is used.

[27]Dry it in layers[28].

Make the outside mould of plaster, to
save time in drying and the expense in
wood; and with this plaster enclose the
irons [props] both outside and inside to a
thickness of two fingers; make terra cotta.

And this mould can be made in one day;
half a boat load of plaster will serve you.

[42]Good.

Dam it up again with glue and clay, or
white of egg, and bricks and rubbish.

C. A. 213*b*; 628*b*]   712.

Tutti · i capi de2lle chiavarde.   All the heads of the large nails.

. . falla. 7. grosseza. 8. ecquella · cosua . . ec. 9. ella richuoci . . dove attochare. 11. pezi. 12. pezi. 13. chettu . .
vesstire . . chavallo. 14. quādo se fini. 15. chettu . . chavare ricomettere. 16. al p"o" locho cholli . . cōtrassegni.
17. infralla chappa elmasscio cioe [di]. 18. uachuo dove asstare . . liquefacto ecquesti. 19. lisspati. 20. dallalla chappa
chon . . disstātia . . quessto. 22. tera sie. 27. sechalla soli. 28. assu oli. 31. sechare. 32. espesa. 36. rosseza fatterra.
38. ecquesta. 39. farai nūdi vna me. 43. ritasa. 44. etterra 47. ssume.
712. 1—2 R. 1. tucti i chapi.

711. See Pl. LXXV. The figure "40," close
to the sketch in the middle of the page between
lines 16 and 17 has been added by a collector's
hand.

In the original, below line 21, a square piece
of the page has been cut out about 9 centimètres
by 7 and a blank piece has been gummed into the
place.

Lines 22—24 are written on the margin. l. 27 and
28 are close to the second marginal sketch. l. 42 is a
note written above the third marginal sketch and on

the back of this sheet is the text given as No. 642.
Compare also No. 802.

712. See Pl. LXXVI, No. 1. This drawing has
already been published in the "*Saggio delle Opere di
L. da Vinci.*" Milano 1872, Pl. XXIV, No. 1. But,
for various reasons I cannot regard the editor's
suggestions as satisfactory. He says: "*Veggonsi le
armature di legname colle quali forse venne sostenuto il
modello, quando per le nozze di Bianca Maria Sforza con
Massimiliano imperatore, esso fu collocato sotto un arco
trionfale davanti al Castello.*"

W. XII.]   **713.**

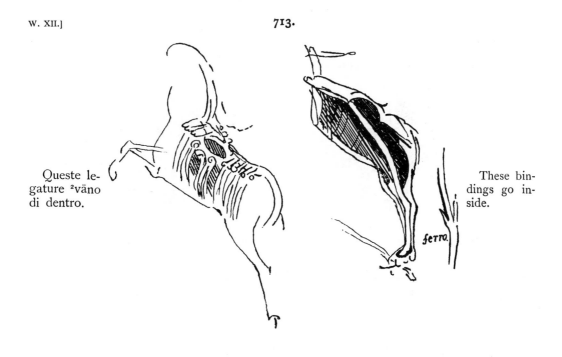

Queste le-
gature ²vāno
di dentro.

These bin-
dings go in-
side.

W. XIII   **714.**

Sale fatto di sterco vmano
bruciato ²e calcinato e fatto-
ne liscia e que³lla distesa
al lēto foco, e tutti li ster⁴chi
in simile modo fanno sale, e
quelli ⁵sali destillati·sono molto
penetrāti.

Salt may be made from human
excrements, burnt and calcined,
made into lees and dried slowly
at a fire, and all the excrements
produce salt in a similar way
and these salts when distilled, are
very strong.

714. 1. stercho. 2. chalcinato effatto neliscia ecque. 3. disecha allēto focho ettutti lisster. 4. quali. 5. desstilati.

714. VASARI repeatedly states, in the fourth chapter of his *Introduzione della Scultura*, that in preparing to cast bronze statues horse-dung was frequently used by sculptors. If, notwithstanding this, it remains doubtful whether I am justified in having introduced here this text of but little interest, no such doubt can be attached to the sketch which accompanies it.

W. XII.]   715.

MODO DI RICUOCERE.   METHOD OF FOUNDING AGAIN.

²Questo si potrebbe fare fatto ³il for-   This may be done when the furnace is

nello ⁴ferma e pillata.   made [4] strong and bruised.

W. H. 64.]   716.

Models for
the horse of
the Sforza
monument
(716—718).

Ginnetto · grosso · di messer Galeazzo.   Messer Galeazzo's big genet.

W. H. IV.]   717.

Siciliano di messer Galeazzo.   Messer Galeazzo's Sicilian horse.

C. A. 286 b ; 870 a]   718.

Misura del siciliano, la ganba dirieto,   Measurement of the Sicilian horse the leg
²in faccia, alzata e distesa.   from behind, seen in front, lifted and extended.

C. A. 382 a ; 1182 a]   719.

Occasional
references
to the Sforza
monument
(719—724).

Ancora si potrà dare opera al cauallo di   Again, the bronze horse may be taken in
bronzo che sarà gloria īmortale e eterno   hand, which is to be to the immortal glory and
onore della ²felice memoria del signore   eternal honour of the happy memory of the
vostro padre e della īclyta casa Sfor-   prince your father, and of the illustrious
zesca.   house of Sforza.

C. 15 b (1)]   720.

A di 23 d'aprile 1·4·90 comīciai   On the 23rd of April 1490 I began this
questo libro e ricomīciai · il cavallo.   book, and recommenced the horse.

---

715. 1. richuocere. 2. potre. 4. pilata.   **716.** 1. gianecto . . galeaz.
717. 1. ciciliano . . meser galeazo.   **718.** 1. ciciliano. 2. alza.
719. 1—2 *written from left to right.* 1. Anchora si potera . . honore dela. 2. S"gre" vost . . dela.
720. chomīciai . . richomīciai.

715. This note in l. 4 is written below the sketches.   San Severino, the famous captain who married Bianca
716. 717. These notes are by the side of a   the daughter of Ludovico il Moro.
drawing of a horse with figured measurements.   **719.** The letter from which this passage is here
718. There is no sketch belonging to this pas-   extracted will be found complete in section XXI.
sage. Galeazzo here probably means Galeazzo di   (see the explanation of it, on page 2).

Leic. 9 *b*]   **721.**

Vedesi in nelle montagnie di Parma e Piacētia la moltitudine di nichi e coralli ²intarlati ancora appiccati alli'sassi, de' quali, quand'io facevo il grā ³cavallo di Milano, me ne fu portato vn grā sacco ne⁴lla mia fabrica da cierti villani che in tal loco trovati.

There is to be seen, in the mountains of Parma and Piacenza, a multitude of shells and corals full of holes, still sticking to the rocks, and when I was at work on the great horse for Milan, a large sackful of them, which were found thereabout, was brought to me into my workshop, by certain peasants.

C. A. 316*a*; 958*a*]   **722.**

Credetelo a me, Leonardo fiorētino che fa il cauallo del duca Francesco di brōzo che non ne bisognia fare stima, ²perchè à che fare il tenpo di sua vita·, e dubito che per l'essere si grāde opera, che non la finirà mai.

Believe me, Leonardo the Florentine, who has to do the equestrian bronze statue of the Duke Francesco that he does not need to care about it, because he has work for all his life time, and, being so great a work, I doubt whether he can ever finish it.

C. A. 328*b*; 983*a*]   **723.**

Del cauallo nō dirò niēte perchè cogniosco·i tēpi.

Of the horse I will say nothing because I know the times.

C. A. 272*b*; 833*a*]   **724.**

Del marmo operasi dieci añi; ²io nō vo' aspettare che 'l mio pa³gamēto passi il termine del ⁴fine della opera mia.

During ten years the works on the marbles have been going on I will not wait for my payment beyond the time, when my works are finished.

C. A. 176*b*; 533*a*]   **725.**

SEPULCRO DI MESSER GIOVĀNI JACOMO DA TREVULZO.

THE MONUMENT TO MESSER GIOVANNI JACOMO DA TREVULZO.

²Spesa della ³manifattu⁴ra e materi⁵a del cauallo.

[2] Cost of the making and materials for the horse [5].

The project of the Trivulzio monument.

721. 1. in nelle . . mvltitudine. 2. apichati . . sacho. 3. fabricha.
722. 1. me saluo [quel] | "lonar fiorētino" cheffa il chauallo . . franc"o" "di brōzo" chēnone. 2. lesere . . nella.
724. 1. marmoperassi. 2. inōvo. 3. ghamēto. 4. dela.
725. 1. giovāni iacomo da trevlsa. 3. manifatu. 7. inel . . ellegrame ella. 11. soma. 15. pezo. 16. lungha br 4 ellargho br.

722. This passage is quoted from a letter to a committee at Piacenza for whom Leonardo seems to have undertaken to execute some work. The letter is given entire in section XXI.; in it Leonardo remonstrates as to some unreasonable demands.

723. This passage occurs in a rough copy of a letter to Ludovico il Moro, without date (see below among the letters).

724. This possibly refers to the works for the pedestal of the equestrian statue concerning which we have no farther information in the MSS. See p. 6.

725. In the original, lines 2—5, 12—14, 33—35, are written on the margin. This passage has been

recently published by G. GOVI in Vol. V, Ser. 3ª, of *Transunti*, *Reale Accademia dei Lincei*, sed. del 5 *Giugno*, 1881, with the following introductory note: "*Desidero intanto che siano stampati questi pochi frammenti perchè so che sono stati trascritti ultimamente, e verranno messi in luce tra poco fuori d'Italia. Li ripubblichi pure chi vuole, ma si sappia almeno che anche tra noi si conoscevano, e s'eran raccolti da anni per comporne, quando che fosse, una edizione ordinata degli scritti di Leonardo.*"

The learned editor has left out line 22 and has written 3 *piè* for 8 *piedi* in line 25. There are other deviations of less importance from the original.

⁶Vno corsiero grāde al naturale coll'omo sopra vuole per la spesa del metallo . . . . duc. 500.

⁷E per la spesa del ferramēto che ua in nel modello e carboni e legname e la fossa per gittarlo ⁸e per serrare la forma, e col fornello doue si de' gittare duc. 200.

⁹Per fare il modello di terra e poi di cera . . . . duc. 432.

¹⁰E per li lauorāti che lo netterāno quādo fia gittato . . . . . . duc. 450.

¹¹In somma sono . . . . . duc. 1582.

¹²Spesa de' m¹³armi della ¹⁴sepul·tura.

¹⁵Spesa del marmo secōdo il disegnio; jl pezzo del marmo che ua sotto il cauallo ¹⁶ch'è lungo braccia 4 e largo braccia 2 e oncie 2 e grosso oncie 9, cētinara 58, a L. 4 e S. 10 per cētinaro . . . . duc. 58.

¹⁷E per 13 braccia di cornice e ō 6, larga ō 7, e grossa ō 4, cēt. 24, duc. 24.

¹⁸E per lo fregio e architrave ch'è lungo br. 4 e ō 6 ·, largo br. 2 e grosso ō 6, cēt 20 . . . . . . duc. 20.

¹⁹E per li capitelli fatti di metallo, che sono 8, vaño ī tavola ō 5, e grossi ō 2, a prezzo di ²⁰ducati 15 per ciascuno montano . . . . duc. 120.

²¹E per 8 colonne di br. 2 e ō 7, grosse ō 4 e ¹/₂ · cētinara 20 . . duc. 20.

²²E per 8 base che sono in tauola ō 5 e ¹/₂ e alte ō 2 cent. 5 . . duc. 5.

²³E per la pietra dou' è su la sepultura, lūga br. 4 e ō 10, larga br. 2 e ō 4 e ¹/₂ ²⁴centinara 36 . . . duc. 36.

²⁵E per 8 piedi di piedistalli che uā lunghi br. 8 e larghi ō 6 e ¹/₂ grossi ō 6¹/₂ ²⁶centinara 20, mōtano . . duc. 20.

²⁷E per la cornice ch'è di sotto, ch'è lūga br. 4 e ō 10, larga br. 2 e ō 5, e grossa ō 4, cēt. 32 . . . duc. 32.

²⁸E per la pietra di che si fa il morto ch'è lunga br. 3 e ō 8, larga br. uno e ō 6, grossa ō 9, cent 30, duc. 30.

²⁹E per la pietra che ua sotto il morto·ch'è lūga br. 3 e ō 4, larga br. uno e ō 2, grossa ō 4¹/₂ . . duc. 16.

³⁰E per le tauole del marmo īterposte infra li piedistalli, che sono 8 e son lūghe br. 9, ³¹larghe ō 9, grosse ō 3 cent 8 . . . . . duc. 8.

³²In somma sono . . . . . duc. 389.

A courser, as large as life, with the rider requires for the cost of the metal, duc. 500.

And for cost of the iron work which is inside the model, and charcoal, and wood, and the pit to cast it in, and for binding the mould, and including the furnace where it is to be cast . . duc. 200.

To make the model in clay and then in wax . . . . duc. 432.

To the labourers for polishing it when it is cast . · . . . . . . duc. 450.

in all . . duc. 1582.

[12]Cost of the marble of the monument[14].

Cost of the marble according to the drawing. The piece of marble under the horse which is 4 braccia long, 2 braccia and 2 inches wide and 9 inches thick 58 hundredweight, at 4 Lire and 10 Soldi per hundredweight . . duc. 58.

And for 13 braccia and 6 inches of cornice, 7 in. wide and 4 in. thick, 24 hundredweight . . . . . . duc. 24.

And for the frieze and architrave, which is 4 br. and 6 in. long, 2 br. wide and 6 in. thick, 29 hundredweight.. duc. 20.

And for the capitals made of metal, which are 8, 5 inches in. square and 2 in. thick, at the price of 15 ducats each, will come to . . . . . duc. 122.

And for 8 columns of 2 br. 7 in., 4 ¹/₂ in. thick, 20 hundredweight duc. 20.

And for 8 bases which are 5 ¹/₂ in. square and 2 in. high 5 hundᵗ. . duc. 5.

And for the slab of the tombstone 4 br. 10 in. long, 2 br. 4¹/₂ in. wide 36 hundredweight . . . . . . duc. 36.

And for 8 pedestal feet each 8 br. long and 6 ¹/₂ in. wide and 6 ¹/₂ in. thick, 20 hundredweight come to . . . duc. 20.

And for the cornice below which is 4 br. and 10 in. long, and 2 br. and 5 in. wide, and 4 in. thick, 32 hundᵗ. . duc. 32.

And for the stone of which the figure of the deceased is to be made which is 3 br. and 8 in. long, and 1 br. and 6 in. wide, and 9 in. thick, 30 hundᵗ. . duc. 30.

And for the stone on which the figure lies which is 3 br. and 4 in. long and 1 br. and 2 in., wide and 4¹/₂ in. thick duc. 16.

And for the squares of marble placed between the pedestals which are 8 and are 9 br. long and 9 in. wide, and 3 in. thick, 8 hundredweight . . . duc. 8.

in all . . duc. 389.

2 e Co egrosso Co 9. 17. 13 br. 18. frego . . lungho . . largho. 19. prezo. 20. ciasscuno. 22. chessono. 25. lungh br. 8 . ellarghi. 28. di ce si . . . br î e ō 6, grosa. 29. larga br î e ō 2 grosa. 30. infra li piedi di stallo che . . lūgh.

[33]Spesa della [34]manifattu[35]ra ne' marmi.

[36]Attorno allo inbasamēto del cauallo vā figure 8 di 25 ducati l' una,
                                        duc. 200.

[37]E nel medesimo inbasamēto ci
vā festoni 8 cō certi altri ornamēti e
di questi [38]ve n' è 4 a prezzo di ducati 15 per ciascuno, e 4 a prezzo
di 8 ducati l' uno . . . . duc. 92.

[39]E per isquadrare dette pietre,
                                        duc.   6.

[40]Ancora pel cornicione che ua
sotto lo inbasamēto del cauallo, ch' è
br. 13 e ō 6 a duc. 2 per br. duc. 27.

[41]E per 12 br. di fregio, a ducati
5 per br. . . . . duc. 60.

[42]E per 12 br. d' architrave, a ducati 1 e 1/2 per br. . . . . . . duc. 18.

[43]E per 3 fioroni che fā soffitta
alla sepultura, a 20 ducati per fiorone,
                                        duc. 60.

[44]E per 8 colonne accanalate, a
8 ducati l' una . . . . duc. 64.

[45]E per 8 base, a un ducato l' una,
                                        duc.   8.

[46]E per 8 piedistalli, dè' quali n' è
4 a 10 duc. l' uno, che uā sopra li
cātoni, e 4 a 6 duc. l' uno . . duc. 64.

[47]E per isquadrare e incorniciare li
piedistalli, a due duc. l' uno, che sono 8,
                                        duc. 16.

[48]E per 6 tavole con figure e trofei,
a 25 ducati l' uno . . . . . . duc. 150.

[49]E per la scorniciatura della
pietra che ua sotto il morto . . .
                                        duc. 40.

[50]Per la figura del morto a farla
bene . . . . duc. 100.

[51]Per 6 arpie colli candelieri, a 25
ducati l' una . . . . duc. 150.

[52]Per isquadrare la pietra dove si
posa il morto e sua incorniciatura
                                        duc. 20.

[53]In somma   duc. 1075.

[54]In somma ogni cosa insieme
giūta sō . . . . duc. 3046.

---

[33]Cost of the work in marble[35].

Round the base on which the horse
stands there are 8 figures at 25 ducats
each . . . . duc. 200.

And on the same base there are 8
festoons with some other ornaments,
and of these there are 4 at the price
of 15 ducats each, and 4 at the price
of 8 ducats each . . . . duc. 92.

And for squaring the stones   duc.   6.

Again, for the large cornice which
goes below the base on which the
horse stands, which is 13 br. and 6 in.,
at 2 duc. per br. . . . . . . duc. 27.

And for 12 br. of frieze at 5 duc.
per br. . . . . duc. 60.

And for 12 br. of architrave at
1 1/2 duc. per br. . . . . duc. 18.

And for 3 rosettes which will be
the soffit of the monument, at 20 ducats each . . . . duc. 60.

And for 8 fluted columns at 8
ducats each . . . . duc. 64.

And for 8 bases at 1 ducat each,
                                        duc.   8.

And for 8 pedestals, of which 4 are
at 10 duc. each, which go above the
angles; and 4 at 6 duc. each . . duc. 64.

And for squaring and carving the
moulding of the pedestals at 2 duc.
each, and there are 8 . . . . duc. 16.

And for 6 square blocks with figures
and trophies, at 25 duc. each . . duc. 150.

And for carving the moulding of
the stone under the figure of the
deceased . . . . duc. 40.

For the statue of the deceased, to
do it well . . . . duc. 100.

For 6 harpies with candelabra, at 25
ducats each . . . . duc. 150.

For squaring the stone on which
the statue lies, and carving the moulding . . . . duc. 20.

                    in all . . duc. 1075.

The sum total of every thing added
together amount to . . . . . . duc. 3046.

G. 43 a]   726.

ZECCA DI ROMA.   MINT AT ROME.

[2]Puosi ancora fare sanza molla; [3]Ma
sempre il maschio di sopra debbe [4]stare
congiunto alla parte della gu[5]aina mobile;

It can also be made without a spring. The mint of
But the screw above must always be joined   Rome.
to the part of the movable sheath:

---

31. larghi. 36. va. 37. li va fesso 8 cō . . queste. 38. ciascuna . . luna. 39. issguadare. 40. cornicone. 41. frego.
46. piedistalle. 47. issguadrare esscornicare lipiedisstallo . . chessono . . luma. 48. trufei. 50. affarla. 52. essa scornica-
tura. 54. soma ōnicossa . . gūta so duc.

726. See Pl. LXXVI. This passage is taken from a note book which can be proved to have been
used in Rome.

⁶Tutte le monete che ⁷non àño ɟl cierchio ⁸intero, non sieno acci⁹ettate per
buone, e a ¹⁰fare la perfectione del lor
¹¹cierchio è neciessario ¹²che in prima le
mone¹³te siē tutte di perfetto cir¹⁴colo, e
a fare questo ¹⁵e' si debbe in prima fare
vna ¹⁶moneta perfetta in peso ¹⁷e in larghezza e grossez¹⁸za, e di questa tal lar¹⁹ghezza
e grossezza siē fat²⁰te molte lamine, tira-
²¹te per una medesima tra²²fila, le quali re-
sterā²³no a modo di righe, e · ²⁴di queste
tali righe si ²⁵stanpī fuori le monete ²⁶tōde,
a modo che si fā²⁷no i criuelli da casta-
²⁸gnie, e queste mone²⁹te poi si stanpino
nel ³⁰modo sopra detto ecc.

³¹Il vacuo della stanpa ³²sia più largo
da alto ³³che da basso vni³⁴formemente,
³⁵e insēsibile.

³⁶Questo taglia le monete di perfetta
ro³⁷tondità e grossezza e peso e ris³⁸parmia
l'omo che taglia e pesa, e ³⁹rispiarmia l'omo
che fa le monete ⁴⁰tonde; adūque sol passa per li mani ⁴¹del trafilatore e dello
stanpato⁴²re e fa monete bellissime.

All coins which do not have the rim complete, are not to be accepted as good; and
to secure the perfection of their rim it is
requisite that, in the first place, all the
coins should be a perfect circle; and to do
this a coin must before all be made perfect
in weight, and size, and thickness. Therefore have several plates of metal made of
the same size and thickness, all drawn through
the same gauge so as to come out in strips.
And out of [24]these strips you will stamp
the coins, quite round, as sieves are made
for sorting chestnuts[27]; and these coins
can then be stamped in the way indicated
above; &c.

[31]The hollow of the die must be uniformly wider than the lower, but impercep-
tibly[35].

This cuts the coins perfectly round and
of the exact thickness, and weight; and saves
the man who cuts and weighs, and the man
who makes the coins round. Hence it passes
only through the hands of the gauger and of
the stamper, and the coins are very superior.

C. 15b (1)]　　　　　　　　727.

POLUERE DA MEDAGLIE.

²Stoppini · incombustibili · di fungo ridot-
to in poluere, ³stagnio bruciato e tutti i
metalli, ⁴allume scagliuolo, ⁵fumo di fucina
da ottone, ⁶e ciascuna cosa inumidisci con
acquauite o maluagìa ⁷o acieto · forte di
grā, uino bianco ·, o di quella prima acqua
⁸di trementina destillata, o olio, pure che
poco sia ⁹invmidità ·, e gitta in telaroli.

POWDER FOR MEDALS.

The incombustible growth of soot on wicks
reduced to powder, burnt tin and all the
metals, alum, isinglass, smoke from a brass
forge, each ingredient to be moistened,
with aqua vitae or malmsey or strong
malt vinegar, white wine or distilled extract
of turpentine, or oil; but there should be
little moisture, and cast in moulds.

On the coining of medals (727. 728).

Mz. o']　　　　　　　　728.

DELLO INPRŌTARE MEDAGLIE.

Polta di smeriglio mista con acquavite ²o
scaglia di ferro con aceto ·, o cenere di foglie
di noce ·, o cenere ³di paglia sottilmēte trita.

OF TAKING CASTS OF MEDALS.

A paste of emery mixed with aqua vitae, or
iron filings with vinegar, or ashes of walnut
leaves, or ashes of straw very finely powdered.

726. 1. zeccha di roma. 2. Puossi anchora. 3. masscio. 4. chom giunto . . ghu. 9. ectate . . eaf. 10. perfectione. 12. prima
ne mone. 13. perfecto. 14. cholo e affare. 15. e si . . in p"a". 16. perfecta. 18. quessta. 19. sie fac. 24. queste . . sis.
26. chessi. 28. ecqueste. 29. sisstan pino. 30. decto ele. 31. vachuo. 32. larcho. 33. chedda. 36. Quessto. 37. grosseza
eppeso eriss. 38. spiarma . . chettaglia eppesa. 39. rispiarma . . falle. 40. istanpito. 42 effa.
727. 1. stopini inchonbusstibili. 3. brusato ettutti. 4. alume schāgliolo. 6. essciasschuna . . inūmidissci con acq"a". 7. biancho
o di ella prima acq"a". 8. desstillata o holio.
728. 1. polta di smeriglo . . acq"a". 2. ho cenere. 4. inolto [inp] in . . battutto. 5. radopiato [cre] essitiene. 6. accochettal

726. See Pl. LXXVI No. 2. The text of lines
31—35 stands parallel l. 24—27.

Farther evidence of Leonardo's occupations and
engagements at Rome under Pope Leo X. may be
gathered from some rough copies of letters which
will be found in this volume. Hitherto nothing
has been known of his work in Rome beyond some
doubtful, and perhaps mythical, statements in Vasari.

727. The meaning of *scagliuolo* in this passage is
doubtful.

⁴Il diametro si presta inuolto in nel piōbo ·, è battuto con martello ⁵e disteso piv volte; tal piōbo è raddoppiato e si tiene involto nel⁶la carta, acciochè tal poluere nō si versi, e poi fondi il piōbo e la pol⁷vere vi è di sopra al pionbo fonduto, la qual poi sia fregata infra due ⁸piastre d' acciaio tanto si poluerizi bene, di poi lauala coll' acqua da partire ⁹e risoluerassi la negrezza del ferro, e lascierà la poluere netta;

¹⁰Lo smeriglo in pezzi grossi si rompe col metterlo sopra vn panno in mol¹¹ti doppi, e si percuote per fianco col martello, e così se ne va; poi mischia lì ¹²a poco a poco, e poi si pesta cō facilità, e se tu lo tenessi sopra l' ancu¹³dine, mai lo rōperesti, essendo così grosso.

¹⁴Chi macina li smalti debbe fare tale esercitio sopra le pias¹⁵tre d' acciaio, temperato col macinatojo da conio, e poi metter¹⁶lo nell' acqva forte, la qual risolue tutto esso acciaio che si è ¹⁷cōsumato e misto con esso smalto e lo fece nero, onde poi ¹⁸rimā purificato e netto, e se tu lo macini sul porfido, esso ¹⁹porfido si consuma e si mischia collo smalto e lo guasta, ²⁰e l' acqua da partire mai lo lieva da dosso, perchè nō può ²¹risoluere tale porfido.

²²Se volli fare colore bello azzurro risolui lo smalto, fatto ²³col tartaro, e po' li leva il sal da dosso.

²⁴L' ottone vetrificato fa bello rosso.

The diameter is given in the lead enclosed; it is beaten with a hammer and several times extended; the lead is folded and kept wrapped up in parchment so that the powder may not be spilt; then melt the lead, and the powder will be on the top of the melted lead, which must then be rubbed between two plates of steel till it is thoroughly pulverised; then wash it with aqua fortis, and the blackness of the iron will be dissolved leaving the powder clean.

Emery in large grains may be broken by putting it on a cloth many times doubled, and hit it sideways with the hammer, when it will break up; then mix it little by little and it can be founded with ease; but if you hold it on the anvil you will never break it, when it is large.

Any one who grinds smalt should do it on plates of tempered steel with a cone shaped grinder; then put it in aqua fortis, which melts away the steel that may have been worked up and mixed with the smalt, and which makes it black; it then remains purified and clean; and if you grind it on porphyry the porphyry will work up and mix with the smalt and spoil it, and aqua fortis will never remove it because it cannot dissolve the porphyry.

If you want a fine blue colour dissolve the smalt made with tartar, and then remove the salt.

Vitrified brass makes a fine red.

G. 75b]　　　　　　　　729.

STUCCO.

²Fa stucco sopra il gobbo del ...... di giesso, ³il quale sia cōposto di venere e ⁴mercurio, e impasta bene sopra esso gobbo ⁵con equal grossezza di costa di coltello fatta colla ⁶sagoma, e questa copri cō coperchio di canpa⁷na da stillare, e riavrai il tuo vmido cō ⁸che inpastasti, el rimanēte · asciugga bene e poi ī⁹foca e batti over

STUCCO.

Place stucco over the prominence of the .... which may be composed of Venus and Mercury, and lay it well over that prominence of the thickness of the side of a knife, made with the ruler and cover this with the bell of a still, and you will have again the moisture with which you applied the paste. The rest you may dry

On stucco (729. 730).

. . ella pol. 7. bere vi e. 8.ʳpiastre dacaio . . lavolo chollacq“a”. 9. la negredine del ferro ellasciara. 10. lossmeriglo . . chol . . imol. 11. essi perchote per fiancho . . misscagle. 12. a pocho appocho . . essettu. 13. rōperessti . . chosi. 14. lissmalti. 15. chol macintatoio. 16. accaio chesse. 17. missto . . ello. 18. purifichato ennetto essettullo. 19. essimissca collossmalto ello. 20. ellae qua dosso [s] perche nō po. 22. azurro . . lossmalto. 24. vetrifichato.

729. 1. stuccho. 2. fasstucho . . ghobb del . a engui di giesso. 3. cōpossto di erenev e. 4. oirucrem e inpassta . ghobbo. 5. grosseza . . cholla. 6. saghoma ecquessta . . choperchio. 7. dasstillare erriarai. 8. inpasstassti . . assciugha. 9. focha

---

729. In this passage a few words have been written in a sort of cipher—that is to say backwards; as in l. 3 *erenev* for *Venere*, l. 4 *oirucrem* for *Mercurio*, l. 12 *il orreve cō ecarob* for *il everro (?) cō borace*. The meaning of the word before *"di giesso"*

in l. 1 is unknown; and the sense, in which *sagoma* is used here and in other passages is obscure.— *Venere* and *Mercurio* may mean 'marble' and 'lime', of which stucco is composed.

12. The meaning of *orreve* is unknown.

brunisci cō buon brunitoio e fa [10]grosso inverso la costa.

well; afterwards fire it, and beat it or burnish it with a good burnisher, and make it thick towards the side.

STUCCO.

[12]Poluerizza il . . . . cō borace e acqua, in[13]pasta e fa stucco, e poi scalda in mo-do si sec[14]chi, e poi vernica con foco in modo che lustri.

STUCCO.

Powder . . . with borax and water to a paste, and make stucco of it, and then heat it so that it may dry, and then varnish it, with fire, so that it shines well.

C. A. 313 *a*; 951 *a*]   **730.**

STUCCO DA FORMARE.

[2]Togli · butiro parti 6 ·, ciera parti · 2 ·, [3]e tāta farina volatile · che, messa sopra [4]le cose strutte ·, le facci · sode a modo [5]di cera · o di terra · da formare.

STUCCO FOR MOULDING.

Take of butter 6 parts, of wax 2 parts, and as much fine flour as when put with these 2 things melted, will make them as firm as wax or modelling clay.

COLLA.

[7]Togli mastice tremētina stillata [8]e biacca.

GLUE.

Take mastic, distilled turpentine and white lead.

S. K. M. III 50 *a*]   **731.**

DA GITTARE.

On bronze casting generally (731—740).

[2]Il tartaro bruciato e pol[3]verizzato col giesso e gitta[4]to fā che esso · giesso si [5]tiene insieme · poi, ch'è ricot[6]to, e poi · nell' acqua si disfa.

TO CAST.

Tartar burnt and powdered with pla-ster and cast cause the plaster to hold to-gether when it is mixed up again; and then it will dissolve in water.

S. K. M. III. 53 *a*]   **732.**

PER GITTARE BRŌZO · IN GIESSO.

[2]Togli per ogni 2 scodelle · di giesso una di [3]corno di bo bruciato e mischia īsieme [4]e gitta.

TO CAST BRONZE IN PLASTER.

Take to every 2 cups of plaster 1 of ox-horns burnt, mix them together and make your cast with it.

S. K. M. II.1 95 *a*]   **733.**

Quādo voi gittare di ciera, abbrucia la schiuma [2]con una candela, e'l gietto verrà sanza busi.

When you want to take a cast in wax, burn the scum with a candle, and the cast will come out without bubbles.

S. K. M. III. 55 *b*]   **734.**

2 ōcie di giesso da libbra [2]di metallo; [3]noce che fa simile alla [4]curva.

2 ounces of plaster to a pound of metal;— walnut, which makes it like the curve.

. . brunissci cō biō brunitoio effa. 10. chossta. 11. stuccho. 12. il orreve cō ecarob e acq"a" in. 13. passta effa stucho eppoi scal"d"a. 14. eppoi vernicha con vocho . . lusstri.

730. 1. stucho. 2. toli bituro parte . . parte. 4. chose. 5. tera. 7. tomastice temetina. 8. biaccha.

731. 2. tartero. 3. verizato chol. 4. hesso.. 5. tiene sieme . . rico. 6. acq"a".

732. 1. giesso ḷ di. 3. bruciata e misscia.

733. 1. abrucia. 2. chandela.   **734.** 1. libra.

734. The second part of this is quite obscure.

S. K. M. III. 56*a*]

735.

[Terra asciuta 16 ²libbre, 100 libbre di metallo ³la bagniata terra 20, ⁴di bagniato 100, di metà, ⁵che cresce 4 libbre d'acqua, ⁶una di cera, una libbra di me⁷tallo, alquāto māco, ⁸cimatura cō terra, ⁹misura per misura.]

[Dried earth 16 pounds, 100 pounds of metal wet clay 20,—of wet 100,—half,—which increases 4 lbs. of water,—1 of wax, 1 lb. of metal, a little less,—the scrapings of linen with earth, measure for measure.]

H.² 52*b*]

736.

Tal fia il gietto ²qual fia la stāpa.

Such as the mould is, so will the cast be.

Tr. 52]

737.

COME SI DEBBONO PULIRE I GIETTI.

²Farai uno mazzo · di fila · di ferro, grosso · come spaghetto, ³e coll' acqua fregherai, tenēdo sotto uno tinello, acciò nō facci ⁴fāgo sotto.

HOW CASTS OUGHT TO BE POLISHED.

Make a bunch of iron wire as thick as thread, and scrub them with [this and] water; hold a bowl underneath that it may not make a mud below.

COME SI DE' LEUARE I RICCI DEL BRŌZO.

⁶Farai uno · palo di ferro che sia a uso d'uno largo · scarpello, ⁷e cō quello fregherai · su per quelle · creste · del brōzo, che rimarrāno ⁸sopra · i gietti delle bōbarde, che diriuano dalle schiappature della ⁹forma, · ma fa che 'l palo · pesi · bene ·, e' colpi sieno lūghi e grādi.

HOW TO REMOVE THE ROUGH EDGES FROM BRONZE.

Make an iron rod, after the manner of a large chisel, and with this rub over those seams on the bronze which remain on the casts of the guns, and which are caused by the joins in the mould; but make the tool heavy enough, and let the strokes be long and broad.

FACILITÀ DI FONDERE.

¹¹Allega · prima · una parte del metallo alla · manica, di poi lo metti ī fornace, ¹²e questo farà prīcipio · col suo bagnio al fondere del rame.

TO FACILITATE MELTING.

First alloy part of the metal in the crucible, then put it in the furnace, and this being in a molten state will assist in beginning to melt the copper.

PER PROVEDERE AL RAME CHE SI FREDDASSE NELLA FORNACE.

¹⁴Quando · il rame · si fredasse nella fornace fa · che subito ·, quādo tu te n'avedi, ¹⁵di tagliarlo cō frugatojo · mētre ch' eli è · ī paniccia ·, overo se fusse ¹⁶īteramēte · raffreddato, taglialo, come si fa il piōbo, cō larghi e grossi scar¹⁷pelli.

TO PREVENT THE COPPER COOLING IN THE FURNACE.

When the copper cools in the furnace, be ready, as soon as you perceive it, to cut it with a long stick while it is still in a paste; or if it is quite cold cut it as lead is cut with broad and large chisels.

735. 1. assciutta. 2. libre 100 lbbre. 5. cressie. 4. librdacq"a". 6. ī di . . ī libra.
737. 1. debe. 2. fara ī mazo . . spagetto. 3. echollacq"a" frecherai . . ī tinello. 6. ī palo . . chessia . . largho. 7. chō . . rimā. 8. isciappature. 9. maffa . . chalpi. 11. ī parte . . manicha. 12. ecquesto . . chol . . derame. 13. chessi fredassi. 14. chessubito. 15. chō . . imētre . . overo [mēte] seffussi. 16. raffredo taglalo chome . . chō chargi . . schar. 18. affare ī. 19. affare ī . libre fallo . . cho 2006 libr. 20. ciasschuno . . libr.

735. The translation is given literally, but the meaning is quite obscure.

SE AVESSI A FARE VNO GRĀ GIETTO.

[19]Se avessi a fare uno gietto di cento mila · libbre, falo cō · 2 · fornelli con 2000 libbre [20]per ciascuno · o īsino . in 3000 libbre il piv.

IF YOU HAVE TO MAKE A LARGE CAST.

If you have to make a cast of a hundred thousand pounds do it with two furnaces and with 2000 pounds in each, or as much as 3000 pounds at most.

Tr. 53]   **738.**

¶ COME FARE BENE A RŌPERE VNA GRĀ MASSA DI BRŌZO. ¶

[2]Se volli rōpere · una · grā · massa · di brōzo · sospēdilo · prima, [3]poi · lì fa da 4 · lati · uno muro · a vso di truogo · di mattoni, e fa lì grā foco ·, [4]e quādo è bē rosso, dali · uno colpo con vno [5]grā peso levato · in alto cō grā forza.

HOW TO PROCEED TO BREAK A LARGE MASS OF BRONZE.

If you want to break up a large mass of bronze, first suspend it, and then make round it a wall on the four sides, like a trough of bricks, and make a great fire therein. When it is quite red hot give it a blow with a heavy weight raised above it, and with great force.

Tr. 54]   **739.**

¶ DEL FARE VNIRE IL PIŌBO CON ALTRO · METALLO. ¶

[2]Se volessi per masseritia · mettere · il piōbo · nel metallo · e per sopire . alla soma [3]dello stagnio · che si · richiede · nel metallo ·, allega · prima · il piōbo · collo [4]stagnio · e poi metti sopra · il rame fōduto.

TO COMBINE LEAD WITH OTHER METAL.

If you wish for economy in combining lead with the metal in order to lessen the amount of tin which is necessary in the metal, first alloy the lead with the tin and then add the molten copper.

¶ COME SI DEBE · FONDERE IN UNO FORNELLO. ¶

[6]Il fornello · de' essere · īfra 4. pilastri bē fōdati.

HOW TO MELT [METAL] IN A FURNACE.

The furnace should be between four well founded pillars.

¶ DELLA GROSSEZZA DELLA CAPPA. ¶

[8]La cappa nō debe · prevalicare · la grossezza · di 2 · dita ·, e debesi interrare · [9]in quatro volte . sopra · la terra · sottile · e poi bene armare, [10]e sia · sola · mēte · ricotta · di dētro · e dato · poi · sottilmēte · di cenere · e bouina.

OF THE THICKNESS OF THE COATING.

The coating should not be more than two fingers thick, it should be laid on in four thicknesses over fine clay and then well fixed, and it should be fired only on the inside and then carefully covered with ashes and cow's dung.

DELLA GROSSEZZA DELLA BŌBARDA.

[12]La bōbarda · de' essere da 600 libbre di ballotta · ī su, cō questa regola; [13]farai la misura del diametro della · ballotta · e quel-

OF THE THICKNESS OF THE GUN.

The gun being made to carry 600 lbs. of ball and more, by this rule you will take the measure of the diameter of the ball and

---

738. 1. be a . . î grā. 2. î grā. 3. î muro . . effa . . focho. 4. ecquādo . . dalli î colpi chon.

739. 1. chol. 2. e per soperire. 3. chessi . . cholo. 4. eppoi . . arame. 5. fondere î fornello. 7. grosseza . . chappa. 8. chappa . . prevalichare la grosseza debessi. 9. gutro . . soctile. 10. essia . . riçhotta. 11. grosseza. 12. libr. 13. ba"lo"ta . . dia-

la · diuidi · ī 6 · parti, ¹⁴e una d'esse parti·
fia la grossezza · dināzi e la metà sēpre ·
piv rieto, ¹⁵e se la ballotta fia di libbre 7oo,
¹/₇ del · diametro della ballotta fia la sua
¹⁶grossezza · dināzi ·, e se la ballotta · fia
8oo ·, l'ottavo del suo diametro ¹⁷dināzi, e
se 9oo · ¹/₈ e ¹/₂ | e se 1ooo ¹/₉.

DELLA LŪGHEZZA DELLA TRŌBA DELLA BŌBARDA.

¹⁹Se voi · ch'ella · gitti · una ballotta · di
pietra · fa la lūghezza della trōba ²⁰in 6 · o
insino ī 7 ballotte ·, e se la · ballotta · fusse
di ferro ·, fa ²¹detta trōba · īsino in · 12 ballotte ·, e se la ballotta · fusse di ²²piōbo ·
farai la insino · in diciotto · ballotte, dico
quādo la bōbarda ²³avesse · la bocca · atta
· a ricieuere · in se da 6oo libr · di ballotta
di pietra ī su.

DELLA GROSSEZZA DE' PASSA·VOLANTI.

²⁵La grossezza dināzi de' passavolanti ·
nō deve passare dalla · metà ²⁶īsino · al
terzo del diametro della ballotta, E la lūghezza da 3o īsino ī 36 ²⁷ballotte.

divide it into 6 parts and one of these parts
will be its thickness at the muzzle; but at the
breech it must always be half. And if the ball
is to be 7oo lbs., ¹/₇th of the diameter of
the ball must be its thickness in front; and
if the ball is to be 8oo, the eighth of its
diameter in front; and if 9oo, ¹/₈th and
¹/₂ [³/₁₆], and if 1ooo, ¹/₉th.

OF THE LENGTH OF THE BODY OF THE GUN.

If you want it to throw a ball of stone,
make the length of the gun to be 6, or as
much as 7 diameters of the ball; and if the
ball is to be of iron make it as much as
12 balls, and if the ball is to be of lead,
make it as much as 18 balls. 'I mean
when the gun is to have the mouth fitted
to receive 6oo lbs. of stone ball, and
more.

OF THE THICKNESS OF SMALL GUNS.

The thickness at the muzzle of small guns
should be from a half to one third of the diameter of the ball, and the length from 3o
to 36 balls.

Tr. 55]   **740.**

¶DELLO · ILLOTARE · IL FORNELLO DI DĒTRO.¶

²Il fornello · debbe ināzi · che tu · īforni
il metallo · essere · illotato di terra di
Valenza, ³e sopra quella · cienere.

¶DEL RISTORARE · IL METALLO, QUĀDO · RIVOLESSE FREDDARE.¶

⁵Quādo · tu · vedi il brōzo volersi cō-
gielare · tolli legnie di salice, schiappate
⁶sottilmēte, e cō quelle · fa · foco.

¶LA CAGIONE DEL CŌGIELARSI.¶

⁸Dico · la cagione · d'essa cōgielatione
derivar · spesse volte · da troppo foco ⁹e
ancora da legnie · mal secche.

¶A CONOSCIERE LA DISPOSITIONE DEL FOCO.¶

¹¹Il foco · conoscierai, quādo fia bono e
vtile ·, alle fiame · chiare, e se uedrai ¹²le

OF LUTING THE FURNACE WITHIN.

The furnace must be luted before you
put the metal in it, with earth from Valenza,
and over that with ashes.

OF RESTORING THE METAL WHEN IT IS BECO-MING COOL.

When you see that the bronze is congealing
take some willow-wood cut in small chips
and make up the fire with it.

THE CAUSE OF ITS CURDLING.

I say that the cause of this congealing
often proceeds from too much fire, or from
ill-dried wood.

TO KNOW THE CONDITION OF THE FIRE.

You may know when the fire is good
and fit for your purpose by a clear flame,

---

mitro. 14. e ī . . grosseza . . ella. 15. esse . . di br 7oo . . balotta . . diamitro. 16. grosseza . . sella . . diamitro. 17. esse
. . | e ese. 18. lūgeza. 19. ī ballotta . . lūgeza. 20. essella . . fussi. 21. essela . . fussi. 23. avesse . la bocha. 24. gro-
sseza. 25. grosseza . . debono. 26. diamitro . . lūgeza.
740. 1. ilotare. 2. chetti . . tera di ualēza. 4. uolessi fredare. 5. chōgielare . . sciapate. 6. chō. 8. dicho la chagione .. dirivar.
9. anchora . . seche. 10. focho. 11. conosscierai . . ale . . esse uederai. 12. effinire co. 13. arai . . acq"a". 14. alegare.

740. l. 2. *Terra di Valenza.*—Valenza is **north** of Alessandria on the Po.

pūte · d'esse · fiāme turbe e finire cō molto · fumo ·, nō te ne fidare, e massime [13] quādo · avrai il bagnio · quasi · in acqua.

¶ DELLO ALLEGARE IL METALLO. ¶

[15] Il metallo · si uole fare vniversalmēte nelle bōbarde cō · 6 · o uisino 8 [16] per ciēto ·, cioè 6 di stagnio · sopra · ciēto · di rame, e quāto meno ve ne metti, [17] piv sicura fia · la bōbarda.

¶ QUĀDO SI DEBE ACCŌPAGNIARE · LO STAGNIO COL RAME. ¶

[19] Lo stagnio · col rame si debbe · mettere · quādo · ài il rame cōdotto in acqua.

¶ COME SI DEBE AVMĒTARE IL FONDERE. ¶

[21] Il fondere fia da te avmētato · quādo sarà cōdotto il rame in ²/₃ [22] in acqua ·, allora · con v̄ legnio di castagnio ispesso rimaneggerai il rima[23]nēte del rame ancora ītero · īfra la · parte · fonduta.

and if you see the tips of the flames dull and ending in much smoke do not trust it, and particularly when the flux metal is almost fluid.

OF ALLOYING THE METAL.

Metal for guns must invariably be made with 6 or even 8 per cent, that is 6 of tin to one hundred of copper, for the less you put in, the stronger will the gun be.

WHEN THE TIN SHOULD BE ADDED TO THE COPPER.

The tin should be put in with the copper when the copper is reduced to a fluid.

HOW TO HASTEN THE MELTING.

You can hasten the melting when ²/₃ds of the copper is fluid; you can then, with a stick of chestnut-wood, repeatedly stir what of copper remains entire amidst what is melted.

15. metalo. 17. sichura. 18. acōpagniare . . chol. 19. acq"a". 21. datte. 22. chastagnio . . rimanerai.

Introductory Observations on the Architectural Designs (XII), and Writings on Architecture (XIII).

Until now very little has been known regarding Leonardo's labours in the domain of Architecture. No building is known to have been planned and executed by him, though by some contemporary writers incidental allusion is made to his occupying himself with architecture, and his famous letter to Lodovico il Moro,—which has long been a well-known document,—in which he offers his service as an architect to that prince, tends to confirm the belief that he was something more than an amateur of the art. This hypothesis has lately been confirmed by the publication of certain documents, preserved at Milan, showing that Leonardo was not only employed in preparing plans but that he took an active part, with much credit, as member of a commission on public buildings; his name remains linked with the history of the building of the Cathedral at Pavia and that of the Cathedral at Milan.

Leonardo's writings on Architecture are dispersed among a large number of MSS., and it would be scarcely possible to master their contents without the opportunity of arranging, sorting and comparing the whole mass of materials, so as to have some comprehensive idea of the whole. The sketches, when isolated and considered by themselves, might appear to be of but little value; it is not till we understand their general purport, from comparing them with each other, that we can form any just estimate of their true worth.

Leonardo seems to have had a project for writing a complete and separate treatise on Architecture, such as his predecessors and contemporaries had composed—Leon Battista Alberti, Filarete, Francesco di Giorgio and perhaps also Bramante. But, on the other hand, it cannot be denied that possibly no such scheme was connected with the isolated notes and researches, treating on special questions, which are given in this work; that he was merely working at problems in which, for some reason or other he took a special interest.

A great number of important buildings were constructed in Lombardy during the period between 1472 and 1499, and among them there are several by unknown architects, of so high an artistic merit, that it is certainly not improbable that either Bramante or Leonardo da Vinci may have been, directly or indirectly, concerned in their erection.

Having been engaged, for now nearly twenty years, in a thorough study of Bramante's life and labours, I have taken a particular interest in detecting the distinguishing marks of his style as compared with Leonardo's. In 1869 I made researches about the architectural drawings of the latter in the Codex Atlanticus at Milan, for the purpose of finding out, if possible the original plans and sketches of the churches of Santa Maria delle Grazie at Milan, and of the Cathedral at Pavia, which buildings have been supposed to be the work both of Bramante and of Leonardo. Since 1876 I have repeatedly examined Leonardo's architectural studies in the collection of his manuscripts in the Institut de France, and some of these I have already given to the public in my work on "Les Projets Primitifs pour la Basilique de St. Pierre de Rome", Pl. 43. In 1879 I had the opportunity of examining the manuscript in the Palazzo Trivulzio at Milan, and in 1880 Dr Richter showed me in London the manuscripts in the possession of Lord Ashburnham, and those in the British Museum. I have thus had opportunities of seeing most of Leonardo's architectural drawings in the original, but of the manuscripts themselves I have deciphered only the notes which accompany the sketches. It is to Dr Richter's exertions that we owe the collected texts on Architecture which are now published, and while he has undertaken to be responsible for the correct reading of the original texts, he has also made it his task to extract the whole of the materials from the various MSS. It has been my task to arrange and elucidate the texts under the heads which have been adopted in this work. MS. B. at Paris and the Codex Atlanticus at Milan are the chief sources of our knowledge of Leonardo as an architect, and I have recently subjected these to a thorough re-investigation expressly with a view to this work.

A complete reproduction of all Leonardo's architectural sketches has not, indeed, been possible, but as far as the necessarily restricted limits of the work have allowed, the utmost completeness has been aimed at, and no efforts have been spared to include every thing that can contribute to a knowledge of Leonardo's style. It would have been very interesting, if it had been possible, to give some general account at least of Leonardo's work and studies in engineering, fortification, canal-making and the like, and it is only on mature reflection that we have reluctantly abandoned this idea. Leonardo's occupations in these departments have by no means so close a relation to literary work, in the strict sense of the word as we are fairly justified in attributing to his numerous notes on Architecture.

Leonardo's architectural studies fall naturally under two heads:

I. Those drawings and sketches, often accompanied by short remarks and explanations, which may be regarded as designs for buildings or monuments intended to be built. With these there are occasionally explanatory texts.

II. Theoretical investigations and treatises. A special interest attaches to these because they discuss a variety of questions which are of practical importance to this day. Leonardo's theory as to the origin and progress of cracks in buildings is perhaps to be considered as unique in its way in the literature of Architecture.

HENRY DE GEYMÜLLER.

XII.

Architectural Designs.

I. Plans for towns.

A. Sketches for laying out a new town with a double system of high-level and low-level road-ways.

Pl. LXXVII, No. 1 (MS. B, 15ᵇ). A general view of a town, with the roads outside it sloping up to the high-level ways within.

Pl. LXXVII, No. 3 (MS. B, 16ᵇ, see No. 741; and MS. B, 15ᵇ, see No. 742) gives a partial view of the town, with its streets and houses, with explanatory references.

Pl. LXXVII, No. 2 (MS. B, 15ᵇ; see No. 743). View of a double staircase with two opposite flights of steps.

Pl. LXXVIII, Nos. 2 and 3 (MS. B, 37ᵃ). Sketches illustrating the connection of the two levels of roads by means of steps. The lower galleries are lighted by openings in the upper road way.

B. Notes on removing houses (MS. Br. M., 270ᵇ, see No. 744).

B. 16a]   **741.**

Le strade · m · sono · piv · alte · che le strade · p · s · braccia 6., e ciascuna ²strada · de' essere larga braccia 20, e avere ¹/₂ braccio di calo dalle stremità ³al mezzo, e in esso mezzo sia a ogni braccio uno braccio di ⁴fessura, largo uno dito, dove l'acqua che

The roads *m* are 6 braccia higher than the roads *p s,* and each road must be 20 braccia wide and have ¹/₂ braccio slope from the sides towards the middle; and in the middle let there be at every braccio an opening, one braccio long and one finger wide, where the rain water may run off into

741. 1. strade . [m] M . . chelle. 2. largbr . . chalo. 3. mezo [eda esse stremita einesso mezo . . br unobr. 4. deba. 6. largeza

pioue debba scolare nelle ca⁵ve fatte al medesimo piano di $p \cdot s \cdot$, e da ogni stremità della ⁶larghezza di detta strada · sia · uno · portico di larghezza di braccia 6 ī sul ⁷le colonne, e sappi che, chi volesse andare per tutta la terra per le ⁸strade alte, potrà a suo acconcio usarle, e chi volesse andare ⁹per le basse, ancora il simile; per le strade alte non devono andare ¹⁰carri, nè altre simili cose, anzi siano solamēte per li giēteli o¹¹mini; per le basse deono andare i carri e altre some al uso ¹²e commodità del popolo · ; l'una casa de' volgiere le schiene ¹³all'altra ·, lasciādo la strada bassa in mezzo, ed agli usci · n ¹⁴si mettano le vettovaglie, come legnie, vino e simili cose; per le ¹⁵vie sotterrane si de' votare destri, stalle e simili cose fetide ¹⁶dall'uno arco all'altro

hollows made on the same level as $p\ s$. And on each side at the extremity of the width of the said road let there be an arcade, 6 braccia broad, on columns; and understand that he who would go through the whole place by the high level streets can use them for this purpose, and he who would go by the low level can do the same. By the high streets no vehicles and similar objects should circulate, but they are exclusively for the use of gentlemen. The carts and burdens for the use and convenience of the inhabitants have to go by the low ones. One house must turn its back to the other, leaving the lower streets between them. Provisions, such as wood, wine and such things are carried in by the doors n, and privies, stables and other fetid matter must be emptied away underground. From one arch to the next

B. 5ᵇ]   **742.**

de' essere braccia 300, cioè ciascuna via che ricieve il lume dalle fessu²re delle strade di sopra, e a ogni arco de' essere una scala a luma³ca tōda, perchè ne' cātoni delle quadre si piscia, e larga, e nella ⁴prima uolta sia vn uscio ch'entri ī destri e pisciatoi comuni, e per ⁵scala si disciēda dalla · strada alta · alla bassa, · e le strade ⁶alte si comīcino fori delle porte, e givnte a esse porte abbia⁷no conposto l'altezza di braccia 6; Fia fatta detta terra o presso ⁸a mare o altro fiume grosso, acciocchè le brutture della ⁹città, menate dall'acqua sieno portate · via.

must be 300 braccia, each street receiving its light through the openings of the upper streets, and at each arch must be a winding stair on a circular plan because the corners of square ones are always fouled; they must be wide, and at the first vault there must be a door entering into public privies and the said stairs lead from the upper to the lower streets and the high level streets begin outside the city gates and slope up till at these gates they have attained the height of 6 braccia. Let such a city be built near the sea or a large river in order that the dirt of the city may be carried off by the water.

B. 15ᵇ]   **743.**

Modo di scale | le scale · $c \cdot d$ · discendono j̄ $f \cdot g \cdot$, e ²similmēte $f \cdot g \cdot$ ² disciēde j̄ · $h \cdot k$.

The construction of the stairs: The stairs $c\ d$ go down to $f\ g$, and in the same way $f\ g$ goes down to $h\ k$.

Br. M. 270ᵇ]   **744.**

MUTATIONE DI CASE.

ON MOVING HOUSES.

²Le case sieno trasmutate e messe per ordine, ³e questo cō facilità si farà, ⁴per-

Let the houses be moved and arranged in order; and this will be done with facility

---

. . î portico di largeza di br . . īsu. 7. le colone essapiche . . volessi . . tera. 8. assuo anchoncio . . volessi. 9. no de antare. 10. cari . . simile . . sia. 11. cari. 12. chomodita . . chasa . . lesciene. 13. lassciādo . . imezo edal ussi. 14. mettino le vetto vaglio . . essimili. 15. socterane . . essimile. 16. archo allaltro 5.
742. 1. br . 300 . . ciaschuna . . ilume. 2. ī schala. 3. cātō dele . . pisia a e. 4. piscatoi. 5. schala . . | elle |. 6. abbi. 7. chonposte lalteza . . facta decta tera. 8. mere . . acioche le bructure. 9. cicta.
743. 1. disciēdano . . essimilemēte.
744. 1. chase. 2. chase. 3. ecquesto cō facilita (?). 5. eppoi. 6. cōmettano. 11. chase . . novela.

chè tali case son prima fatte [5]di pezzi sopra le piazze, e poi [6]si cōmettono insieme
colli lor [7]legniami nel sito dove si debbono
[8]stabilire.

because such houses are at first made in
pieces on the open places, and can then be
fitted together with their timbers in the site
where they are to be permanent.

[9]Li omini del pae[10]se abitino le nuo-
[11]ve case in parte, [12]quando nō v'è la
cor[13]te.

[9] Let the men of the country [or the
village] partly inhabit the new houses when
the court is absent[12].

744. On the same page we find notes referring
to Romolontino and Villafranca with a sketch-map
of the course of the "Sodro" and the "(Lo)era" (both
are given in the text farther on). There can hardly
be a doubt that the last sentence of the passage

given above, refers to the court of Francis I. King of
France.—L.9—13 are written inside the larger sketch,
which, in the original, is on the right hand side of
the page by the side of lines 1—8. The three
smaller sketches are below.   J. P. R.

II. *Plans for canals and streets in a town.*

*Pl. LXXIX, 1. and 2, (MS. B, 37 b, see No. 745, and MS. B. 36 a,
see No. 746). A Plan for streets and canals inside a town, by which the
cellars of the houses are made accessible in boats.*

*The third text given under No. 747 refers to works executed by Leo-
nardo in France.*

B. 37 b]   745.

La fāccia *a* ²*m* darà il lume ³alle stā-
⁴ze; ⁵*a · e ·* sarà · braccia 6 ·, *a · b* fia braccia ·
8 ·, *b · e* fia braccia 30; acciochè le stanze
sotto i portici siano ⁶luminose ·, *c · d · f ·*
fia il loco donde se vadi a scaricare le navi
in nel⁷le case; A volere che questa cosa ·
abbia effetto bisogna che la inondatione
⁸de' fiumi non mādasse l' acqua alle canove; è neciessario elegiere sito accomo-
dato, ⁹come porsi uicino a vno fiume, il
quale ti dia i canali, che nō si possino nè
per ¹⁰inōdatione o secchezza delle acque
dare mutatione alle altezze d'esse acque,
¹¹e il modo è qui di sotto figurato, e facciasi eletione di bel fiume che nō intorbidi,
nè ¹²per pioggia, come Tesino Adda e
molti altri; il modo che l'acque senpre

The front *a m* will give light to the
rooms; *a e* will be 6 braccia—*a b* 8 braccia
—*b e* 30 braccia, in order that the rooms
under the porticoes may be lighted; *c d f*
is the place where the boats come to the
houses to be unloaded. In order to render
this arrangement practicable, and in order
that the inundation of the rivers may not
penetrate into the cellars, it is necessary to
chose an appropriate situation, such as a spot
near a river which can be diverted into
canals in which the level of the water will
not vary either by inundations or drought.
The construction is shown below; and make
choice of a fine river, which the rains do
not render muddy, such as the Ticino, the
Adda and many others. [12]The construction

745. 2. ilume. 5. br . 6 . . br . 8 . . chelle . . socto. 6. donde [si dia lum] se . . asscharicare . . ine. 7. chuesta . . abbi
effecto bisognia accio chella nōdatione. 8. mādassi . . achomodato. 9. vissino. 10. rinōdatione ossecheza . . alteze. 11. el
modo . . soto . . effaci . . nōnintorbidine. 12. per piogie chome tesino adda . . chellacque. 13. alteza . . disocto. 14. tera
. . sare . . disfaciesino.

745. L. 1—4 are on the left hand side and within
the sketch given on Pl. LXXIX, No. 1. Then follows
after line 14, the drawing of a sluicegate—*conca*—of
which the use is explained in the text below it.

12 *Tesino, Adda e molti altri, i.e.* rivers coming
from the mountains and flowing through lakes.

On the page 38 a, which comes next in the original
MS. is the sketch of an oval plan of a town over
which is written *"modo di canali per la città"* and
through the longer axis of it *"canale magior"* is written
with *"Tesino"* on the prolongation of the canal.

J. P. R.

stieno [13]a un altezza sarà una cōca, come qui disotto, la quale fia all' entrare della [14]terra, e meglio alquāto dētro aciochè nimici nō la disfacciessino.

to oblige the waters to keep constantly at the same level will be a sort of dock, as shown below, situated at the entrance of the town; or better still, some way within, in order that the enemy may not destroy it[14].

B. 36 a]   **746.**

Tanto sia larga la stra[2]da ·, quanto è la universale [3]altezza delle case.

Let the width of the streets be equal to the average height of the houses.

Br. M. 270 b]   **747.**

Il fiume di ' mezzo [2]nō ricieva acqua [3]torbida, ma tale ac[4]qua vada per li fossi [5]di fori della terra [6]con 4 molina nell' ē[7]trata e 4 nella u[8]scita, e questo si fa[9]rà col ringorgare l'acqua [10]di sopra a Romo-lontino;

[11]Facciāsi fonti [12]in cia-[13]scuna piazza.

The main underground chan-nel does not receive turbid water, but that water runs in the ditches outside the town with four mills at the entrance and four at the outlet; and this may be done by damming the water above Romorantin.

[11]There should be foun-tains made in each piazza[13].

746. 3. alteza . . chase.
747. 1. el . . mezo. 3. mattale. 7. nella vs. 8. ecquesto. 9. ringhorghare. 12. [chome] in cias. 13. piaza.

747. In the original this text comes immediately after the passage given as No. 744. The remainder of the writing on the same page refers to the con-struction of canals and is given later, in the "Topo-graphical Notes".

10. *Romolontino* is Romorantin, South of Orleans in France.

Lines 1—11 are written to the right of the plan lines 11—13 underneath it.   J. P. R.

III. Castles and Villas.

A. Castles.

Pl. LXXX, No. 1 (P. V. fol. 39ᵇ; No. d'ordre 2282). The fortified place here represented is said by Vallardi to be the "castello" at Milan, but without any satisfactory reason. The high tower behind the "rivellino" ravelin—seems to be intended as a watch-tower.

Pl. LXXX, No. 2 (MS. B, 23ᵇ). A similarly constructed tower probably intended for the same use.

Pl. LXXX, No. 3 (MS. B). Sketches for corner towers with steps for a citadel.

Pl. LXXX, No. 4 (W. XVI). A cupola crowning a corner tower; an interesting example of decorative fortification. In this reproduction of the original pen and ink drawing it appears reversed.

B. Projects for Palaces.

Pl. LXXXI, No. 2 (MS. C. A, 75ᵇ; 221ᵃ, see No. 748). Project for a royal residence at Amboise in France.

Pl. LXXXII, No. 1 (C. A 308ᵃ; 939ᵃ). A plan for a somewhat extensive residence, and various details; but there is no text to elucidate it; in courts are written the three names:

Sām arch o *(St. Mark)*   cosi mo *(Cosmo)*   giovā nino *(John)*,

C. Plans for small castles or Villas.

The three following sketches greatly resemble each other.
Pl. LXXXII, No. 2 (MS. K³ 36ᵇ; see No. 749).

Pl. LXXXII, No. 3 (MS. B 60ᵃ; see No. 750).

Pl. LXXXIII (W. XVII). The text on this sheet refers to Cyprus (see Topographical Notes No. 1103), but seems to have no direct connection with the sketches inserted between.

Pl. LXXXVIII, Nos. 6 and 7 (MS. B, 12ᵃ; see No. 751). A section of a circular pavilion with the plan of a similar building by the side of it. These two drawings have a special historical interest because the text written below mentions the Duke and Duchess of Milan.

The sketch of a villa on a terrace at the end of a garden occurs in C. A. 150; and in C. A. 77ᵇ; 225ᵇ is another sketch of a villa somewhat resembling the Belvedere *of Pope Innocent VIII, at Rome. In C. A. 62ᵇ; 193ᵇ there is a* Loggia.

Pl. LXXXII, No. 4 (C. A. 387ᵃ; 1198ᵃ) is a tower-shaped Loggia *above a fountain. The machinery is very ingeniously screened from view.*

C. A. 75ᵇ; 221ᵃ]   **748.**

[Il palazzo del principe de' auere dināti vna piazza.]

²Le abitationi doue s'abbia a ballare o fare diuersi ³salti o uari movimēti con moltitudine di gente sieno ter⁴rene, perchè già n'ò veduto ruinare colla morte di ⁵molti; E sopra tutto fa che ogni muro, per sottile che ⁶sia, abbia fondamēto in terra o sopra archi bene ⁷fondati.

⁸Sieno li mezzanelli delli abitacoli ⁹diuisi da muri fatti di stretti mat¹⁰toni e sanza legniami per ri¹¹spetto del fuoco. ¹²Tutti li neciessari abbino esalatio¹³ne per le grossezze de' muri, e in ¹⁴modo che spirino per li tetti.

¹⁵Li mezzanelli sieno in volta, le quali ¹⁶sarà tanto più forti quāto e' sarā mi¹⁷nori.

¹⁸Le catene di quercia siē rinchi¹⁹use per li muri acciò nō siē offese ²⁰da foco.

The Palace of the prince must have a piazza in front of it.

Houses intended for dancing or any kind of jumping or any other movements with a multitude of people, must be on the ground-floor; for I have already witnessed the destruction of some, causing death to many persons, and above all let every wall, be it ever so thin, rest on the ground or on arches with a good foundation.

Let the mezzanines of the dwellings be divided by walls made of very thin bricks, and without wood on account of fire.

Let all the privies have ventilation [by shafts] in the thickness of the walls, so as to exhale by the roofs.

The mezzanines should be vaulted, and the vaults will be stronger in proportion as they are of small size.

The ties of oak must be enclosed in the walls in order to be protected from fire.

748. 1. palazo. 2. abitationini . . abballare offare. 3. chomoltitudine. 4. rrene . . cholla. 5. Essopra tucto . . persottile. 6. ossópra arachi. 8. mezanelli . . abitacholi. 9. mac. 10. tono essanza . . ris. 11. fuocho. 12. Tucti. 13. grosseze. 14. chesspirino . . tecti. 15. mezanelli. 18. chatene diquercie. 20. focho. 21. Lesstāze . . adesstri. 23. il ferore non isspiri.

748. The remarks accompanying the plan reproduced on Pl. LXXXI, No. 2 are as follows: Above, to the left: *"in a angholo stia la guardia de la sstalla"* (in the angle *a* may be the keeper of the stable). Below are the words *"strada dābosa"* (road to Ámboise), parallel with this *"fossa br 40"* (the moat 40 braccia) fixing the width of the moat. In the large court surrounded by a portico *"in terre No. — Largha br.80 e lügha br 120."* To the right of the castle is a large basin for aquatic sports with the words *"Giostre colle nave cioè li giostrā li stieno sopra le na"* (Jousting in boats that is the men are to be in boats).   J. P. R.

²¹Le stāze d'andare a' destri sieno ²²molte che entrino l'una nell' al²³tra, acciochè il fiero odore non spiri per ²⁴le abitationi, e tutti li loro usci ²⁵si serrino colli cōtrapesi.

²⁶La massima diuisione della frōte di que²⁷sto palazzo è in due parti, cioè che la larghez²⁸za della corte sia la metà di tutta la predetta ²⁹fronte; La 2ª ...

The privies must be numerous and going one into the other in order that the stench may not penetrate into the dwellings, and all their doors must shut off themselves with counterpoises.

The main division of the façade of this palace is into two portions; that is to say the width of the court-yard must be half the whole façade; the 2nd ...

K.3 36b]   749.

Largo per ogni lato br. 30; l'entrata da ²basso è in una sala larga braccia 10 e ³lunga braccia 30 e a 4 camere cō sua cami⁴ni.

30 braccia wide on each side; the lower entrance leads into a hall 10 braccia wide and 30 braccia long with 4 recesses each with a chimney.

B. 60a]   750.

Il primo grado sia · tutto ²ripieno.

The first storey [or terrace] must be entirely solid.

B. 12a]   751.

Padiglione del giardino della duchessa ²di Milano.

Fondamēto del padiglione ch'è nel ⁴mezzo del laberinto del duca di Milano.

The pavilion in the garden of the Duchess of Milan.

The plan of the pavilion which is in the middle of the labyrinth of the Duke of Milan.

---

24. li . . ettutti . . vssci. 25. cholli chōtrappesi. 26. ques. 26. chella larghe.

749. 1. Largho . . dab. 2. basso [e ino] e in . . la"r"gha br . 10 el. 3. lungha br 30.

751. 1. zardino. 3. del [z]. 4. mezo.

---

749. On each side of the castle, Pl. LXXXII. No. 2 there are drawings of details, to the left "*Camino*" a chimney, to the right the central lantern, sketched in red "8 *lati*" *i. e.* an octagon.

751. This passage was first published by AMORETTI in *Memorie Storiche* Cap. X: *Una sua opera da riportarsi a quest' anno fu il bagno fatto per la duchessa Beatrice nel parco o giardino del Castello. Lionardo non solo ne disegnò il piccolo edifizio a foggia di padiglione, nel cod. segnato Q. 3, dandone anche separatamente la pianta; ma sotto vi scrisse: Padiglione del giardino della duchessa; e sotto la pianta: Fondamento del padiglione ch'è nel mezzo del labirinto del duca di Milano; nessuna data è presso il padiglione, disegnato nella pagina 12, ma poco sopra fra molti circoli intrecciati vedesi = 10 Luglio 1492 = e nella pagina 2 presso ad alcuni disegni di legumi qualcheduno ha letto Settembre 1482 in vece di 1492, come dovea scriverevi, e probabilmente scrisse Lionardo.*

The original text however hardly bears the interpretation put upon it by AMORETTI. He is mis-

taken as to the mark on the MS. as well as in his statements as to the date, for the MS. in question has no date; the date he gives occurs, on the contrary, in another note-book. Finally, it appears to me quite an open question whether Leonardo was the architect who carried out the construction of the dome-like Pavilion here shown in section, or of the ground plan of the Pavilion drawn by the side of it. Must we, in fact, suppose that "*il duca di Milano*" here mentioned was, as has been generally assumed, Ludovico il Moro? He did not hold this title from the Emperor before 1494; till that date he was only called *Governatore* and Leonardo in speaking of him, mentions him generally as "*il Moro*" even after 1494. On January 18, 1491, he married Beatrice d'Este the daughter of Ercole I, Duke of Ferrara. She died on the 2nd January 1497, and for the reasons I have given it seems improbable that it should be this princess who is here spoken of as the "*Duchessa di Milano*". From the style of the handwriting it appears to me to be beyond

B. 19*b*]   **752.**

Il terreno · che si cava · dalle · canove ²si
debe elevare da cāto tāto · in alto che ³fac-
cia un orto ·, che sia alto quāto la sala, ⁴ma
fa che tra'l terreno dell' orto e'l muro
⁵della casa sia uno · intervallo, acciò che
⁶l'umido nō guasti i muri maestri.

The earth that is dug out from the cellars
must be raised on one side so high as to
make a terrace garden as high as the level
of the hall; but between the earth of the
terrace and the wall of the house, leave an
interval in order that the damp may not spoil
the principal walls.

752. 1. tereno chessi chava delle chanove.   2. ellevare da chāto.   3. chessia.   4. chettral tereno.   5. chasa.   6. maesstri.

all doubt that the MS. B, from which this passage
is taken, is older than the dated MSS. of 1492 and
1493. In that case the Duke of Milan here mentioned would be Gian Galeazzo (1469—1494) and
the Duchess would be his wife Isabella of Aragon,
to whom he was married on the second February
1489.   J. P. R.

IV. Ecclesiastical Architecture.

A. General Observations.

B. 39 b]

753.

Senpre vno edifitio vole · essere ²spiccato dintorno a volere dimostra³re la sua vera forma.

A building should always be detached on all sides so that its form may be seen.

Ash. II. 8 b]

754.

Qui nō si può nè si debe fare ²cāpanile, anzi debe ³stare separato come à il do⁴mo e Sā Giovanni di Firēze·, ⁵e così il domo di Pisa · che mo⁶stra il cāpanile per se dispicca⁷to ī circa e così il domo, e o⁸gni vno per se può mostrare la sua ⁹perfettione, e chi lo uolesse pure ¹⁰fare colla chiesa, faccia la lā¹¹terna scusare cāpanile ¹²come è la chiesa di Chiaravalle.

Here there cannot and ought not to be any *campanile;* on the contrary it must stand apart like that of the Cathedral and of San Giovanni at Florence, and of the Cathedral at Pisa, where the campanile is quite detached as well as the dome. Thus each can display its own perfection. If however you wish to join it to the church, make the lantern serve for the campanile as in the church at Chiaravalle.

753. 2. ispichato.
754. 1. po nessi. 2. chãpanile. 3. chome. 4. essãgiovani. 6. chãpanile . . displicha. 7. circho e chosi. 8. po. 9. perfectione. 10. colla. 11. schusare chãpanile.

753. The original text is reproduced on Pl. XCII, No. 1 to the left hand at the bottom.

754. This text is written by the side of the plan given on Pl. XCI. No. 2.

12. The Abbey of Chiaravalle, a few miles from Milan, has a central tower on the intersection of the cross in the style of that of the Certosa of Pavia, but the style is mediaeval (A. D. 1330). Leonardo seems here to mean, that in a building, in which the circular form is strongly conspicuous, the campanile must either be separated, or rise from the centre of the building and therefore take the form of a lantern.

B. 18 *b*]

755.

A nessuna chiesa sta [2]bene vedere tetti, āzi [3]sia rappianato e per ca[4]nali l'acqua discē[5]da ai condotti fatti nel [6]fregiō.

It never looks well to see the roofs of a church; they should rather be flat and the water should run off by gutters made in the frieze.

755. 3. rapianato . . cha. 4. la ch . gua dissie. 5. chondotti.

755. This text is to the left of the domed church reproduced on Pl. LXXXVII, No. 2.

B. The theory of Dome Architecture.

This subject has been more extensively treated by Leonardo in drawings than in writing. Still we may fairly assume that it was his purpose, ultimately to embody the results of his investigation in a "Trattato delle Cupole." The amount of materials is remarkably extensive. MS. B is particularly rich in plans and elevations of churches with one or more domes—from the simplest form to the most complicated that can be imagined. Considering the evident connexion between a great number of these sketches, as well as the impossibility of seeing in them designs or preparatory sketches for any building intended to be erected, the conclusion is obvious that they were not designed for any particular monument, but were theoretical and ideal researches, made in order to obtain a clear understanding of the laws which must govern the construction of a great central dome, with smaller ones grouped round it; and with or without the addition of spires, so that each of these parts by itself and in its juxtaposition to the other parts should produce the grandest possible effect.

In these sketches Leonardo seems to have exhausted every imaginable combination.[1] The results of some of these problems are perhaps not quite satisfactory; still they cannot be considered to give evidence of a want of taste or of any other defect in Leonardo's architectural capacity. They were no doubt intended exclusively for his own instruction, and, before all, as it seems, to illustrate the features or consequences resulting from a given principle.

---

[1] In MS. B, 32 ^{b} (see Pl. C III, No. 2) we find eight geometrical patterns, each drawn in a square; and in MS. C.A., fol. 87 to 98 form a whole series of patterns done with the same intention.

I have already, in another place,[1] pointed out the law of construction for buildings crowned by a large dome: namely, that such a dome, to produce the greatest effect possible, should rise either from the centre of a Greek cross, or from the centre of a structure of which the plan has some symmetrical affinity to a circle, this circle being at the same time the centre of the whole plan of the building.

Leonardo's sketches show that he was fully aware, as was to be expected, of this truth. Few of them exhibit the form of a Latin cross, and when this is met with, it generally gives evidence of the determination to assign as prominent a part as possible to the dome in the general effect of the building.

While it is evident, on the one hand, that the greater number of these domes had no particular purpose, not being designed for execution, on the other hand several reasons may be found for Leonardo's perseverance in his studies of the subject.

Besides the theoretical interest of the question for Leonardo and his Trattato *and besides the taste for domes prevailing at that time, it seems likely that the intended erection of some building of the first importance like the Duomos of Pavia and Como, the church of Sta. Maria delle Grazie at Milan, and the construction of a Dome or central Tower* (Tiburio) *on the cathedral of Milan, may have stimulated Leonardo to undertake a general and thorough investigation of the subject; whilst Leonardo's intercourse with Bramante for ten years or more, can hardly have remained without influence in this matter. In fact now that some of this great Architect's studies for S. Peter's at Rome have at last become known, he must be considered henceforth as the greatest master of Dome-Architecture that ever existed. His influence, direct or indirect even on a genius like Leonardo seems the more likely, since Leonardo's sketches reveal a style most similar to that of Bramante, whose name indeed, occurs twice in Leonardo's manuscript notes. It must not be forgotten that Leonardo was a Florentine; the characteristic form of the two principal domes of Florence, Sta. Maria del Fiore and the Battisterio, constantly appear as leading features in his sketches.*

The church of San Lorenzo at Milan, was at that time still intact. The dome is to this day one of the most wonderful cupolas ever constructed, and with its two smaller domes might well attract the attention and study

[1] Les Projets Primitifs pour la Basilique de St. Pierre de Rome, par Bramante, Raphael etc., Vol. I, p. 2.

of a never resting genius such as Leonardo. A whole class of these sketches betray in fact the direct influence of the church of S. Lorenzo, and this also seems to have suggested the plan of Bramante's dome of St. Peter's at Rome.

In the following pages the various sketches for the construction of domes have been classified and discussed from a general point of view. On two sheets: Pl. LXXXIV (C. A. 354ᵇ; 118ᵃ) and Pl. LXXXV, Nos. 1—11 (Ash. II, 6ᵇ) we see various dissimilar types, grouped together; thus these two sheets may be regarded as a sort of nomenclature of the different types, on which we shall now have to treat.

1. Churches formed on the plan of a Greek cross.

Group I.

Domes rising from a circular base.

The simplest type of central building is a circular edifice.

Pl. LXXXIV, No. 9. Plan of a circular building surrounded by a colonnade.

Pl. LXXXIV, No. 8. Elevation of the former, with a conical roof.

Pl. XC. No. 5. A dodecagon, as most nearly approaching the circle.

Pl. LXXXVI, No. 1, 2, 3. Four round chapels are added at the extremities of the two principal axes;—compare this plan with fig. 1 on p. 44 and fig. 3 on p. 47 (W. P. 5·^{b}) where the outer wall is octagonal.

Group II.

Domes rising from a square base.

The plan is a square surrounded by a colonnade, and the dome seems to be octagonal.

Pl. LXXXIV. The square plan below the circular building No. 8, and its elevation to the left, above the plan: here the ground-plan is square, the upper storey octagonal. A further development of this type is shown in two sketches C. A. 3^a (not reproduced here), and in

Pl. LXXXVI, No. 5 (which possibly belongs to No. 7 on Pl. LXXXIV.

Pl. LXXXV, No. 4, and p. 45, Fig. 3, a Greek cross, repeated p. 45, Fig. 3, is another development of the square central plan.

The remainder of these studies show two different systems; in the first the dome rises from a square plan,—in the second from an octagonal base.

Group III.

Domes rising from a square base and four pillars.[1]

a) First type. *A Dome resting on four pillars in the centre of a square edifice, with an apse in the middle, of each of the four sides.   We have eleven variations of this type.*

aa)   Pl. LXXXVIII, No. 3.

bb)   Pl. LXXX, No. 5.

cc)   Pl. LXXXV, Nos. 2, 3, 5.

dd)   Pl. LXXXIV, No. 1 and 4 beneath.

ee)   Pl. LXXXV, Nos. 1, 7, 10, 11.

b) Second type. *This consists in adding aisles to the whole plan of the first type; columns are placed between the apses and the aisles; the plan thus obtained is very nearly identical with that of S. Lorenzo at Milan.*

Fig. 1 on p. 56. (MS. B, 75ᵃ) shows the result of this treatment adapted to a peculiar purpose about which we shall have to say a few words later on.

Pl. XCV, No. 1, shows the same plan but with the addition of a short nave.   This plan seems to have been suggested by the general arrangement of S. Sepolcro at Milan.

MS. B. 57ᵇ (see the sketch reproduced on p. 51).   By adding towers in the four outer angles to the last named plan, we obtain a plan which bears the general features of Bramante's plans for S. Peter's at Rome.[2]   (See p. 51 Fig. 1.)

Group IV.

Domes rising from an octagonal base.

This system, developed according to two different schemes, has given rise to two classes with many varieties.

In a) On each side of the octagon chapels of equal form are added.

In b) The chapels are dissimilar; those which terminate the principal axes being different in form from those which are added on the diagonal sides of the octagon.

a. First Class.

The Chapel "degli Angeli," at Florence, built only to a height of about 20 feet by Brunellesco, may be considered as the prototype of this group; and, indeed it probably suggested it.   The fact that we see in MS. B. 11ᵇ

---

[1] *The ancient chapel San Satiro, via del Falcone, Milan, is a specimen of this type.*

[2] *See* Les projets primitifs *etc., Pl. 9—12.*

(Pl. XCIV, No. 3) by the side of Brunellesco's plan for the Basilica of Sto. Spirito at Florence, a plan almost identical with that of the Capella degli Angeli, *confirms this supposition. Only two small differences, or we may say improvements, have been introduced by Leonardo. Firstly the back of the chapels contains a third niche, and each angle of the Octagon a folded pilaster like those in Bramante's* Sagrestia di S. M. presso San Satiro *at Milan, instead of an interval between the two pilasters as seen in the Battistero at Florence and in the Sacristy of Sto. Spirito in the same town and also in the above named chapel by Brunellesco.*

The first set of sketches which come under consideration have at first sight the appearance of mere geometrical studies. They seem to have been suggested by the plan given on page 44 Fig. 2 (MS. B, 55ª) in the centre of which is written "Santa Maria in perticha da Pavia", *at the place marked A on the reproduction.*

a) (MS. B, 34ᵇ, page 44 Fig. 3). In the middle of each side a column is added, and in the axes of the intercolumnar spaces a second row of columns forms an aisle round the octagon. These are placed at the intersection of a system of semicircles, of which the sixteen columns on the sides of the octagon are the centres.

b) The preceding diagram is completed and becomes more monumental in style in the sketch next to it (MS. B, 35ª, see p. 45 Fig. 1). An outer aisle is added by circles, having for radius the distance between the columns in the middle sides of the octagon.

c) (MS. B, 96ᵇ, see p. 45 Fig. 2). Octagon with an aisle round it; the angles of both are formed by columns. The outer sides are formed by 8 niches forming chapels. The exterior is likewise octagonal, with the angles corresponding to the centre of each of the interior chapels.

Pl. XCII, No. 2 (MS. B. 96ᵇ). Detail and modification of the preceding plan—half columns against piers—an arrangement by which the chapels of the aisle have the same width of opening as the inner arches between the half columns. Underneath this sketch the following note occurs: questo vole · avere 12 facce · cō 12 tabernaculi · come · a · b. *(This will have twelve sides with twelve tabernacles as* a b.*) In the remaining sketches of this class the octagon is not formed by columns at the angles.*

The simplest type shows a niche in the middle of each side and is repeated on several sheets, viz: MS. B 3; MS. C.A. 354ᵇ (see Pl. LXXXIV, No. 11), and MS. Ash II 6ᵇ; (see Pl. LXXXV, No. 9 and the elevations No. 8; Pl. XCII, No. 3; MS. B. 4ᵇ [not reproduced here] and Pl. LXXXIV, No. 2).

Fig. 1.

Fig. 2.   Fig. 3.

Fig. 1.

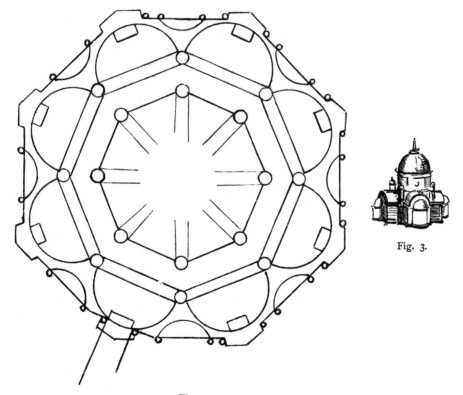

Fig. 3.

Fig. 2.

*Pl. XCII, 3 (MS. B, 56ᵇ) corresponds to a plan like the one in MS.
B 35ᵃ, in which the niches would be visible outside or, as in the following sketch, with the addition of a niche in the middle of each chapel.*

*Pl. XC, No. 6. The niches themselves are surrounded by smaller niches
(see also No. 1 on the same plate).*

Octagon expanded on each side.

A. by a square chapel:
   MS. B. 34ᵇ (not reproduced here).
B. by a square with 3 niches:
   MS. B. 11ᵇ (see Pl. XCIV, No. 3).
C. by octagonal chapels:
   a) MS. B, 21ᵃ; Pl. LXXXVIII, No. 4.
   *b) No. 2 on the same plate. Underneath there is the remark: "quest'è
      come le 8 cappele àno a essere facte" (this is how the eight chapels
      are to be executed).*
   *c) Pl. LXXXVIII, No. 5. Elevation to the plans on the same sheet,
      it is accompanied by the note: "ciasscuno de' 9 tiburi no' uole · passare
      l'alteza · di · 2 · quadri" (neither of the 9 domes must exceed the
      height of two squares).*
   *d) Pl. LXXXVIII, No, 1, Inside of the same octagon.
      MS. B, 30ᵃ, and 34ᵇ; these are three repetitions of parts of the
      same plan with very slight variations.*
D. by a circular chapel:
   *MS. B, 18ᵃ (see Fig. 1 on page 47) gives the plan of this arrangement in
   which the exterior is square on the ground floor with only four of the
   chapels projecting, as is explained in the next sketch.*
   *Pl. LXXXIX, MS. B, 17ᵇ. Elevation to the preceding plan sketched on
   the opposite side of the sheet, and also marked A. It is accompanied by
   the following remark, indicating the theoretical character of these studies:
   questo · edifitio · anchora · starebbe · bene affarlo dalla linja · a · b · c · d ·
   insù. ("This edifice would also produce a good effect if only the part above
   the lines a b, c d, were executed").*
   *Pl. LXXXIV, No. 11. The exterior has the form of an octagon, but the
   chapels project partly beyond it. On the left side of the sketch they
   appear larger than on the right side.*
   Pl. XC, No. 1, (MS. B, 25ᵇ); Repetition of Pl. LXXXIV, No. 11.
   *Pl. XC, No. 2. Elevation to the plan No. 1, and also to No. 6 of the
   same sheet.*

Fig. 1.

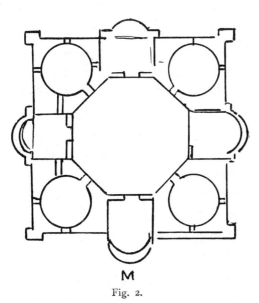

Fig. 2.

Fig. 3.

E. By chapels formed by four niches:

Pl. LXXXIV, No. 7 (the circular plan on the left below) shows this arrangement in which the central dome has become circular inside and might therefore be classed after this group.[1]

The sketch on the right hand side gives most likely the elevation for the last named plan.

F. By chapels of still richer combinations, which necessitate an octagon of larger dimensions:

Pl. XCI, No. 2 (MS. Ash. II. 8ᵇ)[2]*; on this plan the chapels themselves appear to be central buildings formed like the first type of the third group. Pl. LXXXVIII, No. 3.*

Pl. XCI, No. 2 above; the exterior of the preceding figure, particularly interesting on account of the alternation of apses and niches, the latter cantaining statues of a gigantic size, in proportion to the dimension of the niches.

b. Second Class.

Composite plans of this class are generally obtained by combining two types of the first class—the one worked out on the principal axes, the other on the diagonal ones.

MS. B. 22 shows an elementary combination, without any additions on the diagonal axes, but with the dimensions of the squares on the two principal axes exceeding those of the sides of the octagon.

In the drawing W. P. 5ᵇ (see page 44 Fig. 1) the exterior only of the edifice is octagonal, the interior being formed by a circular colonnade; round chapels are placed against the four sides of the principal axes.

The elevation, drawn on the same sheet (see page 47 Fig. 3), shows the whole arrangement which is closely related with the one on Pl. LXXXVI No. 1, 2.

MS. B. 21ᵃ shows:

a) four sides with rectangular chapels crowned by pediments Pl. LXXXVII No. 3 (plan and elevation);

b) four sides with square chapels crowned by octagonal domes. Pl. LXXXVII No. 4; the plan underneath.

MS. B. 18ᵃ shows a variation obtained by replacing the round chapels in the principal axes of the sketch MS. B. 18ᵃ by square ones, with an

---

[1] *This plan and some others of this class remind us of the plan of the Mausoleum of Augustus as it is represented for instance by Durand. See* Cab. des Estampes, Bibliothèque Nationale, Paris, Topographie de Rome, V, 6, 82.

[2] *The note accampanying this plan is given under No.* 754.

apse. Leonardo repeated both ideas for better comparison side by side, see page 47. *Fig.* 2.

Pl. LXXXIX (MS. B. 17*[b]). Elevation for the preceding figure. The comparison of the drawing marked M with the plan on page* 47 *Fig.* 2, *bearing the same mark, and of the elevation on Pl. LXXXIX below (marked A) with the corresponding plan on page* 47 *is highly instructive, as illustrating the spirit in which Leonardo pursued these studies.*

Pl. LXXXIV No. 12 *shows the design Pl. LXXXVII No.* 3 *combined with apses, with the addition of round chapels on the diagonal sides.*

Pl. LXXXIV No. 13 *is a variation of the preceding sketch.*

Pl. XC No. 3. *MS. B.* 25*[b]. The round chapels of the preceding sketch are replaced by octagonal chapels, above which rise campaniles.*

Pl. XC No. 4 *is the elevation for the preceding plan.*

Pl. XCII No. 1. *(MS. B.* 39*[b].); the plan below. On the principal as well as on the diagonal axes are diagonal chapels, but the latter are separated from the dome by semicircular recesses. The communication between these eight chapels forms a square aisle round the central dome.*

Above this figure is the elevation, showing four campaniles on the angles.[1]

Pl. LXXXIV No. 3. *On the principal axes are square chapels with three niches; on the diagonals octagonal chapels with niches. Cod. Atl.* 340*[b] gives a somewhat similar arrangement.*

MS. B. 30. *The principal development is thrown on the diagonal axes by square chapels with three niches; on the principal axes are inner recesses communicating with outer ones.*

The plan Pl. XCIII No. 2 *(MS. B.* 22) *differs from this only in so far as the outer semicircles have become circular chapels, projecting from the external square as apses; one of them serves as the entrance by a semicircular portico.*

The elevation is drawn on the left side of the plan.

MS. B. 19. *A further development of MS. B.* 18, *by employing for the four principal chapels the type Pl. LXXXVIII No.* 3, *as we have already seen in Pl. XCI No.* 2; *the exterior presents two varieties.*

a) The outer contour follows the inner.[2]

b) It is semicircular.

Pl. LXXXVII No. 2 *(MS. B.* 18*[b]) Elevation to the first variation MS. B.* 19. *If we were not certain that this sketch was by Leonardo, we might feel tempted to take it as a study by Bramante for St. Peter's at Rome.*[3]

---

[1] *The note accompanying this drawing is reproduced under No.* 753.

[2] *These chapels are here sketched in two different sizes; it is the smaller type which is thus formed.*

[3] *See* Les projets primitifs Pl. 43.

MS. P. V. 39^b. In the principal axes the chapels of MS. B. 19, and semicircular niches on the diagonals. The exterior of the whole edifice is also an octagon, concealing the form of the interior chapels, but with its angles on their axes.

Group V.

Suggested by San Lorenzo at Milan.

In MS. C. A. 266 II^b, 812^b there is a plan almost identical with that of San Lorenzo.— The diagonal sides of the irregular octagon are not indicated. If it could be proved that the arches which, in the actual church, exist on these sides in the first story, were added in 1574 by Martimo Bassi, then this plan and the following section would be still nearer the original state of San Lorenzo than at present. A reproduction of this slightly sketched plan has not been possible. It may however be understood from Pl. LXXXVIII No. 3, by suppressing the four pillars corresponding to the apses.

Pl. LXXXVII No. 1 shows the section in elevation corresponding with the above-named plan. The recessed chapels are decorated with large shells in the halfdomes like the arrangement in San Lorenzo, but with proportions like those of Bramante's Sacristy of Santa Maria presso S. Satiro.

MS. C. A. 266; a sheet containing three views of exteriors of Domes. On the same sheet there is a plan similar to the one above-named but with uninterrupted aisles and with the addition of round chapels in the axes (compare Pl. XCVII No. 3 and page 44 Fig. 1), perhaps a reminiscence of the two chapels annexed to San Lorenzo.— Leonardo has here sketched the way of transforming this plan into a Latin cross by means of a nave with side aisles.

Pl. XCI No. 1. Plan showing a type deprived of aisles and comprised in a square building which is surrounded by a portico. It is accompanied by the following text:

Ash. II. 7 *a*]   756.

Questo edifitio è abitato di sotto · e di sopra come · è san Sepulcro, ²ed è sopra come sotto, saluo che 'l di sopra · al tiburio · c · d · e'l di sotto ³al tiburio a · b · e quãdo

This edifice is inhabited [accessible] below and above, like San Sepolcro, and it is the same above as below, except that the upper story has the dome c d; and the

756. 1. socto . . chome . . sansepulchro. 2. chome. 3. a . b . e ecquãdo. 4. nela . . socto. 4. chali 10 schalini. 5. schalini . .

756. The church of San Sepolcro at Milan, founded in 1030 and repeatedly rebuilt after the middle

of the XVIth century, still stands over the crypt of the original structure.

entri nella chiesa di sotto, [4]tu cali 10 scalini, e quãdo mõti in quello di sopra tu sali
20 [5]scalini, che a $^1/_3$ l'uno fãno 10 braccia,
e questo è lo spatio ch'è [6]iñfra i piani
dell'una e l'altra chiesa.

lower has the dome *a b*, and when you
enter into the crypt, you descend 10 steps,
and when you mount into the upper you
ascend 20 steps, which, with $^1/_3$ braccio for
each, make 10 braccia, and this is the height
between one floor of the church and the other.

10. br . e.   11. ellaltra.

*Above the plan on the same sheet is a view of the exterior. By the aid
of these two figures and the description, sections of the edifice may easily
be reconstructed. But the section drawn on the left side of the building
seems not to be in keeping with the same plan, notwithstanding the explanatory note written underneath it:* "dentro il difitio di sopra" *(interior of
the edifice above)*[1].

*Before leaving this group, it is well to remark that the germ of it
seems already indicated by the diagonal lines in the plans Pl. LXXXV
No. 11 and No. 7. We shall find another application of the same type to
the Latin cross in Pl. XCVII No. 3.*

[1] *The small inner dome corresponds to* a b *on the plan —it rises from the lower church into the upper—,
above, and larger, rises the dome* c d. *The aisles above and below thus correspond* (è di sopra come di sotto,
salvoche etc.). *The only difference is, that in the section Leonardo has not taken the trouble to make the form
octagonal, but has merely sketched circular lines in perspective.*   J. P. R.

2. Churches formed on the plan of a Latin cross.

We find among Leonardo's studies several sketches for churches on the plan of the Latin cross; we shall begin by describing them, and shall add a few observations.

A. Studies after existing Monuments.

Pl. XCIV No. 2. (MS. B. 11ᵇ.) Plan of Santo Spirito at Florence, a basilica built after the designs of Brunellesco.—Leonardo has added the indication of a portico in front, either his own invention or the reproduction of a now lost design.

Pl. XCV No. 2. Plan accompanied by the words: "A è santo sepolcro di milano di sopra" *(A is the upper church of S. Sepolcro at Milan); although since Leonardo's time considerably spoilt, it is still the same in plan.*

The second plan with its note: "B è la sua parte socto tera" *(B is its subterranean part [the crypt]) still corresponds with the present state of this part of the church as I have ascertained by visiting the crypt with this plan. Excepting the addition of a few insignificant walls, the state of this interesting part of the church still conforms to Leonardo's sketch; but in the Vestibolo the two columns near the entrance of the winding stairs are absent.*

B. Designs or Studies.

Pl. XCV No. 1. Plan of a church evidently suggested by that of San Sepolcro at Milan. The central part has been added to on the principle of the second type of Group III. Leonardo has placed the "coro" *(choir) in the centre.*

Pl. XCVI No. 2. In the plan the dome, as regards its interior, belongs to the First Class of Group IV, and may be grouped with the one in MS. B. 35ᵃ. The nave seems to be a development of the type represented in Pl. XCV No. 2, B. by adding towers and two lateral porticos[1].

On the left is a view of the exterior of the preceding plan. It is accompanied by the following note:

B. 24 a]   757.

Questo · edifitio è abitato di sopra e di sotto; ²di sopra · si va · per li campanili · e uassi sù per lo piano ³dove sono fondati · i · 4 · tiburi, e detto piano ⁴à uno parapetto dinãzi, e di detti tiburi nessuno ⁵ne riesce in chiesa, anzi sono separati ī tutto.

This building is inhabited below and above; the way up is by the campaniles, and in going up one has to use the platform, where the drums of the four domes are, and this platform has a parapet in front, and none of these domes communicate with the church, but they are quite separate.

757. 4. a ī parapecto. 5. neriessie . . tucto.

Pl. XCVI No. 1 (MS. C. A. 16ᵇ; 65ᵃ). Perspective view of a church seen from behind; this recalls the Duomo at Florence, but with two campaniles[2].

Pl. XCVII No. 3 (MS. B. 52ᵃ). The central part is a development of S. Lorenzo at Milan, such as was executed at the Duomo of Pavia. There is sufficient analogy between the building actually executed and this sketch to suggest a direct connection between them. Leonardo accompanied Francesco di Giorgio[3] *when the latter was consulted on June 21ˢᵗ, 1490 as to this church; the fact that the only word accompanying the plan is: "sagrestia", seems to confirm our supposition, for the sacristies were added only in 1492, i. e. four years after the beginning of the Cathedral, which at that time was most likely still sufficiently unfinished to be capable of receiving the form of the present sketch.*

Pl. XCVII No. 2 shows the exterior of this design. Below is the note: edifitio al proposito del fõdameto figurato di socto (*edifice proper for the ground plan figured below*).

Here we may also mention the plan of a Latin cross drawn in MS. C. A. fol. 266 (see p. 50).

Pl. XCIV No. 1 (MS. L. 15ᵇ). External side view of Brunellesco's Florentine basilica San Lorenzo, seen from the North.

Pl. XCIV No. 4 (V. A. V, 1). Principal front of a nave, most likely of a church on the plan of a Latin cross. We notice here not only the

[1] *Already published in* Les projets primitifs *Pl. XLIII.*
[2] *Already published in the* Saggio *Pl. IX.*
[3] *See* MALASPINA, il Duomo di Pavia. *Documents.*

principal features which were employed afterwards in Alberti's front of
S. Maria Novella, but even details of a more advanced style, such as
we are accustomed to meet with only after the year 1520.

In the background of Leonardo's unfinished picture of St. Jerome
(Vatican Gallery) a somewhat similar church front is indicated (see the
accompanying sketch).

The view of the front of a temple, apparently a dome in the centre of
four corinthian porticos bearing pediments (published by Amoretti Tav. II. B
as being by Leonardo), is taken from a drawing, now at the Ambrosian
Gallery. We cannot consider this to be by the hand of the master.

C. Studies for a form of a Church most proper for preaching.

The problem as to what form of church might answer the require-
ments of acoustics seems to have engaged Leonardo's very particular attention.
The designation of "teatro" given to some of these sketches, clearly shows
which plan seemed to him most favourable for hearing the preacher's voice.

Pl. XCVII, No. 1 *(MS. B, 52).* Rectangular edifice divided into three
naves with an apse on either side, terminated by a semicircular theatre with
rising seats, as in antique buildings. The pulpit is in the centre. Leonardo
has written on the left side of the sketch: "teatro da predicare" *(Theatre
for preaching).*

MS. B, 55ª *(see page 56, Fig. 1).* A domed church after the type of
Pl. XCV, No. 1, shows four theatres occupying the apses and facing the
square "coro" *(choir),* which is in the centre between the four pillars of the
dome.[1] The rising arrangement of the seats is shown in the sketch above.
At the place marked B Leonardo wrote teatri per uldire messa *(rows of
seats to hear mass),* at T teatri, and at C coro *(choir).*

In *MS. C.A.* 260, are slight sketches of two plans for rectangular
choirs and two elevations of the altar and pulpit which seem to be in connection with these plans.

In *MS. Ash II,* 8ª *(see p. 56 and 57. Fig. 2 and 3).* "Locho dove si predica" *(Place for preaching).* A most singular plan for a building. The
interior is a portion of a sphere, the centre of which is the summit of
a column destined to serve as the preacher's pulpit. The inside is somewhat

---

[1] *The note* teatro de predicar, *on the right side is, I believe, in the handwriting of Pompeo Leoni.* J. P. R.

Fig. 1.

Fig. 2.

like a modern theatre, whilst the exterior and the galleries and stairs recall the ancient amphitheatres.

Page 57, Fig. 4. A plan accompanying the two preceding drawings. If this gives the complete form Leonardo intended for the edifice, it would

Fig. 3.

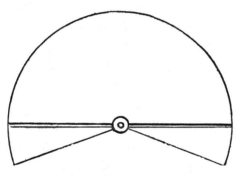

Fig. 4.

have comprised only about two thirds of the circle. Leonardo wrote in the centre "fondamento", *a word he often employed for plans, and on the left side of the view of the exterior:* locho dove si predicha *(a place for preaching in).*

D. Design for a Mausoleum.

Pl. XCVIII (P. V., 182. No. d'ordre 2386). In the midst of a hilly landscape rises an artificial mountain in the form of a gigantic cone, crowned by an imposing temple. At two thirds of the height a terrace is cut out with six doorways forming entrances to galleries, each leading to three sepulchral halls, so constructed as to contain about five hundred funeral urns, disposed in the customary antique style. From two opposite sides steps ascend to the terrace in a single flight and beyond it to the temple above. A large circular opening, like that in the Pantheon, is in the dome above what may be the altar, or perhaps the central monument on the level of the terrace below.

The section of a gallery given in the sketch to the right below shows the roof to be constructed on the principle of superimposed horizontal layers, projecting one beyond the other, and each furnished with a sort of heel, which appears to be undercut, so as to give the appearance of a beam from within. Granite alone would be adequate to the dimensions here given to the key stone, as the thickness of the layers can hardly be considered to be less than a foot. In taking this as the basis of our calculation for the dimensions of the whole construction, the width of the chamber would be about 25 feet but, judging from the number of urns it contains—and there is no reason to suppose that these urns were larger than usual—it would seem to be no more than about 8 or 10 feet.

The construction of the vaults resembles those in the galleries of some etruscan tumuli, for instance the Regulini Galeassi tomb at Cervetri (lately discovered) and also that of the chamber and passages of the pyramid of Cheops and of the treasury of Atreus at Mycenae.

The upper cone displays not only analogies with the monuments mentioned in the note, but also with Etruscan tumuli, such as the Cocumella tomb at Vulci, and the Regulini Galeassi tomb[1]. *The whole scheme is one of the most magnificent in the history of Architecture.*

It would be difficult to decide as to whether any monument he had seen suggested this idea to Leonardo, but it is worth while to enquire, if any monument, or group of monuments of an earlier date may be supposed to have done so.[2]

[1] *See* FERSGUSON, *Handbook of Architecture, I,* 291.

[2] *There are, in Algiers, two Monuments, commonly called* "Le Madracen" *and* "Le tombeau de la Chrétienne," *which somewhat resemble Leonardo's design. They are known to have served as the Mausolea of the Kings of Mauritania. Pomponius Mela, the geographer of the time of the Emperor Claudius, describes them as having been* "Monumentum commune regiae gentis." *See* Le Madracen, Rapport fait par M. le Grand Rabbin AB. CAHEN, Constantine 1873—Mémoire sur les fouilles executées au Madras'en . . par le Colonel BRUNON, Constantine 1873.—Deux Mausolées Africains, le Madracen et le tombeau de la Chrétienne par M. J. DE LAURIÈRE, Tours 1874.—Le tombeau de la Chrétienne, Mausolée des rois Mauritaniens par M. BERBRUGGER, Alger 1867.—*I am indebted to M. LE BLANC, of the Institut, and M. LUD. LALANNE, Bibliothécaire of the Institut for having first pointed out to me the resemblance between these monuments; while M. ANT. HÉRON DE VILLEFOSSE of the Louvre was kind enough to place the abovementioned rare works at my disposal. Leonardo's observations on the coast of Africa are given later in this work. The Herodium near Bethlehem in Palestine* (Jebel el Fureidîs, *the Frank Mountain*) *was, according to the latest researches, constructed on a very similar plan. See* Der Frankenberg, von Baurath C. SCHICK in Jerusalem, Zeitschrift des Deutschen Palästina-Vereins, *Leipzig* 1880, *Vol. III, pages* 88—99 *and Plates IV and V.* J. P. R.

E. Studies for the Central Tower, or Tiburio of Milan Cathedral.

Towards the end of the fifteenth century the Fabbricceria del Duomo *had to settle on the choice of a model for the crowning and central part of this vast building. We learn from a notice published by G. L. Calvi[1] that among the artists who presented models in the year* 1488 *were: Bramante, Pietro da Gorgonzola, Luca Paperio (Fancelli), and Leonardo da Vinci.—*

Several sketches by Leonardo refer to this important project:

Pl. XCIX, No. 2 *(MS. S. K. III, No.* 36ᵃ*) a small plan of the whole edifice.— The projecting chapels in the middle of the transept are wanting here. The nave appears to be shortened and seems to be approached by an inner* "vestibolo".—

Pl. C, No. 2 *(Tr.* 21*). Plan of the octagon tower, giving the disposition of the buttresses; starting from the eight pillars adjoining the four principal piers and intended to support the eight angles of the Tiburio. These buttresses correspond exactly with those described by Bramante as existing in the model presented by Omodeo.[2]*

Pl. C, 3 *(MS. Tr.* 16*). Two plans showing different arrangements of the buttresses, which seem to be formed partly by the intersection of a system of pointed arches such as that seen in*

Pl. C, No. 5 *(MS. B,* 27ᵃ*) destined to give a broader base to the drum. The text underneath is given under No.* 788.

MS. B, 3*—three slight sketches of plans in connexion with the preceding ones.*

[1] G. L. Calvi, Notizie sulla vita e sulle opere dei principali architetti scultori e pittori che fiorirono in Milano, *Part III,* 20. *See also:* H. de Geymüller, Les projets primitifs *etc. I,* 37 *and* 116—119.— *The Fabbricceria of the Duomo has lately begun the publication of the archives, which may possibly tell us more about the part taken by Leonardo, than has hitherto been known.*

[2] *Bramante's opinion was first published by* G. Mongeri, Arch. stor. Lomb. *V, fasc.* 3 *and afterwards by me in the publication mentioned in the preceding note.*

Pl. XCIX, No. 1 (MS. Tr. 15) contains several small sketches of sections and exterior views of the Dome; some of them show buttress-walls shaped as inverted arches. Respecting these Leonardo notes:

Tr. 15]   **758.**

L'arco rivescio è migliore per fare
²spalla che l'ordinario, perchè il rovescio
³trova · sotto · se · muro resistēte alla sua
⁴debolezza, e l'ordinario nō trova nel suo
⁵debole se non aria.

The inverted arch is better for giving a shoulder than the ordinary one, because the former finds below it a wall resisting its weakness, whilst the latter finds in its weak part nothing .but air.

758. 1. larcho. 2. isspalla . . riverscio. 4. deboleza ellordinario.

Three slight sketches of sections on the same leaf—above those repro-duced here—are more closely connected with the large drawing in the centre of

Pl. C, No. 4 (MS, Tr. 41) which shows a section of a very elevated dome, with double vaults, connected by ribs and buttresses ingeniously dis-posed, so as to bring the weight of the lantern to bear on the base of the dome.

A sketch underneath it shows a round pillar on which is indicated which part of its summit is to bear the weight: "il pilastro sarà charicho in · a · b." *(The column will bear the weight at* a b.*) Another note is above on the right side:* Larcho regierà tanto sotto asse chome di sopra ⁵e *(The arch supports as much below it [i. e. a hanging weight] as above it).*

Pl. C, No. 1 (C. A. 303ᵃ). Larger sketch of half section of the Dome, with a very complicated system of arches, and a double vault. Each stone ¹ˢ *shaped so as to be knit or dovetailed to its neighbours. Thus the inside of the Dome cannot be seen from below.*

MS. C. A. 303ᵇ. A repetition of the preceding sketch with very slight modifications.

Fig. 1.

Fig. 2.

MS. Tr. 9 (see Fig. 1 and 2). Section of the Dome with reverted buttresses between the windows, above which iron anchors or chains seem to be intended. Below is the sketch of the outside.

Pl. XCIX, No. 3 *(C. A.,* 262ᵃ*) four sketches of the exterior of the Dome.*

C. A. 12. *Section, showing the points of rupture of a gothic vault, in evident connection with the sketches described above.*

It deserves to be noticed how easily and apparently without effort, Leonardo manages to combine gothic details and structure with the more modern shape of the Dome.

The following notes are on the same leaf, oni cosa pōderosa, *and* oni cosa pōderosa desidera de(scendere); *farther below, several multiplications most likely intended to calculate the weight of some parts of the Dome, thus* 16 × 47 = 720; 720 × 800 = 176000, *next to which is written:* peso del pilastro di 9 teste *(weight of the pillar 9 diameters high).*

Below: 176000 × 8 = 1408000; *and below:*

Semjliō e se cē 80 (?) il peso del tiburio

(six millions six hundred (?) 80 the weight of the Dome),

Bossi hazarded the theory that Leonardo might have been the architect who built the church of Sta. Maria delle Grazie, but there is no evidence to support this, either in documents or in the materials supplied by Leonardo's manuscripts and drawings. The sketch given at the side shows the arrangement of the second and third socle on the apses of the choir of that church; and it is remarkable that those sketches, in MS. S. K. M. II², 2ᵃ and 1ᵇ, occur with the passage given in Volume I as No. 665 and 666 referring to the composition of the Last Supper in the Refectory of that church.

F. The Project for lifting up the Battistero of Florence and setting it on a basement.

Among the very few details Vasari gives as to the architectural studies of Leonardo, we read: "And among these models and designs there was one by way of which he showed several times to many ingenious citizens who then governed Florence, his readiness to lift up without ruining it, the church of San Giovanni in Florence (the Battistero, opposite the Duomo) in order to place under it the missing basement with steps; he supported his assertions with reasons so persuasive, that while he spoke the undertaking seemed feasable, although every one of his hearers, when he had departed, could see by himself the impossibility of so vast an undertaking."[1]

In the MS. C. A. fol. 293, there are two sketches which possibly might have a bearing on this bold enterprise. We find there a plan of a circular or polygonal edifice surrounded by semicircular arches in an oblique position. These may be taken for the foundation of the steps and of the new platform. In the perspective elevation the same edifice, forming a polygon, is shown as lifted up and resting on a circle of inverted arches which rest on an other circle of arches in the ordinary position, but so placed that the inverted arches above rest on the spandrels of the lower range.

What seems to confirm the supposition that the lifting up of a building is here in question, is the indication of engines for winding up, such as jacks, and a rack and wheel. As the lifting apparatus represented on this sheet does not seem particularly applicable to an undertaking of such magnitude, we may consider it to be a first sketch or scheme for the engines to be used.

[1] *This latter statement of Vasari's must be considered to be exaggerated. I may refer here to some data given by* LIBRI, Histoire des sciences mathématiques en Italie (II, 216, 217): "On a cru dans ces derniers temps faire un miracle en mécanique en effectuant ce transport, et cependant dès l'année 1455, Gaspard Nadi et Aristote de Fioravantio avaient transporté, à une distance considérable, la tour de la Magione de Bologne, avec ses fondements, qui avait presque quatre-vingts pieds de haut. Le continuateur de la chronique de Pugliola dit que le trajet fut de 35 pieds et que durant le transport auquel le chroniqueur affirme avoir assisté, il arriva un accident grave qui fit pencher de trois pieds la tour pendant qu'elle était suspendue, mais que cet accident fut promptement reparé (Muratori, Scriptores rer. ital. Tom. XVIII, col. 717, 718). Alidosi a rapporté une note où Nadi rend compte de ce transport avec une rare simplicité. D'après cette note, on voit que les opérations de ce genre n'étaient pas nouvelles. Celle-ci ne coûta que 150 livres (monnaie d'alors) y compris le cadeau que le Légat fit aux deux mécaniciens. Dans la même année, Aristote redressa le clocher de Cento, qui penchait de plus de cinq pieds (Alidosi, instruttione p. 188 — Muratori, Scriptores rer. ital., tom. XXIII, col. 888. — Bossii, chronica Mediol., 1492, in-fol. ad ann. 1455). On ne conçoit pas comment les historiens des beaux-arts ont pu négliger de tels hommes." J. P. R.

G. *Description of an unknown Temple.*

Per dodici gradi di scale al magno tempio si saliva, il quale otto cento braccia circundaua, e con ottāgulare ²figura era fabricato, e sopra li otto anguli otto gran base si posauano a un braccio e mezzo, e grosse 3, ³e lunghe 6 nel suo sodo, coll'angolo in mezzo, sopra delle quali si fondauano 8 grā pilastri: sopra del sodo della basa si le⁴vava per ispatio di 24 braccia, e nel suo termine erano stabiliti 8 capitelli di 3 braccia l'uno, e largo 6, sopra di questi se⁵guiva architraue fregio e cornice con altezza di 4 braccia e ¹/₂, il quale per retta linia ⁶dall' un pilastro all' altro s'astendea, e così con circuito d'otto cento braccia il tempio circundava infra l' ū ⁷pilastro e l'altro; per sostentacolo di tal mēbro erano stabiliti dieci gran coloñe dell' altezza de' pilastri e cō ⁸grossezza di 3 braccia sopra le base, le quali erā alte vn braccio e ¹/₂.

⁹Salivasi a questo tenpio per 12 gradi di scale, il quale tempio era sopra il dodecimo grado fondato in figura ottan¹⁰gulare, e sopra ciascuno angulo nasceva vn gran pilastro; e infra li pilastri erano inframessi ¹¹dieci

Twelve flights of steps led up to the great temple, which was eight hundred braccia in circumference and built on an octagonal plan. At the eight corners were eight large plinths, one braccia and a half high, and three wide, and six long at the bottom, with an angle in the middle; on these were eight great pillars, standing on the plinths as a foundation, and twenty four braccia high. And on the top of these were eight capitals three braccia long and six wide, above which were the architrave frieze and cornice, four braccia and a half high, and this was carried on in a straight line from one pillar to the next and so, continuing for eight hundred braccia, surrounded the whole temple, from pillar to pillar. To support this entablature there were ten large columns of the same height as the pillars, three braccia thick above their bases which were one braccia and a half high.

The ascent to this temple was by twelve flights of steps, and the temple was on the twelfth, of an octagonal form, and at each angle rose a large pillar; and between the pillars were placed ten columns of the

---

759. 1. di sala al . . otāgulare. 2. posaua alte v br e mezo. 3. ellungha . . collangholo imezo . . fondaua. 4. ne di 24 br e . . era stabilito . . di 3 br . luno . . "elargo 6". 5. alteza di 4 br e 1/2 [el simile] il quale. 6. pilastra . . circuito dotto cento br . . infrallū. 7. ellaltro per sostentachulo . . era stabilito . . colone dellalteza. 8. grossezza di 3 br . . vnbr. 9. acquesto . . disscale . . dode | "cimo" . . otta. 10: tangulare [e inf] e sopra . . infralli . . era inframeso. 11. cola . . alteza . . 28

---

759. Either this description is incomplete, or, as seems to me highly probable, it refers to some ruin. The enormous dimensions forbid our supposing this to be any temple in Italy or Greece. Syria was the native land of colossal octagonal buildings, in the early centuries A. D. The Temple of Baalbek, and others are even larger than that here described.

J. P. R.

colonne colla medesima altezza de' pilastri, i quali si levauā sopra del pauimēto · 28 braccia e ¹/₂ ; sopra ¹²di questa medesima altezza si posaua architraue fregio e cornice con lunghezza d'otto cēto braccia, e cignea ¹³il tenpio a vna medesima altezza circuiua dentro a tal circuito sopra il medesimo piano; in giro in centro del tempio per spatio di 24 braccia nascono ¹⁴le conrispondentie delli 8 pilastri delli angoli, e delle colonne poste a esse prime faccie, e si ¹⁵leuauano alla medesima altezza sopra detta, e sopra tal pilastri li architraui perpetui ¹⁶ritornavano sopra li primi detti pilastri e colonne.

same height as the pillars, rising at once from the pavement to a height of twenty eight braccia and a half; and at this height the architrave, frieze and cornice were placed which surrounded the temple having a length of eight hundred braccia. At the same height, and within the temple at the same level, and all round the centre of the temple at a distance of 24 braccia farther in, are pillars corresponding to the eight pillars in the angles, and columns corresponding to those placed in the outer spaces. These rise to the same height as the former ones, and over these the continuous architrave returns towards the outer row of pillars and columns.

br e ¹ 2. 12. ,di queste sta . . alteza . . frego e corice cho collungeza dotto cēto br cigea. 13. alteza . . attal . . piano | "iciero il centro del tenpio per ispatio di 24 br . nasscie. 14. e delle [ottamta] colone . . facce essi. 15. alteza sopra [di que] detta.

V. Palace architecture.

But a small number of Leonardo's drawings refer to the architecture of palaces, and our knowledge is small as to what style Leonardo might have adopted for such buildings.

Pl. CII No. 1 (W. XVIII). A small portion of a façade of a palace in two stories, somewhat resembling Alberti's Palazzo Rucellai.—Compare with this Bramante's painted front of the Casa Silvestri, and a painting by Montorfano in San Pietro in Gessate at Milan, third chapel on the left hand side and also with Bramante's palaces at Rome. The pilasters with arabesques, the rustica between them, and the figures over the window may be painted or in sgraffito. The original is drawn in red chalk.

Pl. LXXXI No. 1 (MS. Tr. 42). Sketch of a palace with battlements and decorations, most likely graffiti; the details remind us of those in the Castello at Vigevano.[1]

MS. Mz. 0", contains a design for a palace or house with a loggia in the middle of the first story, over which rises an attic with a Pediment reproduced on page 67. The details drawn close by on the left seem to indicate an arrangement of coupled columns against the wall of a first story.

Pl. LXXXV No. 14 (MS. S. K. M. III 79ª) contains a very slight

---

[1] *Count* GIULIO PORRO, *in his valuable contribution to the* Archivio Storico Lombardo, Anno VIII, Fasc. IV (31 Dec. 1881): Leonardo da Vinci, Libro di Annotazioni e Memorie, *refers to this in the following note:* "Alla pag. 41 vi è uno schizzo di volta ed accanto scrisse: 'il pilastro sarà charicho in su 6' e potrebbe darsi che si riferisse alla cupola della chiesa delle Grazie tanto più che a pag. 42 vi è un disegno che rassomiglia assai al basamento che oggi si vede nella parte esterna del coro di quella chiesa." *This may however be doubted. The drawing, here referred to, on page* 41 *of the same manuscript, is reproduced on Pl. C No.* 4 *and described on page* 61 *as being a study for the cupola of the Duomo of Milan.*   J. P. R.

sketch in red chalk, which most probably is intended to represent the façade of a palace. Inside is the short note 7 he 7 (7 and 7).

MS. J² 8ᵃ (see pages 68 Fig. 1 and 2) contains a view of an unknown palace. Its plan is indicated at the side.

In MS. Br. M. 126ᵃ (see Fig. 3 on page 68) there is a sketch of a house, on which Leonardo notes: casa con tre terrazi *(house with three terraces).*

Pl. CX, No. 4 (MS. L. 36ᵇ) represents the front of a fortified building drawn at Cesena in 1502 (see No. 1040).

Fig. 2.   Fig. 1.

Fig. 3.

Here we may also mention the singular building in the allegorical composition represented on Pl. LVIII in Vol. I. In front of it appears the head of a sphinx or of a dragon which seems to be carrying the palace away.

The following texts refer to the construction of palaces and other buildings destined for private use:

On the proportions of a court yard. La corte de' auere le parieti ²per l'al-tezza la metà della sua ³larghezza, cioè se la corte ⁴sarà braccia 40, la casa deve essere ⁵alta 20 nelle parieti di tal ⁶corte, e tal corte vol essere ⁷larga per la metà di tutta la ⁸facciata.

In the courtyard the walls must be half the height of its width, that is if the court be 40 braccia, the house must be 20 high as regards the walls of the said courtyard; and this courtyard must be half as wide as the whole front.

760. 1. pariete. 2. lalteza. 3. largezza coe sella. 4. br 40 . la casa e essere. 5. alte . . pariete. 6. volerssere. 7. faccata.

760. See Pl. CI, no. 1, and compare the dimensions here given, with No. 748 lines 26—29; and the drawing belonging to it Pl. LXXXI, no. 2.

B. 39 *a*]   **761.**

PER FARE VNA POLITA STALLA.

[2]Modo · come · si de' · componere · vna · stalla: Dividerai in prima la sua lar[3]ghezza · in parti · 3 · e la sua lunghezza è libera·, e le · 3 · dette divisioni [4]sieno equali e di larghezza di braccia 6 per ciascuna, e alte 10, e la parte di mezzo [5]sia in uso · de' maestri di stalla ·, le 2 da cāto per i cavagli, de' quali ciascuno ne de' [6]pigliare per larghezza braccia 6 ·, lūghezza braccia 6, e alte piv dinanti · che dirieto · ¹/₂ · braccio; [7]la mangiatoia sia alta da terra braccia 2, il principio della rastrelliera [8]braccia · 3 · e l'ultimo · braccia 4 ·; Ora · a volere atenere · quello ch'io prometto, cioè di [9]fare detto sito cōtro allo universale vso · pulito e netto · inquāto al · di sopra [10]della stalla·, cioè dove sta il fieno ·, debe detto loco avere nella sua testa di fori vna [11]finestra alta 6 · e larga · 6, donde con vn facil modo si cōduca il fieno su detto [12]solaro, come appare nello strumēto *E*·, e sia collocata ī un sito di larghez[13]za di braccia 6, e lungo quāto la stalla, come appare in · *k·p·* e l'altre 2 parti [14]che mettano in mezzo · questa, ciascuna sia diuisa in 2 parti, le dua diverso il fieno sia[15]no braccia 4 ·, *p · s* ·, solo allo ofitio e andamento de' ministri d'essa stalla, l'altre [16]2 che confinano colle parieti murali · sieno di braccia 2, come appare in *s · k* ·, [17]e queste sieno allo ofitio di dare · il feno alle māgiatoie · per condotti stretti nel [18]principio e larghi sulle māgiatoie, acciò che'l feno nō si fermi infra via, sieno [19]bene ītonicati e politi, figurati dov'è segnato *4*. *f · s* ·; in quanto al dare [20]bere siano le māgiatoie di pietra, sopra le quali sia l'acqua, si chè si possino [21]scoprire le māgiatoie come si scoprono le casse, alzādo i coperchi loro.

FOR MAKING A CLEAN STABLE.

On the dispositions of a stable.

The manner in which one must arrange a stable. You must first divide its width in 3 parts, its depth matters not; and let these 3 divisions be equal and 6 braccia broad for each part and 10 high, and the middle part shall be for the use of the stablemasters; the 2 side ones for the horses, each of which must be 6 braccia in width and 6 in length, and be half a braccio higher at the head than behind. Let the manger be at 2 braccia from the ground, to the bottom of the rack, 3 braccia, and the top of it 4 braccia. Now, in order to attain to what I promise, that is to make this place, contrary to the general custom, clean and neat: as to the upper part of the stable, i. e. where the hay is, that part must have at its outer end a window 6 braccia high and 6 broad, through which by simple means the hay is brought up to the loft, as is shown by the machine *E*; and let this be erected in a place 6 braccia wide, and as long as the stable, as seen at *k p*. The other two parts, which are on either side of this, are again divided; those nearest to the hay-loft are 4 braccia, *p s*, and only for the use and circulation of the servants belonging to the stable; the other two which reach to the outer walls are 2 braccia, as seen at *s k*, and these are made for the purpose of giving hay to the mangers, by means of funnels, narrow at the top and wide over the manger, in order that the hay should not choke them. They must be well plastered and clean and are represented at *4 f s*. As to the giving the horses water, the troughs must be of stone and above them [cisterns of] water. The mangers may be opened as boxes are uncovered by raising the lids.

761. 2. chome . . chomponere . . isstalla. 3. geza in parte. 3. ella . . lungeza . . decte· 4. largeza di br 6 . . mezo. 6. largeza br . 3 ellūgeza br 6 . . 1/2 br. 7. la mangiatoria sialta dacterra br . 2 . [larastella era] il . . dela rastelliera. 8. br . 3 . ellultimo br 4 . . attenere . . promecto. 9. decto . . necto. 10. feno . . decto . . nela. 11. feno. 12. apare . . essia colocata . . large. 13. br 6 . . apare in K. p. laltre e laltre. 14. metano imezo . . si diuisa . . feno. 15. no br 4 "p . s" . . ofitio [de mini si ribe] e andamento. 16. 2 che che chonfinano chole pariete . . br 2 . . apare. 17. ecqueste . . māgiatore . per condocti strecti. 18. sule māgiatore acio. 20. le māgiatore . . sia la sichessi. 21. māgiatore chome si schoprano.

761. See Pl. LXXVIII, No. 1.

B. 28b]   762.

MODO COME SI FANNO ²L'ARMATURE PER FARE   THE WAY TO CONSTRUCT A FRAME-WORK FOR
        ³ORNAMĒTO ⁴DI EDIFITI.   DECORATING BUILDINGS.

Decorations ⁵Modo come si debbono ⁶mettere le per-   The way in which the poles ought to be
for feasts. tiche ⁷per legare i mazzuoli ⁸de' ginepri   placed for tying bunches of juniper on to
sopra esse ⁹pertiche, le quali sono ¹⁰confitte   them. These poles must lie close to the frame-
sopra l'ar¹¹matura della vol¹²ta e lega essi   work of the vaulting and tie the bunches on
ma¹³zzuoli con salci e ¹⁴sù per fare cimerosa   with osier withes, so as to clip them even
¹⁵colle forbici e la¹⁶vora le cō salci;   afterwards with shears.
    ¹⁷Sia da l'u¹⁸no all' altro ¹⁹cerchio uno   Let the distance from one circle to another
²⁰ ¹/₂ braccio e 'l gi²¹nepro si de' ²²regiere   be half a braccia; and the juniper [sprigs]
col²³le cime in giv ²⁴cōmīciādo ²⁵di sotto;   must lie top downwards, beginning from below.
    ²⁶A questa colonna si lega ²⁷d'intorno   Round this column tie four poles to
4 pertiche, dintor²⁸no alle quali s'inchioda   which willows about as thick as a finger must
²⁹vinchi grossi uno dito · e poi ³⁰si fa da   be nailed and then begin from the bottom
piè e vassi in alto legā³¹do mazzuoli di   and work upwards with bunches of juniper
cime di ³²ginepro colle cime j̄ ba³³ssò cioè   sprigs, the tops downwards, that is upside
sotto sopra.   down.

Br. M. 192a]   763.

Sia lasciata cadere l'acqua ²in   The water should be allowed to

tutto il cerchio di *a · b*.   fall from the whole circle *a b*.

762. 1. fa. 2. larmadure. 5. debe. 7. mazoli. 10. chõfitte. 11. madura. 13. coli chon salcie[l]e. 16. cosalci. 19. cierchio ĩ.
    20. ¹/₂ br. 22. cho. 26. acquesta. 28. ale. 29. ĩ dito. 31. mazoli di [gin] cime. 32. cholle.
763. 1. lacq"a". 2. totto il cierchio.

    762. See Pl. CII, No. 3. The words here given   763. Other drawings of fountains are given on
as the title line, lines 1—4, are the last in the ori-   Pl. CI (W. XX); the original is a pen and ink drawing
ginal MS.—Lines 5—16 are written under fig. 4.   on blue paper; on Pl. CIII (MS. B.) and Pl. LXXXII.

VI. Studies of architectural details.

Several of Leonardo's drawings of architectural details prove that, like other great masters of that period, he had devoted his attention to the study of the proportion of such details. As every organic being in nature has its law of construction and growth, these masters endeavoured, each in his way, to discover and prove a law of proportion in architecture. The following notes in Leonardo's manuscripts refer to this subject.

Fig. 1.

Fig. 2.

MS. S. K. M. III, 47[b] (see Fig. 1). A diagram, indicating the rules as given by Vitruvius and by Leon Battista Alberti for the proportions of the Attic base of a column.

MS. S. K. M. III 55[a] (see Fig. 2). Diagram showing the same rules.

S. K. M. III. 48 a]   **764.**

B toro superiore	toro superiore
[2]**B** nestroli	astragali quadre
[3]**B** orbiculo	. . troclea
[4]**B** nestroli	astragali quadre
[5]**B** toro ĩferiore	. toro ĩferiore
[6]**B** latastro	. plintho

L. 19 b; 20 a]   **765.**

SCALE D' URBINO.

[3]Il latastro deve [4]essere largo quā[5]to la grossezza di qua[6]lūque muro dove [7]tale latastro s' ap[8]poggia.

STEPS OF URBINO.

The plinth must be as broad as the thickness of the wall against which the plinth is built.

C. A. 318 a; 961 a]   **766.**

I nostri antichi architettori . . . . comīciando in prima dagli Egitti, i quali secōdo che descrive Diodoro Sicolo [2]furō i primi edificatori e componitori di città grandissime e di castelli ed edifizi publici e privati di forma, grandezza [3]e qualità · per le quali i loro antecedēti riguardevoli con stupefazione e maraviglia [4]le eleuate e grandissime macchine parēdo loro . . . .

[5]La colonna ch'à la sua grossezza nel terzo . . . . [6]quella che fusse sottile nel mezzo ronperassi nelle..; [7]quella ch'è di pari grossezza e di pari fortezza è migliore per l'edifizio, [8]seconda di bontà sarà quella ch'à la maggior grossezza dov' ella si cōgivgnie colla [9]basa.

The ancient architects . . . . . . beginning with the Egyptians (?) who, as Diodorus Siculus writes, were the first to build and construct large cities and castles, public and private buildings of fine form, large and well proportioned . . . . .

The column, which has its thickness at the third part . . . . The one which would be thinnest in the middle, would break...; the one which is of equal thickness and of equal strength, is better for the edifice. The second best as to usefulness will be the one whose greatest thickness is where it joins with the base.

764. 1. toro superio . . super. 2. nexstroli. 3. torclea. 5. inferior . . ĩferi. 6. [plato] plinto.

765. 2. [il muro]. 3, illatasstro debbe. 4. [g] largo. 5. grosseza di qu"a". 7. latastro. 8. pogga.

766. 1—.. *written from left to right.* 1. nosstri . . otalecine chomīciando . . daglitii˙. . sechōdo . . desscriue . . sicholo. 2. edi˙ fichatori e chomponitori di cita . . chasstella. 4. grandeza . . anticiedēti [gestupessani che] righuardevoli chonnistupefazione . . loro; *here the text breaks off.* 5. cholonna . . groseza terzo qui . ve ana aroper se (?) 6. . . mezo . . nelle 2 ispasia.

764. No explanation can be offered of the meaning of the letter B, which precedes each name. It may be meant for *basa* (base). Perhaps it refers to some author on architecture or an architect (Bramante?) who employed the designations, thus marked for the mouldings.

3. *troclea.* Philander: *Trochlea sive trochalia aut rechanum.*

6. *Laterculus* or *latastrum* is the Latin name for *Plinthus* (πλίνθος), but Vitruvius adopted this Greek name and "latastro" seems to have been little

in use. It is to be found besides the text given above, as far as I am aware, only on two drawings of the Uffizi Collection, where, in one instance, it indicates the *abacus* of a Doric capital.

765. See Pl. CX No. 3. The hasty sketch on the right hand side illustrates the unsatisfactory effect produced when the plinth is narrower than the wall.

766. See Pl. CIII, No. 3, where the sketches belonging to lines 10—16 are reproduced, but reversed. The sketch of columns, here reproduced by a wood cut, stands in the original close to lines 5—8.

¹⁰Il capitello à a essere ɉ questo formato, dividi la sua grossezza da capo ɉ 8 d' ū piè ····· ¹¹e fa che sia alto ⁵/₇ e verrà a essere quadro, dipoi dividi l'altezza ɉ 8, come facesti la colonna, di poi poni ¹/₈ l'uovolo ¹²e un altro ottavo la grossezza della tavola che sta di sopra al capitello; ¹³i corni della tavola del capitello àno a sportare fuori dalla maggior larghezza della cāpana ²/₇ ¹⁴ cioè settimi del di sopra della cāpana che tocca a ciascū corno di sporto ¹/₇ · ¹⁵e la mozzatura de' corni vuole essere largha quāt' è alta, cioè ¹/₈ ; ɉl resto degli ornamēti lascio ¹⁶jn libertà degli scultori; ¹⁷ma per tornare alle colonne, e provare la ragione secondo la forma di lor fortezza ¹⁸o debolezza, dico così, che quādo le linie si partiranno dalla sommità della ¹⁹colonna e termineranno nel suo nascimēto e la lor uia e lūghezza sia di pari ²⁰distanzia o latitudine, dico che questa colonna . . . .

The capital must be formed in this way. Divide its thickness at the top into 8; at the foot make it ⁵/₇, and let it be ⁵/₇ high and you will have a square; afterwards divide the height into 8 parts as you did for the column, and then take ¹/₈ for the echinus and another eighth for the thickness of the abacus on the top of the capital. The horns of the abacus of the capital have to project beyond the greatest width of the bell ²/₇, i.e. sevenths of the top of the bell, so ¹/₇ falls to the projection of each horn. The truncated part of the horns must be as broad as it is high. I leave the rest, that is the ornaments, to the taste of the sculptors. But to return to the columns and in order to prove the reason of their strength or weakness according to their shape, I say that when the lines starting from the summit of the column and ending at its base and their direction and length . . ., their distance apart or width may be equal; I say that this column . . . .

Ash. III. 13*b*]　　　　　　　**767.**

Il cilindro d'vn corpo di figura colō²nale, e le sua opposité fronti sō due cierchi ³d'interpositione paralella ⁴e infra li lor ciētri s'estēde una linia ⁵retta, che passa per il mezzo della grossezza ⁶del cilindro e termina nelli ciētri ⁷d'essi cierchi, la quale linia dalli antichi è detta axis.

The cylinder of a body columnar in shape and its two opposite ends are two circles enclosed between parallel lines, and through the centre of the cylinder is a straight line, ending at the centre of these circles, and called by the ancients the axis.

H.3 73*b*]　　　　　　　**768.**

〜 *a* · *b* · ¹/₃ di · *n* · *m* · ; ²*m* · *o* ¹/₆ di *r o*; ³l'ovo sporta ¹/₆ di *r* · *o*; ⁴ *s* · 7 ¹/₅ di *r* · *o* ⁵*a* · *b* si diuida in 9 e ¹/₂ ⁶l'abaco è ³/₉; ⁷ovo ⁴/₉; ⁸fusaiolo e listello ²/₉ e ¹/₂.

a b is ¹/₃ of *n m*; *m o* is ¹/₆ of *r o*. The ovolo projects ¹/₆ of *r o*; *s* 7¹/₅ of *r o*, *a b* is divided into 9¹/₂; the abacus is ³/₉ the ovolo ⁴/₉, the bead-moulding and the fillet ²/₉ and ¹/₂.

7. grosseza . . forteza. 8. sechonda . . magior grosseza dovela . . chōgivgnie cholla. 10. chapitello . . grosseza da chapo ɉ 7 | 8 dupie ne me 5/7. 11. evera . . lalteza . . chome . . cholona . . poni 1/8 luovolo. 12. grosseza dalla . . chessta . . chapitello. 13. i chorni . . chapitello . . assorportera . . della magior largheza . . chāpana. 14. cio settimi . . chāpana che tocha a ciasschū chorno dissporto 1/7. 15. mozatura de de chorni . . essre largha . . ɉ resto. 16. ischultori . . 17. cholonne . . sechondo . . forteza. 18. deboleza dicho chosi che quādo [che qual] le. 19. cholonna ettermineranno . . nasscimēto ella . . ellūgheza. 20. l disstanzia . . dicho . . cholonna. *Here the text breaks off.*

767. 1. El chilindro . . chorpo . . cholō. 2. elle . . fronte. 3. dinterpositio paraḷella · e infra li lor ciētri. 4. sastēde . . linia pa. 5. mezo . . grossetta. 6. chilindro ottermina. 7. linia di detta. 8. linia cietrale e dalli . . assis.

768. 1—8 R. 6. labaco he. 7. hovo. 8. fesaiolo.

767. Leonardo wrote these lines on the margin of a page of the Trattato di Francesco di Giorgio, where there are several drawings of columns, as well as a head drawn in profile inside an outline sketch of a capital.

768. See Pl. LXXXV, No. 16. In the original the drawing and writing are both in red chalk.

Pl. LXXXV No. 6 (MS. Ash. II 6^b) contains a small sketch of a capital with the following note, written in three lines: I chorni del capitelo deono essere la quarta parte d'uno quadro *(The horns of a capital must measure the fourth part of a square).*

MS. S. K. M. III 72^b contains two sketches of ornamentations of windows.

In MS. C. A. 308^a; 938^a (see Pl. LXXXII No. 1*) there are several sketches of columns. One of the two columns on the right is similar to those employed by Bramante at the Canonica di S. Ambrogio. The same columns appear in the sketch underneath the plan of a castle. There they appear coupled, and in two stories one above the other. The archivolts which seem to spring out of the columns, are shaped like twisted cords, meant perhaps to be twisted branches. The walls between the columns seem to be formed out of blocks of wood, the pedestals are ornamented with a reticulated pattern. From all this we may suppose that Leonardo here had in mind either some festive decoration, or perhaps a pavilion for some hunting place or park. The sketch of columns marked "35" gives an example of columns shaped like candelabra, a form often employed at that time, particularly in Milan, and the surrounding districts for instance in the Cortile di Casa Castiglione now Silvestre, in the cathedral of Como, at Porta della Rana &c.*

G. 52 a]   **769.**

DELLI ARCHITRAVI DI UNO ²E DI PIÙ PEZZI.	CONCERNING ARCHITRAVES OF ONE OR SEVERAL PIECES.

³L'architrave di più pezzi è più potēte che quel d'ū ⁴sol pezzo, essendo essi pezzi colle lor lunghezze situati ⁵per inverso il cētro del mōdo; pruovasi perchè ⁶le pietre ànno il neruo overo tiglio gienerato per il tra⁷verso, cioè per il uerso delli orizzonti opposti d'un mede⁸simo emisperio, e questo è contrario al tiglio delle ⁹piāte le quali ànno . . .

An architrave of several pieces is stronger than that of one single piece, if those pieces are placed with their length in the direction of the centre of the world. This is proved because stones have their grain or fibre generated in the contrary direction *i. e.* in the direction of the opposite horizons of the hemisphere, and this is contrary to fibres of the plants which have . . .

769. 1. di î. 2. eddi 4. 3. eppiu . . che cquel. 4. pezo . . cholle . . lungheza. 7. orizonti opopositi. 8. ecquesto e chontrario.

769. The text is incomplete in the original.

The Proportions of the stories of a building are indicated by a sketch in MS. S. K. M. II² 11^b (see Pl. LXXXV No. 15*). The measures are written on the left side, as follows:* br 1^{1}|_{2}—6^{3}|_{4}—br ^{1}|_{12}—2 br—9 e ^{1}|_{2}—1^{1}|_{2}—br 5—ō 9—ō 3 *[br = braccia; ō = oncie].*

Pl. LXXXV No. 13 *(MS. B. 62^a) and Pl. XCIII No.* 1. *(MS. B. 15^a) give a few examples of arches supported on piers.*

XIII.

Theoretical writings on Architecture.

Leonardo's original writings on the theory of Architecture have come down to us only in a fragmentary state; still, there seems to be no doubt that he himself did not complete them. It would seem that Leonardo entertained the idea of writing a large and connected book on Architecture; and it is quite evident that the materials we possess, which can be proved to have been written at different periods, were noted down with a more or less definite aim and purpose. They might all be collected under the one title: "Studies on the Strength of Materials". Among them the investigations on the subject of fissures in walls are particularly thorough, and very fully reported; these passages are also especially interesting, because Leonardo was certainly the first writer on architecture who ever treated the subject at all. Here, as in all other cases Leonardo carefully avoids all abstract argument. His data are not derived from the principles of algebra, but from the laws of mechanics, and his method throughout is strictly experimental.

Though the conclusions drawn from his investigations may not have that precision which we are accustomed to find in Leonardo's scientific labours, their interest is not lessened. They prove at any rate his deep sagacity and wonderfully clear mind. No one perhaps, who has studied these questions since Leonardo, has combined with a scientific mind anything like the artistic delicacy of perception which gives interest and lucidity to his observations.

I do not assert that the arrangement here adopted for the passages in question is that originally intended by Leonardo; but their distribution into five groups was suggested by the titles, or headings, which Leonardo himself prefixed to most of these notes. Some of the longer sections perhaps should not, to be in strict agreement with this divi-

sion, have been reproduced in their entirety in the place where they occur. But the comparatively small amount of the materials we possess will render them, even so, sufficiently intelligible to the reader; it did not therefore seem necessary or desirable to subdivide the passages merely for the sake of strict classification.

The small number of chapters given under the fifth class, treating on the centre of gravity in roof-beams, bears no proportion to the number of drawings and studies which refer to the same subject. Only a small selection of these are reproduced in this work since the majority have no explanatory text.

I.

ON FISSURES IN WALLS.

Br. M. 157 a]

770.

Fa prima il trattato delle cause giene-ratrici del²le rotture de' muri, e poi il trattato de'rimedi separato.

³Li fessi paralelli sono vniversalmēte gienerati ⁴in quelli edifiti che si edificano in lochi montuosi, li ⁵quali sien cōposti di pietre faldate con obbliquo ⁶faldamēto, e perchè in tale obbliquità spesso penetra ⁷acqua e altra vmidità portatricie di cierta terra ⁸vntuosa e sdrucciolante ·, e perchè tali falde nō sono ⁹continuate insino al fon-do delle valli, ¹⁰tali pietre si muovono per la loro obli¹¹quità e mai termināo il moto insin ¹²che discendono al fondo della valle, ¹³portando con seco a vso di barca ¹⁴quella parte dello edifitio che per lo¹⁵ro si separa dal suddetto rimanēte;

¹⁶Il rimedio di questo è il fondare spes-¹⁷si pilastri sotto il muro che si move, ¹⁸e con archi dall' uno all' altro e be¹⁹ne ab-barbicati, e questi tali ²⁰pilastri sieno fun-da²¹ti e fermi ²²nelle falde le quali non sieno rotte;

²³Per trovare la parte stabile delle sopra dette falde è neciessario fare vn ²⁴pozzo sotto il piè del muro cō grā profondità in-fra esse falde ²⁵e di tal pozzo pulirne cō piana superfitie la larghezza d'un palmo

First write the treatise on the causes of the giving way of walls and then, separately, treat of the remedies.

Parallel fissures constantly occur in buildings which are erected on a hill side, when the hill is composed of stratified rocks with an oblique stratification, because water and other moisture often penetrates these oblique seams carrying in greasy and slippery soil; and as the strata are not con-tinuous down to the bottom of the valley, the rocks slide in the direction of the slope, and the motion does not cease till they have reached the bottom of the valley, carrying with them, as though in a boat, that portion of the building which is separated by them from the rest. The remedy for this is always to build thick piers under the wall which is slipping, with arches from one to another, and with a good scarp and let the piers have a firm foundation in the strata so that they may not break away from them.

In order to find the solid part of these strata, it is necessary to make a shaft at the foot of the wall of great depth through the strata; and in this shaft, on the side from which the hill slopes, smooth and flatten a

770. 1. chause. 3. [di] sono. 4. chessi edifichano illochi. 5. chōposti . . chon obbriquo. 8. essdrucciolente. 9. chontinovate. 10. tale . . simovan. 12. cheddisciendano. 13. chonsecho . . barcha. 16. Irimedio . . spe. 17. pilasstri . . chessi. 18. chon. 19. abarbatiati esti. 20. pilasstri. 21. effermi. 22. rutte. 23. per [del]. 24. pozzo [no] sotto . . chō. 25. pozo . . chō . .

770. See Pl. CIV.

²⁶dalla sōmità insino al fondo da quel lato, donde il mōte discēde, ²⁷e in capo d'alquāto tempo questa parte pulita, che si fecie nella pa²⁸riete del pozzo, mostrerà manifesto segnio qual parte del mōte si move.

space one palm wide from the top to the bottom; and after some time this smooth portion made on the side of the shaft, will show plainly which part of the hill is moving.

Br. M. 157 b]   771.

Mai le fessure de' muri ²sarā paralelle, fuor che se la ³parte del muro, la quàl ⁴si separa dal suo rimanēte, ⁵non discēda.

The cracks in walls will never be parallel unless the part of the wall that separates from the remainder does not slip down.

QUALE REGOLA È QUELLA CHE FA ⁷LI EDIFITI PERMANĒTI.

WHAT IS THE LAW BY WHICH BUILDINGS HAVE STABILITY.

⁸La permanētia delli edifiti è la regola contra⁹ria alle 2 anteciedēti, cioè che le muraglie ¹⁰sieno eleuate in alto tutte equalmēte con e quali ¹¹gradi, che abbraccino l'intera circuitione dello ¹²edifitio colle intere grossezze di qualunque sorte di ¹³muri, e ancora che il muro sottile secchi più pre-¹⁴sto che il grosso, e' nō si avrà a rōpere per il peso che lui ¹⁵possa acquistare dall'una all'altra giornata, perchè, ¹⁶se il suo duplo seccassi in una giornata il dop¹⁷pio seccherà in due o circa, si uerrà ragguagliādo ¹⁸cō piccola differētia di peso in piccola differētia di tēpo.

The stability of buildings is the result of the contrary law to the two former cases. That is to say that the walls must be all built up equally, and by degrees, to equal heights all round the building, and the whole thickness at once, whatever kind of walls they may be. And although a thin wall dries more quickly than a thick one it will not necessarily give way under the added weight day by day and thus, [16] although a thin wall dries more quickly than a thick one, it will not give way under the weight which the latter may acquire from day to day. Because if double the amount of it dries in one day, one of double the thickness will dry in two days or thereabouts; thus the small addition of weight will be balanced by the smaller difference of time [18].

¹⁹Dicie l'aversario ²⁰che a becca²¹tello disciēde.

The adversary says that a which projects, slips down.

²²E qui dicie l'auersario ²³che r disciēde e non e.

And here the adversary says that r slips and not c.

PRONOSTICI DELLE CAVSE ²⁵DELLE FESSURE DI QUALŪCHE ²⁶MURO.

HOW TO PROGNOSTICATE THE CAUSES OF CRACKS IN ANY SORT OF WALL.

²⁷Quella parte del muro che nō disciēde riserua ²⁸in se l'obbiquità del beccatello, copritore dell'o²⁹bliquità del muro da lui discesa.

The part of the wall which does not slip is that in which the obliquity projects and overhangs the portion which has parted from it and slipped down.

DE'SITI DE'FONDAMĒTI E IN QUAL ³¹LOCO SŌ CAVSA DELLE RUINE.

ON THE SITUATION OF FOUNDATIONS AND IN WHAT PLACES THEY ARE A CAUSE OF RUIN.

³²Quando la fessura del muro è più larga di sopra ³³che di sotto elli è manifesto segnio che la mu³⁴raglia à la causa della ruina remota dal perpē³⁵diculare d'essa fessura.

When the crevice in the wall is wider at the top than at the bottom, it is a manifest sign, that the cause of the fissure in the wall is remote from the perpendicular line through the crevice.

larcheza. 26. dacquel .. dissciēde. 27. chapo dalquāto lento questa .. chessi. 28. mossterra .. mōte si m\\\\\. 771. 2. paralelle .. chella. 3. par del. 5.disscēda. 6. reghola ecquella cheffa. 8. edifiti[e] .. ella reghola. 9. chelle. 10. che qual .. cho quali. 11. abbraccino .. circhuitione. 12. cholle .. q aluche sorte. 13. anchora .. sechi. 14. ara .. chellui. 15. acquisstare. 16. il sudduplo sechassi innuna. 17. sechera .. circha . ragualgliādo. 18. cho pichola diferētia .. pichola diferētia. 20. becha. 22. ecqui. 24. chause. 25. delle [mu]. 27. [I] Quella .. nō [si move] "disciēde". 28. bechatello copritricio dello. 29. delei disciesa. 31. locho sō chavsa. 32. largha. 33. chella. 34. alla chausa. 35. dichulare.

Br. M. 138a]   772.

Br. M. 138a]

DELLE FESSURE DE'MURI, LE QUALI
SŌ ²LARGHE DA PIÈ E STRETTE DA CA³PO E
LOR CAUŞA.

⁴Quel muro senpre si fende che ⁵non si
secca vniformemēte ⁶con equal tēpo;

⁷E quel muro d'uniforme gros⁸sezza nō si
secca con equal ⁹tēpo, il quale non è in cō-
tat¹⁰to d'equal mezzo; come se ¹¹vna parte
d'un muro fusse edi¹²ficata in cōtatto d'ū
monte ¹³vmido e 'l rimanente restasse ¹⁴in
contatto dell'aria, che allo¹⁵ra il rimanēte
si ristrigne per ¹⁶ciascun verso e l'umido si
man¹⁷tiene nella sua prima grādezza, ¹⁸e
allora·quel che s'asciuga ¹⁹nell'aria, restrignie e diminui²⁰scesi, e quel che è inu-
midito nō ²¹si asciuga e volentieri si rō²²pe
al secco dall'umido perchè es²³so vmido
non à tenacità da ²⁴seguitare il moto di
quel che al cō²⁵tinuo si secca.

DELLI FESSI ARCATI LARGHI DI SOPRA
²⁷E STRETTI DI SOTTO.

²⁸Quelli fessi arcati larghi di sopra
²⁹e stretti di sotto nascono nelle ³⁰porte
rimurate che calā più ne³¹l'altezza che nella
larghezza loro ³²per tanto quāto l'altezza
è maggiore ³³che nella larghezza e per
quāto le com³⁴messure della calcina son
piv numerosi ³⁵in nell'altezza che nella
larghezza.

³⁶Il fesso diminuisce ³⁷tanto meno in
r o ³⁸che in m n, quāto ³⁹infra r o è mē
ma⁴⁰teria che in n m.

⁴¹Ogni fessura fatta ⁴²ī loco cōcavo
è larga ⁴³di sotto, e stretta di sopra, ⁴⁴e
questo nascie, come ⁴⁵mostra b c d da lato
figu⁴⁶rato.

⁴⁷pᵃ ¶Ciò che si inumidi⁴⁸sce cresce per
tāto ⁴⁹quāto è l'umido ac⁵⁰quistato.¶

⁵¹2ᵃ ¶E ogni cosa umi⁵²da si restrignie
nel⁵³lo asciugare per tā⁵⁴to quanto è l'umido
⁵⁵che da lei si diuide.¶

OF CRACKS IN WALLS, WHICH ARE WIDE AT
THE BOTTOM AND NARROW AT THE TOP AND
OF THEIR CAUSES.

That wall which does not dry uniformly
in an equal time, always cracks.

A wall though of equal thickness will
not dry with equal quickness if it is not
everywhere in contact with the same
medium. Thus, if one side of a wall were
in contact with a damp slope and the other
were in contact with the air, then this latter
side would remain of the same size as before;
that side which dries in the air will shrink
or diminish and the side which is kept damp
will not dry. And the dry portion will break
away readily from the damp portion because
the damp part not shrinking in the same proportion does not cohere and follow the movement of the part which dries continuously.

OF ARCHED CRACKS, WIDE AT THE TOP, AND
NARROW BELOW.

Arched cracks, wide at the top and
narrow below are found in walled-up
doors, which shrink more in their height
than in their breadth, and in proportion as
their height is greater than their width,
and as the joints of the mortar are
more numerous in the height than in the
width.

The crack diminishes less in r o than in
m n, in proportion as there is less material
between r and o than between n and m.

Any crack made in a concave wall is
wide below and narrow at the top; and this
originates, as is here shown at b c d, in
the side figure.

1. That which gets wet increases in
proportion to the moisture it imbibes.

2. And a wet object shrinks, while drying,
in proportion to the amount of moisture which
evaporates from it.

772. 2. dappiedi esstrtte da cha. 3. ellor chausa. 5. secha. 6. chon. 7. Ecquel . . gro. 8. secha chon. 9. chōta. 10. del
qual mezo comesse. 11. fussi. 12. fichato. 13. resstassi. 14. chontatto. 15. sirisstrignie. 16. cias chun . . ellumido
17. grādeza. 18. [il] quel chesasscuigha. 19. restringnie. 20. ecquel . . īnumidito. 21. assciugha. 22. secho. 23. nona[re.
tenacita. 24. chō. 25. secha. 26. delli . . archati. 27. esstretti. 28. archati. 29. esstretti . . nasschano. 30. chalā.
31. lalteza . . largheza. 32. magiore. 33. larghezza . . lecho. 34. mesurie. 35. larghezza. 36. diminuisscie. 38. quādo.
41. Ōni . . tātta. 42. locho chōchavo ellargha. 43. esstretta. 44. ecquesto nasscie. 45. dallato fighu. 47. chessi inumidis.
48. scie cresscie. 49. ellumido. 51. chosa. 53. llo asscuigrare. 54. ellumido. 55. dallei.

772. The text of this passage is reproduced in
facsimile on Pl. CVI to the left. L. 36—40 are written
inside the sketch No. 2. L. 41—46 are partly written
over the sketch No. 3 to which they refer.

Br. M. 158 a] 773.

DELLA CAVSA DEL RONPERE DELLI EDIFITI PUBLICI E PRIVATI.

OF THE CAUSES OF FISSURES IN [THE WALLS OF] PUBLIC AND PRIVATE BUILDINGS.

[2] Romponsi li muri per fessure, che ànno del diretto e alcune che [3] ànno dello obbliquo; le rotture che ànno del diretto [4] son gienerate dalli muri novi [5] in cōgiūtiō de' muri vecchi diiitti o cō morse giūte alli [6] muri vecchi, perchè tali morse, nō potendo resistere allo [7] insopportabile peso del muro a lor' cōgiūto, è necies [8] sario a quelle ronpersi e dar loco al disciēso del predet [9] to muro novo, il quale cala vn braccio per ogni 10 braccia, o più [10] o meno, secondo la maggioi ε o minore soma di calcina [11] interposta infra le pietre murate e cō calcina più [12] o mē liquida; E nota che senpre si debbe īprima fare [13] li muri e poi vestirli delle pietre che li àno a vestire, [14] perchè se così nō si faciesse, il muro facciēdo maggiore calo che [15] la crosta di fori, e' sarebbe neciessario che le morse fatte [16] nelli lati de' muri si rōpessino; perchè le pietre che vestono li mu [17] ri, essendo di maggiore grandezza che le pietre da quel [18] le vestite, è neciessario che ricievino minor quātità di calcina [19] nelle loro comessure e per cōsegueza faccino minore calo, [20] il che accadere nō può, essendo murate tali croste poi ch'el mu [21] ro è secco.

[22] a b muro nuo [23] vo, · c · è muro vechio [24] che già à fatto il calo, [25] e lo a · b fa il calo poi, [26] bēchè a, essēdo fonda [27] to sopra il c muro [28] vechio, nō si può in nes [29] sū modo rōpere per ave [30] re stabile fondamēto [31] sopra del muro ve [32] chio, ma sol si ronpe [33] rà il rimanēte del mu [34] ro nvovo b cō [35] ciosia ch'elli è murato di [36] sopra dalla sommità del edifitio insino al fondo, [37] faciēdo il rimanēte del muro nuovo beccatello [38] sopra il muro che disciēde.

The walls give way in cracks, some of which are more or less vertical and others are oblique. The cracks which are in a vertical direction are caused by the joining of new walls, with old walls, whether straight or with indentations fitting on to those of the old wall; for, as these indentations cannot bear the too great weight of the wall added on to them, it is inevitable that they should break, and give way to the settling of the new wall, which will shrink one braccia in every ten, more or less, according to the greater or smaller quantity of mortar used between the stones of the masonry, and whether this mortar is more or less liquid. And observe, that the walls should always be built first and then faced with the stones intended to face them. For, if you do not proceed thus, since the wall settles more than the stone facing, the projections left on the sides of the wall must inevitably give way; because the stones used for facing the wall being larger than those over which they are laid, they will necessarily have less mortar laid between the joints, and consequently they settle less; and this cannot happen if the facing is added after the wall is dry.

a b the new wall, c the old wall, which has already settled; and the part a b settles afterwards, although a, being founded on c, the old wall, cannot possibly break, having a stable foundation on the old wall. But only the remainder b of the new wall will break away, because it is built from top to bottom of the building; and the remainder of the new wall will overhang the gap above the wall that has sunk.

773. 1. chausa . . pubbici. 2. ronpasi . . alchune. 3. rocture. 4. novi [murati in tēpo brevissimo]. 5. in chōgiūtiō de muri [no] ve "echi" . . chō. 7. allor chōgiūto. 8. acquelle . . locho al disscièso. 9. chala vn br per ogni 10 br . oppiu 10. sechondo . . ōminore . . chalcina. 11. interpossta infralle . . chō chalcina. 12. ōmē . . chessenpre. 13. eppoi vesstirl. chelli . avesstire. 14. chosi . . faciessi . . magiore chalo chel. 15. lacrossta . . farebe . . chelle. 16. vesstano. 17. esendo . . chelle . . dacque. 18. vesstite . . chalcina. 19. chomessure e per chōseghuēza . . chalo. 20. achadere . . murato tale crosste. 21. essecho. 22. muro [vechio] nuo. 24. affatto il chalo. 25. ello . . chalo. 30. fondamē. 34. chō. 30. cio chelli. 37. bechatello. 38. \\\\\\il muro cheddisciēde.

Br. M. 159 b]					**774.**

Torre nova fundata ²sopra la
vecchia in parte.

A new tower founded partly on old
masonry.

Br. M. 157 b]					**775.**

DELLE PIETRE CHE SI DIS²GIŪGONO DALLA LOR
CALCINA.

OF STONES WHICH DISJOIN THEMSELVES FROM
THEIR MORTAR.

³Le pietre d'equal numero nella loro altezza, mu⁴rate con equal quātità di calcina, fāno equal ⁵calo nella partita dell'umido che mollifi⁶cò essa calcina.

⁷Per lo passato si prvova che la poca quātità ⁸del muro nuovo interposta infra A · n farà po⁹co calo rispetto alla quātità del medesimo mu¹⁰ro che s'interpone infra c d, e tal fia la pro¹¹portione che ànno infra loro le raretà delle ¹²dette calcine qual' è la proportiōe delli ¹³nvmeri over delle quātità delle calcine interpo¹⁴ste nelle cōmessure delle pietre murate so¹⁵pra le varie altezze delli muri vechi.

Stones laid in regular courses from bottom to top and built up with an equal quantity of mortar settle equally throughout, when the moisture that made the mortar soft evaporates.

By what is said above it is proved that the small extent of the new wall between A and n will settle but little, in proportion to the extent of the same wall between c and d. The proportion will in fact be that of the thinness of the mortar in relation to the number of courses or to the quantity of mortar laid between the stones above the different levels of the old wall.

A. 53 a]					**776.**

Questo · muro · si rōperà · sotto · l'arco e · f perchè · i sette · quadrelli ²integri · nō sono · soffitiēti · a sostenere il piè · dell'arco sopra · postoli ³e rōperannosi questi · 7 · quadrelli · nel mezzo · apūto come · appare in · a · b; ⁴la ragione si è · che il quadrello · a · à solamēte · sopra · se il peso a · k ⁵e l'ultimo · quadrello · sotto · l'arco · à sopra · se il peso c · d, x · a; ⁶c · d · pare che facci fare · for-

This wall will break under the arch e f, because the seven whole square bricks are not sufficient to sustain the spring of the arch placed on them. And these seven bricks will give way in their middle exactly as appears in a b. The reason is, that the brick a has above it only the weight a k, whilst the last brick under the arch has above it the weight c d x a.

---

774. 2. sopra il vechio.
775. 1. chessi. 2. giūghano . . chalcina. 3. puetre. 4. chon . . chalcina. 8. cho . . chalcina. 7. la passata . . chella pocha. 9. pocho chalo risspecto. 10. chessinterpone . . ettal. 11. portione [di] che anno infralloro. 12. chalcine. 13. chalcine. 14. ste . . chōmesure.
776. 1. Quessto . . larcho [c] e . f. 2. assosstenere . . archo . . posstoli. 3. e rōperanosi . quesste . . mezo . . chome apare. 6. larcho. 7. cheffacci . . archo uerlasspalla. 8. archo. 9. chome . . dopio.

775. See Pl. CV, No. 1. The top of the tower is wanting in this reproduction, and with it the letter n which, in the original, stands above the letter A over the top of the tower, while c stands perpendicularly over d.

za · all'arco · verso la spalla nel pūto · *p* ·, [7]ma il peso · *p* · *o* · lì fa resistētia ·, ōde tutto · il peso · ne va · nella radice dell'arco; [8]adū-

c d seems to press on the arch towards the abutment at the point *p* but the weight *p o* opposes resistence to it, whence the whole

que fa · la radice delli archi · come · 7 · 6, ch'è · più · forte il doppio che · *x* · *z*.

pressure is transmitted to the root of the arch. Therefore the foot of the arch acts like 7 6, which is more than double of *x z*.

ON FISSURES IN NICHES.

Br. M. 158 a]

DELLE ROTTURE DELLI NICHI.

[2]L'arco fatto del semicircolo, il quale fia carico nelli [3]due oppisiti terzi della sua curvità, rōperà in [4]cinque lochi della sua curvità; provasi e sieno li pe[5]si *n m*, li quali rompono esso arco *a · b · f ·*, dico per lo [6]passato come *c a* stremi sono equalmēte aggravati dal peso *n*, [7]seguita per la 5ª che l'arco ronperà nella parte più remota dalle [8]due potentie che lo premono, il quale è il mezzo *e ·*, e altre[9]tanto intēdo aver detto dell'arco opposito *d g b*; adū[10]que *n m* pesi vēgono

a discēdere, e disceder nō posso[11]no per la 7ª che non si faccī più vicini, e avicinar nō si pos[12]sono, se l'arco che infra lor s'interpone non avicini li sua [13]stremi, li quali nō si possono accostare sanza rottura del [14]suo mezzo; adūque l'arco si ronperà in 2 lochi come fu primo [15]posto ecc.

[16]Domāda del peso dato in *a*, che parte ne risponde ī · *n* · [17]*f* linia, e cō che peso s'à a vinciere il peso posto in *f*.

ON FISSURES IN NICHES.

An arch constructed on a semicircle and bearing weights on the two opposite thirds of its curve will give way at five points of the curve. To prove this let the weights be at *n m* which will break the arch *a*, *b, f*. I say that, by the foregoing, as the extremities *c* and *a* are equally pressed upon by the thrust *n*, it follows, by the 5th, that the arch will give way at the point which is furthest from the two forces acting on them and that is the middle *e*. The same is to be understood of the opposite curve, *d g b*; hence the weights *n m* must sink, but they cannot sink by the 7th, without coming closer together, and they cannot come together unless the extremities of the arch between them come closer, and if these draw together the crown of the arch must break; and thus the arch will give way in two places as was at first said &c.

I ask, given a weight at *a* what counteracts it in the direction *n f* and by what weight must the weight at *f* be counteracted.

777. 1. rocture. 2. semil . . charicho. 3. churvita. 4. churvita prosi essieno. 5. ronpano . . archo . . per la. 6. passata chome ca"stremi" sono ecqualmēte agravati. 7. seguita "per la 5ª chellarcho." 8. chello priemano . . altrec. 9. archo ·.. addū. 10. vēghano addisscīēdere e disscīēder nō possa. 12. sano dellarcho che infrallor. 13. achosstare. 14. larcho . . chome fu pr"o" . ne rissponde. 17. chō . . possto.

Br. M. 141 _b_]   **778.**

DELLA DIMINUITIONE DE' CORPI VMIDI ²DI
GROSSEZZA O LARGHEZZA DIFFORME.

³La finestra _a_ è causa della rottura del
_b_ e questa tal rot⁴tura è aumētata dal peso
_n m_, il quale più si ficca ovvero penetra
intra la ter⁵ra che ricieve il suo fondamēto,
che nō fa la leuità del _b_ ·, e ancora il fō-
⁶damēto vechio che sta sotto _b_ à fatto il
calo, il che fatto non aveā li pi⁷lastri _n m_ ·
e la parte _b_ non disciēde perpendiculare,
anzi si gitta info⁸ri per obbliquo e non
si può per l'aversario gittare in dētro,
perchè tal parte disuni⁹ta dal tutto è più
larga di fori che di dentro e li labri del
rimanente ¹⁰e della medesima figura, e se
tal parte disunita avesse a ētrare in dentro, ¹¹il maggiore entrerebbe nel minore, il che sarebbe inpossibile; adunque
¹²è cōcluso che per necessità la parte
di tale emiciclo si disuniscie dal tutto
col ¹³gittarsi colla parte inferiore infori
e non indētro come vole ¹⁴l'auersario
ecc.

¹⁵Quando le tribune intere o mezze
¹⁶sarā di sopra vinte da superchio peso, al-
¹⁷lora le sue volte si aprirāno ¹⁸cō apritura
diminuitiva ¹⁹dalla parte di sopra e larga
di sot²⁰to e stretta dalla parte di dentro e
²¹larga di fuori, a similitudine della ²²scorza
del pomo ovvero melarācia ²³divisa in molte
parti per la sua lūghez²⁴za, chè quāto ella
sarà premuta dal²⁵le opposite parti della
sua lūghezza, ²⁶quella parte delle giūture
più si a²⁷prirà, che fia più distāte alla causa
²⁸che la preme ·, e per questo mai si ²⁹deb-
bono caricare li archi delle volte ³⁰di qualunche emiciclo dalli archi dello ³¹suo
edifitio massimo, perchè quel che ³²più
pesa più prieme sopra ciò che li è di³³sotto,
e più disciende sopra li sua fon³⁴damēti, il
che interuenire nō può ³⁵alle cose più lieui
come sono li emi³⁶cicli predetti.

ON THE SHRINKING OF DAMP BODIES OF
DIFFERENT THICKNESS AND WIDTH.

The window _a_ is the cause of the crack
at _b;_ and this crack is increased by the
pressure of _n_ and _m_ which sink or penetrate
into the soil in which foundations are built
more than the lighter portion at _b_. Besides,
the old foundation under _b_ has already
settled, and this the piers _n_ and _m_ have not
yet done. Hence the part _b_ does not settle
down perpendicularly; on the contrary, it is
thrown outwards obliquely, and it cannot
on the contrary be thrown inwards, because a portion like this, separated from
the main wall, is larger outside than inside
and the main wall, where it is broken, is of
the same shape and is also larger outside
than inside; therefore, if this separate portion
were to fall inwards the larger would have
to pass through the smaller—which is impossible. Hence it is evident that the portion
of the semicircular wall when disunited
from the main wall will be thrust outwards,
and not inwards as the adversary says.

When a dome or a half-dome is crushed
from above by an excess of weight the vault
will give way, forming a crack which diminishes towards the top and is wide below,
narrow on the inner side and wide outside;
as is the case with the outer husk of a
pomegranate, divided into many parts lengthwise; for the more it is pressed in the
direction of its lengtn, that part of the joints
will open most, which is most distant from
the cause of the pressure; and for that reason
the arches of the vaults of any apse should
never be more loaded than the arches of
the principal building. Because that which
weighs most, presses most on the parts below, and they sink into the foundations; but
this cannot happen to lighter structures like
the said apses.

---

778. 1. chorpi. 2. "ollarghezza". 3. finesstra . . chausa . . roctura . . ecquesta . . roc. 4. ficha over . . intralla. 5. anchora
6. chessta ·. . affatto il chalo. 7. lasstri n . m . ella . . dissciēde per pēdichulare . . infor. 8. po. 9. eppiu largha . .
cheddi dentro [ess] elli. 10. fighura essettal . . avessi. 11. enterrebbe . . addunque. 12. e chōcluso . . disunisscie . . chol.
13. gittari [dap] cholla . . inferiore [di] inforienone . . chome. 15. trebune . . omeze. 17. apirrāno [chōta]. 18. [tama]
chō. 19. ellargha. 20. esstrēta . . dentro el. 21. largha . . assimilitudine. 22. over. 23. imolte parte. 24. sara permuta.
25. parte . . lūgheza. 26. quela. 27. pirra cheffia . . chausa. 28. chella . . quessto. 29. debbe charichare. 32. sopra chilli
edi. 33. dissciende. 35. chose . . chome. 36. predecti. 37. quessti . . chubi. 38. ho. 39. chubo. 40. chubo b sosspeso. 41. in-

---

778. The figure on Pl. CV, No. 4 belongs to
the first paragraph of this passage, lines 1—14;
fig. 5 is sketched by the side of lines 15—and

following. The sketch below of a pomegranate
refers to line 22. The drawing fig. 6 is, in the
original, over line 37 and fig. 7 over line 54.

[37] Qual di questi due cubi dimi[38]nuirà più vniformeméte, o [39] il cvbo *A* posato sopra il pavi[40]méto, o'l cubo *b* sospeso [41] infra l'aria, essédc l'uno [42] e l'altro cubo equali in peso [43] e in quantità e di terra mista [44] con equale vmidità? —

[45] Quel cubo che si posa sopra [46] il paviméto più diminui[47]scie della sua altezza che per la [48] sua larghezza, il che [49] far nō può il cubo ch'è di [50] sopra e sospeso infra l'aria; [51] pruovasi così; il cubo po[52]sato sopra questa medesima [53] sta meglio qui di sotto.

[54] Il fine delli dua cilindri di [55] terra fresca cioè *a b* sa[56]rā le figure piramidali di [57] sotto *c d* ‖ provasi co[58]sì : il cilindro *a*, posato [59] sopra il suo paviméto per esse[60]re lui di terra assai mista [61] coll'umido, va ca-lādo me[62]diante il suo peso che da di se [63] alla sua basa, e tāto più ca[64]lerà e ingrosserà, quāto e'sa[65]rà colle sua parti più presso [66] alla sua basa, perchè lì si cari[67]ca il suo tutto ecc; E si[68]mile farà il peso *b*, il quale pi[69]ù s'astéderà, quāto elli à maggi[70]or peso sotto se, la qual maggiorità [71] è ne'cōfini del suo sostétaculo.

Which of these two cubes will shrink the more uniformly: the cube *A* resting on the pavement, or the cube *b* suspended in the air, when both cubes are equal in weight and bulk, and of clay mixed with equal quantities of water?

The cube placed on the pavement diminishes more in height than in breadth, which the cube above, hanging in the air, cannot do. Thus it is proved. The cube shown above is better shown here below.

The final result of the two cylinders of damp clay that is *a* and *b* will be the pyramidal figures below *c* and *d*. This is proved thus: The cylinder *a* resting on block of stone being made of clay mixed with a great deal of water will sink by its weight, which presses on its base, and in proportion as it settles and spreads all the parts will be somewhat nearer to the base because that is charged with the whole weight, &c.; and the case will be the same with the weight of *b* which will stretch lengthwise in proportion as the weight at the bottom is increased and the greatest tension will be the neighbourhood of the weight which is suspended by it.

---

frallaria essē luno. 44. ellaltro chub. 43. missta. 44. chon. 45. chubo chessi. 47. alteza. 48. [che] il che. 49. chubo. 50. essosspeso. 51. chosi il chubo. 54. chilindri. 55. fressca. 56. ra le. 57. socto . . cho. 58. chilindro. 60. missta. 61. chollumido va chalādo. 63. ettāto piu cha. 64. ēgrossera. 65. cholle . . parte. 66. chari. 67. cha . . Essi. 69. sasstēdera . . magi. 70. laqqual magiorita. 71. cne chōfusi . sostētachulo.

III.

ON THE NATURE OF THE ARCH.

CHE COSA È ARCO.

[2]Arco non è altro che una fortezza · cavsata da due debolezze, īpero[3]chè l'arco negli edifiti è cōposto di 2 quarti · di circulo, i quali [4]quarti cir-culi, ciascuno debolissimo per se, desi-derā cadere, e opponē[5]dosi alla ruina l'uno dell'altro de' due debolezze, si cōver-tono in vni[6]ca fortezza.

WHAT IS AN ARCH?

The arch is nothing else than a force originated by two weaknesses, for the arch in buildings is composed of two segments of a circle, each of which being very weak in itself tends to fall; but as each opposes this tendency in the other, the two weaknesses combine to form one strength.

DELLA QUALITÀ DEL PESO DELLI ARCHI.

[8]Poichè l'arco fia · cōposto ·, quello · ri-mane in equilibrio, īpero[9]chè tāto spī-gie · l'uno · l'altro · quāto l'altro l'uno ·, e se pesa piv l'uno [10]quarto circulo · che l'altro ·, quivi fia leuata e negata la permanēza, [11]imperochè 'l maggiore vīcierà · il minore peso.

OF THE KIND OF PRESSURE IN ARCHES.

As the arch is a composite force it remains in equilibrium because the thrust is equal from both sides; and if one of the segments weighs more than the other the stability is lost, because the greater pressure will out-weigh the lesser.

DEL CARICO DATO AGLI ARCHI.

[13]Dopo il peso equale de' quarti circuli è neciessario dare loro equale [14]peso di sopra, altremēti si corre-rebbe nel sopra · detto errore.

OF DISTRIBUTING THE PRESSURE ABOVE AN ARCH.

Next to giving the segments of the circle equal weight it is neces-sary to load them equally, or you will fall into the same defect as before.

---

779. 1. chosa e archo. 2. archo . . ī forteza . . deboleze. 3. larcho . . chōposto . . circhuli. 4. circhuli ciaschuno . debolisimo . . chadere eoponē. 5. deboleze . . chōuertano. 6. cha forteza. 7. dela . . deli. 8. chōposto quelo . . equilibra. 9. chettāto . . esse e pesa. 10. circhulo . . premanēza. 11. magiore. 12. charicho dati ali. 13. circhuli. 14. chorerebe . . erore

DOVE L'ARCO SI RŌPE.

[16] L'arco si rōperà j̄ quella · parte che passa · il suo mezzo sotto il cietro.

WHERE AN ARCH BREAKS.

An arch breaks at the part which lies below half way from the centre.

SECŌDO RŌPIMETO DELL'ARCO.

[18] Se 'l superchio · peso · fia posto ī mezzo · l'arco nel pūto · *a* ·, quello desi[19]dera cadere · in · *b* ·, e ronpesi ne' $2/3$ della sua altezza in . *c* · *e*, [20]e tāto fia più potēte · *g* · *e* che *e* · *a* · quanto [21] *m* · *o* · entra in · *m* · *n*.

SECOND RUPTURE OF THE ARCH.

If the excess of weight be placed in the middle of the arch at the point *a*, that weight tends to fall towards *b*, and the arch breaks at $2/3$ of its height at *c e*; and *g e* is as many times stronger than *e a*, as *m o* goes into *m n*.

D'UN ALTRA CAGIONE DI RUINA.

[23] L'arco verrà · ancora · meno · per essere sospīto da traverso, inpero[24]chè quādo il carico nō si dirizza ai piè del'arco, [25] l'arco poco dura.

ON ANOTHER CAUSE OF RUIN.

The arch will likewise give way under a transversal thrust, for when the charge is not thrown directly on the foot of the arch, the arch lasts but a short time.

A. 50 *b*]   **780.**

DELLA FORTEZZA DELL'ARCO.

[2] Il modo di fare l'arco permanēte si è a rienpiere i sua angoli · di buono ripieno [3] insino · al suo raso overo · culmine.

ON THE STRENGTH OF THE ARCH.

The way to give stability to the arch is to fill the spandrils with good masonry up to the level of its summit.

[4] DEL CARICARE SOPRA L'ARCO TŌDO.

ON THE LOADING OF ROUND ARCHES.

[5] DEL CARICARE L'ARCO · ACUTO BENE.

ON THE PROPER MANNER OF LOADING THE POINTED ARCH.

[6] DELLO INCŌVENIÉTE CHE SEGUITA A CARICARE [7] L'ARCO ACUTO SUL SUO MEZZO.

ON THE EVIL EFFECTS OF LOADING THE POINTED ARCH DIRECTLY ABOVE ITS CROWN.

15. larcho. 16. larcho . . mezo [da]. 17. sechōdo . . archo. 18. imezo larcho . . quelo. 19. chadere . . dela . . alteza. 20. [c . in n che in . e] g . e. 22. chagione. 23. larcho vera . anchora . . esserre. 24. charicho . . diriza . . archo. 25. larcho pocho.

780. 1. dela forteza delarcho. 2. larcho. 3. chulmine. 4. charichare . . larcho. 5. charichare larcho achuto. 6. delo inchōveniēte . . charichare. 7. larcho achuto . . mezo. 8. dano . . larcho achuto. 9. charichato sopra a sua fiāchi. 10. larcho

[8]DEL DANNO CHE RICIEVE L'ARCO ACUTO A ESSERE [9]CARICATO SOPRA I SUOI FIÃCHI.

ON THE DAMAGE DONE TO THE POINTED ARCH BY THROWING THE PRESSURE ON THE FLANKS.

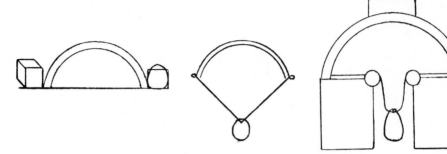

[10]L'arco · poco · curvo fia sicuro per se, [11]ma se fia carico ·, le spalle · bisognia [12]bene · armare; [13]l'arco d'assai curvità fia per se debole, [14]e piv forte se fia carico e farà poca noia [15]alle sue spalle ·, e lui · rōperà · in o · p.

An arch of small curve is safe in itself, but if it be heavily charged, it is necessary to strengthen the flanks well. An arch of a very large curve is weak in itself, and stronger if it be charged, and will do little harm to its abutments, and its places of giving way are o p.

A. 51 a]   781.

DEL RIPARO A TERREMOTI.

ON THE REMEDY FOR EARTHQUAKES.

[2]L'arco il quale mā[3]derà il peso per-pēdicu[4]lare alle sue radici [5]farà il suo · ofitio

The arch which throws its pressure perpendicularly on the abutments will fulfil

per [6]qualūque verso si stia, [7]o rovescio, o a giacere, [8]o ritto.

[9]¶L'arco · nō si rōperà · se la · corda del'arco di fori · nō toccherà l'arco di den-tro¶; [10]Questo · appare per isperiēza, chè ogni · volta che la corda · a · o · n dell'arco [11]di fori · n · r · a · toccherà · l'arco di dentro · x · b · y ·, l'arco darà prīcipio a sua [12]debo-lezza ·, e tāto si farà · piv · debole · quāto l'arco · di dētro · rōperà dessa · corda.

[13]Quell'arco · il quale fia · carico dal'una de'lati, [14]il peso si caricherà · sulla sōmità

its function whatever be its direction, upside down, sideways or upright.

The arch will not break if the chord of the outer arch does not touch the inner arch. This is manifest by experience, because whenever the chord a o n of the outer arch n r a approaches the inner arch x b y the arch will be weak, and it will be weaker in proportion as the inner arch passes beyond that chord. When an arch is loaded only on one side the thrust will press on the top of the other side and be transmitted

pocho . . sichuro. 11. charicho lesspali. 13. larcho . . churvita. 14. epiv seffia charicho effara . . 15. ellui.
781. 2. larcho. 3. perpēdichu. 6. Qulūque "r" so. 7. oadiacere. 9. larcho . . chorda delarcho . . tochera larcho. 10. apare chorda . . archo. 11. tochera larcho . . assua. 12. deboleza ettāto . . larcho . . chorda. 13. archo . . charicho. 14. chari-

780. Inside the large figure on the right is the note: *Da pesare la forza dell' archo.*

del'altro mezzo·, e pas¹⁵serà
il peso·per īsino·al suo·fon-
damēto·, e rōperà·in quella ¹⁶par-
te che fia·piv·lontana·dai sua·
stremi·e dalla sua corda.

to the spring of the arch on that
side; and it will break at a point
half way between its two extremes, where it is farthest from
the chord.

H.¹ 35 b]

782.

La quātità cōtinua,
che per forza in arco
²fia piegata, spīgie per
la linia, ōde deside³ra
tornare.

A continuous body
which has been forcibly
bent into an arch, thrusts
in the direction of the
straight line, which it
tends to recover.

H.¹ 36 a]

783.

L'arco di quātità discreta
fa forza ²per linia obliqua,
cioè il triangulo ³c n b nō
sēte peso.

In an arch judiciously
weighted the thrust is oblique,
so that the triangle c n b
has no weight upon it.

S. K. M. II.² 67 b]

784.

Domando qui che ²pesi fieno quelli
³ de'contrapesi a fa⁴re resistētia alla ru⁵ina·
di ciascun arco?

I here ask what weight will be needed to
counterpoise and resist the tendency of each
of these arches to give way?

chera sula somita . . mezo e pa.   15. quela.   16. cheffia . . dala.
782. 1—3 R.   1. archo.   2. fie.   **783.** 1—3 R.   1. larcho.   **784.** 2. hce pesi.   3. affa.   4. resisētia.

784. The two lower sketches are taken from the MS. S. K. M. III, 10ᵃ; they have there no explanatory text.

Br. M. 158*b*]   785.

DELLA POTĒTIA DELL'ARCO NELL'ARCHITETTURA.

²La permanēza dell'arco fabbricato dallo architetto con³siste nella corda e nelle spalle sue.

DELLA SITUATIONE DELLA CORDA NEL SOPRA DETTO ARCO.

⁵La situatione della corda à equale necessità nel princi⁶pio dell'archo, e nel fine della rettitudine del pilastro ⁷dove si posa; pruovasi per la 2ª delli sostētaculi che dicie: ⁸Quella parte del sostentaculo manco resiste che è più remota dal fer⁹mamēto del suo tutto; adunque essendo la ¹⁰sōmità del pilastro vltima remotione dal suo fermamēto, e 'l si¹¹mile accadēdo nelli oppositi stremi dell'arco, che sono vl¹²tima distantia dal mezzo, suo vero fermamēto, noi abbiā con¹³cluso, che tal corda *a b* di neciessità richiede la situatione delli ¹⁴sua oppositi stremi infra li 4 oppositi stremi predetti;

¹⁵Dicie l'auersario che tale arco vole essere più che mezzo ¹⁶tondo, e allora non avrà bisognio di corda perchè tali stremi ¹⁷nō spignerāno infuori, ma indentro, come si di¹⁸mostra nello ecciesso *a·c·b·d*; Qui si risponde, tale ¹⁹inventione essere trista per 5 cause, e la prima è inquanto ²⁰alla fortezza, perchè è provato ꞁl parallelo cir²¹culare, essendo cōposto di due semicirculi, ·sol rōpersi dove ²²tali semicirculi insieme si congiūgono, come mo²³stra la figura *n m;* oltre a di questo seguita, ch'egli è mag²⁴giore spatio infra li stremi del semicirculo che infra le pa²⁵rieti delli muri; terza è che 'l peso posto per cōtro alla fortezza ²⁶dell'arco diminuiscie tanto di peso, quāto le poste dell'arco ²⁷sono più larghe che detto spatio interposto infra li pilastri, 4ª è ²⁸che li pilastri indeboliscono per tāto quāto la parte loro

ON THE STRENGTH OF THE ARCH IN ARCHITECTURE.

The stability of the arch built by an architect resides in the tie and in the flanks.

ON THE POSITION OF THE TIE IN THE ABOVE NAMED ARCH.

The position of the tie is of the same importance at the beginning of the arch and at the top of the perpendicular pier on which it rests. This is proved by the 2nd "of supports" which says: that part of a support has least resistance which is farthest from its solid attachment; hence, as the top of the pier is farthest from the middle of its true foundation and the same being the case at the opposite extremities of the arch which are the points farthest from the middle, which is really its [upper] attachment, we have concluded that the tie *a b* requires to be in such a position as that its opposite ends are between the four above-mentioned extremes.

The adversary says that this arch must be more than half a circle, and that then it will not need a tie, because then the ends will not thrust outwards but inwards, as is seen in the excess at *a c, b d.* To this it must be answered that this would be a very poor device, for three reasons. The first refers to the strength of the arch, since it is proved that the circular parallel being composed of two semicircles will only break where these semicircles cross each other, as is seen in the figure *n m;* besides this it follows that there is a wider space between the extremes of the semicircle than between the plane of the walls; the third reason is that the weight placed to counterbalance the strength of the arch diminishes in proportion as the piers of the arch are wider than the space between the piers. Fourthly in proportion as the parts at *c a b d* turn outwards, the piers are weaker to support the arch above them. The 5th is that all the material and weight of the

785. 1. dellarcho. 2. premanēza dellarcho fabrichato . . architettoch ꞁꞁꞁꞁꞁ. 3. chorda. 4. chorda . . archo. 5. chorda allaq"a" neciessita. 6. rectitudine del pilasstro. 7. dovessi . . pella . . sostētachuli cheddicie. 8. sostentachulo mā. 9. tucto . . essendo [la somita delli] la. 10. somita . . pilasstro . . repotione. 11. achadēdo [nellarcho] nelli . . archo chessono . . chon. 13. chluso chettal chorda "a b" di. 14. infralli . . predecti. 15. chettale archo. 16. ara . . chorda. 17. nō [gitteranno] inspignierāno . . indrēto. 18. mosstra . . rispotale. 19. trissta per "5" [tre] chause ella . . e inꝗ. 20. provato [larcho sol] ꞁl. 21. chulare . . chōposto . . semice . . 22. semicirchuli . . chongiūghano . . mos. 23. fighura . . questto . . ema. 24. infralli . . semics . . infralle. 25. riete . . posto perchōtro. 26. archo diminuisscie . . posste dellarcho. 27. e piu largha . . interposto infralli pilasstri ꞁꞁꞁꞁꞁ. 28. ꞁꞁꞁꞁ elli pilasstri indebolisschano. 29. larcho . . la 5ᵃ he. 30. chettutta.

c a ²⁹*b d* si piegha indirieto nel ritenere sopra di se l'arco; la 5ª è ³⁰che tutta la spesa e 'l peso dell'arco che eccede il mezzo tondo ³¹è inutile e dañoso, ed è qui da notare, che il peso ³²sopra posto all'archo rōperà cō più facilità l'arco in *a b* trouā³³do la curuatura dell'ecciesso che al mezzo circulo s'agiugnie ³⁴che essendo dirieto il pilastro insino al cōtatto del semicirculo.

arch which are in excess of the semicircle are useless and indeed mischievous; and here it is to be noted that the weight placed above the arch will be more likely to break the arch at *a b*, where the curve of the excess begins that is added to the semicircle, than if the pier were straight up to its junction with the semicircle [spring of the arch].

LARCHO IL QUALE È CARICO SOPRA IL SUO MEZZO RŌPERÀ ³⁶NEL SUO QUARTO DESTRO E SINISTRO.

AN ARCH LOADED OVER THE CROWN WILL GIVE WAY AT THE LEFT HAND AND RIGHT HAND QUARTERS.

³⁷Prouasi per la 7ª di questo che dicie ³⁸¶le opposite stremità delli sostētaculi sono equalmēte agra³⁹vate dal peso che per lor si sospēde; adūque il peso dato in *f* si ⁴⁰sēte in *b c* cioè mezzo per ciascuno stremo, e per la terza che dicie: ⁴¹Quella parte del sostētacolo d'equal potētia più presto si rompe ⁴²che è più distante al suo fermamēto, ōde seguita che . . . . ⁴³per essere *d* equalmente distāte al *f e* ferma . . . . . .

This is proved by the 7th of this which says: The opposite ends of the support are equally pressed upon by the weight suspended to them; hence the weight shown at *f* is felt at *b c*, that is half at each extremity; and by the third which says: in a support of equal strength [throughout] that portion will give way soonest which is farthest from its attachment; whence it follows that *d* being equally distant from *f*, *e* . . . . .

³⁵Se l'armadura dell'ar³⁶co nō cala insieme ³⁷col calo dell'arco, la cal³⁸cina nel seccarsi restri³⁹gnie in se medesima e ⁴⁰si spicca dall'ū de'matto⁴¹ni, alli quali ella per col⁴²legarli è interpo⁴³sta, e così li lascia dis⁴⁴legati, per la qual co⁴⁵sa la uolta resta disu⁴⁶nita e le pioggie in brie⁴⁷ve la ruinano.

If the centering of the arch does not settle as the arch settles, the mortar, as it dries, will shrink and detach itself from the bricks between which it was laid to keep them together; and as it thus leaves them disjoined the vault will remain loosely built, and the rains will soon destroy it.

A. 49*b*]   **786.**

DELLA · FORTEZZA · E QUALITÀ · DELLI ARCHI, E DOVE SONO FORTI ²O DEBOLI · E COSÌ LE COLONNE.

ON THE STRENGTH AND NATURE OF ARCHES, AND WHERE THEY ARE STRONG OR WEAK; AND THE SAME AS TO COLUMNS.

¶³Quella · parte dell'arco che fia · piv · piana, farà minore resistētia ⁴al peso · sopra · postoli. ¶

That part of the arch which is nearer to the horizontal offers least resistance to the weight placed on it.

archo . . eciede. 31. [dellarcho] e inutile. 32. possto . . larcho. 33. churuatura . . mezo circhulo. 34. pilasstro . . chō-tatto. 35. charicho . . mezo. 36. desstro essinisstro. 37. cheddicie. 18. sosstētachuli seno. 40. ciasscuno. 41. sosstē-tacholo . . si r\||||||||. 42. disstante . . seghuita che\||||||||. 43. deq distante al f e ferma ||||||||||||. 36. cho nō chala. 37. chol chalo dell archo. 38. secharsi. 40. sispicha. 41. chol. 42. legharsi. 43. e chosi. 44. leghati . . qual che. 45. la la . . ressta. 46. elle. 47. ve le.
786. 1. forteza. 2. chosi le cholone. 3. archo cheffia. 6. chalando chaccia. 7. ciaschuno ¹/₂ archo. 8. echosi. 11. ciasschuno

5Quando · ןl triāgolo · *a z n* 6calando caccia indirieto · 7ן ²/₃ di ciascuno ¹/₂ arco 8cioè *a . s* · e così *z · m*, ela 9ragiō si è che *a* · piōba sopra · *b*, 10e così *z* · sopra *f*.

When the triangle *a z n*, by settling, drives backwards the ²/₃ of each ¹/₂ circle that is *a s* and in the same way *z m*, the reason is that *a* is perpendicularly over *b* and so likewise *z* is above *f*.

11Ciascuno ¹/₂ · arco ·, sendo vinto · dal superchio · peso ·, si ronperà ne ²/₃ della 12sua · altezza ·, la quale · parte · risponde · per perpēdiculare · linia · sopra · il mezzo della sua 13basa · come · appare · in · *a · b*; E questo accade chè'l pe o · desidera cadere 14e passare pel · pūto · *r* ·; E s'egli desiderasse cōtra sua · natura cade15re dal pūto · *s* ·, l'arco · *n · s* · si rōperebbe · nel suo · mezzo · appūto 16e se l'arco · *n · s* · fusse d'ū solo legnio, il peso posto in · *n* · desidereb17be cadere in · *m* · e ronperebbesi in mezzo ¹/₂ · all'arco *e · m* ·, altremēti si rōperà nel terzo 18di sopra nel pūto 19*a* ·, perchè da · *a · n* · 20è l'arco · piv pia21no, che non è da 22*a · o* e che no23n è da *o · s*; 24e tanto · quāto 25*p · t* · è maggio26re che *t · n* · 27tanto fia piv for28te · *a · o* · che 29non è *a · n* ·; 30e similmēte 31tanto fia piv 32forte · *s · o* · che 33*o · a* · quāto · 34*r · p* · fia maggi35ore · che *p t*.

Either half of an arch, if overweighted, will break at ²/₃ of its height, the point which corresponds to the perpendicular line above the middle of its bases, as is seen at *a b;* and this happens because the weight tends to fall past the point *r*.—And if, against its nature it should tend to fall towards the point *s* the arch *n s* would break precisely in its middle. If the arch *n s* were of a single piece of timber, if the weight placed at *n* should tend to fall in the line *n m*, the arch would break in the middle of the arch *e m*, otherwise it will break at one third from the top at the point *a* because from *a* to *n* the arch is nearer to the horizontal than from *a* to *o* and from *o* to *s*, in proportion as *p t* is greater than *t n*, *a o* will be stronger than *a n* and likewise in proportion as *s o* is stronger than *o a*, *r p* will be greater than *p t*.

36Quel arco · che fia · raddoppiato · nella quadratura della sua · grossezza 37regierà · quattro · tanti · peso quanto · regieva · lo scēpio ·, tanto · piv · 38quanto · il diamitro della · sua · grossezza · entra · mē · numero · di uolte nella 39sua · lunghezza, Cioè · se la · grossezza dell'arco scēpio entra · 10 40volte nella sua · lūghezza, la grossezza · del arco duplicato · ētrerà 5 volte 41nella · sua · lūghezza ·; Adūque entrādo la metà meno la grossezza de 42l'arco · duplicato · nella sua · lunghezza · che nō fa quella de43l'arco · scēpio · nella · sua ·, è ragionevol cosa che regga la metà piv 44peso che nō gli toccherebbe, se fusse alla proportione dell'ar45co · scēpio; Onde essendo quest'arco dupplicato per 4 volte la quā46tità del'arco scēpio, parrebbe che dovesse regiere 4 tāti piv peso, 47e la sopra detta regola dimostra che ne sostiene · 8 cotāti appūto.

The arch which is doubled to four times of its thickness will bear four times the weight that the single arch could carry, and more in proportion as the diameter of its thickness goes a smaller number of times into its length. That is to say that if the thickness of the single arch goes ten times into its length, the thickness of the doubled arch will go five times into its length. Hence as the thickness of the double arch goes only half as many times into its length as that of the single arch does, it is reasonable that it should carry half as much more weight as it would have to carry if it were in direct proportion to the single arch. Hence as this double arch has 4 times the thickness of the single arch, it would seem that it ought to bear 4 times the weight; but by the above rule it is shown that it will bear exactly 8 times as much.

¹/₂ · archo. 12. alteza . . rispōde perpēdichulare . . mezo dela. 13. chome apare . . Ecquesto achade . . chadere. 14. Essegli desiderassi . . chōtra . . chade. 15. larcho . . rōperebe . . apūto. 16. esselarcho [in] fussi . . desidere. 17. be chadere eronprrebesi in ¹/₂ archo. 20. elarcho. 25. magio. 30. essimilmēte. 34. magi. 36. archo . cheffia radopiato . . grosseza. 37. losscēpio . Ettanto. 38. grosseza. 39. lungeza . . sella grosseza dellarcho duplichato ētera. 40. volte ila . . lūgeza la grosseza . . archo duplichato ētera. 41. nela . . lūgeza . . grosseza. 42. larcho duplichato . . lungeza che nō fa che nō fa. 43. larcho . . chosa che rega. 44. peso [ap] che . . tocherebe [ali] sefuss·ssi ala. 45. cho . . archo duplichato. 46. archo . . parebe . . dovessi. 47. chōtāli apūto. 48. cheffia charicho . . diseghuale . . vera. 49. mācho. 50. cholona . . cha

QUEL PILASTRO CHE FIA CARICO DI PIV DI-
SEGUALE [49]PESO VERRÀ PIV PRESTO AL MĀCO.

THAT PIER, WHICH IS CHARGED MOST UN-
EQUALLY, WILL SOONEST GIVE WAY.

[50]La colonna *c · b ·* per l'essere carica
d'equale · somma fia · piv · permanēte, [51]e l'altre · 2 di fori · àño
bisognio di tāto peso dal loro
ciētro infori [52]quāt'è · dal loro ·
ciētro indētro · cioè dal ciētro
della colonna insino a mezzo l'arco.

The column *c b*, being charged with an
equal weight, [on each side] will be
most durable, and the other two outward columns require on the part outside of their centre as much pressure
as there is inside of their [l]centre,
that is, from the centre of the column, towards the middle of the arch.

[53]Li archi che stano per forza di catene
nō fieno permanēti.

Arches which depend on chains for their
support will not be very durable.

L'ARCO · FIA DI PIV LŪGA PERPETUITÀ ·, IL
QUALE AVRÀ BONO CONTRARIO AL SUO
SPĪGIERE.

THAT ARCH WILL BE OF LONGER DURATION
WHICH HAS A GOOD ABUTMENT OPPOSED TO
ITS THRUST.

[55]L'arco per se desidera cadere, e se l'arco fia 30 braccia e lo īteruallo
ch'è infra i mvri [56]che lo so-
stēgono sia · 20 ·, noi sappiamo che 30 nō passerà per
20, se 20 nō si [57]fa ancora
lui · 30 ·; ōde sendo vinto
l'arco dal superchio · peso · si
dirizza e i mvri [58]male resitēti
l'aprono e dāno l'entrata infra loro spatio alla ruina
del' arco; [59]Ma se tu nō uolessi mettere al-
l'arco la sua corda di ferro, li debbi fare
tali [60]spalle che facciano · resistētia al suo
spingiere, la qual cosa · farai così : carica
[61]li angoli *m · n ·* di pietre che le linie delle
loro givnture se dirizzino al cientro [62]del
circulo del'arco, E la ragione, che sarà
l'arco permanēte, fia questa, Noi [63]sap-
piamo chiaro che chi carica · l'arco nel
quarto suo · *a · b* di superchio peso che'l
[64]muro · *f · g ·* fia sospinto, perchè l'arco si
uorrà dirizzare; E chi caricasse l'altro
quarto [65]*b · c ·* ch'eli tirerebbe il mvro ·
f · g · indētro, se nō fusse la linia delle
pietre [66]*x y* che fa sostegnio.

The arch itself tends to fall. If the arch be
30 braccia and the interval be-
tween the walls which carry it
be 20, we know that 30 cannot
pass through the 20 unless 20
becomes likewise 30. Hence
the arch being crushed by the
excess of weight, and the walls
offering insufficient resistance,
part, and afford room between
them, for the fall of the arch.
But if you do not wish to strengthen the arch
with an iron tie you must give it such
abutments as can resist the thrust; and you
can do this thus: fill up the spandrels *m n*
with stones, and direct the lines of the joints
between them to the centre of the circle
of the arch, and the reason why this makes
the arch durable is this. We know very
well that if the arch is loaded with an excess of weight above its quarter as *a b*, the
wall *f g* will be thrust outwards because the
arch would yield in that direction; if the
other quarter *b c* were loaded, the wall *f g*
would be thrust inwards, if it were not for
the line of stones *x y* which resists this.

S. K. M. II.2 66*b*]   787.

FONDAMĒTO.

PLAN.

[2]Qui si dimostra · come li archi [3]fatti ne'
lati dell'ottāgolo spingo[4]no i pilastri delli

Here it is shown how the arches made
in the side of the octagon thrust the piers

---

richa . . soma . . premanēte. 51. ano . . tādo . . daloro. 52. daloro . . cholona . . mezo. 53. stano . . chatene. 54. larcho . .
ara . . chontrario. 55. larcho . . chadere Esselarcho . . 30 br . . īterualo. 56. sostēgano . . sapiano. 57. anora . . larcho
. . diriza. 58. laprano edano . . ala . . archo. 59. Massettu . . archo . . chorda. 60. spale cheffacino . . chosa . . charicha. 61. chelle . . dele . . dirizino. 62. circhulo . . archo . larcho . . premanēte. 63. sapiano . . chariche larcho.
64. larcho si uora dirizare . . charichassi. 65. tirerebe . . fussi. 66. cheffa.
787. 2. dimosstra chome. 3. caciarlo.

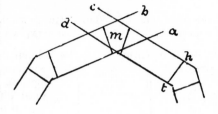

angoli infori, [5]come si dimostra nella linia · *h* · *c* [6]e nella linia *t d* che spingono [7]il pilastro · *m* · in fori, cioè si [8]sforzano cacciarlo dal ciētro di tale [9]ottangolo.

of the angles outwards, as is shown by the line *h c* and by the line *t d* which thrust out the pier *m*; that is they tend to force it away from the centre of such an octagon.

B. 27 a]   788.

La speriēza · che vn peso posto sopra vno arco nō si carica tutto sopra alle sua colon[2]ne, anzi quāto è maggior peso fraposto sopra l'archi ·, tanto mē pesa [3]l'arco il peso alle colōne; la sperienza siè questa: sia messo vn omo [4]sopra le stadere in mezzo la trōba d'uno pozzo; fa dipoi che questo allarghi le mani [5]e piedi infra le parieti di detto pozzo ·, vedrai questo pesare alla stadera mol[6]to meno ·; da li vno peso alle spalle, uedrai per speriēza quāto maggior [7]peso ti darà, maggiore forza farà in aprire le braccia e ganbe, e piv pō[8]dare nelle parieti, e piv mācare il pōdo alle stadere.

An Experiment to show that a weight placed on an arch does not discharge itself entirely on its columns; on the contrary the greater the weight placed on the arches, the less the arch transmits the weight to the columns. The experiment is the following. Let a man be placed on a steel yard in the middle of the shaft of a well, then let him spread out his hands and feet between the walls of the well, and you will see him weigh much less on the steel yard; give him a weight on the shoulders, you will see by experiment, that the greater the weight you give him the greater effort he will make in spreading his arms and legs, and in pressing against the wall and the less weight will be thrown on the steel yard.

788. 1. archo . . carica tu sopra . . colo. 2. magior. 3. larcho el . . cholone . . questa si mezzo. 4. imezo . . pozo. 5. pozo . . ala. 6. spalli . . isperieza . . magior. 7. darai magiore. 8. pariete . . māchare.

IV.

ON FOUNDATIONS, THE NATURE OF THE GROUND AND SUPPORTS.

Br. M. 138 a]

789.

La prima parte neciessarissima è la loro permanētia.

[2] Delli fondamēti che ànno le mēbrifica-tioni componi[3]trici delli tēpli e altri edi-fiti publici, tal proporti[4]one deve essere da profondità a profondità quale [5]è da peso a peso che scaricare si deve sopra essi mē[6]bri.

[7] Ogni parte della pro[8]fondità, che à la terra [9]per alquāto spatio, è [10]fatta a suoli, e [o][11]gni suolo è cōposto di [12]parti, più grave [13]e piv leue l'una chel'al[14]tra; nel pro-fondarsi è più grave, e questo si prova, [15]perchè questi tali soli sō cō[17]posti dalle turbulentie [16]delle acque scaricate ī [18]mare dal corso de' fiumi, [19]che in quello ver-sano, [20]delle quali turbulentie [21]la parte più grave fu [22]quella che prima [23]si scaricò successiva[24]mēte, e questo fa l'ac[25]qua, dov' ella si ferma, le[26]vādo prima dove es[27]sa si move; E di que[28]sti tali soli di terra [29]si manifesta nelli lati [30]di fiumi che coi lor con[31]tinui corsi ànno secati [32]e partiti con grā pro[33]fondità di tagli l'ū mō[34]te dall'al-tro, doue per li [35]ghiajosi soli l'acque so[36]no scolate e per questo [37]la materia si è sec-

The first and most important thing is stability.

As to the foundations of the component parts of temples and other public buildings, the depths of the foundations must bear the same proportions to each other as the weight of material which is to be placed upon them.

Every part of the depth of earth in a given space is composed of layers, and each layer is composed of heavier or lighter materials, the lowest being the heaviest. And this can be proved, because these layers have been formed by the sedi-ment from water carried down to the sea, by the current of rivers which flow into it. The heaviest part of this sediment was that which was first thrown down, and so on by degrees; and this is the action of water when it becomes stagnant, having first brought down the mud whence it first flowed. And such layers of soil are seen in the banks of rivers, where their constant flow has cut through them and divided one slope from the other to a great depth; where in gra-velly strata the waters have run off, the ma-

789. 1. ella loro permanentia. 2. chean le mēbrificationi chonponi. 3. pubblici. 4. debbe . dapprofondita approfondita. 5. dap-peso . . chesscarichare si debbe. 8. alla. 9. spatiotio. 10. faetata assuoli. 11. chōpossto. 12. parte . . grave [opi]. 13. eppiv lievi luna chellal. 14. tra "nel grave" ecquesto si prove. 15. quessti. 16. turbbulentie. 17. scharichate. 21. fuc. 22. prim"a". 23. sisscharicho. 24. ecquesto fallac. 25. ferme. 29. manifessta. 30. cholor chon. 31. chorsi an seghati. 32. esspartiti. 34. dallaltre. 35. gliorosi. 37. se secha. 38. chōvertita. 40. fāgho. 41. ecquesto. 43. tereste. 45. chosi de chōverso.

cata ³⁸ e coüertita in dura ³⁹ pietra, e massime
di ⁴⁰ quel fāgo, che era più ⁴¹ sottile, e questo
ci ⁴² fa cōcludere, che ogni par⁴³te della terrestre superfitie fu ⁴⁴ già ciētro della terra e
⁴⁵ così de cōverso ecc.

terials have, in consequence, dried and been
converted into hard stone, and this happened
most in what was the finest mud; whence
we conclude that every portion of the surface of the earth was once at the centre of
the earth, and *vice versa* &c.

A. 50 a]

790.

¶ Quella parte del fondamēto delli edifiti
che piv pesa ² piv si ficca · e lascia in alto
il piv leggiero disunito da se; ¶ ³ ¶ E quel terreno ch'è piv · premvto, sendo poroso ·, piv
acconsente; ¶ ⁴ Senpre tu · devi · fare i fondamēti che sportino egualmēte fori del
⁵ carico · de'lor mvri e pilastri come appare
· in *m · a · b* ·, e se ⁶ farai · come · molti fanno,
cioè di fare uno fondamēto d'equale ⁷ larghezza · in sino alla superfitie · della terra,
e di sopra li danno diseguale ⁸ carico come

The heaviest part of the foundations of
buildings settles most, and leaves the
lighter part above it separated from it.

And the soil which is most pressed, if
it be porous yields most.

You should always make the foundations
project equally beyond the weight of the walls
and piers, as shown at *m a b*. If you do
as many do, that is to say if you make a
foundation of equal width from the bottom
up to the surface of the ground, and charge

si dimostra in · *b · e* · e in *e · o*, la parte del
fonda⁹mēto · *b · e*, perchè è piena dal pilastro del cātone ·, piv pesa e piv spīgie ¹⁰ in
basso il suo fōdamēto che nō fa il muro ·
e · o che non occupa ¹¹ interamēte il suo
fōdamēto, e però meno spegnie e mē si
ficca, ¹² onde ficcādosi il pilastro *b · e* · e si
diunisce e parte dal mv¹³ro · *e · o* · come si
uede nel piv delli edifiti che sono spicati
intorno · a detti pilastri.

it above with unequal weights, as shown at
b e and at *e o*, at the part of the foundation
at *b e*, the pier of the angle will weigh most
and thrust its foundation downwards, which
the wall at *e o* will not do; since it does not
cover the whole of its foundation, and therefore thrusts less heavily and settles less. Hence,
the pier *b e* in settling cracks and parts
from the wall *e o*. This may be seen in most
buildings which are cracked round the piers.

A. 53 a]

791.

La finestra · *a* · sta bene sotto
² la finestra *c* · e la finestra ³ · *b* ·
sta · male · sotto · lo spatio ⁴ · *d* ·,
perchè detto · spatio · è sanza
⁵ sostegnio · e fondamēto, ⁶ si chè
ricordati di nō rōpere ⁷ mai sotto
· li spati · delle finestre.

The window *a* is well placed
under the window *c*, and the window *b* is badly placed under the
pier *d*, because this latter is without
support and foundation; mind therefore never to make a break under
the piers between the windows.

790. 1. Quela. 2. ficha . ellasscia . . el . . legieri . dasse. 3. Ecquel tereno . . achōsēte. 4. debi . . chessportino. 5. pilasstri
chome apare . . esse. 6. chome . . ī̊ fondamēto [equi] de quale. 7. largeza . . ala . . delatera . . dano. 8. charicho.
9. chātone. 10. baso . . none ochupa. 11. ficha. 12. fi[g] chādosi . . disunisscie. 13. chome . . chessono spichati. 14. pilasstri.
791. 2. ella. 3. sotto [la finestra] lo spatio. 5. effondamēto. 6. richordati.

A. 48 *b*]   **792.**

DEL SOSTĒTACULO.

[2]Il pilastro moltiplicato per grossezza · crescierà tanto piv che la sua debita potētia [3]quāto · e' māca · della ragionevole altezza.

ESĒNPLO.

[5]Se uno pilastro · debe · essere · alto · 9 · grossezze ·, cioè · che s'egli · sarà · grosso · uno braccio, la regola [6]lo pone di · 9 · braccia ·; se ne collegherai · 100 · insieme · per grossezza · fia grosso braccia 10 e alto · 9, [7]e se il primo pilastro regieva 10000 libbre, perchè questo secōdo non è alto se non è circa [8]a una grossezza, e mācādoli · 8 parti della lunghezza · e' regierà · piv otto volte, [9]cioè ogni · pilastro collegato · li toccerà a regiere piv 8 volte che dislegato, cioè [10]che se prima regieva dieci mila libbre ·, adesso ne sosterrà 90 mila.

OF THE SUPPORTS.

A pillar of which the thickness is increased will gain more than its due strength, in direct proportion to what its loses in relative height.

EXAMPLE.

If a pillar should be nine times as high as it is broad—that is to say, if it is one braccio thick, according to rule it should be nine braccia high—then, if you place 100 such pillars together in a mass this will be ten braccia broad and 9 high; and if the first pillar could carry 10000 pounds the second being only about as high as it is wide, and thus lacking 8 parts of its proper length, it, that is to say, each pillar thus united, will bear eight times more than when disconnected; that is to say, that if at first it would carry ten thousand pounds, it would now carry 90 thousand.

---

792. 1. sosstētachulo. 2. pilasstro mvltiplichato per grosseza cressciera . tanto "piv che". 3. mācha . . alteza. 5. Se î . . grosseze . . chesseli . . î br . [de] la. 6. 9 br . . cholegerai . . grosseza . br. 10. 7. esse . . lbr . . ṣechōdo . . circha. 8. a î grosseza e māchādoli . . dela lungeza. 9. cholegato . . tochera. 10. chesse . . mila lbr . . sostera.

ON THE RESISTANCE OF BEAMS.

S. K. M. II.¹ 72 *a*] **793.**

²Quell'angolo sa³rà di piv resistē⁴tia che fia piv a⁵cuto e 'l piv ottu⁶so fia piv debole.

That angle will offer the greatest resistance which is most acute, and the most obtuse will be the weakest.

PALCO DOPPIO.

S. K. M. III.¹ 90 *b*] **794.**

Se i travi e'l peso *o* fia · 100 · libre, ²quāto · peso · sarà · in *a · b* · a fa³re resistētia · a esso · peso · che ⁴nō caggia in basso?

If the beams and the weight *o* are 100 pounds, how much weight will be wanted at *a · b* to resist such a weight, that it may not fall down?

A. 53 *a*] **795.**

DELLA LUNGHEZZA DELLE TRAVI.

ON THE LENGTH OF BEAMS.

²Quella · trave · che fia lūga · piv · che le 20 sua ³maggiori grossezze, fia poco permanēte e rōperasi in ¹/₂; ⁴e ricordati che

That beam which is more than 20 times as long as its greatest thickness will be of brief duration and will break in half; and

793. 4. cheffia. 5. piotu.   794. 1—4 R. 2. affa. 3. resisstētia. 4. chaggio.

793. The three smaller sketches accompany the text in the original, but the larger one is not directly connected with it. It is to be found on fol. 89ª of the same Manuscript and there we read in a note, written underneath, *coverchio della perdicha del castello* (roof of the flagstaff of the castle).—Compare also Pl. XCIII, No. 1.

la parte ch'ētra nel mvro, sia penetrata
[5] di pece calda e fasciata d'asse di quercia,
ācor essa penetrata; [6]Ogni trave vole passare i sua muri e esser ferma di là da essi
mv[7]ri cō soffitiēti catene, perchè spesso si
vede per terremoti le tra-
vi usci[8]re de'mvri e rovi-
nare poi i mvri e solari;
dove, se sono īcatenate,
[9]terranno · i mvri · in · sieme fermi, e i mvri fermano · i solari.

[10]Ancora ti ricorda · che tu · nō faci mai
i smalti · sopra legni[11]ame, imperochè nel
cresciere e discresciere · che fa il legname
[12]per l'umido · e secco, spesse volte cre-
pano detti solai e crepa[13]te le loro diuisioni
· a poco a poco si fāno in poluere e fāno
[14]brutta evidētia.

[15]Ancora ti ricordo nō facci solari soste-
nvti da archi [16]e travi, imperochè col tēpo il
solaro, ch'è sostenvto dalle tra[17]vi, cala alquāto in nel suo · mezzo, e quella parte
[18]del solaro, ch'è sostenuta dal arco, resta
nel suo loco, onde [19]J solari che sono soste-
nvti da 2 varie nature di sostēta[20]culi paiono
col tēpo fatti a còlli.

remember, that the part built into the wall
should be steeped in hot pitch and filleted
with oak boards likewise so steeped. Each
beam must pass through its walls and be
secured beyond the walls with sufficient
chaining, because in con-
sequence of earthquakes
the beams are often seen
to come out of the walls
and bring down the walls
and floors; whilst if they are chained they will
hold the walls strongly together and the
walls will hold the floors. Again I remind
you never to put plaster over timber.
Since by expansion and shrinking of
the timber produced by damp and dryness
such floors often crack, and once cracked
their divisions gradually produce dust and
an ugly effect. Again remember not to
lay a floor on beams supported on arches;
for, in time the floor which is made on
beams settles somewhat in the middle
while that part of the floor which rests on
the arches remains in its place; hence, floors
laid over two kinds of supports look, in
time, as if they were made in hills [19].

795. 1. dela lungeza. 2. cheffia . . pivi . chele [10] 20. 3. magiori grosseze . . pocho. 4. richordoti. 5. chalda . . essa *is wanting.* 7. chō soffitiēte chatene . . tremoti . . ussci. 8. īchatenate. 9. terano . . e e mvri. 10. Anchora ti richordo chettu. 11. cresciere e disscresciere cheffa ilegname. 12. essecho . . isspesse . . detti soli e crep. 13. ti le . . apocho apocho . . effano. 15. Anchora ti richordo nō faci. 16. ettrav . . chol . . dale. 17. chola . . inel . . mezo [che elp] eqlle parte. 18. sostenta . . archo . . locho. 19. propositione J solari chessone. 20. ch chili paiano chol . . acholli. *The word* propositione *written on the margin near line* 19 *has apparently nothing to do with this text, but M. Ravaisson, in his edition of MS. A. has been misled by it to take* j solari (*line* 18) *for the beginning of a new paragraph.*

795. 19. M. RAVAISSON, in his edition of MS. A gives a very different rendering of this passage translating it thus: *Les planchers qui sont soutenus par deux différentes natures de supports paraissent avec le temps faits en voûte* [*a cholli*].

Remarks on the style of Leonardo's architecture.

A few remarks may here be added on the style of Leonardo's architectural studies. However incomplete, however small in scale, they allow us to establish a certain number of facts and probabilities, well worthy of consideration.

When Leonardo began his studies the great name of Brunellesco was still the inspiration of all Florence, and we cannot doubt that Leonardo was open to it, since we find among his sketches the plan of the church of Santo Spirito[1] and a lateral view of San Lorenzo (Pl. XCIV No. 1), a plan almost identical with the chapel Degli Angeli, only begun by him (Pl. XCIV, No. 3) while among Leonardo's designs for domes several clearly betray the influence of Brunellesco's Cupola and the lantern of Santa Maria del Fiore[2].

The beginning of the second period of modern Italian architecture falls during the first twenty years of Leonardo's life. However the new impetus given by Leon Battista Alberti either was not generally understood by his contemporaries, or those who appreciated it, had no opportunity of showing that they did so. It was only when taken up by Bramante and developed by him to the highest rank of modern architecture that this new influence was generally felt. Now the peculiar feature of Leonardo's sketches is that, like the works of Bramante, they appear to be the development and continuation of Alberti's.

[1] *See Pl. XCIV, No. 2. Then only in course of erection after the designs of Brunellesco, though he was already dead; finished in* 1481.

[2] *A small sketch of the tower of the Palazzo della Signoria (MS. C. A.* 309) *proves that he also studied mediaeval monuments.*

But a question here occurs which is difficult to answer. Did Leonardo, till he quitted Florence, follow the direction given by the dominant school of Brunellesco, which would then have given rise to his "First manner", or had he, even before he left Florence, felt Alberti's influence—either through his works (Palazzo Ruccellai, and the front of Santa Maria Novella) or through personal intercourse? Or was it not till he went to Milan that Alberti's work began to impress him through Bramante, who probably had known Alberti at Mantua about 1470 and who not only carried out Alberti's views and ideas, but, by his designs for St. Peter's at Rome, proved himself the greatest of modern architects. When Leonardo went to Milan Bramante had already been living there for many years. One of his earliest works in Milan was the church of Santa Maria presso San Satiro, Via del Falcone[1].

Now we find among Leonardo's studies of Cupolas on Plates LXXXIV and LXXXV and in Pl. LXXX several sketches which seem to me to have been suggested by Bramante's dome of this church.

The MSS. B and Ash. II contain the plans of S. Sepolcro, the pavilion in the garden of the duke of Milan, and two churches, evidently inspired by the church of San Lorenzo at Milan.

MS. B. contains besides two notes relating to Pavia, one of them a design for the sacristy of the Cathedral at Pavia, which cannot be supposed to be dated later than 1492, and it has probably some relation to Leonardo's call to Pavia June 21, 1490[2]. These and other considerations justify us in concluding, that Leonardo made his studies of cupolas at Milan, probably between the years 1487 and 1492 in anticipation of the erection of one of the grandest churches of Italy, the Cathedral of Pavia. This may explain the decidedly Lombardo-Bramantesque tendency in the style of these studies, among which only a few remind us of the forms of the cupolas of S. Maria del Fiore and of the Baptistery of Florence. Thus, although when compared with Bramante's work, several of these sketches plainly reveal that master's influence, we find, among the sketches of domes, some, which show already Bramante's classic style, of which the Tempietto of San Pietro in Montorio, his first building executed at Rome, is the foremost example[3].

On Plate LXXXIV is a sketch of the plan of a similar circular building; and the Mausoleum on Pl. XCVIII, no less than one of the pedestals for the statue of Francesco Sforza (Pl. LXV), is of the same type.

---

1 *Evidence of this I intend to give later on in a Life of Bramante, which I have in preparation.*

2 *The sketch of the plan of Brunellesco's church of Santo Spirito at Florence, which occurs in the same Manuscript, may have been done from memory.*

3 *It may be mentioned here, that in 1494 Bramante made a similar design for the lantern of the Cupola of the Church of Santa Maria delle Grazie.*

The drawings *Pl. LXXXIV No.* 2, *Pl. LXXXVI No.* 1 and 2 and the ground floor of the building in the drawing *Pl. XCI No.* 2, with the interesting decoration by gigantic statues in large niches, are also, I believe, more in the style Bramante adopted at Rome, than in the Lombard style. Are we to conclude from this that Leonardo on his part influenced Bramante in the sense of simplifying his style and rendering it more congenial to antique art? The answer to this important question seems at first difficult to give, for we are here in presence of Bramante, the greatest of modern architects, and with Leonardo, the man comparable with no other. We have no knowledge of any buildings erected by Leonardo, and unless we admit personal intercourse—which seems probable, but of which there is no proof—, it would be difficult to understand how Leonardo could have affected Bramante's style. The converse is more easily to be admitted, since Bramante, as we have proved elsewhere, drew and built simultaneously in different manners, and though in Lombardy there is no building by him in his classic style, the use of brick for building, in that part of Italy, may easily account for it.

Bramante's name is incidentally mentioned in Leonardo's manuscripts in two passages (*Nos.* 1414 and 1448). On each occasion it is only a slight passing allusion, and the nature of the context gives us no due information as to any close connection between the two artists.

It might be supposed, on the ground of Leonardo's relations with the East given in sections XVII and XXI of this volume, that some evidence of oriental influence might be detected in his architectural drawings. I do not however think that any such traces can be pointed out with certainty unless perhaps the drawing for a Mausoleum, *Pl. XCVIII.*

Among several studies for the construction of cupolas above a Greek cross there are some in which the forms are decidedly monotonous. These, it is clear, were not designed as models of taste; they must be regarded as the results of certain investigations into the laws of proportion, harmony and contrast.

The designs for churches, on the plan of a Latin cross are evidently intended to depart as little as possible from the form of a Greek cross; and they also show a preference for a nave surrounded with outer porticos.

The architectural forms preferred by Leonardo are pilasters coupled (*Pl. LXXXII No.* 1) or grouped (*Pl. LXXX No.* 5 and *XCIV No.* 4), often combined with niches. We often meet with orders superposed, one in each story, or two small orders on one story, in combination with one great order (*Pl. XCVI No.* 2).

The drum (tamburo) of these cupolas is generally octagonal, as in the cathedral of Florence, and with similar round windows in its sides. In Pl. LXXXVII No. 2 it is circular like the model actually carried out by Michael Angelo at St. Peter's.

The cupola itself is either hidden under a pyramidal roof, as in the Baptistery of Florence, San Lorenzo of Milan and most of the Lombard churches (Pl. XCI No. 1 and Pl. XCII No. 1); but it more generally suggests the curve of Sta Maria del Fiore (Pl. LXXXVIII No. 5; Pl. XC No. 2; Pl. LXXXIX, M; Pl. XC No. 4, Pl. XCVI No. 2). In other cases (Pl. LXXX No. 4; Pl. LXXXIX; Pl. XC No. 2) it shows the sides of the octagon crowned by semicircular pediments, as in Brunellesco's lantern of the Cathedral and in the model for the Cathedral of Pavia.

Finally, in some sketches the cupola is either semicircular, or as in Pl. LXXXVII No. 2, shows the beautiful line, adopted sixty years later by Michael Angelo for the existing dome of St. Peter's.

It is worth noticing that for all these domes Leonardo is not satisfied to decorate the exterior merely with ascending ribs or mouldings, but employs also a system of horizontal parallels to complete the architectural system. Not the least interesting are the designs for the tiburio (cupola) of the Milan Cathedral. They show some of the forms, just mentioned, adapted to the peculiar gothic style of that monument.

The few examples of interiors of churches recall the style employed in Lombardy by Bramante, for instance in S. Maria di Canepanuova at Pavia, or by Dolcebuono in the Monastero Maggiore at Milan (see Pl. CI No. 1 [C. A. 181ᵇ; 546ᵇ]; Pl. LXXXIV No. 10).

The few indications concerning palaces seem to prove that Leonardo followed Alberti's example of decorating the walls with pilasters and a flat rustica, either in stone or by graffitti (Pl. CII No. 1 and Pl. LXXXV No. 14).

By pointing out the analogies between Leonardo's architecture and that of other masters we in no way pretend to depreciate his individual and original inventive power. These are at all events beyond dispute. The project for the Mausoleum (Pl. XCVIII) would alone suffice to rank him among the greatest architects who ever lived. The peculiar shape of the tower (Pl. LXXX), of the churches for preaching (Pl. XCVII No. 1 and pages 56 and 57, Fig. 1—4), his curious plan for a city with high and low level streets (Pl. LXXVII and LXXVIII No. 2 and No. 3), his Loggia with fountains (Pl. LXXXII No. 4) reveal an originality, a power and facility of invention for almost any given problem, which are quite wonderful.

In addition to all these qualities he propably stood alone in his day in one department of architectural study,—his investigations, namely, as to the resistance of vaults, foundations, walls and arches.

As an application of these studies the plan of a semicircular vault (Pl. CIII No. 2) may be mentioned here, disposed so as to produce no thrust on the columns on which it rests: volta ī botte e non ispignie īfori le colone. *Above the geometrical patterns on the same sheet, close to a circle inscribed in a square is the note:* la ragiō d'una volta cioè il terzo del diamitro della sua . . . del tedesco in domo.

There are few data by which to judge of Leonardo's style in the treatment of detail. On Pl. LXXXV No. 10 and Pl. CIII No. 3, we find some details of pillars; on Pl. CI No. 3 slender pillars designed for a fountain and on Pl. CIII No. 1 MS. B, is a pen and ink drawing of a vase which also seems intended for a fountain. Three handles seem to have been intended to connect the upper parts with the base. There can be no doubt that Leonardo, like Bramante, but unlike Michael Angelo, brought infinite delicacy of motive and execution to bear on the details of his work.

XIV.

Anatomy, Zoology and Physiology.

Leonardo's eminent place in the history of medicine, as a pioneer in the sciences of Anatomy and Physiology, will never be appreciated till it is possible to publish the mass of manuscripts in which he largely treated of these two branches of learning. In the present work I must necessarily limit myself to giving the reader a general view of these labours, by publishing his introductory notes to the various books on anatomical subjects. I have added some extracts, and such observations as are scattered incidentally through these treatises, as serving to throw a light on Leonardo's scientific attitude, besides having an interest for a wider circle than that of specialists only.

VASARI expressly mentions Leonardo's anatomical studies, having had occasion to examine the manuscript books which refer to them. According to him Leonardo studied Anatomy in the companionship of Marc Antonio della Torre "aiutato e scambievolmente aiutando."—This learned Anatomist taught the science in the universities first of Padua and then of Pavia, and at Pavia he and Leonardo may have worked and studied together. We have no clue to any exact dates, but in the year 1506 Marc Antonio della Torre seems to have not yet left Padua. He was scarcely thirty years old when he died in 1512, and his writings on anatomy have not only never been published, but no manuscript copy of them is known to exist.

This is not the place to enlarge on the connection between Leonardo and Marc Antonio della Torre. I may however observe that I have not been able to discover in Leonardo's manuscripts on anatomy any mention of his younger contemporary. The few quotations which occur from writers on medicine—either of antiquity or of the middle ages are printed in Section XXII. Here and there in the manuscripts mention is made of an anonymous "adversary" (avversario) whose views are opposed and refuted by Leonardo, but there is no ground for supposing that Marc Antonio della Torre should have been this "adversary".

Only a very small selection from the mass of anatomical drawings left by Leonardo have been published here in facsimile, but to form any adequate idea of their scientific merit they should be compared with the coarse and inadequate figures given in the published books of the early part of the XVI. century.

William Hunter, the great surgeon—a competent judge—who had an opportunity in the time of George III. of seeing the originals in the King's Library, has thus recorded his opinion: "I expected to see little more than such designs in Anatomy as might be useful to a painter in his own profession. But I saw, and indeed with astonishment, that Leonardo had been a general and deep student. When I consider what pains he has taken upon every part of the body, the superiority of his universal genius, his particular excellence in mechanics and hydraulics, and the attention with which such a man would examine and see objects which he has to draw, I am fully persuaded that Leonardo was the best Anatomist, at that time, in the world . . . Leonardo was certainly the first man, we know of, who introduced the practice of making anatomical drawings" (Two introductory letters. London 1784, pages 37 and 39).

The illustrious German Naturalist Johan Friedrich Blumenbach esteemed them no less highly; he was one of the privileged few who, after Hunter, had the chance of seeing these Manuscripts. He writes: Der Scharfblick dieses grossen Forschers und Darstellers der Natur hat schon auf Dinge geachtet, die noch Jahrhunderte nachher unbemerkt geblieben sind" *(see* Blumenbach's medicinische Bibliothek, *Vol. 3, St. 4, 1795, page 728).*

These opinions were founded on the drawings alone. Up to the present day hardly anything has been made known of the text, and, for the reasons I have given, it is my intention to reproduce here no more than a selection of extracts which I have made from the originals at Windsor Castle and elsewhere. In the Bibliography of the Manuscripts, at the end of this volume a short review is given of the valuable contents of these Anatomical note books which are at present almost all in the possession of her Majesty the Queen of England. It is, I believe, possible to assign the date with approximate accuracy to almost all the fragments, and I am thus led to conclude that the greater part of Leonardo's anatomical investigations were carried out after the death of della Torre.

Merely in reading the introductory notes to his various books on Anatomy which are here printed it is impossible to resist the impression that the Master's anatomical studies bear to a very great extent the stamp of originality and independent thought.

I.

ANATOMY.

W. An. IV. 167 a]

796.

Voglio far miraculi;—²abbi mē che li altri o³mini più quieti, e ⁴quelli che vogliono ar⁵ricchirsi in ū dì; vivi ⁶nel lungo tēpo in ⁷grā povertà, co⁸me interviene e ⁹interverrà in etter¹⁰no alli alchimisti, ¹¹cercatori di cre¹²are oro e argēto, ¹³e all' īgegnieri che ¹⁴vogliono che l'a¹⁵cqua morta dia ¹⁶vita motiua ¹⁷a se medesima ¹⁸con cōtinuo ¹⁹moto, ²⁰e al sōmo stol²¹to negromante ²²e īcantatore.

²³E tu che dici, esser me²⁴glio il uedere fare ²⁵l'anatomia, che uede²⁶re tali disegni, dire²⁷sti bene, se fusse ²⁸possibile vedere tu²⁹tte queste cose che ³⁰in tal disegni si di³¹mostrano in una ³²sola figura, nella ³³quale con tutto il tu³⁴o ingenio nō vedra³⁵i, e non avrai la no³⁶titia, se nō d'alquā³⁷te poche vene, del³⁸le · quali io, per aver³⁹ne · vera · e piena ⁴⁰notitia, ò disfatti ⁴¹piv di dieci co⁴²rpi vmani, ⁴³di-

I wish to work miracles;—it may be that I shall possess less than other men of more peaceful lives, or than those who want to grow rich in a day. I may live for a long time in great poverty, as always happens, and to all eternity will happen, to alchemists, the would-be creators of gold and silver, and to engineers who would have dead water stir itself into life and perpetual motion, and to those supreme fools, the necromancer and the enchanter.

[23]And you, who say that it would be better to watch an anatomist at work than to see these drawings, you would be right, if it were possible to observe all the things which are demonstrated in such drawings in a single figure, in which you, with all your cleverness, will not see nor obtain knowledge of more than some few veins, to obtain a true and perfect knowledge of which I have dissected more than ten human bodies, destroying

A general
introduction

---

796. 3. quieti ecq. 4. voliano a. 5. richire nūdi. 6. lungho. 9. intervera. 10. archimisti. 14. voglia. 15. ċq"a" morta. 17. asse. 20. somo. 23. "e" ettu che di. 27. fussi. 31. mosstrano. 35. e non arai. 37. vene de. 43. destrugendo.

796. Lines 1—59 and 60—89 are written in two parallel columns. When we here find Leonardo putting himself in the same category as the Alchemists and Necromancers, whom he elsewhere mocks at so bitterly, it is evidently meant ironically. In the same way Leonardo, in the introduction to the Books on Perspective sets himself with transparent satire on a level with other writers on the subject.

Line 23 and the following seem to be directed against students of painting and young artists rather than against medical men and anatomists.

struggendo ogni ⁴⁴altri mēbri, consu⁴⁵mando con minutis⁴⁶sime particule ⁴⁷tutta la carne che ⁴⁸d'intorno a esse ⁴⁹vene si trovaua, ⁵⁰sanza insangui⁵¹narle, se non d'ī⁵²sensibile insan⁵³guinamēto delle vene capillari; ⁵⁴e vn sol corpo nō ⁵⁵bastava a tanto tēpo, che biso⁵⁶gnava procedere di mano in mano ⁵⁷in tanti corpi, che si finisca la inte⁵⁸ra cognitione; le qual repli⁵⁹cai 2 volte per vedere le differentie.

⁶⁰E se tu avrai l'amore a tal cosa, ⁶¹tu sarai forse inpedito dallo ⁶²stomaco, e se questo nō ti inpedi⁶³sce, tu sarai forse inpedito dal⁶⁴la paura coll' abitare nelli tē-⁶⁵pi notturni in cōpagnia di tali ⁶⁶morti squadrati e scorticati e ⁶⁷spaventevoli a vederli; e se que⁶⁸sto nō t'īpedisce, forse ti māche⁶⁹rà il disegnio bono, il quale s'appa⁷⁰rtiene a tal figuratione; E ⁷¹se tu avrai il disegnio e' nō sarà ⁷²accōpagnato dalla prospettiva, ⁷³e se sarà accōpagnato ⁷⁴e'ti mācherà l'ordine ⁷⁵delle dimostratiō ⁷⁶geometriche e l'ordine ⁷⁷delle calculation delle ⁷⁸forze e valimēto de' ⁷⁹muscoli; e forse ti ⁸⁰mācherà la patiētia che ⁸¹tu nō sarai diligēte; Delle ⁸²quali se in me tutte queste ⁸³cose sono state o no, ⁸⁴i cēto 20 libri da me ⁸⁵conposti ne darà sentē-⁸⁶tia del sì o del no, nelli ⁸⁷quali nō sono stato inpedi⁸⁸to nè d'auaritia o negligētia, ⁸⁹ma sol dal tenpo ∥ vale.

all the other members, and removing the very minutest particles of the flesh by which these veins are surrounded, without causing them to bleed, excepting the insensible bleeding of the capillary veins; and as one single body would not last so long, since it was necessary to proceed with several bodies by degrees, until I came to an end and had a complete knowledge; this I repeated twice, to learn the differences [59].

And if you should have a love for such things you might be prevented by loathing, and if that did not prevent you, you might be deterred by the fear of living in the night hours in the company of those corpses, quartered and flayed and horrible to see. And if this did not prevent you, perhaps you might not be able to draw so well as is necessary for such a demonstration; or, if you had the skill in drawing, it might not be combined with knowledge of perspective; and if it were so, you might not understand the methods of geometrical demonstration and the method of the calculation of forces and of the strength of the muscles; patience also may be wanting, so that you lack perseverance. As to whether all these things were found in me or not[84], the hundred and twenty books composed by me will give verdict Yes or No. In these I have been hindered neither by avarice nor negligence, but simply by want of time. Farewell [89].

W. A. II. 36 *a* (21)]

DELL'ORDINE DEL LIBRO.

OF THE ORDER OF THE BOOK.

Plans and suggestions for the arrangement of materials (797—802).

²Questa · opera · si deve prīcipiare alla · cōciettione · dell'omo ., e devi descrivere · il modo della matrice, ³e come il putto · l'a-bita ·, e in che grado · lui risegga · ī quella·, e 'l modo · dello vivificarsi e cibarsi, ⁴e 'l suo · accrescimēto ·, e che · interuallo · sia ·

This work must begin with the conception of man, and describe the nature of the womb and how the foetus lives in it, up to what stage it resides there, and in what way it quickens into life and feeds. Also its growth and what interval there is between

44. consi. 45. minuti. 46. partichule. 53. capillar "e"(?). 54. e [altrettāte] e vn. 55. attanto tēpo che. 56. imano. 57. corpi che si finissimi la inte. 58. cognitione le qual [s] ripri. 59. cai [1] "2" volte . . diferentie. 60. essettu arai. 66. squartati. 68. nōtipedisce. 69. qual sapa. 70. attal. 71. settu arai. 72. acōpagnato. 73. esse . . acōpagnato. 76. geometrice. 79. efforse. 82. seime. 83. onno [lili]. 84. iccēto 20. 86. tia [di] del. 88. negli ētia. 89. d·l [dalla ve] tenpo.
797. 2. debe. 2. e disscrivere. 3. chome il pucto . . risega . . uiuicharsi. 4. acresscimēto . . da ī grado da cresscimēto . a. ī.

84. Leonardo frequently, and perhaps habitually, wrote in note books of a very small size and only moderately thick; in most of those which have been preserved undivided, each contains less than fifty leaves. Thus a considerable number of such volumes must have gone to make up a volume of the bulk of the 'Codex Atlanticus' which now contains nearly 1200 detached leaves. In the passage under consideration, which was evidently written at a late

period of his life, Leonardo speaks of his Manuscript note-books as numbering 120; but we should hardly be justified in concluding from this passage that the greater part of his Manuscripts were now missing (see *Prolegomena*, Vol. I, pp. 5—7).

797. The meaning of the word *nervo* varies in different passages, being sometimes used for *muscolo* (muscle).

da · uno grado d'accrescimēto · a · uno · altro, e che cosa lo spigna fori [5]del corpo · della madre ·, e per che · cagione qualche · uolta · lui · uēga fori · dal uētro di sua madre iñāti al debito [6]tēpo.

[7]Poi discriuerai quali mēbra sieno · quelle · che crescono · poi · che'l putto è nato · piv che l'altre, [8]e da la misura d'ū putto · d'un anno.

[9]Poi discrivi l'omo crescivto e la fēmina · e sue · misure · e nature di complessione colore [10]e fisonomie.

[11]Di poi descrivi com'egli è cōposto · di uene ·, nerui ·, muscoli e ossa; Questo farai nell'ultimo del libro; [12]di poi figura · in · 4 storie · quattro vniversali casi delli omini, · cioè letitia con uari atti di ridere, [13]e figura · la cagiō · del riso ·; piāto in vari modi colla · sua · cagione ·; cōtētione cō uari movi[14]mēti d'uccisione ·, fughe ·, pavre ·, ferocità ·, ardimēti, micidi · e tutte cose appartenēti a simil casi; [15]di poi figura · vna fatica cō tirare, spiegniere · portare, fermare, sostenere e simili [16]cose;

[17]Di poi discriui attitudine · e movimēto; [18]di poi prospettiva · per l'ofitio e effetti dell'ochio e dell' udito,—dirai di mvsicha—e descrivi delli altri sēsi.

[19]Di poi discrivi la natura · de' sensi.

[20]Questa figura strumētale dell'omo dimostreremo in .. figure, delle [21]quali le 3 prime saranno la ramificatione delle ossa, cioè vna dināzi · che [22]dimostri l'altitudine de' siti e figure delli ossi, la seconda sarà veduta in [23]proffilo e mostrerà la profondità del tutto e delle parti e loro sito; La 3ª [24]figura fia dimostratrice delle ossa dalla parte dirieto; Di poi faremo [25]3 altre figure ne' simili aspetti colle ossa segate, nelle quali si vedranno le lor [26]grossezze e uacuità; 3 altre figure faremo dell' ossa intere e de' nerui che na[27]scono dalla nuca, e in che mēbra ramificano; E 3 altre de'ossa e vene e do[28]ve ramificano, poi 3 con muscoli e 3 con pelle, e figure propor-[29]tionate, e 3 della femina per dimostrare matrice e vene mestruali, [30]che vanno alle poppe.

one stage of growth and another. What it is that forces it out from the body of the mother, and for what reasons it sometimes comes out of the mother's womb before the due time.

Then I will describe which are the members, which, after the boy is born, grow more than the others, and determine the proportions of a boy of one year.

Then describe the fully grown man and woman, with their proportions, and the nature of their complexions, colour, and physiognomy.

Then how they are composed of veins, tendons, muscles and bones. This I shall do at the end of the book. Then, in four drawings, represent four universal conditions of men. That is, Mirth, with various acts of laughter, and describe the cause of laughter. Weeping in various aspects with its causes. Contention, with various acts of killing; flight, fear, ferocity, boldness, murder and every thing pertaining to such cases. Then represent Labour, with pulling, thrusting, carrying, stopping, supporting and such like things.

Further I would describe attitudes and movements. Then perspective, concerning the functions and effects of the eye; and of hearing—here I will speak of music—, and treat of the other senses.

And then describe the nature of the senses.

This mechanism of man we will demonstrate in ... figures; of which the three first will show the ramification of the bones; that is: first one to show their height and position and shape: the second will be seen in profile and will show the depth of the whole and of the parts, and their position. The third figure will be a demonstration of the bones of the backparts. Then I will make three other figures from the same point of view, with the bones sawn across, in which will be shown their thickness and hollowness. Three other figures of the bones complete, and of the nerves which rise from the nape of the neck, and in what limbs they ramify. And three others of the bones and veins, and where they ramify. Then three figures with the muscles and three with the skin, and their proper proportions; and three of woman, to illustrate the womb and the menstrual veins which go to the breasts.

altro .. chosu .. spiga. 5. chorpo .. chagione .. uega .. del. 7. cresscano ēnato. 9. ella .. essue .. chōprlessione chollore effisosomie. 11. desscrivi chom eli e chōposto .. musscoli. 12. chasi .. chouari. 13. effigura la chagiō . de riso .. cholla .. chagione . chōtetione cho. 14. ucisione . fuge .. ettutte chose apartenēti assimil chasi. 15. faticha chō .. sosstenere essimili. 16. chose. 18. lofitio effetti .. della uldito .. musicha .. sesi. 19. de . 2 . "sensi" sensi. 20. dimōsterreno. 22. effigure .. sechonda. 23. mossterra. 24. delle [ner] ossa .. faren. 20. asspetti .. segate .. uetra le. 26. gosseze e uachuita .. fareno. 27. scā della nucha .. ramifichino. 28. ramifichino .. mvsscoli .. effigure. 29. tionati .. mestruale.

ORDINE DEL LIBRO.

[2] Questa mia figuratione del corpo vmano ti sarà dimostra nō altre[3]menti, che se tu auessi l'omo naturale ināti, e la ragō si è, che se tu vuoi be[4]ne conoscere le parti dell'omo anatomizzato, tu lo vuoi ·—o l'o-chio tuo—per di[5]versi aspetti, quello cōside-rando di sotto, e di sopra, e dalli lati, vol-tando[6]lo e cercando l'origine di ciascū mēbro, e ī tal modo la notomia na[7]turale à soddisfatta alla tua notitia; Ma tu ài a intēdere, che tal noti[8]tia nō ti lascia sad-disfatto, cōciosiachè la grādissima confusione che [9]resulta della mistione di pañiculi misti cō uene, arterie, nerui, corde, [10]muscoli, ossi, sangue, il quale tignie di se ogni parte d'un medesimo colo[11]re, e le vene, che di tal sangue si votano non sono conosciute per la lor dimi[12]nutione, e la integrità delli pannicoli, nel cercare le parti che dentro a [13]loro s'includono, si viene a rompere, e la lor trasparētia, tinta di sangue, [14]nō ti lascia conoscere le parti coperte da loro per la similitu[15]dine del lor colore insanguinato, e nō puoi avere la notitia dell'ū che tu [16]nō cōfonda e distrugga l'altro; | adunque è necessario fare più notomie, [17]delle quali 3 te ne bisognia per auere piena notitia delle vene e arterie, [18]distruggēdo con sōma diligentia tutto il rimanēte, e altre 3 per auere la notitia [19]delli pannicoli, e 3 per le corde e muscoli e legamēti, e 3 per li ossi e car[20]tilagini, e 3 per la notomia delle ossa, le quali s'ànno a segare e dimo-[21]strare, quale è buso e quale no, quale è midolloso, quale è spugno[22]so, e quale è grosso dal fori al dentro, e quale è sottile, e alcuno à in al[23]cuna parte grā sottiglezza, e in alcuna è grosso, e in alcuna busa, o

THE ORDER OF THE BOOK.

This depicting of mine of the human body will be as clear to you as if you had the natural man before you; and the reason is that if you wish thoroughly to know the parts of man, anatomically, you—or your eye— require to see it from different aspects, considering it from below and from above and from its sides, turning it about and seeking the origin of each member; and in this way the natural anatomy is sufficient for your comprehension. But you must understand that this amount of knowledge will not continue to satisfy you; seeing the very great confusion that must result from the combination of tissues, with veins, ar-teries, nerves, sinews, muscles, bones, and blood which, of itself, tinges every part the same colour. And the veins, which dis-charge this blood, are not discerned by rea-son of their smallness. Moreover integrity of the tissues, in the process of the inves-tigating the parts within them, is inevitably destroyed, and their transparent substance being tinged with blood does not allow you to recognise the parts covered by them, from the similarity of their blood-stained hue; and you cannot know everything of the one with-out confusing and destroying the other. Hence, some further anatomy drawings be-come necessary. Of which you want three to give full knowledge of the veins and ar-teries, everything else being destroyed with the greatest care. And three others to dis-play the tissues; and three for the sinews and muscles and ligaments; and three for the bones and cartilages; and three for the anatomy of the bones, which have to be sawn to show which are hollow and which are not, which have marrow and which are spongy, and which are thick from the out-side inwards, and which are thin. And some are extremely thin in some parts and thick in others, and in some parts hollow or filled up with bone, or full of marrow, or spongy. And all these conditions are sometimes found

---

798. 2. Quessta. 3. chessettu . . ella . . chessettu. 4. conoscere le parte . . natomizate tu lo voli ollui ollochio. 5. asspetto. 6. ec-cerchando . . ciasscū. 7. turale ta sadidisfatto . . chettal. 8. lasscia . . cōcosia chella . . chonfusione. 9. della . . pañi-chuli. 10. musscoli . . dumedesimo. 11. elle . . cognosscute. 12. nuitione ella . . pannichuli nel cierchare le parte . . al. 13. sincludano . si uēgano . . ella . . trassparētia. 14. lasscia cognossciere le parte [che son sotto a] coperte dalloro per almilitu. 15. poi . . chettu. 16. desstruggha . . natomie. 18. desstrugēdo . . soma. 19. pannichuli . . musscoli ellegamēti e 3 e 3. 20. e [1̊] 3 per la natomia . . assegare e dimos. 21. quale he spugn"a". 22. ecqua le he . . essottile . . innal. 23. chuna . . sottiglieza . alchuna . . alchuna. 24. osspugnosa e chosi . . sarano. 25. nūmēdesimo. 26. essuo. 28. as-

piena ^{24}d'osso, o midollosa, o spugnosa; e
così tutte queste cose sarāno alcuna volta
tro^{25}vate in un medesimo osso, e alcuno
osso fia che non à nessuna; e 3 te ne bisog-
^{26}na fare per la donna, nella quale è grā mis-
terio, mediante la · matrice e suo feto; ^{27}a-
dunque per il mio disegnio ti fia noto ogni
parte e ogni tutto mediante la di^{28}mostratione
di 3 diuersi aspetti di ciascuna parte, perchè
quando tu avrai vedu^{29}to alcun mēbro dalla
parte dinanzi con qualche neruo, corda, o
vena che ^{30}nasca dalla opposita parte, ti fia
dimostro il medesimo mēbro volto per lato
^{31}o dirieto-; non altremēti che se tu auessi
in mano il medesimo mēbro e andas^{32}si lo
voltādo di parte in parte insino a tanto
che tu auessi piena notitia di quel^{33}lo che
tu desideri sapere, e così similmēte ti fia
posto inanti in tre o ^{34}4 dimostrationi di
ciascū mēbro per diuersi aspetti in modo che
tu resterai con^{35}vera e piena notitia di quello
che tu vuoi sapere della figura dell' omo.

^{36}Adunque qui con 12 figure intere ti
sarà mostrata la cosmografia del minor
^{37}mōdo col medesimo ordine che ināzi a
me fu fatto da Tolomeo nella sua cosmo-
^{38}grafia, e così diuidero poi quelle in
mēbra, come lui diuise il tutto in provincie; ^{39}e poi dirò l'ufitio delle parti per
ciascū verso, mettēdoti dināti alli ochi la
notitia ^{40}di tutta la figura e valitudine del-
l'omo inquāto a moto locale mediante le
sue parti, ^{41}E così piacesse al nostro autore
che io potessi dimostrere la natura delli
omini e lo^{42}ro costumi nel modo che io
descrivo la sua figura.

^{43}E ricordoti che la notomia delli nerui non ti darà la situatione della loro rami-
^{44}ficatione, nè in quali muscoli essi si ramificano · mediante li corpi disfatti in acqua
^{45}corrēte, o in acqua di calcina, perchè,
ancorachè ti rimāga la origine de'lor nas-
scimenti ^{46}sanza tale acqua come coll' acqua, le ramificationi loro pel corso del-
l'acqua si ^{47}vengono a vnire, non altremēti
che sì fascia il lino o canapa pettinata per
filare, ^{48}tutto in vn fascio in modo che inpossibile è a ritrovare in quali muscoli o
cō quale ^{49}o cō quāte ramificationi li nerui
s'infondino ne' predetti muscoli.

in one and the same bone, and in some
bones none of them. And three you must
have for the woman, in which there is
much that is mysterious by reason of the
womb and the foetus. Therefore by my
drawings every part will be known to you,
and all by means of demonstrations from
three different points of view of each part;
for when you have seen a limb from the
front, with any muscles, sinews, or veins
which take their rise from the opposite side,
the same limb will be shown to you in a
side view or from behind, exactly as if you
had that same limb in your hand and were
turning it from side to side until you
had acquired a full comprehension of all
you wished to know. In the same way there
will be put before you three or four demonstrations of each limb, from various points
of view, so that you will be left with a true
and complete knowledge of all you wish to
learn of the human figure[35].

Thus, in twelve entire figures, you will
have set before you the cosmography of this
lesser world on the same plan as, before
me, was adopted by Ptolemy in his cosmography; and so I will afterwards divide them
into limbs as he divided the whole world
into provinces; then I will speak of the function of each part in every direction, putting
before your eyes a description of the whole
form and substance of man, as regards his
movements from place to place, by means
of his different parts. And thus, if it
please our great Author, I may demonstrate
the nature of men, and their customs in the
way I describe his figure.

And remember that the anatomy of the
nerves will not give the position of their
ramifications, nor show you which muscles
they branch into, by means of bodies dissected in running water or in lime water;
though indeed their origin and starting point
may be seen without such water as well as
with it. But their ramifications, when under
running water, cling and unite—just like flat
or hemp carded for spinning—all into a skein,
in a way which makes it impossible to trace
in which muscles or by what ramification the
nerves are distributed among those muscles.

spetti . . quanto . . arai. 30. parte [tu] eti . . per lalo. 31. chessettu . . imano. 32. attanto chettu. 33. llo chettu . .
possto. 34. asspetti . . chettu. 35. chettu voi. 36. mosstro la cossmografia. 37. fuffatto dattolomeo . . cossmo. 38. imēbra
. . province. 39. ciasscū. 40. lochale . . parte. 41. Eccosi piacessi . . altore . . dimosstrare. 42. cosstumi . . desscrivo.
43. cholla dilora. 44. facione . . musscoli . . ramifichino. 45. corēte o in acq"a" . . rimāgha. 46. tale acq "a" . .
ramificatione. 47. vengono chessi facci . . chanapa. 48. fasscio. 49. ramificatione . . mvsscoli.

798. 35. Compare Pl. CVII. The original drawing at Windsor is 28^{1}/$_{2}$ ✕ 19^{1}/$_{2}$ centimètres. The
upper figures are slightly washed with Indian ink. On the back of this drawing is the text No. 1140.

ORDINE DI NOTOMIA.

[2]Fa prima l'ossa come dire le braccia, e poni il motore dalla spalla al [3]gomito per tutte le linie; Di poi dal gomito al braccio; Di poi dal [4]braccio alla mano e dalla mano alli diti.

[5]E nel · braccio porrai li motori de' diti che s'aprono, e [6]questi nella lor dimostratione porrai soli; nella 2ª dimo-[7]stratione vestirai questi muscoli delli secondi motori de' diti, [8]e così farai a grado a grado per non confondere: ma primo po[9]ni sopra dell' ossa quelli muscoli che con essi ossa si congiungono, [10]sanza altra confusione d'altri muscoli, e con quelli porrai [11]li nerui e uene, che li nutriscono, auendo prima fatto l'albero delle ue[12]ne e nerui sopra delle senplici ossa.

THE ARRANGEMENT OF ANATOMY.

First draw the bones, let us say, of the arm, and put in the motor muscle from the shoulder to the elbow with all its lines. Then proceed in the same way from the elbow to the wrist. Then from the wrist to the hand and from the hand to the fingers.

And in the arm you will put the motors of the fingers which open, and these you will show separately in their demonstration. In the second demonstration you will clothe these muscles with the secondary motors of the fingers and so proceed by degrees to avoid confusion. But first lay on the bones those muscles which lie close to the said bones, without confusion of other muscles; and with these you may put the nerves and veins which supply their nourishment, after having first drawn the tree of veins and nerves over the simple bones.

Comīcia la notomia alla testa e finiscila nella piāta del piede.

Begin the anatomy at the head and finish at the sole of the foot.

3 · uomini finiti, [2]3 · con ossa e nerui, [3]3 · con ossa senplici; [4]Queste sono 12 dimo[5]strationi di figure ī[6]tere.

3 men complete, 3 with bones and nerves, 3 with the bones only. Here we have 12 demonstrations of entire figures.

Quādo · tu · ài · finito di [2]crescere l'omo · tu [3]farai · la statua · cō tu[4]tte · sue misure · [5]superfitiali.

When you have finished building up the man, you will make the statue with all its superficial measurements.

---

799. 2. le br e. 3. al br. 4. br alla. 5. nel br. porrai . . chessaperano. 6. cquesti. 7. musscoli. 9. musscoli . . chon . . chongunghano. 10. musscoli. 11. chelli notrisscano . . p "a" fatto. 12. ennerui.
800. effiniscila.
801. 1. homini. 2. chon. 3. ssenplici. 6. tiere.   **802.** 2. cressciere . . ettu. 3. lasstatua . chō.

---

802. *Cresciere l'omo.* The meaning of this expression appears to be different here and in the passage C. A. 157ª, 468ª (see No. 526, Note I. 2). Here it can hardly mean anything else than modelling, since the sculptor forms the figure by degrees, by adding wet clay and the figure consequently increases or grows. *Tu farai la statua* would then mean, you must work out the figure in marble. If this interpretation is the correct one, this passage would have no right to find a place in the series on anatomical studies. I may say that it was originally inserted in this connection under the impression that *di cresciere* should be read *descrivere.*

W. An. III, XXII] 803.

Farai tutti li moti dell' ossa ²colle giunture loro dopo ³la dimostratione delle pri⁴me tre figure dell' ossa, e⁵questo si deve fare nel primo ⁶libro.

You must show all the motions of the bones with their joints to follow the demonstration of the first three figures of the bones, and this should be done in the first book.

Plans for the representation of muscles by drawings (803—809).

W. XXIII] 804.

Ricordoti che per farti certo del nascimento di qualunche muscolo, che tu tiri ²la corda, partorita da esso muscolo, in modo che tu veda movere esso ³muscolo e 'l suo nascimēto sopra delle · legature delli ossi.

Remember that to be certain of the point of origin of any muscle, you must pull the sinew from which the muscle springs in such a way as to see that muscle move, and where it is attached to the ligaments of the bones.

NOTANDO.

NOTE.

⁵Tu non farai mai se nō confusione nella di⁶mostratione de' muscoli e lor siti, nascimēti ⁷e fini, se prima non fai vna dimostratione di ⁸muscoli sottili a uso di fila di refe, e così potrai ⁹figurare l'un· sopra dell' altro, come li a situati la ¹⁰natura, e così li potrai nominare secōdo il mēbro ¹¹al quale lor seruono, cioè il motore della pū¹²ta del dito grosso e del suo osso di mezzo o del primo ecc; ¹³e dato che tu ài tale notitia, figurerai al lato a ¹⁴questa · la uera forma e quātità e sito di ciascū muscolo; ¹⁵ma ricordati di fare li fili, che insegniano li muscoli, neg¹⁶li medesimi siti che son le linie centrali di ciascū mu¹⁷scolo, e così tali fili dimostreranno la figura della ganba ¹⁸e la loro distantia spedita e nota.

¹⁹Ho spogliato di pelle vno il quale per una mala²⁰ttia s'era tanto diminuito che li muscoli erā ²¹consumati e restati a uso di pellicola sottile, ²²in modo che le corde in scābio del conuertirsi ²³in muscolo si convertivano in larga pelle, ²⁴e quādo l'ossa erā uestite di pelle, poco acqui²⁵stauā della lor naturale grossezza.

You will never get any thing but confusion in demonstrating the muscles and their positions, origin, and termination, unless you first make a demonstration of thin muscles after the manner of linen threads; and thus you can represent them, one over another as nature has placed them; and thus, too, you can name them according to the limb they serve; for instance the motor of the point of the great toe, of its middle bone, of its first bone, &c. And when you have the knowledge you will draw, by the side of this, the true form and size and position of each muscle. But remember to give the threads which explain the situation of the muscles in the position which corresponds to the central line of each muscle; and so these threads will demonstrate the form of the leg and their distance in a plain and clear manner.

I have removed the skin from a man who was so shrunk by illness that the muscles were worn down and remained in a state like thin membrane, in such a way that the sinews instead of merging in muscles ended in wide membrane; and where the bones were covered by the skin they had very little over their natural size.

803. 2. gunture. 3. dimosstratione. 4. ecq. 5. defare.

804. 1. nasscimēto . . chettu. 2. corta. 3. musscolo..nasscimēto. 6. mosstratione . . musscoli ellor . . nasscimēti. 7. effini . . dimosstratione. 8. musscoli. 10. mēbr. 11. seruano coe . . motore [delluli]. 12. mezo. 13. chettu. 14. cquessta . . essito . . mussolo. 15. musscoli ne. 16. le medesimi . . chesson . . ciasscū. 17. dimosterā. 18. ella . . disstantia . . e note. 19. hosspogliato. 20. chelli musscoli. 21. cresstati. 22. chelle corde niscābio. 23: musscolo . . largha. 24. pocho. 25. grosseza.

804. The photograph No. 41 of Grosvenor Gallery Publications: a drawing of the muscles of the foot, includes a complete facsimile of the text of this passage.

W. An. I. 1 *b*]

805.

Quale nervo è cagione del moto dell'ochio a fare·che 'l moto dell'un ochio tiri l'altro.

²¶Del chiudere le ciglia, ³dello alzare le ciglia, ⁴dello abbassare le ciglia,¶ ⁵¶dello chiudere li ochi, ⁶dello aprire li ochi,¶ ⁷¶dello alzare le narici, ⁸del aprire le labra cō dēti·serrati, ⁹dello·appūtare·le labra, ¹⁰del ridere, ¹¹del maravigliarsi.

¹²A discriuere il principio dell'omo quādo elli si cavsa·nella matrice, ¹³e perchè uno putto nō uiue·d'otto·mesi; ¹⁴che cosa è starnvto, ¹⁵che cosa è sbadiglio, ¹⁶malmaestro, ¹⁷spasimo, ¹⁸paralitico, ¹⁹tremito di freddo, ²⁰sudore, ²¹stāchezza, ²²fame, ²³sonno, ²⁴sete, ²⁵lussuria.

²⁶¶Del neruo·ch'è cagione del moto della spalla al gomito, ²⁷del moto che è dal gon ito alla mano, ²⁸dalla givntura·della·mano·al nascimēto de'diti, ²⁹dal nascimēto de'diti·al loro·mezzo ³⁰e dal mezzo all'ultimo nodo.¶

³¹Del neruo che è cagione del moto della coscia, ³²e dal ginochio al piè, e dalla givntura del piè ai diti ³³e così ai lor mezzi, ³⁴e del girare d'essa ganba.

Which nerve causes the motion of the eye so that the motion of one eye moves the other?

Of frowning the brows, of raising the brows, of lowering the brows,—of closing the eyes, of opening the eyes,—of raising the nostrils, of opening the lips, with the teeth shut, of pouting with the lips, of smiling, of astonishment.—

Describe the beginning of man when it is caused in the womb and why an eight months child does not live. What sneezing is. What yawning is. Falling sickness, spasms, paralysis, shivering with cold, sweating, fatigue, hunger, sleepiness, thirst, lust.

Of the nerve which is the cause of movement from the shoulder to the elbow, of the movement from the elbow to the hand, from the joint of the hand to the springing of the fingers. From the springing of the fingers to the middle joints, and from the middle joints to the last.

Of the nerve which causes the movement of the thigh, and from the knee to the foot, and from the joint of the foot to the toes, and then to the middle of the toes and of the rotary motion of the leg.

F. 95 *b*]

806.

ANATOMIA.

²Quali nerui over corde della mano sō ³quelle che accostano e discostano li ⁴diti della mano e de'piedi l'un dall'altro?

ANATOMY.

Which nerves or sinews of the hand are those which close and part the fingers and toes latteraly?

W. 238 *b*]

807.

Scuopri a grado a grado tutte le parti dinanti dell'omo ²nel fare la tua notomia, e così insino in sull'osso; ³descritione de' mēbra della vita e lor trauagliamēti.

Remove by degrees all the parts of the front of a man in making your dissection, till you come to the bones. Description of the parts of the bust and of their motions.

K.3 28 *a*]

808.

Fa la notomia della gā²ba insino al fiāco per ³tutti i versi e per tutti li ⁴atti e in

Give the anatomy of the leg up to the hip, in all views and in every action and in

---

805. 1. chagione . . affare. 7. anarise. 8. cho . . serati. 12. [facci] a desscrivere . . chausa. 13. î putto. 14. chosa esstarnuto. 15. chosa essbaviglio. 16. malmaesstro. 18. parleticho. 19. frede. 21. stācheza. 26. chagione . . dalla. 28. nassimēto. 29. nassimēto . . mezo. 30. mezo. 31. chagione . . cosscia. 33. mezi.
806. 1. anotamia. 3. quelle che achostano e disscostano.   **807.** 1. parte. 3. discretiō de mēbr . . vite ellor.
808. 1—9 R. 2. fiācho. 7. lle. 8. seghate . . gro.

808. A straightened leg in profile is sketched by the side of this text.

tutte le spoglie, [5]vene, arterie, nerui, [6]corde e mvscoli, pel[7]le e ossa, e poi dell'ossa [8]segate per uedere la gros[9]sezza dell' ossa.

every state; veins, arteries, nerves, sinews and muscles, skin and bones; then the bones in sections to show the thickness of the bones.

W. A. II. 76 b]

809.

Farai regola e misura di ciascun muscolo, [2]e renderai ragione di tutti li loro vfiti, e in che mo[3]do s'adoperano e che li muove ecc.

[4]Farai prima la spina del dosso, di poi va vestendo [5]a gradi l'un sopra dell' altro di ciascū di questi musco[6]li, e poni li nervi all'arterie e vene a ciascun [7]muscolo per se, e oltre a di questo nota a quā[8]ti spondili si congiūgono, e che intestini sono [9]loro a riscōtro e che ossi e altri strumēti orga[10]nici ecc.

[11]Le parti più alte de' magri son più alte nelli mu[12]scolosi, e similmēte ne' grassi; Ma la differētia, che è [13]dalla figura de' muscoli che ànno li grossi a rispetto [14]delli muscolosi, sarà qui di sotto descritta.

Make the rule and give the measurement of each muscle, and give the reasons of all their functions, and in which way they work and what makes them work &c.

[4]First draw the spine of the back; then clothe it by degrees, one after the other, with each of its muscles and put in the nerves and arteries and veins to each muscle by itself; and besides these note the vertebrae to which they are attached; which of the intestines come in contact with them; and which bones and other organs &c.

The most prominent parts of lean people are most prominent in the muscular, and equally so in fat persons. But concerning the difference in the forms of the muscles in fat persons as compared with muscular persons, it shall be described below.

On corpulency and leanness (809—811).

W. An IV. 7 (A. A)]

810.

Descriui quali mu[2]scoli si perdono nello ī[3]grossare, e nel dimagra[4]re quali muscoli si sco[5]prono.

[6]E nota che quel loco del[7]la superfitie del grasso [8]che sarà più cōcauata, [9]quādo si disgrassa fia [10]più eleuato.

[11]Doue li muscoli [12]si separano l'ū dal[13]l'altro, farai p[14]roffili, e doue s'[15]appiccano insieme . . .

Describe which muscles disappear in growing fat, and which become visible in growing lean.

And observe that that part which on the surface of a fat person is most concave, when he grows lean becomes more prominent.

Where the muscles separate one from another you must give profiles and where they coalesce . . .

W. 239 (= W. L. 131)]

811.

DE FIGURA VMANA.

[2]Qual parte è quella nell'omo che nel suo ingrassa[3]re mai cresce carne?

[4]Quale è quella parte che nel dimagrare dell' omo [5]mai nō dimagra con dimagratiō troppo sēsibile? [6]infra le parti che ingrassano qual' è quella che più [7]ingrassa?

OF THE HUMAN FIGURE.

Which is the part in man, which, as he grows fatter, never gains flesh?

Or what part which as a man grows lean never falls away with a too perceptible diminution? And among the parts which grow fat which is that which grows fattest?

809. 1. reghola . . ciasscū musscolo. 3. he chilli. 4. lasspina . . vavesstendo. 5. hagradi . . ciasscū di quessti. 6. ciasscū. 7. musscholo . . addi quessto . . acquā. 8. chongiūghano . . intestini. 9. arrisscōtro . . orgha. 11. parte . . mus. 12. scholosi essimilmēte . . Malla diferētia. 13. musscoli che āli . . aris specto. 14. musscholosi . . disocto desscrcta.

810. 2. perdano. 4. musscoli. 5. prano. 6. que lochi. 7. lla. 8. chessara. 9. dissgrassa. 11. musscoli. 15. apichano.

811. 3. cressce. 4. ecquella. 6. infralle parte. 8. infralle parte . . chessi. 10. musscoli . . di ma. 11. gore grosseza. 12. affi-

809. The two drawings given on Pl. CVIII no. I come between lines 3 and 4. A good and very early copy of this drawing without the written text exists in the collection of drawings belonging to Christ's College Oxford, where it is attributed to Leonardo.

⁸Infra le parti che dimagrano qual'è quella che si fa ⁹più magra?

Among those which grow lean which is that which grows leanest?

¹⁰Degli omini potēti in forze quali muscoli son di mag¹¹giore grossezza e più eleuati?

In very strong men which are the muscles which are thickest and most prominent?

¹²Tu ài a figurare nella tua anatomia tutti li gradi ¹³delle mēbra dalla creatiō dell'omo insino alla sua ¹⁴morte, e insino alla morte dell'osso, e qual parte d'esso ¹⁵prima si cōsuma e qual più si cōserua.

In your anatomy you must represent all the stages of the limbs from man's creation to his death, and then till the death of the bone; and which part of him is first decayed and which is preserved the longest.

¹⁶E similmente dall'ultima magrezza all'ultima grassezza.

And in the same way of extreme leanness and extreme fatness.

S. K. M. III. 66 a]

812.

NOTOMIA.

²I membri semplici · sono · vndici · cioè ³cartilagine · ossi · nerui · vene, ⁴arterie · pannicoli · legamēti e ⁵corde, cotica e carne e grasso.

The divisions of the head (812. 813).

ANATOMY.

There are eleven elementary tissues:—
Cartilage, bones, nerves, veins, arteries, fascia, ligament and sinews, skin, muscle and fat.

DEL CAPO.

⁷Le parti del uaso del capo · sono 10: cioè ⁸5 · contenēti · e 5 · cōtenute; le contenēti ⁹sono: capegli · cotica · carne ¹⁰muscolosa · panniculo · grosso · e 'l ¹¹craneo · || le contenvte son queste : du¹²ra madre · pia madre · cieruello | diso¹³tto ritorna la pia e dura madre che dentro ¹⁴a se rinchiudono il cieruello ·, poi la rete ¹⁵mirabile · poi è l'osso, fondamēto del celabro ¹⁶e donde · nascono li nerui.

OF THE HEAD.

The divisions of the head are 10, viz. 5 external and 5 internal, the external are the hair, skin, muscle, fascia and the skull; the internal are the dura mater, the pia mater, [which enclose] the brain. The pia mater and the dura mater come again underneath and enclose the brain; then the rete mirabile, and the occipital bone, which supports the brain from which the nerves spring.

S. K. M. III. 65 b]

813.

a capelli
n cotica
c carne musculosa
m pañiculo · grosso
⁵*o* craneo cioè osso
b dura madre
d pia · madre
f ciervello
¹⁰*r* · pia madre · di sotto
t · dura · madre
l · rete mirabile
s · osso fondamēto.

a. hair
n. skin
c. muscle
m. fascia
o. skull *i. e.* bone
b. dura mater
d. pia mater
f. brain
r. pia mater, below
t. dura mater
l. rete mirablile
s. the occipitul bone.

gurare. 15. ecqual. 16. essimilmente . . magreza . . graseza.
812. 3. hossi. 4. pannichuli . . he. 5. codigahe. 8. he 5 cōtenute. 9. codiga. 10. musscolosa. 14. asse ringiugano. 15. ellosso. 16. nasscie.
813. 2. codiga. 6. [f cieruello].

813. See Pl. CVIII, No. 3.

W. An. II. 37 a]   **814.**

Causa dell'alitare, ²causa del moto del core, ³causa del uomito, ⁴causa del discēdere il ⁵cibo dallo stomaco, ⁶causa del votare li ī⁷testini;

⁸Causa del moto delle ⁹superfluità per le inte¹⁰stini;

¹¹Causa dello inghiottire, ¹²causa dello tossire, ¹³causa dello sbadigliare, ¹⁴causa dello starnuto, ¹⁵causa dell'adormētamē¹⁶to di diuerse mēbra;

¹⁷Causa del perdere il sēso ¹⁸ad alcū mēbro;

¹⁹Causa del solletico;

²⁰Causa della lussuria e al²¹tre necessità del corpo, ²²causa dell'orinare, ²³e così di tutte le lotioni natu²⁴rali del corpo.

Of the cause of breathing, of the cause of the motion of the heart, of the cause of vomiting, of the cause of the descent of food from the stomach, of the cause of emptying the intestines.

Of the cause of the movement of the superfluous matter through the intestines.

Of the cause of swallowing, of the cause of coughing, of the cause of yawning, of the cause of sneezing, of the cause of limbs getting asleep.

Of the cause of losing sensibility in any limb.

Of the cause of tickling.

Of the·cause of lust and other appetites of the body, of the cause of urine and also of all the natural excretions of the body.

Physiological problems (814. 815).

W. An. III. 230 a (·S·)]   **815.**

Le lagrime ²vengono dal ³core e nō dal ⁴ceruello.

⁵Difinisci tutte ⁶le parti di che si cō-⁷pone il corpo, co⁸minciādosi dalla ⁹cute colla sua so¹⁰praveste, la qual ¹¹è spesso spiccata ¹²mediante il sole.

The tears come from the heart and not from the brain.

Define all the parts, of which the body is composed, beginning with the skin with its outer cuticle which is often chapped by the influence of the sun.

814. 5. dello stomacho. 6. otare le ī. 7. testine. 9. super fruita. 10. stine. 11. delle ingiottire. 13. isbauiglare. 14. isstarnuto. 23. tutte lutioni.

815. 2. vengano. 5 difinisscitute. 6. parte. 8. mincādosi. 9. cutic. 10. pravessta. 11. spicha.

814. By the side of this text stands the pen and ink drawing reproduced on Pl. CVIII, No. 4; a skull with indications of the veins in the fleshy covering.

II.

ZOOLOGY AND COMPARATIVE ANATOMY.

W. An. I. 173*b*]

816.

The divisions of the animal kingdom (816. 817).

Uomo | la descritione dell'omo, nella qual si contengono quelli che son qua²si di simile spetie come babbuino, scimmia e simili che sō molti.
³ *Leone* | e suoi seguaci come pantieri, leonze, tigri, liopardi, lupi, cervie⁴ri, gatti di Spagna, gannetti e gatti comvni e simili.
⁵ *Cavallo* e sua seguaci come mulo, asino e simili che ànno dēti sopra e di sotto.
⁶ *Toro* | e sua seguaci cornvti e sanza denti di sopra come bufolo, ceruio, daino ⁷capriolo, pecore, capre, stambecchi, mvcheri, camozze, giraffe.

Man. The description of man, which includes that of such creatures as are of almost the same species, as Apes, Monkeys and the like, which are many,
The Lion and its kindred, as Panthers. Wildcats (?) Tigers, Leopards, Wolfs, Lynxes, Spanish cats, common cats and the like.
The Horse and its kindred, as Mule, Ass and the like, with incisor teeth above and below.
The Bull and its allies with horns and without upper incisors as the Buffalo, Stag Fallow Deer, Wild Goat, Swine, Goat, wild Goats Muskdeers, Chamois, Giraffe.

W. An. II. 206*b* (I)]

817.

Scrivi le varietà ²delli intestini de³lla spetie vma⁴na, scimie e si⁵mili; Di poi in ⁶che si uaria la spe⁷tie leonina, di ⁸poi la bovina, ⁹e vltimo li uccelli, ¹⁰ e vsa tal descrit¹¹tione a uso di ¹²discorso.

Describe the various forms of the intestines of the human species, of apes and such like. Then, in what way the leonine species differ, and then the bovine, and finally birds; and arrange this description after the manner of a disquisition.

---

816. homo la . . contiene . . chesson. 2. essimili. 3. essua seguace . . tigre. 4. gannetti . . essimili. 5. chavallo . . [cervio] essimili cano. 6. essanza. 7. pechore . . stanbeche mvcheri
817. 2. delli intestini. 4. essi. 7. elonina. 9. ucielli. 10. discrip.

---

816. 3. *Leonza*—wild cat? "*Secondo alcuni, lo stesso che Leonessa; e secondo altri con più certezza, lo stesso che Pantèra.*" FANFANI, *Vocabolario* page 858.

W. A. IV. 153 b]

818.

Fa ti dare vna secōdina delli ²vitelli quādo nascono e nota ³la figura de' cotiledoni, se riser⁴vano li cotiledoni mas⁵chi o femminei.

Procure the placenta of a calf when it is born and observe the form of the cotyledons, if their cotyledons are male or female.

Miscellaneous notes on the study of Zoology (818—821).

W. An. IV. 167 a]

819.

Scrivi la lingua del picchio ²e la mascella del cocodrillo.

Describe the tongue of the woodpecker and the jaw of the crocodile.

G. 64 b]

820.

Volare della 4ª spetie ²di parpaglioni divo³ratori delle formiche alate; ⁴delle tre principali situationi ⁵che fanno l' ali delli vccielli che discēdono.

Of the flight of the 4ᵗʰ kind of butterflies that consume winged ants. Of the three principal positions of the wings of birds in downward flight.

M. 67 a]

821.

Che modo fa la coda del pescie a so-spin²giere il pescie innāzi, e così l'anguilla, ³biscia e mignatta.

Of the way in which the tail of a fish acts in propelling the fish; as in the eel, snake and leech.

W. An. IV. 157 a (B)]

822.

DELLA MANO DI DENTRO.

OF THE PALM OF THE HAND.

²Farai poi vn discor³so delle mani di ciascu⁴n animale per mostrare ⁵in che si uariano, come nell' orso che ⁶agiugne la legatura de⁷lle corde de' diti del piè ⁸sopra il collo d' esso piè.

Then I will discourse of the hands of each animal to show in what they vary; as in the bear, which has the ligatures of the sinews of the toes joined above the instep.

Comparative study of the structure of bones and of the action of muscles (822—826).

W. XXIV ('55')]

823.

Dimostratione secōda ²interposta infra l'anato³mia e 'l uiuo.

⁴Figurerai a questo p⁵aragone le gambe de' ra⁶nocchi, le quali ànno gran ⁷similitudine colle ganbe ⁸dell'omo si nell'ossa come ⁹ne' suoi muscoli; di poi ¹⁰seguirai le gābe dirieto ¹¹della lepre, le quali son ¹²molto muscolose e di ¹³muscoli spediti, perchè nō ¹⁴sono inpedite da grasse¹⁵zza.

A second demonstration inserted between anatomy and [the treatise on] the living being.

You will represent here for a comparison, the legs of a frog, which have a great resemblance to the legs of man, both in the bones and in the muscles. Then, in continuation, the hind legs of the hare, which are very muscular, with strong active muscles, because they are not encumbered with fat.

---

818. 1. fatti. 2. nascano. 3. cotilidoni. 4. cotilidoni mass. 5. ci offeminine.
819. lingha . . pichio. 2. ella masscella.   **820.** 5. cheffa . . discēda.
821. 1. pescie assosspī. 2. pesscio . . languila. 3. bisscia e migmatta.   **822.** 6. agugne la lecatura.
823. 4. acquessto. 6. nochi. 8. com"e". 9. musscoli. 12. molte.

820. 4. A passing allusion is all I can here permit myself to Leonardo's elaborate researches into the flight of birds. Compare the observations on this subject in the Introduction to section XVIII and in the Bibliography of Manuscripts at the end of the work.

821. A sketch of a fish, swimming upwards is in the original, inserted above this text.—Compare No. 1114.

823. This text is written by the side of a drawing in black chalk of a nude male figure, but there is no connection between the sketch and the text.

824.

K.3 29*b*]

Qui fo ricordo ²di dimostrare la dif-³ferentia ch'è dall'o⁴mo al cauallo, e simil-⁵mente delli altri ani⁶mali; e prima ⁷comin-cerò all'ossa, e proseguirò ⁸tutti li muscoli che sanza corde na⁹scono e finiscono nelle ossa, ¹⁰e poi di quelli che cō corda na-¹¹scono e finiscono nell'ossa, e poi di quelle ¹²che con una sola corda da v̄ can-to.

Here I make a note to demonstrate the difference there is between man and the horse and in the same way with other animals. And first I will begin with the bones, and then will go on to all the muscles which spring from the bones without tendons and end in them in the same way, and then go on to those which start with a single tendon at one end.

825.

E. 16*a*]

Nota delle piegatu²re delle giūtu³re, e in che mo⁴do cresce la ⁵carne sopra di ⁶loro nelli ⁷lor piegamē⁸tio e stendimē⁹ti; e di questa ¹⁰īportātissima ¹¹notitia fa uno ¹²particulare ¹³trattato | nel¹⁴la descritione ¹⁵de' movimēti ¹⁶delli animali ¹⁷di quattro pi¹⁸edi, infra li ¹⁹quali è l'omo ²⁰che ācora lui ²¹nella infātia ²²va cō 4 piedi.

Note on the bendings of joints and in what way the flesh grows upon them in their flexions or extensions; and of this most important study write a separate treatise: in the description of the movements of animals with four feet; among which is man, who likewise in his infancy crawls on all fours.

826.

C. A. 292 *a*; 888 *a*]

DELLO · ANDARE DELL'OMO.

²L'andare dell'omo · è sempre a uso dell'universale andare delli animali di 4 piedi, imperochè siccome essi ³movono · i loro · piedi in croce a vso del trotto del cauallo, così l'omo in croce si move le sue 4 · mēbra, cioè ⁴se caccia · īnāti il piè destro per caminare, egli caccia ināzi cō quello il braccio · sinistro, e sempre così seguita.

OF THE WAY OF WALKING IN MAN.

The walking of man is always after the universal manner of walking in animals with 4 legs, inasmuch as just as they move their feet crosswise after the manner of a horse in trotting, so man moves his 4 limbs crosswise; that is, if he puts forward his right foot in walking he puts forward, with it, his left arm and vice versa, invariably.

---

824. 2. la di. 4. essimil. 6. e p"a". 7. epposseguiro. 8. musscoli. 9. scano effiniscano. 10. eppoi. 11. scano effinisscano . . he poi. 12. [q] che.

825. 1. "nota" delle pieghatu. 4. cressca. 5. charne. 7. pieghamē. 8. esstendimē: 9. quessta. 12. partichulare. 13. tractato. 14. lla desscritione. 18. infralli. 19. ellomo. 20. āchora.

826. 2. essenpre . . inperochessichome. 3. movano illoro . . chauallo . chosi. 4. chaccia . . desstro . . chaminare . . chaccia . chō . . sinisstro essepr.

824. See Pl. CVIII, No. 2.

III.

PHYSIOLOGY.

W. An. IV. 173 a] **827.**

Ho trovato nella compositione del corpo
vmano che, come in tutte ²le compositioni
delli animali, esso è di piv ottusi e grossi
sentiméti; ³così è composto di struméto
manco ingegnoso e di lochi māco ⁴capaci
a ricevere la uirtù de' sensi; ò veduto nella
spetie leoni⁵na il senso dell'odorato auere
parte della sustantia del celabro, e discē-
⁶dere li narici, capace ricettaculo contro al
senso dello odorato, ⁷il quale entra infra
grā nvmero di saccoli cartilaginosi con
assai ⁸vie contro all'avenimento del predetto
celabro.

⁹Li ochi della spetie leonina ànno gran
parte della lor testa per lor ¹⁰ricettacolo,
e li nerui ottici inmediate congiugnersi col
celabro; il che al¹¹li omini si uede in contrario, perchè le casse delli ochi sono vna
picco¹²la parte del capo, e li nerui ottici
sono sottili e lunghi e deboli, e per debo-
¹³le operatione si uede di loro il dì, e peggio
la notte, e li predetti animali ¹⁴vedono
in nella notte che 'l giorno; ¹⁵e 'l segno se
ne vede, perchè predano di notte ¹⁶e dormono il giorno come fāno ancora li uccelli
notturni.

I have found that in the composition of Comparative study of the organs of sense in men and animals. the human body as compared with the bodies
of animals the organs of sense are duller
and coarser. Thus it is composed of less
ingenious instruments, and of spaces less
capacious for receiving the faculties of sense.
I have seen in the Lion tribe that the sense
of smell is connected with part of the substance of the brain which comes down the
nostrils, which form a spacious receptacle for the sense of smell, which enters
by a great number of cartilaginous vesicles
with several passages leading up to where
the brain, as before said, comes down.

The eyes in the Lion tribe have a large
part of the head for their sockets and the
optic nerves communicate at once with the
brain; but the contrary is to be seen in
man, for the sockets of the eyes are but a
small part of the head, and the optic nerves
are very fine and long and weak, and by the
weakness of their action we see by day but
badly at night, while these animals can see as
well at night as by day. The proof that they
can see is that they prowl for prey at night
and sleep by day, as nocturnal birds do also.

827. 1. ottrovato . . conpositone . . cho·ne. 3. chosi e conpossto . . mancho . . mancho. 4. chapaci. 5. nel senso . . susstantia
del celabro discē. 6. ricettachulo. 7. sachuli chartilaginosi. 9. tessta. 10. ricettachulo elli . . ottitti . . congugnersi.
11. lli . . chasse . . picho. 12. elli . . ellunghi. 13. eppeggo . . elli. 14. vegan inela . . gorno. 15. dormano il gorno
. . fano . . ucelli.

H.2 38 a]   **828.**

¶Tutte · le cose vedute parrāno ²mag-
giori · di mezza notte, che · di ³mezzo · dì ·
e maggiori di mattina che ⁴di mezzodì. ¶
⁵Questo · accade · perchè · la pupilla ⁶del-
l'ochio · è · minore · assai di mezzo ⁷dì · che
di nessuno · altro tenpo.
⁸Tanto · quāto · è · maggiore · l'ochio
⁹over · pupilla del gufo a proportione ¹⁰dello
· animale, che non è · quella · dell'o¹¹mo ·,
tanto piv · lume vede di notte che ¹²nō · fa
· l'omo; ōde di mezzo · dì nō vede ni¹³ente ·,
se lui nō · diminuisce · sua · pupil¹⁴la ·, e similmēte · vede di notte le cose mag¹⁵giori ·
che di dì.

Every object we see will appear larger
at midnight than at midday, and larger in
the morning than at midday.

This happens because the pupil of the
eye is much smaller at midday than at any
other time.

In proportion as the eye or the pupil of
the owl is larger in proportion to the animal
than that of man, so much the more light
can it see at night than man can; hence at
midday it can see nothing if its pupil does
not diminish; and, in the same way, at night
things look larger to it than by day.

G. 44 a]   **829.**

DELLI OCHI DELLI ANIMALI.

²Li ochi di tutti li animali àño le ³lor
popille, le quali per loro medesime cres-
⁴cono e diminuiscono secōdo il mag⁵giore
e minore lume del sole o altro ⁶chiarore;
Ma nelli uccelli fa maggio⁷re differētia, e
massima nelli nottur⁸ni, come gufi, barba-
gianni, e all'ochi ⁹che son di spetie di
civetta; a questi cresce ¹⁰la popilla in modo
che quasi occupa tut¹¹to l'ochio, e diminuisce insino alla grā¹²dezza d'ū grā di
miglio e sempre osser¹³va figura circulare;
Ma la spe¹⁴tie leonina come pātere,
pardi, ¹⁵leōze, tigri, lupi, cieruieri,
gatti di Spa¹⁶gnia e altri simili diminuiscono ¹⁷la lucìe dal perfetto circulo
¹⁸alla figura biāgolare, cioè questa ¹⁹è
come si dimostra in margine; Ma l'uomo ²⁰per avere più debole vista
che nessuno altro a²¹nimale, meno è
offeso dalla superchia luce, ²²e mē s'av-
mēta nelli lochi tenebrosi; ma ²³alli ochi
delli detti animali notturni,—al ²⁴gufo vcciello cornuto, il quale è 'l ²⁵massimo nella
spetie delli vccelli nottur²⁶ni: a questo · s'au-
mēta tanto la uirtù vi²⁷siva, che nel minimo

OF THE EYES IN ANIMALS.

The eyes of all animals have their pupils
adapted to dilate and diminish of their own
accord in proportion to the greater or less
light of the sun or other luminary. But in
birds the variation is much greater; and
particularly in nocturnal birds, such as horned owls, and in the eyes of one species of
owl; in these the pupil dilates in such a way
as to occupy nearly the whole eye, or
diminishes to the size of a grain of millet,
and always preserves the circular form. But

in the Lion tribe, as panthers, pards,
ounces, tigers, lynxes, spanish cats
and other similar animals the pupil diminishes from the perfect circle to the
figure of a pointed oval such as is
shown in the margin. But man having
a weaker sight than any other animal
is less hurt by a very strong light and
his pupil increases but little in dark places;
but in the eyes of these nocturnal animals, the
horned owl—a bird which is the largest of
all nocturnal birds— the power of vision
increases so much that in the faintest nocturnal light (which we call darkness) it sees

829. Compare No. 24, lines 8 and fol.

lume notturno (il [28]quale da noi dimādasi tenebre) vede assai cō [29]più vigore che noi nello splendore del [30]mezzo giorno, nel quale tali vccielli stā [31]nascosti in lochi tenebrosi; e se pur [32]sō costretti u[33]scire all'a[34]ria allumina[35]ta dal sole, elli' [36]diminuiscono [37]tāto la lor po[38]pilla che la po[39]tentia visiua [40]diminuisce [41]insieme colla [42]quātità di tale [43]lucie.

[44]Fa notomia [45]di vari ochi, [46]e vedi quali [47]sō li muscoli [48]ch'aprono e [49]serrano le pre[50]dette popille [51]delli ochi del[52]li animali.

with much more distinctness than we do in the splendour of noon day, at which time these birds remain hidden in dark holes; or if indeed they are compelled to come out into the open air lighted up by the sun, they contract their pupils so much that their power of sight diminishes together with the quantity of light admitted.

Study the anatomy of various eyes and see which are the muscles which open and close the said pupils of the eyes of animals.

Br. M. 64 b]   830.

a b n è il coperchio di sotto che chiude [2]l'ochio di sotto in sù con coperchio oppaco, [3]c n b chiude l'ochio dinanzi īdirieto [4]con coperchio transparēte.

[5]Chiudesi sotto in sù [6]perchè da alto disciē[7]de.

[8]Quando l'ochio delli uccelli si chiude [9]colle sue due copriture, esso chiu[10]de prima la secondina la qual [11]chiude dal lagrimatoio alla co[12]da d'esso ochio, e la prima si chi[13]vde da basso in alto, e que[14]sti due moti interseghati occupano [15]in prima dal lacrimatoio, perchè già abbiamo veduto che [16]dinanzi e di sotto si sono assicurati, e sol serba[17]no la parte di sopra per li pericoli delli uccelli ra[18]paci che discendono di sopra e dirieto; e sco[19]prano prima il pannicolo di verso la coda, [20]perchè se 'l nemico viene dirieto, egli à la como[21]dità del fugire innāzi, e ancora tiene [22]il pannicolo detto secondino e traspa[23]rente, perchè se non avesse tale scudo, e' nō [24]potrebbe tener li ochi aperti cōtro al [25]vēto che percuote l'ochio nel furo[26]re del suo velocie volare; E la sua [27]popilla crescie e discrescie nel uedere [28]minore o maggiore lume cioè splēdore.

a b n is the membrane which closes the eye from below, upwards, with an opaque film, c n b encloses the eye in front and behind with a transparent membrane.

It closes from below, upwards, because it [the eye] comes downwards.

When the eye of a bird closes with its two lids, the first to close is the nictitating membrane which closes from the lacrymal duct over to the outer corner of the eye; and the outer lid closes from below upwards, and these two intersecting motions begin first from the lacrymatory duct, because we have already seen that in front and below birds are protected and use only the upper portion of the eye from fear of birds of prey which come down from above and behind; and they uncover first the membrane from the outer corner, because if the enemy comes from behind, they have the power of escaping to the front; and again the muscle called the nictitating membrane is transparent, because, if the eye had not such a screen, they could not keep it open against the wind which strikes against the eye in the rush of their rapid flight. And the pupil of the eye dilates and contracts as it sees a less or greater light, that is to say intense brilliancy.

H.3 61 a]   831.

¶ L'ochio che di notte s'interporrà infra 'l lume e l'ochio [2]della gatta, vedrà esso occhio parere di foco. ¶

If at night your eye is placed between the light and the eye of a cat, it will see the eye look like fire.

assai chō. 29. vighore. 31. nasscosti inochi . . esseppur. 32. cosstretti vs. 33. allalla. 36. diminuiscā. 38. chella. 40. diminuissie. 41. cholla. 47. musscoli. 48. aprano es.

830. 2. socto . . oppacho. 4. chon choperchio transsparēte. 6. disciē. 7. da. 8. vcielli. 9. cholle . . chopriture. 12. ella. 13. di basso . . ecque. 14. interseghati ochupano. 15. dalacrimatoio . . giaā ueduto. 16. assichurati.! 17. pericholi. 18. dissciendono . . diriecto essco. 19. panitolo . . choda. 20. nemicho . . diriecto. 22. trāsspa. 23. auessi. 25. perchuote. 26. Ella. 27. cresscie e disscresscie. 28. magiore.

831. 1. ellochio. 2. vedera . . focho.

832.

W. An. IV. 184 *a* (7)]

Remarks on the organs of speech (832. 833).

La lingua è trouata auere 24 muscoli li quali rispondono alli sei muscoli di che è ²conposta la quātità della lingua che si move per la bocca.

³E quando *a o v* si pronūtiano con ⁴intelligibile e spedita pronū-tia, egli è ⁵necessario che nella continua lor ⁶pronūtiatione sanza intermissiō di tēpo, che ⁷l'apritura de' labri si uadi al cōtinuo restri-⁸gnendo, cioè larghi sarāno nel dire *a,* pi⁹ù stretti nel dire *o,* e assai piv stretti nel pr¹⁰onun-tiare *v.*

¹¹Prouasi come tutte le uo-¹²cali son pronūtiate colla ¹³parte ultima del pala¹⁴to mobile, il quale copre l'e¹⁵piglotta.

a	*e*	*i*	*o*	*u*
ba	*be*	*bi*	*bo*	*bu*
ca	*ce*	*ci*	*co*	*cu*
da	*de*	*di*	*do*	*du*
fa	*fe*	*fi*	*fo*	*fu*
ga	*ge*	*gi*	*go*	*gu*
la	*le*	*li*	*lo*	*lu*
ma	*me*	*mi*	*mo*	*mu*
na	*ne*	*ni*	*no*	*nu*
pa	*pe*	*pi*	*po*	*pu*
qa	*qe*	*qi*	*qo*	*qu*
ra	*re*	*ri*	*ro*	*ru*
sa	*se*	*si*	*so*	*su*
ta	*te*	*ti*	*to*	*tu*

The tongue is found to have 24 muscles which correspond to the six muscles which compose the portion of the tongue which moves in the mouth.

And when *a o u* are spoken with a clear and rapid pronunciation, it is necessary, in order to pronounce continuously, without any pause between, that the opening of the lips should close by degrees; that is, they are wide apart in saying *a,* closer in saying *o,* and much closer still to pronounce *u.*

It may be shown how all the vowels are pronounced with the farthest portion of the false palate which is above the epiglottis.

833.

W. XXI]

Se tirerai il fiato pel na²so e lo vorrai mādar fori ³per la bocca, tu sentirai il sono ⁴che fa il tramezzo cioè il ⁵pānicolo in ...

If you draw in breath by the nose and send it out by the mouth you will hear the sound made by the division that is the membrane in[5] ...

834.

C. A. 89 *a*; 258 *a*]

DELLA NATURA DEL UEDERE.

On the conditions of sight (834. 835).

²Dico · jl uedere · essere operato da tutti li animali · mediāte · la luce; e se alcuno cōtra questo ³allegherà · jl uedere · delli animali notturni, dirò · questo · medesima-mēte essere · sottoposto · a simile · natura; jpero⁴chè · chiaro · si cōprēde ·, j sensi · ricievēdo · le similitudini delle cose · nō mā-dano · fori di loro alcuna virtù; ⁵anzi me-diāte l'aria, che si trova īfra l'obietto e 'l sēso ·, jncorpora · j se le spetie delle · cose ·, e per lo cōtatto, ⁶che à · col sēso, le porgie a quello; se li obietti o per sono · o per odore mādano le potētie spirituali all'orechio ⁷o al naso ·, qui nōn è neciessario nè si adopera la luce ·; le forme delli obietti non

OF THE NATURE OF SIGHT.

I say that sight is exercised by all animals, by the medium of light; and if any one adduces, as against this, the sight of nocturnal animals, I must say that this in the same way is subject to the very same natural laws. For it will easily be understood that the senses which receive the images of things do not project from themselves any visual virtue[4]. On the contrary the atmospheric medium which exists between the object and the sense incorporates in itself the figure of things, and by its contact with the sense transmits the object to it. If the object—whether by sound or by odour—presents its spiritual force to the ear or the nose, then light is not required and does not act. The forms of objects do not send their images into

---

832. 1. musscole . . risspondano . . musscoli. 2. conposta . . boccha. 3. linghua chessi perbocha. 4. Essecquando . . cho. 4. esspedita. 7. dellabri . . resstri. 8. coe. 12. chali. 13. lla. 15. piglotto.

833. 1. settirarai. 2. ello. 3. bocha tusscutirai. 4. cheffa il tramazzo. 5. pānicholo.

834. 1. operato [mediāte la lu] dattutti . . esse. 3. alegera . . sotto . posti . assimile. 4. cōplēde . . similitudine . . alchuna. 5. ānti . . chessi . . jnchorpora . . chōtatto. 6. chol . . acquelo . . per [romore] "sono" per . . māda . per la. 7. nessi

833. 5. The text here breaks off. 　**834.** 4. Compare No. 68. 8. See No. 58—67.

ētrano per similitudine jfra l'aria, [8] se quelli · nō sono · lvminosi ·; essēdo così l'ochio nō la può ricievere da quell'aria che nō l'à e che tocca la sua superfitie; [9] se tu volessi dire di molti animali · j quali · predano di notte ·, dico che quando in questi manca la poca luce [10] che basta · alla natura · de' loro · ochi ·, che questi s'aivtano colla · potētia dello · udito · e dello odorato, [11] i quali nō sono · īpediti · dalle tenebre ·, e de' quali avāzano di grā lūga · l'omo ·; Se porrai mēte · a una gatta [12] di giorno · saltare · īfra molte vasellamēti ·, vedrai · quelli rimanere salui, e se farai questo medesimo [13] di notte, ronperā ne · assai ·; li vccelli notturni · nō volano ·, se nō lucie · tutta o ī parte la luna, āzi si pasco[14]no jfra il coricare · del sole · e la · ītera oscurità della notte; —

[15] Nessuno corpo · si può · cōprendere sāza lume e ōbra; lume e ōbra sono causate dalla luce.

the air if they are not illuminated[8]; and the eye being thus constituted cannot receive that from the air, which the air does not possess, although it touches its surface. If you choose to say that there are many animals that prey at night, I answer that when the little light which suffices the nature of their eyes is wanting, they direct themselves by their strong sense of hearing and of smell, which are not impeded by the darkness, and in which they are very far superior to man. If you make a cat leap, by daylight, among a quantity of jars and crocks you will see them remain unbroken, but if you do the same at night, many will be broken. Night birds do not fly about unless the moon shines full or in part; rather do they feed between sun-down and the total darkness of the night.

No body can be apprehended without light and shade, and light and shade are caused by light.

G. 90a]

835.

PERCHÈ NELLI OMINI ATTĒPATI [2] IL UEDERE È MEGLIO DISCOSTO.

WHY MEN ADVANCED IN AGE SEE BETTER AT A DISTANCE.

[3] Il uedere è meglio discosto che da pres[4]so in quelli omini, li quali s'attēpano, [5] perchè vna medesima cosa [6] māda di se minore inpressione nell'oc[7]chio, essendo remota che quādo li è vi[8]cina.

Sight is better from a distance than near in those men who are advancing in age, because the same object transmits a smaller impression of itself to the eye when it is distant than when it is near.

C. At. 89a; 258a]

836.

Il sēso comune è quello · che givdica · le cose · a · lui · date dalli altri sensi; [2] Li antichi · speculatori · àno · cōcluso · che quella · parte del giuditio · che è data all'omo, sia causata [3] da vno · strumēto ·, al quale referiscono · li altri 5 · mediāte la īpressiva, e a detto · strumēto · àno posto nome sēso · comvne, [4] e dicono questo sēso · essere situato · in mezzo · il capo jfra la īpressiva · e la memoria; E questo nome di sēso [5] comvne dicono solamēte ·, perchè è

The Common Sense, is that which judges of things offered to it by the other senses. The ancient speculators have concluded that that part of man which constitutes his judgment is caused by a central organ to which the other five senses refer everything by means of impressibility; and to this centre they have given the name Common Sense. And they say that this Sense is situated in the centre of the head between Sensation and Memory. And this name of Common Sense

The seat of the common sense.

---

comvne · judice · delli altri · 5 sēsi, cioè vedere · udire · toccare · gustare e odorare;
⁶Il senso · comvne · si move mediāte la
īpressiva ch'è posta · ī mezzo jfra lui e i
sēsi; la inpressiua si move ⁷mediāte le similitudini delle cose · a lei date · dalli strumēti · superfitiali cioè sēsi, i quali sono posti
ī mezzo ⁸jfra le cose esteriori e la īpressiva ·, e similmēte i sēsi si movono mediāte
li obietti; ⁹le · circōstanti · cose · mādano le
loro · similitudini · ai sēsi; e i sensi le trās-
feriscono alla īpressiva; ¹⁰la īpressiva le
māda al sēso comvne ·, e da quello · sono
stabilite nella memoria ·, e lì · sono · piv ·
o meno ¹¹retenute · secōdo la īportātia o
potētia della · cosa · data ·; Quello · senso ·
è piv veloce nel suo ¹²ofitio, jl quale · è
piv · uicino · alla · impressiva ·, e l'ochio ·
superiore · è prīcipe · delli altri ·, ¹³del quale
· solo · tratteremo e li altri lascieremo · per
nō ci · allūgare · dalla nostra · materia ·; dice
la speriēza ¹⁴che l'ochio · s'astēde · j · 10 ·
varie nature · d' obietti · cioè · luce · e tenebre,
· l'una · cagione dell'altre 9 ·, e l'altra · priva-
tione: ¹⁵colore · e corpo · figura · e sito ·
remotione · e propīquità · moto e quiete.

is given to it solely because it is the common judge of all the other five senses *i. e.*
Seeing, Hearing, Touch, Taste and Smell.
This Common Sense is acted upon by means
of Sensation which is placed as a medium
between it and the senses. Sensation is acted upon by means of the images of things
presented to it by the external instruments,
that is to say the senses which are the
medium between external things and Sensation. In the same way the senses are
acted upon by objects. Surrounding things
transmit their images to the senses and
the senses transfer them to the Sensation. Sensation sends them to the Common Sense, and by it they are stamped
upon the memory and are there more or
less retained according to the importance
or force of the impression. That sense is
most rapid in its function which is nearest
to the sensitive medium and the eye, being
the highest is the chief of the others. Of
this then only we will speak, and the
others we will leave in order not to make
our matter too long. Experience tells us that
the eye apprehends ten different natures of
things, that is: Light and Darkness, one
being the cause of the perception of the
nine others, and the other its absence:—
Colour and substance, form and place, distance and nearness, motion and stillness[15].

W. An. IV. 184*a* (7)]   **837.**

On the ori-
gin of the
soul.

Ancorachè lo ingiegnio ²vmano faccia
īuētioni va³rie, rispōdēdo cō uari ⁴strumēti
a ū medesimo ⁵fine, mai esso trove⁶rà
inuentione più ⁷bella, nè più facile, nè ⁸più
brieue della natu⁹ra, perchè nelle suē in-
¹⁰venzioni nulla mā¹¹ca e nullo è superflu-
¹²o, e non va cō contra¹³pesi, quādo essa
fa le ¹⁴mēbra atti al moto nel¹⁵li corpi delli
animali; ¹⁶Ma ui mette dentro l'a¹⁷nima
d'esso corpo cōpo¹⁸nitore, cioè l'anima
del¹⁹la madre che prima ²⁰conpone nella
ma²¹trice la figura dell' o²²mo; e al tenpo
debito ²³desta l'anima, che di quel ²⁴deve
essere abitatore, ²⁵la qual prima restau²⁶a
dormētata e in tutela ²⁷dell' anima della

Though human ingenuity may make various inventions which, by the help of various machines answering the same end, it
will never devise any inventions more beautiful, nor more simple, nor more to the purpose than Nature does; because in her inventions nothing is wanting, and nothing is
superfluous, and she needs no counterpoise
when she makes limbs proper for motion in
the bodies of animals. But she puts into
them the soul of the body, which forms them
that is the soul of the mother which first
constructs in the womb the form of the man
and in due time awakens the soul that is
to inhabit it. And this at first lies dormant

chose . . dali . . sēsiggugali . . mezo. 8. Infralle . . isteriori ella īpressiua essimilemēte . . movano . . obietti le similitudine. 9. delle circhūstanti chose . . similitudine a sēsie sensi . . trāsferischano . . īprēsiua. 10. īprēsiua la . . dacquello . .
elli. 11. sechōdo. 12. uisino . ala inprēsiua . . deli. 13. trattereno e laltri lasciereno . . dala. 14. chagne . . ellaltra.
15. chorpo . . essito . . ecquiete.
837. 1. chello. 2. vmano inīuētioni. 5. trover. 11. cha e nulla. 13. fa il. 14. mēbr. 16. coe. 23. dessta. 24. debbe. 25. resta[ui].

836. 15. Compare No. 23.

madre, [28]la quale la nutrisce e vivifi[29]ca per la vena ombelica[30]le, con tutti li sua mē[31]bri spirituali, e così segu[32]irà insino che tale ombe[33]lico lì è giunto colla se-[34]condina e li cotilido[35]ni per la quale il figlo[36]lo si unisce colla madre; [37]e questi son causa che v[38]na volontà, vn sommo desi [39]derio, vna paura che [40]abbia la madre, o altro [41]dolor mētale à potēti[42]a più nel figliolo che nel[43]la madre, perchè spesse sono [44]le volte, che il figlio ne per[45]de la vita ecc.

[46]Questo discor[47]so nō ua qui, [48]ma si r[49]ichiede [50]nella cō[51]positiō [52]delli cor[53]pi anima[54]ti; — E il resto della difinitione dell' anima lascio nel[55]le mēti de' frati, padri de' popoli, li quali per inspira[56]tione sanno tutti li segreti.

[57]Lascio star le lettere incoronate, per-chè sō sōma verità.

and under the tutelage of the soul of the mother, who nourishes and vivifies it by the umbilical vein, with all its spiritual parts, and this happens because this umbilicus is joined to the placenta and the cotyledons, by which the child is attached to the mother. And these are the reason why a wish, a strong craving or a fright or any other mental suffering in the mother, has more influence on the child than on the mother; for there are many cases when the child loses its life from them, &c.

This discourse is not in its place here, but will be wanted for the one on the composition of animated bodies—and the rest of the definition of the soul I leave to the imaginations of friars, those fathers of the people who know all secrets by inspiration.

[57]I leave alone the sacred books; for they are supreme truth.

W. An. II. 202 a (·B·)]

838.

COME · I · 5 SENSI · SONO · OFITIALI · DELL'ANIMA.

[2]L'anima · pare · risedere · nella parte juditiale, · e la · parte · juditiale pare essere [3]nel loco · doue · concorrono · tutti i sēsi ·, il quale è detto · senso comvne, e non è tutta [4]per tutto · il corpo ·, come molti · àño · creduto ·, anzi · tutto in nella · parte ·, inpercchè se ella [5]fusse · tutta per tutto · e tutta · in ogni · parte ·, non era · necessario · li stru[6]mēti · de' sensi fare infra loro · uno · medesimo cōcorso a uno · solo loco ·, anzi · basta[7]va · che l'ochio operasse · l'ufitio · del sentimēto · sulla · sua superfitie · e nō mandare per la uia [8]delli nerui · ottici la similitudine · delle cose · vedute · al sēso ·, che l'anima · alla · sopra [9]detta ragione le poteua comprēdere · in essa · superfitie del'o-

HOW THE FIVE SENSES ARE THE MINISTERS OF THE SOUL.

The soul seems to reside in the judgment, and the judgment would seem to be seated in that part where all the senses meet; and this is called the Common Sense and is not all-pervading throughout the body, as many have thought. Rather is it entirely in one part. Because, if it were all-pervading and the same in every part, there would have been no need to make the instruments of the senses meet in one centre and in one single spot; on the contrary it would have sufficed that the eye should fulfil the function of its sensation on its surface only, and not transmit the image of the things seen, to the sense, by means of the optic nerves, so that the soul—for the reason given above—may perceive it in the surface of the eye. In the same way as to the sense of hearing, it would have sufficed if the voice had mere-

On the relations of the soul to the organs of sense.

---

28. la qual nutrisscie vivifi. 29. cha . . vnbilica. 30. le sua. 32. chettale vnbi. 33. licho. 34. elli. 36. unisscie colla ma 37. ecquesti. 38. somo. 42. che ne. 43. spesse so. 45. della uita ecc. 54. dellania lasscio ne. 55. le mēte . . ispirita 56. tatione san. 57. Lascia *doubtful* . . soma. ·

838. 2. ella. 3. lọcho . . chonchorano . chomvne . . ettuta. 4. chorpo chome . . inela . . ssella. 5. fussi tutta [in ogni] per tutto . ettutta . . neciessario . fare li. 6. infralloro .î. . . chōchorso a . î . . locho. 7. operassi . . del [suo] sentimēto. 8. ottiti [il] la . . chose . . chellanima. 9. conplēdere.· 10. Essimilmēte il . . dellavldito . . risonassi . . chōchaue. 11. cho-

---

837. 57. *lettere incoronate.* By this term Leonardo probably understands not the Bible only, but the works of the early Fathers, and all the books recognised as sacred by the Roman Church.

chio ·; ¹⁰E similmēte al sēso · dell' udito · bastaua solamēte · la uoce · risonasse nelle cōcaue porosità ¹¹dell' osso · petroso · che sta · dentro · all'orechio ·, e nō fare da esso · osso al sēso comune altro ¹²trāsito · dove · essa s'abbocca, e abbia a discorrere · al comune givditio; ¹³Il senso dell' odorato · ācora lui si uede · essere dalla neciessità · costretto · a cōcorrere a detto ¹⁴juditio; ¹⁵Il tatto passa · per le corde forate, ed è portato · a esso sēso ·; le quali corde si uanno ¹⁶spargiēdo · con īfinita · ramificatione · in nella pelle · che circūda · le corporee mēbra ¹⁷e visciere ·; ¹⁸Le corde perforate portano il comādamēto · e sentimēto alli mēbri ofitiali, ¹⁹le quali · corde e nerui · infra · i muscoli · e lacierti ²⁰comādano · a quelli · il mouimēto ·; quelli ubidiscono, e tale·. obediētia si ²¹mette in atto · collo sgōfiare ·, imperochè 'l gōfiare · raccorta · le loro · lunghezze e tirasi dirieto · i nerui, ²²i quali · si tessono per le particule de' mēbri; essendo infusi nelli · stremi de' diti, ²³portano · al sēso · la cagione del loro · cōtatto;

²⁴I nerui · coi loro · muscoli · servono · alle corde · come · i soldati · a cōdottieri ·, e le corde ²⁵seruono · al senso comune · come i cōdottieri al capitano ·; ²⁶adūque · la givntura delli ossi · obbediscie · al neruo ·, e 'l neruo · al muscolo e 'l muscolo alla corda, ²⁷e la corda al senso comune ·, e'l sēso comune · è sedia · dell' anima ·, e la · memoria è sua ²⁸munitione · e la · impressiva · è sua · referēdaria; ²⁹come il senso · serve · all' anima · e nō l'anima al senso ·, e dove · māca · il senso ofitiale dell' anima ³⁰all' anima ·, māca in questa vita · la totalità dell'ufitio · d' esso · sēso, come appare nel ³¹mvto e l' orbo nato.

ly sounded in the porous cavity of the indurated portion of the temporal bone which lies within the ear, without making any farther transit from this bone to the common sense, where the voice confers with and discourses to the common judgment. The sense of smell, again, is compelled by necessity to refer itself to that same judgment. Feeling passes through the perforated cords and is conveyed to this common sense. These cords diverge with infinite ramifications into the skin which encloses the members of the body and the viscera. The perforated cords convey volition and sensation to the subordinate limbs. These cords and the nerves direct the motions of the muscles and sinews, between which they are placed; these obey, and this obedience takes effect by reducing their thickness; for in swelling, their length is reduced, and the nerves shrink which are interwoven among the particles of the limbs; being extended to the tips of the fingers, they transmit to the sense the object which they touch.

The nerves with their muscles obey the tendons as soldiers obey the officers, and the tendons obey the Common [central] Sense as the officers obey the general. [27]Thus the joint of the bones obeys the nerve, and the nerve the muscle, and the muscle the tendon and the tendon the Common Sense. And the Common Sense is the seat of the soul[28], and memory is its ammunition, and the impressibility is its referendary since the sense waits on the soul and not the soul on the sense. And where the sense that ministers to the soul is not at the service of the soul, all the functions of that sense are also wanting in that man's life, as is seen in those born mute and blind.

W. An. II. 202 *b* ('·B·)]　　　　　**839.**

COME · I NERUI OPERANO QUALCHE UOLTA PER LORO ²SANZA · COMĀDAMĒTO DELLI ALTRI OFITIALI DELL' ANIMA.

HOW THE NERVES SOMETIMES ACT OF THEMSELVES WITHOUT ANY COMMANDS FROM THE OTHER FUNCTIONS OF THE SOUL.

On involuntary muscular action.

³Questo · chiaramēte · apparisce ·, inperochè tu · vedrai · movere · ai paraletici e a

This is most plainly seen; for you will see palsied and shivering persons move,

mvne. 12. essaboca . abbia dischorere . al chomune givditio [lodor]. 13. āchora . . chōstretto a chōchorrere. 14. jvditio [il] gusto el tatto. 15. Il tutto nō passa elli per le chorde . . chorde si uano [di]. 16. sprgiēdo chōn . . ramifichatione inella . . circhūda le chorporee. 18. [j nervi] "le corde" . . portano [il sentimento] il chomādamēto essentimēto. 19. chorde . . musscoli. 20. acquelli . . queli obediscano [chollosco] ettale. 21. chollo schōfiare ipero chel . . rachorta . . lungeze ettirasi. 22. tessano . partichule. 23. chagione . . chōtatto. 24. choi . . mvsscoli . . servno . . chorde chome chōdottieri . elle chorde. 25. seruano . . chomvne chome i chōdotieri al chapitano el sēso chomvne serve. 26. [adunque il neruo . serue . al mvsscolo el mvsscolo]. 27. musscholo el mvsscolo . . chorda. 28. ella chorda . . chomvne . . chomvne essedia . . ella . . essua. 29. amvnitione . ella inpresiua essua referēdaria [e il chore essuo]. 30. chome . . de all . . mācha. 31. mācha . . apare. 32. ellorbo.

839. 1. chome. 2. chomādamēto. 3. aparisscie inperro . chettu vederai . . fredolleti. 4. chome. 5. chon . . essi . benbri . .

838. The peculiar use of the words *nervo, muscolo, corda, senso comune,* which are here literally rendered by nerve, muscle cord or tendon and Common Sense may be understood from lines **27** and **28**.

freddolosi, ⁴e assiderati · le loro\ · tremāti · mēbra come · testa · e mani · sanza · liciēza · dell' anima ·, la quale ⁵anima cō tutte · sue · forze nō potrà · vietare a essi . menbri · che nō tremino; Questo medesimo ⁶accade nel malcaduco e ne' mēbra tagliati come code di lucierte; ⁷la idea · over imaginatiua · è · timone e briglia de' sensi ·, imperochè la cosa im̄aginata ⁸move il sēso; ⁹preimaginare · è lo imaginare le cose che saranno; ¹⁰post-imaginare è imaginare · le cose passate.

and their trembling limbs, as their head and hands, quake without leave from their soul and their soul with all its power cannot prevent their members from trembling. The same thing happens in falling sickness, or in parts that have been cut off, as in the tails of lizards. The idea or imagination is the helm and guiding-rein of the senses, because the thing conceived of moves the sense. Pre-imagining, is imagining the things that are to be. Post-imagining, is imagining the things that are past.

Tr. 14.

840.

4 sono le potentie : memoria · e intelletto, lascibili · e cōcupiscibili, ²le 2 prime son ragionevoli e l'altre sēnsuali; ³I 3 sensi vedere, udire, odorato sono di poca proibitione ·, tato e gusto⁴no; l'odorato · mena · con seco · il gusto · nel cane e altri · golosi animali.

There are four Powers: memory and intellect, desire and covetousness. The two first are mental and the others sensual. The three senses: sight, hearing and smell cannot well be prevented; touch and taste not at all. Smell is connected with taste in dogs and other gluttonous animals. Miscellaneous physiological observations (840—842).

W. A. IV. 151*b*]

841.

Jo scopro alli omini l'origine ²della prima · o forse secōda cagione del loro essere.

I reveal to men the origin of the first, or perhaps second cause of their existence.

H.I 32*a*]

842.

Lussuria è cavsa della gienera²tione.

³Gola è mātenimēto della vita, ⁴pavra over timore è prolūga⁵mēto di uita e ⁶salvamēto dello strumē⁷to.

Lust is the cause of generation.

Appetite is the support of life. Fear or timidity is the prolongation of life and preservation of its instruments.

W. An. II. 43*b* (8)]

843.

COME IL CORPO DELL'ANIMALE AL CONTINUO ²MORE E RINASCIE.

HOW THE BODY OF ANIMALS IS CONSTANTLY DYING AND BEING RENEWED.

Il corpo di qualunche cosa la qual si nutrica, al con⁴tinuo muore e al continuo rinasce, perchè entrare ⁵non può nutrimēto se non in quelli lochi, dove il passato ⁶nutrimēto è spirato, e s'elli è spirato elli più nō à ⁷vita, e se tu nō li rendi nutrimēto equa⁸le al nutrimēto partito, allora

The body of any thing whatever that takes nourishment constantly dies and is constantly renewed; because nourishment can only enter into places where the former nourishment has expired, and if it has expired it no longer has life. And if you do not supply nourishment equal to the nourishment The laws of nutrition and the support of life (843—848).

trie mino Questo medessi. 6. achade . . mal chaducho . . mēbr . . chome chode. 7. e ētimone . . inpero chella chosa. 9. premaginare . . chose . chessaranno. 10. posimaginare . . chose.

840. .1. lascibili e chōcupiscibili. 2. ellaltre. 3. de [2] 3 sensi . . vldire . . pocha . . tato. 4. chōseco . . chane . . golos.

841. 1. schopro. 2. della loro "prima offorse secōdo" sechonda chagione di loro.

842. 1—7 R. 1. chausa. 6. delo e saluamēto.

843. 1. chorpo . . chontinuo . . chosa . . nutricha . . chon. 4. chontinuo rinasscie. 5. sēnon. 6. esspirato esselli he . . nō[nu]. 7. [trusscie] vita essectu. 8. mancha. 9. valtudine essettulli . . tuc. 10. ressta desstructa Massettu. 11. des-la vita manca di su⁹a valetūdine, e se tu li leui esso nutrimento, la uita in tut¹⁰to resta distrutta; Ma se tu ne rēdi tanto quanto si ¹¹ne distrugge alla giornata, allora tanto rinasce di ¹²uita, quanto se ne consuma a similitudine del lume ¹³della candela col nutrimēto datoli dall'omore ¹⁴d'essa candela, il quale lume ancora lui al con¹⁵tinuo con velocissimo socorso restaura di sotto, ¹⁶quāto di sopra se ne consuma morendo, e di splendi¹⁷da lucie si converte morēdo in tenebroso fumo, la qual ¹⁸morte è continua, siccome è cōtinuo esso fumo, e la cō¹⁹tinuità di tal fumo · è equale al cōtinuato nutrimēto, ²⁰e in instante tutto il lume è morto e tutto rigienerato insie²¹me col moto del nutrimento suo.

which is gone, life will fail in vigour, and if you take away this nourishment, the life is entirely destroyed. But if you restore as much is destroyed day by day, then as much of the life is renewed as is consumed, just as the flame of the candle is fed by the nourishment afforded by the liquid of this candle, which flame continually with a rapid supply restores to it from below as much as is consumed in dying above: and from a brilliant light is converted in dying into murky smoke; and this death is continuous, as the smoke is continuous; and the continuance of the smoke is equal to the continuance of the nourishment, and in the same instant all the flame is dead and all regenerated, simultaneously with the movement of its own nourishment.

W. An. III. 241a]   844.

¶Come tu ài descritto il rè delli animali — ma io meglio direi dicēdo ²rè delle bestie · essendo tu la maggiore—perchè non li ài uccisi, acciò che possino poi darti ³li lor figlioli in benifitio della tua gola colla quale tu ài tē⁴tato farti sepultura di tutti li animali, e più oltre direi, se'l ⁵dire il uero mi fusse integramēte lecito; Ma non usciamo ⁶delle cose vmane, dicendo vna somma scelerata⁷gine, la qual non accade nelli animali terrestri, ⁸inperochè in quelli nō si trovano animali che māgino della loro ⁹spetie se nō per mācamēto di celabro (in poche infra loro, e de'ma¹⁰dri come infra li omini, bēchè nō sieno in tāto numero); ¹¹e questo non accade se nō nel¹²li

King of the animals—as thou hast described him—I should rather say king of the beasts, thou being the greatest—because thou hast spared slaying them, in order that they may give thee their children for the benefit of the gullet, of which thou hast attempted to make a sepulchre for all animals; and I would say still more, if it were allowed me to speak the entire truth[5]. But we do not go outside human matters in telling of one supreme wickedness, which does not happen among the animals of the earth, inasmuch as among them are found none who eat their own kind, unless through want of sense (few indeed among them, and those being mothers, as with men, albeit they be not many in number); and this happens only among the rapacious animals, as with the leonine species, and leo-

struggie . . rinasscie. 12. chonsuma assimilitudine. 13. socto della chandela chol. 14. chandela . . anchora . . chon. 15. chon velocissimo [vita] "sochorso" . . socto. 16. chonsuma. 17. chonverte . . tenebro. 18. chontinua sichome chontinuo . . ella. 19. chōtinuato. 20. e i ni state . . ettutto. 21. chol.
844. 1. isscritto . . ma i . . dirai. 2. bestie "essendo tu la magore" | perche no li ai uticcoche ti possin. 3. figloli . . ai te. 5. fussi . . none vssciā. 6. disscendo . . soma isscelerati. 7. gine . . soma isscelerati . . achade . . terresti. 8. trova. 10. numero)e. 11. [alcvna volta] ecquesto none achade . . ne. 12. leonina [che sspessa]. 13. si māgia che] . . cerveri

844. We are led to believe that Leonardo himself was a vegetarian from the following interesting passage in the first of Andrea Corsali's letters to Giuliano de' Medici: *Alcuni gentili chiamati Guzzarati non si cibano di cosa alcuna che tenga sangue, nè fra essi loro consentono che si noccia ad alcuna cosa animata, come il nostro Leonardo da Vinci.*

5—18. Amerigo Vespucci, with whom Leonardo was personally acquainted, writes in his second letter to Pietro Soderini, about the inhabitants of

the Canary Islands after having stayed there in 1503: *"Hanno una scelerata libertà di viuere; . . . . si cibano di carne humana, di maniera che il padre māgia il figliuolo, et all'incontro il figliuolo il padre seĩondo che a caso e per sorte auiene. Io viddi vn certo huomo sceleratissimo che si vantaua, et si teneua a non piccola gloria di hauer mangiato più di trecento huomini. Viddi anche vna certa città, nella quale io dimorai forse ventisette giorni, doue le carni humane, hauendole salate, eran appicate alli traui, si come noi alli traui di cucina* animali rapaci, come nella spetie leonina [13]e pardi, pardere, cervieri, gatte e simili, [14]li quali alcuna volta si māgiano i figlioli; ma tu oltre [15]alli figlioli ti māgi il padre, madre, fratelli e amici, e nō [16]ti basta questo, chè tu vai a caccia per le altrui isole, pi-[17]gliando li altri omini e questi mezzo nudi il mēbro e li testi[18]culi fai ingrassare e te li cacci giù per la tua gola; or [19]non produce la natura tāti senplici, che tu ti possa satia[20]re? e se nō ti cōtenti de' senplici, non puoi tu cō la mistiō [21]di quelli fare infiniti conposti, come scrisse il Platina [22]e li altri autori di gola? ¶

pards, panthers lynxes, cats and the like, who sometimes eat their children; but thou, besides thy children devourest father, mother, brothers and friends; nor is this enough for thee, but thou goest to the chase on the islands of others, taking other men and these half-naked, the . . . . and the . . . . thou fattenest, and chasest them down thy own throat[18]; now does not nature produce enough simples, for thee to satisfy thyself? and if thou art not content with simples, canst thou not by the mixture of them make infinite compounds, as Platina wrote[21], and other authors on feeding?

H.[2] 41 b]　　　　　　　**845.**

Facciamo nostra vita coll' al[2]trui · morte. [3]In nella cosa morta rimā vi[4]ta dissensata, la quale ri[5]cōgiūta alli stomachi de' vi[6]ui ripiglia uita sēsitiva [7]e ītellettiva.

Our life is made by the death of others. In dead matter insensible life remains, which, reunited to the stomachs of living beings, resumes life, both sensual and intellectual.

S. K. M. III, 74 a]　　　　　　　**846.**

La natura pare qui in molti [2]o di molti animali stata più pre[3]sto crudele matrignia che ma[4]dre, e d'alcuni nō matrignia [5]ma pietosa madre.

Here nature appears with many animals to have been rather a cruel stepmother than a mother, and with others not a stepmother, but a most tender mother.

C. A. 75 b; 219 b]　　　　　　　**847.**

L'omo e li animali sono propi trāsito e condotto di cibo, sepoltura · d'animali · albergo de' morti, facciēdo a se vna [2]dell'altrui morte guaina di corrutione!

Man and animals are really the passage and the conduit of food, the sepulchre of animals and resting place of the dead, one causing the death of the other, making themselves the covering for the corruption of other dead [bodies].

---

chatte essimili. 14. māgano i figloli, mattu. 15. figloli. 16. bassta . . chaccia. 17. meznudi. 18. ettelli caccigu. 19. chet-tutti. 20. esse nō . . poi. 22. elli . . altori.
845. 1—7 R. 1. faciano nosstra . . choll. 3. jnella. 4. disensata. 5. stomaci. 7. ētellectiva.
846. 1. immolti. 5. piatosa.
847. 1. elli . . propi "trāsitoe" chondotto . . morti [animali] faciēdo asse. 2. morte [pigliando piacere dellaltri miserie] guaina di chorutione.

appicchiamo le carni di cinghali secche al sole o al fumo, et massimamente salsiccie, et altre simil cose: anzi si marauigliauano grādemēte che noi non māgiassimo della carne de nemici, le quali dicono muouere appetito, et essere di marauiglioso sapore, et le lodano come cibi soaui et delicati (Lettere due di Amerigo Vespucci Fiorentino drizzate al *magnifico Pietro Soderini, Gonfaloniere della eccelsa Republica di Firenze;* various editions).

21. *Come scrisse il Platina* (Bartolomeo Sacchi, a famous humanist). The Italian edition of his treatise *De arte coquinaria*, was published under the title *De la honestra voluptate, e valetudine, Venezia* 1487.

F. 1 a]   **848.**

La morte ne' vecchi sanza febre si causa dalle ²uene che uā dalla milza alla porta del fega³to e s'ingrossan tanto di pelle ch'elle si richi⁴udono e non danno più transito al san⁵gue che li nutrica.

⁶Il continuo corso che fa il sangue per le sue ⁷uene fa che tali vene s'ingrossano e fanno⁸si callose in tal modo che al fine si riserra⁹no e proibiscono il corso al sangue.

On the circulation of the blood (848—850).

Death in old men, when not from fever, is caused by the veins which go from the spleen to the valve of the liver, and which thicken so much in the walls that they become closed up and leave no passage for the blood that nourishes it.

[6]The incessant current of the blood through the veins makes these veins thicken and become callous, so that at last they close up and prevent the passage of the blood.

Leic. 21 b]   **849.**

Raggirāsi l'acque con cōtinvo moto dall'infime profondità de' mari alle altissimę somità de' mōti, non osseruando ²la natura delle cose graui, e in questo caso fanno come il sangue delli animali che sempre si ³moue dal mare del core e scorre alla sōmità delle loro teste, e che quiui rōpōsi le uene ·, ⁴come si uede una vena rotta nel naso, che tutto il sangue da basso si leua alla altezza della rotta vena; — ⁵Quando l'aqua escie dalla rotta vena della terra essa osserua la natura delle altre cose piy ⁶graui che l'aria, onde senpre cerca i lochi bassi.

The waters return with constant motion from the lowest depths of the sea to the utmost height of the mountains, not obeying the nature of heavier bodies; and in this they resemble the blood of animated beings which always ·moves from the sea of the heart and flows towards the top of the head; and here it may burst a vein, as may be seen when a vein bursts in the nose; all the blood rises from below to the level of the burst vein. When the water rushes out from the burst vein in the earth, it obeys the law of other bodies that are heavier than the air since it always seeks low places.

W. A. III. 226 a (·M·)]   **850.**

Come il sangue che torna indirieto, ²quādo il core si riapre, non è quel che ³riserra le porte del core.

That the blood which returns when the heart opens again is not the same as that which closes the valves of the heart.

Br. M. 147 b]   **851.**

Fattevi dare la difinitione e riparo del caso secondo . . . . ² . . . . . e vedrete che omini son eletti per medici di mala³tie da loro non conosciute.

Some notes on medicine (851—855).

Make them give you the definition and remedies for the case . . . and you will see that men are selected to be doctors for diseases they do not know.

848. 1. vechi. 2. miza. 3. to singrossan. 4. vdano . . transitu. 5. chelli nutricha. 6. cheffa. 7. chettali . . effan. 8. risera.
    9. proibisscano . . sanghue.
849. 1. Ragirāsi. 2. fa . . animati. 3. move [dal lago] "dal mare" del . . tesste . . echi quiui rōpasi. 4. chettutto . . alteza . .
    ve"na". 5. esscie. 6. grave chellaria . cercha.
850. 1. chettorna . . de porte.
851. 1. fatevi . . caso al scō e al. 2. laltro e vedrete. 3. dallor . . conossciute.

849. From this passage it is quite plain that Leonardo had not merely a general suspicion of the circulation of the blood but a very clear conception of it. Leonardo's studies on the muscles of the heart are to be found in the MS. W. An. III. but no information about them has hitherto been made public. The limits of my plan in this work exclude all purely anatomical writings, therefore only a very brief excerpt from this note book can be given here. WILLIAM HARVEY (born 1578 and Professor of Anatomy at Cambridge from 1615) is always considered to have been the discoverer of the circulation of the blood. He studied medicine at Padua in 1598, and in 1628 brought out his memorable and important work: *De motu cordis et sanguinis*.

W. XIII δ]

852.

Medicina da grattature insegniomela l'araldo [2]del rè di Frācia: oncie 4 ciera nova, ōcie 4, [3]pece greca, ōcie 2 inciēso e ogni cosa [4]stia separata, e fondi la ciera, e poi vi metti den[5]tro l'inciēso, e poi la pece; fa ne pe[6]verada e metti sopr'al male.

A remedy for scratches taught me by the Herald to the King of France. 4 ounces of virgin wax, 4 ounces of colophony, 2 ounces of incense. Keep each thing separate; and melt the wax, and then put in the incense and then the colophony, make a mixture of it and put it on the sore place.

Tr. 7]

853.

¶Medicina è ripareggiamēto de' dise-quali elemēti; ¶[2]malattia è discordanza d'elemēti īfusi nel uitale.corpo.

Medicine is the restoration of discordant elements; sickness is the discord of the ele-ments infused into the living body.

Tr. 49]

854.

A chi da noia il uomito al nauicare debba bere sugo [2]d'assētio.

Those who are annoyed by sickness at sea should drink extract of wormwood.

C. A. 77 δ; 225 δ]

855.

Se vuoi star sano esser a questa nor-ma; [2]nō māgiar sanza voglia . . . . [3]mastica bene; e per quel che niēte ritiene, [4]sia bē cotto e di semplice forma; [5]chi medicina piglia mal s'informa.

To keep in health, this rule is wise: Eat only when you want and relish food. Chew thoroughly that it may do you good. Have it well cooked, unspiced and undis-guised. He who takes medicine is ill advised.

W. An. III, XXV]

856.

Insegnioti di conse[2]rvare la sanità [3]la qual cosa tanto [4]più ti riuscirà, [5]quāto più da fisici [6]ti guarder[7]ai; [8]perchè le sue cō [9]positioni sō [10]di spetie d'al[11]chimia.

I teach you to preserve your health; and in this you will succed better in proportion as you shun physicians, because their medicines are the work of alchemists.

852. 4. sta seperata . . metti\|\|\|\|\. 5. effane. 6. mal.
854. al uomito il nauicare deba. 2. dasentio.
855. 1. uoi strasano. 2. voglia ecci \|\|\ ellette. 3. masstica . . ecquel. 4. chotto.
856. 1. e ingegniati. 4. riusscira. 9. positione. 10. spetie dar. 12. ella. 13. qual. 14. nonemē. 15. numero. 16. de libri.
  17. che sia dime. 18. dicina. *The meaning of these short lines 12—18 is doubtful.*

855. This appears to be a sketch for a poem.
856. This passage is written on the back of the drawing Pl. CVIII. Compare also No. 1184.

Héliog. Dujardin.

Imp. Eudes.

Héliog. Dujardin.

Imp. Eudes.

Héliog. Dujardin.

Imp. Eudes.

Héliog: Dujardin.

Imp. Eudes.

Héliog. Dujardin.

Imp. Eudes.

Heliog: Dujardin.

Imp. Eudes.

1

2

2

manera des caleva

8

3

10

Imp. Eudes.

1

2

1

2

5

4

Heliog. Dujardin.

Imp. Eudes.

Héliog. Dujardin.

Plate LXXXII is reproduced on the following two pages.

Héliog Dujardin.

Imp. Eudes.

2

1

4

3

5

6

PL. XCV.

Héliog. Dujardin.

Imp. Eudes.

XV.

Astronomy.

Ever since the publication by Venturi in 1797 and Libri in 1840 of some few passages of Leonardo's astronomical notes, scientific astronomers have frequently expressed the opinion, that they must have been based on very important discoveries, and that the great painter also deserved a conspicuous place in the history of this science. In the passages here printed, a connected view is given of his astronomical studies as they lie scattered through the manuscripts, which have come down to us. Unlike his other purely scientific labours, Leonardo devotes here a good deal of attention to the opinions of the ancients, though he does not follow the practice universal in his day of relying on them as authorities; he only quotes them, as we shall see, in order to refute their arguments. His researches throughout have the stamp of independent thought. There is nothing in these writings to lead us to suppose that they were merely an epitome of the general learning common to the astronomers of the period. As early as in the XIVth century there were chairs of astronomy in the universities of Padua and Bologna, but so late as during the entire XVIth century Astronomy and Astrology were still closely allied.

It is impossible now to decide whether Leonardo, when living in Florence, became acquainted in his youth with the doctrines of Paolo Toscanelli the great astronomer and mathematician (died 1482), of whose influence and teaching but little is now known, beyond the fact that he advised and encouraged Columbus to carry out his project of sailing round the world. His name is nowhere mentioned by Leonardo, and from the dates of the manuscripts from which the texts on astronomy are taken, it seems highly probable that Leonardo devoted his attention to astronomical studies less in his youth than in his later years. It was evidently his purpose to treat of Astronomy in a connected form and in a separate work (see the beginning of Nos. 866 and 892; compare also No. 1167). It is quite in accordance with his general scientific thoroughness that he should propose to write a special treatise on Optics as an introduction to Astronomy (see Nos. 867 and 877). Some of the chapters belonging to this Section bear the title

"Prospettiva" *(see Nos. 869 and 870), this being the term universally applied at the time to Optics as well as Perspective (see Vol. I, p. 10, note to No. 13, l. 10).*

At the beginning of the XVIth century the Ptolemaic theory of the universe was still universally accepted as the true one, and Leonardo conceives of the earth as fixed, with the moon and sun revolving round it, as they are represented in the diagram to No. 897. He does not go into any theory of the motions of the planets; with regard to these and the fixed stars he only investigates the phenomena of their luminosity. The spherical form of the earth he takes for granted as an axiom from the first, and he anticipates Newton by pointing out the universality of Gravitation not merely in the earth, but even in the moon. Although his acute research into the nature of the moon's light and the spots on the moon did not bring to light many results of lasting importance beyond making it evident that they were a refutation of the errors of his contemporaries, they contain various explanations of facts which modern science need not modify in any essential point, and discoveries which history has hitherto assigned to a very much later date.

The ingenious theory by which he tries to explain the nature of what is known as earth shine, the reflection of the sun's rays by the earth towards the moon, saying that it is a peculiar refraction, originating in the innumerable curved surfaces of the waves of the sea may be regarded as absurd; but it must not be forgotten that he had no means of detecting the fundamental error on which he based it, namely: the assumption that the moon was at a relatively short distance from the earth. So long as the motion of the earth round the sun remained unknown, it was of course impossible to form any estimate of the moon's distance from the earth by a calculation of its parallax.

Before the discovery of the telescope accurate astronomical observations were only possible to a very limited extent. It would appear however from certain passages in the notes here printed for the first time, that Leonardo was in a position to study the spots in the moon more closely than he could have done with the unaided eye. So far as can be gathered from the mysterious language in which the description of his instrument is wrapped, he made use of magnifying glasses; these do not however seem to have been constructed like a telescope—telescopes were first made about 1600. As LIBRI pointed out (Histoire des Sciences mathématiques III, 101) *Fracastoro of Verona (1473—1553) succeeded in magnifying the moon's face by an arrangement of lenses (compare No. 910, note), and this gives probability to Leonardo's invention at a not much earlier date.*

I.

THE EARTH AS A PLANET.

Br. M. 176a]

857.

Linia d' equalità, ²linia dell' orizzōte, ³linia giacēte, ⁴linia equigiacēte;

⁵Queste linie sō quelle ⁶che con sua stremi sō ⁷equidistanti al cē⁸tro del mondo.

The equator, the line of the horizon, the ecliptic, the meridian:

These lines are those which in all their parts are equidistant from the centre of the globe.

The earth's place in the universe (857. 858).

F. 41b]

858.

Come la terra non è nel mezzo del cerchio del ²sole, nè nel mezzo del mōdo, ma è ben nel mez³zo de' sua elemēti, conpagni e vniti cō lei, e chi ⁴stesse nella luna, quād' ella insieme col sole ⁵è sotto a noi, questa nostra terra coll' ele⁶mento dell' acqua parrebbe e farebbe ofitio tal ⁷qual fa la luna a noi.

The earth is not in the centre of the Sun's orbit nor at the centre of the universe, but in the centre of its companion elements, and united with them. And any one standing on the moon, when it and the sun are both beneath us, would see this our earth and the element of water upon it just as we see the moon, and the earth would light it as it lights us.

Br. M. 151a]

859.

La forza da carestia · o · douitia · è gienerata; ²questa è figliola del moto · materiale · e nepote ³ del moto · spirituale ·, e madre e origine del peso; ⁴e esso peso è finito nell' elemēto dell' acqua e terra, ⁵e essa ·

Force arises from dearth or abundance; it is the child of physical motion, and the grand-child of spiritual motion, and the mother and origin of gravity. Gravity is limited to the elements of water and

The fundamental laws of the solar system (859—864).

---

857. 2. dorizōte. 6. che cho. 7. nequidistante.

858. 1. mezo. 2. mezo. 4. stessi. 5. essotto annoi . . nosta. 6. acq"a" parebbe effarebe. 7. annoi.

859. 1. odouitia. 2. effigliola . . enepo. 4. chesso . . heffinito . . ettera. 5. chessa . . he. 6. mouerebbe . . potessi. 7. hessa

---

859. Only part of this passage belongs, strictly speaking, to this section. The principle laid down in the second paragraph is more directly connected with the notes given in the preceding section on Physiology.

forza · è infinita, perchè con essa infiniti
⁶mōdi si mouerebbero ·, se strumēti farsi
potessero, ⁷doue essa forza gienerare si
potesse.

⁸La forza col moto materiale e 'l peso
colla percussione ⁹son le quattro accidētali
potētie, colle quali tutte l' opere ¹⁰de' mortali ànno loro essere e lor morte;

¹¹La forza · dal moto · spirituale · à origine; il quale moto, ¹²scorrēdo · per le mēbra
degli animali · sensibili ·, ingrossa ¹³i muscoli
di quelli ·, onde ingrossati · essi muscoli si
uē¹⁴gono a raccortare e trarsi dirieto i nervi
che con essi ¹⁵sō cōgiunti ·, e di qui si causa
la forza per le mēbra umane.

¹⁶La qualità e quātità delle forze · d'uno
uomo potrà ¹⁷partorire · altra forza ·, la quale
sarà proportio¹⁸nevolmēte tanto maggiore
quāto essa sarà di piv ¹⁹lūgo moto, l'una
che l'altra.

earth; but this force is unlimited, and
by it infinite worlds might be moved if
instruments could be made by which the
force could be generated.

Force, with physical motion, and gravity, with resistance are the four external powers on which all actions of mortals
depend.

Force has its origin in spiritual motion;
and this motion, flowing through the limbs
of sentient animals, enlarges their muscles.
Being enlarged by this current the muscles
are shrunk in length and contract the tendons
which are connected with them, and this is
the cause of the force of the limbs in man.

The quality and quantity of the force
of a man are able to give birth to other
forces, which will be proportionally greater
as the motions produced by them last
longer.

860.

Br. M. 175*a*]

Il peso · *o* · perchè non resta nel suo
sito? ²non resta perchè non à resistētia;
e dō³de si moverà? Moverassi · inverso il
⁴centro; e perchè nō per altre linie? perchè ⁵il peso, che non à resistentia, discien-
derà ⁶in basso per la uia piv brieve, e 'l
più bas⁷so sito è il ciētro del mondo; e
perchè lo sa ⁸così tal peso trovarlo con
tanta breuità? ⁹perchè non va come insensibile prima ¹⁰vagando per diverse linie.

Why does not the weight *o* remain in its
place? It does not remain because it has no
resistance. Where will it move to? It will
move towards the centre [of gravity]. And
why by no other line? Because a weight
which has no support falls by the shortest
road to the lowest point which is the centre
of the world. And why does the weight know
how to find it by so short a line? Because it
is not independant and does not move about
in various directions.

861.

F. 22*b*]

Movasi la terra da che parte voglia,
²mai la superfitie dell'acqua uscirà fori
della ³sua spera, ma senpre
sarà equidistante al ⁴centro del
mondo;

⁵¶Dato che la terra · si ri-
movessi dal centro ⁶del mondo, che farebbe l'acqua?¶

⁷Resterebbe intorno a esso
centro ⁸con equal grossezza,
ma minore diami⁹tro, che
quando ella auea la terra in
corpo.

Let the earth turn on which side it may
the surface of the waters will never move
from its spherical form, but will
always remain equidistant from
the centre of the globe.

Granting that the earth might
be removed from the centre of
the globe, what would happen
to the water?

It would remain in a sphere
round that centre equally thick,
but the sphere would have a
smaller diameter than when it
enclosed the earth.

. . potessi. 9. quatro. 10. ellor. 12. scorēdo. 13. musscoli di quelle . . musscoli. 14. gano aracortare. 16. ecquātita
. . homo. 18. magiore. 19. luna cellaltra.

860. 4. cientro he. 8. chon. 9. perche nona come [in gi] insensibile prima. 10. vagando per diuerse linie.

861. 2. acq"a" vsscirà. 5. chella. 6. cheffarebbe.

860. This text and the sketch belonging to it,
are reproduced on Pl. CXXI.

861. Compare No. 896, lines 48—64; and
No. 936.

F. 11 b]

862.

Se la terra delli antipodi che sostiene ²l'oceano s'inalzasse, e si scoprisse assai ³fori d'esso mare, essendo quasi pia⁴na, in che modo sarebbe poi col tēpo ⁵a creare li mōti e le valli.

⁶E li sassi di diuerse falde?

Supposing the earth at our antipodes which supports the ocean were to rise and stand uncovered, far out of the sea, but remaining almost level, by what means afterwards, in the course of time, would mountains and vallies be formed?

And the rocks with their various strata?

Tr. 28]

863.

Ogni omo senpre si troua nel mezzo del mōdo e sotto il mezzo ²del suo · emisperio, e sopra il ciētro d'esso mōdo.

Each man is always in the middle of the surface of the earth and under the zenith of his own hemisphere, and over the centre of the earth.

Leic. 1 a]

864.

Ricordo come io ho' in prima a dimo-²strare la distantia del sole dalla terra, ³e con ū de' sua razzi passati per ispi⁴racolo in loco oscuro ritrovare ⁵la sua quātità vera, e oltre a ⁶di questo per lo mezzo della spera del ⁷l'acqua ritrovare la grādezza della terra.¶

⁸Qui si dimostra come, quā⁹do il sole è nel mezzo del nostro ¹⁰emisperio, che li antipodi ¹¹orientali cogli occidentali ue¹²dono in un medesimo tenpo cias¹³cun per se spechiare il sole nelle ¹⁴loro acque, e 'l simile quelli del po¹⁵lo artico col antartico, se abi¹⁶tatori ui sono.

Mem.: That I must first show the distance of the sun from the earth; and, by means of a ray passing through a small hole into a dark chamber, detect its real size; and besides this, by means of the aqueous sphere calculate the size of the globe . . .

Here it will be shown, that when the sun is in the meridian of our hemisphere[10], the antipodes to the East and to the West, alike, and at the same time, see the sun mirrored in their waters; and the same is equally true of the arctic and antarctic poles, if indeed they are inhabited.

C. A. 111 b; 345 b]

865.

Come la terra è una stella.

That the earth is a star.

How to prove that the earth is a planet (865—867).

F. 56 a]

866.

Tu nel tuo discorso ài a cōcludere ²la terra essere vna stella quasi si³mile alla luna, ⁴e la nobiltà del nostro mōdo;

⁵E così farai vn discorso delle grā⁶dezze di molte stelle, secōdo li autori.

In your discourse you must prove that the earth is a star much like the moon, and the glory of our universe; and then you must treat of the size of various stars, according to the authors.

---

862. 1. sella. 2. sinalzassi . . scoprissi essi. 5. elle. 6. elli.　　**863.** 1. mezo . . essotto il mezo.
864. 1. chome . . in p"a" a dimō. 2. disstantia. 3. razi. 4. rachulo illocho osscuro. 6. mezo. 7. grādeza. 8. dimosstra chome. 9. mezo . . nosstro. 10. emissperio chelli antipodi di. 11. horientali. 12. gano nun. 13. scun. 14. acque . . quelgli. 15. articho chol antarticho.
865. R.　　　**866.** 1. tutto tuo discorsa a cō cludere. 3. luna [e cosi proverra]. 6. altori.

864. 10. 11. *Antipodi orientali cogli occidentali.* The word *Antipodes* does not here bear its literal sense, but—as we may infer from the simultaneous reference to inhabitants of the North and South— is used as meaning men living at a distance of 90 degrees from the zenith of the rational horizon of each observer.

F. 25 b]

867.

ORDINE DEL PROVARE LA TERRA ESSERE [2] VNA STELLA.

[3] Inprima definisci l'ochio, poi mostra come il bat[4]tere d'alcuna stella viene dall'ochio, e perchè il battere [5] d'esse stelle è più nell'una che nell'altra, e come li [6] razzi delle stelle nascono dall'ochio, e dì, che se 'l batte[7]re delle stelle fusse come pare nelle stelle, che tal bat[8]timēto mostra d'essere di tanta dilatatione, quāt'è [9] il corpo di tale stella; essendo adūque maggiore della ter[10]ra che tal moto fatto in istante sarebbe troppo veloce [11] a raddoppiare la grādezza di tale stella; Di poi pro[12]va come la superfitie dell'aria ne' cō- fini del foco, e [13] la superfitie del foco nel suo termine è quel[14]la, nella qual penetrādo li razzi solari portano la [15] similitudine di corpi celesti grāde nel lor leua[16]re, e però è pic- cola, essendo esse nel mezzo del celo; [17] sia la terra $a \mid n\ d\ m$ sia [18] la superfitie dell'aria che [19] confina colla spera del [20] foco; · $h\ f\ g$ · sia il corso [21] della luna o vuoi del sole; [22] dico che quādo il sole appari[23]sce al' orizzōte g, che lì sono ueduti [24] li sua razzi passare per la superfitie [25] dell'aria infra āgoli inequali cioè $o\ m$, il che non è in $d\ k$, e ācora [26] passa per maggiore grossezza d'aria; tutto $e\ m$ è aria più spessa.

THE METHOD OF PROVING THAT THE EARTH IS A STAR.

First describe the eye; then show how the twinkling of a star is really in the eye and why one star should twinkle more than another, and how the rays from the stars originate in the eye; and add, that if the twinkling of the stars were really in the stars —as it seems to be—that this twinkling appears to be an extension as great as the diameter of the body of the star; therefore, the star being larger than the earth, this motion effected in an instant would be a rapid doubling of the size of the star. Then prove that the surface of the air where it lies contiguous to fire, and the surface of the fire where it ends are those into which the solar rays penetrate, and transmit the images of the heavenly bodies, large when they rise, and small, when they are on the meridian. Let a be the earth and $n\ d\ m$ the surface of the air in contact with the sphere of fire; $h\ f\ g$ is the orbit of the moon or, if you please, of the sun; then I say that when the sun appears on the horizon g, its rays are seen passing through the surface of the air at a slanting angle, that is $o\ m$; this is not the case at $d\ k$. And so it passes through a greater mass of air; all of $e\ m$ is a denser atmosphere.

W. XXVI]

The principles of astronomical perspective (868—873).

868.

Infra 'l sole · e noi è tenebre, e però l'aria pare azzurra.

Beyond the sun and us there is darkness and so the air appears blue.

E. 15 b]

869.

PROSPETTIVA.

[2] Possibile è fare che l'ochio nō uedrà [3] le cose remote molto diminuite, come fa

PERSPECTIVE.

It is possible to find means by which the eye shall not see remote objects as much

---

867. 3. difinissci. 4. piene . . il bat. 6. razi . . nasscā . . e di chessel bate. 7. fussi . . tal ba. 9. magor. 10. istante sare trovo veloce. 11. radopiare la grādeza. 12. foco el. 15. lla superfitie . . focho . . ecquel. 14. razi . . portāta. 16. eppero e pichole . . mezo. 20. foco. 21. della nuna ouoi. 22. apari. 23. orizōte g chele veduto. 24. razi. 25. coe o m il ce non . . acora. 26. magore grosseza.

868. ettenebre . . azura.

869. 1. prosspettiva. 2. he fare chellochio . . uedera. 3. chome ffa. 4. presspettiva naturale [le spe] le. 5. le diminuisschano.

868. Compare Vol. I, No. 301.

⁴la prospettiva naturale, le quali ⁵diminui-
scono mediante la curuità del⁶l'ochio, che
è costretto a tagliare sopra di ⁷se le piramidi di qualunche spetie che viene al ⁸ochio
· infra angoli retti sperici; Ma ⁹l'arte, che
io insegnio qui in margine, ta¹⁰glia
esse piramidi con angoli ret¹¹ti vicino alla superfitie di tal popilla;
Ma ¹²la convessa popilla dell'occhio
piglia sopra ¹³di se tutto il nostro
emisperio, e que¹⁴sta mostrerà solo
una stella; ma doue ¹⁵molte piccole stelle si ricevono per similitu¹⁶dine
nella superfitie della popilla, ¹⁷le quali
stelle son minime, questa di¹⁸mostrerà vna
sola stella, ma fia grāde; ¹⁹E così la luna
di maggiore grādezza, e le su²⁰e macule
di più nota figura; A questo ²¹nostro ochio
si debbe fare v̄ uetro pieno di ²²quell'acqua
di che si fa mētione ²³nel 4 del libro 113
delle cose naturali, ²⁴la quale acqua fa
parere spogliate di ²⁵vetro quelle cose
che son congielate nel²⁶le palle del uetro
cristallino.

DELL'OCHIO.

²⁸Infra li corpi minori della popilla del-
l'ochio ²⁹quella fia manco nota a essa popilla, ³⁰la quale le sarà più vicina ‖ E con
questa ³¹speriētia ci si è fatto noto che la
virtù visiva nō ³²si riducie in pūto perchè
se la ecc.;

³³Leggi ī margine.

³⁴Quella cosa si ³⁵dimostra maggi³⁶ore,
che uiene ³⁷all'ochio cō più ³⁸grosso angolo.

³⁹Ma le spetie delli ob⁴⁰bietti, che cō-
cor⁴¹rono alla popilla ⁴²dell'ochio, si con-
par⁴³tono sopra tal popi⁴⁴lla nel medesimo
⁴⁵modo, ch'elle son cō⁴⁶partite infra l'aria;
⁴⁷e la prova di ques⁴⁸to è in se⁴⁹guito;
quādo noi ⁵⁰riguardiamo il ⁵¹cielo stellato
⁵²sanza por la ui⁵³sta più a una stel⁵⁴la
che all'altra, ⁵⁵che allora ci si mo⁵⁶stra il
cielo semina⁵⁷to di stelle, e sō pro⁵⁸portio-
nate nell'ochio ⁵⁹siccome lo sono in ⁶⁰cielo,
e così li loro ⁶¹spati fanno il simile.

diminished as in natural perspective, which
diminishes them by reason of the convexity
of the eye which necessarily intersects,
at its surface, the pyramid of every image
conveyed to the eye at a right angle on its
spherical surface. But by the method
I here teach in the margin[9] these
pyramids are intersected at right
angles close to the surface of the
pupil. The convex pupil of the eye
can take in the whole of our hemisphere, while this will show only a
single star; but where many small stars transmit their images to the surface of the pupil
those stars are extremely small; here only
one star is seen but it will be large. And
so the moon will be seen larger and its
spots of a more defined form[20]. You must
place close to the eye a glass filled with the
water of which mention is made in number
4 of Book 113 "On natural substances"[23];
for this water makes objects which are enclosed in balls of crystalline glass appear
free from the glass.

OF THE EYE.

Among the smaller objects presented to
the pupil of the eye, that which is closest to
it, will be least appreciable to the eye. And
at the same time, the experiments here made
with the power of sight, show that it is not
reduced to speck if the &c.[32].

Read in the margin.

[34]Those objects are seen largest which
come to the eye at the largest angles.

But the images of the objects conveyed
to the pupil of the eye are distributed to
the pupil exactly as they are distributed in
the air: and the proof of this is in what
follows; that when we look at the starry sky,
without gazing more fixedly at one star than
another, the sky appears all strewn with stars;
and their proportions to the eye are the same
as in the sky and likewise the spaces between
them[61].

6. chosstretta attagliare. 7. piramide . . spetie viene. 8. llochio . . angholi. 10. lia [le] esse piramide chon angholi.
12. delloccio pigli. 13. mostro omissperio ecques. 14. mossterra. 15. pichole . . riciev. 16. popille [qu]. 17. stielle . .
quista e di. 18. mossterra . . maffia. 19. chosi . . magiore grādeza elle. 20. machule. 22. acqua [che] di . . mētione [de].
23. chose. 24. aqua. 25. chose chesson. 26. crisstallino. 28. Infralli chorpi. 29. mancho. 29. a essa [ochu] popilla.
30. chon questa [no]. 31. ci se . . chella. 32. sella. 33. [Quella u]. 34. chosa. 35. dimosstra magi. 37. chō. 38. grosse
anghole. 39. Malle setie. 40. biecto che chōchor. 41. rano. 42. chonpa"r". 43. tano. 44. chō. 45. chō. 46. infrallari"a". 47. ella.
48. sto [cm] ciē inse. 49. quasa quādo. 50. righuardiamo. 52. la ui. 53. ta. 58. ochi"o". 59. si chomelle. 60. chosi.

869. 9. 32. *in margine:* lines 34—61 are, in the
original, written on the margin and above them is
the diagram to which Leonardo seems to refer
here.

20 and fol. Telescopes were not in use till a
centu r later. Compare No. 910 and page 136.

23. *libro* 113. This is perhaps the number of a
book in some library catalogue. But it may refer,
on the other hand, to one of the 120 Books mentioned in No. 796. l. 84.

32. Compare with this the passage in Vol. I,
No. 52, written about twenty years earlier.

F. 60 b]   **870.**

PROSPETTIVA.

²Delle cose remosse dall'ochio con e-quale di³stantia, quella parrà esser mē dimin⁴vita che prima era più.

⁵Delle cose remosse dall'ochio con equal di⁶stantia dal lor primo sito quella mē diminuisce ⁷che prima era più distante da esso ochio; E tal ⁸fia la proportione della diminuitione, qual fù ⁹la proportione delle distantie ch'esse aveā da¹⁰l'ochio auanti il loro moto.

¹¹Come dire il corpo *t* e 'l corpo *e* e ¹²che la proportiō delle lor distantie dall'ochio *a* ¹³è quītupla; io rimovo ciascū dal suo sito ¹⁴e lo fo più distante dal-

PERSPECTIVE.

Among objects moved from the eye at equal distance, that undergoes least diminution which at first was most remote.

When various objects are removed at equal distances farther from their original position, that which was at first the farthest from the eye will diminish least. And the proportion of the diminution will be in proportion to the relative distance of the objects from the eye before they were removed.

That is to say in the object *t* and the object *e* the proportion of their distances from the eye *a* is quintuple. I remove each from its place and set it farther from the eye by one of the 5 parts

l'ochio vno d'essi 5' in che è ¹⁵diuisa la propositione; accade dūque che il più vicino ¹⁶all'ochio avrà doppiata la distantia, e per la penulti¹⁷ma di questo esso è diminuto la metà del suo tutto, ¹⁸e 'l corpo *e* per lo medesimo moto è diminuito ¹/₅ ¹⁹d'esso suo tutto; adūque per la detta penultima ²⁰è vero quel che in questa vltima s'è proposto; ²¹e questo dico per li moti de' corpi celesti ²²in 3500 miglia di distātia che piv essē²³do in oriēte che sopra di noi, non crescono o diminuiscono ²⁴con sensibile dimostratione.

into which the proposition is divided. Henc it happens that the nearest to the eye ha doubled the distance and according to the last proposition but one of this, is diminished by the half of its whole size; and the body *e*, by the same motion, is diminished ¹/₅ of its whole size. Therefore, by that same last proposition but one, that which is said in this last proposition is true; and this I say of the motions of the celestial bodies which are more distant by 3500 miles when setting than when overhead, and yet do not increase or diminish in any sensible degree.

Br. M. 174 b]   **871.**

a b è lo spiraculo donde ²passa il sole, e se tu po³tessi misurare la grossezza de' ⁴razzi solari in *n m*, tu po⁵tresti por bene le uere linie ⁶del concorso d'essi razzi solari, ⁷stante lo spechio in · *a b*, e ⁸poi fare i

a b is the aperture through which the sun passes, and if you could measure the size of the solar rays at *n m*, you could accurately trace the real lines of the convergence of the solar rays, the mirror being at *a b*, and then show the reflected rays at

870. 1. prespectiva. 2. remosse "dallochio" [dellor sito cone] quala di. 4. che p"a"era . . 5. chon . . dis. 6. p"o"sito qualla . . diminuissce. 7. che p"a" . . Ettal. 10. iloro. 11. corpo e che e. 12. chella. 13. ciasscū del. 14. ellolofo . . inche. 15. la pro "ne" achade . . che piu. 16. ara dopiato. 20. preposto. 21. ecquesto . . celestiche. 22. [1500 in] 3500 . . distātia cheli ā piv. 23. crescano o diminuiscano.

871. 1. ellosspiraculo. 2. essettu. 3. grossezza. 4. razi. 6. razi. 7. losspechio. 8. razi refressi. 10. chettu uoli poi torre razzi reflessi infra āᵍgoli equali inuerso · *n m* · ¹⁰ma poi che tu vuoi torre in ¹¹*n m* · togli dentro allo spiracu¹²lo in *c d* che si possan misura¹³re nella percussione del razzo solare, ¹⁴e poi poni il tuo spechio nella distā¹⁵tia *a b* ·, e lì fa cadere i razzi *d b, c a*; poi ¹⁶risaltare infra angoli equali in uer¹⁷so *c d* · e questo è il uero modo; ¹⁸ma ti bisognia operare tale spe¹⁹chio nel medesimo mese e medesi²⁰mo dì e ora e pūto, e farà meglio ²¹che di nessū tempo, perchè in tal distantia ²²di sole si causò tal piramide.

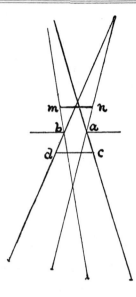

equal angles to *n m*; but, as you want to have them at *n m*, take them at the inner side of the aperture at *cd*, where they may be measured at the spot where the solar rays fall. Then place your mirror at the distance *a b*, making the rays *d b, c a* fall and then be reflected at equal angles towards *c d*; and this is the best method, but you must use this mirror always in the same month, and the same day, and hour and instant, and this will be better than at no fixed time because when the sun is at a certain distance it produces a certain pyramid of rays.

G. 3*b*]

872.

a parte del corpo ō²broso *n* vede tutta la pa³rte dell'emisferio *b c d e f* ⁴e nō ui vede parte alcuna ⁵della oscurità della terra; ⁶e 'l simile accade nel punto *o*; adunque lo spatio *a* · *o* · è ⁷tutto d'una medesima chiarezza, in *s* vede sol 4 gra- ⁸di dell'emisperio *d e f g h* ·, e vi vede tutta la terra ⁹*s h* che la fa più oscura quāto darà la calculatione.

a, the side of the body in light and shade *n*, faces the whole portion of the hemisphere *b c d e f*, and does not face any part of the darkness of the earth. And the same occurs at the point *o*; therefore the space *a o* is throughout of one and the same brightness, and *s* faces only four degrees of the hemisphere *d e f g h*, and also the whole of the earth *s h*, which will render it darker; and how much must be demonstrated by calculation.

A. 64*b*]

873.

PRUOVA DELL'ACCRESCIMĒTO DEL SOLE ²IN NEL OCCIDĒTE.

THE REASON OF THE INCREASED SIZE OF THE SUN IN THE WEST.

³Alcuni · matematici · dimostrano · il sole · cresciere nel ponēte ·, perchè l'ochio · sēpre lo uede per aria di maggiore grossezza, ⁴allegādo che le · cose uiste nella · nebbia e nel acqua pajono maggiori: ai quali · io rispōdo di no, inperochè le cose viste īfra la

Some mathematicians explain that the sun looks larger as it sets, because the eye always sees it through a denser atmosphere, alleging that objects seen through mist or through water appear larger. To these I reply: No; because objects seen through a mist are

---

11. allosspiracu.　12. chessi.　13. razo.　15. elli . . razi; *in the margin*: "d b" c a.　17. ecquesto.　18. matti.　20. effara. 872. 1. in a.　5. asscurita.　6. achade . . losspatio a . o . ed.　9. chella . . osscura. 873. 1. dellacresscimēto.　2. inel ocidēte.　3. raria . . magiore grosseza.　4. alegādo chelle chose . . nebia | "e nel acqᵘ" paro

872. This passage, which has perhaps a doubtful right to its place in this connection, stands in the Manuscript between those given in Vol. I as No. 117 and No. 427.

nebbia sō simi⁵li per colore alle lōtane ·, e nōn essendo simili per diminvitione appariscono di maggiore grādezza; Ancora nessuna cosa ⁶crescie · in acqua · piana, e la pruova ne farai a lucidare vn asse mezza sotta l' acqua; Ma la ragione che 'l sol ⁷crescie · si è che | Ogni corpo luminoso quāto piv s'allōtana, piv pare grāde.

similar in colour to those at a distance; but not being similarly diminished they appear larger. Again, nothing increases in size in smooth water; and the proof of this may be seen by throwing a light on a board placed half under water. But the reason why the sun looks larger is that every luminous body appears larger in proportion as it is more remote.

F. 94 *b*]   **874.**

On the luminosity of the Earth in the universal space (874—878).

Il libro mio s'astēde a mostrare, ²come l'oceā colli altri mari ³fa mediāte il sole splēde⁴re il nostro mōdo a modo ⁵di luna e a più remoti pa⁶re stella e questo provo;
⁷Dimostra prima come ogni lume remoto da⁸ll'ochio fa razzi, li quali pare che accrescino la figu⁹ra di tal corpo luminoso e di questo ne segui¹⁰ta che 2 . . . .
¹¹Luna frigida ¹²e vmida.
¹³L'acqua è frigi¹⁴da e vmida; ¹⁵tale influēti¹⁶a da il nostro ¹⁷mare alla lu¹⁸na qual la luna ¹⁹a noi.

In my book I propose to show, how the ocean and the other seas must, by means of the sun, make our world shine with the appearance of a moon, and to the remoter worlds it looks like a star; and this I shall prove.

Show, first that every light at a distance from the eye throws out rays which appear to increase the size of the luminous body; and from this it follows that 2 . . [10].
[11]The moon is cold and moist.
Water is cold and moist. Thus our seas must appear to the moon as the moon does to us.

Br. M. 25 *a*]   **875.**

L'onde dell'acqua crescono il simulacro della cosa che ²in lor si specchia.
³*a* sia il sole, *n m* sia l'acqua inōdata, *b* è 'l simulacro ⁴del sole, quando l'acqua nō fusse inondata; *f* sia l'ochio ⁵che uede esso simulacro in tutte l'onde che si rinchiudo⁶no nella basa del triangolo *c e f*; adunque il sole ⁷che nella superfitie sanza onde occupava l'acqua *c d*, ora ⁸nella superfitie inondata occupa tutta l'acqua *c e* (come è ⁹prouato nel 4

The waves in water magnify the image of an object reflected in it.

Let *a* be the sun, and *n m* the ruffled water, *b* the image of the sun when the water is smooth. Let *f* be the eye which sees the image in all the waves included within the base of the triangle *c e f*. Now the sun reflected in the unruffled surface occupied the space *c d*, while in the ruffled surface it covers all the watery space *c e* (as is proved in the 4th of my

magiore . . llechose . . nebia. 5. le per cholore ale . . esendo simile . . aparischano . . magiore grādeza Anchora nesuna chosa. 6. acq"a" . . meza . . lacq"a" Malla. 7. cresscie . . chorpo.
874. 1. libro mio (il *is wanting*). 5. e "a" piu. 6. ecquesto. 7. ōni lume. 8. razi . . acresscino. 11. fregida. 13. Lacq"a". 15. infruēti.
875. 1. aq"a" cresscano. 2. sisspechia. 3. lacq"a". 4. lacq"a" . . fussi. 5. chessi rinchiuda. 7. ocupava lacq"a" . . or"a".

873. Lines 5 and 6 are thus rendered by M. Ravaisson in his edition of MS. A. "*De même, aucune chose ne croît dans l'eau plane, et tu en feras l'expérience en calquant un ais sous l'eau.*"—Compare the diagrams in Vol. I, p. 114.
874. 10. Here the text breaks off; lines 11 and fol. are written in the margin.
875. In the original sketch, inside the circle in

the first diagram, is written *Sole* (sun), and to the right of it *luna* (moon). Thus either of these heavenly bodies may be supposed to fill that space. Within the lower circle is written *simulacro* (image). In the two next diagrams at the spot here marked *L* the word *Luna* is written, and in the last *sole* is written in the top circle at *a*.

della mia prospettiva), e tanto più occupe-
[10]rebbe d' acqua quanto esso simulacro fusse
più distāte dal' ochio.

[11] ¶ Il simulacro del sole si dimostrerà
piv lucido nell' onde mi[12]nute che nelle onde
grandi ¶; E questo accade perchè le simili-
[13]tudini over simulacri del sole sono più
spesse nell' onde minute [14] che nelle grandi,
e li più spessi splendori rendono maggiore
[15] lume che li splendori più rari.

[16] L' onde intersegate a uso di scorza di
pigna rendono il si[17]mulacro del sole di
grandissimo splendore, [18] e questo accade
perchè tanto son li simulacri quanto son
li gio[19]ghi del' onde vedute dal sole, e

"Perspective") [9] and it will cover more of
the water in proportion as the reflected image
is remote from the eye [10].

The image of the sun will be more
brightly shown in small waves than in large
ones — and this is because the reflections or
images of the sun are more numerous in the
small waves than in large ones, and the more
numerous reflections of its radiance give a
larger light than the fewer.

Waves which intersect like the scales of
a fir cone reflect the image of the sun with
the greatest splendour; and this is the case
because the images are as many as the
ridges of the waves on which the sun

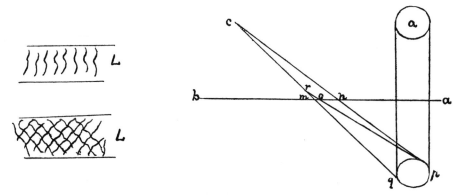

l' onbre che infra esse onde s' inter[20]pongono
sōn piccole e di poca oscurità, e li splendori di tanti [21] simulacri insieme s' infondono
nelle similitudini che di lor [22] viene all' ochio,
in modo tale che esse ōbre sono insen-
sibili ; ¶
[23] Quel simulacro del sole occuperà
[24] più lochi nella superfitie dell' acqua, che
[25] sarà più distante dall' ochio che lo uede ;

[26] a sia il sole, p q è il simulacro d' esso
[27] sole, a b è la superfitie dell' acqua doue
il sol [28] si spechia, r sia l' ochio che uede
esso si[29]mulacro nella superfitie dell' acqua
occupare [30] lo spatio o m ; c è l' occhio
più remoto [31] da essa superfitie dell' acqua,
e così dal simulacro, onde esso simulacro
[32] occupa maggiore spatio d' acqua, — quāto
è lo spatio n o.

shines, and the shadows between these waves
are small and not very dark; and the radiance
of so many reflections together becomes
united in the image which is transmitted to
the eye, so that these shadows are imperceptible.

That reflection of the sun will cover most
space on the surface of the water which is
most remote from the eye which sees it.

Let a be the sun, p q the reflection of
the sun; a b is the surface of the water, in
which the sun is mirrored, and r the eye
which sees this reflection on the surface of
the water occupying the space o m. c is the
eye at a greater distance from the surface
of the water and also from the reflection;
hence this reflection covers a larger space of
water, by the distance between n and o.

8. ochupa. 9. prosspectiva) ettanto . . ochupe. 10. dacq"a" . . fussi. 11. dimosterra. 12. achade chelle. 13. tudine.
14. elli . . rendan magore. 15. chelli. 16. disscorsa di pina rendano [loss] il si. 17. plendore [e chiareza]. 18. ecquesto
achade. 19. ellonbre. 20. pongono . . pichole . . pocha osscurita elli. 21. sinfondano . . similitudine. 23. sole [se]
ochupera. 25. chel uede. 27. ella. 28. sisspechia. 29. acq"a" ocupare. 30. Losspatio . . elloccio. 32. ochupa magore
. . ello.

9. *Nel quarto della mia prospettiva.* If this reference
is to the diagrams accompanying the text — as is
usual with Leonardo — and not to some particular
work, the largest of the diagrams here given

must be meant. It is the lowest and actually the
fifth, but he would have called it the fourth, for the
text here given is preceded on the same page of
the manuscript by a passage on whirlpools, with

Br. M. 28 a]   876.

Ĵpossibile è ²che tan³to quāto il sole allumina ⁴dello spechio sperico, ⁵tāto d'esso spechio ab⁶bia a risplendere, ⁷se già esso spechio ⁸non fusse ōdāte o globulē⁹to;

¹⁰Vedi qui il so¹¹le allumina¹²re la luna, s¹³pecchio speri¹⁴co, e tan¹⁵to quāto es¹⁶so sole ne ¹⁷uede, tāto ne ¹⁸fa splēdere;

¹⁹Qui si concluderà che ciò che della luna ²⁰splende è acqua simile a quella deg-²¹li nostri mari, e così inōdata, ciò ²²che di lei non splende sone isole e ter²³ra ferma.

It is impossible that the side of a spherical mirror, illuminated by the sun, should reflect its radiance unless this mirror were undulating or filled with bubbles.

You see here the sun which lights up the moon, a spherical mirror, and all of its surface, which faces the sun is rendered radiant.

Whence it may be concluded that what shines in the moon is water like that of our seas, and in waves as that is; and that portion which does not shine consists of islands and terra firma.

²⁴Questa dimostratione di tanti · corpi sperici interposti infra l'ochio ²⁵e 'l sole è fatta per mostrare che, siccome in ciascuno d'essi ²⁶corpi si uede il simulacro del sole, così si può vedere esso simulacro in cia-²⁷scuna globosità dell' onde del mare; come in molti di questi sperici si ²⁸uedono molti soli, così in molte onde si uedono molti lustri, li quali in molta ²⁹distanzia, ciascū lustro per se, si fanno grādi all' ochio e, così faciēdo ciascu³⁰na onda, si uengono a con-

This diagram, of several spherical bodies interposed between the eye and the sun, is given to show that, just as the reflection of the sun is seen in each of these bodies, in the same way that image may be seen in each curve of the waves of the sea; and as in these many spheres many reflections of the sun are seen, so in many waves there are many images, each of which at a great distance is much magnified to the eye.   And, as this happens with each wave, the spaces

876. 1. he [chellol spechio]. 2. consperico possa] chettan. 4. spericho tā. 6. rissplendere. 7. ga. 8. fussi ōdate o globbule. 13. echio. 14. cho ettan. 19. che co che. 20. acqui . . acquella de. 21. ecco. 22. etter. 24. sperichi. 25. sole [nō] effatta per mosstrare [come] che si come in ciasscuno. 26. po . . in ca. 27. globbosita . . mare c . me. 28. uede . . uede lusstri. 29. ciasscū lusstro . . fa grande . . ciasscu. 30. lesspati . . infrallonde. 31. cagone. 32. elle parte onbro. 33. chettale . . none e . . in ese.

the diagram belonging to it also reproduced here. The words *della mia prospettiva* may therefore indicate that the diagram to the preceding chapter treating on a heterogeneal subject is to be excluded. It is a further difficulty that this diagram belongs properly to lines 9—10 and not to the preceding

sentence. The reflection of the sun in water is also discussed in the Theoretical part of the Book on Painting; see Vol. I, No. 206, 207.

876. In the original, at letter *A* in the diagram "*Sole*" (the sun) is written, and at *o* "*occhio*" (the eye).

sumare gli spati interposti infra l' onde, [31] e per questa tal cagione e' pare tutto vn sole continuato nelli molti soli [32] spechiati nelle molte onde, e le parti onbrose miste colle spetie luminose [33] fan che tale splendore non è lucido come quel del sole in esse ōde spechia [34] to.

interposed between the waves are concealed; and, for this reason, it looks as though the many suns mirrored in the many waves were but one continuous sun; and the shadows, mixed up with the luminous images, render this radiance less brilliant than that of the sun mirrored in these waves.

F. 77 *b*]   877.

Questa avrà ināzi a se il trattato de' [2] onbra e lumi.

[3] Li stremi della luna sarā più alluminati e si dimostre [4] ran più luminosi, perchè in quelli non appare se nō le sō- [5] mità dell' ōde delle sue acque.

This will have before it the treatise on light and shade.

The edges in the moon will be most strongly lighted and reflect most light, because, there, nothing will be visible but the tops of the waves of the water[5].

W. X]   878.

Il sole parirà maggiore nell' acqua movente e ōdeggiäte [2] che nella ferma: esemplo del lume visto sopra le corde [3] del monocordo.

The sun will appear larger in moving water or on waves than in still water; an example is the light reflected on the strings of a monochord.

877. 1. ara . . asse. 2. ellumi. 3. dimoste. 4. apare.   **878.** 1. magiore . . ōdegiato. 2. essenplo . . chorde.

877. 5. I have thought it unnecessary to reproduce the detailed explanation of the theory of reflection on waves contained in the passage which follows this.

II.

THE SUN.

F. 5*a*] 879.

Laude del sole.

IN PRAISE OF THE SUN.

The question of the true and of the apparent size of the sun (879—884).

[2] Se guarderai le stelle sanza razzi (come si fa a veder[3]le per un piccolo foro fatto colla strema pūta da[4]la sottile aguglia, e questo posto quasi a toccare l'ochio), [5] tu uedrai esse stelle essere tanto minime che nul[6]la cosa pare essere minore, e uera-mēte la lūga. di[7]stātia le fa ragionevol-mente diminuire, ancorachè [8] molte vi sono che son moltissime volte maggiori che la [9] stella cioè la terra coll'acqua·; ora pensa quel che par[10]rebbe essa nostra stella in tāta distantia, e conside[11]ra poi, quāte stelle si metterebbero e per longitudine e la[12]ti-tudine infra esse stelle, le quali sono semi-na[13]te per esso spatio tenebroso; mai nō posso fare [14] ch'io non biasimi molti di quelli antichi, li quali disse[15]ro che 'l sole non avea altra grādezza che quella che [16] mostra, īfra quali fu Epicuro, e credo che caua[17]si tale ragione da vn lume posto in questa nostra a[18]ria, equidistāte al cētro; chi lo uede, non lo uede mai di[19]minuito di grādezza in nessuna distātia; e le ragi-

If you look at the stars, cutting off the rays (as may be done by looking through a very small hole made with the extreme point of a very fine needle, placed so as almost to touch the eye), you will see those stars so minute that it would seem as though nothing could be smaller; it is in fact their great distance which is the reason of their dimi-nution, for many of them are very many times larger than the star which is the earth with water. Now reflect what this our star must look like at such a distance, and then con-sider how many stars might be added—both in longitude and latitude—between those stars which are scattered over the darkened sky. But I cannot forbear to condemn many of the ancients, who said that the sun was no larger than it appears; among these was Epicurus, and I believe that he founded his reason on the effects of a light placed in our atmosphere equidistant from the centre of the earth. Any one looking at it never sees it dimini-shed in size at whatever distance; and the rea-

879. 1. lalde. 2. razi. 3. picholo. 4. acuchia ecque posto . . attocare. 6. lūgha dis. 7. stātia dalloro ragionevole diminuire ne anchora che. 8. magore chella. 9. coe . . aq"a" . . che pa. 11. metterebbe e per . . ella. 14. quali diso. 15. no chel sole . . grādeza. 16. mostra [alla] īfra. 18. noluede. 19. minuto . . grādeza inessuna . . elle.

879—882. What Leonardo says of Epicurus—who according to LEWIS, *The Astronomy of the ancients*, and MÄDLER, *Geschichte der Himmelskunde*, did not devote much attention to the study of ce-

lestial phenomena—, he probably derived from Book X of Diogenes Laertius, whose *Vitae Philosophorum* was not printed in Greek till 1533, but the Latin translation appeared in 1475.

F. 4*b*]

880.

oni della sua grandezza e virtù le riseruo nel [2]4° libro; ma bē mi maraviglio che Socrate biasi[3]masse questo tal corpo, e che dicesse quello esse[4]re a similitudine di pietra infocata, e certo, chi [5]l'oppose di tal errore poco peccò; Ma io vorrei [6]avere vocabuli che mi seruissero a biasimare quel-[7]li che vogliono laudare più lo adorare li omini che [8]tal sole, nō uedēdo nell'uniuerso corpo [9]di maggiore magnitudine e virtù di quello; e 'l [10]suo lume allumina tutti li corpi celesti che per l'u[11]niverso si cōpartono; tutte l'anime discēdono da lui, [12]perchè il caldo ch'è in nelli animali viui viē dall'ani-[13]me, e nessuno altro caldo nè lume è nell' u[14]niverso, come mostrerò nel 4° libro, e cier[15]to costoro che ànno voluto adorare uomimi per i dei [16]come Giove Saturno Marte e simili ànno fatto grā[17]dissimo errore, vedēdo che ancorachè l'omo fus[18]se grande quāto il nostro mōdo, che parrebbe simi[19]le a vna minima stella, la qual pare vn pūto nell'uni[20]verso, e ancora vedendo essi omini mortali e [21]putridi e corruttibili nelle lor sepolture.

[22]Luspera (?) [23]e Marcello [24]lauda cō m[25]olti altri [26]esso sole.

sons of its size and power I shall reserve for Book 4. But I wonder greatly that Socrates[2] should have depreciated that solar body, saying that it was of the nature of incandescent stone, and the one who opposed him as to that error was not far wrong. But I only wish I had words to serve me to blame those who are fain to extol the worship of men more than that of the sun; for in the whole universe there is nowhere to be seen a body of greater magnitude and power than the sun. Its light gives light to all the celestial bodies which are distributed throughout the universe; and from it descends all vital force, for the heat that is in living beings comes from the soul [vital spark]; and there is no other centre of heat and light in the universe as will be shown in Book 4; and certainly those who have chosen to worship men as gods—as Jove, Saturn, Mars and the like—have fallen into the gravest error, seeing that even if a man were as large as our earth, he would look no bigger than a little star which appears but as a speck in the universe; and seeing again that these men are mortal, and putrid and corrupt in their sepulchres.

Marcellus[23] and many others praise the sun.

F. 6*a*]

881.

Forse Epicuro vide le ōbre delle colonne ripercosse nelli an[2]tiposti muri essere equali al diametro della colōna [3]donde si partì a

Epicurus perhaps saw the shadows cast by columns on the walls in front of them equal in diameter to the columns from which the

880. 1. grandeza. 3. massi..dicessi. 4. assimilitudine. 5. loponi . . erore . . pecho. 6. seruissino abbiasimare que. 7. che vollō laldare. 9. magore. 11. cōpartano . . discēdā dallui. 12. inelli. 13. nellume enellu. 14. mosterro. 15. che an . . homini . . iddei. 16. gove saturno marte essimili an. 17. che anchorachellomo fu. 18. si grande . . parebe. 19. stela. 21. pitridi e curuttibili. *Lines 22—26 are written on the margin.* 22. luspera (?). 24. lalda.
881. 1. ripercose. 2. diametro 3. esendo . . paralella. 5. gudicare. 6. fussi. 8. colona . . sauide. 11. fussi . . lesstelle. 12. sarebō.

880. 2. *Socrates*; I have little light to throw on this reference. Plato's Socrates himself declares on more than one occasion that in his youth he had turned his mind to the study of celestial phenomena (Μετέωρα) but not in his later years (see G. C. LEWIS, *The Astronomy of the ancients*, page 109; MÄDLER, *Geschichte der Himmelskunde*, page 41). Here and there in Plato's writings we find incidental notes on the sun and other heavenly bodies. Leonardo may very well have known of these, since the Latin version by Ficinus was printed as early as 1491; indeed an undated edition exists which may very likely have appeared between 1480—90.

There is but one passage in Plato, Epinomis (p. 983) where he speaks of the physical properties of the sun and says that it ĩs larger than the earth.

Aristotle who goes very fully into the subject says the same. A complete edition of Aristotele's works was first printed in Venice 1495—98, but a Latin version of the Books *De Coelo et Mundo* and *De Physica* had been printed in Venice as early as in 1483 (H. MÜLLER-STRÜBING).

23. I have no means of identifying *Marcello* who is named in the margin. It may be Nonius Marcellus, an obscure Roman Grammarian of uncertain date (between the IInd and V[th] centuries A. C.) the author of the treatise *De compendiosa doctrina per litteras ad filium* in which he treats *de rebus omnibus et quibusdam aliis*. This was much read in the middle ages. The *editio princeps* is dated 1470 (H. MÜLLER-STRÜBING).

881. In the original the writing is across the diagram.

tale ōbra; essendo adunque il cōco⁴rso dell'ōbre paralello dall'suo nascimēto al suo fine, ⁵li parue da giudicare che 'l sole an-⁶cora lui fusse frōte di tal paralel⁷lo, e per cōseguēza non essere piv gros⁸so di tal colonna, e nō s'avvide che tal ⁹diminuitione

shadows were cast; and the breadth of the shadows being parallel from beginning to end, he thought he might infer that the sun also was directly opposite to this parallel and that consequently its breadth was not greater than that of the column; not perceiving that the diminution in the shadow was

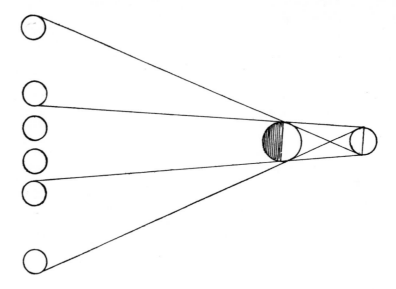

d'ōbra era insēsibile ¹⁰per la lunga distantia del sole; ¹¹se 'l sole fusse minore della terra, le stelle ¹²di grā parte del nostro emisperio sarebbero sā¹³za lume; cōtro a Epicuro che dice, tāto è ¹⁴grāde il sole, quāto e' pare.

insensibly slight by reason of the remoteness of the sun. If the sun were smaller than the earth, the stars on a great portion of our hemisphere would have no light, which is evidence against Epicurus who says the sun is only as large as it appears.

F. 8 *b*]

882.

Dice Epicuro il sole essere tāto quāto esso si dimostra; a²dunque e' pare essere vn piè, e così l'abbiamo a tenere; ³seguirebbe che la luna quād'ella fa oscurare il sole, il so⁴le non l'avāzerebbe di grādezza come e' fa, onde, sendo ⁵la luna minor del sole, essa luna sarebbe meno d'un piede, ⁶e per conseguēza quando il nostro mōdo fa oscurare la lu⁷na, sarebbe minore a un dito del piedi, conciò sia se 'l so⁸le è un piede, e la nostra terra fa onbra piramidale in⁹verso la luna, egli è necessario che sia maggiore il lumi¹⁰noso, causa della piramide ōbrosa, che l'opaco, causa d'essa ¹¹piramide.

Epicurus says the sun is the size it looks. Hence as it looks about a foot across we must consider that to be its size; it would follow that when the moon eclipses the sun, the sun ought not to appear the larger, as it does. Then, the moon being smaller than the sun, the moon must be less than a foot, and consequently when our world eclipses the moon, it must be less than a foot by a finger's breadth; inasmuch as if the sun is a foot across, and our earth casts a conical shadow on the moon, it is inevitable that the luminous cause of the cone of shadow must be larger than the opaque body which casts the cone of shadow.

882. 2. labiamo attenere. 3. seguirebe chella. 4. nollauāzerebbe . . grādeza chome. 5. medun piedi. 6. chonsequēza . . osscurar. 7. concosia. 8. piedi ella. 9. luna "la" egli . . magore. 10. caua della.

F. 10 δ]   **883.**

Misura quāti soli si metterebbero ²nel corso suo di 24 ore.

³Fa vn circulo e voltalo a mezzodì, come sō ⁴li orilogi da sole, e metti vna bacchetta in ⁵mezzo, in modo che la sua lūghezza si di⁶rizzi al cētro di tal cerchio, e nota l'on⁷bra che fa il sole d'essa bacchetta sopra la ⁸circūferentia di tale cerchio, che sarà ⁹l'onbra larga, diciamo tutto *a n*; ora ¹⁰misura quante volte tale ōbra entra in ¹¹tale circūferētia di cerchio, e tāte vol¹²te fia il numero che 'l corpo solare entrerà nel ¹³corso suo in 24 ore; e qui si potrà ¹⁴vedere, se Epicuro disse, che 'l sole era ¹⁵tanto grande quāto esso parea | che, pa-¹⁶rendo il diametro del sole vna misura ¹⁷pedale, e che esso sole entrasse mille ¹⁸volte nel suo corso di 24 ore, egli avre-¹⁹bbe corso mille piedi, cioè 300 braccia che ²⁰è vn sesto di miglio; ora ecco che 'l cor²¹so del sole infra dì e notte sarebbe ²²la sesta parte d'ū miglio, ²³e questa venerabile lumaca del sole av²⁴rebbe caminato 25 braccia per ora.

To measure how many times the diameter of the sun will go into its course in 24 hours.

Make a circle and place it to face the south, after the manner of a sundial, and place a rod in the middle in such a way as that its length points to the centre of this circle, and mark the shadow cast in the sunshine by this rod on the circumference of the circle, and this shadow will be—let us say— as broad as from *a* to *n*. Now measure how many times this shadow will go into this circumference of a circle, and that will give you the number of times that the solar body will go into its orbit in 24 hours. Thus you may see whether Epicurus was [right in] saying that the sun was only as large as it looked; for, as the apparent diameter of the sun is about a foot, and as that sun would go a thousand times into the length of its course in 24 hours, it would have gone a thousand feet, that is 300 braccia, which is the sixth of a mile. Whence it would follow that the course of the sun during the day would be the sixth part of a mile and that this venerable snail, the sun will have travelled 25 braccia an hour.

F. 0″]   **884.**

Possidonius cōpose libri della grādezza del sole.

Posidonius composed books on the size of the sun.

G. 34 a]   **885.**

DELLA PROVA CHE 'L SOLE È CAL²DO PER NATURA E NŌ PER VIRTÙ.

OF THE PROOF THAT THE SUN IS HOT BY NATURE AND NOT BY VIRTUE.

³Che 'l sol sia in se caldo per natura e nō per vir⁴tù, si dimostra manifestamēte

That the heat of the sun resides in its nature and not in its virtue [or mode of   Of the nature of Sunlight.

---

883. 1. metterebbe. 3. mezodi. 4. dassole . . bachetta. 5. mezo . . chella. 5. lūgeza. 6. rizi. 7. cheffa. 8. cercio chessara. 9. largha. 11. ettāte. 12. il n"o" chel . . entera. 13. ecqui. 16. diamitro. 17. entrassi. 18. egliare. 19. coe 300 br . che. 20. miglo ora e che chel corso. 21. serebbela. 22. minato la sesta. 23. che questa . . lumacha del sole a. 24. rebe . . 25. br per.

885. 1—47 R. 1. grādeza. 4. manifestamēti. 5. sprendore. 6. po. 8. razi refre. 9. delli. 11. eldore chellochio nol possa

---

884. Poseidonius of Apamea, commonly called the Rhodian, because he taught in Rhodes, was a Stoic philosopher, a contemporary and friend of Cicero's, and the author of numerous works on natural science, among them: Φυσικὸς λόγος, περὶ κόσμου, περὶ μετεώρων.

Strabo quotes no doubt from one of his works, when he says that Poseidonius explained how it was that the sun looked larger when it was rising or setting than during the rest of its course (III, p. 135).

Kleomedes, a later Greek Naturalist also mentions this observation of Poseidonius' without naming the title of his work; however, as Kleomedes' Cyclia Theorica was not printed till 1535, Leonardo must have derived his quotation from Strabo. He probably wrote this note in 1508, and as the original Greek was first printed in Venice in 1516, we must suppose him to quote here from the translation by Guarinus Veronensis, which was printed as early as 1471, also at Venice (H. MÜLLER-STRÜBING).

per [5]lo splendore del corpo solare, nel [6]qual nō si può fermare l'ochio vmano, [7]e oltre a di questo manifestissima[8]mēte lo dimostrano li sua razzi refle[9]ssi dalli spechi concavi, li quali, quā[10]do la lor percussione sarà di tāto sp[11]lendore, che l'occhio non lo possa soppo[12]rtare, allora essa percussione [13]avrà splendore simile al sole nel [14]suo propio sito; e che sia vero, pro[15]vo che se tale spechio à la sua [16]cōcavità tal qual si richiede alla [17]generatione di tale razzo, allora [18]nessuna cosa creata reggerà [19]alla caldezza di tale percussione [20]di razzo reflesso d'alcuno spechio; [21]e se tu dirai che lo spechio anco[22]ra lui è freddo e gitta i razzi caldi, io [23]ti rispondo, che 'l razzo viē dal sole ed è [24]il razzo [25]dello spec[26]chio conca[27]vo, passa[28]to [29]a traver-[30]so della [31]finestra.

action] is abundantly proved by the radiance of the solar body on which the human eye cannot dwell and besides this no less manifestly by the rays reflected from a concave mirror, which—when they strike the eye with such splendour that the eye cannot bear them—have a brilliancy equal to the sun in its own place. And that this is true I prove by the fact that if the mirror has its concavity formed exactly as is requisite for the collecting and reflecting of these [rays, no created being could endure the heat that strikes from the reflected rays of such a mirror. And if you argue that the mirror itself is cold and yet send forth hot rays, I should reply that those rays come really from the sun and that it is the ray of the concave mirror after having passed through the window.

W. L. 132 a]

886.

Il sole nō si move.

The sun does not move.

Ash. I. 19 a]

887.

PRUOVA · COME QUĀTO PIV · SARAI PRESSO ALLA CAGI[2]ONE · DE' RAZZI DEL SOLE ·, PIV TI PARRÀ MAGGIORE IL SOLE [3]SPECHIATO SUL MARE.

PROOF THAT THE NEARER YOU ARE TO THE SOURCE OF THE SOLAR RAYS, THE LARGER WILL THE REFLECTION OF THE SUN FROM THE SEA APPEAR TO YOU.

[4]Se il sole adopera il suo splendore col suo ciētro [5]a fortificare la potētia di tutto il corpo, è ne[6]ciessario · che i sua razzi, quāto piv · s'alontanano da lui, piv si uadino [7]aprēdo: se così è, tu che sei col ochio presso all'acqua · che spechia il sole, [8]vedi una minima parte de' razzi del sole portare sulla superfitie [9]del'acqua la forma d'esso sole spechiato ·, e se tu sarai presso al sole, [10]come sarebbe quādo il sole è ī mezzodì e 'l mare sia per ponēte, ved[11]rai il sole spechiarsi sù detto mare di grādis-

[4]If it is from the centre that the sun employs its radiance to intensify the power of its whole mass, it is evident that the farther its rays extend, the more widely they will be divided; and this being so, you, whose eye is near the water that mirrors the sun, see but a small portion of the rays of the sun strike the surface of the water, and reflecting the form of the sun. But if you were near to the sun—as would be the case when the sun is on the meridian and the sea to the westward—you would see the sun, mirrored in the

sopo. 12. percussione ar. 13. ara. 15. va chesse tale .. alla. 17. razo. 18. regiera. 20. refresso. 21. essettu .. chello. 22. fredo .. razi. 23. razo. 24. razo. 28. to [per il fo]. *Lines 32—47 are much effaced and some words remain doubtful:* 32. delle stan (?). 33. cedove. 34. sō tundu (?). 35. si \\\\\\\\\. 36. non aqst (= *aquisterà?*). 37. caldeza ne. 38. ancora \\\\\\\\. 39. passādo per la. 40. spera del co. 41. simulacro. 42. alla su. 43. a cavsa e. 44. passi per ele. 45. mēto (?) pa. 46. sar si vo. 47. glia.

886. El sol.

887. 2. razi .. para magiore. 4. splendre. 5. a forzifichato dala .. chorpo. 6. razi. 7. che se chol .. preso. 8. vedi ī. parte [del sole] de razi .. sula. 9. esse tussarai. 10. sarebe .. mezodi .. vede. 12. razi. 13. perco .. magiore

886. This sentence occurs incidentally among mathematical notes, and is written in unusually large letters.
887. Lines 4 and fol. Compare Vol. I, Nos. 130, 131.

sima forma, perchè, [12]essēdo tu più presso al sole ·, l' ochio tuo, pigliādo i razzi presso al pūto, [13]ne piglia piv, e perciò ne resulta maggiore splēdore, e per questa ca[14]gione si potrebbe provare la luna essere mare che spe[15]chia · il sole ·, e quello che nō risplēde fia terra.

sea, of a very great size; because, as you are nearer to the sun, your eye taking in the rays nearer to the point of radiation takes more of them in, and a great splendour is the result. And in this way it can be proved that the moon must have seas which reflect the sun, and that the parts which do not shine are land.

Br. M. 78*b*]

888.

Togli la misura [2]del sole in solstitio [3]a mezzo giugnio.

Take the measure of the sun at the solstice in mid-June.

A. 64*a*]

889.

PERCHÈ · IL SOLE · PARE MAGGIORE NEL TRA[2]MŌ-TARE · CHE DI MEZZO GIORNO CHE CI È PRESSO.

[3]Ogni corpo ch'è visto per curvo mezzo [4]apparisce di maggiore forma, che non è.

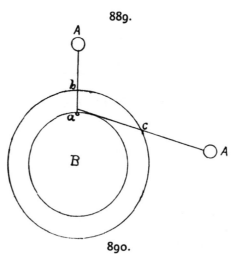

WHY THE SUN APPEARS LARGER WHEN SETTING THAN AT NOON, WHEN IT IS NEAR TO US.

Every object seen through a curved medium seems to be of larger size than it is.

C. A. 234*b*; 704*a*]

890.

Perchè l'ochio è piccolo, esso non può vedere [2]il sole in simvlacro, se nō piccolo; [3]Se l'occhio fusse equale al sole, esso vedrebbe [4]nell'acque, dato che le fussī [5]piane, il simulacro del sole equa[6]le al uero corpo del sole.

Because the eye is small it can only see the image of the sun as of a small size. If the eye were as large as the sun it would see the image of the sun in water of the same size as the real body of the sun, so long as the water is smooth.

Tr. 12]

891.

MODO DI VEDERE · IL SOLE ECLISSATO SANZA · PASSIONE · DELL'OCHIO.

[2]Tolli · vna carta · e falle busi con una agucchia, e per es[3]si busi · riguarda · il sole.

A METHOD OF SEEING THE SUN ECLIPSED WITHOUT PAIN TO THE EYE.

Take a piece of paper and pierce holes in it with a needle, and look at the sun through these holes.

14. potrebe. 15. ecquella.
888. 1. to la. 2. sostiṭio. 3. [a me] stitio a mezo gugnio.
889. 1. magiore. 2. megogorno checepresso. 3. chorpo . . churvo mezo. 4. aparisscie di magiore.
890. 1. picholo . . po. 2. dere il . . picholo. 3. Sellochio fussi. 4. aque . . chelle.
891. 1. da vedere. 2. charta . . chon aguchia epere.

889. At A is written *sole* (the sun), at B *terra* (the earth).

III.

THE MOON.

892.

DELLA LUNA.

[2]Volendo io trattare della essentia della luna · è neciessario in prima [3]descriuere la prospettiva delli spechi piani, cōcaui e cōuessi; [4]e prima che cosa è razzo luminoso, e come si piega per varie nature [5]di mezzi; Dipoi dove il razzo riflesso è più potēte,

OF THE MOON.

As I propose to treat of the nature of the moon, it is necessary that first I should describe the perspective of mirrors, whether plane, concave or convex; and first what is meant by a luminous ray, and how it is refracted by various kinds of media; then, when a reflected ray is most powerful, whether

o nell' esser l'angolo [6]della incidentia acuto retto o ottuso, o nelle cōuessità o piano o [7]cōcavità, o da corpo dēso e trasparēte; Oltre a · questo, [8]come li razzi solari, che percuotono l'onde marine, si dimostrano al

when the angle of incidence is acute, right, or obtuse, or from a convex, a plane, or a concave surface; or from an opaque or a transparent body. Besides this, how it is that the solar rays which fall on the waves of the sea, are seen by the eye of the same

---

892. 2. tractare. 3. desscriuere . . presspectiva . . cōchaui e chōuissi [e che]. 4. chosa errazzo . . chome . . piegha. 5. mezi . . refresso eppiu potēte o nell esser lato. 6. achuta retta o hottusa ho . . pioni ho. 7. chōchavita adda chorpo . . ettrasparete . . addiquesto. 8. chome li razi . . perchotano. 9. llochio . . largheza . . āghol . soma. 10. orizōte . . mācha chettale. 11. fresso . . fighura . . chosseghuē. 12. disstātia . . largheza āchora. 13. nosstro . . dimosstri parallela. 15. he

892. In the diagram Leonardo wrote *sole* at the place marked *A*.

⁹l'ochio in tanta larghezza nell'āgolo dell'o-
chio quanto nell'ultima somma ¹⁰dell'ōde
all'orizzōte, e per questo nō māca che
tale splendore solare ri¹¹flesso dall'ōde ma-
rittime nō sia di figura piramidale e per
conseguē¹²za in ogni grado di distātia non
acquisti gradi di larghezza ācorachè ¹³in-
quāto al nostro vedere si dimostri paralello.

¹⁴1ᵃ¶Nessū lievissimo ¹⁵è opaco;¶

¹⁶2ᵃ¶Nessū più lieve sta ¹⁷sotto al mē
lieve;¶

¹⁸3ᵃ¶Se la luna à sito ¹⁹in mezzo ai
sua ele²⁰mēti o no;

²¹e s'ella non à sito ²²particulare co-
²³me la terra nelli sua ²⁴elemēti, perchè nō ca²⁵de al cientro de' nostri ²⁶ele-
mēnti?

²⁷E se la luna non è ²⁸in mezzo alli
sua elemē²⁹ti e nō discēde, ³⁰adūque ella
è più ³¹lieve che altro elemē³²to;

³³E se la luna è più lie³⁴ve che altro
elemēto, per³⁵chè è solida e nō traspare.

³⁶¶Delle cose di varie grādezze che,
poste in varie distātie, ³⁷si mostrano e-
quali, tal proportione fia da distātia a
distā³⁸tia, qual fia da magnitudine a magnitudine.¶

width at the angle nearest to the eye, as at
the highest line of the waves on the horizon;
but notwithstanding this the solar rays reflected from the waves of the sea assume the
pyramidal form and consequently, at each
degree of distance increase proportionally in
size, although to our sight, they appear as
parallel.

1ˢᵗ. Nothing that has very little weight is
opaque.

2ᵈˡʸ. Nothing that is excessively weighty
can remain beneath that which is heavier.

3ᵈˡʸ. As to whether the moon is situated
in the centre of its elements or not.

And, if it has no proper place of its
own, like the earth, in the midst of its elements, why does it not fall to the centre of
our elements [26]?

And, if the moon is not in the centre
of its own elements and yet does not fall, it
must then be lighter than any other element.

And, if the moon is lighter than the other
elements why is it opaque and not transparent?

When objects of various sizes, being
placed at various distances, look of equal
size, there must be the same relative proportion
in the distances as in the magnitudes of the
objects.

F. 93ᵃ]   893.

DELLA LUNA E SE ELLA È PULITA E
SPERICA.

²Il simulacro del sole in lei è potētē-
men³te luminoso ed è in piccola parte della
su⁴a superfitie; E la prova vedrai a tor⁵re
vna palla d'oro brunito, posta nel⁶le tenebre, con vn lume da lei remoto, ⁷il quale
ancorachè esso allumini circa ⁸la metà d'essa
palla, l'ochio non lo uede, se nō ⁹in piccola
parte della sua superfitie, e tut¹⁰to il resto
di tal superfitie spechia le tenebre ¹¹che
la circūdano, e per questo in lei solo appa-
¹²risce il simulacro del lume e tutto il re¹³sto
rimane invisibile, stando l'ochio remo¹⁴to
da tal palla; Questo medesimo interue-
¹⁵rrebbe nella superfitie della luna, essendo
po¹⁶lita, lustra e densa, come son corpi
che spe¹⁷chiano;

OF THE MOON AND WHETHER IT IS POLISHED
AND SPHERICAL.

The image of the sun in the moon is
powerfully luminous, and is only on a small
portion of its surface. And the proof may
be seen by taking a ball of burnished gold
and placing it in the dark with a light at
some distance from it; and then, although
it will illuminate about half of the ball, the
eye will perceive its reflection only in a small
part of its surface, and all the rest of the surface
reflects the darkness which surrounds it; so
that it is only in that spot that the image of the
light is seen, and all the rest remains invisible,
the eye being at a distance from the ball. The
same thing would happen on the surface of the
moon if it were polished, lustrous and opaque, like all bodies with a reflecting surface.

oppacho. 18. sella . . assito. 20. onno. 21. essella. 22. partichulare cho. 24. cha. 25. nosstri. 27. essella. 28. imezzo.
29. dissciēde. 30. eppiu. 33. essella . . eppiu. 35. solita . . trasspare. 36. delle chose . . grādezze [chessendo] posste.
37. disstātia adisstā.

893. 1. esselle. 2. illei. 3. pichola. 4. attor. 6. dallei. 8. noluede. 9. pichola . . ettu. 11. chella circūda . . illei . . apa.
12. ettutto. 14. dattal. 15. rebe. 16. lusstra . . chessspe. 19. settu. 21. inî. 24. pa. 27. cheffa. 30. col inel si. 34. po.

26. The problem here propounded by Leonardo
was not satisfactorily answered till Newton in 1682
formulated the law of universal attraction and gravitation. Compare No. 902, lines 5—15.

¹⁸Prova tu ¹⁹come, se tu ²⁰stessi nella ²¹luna o in una ²²stella, ²³la nostra ²⁴terra ti par²⁵rà far l'u²⁶fitio col so²⁷le che fa la ²⁸luna;

²⁹E prova ³⁰come in nel si³¹mulacro ³²del sole nel ³³mare nō ³⁴può parere ³⁵vn sole co³⁶me pare in u³⁷no spechio pi³⁸ano.

Show how, if you were standing on the moon or on a star, our earth would seem to reflect the sun as the moon does.

And show that the image of the sun in the sea cannot appear one and undivided, as it appears in a perfectly plane mirror.

Ash. I. 19 a]

894.

Come l'onbre si cōfondono per lūnga distātia, ² si prvova nel' ōbra della luna che mai ³ si vede.

How shadows are lost at great distances, as is shown by the shadow side of the moon which is never seen.

Br. M. 28 a]

895.

O la luna à lume da se ²o no; s'ell' à lume da se, per³chè non risplende sanza ⁴l'aiuto del sole? e s'ella ⁵non à lume da se, ne-cies⁶sità la fa spe-chio sperico; ⁷e se ella è spechio, non è prova⁸to in prospettiua ¶che '1 sim⁹ula-cro d'uno obbiet-to lumi¹⁰noso nō sarà mai equale alla ¹¹parte di quello spechio che da esso lu-minoso è ¹²allu-minato?¶e se così è, come ¹³mostra qui la figura in r s, dō¹⁴de uiē tanta quantità di splendo¹⁵re che à il plenilunio, che noi ve¹⁶diamo nella quinta deci-ma della ¹⁷luna?

Either the moon has intrinsic luminosity or not. If it has, why does it not shine without the aid of the sun? But if it has not any light in itself it must of neces-sity be a spherical mirror; and if it is a mirror, is it not proved in Per-spective that the image of a lumi-nous object will never be equal to the extent of sur-face of the reflec-ting body that it illuminates? And if it be thus [13], as is here shown at r s in the figure, whence comes so great an extent of radiance as that of the full moon as we see it, at the fifteenth day of the moon?

35. vn sole. 36. pare nū 37. no spechio. 38. anano.
894. 1. chōfondono. 2. dela.
895. 1. Olla . . allume dasse. 2. onno. 3. risplde. 4. essella. 6. dasse. 8. essello spechio, 9. prosspectiva. 13. parte "di quello spechio" che . . he. 13. esse.

894. Compare also Vol. I, Nos. 175—179.
895. 13. At A, in the diagram, Leonardo wrote "sole" (the sun), and at B "luna o noi terra" (the moon or our earth). Compare also the text of No. 876.

Br. M. 94 b]   896.

DELLA LUNA.

²La luna non à lume da se, se nō
quāto ne vede il sole tanto l'allumina,
³della qual luminosità tanto ne vediamo
quāto è quella che vede noi; ⁴E la sua
notte ricieve tanto di splēdore, quāto è
quello che li pre⁵stano le nostre acque nel
refletterli il simulacro del sole, che in
⁶tutte quelle che vedono il sole e la luna,
si spechia; ⁷La pelle over superfitie del-
l'acqua, di che si cōpone il mare della luna
e il ⁸mare della nostra terra, è senpre
rugoso, ⁹o poco o assai, o più, o meno, e
tale rugosità è cavsa di dila¹⁰tare l'innumerabili simulacri del sole, che nei colli e
cōcavità e la¹¹ti e frōti delle innumerabili
rughe si spechiano, cioè in tāti vari siti di
ciascuna ¹²ruga quāto son vari li siti che
ànno li ochi che le vedono, ɉl che ac¹³ca-
dere nō potrebbe, se la spera dell' acqua,
che ɉ grā parte di se veste la ¹⁴luna fusse
d'uniforme spericità, perchè allora il simulacro del ¹⁵sole sarebbe uno a ciascuno
occhio, e la sua reflessione sarebbe particu-
¹⁶lare e senpre sarebbe splēdore sperico,
come manifestamē¹⁷te ci assegnano le palle
dorate, poste nelle sommità delli alti edifiti; Ma ¹⁸se tali palle dorate fussino rugose
o globulēti come son le mo¹⁹re, frutti neri
conposti di minute globosità rotonde, allora
ciascuna delle parti d'essa ²⁰globosità, vedute dal sole e dall'ochio, mostrerà a esso
ochio il lustro ²¹gienerato dal simulacro
d'esso sole, e così in ū medesimo corpo si
ue²²drebbero molti minimi soli, li quali
spesse sō le volte che per lunga distātia
²³si uniscono e paiono cōtinuati; E 'l lustro
della luna nuova è più lucido e più ²⁴potēte
che quādo è in plenilunio, e questo si ca-
²⁵vsa perchè l'angolo della incidētia è molto
più ottuso nella luna nuo²⁶va che nella
vecchia, doue tali angoli sono acutissimi;
e l'onde della ²⁷luna spechiano il sole così
nelle lor ualli come nelli colli, e li lati
²⁸restano oscuri ·; ma ne' lati della luna li
fondi dell'onde non ²⁹vedono il sole, ma

OF THE MOON.

The moon has no light in itself; but so
much of it as faces the sun is illuminated, and
of that illumined portion we see so much
as faces the earth. And the moon's night
receives just as much light as is lent it by our
waters as they reflect the image of the sun,
which is mirrored in all those waters which
are on the side towards the sun. The outside or surface of the waters forming the
seas of the moon and of the seas of our
globe is always ruffled little or much,
or more or less—and this roughness causes
an extension of the numberless images of
the sun which are repeated in the ridges and
hollows, the sides and fronts of the innumerable waves; that is to say in as many
different spots on each wave as our eyes
find different positions to view them from.
This could not happen, if the aqueous sphere
which covers a great part of the moon were
uniformly spherical, for then the images of
the sun would be one to each spectator,
and its reflections would be separate and
independent and its radiance would always
appear circular; as is plainly to be seen in
the gilt balls placed on the tops of high
buildings. But if those gilt balls were rugged
or composed of several little balls, like mul-
berries, which are a black fruit composed of
minute round globules, then each portion of
these little balls, when seen in the sun,
would display to the eye the lustre resulting
from the reflection of the sun, and thus, in
one and the same body many tiny suns
would be seen; and these often combine at a
long distance and appear as one. The lustre of
the new moon is brighter and stronger, than
when the moon is full; and the reason of
this is that the angle of incidence is more
obtuse in the new than in the full moon, in
which the angles [of incidence and reflection]
are highly acute. The waves of the moon
therefore mirror the sun in the hollows of
the waves as well as on the ridges, and the
sides remain in shadow. But at the sides

896. 2. dasse. 3. vedano . . ecquella . . vede. 4. Ella . . chelli pres. 5. nosstre acque . . refretterli. 6. vedano . . elluna si
sspechia. 7. dichessi . . luna edel. 8. [la nostra luna] mare . . nosstra . . essenpre rughoso. 9. oppocho . . oppiu ōmeno
ettale rughosita e chausa. 10. ine cholli e chōchavita ellati. 11. ti effrote "delle inumerabili" rughe sisspechiano . . ciasscuna. 12. rugha . . che āli . . chelle vedano. 13. chadere . . sella . . achq"a" ·, vesste. 14. luno fussi. 15. uno "accias
cuno ochio" ella . . refressione . . partichu. 16. essenpre . . spericho chome. 17. asegnia. 18. ssettali . . rughose o
globbulēti chome. 19. "neri" chonposti . . "rotonde" allora ciasscuna "delle parte". 20. globbosita . . mossterra. 21. chosi
nūn . . chorpo. 22. derebbe . . lungha disstātia. 23. vnisschono eppaiano chōtinuati . . eppiu cido epiu. 24. pleniunnio
ecquesto . . cha. 25. langholo. 26. vechia . . tale angholi . . achutissimi ellonde. 27. chosi . . chome . . cholli elli.
28. resstano osschuri. 29. vedano . . massolo vede . . quessto. 30. choll . . ettal. 31. elluminose chosi . . infussi venghano.

solo uedono le cime d'esse ōde, e per
questo li simu³⁰lacri son più rari e più
misti coll'onbre delle valli, e tal mistione
³¹delle spetie ōbrose e luminose, così insieme infuse, vengono all'o³²chio cō poco
splēdore, e nelli stremi sarā piv oscure per
essere ³³la curuità de' lati di tale ōde in-
suffitiēte a riflettere all'ochio li ri³⁴cievuti
razzi; La luna nova per natura riflette li
³⁵razzi solari più inverso l'ochio per tali

ōde streme, ³⁶che per nessuno altro loco,
come mostra la figura della luna che
³⁷percuōtēdo con razzi *a* nell'onda *b* riflette
in *b d*, dou' è situa³⁸to l'ochio *d*; E questo
accadere nō può nel plenilunio dove ³⁹il
razzo solare, stando all'occidēte, percuote
l'onde streme della ⁴⁰luna all'oriēte dal *n*
in *m*, e non riflette inverso l'oc⁴¹chio occi-
dētale, ma risalta all'oriēte, poco piegādo
la rettitu⁴²dine d'esso razzo solare, e così
l'angolo della incidētia è grossissimo.

⁴³La luna è corpo opa⁴⁴co e solido, e se
per lo a⁴⁵versario ella fusse trāspa⁴⁶rente, ella
nō ricieverebbe ⁴⁷il lume del sole.

⁴⁸Il rossume over tu-orlo dell'o⁴⁹vo sta ⁵⁰in
mezzo al suo al⁵¹bume sanza discēdere ⁵²d'alcuna
parte, ed è pi⁵³v lieve o
più grave o equale d'esso ⁵⁴albume; e s'elli è
più li⁵⁵eve egli doverebbe surgie⁵⁶re sopra
tutto l'albume e ⁵⁷fermarsi in cōtatto del-

of the moon the hollows of the waves do
not catch the sunlight, but only their crests;
and thus the images are fewer and more
mixed up with the shadows in the hollows;
and this intermingling of the shaded and
illuminated spots comes to the eye with a
mitigated splendour, so that the edges will
be darker, because the curves of the sides
of the waves are insufficient to reflect to the
eye the rays that fall upon them. Now
the new moon naturally reflects the solar
rays more directly towards the eye from the

crests of the waves than from any other part,
as is shown by the form of the moon, whose
rays *a* strike the waves *b* and are reflected
in the line *b d*, the eye being situated at *d*.
This cannot happen at the full moon, when
the solar rays, being in the west, fall on the
extreme waters of the moon to the East
from *n* to *m*, and are not reflected to the
eye in the West, but are thrown back eastwards, with but slight deflection from the
straight course of the solar ray; and
thus the angle of incidence is very wide
indeed.

The moon is an opa-
que and solid body and
if, on the contrary, it
were transparent, it would
not receive the light of
the sun.

The yellow or yolk
of an egg remains in the
middle of the albumen,
without moving on either
side; now it is either lighter
or heavier than this albumen, or equal to it; if
it is lighter, it ought to rise above all the
albumen and stop in contact with the shell

32. chō pocho .. osschure. 33. churuita .. arefrettere. 34. razza da qual chosa la luna .. refrette. 35. razi .. tale. 36. locho .. mosstra la fighura. 37. percho tendo cho razi *b* e rēfrette. 38. Ecquesto achadere .. dove || o. 39. razo solare [que] perchote stando allocidēte perchote lonte. 40. refrette. 41. pocho pieghādo. 42. chosi langholo. 43. chorpo. 44. cho essolido esse. 45. e fussi. 46. enō. 49. sta [in in al piu delle]. 50. [volte] in. 51. disscēdere. 52. dalchuna. 53. greve "o equale" desso. 54. esselli. 55. eve edovere vesurgie. 57. chōtratto. 58. la [sua scho] schorza. 59. hovo

896. 48—64. Compare No. 861.

⁵⁸la scorza d'es⁵⁹so uovo, e s'elli è più ⁶⁰grave doverebbe di⁶¹sciēdere, e s'egli è equa⁶²le così potrebbe stare ⁶³nell' v̄ delli stremi, co⁶⁴me in mezzo o disotto;

⁶⁵L'īnvmerabili simulacri ⁶⁶che dalle innumerabili onde del ma⁶⁷re reflettono li sola⁶⁸ri razzi, in esse onde percos⁶⁹si, son causa di rē⁷⁰dere cōtinuato e larghissi⁷¹mo splēdore sopra la superfitie ⁷² del mare.

of the egg; and if it is heavier, it ought to sink, and if it is equal, it might just as well be at one of the ends, as in the middle or below[54].

The innumerable images of the solar rays reflected from the innumerable waves of the sea, as they fall upon those waves, are what cause us to see the very broad and continuous radiance on the surface of the sea.

Br. M. 104 a]   **897.**

[Come nō si può spechiare il sole nel corpo ²della luna, essendo spechio colmo,

That the sun could not be mirrored in the body of the moon, which is a convex mirror,

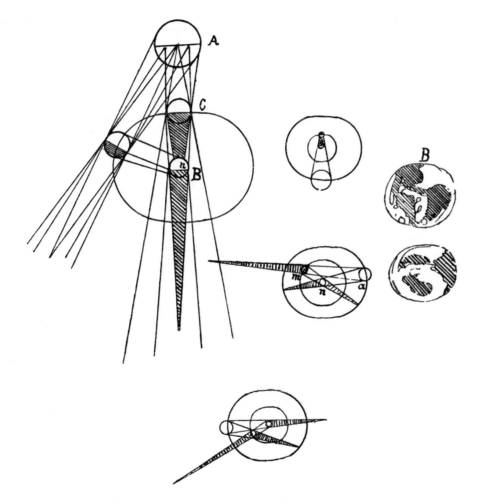

esselli. 60. dis. 61. esselli. 62. chosi. 63. cho. 64. dissotto. 66. cheddalle. 67. refrettano dalli. 68. razi . . perchos. 69. se son quelli chausa. 70. chōtinuato ellarghissi.

897. 1. po. 3. chettantọ . . nalumina. 4. nesspechi. 5. avessi la superfitie che atta asspechiare. 6. cheffussi. 7. emmosso dal-

897. In the original diagrams *sole* is written at the place marked *A; luna* at *C*, and *terra* at the two spots marked *B*.

in mo³do che tanto quanto esso sol ne
allumina, ⁴tanto essa luna ne specchia, se
già tal luna ⁵non avesse la superfitie alta
a specchiare, ⁶che fusse rugosa, a vso di
superfitie di mare, ⁷quando in parte è
mossa dal uento]·

⁸[L' onde dell' acqua crescono ⁹il simulacro della cosa ¹⁰in lei specchiata].

¹¹Quest' onde fanno per o¹²gni linia a
similitu¹³dine della spoglia del¹⁴la pina.

¹⁵Queste son 2 figure sicchè¹⁶faraile
l'una diversa dall' altra, ¹⁷coll' acqua
¹⁸ondeggiante e coll' acqua piana.

¹⁹Inpossibil'è ²⁰che per alcuna distantia
il ²¹simulacro del sole, ²²fatto nella superfitie ²³del corpo sperico, occupi ²⁴la metà
d'esso sperico;

²⁵Qui tu ài a provare, come la terra fa
tutti ²⁶questi medesimi ofiti inverso la luna
che ²⁷la luna inverso la terra;

²⁸Nō luce la luna col suo lume riflesso
come ²⁹fa il sole, perchè il lume della luna
non piglia ³⁰il lume del sole continuo in
nel³¹la superfitie, ma in sù colmi e cavi
del³²le onde delle acque, e per esser tal
sole nella ³³luna cōfusamente spechiato per
le mi³⁴stioni' delle onbre, che sono infra
³⁵l'onde che lustrano, perciò non è ³⁶il suo
lume lucido e chiaro ³⁷com'è 'l sole.

³⁸Terra infra la luna in quīta decima e
il sole; ³⁹Qui il sole è nel levante e la luna
in ponente in quīta decima; ⁴⁰luna infra
la terra in quīta decima e il sole; ⁴¹Qui è
la luna che à il sole per ponēte e la terra
per levāte.

in such a way as that so much of its surface
as is illuminated by the sun, should reflect the sun unless the moon had a surface adapted to reflect it—in waves and
ridges, like the surface of the sea when its surface is moved by the wind.

The waves in water multiply the image
of the object reflected in it.

These waves reflect light, each by its own
line, as the surface of the fir cone does [14].

These are 2 figures one different from
the other; one with undulating water and the
other with smooth water.

It is impossible that at any distance the
image of the sun cast on the surface of a
spherical body should occupy the half of
the sphere.

Here you must prove that the earth produces all the same effects with regard to the
moon, as the moon with regard to the earth.

The moon, with its reflected light, does
not shine like the sun, because the light of
the moon is not a continuous reflection of
that of the sun on its whole surface, but
only on the crests and hollows of the waves
of its waters; and thus the sun being con-
fusedly reflected, from the admixture of the
shadows that lie between the lustrous waves,
its light is not pure and clear as the sun is.

[38] The earth between the moon on the
fifteenth day and the sun. [39] Here the
sun is in the East and the moon on the
fifteenth day in the West. [40] The moon
on the fifteenth [day] between the earth and
the sun. [41] Here it is the moon which has
the sun to the West and the earth to the East.

A. 64a]   **898.**

CHE COSA · È LA LUNA.   WHAT SORT OF THING THE MOON IS.

²La luna non è · luminosa · per se, ma
bene è atta · a ricievere la natura · della ·
luce ³a similitudine · dello · spechio · e del-
l'acqua · o altro · corpo · lucido ·, e crescie nel-
l'oriēte ⁴e occidēte · come · il sole · e gli altri
pianeti ·; E la ragione · si è · che ogni · corpo

The moon is not of itself luminous, but
is highly fitted to assimilate the character of
light after the manner of a mirror, or of
water, or of any other reflecting body; and it
grows larger in the East and in the West,
like the sun and the other planets. And
the reason is that every luminous body looks

uencto. 8. acq"a" cresccano. 10. illei. 12. assimilitu. 13. spoglia de siche. 16. fara le luna disspersi. 17. acqua [ondosa]
18. ondegiante dallacq"a". 21. siimularcro. 23. ochupi. 28. refresso. 32. acq"e". 34. chessono. 35. lusstrano pero.
38. infralla . . decima il sole. 39. Ogni el . . "po"nente ella luna illeuante. 40. infralla . . decima il sole. 41. ella per-
leuāte ella terra per ponēte.
898. 1. chosa ella. 2. nōne. 3. assimilitudine . . acq"a" . . cho"r"po . . ecresscie. 4. chome . . chorpo. 5. cresscie Chiaro . .

14. See the diagram p. 145.
38. This refers to the small diagram placed between B and B. — 39. See the diagram below the
one referred to in the preceding note.

40. 41. Refers to the diagram below the others.
898. This text has already been published by
LIBRI: *Histoire des Sciences*, III, pp. 224, 225.

· luminoso ⁵quāto piv . s'allontana · piv čresce ·; Chiaro · si
può · cōprēdere · che · ogni pianeta e stel⁶la · è piv lontano ·
da noi nel ponēte che quādo ·
ci è · sopra · capo ·, circa · 3500, per
la pruova se⁷gniata · da parte ·,
e se uedi spechiare · il sole o la
luna nell'acqua che ti sia · vicina,
⁸paratti in detta
acqua della grā-
dezza che ti · pare
· in cielo; E se
t'allontanerai·vno
⁹miglio · parrà
maggiore 100 vol-
te, e se lo vedrai
spechiare · ī mare
¹⁰nel tramōtare · il sole · spechiato · ti · parrà grāde · piv di · 10 ·
miglia, per¹¹chè occuperà · in detta spechiatione · piv · di 10 miglia
· di marina ·, e se tu fussi ¹²dov'è
la luna · parrebbe ti · esso · sole
spechiarsi · in tāto · mare · quāto
egli¹³n'allumina · alla giornata ·, e
la terra · parrebbe infra detta ·
aqua come pajono · le ¹⁴macchie
scure che sono · in nella · luna ·,
la quale stādo in terra · si dimostra ta¹⁵le agli omini, qual
farebbe agli omini che abitassi-
no · nella luna il nostro ¹⁶mon-
do · appūto.

larger in proportion as it is remote. It is easy to understand
that every planet and star is
farther from us when in the
West than when it is overhead,
by about 3500 miles, as is proved on the margin [7], and if you
see the sun or moon mirrored in
the water near to you, it looks
to you of the same
size in the water
as in the sky. But
if you recede to the
distance of a mile,
it will look 100
times larger; and
if you see the sun
reflected in the sea
at sunset, its image would look
to you more than 10 miles long;
because that reflected image extends over more than 10 miles
of sea. And if you could stand
where the moon is, the sun would
look to you, as if it were reflected from all the sea that it illuminates by day; and the land amid
the water would appear just like
the dark spots that are on the
moon, which, when looked at
from our earth, appears to men
the same as our earth would appear to any men who might dwell
in the moon.

DELLA QUALITÀ · DELLA · LUNA.

¹⁸La luna quādo · è tutta · lu-
minata · al nostro vedere, noi vediamo tutto il suo ¹⁹giorno, e
allora per riflessione de' razzi
del sole, percossi in lei e risal-
tati a noi, ²⁰l'ocieano · suo · ci
gitta · meno vmidità, e quāto mē
è luce piv noce.

OF THE NATURE OF THE MOON.

When the moon is entirely lighted up to our sight, we see its
full daylight; and at that time,
owing to the reflection of the solar rays which fall on it and are
thrown off towards us, its ocean
casts off less moisture towards us;
and the less light it gives the
more injurious it is.

Leic. 30 a]   899.

DELLA LUNA.

²Dico che non avendo la luna lume da se, essendo luminosa, egl' è necessario che tale
lume ³sia causato da altri.

OF THE MOON.

I say that as the moon has no
light in itself and yet is luminous,
it is inevitable but that its light
is caused by some other body.

---

chōplēdere . . esste. 6. da "noi" . . chapo . circha. 7. esse . . oluna . . chetti. 8. acq"a" . . grādeza chetti . . Essettalonta-
nera. 9. parira magiore . . essello vederai . . mare [il sole]. 10. [spe] nel . . para. 11. ochopera . . essettu. 12. parebbeti
. . inquāto. 13. nalumina . . ellatera parebe . . achva chome pare. 14. mache schure chessono inella . . qual. 15. farebe
alla. 16. acpūto. 19. refressione razi . . perchossi illei.   899. 2. dicho . . dasse . . chettale. 3. sie chausato.

Line 7 refers to the first diagram.—A = *sole* (the sun), B = *terra* (the earth), C = *luna* (the moon).

Leic. 36 b]   **900.**

DELLA LUNA.

Tutte le cōtradizioni dell' auersario a
dir che nella lunā non è acqua.

OF THE MOON.

All my opponent's arguments to say that
there is no water in the moon.

Leic. 1 b]   **901.**

Risposta a maestro Andrea da Imola,
che disse come li razzi solari riflessi dal
corpo dello spechio convesso si confondono
[2] e si consumano in brieue spatio, e che per
questo si negaua al tutto la parte luminosa
della luna non essere di natu[3]ra di spechio,
e per consequenza non essere nato tale
lume dalla innvmerabile moltitudine del-
l'onde di quel [4]mare, il quale io proponeuo
essere quella parte della luna che s'allumi-
naua per li razzi solari;

[5] o p · sia il corpo del sole, c n s sia la
luna, b sia l'ochio, che in sù la basa c n
del cateto c n m vede spechia[6]re il corpo
del sole infra li equali angoli c n, e 'l simile
fa remouendosi l'ochio da b in a.

Answer to Maestro Andrea da Imola, who
said that the solar rays reflected from a
convex mirror are mingled and lost at a short
distance; whereby it is altogether denied that
the luminous side of the moon is of the
nature of a mirror, and that consequently
the light is not produced by the innumerable multitude of the waves of that sea,
which I declared to be the portion of the
moon which is illuminated by the solar
rays.

Let $o\,p$ be the body of the sun, $c\,n\,s$ the
moon, and b the eye which, above the base
$c\,n$ of the cathetus $c\,n\,m$, sees the body
of the sun reflected at equal angles $c\,n$; and
the same again on moving the eye from b to a.

Leic. 2 a]   **902.**

DELLA LUNA.

¶[2]Nessun denso è piv̀ lieue che l'aria.

[3]Avendo noi provato come la parte
della luna che risplende è acqua, che
spechia il corpo del sole, [4]la quale ci riflette lo splendore da lui riceuuto; E come,
se tale acqua fusse sanza ōde, ch'ella [5]pic-
cola si dimostrerebbe, ma di splendore
quasi simile al sole; Al presente bisognia
provare, se essa [6]luna è corpo grave o lieve,
inperochè se fusse grave, — confessando che
dalla terra in sù in ogni grado d'altez[7]za
s'acquista gradi di leuità, cōciosiachè
l'acqua è più lieue che la terra, e l'aria
che l'acqua, e'l foco che l'aria, e così
[8]seguitando successiuamēte, — e'parrebbe che,
se la luna auesse densità com'ella à, ch'ella
auesse gravità, e avēdo [9]gravità che lo

Explanation of the lumen cinereum in the moon.

OF THE MOON.

No solid body is less heavy than the atmosphere.

Having proved that the part of the moon
that shines consists of water, which mirrors
the body of the sun and reflects the radiance
it receives from it; and that, if these waters
were devoid of waves, it would appear
small, but of a radiance almost like the sun;
—[5] It must now be shown whether the
moon is a heavy or a light body: for, if it
were a heavy body—admitting that at every
grade of distance from the earth greater
levity must prevail, so that water is lighter
than the earth, and air than water, and fire
than air and so on successively—it would seem
that if the moon had density as it really has,
it would have weight, and having weight,
that it could not be sustained in the space

900. 2. acqu"a".

901. 1. razi . . refressi . . chonvesso . . confondeano.   2. essi.   3. disspechio e per chonseguenza . . inumerabile.   4. chessa-
luminava . . razi . . lochio di.

902. 2. chellaria.   3. chome . . rissplende.   4. refrette . . dallui riceuuti . . ssettale acq"a" fussi . . chel.   5. pichola . . dimoster-
"r"ebe.   6. ollieue . . fussi . . dalte.   7. concosiachellacq"a" . . piv . . chella . . chellacq"a" . . focho chellaria.   8. eparebe
chessella auessi . . chomella chella auessi . . av̄do.   9. chello . . ouessa . . nolla potessi sosstenere . . chon . . auessi a disscendere.

900. The objections are very minutely noted
down in the manuscript, but they hardly seem to
have a place here.

901. The large diagram on the margin of page
161 belongs to this chapter.

902. 1. On the margin are the words *tola romantina, tola = ferro stagnato* (tinned iron); *romantina*
is some special kind of sheet-iron no longer known
by that name.

spatio, ove essa si troua, non la potesse sostenere, e per conseguēza avesse a discendere [10]inverso il centro dell' universo, e congiugnersi colla terra, e se nō lei, al māco le sue acque aues[11]sino a cadere e spogliarla di se e cadere inverso il cētro e lasciar di se la luna spogliata e sanza lu[12]stro; ōde, nō seguitando quel che di lei la ragione ci promette, egli è manifesto segno che tal luna è vestita de' sua [13]elemēti, cioè acqua, aria e foco, e così in se, per se si sostenga in quello spatio come fa la nostra ter[14]ra coi sua elemēti in quest' altro spatio, e che tale ofitio faccino le cose gravi ne' sua elemē[15]ti, qual fanno l'altre cose gravi nelli elemēti nostri.

[16]Quando l'ochio in oriēte vede la luna in occidente vicina al tramōtato sole, esso la vede [17]colla sua parte onbrosa circundata da parte luminosa, del quale lume la parte laterale [18]e superiore deriua dal sole, e la parte inferiore deriva dallo oceano occidentale, il qual [19]ancora lui riceue li razzi solari e li riflette nelli inferiori mari della luna, e ancora per [20]tutta la parte ōbrosa · della luna dà tanto di splendore, qual' è quel che dà la luna alla terra nella mez[21]zanotte, e perciò nō resta integralmēte scura, e di qui à alcuno creduto, che la [22]luna abbia in parte lume da se oltre a quel che gli è dato dal sole, il quale lume diriua dalla āti[23]detta causa delli nostri mari alluminati dal sole.

[24]Ancora si potrebbe dire che'l cerchio dello splendore

where it is, and consequently that it would fall towards the centre of the universe and become united to the earth; or if not the moon itself, at least its waters would fall away and be lost from it, and descend towards the centre, leaving the moon without any and so devoid of lustre. But as this does not happen, as might in reason be expected, it is a manifest sign that the moon is surrounded by its own elements: that is to say water, air and fire; and thus is, of itself and by itself, suspended in that part of space, as our earth with its element is in this part of space; and that heavy bodies act in the midst of its elements just as other heavy bodies do in ours[15].

When the eye is in the East and sees the moon in the West near to the setting sun, it sees it with its shaded portion surrounded by luminous portions; and the lateral and upper portion of this light is derived from the sun, and the lower portion from the ocean in the West, which receives the solar rays and reflects them on the lower waters of the moon, and indeed affords the part of the moon that is in shadow as much radiance as the moon gives the earth at midnight. Therefore it is not totally dark, and hence some have believed that the moon must in parts have a light of its own besides that which is given it by the sun; and this light is due, as has been said, to the abovementioned cause,—that our seas are illuminated by the sun.

Again, it might be said that the circle of radiance

---

10. congugnersi . . esse . . mācho. 11. chadere . . ellasscia . . spoglata essanza lus. 12. ragon . . "segno" chettal. 13. coe . . effocho echosi . . sostengha. 14. rra cosua . . chettale . . grave. 15. nosstri. 16. ochidento . . vede [la luna]. 17. circhundata . . luminoso. 18. essuperiore . . ella. 19. razzi . . elli refrette. 20. dissplendore . . nella me. 21. perco . . integralmēte [luminosa e di] "[onb]os" osscura . . alchuna . . chella. 22. parte di lume dasse . . accquel chelle. 23. chavsa nosstri. 24. Anchora si p"r"otrebbe . . cheff. 25. occidente . . dirivassi . . choll ochio essituato. 26. dimosstra. 27. Al-

---

15. This passage would certainly seem to establish Leonardo's claim to be regarded as the original discoverer of the cause of the ashy colour of the new moon (*lumen cinereum*). His observations

che fa la luna, quand' el' è col sole in ²⁵occi-
dente, dirivasse dal sole integralmente ·,
quando essa col sole e coll' ochio è situata
nel ²⁶modo che qui disopra si dimostra.

²⁷Alcuni potrebbero dire che
l' aria, elemēto della luna, pigliando il lume del sole, come
fa la no²⁸stra spera dell' aria,
fusse quella che finisce il cerchio luminoso al corpo della
luna.

²⁹Alcuni àn creduto che la
luna abbia alquanto di lume da
se, la quale ope³⁰nione è falsa,
perchè l' ànno fondata sopra quel
chiarore che si uede in mezzo ali

³¹corni quando la luna è nova, la quale
alli confini dello splendore pare oscura,
³²e al confine della oscurità · del campo
pare si chiara, che molti credono essere
³³vn cerchio di nouo splendore, che finisca
di circundare, doue le punte de' corni ³⁴al-
luminati dal sole terminano il loro splendore; e questa varietà di campo nasce
³⁵perchè quella parte d' esso campo, che
termina colla parte luminosa della luna,
per tal ³⁶paragone di splendore si dimonstra piv oscura che non è, e quella parte di
sopra, doue ³⁷pare vn pezzo di cerchio
luminoso d' uniforme larghezza, nasce chè
quiui la luna, essendo più chiara che
³⁸il mezzo over il campo, oue essa si troua,
pel paragō di tale oscurità si dimostra in
tale confine piv lu³⁹minosa che non è, la
qual luminosità in tal tenpo nasce dal
nostro oceano colli altri mediterrani ⁴⁰che
in quel tēpo è alluminato dal sole che già
è tramōtato, in modo che il mare allora fa
tale ofitio alla ⁴¹parte oscura della luna,
qual fa la luna in quīta decima a noi,

shown by the moon when it and the sun
are both in the West is wholly borrowed
from the sun, when it, and the sun, and
the eye are situated as is shown above.

Some might say that the air
surrounding the moon as an element, catches the light of the
sun as our atmosphere does, and
that it is this which completes
the luminous circle on the body
of the moon.

Some have thought that the
moon has a light of its own, but
this opinion is false, because they
have founded it on that dim light
seen between the hornes of the
new moon, which looks dark where it is close
to the bright part, while against the darkness
of the background it looks so light that many
have taken it to be a ring of new radiance
completing the circle where the tips of the
horns illuminated by the sun cease to shine[34].
And this difference of background arises from
the fact that the portion of that background
which is conterminous with the bright part
of the moon, by comparison with that brightness looks darker than it is; while at the
upper part, where a portion of the luminous
circle is to be seen of uniform width, the result is that the moon, being brighter there
than the medium or background on which it
is seen by comparison with that darkness it
looks more luminous at that edge than it is.
And that brightness at such a time itself is derived from our ocean and other inland-seas.
These are, at that time, illuminated by the
sun which is already setting in such a way as
that the sea then fulfils the same function
to the dark side of the moon as the moon
at its fifteenth day does to us when the

---

chuni potrebono . . chellaria . . piglando ilume. 28. fussi . . finissi. 29. alchuni . . chella . . dasse. 30. effalsa . . fondato
. . chessi . . mezo. 31. quandella . . il quale alli . . osscuro. 32. osscurita . . molte credano . . 33. finissca di circhundare.
34. ecquesta . . canpo nassce. 35. chettermina. 36. hosscura . . nonne ecquella. 37. pezo . . largeza nassce. 38. mezo over
chanpo. 39. nassce . . occeana coli . . mediterani. 40. ga. 41. osscura . . annoi quādel . . ettal. 42. dacquel pocho . .

---

however, having hitherto remained unknown to
astronomers, Moestlin and Kepler have been credited
with the discoveries which they made independently
a century later.

Some disconnected notes treat of the same subject in MS. C. A. 239ᵇ; 718ᵇ and 719ᵇ: "*Perchè la
luna cinta della parte alluminata dal sole in ponente,
tra maggior splendore in mezzo a tal cerchio, che quando
essa eclissava il sole. Questo accade perchè nell' eclissare
il sole ella ombrava il nostro oceano, il qual caso non
accade essendo in ponente, quando il sole alluma esso
oceano.*" The editors of the "*Saggio*" who first published this passage (page 12) add another short

one about the seasons in the moon which I confess not to have seen in the original manuscript:
"*La luna ha ogni mese un verno e una state, e ha
maggiori freddi e maggiori caldi, e i suoi equinozii son
più freddi de' nostri.*"

23. 24. The larger of the two diagrams reproduced
above stands between these two lines, and the smaller
one is sketched in the margin. At the spot marked *A*
Leonardo wrote *corpo solare* (solar body) in the larger
diagram and *Sole* (sun) in the smaller one. At *C
luna* (moon) is written and at *B terra* (the earth).

34. See Pl. CVIII, No. 5.

quando il sol'è tramōtato, e tal propor-
[42]tione è da quel poco lume che à la parte
oscura della luna alla chiarezza della parte
alluminata, qual è dalla . . .

[43]Se uoi vedere [44]quanto la parte [45]on-
brosa della luna [46]sia più chiara che'l
[47]canpo, ove tal luna si [48]truova, occupa
col[49]la mano, o con altro [50]obietto più distāte [51]all'ochio, la parte lu[52]minosa della
luna.

sun is set. And the small amount of light
which the dark side of the moon receives
bears the same proportion to the light of
that side which is illuminated, as that . . . [42].

If you want to see how much brighter
the shaded portion of the moon is than the
background on which it is seen, conceal the
luminous portion of the moon with your
hand or with some other more distant object.

F. 84 a]

903.

MACULE DELLA LUNA.

[2]Alcuni dissero leuarsi da essa vapori
a modo di [3]nugoli e interporrsi infra la
luna e li ochi no[4]stri; il che, se così fusse,
mai tali macule sare[5]bbero stabili nè di
siti nè di figura, e vedendo la [6]luna in
diuersi aspetti, ancor che tal macule [7]nō
fossero variate, esse muterebbero figura
come [8]fa quella cosa che si vede per più
versi.

THE SPOTS ON THE MOON.

Some have said that vapours rise from
the moon, after the manner of clouds and
are interposed between the moon and our
eyes. But, if this were the case, these spots
would never be permanent, either as to
position or form; and, seeing the moon
from various aspects, even if these spots did
not move they would change in form, as objects do which are seen from different sides.

On the spots
in the moon
(903—907).

F. 84 b]

904.

DELLE MACHIE DELLA LUNA.

[2]Altri dissero che la luna era conposta
di parti più [3]o mē transparenti, come se
una parte fusse a modo [4]d'alabastro, e
alcuna altra a modo di cristallo o vetro,
[5]che ne seguirebbe che 'l sole, ferēdo colli
sua razzi [6]nella parte mē transparēte, il
lume rimarrebbe in [7]superfitie, e così la
parte più densa resterebbe allu[8]minata, e
la parte transparēte mostrerebbe le [9]onbre
delle profondità sue oscure, e così si cōpo-
[10]ne la qualità della luna; e questa opinione è [11]piaciuta a molti filosofi, e massime
a Aristotele, e [12]pure ella è falsa opinione,
perchè ne' di[13]versi aspetti, che si trovano
spesso la luna e il so[14]le alli nostri occhi,
noi vedremmo variare tal ma[15]cule, e quando

OF THE SPOTS ON THE MOON.

Others say that the moon is composed
of more or less transparent parts; as though
one part were something like alabaster and
others like crystal or glass. It would
follow from this that the sun casting its rays
on the less transparent portions, the light
would remain on the surface, and so the
denser part would be illuminated, and the
transparent portions would display the shadow
of their darker depths; and this is their
account of the structure and nature of the
moon. And this opinion has found favour
with many philosophers, and particularly with
Aristotle, and yet it is a false view—for, in
the various phases and frequent changes of
the moon and sun to our eyes, we should
see these spots vary, at one time looking
dark and at another light: they would be
dark when the sun is in the West and the

alla . . osscura . . ciareza. 48. ochupi. 49. chon. 50. distāte ochu. 51. pì all.

903. 2. disse. 3. interprsi infralla . . elli . . nos. 4. fussi . . tal. 5. bon stabili. 6. chettal. 7. fusi variate . . muterebō.
8. chessi.

904. 2. chella . . parte. 3. transsparenti . . fussi. 5. cēne . . coli. 6. rimarebbe. 7. resterrebbe. 8. ella . . mosterrebbe.
9. osscure. 10. ecquesto openione. 11. piacuta . . massime aristotie e. 12. puere . . oppennione perche inne de. 13. asspetti
trauāno . . esso. 14. vederem. 15. ecquando . . farebono osscure ecquando. 16. in o. 17. ella . . mezo. 18. transparēte

42. Here the text breaks off; lines 43—52 are written on the margin.

si farebbono oscure, e quãdo chi[16]are; scure si farebbono, quãdo il sole è in oc[17]cidēte e la luna nel mezzo del celo, chè allora le [18]cõcauità transparēti piglierebbono l'onbre in[19]sino alle sommità de' labbri di tal cõcauità trãs[20]parēti, perchè il sole nõ potrebbe penetrare li [21]sua razzi dentro alle boche di tali cõcauità, [22]le quali parrebbono chiare nel plenilunio, [23]doue la luna in oriẽte guarda il sole all'occidē[24]te; allora il sole alluminerebbe insino ne' fõ[25]di di tali transparẽtie, e così, nõ generãdosi [26]onbre, la luna non ci mostrerebbe in tal tenpo [27]le predette machie, e così ora piv ora meno, [28]secondo le mutatiõ del sol dalla luna e della lu[29]na dai lochi nostri, come di sopra dissi.

moon in the middle of the sky; for then the transparent hollows would be in shadow as far as the tops of the edges. of those transparent hollows, because the sun could not then fling his rays into the mouth of the hollows, which however, at full moon, would be seen in bright light, at which time the moon is in the East and faces the sun in the West; then the sun would illuminate even the lowest depths of these transparent places and thus, as there would be no shadows cast, the moon at these times would not show us the spots in question; and so it would be, now more and now less, according to the changes in the position of the sun to the moon, and of the moon to our eyes, as I have said above.

F. 85a]   905.

DELLE MACULE DELLA LUNA.

[2]Si è detto che le macule della luna son create in essa luna, [3]da essere in se di uaria rarità e dēsità, il che se così fusse, [4]nell'eclissi della luna i razzi solari penetrebbono per [5]alcuna parte della predetta rarità, e, nõ si ueden[6]do tale effetto, detta opinione è falsa;

[7]Altri dicono che la superfitie della luna, essendo tersa [8]e pulita, che essa, a similitudine di spechio, riceue in [9]se la similitudine della terra; Questa openione [10]è falsa, conciosiachè la terra, scoperta dall'acqua, per diuer[11]si aspetti à diuerse figure; adunque, quando la luna [12]è all'oriẽte, essa specchierebbe altre machie, che quã[13]do essa ci è di sopra, o quãdo essa è in occidẽte; però [14]le machie della luna, come si uede nel plenilunio, [15]mai si uariano nel moto da lei fatto nel nostro emi[16]sperio; 2ᵃ ragione è, che la cosa specchia[17]ta nella convessità piglia piccola parte d' es[18]so spechio, com'è provato in prospettiua; 3ᵃ ragione [19]li è, che nel plenilunio la luna vede solo il mezzo [20]della

OF THE SPOTS ON THE MOON.

It has been asserted, that the spots on the moon result from the moon being of varying thinness or density; but if this were so, when there is an eclipse of the moon the solar rays would pierce through the portions which were thin as is alleged [5]. But as we do not see this effect the opinion must be false.

Others say that the surface of the moon is smooth and polished and that, like a mirror, it reflects in itself the image of our earth. This view is also false, inasmuch as the land, where it is not covered with water, presents various aspects and forms. Hence when the moon is in the East it would reflect different spots from those it would show when it is above us or in the West; now the spots on the moon, as they are seen at full moon, never vary in the course of its motion over our hemisphere. A second reason is that an object reflected in a convex body takes up but a small portion of that body, as is proved in perspective [18]. The third reason is that when the moon is full, it only faces half the hemisphere of the

905. 3—5. *Eclissi.* This word, as it seems to me, here means eclipses of the sun; and the sense of the passage, as I understand it, is that by the foregoing hypothesis the moon, when it comes between the sun and the earth must appear as if pierced,—we may say like a sieve.

18. *come è provato.* This alludes to the accompanying diagram.

spera della terra alluminata, nella quale [21]l'oceano colle altre acque risplendono, e la terra [22]fa macule in esso splendore, e così si uedrebbe [23]la metà della nostra terra cinta dallo splendo[24]re del mare alluminato dal sole, e nella luna tal [25]similitudine sarebbe minima parte d'essa luna; [26]4ª è che la cosa splendida non si spechia nell'al[27]tra splendida; adunque il mare, pigliando splendo[28]re dal sole, siccome fa la luna, e' nō si potrebbe in lei spe-[29]chiare tal terra, che ancora specchiar non vi si vedesse [30]particularmēte il corpo del sole e di ciascuna stel[31]la a lei opposta.

illuminated earth, on which only the ocean and other waters reflect bright light, while the land makes spots on that brightness; thus half of our earth would be seen girt round with the brightness of the sea lighted up by the sun, and in the moon this reflection would be the smallest part of that moon. Fourthly, a radiant body cannot be reflected from another equally radiant; therefore the sea, since it borrows its brightness from the sun,—as the moon does—, could not cause the earth to be reflected in it, nor indeed could the body of the sun be seen reflected in it, nor indeed any star opposite to it.

Br. M. 19 a]

906.

Se terrai osseruate le particule delle machie della luna, [2]tu troverai in quelle spesse uolte gran varietà, e di questo [3]ò fatto pruova io medesimo disegnādole; E questo nasce da nuvo[4]li che si leuano dall'acque d'essa luna, li quali s'interpongo-[5]no infra 'l sole e essa acqua, e colla loro onbra tolgo[6]no i razzi del sole a tale acqua, onde essa acqua viene a ri[7]manere oscura, per non potere spechiare il corpo solare.

If you keep the details of the spots of the moon under observation you will often find great variation in them, and this I myself have proved by drawing them. And this is caused by the clouds that rise from the waters in the moon, which come between the sun and those waters, and by their shadow deprive these waters of the sun's rays. Thus those waters remain dark, not being able to reflect the solar body.

Leic. 5 a]

907.

Come le mac[2]chie della luna [3]son variate da [4]quel che già fu[5]rō, per causa del [6]corso delle sue [7]acque.

How the spots on the moon must have varied from what they formerly were, by reason of the course of its waters.

C. A. 341 b; 1055 a]

908.

DE' CIERCHI DELLA LUNA.

[2]Jo · truouo · che quelli · cierchi ·, li quali · par che di notte circūdino la luna · di uarie grādezze e grossezze, [3]sono · causati da uarie · qualità di grossezze d'umori, i quali in varie altezze infra la luna e li ochi [4]nostri sono situati ·; E quel cierchio maggiore è mē rosso · ed è nella prima parte più bassa di detti [5]umori, il secondo minore è piv alto, e pare piv rosso, perch'è visto per

OF HALOS ROUND THE MOON.

I have found, that the circles which at night seem to surround the moon, of various sizes, and degrees of density are caused by various gradations in the densities of the vapours which exist at different altitudes between the moon and our eyes. And of these halos the largest and least red is caused by the lowest of these vapours; the second, smaller one, is higher up, and looks redder because it is

On the moon's halo.

dano ell̄. 24. aluminato. 25. luna c. 26. 4ªhe chella . . splendida no si . . 27. splendita . . piglando. 28. si come fa la luna e nō . . illei. 29. speciar . . vedessi. 30. sole di ciasscuna. 31. allei opposita.

906. 1. Setterrai. 2. troverrai. 3. offatto . . "disegnādole" Ecquesto nassce da nugho. 4. chessi . . sinterponga. 5. cholla . . tolgho. 6. razi . . attale . . arri. 7. osscura.

907. 4. ga.

908. 2. circhūdino . . grādeze e rosseza. 3. chausati . . grosseze domori . . alteze infralla . . elli. 4. nosstri . . Ecquel . .

2 umori ·; e così quanto [6]piv alti sieno, minori e piv rossi appariràno, perchè infra l'ochio e quello fiã piv solidi umori, [7]e per questo si pruova che doue apparisce maggiore rossore · lì è piv somma d'umori.

seen through two vapours. And so on, as they are higher they will appear smaller and redder, because, between the eye and them, there is thicker vapour. Whence it is proved that where they are seen to be reddest, the vapours are most dense.

W. XXVII]

909.

On instruments for observing the moon (909. 910).

Come tu vuoi prouare, la luna mostrarsi [2]maggiore che essa non è, giugnendo all'orizzonte; [3]tu torrai vn ochiale colmo da una superfitie [4]e concauo dalla superfitie opposita, e tieni [5]l'ochio dal concavo, e guarda l'obbietto fori [6]della superfitie conuessa, e così [7]avrai fatto vn vero simile [8]all'aria, che si include in[9]fra la spera del foco e de[10]lla acqua, la quale aria è [11]concaua diuerso la terra e [12]conuessa diuerso il foco.

If you want to prove why the moon appears larger than it is, when it reaches the horizon; take a lens which is highly convex on one surface and concave on the opposite, and place the concave side next the eye, and look at the object beyond the convex surface; by this means you will have produced an exact imitation of the atmosphere included beneath the sphere of fire and outside that of water; for this atmosphere is concave on the side next the earth, and convex towards the fire.

C. A. 187 a; 561 a]

910.

Fa ochiali da vedere [2]la luna grande.

Construct glasses to see the moon magnified.

---

magiore . . edella prima. 5. omori . . sechondo . . vissto . . omori e chosi. 6. infrallochio ecquello . . solidomori. 7. apariscie magiore . . domori.

909. 1. volli . . mosstrare. 2. magore . . gngnendo. 4. conchauo . . ettieni. 6. chonuessa e chosi. 7. arai. 8. chessi. 9. fralla . . focho chede. 12. focho.

---

910. See the Introduction, p. 136, Fracastoro ays in his work Homocentres: *"Per dua specilla ocularia si quis perspiciat, alteri altero superposito, majora multo et propinquiora videbit omnia.—Quin imo*

quaedam specilla ocularia fiunt tantae densitatis, ut si per ea quis aut lunam, aut aliud siderum spectet, adeo propinqua illa iudicet, ut ne turres ipsas excedant" (sect. II c. 8 and sect. III, c. 23).

VI.

THE STARS.

On the light of the stars (911—913).

F. 5 *b*]   **911.**

Veggonsi le stelle di notte e nō di dì, per esser noi sotto ²la grossezza dell'aria, la quale è piena d'infinite particu³le d'umidità, le quali, ciascuna per se quādo è percossa ⁴dalli razzi del sole, rendono splendore, e così l'in⁵nvmerabili splēdori occupano esse stelle, e se ⁶tale aria nō fusse, il celo senpre ci mostrerebbe ⁷le stelle nelle sua tenebre.

The stars are visible by night and not by day, because we are beneath the dense atmosphere, which is full of innumerable particles of moisture, each of which independently, when the rays of the sun fall upon it, reflects a radiance, and so these numberless bright particles conceal the stars; and if it were not for this atmosphere the sky would always display the stars against its darkness.

F. 57 *a*]   **912.**

SE LE STELLE ÀNNO LUME DAL SOLE O DA SE.

²Dicono di auere il lume da se, allegando ³che se Venere e Mercurio non avessino ⁴il lume da se, quādo essa s'interpone infra ⁵l'ochio nostro e 'l sole, esse oscurerebbero tan⁶to d'esso sole, quāto esse ne coprono al ochio ⁷nostro; E quest'è falso, perch'è prouato ⁸come l'onbroso, posto nel luminoso, è cinto e coper⁹to tutto da razzi laterali del rimanēte di tal lu¹⁰minoso, e così resta inuisibile, come si

WHETHER THE STARS HAVE THEIR LIGHT FROM THE SUN OR IN THEMSELVES.

Some say that they shine of themselves, alledging that if Venus and Mercury had not a light of their own, when they come between our eye and the sun they would darken so much of the sun as they could cover from our eye. But this is false, for it is proved that a dark object against a luminous body is enveloped and entirely concealed by the lateral rays of the rest of that luminous body and so remains invisible. As may be seen

---

911. 1. vegāsi lesselle. 2. grosseza. 3. ciasscuna . . rende. 4. cossi. 5. ochupano . . esse. 6. fussi . . mosterrebbe. 7. lesstelle.
912. 1. ā lume. 2. dicano di havere . . dasse. 3. uenere e merchurio nōn auessi. 4. illume dasse . . infral. 5. oscurerebō.
6. coprano. 9. razi. 12. ilūga. 13. ochupano. 15. acade. 16. esieno . . non o. 18. nosstro. *Lines* 19 *and* 20 *are written*

911. See Vol. .I, No. 296, which also refers to starlight.

912. From this and other remarks (see No. 902,

l. 34 &c.) it is clear that Leonardo was familiar with the phenomena of Irradiation.

di[11]mostra : quando il sole è veduto per la ra[12]mificatione delle piāte sanza foglie in lūga di[13]stantia, essi rami non occupano parte al[14]cuna d'esso sole alli ochi nostri; jl simile [15]accade a' predetti pianeti, li quali ancora [16]che da se sieno sanza luce, eglino non oc[17]cupano, com'è detto, parte alcuna del sole [18]all'ochio nostro.

when the sun is seen through the boughs of trees bare of their leaves, at some distance the branches do not conceal any portion of the sun from our eye. The same thing happens with the above mentioned planets which, though they have no light of their own, do not—as has been said—conceal any part of the sun from our eye[18].

Seconda [20]prova.

Second argument.

[21]Dicono le stelle nella notte parere lucidissime [22]quāto più ci sō superiori, e che, se esse nō auessino lume [23]da se, che l'ombra che fa la terra, che s'interpone [24]fra loro e 'l sole, verrebbe a scurarle, non vedē[25]do esse, nè sēdo vedute dal corpo solare; Ma [26]questi non ànno considerato, che l'onbra piramidale de[27]lla terra non aggiugne infra troppe stelle, e in [28]quelle ch'ella aggiugne, la piramide è tanto dimi[29]nuita, che poco occupa del corpo della stella; e 'l ri[30]manēte è alluminato dal sole.

Some say that the stars appear most brilliant at night in proportion as they are higher up; and that if they had no light of their own, the shadow of the earth which comes between them and the sun, would darken them, since they would not face nor be faced by the solar body. But those persons have not considered that the conical shadow of the earth cannot reach many of the stars; and even as to those it does reach, the cone is so much diminished that it covers very little of the star's mass, and all the rest is illuminated by the sun.

F. 60 a]

913.

Perchè li pianeti appariscono maggiori [2]in oriēte che sopra di noi, che dovrebbe [3]essere il contrario, essendo [4]3500 miglia più vicini a noi, essendo [5]nel mezzo del celo, che essendo al-l'o[6]rizzōte.

[7]Tutti li gradi delli elemēti, donde passa-[8]no le spetie de' corpi celesti, [9]che vengono all'ochio, sono [10]equali, e li angoli, [11]donde li penetra [12]la linia cē-trale di tali spetie, so-no [13]inequali, e la di-stantia è [14]maggiore, come mostra l'eccesso a b so[15]pra a d, e per la 9ª del 7° la gran-dezza [16]d'essi corpi celesti nell'orizzonte è provata.

Why the planets appear larger in the East than they do overhead, whereas the contrary should be the case, as they are 3500 miles nearer to us when in mid sky than when on the horizon.

All the degrees of the elements, through which the images of the celestial bodies pass to reach the eye, are equal curves and the angles by which the central line of those images passes through them, are unequal angles [13]; and the distance is greater, as is shown by the excess of a b beyond a d; and the enlargement of these celestial bodies on the horizon is shown by the 9th of the 7th.

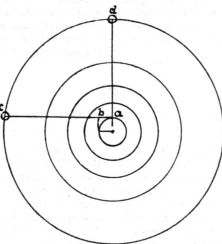

on the margin. 20. pruoua. 21. Dicano. 22. superiore e chesselle nō auesino. 23. che obra cheffa . . chessinterpone. 24. le verebe asscurare. 25. nessēdo. 26. nōnā . . chellonbra. 27. nōnagugne . . stelle ege. 28. chellagugnie . . ettanto. 29. ochupa. 30. aluminato.

913. 1. apariscā magori. 2. douerebbe. 5. mezo. 6. rizōte. 7. gradi | ' delli elemēti". 9. vengano. 10. cului elli angoli [della luna]. 11. [contra le di] donde li. 12. tale. 13. nequali ella. 14. magore . . ecesso. 15. grandeza. 16. orizonte.

913. l. 13. inequali, here and elsewhere does not mean unequal in the sense of not being equal to each other, but angles which are not right angles.

Br. M. 279 *b*] 914.

Per uedere la natura delli pi²aneti apri il tetto e mo³stra alla basa vn sol pia⁴neta, e 'l moto reflesso da ⁵tale basa dirà la comples⁶sione del predetto pianeta, ⁷ma fa che tal basa nō ne ⁸veda più d'uno per uolta.

To see the real nature of the planets Observations on the stars. open the covering and note at the base [4] one single planet, and the reflected movement of this base will show the nature of the said planet; but arrange that the base may face only one at the time.

E. o'] 915.

Tullius de Diuinatione ²ait Astrologiam fuisse ³adinuentā ante trojanum ⁴bellū Quingentis septua⁵ginta milibus añorum.
57000.

Cicero says in [his book] De Divinatione On history of astro- that Astrology has been practised five nomy. hundred seventy thousand years before the Trojan war.
57000.

Br. M. 173 *b* (190 *b*)] 916.

Benchè il tenpo · sia annumerato infra le continue ²quātità, esso, per essere inuisibile e sanza corpo, non cade integralmēte sotto la ³geometrica potentia, la quale lo diuide per figure e corpi d'infinita varietà, ⁴come continuo nelle cose uisibili e corporee far si uede; Ma sol co' sua primi ⁵principi si cōuiene ·, cioè col punto e colla linia ·; ɉl punto nel tempo è da ⁶essere equiparato · al suo instante, e la linia à similitudine colla lūghez⁷za d'una quantità d'un tempo, e siccome i pūti sō principio e fine della predet⁸ta linia ·, così li instanti

Although time is included in the class of Of time and its divisions Continuous Quantities, being indivisible and (916—918). immaterial, it does not come entirely under the head of Geometry, which represents its divisions by means of figures and bodies of infinite variety, such as are seen to be continuous in their visible and material properties. But only with its first principles does it agree, that is with the Point and the Line; the point may be compared to an instant of time, and the line may be likened to the length of a certain quantity of time, and just as a line begins and terminates in a point, so such a space of time.

914. 4. refresso. 5. compless. 8. duna.
916. 1. anvmerato infralle 3. geometricha | "potentia" . . diuide . . chorpi difinita. 4. uisibile . . farsi e uede Massol. 5. coe . . cholla. 6. Ella . . "a" . . cholla lūggez. 7. "duna quantita" dun . . essicome . . effine. 8. instancti . . prcipio . . Esse.

914. 4. *basa.* This probably alludes to some instrument, perhaps the Camera obscura.
915. The statement that CICERO, *De Divin.* ascribes the discovery of astrology to a period 57000 years before the Trojan war I believe to be quite erroneous. According to ERNESTI, *Clavis Ciceroniana*, CH. G. SCHULZ (*Lexic. Cicer.*) and the edition of *De Divin.* by GIESE the word Astrologia occurs only twice in CICERO: *De Divin. II*, 42. *Ad Chaldæorum monstra veniamus, de quibus Eudoxus, Platonis auditor, in astrologia judicio doctissimorum hominum facile princeps, sic opinatur (id quod scriptum reliquit): Chaldæis in prædictione et in notatione cujusque vitæ*

ex natali die minime esse credendum." He then quotes the condemnatory verdict of other philosophers as to the teaching of the Chaldaeans but says nothing as to the antiquity and origin of astronomy. CICERO further notes *De oratore* I, 16 that Aratus was *"ignarus astrologiæ"* but that is all. So far as I know the word occurs nowhere else in CICERO; and the word *Astronomia* he does not seem to have used at all. (H. MÜLLER-STRÜBING.)
916. This passage is repeated word for word on page 190 *b* of the same manuscript and this is accounted for by the text in Vol. I, No. 4. Compare also No. 1216.

sō termine e principio di qualūche dato spatio di tenpo;—e se [9]la linia è diuisibile in īfinito, lo spatio d'ū tenpo di tal diuisione non è alieno, [10]e se le parti diuise della linia sono proportionabili infra se, ancora le parti del tenpo [11]saraño proportionabili infra loro.

begins and terminates in an instant. And whereas a line is infinitely divisible, the divisibility of a space of time is of the same nature; and as the divisions of the line may bear a certain proportion to each other, so may the divisions of time.

Br. M. 176 a]

917.

Scriui la qualità del [2]tenpo, separata dalla [3]geometrica.

Describe the nature of Time as distinguished from the Geometrical definitions.

Br. M. 191 a]

918.

Fa che vn ora sia diui[2]sa in 3000 parti, e [3]questo farai coll'oriolo [4]alleggerēdo o aggravādo [5]il cōtrapeso.

Divide an hour into 3000 parts, and this you can do with a clock by making the pendulum lighter or heavier.

10. esselle parte. 11. infralloro.
917. 2. seperata. 3. geometricha.   **918.** 3. cquesto. 4. allegerēdo o agravādo.

XVI.

Physical Geography.

Leonardo's researches as to the structure of the earth and sea were made at a time, when the extended voyages of the Spaniards and Portuguese had also excited a special interest in geographical questions in Italy, and particularly in Tuscany. Still, it need scarcely surprise us to find that in deeper questions, as to the structure of the globe, the primitive state of the earth's surface, and the like, he was far in advance of his time.

The number of passages which treat of such matters is relatively considerable; like almost all Leonardo's scientific notes they deal partly with theoretical and partly with practical questions. Some of his theoretical views of the motion of water were collected in a copied manuscript volume by an early transcriber, but without any acknowledgment of the source whence they were derived. This copy is now in the Library of the Barberini palace at Rome and was published under the title: "De moto e misura dell' acqua," by FRANCESCO CARDINALI, *Bologna* 1828. *In this work the texts are arranged under the following titles:* Libr. I. Della spera dell' acqua; Libr. II. Del moto dell' acqua; Libr. III. Dell' onda dell' acqua; Libr. IV. Dei retrosi d' acqua; Libr. V. Dell' acqua cadente; Libr. VI. Delle rotture fatte dall' acqua; Libr. VII Delle cose portate dall' acqua; Libr. VIII. Dell' oncia dell' acqua e delle canne; Libr. IX. De molini e d' altri ordigni d' acqua.

The large number of isolated observations scattered through the manuscripts, accounts for our so frequently finding notes of new schemes for the arrangement of those relating to water and its motions, particularly in the Codex Atlanticus: I have printed several of these plans as an introduction to the Physical Geography, and I have actually arranged the texts in accordance with the clue afforded by one of them which is undoubtedly one of the latest notes referring to the subject (No. 920). The text given as No. 930 which is also taken from a late note-book of Leonardo's, served as a basis for the arrangement of the first of the seven books—or sections—, bearing the title: Of the Nature of Water (Dell' acque in se).

As I have not made it any part of this undertaking to print the passages which refer to purely physical principles, it has also been necessary to exclude those practical researches which, in accordance with indications given in 920, ought to come in as Books 13, 14 and 15. I can only incidentally mention here that Leonardo—as it seems to me, especially in his youth—devoted a great deal of attention to the construction of mills. This is proved by a number of drawings of very careful and minute execution, which are to be found in the Codex Atlanticus. Nor was it possible to include his considerations on the regulation of rivers, the making of canals and so forth (No. 920, Books 10, 11 and 12); but those passages in which the structure of a canal is directly connected with notices of particular places will be found duly inserted under section XVII (Topographical notes). In Vol. I, No. 5 the text refers to canal-making in general.

On one point only can the collection of passages included under the general heading of Physical Geography claim to be complete. When comparing and sorting the materials for this work I took particular care not to exclude or omit any text in which a geographical name was mentioned even incidentally, since in all such researches the chief interest, as it appeared to me, attached to the question whether these acute observations on the various local characteristics of mountains, rivers or seas, had been made by Leonardo himself, and on the spot. It is self-evident that the few general and somewhat superficial observations on the Rhine and the Danube, on England and Flanders, must have been obtained from maps or from some informants, and in the case of Flanders Leonardo himself acknowledges this (see No. 1008). But that most of the other and more exact observations were made, on the spot, by Leonardo himself, may be safely assumed from their method and the style in which he writes of them; and we should bear it in mind that in all investigations, of whatever kind, experience is always spoken of as the only basis on which he relies. Incidentally, as in No. 984, he thinks it necessary to allude to the total absence of all recorded observations.

I.

INTRODUCTION.

Leic. 5a]

919.

Questi libri contēgono in ne' primi ² della natura dell' acqua in se ne' ³ sua moti, li altri contēgono delle ⁴ cose fatte dai sua corsi, ⁵ che mv⁶tano il mondo di centro e di figura.

These books contain in the beginning: Of the nature of water itself in its motions; the others treat of the effects of its currents, which change the world in its centre and its shape.

Schemes for the arrangement of the materials (919—928).

Leic. 15b]

920.

DIVISIŌ DEL LIBRO.

Libro p° dell' acque in se,
libro 2° del mare,
libro 3° delle uene,
⁵libro 4° de' fiumi;
libro 5° delle nature de' fōdi,
libro 6 delli obbietti,
libro 7 delle ghiaje,
libro 8° della superfitie del'acqua,
¹⁰libro 9 delle cose che in quella
son messe;
libro 10° de' ripari de' fiumi,
libro 11° delli condotti,
libro 12 de' canali,
libro 13 delli strumēti volti dall'acqua,
¹⁵libro 14 del far mōtare l'acque,
libro 15 delle cose cōsumate dall'acque.

DIVISIONS OF THE BOOK.

Book 1 of water in itself.
Book 2 of the sea.
Book 3 of subterranean rivers.
Book 4 of rivers.
Book 5 of the nature of the abyss.
Book 6 of the obstacles.
Book 7 of gravels.
Book 8 of the surface of water.
Book 9 of the things placed
therein.
Book 10 of the repairing of rivers.
Book 11 of conduits.
Book 12 of canals.
Book 13 of machines turned by water.
Book 14 of raising water.
Book 15 of matters worn away by water.

919 .1. cōtēgano. 3. cōtēgano. 4. dae sua.
920. 8. giare. 9. delle . . acq"a". 10. quella. 16. dell cose . . acq"e".

Leic. 9a]

921.

Farai prima un libro ²che tratti de' lochi ³occupati dall' acque ⁴dolci, e 'l 2° dal⁵l' acque salse, e 'l ⁶3° come, per la par-⁷tita di quelle, queste ⁸nostre parti son ⁹fatte piv lieui, e ¹⁰per consequēza piv ¹¹remosse dal cen¹²tro del mōdo.

First you shall make a book treating of places occupied by fresh waters, and the second by salt waters, and the third, how by the disappearance of these', our parts of the world were made lighter and in consequence more remote from the centre of the world.

F. 87b]

922.

Descriui in prima tutta l' acqua in ciascuno suo moto, di poi ²descriui tutti li sua fondi e le lor materie, senpre al³legando le propositioni delle predette acque, e fia bu⁴ono ordine, che altrimēti l' opera sarebbe cō-fusa.

⁵Descriui tutte le figure che fa l' acqua dalla sua ⁶maggiore alla sua minore onda ·e le lor cause.

First write of all water, in each of its motions; then describe all its bottoms and their various materials, always referring to the propositions concerning the said waters; and let the order be good, for otherwise the work will be confused.

Describe all the forms taken by water from its greatest to its smallest wave, and their causes.

F. 88a]

923.

Libro 9 de' surgimenti accidentali dell'acqua.

Book 9, of accidental risings of water.

F. 90b]

924.

Ordine del libro.

²Poni nel principio ciò che può fare vn fiume.

The order of the book.

Place at the beginning what a river can effect.

Br. M. 35a]

925.

Libro d' abbattere li eserciti · col' impeto de' diluui fatti dall' acque disgorgate,

²Libro che l' acque cōducino a salua-mento li legniami tagliati ne' mōti,

³Libro delle barche condotte contro all' inpeto de' fiumi,

⁴Libro dell' alzare li gran ponti col senplice accrescimēto dell' acque,

⁵Libro del riparare all' inpeto de' fiumi che le città da quelli nō siē percosse.

A book of driving back armies by the force of a flood made by releasing waters.

A book showing how the waters safely bring down timber cut in the mountains.

A book of boats driven against the impetus of rivers.

A book of raising large bridges higher. Simply by the swelling of the waters.

A book of guarding against the impetus of rivers so that towns may not be damaged by them.

---

921. 1. p"a" vn libr. 3. ochupati. 7. quele. 8. parte.
922. 1. scriui in p"a" . . lacq"a" . . ciasscuno. 2. desscriui . . elle. 4.· altremēti. 5. cheffa lacq"a". 6. magore . . elle.
923. acq"a".
924. 2. co che po.
925. *The head of each line is marked by the letter* d *which is crossed out.* 1. dabatter . . chol inpito . . dilumi . . dellacq"a" discorghate. 2. chellacque . . assaluamento. 4. acresscimēto. 5. chelle cita dacquelli . . percossi.

Br. M. 35*b*]　　　　　　　　926.

Libro della dispositiō de' fiumi a cō-
seruatiō dell'argine sue,

²Libro delli monti, che si spiccherāno,
e fiā la terra sotto il nostro emisperio
scoperta dall'acqua,

³Libro del terreno portato dal'acqua a
riēpiere la grā profondità de' pelaghi,

⁴Libro de' modi che la fortuna per se
netti li riēpiuti porti del mare,

⁵Libro dell'argine de' fiumi e lor permanentia,

⁶Libro del fare che li fiumi con lor corso
tēgin netti li fondi loro per le città dōde
passano,

⁷Libro del fare o rifondare li ponti sopra
li fiumi,

⁸Libro di ripari che farsi debbō alli
muri e argini de' fiumi percossi dall'acqua,

⁹Libro del generare li colli dall'arena
o ghiaja sopra le gran profondità dell'acque.

A book of the ordering of rivers so as to
preserve their banks.

A book of the mountains, which would
stand forth and become land, if our hemisphere were to be uncovered by the water.

A book of the earth carried down by the
waters to fill up the great abyss of the seas.

A book of the ways in which a tempest may
of itself clear out filled up sea-ports.

A book of the shores of rivers and of
their permanency.

A book of how to deal with rivers, so
that they may keep their bottom scoured by
their own flow near the cities they pass.

A book of how to make or to repair
the foundations for bridges over the rivers.

A book of the repairs which ought to
be made in walls and banks of rivers where
the water strikes them.

A book of the formation of hills of sand
or gravel at great depths in water.

Br. M. 122 *a*]　　　　　　　　927.

L'acqua dà principio al moto suo,

²Libro liuellamenti d'acque per diuersi
modi,

³Libro del discostare li fiumi dai lochi
da loro offesi,

⁴Libro del dirizzar li fiumi che occupano superchio terreno,

⁵Libro del diuidere li fiumi in molti
rami e farli guadabili,

⁶Libro dell'acque che cō diuersi moti
passā pe' pelaghi loro,

⁷Libro del profondare li letti alli fiumi
cō uari corsi d'acque,

⁸Libro di disporre li fiumi ī modo che
li piccoli prīcipj de' sua danni non accrescino,

⁹Libro de' uari moti dell'acque che
passan per diuerse figure di canali,

¹⁰Libro del fare che li piccoli fiumi non
pieghino il maggiore percosso dalle loro
acque,

¹¹Libro della maggior bassezza che
trouar si possa nella corrēte della superfitie de' fiumi,

Water gives the first impetus to its
motion.

A book of the levelling of waters by
various means.

A book of diverting rivers from places
where they do mischief.

A book of guiding rivers which occupy
too much ground.

A book of parting rivers into several
branches and making them fordable.

A book of the waters which with various
currents pass through seas.

A book of deepening the beds of rivers
by means of currents of water.

A book of controlling rivers so that the
little beginnings of mischief, caused by them,
may not increase.

A book of the various movements of waters
passing through channels of different forms.

A book of preventing small rivers from
diverting the larger one into which their
waters run.

A book of the lowest level which can
be found in the current of the surface of
rivers.

---

926. 2. chessi spich[a] erāno effia la terra "sotto il nostro emisperio" scoperta dellacqua. 3. terē. 4. perse nettili riēpiuti porta del mare. 5. ellor premanentia. 6. chelli . . collor . . tēginetti . . fondi "lor". 7. orrifondare. 8. cheffarsi. 9. ghi-
ara . . acq"e".

927. 1. ||||||||||||||||| gito dobliquita Lacq"a". 2—13. *Each line is headed by an* L, *meaning* Libro. 3. discostare . . dalloro. 4. diri-
zar . . ce ochupan. 5. effarli. 6. chō. 7. chō . . chorsi. 8. di sporre . . chelli picholi . . accresscino. 9. acq"e" . .
chanali. 10. chelli picholi . . magore perchosso. 11. dalla maggor basseza . . corēte. 12. pellalte.

¹²Libro dell'origine de' fiumi che versā per l'alte cime de' monti,

A book of the origin of rivers which flow from the high tops of mountains.

¹³Libro della uarietà de' moti dell'acque ne' lor fiumi.

A book of the various motions of waters in their rivers.

[1] Della inequalità della concauità del nauilio,

[1] Of inequality in the concavity of a ship.

²[1] Libro della inequalità della curuità de' lati de' nauili,

[1] A book of the inequality in the curve of the sides of ships.

³[1] Libro della inequalità del sito del timone,

[1] A book of the inequality in the position of the tiller.

⁴[1] Libro della inequalità della carena de' nauili,

[1] A book of the inequality in the keel of ships.

⁵[2] Libro della uarietà delli spiraculi donde l'acqua si uersa,

[2] A book of various forms of apertures by which water flows out.

⁶[3] Libro dell'acqua inclusa ne' vasi insieme coll'aria e sua moti,

[3] A book of water contained in vessels with air, and of its movements.

⁷[4] Libro del moto dell'acqua per le cicognole,

[4] A book of the motion of water through a syphon.

⁸[5] Libro delli scontri e concorsi dell'acque venute da diuersi aspetti,

[5] A book of the meetings and union of waters coming from different directions.

⁹[6] Libro delle varie figure delli argini traversati dalli fiumi,

[6] A book of the various forms of the banks through which rivers pass.

¹⁰[7] Libro delle uarie secche generate sotto le chiuse de' fiumi,

[7] A book of the various forms of shoals formed under the sluices of rivers.

¹¹[8] Libro delle torture e pieghamēti delle corrēti de' fiumi,

[8] A book of the windings and meanderings of the currents of rivers.

¹²[9] Libro de' uari siti donde si de' trar l'acqua de' fiumi,

[9] A book of the various places whence the waters of rivers are derived.

¹³[10] Libro delle figure dell'argini de' fiumi e lor permanētia,

[10] A book of the configuration of the shores of rivers and of their permanency.

¹⁴[11] Libro dell'acqua cadente perpēdicularmente sopra diuersi obbietti,

[11] A book of the perpendicular fall of water on various objects.

¹⁵[12] Libro del corso dell'acqua inpedito in diuersi siti,

[12] A book of the course of water when it is impeded in various places.

¹⁶[12] Libro delle uarie figure delli obbietti che impediscono il corso del acque,

[12] A book of the various forms of the obstacles which impede the course of waters.

¹⁷[13] Libro delle concauità e globosità fatte dal fondo ītorno a vari obbietti,

[13] A book of the concavity and globosity formed round various objects at the bottom.

¹⁸[14] Libro del condurre li canali navigabili sopra o sotto li fiumi che l'ītersegano,

[14] A book of conducting navigable canals above or beneath the rivers which intersect them.

¹⁹[15] Libro delli terreni che beono le acque de' canali e lor ripari,

[15] A book of the soils which absorb water in canals and of repairing them.

²⁰[16] Libro della creatiō de' corsi de' fiumi che votano il letto de' fiumi riēpiuti di terreno.

[16] A book of creating currents for rivers, which quit their beds, [and] for rivers choked with soil.

928. 4. charena. 5. spirachuli . . lacq"a". 6. essua. 7. cicognuole. 8. acq"e" . . di . . asspetti. 9. delle . . traversate alli. 10. secche [fatte sotto] generate. 11. chorrēti. 12. lacque. 13. fighure dellargine . . ellor premanētia. 14. chadende perpēdichulare. 15. acq"a". 16. chenpedisscano . . aeq"e". 17. globbosita. 18. condure . . navichabili . . ossotto . . chellītersegano. 19. beano . . chanali ellor.

928. 1. The first line of this passage was added subsequently, evidently as a correction of the following line. 7. *cicognole*, see No. 966, 11, 17.

A. 55*b*]

929.

COMICIAMĒTO DEL TRATTATO DEL'ACQUA.

²L'omo è detto · da li antiqui · mōdo minore ·, e cierto la ditione · d'esso · nome è bene collocata, ³impero · chè, sicchome · l'omo · è cōposto · di terra ·, acqua ·, aria · e foco ·, questo corpo · della · terra ⁴è il simiglante ·; se l'omo · à in se · ossi, sostenitori e armadura · della carne ·, jl mōdo à i sassi, ⁵sostenitori della · terra; se l'omo à in se il lago · del sangue, doue crescie · e discrescie il polmo⁶ne · nello · alitare ·, jl corpo della terra à il suo oceano mare ·, il quale ancora · lui crescie ⁷e discrescie ogni · sei · ore · per lo alitare · del mōdo ·; se dal detto · lago di sangue · diriuano ve⁸ne ·, che si vanno ramificādo · per lo corpo · vmano ·, similmēte il mare oceano enpie ⁹il corpo della terra · d'infinite vene d'acqua; mancano al corpo della terra · i nerui, i quali nō ui ¹⁰sono ·, perchè i nervi sono fatti al proposito · del movimēto ·, e il mōdo sendo di perpetua stabilità, ¹¹non accade movimēto e, nō accadēdo movimēto, i nervi · nō ui sono · neciessari; Ma ī tutte ¹²l'altre · cose · sono · molto simili.

THE BEGINNING OF THE TREATISE ON WATER.

By the ancients man has been called the world in miniature; and certainly this name is well bestowed, because, inasmuch as man is composed of earth, water, air and fire, his body resembles that of the earth; and as man has in him bones the supports and framework of his flesh, the world has its rocks the supports of the earth; as man has in him a pool of blood in which the lungs rise and fall in breathing, so the body of the earth has its ocean tide which likewise rises and falls every six hours, as if the world breathed; as in that pool of blood veins have their origin, which ramify all over the human body, so likewise the ocean sea fills the body of the earth with infinite springs of water. The body of the earth lacks sinews and this is, because the sinews are made expressly for movements and, the world being perpetually stable, no movement takes place, and no movement taking place, muscles are not necessary.—But in all other points they are much alike.

General introduction.

929. 1. acq"a".   2. cholochata.   3. impero . chessi . chome . . chōposto di tera . acq"a" . . effocho . . chorpo . . tera.   4. sellomo . . osso . . charne.   5. ssisotenitori . . lacho.   6. tera . . occicano . . anchora . . cresscie.   7. diriua ve.   8. chessi vano ramifichādo . . chorpo . . [C] similmēte . . occieano.   9. dacq"a" mancha . . tera.   11. achade . . achadēdo.   12. chose.

I.

OF THE NATURE OF WATER.

E. 12a]   930.

ORDINE DEL PRIMO LIBRO DELLE ACQUE.

The arrangement of Book I.

²Difinisci prima che cosa è altezza e bassezza   anzi come sō situati ³ li elemēti l'ū'dentro all'altro; Di poi che cosa è gravità dē⁴sa e che è gravità liquida, ma prima che cosa è in se gravi⁵tà e leuità·; Di poi descrivi perchè l'acqua si move e perchè ter⁶mina il moto suo, poi perchè si fa più tarda o velocie, oltre ⁷ a questo come ella senpre disciēde, essendo in cōfine d'ari⁸a più bassa di lei | E come l'acqua si leua in aria mediante ⁹ il calore del sole e poi · ricade in pioggia·; ancora perchè l'acqua ¹⁰ surgie dalle cime de' monti e se l'acqua di nessuna vena più alta ¹¹ che l'oceano mare può uersare acqua più alta che la superfitie ¹² d'esso·oceano·; E come tutta · l'acqua che torna all'oceano è più alta ¹³ della spera dell'acqua | e come l'acqua delli mari equinotiali è più alta ¹⁴ che le acque settētrionali, ed è più alta sotto il corpo del sole ¹⁵ che in nessuna parte del circulo equinotiale | come si speri¹⁶mēta sotto il calore dello stizzo infocato, l'acqua che mediā¹⁷te tale stizzo bolle e l'acqua circustāte al ciētro di tal bol¹⁸lore senpre

THE ORDER OF THE FIRST BOOK ON WATER.

Define first what is meant by height and depth; also how the elements are situated one inside another.   Then, what is meant by solid weight and by liquid weight; but first what weight and lightness are in themselves.   Then describe why water moves, and why its motion ceases; then why it becomes slower or more rapid; besides this, how it always falls, being in contact with the air but lower than the air.   And how water rises in the air by means of the heat of the sun, and then falls again in rain; again, why water springs forth from the tops of mountains; and if the water of any spring higher than the ocean can pour forth water higher than the surface of that ocean.   And how all the water that returns to the ocean is higher than the sphere of waters.   And how the waters of the equatorial seas are higher than the waters of the North, and higher beneath the body of the sun than in any part of the equatorial circle; for experiment shows that under the heat of a burning brand the water near the brand boils, and the water surrounding this ebullition always sinks with

930. 1. p"o" libro. 2. p"a" che chosa he . . ebbasseza. 3. chosa. 4. chosa. 5. elleuita. 7. addi questo chomella . . cōtino. 8. chome. 9. chalore . . eppoi richade . . anchora. 10. delle cime . . essellacqua. 11. chelloccieano . . chella. 12. occieano . . chome . . chettorna . . accieano eppiu. 13. [desso] della . . chome . . ecquinotiali eppiu. 14. chelle. 15. inessuna . . circhulo . . sissperi. 16. chalore . . infochato. 17. talle . . ellacqua circhustāte. 18. dissciende . . circhulare e chome.

disciende con onda circulare e come l'acque ¹⁹settētrionali son piv basse che li altri mari e tāto più, quā²⁰to esse son piv fredde, insin che si convertono in ghiaccio.

a circular eddy. And how the waters of the North are lower than the other seas, and more so as they become colder, until they are converted into ice.

C 26 *b* (4)]

CHE COSA È ACQUA.

²Acqua è infra i quatro elemēti il secōdo mē grave e di seconda volubilità.·

931.

OF WHAT IS WATER.

Among the four elements water is the second both in weight and in instability.

Definitions (931. 932).

I.² 24 *a* and *b*]

PRINCIPIO DEL LIBRO DELL'ACQUE.

²Pelago è detto quello, il quale à figura larga ³e profōda; ⁴nel quale l'acque stanno con poco moto.

932.

THE BEGINNING OF THE BOOK ON WATER.

Sea is the name given to that water which is wide and deep, in which the waters have not much motion.

Leic. 34 *b*]

933.

Li centri della spericità dell'acqua sono due: l'uno è della vniuersale acqua, l'altro è particulare; ²l'vniuersale è quello, il quale serue a tutte l'acque sanza moto, che sono in se in grā quātità, ³come canali, fossi, viuai, fonti, pozzi, fiumi morti, laghi, paduli, stagni e mari, li quali, ancorachè sieno di uarie altezze ciascuno per se, àno li termini delle lor superfitie equi⁴distanti al centro del mondo, come sono i laghi posti nelle cime delli alti mōti come sopra ⁵Pietra Pana e Lago della Sibilla a Norcia, e tutti li laghi che dā principio a grandi fiumi, come Tesino ⁶dal Lago Maggiore, Adda dal lago di Como, Mincio dal lago di Garda e Reno dal lago di Costan⁷tia | e di Coira e dal lago di Lucerne, e come Tigron, il quale passa per la Minore Asia, il quale ne porta ⁸con seco l'acqua di 3 paduli, l'un dopo l'altro, di uarie altezze, de' quali il piv alto è Munace, el mezzano è Pallas ⁹e 'l più basso è Triton; ancora el Nilo diriua da 3 altissimi paduli in Etiopia.

The centres of the sphere of water are two, one universal and common to all water, the other particular. The universal one is that which is common to all waters not in motion, which exist in great quantities. As canals, ditches, ponds, fountains, wells, dead rivers, lakes, stagnant pools and seas, which, although they are at various levels, have each in itself the limits of their superficies equally distant from the centre of the earth, such as lakes placed at the tops of high mountains; as the lake near Pietra Pana and the lake of the Sybil near Norcia; and all the lakes that give rise to great rivers, as the Ticino from Lago Maggiore, the Adda from the lake of Como, the Mincio from the lake of Garda, the Rhine from the lakes of Constance and of Chur, and from the lake of Lucerne, like the Tigris which passes through Asia Minor carrying with it the waters of three lakes, one above the other at different heights of which the highest is Munace, the middle one Pallas, and the lowest Triton; the Nile again flows from three very high lakes in Ethiopia.

Of the surface of the water in relation to the globe (933—936).

19. chelli . . ettāto. 20. chessi chonvertano in diaccio.

931. 1. chosa . . sechōdo. 2. grieve . . sechonda.   **932.** 2. pellago . . affigura.

933. 1. Lli centri . . acq"a" . . partichulare. 2. deluniversale . . attutte lacque . . chessono. 3. cannali fossi "viuai fonti pozi' fiumi . . quali "ancorche sieno di uarie alteze ciascun per se" ano. 4. distante . . illaghi. 5. pietra pana ellago . . sibilla a norca ettutti. 6. [adda da] dal . . magore . . lagho . . como [adice] "menzo" dal lagho . . erreno . . gostan. 7. eurio lacho . . Trigon . . minore africha il quane ne. 8. consecholacq"a" . . alteze . . mezano he. 9. di.

932. Only the beginning of this passage is here given, the remainder consists of definitions which have no direct bearing on the subject.

933. 5. *Pietra Pana*, a mountain near Florence. If for Norcia, we may read Norchia, the remains of

the Etruscan city near Viterbo, there can be no doubt that by '*Lago della Sibilla*'—a name not known elsewhere, so far as I can learn—Leonardo meant *Lago di Vico* (Lacus Ciminus, Aen. 7).

A. 58 *b*]   **934.**

DEL CIĒTRO DELL OCIEANO · MARE.

²Il ciētro della spera · dell'acqua · è il centro · vero · della rotōdita del nostro mōdo, · il quale si cōpone ³infra · acqua e terra · in forma · rotōda ·; Ma se tu · volessi trovare · il ciētro dello · elemēto della ⁴terra ·, questo · è cōtenuto · per equidistāte · spatio · dalla superfitie · dell'oceano · mare ·, e nō dalla ⁵equidistante · superfitie · della · terra ·, perchè chiaro · si comprende · questa palla · della · terra non ⁶avere · niente · di perfetta · rotōdità ·, se non è · in quella · parte dou'è mare · o paduli o altre acque mor⁷te, e qualunque · parte · d'essa · terra che escie · fori · d'esso mare, s'allontana · dal suo · ciētro.

OF THE CENTRE OF THE OCEAN.

The centre of the sphere of waters is the true centre of the globe of our world, which is composed of water and earth, having the shape of a sphere. But, if you want to find the centre of the element of the earth, this is placed at a point equidistant from the surface of the ocean, and not equidistant from the surface of the earth; for it is evident that this globe of earth has nowhere any perfect rotundity, excepting in places where the sea is, or marshes or other still waters. And every part of the earth that rises above the water is farther from the centre.

E. 4 *b*]   **935.**

DEL MARE CHE MUTA ²IL PESO DELLA TERRA.

³Li nichi, ostrighe e altri simili animali, ⁴che nascono nelli fanghi marini, ci testifi-⁵cano la mutatiō della terra intorno al ⁶ciētro de' nostri elemēti; pruovasi così: ⁷Li fiumi reali senpre corrono con torbidu-⁸me, tinto dalla terra, che per lor si leua mediāte la cō⁹fregatiō delle sue acque sopra il fondo e nelle sue ¹⁰riue, e tal cōsumati-one scopre le fronti de' gradi ¹¹fatti a' suoli di quelli nichi, che stan nella superfitie ¹²del fango marino, li quali in tal sito nascierono, quā¹³do l'acque salse li coprivano, e questi tali gradi erano ri¹⁴coperti di tenpo in tenpo dalli fanghi di uarie grossez¹⁵ze o condotti al mare dalli fiumi cō diluvi di diverse grā¹⁶dezze; e così tali fāghi furono composti in tāta altezza, che dal fondo si ¹⁷scopriua all'aria; Ora questi tali fondi sono in tāta ¹⁸altezza che son fatti colli, o alti mōti, e li fiumi, ¹⁹consuma²⁰tori de' lati ²¹d'essi monti, ²²scoprono ²³li gradi d'es²⁴si nichi, e co²⁵sì il leni²⁶ficato lato ²⁷della terra ²⁸al cōtinuo ²⁹s'inalza, e ³⁰li antipo³¹di s'accosta³²no più al ³³ciētro del ³⁴mondo, ³⁵e li anti³⁶chi fondi del ³⁷mare son fatti ³⁸gioghi di monti.

OF THE SEA WHICH CHANGES THE WEIGHT OF THE EARTH.

The shells, oysters, and other similar animals, which originate in sea-mud, bear witness to the changes of the earth round the centre of our elements. This is proved thus: Great rivers always run turbid, being coloured by the earth, which is stirred by the friction of their waters at the bottom and on their shores; and this wearing disturbs the face of the strata made by the layers of shells, which lie on the surface of the marine mud, and which were produced there when the salt waters covered them; and these strata were covered over again from time to time, with mud of various thickness, or carried down to the sea by the rivers and floods of more or less extent; and thus these layers of mud became raised to such a height, that they came up from the bottom to the air. At the present time these bottoms are so high that they form hills or high mountains, and the rivers, which wear away the sides of these mountains, uncover the strata of these shells, and thus the softened side of the earth continually rises and the antipodes sink closer to the centre of the earth, and the ancient bottoms of the seas have become mountain ridges.

934. 1. eccicono. 2. dellacq"a" .. retōdita .. nosstro .. qualle .. chōpone. 3. acq"a" ecterra .. retōda Massettu .. ellemēto. 4. quessto e chōtenuto .. equidisstante .. occieano. 5. equidisstanto .. chonplende questa .. nōna. 6. retōdita. 7. ecqualumque .. terra esscie.

935. 3. osstrighe. 4. nasschano .. tessti. 5. chano. 6. nosstri. 7. senpre [stanno] corā torbidi. 8. medinte la terra. 9. freghatiō .. accque .. nelle sine. 10. rive ettal .. sconpre .. fronte. 11. assuoli .. chesstan. 12. fangho .. nasscicrono. 13. ecquessti .. era ri. 14. grosse. 15. indotti. 16. faghi conpossti .. alteza. 17. quessti. 18. alteza .. elli fiumi. 22. scoprano. 24. echo. 25. si [l] illeni. 26. fichato. 29. el sacosstā. *Lines* 19—38 *are written on the margin.*

Leic. 10 b]   936.

Faccia mutatiō la terra colla sua gravezza, quāte farsi ²voglia, che mai la
superfitie della spera dell'acqua nō si
partirà dalla sua equidistātia col centro del
mōdo.

Let the earth make whatever changes
it may in its weight, the surface of the
sphere of waters can never vary in its
equal distance from the centre of the
world.

Leic. 35 b]   937.

SE LA TERRA È MĒ CHE L'ACQUA.

WHETHER THE EARTH IS LESS THAN THE WATER.

²Dicono alcuni esser vero, che la terra,
ch'è scoperta dalle acque, sia molto
minore che quella che da esse acqu'è
coperta; ³Ma che considerando la
grossezza di 7000 miglia di diametro,
che à · essa terra, e' si può concludere
l'acqua essere di ⁴poca profondità.

Some assert that it is true that the earth,
which is not covered by water is
much less than that covered by water. But considering the size of 7000
miles in diameter which is that of
this earth, we may conclude the
water to be of small depth.

*Of the pro-
portion of
the mass of
water to that
of the earth
(937. 938).*

Leic. 36 a]   938.

DELLA TERRA IN SE.

OF THE EARTH.

²L'alzarsi tanto le cime de' monti sopra
la spera dell'acqua può esser diriuato, perchè
il loco grandissimo ³della terra, il quale

The great elevations of the peaks of the
mountains above the sphere of the water
may have resulted from this that: a very

era ripieno d'acqua,
cioè la grandissima
cauerna, douette ca-
dere ⁴assai della sua
volta inuerso il centro
del mondo, trovandosi
ispiccata mediante il
corso de⁵lle uene che
al continuo consuma-
no il loco donde pas-
sano.
⁶Profondamēto di paesi ⁷come nel
Mare Morto di So⁸ria cioè Sodoma e Go-
morra.
⁹È necessario che l'acqua sia più che
la terra, e la parte scoperta del mare nō

large portion of the earth
which was filled with
water that is to say
the vast cavern inside
the earth may have fal-
len in a vast part of
its vault towards the
centre of the earth, being
pierced by means of the
course of the springs
which continually wear
away the place where they pass.
Sinking in of countries like the Dead Sea
in Syria, that is Sodom and Gomorrah.
It is of necessity that there should be more
water than land, and the visible portion of

936. 1. facia . . graveza. 2. dellacq"a".
937. 1. Sella . . chellacq"a". 2. dicano . . chella. 3. groseza . . diamitro . . po con chludere lacqua per essere. 4. pocha.
938. 2. lasspera . . ilocho. 3. coe. 4. isspichata. 5. iloco. 8. coe soddoma e gamora. 9. chellacq"a" . . chella terra ella . .
dell . . dimosstra.

938. The small sketch below on the left, is placed in the original close to the text referring to the
Dead Sea.

lo dimostra, onde bisognia che [10]molta acqua sia dentro alla terra, sanza quella ch'è infusa nella bassa aria e che scorre [11]per li fiumi e uene.

the sea does not show this; so that there must be a great deal of water inside the earth, besides that which rises into the lower air and which flows through rivers and springs.

F. 27 a]

939.

FIGURA D'ELEMĒTI.

The theory of Plato.

[2]Della figura delli elemēti, e prima contro a chi nega [3]l'opinione di Platone, che dicono che se essi elemēti vestis[4]sero l'un l'altro, colle figure che mette Platone, che si ca[5]vserebbe vacuo infra l'uno e l'altro; e non è vero, e [6]qui lo provo, ma prima bisognia proporre alcuna cō[7]clusione: Non è neciessario che nessuno ele[8]mento, che veste l'ū l'altro, sia d'equ 1 grossezza in tu[9]tta la sua quantità infra la parte che ueste e quel[10]la ch'è uestita; Noi uediamo la spera dell'acqua ma[11]nifestamēte essere di uarie grossezze dal-la sua [12]superfitie al fondo, e che, nō che essa vestisse [13]la terra

quando fusse di figura cuba cioè di 8 an-goli come [14]vole Platone, essa veste la terra che à innumerabili [15]angoli di scogli coperti dall'acqua e varie globosità e cō-[16]cavità, e non si genera vacuo infra l'ac-qua e la terra; Ancora l'aria veste la spera dell'acqua [17]insieme colli monti e valli che superano essa spera, e nō [18]ri-mane vacuo infra la terra e l'aria, sicchè, chi disse [19]generarsi vacuo, ebbe tristo di-scorso.

[20]A Platō si rispōde che la superfitie [21]delle figure che avrebbero li elemēti, [22]che lui pone, non potrebbero sta[23]re.

THE FIGURES OF THE ELEMENTS.

Of the figures of the elements; and first as against those who deny the opinions of Plato, and who say that if the elements include one another in the forms attributed to them by Plato they would cause a va-cuum one within the other. I say it is not true, and I here prove it, but first I desire to propound some conclusions. It is not necessary that the elements which include each other should be of corresponding magni-tude in all the parts, of that which includes and of that which is inclu-ded. We see that the sphere of the waters varies conspicuously in mass from the surface to the bottom, and that, far from investing the earth when that in the form of a cube that is of 8 angles as Plato will have it, that it invests the earth which has innumerable angles of rock covered by the water and various prominences and concavi-ties, and yet no vacuum is generated between the earth and water; again, the air invests the sphere of waters together with the moun-tains and valleys, which rise above that sphere, and no vacuum remains between the earth and the air, so that any one who says a vacuum is generated, speaks foolishly.

But to Plato I would reply that the sur-face of the figures which according to him the elements would have, could not exist.

A. 58 δ]

940.

PRUOVA · COME · LA TERRA · NON È · TŌDA, [2]E, NON ESSENDO TŌDA, NŌ PUÒ AVER COMVNE · CETRO.

That the flow of rivers proves the slope of the land.

[3]Noi · vediamo · il Nilo · partirsi dalle · meridiane · regioni · e rigare · diuerse pro-vincie, corrēdo [4]inverso · settentrione · per

PROVES HOW THE EARTH IS NOT GLOBULAR AND NOT BEING GLOBULAR CANNOT HAVE A COMMON CENTRE.

We see the Nile come from Southern regions and traverse various provinces, run-ning towards the North for a distance of

939. 1. p"a" contro . . niegha. 3. lopēnione . . dicano chesse . . vessti. 4. sm lūlaltro cholle. 5. vserebe . . ellaltro ilenone vere. 6. sna p"a". 8. grosseza. 9. infralla . . ecquel. 10. lasspera dellacq"a". 11. grosseze. 12. vestissi [il cubo] 13. quande fussi . . cubo "cee di 8 angoli" come. 14. esse . . inunbili. 15. acq"a". 16. cavita "e non sigenera vacuo infra lacqua ella terra" Ancora laria che veste. 17. cholli. 18. ellaria siche. 20. chella. 21. arebō. 22. chellui . . potrebono.

940. 1. chome . . tera . . po avr chomune. 3. vedemo . . delle . . chorēdo. 4. settantrione . . isspatio . . miglia "e vessare

ispatio · di 3000 · miglia e versare nelle
mediterrane ōde ai liti d'Egitto, e se noi ·
vogliamo · dare a questo · di calo quelle
⁵dieci · braccia per miglio ·, le quali comv-
nalmēte · si concede · alla · vniversalità · del
corso · de' fiumi, ⁶noi troveremo · il Nilo ·
avere il suo · fine piv basso · che 'l prīcipio
· miglia dieci ·; ⁷Ancora · vediamo il Reno,
Rodano e Danvbio · partirsi dalle germaniche · parti, quasi ciētro ⁸d'Evropa ·, e l'uno
a Oriēte, l'altro a settētrione ·, e l'ultimo ·
a meridiani mari fa suo corso; ⁹se tu cōsi-
derai · bene tutto, vedrai le pianvre d'Europa
fare vno cōcorso molto ¹⁰piv · elevato ·,
che nō sono · l'alte cime de' marittimi mōti;
or pēsa, quāto le loro cime ¹¹si trovano ·
piv · alte · che liti marini.

3000 miles and flow into the Mediterranean
by the shores of Egypt; and if we will give
to this a fall of ten braccia a mile, as is
usually allowed to the course of rivers in
general, we shall find that the Nile must
have its mouth ten miles lower than its source.
Again, we see the Rhine, the Rhone and
the Danube starting from the German parts,
almost the centre of Europe, and having a
course one to the East, the other to the
North, and the last to Southern seas.
And if you consider all this you will see
that the plains of Europe in their aggregate are much higher than the high peaks
of the maritime mountains; think then how
much their tops must be above the sea
shores.

A. 55ᵇ]   **941.**

DEL CALDO CHE NEL MŌDO · È.

²Dov'è · vita lì è calore ·, e dou'è · calore · vitale, quiui è mouimēto · d'umori;
³Questo · si pruova, · inperochè si uede · per
effetto · che · il caldo · dello elemēto · del
foco · senpre · tira · a se ⁴li umidi · vapori · e
folte nebbie e spessi · nuvoli ·, i quali · spic-
cano da' mari e altri · paduli · e fiumi e
vmide ⁵valli, e quelle tirādo · a poco a poco
· insino · alla · fredda · regione, quella prima
parte si ferma, ⁶perchè · il caldo · e vmido
nō si affà · col freddo · e secco; onde · ferma
la prima parte lì assetta l'altre ⁷parti, e
così, aggiugniēdosi parte cō parte ·, si fa ·
spesse · e oscure nvbole ·; e spesso sono
⁸remosse e portate da vēti d'una · in altra
regione; dove per la densità loro fanno sì
spessa gravezza, ⁹che cadono · cō spessa ·
pioggia ·; e se 'l caldo · del sole s'aggivgnie ·
alla potētia dello elemēto ¹⁰del foco ·, i
nvuoli fieno tirati piv · alti e trovano · piv
freddo, in nel quale sì ghiacciano e cavsasi
¹¹tēpestosa · grādine ·; Ora · quel medesimo
· caldo ·, che tiene · sì grā peso · d'acqua ·,
come si uede ¹²piovere de' nvvoli, sveglie
l'acque di basso · in alto · dalle base delle
mōtagnie, e cōduciele, e tienle ¹³dētro ·
alle · cime delle mōtagnie,—le quali, trovādo qualche fessura, al · continuo vsciēdo,
¹⁴causā i fiumi.

OF THE HEAT THAT IS IN THE WORLD.

Where there is life there is heat, and where
vital heat is, there is movement of vapour.
This is proved, inasmuch as we see that
the element of fire by its heat always draws
to itself damp vapours and thick mists as
opaque clouds, which it raises from seas as
well as lakes and rivers and damp valleys; and
these being drawn by degrees as far as the
cold region, the first portion stops, because
heat and moisture cannot exist with cold
and dryness; and where the first portion stops
the rest settle, and thus one portion after
another being added, thick and dark
clouds are formed. They are often wafted
about and borne by the winds from one
region to another, where by their density
they become so heavy that they fall in thick
rain; and if the heat of the sun is added to
the power of the element of fire, the clouds
are drawn up higher still and find a greater
degree of cold, in which they form ice and
fall in storms of hail. Now the same heat
which holds up so great a weight of water
as is seen to rain from the clouds, draws
them from below upwards, from the foot of
the mountains, and leads and holds them
within the summits of the mountains, and
these, finding some fissure, issue continuously
and cause rivers.

*Theory of
the elevation
of water
within the
mountains.*

nelle mediterane ōde a liti e se .. degitto acquessto di cholo qualle. 5. dieci br .. quale chomvnemēte .. chonciede. 6. no
trovrremo .. prēcipio ... diecip. 7. vedemo .. delle. 8. elluno .. assettātrione .. chorso. 9. settu chōsiderai · be
verai [levr] le .. deropia .. chōchorso. 10. cime.
941. 1. chaldo. 2. vita | "li" e chalore .. quiue .. domori [Esse l chaldo move lumido "il freddo lo ferma". 3. chaldo .. focho
.. asse. 4. effolte nebie esspessi nuboli .. spicha de .. effiumi. 5. quele .. apocho apocho .. freda regione [i] e. 6. chaldo .. chol .. essecho .. li assetta laltre. 7. chosi agiugnēdo .. chō .. osschure .. esspesso sono [portale]. 8. fano
. graueza. 9. chadano chōispessa piogia esselchaldo .. sagivgnie. 10. focho .. fredo inel .. diacciano e chavsasi.
11. chaldo chettiene .. chome. 12. nvboli [tienè] disuelle .. delle mōtagnie e chōducie le ettielle. 13. mōtagnie le quali
.. li chontinui vssciēdo. 14. chausano i fiumi.

DEL MARE CHE A MOLTI [2]SENPLICI PAR PIÙ ALTO [3]CHE LA TERRA CHE GLI FA LITI.

OF THE SEA, WHICH TO MANY FOOLS APPEARS TO BE HIGHER THAN THE EARTH WHICH FORMS ITS SHORE.

The relative height of the surface of the sea to that of the land (942—945).

[4]*b d* è vna pianvra, donde corre [5]vn fiume al mare, la qual pianu[6]ra à per termine esso mare; e per[7]chè in vero essa terra scoperta nō [8]è nel sito dell' e-qualità, — perchè, seco[9]sì fusse, il fiume non avrebbe mo[10]to—-, onde, moven-dosi, questo sito [11]à piutosto da essere detto spiagg[12]ia che pianvra; e così essa pia[13]nura *d b* termina in tal modo [14]colla spera dell' acqua che, chi la produ[15]cesse in continua rettitudine in *b a*, [16]essa entrerebbe sotto il mare, e [17]di qui nasce che 'l mar *a c b* pare più alto che la terra discoperta.

[18]Naturalmēte nes[19]suna parte della [20]terra discoperta da [21]l'acqua fia mai [22]più bassa che la [23]superfitie della [24]spera d'essa acqua.

b d is a plain through which a river flows to the sea; this plain ends at the sea, and since in fact the dry land that is un-covered is not perfectly level—for, if it were, the river would have no motion—as the river does move, this place is a slope rather than a plain; hence this plain *d b* so ends where the sphere of water begins that if it were extended in a continuous line to *b a* it would go down beneath the sea, whence it follows that the sea *a c b* looks higher than the dry land.

Obviously no portions of dry land left uncovered by water can ever be lower than the surface of the watery sphere.

D'ALCUNI CHE DICONO · L'ACQUA ESSERE · PIV · ALTA · CHE LA TERRA · SCOPERTA.

OF CERTAIN PERSONS WHO SAY THE WATERS WERE HIGHER THAN THE DRY LAND.

[2]Cierto · non poca · ammiratione · mi da · la comvne · opinione fatta cōtro · al uero dallo vniversale [3]cōcorso · de' givditi · delli omini ·, e questo · è che tutti · s'accordano · che la superfitie · del mare [4]sia · piv · alta · che l'altissime · cime delle · mōtagnie ·, alle-gādo molte · vane e puerili · ragioni, [5]cōtro ai quali · io n'allegherò · solo · vna · senplie e brieve ragione ·; Noi vediamo chiaro, che [6]se si toglie · via · l'argine · al mare ·, che lui · vestirà · la terra e faralla di per-fetta rotōdità; [7]or cōsidera · quāta · terra si leuerebbe a fare che l'ōde marine coprissino [8]il mōdo; adūque ciò, che si leuasse, sarebbe piv · alto · che la riua del mare.

Certainly I wonder not a little at the common opinion which is contrary to truth, but held by the universal consent of the judgment of men. And this is that all are agreed that the surface of the sea is higher than the highest peaks of the mountains; and they allege many vain and childish reasons, against which I will allege only one simple and short reason: We see plainly that if we could remove the shores of the sea, it would invest the whole earth and make it a perfect sphere. Now, consider how much earth would be carried away to enable the waves of the sea to cover the world; there-fore that which would be carried away must be higher than the sea-shore.

942. 2. senpici par pu. 3. chella . . chelli. 4. a d e vna. 5. lacqual. 6. essesso. 9. fussi . . arebbe. 14. dellacq"a". 15. cessi. 16. enterebbe. 17. nassce. *On the margin is written:* cella tera
di scoperta.

Lines 18—24 are also written on the margin. 18. ne. 22. chella. 24. acq"a".

943. 1. dichano lacq"a" . . chella. 2. pocha amiratione . . chomvne oppenione fatto chōtra. 3. chōchorso . . ecquesto e chet-tutti sachordano chella. 4. chellaltissime . . ragione. 5. nalegero . . vedemo. 6. tolglie . . chellui vesstira effaralla . . retōdita. 7. chōsidera [vn pccha] . . affare chellōde . . choprissino. 8. chessi leuassi . . chella.

A. 56a]   944.

OPINIONE D'ALCUNI · CHE DICONO · CHE L'AC-
QUA D' ALCUNI ²MARI È PIV ALTA CHE LE PIV
ALTE SOMMITÀ DE'MŌTI, ³E PERÒ · SIA SOSPĪTA
L'ACQUA · A ESSE SŌMITÀ.

THE OPINION OF SOME PERSONS WHO SAY THAT
THE WATER OF SOME SEAS IS HIGHER THAN THE
HIGHEST SUMMITS OF MOUNTAINS; AND NEVER-
THELESS THE WATER WAS FORCED UP TO
THESE SUMMITS.

⁴L'acqua nō si moverà · da loco a loco
· se la bassezza · non la tira; E per corso
⁵naturale · nō potrà · mai · ritornare · a altezza
· simile · al primo loco, do⁶ve
nel uscire de' mōti si mostrò
· al cielo ·; E quella · parte
del mare ·, che ⁷cō falsa ·
imaginatione · tu · diciesti · essere si alta ·, che uersaua ·
per le cime · de⁸li alti · mōti,
· per tāti seculi · sarebbe · cō-
sumata · e uersata per l'uscita
d'esse ⁹mōtagnie; Tu puoi
bene pēsare · che tāto tēpo
che Tigris ed Eufrates

Water would not move from place to
place if it were not that it seeks the lowest
level and by a natural consequence it never
can return to a height like that
of the place where it first on
issuing from the mountain
came to light. And that portion of the sea which, in your
vain imagining, you say was
so high that it flowed over the
summits of the high mountains,
for so many centuries would be
swallowed up and poured out
again through the issue from
these mountains. You can well imagine that
all the time that Tigris and Euphrates

A. 56b]   945.

ànno · versato · per le · sommità de' mōti
· Armeni ·, che si può · credere · che tutta
l'acqua dell'ocieano ²sia · moltissime · volte
· passata · per dette · bocche ·; or non credi tu che 'l Nilo · abbi messo · piv ³acqua ·
ī mare · che non è · al presente tutto lo elemēto · dell' acqua ·? cierto · sì; · e se detta ·
acqua ⁴fusse · caduta fori di questo · corpo
· della terra ·, questa machina · sarebbe già
lūgo tēpo ⁵stata sāza acqua, sichè si può
cōcludere · che l'acqua vadi dai fiumi al
mare e dal mare ⁶ai fivmi, senpre così
raggirādo e voltādosi, e che tutto · il mare
· e i fivmi sieno passati per la bocca del
Nilo infinite volte.

have flowed from the summits of the
mountains of Armenia, it must be believed
that all the water of the ocean has passed
very many times through these mouths.
And do you not believe that the Nile must
have sent more water into the sea than at
present exists of all the element of water?
Undoubtedly, yes. And if all this water
had fallen away from this body of the earth,
this terrestrial machine would long since
have been without water. Whence we may
conclude that the water goes from the rivers
to the sea, and from the sea to the rivers, thus
constantly circulating and returning, and that
all the sea and the rivers have passed through the
mouth of the Nile an infinite number of times.

944. 1. Opemione dalchuni che dichano chellacqua dalchuni. 2. alta [che alchu] chelle . . somita. 4. Lacq"a" . . dalocho al-
locho sella bassezza . . chorso. 5. alteza . . locho. 6. usscire . . Ecquella. 7. chō . . dicievi. 8. tāte sechuli sarebe chō
sumata . . lusscita. 9. mōtagnia . . chettāto . . chettigris.

945. 1. mōti ermini che si po . . che | "tutta"llacq"a". 2. boche . . abi. 3. imare . . e "al presēte" tutto . . esse. 4. fussi
chaduta . . chorpo . . tera . . sarebe. 5. chōchiudere. 6. ragirādo . . chettutto . . sia pasato . . bocha; *the last two words*
infinite volte *are written on the margin.*

945. *Mōti Armeni, Ermini* in the original, in M.
RAVAISSON's transcript "*monti ernini [le loro ruine?]*".
He renders this "*Le Tigre et l'Euphrate se sont dé-
versés par les sommets des montagnes [avec leurs eaux
destructives?] on peut cro're*" &c. Leonardo always
writes *Ermini, Erminia,* for *Armeni, Armenia* (Arabic:

Irminiah). M. RAVAISSON also deviates from the
original in his translation of the following passage: "*Or tu ne crois pas que le Nil ait mis plus
d'eau dans la mer qu'il n'y en a à présent dans tout
l'élément de l'eau. Il est certain que si cette eau était
tombée*" &c.

II.

ON THE OCEAN.

946.

PERCHÈ L'ACQUA È SALSA.

Refutation of Pliny's theory as to the saltness of the sea (946. 947).

[2]Dicie Plinio nel 2° suo libro, al 103 ca[3]pitolo, che l'acqua del mare è salata per- chè [4]l'ardore del sole secca l'umi[5]do e quello succia, e questo al mare, che [6]molto s'allarga, dà sapore di sale; [7]Ma questo nō si cōciede, perchè se la salsedine [8]del mare avesse cavsa dallo ardore del sole, [9]e' non è dubbio che tanto maggiormente li laghi, stagni e paduli [10]sarebbono più insalati, quāto [11]le loro acque son manco mobili e di [12]minore profondità, e la esperiēzia ci mo[13]stra il contrario; tali paduli ci mostrā [14]le loro acque essere al tutto private di sal[15]sedine; Ancora s'assegnia da Plinio nel medesimo[16]capitolo che tal salsedine

WHY WATER IS SALT.

Pliny says in his second book, chapter 103, that the water of the sea is salt because the heat of the sun dries up the moisture and drinks it up; and this gives to the wide stretching sea the savour of salt. But this cannot be admitted, because if the saltness of the sea were caused by the heat of the sun, there can be no doubt that lakes, pools and marshes would be so much the more salt, as their waters have less motion and are of less depth; but experience shows us, on the contrary, that these lakes have their waters quite free from salt. Again it is stated by Pliny in the same chapter that this saltness might originate,

---

946. 1. essalsa. 2. a 103 capitoli. 3. chellacqua . . essalata. 4. [li razi solari] Lardore . . secha "abrōzre e (?)" lumi. 5. ecquello . . ecquesto. 6. sallargha . . sale | [Qui]. 7. Macquesto . . sella. 8. avessi chausa dello. 9. chelli "tanto magiormente" laghi. 10. [dove lacque] sarebbono. 11. [le] le . . mancho . . eddi. 12. ella . . mos. 13. in chontrario . . mosstrā. 14. tucto. 15. Acora sasegnia [nel me]. 16. chapitolo chettal. 17. nassciere . . leuato | "ne ogni" porte. 18. dolcie [dellacq"a" ressta lasspra]

---

946. See PLINY, Hist. Nat. II, CIII [C]. *Itaque Solis ardore siccatur liquor: et hoc esse masculum sidus accepimus, torrens cuncta sorbensque.* (cp. CIV.) *Sic mari late patenti saporem incoqui salis, aut quia exhausto inde dulci tenuique, quod facillime trahat vis ignea, omne asperius crassiusque linquatur: ideo summa aequorum aqua dulciorem profundam; hanc esse veriorem causam, quam quod mare terrae sudor sit aeternus: aut quia plurimum ex arido misceatur illi vapore: aut quia terrae natura sicut medicatas aquas inficiat . .* (cp. CV): *altissimum mare XV. stadiorum Fabianus tradit. Alii n Ponto coadverso Coraxorum gentis (vocant Βαθέα Ponti) trecentis fere a continenti stadiis immensam altitudinem maris tradunt, vadis nunquam repertis.* (cp. CVI [CIII]) *Mirabilius id faciunt aquae dulces, juxta mare, ut fistulis emicantes. Nam nec aquarum natura a miraculis cessat. Dulces mari invehuntur, leviores haud dubie. Ideo et marinae, quarum natura gravior, magis invecta sustinent. Quaedam vero et dulces inter se supermeant alias.*

¹⁷potrebbe nasciere, perchè, leuatone ogni ¹⁸dolce e sottile ¹⁹parte, la qual facilmēte il caldo a se ti²⁰ra, rimane la parte più aspra e più ²¹grossa, e per questo l'acqua, che è nella su²²perfitie, è più dolcie che nel fōdo; ²³a questa si cōtradice colle medesime ²⁴sopradette ragioni, cioè che il medesimo ac²⁵caderebbe alli paduli e altre acque che per il cal²⁶do s'asciugano; Ācora fu detto che ²⁷la salsedine del mare è sudore della terra; ²⁸a questo si rispōde che tutte le uene dell'acque ²⁹che penetrano la terra, sarebbono insalate; Ma ³⁰si cōclude la salsedine del mare esser nata ³¹dalle molte vene d'acqua le quali nel ³⁴penetrare la ter³⁵ra trovano ³⁶le mini-³⁷ere del sale, e ³⁸quelle in parte ³⁹si soluono e por⁴⁰tā seco all' o⁴¹cieano e li altri ⁴²mari, d'ō⁴³de mai ¶li nuvo⁴⁴li, seminatori ⁴⁵d'elli fiumi¶ ⁴⁶lo leuano; ed e' sarebbe ⁴⁷più salato il ma⁴⁸re alli nostri tē⁴⁹pi che mai per ⁵⁰alcun altro tē⁵¹po fusse, e se per ⁵²l'auersario si di⁵³cesse, che il tenpo ⁵⁴infinito secchereb⁵⁵be over cōgielereb⁵⁶be il mare in sa⁵⁷le, a questo ⁵⁸si risponde, che ⁵⁹tal sale si rē⁶⁰de alla terra ⁶¹colla liberatione ⁶²d'essa terra, che ⁶³s'inalza col suo ⁶⁴acquistato sale, ⁶⁵e li fiumi lo rendo-⁶⁶no alla sōmersa terra.

because all the sweet and subtle portions which the heat attracts easily being taken away, the more bitter and coarser part will remain, and thus the water on the surface is fresher than at the bottom [22]; but this is contradicted by the same reason given above, which is, that the same thing would happen in marshes and other waters, which are dried up by the heat. Again, it has been said that the saltness of the sea is the sweat of the earth; to this it may be answered that all the springs of water which penetrate through the earth, would then be salt. But the conclusion is, that the saltness of the sea must proceed from the many springs of water which, as they penetrate into the earth, find mines of salt and these they dissolve in part, and carry with them to the ocean and the other seas, whence the clouds, the begetters of rivers, never carry it up. And the sea would be salter in our times than ever it was at any time; and if the adversary were to say that in infinite time the sea would dry up or congeal into salt, to this I answer that this salt is restored to the earth by the setting free of that part of the earth which rises out of the sea with the salt it has acquired, and the rivers return it to the earth under the sea.

G. 49a]   947.

Terza e vlti²ma ragione di³remo, il sale ⁴essere in tutte ⁵le cose create ⁶e questo c' ī⁷segniano ⁸le acque passa⁹te per tutte le ci¹⁰eneri e calci¹¹ni delle cose ¹²bruciate, e le ¹³orine di qua¹⁴lūche anima¹⁵le e le super¹⁶fluità usci¹⁷te de' lor cor¹⁸pi e le terre, ¹⁹nelle quali si ²⁰cōuertono ²¹le corrutioni ²²di tutte le cose.

²³Ma a dire meglio, essendo dato il mōdo eterno, egli è neciessario ²⁴che li sua popoli sieno ācora loro eterni; ōde ²⁵eternalmēte fu e sarebbe la spetie vmana cōsu²⁶matricie del sale; e se tutta la massa

For the third and last reason we will say that salt is in all created things; and this we learn from water passed over the ashes and cinders of burnt things; and the urine of every animal, and the superfluities issuing from their bodies, and the earth into which all things are converted by corruption.

But,—to put it better,—given that the world is everlasting, it must be admitted that its population will also be eternal; hence the human species has eternally been and would be consumers of salt; and if all the mass of the earth were to be turned into salt, it

essottile. 19. chaldo asseti. 20. asspra. 22. fōdo ‖ contro. 23. acquessta si cōtraddicie cholle. 25. chaderebbe . . chal. 26. sasscingano Āchora fuddetto. 27. essudore. 28. acquessto . . chettutte. *Lines* 32—66 *are written on the margin.* 32. ¶finiscie quel che. 33. mācha di socto.¶ 35. trovano [le ve]. 36. [ne del 5] le. 40. secho alloc. 41. elli. 42. mari [dove] dō. 43. de mai (li nuvo. 45. delli fiumi) mai. 46. nō leuano ede "sare". 48. nosstri. 50. alchū. 51. fussi esse. 53. ciessi. 54. sechere. 55. cōgielere. 57. acquesto. 59. sare. 61. cholla. 65. elli . . rēda. 66. somersa.

947. 3. direno . . sale es. 5. chose. 6. ecquessto. 7. segnia [l'echo]. 10. enere e chalci. 11. ne. 12. elle. 15. elle. 16. fruita vssci. 17. de de. 18. elle. 19. nelle. 20. cōuertano. *Lines* 1—27 *are written on the margin along the text no* 1201, *under which is the text of lines* 23—39, *parallel with the lines* 40—60. 23. essendo | "dato" il mōdo "etterno", egli. 24. chelli . . āchora . . ecterni. 25. etternalmēte . . essarebbe lasspetie . . cōsu. 26. essettutta. 27. bassterebbe. 28. chonfessare | o

22. Compare No. 948.

della terra fas[27]si sale, non basterebbe alli cibi vmani, per la qual [28]cosa ci bisognia confessare, o che la spetie del sale [29]sia eterna īsieme col mōdo, o che quella [30]mora e rinasca insieme cogli omini d'essa di[31]voratori; Ma se la esperiēza c'insegnia quel [32]non avere morte come per il foco si manife[33]sta, il qual non la cōsuma, e per l'acqua che di tāto si [34]sala di quāto ella in se ne risolue, evaporādo l'a[35]qua, sempre il sale resta nella prima quātità; [36]deve passare per li corpi vmani che in orina, [37]o sudore, o altre superfluità fia ritrovato, e ques[38]to è il sale che ogni anno si porta alle città; adūque [39]cavasi il sale de' lochi, dov'è piscia;—li porci e li vēti marini sō salati;—

[40]Diremo che la [41]pioggia pene[42]tratrice della [43]terra sia que[44]lla, ch'è sotto [45]alli fonda[46]mēti delle cit[47]tà e popoli, [48]e sia quella che [49]per li meati del[50]la terra rē[51]da la salsedi[52]ne leuata dal [53]mare, e che [54]la mutatiō [55]del mare, sta[56]to sopra tutti [57]li monti, lo la[58]sci per le minie[59]re ritrovate [60]in essi monti ecc.

would not suffice for all human food [27]; whence we are forced to admit, either that the species of salt must be everlasting like the world, or that it dies and is born again like the men who devour it. But as experience teaches us that it does not die, as is evident by fire, which does not consume it, and by water which becomes salt in proportion to the quantity dissolved in it,—and when it is evaporated the salt always remains in the original quantity—it must pass through the bodies of men either in the urine or the sweat or other excretions where it is found again; and as much salt is thus got rid of as is carried every year into towns; therefore salt is dug in places where there is urine.—Sea hogs and sea winds are salt.

We will say that the rains which penetrate the earth are what is under the foundations of cities with their inhabitants, and are what restore through the internal passages of the earth the saltness taken from the sea; and that the change in the place of the sea, which has been over all the mountains, caused it to be left there in the mines found in those mountains,&c.

Leic. 21 b]   **948.**

The characteristics of sea water (948. 949).

L'acque de' mari salati son dolci nelle sua grā profondità.

The waters of the salt sea are fresh at the greatest depths.

G. 38 a]   **949.**

COME L'OCEANO NŌ PE[2]NETRA INFRA LA TERRA.

[3]L'oceano nō penetra infra la terra, e que[4]sto c'insegniano le molte e varie vene d'acque dol[5]ci, le quali in diuersi lochi d'esso oceano pene[6]trano dal fondo alla sua superfitie; Ancora il me[7]desimo dimostrano li pozzi fatti dopo lo spa[8]tio d'ū miglio remoti dal detto ocieano, [9]li quali s'enpiano d'acqua dolcie, e questo ac[10]cade perchè l'acqua dolcie è più sottile che l'ac[11]qua salata, e per cōseguēza più penetra[12]tiva.

[13]Qual pesa più, [14]o l'acqua ghiac[15]ciata o la nō [16]ghiacciata?

THAT THE OCEAN DOES NOT PENETRATE UNDER THE EARTH.

The ocean does not penetrate under the earth, and this we learn from the many and various springs of fresh water which, in many parts of the ocean make their way up from the bottom to the surface. The same thing is farther proved by wells dug beyond the distance of a mile from the said ocean, which fill with fresh water; and this happens because the fresh water is lighter than salt water and consequently more penetrating.

Which weighs most, water when frozen or when not frozen?

chella. 29. etterna . . chol . . checquella. 30. rinascca . . chogli. 31. Massella esisperiēza. 32. focho. 33. nolla. 35. sepre . . ressta. 36. ne vale passare. 37. ritrorato ecq"a". 38. ōni. 39. pisscia. 40. direno chelle. 41. piogie. 42. tratrici. 43. sien. 44. lla. 46. delli ci. 48. sie quella che. 49. de. 60. nessi.

949. loccieano. 2. infralla. 3. loccieano . . infralla . . ecques. 4. cinsegnia . . euuarie. 5. occieano "pe" nene. 7. dimostrano li pozi . . losspa. 8. miglio [li quali] remōti. 9. ecquessto. 10. chade . . chellac. 11. piu [soct] penetra. *Lines* 13—16 *are written on the margin.* 14. diac. 15. olla. 16. diacciata. 17. dole. 18. chella. 20. chellacqua . . chōtro.

947. l. 27. That is, on the supposition that salt, once consumed, disappears for ever.

PIÙ PENETRA L'ACQUA DOLCE CŌTRO [18]AL-
L'ACQUA SALSA, CHE LA SALSA CŌTRO AL[19]LA
DOLCIE.

[20]Che l'acqua dolcie penetri più cōtro
all'ac[21]qua salsa, che essa salsa cōtro alla
dolcie, ci [22]lo manifesta vna sottil tela asci-
utta e [23]vechia, pendente con equal bassezza [24]colli sua oppositi stremi nelle due
varie [25]acque, delle quali le lor superfitie
siē [26]d'equal bassezza, e allor si vedrà ele-
var[29]si in alto infra essa pezza tanto più
l'acqua [28]dolcie, che la salsa, quanto la
dolcie è più [29]lieve che essa salsa.

FRESH WATER PENETRATES MORE AGAINST SALT
WATER THAN SALT WATER AGAINST FRESH
WATER.

That fresh water penetrates more against
salt water, than salt water against fresh is
proved by a thin cloth dry and old,
hanging with the two opposite ends equally
low in the two different waters, the surfaces
of which are at an equal level; and it will
then be seen how much higher the fresh
water will rise in this piece of linen than the
salt; by so much is the fresh lighter than
the salt.

C. A. 157*b*; 466*a*]　　　**950.**

Tutti li mari mediterrani e li [2]golfi
d'essi mari sō fatti da fi[3]vmi che versano
in mare.

All inland seas and the gulfs of those
seas, are made by rivers which flow into
the sea.

On the for-
mation of
Gulfs
(950. 951).

C. A. 83*b*; 240*b*]　　　**951.**

QUI SI RENDE RAGIONE DELLI EFFETTI FATTI
DALLE ACQUE NEL PROPOSITO SITO.

[2]Tutti li laghi e tutti li golfi del mare
e tutti li mari mediterrani nascono dalli
fiumi, che in quelli spā[3]dono le loro acque,
e dalli impedimēti della loro declinatione
[4]nel Mare Mediterrano, diuisore d'Africa
dall'Europa, e dell'Europa dall'Asia, mediāte il Nilo e Tanai che in [5]lui versano
le loro acque; Si domāda, quale inpedi-
mēto è maggiore a proibire il corso delle
sue acque, che nō si renda all'oceano.

HERE THE REASON IS GIVEN OF THE EFFECTS
PRODUCED BY THE WATERS IN THE ABOVE MEN-
TIONED PLACE.

All the lakes and all the gulfs of the sea
and all inland seas are due to rivers which
distribute their waters into them, and from im-
pediments in their downfall into the Mediterranean—which divides Africa from Europe
and Europe from Asia by means of the Nile
and the Don which pour their waters into it.
It is asked what impediment is great enough to stop the course of the waters
which do not reach the ocean.

Ash. III. 25*a*]　　　**952.**

DE ONDA.

[2]L'onda del mare
senpre ruina [3]dinan-
ti alla sua basa, e
quella par[4]te del col-
mo si troverà più
bassa che [5]prima era
più alta.

OF WAVES.

A wave of the
sea always breaks in
front of its base,
and that portion of
the crest will then be
lowest which before
was highest.

On the en-
croachments
of the sea on
the land and
vice versa
(952—954).

21. dolcie cie. 22. assciuta eo. 23. pendente [cholli] chon. 24. cholli. 26. vedra mē eleua "r". 27. si [eleua] in . . tantu.
28. chella . . he piu.
950. 1. elli. 2. gholfi.
951. 1. effecti..delle. 2. ettuttili gholfi . . etti ttutti . . nasschano. 3. Dano le . . ed dalli la pedimēti. 4. mediterano . . ettanai
che il. 5. domāde . . occieano.
952. 2. Londa [delle] del. 3. ecquella. 4. cholmo. 5. alta sara poi piu bas.

952. The page of FRANCESCO DI GIORGIO'S
Trattato, on which Leonardo has written this remark,
contains some notes on the construction of dams,
harbours &c.

Leic. 20 a]   953.

Come le riue del ma²re al continvo acquistano terreno inuerso il mezzo del mare; Come li scogli e promontori ³ de' mari al continvo ruinano e si consumano; Come i mediterrani scopriranno i lor fondi all'aria e sol ri⁴serberanno il canale al maggior fiume, che dentro vi metta, il quale correrà all'oceano e iui uerse⁵rà le sue acque insieme con quelle di tutti i fiumi, che cō seco s'accōpagnano.

That the shores of the sea constantly acquire more soil towards the middle of the sea; that the rocks and promontories of the sea are constantly being ruined and worn away; that the Mediterranean seas will in time discover their bottom to the air, and all that will be left will be the channel of the greatest river that enters it; and this will run to the ocean and pour its waters into that with those of all the rivers that are its tributaries.

Leic. 27 b]   954.

Come il fiume del Po in brieve tenpo secca il mare Adriano nel ² medesimo modo ch'elli asseccò grā parte di Lonbardia.

How the river Po, in a short time might dry up the Adriatic sea in the same way as it has dried up a large part of Lombardy.

C. A. 162 b; 482 a]   955.

The ebb and flow of the tide (955—960)

¶ Dove è maggior quātità d'acqua, ² quivi è maggior flusso e riflusso; e 'l ³ contrario fa nelle acque strette. ¶
⁴ Guarda se 'l mare è nella soma cre-scie⁵te quādo la luna è nel mezzo del tuo emi⁶sphero.

Where there is a larger quantity of water, there is a greater flow and ebb, but the contrary in narrow waters.
Look whether the sea is at its greatest flow when the moon is half way over our hemisphere [on the meridian].

Leic. 17 b]   956.

Se 'l flusso e riflusso nasce dalla luna o sole, overo è l'ali²tare di questa terrestre machina; Come il flusso e riflusso è vario in diuersi paesi e mari.

Whether the flow and ebb are caused by the moon or the sun, or are the breathing of this terrestrial machine. That the flow and ebb are different in different countries and seas.

Leic. 5 a]   957.

Libro 9° delli scontri de' fiumi e lor flusso e riflusso; e la medesima ² causa lo crea nel mare per causa dello stretto di Gibiltar, e ancora accade per le uoragini.

Book 9 of the meeting of rivers and their flow and ebb. The cause is the same in the sea, where it is caused by the straits of Gibraltar. And again it is caused by whirlpools.

953. 2. acquisstano . . mezo . . liscogli. 3. essi chonsumano Come e . . scopiranno . . essol. 4. magor. 5. cōsecho sacōpagnano.
954. 1. secha. 2. assecho.
955. 1. he magior. 2. frusso e refrusso. 4. gharda. 5. mezo.
956. 1. frusso e refrusso nassce. 2. tereste . . frusso e refrusso.
957. 1. isscontri . . ellor frusso e refrusso ella. 2. chausa . . strett[i] o di gibiltar . . achade . . voragine.

956. 1. Allusion may here be made to the my-thological explanation of the ebb and flow given in the Edda. Utgardloki says to Thor (Gylfaginning 48): "When thou wert drinking out of the horn, and it seemed to thee that it was slow in emptying a wonder befell, which I should not have believed possible: the other end of the horn lay in the sea, which thou sawest not; but when thou shalt go to the sea, thou shalt see how much thou hast drunk out of it. And that men now call the ebb tide."
Several passages in various manuscripts treat of the ebb and flow. In collecting them I have been guided by the rule only to transcribe those which named some particular spot.

958.

DEL FLUSSO E RIFLUSSO.

[2]Tutti li mari ànno il lor flusso e riflusso in v̄ medesimo tempo, ma pare variarsi, perchè li giorni nō co[3]minciano in vn medesimo tenpo in tutto l'universo, cōciosiachè, quādo nel nostro emisperio è mezzo [4]giorno, nell' opposito emisperio è mezzanotte ·, e nelle congiuntioni oriētali dell' uno e del' altro emispe[5]rio comincia la notte che corre dirieto al giorno, e nelle congiūtioni occidentali d'essi emisperi comincia [6]il giorno che seguita la notte dalla sua opposita parte ·; adunque è conchiuso che, ancora che 'l [7]detto accrescimēto e diminvitione delle altezze de' mari sien fatte in vn [8]medesimo tenpo, essi mostrano variarsi per le già dette cagioni; sono adunque sōmerse le acque [9]nelle uene partite dai fondi de' mari, le quali ramificano dentro al corpo della terra, e rispondono [10]al nascimento de' fiumi ·, i quali al continvo tolgono dal fondo il mare al mare andato; è tolto innvme[11]rabili volte nella superfitie un mare al mare; E se tu volessi, che la luna, apparendo all'orientale parte [12]del Mare Mediterrano, comīciasse ad attrarre a se l'acque del mare, ne seguirebbe che inmediate [13]se ne vedrebbe la speriēza al fine oriētale di tal mare predetto; Ancora essendo il Mar Medi[14]terrano circa alla ottava parte della circūferenza della spera dell acqua, per essere lui [15]lungo 3 mila miglia, e 'l flusso e riflusso nō fa se nō 4 volte in 24 ore, e' nō s'accorderebbe tale [16]effetto col tenpo d'esse 24 ore, se esso Mare Mediterrā nō fusse lungo semila miglia, perchè [17]se lo spogliamēto di tanto mare avesse a passare per lo stretto di Gibiltar nel correr dietro [18]alla luna, e' sarebbe si grāde il corso delle acque per tale stretto, e s'alzerebbe in tāta altezza, [19]che dopo esso stretto farebbe tal corso, che per molte miglia infra l'oceano farebbe inōdatione e bolli[20]mēti grandissimi, per la qual cosa sarebbe inpossibile passarui, e dopo questo · subito l'ocea[21]no rēderebbe colla medesima furia l'acque ricevute, dōnde esso le riceve;

OF THE FLOW AND EBB.

All seas have their flow and ebb in the same period, but they seem to vary because the days do not begin at the same time throughout the universe; in such wise as that when it is midday in our hemisphere, it is midnight in the opposite hemisphere; and at the Eastern boundary of the two hemispheres the night begins which follows on the day, and at the Western boundary of these hemispheres begins the day, which follows the night from the opposite side. Hence it is to be inferred that the above mentioned swelling and diminution in the height of the seas, although they take place in one and the same space of time, are seen to vary from the above mentioned causes. The waters are then withdrawn into the fissures which start from the depths of the sea and which ramify inside the body of the earth, corresponding to the sources of rivers, which are constantly taking from the bottom of the sea the water which has flowed into it. A sea of water is incessantly being drawn off from the surface of the sea. And if you should think that the moon, rising at the Eastern end of the Mediterranean sea must there begin to attract to herself the waters of the sea, it would follow that we must at once see the effect of it at the Eastern end of that sea. Again, as the Mediterranean sea is about the eighth part of the circumference of the aqueous sphere, being 3000 miles long, while the flow and ebb only occur 4 times in 24 hours, these results would not agree with the time of 24 hours, unless this Mediterranean sea were six thousand miles in length; because if such a superabundance of water had to pass through the straits of Gibraltar in running behind the moon, the rush of the water through that strait would be so great, and would rise to such a height, that beyond the straits it would for many miles rush so violently into the ocean as to cause floods and tremendous seething, so that it would be impossible to pass through. This agitated ocean would afterwards return the waters it

---

958. 1. frusso e refrusso. 2. frusso e refrusso nv̄ . . gorni nō cho- 3. mincano. 3. concosia . . nosstro ·: mez. 4. gorno . . oposito . . mezanotte . . conguntioni . . emisspe. 5. cominca . . gorno . . congūtioni ocidentali . . comica. 6. gorno . . oposita. 7. acresscimēto . . dellellalteze de mari ancora chelle . . nvn. 8. mostra . . chagoni . . somerse. 9. defondi ramifichano . . rispondano. 10. nasscimento De . . tolgano "del fondo" [e rendano] il . . andato "e tolto" invmerabili volte "nella superfitie" umare . . Essettu . . chella . . aparendo. 12. mediterano comicassi . . asse. 13. lassperiēza . . mare "predetto". 14. terano circha . . acqu"a". 15. lungho . . frusso e refrusso . . sacorderebe. 16. mediterā fussi lungho. 17. sello . . avessi . . dirie. 18. sarebe . . essalzerebe. 19. hesso . . infrall . . ebbolli. 21. rederebbe . . riceve . . echoche. 22. passerebe . .

ecco che adūque mai si ²²passerebbe per tale stretto·, e la speriēza mostra che d'ogni ora vi si passa, saluo che quādo il uento ²³viē per la linia della corrēte, allora il riflusso forte s'aumēta·; Il mare non alza l'acqua nelli ²⁴stretti che ànno vscita ma ben s'ingorga e si ritarda dināti a quelli·, onde con furioso moto ²⁵poi ristora il tempo del suo ritardamēto insino al fin del suo moto riflesso.

had received with equal fury to the place they had come from, so that no one ever could pass through those straits. Now experience shows that at every hour they are passed in safety, but when the wind sets in the same direction as the current, the strong ebb increases [23]. The sea does not raise the water that has issued from the straits, but it checks them and this retards the tide; then it makes up with furious haste for the time it has lost until the end of the ebb movement.

Leic. 13 a]   959.

Come jl flusso e riflusso non è generale, perchè ²in riuiera di Genova non fa niēte, a Vinegia due braccia, tra la Inghilterra e Fiandra fa 18 braccia; ³Come per lo stretto di Sicilia la corrēte è grādissima, perchè di lì passā tutte l'acque de' fiumi che uersā ⁴nel Mare Adriatico.

That the flow and ebb are not general; for on the shore at Genoa there is none, at Venice two braccia, between England and Flanders 18 braccia. That in the straits of Sicily the current is very strong because all the waters from the rivers that flow into the Adriatic pass there.

Leic. 35 a]   960.

Nelle parti occidentali·, appresso alla Fiandra, il mare cresce e māca ogni 6 ore circa 20 braccia, ²e 22 quādo la luna è in suo fauore, ma le 20 braccia è il suo ordinario, il quale ordinario manifestamēte si uede ³non essere per cavsa della luna; Questa varietà del crescere e discrescere del mare ogni 6· ore può ⁴accadere per le ringorgationi delle acque, le quali son condotte nel Mare Mediterrano da quella quantità de' fiu⁵mi dell'Africa Asia ed Evropa, che in esso mare versano le loro acque, le quali per lo stretto di Gibiltar infra Abila

In the West, near to Flanders, the sea rises and decreases every 6 hours about 20 braccia, and 22 when the moon is in its favour; but 20 braccia is the general rule, and this rule, as it is evident, cannot have the moon for its cause. This variation in the increase and decrease of the sea every 6 hours may arise from the damming up of the waters, which are poured into the Mediterranean by the quantity of rivers from Africa, Asia and Europe, which flow into that sea, and the waters which are given to it by those rivers; it pours them to the ocean

ella . . ora usi passa. 23. refrusso . . lacq"a". 24. vscita [ne in quelli] ma ben siningorgha "essiritarda . . acquelli onde poi con. 25. tenpo [cheche] del . . refresso.

959. 1. frusso e refrusso. 2. genva . . uinegia due br tralla ingilterra . . 18 br. 3. cicilia lacorēte. 4. adriatico.

960. 1. parte hoccidentale . . cressce "e mācha . . circha 20 bra. 2. 20 br quale "ordinario". 3. chavsa . . cressciere e discresscere . . ore po. 4. achadere . . mediterano da "quella". 5. africha . . versano "le loro acque" le . . abile e calpe.

958. 23. In attempting to get out of the Mediterranean, vessels are sometimes detained for a considerable time; not merely by the causes mentioned by Leonardo but by the constant current flowing eastwards through the middle of the straits of Gibraltar.

959. A few more recent data may be given here to facilitate comparison. In the Adriatic the tide rises 2 and ¹/₂ feet, at Terracina 1¹/₄. In the English channel between Calais and Kent it rises from 18 to 20 feet. In the straits of Messina it rises no more than 2 ¹/₂ feet, and that only in stormy weather, but the current is all the stronger. When Leo-

nardo accounts for this by the southward flow of all the Italian rivers along the coasts, the explanation is at least based on a correct observation; namely that a steady current flows southwards along the coast of Calabria and another northwards, along the shores of Sicily; he seems to infer, from the direction of the fiist, that the tide in the Adriatic is caused by it.

960. 5. *Abila*, Lat. *Abyla*, Gr. 'Aβύλη, now *Sierra Ximiera* near Ceuta; *Calpe*, Lat. *Calpe*. Gr. Κάλπη, now Gibraltar. Leonardo here uses the ancient names of the rocks, which were known as the Pillars of Hercules.

e Calpe [6]promōtori rende all'occeano le acque che da essi fiumi li son date, ɉl quale oceano, astendendosi [7]infra le isole d'Inghilterra e l'altre più settētrionali, si uiene a ringorgare e tenere in collo per diuersi golfi, [8]li quali, essendo tali mari discostatisi colla lor superfitie dal centro del mōdo·, ànno acquistato peso, il quale, [9]poichè supera la potentia dell'avenimēto delle acque che lo cavsauano, essa acqua ripiglia im[10]peto in contrario al suo avenimēto, e fa impeto contro alli stretti, che li davano l'acque e massime fa [11]contra lo stretto di Gibiltar, il quale per alquāto spatio di tenpo rimā ringorgato e viene a riseruarsi tut[12]te l'acque che di novo in tal tenpo li sō date dalli già detti fiumi, e questa mi pare una delle ragioni che [13]si potrebbe assegnare della causa d'esso flusso e riflusso, come nella 21ª del 4ª della mia teori[14]ca è provato.

through the straits of Gibraltar, between Abila and Calpe[5]. That ocean extends to the island of England and others farther North, and it becomes dammed up and kept high in various gulfs. These, being seas of which the surface is remote from the centre of the earth, have acquired a weight, which as it is greater than the force of the incoming waters which cause it, gives this water an impetus in the contrary direction to that in which it came and it is borne back to meet the waters coming out of the straits; and this it does most against the straits of Gibraltar; these, so long as this goes on, remain dammed up and all the water which is poured out meanwhile by the aforementioned rivers, is pent up [in the Mediterranean]; and this might be assigned as the cause of its flow and ebb, as is shown in the 21st of the 4th of my theory.

6. asslendendosi.   7. infralle isola digilterra ellaltre . . settātrionali . . ettenere.   8. cholla . . del mō . ano.   9. chello . . ripiglia ē.   10. peto . . inpito . . chelli.   12. ta lacq"a`' . . ga detti . . ecquesti . . chausa . . frusso e refrusso comi.   14. cha e.

III.

SUBTERRANEAN WATER COURSES.

C. A. 157 *b*; 466 *a*]

961.

Theory of the circulation of the waters (961. 962).

Grādissimi fiumi corrono ²sotto terra.

Very large rivers flow under ground.

Leic. 31 *a*]

962.

Qui s'à a īmagina²re la terra ³segata pel mez⁴zo, e vedrannosi ⁵le pro-fondità ⁶del mare e della ⁷terra; ⁸le uene si partono ⁹da' fondi de' ma¹⁰ri e tessono la ¹¹terra, e si leua¹²no alla sommità ¹³de' mōti, e riuer¹⁴sano per li fiumi e ¹⁵ritor-nano al ma¹⁶re.

This is meant to represent the earth cut through in the middle, showing the depths of the sea and of the earth; the waters start from the bottom of the seas, and ramifying through the earth they rise to the summits of the mountains, flowing back by the rivers and returning to the sea.

Leic. 21 *b*]

963.

Observations in support of the hypothe-sis (963—969).

Raggirasi l'acqua con cōtinvo moto dal-l'infime profondità de' mari alle altissime sōmità de' mōti, non osseruando ²la natura delle cose graui, e in questo caso fanno come il sangue delli animali, che sempre si ³moue dal mare del core e scorre alla sōmità delle loro teste, e quiui rōponsi le uene, come si uede ⁴una vena rotta nel naso, che tutto il sangue da basso si leua

The waters circulate with constant motion from the utmost depths of the sea to the highest summits of the mountains, not obeying the nature of heavy matter; and in this case it acts as does the blood of animals which is always moving from the sea of the heart and flows to the top of their heads; and here it is that veins burst—as one may see when a vein bursts in the nose, that all the blood

961. 1. corā.

962. 4. uedrassi. 7. [e come]. 8. partā. 10. ettessano. 11. essi.

963. 1. Rogirāsi. 2. fa . . animati. 3. move [dal lago] "dal mare" del . . tesste . . e chi quiui rōpasi. 4. chettutto . . àlteza

963. The greater part of this passage has been given as No. 849 in the section on Anatomy.

alla altezza della rotta vena; ⁵ Quando l'acqua escie della rotta vena della terra, essa osserua la natura dell'altre cose piv gravi ⁶che l'aria, onde senpre cerca i lochi bassi. ⁷Vaño ⁸le uene scorrēdo con īfinita ramificatione pel corpo della terra.

from below rises to the level of the burst vein. When the water rushes out of a burst vein in the earth it obeys the nature of other things heavier than the air, whence it always seeks the lowest places. [7] These waters traverse the body of the earth with infinite ramifications.

Br. M. 233 δ]

964.

Quella cavsa, che move li umori in tutte le spetie de' corpi · animati e che cō quelle soccorre a ogni lesione, ²move l'acqua ·dall'infima profōdità del mare alla soma altezza de' mōti, ³e come l'acqua si leua dalle ⁴inferiori parti della vite all'alte tagliature.

The same cause which stirs the humours in every species of animal body and by which every injury is repaired, also moves the waters from the utmost depth of the sea to the greatest heights.

Br. M. 236 δ]

965.

L'acqua è proprio quella che per vitale umore ²di questa · arida terra · è dedicata·, e ³quella cavsa che la move · per le sue rami⁴ficate vene · cōtro al natural corso del-⁵le cose gravi ·, è proprio quella che mo⁶ve · li umori · in tutte le spetie de' corpi ⁷animati; Ma quella, con sōma āmi⁸ratiō de' sua contem-planti, dall'infima pro⁹fondità del mare · all'altissime somità ¹⁰de' mōti si leua, e per le rotte · vene ver¹¹sando · al basso mare · ritorna, · e di novo ¹²con celerità · sormōta, e all' · āti-detto de¹³sceso · ritorna ·, così dalle parti intrī¹⁴siche · al-l'esteriori ·, così dalle infime alle ¹⁵superiori, voltādo · quādo con naturale cor¹⁶so ruina ·, così insieme cōgiunta, cō ¹⁷cōtinua revolutione, ¹⁸per li terrestri meati si ua raggirādo.

It is the property of water that it con-stitutes the vital human of this arid earth; and the cause which moves it through its ramified veins, against the natural course of heavy matters, is the same property which moves the humours in every spe-cies of animal body. But that which crowns our wonder in contemplating it is, that it rises from the utmost depths of the sea to the highest tops of the mountains, and flowing from the opened veins returns to the low seas; then once more, and with extreme swiftness, it mounts again and returns by the same descent, thus rising from the inside to the outside, and going round from the lowest to the high-est, from whence it rushes down in a natural course. Thus by these two move-ments combined in a constant circulation, it travels through the veins of the earth.

G. 70 a]

966.

SE L'ACQUA PUÒ MŌTARE DAL MARE ²ALLE CIME DELLI MONTI.

WHETHER WATER RISES FROM THE SEA TO THE TOPS OF MOUNTAINS.

³Il mare oceano nō può penetrare ⁴dalle radici alle cime de' mōti che con lui ⁵con-

The water of the ocean cannot make its way from the bases to the tops of the mountains

. . ve "ne". 5. esscie. 6. grave chellaria . . cercha.
964. 1. socore . . lesione. 2. frofōdita . . alteza. 3. come [il sangue] lacq"a". 4. tagliature de. *here the text breaks off.*
965. 1. lacq"a" . . omore. 2. quessta . . dedichata. 4. chōtro · de. 5. chose. 6. omori . . lesspetie. 7. che chōsoma ami. 8. contenplanti | "e che" dall. 10. rocte. 12. cono celerita . . dis. 13. scienso. 15. cho. 17. cōtinua revoluitione siua [ragirādo]. 18. teresti . . ragirādo.
966. 1. sellacq"a" mōtare. 3. occieano. 4. radicie . . collui. 5. sul si leua quato la seccita. 6. Esse. 7. cheppienetra.

finano, ma solo si leua quãdo la secchità
[6]del mõte ne tira; E se per l'aversario la
[7]pioggia, che penetra dalla cima del monte
[8]alle radici sua, che col mare confinano,
discẽ[9]de e mollifica la spiaggia opposta
del me[10]desimo monte e tira al continuo,
si come [11]fa la cicogniola che versa per il
suo lato più lũ[12]go, fusse quella che tira
in alto l'acqua del [13]mare; come se *s n*
fusse la pelle del ma[14]re, e la pioggia discende dalla cima del mõ[15]te *a* allo *n* da
vn lato e dall'altro lato di[16]scẽde
da *a* allo *m*, sanza dubbio que[17]sto
sarebbe il modo dello stillare a
feltro o [18]come si fa per la canna
detta cico[19]gniola, e senpre l'acqua che à mollificato [20]il monte
per la gran pioggia, che discende
dal[21]li due oppositi lati, tirerebbe a sè al
lato [22]più lũgo la pioggia *a n* insieme
coll' acqua [23]del mare perpetuamẽte, se il
lato del mõte [24]*a m* fusse più lũgo che
l'altro *a n*, il che essere [25]nõ può, perchè
nessuna parte di terra che nõ [26]sia sõ-
mersa dall' oceano sarà più bassa [27]d'esso
oceano ecc.

which bound it, but only so much rises as
the dryness of the mountain attracts. And if,
on the contrary, the rain, which penetrates from the summit of the mountain to
the base, which is the boundary of the sea,
descends and softens the slope opposite to
the said mountain and constantly draws the
water, like a syphon[11] which pours through
its longest side, it must be this which
draws up the water of the sea; thus if *s n* were
the surface of the sea, and the rain descends
from the top of the mountain *a* to *n*
on one side, and on the other sides
it descends from *a* to *m*, without a
doubt this would occur after the
manner of distilling through felt, or
as happens through the tubes called
syphons[17]. And at all times the
water which has softened the mountain, by
the great rain which runs down the two
opposite sides, would constantly attract the
rain *a n*, on its longest side together with the
water from the sea, if that side of the
mountain *a m* were longer than the other *a*
n; but this cannot be, because no part of the
earth which is not submerged by the ocean
can be lower than that ocean.

A. 55*b*]   **967.**

DELLE VENE DEL'ACQUA SOPRA · LE CIME DELLE MÕTAGNIE.

[2]Chiaro · apparisce · che tutta la · superfitie dell'ocieano ·, quãdo non à fortuna ·, è
di pari distãtia [3]al ciẽtro · della · terra ·, e
che le cime delle mõtagnie sono piv
lontane · da esso [4]ciẽtro · quãto · elle s'alzano
· sopra alla superfitie d'esso · mare ·; Adũ-
que se 'l corpo della [5]terra non avesse similitudine · coll'omo, sarebbe · inpossibile · che
l'acqua · del mare, essendo tãto [6]piv · bassa
· che le mõtagnie ·, ch'ella potesse · di sua
natura · salire · alle · sommità · d'esse mõtagnie; [7]Onde · è da credere · che quella · cagione ·, che tiene il sangue · nella · sõmità
della · testa · dell'omo, [8]quella · medesima ·
tenga l'acqua · nella · sommità · de' monti.

OF SPRINGS OF WATER ON THE TOPS OF MOUNTAINS.

It is quite evident that the whole surface
of the ocean—when there is no storm—is at
an equal distance from the centre of the
earth, and that the tops of the mountains
are farther from this centre in proportion as
they rise above the surface of that sea;
therefore if the body of the earth were
not like that of man, it would be impossible
that the waters of the sea—being so much
lower than the mountains—could by their
nature rise up to the summits of these
mountains. Hence it is to be believed that
the same cause which keeps the blood at
the top of the head in man keeps the water
at the summits of the mountains.

8. chol . . chonfina disciē. 9. mollifiche. 10. ettira. 12. gho fussi . . chettira. 13. chome . . fusse. 14. ella . . disciende alla. 15. da ullato. 16. disciẽde . . dubbio che. 17. affeltro. 18. chome . . lla channa [decta]. 19. essenpre . . mollifi-chato. 20. cheddisciẽde. 21. asse il lato. 22. lũgho . . chollacq"a". 23. sellatto. 24. fussi . . lũgho chellaltro. 26. o'cieano. 27. occieano.

967. 1. acq"a". 2. aparisscie . . chella "tutta". 3. tera e chelle . . mõtagni "e" . . esso [mare]. 4. sopa . . chorpo. 5. tera . . avessi . . choll . . chellacqua. 7. checquella chagione . chettiene . . somita. 8. lacq"a".

966. 11, 17. Cicognola, Syphon. See Vol. I, Pl. XXIV, No. 1.
967. 968. This conception of the rising of the

blood, which has given rise to the comparison, was recognised as erroneous by Leonardo him-self at a later period. It must be remembered that

A. 56 a]   **968.**

DELLA CŌFERMATIONE PERCHÈ L'ACQUA È NELLE · SOM̄ITÀ DE' MŌTI.

[2]Dico · che siccome · il naturale · calore · tiene il sāgue nelle uene · alla sommità dell'omo, [3]e quādo lo · omo · è morto, esso sangue · freddo · si riduce [4]ne' lochi · bassi ·, e, quādo · il sole · riscalda · la testa all'omo, [5]moltiplica · e sopraviene tāto sangue con omori ·, che forzādo · le uene [6]gienera · spesso · dolori · di testa ·, similemēte le uene ·, che vanno ramificādo [7]per il · corpo · della · terra · e per lo · naturale · calore, · ch'è sparso per tutto · il cōti[8]nēte · corpo ·, l'aqua · sta · per le uene · eleuate · all'alte cime de' mōti; È quel[9]la · acqua ·, che passasi · per uno · condotto mvrato · nel corpo d'essa · mōtagnia, [10]come · cosa · morta · non uscirà · dalla · sua · prima · bassezza ·, perchè non è [11]riscaldata · dal uitale · calore della · prima · vena ·; ancora · il calore [12]dell'elemēto del fuoco ·, e il giorno · il caldo del sole ·, ànno potētia di suegliere [13]l'umidità · de' bassi lochi · de' mōti e tirare in alto · nel medesimo · modo ch'ella [14]tira. i nvvoli · e sueglie · la loro · vmidità · dal letto del mare.

IN CONFIRMATION OF WHY THE WATER GOES TO THE TOPS OF MOUNTAINS.

I say that just as the natural heat of the blood in the veins keeps it in the head of man,—for when the man is dead the cold blood sinks to the lower parts—and when the sun is hot on the head of a man the blood increases and rises so much, with other humours, that by pressure in the veins pains in the head are often caused; in the same way veins ramify through the body of the earth, and by the natural heat which is distributed throughout the containing body, the water is raised through the veins to the tops of mountains. And this water, which passes through a closed conduit inside the body of the mountain like a dead thing, cannot come forth from its low place unless it is warmed by the vital heat of the spring time. Again, the heat of the element of fire and, by day, the heat of the sun, have power to draw forth the moisture of the low parts of the mountains and to draw them up, in the same way as it draws the clouds and collects their moisture from the bed of the sea.

Leic. 11 a]   **969.**

Come molte vene d'acqua salata si trovano fortemēte distanti dal [2]mare, e questo potrebbe accadere, perchè tal uena passasse per qualche miniera di sale come quella d'Ungheria, che si caua [3]il sale per le grandissime cave, come quasi cavano le pietre.

That many springs of salt water are found at great distances from the sea; this might happen because such springs pass through some mine of salt, like that in Hungary where salt is hewn out of vast caverns, just as stone is hewn.

---

968. 1. chōfermatione . . lacq"a". 2. dicho chessichome . . chalore tie "il sāgue" leuene . ala somita. 3. [cho] e quādo [esso] "lo" omo . . fredo. 4. bassi [chosi] echauādo il . . risschalda [il n] la. 5. molti pricha essopraviene . . chon . . chefforzādo. 6. vano ramifichādo. 7. lochorpo . . tera . . chalori chessparso . . chōti. 8. chorpo . . elleuate . . Ecque. 9. per ī chondotto . . chorpo. 10. chome chosa . . vsscira della . . basseza . nōne. 11. rischaldata . . chalore anchora il chalore. 12. focho . . chaldo . sole a . dissuegliere. 13. lochi "de mōti" ettirare. 14. nvboli essueglie . . delletto.

969. 1. trova . . distante . . da. 2. ecquesto . . achadere . . passasi . . chessi. 3. quasi caua.

---

the MS. *A*, from which these passages are taken, was written about twenty years earlier than the MS. Leic. (Nos. 963 and 849) and twenty-five years before the MS. W. An. IV.

There is, in the original a sketch with No. 968 which is not reproduced. It represents a hill of the same shape as that shown at No. 982. There

are veins, or branched streams, on the side of the hill, like those on the skull Pl. CVIII, No. 4.

969. The great mine of Wieliczka in Galicia, out of which a million cwt. of rock-salt are annually dug out, extends for 3000 mètres from West to East, and 1150 mètres from North to South.

IV.

OF RIVERS.

970.

DELLE DIRIUATIONI DE' FIUMI.

On the way in which the sources of rivers are fed.

²Il corpo della terra, a similitudine de' corpi deli animali, è tessuto di ramificationi di uene, le quali son tutte insieme cōgiunte, ³e soñ constituite a nvtrimento e viuificatione d'essa terra e de' sua creati ·; partono dalle profondità del mare, e a quelle dopo molta revolutio⁴ne ànno a tornare per li fiumi creati dalle alte rotture d'esse uene; e se tu volessi dire, le pio⁵ve il uerno o la resolutione della neue l'estate essere causa del nascimento de' fiumi, e' si ti potrebbe allegare ⁶li fiumi, che ànno origine ne' paesi focosi dell'Africa, nella quale non piove e meno nevica, perchè il superchio ⁷caldo senpre risolue in aria tutti li nuvoli, che da uēti in là son sospinti; e se tu dicessi che tali fiumi, che uē⁸gono grossi il Luglio e 'l Agosto, son delle nevi che si risoluono il Maggio e 'l Giugnio per l'appressamēto del sole alle ne⁹ui delle montagnie di Scitia, e che tali resolutioni si riducono in certe valli e fanno laghi, doue poi entrano per le ¹⁰vene e caue sotterane, le

OF THE ORIGIN OF RIVERS.

The body of the earth, like the bodies of animals, is intersected with ramifications of waters which are all in connection and are constituted to give nutriment and life to the earth and to its creatures. These come from the depth of the sea and, after many revolutions, have to return to it by the rivers created by the bursting of these springs; and if you chose to say that the rains of the winter or the melting of the snows in summer were the cause of the birth of rivers, I could mention the rivers which originate in the torrid countries of Africa, where it never rains—and still less snows—because the intense heat always melts into air all the clouds which are borne thither by the winds. And if you chose to say that such rivers, as increase in July and August, come from the snows which melt in May and June from the sun's approach to the snows on the mountains of Scythia[9], and that such meltings come down into certain valleys and form lakes, into which they enter by springs and subter-

970. 1. assimi . . ettessudi di ramifichatione . . cōgunte. 3. consstit ite "a nvtrimento" e viuifichatione . . terra | "e de sua creati" essi partano delle . . acquelle. 4. ano attornare . . essettu. 5. olla . lastate . . chausa . . nasscimento . . portrebbe. 6. fochosi africha . . nevicha. 7. chaldo . . nvoli . . illa . . sosspinte . . essettu . . chettali. 8. gano . . ellagosto . . chessi . . lapressamēto . . mago . . gugnio. 9. disscitia . . riduchano . . effano lagh. 10. riescano . . effalso inperochelle . . las. 11. chellorigine . . concosia chella.

970. 9. Scythia means here, as in Ancient Geography, the whole of the Northern part of Asia as far as India.

quali riescono poi all' origine del Nilo, questo è falso, inperochè è piv bassa la [11]Scitia che l' origine del Nilo, conciosiachè la Scitia è presso al mare di Pōto a 400 miglia, e l' origine del Nilo è [12]remoto 3000 miglia dal mare d' Egitto, ove versā le sue acque.

ranean caves to issue forth again at the sources of the Nile, this is false; because Scythia is lower than the sources of the Nile, and, besides, Scythia is only 400 miles from the Black sea and the sources of the Nile are 3000 miles distant from the sea of Egypt into which its waters flow.

Leic. 5a]

971.

Libro 9° delli scontri de' fiumi e lor flusso e riflusso, e la medesima [2]causa lo crea nel mare per causa dello stretto di Gibilterra, e ancora accade per le uoragini;

[3]Se due fiumi insieme si scontrano per vna medesima linia, la qual sia retta, poi infra 2 angoli retti [4]pigliano insieme lor corso, e' seguirà il flusso e riflusso · ora a l' uno fiume, ora all' altro, avanti [5]che sieno · vniti e massime, se l' uscita nella loro vnitione nō sarà piv veloce, che quād' erā disuniti; [6]Qui accadono 4 casi.

Book 9, of the meeting of rivers and of their ebb and flow. The cause is the same in the sea, where it is caused by the straits of Gibraltar; and again it is caused by whirlpools.

[3] If two rivers meet together to form a straight line, and then below two right angles take their course together, the flow and ebb will happen now in one river and now in the other above their confluence, and principally if the outlet for their united volume is no swifter than when they were separate. Here occur 4 instances.

The tide in estuaries.

Leic. 15a]

972.

Quando il fiume minore versa le sue acque nel maggiore, il quale maggiore corra dall' opposita [2]riua, allora il corso del fiume minore piegherà il suo corso inverso l' auenimēto del fiume [3]maggiore; e questo accade perchè, quando esso maggiore fiume enpie d' acqua tutto il suo letto, e' [4]glì viene a fare ritroso sotto la bocca di tal fiume, e così spingnie cō seco l' acqua versata dal fi[5]vme minore; Quando il fiume minore versa le sue acque nel fiume maggiore, il quale [6]abbia la corrente alla foce del minore, allora le sue acque si piegheranno inverso la fu[7]ga del fiume maggiore.

When a smaller river pours its waters into a larger one, and that larger one flows from the opposite direction, the course of the smaller river will bend up against the approach of the larger river; and this happens because, when the larger river fills up all its bed with water, it makes an eddy in front of the mouth of the other river, and so carries the water poured in by the smaller river with its own. When the smaller river pours its waters into the larger one, which runs across the current at the mouth of the smaller river, its waters will bend with the downward movement of the larger river.

On the alterations, caused in the courses of rivers by their confluence (972—974).

971. 1. isscontri . . ellor frusso e refrusso alta. 2. chausa . . strett [i] o di gibiltar . . achade . . uoragine. 3. retta e poi. 4. piglino . . refrusso. 5. chessieno . . lusscita nedella. .6. achade 4 chasi.

972. 1. magore il cqual "magore" corra "dall oposita riua" [remoto dalla sua]. 2. piegera. 3. magore ecquesto acchade . . magor . . letto el. 4. affare retroso . . bocha. 5. magore. 6. minor [fiume] allora . . piegeranno. 7. magore.

971. The first two lines of this passage have already been given as No. 957. In the margin, near line 3 of this passage, the text given as No. 919 is written.

972. In the original sketches the word *Arno* is written at the spot here marked *A*, at *R. Rifredi*, and at *M. Mugnone*.

Leic. 16 b]

973.

Quando le piene de' fiumi sō ²diminuite ·, allor li angoli acuti, che si generā nelle congiuntioni de' sua rami, si fanno piv cor³ti nelli lor lati e più grossi nelle lor punte, come sia la corrente *a n*, e la corrente *d n*, ⁴le quali si congiunghino insieme in · *n*, quando il fiume è nelle sue gran piene; dico che, quando sia ⁵nella predetta dispositione ·, che se *d n* avanti la piena era piv basso che *a n*, che nel tempo della piena ⁶*d n* sarà piē di rena e fango, il quale nel calare delle acque *d n* porterà uia il fango e rimar⁷rà col fondo basso, e 'l canale *a n*, trovandosi alto, scolerà le sue acque nel basso *d n* e consumerà tutta ⁸la punta del renaio *b c n*, e così rimarrà l'angolo *a c d* piv grosso che l'angolo *a n d*, e di lati più corti, come ⁹prima dissi.

When the fulness of rivers is diminished, then the acute angles formed at the junction of their branches become shorter at the sides and wider at the point; like the current *a n* and the current *d n*, which unite in *n* when the river is at its greatest fulness. I say, that when it is in this condition if, before the fullest time, *d n* was lower than *a n*, at the time of fulness *d n* will be full of sand and mud. When the water *d n* falls, it will carry away the mud and remain with a lower bottom, and the channel *a n* finding itself the higher, will fling its waters into the lower, *d n*, and will wash away all the point of the sand-spit *b n c*, and thus the angle *a c d* will remain larger than the angle *a n d* and the sides shorter, as I said before.

G. 48 a]

974.

Aqua.

DEL MOTO D'Ū SUBITO ENPITO FATTO ³DA UN FIUME SOPRA IL SUO LETTO ASCIUTTO.

⁴Tanto è più tardo o velocie il corso dell'acqua, ⁵data dallo isboccato lago al secco fivme, quā⁶to esso fiume fia più largo o piv stretto, over ⁷più piano o cupo in un loco che in un altro, ⁸per quel che è proposto: il flusso e ri⁹flusso del mare che dallo oceano entra nel Me¹⁰diterraneo Mare e de' fiumi, che giostrano ¹¹con lui, alzano tanto più o meno le loro acque, ¹²quanto tal mare è piv o meno stretto.

Water.

OF THE MOVEMENT OF A SUDDEN RUSH MADE BY A RIVER IN ITS BED PREVIOUSLY DRY.

In proportion as the current of the water given forth by the draining of the lake is slow or rapid in the dry river bed, so will this river be wider or narrower, or shallower or deeper in one place than another, according to this proposition: the flow and ebb of the sea which enters the Mediterranean from the ocean, and of the rivers which meet and struggle with it, will raise their waters more or less in proportion as the sea is wider or narrower.

C. A. 362 b; 1134 b]

975.

Whirlpools. Voragine, cioè caverne, ²cioè residui d'acque pre³cipitose.

Whirlpools, that is to say caverns; that is to say places left by precipitated waters.

---

973. 2. conguntione. 3. corente . . ella corente. 4. congunghino . . dicho. 5. predecta disspositione chesse. 6. effango . . rima. 8. cori rimara lanolo . . groso.

974. 3. da u . . assciucto. 4. eppiu . . chorpo . . acq"a". 5. isbochato lagho . . secho. 6. largho . . strecto. 7. ochupo nū locho che inu. 8. propossto . . e re. 9. frusso . . dello occieano. 10. mediterano . . giosstrano. 11. chō. 12. eppiu . . strecto.

975. 2. coe residii. 3. cipitosa.

973. Above the first sketch we find, in the original, this note: *"Sopra il pōte rubaconte alla torricella";* and by the second, which represents a pier of a bridge, *"Sotto l'ospedal del ceppo."*

974. In the margin is a sketch of a river which winds so as to form islands.

G. 49*b*]

976.

DELLA VIBRATIONE DELLA TERRA.

[2] Li corsi sotterranei [3] delle acque, sicome quelli che son fatti infra [4] l'aria e la terra, son quelli che al continuo [5] cōsumano e profondano li letti del[6]li lor corsi.

OF THE VIBRATION OF THE EARTH.

On the alterations in the channels of rivers.

The subterranean 'channels of waters, like those which exist between the air and the earth, are those which unceasingly wear away and deepen the beds of their currents.

Leic. 6*b*]

977.

Il fiume che esce de' mōti pone gran quātità di sassi grossi in nel suo ghiareto, i quali fatti sono ancora [2] con parte de' sua angoli e lati, e nel processo del corso conduce pietre minori con angoli piv cōsumati, cioè le grā [3] pietre fa minori, e piv oltre pō ghiaia · grossa, e poi minvta ·, e seguita rena grossa, e poi minvta, dipoi procede [4] litta grossa, e poi piv sottile, e così seguēdo giugne al mare l'acqua turba di rena e di litta; la rena scarica sopra de' [5] liti marini per il rigurgitamēto dell' ōde salse, e segue la litta di tanta sottilità che par di natura d'acqua, la qual non si fer[6]ma sopra de' marī liti, ma ritorna indietro coll' acqua per la sua leuità, perch'è nata di foglie marcie e d'altre cose leuissime, si [7] che, essendo quasi, com'è detto, di natura d'acqua, essa poi in tenpo di bonaccia si scarica e si ferma sopra del [8] fondo del mare, ove per la sua sottilità si condensa e resiste all'onde che sopra vi passano per la sua lubricità, e [9] qui stanno i nichi e quest'è terra bianca da far boccali.

The origin of the sand in rivers (977. 978).

A river that flows from mountains deposits a great quantity of large stones in its bed, which still have some of their angles and sides, and in the course of its flow it carries down smaller stones with the angles more worn; that is to say the large stones become smaller. And farther on it deposits coarse gravel and then smaller, and as it proceeds this becomes coarse sand and then finer, and going on thus the water, turbid with sand and gravel, joins the sea; and the sand settles on the sea-shores, being cast up by the salt waves; and there results the sand of so fine a nature as to seem almost like water, and it will not stop on the shores of the sea but returns by reason of its lightness, because it was originally formed of rotten leaves and other very light things. Still, being almost—as was said—of the nature of water itself, it afterwards, when the weather is calm, settles and becomes solid at the bottom of the sea, where by its fineness it becomes compact and by its smoothness resists the waves which glide over it; and in this shells are found; and this is white earth, fit for pottery.

Leic. 31*b*]

978.

Tutte l'uscite dell'acque dal monte nel mare portā cō seco li sassi del monte in es[2]so mare, e per la inōdatione dell'acque marine contro alli sua monti, esse pietre erā ributta[3]te inverso il mōte, e nell'ādare e nel ritornare indietro delle acque al mare, le pietre insieme cō quel[4]la tornavano, e nel ritornare li angoli loro insieme si percuoteano, e come parte men [5] resistente alle percosse si cōsumavano e facean le pietre sanza angoli, in figu[6]ra rotonda ·, come ne' liti dell' Elsa si dimostra, e quelle rimanevā piv grosse, che manco sarā remosse [7] dal lor

All the torrents of water flowing from the mountains to the sea carry with them the stones from the hills to the sea, and by the influx of the sea-water towards the mountains; these stones were thrown back towards the mountains, and as the waters rose and retired, the stones were tossed about by it and in rolling, their angles hit together; then as the parts, which least resisted the blows, were worn off, the stones ceased to be angular and became round in form, as may be seen on the banks of the Elsa. And those remained larger which were less removed

976. 1. viberatio. 2. supterrani [e super accquelli]. 3. so fatti infral. 4. ella. 6. chorsi.

977. 1. essce . . inel. 2. ellati . . agoli . . coe. 3. grosa e po . . grosa prociede. 4. lita . . gugne . . lita . . scaricha. 5. per e . ricitramēto . . lita . . dachq"a". 6. indirieta collo per . . marce. 7. bonacca . . scaricha essi. 9. ecquest . biancha daffar bochali.

978. 1. lusscite dellacq"e" . . secho . in e. 2. rebutta. 3. mōde "e nellādare" e . . indirieto. 4. toravano . . perchoteano. 5. perchose . . effacean. 6. ritonda "come ne liti dellebba si dimosstra" ecquella rimanē . . mancho. 7. nasscimēto. 8. locho

nascimēto; e così quella si facea minore, che piv si rimouea dal predet[8]to loco, in modo che nel procedere ella si cōuerte in ghiaja minvta, e poi in rena [9]e in vltimo in fango ·; dipoi che 'l mare si discosta dalli predetti monti·, la salsedine lascia[10]ta dal mare con altro umore della terra à fatta vna collegatione a essa ghiaja e rena, che la [11]ghiaja in sasso e la rena in tufo s'è convertita; E di questo si uede l'esenplo [12]in Adda all'uscire de' monti di Como e in Tesino, Adige, Oglio dall'alpi de' Tedeschi, e il si[13]mile d'Arno dal monte Albano intorno a Mōte Lupo e Capraia, doue li sassi grandissimi son tutti [14]di ghiaia cōgelata di diuerse pietre e colori.

from their native spot; and they became smaller, the farther they were carried from that place, so that in the process they were converted into small pebbles and then into sand and at last into mud. After the sea had receded from the mountains the brine left by the sea with other humours of the earth made a concretion of these pebbles and this sand, so that the pebbles were converted into rock and the sand into tufa. And of this we see an example in the Adda where it issues from the mountains of Como and in the Ticino, the Adige and the Oglio coming from the German Alps, and in the Arno at Monte Albano [13], near Monte Lupo and Capraia where the rocks, which are very large, are all of conglomerated pebbles of various kinds and colours.

.. procedere in si .. giara. 9. fangho .. disscosste .. lasscia. 10. ta del .. altromore .. affatto .. giara errena chella. 11. giara .. ella .. chonvertita. 12. inada .. .. adice oglio e adriano dell alpi .. tedesci el si .. 13. darno del. 14. cholori.

978. 13. At the foot of *Monte Albano* lies Vinci, the birth place of Leonardo. Opposite, on the other bank of the Arno, is *Monte Lupo*.

ON MOUNTAINS.

C. A. 157 b; 466 a]

979.

¶Li mōti son fatti dalli cor²si de' fiumi;¶

³¶Li mōti son disfatti dalli cor⁴si de' fiumi.¶

Mountains are made by the currents of rivers.

Mountains are destroyed by the currents of rivers.

The formation of mountains (979—983).

Leic. 10 a]

980.

Come le ²radici settentrionali di qualunche alpe · non sono ancora petrificate; e questo si vede ma³nifestamente doue i fiumi, che le tagliano, corrano inverso settentrione, li quali tagliā ⁴ nell' altezze de' mōti le falde delle pietre viue, e nell' congiugniersi colle pianure le predette falde ⁵ son tutte di terra da fare boccali ·, come si dimostra in Val di Lamona al fiume Lamona nel⁶l' uscire del Mōte Appenino fargli le predette cose nelle sue rive;

Come li fiumi ànno tutti segati ⁷ e diuisi li menbri delle grand' alpi l'uno dall'altro, e questo si manifesta per lo ordine delle ⁸ pietre faldate, chè dalla sommità del monte insino al fiume si vedono le corrispōdenze delle falde essere ⁹ così da l'un de' lati del fiume come dall'altro; Come

That the Northern bases of some Alps are not yet petrified. And this is plainly to be seen where the rivers, which cut through them, flow towards the North; where they cut through the strata in the living stone in the higher parts of the mountains; and, where they join the plains, these strata are all of potter's clay; as is to be seen in the valley of Lamona where the river Lamona, as it issues from the Appenines, does these things on its banks.

That the rivers have all cut and divided the mountains of the great Alps one from the other. This is visible in the order of the stratified rocks, because from the summits of the banks, down to the river the correspondence of the strata in the rocks is visible on either side of the river. That the

---

979. 3. dissfacti . . chor.
980. 2. radice . . petrifichate ecquesto. 3. chelle . . chorrane . . settantrione. 4. alteze . . congugnersi cholle. 5. daffare bochali . . lumona fare al. 6. lusscire . . farli . . fiumi an. 7. alpe . . ecquesto. 8. somita . . vede . . conrisspōdenze. 9. tutti

le pietre faldate de' monti · son tutti i gradi [10]de' fanghi posati l'un sopra l'altro per le inōdationi de' fiumi; Come le diuerse grossezze delle falde del[11]le pietre son create da diuerse inondationi de' fiumi, cioè maggiore ondatione o minore.

stratified stones of the mountains are all layers of clay, deposited one above the other by the various floods of the rivers. That the different size of the strata is caused by the difference in the floods—that is to say greater or lesser floods.

L. 76 a]

981.

Le sommità de' monti per [2]lungo tenpo senpre s'i[3]nalzano;

[4]I lati opposti de' mō[5]ti senpre s'auicinano; [6]le profondità delle ualli, [7]le quali son sopra la [8]spera dell'acqua, per lungo [9]tenpo senpre [10]s'appropinquano al cē[11]tro del mondo;

[12]In equal tēpo molto pi[13]v si profondano le ual[14]li che non s'alzano i mō[15]sti;

[16]Le base de' monti senpre [17]si fanno piv strette;

[18]Quanto [19]la ualle piv si pro[20]fonda, piv si consu[21]ma ne' sua lati in [22]più brieue tenpo.

The summits of mountains for a long time rise constantly.

The opposite sides of the mountains always approach each other below; the depths of the valleys which are above the sphere of the waters are in the course of time constantly getting nearer to the centre of the world.

In an equal period, the valleys sink much more than the mountains rise.

The bases of the mountains always come closer together.

In proportion as the valleys become deeper, the more quickly are their sides worn away.

Br. M. 30 b]

982.

In ogni concauità delle cime de' monti senpre si trover[2]anno li piegamēti delle falde delle pietre.

In every concavity at the summit of the mountains we shall always find the divisions of the strata in the rocks.

C. A. 124 b; 383 a]

983.

DEL MARE CHE CIGNE LA TERRA.

[2]Jo truouo il sito della terra essere ab antico · nelle sue pianure tutto [3]occupato e coperto dall'acque salse ecc.

OF THE SEA WHICH ENCIRCLES THE EARTH.

I find that of old, the state of the earth was that its plains were all covered up and hidden by salt water.

e gradi. 10. gosseze. 11. coe magore . . ōminore.
981. 1. somita. 7. la 5. 8. acq"a". 9. senpre [sabb]. 17. strecte. 20. consū. 21. made sua.
982. 2. ra li.
983. 1. ce cignie. 2. abbanticho . . tucto. 3. ochupato e choperto.

983. This passage has already been published by Dr. M. JORDAN: Das Malerbuch des L. da Vinci, Leipzig 1873, p. 86. However, his reading of the text differs from mine.

Leic. 31 *a*]

984.

Perchè molto sō ²piv antiche le ³cose che le lette⁴re, non è maravi⁵glia, se alli nostri ⁶giorni non appari⁷sce scrittura de-⁸lli predetti ma⁹ri essere occupa¹⁰tori di tanti pa¹¹esi; ¹²e se pure alcuna ¹³scrittura apparia, ¹⁴le guerre, l'incēdi, li diluvi dell'acque ¹⁵le mutationi delle ¹⁶lingue e delle leggi ¹⁷ànno cōsumato ¹⁸ogni antichità, ma ¹⁹a noi bastano le testi²⁰monianze delle co-²¹se nate nelle acque ²²salse ritrouarsi ²³nelli alti mōti, ²⁴lontani dalli mari ²⁵d'allora.

Since things are much more ancient than letters, it is no marvel if, in our day, no records exist of these seas having covered so many countries; and if, moreover, some records had existed, war and conflagrations, the deluge of waters, the changes of languages and of laws have consumed every thing ancient. But sufficient for us is the testimony of things created in the salt waters, and found again in high mountains far from the seas.

The authorities for the study of the structure of the earth.

984. 3. chelle. 6. gorni non aparis. 7. sciptura del. 9. ocupa. 11. [esi essettu]. 12. esse. 15. "li diluui dellacque" le muta-tioni. 16. legi. 19. basta. 20. monātie. 26. talor.

VI.

GEOLOGICAL PROBLEMS.

Leic. 3 a] **985.**

In questa tua opera tu ài ɟn prima a provare, come li nichi in mille braccia d'altura nō ui furō ²portati dal diluuio, perchè si uedono a ū medesimo liuello, e si vedono auāzare assai mōti sopra ³esso liuello, e a dimādare se 'l ḍiluvio fù per piogga o per ringorgamēto di mare, e poi ài ⁴a mostrare, che nè per pioggia che ingrossi i fiumi, nè per rigonfiamēto d'esso mare; li nichi, come cosa ⁵grave, non sono sospinti dal mare alli mōti, nè tirati a se dalli fiumi cōtro al corso delle ⁶loro acque.

In this work you have first to prove that the shells at a thousand braccia of elevation were not carried there by the deluge, because they are seen to be all at one level, and many mountains are seen to be above that level; and to inquire whether the deluge was caused by rain or by the swelling of the sea; and then you must show how, neither by rain nor by swelling of the rivers, nor by the overflow of this sea, could the shells—being heavy objects—be floated up the mountains by the sea, nor have carried there by the rivers against the course of their waters.

C. A. 152 a; 452 a] **986.**

DUBITATIONE.

A DOUBTFUL POINT.

Doubts about the deluge.

²Mouesi qui vn dubbio e questo è, se 'l ³diluvio, venuto al tenpo di Noè, fù vni-⁴versale o no; E qui parrà di no, per le

Here a doubt arises, and that is: whether the deluge, which happened at the time of Noah, was universal or not. And it would

---

985. 1. quessta . . br daltura. 2. perchessi uedano . . e uedesi. 4. mosstrare . . piogga chengrossi . . chome. 5. sosspinti . . asse . . chorso. 6. accq"e".

986. 2. ecquesso. 4. onno. 5. chessi . . abbian "nella bibbia. 6. chonpossto. 7. nocte . . pio. 8. chettal piogg. 9. ghomiti.

985. The passages, here given from the MS. Leic., have hitherto remained unknown. Some preliminary notes on the subject are to be found in MS. *F* 80ᵃ and 80ᵇ; but as compared with the fuller treatment here given, they are, it seems to me, of secondary interest. They contain nothing

that is not repeated here more clearly and fully. LIBRI, *Histoire des Sciences mathématiques III*, pages 218—221, has printed the text of *F* 80ᵃ and 80ᵇ, therefore it seemed desirable to give my reasons for not inserting it in this work.

⁵ragioni che si assegnieranno; Noi abbiamo nella bibbia, ⁶che il predetto diluvio fù conposto di 40 ⁷dì e 40 notti di continua e vniversa piog⁸gia, e che tal pioggia alzò dieci ⁹gomiti sopra al più alto mõte dell'univer¹⁰so; E se così fù, che la pioggia fusse vniver¹¹sale, ella vestì di se la nostra ter¹²ra di figura sperica; È la superfi¹³tie sperica in ogni sua parte equalmen¹⁴te distante dal ciẽtro della sva spe¹⁵ra, onde la spera del'acqua, trovandosi ¹⁶nel modo della detta conditione, elli è ¹⁷inpossibile, che l'acqua sopra di lei si mova, ¹⁸perchè l'acqua in se non si move, s'ella non ¹⁹disciẽde; addunque l'acqua di tanto dilu²⁰vio come si partì, se qui è provato, non a²¹ver moto? e s'ella si partì, come si mosse, ²²se ella non ādava allo insù? e qui ne mãcano²³ le ragiõ naturali, õde bisognia per soccor-²⁴so di tal dvbitatione chiamare il mira-²⁵colo per aiuto, o dire che ²⁶tale acqua fu vaporata dal calore del sole.

seem not, for the reasons now to be given: We have it in the Bible that this deluge lasted 40 days and 40 nights of incessant and universal rain, and that this rain rose to ten cubits above the highest mountains in the world. And if it had been that the rain was universal, it would have covered our globe which is spherical in form. And this spherical surface is equally distant in every part, from the centre of its sphere; hence the sphere of the waters being under the same conditions, it is impossible that the water upon it should move, because water, in itself, does not move unless it falls; therefore how could the waters of such a deluge depart, if it is proved that it has no motion? and if it departed how could it move unless it went upwards? Here, then, natural reasons are wanting; hence to remove this doubt it is necessary to call in a miracle to aid us, or else to say that all this water was evaporated by the heat of the sun.

Leic. 8 *b*]   **987.**

DEL DILUUIO E DE' NICHI MARINI.

²Se tu dirai che li nichi, che per li confini d'Italia lontano dalli mari in tāta altezza si ueggono ³alli nostri tempi, siano stati per causa del diluuio che lì li lasciò, io ti rispõdo che, credendo tu che ⁴tal diluuio superasse il piv alto monte 7 cubiti, come scrisse chi li misurò, tali nichi che senpre ⁵stanno vicini ai liti del mare, e' doueano restare sopra tali mõtagnie, e nõ si poco sopra le radi⁶ci de' monti per tutto a vna medesima altezza a suoli a suoli; E se tu dirai che, essendo tali ⁷nichi vaghi di stare vicini alli liti marini e che, crescẽdo in tāta altezza, che li nichi si ⁸partirono da esso lor primo sito e seguitarono l'accrescimẽto delle acque insino alla lor ⁹soma altezza, Qui si risponde chè, sendo il nichio anima-

OF THE DELUGE AND OF MARINE SHELLS.

If you were to say that the shells which are to be seen within the confines of Italy now, in our days, far from the sea and at such heights, had been brought there by the deluge which left them there, I should answer that if you believe that this deluge rose 7 cubits above the highest mountains— as he who measured it has written—these shells, which always live near the sea-shore, should have been left on the mountains; and not such a little way from the foot of the mountains; nor all at one level, nor in layers upon layers. And if you were to say that these shells are desirous of remaining near the margin of the sea, and that, as it rose in height, the shells quitted their first home, and followed the increase of the waters up to their highest level; to this I answer, that the cockle is an animal of not more rapid movement than the snail is out of water, or even somewhat

That marine shells could not go up the mountains.

---

10. chosi . . chella piggia fussi. 12. fighura sperica Ella. 13. sperica nogni. 14. disstante al. 16. chonditione. 17. chellacqua . . mov "a". 20. chome. 21. essella . . chome. 22. ecquimãca. 23. sochor. 25. cholo [per sochorso] per . . oddire. 26. chalar.

987. 1. 8 del. 2. settu . . chelli . . luntano dalì . . alteza si uegghano. 3. nosstri tenpi sia stato . . chausa . . lasscio . . rispõde. 4. diluio superassi . . chessenpre. 5. aliti del mare doueano . . pocho . . li radi. 6. ce de . . assuoli assuoli Essettu. 7. cresscẽdo . . alteza che'li. 8. partirano . . lor p' o'' sito esseguitorno lacresscimẽto. 9. alteza . . chessendo. 10. chessi

[10]le di non più veloce moto, che si sia la lumaca, fori dell'acqua, e qualche cosa più tarda perchè nō nota, ā[11]zi si fa vn solco per l'arena mediante i lati di tal solco ove s'appoggia, caminerà il dì dalle 3 alle 4 . braccia; [12]adunque questo cō tale moto nō sarà caminato dal mare Adriano insino in Mōferrato di Lon[13]bardia, chè v'è 250 miglia di distantia, in 40 giorni, come disse chi tenne cōto d'esso tenpo; e se tu dici che [14]l'onde ve li portarono, essi per la lor gravezza non si reggono, se nō sopra il suo fondo·; e se questo nō mi [15]concedi, cōfessami al meno ch'elli aueano a rimanere nelle cime de' piv alti mōti e ne' laghi che in[16]fra li mōti si serrano, come lago di Lario o di Como, e 'l Maggiore, e di Fiesole, e di Perugia e simili;

[17]E se tu dirai che li nichi son [18]portati dall'onde, essēdo voti e morti, io dico che, dove andauano li morti, poco si rimoueuano da'uiui, e in que[19]ste montagnie sono trovati tutti i uiui che si cognoscono che sono colli gusci appaiati, e sono [20]in vn filo doue non è nessun de' morti, e poco piv alto è trovato doue eran gittati dall'ō[21]de tutti li morti colle loro scorze separate, apresso a dove li fiumi cascavano in [22]mare in grā profondità; come Arno, che cadea dalla Gonfolina apresso a [23]Mōte Lupo e quiui lasciaua la ghiaja, la quale ancor si uede, che si è insieme ricōgielata e di pie[24]tre di uari paesi nature e colori e durezze se n'è fatto vna sola congelatione, e poco più oltre la congelatione dell'are[25]na s'è fatta tufo, dou'ella s'agiraua inverso Castel Fiorētino, più oltre si scaricava il fango, [26]nel quale abitavano i nichi, il quale s'inalzava a gradi, secondo che le piene d'Arno torbido [27]in quel mare versauano, e di tempo in tempo s'inalzaua il fondo al mare, ɉl quale a gradi [28]producea essi nichi, come si mostra nel taglio di Colle Gonzoli, dirupato dal fiume d'Arno, [29]che il suo piede consuma, nel qual taglio si

slower; because it does not swim, on the contrary it makes a furrow in the sand by means of its sides, and in this furrow it will travel each day from 3 to 4 braccia; therefore this creature, with so slow a motion, could not have travelled from the Adriatic sea as far as Monferrato in Lombardy [13], which is 250 miles distance, in 40 days; which he has said who took account of the time. And if you say that the waves carried them there, by their gravity they could not move, excepting at the bottom. And if you will not grant me this, confess at least that they would have to stay at the summits of the highest mountains, in the lakes which are enclosed among the mountains, like the lakes of Lario, or of Como and il Maggiore [16] and of Fiesole, and of Perugia, and others.

And if you should say that the shells were carried by the waves, being empty and dead, I say that where the dead went they were not far removed from the living; for in these mountains living ones are found, which are recognisable by the shells being in pairs; and they are in a layer where there are no dead ones; and a little higher up they are found, where they were thrown by the waves, all the dead ones with their shells separated, near to where the rivers fell into the sea, to a great depth; like the Arno which fell from the Gonfolina near to Monte Lupo [23], where it left a deposit of gravel which may still be seen, and which has agglomerated; and of stones of various districts, natures, and colours and hardness, making one single conglomerate. And a little beyond the sandstone conglomerate a tufa has been formed, where it turned towards Castel Florentino; farther on, the mud was deposited in which the shells lived, and which rose in layers according to the levels at which the turbid Arno flowed into that sea. And from time to time the bottom of the sea was raised, depositing these shells in layers, as may be seen in the cutting at Colle Gonzoli, laid open by

. . lumacha . . ecqualche . . tarda. 11. solcho . . sapogia chaminera . . 4 br. 12. chaminato . . i mōferato. 13. gorni . . tene . . essettu di che. 14. portorono . . regano. 15. cedi. 16. fralli . . magore . . peruga. 17. Esse tu dirai dirai chelle. 18. dicho . . andaua . . pocho. 19. cognoscano . . cholli gussci . . essono. 20. in vnn . . pocho. 21. cholle . . chasscavano. 22. gra . . chadea della Golfolina. 23. giara . . chesse insieme . ricōgielata. 24. nari "paesi" nature "e colorie dureze" se ne fatto . . gongelatione . . pocho. 25. seffatto . . invero chastel . . scharichava il fango. 26. abitava . . chelle

987. 13. *Monferrato di Lombardia.* The range of hills of Monferrato is in Piedmont, and Casale di Monferrato belonged, in Leonardo's time, to the Marchese di Mantova.

16. *Lago di Lario.* Lacus Larius was the name given by the Romans to the lake of Como. It is evident that it is here a slip of the pen since the

the words in the MS. are: "*Come Lago di Lario o 'l Magore e di Como.*" In the MS. after line 16 we come upon a digression treating of the weight of water; this has here been omitted. It is 11 lines long.

23. *Monte Lupo,* compare 970, 13; it is between Empoli and Florence.

uedono manifestamēte li predetti gradi de' nichi in ³⁰fango azzureggiante, e ui si trova di uarie cose marine; E si è alzata la terra del nostro ³¹emisperio per tanto più che nō solea, per quāto ella si fece più lieue delle acque, che le manca³²rono per il taglio di Calpe e d'Abila, e altrettanto piv s'è alzata, perchè il peso dell'acque, che di qui mā³³carono, s'aggiunsero · alla terra volta all'altro emisperio, E se li nichi fussero stati ³⁴portati dal Torbido diluuio, essi si sarebbero misti, separatamente l'un dal'altro, infra 'l fango e non ³⁵con ordinati gradi a suoli, come alli nostri tenpi si vede.

the Arno which is wearing away the base of it; in which cutting the said layers of shells are very plainly to be seen in clay of a bluish colour, and various marine objects are found there. And if the earth of our hemisphere is indeed raised by so much higher than it used to be, it must have become by so much lighter by the waters which it lost through the rift between Gibraltar and Ceuta; and all the more the higher it rose, because the weight of the waters which were thus lost would be added to the earth in the other hemisphere. And if the shells had been carried by the muddy deluge they would have been mixed up, and separated from each other amidst the mud, and not in regular steps and layers— as we see them now in our time.

Leic. 9 a]

988.

Di quelli che dicono che i nichi sono per molto spatio e nati remoti dalli mari · per la natura del sito e de' cieli, ²che dispone e influiscie tal loco a simile creatione d'animali ·; a costor si risponderà che, se tale influētia ³d'animali nō potrebbe accadere in vna sola linia, se nō animali di medesima sorte e età, e non il uechio col gio⁴vane, e nō alcun col coperchio e l'altro essere sanza sua copritura, e nō l'uno esser rotto e l'altro intero, ⁵e nō l'uno ripieno di rena marina e rottame minvto e grosso d'altri nichi dentro alli nichi ⁶interi, che lì son rimasti aperti, e nō le boche de' granchi sanza il rimanēte del suo tutto, e non li ni⁷chi d'altre spetie appicati con loro in forma d'animale che sopra di quelli si mouesse, perchè ancora resta ⁸il uestigio del suo andamento sopra la scorza che lui già, a uso di tarlo sopra il legname, andò cōsumādo; ⁹nō si troverebbero infra loro ossa e denti di pescie, li quali alcuni dimandano saette e altri lingue di ser¹⁰penti,

As to those who say that shells existed for a long time and were born at a distance from the sea, from the nature of the place and of the cycles, which can influence a place to produce such creatures—to them it may be answered: such an influence could not place the animals all on one line, except those of the same sort and age; and not the old with the young, nor some with an operculum and others without their operculum, nor some broken and others whole, nor some filled with sea-sand and large and small fragments of other shells inside the whole shells which remained open; nor the claws of crabs without the rest of their bodies; nor the shells of other species stuck on to them like animals which have moved about on them; since the traces of their track still remain, on the outside, after the manner of worms in the wood which they ate into. Nor would there be found among them the bones and teeth of fish which some call arrows and others serpents' tongues, nor would so many

The marine shells were not produced away from the sea.

piane. 27. quell . . versaua. 28. deripato. 29. piede . . taglo si vede. 30. fangho azuregante . . Essi alzato . . nosstro. 31. emisperio . . mancho. 32. perl . . calpe dattile . . perche[la] il. 33. chorono sagunsono . . emissperio Esselli . . futtino. 34. portadi . . essi saren misti . . fangho ennō. 35. assuoli.
93}. 1. dicano che michi. 2. infruisscie . . locho assimile . . risodera chesse . . infruētia. 3. po achadere . . enone il . . col go. 4. ellaltro esere colla sua . . ellaltro. 6. chelli . . rimassti . . rimanē dal . . e none. 7. colloro apichati . . mouessi. 8. lasscorza chellui ga. 9. troverra infrallaro . . pesscie. 10. troverra. 11. auebe . . stano . . elle cose. 12. sariano . . alteza . . ga a

e nō si troverebbero tanti mēbri di diuersi animali insieme vniti se lì da liti marini gittati nō fussino, [11] e 'l diluuio lì nō gli avrebbe portati, perchè le cose gravi più del'acqua nō stanno a galla sopra l'acqua, e le cose pre[12]dette nō sariano in tanta altezza, se già a nuoto ivi sopra dell'acque portate non furono, la qual cosa è inpossi[13]bile per la lor gravezza; Dove le uallate non ricievono le acque salse del mare, quiui i nichi mai non si [14]vedono, come manifesto si uede nella gran valle d'Arno di sopra alla Gonfolina, sasso per antico vnito [15]con Monte Albano in forma d'altissimo argine, il quale tenea ringorgato tal fiume in modo che prima che versasse nel mare, [16]il quale era dopo ai piedi di tal sasso, conponea 2 grandi laghi, de' quali il primo è, dove oggi si uede fiorire la città di Fiorē[17]ze insieme con Prato e Pistoia, e Monte Albano seguiva il resto dell'argine insin doue oggi è posto Serravalle·; dal Val d'Arno [18]di sopra insino Arezzo si creava vno secondo lago, il quale nell'ātidetto lago versaua le sue acque, [19]chiuso circa dove oggi si uede Girone, e occupaua tutta la detta valle di sopra per ispatio di 40 miglia [20]di lūghezza; questa valle riceue sopra il suo fondo tutta la terra portata dall'acqua da quella intorbidata, la quale [21]ancora si uede a' piedi di Prato Magno restare altissima, doue li fiumi nō l'ànno consumata, e infra essa terra si uedono le pro[22]fonde segature de' fiumi che quiui son passati, li quali discēdono dal grā mōte di Prato Magno, nelle quali [23]segature nō si uede vestigio alcuno di nichi e di terra marina; questo lago si congiugnea col lago di Perugia;

[24]Gran somma di nichi si uede doue li fiumi versano in mare, perchè in tali siti l'acque non so[25]no tante salse per la mistion dell'acque dolci che con quelle s'uniscono·, e 'l segnio di ciò si vede doue per antico li Mo[26]nti Appenini versauano li lor fiumi nel mare Adriano, li quali in gran parte mostrano infra li mōti grā [27]somma di nichi insieme coll azzurigno terreno di mare,

portions of various animals be found all together if they had not been thrown on the sea shore. And the deluge cannot have carried them there, because things that are heavier than water do not float on the water. But these things could not be at so great a height if they had not been carried there by the water, such a thing being impossible from their weight. In places where the valleys have not been filled with salt sea water shells are never to be seen; as is plainly visible in the great valley of the Arno above Gonfolina; a rock formerly united to Monte Albano, in the form of a very high bank which kept the river pent up, in such a way that before it could flow into the sea, which was afterwards at its foot, it formed two great lakes; of which the first was where we now see the city of Florence together with Prato and Pistoia, and Monte Albano. It followed the rest of its bank as far as where Serravalle now stands. From the Val d'Arno upwards, as far as Arezzo, another lake was formed, which discharged its waters into the former lake. It was closed at about the spot where now we see Girone, and occupied the whole of that valley above for a distance of 40 miles in length. This valley received on its bottom all the soil brought down by the turbid waters. And this is still to be seen at the foot of Prato Magno; it there lies very high where the rivers have not worn it away. Across this land are to be seen the deep cuts of the rivers that have passed there, falling from the great mountain of Prato Magno; in these cuts there are no vestiges of any shells or of marine soil. This lake was joined with that of Perugia [23].

A great quantity of shells are to be seen where the rivers flow into the sea, because on such shores the waters are not so salt owing to the admixture of the fresh water, which is poured into it. Evidence of this is to be seen where, of old, the Appenines poured their rivers into the Adriatic sea; for there in most places great quantities of shells are to be found, among the mountains, together

noto . . inposi. 13. graveza. 14. vidone . . vale. 15. "con monte albano" in forma . . daltissima argine [il quale] tenea . . versassi nel ma. 16. apiedi . . il p"o"e dove ogi si uide "fruire" la. 17. ze "insieme con" prato . . il re"sto" . . ogi . . ualdarno. 18. arezo . . lagho . . ati detto. 19. chircha . . ochupaua. 20. di lūgeza . 20 tera porta dallacque di . 21. acora . . al "tissima" . . nō lan. 22. si uede . . disscēdano. 23. alchuno . . terra [azurigma come] "marina" questo . . congugnea collacho di peruga. 24. soma. 25. suniscano . . dicosi . . anticho. 26. nti appenini . . moti. 27. chollazurigno terē . .

23. See Pl. CXIII.

e tutti li sassi, che di tal loco si cauano, son pieni di nichi; [28]Il medesimo si conoscie auere fatto Arno, quando cadea dal sasso della Gonfolina nel mare, [29]che dopo quella non troppo basso si trovaua, perchè a quelli tempi superaua l'altezza di San Miniato al Tedesco, [30]perchè nelle somme altezze di quello si uedono le ripe piene di nichi e ostriche dentro alle sue mvra; non si distesero li ni[31]chi inverso Val di Nievole, perchè l'acque dolci d'Arno in là non si astendeano;

Come li nichi nō si [32]partirono dal mare per diluuio, perchè l'acque, che di uerso la terra veniuano, ācora che esse tirassino il mare [33]inverso la terra, esse erā quelle che percuoteano il suo fondo, perchè l'acqua, che viene diuerso la terra, à [34]più corso che quella del mare, e per cōseguenza è piv potente, entra sotto l'altra acqua del mare [35]e rimove il fondo e accompagnia con seco tutte le cose mobili che in quella trova, come son i predetti [36]nichi e altre simili cose, e quanto l'acqua, che viē di terra, è piv torbida che quella del mare, tā[37]to piv si fa potente e grave che quella; adunque io nō ci vedo modo di tirare i predetti nichi tanto in[38]fra terra, se quiui nati nō fussino; se tu mi dicessi, il fiume Loira, che passa per la Francia, [39]nell'accrescimēto del mare si copre piv di ottanta miglia di paese, perchè è loco di grā pia[40]nvra, e 'l mare s'alza circa braccia 20, e nichi si · uengono a trovare in tal pianvra, disco[41]sta dal mare essa 80 miglia, qui si rispōde che 'l flusso e reflusso ne' nostri mediterrani [42]mari nō fanno tanta varietà, perchè in Genovese nō uaria nvlla, a Vinegia poco, in A[43]frica poco, e dove poco varia, poco occupa di paese;

Senpre la corrēte dell'acqua de' fiumi [44]s'inōda sopra del loco doue li è inpedito il corso ·; ancora doue essa si ristrignie per passare sotto [45]li archi de' ponti.

with bluish marine clay; and all the rocks which are torn off in such places are full of shells. The same may be observed to have been done by the Arno when it fell from the rock of Gonfolina into the sea, which was not so very far below; for at that time it was higher than the top of San Miniato al Tedesco, since at the highest summit of this the shores may be seen full of shells and oysters within its flanks. The shells did not extend towards Val di Nievole, because the fresh waters of the Arno did not extend so far.

That the shells were not carried away from the sea by the deluge, because the waters which came from the earth although they drew the sea towards the earth, were those which struck its depths; because the water which goes down from the earth, has a stronger current than that of the sea, and in consequence is more powerful, and it enters beneath the sea water and stirs the depths and carries with it all sorts of movable objects which are to be found in the earth, such as the above-mentioned shells and other similar things. And in proportion as the water which comes from the land is muddier than sea water it is stronger and heavier than this; therefore I see no way of getting the said shells so far in land, unless they had been born there. If you were to tell me that the river Loire[38], which traverses France, covers when the sea rises more than eighty miles of country, because it is a district of vast plains, and the sea rises about 20 braccia, and shells are found in this plain at the distance of 80 miles from the sea; here I answer that the flow and ebb in our Mediterranean Sea does not vary so much; for at Genoa it does not rise at all, and at Venice but little, and very little in Africa; and where it varies little it covers but little of the country.

The course of the water of a river always rises higher in a place where the current is impeded; it behaves as it does where it is reduced in width to pass under the arches of a bridge.

---

ettutti. 28. conosscie . . fatto [il ual darno] arno . . chadea del . . golfolina. 29. tropo . . acquelli tenpi . . lalteza di saminiato. 30. some alteze . . uede . . osstrighe . . distesono. 31. nievole per lacque . . asstendeano. 32. partirō del . . lache che diuerso terra veniuano al mare ancora e esse. 33. inverso terra . . peroteano . . vie diuersō tera | a. 34. checquella . . acq"a" . . 35. aconpagnia consecho . . mobile . . son e prede. 36. ecquanto . . checquella. 37. adunque i nō ci vego . . e predetti. 38. fɪatterra . . settu . . era . . franca. 39. acresscimēto . . ellocho. 40. circha br 20 e . . uengano attrorare . . discos. 41. sto dal . . esse . . risspōde . . frusso e refrusso . . medi terani. 42. nola . . pocho. 43. pocho . . pocho . . pocho schupa . . correte. 44. locho douele . . corso. | anchora.

---

38. Leonardo has written Era instead of Loera or Loira—perhaps under the mistaken idea that *Lo* was an article.

Leic. 9 *b*]   ,989.

CONFUTATIONE CH'È CONTRO COLOR CHE DI-
CONO, I NICHI ESSER PORTATI PER MOLTE GIOR-
NATE DISTANTI DALLI MARI PER CAUSA DEL
DILUUIO [2]TANT'ALTO CHE SUPERASSE TALE
ALTEZZA.

Further
researches
(989—991).
[3]Dico che il diluuio non potè portare
le cose nate dal mare alli mōti, se già il
mare gonfiando nō creasse inōdazione [4]in-
sino alli lochi sopradetti, la qual gonfia-
tione accadere nō può, perchè si darebbe
vacuo, e se tu diciessi l'aria quiui [5]riem-
pierebbe ·, noi abbiamo concluso il grave
non si sostenere sopra il lieue, onde per
neciessità si cō[6]clude, esso diluuio essere
cavsato dall'acque piovane, e se così è,
tutte esse acque corrono al mare, [7]e nō
corre il mare alle montagnie, e se elle corrono al mare, esse spingono li nichi dal
lito del mare, e nō le [8]tirano a se; E se
tu dicessi, poichè 'l mare alzò per l'acque
piovane, portò essi nichi a tale altezza,
[9]già abbiamo detto che le cose piv gravi
dell'acqua nō notā sopra di lei, ma stāno
nei fondi, dalle quali nō si [10]rimovono, se
nō per cavsa di percussiō d'onda ·; E se tu
dirai che l'onde le portassino in tali lochi
alti, noi abbiamo [11]prouato che l'onde nelle
grā profondità tornano in contrario nel
fondo al moto di sopra, la qual cosa [12]si
manifesta per lo intorbidare del mare dal
terreno tolto vicino alli liti; Muovesi la
cosa piv lieue che l'[13]acqua insieme colla
sua onda, ed è lasciata nel piv alto sito
della riva dalla piv alta onda; Muouesi la
cosa [14]più grave che l'acqua ·, sospinta
dalla sua ōda nella superfitie e dal fondo
suo ‖ e per queste due conclusioni, che ai
lochi [15]sua · sarā provate a pieno, noi con-
cludiamo che l'onda superfitiale nō può
portare nichi, per essere più grievi che
[16]l'acqua;
[17]Quando il diluuio auesse avto a portare li nichi trecento e quattro cento mi-
[18]glia distanti dalli mari, esso li avrebbe
portati misti con diuerse nature insieme
ammontati, e noi vediamo in [19]tal distantie
l'ostriche tutte insieme, e le conchilie, e li
pesci calamai, e tutti li altri nichi, che
stanno insieme a congre[20]gatione, essere

A CONFUTATION OF THOSE WHO SAY THAT
SHELLS MAY HAVE BEEN CARRIED TO A DISTANCE
OF MANY DAYS' JOURNEY FROM THE SEA BY THE
DELUGE, WHICH WAS SO HIGH AS TO BE ABOVE
THOSE HEIGHTS.

I say that the deluge could not carry objects,
native to the sea, up to the mountains, unless
the sea had already increased so as to create
inundations as high up as those places; and
this increase could not have occurred because
it would cause a vacuum; and if you were
to say that the air would rush in there, we
have already concluded that what is heavy
cannot remain above what is light, whence of
necessity we must conclude that this deluge
was caused by rain water, so that all these
waters ran to the sea, and the sea did not run
up the mountains; and as they ran to the sea,
they thrust the shells from the shore of the sea
and did not draw them towards themselves. And
if you were then to say that the sea, raised
by the rain water, had carried these shells
to such a height, we have already said that
things heavier than water cannot rise upon
it, but remain at the bottom of it, and do
not move unless by the impact of the waves.
And if you were to say that the waves had
carried them to such high spots, we have
proved that the waves in a great depth move
in a contrary direction at the bottom to the
motion at the top, and this is shown by the
turbidity of the sea from the earth washed
down near its shores. Anything which is
lighter than the water moves with the waves,
and is left on the highest level of the highest
margin of the waves. Anything which is
heavier than the water moves, suspended in
it, between the surface and the bottom; and
from these two conclusions, which will be
amply proved in their place, we infer that the
waves of the surface cannot convey shells,
since they are heavier than water.

If the deluge had to carry shells three
hundred and four hundred miles from the
sea, it would have carried them mixed with
various other natural objects heaped together;
and we see at such distances oysters all
together, and sea-snails, and cuttlefish, and
all the other shells which congregate together,

989. 1. dicano . . gornate . . chausa. 2. tantalta . . superassi. 3. Dicho che diluuio no po | "te" . . cose "nate" del . . creassi
. . achadere . . po . . dare vachuo. 5. rienpierebe . . abiā . . greve. 6. esse chosi . . corrano. 7. esselle corrano . . del
lito. 8. asse Esse . . attale alteza. 9. abiā . . chelle . . grav . stano in fondo delle 10. removano . . . Essettu . . abiā.
11. chellonde . . provondita. 12. del terē . . chella. 13. acq"a" . . lasscciata. 14. chellacqua . sospinte . . e del. 15. che-
llonda . . po. 17. auesse. 18. disstanti . . arebbe . . chon . . amōtati. 19. losstriche . . elli conchili elli . . chalamai

trovati tutti insieme morti, e li nichi soletari trovarsi distanti l'uno dall'altro, come ne' liti marittimi ²¹tutto il giorno vediamo; E se noi troviamo l'ostriche insieme apparētate grādissime, infra le quali assai vedi quelle ²²che ànno ancora il coperchio congiunto, a significare che qui furono lasciate dal mare, che ancor viveano quando fù ²³tagliato lo stretto di Gibilterra; Vedesi in nelle montagnie di Parma e Piacētia le moltitudini di nichi e coralli ²⁴intarlati, ancora appiccati alli sassi, de' quali, quand'io facevo il grā cavallo di Milano, me ne fù portato vn grā sacco ne²⁵lla mia fabbrica da certi villani, che in tal loco furō trovati, fralli quali ve n'era assai delli conseruati nella prima bōtà;

²⁶Truovāsi sotto terra e sotto li profondi cavamenti de' lastroni li legniami delle traui lauorati, fatti già neri, li qua²⁷lì furō trovati a mio tenpo in quel di Castel Fiorētino·, e questi in tal loco profondo v'erano prima che la litta gittata ²⁸dall'Arno nel mare, che quiui copriva, fusse abbandonata in tant' altezza, e che le pianure del Casentino fussī tanto abbassate ²⁹dal terrē che ànno al continuo di lì sgonberato;

³⁰E se tu dicessi, tali ³¹nichi essere crea³²ti e creano a cō³ tinvo in simili lochi per la natura del ³⁴sito e de' cieli, che qui³⁶vi influisce, questa ³⁷tale openione non ³⁸sta in cervelli di trop³⁹po discorso, perchè qui⁴⁰vi s'envmerā li anni ⁴¹del loro accrescimento ⁴²sulle loro scorze, e se ne ⁴³vedono piccoli e grādi, ⁴⁴i quali sanza cibo nō cre⁴⁵scerebbero e non si cibarebbero sā⁴⁶za moto, e quivi mouere nō si po⁴⁷teano.

all to be found together and dead; and the solitary shells are found wide apart from each other, as we may see them on sea-shores every day. And if we find oysters of very large shells joined together and among them very many which still have the covering attached, indicating that they were left here by the sea, and still living when the strait of Gibraltar was cut through; there are to be seen, in the mountains of Parma and Piacenza, a multitude of shells and corals, full of holes, and still sticking to the rocks there. When I was making the great horse for Milan, a large sack full was brought to me in my workshop by certain peasants; these were found in that place and among them were many preserved in their first freshness.

Under ground, and under the foundations of buildings, timbers are found of wrought beams and already black. Such were found in my time in those diggings at Castel Fiorentino. And these had been in that deep place before the sand carried by the Arno into the sea, then covering the plain, had been raised to such a height; and before the plains of Casentino had been so much lowered, by the earth being constantly carried down from them.

[30]And if you were to say that these shells were created, and were continually being created in such places by the nature of the spot, and of the heavens which might have some influence there, such an opinion cannot exist in a brain of much reason; because here are the years of their growth, numbered on their shells, and there are large and small ones to be seen which could not have grown without food, and could not have fed without motion—and here they could not move[47].

Leic. 10 a]

990.

Come ²nelle falde, infra l'una e l'altra si trovano ancora li andamēti delli lonbrici, che caminavano infra esse ³quādo non erano ancora asciutte; Come tutti li fanghi marini ritengono ancora de' nichi ⁴ed è petrificato il nichio insieme col fango; della

That in the drifts, among one and another, there are still to be found the traces of the worms which crawled upon them when they were not yet dry. And all marine clays still contain shells, and the shells are petrified together with the clay. From their firmness and unity some persons will have it that these animals were carried up to

ettutti. 20. elli trovare . . lunoall. 21. gorno . . Esse . . losstriche . . aparētadi grādissimi infralle quale. 22. anchora . . congunto . . assignificare . . lassciate . . ancoravveano. 23. losstretto di gibiltar . . inelle . . moltitudinede. 24. apichati . . ne nefu . . sachone. 25. fabricha . . nella p"a" bōta. 26. essotto . . ga neri. 27. ecquesti . . profondor "o"no . . chella lita gitta. 28. copria fussi abondata . . alteza e chelle . . tante abassate. 29. del . . sgonbera 30. essettu. 31. niche. 33. nvo. 36. infruisscie. 37. none. 38. di tro. 41. deloro acresscimento. 42. sule. 43. vede picoli. 45. bono e non si ciborō. 47. trono.

990. 2. infraliuna allaltra . . trova anchora. 3. neuera . . asscutta . . fangh . . ritengano. 4. essenplicita . . uogliano chettal.

989. 30—47. These lines are written in the margin.

stoltitia e senplicità di quelli, che uogliono che ta[5]li animali fussino alli lochi distanti dai mari portati dal diluvio; Come altra setta d'ignoranti [6]affermano la natura, o i celi auerli in tali lochi creati · per īflussi celesti, come in quelli [7]nō si trovassino l'ossa de' pesci cresciuti cō lūghezza di tenpo, come nelle scorze de' nichi e lumache nō si potesse [8]annvmerare li anni o i mesi della lor uita, come nelle corna de' buoi e de' castroni e nella ramificatione de[9]lle piante, che nō furō mai tagliate in alcuna parte ; E auendo con tali segni dimostrato e la lunghezza della lor uita [10]essere manifesta, ecco bisognio confessare, che tali animali nō uiuino sanza moto per cercare [11]il loro cibo e in loro non si uede strumēto da penetrare la terra e 'l sasso, ove si trovano rinchiusi · ; [12]Ma in che modo si potrebbe trovare in vna grā lumaca i rottami e parte di molt' altre sorti di nichi di uarie na[13]ture, se ad essa, sopra de' liti marini già morta, non li fussino state gittate dalle onde del mare, come dell' al[14]tre cose lieui, che esso gitta a terra ? Perchè si truova tanto rottame e nichi interi fra falda e falda di pie[15]tra, se già quella sopra del lito nō fusse stata ricoperta da una terra rigittata dal mare, la qual poi si uenne pe[16]trificando ? E se 'l diluvio predetto li auesse in tali siti dal mare portato, tu troveresti essi nichi in nel termi[17]ne d'una sola falda, e non al termine di molte ; deuonsi poi annvmerare le uernate delli ā[18]ni, che 'l mare mvltiplicaua le falde dell' arena e fango, portatoli da fiumi vicini, e ch' elli scaricava in sui liti sua, e se [19]tu volessi dire, che piv diluui fussino stati a produrre tali falde e nichi infra loro, e' bisognierebbe, [20]che ancora tu affermassi ogni āno essere vn tal diluuio accaduto ; Ancora infra li rot[21]tami di tal nichi si prosume in tal sito essere spiaggia di mare, doue tutti i nichi son gittati rotti e diuisi e nō [22]mai appaiati, come infra 'l mare viui si trovano con due gusci, che fan coperchio l'uno all' altro ; E infra [23]le falde della riuiera e de' liti marittimi son trovati de' rottami ; E dentro alli termini delle pietre son trovati [24]rari e appaiati de' gusci, come quelli che furō lasciati dal mare sotterrati viui dentro al fango, il qual [25]poi si seccò e col tenpo petrificò.

places remote from the sea by the deluge. Another sect of ignorant persons declare that Nature or Heaven created them in these places by celestial influences, as if in these places we did not also find the bones of fishes which have taken a long time to grow ; and as if, we could not count, in the shells of cockles and snails, the years and months of their life, as we do in the horns of bulls and oxen, and in the branches of plants that have never been cut in any part. Besides, having proved by these signs the length of their lives, it is evident, and it must be admitted, that these animals could not live without moving to fetch their food ; and we find in them no instrument for penetrating the earth or the rock where we find them enclosed. But how could we find in a large snail shell the fragments and portions of many other sorts of shells, of various sorts, if they had not been thrown there, when dead, by the waves of the sea like the other light objects which it throws on the earth? Why do we find so many fragments and whole shells between layer and layer of stone, if this had not formerly been covered on the shore by a layer of earth thrown up by the sea, and which was afterwards petrified? And if the deluge before mentioned had carried them to these parts of the sea, you might find these shells at the boundary of one drift but not at the boundary between many drifts. We must also account for the winters of the years during which the sea multiplied the drifts of sand and mud brought down by the neighbouring rivers, by washing down the shores; and if you chose to say that there were several deluges to produce these rifts and the shells among them, you would also have to affirm that such a deluge took place every year. Again, among the fragments of these shells, it must be presumed that in those places there were sea coasts, where all the shells were thrown up, broken, and divided, and never in pairs, since they are found alive in the sea, with two valves, each serving as a lid to the other; and in the drifts of rivers and on the shores of the sea they are found in fragments. And within the limits of the separate strata of rocks they are found, few in number and in pairs like those which were left by the sea, buried alive in the mud, which subsequently dried up and, in time, was petrified.

---

5. fossi inali .. diluio. ī frussi. 7. trovassi .. cressciuti .. lugeza .. pote. 8. anvmerare .. casstroni .. del. 9. signi dimostro o la lungeza. 10. ecci biṡognia chettali. 11. illor nosi. 12. nvna gra lumacha .. altre sotte. 13. ture e essa sopa de .. morta nolli .. comellā. 14. esso .. atterra. 15. fussi .. uno. 16. trifichando . Essel diluio .. auessi .. troverresti hessi .. inel. 17. nōne .. di [qualunche falda] "di molte" deuensi po anvmerare [li ani] le uernate. 18. del [fango] "larena effangho" portatoli .. insu liti .. esset. 19. ennichi infralloro. 20. ongni .. tatal .. acaduto [e che tenessi] Ancora infralii. 21. spiagia. 22. apaiati .. gussci cheffan .. infralle. 24. apaiati di gussci .. lassciati sollerati. 25. secho .. petrificho.

Leic. 10 b]

991.

E se tu vuoi dire che tale diluuio fu‐ quello che portò tali nichi fuor de' mari cētinaia di miglia ·, questo nō può acca²dere, essendo stato esso diluuio per cause di pioggie, perchè naturalmente le pioggie spingono i fiumi insieme colle cose da loro ³portate inuerso il mare, e nō tirano inverso de' mōti le cose morte dai liti marittimi ., e se tu dicessi che'l diluvio poi s'al⁴zò colle sue acque sopra de' mōti, il moto del mare fù si tardo col camino suo contro al corso de' fiumi, che non avrebbe ⁵sopra di se tenvto a noto le cose piv gravi di lui, e se pur l'auesse sostenute, esso nel calare l'avrebbe lasciate in diversi ⁶lochi seminate; Ma come accomoderemo noi li coraIli, li quali inverso Mōte Ferrato di Lonbardia esser si tutto⁷dì trovati intarlati appiccati alli scogli, scoperti dalle corrēti de'fiumi? e li detti scogli sono tutti coperti di parentadi ⁸e famiglie d'ostriche, le quali noi sappiamo che nō si movono, ma stā senpre appiccate col' ū de' gusci al sasso, e l'altro apro⁹no per cibarsi d'animaluzzi, che notā per l'acque, li quali, credendo trovar bona pastura, diuentano cibo del predetto nichio; non si ¹⁰trova l'arena mista coll'aliga marina essersi petrificata, poichè l'aliga, che la ramezzaua, venne meno; e di questo ¹¹scopre tutto il giorno il Po nelle ruine delle sue ripe.

And if you choose to say that it was the deluge which carried these shells away from the sea for hundreds of miles, this cannot have happened, since that deluge was caused by rain; because rain naturally forces the rivers to rush towards the sea with all the things they carry with them, and not to bear the dead things of the sea shores to the mountains. And if you choose to say that the deluge afterwards rose with its waters above the mountains, the movement of the sea must have been so sluggish in its rise against the currents of the rivers, that it could not have carried, floating upon it, things heavier than itself; and even if it had supported them, in its receding it would have left them strewn about, in various spots. But how are we to account for the corals which are found every day towards Monte Ferrato in Lombardy, with the holes of the worms in them, sticking to rocks left uncovered by the currents of rivers? These rocks are all covered with stocks and families of oysters, which as we know, never move, but always remain with one of their halves stuck to a rock, and the other they open to feed themselves on the animalcules that swim in the water, which, hoping to find good feeding ground, become the food of these shells. We do not find that the sand mixed with seaweed has been petrified, because the weed which was mingled with it has shrunk away, and this the Po shows us every day in the debris of its banks.

Leic. 20 a]

992.

Perchè sono trovate l'ossa ²de' grā pesci e le ostriche e coralli e altri diuersi nichi e chiocciole sopra l'alte cime de' mōti ma³rittimi nel medesimo modo che si trovā ne' bassi mari?

Why do we find the bones of great fishes and oysters and corals and various other shells and sea-snails on the high summits of mountains by the sea, just as we find them in low seas?

Other problems (992—994).

Leic. 36 a]

993.

Tu ài ora a provare come li nichi nō nascono, se nō in acque salse, quasi tutte le sorte, e che ²li nichi di Lonbardia ànno

You now have to prove that the shells cannot have originated if not iu salt water, almost all being of that sort; and that the shells in Lombardy are at four levels,

991. 1. Essettu volli . . chettale . . for . . po acha. 2. chause di piogie . . piogie spingano . . dallor. 3. morte de liti . . esse . . diluui. 4. sittardo . . arebe [te]. 5. esse . . lauesi sosstenvte . . larebe lassciate. 6. acomodereno. 7. ildi . . "intarlati" apichati alli scolgli . . elli . . scolgli . . parendadi e. 8. sapiano . . movano . . apichate cholū degussci . . apra. 9. danimaluzi . . diuenta. 10. trova egli larena . . cholla . . poichellaliga chella framezaua. 11. gorno.

992. 2. pessci elle osstriche . . cioccole. 993. 1. nasscano. 3. chessabochano.

4 liuelli, e così è per tutti, li quali sono fatti in piv tēpi, e questi ³sono per tutte le ualli che sboccano alli mari.

and thus it is everywhere, having been made at various times. And they all occur in valleys that open towards the seas.

994.

Per le 2 linie de' nicchi bisognia dire che la terra per sdegno ²s'attufasse sotto il mare, e fece il primo suolo, poi il diluuio ³fece il secondo.

From the two lines of shells we are forced to say that the earth indignantly submerged under the sea and so the first layer was made; and then the deluge made the second.

994. 1. nicch . . chellatera. 2. sattu fassi sottollmare effe. 3. fe il sechondo.

994. This note is in the early writing of about 1470—1480. On the same sheet are the passages No. 1217 and 1219. Compare also No. 1339. All the foregoing chapters are from Manuscripts of about 1510. This explains the want of connection and the contradiction between this and the foregoing texts.

VII.

ON THE ATMOSPHERE.

Leic. 20a]

995.

Come la chiarezza dell' aria na²scie dall' acqua che in quella s' è resoluta e fattasi in īsēsibili graniculi, li quali, preso il lume del sole dall' op³posita parte, rēdono la chiarezza che in essa aria si dimonstra, e l'azzurro, che in quella apparisce, nascie ⁴dalle tenebre, che dopo essa aria si nascondono.

That the brightness of the air is occasioned by the water which has dissolved itself in it into imperceptible molecules. These, being lighted by the sun from the opposite side, reflect the brightness which is visible in the air; and the azure which is seen in it is caused by the darkness that is hidden beyond the air.[4]

Constituents of the atmosphere.

Leic. 22b]

996.

Come i retrosi de' uēti a certe ²boche di ualli percuotino sopra delle acque e quelle concauino cō grā cauamēto, e portino ³l'acqua in aria in forma colunnale in color di nugola, e il medesimo vid'io già fare sopra ⁴vn arenaio d' Arno, nel quale fu concauato l'arena più d'una statura d'uomo, e ⁵di quella fu remossa la ghiaja e gittata in disparte per lūgo spatio, e parea per l'aria in forma ⁶di grādissimo canpanile, e cresciena la sommità come i rami di gran pino, e si piegaua ⁷poi nel contatto del retto uēto che passaua sopra li mōti.

That the return eddies of wind at the mouth of certain valleys strike upon the waters and scoop them out in a great hollow, whirl the water into the air in the form of a column, and of the colour of a cloud. And I saw this thing happen on a sand bank in the Arno, where the sand was hollowed out to a greater depth than the stature of a man; and with it the gravel was whirled round and flung about for a great space; it appeared in the air in the form of a great bell-tower; and the top spread like the branches of a pine tree, and then it bent at the contact of the direct wind, which passed over from the mountains.

On the motion of air (996—999).

995. 1. chiareza. 2. sscie .. effattasi .. presi. 3. rēdano la ciareza .. dimosstra ellazurro .. apparissce nasscie .. nasscondano.

996. 1. accerte. 2. percotino .. ecquelle .. chauamēto. 3. colunale .. vidio cia. 4. duome he. 5. giara e gittatta. 6. ecresscieva lasomita .. rāmi di girapino essi.

995. 4. Compare Vol. I, No. 300.

Leic. 23 a]   997.

L'onda dell'aria fa il me²desimo vfitio infra l' elemēto del fuoco ·, che fa l'onda dell'acqua infra l'aria, o l' onda dell'a³rena, cioè terra, infra l'acqua, e sono i lor moti in tal proportione qual è quella de' lor mo⁴tori infra loro.

The element of fire acts upon a wave of air in the same way as the air does on water, or as water does on a mass of sand —that is earth; and their motions are in the same proportions as those of the motors acting upon them.

S. K. M. II.² 19 b]   998.

DE MOTO.

Domādo, se 'l uero moto ²de' nuvoli si può conosciere ³per lo moto delle sue ombre, ⁴e similemēte del moto ⁵del sole.

OF MOTION.

I ask whether the true motion of the clouds can be known by the motion of their shadows; and in like manner of the motion of the sun.

H.3 52 a]   999.

Per cognosciere ²meglio i vēti.

To know better the direction of the winds.

Leic. 34 a]   1000.

The globe an organism.

Nessuna cosa nasce in loco doue nō sia vita sensitiua, vegetatiua e rationale; nascono le penne sopra li uccelli, e si mvtano ogni anno; nascono ²li peli sopra li animali, e ogni anno si mvtano, saluo alcuna parte, come li peli delle barbe de' lioni e gatte e simi³li; nascono l'erbe sopra li prati e le foglie sopra li alberi, e ogn'āno in grā parte si rinovano; adunque potremo dire, ⁴la terra avere anima vegetatiua, e che la sua carne sia la terra, li sua ossi sieno li ordini delle collegationi de' sas⁵si,

Nothing originates in a spot where there is no sentient, vegetable and rational life; feathers grow upon birds and are changed every year; hairs grow upon animals and are changed every year, excepting some parts, like the hairs of the beard in lions, cats and their like. The grass grows in the fields, and the leaves on the trees, and every year they are, in great part, renewed. So that we might say that the earth has a spirit of growth; that its flesh is the soil, its bones the arrangement and connection of the rocks of

997. 2. infrallelemēto . . focho . cheffa. 3. coe . . infrallacqua essono . . quele quella delor.
998. 2. nvvoli spo. 3. obre. 4. essimile.nēte.
999. 1—2 R. 1. cōgnosciere. 2. e vēti.
1000, 1. nascce . . locho . . vita "sensitiua [intellettiva] vigitatiua e ra tĩonale] nassce le pene . . essi . . nassce. 2. alchuna . .
   essimi. 3. nassce . . elle . . potren. 4. vigitatiua e chella . . collegatione. 5. comogano. 6. occeano . . cresscere e dis-

999. In connection with this text I may here mention a hygrometer, drawn and probably invented by Leonardo. A facsimile of this is given in Vol. I, p. 297 with the note: '*Modi di pesare l'arie eddi sa-*

pere quando s'à arrompere il tēpo' (Mode of weighing the air and of knowing when the weather will change); by the sponge "*Spugnea*" is written.
   1000. Compare No. 929.

di che si compongono le mōtagnie, il suo tenerume sono li tufi, il suo sangue sono le uene delle acque, il lago [6]del sangue, che sta dintorno al core, è il mare oceano, il suo alitare e 'l crescere e discrescere del sangue [7]pelli polsi, e così nella terra è il flusso e riflusso del mare, e 'l caldo dell' anima del mondo è il fuoco, [8]ch'è infuso per la terra, e la residenza dell' anima vegetativa sono li fochi, che per diuersi lochi della [9]terra spirano in bagni, e in miniere di solfi, e in vulcani, e Mō Gibello di Sicilia, e altri lochi assai.

which the mountains are composed, its cartilage the tufa, and its blood the springs of water. The pool of blood which lies round the heart is the ocean, and its breathing, and the increase and decrease of the blood in the pulses, is represented in the earth by the flow and ebb of the sea; and the heat of the spirit of the world is the fire which pervades the earth, and the seat of the vegetative soul is in the fires, which in many parts of the earth find vent in baths and mines of sulphur, and in volcanoes, as at Mount Ætna in Sicily, and in many other places.

scresscere. 7. frusso e refrusso . . focho. 8. ella reside dell . . vigitativa. 9. in vulgano . . cicilia.

XVII.

Topographical Notes.

A large part of the texts published in this section might perhaps have found their proper place in connection with the foregoing chapters on Physical Geography. But these observations on Physical Geography, of whatever kind they may be, as soon as they are localised acquire a special interest and importance and particularly as bearing on the question whether Leonardo himself made the observations recorded at the places mentioned or merely noted the statements from hearsay. In a few instances he himself tells us that he writes at second hand. In some cases again, although the style and expressions used make it seem highly probable that he has derived his information from others— though, as it seems to me, these cases are not very numerous—we find, on the other hand, among these topographical notes a great number of observations, about which it is extremely difficult to form a decided opinion. Of what the Master's life and travels may have been throughout his sixty-seven years of life we know comparatively little; for a long course of time, and particularly from about 1482 to 1486, we do not even know with certainty that he was living in Italy. Thus, from a biographical point of view a very great interest attaches to some of the topographical notes, and for this reason it seemed that it would add to their value to arrange them in a group by themselves. Leonardo's intimate knowledge with places, some of which were certainly remote from his native home, are of importance as contributing to decide the still open question as to the extent of Leonardo's travels. We shall find in these notes a confirmation of the view, that the MSS. in which the Topographical Notes occur are in only a very few instances such diaries as may have been in use during a journey. These notes are mostly found in the MSS. books of his later and quieter years, and it is certainly remarkable that Leonardo is very reticent as to the authorities from whom he quotes his facts and observations: For instance, as to the Straits of Gibraltar, the Nile, the Taurus Mountains and the Tigris and Euphrates. Is it likely that he, who declared that in all scientific research, his own experience should be the foundation of his statements (see XIX Philosophy No. 987—991) should here have made an exception to this rule without mentioning it?

As for instance in the discussion as to the equilibrium of the mass of water in the Mediterranean Sea—a subject which, it may be observed, had at that time attracted the interest and study of hardly any other observer. The acute remarks, in Nos. 985—993, on the presence of shells at the tops of mountains, suffice to prove—as it seems to me—that it was not in his nature to allow himself to be betrayed into wide generalisations, extending beyond the limits of his own investigations, even by such brilliant results of personal study.

Most of these Topographical Notes, though suggesting very careful and thorough research, do not however, as has been said, afford necessarily indisputable evidence that that research was Leonardo's own. But it must be granted that in more than one instance probability is in favour of this idea.

Among the passages which treat somewhat fully of the topography of Eastern places by far the most interesting is a description of the Taurus Mountains; but as this text is written in the style of a formal report and, in the original, is associated with certain letters which give us the history of its origin, I have thought it best not to sever it from that connection. It will be found under No. XXI (Letters).

*That Florence, and its neighbourhood, where Leonardo spent his early years, should be nowhere mentioned except in connection with the projects for canals, which occupied his attention for some short time during the first ten years of the XVI*th* century, need not surprise us. The various passages relating to the construction of canals in Tuscany, which are put together at the beginning, are immediately followed by those which deal with schemes for canals in Lombardy; and after these come notes on the city and vicinity of Milan as well as on the lakes of North Italy.*

*The notes on some towns of Central Italy which Leonardo visited in 1502, when in the service of Cesare Borgia, are reproduced here in the same order as in the note book used during these travels (MS. L., Institut de France). These notes have but little interest in themselves excepting as suggesting his itinerary. The maps of the districts drawn by Leonardo at the time are more valuable (see No. 1054 note). The names on these maps are not written from right to left, but in the usual manner, and we are permitted to infer that they were made in obedience to some command, possibly for the use of Cesare Borgia himself; the fact that they remained nevertheless in Leonardo's hands is not surprising when we remember the sudden political changes and warlike events of the period. There can be no doubt that these maps, which are here published for the first time, are original in the strictest sense of the word, that is to say drawn from observations of the places themselves; this is proved by the fact—among others—that we find among his manuscripts not only the finished maps themselves but the rough sketches and studies for them. And it would perhaps be difficult to point out among the abundant contributions to geographical knowledge published during the XVI*th* century, any maps at all approaching these in accuracy and finish.*

The interesting map of the world, so far as it was then known, which is among the Leonardo MSS. at Windsor (published in the 'Archaeologia' Vol. XI) cannot be attributed to the Master, as the Marchese Girolamo d'Adda has sufficiently proved; it has not therefore been reproduced here.

Such of Leonardo's observations on places in Italy as were made before or after his official travels as military engineer to Cesare Borgia, have been arranged in alphabetical order, under Nos. 1034—1054. The most interesting are those which relate to the Alps and the Appenines, Nos. 1057—1068.

Most of the passages in which France is mentioned have hitherto remained unknown, as well as those which treat of the countries bordering on the Mediterranean, which come at the end of this section. Though these may be regarded as of a more questionable importance in their bearing on the biography of the Master than those which mention places in France, it must be allowed that they are interesting as showing the prominent place which the countries of the East held in his geographical studies. He never once alludes to the discovery of America.

I.

ITALY.

C. A. 45 *a*; 140 *a*]　　　　　　　**1001.**

CANALE DI FIREZE.

[2]Facciasi alle Chiane d' Arezzo · tali · cateratte che, māchando · acqua l' estate in Arno ·, il canale nō rimāga · arido; [3]e facciasi esso canale · largo · in fōdo braccia 20 ·, e 30 in bocca, e braccia 2 · s · per l' acqua o 4 ·, perchè dua d' esse braccia reca [4]alli mvlini e li prati ·; questo · bonificherà il paese ·, e Prato, Pistoia e Pisa insieme cō Firēze, faranno l' anno di meglio [5]dugiē-to mila ducati ·, e porgieranno le mani e spesa a esso · aivtorio, e i Lucchesi il simile, perchè il lago di Sesto fia navicabile; [6]fo lo · fare · la uia di Prato · e Pistoia e tagliare Serravalle . e uscire nel lago ·, perchè nō bisognia conche o sostegni i qua[7]li · nō sono · eterni, anzi senpre si sta in esercitio · a operarli e mantenerli.

[8]E sappi che se, cauādo · il canale ·, doue esso è profondo · 4 braccia, si · dā 4 dinari per braccio quadro, in doppia profondità · si [9]dā · 6 dinari, se fai 4 [10]braccia e' sono

CANAL OF FLORENCE.

Sluices should be made in the valley of la Chiana at Arezzo, so that when, in the summer, the Arno lacks water, the canal may not remain dry: and let this canal be 20 braccia wide at the bottom, and at the top 30, and 2 braccia deep, or 4, so that two of these braccia may flow to the mills and the meadows, which will benefit the country; and Prato, Pistoia and Pisa, as well as Florence, will gain two hundred thousand ducats a year, and will lend a hand and money to this useful work; and the Lucchese the same, for the lake of Sesto will be navigable; I shall direct it to Prato and Pistoia, and cut through Serravalle and make an issue into the lake; for there will be no need of locks or supports, which are not lasting and so will always be giving trouble in working at them and keeping them up.

And know that in digging this canal where it is 4 braccia deep, it will cost 4 dinari the square braccio; for twice the depth 6 dinari, if you are making 4 braccia

Canals in connection with the Arno (1001—1008).

1001. 2. alle chiane darezo . . chateratte . . māchando . acqua \ lastate innarno. 3. effacciasi . . br. 20 . . boccha e br. 2 . 5 . per qua . . dua desse br. rua (?) . 4. elli . . quessto . . pisstoia . . chō . . fia lano dimeglio. 5. porgierano le mani "esspesa" . . sessto. 6. folli fare . . ettagliare esscire. 7. etterni . *Lines* 8—15 br. *stands always for* braccia. 8. Essapi chesse chauādo il chanale . . dopia. 9. dinari [onsi in . 7 . si da il doppio . perche . quelle . sechonde 4 br. il tereno e giassmosso e poi perche] seffai 4. 10. dellabri . . ellaltro. 11. esse fussi. 12. cresse solo . î . bancho . . cresscie. 13. viene dinari sei

1001. This passage is illustrated by a slightly sketched map, on which these places are indicated

from West to East: Pisa, Luccha, Lago, Seravalle, Pistoja, Prato, Firenze.

solamēte · 2 · banchi ·, cioè · vno dal fondo · del fosso · alla superfitie de' labri del fosso ·, e l'altro da essi labri ¹¹ alla · somità del mōte · della · terra che d'in sulla · riva · dell'argine · si leua ·; e se fusse di doppia profondità ·, esso argine ¹² cresce solo · uno banco, cioè braccia · 4 ·, che crescie · la metà della · prima spesa, cioè che, dove prima in 2 banchi · si da ¹³ và · dinari · 4 · in 3, si viene a dare · sei · a 2 dinari · per banco, essendo il fosso in fondo braccia · 16; ancora se'l fosso fusse largo braccia 16 ¹⁴ e profōdo · 4 ·, venēdo · a · 4 L · per opera ·, dinari 4 · Milanesi · il braccio quadro ·; il fosso · che in fondo sarà braccia ¹⁵ 32, verrà a stare dinari · 8 il · braccio quadro.

and there are but 2 banks; that is to say one from the bottom of the trench to the surface of the edges of it, and the other from these edges to the top of the ridge of earth which will be raised on the margin of the bank. And if this bank were of double the depth only the first bank will be increased, that is 4 braccia increased by half the first cost; that is to say that if at first 4 dinari were paid for 2 banks, for 3 it would come to 6, at 2 dinari the bank, if the trench measured 16 braccia at the bottom; again, if the trench were 16 braccia wide and 4 deep, coming to 4 lire for the work, 4 Milan dinari the square braccio; a trench which was 32 braccia at the bottom would come to 8 dinari the square braccio.

L. 1 a]   **1002.**

Dal muro d'Arno della ² Giustitia al-l'argine d'Ar³no di Sardigna, dove sono ⁴ i muri alle mulina, è braccia ⁵ 7400, cioè migla 2 ⁶ e braccia 1400, ⁷ e'l di là d'Arno è braccia 5500.

From the wall of the Arno at [the gate of] la Giustizia to the bank of the Arno at Sardigna where the walls are, to the mills, is 7400 braccia, that is 2 miles and 1400 braccia and beyond the Arno is 5500 braccia.

C. A. 284 a; 865 a]   **1003.**

Dirizzare Arno ² di sotto e di sopra; ³ s'auanzerà vn tesoro, ⁴ a tanto per stajoro ⁵ a chi lo vole.

By guiding the Arno above and below a treasure will be found in each acre of ground by whomsoever will.

Br. M. 273 b]   **1004.**

Il muro dalle ² Casaccie si ³ dirizza alla por⁴ta di san Niccolò.

The wall of the old houses runs towards the gate of San Nicolo.

. . bancho "essendo il fosso in fondo braccia 16" anchora . . fusi largho. 14. [e al] e profōdo. 15. verıa dinari.
1002. 2. gusstitia. 4. e br. 5. [8000] 7400 coe. 6. br. 7. br.
1003. 1. dirizare arnno. 4. attanto perisstaioro.   **1004.** 1. mro d lle. 2. casace [con]. 3. diriza. 4. nicolo.

1002. 2. *Giustizia.* By this the Porta della Giustizia seems to be meant; from the XVth to the XVIth centuries it was also commonly known as Porta Guelfa, Porta San Francesco del Renaio, Porta Nuova, and Porta Reale. It was close to the Arno opposite to the Porta San Niccolò, which still exists.

1004. By the side of this text there is an indistinct sketch, resembling that given under No. 973. On the bank is written the word *Casace.* There then follows in the original a passage of 12 lines in which the consequences of the windings of the river are discussed. A larger but equally hasty diagram on the same page represents the shores of the Arno inside Florence as in two parallel lines. Four horizontal lines indicate the bridges. By the side these measures are stated in figures: 1. (at the Ponte alla Carraja): 230—*largho br.* 12 *e* 2 *di spōda e* 14 *di pile e* 4 *pilastri;* 2. (at the Ponte S. Trinità): 188—*largho br.* 15 *e* 2 *di spōde he* 28 *di pilastri for delle spōde e pilastri sō* 2; 3. (at the Ponte vecchio); *pōte lung br.* 152 *e largo;* 4. (at the Ponte alle Grazie): 290 *ellargo* 12 *e* 2 *di spōde e* 6 *di pili.*

There is, in MS. W. L. 212ᵇ, a sketched plan of Florence, with the following names of gates: *Nicholo—Saminiato—Giorgo—Ghanolini—Porta San Fredian—Prato—Faenza—Ghallo—Pinti—Giustitia.*

1005.

Br. M. 274 a]

640 braccia è il muro rotto, [2]e 130 è il muro rimanēte, [3]col mulino [4]300 braccia à rotto dal Bisarno in 4 anni.

The ruined wall is 640 braccia; 130 is the wall remaining with the mill; 300 braccia were broken in 4 years by Bisarno.

1006.

W. L. 226 a]

Nō sanno, perchè Arno [2]non starà mai in ca[3]nale; perchě [4]i fiumi che vi mettono, [5]nella loro entrata pō[6]gono terreno, e dalla oppo[7]sita parte leuano e [8]pieganvi il fiume; [9]6 miglia si fa per Ar[10]no dalla Caprona a Li[11]vorno, e 12 si fa per li [12]stagni che s'avãzano 32 [13]miglia, e 16 dalla Caprona [14]in sù, che fã 48 [15]per Arno da Firenze, [16]avanzasi 16 miglia; a Vico miglia 16, [17]e'l canale à 5; [18]da Firenze a Fucechio miglia 40 per [19]acqua d'Arno.
[20]Miglia 56 · per Arno [21]da Firēze a Vico, [22]e pel canale di Pistoia [23]è miglia 44 · adū[24]que è piv corta 12 [25]miglia per canale che per Arno.

They do not know why the Arno will never remain in a channel. It is because the rivers which flow into it deposit earth where they enter, and wear it away on the opposite side, bending the river in that direction. The Arno flows for 6 miles between la Caprona and Leghorn; and for 12 through the marshes, which extend 32 miles, and 16 from La Caprona up the river, which makes 48; by the Arno from Florence beyond 16 miles; to Vico 16 miles, and the canal is 5; from Florence to Fucechio it is 40 miles by the river Arno.
56 miles by the Arno from Florence to Vico; by the Pistoia canal it is 44 miles. Thus it is 12 miles shorter by the canal than by the Arno.

1007.

Leic. 18 b]

Cōcauità fatta da Mēsola, quãdo Arno è basso e Mē-sola grossa.

The eddy made by the Mensola, when the Arno is low and the Mensola full.

1005. 1. 6400 bre. 2. moro.
1006. 2. nōnistara. 4. mettano. 6. gã terreno e dallopo. 10. caprona alli. 12. savãza. 17. ecanale. 19. acq"a". 24. chorta.

1006. This passage is written by the side of a map washed in Indian ink, of the course of the Arno; it is evidently a sketch for a completer map.

These investigations may possibly be connected with the following documents. *Francesco Guiducci alla Balìa di Firenze. Dal Campo contro Pisa 24 Luglio* 1503 (*Archivio di Stato, Firenze, Lettere alla Balìa;* published by J. GAYE, *Carteggio inedito d'Artisti,* Firenze 1840, *Tom. II,* p. 62): *Ex Castris, Franciscus Ghuiduccius,* 24. *Jul.* 1503. *Appresso fu qui hieri con una di V. Signoria Alexandro degli Albizi insieme con Leonardo da Vinci et certi altri, et veduto el disegno insieme con el ghovernatore, doppo molte discussioni et dubii conclusesi che l'opera fussi molto al proposito, o si veramente Arno volgersi qui, o restarvi con un canale, che almeno viete- rebbe che le colline da nemici non potrebbono essere offese; come tucto referiranno loro a bocha V. S.*

And, *Archivio di Stato, Firenze, Libro d'Entrata e Uscita di cassa de' Magnifici Signori di luglio e agosto* 1503 *a* 51 *T.: Andata di Leonardo al Campo sotto Pisa. Spese extraordinarie dieno dare a di XXVI di luglio L. LVI sol. XIII per loro a Giovanni Piffero; e sono per tanti, asegnia avere spexi in vetture di sei chavalli a spese di vitto per andare chon Lionardo da Vinci a livellare Arno in quello di Pisa per levallo del lito suo.* (Published by MILANESI, *Archivio Storico Italiano, Serie III, Tom. XVI.*) VASARI asserts: *(Leonardo) fu il primo ancora, che giovanetto discorrese sopra il fiume d'Arno per metterlo in canale da Pisa a Fiorenza* (ed. SANSONI, IV, 20).

The passage above is in some degree illustrated by the map on Pl. CXII, where the course of the Arno westward from Empoli is shown.

1007. *Mensola* is a mountain stream which falls into the Arno about a mile and a half above Florence.

A=Arno, I=Isola, M=Mvgone, P=Pesa, N=Me-sola.

Leic. 13a]   **1008.**

Come il fiume, che s'a à piegare d'uno in altro loco, debbe essere lusin²gato e nõ con uiolenza aspreggiato, e a questo fare si de' cauare infra'l fiume alquãto ³di pescaia, e poi di sotto gittarne vna piv inãti, e così si faccia colla 3ª 4ª e 5ª, in modo che'l ⁴fiume inbocchi col canale datoli, o che per tal mezzo si scosti dal loco da lui danneggiato, come ⁵fu fatto in Fiãdra, dettomi da Niccolò di Forzore;

Come si de' vestire di riparo vn argine percosso ⁶dal'acqua, come sotto l'isola de'Cocomeri.

That the river which is to be turned from one place to another must be coaxed and not treated roughly or with violence; and to do this a sort of floodgate should be made in the river, and then lower down one in front of it and in like manner a third, fourth and fifth, so that the river may discharge itself into the channel given to it, or that by this means it may be diverted from the place it has damaged, as was done in Flanders—as I was told by Niccolò di Forsore.

How to protect and repair the banks washed by the water, as below the island of Cocomeri.

Fig. 1.

Fig. 2.

Fig. 3.

Fig. 4.

⁷Põte Rubaconte (Fig. 1); ⁸sotto il Bisticci ⁹e Canigiani (Fig. 2); ¹⁰sopra la pescaia de¹¹lla Givstitia (Fig. 3); ¹²a b è vna secca ¹³a riscõtro doue fi¹⁴niscie l'isola de' Coco¹⁵meri in mezzo d'Ar¹⁶no (Fig. 4).

Ponte Rubaconte (Fig. 1); below [the palaces] Bisticci and Canigiani (Fig. 2). Above the flood gate of la Giustizia (Fig. 3); a b is a sand bank opposite the end of the island of the Cocomeri in the middle of the Arno (Fig. 4).

C. A. 387a; 1197a]   **1009.**

Canals in the Milanese (1009—1013).

Navilio di san Cristoforo di Milano fatto a dì 3 di maggio 1509.

The canal of San Cristofano at Milan made May 3rd 1509.

F. 76b]   **1010.**

DEL CANALE DI MARTESANA.

²Facēdo il canale di Martesana e'si diminuisce ³l'acqua all'Adda, la qual è destribuita in mol⁴ti paesi al seruitio de' prati; Ecco vn rime⁵dio, e questo è di fare molti

OF THE CANAL OF MARTESANA.

By making the canal of Martesana the water of the Adda is greatly diminished by its distribution over many districts for the irrigation of the fields. A remedy for this

---

1008. 1. chessa . . locho. 2. asspreggato e acquessto. 4. inbochi . . mezo si scossti dal locho dallui damegato. 5. nicholo . . percossa. 8. besticci. 9. camigagani. 10. pesscaja. 11. giosstitia. 15. imezo.

1009. crisstofano . . facto addi . . maggo.

1010. 1. martigana. 2. martigana . . diminuissce. 3. imol. 4. Ecci. 5. ecquesto . . checq. 6. beuta datta terra. 8. nessono

---

1008. The course of the river Arno is also discussed in Nos. 987 and 988.

1009. This observation is written above a washed pen and ink drawing which has been published as Tav. VI in the „Saggio." The editors of that work explain the drawing as "uno Studio di bocche per estrazione d'acqua."

1010. "el navilio di Martagano" is also mentioned

in a note written in red chalk, MS. H² 17ª Leonardo has, as it seems, little to do with Lodovico il Moro's scheme to render this canal navigable. The canal had been made in 1460 by Bertonino da Novara. Il Moro issued his degree in 1493, but Leonardo's notes about this canal were, with the exception of one (No. 1343), written about sixteen years later.

fontanili, chè q⁶uell'acqua, che è bevuta dalla terra nō fa ser⁷uitio a nessuno, nè ancora danno, perchè a ⁸nessuno è tolta, e facēdo tali fontanili, l'acqua, ⁹che prima era perduta, ritorna di nouo a rifa¹⁰re seruitio e vtile alli omini.

would be to make several little channels, since the water drunk up by the earth is of no more use to any one, nor mischief neither, because it is taken from no one; and by making these channels the water which before was lost returns again and is once more serviceable and useful to men.

Leic. 18a]

IOII.

Nessuno canale, che esca fori de' fiumi, sarà durabile, se l'acqua del fiume, donde ²nascie, non è integralmēte rinchiusa come il canal di Martisana e quel ch' escie di Tesino.

No canal which is fed by a river can be permanent if the river whence it originates is not wholly closed up, like the canal of Martesana which is fed by the Ticino.

C. A. 139b ; 421b]

1012.

Dal principio del navilio al mo²lino.

³Dal prīcipio del navilio di Briuio al ⁴molino del Travaglia è trabochi 2794, ⁵cioè · braccia 11176, che son più di 3 miglia ⁶e due terzi, e quiui truovo più alto il ⁷navilio che la pelle dell'acqua di

From the beginning of the canal to the mill.

From the beginning of the canal of Brivio to the mill of Travaglia is 2794 trabochi, that is 11176 braccia, which is more than 3 miles and two thirds; and here the canal is 57 braccia higher than the surface

ettolta effacēdo . . lacq"a". 9. primo. 10. omini E . *there the text breaks off*.
IOII. I. chanale . . essca . . sellacqua. 2. nasscie , . rinciusa . . tessino.
IOI2. marligana ecquel . . esscie. 5. br. 11176. 6. ecquini. 7. chella . . dellacq"a' . . br. 57. 8. chalo.

IOI2. The following are written on the sketches: At the place marked *N: navilio da dacquiue* (canal of running water); at *M: molin del Travaglia* (Mill of Travaglia); at *R: rochetta ssanta maria* (small-rock of Santa Maria); at *A: Adda;* at *L: Lagho di Lecho ringorgato alli 3 corni in Adda,—Concha perpetua* (lake

Adda · braccia 57, [8]a dare due ōcie di calo per ogni cēto trabochi, [9]e in tal sito

of the water of the Adda, giving a fall of two inches in every hundred trabochi; and

disegniamo torre la bocha [10]del nostro navilio.

at that spot we propose to take the opening of our canal.

C. A. 233*a*; 700*a*]   **1013.**

¶Se nō ui si da fama che questo sia canale pu²blico, e' sarà necessario pagare il terreno, ³e lo pagherà il rè col lasciare li dazi d'un āno.

If it be not reported there that this is to be a public canal, it will be necessary to pay for the land; and the king will pay it by remitting the taxes for a year.

H.² 43*a*]   **1014.**

NAVILIO.

CANAL.

Estimates and preparatory studies for canals (1014. 1015).

²Jl navilio · che sia · largo in fōdo ³braccia 16 · e in bocca · 20 ·, si potrà dire ⁴in soma · tutto · largo braccia 18 ·, e se sarà ⁵profondo · 4 · braccia ·, a 4 · dinari il quadretto ·, ⁶costerà · il miglio · cavatura · sola ⁷duc. 900 ·, essendo · i quadreti · di ⁸comune · braccio, ma se le · braccia saranno ⁹a vso · di misura · di terra ·, che ogni ¹⁰4 . son 4 . e ¹/₄, e se il miglio s'ī¹¹tēde di tre mila braccia comuni, a tornar · ¹²in braccia · di · terra · le sua 3000 · braccia tor¹³nano · māco ¹/₄, che restano · braccia · ¹⁴2250, che a 4 dinari il · braccio, mōta ¹⁵il miglio ducati 675; a 3 dina¹⁶ri il quadretto mōta il miglio ducati ¹⁷506¹/₄, che la cavatura di 30 mi¹⁸glia di navilio mōta ducati 15187 · ¹/₂.

The canal which may be 16 braccia wide at the bottom and 20 at the top, we may say is on the average 18 braccia wide, and if it is 4 braccia deep, at 4 dinari the square braccia; it will only cost 900 ducats, to excavate by the mile, if the square braccio is calculated in ordinary braccia; but if the braccia are those used in measuring land, of which every 4 are equal to 4¹/₂, and if by the mile we understand three thousand ordinary braccia; turned into land braccia, these 3000 braccia will lack ¹/₄; there remain 2250 braccia, which at 4 dinari the braccio will amount to 675 ducats a mile. At 3 dinari the square braccio, the mile will amount to 506¹/₄ ducats so that the excavation of 30 miles of the canal will amount to 15187 ¹/₂ ducats.

1013. 2. necesario. 3. ello pagera . . lidāti.
1014. 2. chessia. 3. br. 16 . . boccha . . portrà di. 4. tucto . . br. 18 essessara. 5. 4 br. a 4 . di. 6. chosstera. 7. quadrecti.
8. br. massellebr. sarano. 10. ¹/₂ M sseil. 11. mila br. 12. br. di . . comunitornar. 12. 3000 br. 13. restaño br.
14. il ¦br. 16. duc. 17. chella. 18. colasciare duc.

of Lecco overflowing at Tre Corni, in Adda,— a permanent sluice). Near the second sketch, referring to the sluice near Q: *qui la chatena ttalie d'ũ peso* (here the chain is in one piece). At *M* in the lower sketch: *mol⁻ del travaglia, nel cavare la concha il tereno ara chōtrapeso cō cassa d'acqua* (Mill of Travaglia, in digging out the sluice the soil will have as a counterpoise a vessel of water).

1013. 3. *il rè.* Louis XII or Francis I of France. It is hardly possible to doubt that the canals here spoken of were intended to be in the Milanese. Compare with this passage the rough copy of a letter by Leonardo, to the "*Presidente dell' Ufficio regolatore dell' acqua*" on No. 1350. See also the note to No. 745, l. 12.

Br. M. 149 a]   **1015.**

Per fare il grā ²canale, fa prima ³il   To make the great canal, first make the
piccolo e dalli ⁴l'acqua, che colla ⁵rota farà   smaller one and conduct into it the waters
il grāde.   which by a wheel will help to fill the great one.

C. A. 72 b; 211 b]   **1016.**

¶Poni il uero mezzo di Milano.¶   Indicate the centre of Milan.

Mōforte—porta rēsa—porta nova—strada nova—navilio—porta cumana—barco—porta Notes on
giovia—porta vercellina—porta sco Anbrogio—porta Tesinese—torre dell'Imperatore— buildings at
porta Lodovica—acqua.   Milan
                                                                                  (1016—1019).

I.¹ 32 b]   **1017.**

                                         A

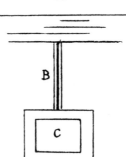

Rifosso di Mila²no;   The moat of Milan.

³Canale ⁴largo 2 ⁵braccia;   Canal 2 braccia wide.

⁶Castello ⁷con fossi ingor-   The castle with the moats
gati;   full.

⁸Ingorgatione ⁹de' fossi del   The filling of the moats of
¹⁰castello di Milā.   the Castle of Milan.

I.¹ 34 a]   **1018.**

            Bagno.   The bath.

²Per iscaldare l'acqua della stufa della   To heat the water for the stove of the
³duchessa torrai 3 parti d'acqua cal¹¹da   Duchess take four parts of cold water to
sopra 4 parti d'acqua fredda.   three parts of hot water.

1015. 1—5 R. 3. picholo. 4. lachq"a" che cholla.
1016. 1. mezo; — barcho — tore delomperatore — porta lodovicha.
1017. 7. co fossi.   1018. 2. lacq"a". 3. torai . . parte dacq"a" chal. 4. dacq"a".

1016. See Pl. CIX. The original sketch is here   noticed. On the sketched Plan of Florence (see
reduced to about half its size. The gates of the   No. 1004 note) Leonardo has written on the margin
town are here named, beginning at the right hand   the following names of gates of Milan: Vercel-
and following the curved line. In the bird's eye   lina — Ticinese — Ludovica — Romana — Orientale —
view of Milan below, the cathedral is plainly recog- Nova—Beatrice—Cumana.—Compare too No. 1448,
nisable in the middle; to the right is the tower of San ll. 5, 12.
Gottardo. The square, above the number 9147, is   1018. *Duchessa di Milano*, Beatrice d'Este, wife of
the Lazzaretto, which was begun in 1488. On the   Ludovico il Moro to whom she was married, in
left the group of buildings of the '*Castello*' will be 1491. She died in June 1497.

L. 15 a]   **1019.**

In domo alla car-
ruco²la del chiodo
della croce;
    ³item.
    ⁴Da mettere il
⁵corpo *v r* ⁶nello . . . .

In the Cathedral at
the pulley of the nail
of the cross.
    Item.
    To place the mass
v r in the . . .

E. 1 a]   **1020.**

DELLA POTENTIA DEL UACUO ²GIENERATO IN
ISTĀTE.

OF THE FORCE OF THE VACUUM FORMED IN
A MOMENT.

³Vidi a Milano v̄a saetta percuotere la
⁴torre della Credenza da quella parte ⁵che
risguarda tramōtana e disciese ⁶con tardo
moto per esso lato, e inmediate ⁷si divise
da essa torre, ⁸e si ualse d'esso ⁹muro uno
spa¹⁰tio di 3 braccia per o¹¹gniv̄o e pro-
¹²fondo due, e ¹³questo muro ¹⁴era grosso
4 braccia, ¹⁵ed era mura¹⁶to di sottili e
¹⁷minuti matto¹⁸ni antichi, ¹⁹e questo fu
ti²⁰rato dal uacu²¹o, che la ²²fiāma della
²³saetta lasciò ²⁴di se ecc.

I saw, at Milan, a thunderbolt fall on
the tower della Credenza on its Northern
side, and it descended with a slow motion
down that side, and then at once parted from
that tower and carried with it and tore away
from that wall a space of 3 braccia wide
and two deep; and this wall was 4 braccia
thick and was built of thin and small old
bricks; and this was dragged out by the
vacuum which the flame of the thunderbolt
had caused, &c.

Leic. 28 a]   **1021.**

Io sono già stato a vedere tal mvltiplicatione (di arie) e già ²sopra a Milano inverso lago Maggiore vidi vna nvuola in

Remarks on
natural phe-
nomena in
and near
Milan
(1021. 1022).

I have already been to see a great
variety (of atmospheric effects). And lately
over Milan towards Lago Maggiore I saw a

1019. 1. charucho. 2. ciodo. 6. nello s *here the text breaks off.*

1020. 1. uachuo. 2. isstāte. 3. perchotere. 4. dacquella. 5. rissghuarda mōtana e dissciesse. 7. torre e porto chonsecho.
    8. essiulse. 10. 3. br. 13. cquesto. 14. 4 br. 18. antichi ec. 19. ecquessto. 20. uachu. 21. chella. 23. lasscio.

1021. 1. mvltiplicatione e ga. 2. magore . . mōtaggnia . . scoli. 3. infochati . . razi . . ga . . orizonte . . rossegaua . .

1019. On this passage AMORETTI remarks *(Memorie Storiche* chap. IX): *Nell'anno stesso lo veggiamo
formare un congegno di caruole e di corde, con cui tras-
portare in più venerabile e più sicuro luogo, cioè nel-
l'ultima arcata della nave di mezzo della metropolitana, la
sacra reliquia del Santo Chiodo, che ivi ancor si venera.
Al fol. 15 del codice segnato Q. R. in 16, egli ci ha lasciata di tal congegno una doppia figura, cioè una di
quattro caruole, e una di tre colle rispettive corde, sog-
giugnandovi: in Domo alla caruola del Chiodo della
Croce.*

AMORETTI's views as to the mark on the MS.
and the date when it was written are, it may be

observed, wholly unfounded. The MS. L, in which
it occurs, is of the year 1502, and it is very un-
likely that Leonardo was in Milan at that time;
this however would not prevent the remark, which
is somewhat obscure, from applying to the Cathedral
at Milan.

1020. With reference to buildings at Milan see
also Nos. 751 and 756, and Pl. XCV, No. 2 (explained on p. 52), Pl. C (explained on pages 60—62).
See also pages 25, 39 and 40.

1021. *di arie* is wanting in the original but may
safely be inserted in the context, as the formation
of clouds is under discussion before this text.

forma di grandissima mōtagnia, piena di scogli ³infocati, perchè li razzi del sole, che già era all'orizzonte che rosseggiava, la tigneano del suo colore, e questa tal nugola ⁴attraeva a se tutti li nvgoli piccoli che intorno li stavano, e la nugola grāde nō si mouea di suo loco, anzi ri⁵seruò nella sua sommità il lume del sole insino a una ora e mezzo di notte, tant'era la sua immēsa grādezza; ⁶e infra due ore di notte gienerò si gran vēto che fu cosa stupēda e inavdita.

cloud in the form of an immense mountain full of rifts of glowing light, because the rays of the sun, which was already close to the horizon and red, tinged the cloud with its own hue. And this cloud attracted to it all the little clouds that were near while the large one did not move from its place; thus it retained on its summit the reflection of the sunlight till an hour and a half after sunset, so immensely large was it; and about two hours after sunset such a violent wind arose, that it was really tremendous and unheard of.

1022.

W. XXVIII.]

A dì 10 di diciembre a ore 15 ²fu appicato il fuoco;
³A dì 18 di dicembre 1511 a ore 15 fu fatto questo ⁴secondo incendio da Suizzeri a Milano ⁵al luogo detto DCXC.

On the 10ᵗʰ day of December at 9 o'clock a. m. fire was set to the place.
On the 18ᵗʰ day of December 1511 at 9 o'clock a. m. this second fire was kindled by the Swiss at Milan at the place called DCXC.

1023.

B. 58 a]

Camini del castello di Pauia, ²año 6 gradi di busi; è dall'uno ³all'altro uno braccio.

The chimneys of the castle of Pavia have 6 rows of openings and from each to the other is one braccio.

Note on Pavia.

ecquesta. 4. asse . . picholi . . locho. 5. somita . . mezo . . imēsu grādeza. 6. stupēte inavldita.
1022. 1—5 (R). 2. apicato . . fuocho. 3. Lore. 4. suizeri. 5. alloguo dicto.
1023. 2. buse. 3. ĩ br.

1022. With these two texts, (l. 1—2 and l. 3—5 are in the original side by side) there are sketches of smoke wreaths in red chalk.

1023. Other notes relating to Pavia occur on p. 43 and p. 53 (Pl. XCVIII, No. 3). Compare No. 1448, 26.

H.² 17 b]   **1024.**

Notes on the
Sforzesca
near Vige-
vano
(1024—1028).

A dì 2 di febraro 1494 alla ²Sforzesca
ritrassi scalini 25 ³di ²/₃ di braccio l'uno,
larghe braccia 8.

On the 2ⁿᵈ day of February 1494.
At Sforzesca I drew twenty five steps, ²/₃
braccia to each, and 8 braccia wide.

H.¹ 38 a]   **1025.**

Vignie di Vigevano ²a dì 20 di marzo
1494.

The vineyards of Vigevano on the 20ᵗʰ
day of March 1494.

H.¹ 1 a]   **1026.**

Da serrare in chiave vno · īcastro ²a
Vigievano.

To lock up a butteris at Vigevano.

Leic. 21 a]   **1027.**

Ancora se la infima parte dell'argine
trauersalmēte opposto al cor²so delle acque
sarà fatto in potenti e larghi gradi a uso
di scala, l'acque ³che nell'abassamento
del lor corso sogliono perpendicularmente
cadere dal ter⁴mine di tale loco in infima
sua bassezza e scalzare i fondamēti d'esso
argine, non po⁵tran più discendere con
colpo di troppa valitudine; e lo esenpio
dico fu a me quella ⁶scala, onde cadea
l'acqua de'prati della Sforzesca di Vige-
uano, sulla quale ui cadea ⁷l'acqua corrēte
in 50 braccia d'altezza.

Again if the lowest part of the bank
which lies across the current of the waters
is made in deep and wide steps, after the
manner of stairs, the waters which, in their
course usually fall perpendicularly from the
top of such a place to the bottom, and wear
away the foundations of this bank can no
longer descend with a blow of too great a
force; and I find the example of this in the
stairs down which the water falls in the
fields at Sforzesca at Vigevano over which
the running water falls for a height of 50
braccia.

Leic. 32 a]   **1028.**

Scala di Vigevano ²sotto la Sforzesca
di 130 ³scaglioni, alti ¹/₄ e lar⁴ghi ¹/₂ braccio, per la qual ⁵cade l'ac-
qua e non ⁶consuma niēte
nell'ul⁷tima percussione, e
per ⁸tale scala è disceso ⁹tanto
terreno che a¹⁰sseccò vn padule, cio¹¹è riempì, e se
n'è fat¹²to praterie da padu¹³
le di grā profondità.

Stair of Vigevano below La Sforzesca,
130 steps, ¹/₄ braccio high and ¹/₂ braccio wide,
down which the water falls, so as
not to wear away anything at the
end of its fall; by these steps
so much soil has come down
that it has dried up a pool;
that is to say it has filled it up
and a pool of great depth has
been turned into meadows.

1024. 1—3 R. 1. allas. 2. sforzesscha . . schalini. 3. di br . . large br.
1025. 1—2 R. 1. vigievine.   1026 1—2 R. 1. asserare. 2. avigievine.
1027. 1. sella . . pare . . oposto. 2. fatti . . ellarghi . . disscala lacqua. 3. 2 . delor soglian . . chadere. 4. tale infima . .
basseza e dissalzare . . desse. 5. disscendere . tropa . . ello . . foame colla. 6. pradi . . sforzessca di uigieuine la qual
ui cadea su. 7. corēte . . br. dalteza.
1028. 1. schala di uigeuine. 2. sforzessa di [100] 130. 3. ellar. 4. ¹/₂ br . . 5. chade. 7. perchussione. 8. dissceso. 10. secho
. . co. 11. rienpivto essene. 12. di padu.

1024. See Pl. CX, No. 2. The rest of the notes on this page refer to the motion of water. On the
lower sketch we read: 4 *br.* (four braccia) and *giara* (for *ghiaja*, sand, gravel).
1025. On one side there is an effaced sketch in red chalk.

Leic. 11 b]

1029.

Come in molti lochi si trovano ve²ne d'acqua che sei ore crescono e sei ore calano, e io per me n'ò veduto vna in sul lago di Como, detta fonte Pli³niana, la quale fa il predetto cresciere e diminuire in modo che, quando uersa, macina due mulini, e quãdo mãca, ⁴cala sì ch'egli è come guardare l'acqua in vn profondo pozzo.

In many places there are streams of Notes on the North Italian lakes (1029—1033). water which swell for six hours and ebb for six hours; and I, for my part, have seen one above the lake of Como called Fonte Pliniana, which increases and ebbs, as I have said, in such a way as to turn the stones of two mills; and when it fails it falls so low that it is like looking at water in a deep pit.

C. A. 211 a; 619 a]

1030.

LAGO DI COMO · ²VAL DI CHIAUENNA.

³Sù pel lago di Como, diuerso la Magnia, è valle Chiauenna doue la Mera fiume mette in esso ⁴lago; qui si truovano mõtagnie · sterili e altissime · con grãdi scogli ·; ĵ queste mõtagnie ⁵li uccielli · d'acqua sono detti marãgoni; qui nascono abeti, larici e pini ·, daini, stãbecchi, camoz⁶zi · e terribili · orsi ·; nõ ci si · può mõtare ·, se non è a 4 piedi ·; vannoci · i villani · a'tẽpi delle ⁷nevi cõ grãdi · ingegni · per fare trabocare gli orsi giv · per esse · ripe; queste ⁸mõtagnie strette mettono in mezzo · il fiume ·, sono a destra e a sinistra per spatio ⁹di miglia 20. tutte a detto modo ·; truovãsi di miglio in miglio bone · osterie ·; su¹⁰per detto fiume · si truovano · cadute · d'acqua di 400 braccia, le quali fanno bel vedere; ¹¹e c'è bõ uiuere · a 4 soldi per scotto ·; per esso fiume si cõduce assai · legniame.

LAKE OF COMO. VALLEY OF CHIAVENNA.

Above the lake of Como towards Germany is the valley of Chiavenna where the river Mera flows into this lake. Here are barren and very high mountains, with huge rocks. Among these mountains are to be found the water-birds called gulls. Here grow fir trees, larches and pines. Deer, wild-goats, chamois, and terrible bears. It is impossible to climb them without using hands and feet. The peasants go there at the time of the snows with great snares to make the bears fall down these rocks. These mountains which very closely approach each other are parted by the river. They are to the right and left for the distance of 20 miles throughout of the same nature. From mile to mile there are good inns. Above on the said river there are waterfalls of 400 braccia in height, which are fine to see; and there is good living at 4 soldi the reckoning. This river brings down a great deal of timber.

VAL SASINA.

¹³Val Sasina · viene diuerso · la Italia .; questa è quasi di simile forma e natura; ¹⁴nascie vi assai mappello ·, e ci sono grã ruine e cadute d'acque.

VAL SASINA.

Val Sasina runs down towards Italy; this is almost the same form and character. There grow here many *mappello* and there are great ruins and falls of water[14].

1029. 1. imolti . . trova. 2. cresscano essei . . chalano . . veduta . . sulago di chomo . . fonte pri. 3. cresciere macina piv mulina . . mãcha. 4. chalisi . . lacqua non . . pozo.

1030. 2. ciauenna. 3. super . . diuer . . ciauenna . . "fiume" mette. 4. truova mõtagni . . chon. 5. dacqua dette . . nasscie . . larice eppini . . stã becche chamo. 6. ze . . teribili . . po . . delli. 7. chõ grãde ingiẽgri . . trabochare. 8. metano . . mezo . . desstra e assinistra . . isspatio. 9. imiglio. 10. truova chadute . . br. le quale. 11. uci bõ . . ischotto per ess . . chõduce. 14. nasscievi . . ecci grã . . ecchadute. 15. valle ditrozzo. 16. ellarici. 17. tessta . . Voltolina elle . . leorme. 18. sepre

---

1029. 2. 3. The fountain is known by this name to this day: it is near Torno, on the Eastern shore of Como. The waters still rise and fall with the flow and ebb of the tide as Pliny described it (Epist. IV, 30; Hist. Nat. II, 206).

1030. 1031. From the character of the handwriting we may conclude that these observations were made in Leonardo's youth; and I should infer from their contents, that they were notes made in anticipation of a visit to the places here described, and derived from some person (unknown to us) who had given him an account of them.

14. The meaning of *mappello* is unknown.

VALLE D'INTROZZO.

[16]Questa valle · produce assai abeti pini e larici ·, è doue Anbrogio Fereri fa [17]venire · il suo legniame ·; in testa · della Valtellina sono le mōtagnie di Bormio, [18]terribili · e piene sēpre di neve; qui nascono ermellini.

VALLEY OF INTROZZO.

This valley produces a great quantity of firs, pines and larches; and from here Ambrogio Fereri has his timber brought down; at the head of the Valtellina are the mountains of Bormio, terrible and always covered with snow; marmots (?) are found there.

A BELLAGGIO.

[20]A riscontro · a Bellaggio · castello è il fiume Latte ·, el quale · cade da alto [21]piv che braccia · 100 dalla vena ·, donde nascie, a piōbo nel lago · cō inestimabile strepito [22]e romore ·; questa vena versa solamēte agosto e settēbre.

BELLAGGIO.

Opposite the castle Bellaggio there is the river Latte, which falls from a height of more than 100 braccia from the source whence it springs, perpendicularly, into the lake with an inconceivable roar and noise. This spring flows only in August and September.

VALTELLINA.

[24]Valtellina ·, com'è detto, valle circūdata d'alti e terribili · mōti, fa [25]vini potēti · e assai ·, e fa tanto bestiame · che da paesani · è concluso · nascierui [25]piv latte che uino ·; questa è la ualle · doue passa Adda, la quale prima corre [27]piv che 40 miglia per la Magnia ·; questo fiume fa il pescie temolo, il quale [28]vive d'argiēto ·, del quale · se ne truova · assai per la sua rena; [29]j questo paese ognivno · può vēdere pane . e vino, e'l uino vale al piv uno soldo [30]il boccale · e la libra della uitella uno soldo, e'l sale 10 dinari, e'l simile il burro, [31]ed è la loro libbra 30 ōcie e l'oua uno soldo la soldata.

VALTELLINA.

Valtellina, as it is called, is a valley enclosed in high and terrible mountains; it produces much strong wine, and there is so much cattle that the natives conclude that more milk than wine grows there. This is the valley through which the Adda passes, which first runs more than 40 miles through Germany; this river breeds the fish *temolo* which live on silver, of which much is to be found in its sands. In this country every one can sell bread and wine, and the wine is worth at most one soldo the bottle and a pound of veal one soldo, and salt ten dinari and butter the same and their pound is 30 ounces, and eggs are one soldo the lot.

C. A. 211*b*; 619*b*]   **1031.**

A BORMIO.

[2]A Bormio sono · i bagni ·;—sopra Como otto miglia · è la Pliniana, [3]la quale · crescie e discrescie ogni 6 · ore, e'l suo crescere fa [4]acqua per 2 mvlina e n'avanza, e'l suo calare fa asciugare la fonte; [5]più su 2 miglia · è Nesso · terra, dove cade uno fiume cō grāde [6]enpito per una grādissima fessura di mōte ·; Queste gite sō da [7]fare nel mese di maggio; E i maggior sassi scoperti che si truovano [8]in questi paesi · sono le mōtagnie di Mādello, vicine alle mōtagnie di [9]Lecco e di Gravidona inverso Bellin-

AT BORMIO.

At Bormio are the baths;—About eight miles above Como is the Pliniana, which increases and ebbs every six hours, and its swell supplies water for two mills; and its ebbing makes the spring dry up; two miles higher up there is Nesso, a place where a river falls with great violence into a vast rift in the mountain. These excursions are to be made in the month of May. And the largest bare rocks that are to be found in this part of the country are the mountains of Mandello 'near to those of Lecco, and

---

nascie. 19. abbellagio. 20. arischontro abbellagio . chastello . . fiume lacci"o" el. 21. nascie a piōbo ne gallo chō inistimabile strepido. 22. erromore. 23. valtolina. 24. chome . . circhūdata . . etteribili. 25. vni . . effa . . besstiame . . paessani . . nasscier ui. 26. ella . . ada . . chore. 27. pessciò temere il. 29. po . . î soldo. 30. bochale ella . . î soldo ell . . burlo. 31. lbra . . elloua.
1031. abormi. 2. abormi . . ella priniana. 3. cresscie e disseresscie ōgni . . cresscière. 4. asscigare. 5. piussu . . tera . . î fiume chō. 7. del .. magio . . magior . . schoperti chessi truovno. 8. visine. 9. leche e di gravidonia . . mglia allecho

zona, a 30 miglia da Lecco, [10]e quelle di ualle di Chiavenna ·, ma la maggiore è quella di Mādello, [11]la quale · à nella · sua basa vna buca diuerso il lago, la quale va sotto [12]200 scalini ·, e qui d'ogni tēpo è ghiaccio · e vēto.

IN VALSASINA.

[14]Ī Valsasina infra · Vimognio et · Introbbio ·, a man destra entrādo per uia di [15]Lecco, si trova la Troggia fiume ·, che cade da uno sasso · altissimo e cadēdo entra [16]sotto terra · e lì finisce · il fiume ·; 3 · miglia · piv là si truouano li edifiti [17]della · vena · del rame · e dello argēto ·, presso a una terra · detta Prato Santo Pietro, [18]e vene di ferro, e cose fantastiche ·; la Grignia è piv alta · mōtagnia ch'abbino [19]questi paesi ed è pelata.

of Gravidona towards Bellinzona, 30 miles from Lecco, and those of the valley of Chiavenna; but the greatest of all is that of Mandello, which has at its base an opening towards the lake, which goes down 200 steps, and there at all times is ice and wind.

IN VAL SASINA.

In Val Sasina, between Vimognio and Introbbio, to the right hand, going in by the road to Lecco, is the river Troggia which falls from a very high rock, and as it falls it goes underground and the river ends there. 3 miles farther we find the buildings of the mines of copper and silver near a place called Pra' Santo Pietro, and mines of iron and curious things. La Grigna is the highest mountain there is in this part, and it is quite bare.

C. A. 270 a; 821 a]　　　　　　　　**1032.**

Il lago di Pusiano [2]versa in nel lago [3]di Segrino e d'Annone [4]e di Sala; [5]Il lago d'Añone ha 22 braccia più alta la pelle [6]della sua acqua che la pelle dell'acqua [7]del lago di Lecco, e 20 braccia è più alto [8]il lago di Pusiano che'l lago d'Añone, [9]le quali, giūte colle braccia 22 dette, fan braccia 42, [10]e quest è la maggiore altezza che abbia la pe[11]lle del lago di Pusiāno sopra la pelle del la[12]go di Lecco.

The lake of Pusiano flows into the lake of Segrino [3] and of Annone and of Sala. The lake of Annone is 22 braccia higher at the surface of its water than the surface of the water of the lake of Lecco, and the lake of Pusiano is 20 braccia higher than the lake of Annone, which added to the afore said 22 braccia make 42 braccia and this is the greatest height of the surface of the lake of Pusiano above the surface of the lake of Lecco.

G. 1 a]　　　　　　　　　　**1033.**

A Santa Maria nella valle [2]di Ravagnate, ne' mōti Briātia sō le pertiche [3]di castagne di 9 braccia e di 14 l'u[2]no in 100. [5]A Varallo di Ponbia presso a Sesto [6]sopra Tesino sono li cotogni biāchi grā[7]di e duri.

At Santa Maria in the Valley of Ravagnate in the mountains of Brianza are the rods of chestnuts of 9 braccia and one out of an average of 100 will be 14 braccia. At Varallo di Ponbia near to Sesto on the Ticino the quinces are white, large and hard.

10. ecquelle . . edavenna malla magiore ecquella. 11. busa. 12. schalini . . diaggio. 14. ualsasina ifra . . desstra. 15. leccho . . trosa . . chade . . da ī . . chadēdo. 16. elli finissce . . pivlla si truova. 17. arzēto . . prascto petro. 18. fero . . chabbi. 19. edie.

1032. 1. ilago di pusiā. 2. inel lagho. 3. di serio e danō. 5. lagho danō . . br . . alto. 6. chella. 7. lagho . . br. eppiu. 8. he il lagho. 8. pustā . . danō br. 20. 9. gute . . br. 22 . . br. 42. 10. ecqueste la magore alteza . . la pel . . Pusiā. 12. gho di lecho.

1033. 1. maria \\\\o nella. 2. di ranvagnā . . briātia. 3. 9 br. e di 14 [et] 7 (?) lu. 4. re (? = no) in 100 di 9 br. 5. a voral di ponbio presso assesto. 6. licatₐni. 7. edduri.

1032. This text has in the original a slight sketch to illustrate it.—3. The statement about the lake Segrino is incorrect; it is situated in the Valle Assina, above the lake of Pusiano.

1033. 2. *Ravagnate* (Leonardo writes *Ravagnā*) in the Brianza is between Oggiono and Brivio, South of the lake of Como. M. Ravaisson avails himself of this note to prove his hypothesis

L. 6 a]   **1034.**

Colōbaia a Urbino a dì 30 ² di luglio   Pigeon-house at Urbino, the 30ᵗʰ day
1502.   of July 1502.

L. 6 b]   **1035.**

Fatta al mare di Piō-   Made by the sea at
bino.   Piombino.

L. 10 b]   **1036.**

Acquapendente è a Oruieto.   Acquapendente is near Orvieto.

L. 15 b]   **1037.**

Rocca di Cesena.   The rock of Cesena.

L. 19 b]   **1038.**

Siena ² a b braccia ³ 4, ⁴ a c braccia ⁵ 10;   Siena, a b 4 braccia, a c 10 braccia.
⁶ Scale d'Urbino.   Steps at [the castle of] Urbino.

L. 33 b]   **1039.**

Campana · di Siena, cioè ² il modo del   The bell of Siena, that is the manner of
suo moto ³ e sito della dinodatura ⁴ del   its movement, and the place of the attachment
battaglio suo.   of the clapper.

1034. 1. du vrbino. 2. luglio 1402.   **1035.** Aquapendente.   **1037.** rocha.   **1038.** 2. l.r.   3. br.
1039. 1. coe. 3. essito.

that Leonardo paid two visits to France. See
Gazette des Beaux Arts, 1881 pag. 528:

*Au recto du même feuillet, on lit encore une note
relative à une vallée "nemonti brigātia"; il me semble
qu'il s'agit bien des monts de Briançon, le Brigantio des
anciens. Briançon est sur la route de Lyon en Italie.
Ce fut par le mont Viso que passèrent, en août 1515,
les troupes françaises qui allaient remporter la victoire de
Marignan.*

*Léonard de Vinci, ingénieur de François Iᵉʳ, comme
il l'avait été de Louis XII, aurait-il été pour quelque
chose dans le plan du célèbre passage des Alpes, qui eut
lieu en août 1515, et à la suite duquel on le vit
accompagner partout le chevaleresque vainqueur? Aurait-
il été appelé par le jeune roi, de Rome où l'artiste était
alors, dès son avénement au trône?*

5. Varallo di Ponbia, about ten miles South of
Arona is distinct from Varallo the chief town in the
Val di Sesia.

1034. An indistinct sketch is introduced with
this text, in the original, in which the word
Scolatoro (conduit) is written.

1035. Below the sketch there are eleven lines
of text referring to the motion of waves.

1036. *Acquapendente* is about 10 miles West of
Orvieto, and is to the right in the map on Pl. CXIII,
near the lake of Bolsena.

1037. See Pl. XCIV No. 1, the lower sketch.
The explanation of the upper sketch is given on p. 29.

1038. See Pl. CX No. 3; compare also No. 765.

1039. The text is accompanied by an indistinct
sketch.

L. 36 b]

1040.

El dì di Sāta Maria mezz'agosto ²a
Cesena 1502.

On St. Mary's day in the middle of August,
at Cesena, 1502.

L. 40 a]

1041.

Scale del cōte d'Urbino, saluatiche.

Stairs of the [palace of the] Count of
Urbino,—rough.

L. 46 b]

1042.

Alla fiera di Scō ²Lorenzo a Cesena,
³1502.

At the fair of San Lorenzo at Cesena.
1502.

L 47 a]

1043.

Finestre da Cesena.

Windows at Cesena.

L. 66 b]

1044.

Porto Cesenatico a dì 6 di set²tenbre
1502, a ore 15;
³In che modo debbono ⁴uscire bastioni
fori delle ⁵mura delle terre per potere
⁶difendere l'argini di fori, ⁷aciò nō sieno
battuti coll'artiglieria.

At Porto Cesenatico, on the 6th of September 1502 at 9 o'clock a. m.
The way in which bastions ought to
project beyond the walls of the towers to
defend the outer talus; so that they may not
be taken by artillery.

L. 67 a]

1045.

La rocca del porto di Cesena sta a
Ce²sena per la 4ª di libeccio.

The rock of the harbour of Cesena is four
points towards the South West from Cesena.

L. 72 a]

1046.

In Romagnia, capo d'ogni grossezza
²d'ingegno, vsano i carri di 4 rote, de qua-
³li ◯ n'àño 2 dinanzi basse e due alte
⁴dirieto, la qual cosa è in gran dis⁵fauore
di moto, perchè in sulle ⁶rote dinanzi si
scarica piv peso, che ⁷in su quelle dirieto,
come mostrai ⁸nella prima del 5° delli
elemēti.

In Romagna, the realm of all stupidity,
vehicles with four wheels are used, of which
◯ the two in front are small and two high
ones are behind; an arrangement which is
very unfavourable to the motion, because
on the fore wheels more weight is laid than
on those behind, as I showed in the first of
the 5th on "Elements".

1040. 1. mezagossto. 2. [4] 502.   1044. 4. vsscire basstioni . . delle.
1045. 1. rocha. 2. pla . . libecco.   1046. 1. grosseza. 2. rote equa. 7. mostai.

1040. See Pl. CX, No. 4.
1041. The text is accompanied by a slight
sketch.

1043. There are four more lines of text which
refer to a slightly sketched diagram.
1044. An indistinct sketch, accompanies this
passage.

L. 77 a]   **1047.**

Uve portate [2]a Ciesena;   Thus grapes are carried at Cesena.
[3]Il numero de' cavatori [4]de' fossi è   The number of the diggers of the ditches
piramidale.   is [arranged] pyramidically.

L. 78 a]   **1048.**

¶ Fassi vn armonia colle diuerse cadute   There might be a harmony of the different
[2]d'acqua, come vedesti alla fonte di   falls of water as you saw them at the
[3]Rimini; come vedesti a dì 8 d'agosto   fountain of Rimini on the 8th day of Au-
[4]1502.¶   gust, 1502.

L. 78 b]   **1049.**

Fortezza d'Urbino.   The fortress at Urbino.

L. 88 b]   **1050.**

Imola vede Bologna a $\frac{5}{8}$ di ponente   Imola, as regards Bologna, is five points
inverso [2]maestro con ispatio di 20 mi-   from the West, towards the North West,
glia;   at a distance of 20 miles.
   [3]Castel san Piero è ueduto da Imola   Castel San Piero is seen from Imola at
in $\frac{1}{2}$ [4]infra ponente e maestro · con ispatio   four points from the West towards the North
di [5]7 miglia;   West, at a distance of 7 miles.
   [6]Faenza sta con Imola tra leuāte e   Faenza stands with regard to Imola be-
scirocco [7]in mezzo giusto a 10 miglia di   tween East and South East at a distance of
spatio; [8]Forlì sta cō Faenza infra scirocco   ten miles. Forli stands with regard to Faenza
e levā[9]te in mezzo giusto con ispatio di 25   between South East and East at a distance of
miglia [10]da Imola e 10 da Faēza;   20 miles from Imola and ten from Faenza.
   [11]Forlimpopoli fa il simile a 25 mi[12]glia   Forlimpopoli lies in the same direction
da Imola;   at 25 miles from Imola.
   [13]Bertinoro sta con Imola a $\frac{5}{8}$ infra   Bertinoro, as regards Imola, is five points
levā[14]te e scirocco a 27 miglia.   from the East towards the South East, at 27 miles.

1047. 1. vue.   1048. 1. chadute. 3. addi.   1049. forteza.
1050. 1. inver. 2. maesstro conisspatio . . migla. 4.· maesstro. 6. faenta . . esscirocho. 7. mezo gussto . . disspatio. 8. furli
    . . scirocho alleuā. 9. mezo gussto. 11. furinpopoli. 13. bertonora. 14. esscirocho.

   1047. A sketch, representing a hook to which two bunches of grapes are hanging, refers to these
first two lines. Cesena is mentioned again Fol. 82 a: *Carro da Cesena* (a cart from Cesena).
   1049. In the original the text is written inside the sketch in the place here marked *n*.

W. L. 229 a] **1051.**

Imola uede Bologna a ⅝ di po²nente · inuerso maestro con di³stantia · di miglia · 20;
⁴Castel · San Piero · è veduto · da Imo⁵la in mezzo infra ponente e mae⁶stro · in distantia di miglia · 7.
⁷Faenza · è veduto da Imola infra leuante ⁸e scirocco in mezzo apunto in distantia ⁹di migla · 10, e 'l simile fa · Forlì con Imo-¹⁰la con distantia di miglia · 20, e Forlimpo-¹¹poli · fa il simile con Forlì con distantia di ¹²miglia 25;
¹³Bertinoro si uede da Imola a ⅖ di leuante ¹⁴inuerso scirocco con distantia di 27 miglia.

Imola as regards Bologna is five points from the West towards the North West at a distance of 20 miles.
Castel San Pietro lies exactly North West of Imola, at a distance of 7 miles.
Faenza, as regards Imola lies exactly half way between the East and South East at a distance of 10 miles; and Forli lies in the same direction from Imola at a distance of 20 miles; and Forlimpopolo lies in the same direction from Forli at a distance of 25 miles.
Bertinoro is seen from Imola two points from the East towards the South East at a distance of 27 miles.

L. 94 b] **1052.**

Da Bōcon²vento alla ³Casa Nova ⁴miglia 10, ⁵dalla Casa No⁶va a Chiusi ⁷miglia · 9 ·, ⁸da Chiusi a Pe⁹rugia, da Peru¹⁰gia a Santa ¹¹Maria degli ¹²Angeli, e poi ¹³a Fuligno.

From Bonconventi to Casa Nova are 10 miles, from Casa Nova to Chiusi 9 miles, from Chiusi to Perugia, from Perugia to Santa Maria degli Angeli, and then to Fuligno.

L. o"] **1053.**

Dì primo d'agosto 1502 ²in Pesaro la libreria.

On the first of August 1502, the library at Pesaro.

1051. *written from left to right.* 1. blogna. 2. inuer maesstro con dis. 4. Chastel. 5. mezo . . emaes. 6. indisstantia . . migla 7. veduta. 7. esscirrocho in mezo appunto in disstantia. 9. furli. 10. chon disstantia di migla . . furlinpo. 11. furli . disstantia. 12. migla. 13. Bernotoro. 14. inver scilocho . . disstantia . . migla.
1052. 1. bōchon. 8. aper. 10. assanta.
1053. 1. di p"o".

1051. Leonardo inserted this passage on the margin of the circular plan, in water colour, of Imola—see Pl. CXI No. 1.—In the original the fields surrounding the town are light green; the moat, which surrounds the fortifications and the windings of the river Santerno, are light blue. The parts, which have come out blackish close to the river are yellow ochre in the original. The dark groups of houses inside the town are red. At the four points of the compass drawn in the middle of the town Leonardo has written (from right to left): *Mezzodì* (South) at the top; to the left *Scirocho* (South east), *levante* (East), *Greco* (North East), *Septantrione* (North), *Maesstro* (North West), *ponente* (West) *Libecco* (South West). The arch in which the plan is drawn is, in the original, 42 centimètres across.

At the beginning of October 1502 Cesare Borgia was shut up in Imola by a sudden revolt of the Condottieri, and it was some weeks before he could release himself from this state of siege (see Gregorovius, *Geschichte der Stadt Rom im Mittelalter*, Vol. VII, Book XIII, 5, 5).
Besides this incident Imola plays no important part in the history of the time. I therefore think myself fully justified in connecting this map, which is at Windsor, with the siege of 1502 and with Leonardo's engagements in the service of Cesare Borgia, because a comparison of these texts, Nos. 1050 and 1051, raise, I believe, the hypothesis to a certainty.
1052. Most of the places here described lie within the district shown in the maps on Pl. CXIII.

1054.

PICTURA.

[2]Scorta sulle sommità e in su' lati [3]de' colli le figure de' terreni e le sue [4]diuisi-

OF PAINTING.

On the tops and sides of hills foreshorten the shape of the ground and its divisions,

oni, e nelle cose uolte a te [5]fa le in propia forma.

but give its proper shape to what is turned towards you.

1055.

Alessandria in Piedmont (1055. 1056).

In Candia di Lonbardia · presso Alessandria della Paglia, facendosi per [2]messer Gualtieri di Candia vno pozzo, fu trovato vno principio di navilio grandissimo sotto terra, circa a braccia 10, e perchè [3]il legname era nero e bello, parue a esso messer Gualtieri di fare allungare tal bocca di pozzo in forma che i termini [4]di tal navilio si scoprissino.

At Candia in Lombardy, near Alessandria della Paglia, in making a well for Messer Gualtieri of Candia, the skeleton of a very large boat was found about 10 braccia underground; and as the timber was black and fine, it seemed good to the said Messer Gualtieri to have the mouth of the well lengthened in such a way as that the ends of the boat should be uncovered.

1054. 3. essere. 4. atte. 5. falle.
1055. 2. pozo . . circha a br. 3. ebbello . . meser . . bocha di pozo. 4. navili si scoprissi.

1054. This passage evidently refers to the making of maps, such as Pl. CXII, CXIII, and CXIV. There is no mention of such works, it is true, excepting in this one passage of MS. L. But this can scarcely be taken as evidence against my view that Leonardo busied himself very extensively at that time in the construction of maps; and all the less since the foregoing chapters clearly prove that at a time so full of events Leonardo would only now and then commit his observations to paper, in the MS. L.

By the side of this text we find, in the original, a very indistinct sketch, perhaps a plan of a position. Instead of this drawing I have here inserted a much clearer sketch of a position from the same MS., L. 82b and 83a. They are the only drawings of landscape, it may be noted, which occur at all in that MS.

1055. 2. *Messer Gualtieri*, the same probably as is mentioned in Nos. 672 and 1344.

1056.

Alessandria della Paglia in Lombardia non à altre pietre ²da far calcina, se nō miste con infinite cose nate in mare, la quale oggi è remota dal mare piv di 200 miglia.

At Alessandria della Paglia in Lombardy there are no stones for making lime of, but such as are mixed up with an infinite variety of things native to the sea, which is now more than 200 miles away.

1057.

Monbracco, sopra Saluzzo,—²sopra la Certosa vn miglo, al piè di mō Viso,—³à vna miniera di pietra ⁴faldata, la quale è biāca ⁵come marmo di Carrara, sanza ⁶macvle, ch' è della durez⁷za del porfido o più; ⁸della quale il conpare ⁹mio, maestro Benedet¹⁰to scultore, à in pro¹¹messo di darmene una ¹²tavoletta per li colori, ¹³a dì 2 di genaro 1511.

At Monbracco, above Saluzzo,—a mile above the Certosa, at the foot of Monte Viso, there is a quarry of flakey stone, which is as white as Carrara marble, without a spot, and as hard as porphyry or even harder; of which my worthy gossip, Master Benedetto the sculptor, has promised to give me a small slab, for the colours, the second day of January 1511. **The Alps** (1057—1062).

1058.

Come son uene che per terremoti o altri accidenti subito nasco²no e subito mācano; E questo accade in vna mōtagnia in Sauoia, doue certi boschi sprofondarono e lasciarono vno ³baratro profondissimo · e lontano circa 4 miglia di lì s'aperse il terreno in certa spiaggia di mōte, e gittò vna ⁴subita inōdatione grossissima d'acqua, la quale nettò tutta vna vallata di terreni lauorativi, vignie e case, e fece ⁵grādissimo danno ovunque discorse.

That there are springs which suddenly break forth in earthquakes or other convulsions and suddenly fail; and this happened in a mountain in Savoy where certain forests sank in and left a very deep gap, and about four miles from here the earth opened itself like a gulf in the mountain, and threw out a sudden and immense flood of water which scoured the whole of a little valley of the tilled soil, vineyards and houses, and did the greatest mischief, wherever it overflowed.

1059.

Riuiera d' Arua presso a Ginevra; ² ¹/₄ di miglio in Sauoia, doue si fa la fiera ³ in San Giovanni nel uillaggio di san Gervagio.

The river Arve, a quarter of a mile from Geneva in Savoy, where the fair' is held on midsummerday in the village of Saint Gervais.

1056. Alesandria . . illonbardia. 2. mista . . il quale.
1057. *Lines* 1, 3—13 *R.* 1. monbracho . . saluzo, 2. a pie . . uiso. 4. biācha. 5. carra"ra"sa. 6. machvle . . dure. 7. obpiu. 8. delle quali. 9. maesstro benedec. 11. messo con darmene.
1058. 1. nasca. 2. essubito . . Ecquesto acade nvna . . bosci profondorono ellasciorono. 3. baladro . . circha . . spiagga. 4. terē . . effece. 5. ovunche.
1059. 2. miglo. 3. batte in san govanni . . uilago . . cervagio.

1057. *Saluzzo* at the foot of the Alps South of Turin.

9. 10. *Maestro Benedetto scultore;* probably some native of Northern Italy acquainted with the place here described. Hardly the Florentine sculptor Benedetto da Majano. Amoretti had published this passage, and M. Ravaisson who gave a French translation of it in the *Gazette des Beaux Arts* (1881, pag. 528), remarks as follows: *Le maître sculpteur que Léonard appelle son "compare" ne serait-il pas Benedetto da Majano, un de ceux qui jugèrent avec lui de la place à donner au David de Michel-Ange, et de qui le Louvre a acquis récemment un buste d'après Philippe Strozzi?*

To this it may be objected that Benedetto da Majano had already lain in his grave fourteen years, in the year 1511, when he is supposed to have given the promise to Leonardo. The colours may have been given to the sculptor Benedetto and the stone may have been in payment for them. From the description of the stone here given we may conclude that it is repeated from hearsay of the sculptor's account of it. I do not understand how, from this observation, it is possible to conclude that Leonardo was on the spot.

1059. An indistinct sketch is to be seen by the text.

Leic. 4 a]   1060.

E questo vedrà come vid'io, chi ādrà
so pra Mōboso, giogo dell'Alpi che diuidono
la Francia dalla Italia, la qual montagnia
à la sua basa che parturisce [3] li 4 fiumi
che rigā per 4 aspetti contrari tutta l'Europa,
e nessuna montagnia à le sue base in simile al[4]tezza; questa si leua in tanta altura
che quasi passa tutti li nuvoli e rare volte
vi cade neve, ma sol grādi[5]ne d'istate
quando li nvvoli sono nella maggiore altezza, e questa grandine vi si cōserua in
modo, che se nō [6]fusse la retà del caderui
e del montarui nvuoli, che non accade 2
volte in vna età, egli ui sarebbe altissima
quātità di ghiaccio inalzato dali gradi della
grādine, il qua[7]le di mezzo luglio vi trouai
grossissimo ·, e vidi l'aria sopra di me tene-
brosa e 'l sole che percotea la mōta[8]gnia
essere piv luminoso quiui assai che nelle
basse pianure, perchè minor grossezza d'aria
s'interpone in[9]fra la cima d'esso monte
e 'l sole.

And this may be seen, as I saw it, by
any one going up[5] Monbroso, a peak of
the Alps which divide France from Italy.
The base of this mountain gives birth to the
4 rivers which flow in four different directions
through the whole of Europe. And no
mountain has its base at so great a height
as this, which lifts itself above almost all the
clouds; and snow seldom falls there, but
only hail in the summer, when the clouds
are highest. And this hail lies [unmelted]
there, so that if it were not for the absorp-
tion of the rising and falling clouds, which
does not happen more than twice in an age, an
enormous mass of ice would be piled up there
by the layers of hail, and in the middle of July
I found it very considerable; and I saw the
sky above me quite dark, and the sun as it
fell on the mountain was far brighter here
than in the plains below, because a smaller
extent of atmosphere lay between the summit
of the mountain and the sun.

Leic. 9 b]   1061.

Truovasi nelle montagnie di Verona la
sua pietra rossa mista tutta di nichi con-
vertiti [2]in essa pietra ·, dalli quali, per la
loro bocca, era gommata la materia d'essa
pietra, ed erano in alcuna parte restati
separati dall'altra massa del sasso che
li circundava; perchè la scorza del nichio
s'era interposta, e nō li auea [4]lasciati
congiugniere; E in alcun altra parte tal
gomma auea petrificate le invecchiate e
quasi la scorza.

In the mountains of Verona the red marble
is found all mixed with cockle shells turned
into stone; some of them have been filled
at the mouth with the cement which is the
substance of the stone; and in some parts
they have remained separate from the mass
of the rock which enclosed them, because
the outer covering of the shell had interposed and had not allowed them to unite
with it; while in other places this cement had
petrified those which were old and almost stripped the outer skin.

C. A. 231 b; 696 a]   1062.

Ponte di Goritia [2] Vilpago.

Bridge of Goertz—Wilbach (?).

1060. 1. ecquesto. 2. gogo . . diuitano la franca . . alla . . parturiscce. 3. alle. 4. nvuoli . . chade. 5. magore . . ecquesta
. . īmodo chesse. 6. fussi "la reta del caderui e del montarui nvuoli" che non achade [del s] . . eta e. 7. mezo . .
grossimo . . tenenebrosa ellsole. 8. luminosi . . grosseza.
1061. 2. delli . . era gornata . . edera. 3. masa . . chelli circhundava . . lasscorza. 4. lassciati congugniere . . goma . . petrificata le invegiate e quasi scorzo.
1062. vilpagho.

1060. I have vainly enquired of every available
authority for a solution of the mystery as to what
mountain is intended by the name Mom boso (Comp.
Vol. I Nos. 300 and 301). It seems most obvious
to refer it to Monte Rosa. *Rosa* is derived from the
Keltic *ros* which survives in Breton and in Gaelic,
meaning, in its first sense, a mountain spur, but which
also—like *Horn*—means a very high peak; thus
Monte Rosa would mean literally the High Peak.

6. *in una età*. This is perhaps a slip of the pen
on Leonardo's part and should be read *estate* (summer).

1062. There is a slight sketch with this text,
Leonardo seems to have intended to suggest, with
a few pen-strokes, the course of the Isonzo and
of the Wipbach in the vicinity of Gorizia (Goerz).
He himself says in another place that he had been
in Friuli (see No. 1077 l. 19).

Leic. 10a]   **1063.**

Quella parte della terra s'è piv alienata dal centro ²del mōdo, la qual s'è fatta piv lieve ·; E quella parte della terra s'è fatta piv lieve, per la quale ³è passato maggior concorso · d'acque, E si è adūque fatta piv lieue quella parte, donde sco⁴la piv numero di fiumi, come l'alpi, che diuidono la Magnia e la Francia dalla Italia, delle quali ⁵escie il Rodano a mezzodì, e il Reno a tramō-tana ·, jl Danubio over Danoia a greco, e 'l Po a leuā⁶te con īnvmerabili fiumi che con loro s'accōpagnano, i quali senpre corrono torbidi, dalla terra ⁷da loro portata, al mare;

Mouōsi al continvo i liti marittimi inverso il mezzo del mare e lo ⁸scacciā dal suo primo sito; Riseruerassi la piv bassa parte del Mediterrano per letto e cor⁹so del Nilo, fiume massimo, che versa in esso mare, E con lui s'accompagnieranno tutti li fiumi sua ¹⁰aderēti, che prima in esso mare le loro acque versar soleano, come far si uede al Po colli aderēti ¹¹sua, li quali prima ver-sauā nel mare · che infra l'Appennino e le Germaniche alpi si era vnito ¹²col Mare Adriatico;

Come le alpi galliche son la piv alta parte dell' Evropa.

That part of the earth which was lightest The Appe-remained farthest from the centre of the nins world; and that part of the earth became (1063—1068). the lightest over which the greatest quantity of water flowed. And therefore that part became lightest where the greatest number of rivers flow; like the Alps which divide Germany and France from Italy; whence issue the Rhone flowing Southwards, and the Rhine to the North. The Danube or Ta-noia towards the North East, and the Po to the East, with innumerable rivers which join them, and which always run turbid with the soil carried by them to the sea.

The shores of the sea are constantly moving towards the middle of the sea and displace it from its original position. The lowest portion of the Mediterranean will be reserved for the bed and current of the Nile, the largest river that flows into that sea. And with it are grouped all its tribu-taries, which at first fell into the sea; as may be seen with the Po and its tributaries, which first fell into that sea, which between the Appenines and the German Alps was united to the Adriatic sea.

That the Gallic Alps are the highest part of Europe.

E. 1b   **1064.**

E di questi ò ri²trovato nelli ³sassi del-l'alto ⁴Appenino e ⁵massime nel ⁶sasso della Ver⁷na.

And of these I found some in the rocks of the high Appenines and mostly at the rock of La Vernia.

E. 80a]   **1065.**

A Parma alla ²Cāpana a dì 25 ³di set-tēbre 1514.

At Parma, at 'La Campana' on the twenty-fifth of October 1514.

1063. 2. lequella .. seffatta. 3. magor choncorso .. Essi adūque. 4. diuidano .. ella franca .. della qual. 5. attramōtana .. danubbio .. tanoia a grecho .. alleu. 6. chon .. cholloro sacōpagniano .. corrā. 7. dallo portata .. movāsi .. mezo .. ello. 8. scaccā del .. mediterano. 9. ineso .. sachonpagniera. 10. solano .. colli aderē. 11. apenino elle .. serava. 12. chol .. adriaticho .. le alpe le .. pivolta.
1064. 1. quessti. 2. trovati. 7. nia.

1064. 6. *Sasso della Vernia.* The frowning rock between the sources of the Arno and the Tiber, as Dante describes this mountain, which is 1269 mètres in height.

This note is written by the side of that given

as No. 1020; but their connection does not make it clear what Leonardo's purpose was in writing it.
1065. 2. *Cāpana*, an Inn.

A note on the petrifactions, or fossils near Parma will be found under No. 989.

C. A. 137 a; 414 a]   **1066.**

Modo di seccare il padule ²di Pion-
bino.

A method for drying the marsh of
Piombino.

K.I 2 a]   **1067.**

Fanno li pastori ²in quel di Roma³gnia
nelle radici ⁴dell' Appēnino certe ⁵gran concauità ne⁶l monte a uso di cor⁷no e da
parte commet⁸tono vn corno, e q⁹uello
piccol corno di¹⁰uēta vn medesimo col¹¹la
già fatta concauità, ō¹²de fa grādissimo
suono.

The shepherds in the Romagna at the
foot of the Apennines make peculiar large
cavities in the mountains in the form of
a horn, and on one side they fasten a horn.
This little horn becomes one and the same
with the said cavity and thus they produce
by blowing into it a very loud noise.

Leic. 31 b]   **1068.**

Vedesi vna vena surgere in Sicilia, la
²quale a certi tenpi dell'anno versa foglie
di castagno in moltitudine, e in Sicilia nō
na³scono castagnie, è adūque necessario
che tal uena esca d'alcū pelago dell'Italia
e va⁴da poi sotto il mare e sbocchi poi in
Sicilia.

A spring may be seen to rise in Sicily
which at certain times of the year throws
out chesnut leaves in quantities; but in
Sicily chesnuts do not grow, hence it is
evident that that spring must issue from some
abyss in Italy and then flow beneath the sea
to break forth in Sicily.

1066. 1. sechare.
1067. 3. radice. 4. apēnino. 5. chonchauita. 7. pare come. 8. tano vn chorno ecq. 9. pichol. 10. chol. 11. ga. 12. sono.
1068. 1. cicilia. 2. accerti . . ano. 3. chasstagno . . moltitudile 3. scie chastagnie . . chettal esscha dalchū pellagho.
       4. día poi essbochi . . cicilia.

1066. There is a slight sketch with this text
in the original. — Piombino is also mentioned in
Nos. 609, l. 55—58 (compare Pl. XXXV, 3, below).
Also in No. 1035.

1067. As to the Romagna see also No. 1046.
1046. The chesnut tree is very common in Sicily. In writing *cicilia* Leonardo meant perhaps
Cilicia.

II.

FRANCE.

C. A. 353 *b*; 1105 *b*]

1069.

ALEMAGNIA.	FRANCIA.	GERMANY.	FRANCE.
2 a. Austria,	a. Picardia,	a. Austria.	a. Picardy.
3 b. Sassonia,	b. Normandia,	b. Saxony.	b. Normandy.
4 c. Norimberga,	c. Delfinato;	c. Nuremberg.	c. Dauphiné.
5 d. Fiandra;	d.	d. Flanders.	

SPAGNIA.	SPAIN.
7 a. Biscaglia,	a. Biscay.
8 b. Castiglia,	b. Castille.
9 c. Galitia,	c. Galicia.
10 d. Portogallo,	d. Portugal.
11 e. Tarragona,	e. Taragona.
12 f. Granada.	f. Granada.

C. A. 358 *b*; 1124 *b*]

1070.

Perpigniana;	Perpignan.
2 Roana,	Roanne.
3 Lione,	Lyons.
4 Parigi,	Paris.
5 Guāto,	Ghent.
6 Brugia,	Bruges.
7 Olanda.	Holland.

1069. *In the original the three columns are parallel.* 1. alamania franca — spognia. 4. nolinberg — dalfinato. 5. flandra. 7. bisscaglia. 8. casstiglia. 11. taragona. 12. granata.
1070. 3. lioñe.

1069. Two slightly sketched maps, one of Europe the other of Spain, are at the side of these notes.
1070. *Roana* does not seem to mean here Rouen in Normandy, but is probably Roanne (Rodumna) on the upper Loire, Lyonnais (Dép. du Loire). This town is now unimportant, but in Leonardo's time was still a place of some consequence.

Leic. 27 b]   1071.

Come in Bordea presso a Guascognia   At Bordeaux in Gascony the sea rises
alza il mare circa a 40 braccia pel suo   about 40 braccia before its ebb, and the
reflus²so, e 'l suo fiume ringorga l'acque river there is filled with salt water for more
salze piv di cento cinquāta miglia, e li   than a hundred and fifty miles; and the
nauili, che ³si debbono calafatare, restano vessels which are repaired there rest high
alti sopra vn alto collo sopra dello abassato and dry on a high hill above the sea at
mare.   low tide.

Leic. 34 b]   1072.

El Rodano esce dal lago di Ginevra e   The Rhone issues from the lake of
corre prima ²a ponente, e poi a mezzodì,   Geneva and flows first to the West and then
con corso di 400 miglia, e versa le sue   to the South, with a course of 400 miles
acque nel mare mediterrano.   and pours its waters into the Mediterranean.

K.3 20 a]   1073.

c d giardino di Bles;   c d is the garden at
²a b è il cōdotto di   Blois; a b is the con-
Bles, fatto ī ³Frācia   duit of Blois, made in
da Fra Giocōdo, b c   France by Fra Giocon-
è il ⁴mācamēto dell'al-   do, b c is what is want-
tezza di tal cō⁵dotto,   ing in the height of
c d è l'altezza del   that conduit, c d is the
giar⁶dino di Bles, e f   height of the garden at
è la caduta ⁷della ci-   Blois, e f is the siphon
cognola, b c, e f, f g   of the conduit, b c, e
⁸è dove tal cicognola   f, f g is, where the si-
versa nel ⁹fiume.   phon discharges into the
                                                                       river.

1071. 1. guasscogna . . circha a 40 br . . refru.   2. elli.   3. deano . . chollo.
1072. 1. essce del lagho.   2. mezodi . . mediterano.

1071. 2. This is obviously an exaggeration   fille aînée à François, comte d'Angoulême, Louis XII lui
founded on inaccurate information. Half of 150   avait constitué en dot les comtés de Blois, d'Asti, de Coucy,
miles would be nearer the mark.   de Montfort, d'Etampes et de Vertus. Une ordonnance
   1073. The tenor of this note (see lines 2 and 3) de François I. lui laissa en 1516 l'administration du
seems to me to indicate that this passage was not comté de Blois.
written in France, but was written from oral infor-   Le roi fit commencer, dans la même année, les travaux
mation. We have no evidence as to when this   de cette belle partie du château, connue sous le nom
note may have been written beyond the circumstance d'aile de François I, et dont nous avons donné la
that Fra Giocondo the Veronese Architect left France description au commencement de ce livre. Nous trouvons
not before the year 1505. The greater part of the en effet, dans les archives du Baron de Joursanvault,
magnificent Château of Blois has now disappeared. une pièce qui en fixe parfaitement la date. On y lit:
Whether this note was made for a special purpose is "Je, Baymon Philippeaux, commis par le Roy à tenir le
uncertain. The original form and extent of the   compte et fair le payement des bastiments, ediffices et
Château is shown in Androvet, Les plus excellents reparacions que le dit seigneur fait faire en son chastu
Bastiments de France, Paris MDCVII, and it may be de Blois, confesse avoir eu et reçeu . . . la somme de
observed that there is in the middle of the   trois mille livres tournois . . . . le cinquième jour de
garden a Pavilion somewhat similar to that shown juillet, l'an mil cinq cent et seize. P. 24: Les jardins
on Pl. LXXXVIII No. 7.   avaient été décorés avec beaucoup de luxe par les différents
   See S. DE LA SAUSSAYE, Histoire du Château de Blois possesseurs du château. Il ne reste de tous les bâtiments
4ème édition Blois et Paris p. 175: En mariant sa qu'ils y élevèrent que ceux des officiers chargés de l'ad-

Br. M. 269 a]   1074.

Loira fiume ²d'Ambosa.

³Il fiume è più ⁴alto dentro al⁵l'argine
b d che ⁶fuori d'essa ar⁷gine;

⁸Isola dove è ⁹vna parte ¹⁰d'An-
buosa.

¹¹Il fiume Loira che passa per Anbosa
passa per *a b, c d*, e poichè è passato il
pōte, ¹²ritorna contro al suo avenimento
per il canale *d e, b f* in contatto dell'argine
¹³che si interpone infra li due moti contrari del predetto fiume *a b, c d, d e, b f;*
¹⁴di poi si riuolta in giù per il canale *f l,
g h, n m*, e si ricongiugnie col fiume dōde
¹⁵prima si diuise, che passa per *k n*, che
fa *k m, r t;* ma quādo il fiume è ¹⁶grosso,
allora elli corre tutto per uno solo verso,
passādo l'argine *b d.*

The river Loire at Amboise.

The river is higher within the bank *b d*
than outside that bank.

The island where there is a part of
Amboise.

This is the river that passes through
Amboise; it passes at *a b c d*, and when it
has passed the bridge it turns back, against
the original current, by the channel *d e, b f*
in contact with the bank which lies between
the two contrary currents of the said river,
a b, c d, and *d e, b f*. It then turns down
again by the channel *f l, g h, n m*, and
reunites with the river from which it was at first
separated, which passes by *k n*, which makes
k m, r t. But when the river is very full it flows
all in one channel passing over the bank *b d.*

Br. M. 269 b]   1075.

L'acque sieno rin²gorgate sopra ³il termine
di Ro⁴morontino in tā⁵sta altezza, ch'elle ⁶fac-
cino poi nel ⁷loro disciēso mol⁸te molina;

The water may be dammed up above
the level of Romorantin to such a height, that
in its fall it may be used for numerous mills.

1073. 1. gardino. 4. alteza. 5. ellalteza del gar. 6. ella.

1074. 1. Loera. 2. dā[n]bosa. 3. gocōdo. 3. eppiu. 8. fiume era che. 13. chessi . . infralli . . controri . . predecto. 14. ess
richongiugnie. 15. diuise [eppa] che . . cheffa.

1075. 1. Lacqua sia rio. 2. ghorghata. 5. alteza. 7. uo disscieso. 9. uilla. 10. francha. 11. docto a romolō. 12. del

*ministration et de la culture des jardins, et un pavillon
carré en pierre et en brique flanqué de terrasses à chacun
de ses angles. Quoique défiguré par des mesures élevées
sur les terrasses, cet édifice est très-digne d'intérêt par
l'originalité du plan, la décoration architecturale et le
souvenir d'Anne de Bretagne qui le fit construire.* Féli-
bien describes the garden as follows: *Le jardin haut
était fort bien dressé par grands compartimens de toutes
sortes de figures, avec des allées de meuriers blancs et
des palissades de coudriers. Deux grands berceaux de
charpenterie separoient toute la longueur et la largeur du
jardin, et dans les quatres angles des allées, où ces
berceaux se croissent, il y auoit 4 cabinets, de mesme
charpenterie . . . Il y a pas longtemps qu'il y auoit dans
ce mesme jardin, à l'endroit où se croissent les allées du
milieu, un édifice de figure octogone, de plus de 7 thoises
de diamètre et de plus de neuf thoises de haut; avec 4
enfoncements en forme de niches dans les 4 angles des
allées. Ce bastiment . . . . estoit de charpente mais d'un
extraordinairement bien travaillé. On y voyait parti-
culièrement la cordilière qui regnait tout autour en forme
de cordon. Car la Reyne affectait de la mettre non-
seulement à ses armes et a ses chiffres mais de la faire
représenter en divers manières dans tous les ouvrages
qu'on lui faisait pour elle . . . le bastiment estait couvert
en forme de dôme qui dans son milieu avait encore un
plus petit dôme, ou lanterne vitrée au-dessus de laquelle
estait une figure dorée représentant Saint Michel. Les*

*deux dômes estoient proprement couvert d'ardoise et de
plomb doré par dehors; par dedans ils estoient lambrisséz
d'une menuiserie très delicate. Au milieu de ce Salon il
y avait un grand bassin octogone de marbre blanc, dont
toutes les faces estoient enrichies de differentes sculptures,
avec les armes et les chiffres du Roy Louis XII et de la
Reine Anne. Dans ce bassin il y en avait un autre
posé sur un piédestal lequel auoit sept piedz de diamètre.
Il estait de figure ronde à godrons, avec des masques et
d'autres ornements très sçauamment taillés. Du milieu
de ce deuxiesme bassin s'y levoit un autre petit piédestal
qui portait un troisiesme bassin de trois pieds de diamètre,
aussy parfaitement bien taillé; c'estoit de ce dernier bassin
que jallissoit l'eau qui se répendoit en suitte dans les
deux autres bassins. Les beaux ouvrages faits d'un
marbre esgalement blanc et poli, furent brisez par la
pesanteur de tout l'édifice, que les injures de l'air renver-
sèrent de fond en comble.*

1074. See Pl. CXV. Lines 1—7 are above, lines
8—10 in the middle of the large island and the
word *Isola* is written above *d* in the smaller island;
a is written on the margin on the bank of the river
above l. 1; in the reproduction it is not visible.
As may be seen from the last sentence, the observation was made after long study of the river's
course, when Leonardo had resided for some time
at, or near, Amboise.

⁹Il fiume di Villa¹⁰franca sia cō¹¹dotto a Romorō¹²tino, e sia fatto dal suo ¹³popolo, e li legni¹⁴ami, che conpō¹⁵gono le lor case, ¹⁶siē per barche cō¹⁷dotte a Romorō¹⁸tino; e 'l fiume ¹⁹sia ringorga²⁰to in tāta altez²¹za, che l'acqua ²²si possa cō co²³modo discie²⁴so riduciere ²⁵a Romorōtino.

The river at Villefranche may be conducted to Romorantin which may be done by the inhabitants; and the timber of which their houses are built may be carried in boats to Romorantin[18]. The river may be dammed up at such a height that the waters may be brought back to Romorantin with a convenient fall.

Br. M. 269 b]   **1076.**

S'elli è meglio che l'acqua ²vada tutta in alto in una so³la volta, o veramēte in due?

⁴Rispōdesi che in vna sola vol⁵ta la rota nō potreb⁶be sostenere tutta l'acqua ⁷ch'ella leua in due volte, per⁸chè nella mezza volta della ⁹rota leverebbe 100 libbre, ¹⁰e nō più, e s'ell' auesse a leua¹¹re le 200 libbre la uolta inte¹²re, non le leverebbe, se ¹³tal rota nō raddoppiasse il dia¹⁴metro, e raddoppiando tal ¹⁵diametro raddoppiereb¹⁶be il tenpo; adūque è meglio ¹⁷e più comodità di spesa a fare ¹⁸tal rota sub 2ª che 2 la ecc.

¹⁹Il discièso del mozzo non s'ab²⁰bassa insino alla pelle dell'acqua, ²¹perchè toccādo l'acqua diminuireb²²be il peso suo.

²³E se per l'aversario ²⁴s'ingrossasse il ²⁵fugatore dell'ac²⁶qua dieci tan²⁷ti più, che la ²⁸canna dell'²⁹acqua fuggiē³⁰te d'essi, se li ³¹dieci tanti ³²men moto ³³che a questo, ³⁴che vfitio sareb³⁵be il suo? Ri³⁶spōdesi per la 37 9ª di questo ³⁸che dice, che l'acqua ³⁹s'alzerebbe ⁴⁰la decima parte di quel che prima s'alzava ⁴¹nell'altezza di quella canna donde prima sur⁴²gieua.

As to whether it is better that the water should all be raised in a single turn or in two?

The answer is that in one single turn the wheel could not support all the water that it can raise in two turns, because at the half turn of the wheel it would be raising 100 pounds and no more; and if it had to raise the whole, 200 pounds in one turn, it could not raise them unless the wheel were of double the diameter and if the diameter were doubled, the time of its revolution would be doubled; therefore it is better and a greater advantage in expense to make such a wheel of half the size (?) &c.

The going down of the nave of the wheel must not be so low as to touch the surface of the water, because by touching the water its momentum will be lessened.

And if on the contrary the conduit for the water were ten times the size of the pipe for the water escaping from it, and if it had ten times less motion, what would be its office? This is answered by the 9th of this which says that the water would rise in the pipe whence it first flow, to a tenth part of its original height.

Br. M. 270 b]   **1077.**

Se'l fiume *m n*, ramo del fiume Loira, si manda nel ²fiume di Romorontino colle sua acque torbide, esso ī³grasserà le can-

If the river *m n*, an affluant of the river Loire, were turned with its muddy waters, into the river of Romorantin, this would fatten

---

13. elli. 14. conpo. 15. ghano. 17. aremolō. 19. ringhorgha. 21. chellacqua. 23. dissciē. 25. romolōtino.

1076. 1. selli . . chellacq"a". 2. alto nuna. 4. nvna. 6. bono sosstenere . . lacq"a". 7. chella. 8. meza. 10. essellauessi alleua. 12. nolle leverebbe [se el] se. 13. raddopiassi. 14. mitro [e ín] e. 15. [tempo] diamitro raddoppiereb. 17. affare. 19. disscièso . . mozzo nossab. 20. acqu"a". 21. tochādo lacqu"a". 23. Esse. 24. singrossassi. 25. fughatore. 27. chella. 28. channa della. 30. tę dessi se li. 31. dieci tanta. 32. men moto. 33. che acque sto. 34. che vfitio sareb. 35. be il suo Ris. 37. quessto. 38. chellacqua. 40. che p"a". 41. channa donde p"a" sue. 42. giena.

1077. 1. fiume [era] Era | si. 2. romolontino . . torbite. 3. essesso. 5. effara chanale navichabile e merchātile. 11. Quella.

1075. 18. Compare No. 744.

1076. The topographical interest of this passage arises from the circumstance that it is written on the reverse of the sheet on which we find the text relating to Romorantin, No. 1074.

pagnie sopra le quali esso adaque⁴rà, e
rēderà il paese fertile da nutrire li a⁵bi-
tatori, e farà canale navicabile e mer-
cātile.

⁶Modo che ’l fiume ⁷col suo corso ⁸netti
il fondo del ⁹fiume.

¹⁰Per la nona
del 3°; ¹¹Quello
ch’ è più velo¹²cie,
più cōsuma il ¹³suo
fondo, e per la cō-
¹⁴versa: l’acqua ch’ è
più ¹⁵tarda piv la-
scia ¹⁶di quel che
la intorbi¹⁷da;

¹⁸E facciasi il serraglio mobile, che io
or¹⁹dinai nel Friuli, del quale, aperto vna
cāterat²⁰ta, l’acqua che di quella vsciua
cavò il fondo; ²¹addunque nelli diluui de’
fiumi si debbono aprire le cate²²ratte de’molini, acciochè tutto il corso del fiume si
renda per ca²³teratta in ciascū molino; sieno
molte, acciochè . . . . . ²⁴si faccia maggiore īpeto, e così netterà tutto il fiume;
²⁵e infra le due poste de’ moli²⁶ni sia vna
delle dette caterat²⁷te; sia vna d’esse poste
di tal cate²⁸ratte infra l’uno e l’al²⁹tro
molino.

the land which it would water and would
render the country fertile to supply food
to the inhabitants, and would make navigable canals for mercantile purposes.

The way in which the river in its flow
should scour its own channel.

By the ninth of the
third; the more rapid
it is, the more it wears
away its channel; and,
by the converse pro-
position, the slower
the water the more
it deposits that which
renders it turbid.

And let the sluice be movable like the one
I arranged in Friuli [19], where when one sluice
was opened the water which passed through
it dug out the bottom. Therefore when the
rivers are flooded, the sluices of the mills
ought to be opened in order that the whole
course of the river may pass through falls
to each mill; there should be many in order
to give a greater impetus, and so all the
river will be scoured. And below the site
of each of the two mills there may be one
of the said sluice falls; one of them may be
placed below each mill.

C. A. 329*b*; 993*a*] **1078.**

Vno trabocco è quattro braccia e vno
miglio è tre mila d’esse braccia; E ’l braccio si diuide in 12 ōcie; ²e l’acqua de’ canali à di calo in ogni cēto trabocchi 2 delle
dette oncie; adūque 14 oncie ³di calo son
neciessarie a due mila ottocēto braccia di
moto ne’detti canali; seguita che 15 oncie
⁴di calo danno debito moto alli corsi del-
l’acque dei predetti canali, cioè uno braccio
e ¹/₂ ⁵per miglio; E per questo cōcluderemo
che l’acqua che si toglie dal fiume di Villa

A trabocco is four braccia, and one mile
is three thousand of the said braccia. Each
braccio is divided into 12 inches; and the
water in the canals has a fall in every
hundred trabocchi of two of these inches;
therefore 14 inches of fall are necessary in
two thousand eight hundred braccia of
flow in these canals; it follows that 15
inches of fall give the required momentum
to the currents of the waters in the said
canals, that is one braccio and a half in the
mile. And from this it may be concluded
that the water taken from the river of Ville-

14. cheppiu. 15. lasscia. 16. chella. *Lines 6—17 are written in the margin.* 18. effaciasi. 19. nel frigholi del. 20. lacq-
“a"che . . vssciua cav“o”. 21. si debbe apr ||||||||||. 22. ratte demolini . . del fiume si ||||||||||||||. 23. ciasscū . . .
acchiochè ||||||||||. 24. sapra effacci magiore . . tutto if |||||||||||. 25. infralle . . posste. 27. posste. 28. rate molini in-
fralluna ellal. *Lines 25—29 stand in the original above line 18.*
1078. 1. traboccho. 2. br. e î . . El br. [s] si . . ōcie |||||||. 2. ellacqua . . addi chalo . . trabochi . . 14 ō di. 3. di chalo . .
adumila . . br. di moto [de de] ne . . 15 ō di. 4. di chalo . . corsi [de detti o] dell . . de . . cioe î br. 5. quesso

1077. 19. This passage reveals to us the fact that
Leonardo had visited the country of Friuli and that
he had stayed there for some time. Nothing
whatever was known of this previously.

Franca e si ⁶presta al fiume di Romorontino vuole ... Dove l'ū fiume mediante la sua bassezza nō ⁷può entrare nell'altro, è neciessario ringorgarlo in tale altezza che possa disciēdere ⁸in quel che prima era piv alto.

⁹¶Vigilia di Sco Anto¹⁰nio tornai da Romo¹¹rōtino in Ābuosa,¶ ¹²e 'l rè si partì due ¹³dì innanti da Romorō¹⁴tino.

¹⁵Da Romorontino insino al ¹⁶pōte a Sodro | si chiama Soudro; ¹⁷e da esso pōte insino a Tours ¹⁸si chiama Schier.

¹⁹Farai saggio del ²⁰liuello di quel ca²¹nale che si à a cōdur²²re dalla Loira a Romo²³lontino con vn ca²⁴nale largo vn braccio e ²⁵profondo vn braccio.

franche and lent to the river of Romorantin will . . . . . Where one river by reason of its low level cannot flow into the other, it will be necessary to dam it up, so that it may acquire a fall into the other, which was previously the higher.

The eve of Saint Antony I returned from Romorantin to Amboise, and the King went away two days before from Romorantin.

From Romorantin as far as the bridge at Saudre it is called the Saudre, and from that bridge as far as Tours it is called the Cher.

I would test the level of that channel which is to lead from the Loire to Romorantin, with a channel one braccio wide and one braccio deep.

Br. M. 263*b*]   **1079.**

STRADA D'ORLEANS.

² Alla quarta di mezzodì verso scirocco; ³alla terza di mezzodì verso scirocco; ⁴alla quarta di mezzodì verso scirocco; ⁵alla quinta di mezzodì verso scirocco; ⁶Tra libeccio e mezzodì; ⁷a leuante participando di mezzodì; ⁸tra mezzo giorno verso leuante ⅛; ⁹Da poi verso ponente; ¹⁰tra mezzodì e libeccio; ¹¹a mezzodì.

THE ROAD TO ORLEANS.

At ¼ from the South to the South East. At ⅓ from the South to the South East. At ¼ from the South to the South East. At ⅕ from the South to the South East. Between the South West and South, to the East bearing to the South; from the South towards the East ⅛; thence to the West, between the South and South West; at the South.

cōcludereno chellacqua chessi . . franca essi. 6. pressta . . remolontino vole . . . . mediante [la ba] la sua. 7. ringhorgharlo . . alteza . . dissciēdere \\\\\\\ . 12. el re [di fran] si. 13. innanti . *Lines 15—18 are written from left to right.* 15. Romorantino. 17. [po] e da. 20. cha. 21. chessa a chōdur. 22. rre dalliraa remo. 23. cha. 24. largho vn br. 25. vn br.
1079. *written from left to right:* 1. dorléons. 2. de mezo syroccho. 3. de mezo . . syroccho. 4. mezo . . syrocco. 5. mezo . . syrocco. 6. lybeccio e mezodi. 6. mezo. 7. mezo. 8. ponte. 9. mezo . . lybeccio. 10. mezo.

1078. Lines 6—18 are partly reproduced in the facsimile on p. 254, and the whole of lines 19—25.

The following names are written along the rivers on the larger sketch. *era f* (the Loire) *scier f* (the Cher) three times. *Pōte Sodro* (bridge of the Soudre). *Villa francha* (Villefranche) *banco* (sandbank) *Sodro* (Soudre). The circle below shows the position of Romorantin. The words *'orologio del sole'* written below do not belong to the map of the rivers. The following names are written by the side of the smaller sketch-map:—*tors* (Tours), *Abosa* (Amboise) *bres*—for Bles (Blois) *mō rica* \\\\ (Montrichard). *Lione* (Lyons). This map was also published in the 'Saggio' (Milano, 1872) Pl. XXII, and the editors remark: *Forse la linia retta che va da Amboise a Romorantin segna l'andamento proposto d'un Canale, che poi sembra prolungarsi in giù fin dove sta scritto Lione.*

M. Ravaisson has enlarged on this idea in the Gazette des Beaux Arts (1881 p. 530): *Les traces de Léonard permettent d'entrevoir que le canal commençant soit auprès de Tours, soit auprès de Blois et passant par Romorantin, avec port d'embarquement à Villefranche, devait, au delà de Bourges, traverser l'Allier au-dessous des affluents de la Dore et de la Sioule, aller par Moulins jusqu' à Digoin; enfin, sur l'autre rive de la Loire, dépasser les monts du Charolais et rejoindre la Saône auprès de Mâcon.* It seems to me rash, however, to found so elaborate an hypothesis on these sketches of rivers. The slight stroke going to *Lione* is perhaps only an indication of the direction. — With regard to the Loire compare also No. 988. l. 38.

1079. The meaning is obscure; a more important passage referring to France is to be found under No. 744.

1080.

B. 61 *a*]

On the Germans (1080. 1081).

Modo come i Tedeschi ingarbugliano e tessano, serādosi īsieme, ²le loro targhe lunghe cōtro a nemici·, abassandosi e mettēdo ³vna delle teste a terra, tenēdo il resto · in mano.

The way in which the Germans closing up together cross and interweave their broad leather shields against the enemy, stooping down and putting one of the ends on the ground while they hold the rest in their hand.

1081.

B. 63 *b*]

Vsano i Germani · annegare · castellani cō fumo di pivma, solfo ²e risagallo ·, e fanno durare detti fumi 7 e 8 ore; ācora la ³pula del frumēto fa assai e durabil fumo; e letame secco ancor lui, ⁴ma fa sia mischiato colla sāsa, cioè vliue tratte nel' olio, o vuoi morchia ⁵d'olio.

The Germans are wont to annoy a garrison with the smoke of feathers, sulphur and realgar, and they make this smoke last 7 or 8 hours. Likewise the husks of wheat make a great and lasting smoke; and also dry dung; but this must be mixed with olive husks, that is olives pressed for oil and from which the oil has been extracted.

1082.

Leic. 1 *b*]

The Danube.

Come le ualli furō già coperte in grā parte da laghi, inperochè senpre il suo terreno fece argine a fiumi, e da mari, i quali poi colla perseueratione de' fiumi ²segarono li monti, e li fiumi coi lor vagabundi corsi portarono via le altre pianvre incluse dalli mōti, e le segature de' mōti so³no note per le falde delle pietre, che si corrispondono nelle lor tagliature fatte dalli detti corsi de' fiumi; ⁴Il Monte Emus che riga la Tratia e la Dardaria e si congiugne col Monte Sardonius, el quale, seguendo ⁵a ponēte, muta il nome di Sardus in | Rebi nel toccare la Dalmatia, poi seguendo a ponēte riga li Illirici ⁶oggi detta Schiavonia, e mvta nome di | Rebi in | Albanus, e seguendo pure a ponēte si muta nel Mōte Ocra ⁷a tramōtana, e a mezzodì sopra all'Istria si nomina | Caruancas e si congiugne a ponēte sopra l'Italia col Mōte

That the valleys were formerly in great part covered by lakes the soil of which always forms the banks of rivers,—and by seas, which afterwards, by the persistent wearing of the rivers, cut through the mountains and the wandering courses of the rivers carried away the other plains enclosed by the mountains; and the cutting away of the mountains is evident from the strata in the rocks, which correspond in their sections as made by the courses of the rivers [4]. The Hæmus mountains which go along Thrace and Dardania and join the Sardonius mountains which, going on to the westward change their name from Sardus to Rebi, as they come near Dalmatia; then turning to the West cross Illyria, now called Sclavonia, changing the name of Rebi to Albanus, and going on still to the West, they change to Mount Ocra in the North; and to the South above Istria they are named Caruancas; and to the West above Italy they join the Adula, where the Danube rises [8], which stretches to the East and has a

---

1080. 2. chome i tedesci ingarigliano ettessana. 2. large lunge. 3. dele . . attera . . imano.
1081. 1. anegare chastelani. 2. risalgalo effano. 3. elletame secho. 4. ovoi morcha.
1082. 1. laghi "inperche senpre il suo terreno fece argine afiumi" e da mari. 2. segorono . . elli fiumi co . . portorono . . mōti elle. 3. chessi conrisspondano. 4. emus . . tratia ella dardaria essi congvgne . . monte [scardus] sardonius. 5. nel cottare la. 6. sciavonia . . ponente [segue] si muta. 7. attramōtana e mezodi . . isstria . . essi congugne. 8. nasscie il reno

---

1080. Above the text is a sketch of a few lines crossing each other and the words *de ponderibus*. The meaning of the passage is obscure.

1081. There is with this passage a sketch of a round tower shrouded in smoke.

1082. 4. *Emus*, the Balkan; *Dardania*, now Servia.

Adula, [8]doue nascie il Danubio, il quale s'astende a leuante con corso di 1500 miglia, e la sua linia breuissima è circa [9]mille miglia, e altrettanto o circa è'l ramo del Monte Adula mutato ne'predetti nomi di mōti; sta a tramon[10]tana il monte | Carpatus, il quale termina la larghezza della valle del Danubio, la qual, come dissi, s'astende [11]a leuāte cō lunghezza di circa mille miglia, ed è larga doue 200 e doue 300 miglia; questa si mette pel [12]mezzo il Danvbio, primo fiume d'Europa per magnitudine, il qual Danvbio si lascia per mezzo di [13]Austria e Albania e per tramōtana Bauaria, Polonia, Ungheria, Valachia e Bosnia; versaua adunque il Danubio | over | Da[14]noia nel mare di Ponto, il quale s'astendea insino vicino all'Austria e occupaua tutta la pianvra che oggi [15]discorre esso Danvbio, e'l segno dico ne mostrano l'ostriche e li nichi e bovoli e cappe e ossa di grā pesci, che an[16]cora in molti lochi si trouano nell'alte coste de'predetti mōti; ed era tale mare fatto per la ringorgatione delli ra[17]mi del Monte Adula, che s'astendeano a leuante e si congiugneano colli rami del Mōte Tauro, che s'astendono a po[18]nēte, e circa alla Bitinia versaua l'acque d'esso Mare di Pōto nel Propontico, cadendo nel Mare Egeo cioè [19]Mar Mediterrano, doue poi il lungo corso spiccò li rami del Mōte Adula dalli rami del Mōte Tauro; li Mare [20]di Pōto s'abassò e scoperse la Val di Danubio colle prenominate provincie, e tutta l'Asia Minore di là dal monte Ta[21]vro per tramōtana e la pianvra ch'è da Mōte Caucasso al mare di Ponto per ponēte, e la pianura del Ta[22]nai dentro alli monti Rifei cioè a' piedi loro; Ecco che 'l mare di Ponto abbassò circa a braccia 1000 [23]nello scoprire di tanta pianura.

course of 1500 miles; its shortest line is about 1000 miles, and the same or about the same is that branch of the Adula mountains changed as to their name, as before mentioned. To the North are the Carpathians, closing in the breadth of the valley of the Danube, which, as I have said extends eastward, a length of about 1000 miles, and is sometimes 200 and in some places 300 miles wide; and in the midst flows the Danube, the principal river of Europe as to size. The said Danube runs through the middle of Austria and Albania and northwards through Bavaria, Poland, Hungary, Wallachia and Bosnia and then the Danube or Donau flows into the Black Sea, which formerly extended almost to Austria and occupied the plains through which the Danube now courses; and the evidence of this is in the oysters and cockle shells and scollops and bones of great fishes which are still to be found in many places on the sides of those mountains; and this sea was formed by the filling up of the spurs of the Adula mountains which then extended to the East joining the spurs of the Taurus which extend to the West. And near Bithynia the waters of this Black Sea poured into the Propontis [Marmora] falling into the Ægean Sea, that is the Mediterranean, where, after a long course, the spurs of the Adula mountains became separated from those of the Taurus. The Black Sea sank lower and laid bare the valley of the Danube with the above named countries, and the whole of Asia Minor beyond the Taurus range to the North, and the plains from mount Caucasus to the Black Sea to the West, and the plains of the Don this side—that is to say, at the foot of the Ural mountains. And thus the Black Sea must have sunk about 1000 braccia to uncover such vast plains.

---

il quale . . alleuante conchorso . . ella . . circha. 9. circha . . attramon. 10. largeza. 11. alleuāte cō lungeza . . largha [dalle do] doue. 12. mezo . . danvbbio . . danvbbio si lasscia per mezo. 13. vngeria . . ebboxnia . . danubbio over da. 14. sasstendea . . ochupaua. 15. disscorre . . losstriche elli . . e bovoli e chappe . . pessci. 17. chessastendeano alleuante essi congugneano . . taruro chessastendanoal. 18. circha allabettima versauā . . propontico chadendo . . egeocoe. 19. mediterano . spicho. 20. esscoperse la ual di danv | "bbio" . . province ettutta . . minore dala dal. 21. ella . . . chavcaso . . ella. 22. coe . . Ecchochel . . circha a br. 1000. 23. isscoprire.

---

8. *Danubio*, in the original *Reno;* evidently a mistake as we may infer from *come dissi* l. 10 &c.

III.

THE COUNTRIES OF THE WESTERN END OF THE MEDITERRANEAN.

A. 57 a]

1083.

PERCHÈ IL MARE FA LA CORRÈTE
NELLO STRETTO DI SPAGNIA PIV
CH'ALTROVE.

The straits
of Gibraltar
(1083—1085).

² ¶ Il fiume · d'equal profondità · avrà · tanto · piv · fuga ·
nella · minore · larghezza ³che
nella · maggiore·, quanto · la
maggiore · larghezza · avanza ·
la minore; ¶

⁴ Questa · propositione · si
pruova . chiaramēte per ragione
cōferma ⁵dalla sperienza·, jnperochè, quando · per uno canale · d'uno miglio · di larghezza
passe⁶rà uno miglio·di lūghezza d'acqua, dove · il fiume·
fia·largo 5 migli, ciascuno ⁷de
5 migli quadri metterà ¹/₅·
di se · per ristaurare il mi⁸glio ·
quadro d'acqua mācato · nello
pelago, ⁹e dove il fivme · fia ·
lar¹⁰go · 3 · miglia ·, ciascu¹¹no ·
d'essi migli quadri ¹²metterà di
se lo terzo ¹³di sua quātità per
lo mā¹⁴care che fecie il mi¹⁵glio
quadro dello stret¹⁶to ·, come si
dimo¹⁷stra · in · *f · g · h* ¹⁸per lo
miglio · *n.*

WHY THE SEA MAKES A STRONGER
CURRENT IN THE STRAITS OF SPAIN
THAN ELSEWHERE.

A river of equal depth runs
with greater speed in a narrow
space than in a wide one, in
proportion to the difference between the wider and the narrower
one.

This proposition is clearly
proved by reason confirmed
by experiment. Supposing that
through a channel one mile
wide there flows one mile in
length of water; where the river
is five miles wide each of the
5 square miles will require
¹/₅ of itself to be equal to
the square mile of water required in the sea, and where
the river is 3 miles wide each
of these square miles will require the third of its volume
to make up the amount of the
square mile of the narrow part;
as is demonstrated in *f g h* at
the mile marked *n.*

1083. 1. chorēte . . chaltro"ve". 2. ara . . fugha . . largheza. 3. chenella . . quancto . . largheza. 4. [perissperienza] per . .
chōferma. 5. dallissperienza . . per î chanale. 6. ra î miglio di lūgezza dacq"a" . . ciaschuno. 7. ciasscun "de 5"
migli[o] quadr[o] i mettera [per ristaurare il mā] ¹/₅ . di se. 8. dacq"a" māchato . . pelago *4.* 9. *4* e dove. 10. gho
. . ciaschu. 14. chare cheffecie. 15. stre. 16. chome. *Lines 9—18 are written in the margin.*

1083. In the place marked A in the diagram
Mare Mediterano (Mediterranean Sea) is written in
the original. And at B, *stretto di Spagna* (straits
of Spain, *i. e.* Gibraltar). Compare No. 960.

C. A. 212 b; 626 b]   **1084.**

PERCHÈ È MAGGIORE SĒPRE LA CORRĒTE DI
SPAGNIA INVERSO PONĒTE · CHE PER LEUĀTE.

²La ragiō si è ·, che se tu · metterai · insieme · le boche · de'fiumi · che mettono · in
questo · Mare Mediterrano, tu tro³verai ·
essere · maggiore · soma d'acqua · ch'è ·
quella · che uersa · esso · mare per lo stretto
in nell'oceano mare; ⁴tu vedi · l'Africa scaricare · i sua fiumi · che corrono · a tramōtana · inesso mare īfra i quali ⁵è · il Nilo ·,
che riga · 3000 miglia dell'Africa ·, e vi è ·
il · fiume Bagrada, · e 'l Mavretano, e altri
simili; ⁶l'Europa vi versa il Tanai e 'l Danvbio ·, il Po e 'l Rodano, Arno e Teuere,
sichè chiaramente questi fivmi insieme co⁷n
īfiniti fivmi di minor fama · fanno · maggiore · larghezza ɛ profōdità · e corso ·, e
non è il mare stretto 18 miglia ⁸che nel
ultima terra di ponēte · diuide · l'Europa
dal' Africa.

WHY THE CURRENT OF GIBRALTAR IS ALWAYS
GREATER TO THE WEST THAN TO THE EAST.

The reason is that if you put together
the mouths of the rivers which discharge
into the Mediterranean sea, you would find
the sum of water to be larger than that
which this sea pours through the straits into
the ocean. You see Africa discharging its
rivers that run northwards into this sea, and
among them the Nile which runs through
3000 miles of Africa; there is also the
Bagrada river and the Schelif and others.
Likewise Europe pours into it the Don and
the Danube, the Po, the Rhone, the Arno,
and the Tiber, so that evidently these rivers,
with an infinite number of others of less
fame, make its great breadth and depth and
current; and the sea is not wider than 18
miles at the most westerly point of land where
it divides Europe from Africa.

Leic. 10 b]   **1085.**

Il ²seno mediterrano come pelago ri-
cevea l'acque regali del'Africa, Asia ed
Europa, che a esso erano volte, ³e le sue
acque veniano alle piaggie de'monti, che
le circūdavano, e lì faceano argine, e le
cime ⁴dello Apennino stauano in esso mare
in forma d'isole, circūdate dalle acque salse,
⁵e ancora l'Africa dentro al suo Mōte Ata-
lante non mostraua al celo scoperta la
terra delle sue grā pianvre cō circa ⁶a
3000 miglia di lunghezza, e Mēfi risedeua
in sul lito di tal mare, e sopra le pianvre
della Italia, doue oggi ⁷volā li ucielli a
turme, soleano discorrere i pesci a grādi
squadre.

The gulf of the Mediterranean, as an
inland sea, received the principal waters
of Africa, Asia and Europe that flowed
towards it; and its waters came up to the
foot of the mountains that surrounded it and
made its shores. And the summits of the
Apennines stood up out of this sea like islands, surrounded by salt water. Africa again,
behind its Atlas mountains did not expose
uncovered to the sky the surface of its
vast plains about 3000 miles in length, and
Memphis[6] was on the shores of this sea,
and above the plains of Italy, where now
birds fly in flocks, fish were wont to wander
in large shoals.

Leic. 27 b]   **1086.**

Co²me sopra Tunisi è il maggior riflusso che faccia il Mare Mediterrano che
son circa 2 braccia ³e ¹/₂, e a Venezia
cala 2 braccia; e in tutto il resto di tal
Mare Mediterrano cala poco o ni⁴ente.

The greatest ebb made anywhere by the **Tunis.**
Mediterranean is above Tunis, being about two
and a half braccia and at Venice it falls two
braccia. In all the rest of the Mediterranean
sea the fall is little or none.

1084. magiore . . chōrēte . . inver. 2. settu . . mettano. 3. magiore . . dacq"a" . . inell. 4. lafricha scharichare . . chorano
attramōtana . . equali. 5. dellafricha . ini . il fiume bagrada. 6. levropia . . siche ciaro . . cho. 7. fano magiore largeza . . chorso . . moglia. 8. nelūtimatera . . leeropa . . africha.

1085. 1. nel. 2. seno [mediterano] mediterano il quale come pelagho . . regali [di circha 300 fiumi regali] "delafrica asia edeu-
ropa, che acso erano volte". 3. e cholle . . acque veniano ale piagge . . chello . . elli faceano . . elle cime. 4. apennino
[in forma di sole] stauano in eso . . circhūdate. 5. lafricha [non mos] dentro . . attalante no mostraua . . celo "scoperta
la terra de" le sue . . circha. 6. lungeza e mēfi . . sulito . . mare "e sopra" le. 7. [disorā] volā . . atturme solea . .
pessci a grāde.

1086. 2. tuniti . . magor . . refrusso . . mediterano . . circha 2 br. 3. vinegia chala . . meditera . . pocho.

1084. 5. *Bagrada* (Leonardo writes Bragada) in Tunis, now Medscherda; *Mavretano*, now Schelif.
1085. 6. *M̄efi.* Leonardo can only mean here the citadel of Cairo on the Mokattam hills.

F. 61 a]   1087.

Libya. Descriui li mōti de' flessibili aridi, cioè della ²creatione dell'onde della rena portate dal uē³to, e de' sua mōti e colli, come accade nella Li⁴bia; l'esenplo ne vedrai sulli grā renaj ⁵di Po o di Tesino o altri grā fiumi.

Describe the mountains of shifting deserts; that is to say the formation of waves of sand borne by the wind, and of its mountains and hills, such as occur in Libya. Examples may be seen on the wide sands of the Po and the Ticino, and other large rivers.

B. 82 b]   1088.

Majorca. Circūfulgore · è vna macchina navale ·, fu invētione di quelli di Majolica.

Circumfulgore is a naval machine. It was an invention of the men of Majorca.

Ash. II. 12 a]   1089.

The Tyrrhene Sea. Alcuni·nel Mare Tirreno · vsarono questo modo, cioè ²appiccauano vn ācora a l'una delle stremità dell'āteña, ³e dall'altra vna · corda che ī basso s'appiccava a vn ācora, ⁴e nel pugniare attacavano detta · ācora ai remeggi dell'o⁵posito navilio, e per forza d'argano quello mādavano alla bāda ⁶e gittavano sapon tenero e stoppa īpeciata īfocata sulla ⁷prima bāda dou'era l'ācora attaccata, acciochè, per fugir detto ⁸foco, i difenditori d'esso navilio avessino a fugire da l'op⁹posita bāda, e faciēdo così facievano avmēto · allo spugnia¹⁰tore, perchè la galera piv facilmēte per lo cōtrapeso ¹¹andava alla bāda.

Some at the Tyrrhene sea employ this method; that is to say they fastened an anchor to one end of the yard, and to the other a cord, of which the lower end was fastened to an anchor; and in battle they flung this anchor on to the oars of the opponent's boat and by the use of a capstan drew it to the side; and threw soft soap and tow, daubed with pitch and set ablaze, on to that side where the anchor hung; so that in order to escape that fire, the defenders of that ship had to fly to the opposite side; and in doing this they aided to the attack, because the galley was more easily drawn to the side by reason of the counterpoise.

1087 1. desscriui . . fressibili. 3. cholli . .   1088. maccina . . macolica.
1089. 1. tireno. 2. apichauano nācora [chorda che ībaso sapienvavācora] "aluna delle stremita dellatena". 3. chorda . . sapicava. 4. decta āchora ai remigi. 5. ala. 6. stopa īpegolata . . sula. 7. bōda lācoratachata acio. 8. affugire dallo. 9. effaciēdo. 10. galea.

1088. The machine is fully described in the MS. and shown in a sketch.

1089. This text is illustrated in the original by a pen and ink sketch.

IV.

THE LEVANT.

1090.

Truovāsi nelle riue del Mare Mediterrano versare fiumi 300, [2] e porti 40 mila 200,
e esso mare è di lunghezza miglia 3000;
Molte volte s'è accozza[3]to l'accrescimēto
de'mari del riflusso suo e'l soffiare delli
venti occidē[4]tali al diluuio del Nilo, ed alli
fiumi che uersā dal mare di Pōto, ed auere
alzato tanto li mari che sō [5]cō grādissimi diluvi discorsi per molti paesi, · e questi diluui accadono nel tenpo, che 'l sole [6]distrugie
le neui delli alti mōti d'Etiopia che si leuano alla fredda regiō dell'aria, e si[7]mil-
mēte fa l'appressamēto del sole alli mōti
della Sarmatia Asiatica e quella d'Europa,
[8]in modo che l'accozzamēto di queste 3
dette cose sono, e sono state cagione di
grā[9]dissimi diluui, cioè il riflusso del mare,
e li uenti occidentali, e la distrutiō delle
nevi; è ogni cosa [10]ringorgata nella Siria,
Samaria, la Giudea infra Sinai e il Libano,
e 'l resto della Siria infra [11]il Libano e Mōte

On the shores of the Mediterranean 300
rivers flow, and 40, 200 ports. And this sea
is 3000 miles long. Many times has the increase of its waters, heaped up by their back-
ward flow and the blowing of the West winds,
caused the overflow of the Nile and of the rivers
which flow out through the Black Sea, and have
so much raised the seas that they have spread
with vast floods over many countries. And
these floods take place at the time when the
sun melts the snows on the high mountains
of Ethiopia that rise up into the cold regions
of the air; and in the same way the approach
of the sun acts on the mountains of Sarmatia
in Asia and on those in Europe; so that the
gathering together of these three things are,
and always have been, the cause of tremendous
floods: that is, the return flow of the sea with
the West wind and the melting of the snows.
So every river will overflow in Syria, in
Samaria, in Judea between Sinai and the
Lebanon, and in the rest of Syria between
the Lebanon and the Taurus mountains, and
in Cilicia, in the Armenian mountains, and
in Pamphilia and in Lycia within the hills,

The Lavan-
tine Sea

1090. 1. mediterano. 2. porti [5] 40 mila 200 . . langeza . . seacoza. 3. lacresscimēto . . refrusso. 4. del mare . . ponto aveuere.
5. luui disscorsi . . ecquesti . . achagiano. 6. le neue . . chessi . . freda . . essi. 7. lapressamēto . . asiaticha ecquella.
8. chellacogamēto . . chagione. 9. coe il refrusso . . ocidentali ella. 10. soria someria la gudea . . sinai e e libano . .
soria. 11. elibano . . ella cilicia . . mōtermini ella . . litia dentrali. 12. ellegitto . . attalante . . lagho . . chade·

Tauro, e la Cilicia dentro alli mōti Armeni e la Pamfilia e Licia dentro alli mōticelli [12] e l'Egitto insino al mōte Atlante; Il seno di Persia, che già fu lago grādissimo del Tigris e cade[13]a nel mare d'India, ora à consumato il mōte · che li facea argine, e si è ragguagliato coll'altezza [14] dèllo Occeano Indico; E se 'l Mare Mediterrano sequiva il moto suo nel sē d'Arabia, ācor facieva il simile, [15] cioè che si ragguagliava l'altezza Mediterranea colla altezza d'esso Mare Indico.

and in Egypt as far as the Atlas mountains. The gulf of Persia which was formerly a vast lake of the Tigris and discharged into the Indian Sea, has now worn away the mountains which formed its banks and laid them even with the level of the Indian ocean. And if the Mediterranean had continued its flow through the gulf of Arabia, it would have done the same, that is to say, would have reduced the level of the Mediterranean to that of the Indian Sea.

Leic. 31 *a*]

1091.

The Red Sea. (1091. 1092).

Versò l'acqua Mediterrana lungamente pel Mare Rosso, el quale è [2] largo cento miglia e lungo mille cinque cento; è tutto pieno di scogli, e à consumato li la[3]ti del Mōte Sinai, la qual cosa testifica, nō da inōdatione del Mar d'India, che in tali liti percuo[4]tesse, ma da una ruina d'acqua, la qual portaua con seco tutti li fiumi che soprabbon[5]dauano al Mare Mediterrano, e oltre a questo il riflusso del mare; [6] e poi, essendo tagliato nel ponente, 3 mila miglia remoto da questo loco, il mōte Calpe è s[7]piccato dal Mōte Abila, e fu tal taglio fatto bassissimo nelle pianure che si trouauā infra Abila [8] e l'oceano a piè del monte in loco basso, aiutato dal concauamēto di qualche vallata fatta [9] da alcun fiume che quiui passasse; venne Ercole ad aprire il mare nel ponēte, e allora [10] l'acque marine cominciarono a uersare nell'oceano occidentale, e per la grā bassezza, il Mare [11] Rosso rimase piv alto, onde l'acque ànno abbandonato il corso di quiui; senpre ànno poi versa[12]to l'acque per lo Stretto di Spagna.

For a long time the water of the Mediterranean flowed out through the Red Sea, which is 100 miles wide and 1500 long, and full of reefs; and it has worn away the sides of Mount Sinai, a fact which testifies, not to an inundation from the Indian sea beating on these coasts, but to a deluge of water which carried with it all the rivers which abound round the Mediterranean, and besides this there is the reflux of the sea; and then, a cutting being made to the West 3000 miles away from this place, Gibraltar was separated from Ceuta, which had been joined to it. And this passage was cut very low down, in the plains between Gibraltar and the ocean at the foot of the mountain, in the low part, aided by the hollowing out of some valleys made by certain rivers, which might have flowed here. Hercules came to open the sea to the westward and then the sea waters began to pour into the Western Ocean; and in consequence of this great fall, the Red Sea remained the higher; whence the water, abandoning its course here, ever after poured away through the Straits of Spain.

C. A. 321 *b*; 971 *a*]

1092.

La superfitie del Mare Rosso è in liuello coll'oceano.

The surface of the Red Sea is on a level with the ocean.

---

13. chelli . argine edessi ragualgliato . . alteza. 14. indicho Esse . . mediterano. 15. coe chesi racualgliaua laltezza mediteranea . . alteza . . indicho.

1091. 1. mediterana lunghamente. 2. largho . . ellungho . . cinquecento tutto. 3. de mōti sinai . . liti percho. 4. tessi . . consecho . . soprabon. 5. dauono . . mediterano e oltre adſquesto il refrusso. 6. chalpe es. 7. pichato . . abile effu . . chessi trovaua . . abile. 8. ellocceano . . locho . . chonchauamēto. 9. passassi . . erchole. 10. comincorono . . occeano . . perlla . . basseza. 11. lacque anbandonato.

1092. 1. mare [so] rosso e illiuello. 2. chaduta . . esserrato [el] la bocha. 3. mediterano. 4. rīghorghato. 5. fralli . . ghade-

---

1091. 9. Leonardo seems here to mention Hercules half jestingly and only in order to suggest to the reader an allusion to the legend of the pillars of Hercules.

²Può esser caduta vna mōtagnia e, ser-
rato la bocca ³del Mare Rosso, e proibito
l'esito al Mediterrano, e co⁴sì rīgorgato tal
mare abbia per esito il trāsito ī⁵fra li gioghi
Gadetani, perchè similmente abbiā ⁶veduti
alli nostri tēpi cadere v̄ monte di sette
⁷miglia e serrare vna valle e farne lago, e
così sō ⁸fatti la maggior parte de'laghi da
mōti come Lago di ⁹Garda di Como e Lugano, e 'l lago Maggiore; ¹⁰il Mediterrano
poco s'abbassò per il taglio Gaditano ne¹¹li
cōfini della Siria e assai in esso taglio, perchè
pri¹²ma che tal taglio si creasse, esso mare
versaua per scirocco, ¹³e poi s'ebbe a fare
la calata, che corresse a tal Gaditano.

¹⁴In *a* cadea l'acqua ¹⁵del Mediterrano
nel oce¹⁶ano.

¹⁷¶Tutte le pianure che son ¹³dalli
mari · alli mōti, sono ¹⁹già state coperte
dall'acque salse;¶

²⁰¶Ogni valle è fatta dal suo fiu²¹me e
tal proportione è da valle a val²²le, quale
è da fiume a fiume;¶

²³¶Il massimo fiume del nostro mōdo è
²⁴il Mediterrano fiume,¶

²⁵¶che si move dal principio ²⁶del Nilo
all'Oceano occidē²⁷tale,¶

²⁸e la sua suprema altezza ²⁹è nella
Mavretania este³⁰riore, e à di corso 10
mila ³¹miglia, prima chè si ripatrii ³²col suo
Oceano, padre del³³le acque,

³⁴Cioè 3000 il Mediterrano, 3000 ³⁵il
Nilo scoperto, e 3000 il Nilo ³⁶che corre
a oriēte ecc.

A mountain may have fallen and closed
the mouth of the Red Sea and prevented
the outlet of the Mediterranean, and the
Mediterranean Sea thus overfilled had for
outlet the passage below the mountains of
Gades; for, in our own times a similar thing
has been seen[6]; a mountain fell seven
miles across a valley and closed it up and
made a lake. And thus most lakes have been
made by mountains, as the lake of Garda,
the lakes of Como and Lugano, and the Lago
Maggiore. The Mediterranean fell but little
on the confines of Syria, in consequence of the
Gaditanean passage, but a great deal in this
passage, because before this cutting was made
the Mediterranean sea flowed to the South
East, and then the fall had to be made by its
run through the Straits of Gades.

At *a* the water of the Mediterranean fell
into the ocean.

All the plains which lie between the sea
and mountains were formerly covered with
salt water.

Every valley has been made by its own
river; and the proportion between valleys is
the same as that between river and river.

The greatest river in our world is the
Mediterranean river,

which moves from the sources of the
Nile to the Western ocean.

And its greatest height is in Outer Mauritania and it has a course of ten thous-
and miles before it reunites with its ocean,
the father of the waters.

That is 3000 miles for the Mediterranean,
3000 for the Nile, as far as discovered and
3000 for the Nile which flows to the East, &c.

---

tani . . simile abbiā. 6. veduta. 7. serare . . effarne lagho. 8. magiore laghi de mōti . . lagho. 9. gharda [lac] di co:no
ellughano ellagho magiore. 10. mediterano pocho sabasso . . ghaditano. 11. soria. 12. chettal . . scirocho. 13. affare
. . choressi . . Gadetano. 14. chadea. 15. mediteraneo nel. 17. chesson. 19. dallacq. 20. effatta. 21. ettal pro"ne".
22. he daffiume affiume. 23. del "nostro" mōde he. 24. mediterano [fatto] fiume. 25. [di] chessi . . occieano. 28. ella . .
supprema. 29 he . . esste. 32. occieano. 34. mediterano. 36. chorre [da] a oriēte.

1092. See Pl. CXI 2, a sketch of the shores of
the Mediterranean Sea, where lines 11 to 16 may
be seen. The large figures 158 are not in Leonardo's
writing. The character of the writing leads us
to conclude that this text was written later than the
foregoing. A slight sketch of the Mediterranean is
also to be found in MS. I', 47ª.

6. Compare also No. 1336, ll. 30, 35 and 36.—
Paolo Giovio, the celebrated historian (born at

Como in 1483) reports that in 1513 at the foot of
the Alps, above Bellinzona, on the road to Switzer-
land, a mountain fell with a very great noise, in
consequence of an earthquake, and that the mass
of rocks, which fell on the left (Western) side
blocked the river Breno (T. I p. 218 and 345
of D. Sauvage's French edition, quoted in ALEXIS
PERCY, *Mémoire des tremblements de terre de la péninsule italique; Académie Royale de Belgique.* T. XXII).—

C. A. 94 _b_; 276 _a_]   **1093.**

The Nile
(1093—1098).

Adūque cōcluderemo quelle · mōtagnie · essere di maggiore altura, ²sopra · delle . quali · fioccando · l'origine · del Nilo · dai nuvoli · casca.

Therefore we must conclude those mountains to be of the greatest height, above which the clouds falling in snow give rise to the Nile.

B. 61 _b_]   **1094.**

Gli Egiziani, gli Etiopi · e gli Arabi · nel passare il Nilo vsano ai cameli ²appiccare ai lati del busto 2 baghe cioè otri ī questa forma di sotto.
³In queste 4 maglie di re⁴te mettono i piè i cameli ⁵di carriaggi.

The Egyptians, the Ethiopians, and the Arabs, in crossing the Nile with camels, are accustomed to attach two bags on the sides of the camel's bodies that is skins in the form shown underneath.
In these four meshes of the net the camels for baggage place their feet.

Leic. 34 _b_]   **1095.**

Il Tigri passa per l'Asia Minore, il quale ne porta ²con seco l'acqua di 3 paduli, l'un dopo l'altro di uarie altezze, de' quali il piv alto è Munace, e 'l mezzano è Pallas, ³e 'l più basso è Triton; ancora el Nilo diriua di 3 altissimi paduli in Etiopia, il quale cor⁴re a tramōtana e versa nel mare d'Egitto con corso di 4000 miglia, e la sua breuissima e diritta linia ⁵è 3000 miglia; di quel che s'à notitia escie de' mōti della luna con diuersi e incogniti prīcipi, e tro⁶vāsi li detti laghi alti sopra la spera dell'acqua circa a 4000 braccia cioè vn miglio e ¹/₃, a dare ⁷vn braccio di caduta al Nilo per ogni miglio.

The Tigris passes through Asia Minor and brings with it the water of three lakes, one after the other of various elevations; the first being Munace and the middle Pallas and the lowest Triton. And the Nile again springs from three very high lakes in Ethiopia, and runs northwards towards the sea of Egypt with a course of 4000 miles, and by the shortest and straightest line it is 3000 miles. It is said that it issues from the Mountains of the Moon, and has various unknown sources. The said lakes are about 4000 braccia above the surface of the sphere of water, that is 1 mile and ¹/₃, giving to the Nile a fall of 1 braccia in every mile.

Leic. 21 _b_]   **1096.**

Moltissime volte il Nilo e gli altri fiumi di grā ma²gnitudine ànno · versato tutto l'elemēto dell' acqua · e rēduto al mare.

Very many times the Nile and other very large rivers have poured out their whole element of water and restored it to the sea.

1093. 1. [adūque chōcluderemo quelle mōtagnie essere di magiore altura]. 2. [sopra delle quali lorigine del nilo dai nvvoli fiochando cade]. 3. sopra delle quali | "fiochando del nilo . dai nvvoli . cade". 4. chōcuderano . . magiore 5. fiochando . . nvuoli casscha.
1094. 1. egiti. 2. apichare . . bage. 4. mettano. 5. cariagi.
1095. 1. come trigon il quale passa per la minore africha il quane ne. 2. consecho lacq"a" . . alteze . . mezano. 4. attramōtana . . ella sua . . ediritti. 5. he 3000 . . quel chessa notitio esscie. 6. vasi . . soppra lasspera dellacq"a" circha 4000 br. coe. 7. vn br. di.

1094. Unfortunately both the sketches which accompany this passage are too much effaced to be reproduced. The upper represents the two sacks joined by ropes, as here described, the other shows four camels with riders swimming through a river.

1095. 5. _Incogniti principio._ The affluents of the lakes are probably here intended. Compare, as to the Nile, Nos. 970, 1063 and 1084.

Leic. 22 a]　　　　　**1097.**

Perchè il Nilo inōda l'estate e viē da paesi focosi?

Why does the inundation of the Nile occur in the summer, coming from torrid countries?

Leic. 32 b]　　　　　**1098.**

Nō si nega che 'l ²Nilo al continvo ³non ētri torbido ⁴nel mare d'Egitto, ⁵e che tal turbulē⁶tia non sia ca⁷vsata dal terrē, ⁸che esso fiume le⁹ua al continvo da' ¹⁰lochi, onde passa, ¹¹il qual terrē ¹²mai ritorna in ¹³dirieto nel ma¹⁴re che lo ricieue, ¹⁵se nō lo ributta al¹⁶li sua liti; vedi ¹⁷il mare areno¹⁸so dirieto al mō¹⁹te Atlante, doue già ²⁰fu coperto d'acqua ²¹salsa.

It is not denied that the Nile is constantly muddy in entering the Egyptian sea and that its turbidity is caused by soil that this river is continually bringing from the places it passes; which soil never returns in the sea which receives it, unless it throws it on its shores. You see the sandy desert beyond Mount Atlas where formerly it was covered with salt water.

B. 61 b]　　　　　**1099.**

Gli Assiri e quelli di Evbea vsano ai loro cavalli ²portare sacchi da potere a lor posta · ēpiere di uēto, ³i quali portano in scābio di bandella della sella di sopra ⁴e d'accanto, e bene è coperta di piastre di corame cotto, ⁵acciochè 'l saettame non le fora, si che non àno in cvore la ⁶fuga sicura che la uittoria īcierta; vno cavallo ⁷così fatto passa 4 e 5 omini a v̄ bisognio.

The Assyrians and the people of Euboea accustom their horses to carry sacks which they can at pleasure fill with air, and which in case of need they carry instead of the girth of the saddle above and at the side, and they are well covered with plates of cuir bouilli, in order that they may not be perforated by flights of arrows. Thus they have not on their minds their security in flight, when the victory is uncertain; a horse thus equipped enables four or five men to cross over at need.

Customs of Asiatic Nations (1099. 1100).

B. 62 b]　　　　　**1100.**

NAVICULA.

SMALL BOATS.

²Le navicule · apresso · ali Assiri furono fatte di uirghe sottili di salice ³e tessute sopra pertiche pur di salice, ridotte ī forma di barchetta, ilotate ⁴di poluere sottile inbeuerata d'olio, o di tremētina · ridotta ī natura ⁵di fango, la qual facieva resistētia al'acqua, e perchè il pino n'isfendea per ⁶senpre stava fresca ci essere vesti detta sorte di navicule · di pelle bouine ⁷nel passare Sicuris ·, fiume di Spagnia, secōdo ne testifica Lucano;

The small boats used by the Assyrians were made of thin laths of willow plaited over rods also of willow, and bent into the form of a boat. They were daubed with fine mud soaked with oil or with turpentine, and reduced to a kind of mud which resisted the water and because pine would split; and always remained fresh; and they covered this sort of boats with the skins of oxen in safely crossing the river Sicuris of Spain, as is reported by Lucan[7].

1097. lāstade . . dipaesi.

1098. 1. negha. 5. chettal. 6. cha. 9. de. 11. equal. 14. re lo. 15. nollo rebutta. 19. attalante. 20. dacq"a".

1099. 1. ecquelli . . cavagli. 3. schābio. 4. dacanto. 5. acciochel saettumel fora si che non ano inēcare (?) la.
　　　6. uettoria.

1100. 1. navichula. 2. navichula . . sali \\\\\\\. 3. ettessute. 4. o di tue mētina ridotta. 5. alacqua e pechel pinōnis fede aper.
　　　6. fresca ci essere vesti detta sorte di navicule . di pele bouine. 8. lissciti elli . . voliono. 9. aligano li grātici . . bage

1100. 7. See Lucan's Pharsalia IV, 130:
Utque habuit ripas Sicoris camposque reliquit,
Primum cana salix madefacto vimine parvam
Texitur in puppim, calsoque inducto juvenco
Vectoris patiens tumidum supernatat amnem.
Sic Venetus stagnante Pado, fusoque Britannus
Navigat oceano, sic cum tenet omnia Nilus,
Conseritur bibula Memphitis cymbo papyro.

His ratibus transjecta manus festinat utrimque
Succisam cavare nemus &c.

Caesar (de bello civ. I, 54) has the same remark about the Britanni (confirmed by Pliny, hist. nat. IV, 15) which Leonardo here makes about the Assyrians.—This and the foregoing text are illustrated by slight sketches.

⁸L'Ispani ·, li Sciti · e li Arabi ·, quãdo vogliono fare vn subito pōte, ⁹alligano · li graticci fatti di salice sopra le baghe overo otri di pelli bouine, ¹⁰e così passã sicuramente.

The Spaniards, the Scythians and the Arabs, when they want to make a bridge in haste, fix hurdlework made of willows on bags of ox-hide, and so cross in safety.

Leic. 10 b]

1101.

Rhodes 1101. 1102).

Nello ottanta 9 fu vno terremoto nel mar di Atalia presso a Rodi, il quale aperse il mare cioè il fondo, ²nella qual apritura si sommerse tanto diluuio d'acque, che per piv di 3 · ore si scoperse il fondo del mare dall'acque, che ³di quiui si spogliarono, e poi si richiuse al primo grado.

In [fourteen hundred and] eighty nine there was an earthquake in the sea of Atalia near Rhodes, which opened the sea—that is its bottom—and into this opening such a torrent of water poured that for more than three hours the bottom of the sea was uncovered by reason of the water which was lost in it, and then it closed to the former level.

L. o']

1102.

Rodi à dētro 5000 case.

Rhodes has in it 5000 houses.

W. XVII a]

1103.

PEL SITO DI VENERE.

SITE FOR [A TEMPLE OF] VENUS.

Cyprus 1103. 1104).

²Farai le scale da 4 faccie, per le quali si pervenga a un prato fatto dalla natura sopra vn sasso, ³il quale sia fatto vuoto e sostenvto dinanzi con pilastri, e sotto traforato con magno portico, nel⁴li quali uada

You must make steps on four sides, by which to mount to a meadow formed by nature at the top of a rock which may be hollowed out and supported in front by pilasters and open underneath in a large portico,

ovrotri . . pelle. 10. passa.
1101. 1. mare disatalia preso . . aperse "il mare co" el fondo [del mare]. 2. somerse tane diluuio . . mare dellacqua.
3. spogliorono.
1103. 2. lesscale . . pervena . . prato [for] fatto [sopr] dalla. 3. voto essoslenvta . . pilasstrī essotto . . conmagnio porticho, ne.

1101. *Nello ottanto 9*. It is scarcely likely that Leonardo should here mean 89 A D. Dr. H. MÜLLER-STRÜBING writes to me as follows on this subject: "With reference to Rhodes Ross says (*Reise auf den Griechischen Inseln*, III 70 ff. 1840), that ancient history affords instances of severe earthquakes at Rhodes, among others one in the second year of the 138th Olympiad=270 B. C.; a remarkably violent one under Antoninus Pius (A. D. 138—161) and again under Constantine and later. But Leonardo expressly speaks of an earthquake "*nel mar di Atalia presso a Rodi*", which is singular. The town of Attalia, founded by Attalus, which is what he no doubt means, was in Pamphylia and more than 150 English miles East of Rhodes in a straight line. Leake and most other geographers identify it with the present town of Adalia. Attalia is rarely mentioned by the ancients, indeed only by Strabo and Pliny and no earthquake is spoken of. I think therefore you are justified in assuming that Leonardo means 1489"." In the elaborate catalogue of earthquakes in the East by Selale Dshelal eddin Sayouthy

(an unpublished Arabic MS. in the possession of Prof. SCHEFER, (Membre de l'Institut, Paris) mention is made of a terrible earthquake in the year 867 of the Mohamedan Era corresponding to the year 1489, and it is there stated that a hundred persons were killed by it in the fortress of Kerak. There are three places of this name. Kerak on the sea of Tiberias, Kerak near Tahle on the Libanon, which I visited in the summer of 1876—but neither of these is the place alluded to. Possibly it may be the strongly fortified town of Kerak=Kir Moab, to the West of the Dead Sea. There is no notice about this in ALEXIS PERCY, *Mémoire sur les tremblements de terres ressentis dans la péninsule turco-héllenique et en Syrie* (*Mémoires couronnés et mémoires des savants étrangers*, *Académie Royale de Belgique, Tome XXIII*).

1103. See Pl. LXXXIII. Compare also p. 33 of this Vol. The standing male figure at the side is evidently suggested by Michael Angelo's David. On the same place a slight sketch of horses seems to have been drawn first; there is no reason for l'acqua in diuersi vasi di graniti porfidi e serpētini, dentro a emicicli, e spā⁵da l'acqua in se medesimi, e dintorno a tal portico inverso tramōtana sia un lago · con vna isoletta ⁶in mezzo, nella quale sia vn folto e ōbroso bosco; l'acque in testa ai pilastri siē uersate in uasi ai piè ⁷de' sua inbasamēti, de' quali si spargano piccoli riuetti;

⁸Partendosi dalla ⁹riviera di Cilitia inverso meridio si scopre ¹⁰la bellezza dell'isola di Cipri.

in which the water may fall into various vases of granite, porphyry and serpentine, within semi-circular recesses; and the water may overflow from these. And round this portico towards the North there should be a lake with a little island in the midst of which should be a thick and shady wood; the waters at the top of the pilasters should pour into vases at their base, from whence they should flow in little channels.

Starting from the shore of Cilicia towards the South you discover the beauties of the island of Cyprus.

W. XVII*b*]　　　　　　　　　　　1104.

Dalli meridionali lidi di Cilitia si uede per australe la bell'isola ²di Cipri, la qual fu regnio della dea Venere, e molti incitati dalla sua bellezza ³ànno rotte le loro navili e sarte infra li scogli circundati dalle vertiginose ōde; ⁴quiui la bellezza del dolce colle invita i vagabundi navicanti a re⁵crearsi infra le sue fiorite verdure, fralle quali i uēti ragiorādosi enpiono l'i⁶sola e 'l circūstante mare di suaui odori; o quāte naui quiui già son sommerse! o quanti ⁷navili rotti negli scogli! quiui si potrebbero vedere invmerabili navili; chi è rotto e mezzo ⁸coperto dall'arena, chi si mostra da poppa, e chi da prua, chi da carena e chi da costa, e parà ⁹a similitudine d'un giudizio, che voglia risuscitare navili morti; tant'è la somma di quelli, che ¹⁰copre tutto il lito settentrionale; quiui i uenti d'aquilone resonādo fan uari e paurosi ¹¹soniti.

From the shore of the Southern coast of Cilicia may be seen to the South the beautiful island of Cyprus, which was the realm of the goddess Venus, and many navigators being attracted by her beauty, had their ships and rigging broken amidst the reefs, surrounded by the whirling waters. Here the beauty of delightful hills tempts wandering mariners to refresh themselves amidst their flowery verdure, where the winds are tempered and fill the island and the surrounding seas with fragrant odours. Ah! how many a ship has here been sunk. Ah! how many a vessel broken on these rocks. Here might be seen barks without number, some wrecked and half covered by the sand; others showing the poop and another the prow, here a keel and there the ribs; and it seems like a day of judgment when there should be a resurrection of dead ships, so great is the number of them covering all the Northern shore; and while the North gale makes various and fearful noises there.

The Caspian Sea (1105. 1106).

C. A. 256*a*; 773*a*]　　　　　　　　1105.

Scriui a Bartolomeo turco del flusso e ²riflusso del mar di Ponto, e che intenda, ³se tal flusso e riflusso è nel Mare Ircano ⁴over Mare Caspio.

Write to Bartolomeo the Turk as to the flow and ebb of the Black sea, and whether he is aware if there be such a flow and ebb in the Hyrcanean or Caspian sea.

---

4. vada lacque in diuersi [5] vasi . . esspā. 5. attal . . si lago. 6. mezo . . testa a pilastri . . uasi a pie. 7. sparga picholi riuetti. 8. dalla riuiera [di lic di cilitia] partendosi. 9. cilitia [si scopr] inver meridio si co. 10. beleza . . cipri la qua.
1104. 1. dalla riuiera dalli. 2. della sa belleza. 3. an rotte lor navili essarte . . delle ruertinali ōde. 4. belleza del del dolce callo invita [invita] i. 5. infralle . . fral . . enpiano. 6. adori . . ga son somerse. 7. roti nelgli . . potrebe . . roto e mezo 8. arena [altri] chissi . . popa . . charena e qui. 9. assimilitudine dun giudizi che volglia risucitare nvavili . . tantella soma. 10. varie. 11. chopre . . settantironale [sopra] quiui e uenti . . pauro.
1105. 1. turcho . . frusso. 2. refrusso. 3. settal frusso e refrusso. 4. casspio.

assuming that the text and this sketch, which have no connection with each other, are of the same date.

Sito di Venere. By this heading Leonardo appears to mean Cyprus, which was always considered by

the ancients to be the home and birth place of Aphrodite (Κύπρις in Homer).

1105. The handwriting of this note points to a late date.

F. 50 a]   1106.

PERCHÈ L'ACQUA ²È IN SU MŌ³TI.

⁴Dallo stretto di Gibilterra al Tanai è migli⁵a 3500, edè alto vn miglio e ¹/₆, dando vn braccio ⁶per miglio di cala a ogni acqua che si move me⁷diocremēte, e il Mar Caspio è assai più al⁸to; e nessū de' mōti d'Europa si leua vn ⁹miglio sopra la pelle delli nostri mari; adū¹⁰que si potrebbe dire, che l'acqua ch'è nelle ¹¹cime de' nostri mōti, venisse dall'altezza d'essi ¹²mari e de' fiumi che vi versano, che sō più alti.

WHY WATER IS FOUND AT THE TOP OF MOUNTAINS.

From the straits of Gibraltar to the Don is 3500 miles, that is one mile and ¹/₆, giving a fall of one braccio in a mile to any water that moves gently. The Caspian sea is a great deal higher; and none of the mountains of Europe rise a mile above the surface of our seas; therefore it might be said that the water which is on the summits of our mountains might come from the height of those seas, and of the rivers which flow into them, and which are still higher.

F. 68 a]   1107.

The sea of Azov.

Qui seguita che 'l Mare della Tana, che ²confina col Tanai, è la più alta parte ³che abbia il Mare Mediterrano, il qua⁴le è remoto dallo Stretto di Gibilterra ⁵3500 miglia, come mostra la carta da ⁶nauicare; e à di calo 3500 braccia, cioè uno ⁷miglio e ¹/₆; e è più alto adunque que⁸sto mare che mōte che abbia l'occidēte.

Hence it follows that the sea of Azov is the highest part of the Mediterranean sea, being at a distance of 3500 miles from the Straits of Gibraltar, as is shown by the map for navigation; and it has 3500 braccia of descent, that is, one mile and ¹/₆; therefore it is higher than any mountains which exist in the West.

Leic. 31 b]   1108.

The Dardanelles.

In nello stretto di Tratia il Mare di Pō²to senpre versa nel Mare Egeo, e mai l'Egeo in lui, e questo diriua, che 'l Mare Caspio, che cō 400 miglia sta per leuāte colli ³fiumi che ī lui versano, senpre versa per cave sotterrane in esso Mar di Pōto, e 'l simile fa il Tanai ⁴col Danvbio, in modo che senpre esse acque Pōtiche son piv alte che quelle dello Egeo, ⁵e per ciò le piv alte senpre discendono nelle basse, e nō mai le basse nelle alte.

In the Bosphorus the Black Sea flows always into the Egean sea, and the Egean sea never flows into it. And this is because the Caspian, which is 400 miles to the East, with the rivers which pour into it, always flows through subterranean caves into this sea of Pontus; and the Don does the same as well as the Danube, so that the waters of Pontus are always higher than those of the Egean; for the higher always fall towards the lower, and never the lower towards the higher.

1106. 1. lacq"a". 5. 3500 coe on miglio . . vn br. 6. acq"a" chessi. 7. e mar casspio. 9. pele. 10 chellacqua. 11. venissi . . alteza. 12. vivsano.

1107. 2. ella. 3. mediterano. 5. mosstra. 6. navicare che . . 3500 br. coe î. 7. e ¹/₆ che e piu.

1108. 2. ecquestō . . caspio "che cō [3] 400 (?) mili sta per leuāte" colli. 3. cave socterrane. 4. danvbbio . . chessenpre ⁵. perco le . . dissēdano.

1107. The passage before this, in the original, treats of the exit of the waters from Lakes in general.

L. 66a]　　　　　　　　　　**1109.**

Ponte da Pera a Costantinopoli · largo
[2]40 braccia, alto dall' acqua braccia 70,
lungo [3]braccia 600, cioè 400 sopra del
mare, e 200 [4]posa in terra, faciendo di se
spalle a se [5]medesimo.

The bridge of Pera at Constantinople,
40 braccia wide, 70 braccia high above the
water, 600 braccia long; that is 400 over
the sea and 200 on the land, thus making
its own abutments.

Constantinople.

Leic. 28a]　　　　　　　　**1110.**

Se si volterà il fiu[2]me alla rottura piv
[3] inãti, mai ritorne[4]rà nel corpo della [5]terra,
come fa l'Eu[6]frates fiume, e co[7]sì faccia, a
chi a Bo[8]lognia rĩcresce li [9]sua fiumi.

If the river will turn to the rift farther
on it will never return to its bed, as the
Euphrates does, and this may do at Bologna
the one who is disappointed for his rivers.

The Euphrates.

C. A. 94b; 276a]　　　　　　**1111.**

Mons Caucasus · Comedorum · e Paro-
panisi insieme cōgiṽti, [2] che tra Batriana e
India nascono Oxus fiume ·, che in essi mõti
nascie [3]e corre 500 miglia a tramõtana e
altrettãte a ponête e versa le sue acque
nel Mare Ircano [4]e cō seco s'accõpagnia ·
Osus ·, Daagodos ·, Arthamis ·, Xariaspis,
Dragamaim ·, Ocus ·, Margus, [5]fiumi grã-
dissimi; dall'opposita parte uerso mezzodì
· nasce · jl grã fiume · Indo · il quale di[6]rizza
le sue ōde per 600 miglia · inverso meridio,
e per questa linia s'accõpagnia cō seco i
fiumi Xaradrus ·, Bibasis ·, [7]Vadris ·, Vandabal ·, Bislaspus · per leuãte ·, Suastus · e Coe
per ponête ·, e incorporati tali fiumi colle
[8]sue acque si uolta · corrēdo miglia 800 per
ponête ·, e ribattēdosi ne' Mõti Arbeti uno
gomito, e' si volta [9]a mezzodì, per la quale
linia · infra 500 miglia truova il mare d'In-

Mounts Caucasus, Comedorum, and Paro-
pemisidae are joined together between Bactria
and India, and give birth to the river Oxus
which takes its rise in these mountains and
flows 500 miles towards the North and as
many towards the West, and discharges its
waters into the Caspian sea; and is accompanied by the Oxus, Dargados, Arthamis, Xari-
aspes, Dargamaim, Ocus and Margus, all very
large rivers. From the opposite side towards
the South rises the great river Indus which
sends its waters for 600 miles Southwards
and receives as tributaries in this course the
rivers Xaradrus, Hyphasis, Vadris, Vandabal
Bislaspus to the East, Suastes and Coe to
the West, uniting with these rivers, and with
their waters it flows 800 miles to the West;
then, turning back by the Arbiti mountains
makes an elbow and turns Southwards, where

Centrae Asia.

1109. 1. gostantinopoli. 2. 40 br . . br. 70. 3. br. 600 coe. 4. spalle asse.

1111. 1. mō caucassus comedorū. 2. nasscano [oduss] oxus . . nasscie. 3. e chōsecho sacōpagnia. 4. attramōtana. 5. dallo-
posita parte [nass] uer mezodi nasscie. 6. riza . . inver . . sachōpagnia. 7. biilasspus . . suasstus hecoe per . . incho-
porate. 8. chorrendo . . arbeti [assali] î gomito. 9. mezodi . . somergie. 10. nasscie. 11. mezodi. 12. ssciròcho . . he
13. sarabas diaravna (?) e so as esscilo. 14. mare | "indo" per molte boche.

1109. See Pl. CX No. 1. In 1453 by order of
Sultan Mohamed II. the Golden Horn was crossed
by a pontoon bridge laid on barrels (see Joh. Dukas'
History of the Byzantine Empire XXXVIII p. 279).
—The biographers of Michelangelo, Vasari as well
as Condivi, relate that at the time when Michelangelo suddenly left Rome, in 1506, he entertained
some intention of going to Constantinople, there to
serve the Sultan, who sought to engage him, by
means of certain Franciscan Monks, for the purpose
of constructing a bridge to connect Constantinople
with Pera. See VASARI, *Vite* (ed. Sansoni VII, 168):
*Michelangelo, veduto questa furia del papa, dubitando di
lui, ebbe, secondo che si dice, voglia di andarsene in
Gostantinopoli a servire il Turco, per mezzo di certi frati*

*di San Francesco, che desiderava averlo per fare un ponte
che passassi da Gonstantinopoli a Pera.* And CONDIVI,
*Vita di M. Buonaroti chap. 30: Michelangelo allora
vedendosi condotto a questo, temendo dell'ira del papa,
pensò d'andarsene in Levante; massimamente essendo
stato dal Turco ricercato con grandissime promesse per
mezzo di certi frati di San Francesco, per volersene servire
in fare un ponte da Costantinopoli a Pera ed in altri
affari.* Leonardo's plan for this bridge was made
in 1502. We may therefore conclude that at about
that time the Sultan Bajazet II. had either announced
a competition in this matter, or that through his
agents Leonardo had first been called upon to carry
out the scheme.

dia doue per sette · rami · in quello si som-mergie.

[10]Nell' aspetto del medesimo mōte nascie il magnio [11]Gāgie, il quale fiume corre per mezzodì miglia 500 [12]e per scirocco · mille · e · Sarabas · Diarnvna e Soas [13]e Scilo · Cōdranvnda · li faño cōpagnia; [14]versa in mare Indo per molte bocche.

after a course of about 100 miles it finds the Indian Sea, in which it pours itself by seven branches. On the side of the same mountains rises the great Ganges, which river flows Southwards for 500 miles and to the South-west a thousand . . . and Sarabas, Diarnuna, Soas and Scilo, Condranunda are its tributaries. It flows into the Indian sea by many mouths.

C. A. 384 *b*; 1189 *b*]

1112.

On the natives of hot countries.

Li omini nati in [2]paesi caldi amano [3]la notte, perchè li rīfre[4]sca, e àño in odio la [5]luce, perchè li ri-scal[6]da, e però sono del co[7]lore della notte cio[8]è neri | e ne' paesi [9]freddi ogni cosa è [10]per l'opposito.

Men born in hot countries love the night because it refreshes them and have a horror of light because it burns them; and therefore they are of the colour of night, that is black. And in cold countries it is just the contrary.

1112. 2. chaldi amaño. 3. perche le. 6. perosino. 9. cosa he.

1112. The sketch here inserted is in MS. H 3 55 [h].

XVIII.

Naval Warfare.—Mechanical Appliances.—Music.

Such theoretical questions, as have been laid before the reader in Sections XVI and XVII, though they were the chief subjects of Leonardo's studies of the sea, did not exclusively claim his attention. A few passages have been collected at the beginning of this section, which prove that he had turned his mind to the practical problems of navigation, and more especially of naval warfare. What we know for certain of his life gives us no data, it is true, as to when or where these matters came under his consideration; but the fact remains certain both from these notes in his manuscripts, and from the well known letter to Ludovico il Moro (No. 1340), in which he expressly states that he is as capable as any man, in this very department.

The numerous notes as to the laws and rationale of the flight of birds, are scattered through several note-books. An account of these is given in the Bibliography of the manuscripts at the end of this work. It seems probable that the idea which led him to these investigations was his desire to construct a flying or aerial machine for man At the same time it must be admitted that the notes on the two subjects are quite unconnected in the manuscripts, and that those on the flight of birds are by far the most numerous and extensive. The two most important passages that treat of the construction of a flying machine are those already published as Tav. XVI, No. 1 and Tav. XVIII in the "Saggio delle opere di Leonardo da Vinci" (Milan 1872). The passages—Nos. 1120—1125—here printed for the first time and hitherto unknown—refer to the same subject and, with the exception of one already published in the Saggio— No. 1126—they are, so far as I know, the only notes, among the numerous observations on the flight of birds, in which the phenomena are incidentally and expressly connected with the idea of a flying machine.

The notes on machines of war, the construction of fortifications, and similar matters which fall within the department of the Engineer, have not been included in this work, for the reasons given on page 26 of this Vol. An exception has been made in favour of the passages Nos. 1127 and 1128, because they have a more general interest, as bearing on *the important question: whence the Master derived his knowledge of these matters. Though it would be rash to assert that Leonardo was the first to introduce the science of mining into Italy, it may be confidently said that he is one of the earliest writers who can be proved to have known and understood it; while, on the other hand, it is almost beyond doubt that in the East at that time, the whole science of besieging towns and mining in particular, was far more advanced than in Europe. This gives a peculiar value to the expressions used in No.* 1127.

I have been unable to find in the manuscripts any passage whatever which throws any light on Leonardo's great reputation as a musician. Nothing therein illustrates VASARI'S well-known statement: Avvenne che morto Giovan Galeazzo duca di Milano, e creato Lodovico Sforza nel grado medesimo anno 1494, fu condotto a Milano con gran riputazione Lionardo al duca, il quale molto si dilettava del suono della lira, perchè sonasse; e Lionardo portò quello strumento ch'egli aveva di sua mano fabbricato d'argento gran parte, in forma d'un teschio di cavallo, cosa bizzarra e nuova, acciocchè l'armonia fosse con maggior tuba e più sonora di voce; laonde superò tutti i musici che quivi erano concorsi a sonare.

The only notes on musical matters are those given as Nos. 1129 *and* 1130, *which explain certain arrangements in instruments.*

Del moto del mobile,—²del cognoscere quāto ³il navilio si move per ora.

⁴Ánno li nostri antichi vsato diuersi in-⁵giegni per vedere che viaggio faccia v̄ navilio per ci⁶ascuna ora, infra li quali Vitruvio ne po⁷ne vno nella sua opera d'Architettura, il qua⁸le modo è fallace insieme cogli altri; e que⁹sto è vna rota da mulino tocca dall'onde ¹⁰marine nelle sue stremità, e mediante le ¹¹intere sue revolutioni si descriue vna linia ¹²retta che rappresenta la linia circūferē¹³tiale di tal rota ridotta in rettitudine; ¹⁴Ma questa tale inventione non è valida, ¹⁵se nō nelle superfitie piane e immobili de' ¹⁶laghi; Ma se l'acqua si move insieme col ¹⁷navilio con equal moto, allora tal rota re¹⁸sta inmobile, e se l'acqua è di moto più o mē ¹⁹velocie che 'l moto del nauilio, ancora tal ro²⁰ta non à moto equale a quel del navilio, in ²¹modo che tale inventione è di poca valitudine; ²²Ecco vn altro modo fatto colla speriētia d'uno ²³spatio noto da una isola a vn altra, e questo si ²⁴fa con un asse o lieua percossa dal uēto, che la percuote o più o ²⁵men velocie, e questo è in Battista Alberti;

On movements;—to know how much a ship advances in an hour.

The ancients used various devices to ascertain the distance gone by a ship each hour, among which Vitruvius [6] gives one in his work on Architecture which is just as fallacious as all the others; and this is a mill wheel which touches the waves of the sea at one end and in each complete revolution describes a straight line which represents the circumference of the wheel extended to a straightness. But this invention is of no worth excepting on the smooth and motionless surface of lakes. But if the water moves together with the ship at an equal rate, then the wheel remains motionless; and if the motion of the water is more or less rapid than that of the ship, then neither has the wheel the same motion as the ship so that this invention is of but little use. There is another method tried by experiment with a known distance between one island and another; and this is done by a board or under the pressure of wind which strikes on it with more or less swiftness. This is in Battista Alberti [25].

The ship's logs of Vitruvius, of Alberti and of Leonardo

1113. 2. cogniossciere. 4. nosstri. 6. asscuna . . infralli . . vetruvio. 7. darchitettura. 8. effallacie . . ecque. 9. tocha dallonde. 11. desscrive. 12. circhūferē. 13. diridotta. 14. Macquessta. 15. inmobile. 16. Massellacqua. 17. rota reſ. 18. essellacqua. 19. anchora. 20. noña . . acquel. 21. chettale . . pocha. 22. Ecci . . cholla. 23. ecquesto. 24. fa vasse lieva perchossa . . chella perchote eppiuō. 25. ecquesto . . balissta abrt̄i. 26. batissta. 27. albertiche effat. 28. lassperi. 31. issola.

1113. 6. See Vitruvius, *De Architectura lib. X.* C. 14 (p. 264 in the edition of Rose and Müller-Strübing). The German edition published at Bale in 1543 has, on fol. 596, an illustration of the contrivance, as described by Vitruvius.

25. Leon Battista Alberti, *De Architectura lib. V.*, c. 12 treats '*de le navi e parti loro*', but there is no reference to the machine, mentioned by Leonardo. Alberti says here: *Noi abbiamo trattato lungamente in altro luogo de' modi de le navi, ma in questo luogo ne abbiamo detto quel tanto che si bisogna.* To this the following note is added in the most recent Italian edition: *Questo libro è tuttora inedito e porta il titolo, secondo Gesnero di 'Liber navis'.*

²⁶Il modo di Battista ²⁷Alberti è fat²⁸to sopra la speri²⁹entia d'uno spa³⁰tio noto da vn³¹a isola a un altra; ³²Ma tale inventi³³one nō riesce, ³⁴se nō a vn navi-³⁵lio simile a quel ³⁶dove è fatto tale ³⁷speriētia, ma ³⁸bisognia che sia ³⁹col medesimo ⁴⁰carico, e me⁴¹desima vela, ⁴²e medesima situ⁴³atiō di vela, e ⁴⁴medesime grā⁴⁵dezze d'onde; ma ⁴⁶il mio modo ser⁴⁷ve a ogni navi⁴⁸lio, si di remi co⁴⁹me vela, e sia pi-⁵⁰ccolo o grāde, ⁵¹o lūgo e alto, ⁵²o basso, sēpre serve.

Battista Alberti's method which is made by experiment on a known distance between one island and another. But such an invention does not succeed excepting on a ship like the one on which the experiment was made, and it must be of the same burden and have the same sails, and the sails in the same places, and the size of the waves must be the same. But my method will serve for any ship, whether with oars or sails; and whether it be small or large, broad or long, or high or low, it always serves [52].

Leic. 22 *b*]　　　　　　　**1114.**

Methods of staying and moving in water

Come con otricoli l'esercito debbe pas-²sare i fiumi a noto; . . . Del modo del notare de' pesci; del modo ³del lor saltare fori delle acque, come far si uede a delfini, che par cosa marauigliosa for⁴mare salto sopra la cosa che non aspetta, anzi si fugge; Del notare delli animali di lū⁵ga figura, come anguille e simili; Del modo del notar contro alle corēti e grā ⁶cadute de' fiumi; Del modo come notino li pesci di retōda figura; Come li animali ⁷che non ànno lunga fessa non sā notare; Come tutti li altri animali naturalmente sā⁸no notare, auendo li piedi colle dita, saluo che l'omo; In che modo l'omo debbe inpara⁹re a notare; Del modo del riposarsi sopra delle acque; Come l'omo si debbe difen¹⁰dere dalle revertigini over retrosi delle acque che lo tirano in fondo; Come l'omo ti¹¹rato in fondo abbia a cercare del moto riflesso, che lo gitti fori della profondità; Co¹²me si debe passeggiare colle · braccia; come si debbe notare riverscio; Come, e come non ¹³si può star sotto l'acque ·, se non quando si può ritenere lo alitare; Come molti stie¹⁴no con istrumēto alquāto sotto l'acque; Come e perchè io non scrivo il mio modo di ¹⁵star sotto l'acqua, quāto io posso star sanza mangiare, e questo nō publico o diuolgo per le ma¹⁶le nature delli omini, li quali vserebbero li assasinamēti ne' fondi de' mari

How an army ought to cross rivers by swimming with air-bags . . . How fishes swim [2]; of the way in which they jump out of the water, as may be seen with dolphins; and it seems a wonderful thing to make a leap from a thing which does not resist but slips away. Of the swimming of animals of a long form, such as eels and the like. Of the mode of swimming against currents and in the rapid falls of rivers. Of the mode of swimming of fishes of a round form. How it is that animals which have not long hind quartres cannot swim. How it is that all other animals which have feet with toes, know by nature how to swim, excepting man. In what way man ought to learn to swim. Of the way in which man may rest on the water. How man may protect himself against whirlpools or eddies in the water, which drag him down. How a man dragged to the bottom must seek the reflux which will throw him up from the depths. How he ought to move his arms. How to swim on his back. How he can and how he cannot stay under water unless he can hold his breath [13]. How by means of a certain machine many people may stay some time under water. How and why I do not describe my method of remaining under water, or how long I can stay without eating; and I do not publish nor divulge these by reason of the evil nature of men who would use them as

32. Mattale. 33. riesscie. 35. acquel. 36. effatto. 37. esperiētia. 38. chessia. 39. chol. 40. charicho. 45. deze . . M"a". 47. a "o"gni. 48. cho. 49. essia. 50. c"j"colo ogrande stār. 51. do ollūgho. 52. obbasso.

1114. 1. otricolli lessercito . . pa. 2. pessci. 3. adalfini. 4. fuge. 5. essimili De. 6. pessci. 7. nonā. 8. cōlle chellomo riposarsi lomo sopra. 10. delle revertigini. 10. chelli tirano. 11. refresso . . che gitti. 12. passegare colle br . . Come e non. 13. si postar . . quanto si po. 14. isscrivo. 15. quāto iposso . . magare ecquesto. 16. vserebono. 17. son-

52. Leonardo does not reveal the method invented by him.

1114. 2. Compare No. 821.
L. 13—19 will also be found in Vol. I No. 1.

col ronpere [17] i navili in fondo, e sommer-
gierli insieme colli omini che ui son dentro,
e bēchè io insegni [18] delli altri, quelli nō
son di pericolo, perchè di sopra all'acqua
apparisce la bocca della canna, [19] onde
alitano, posta sopra li otri o sughero.

means of destruction at the bottom of the sea,
by sending ships to the bottom, and sinking
them together with the men in them. And
although I will impart others, there is no
danger in them; because the mouth of the
tube, by which you breathe, is above the
water supported on bags or corks[19].

Ash. II. 4 *b*]　　　　　　　　　　**1115.**

Se sarā in pugnia · naui · e · galee ·, essendo vincitori le naui per le loro alte
gaggie, [2] si de' tirare l'antena · per īsino
quasi alla sommità
dell'albero, [3] e abbi
nella stremità di detta
ātena, cioè quella ch'è
sporta sopra [4] il nemi-
co, appiccato v̄a gag-
gietta fasciata, e di
sotto e dītorno uno
[5] grosso materasso
pieno di b̄abagia, ac-

Supposing in a battle between ships and
galleys that the ships are victorious by reason
of the high of their tops, you must haul the yard

up almost to the top
of the mast, and at
the extremity of the
yard, that is the end
which is turned tow-
ards the enemy, have
a small cage fastened,
wrapped up below and
all round in a great
mattress full of cotton

On naval
warfare
(1115. 1116).

ciò nō sia offesa dalle b̄obardelle, [6] poi tira
col'argano ī basso l'opposita parte d'essa
antena, e la gaggia [7] opposita andrà tāto
· in alto ·, ch'ella di grā luga av̄azerà la
gaggia del [8] la nave, e potrassi facilmēte
cacciare li omini che dētro ui sono; [9] ma
bisognia che gli omini che sono nella galea
· vadino dall'opposita banda, [10] acciò · faccino · contrapeso al carico delli omini posti
dētro · alla gaggia [11] della antēna.

so that it may not be injured by the bombs;
then, with the capstan, haul down the opposite end of this yard and the top on the opposite side will go up so high, that it will be far
above the round-top of the ship, and you will
easily drive out the men that are in it. But
it is necessary that the men who are in the
galley should go to the opposite side of it so
as to afford a counterpoise to the weight of
the men placed inside the cage on the yard.

mergierli . . ebēce. 18. aparissce la bocha. 19. ossugero.

1115. 1. sara . . gagie. 2. si de [mettere] tirare . . somita. 3. abi . . ītena . . che [apichata] sporta. 4. apichato v̄a gagietta
fassciatta . . dītorno dino. 6. chol . . ella gagia. 7. oposita andera . . gagia de. 8. chaciare. 9. chessono . . ghalea . ·
daloposita. 10. chontrapeso . . charicho . . gagia. 11. antena.

Se vuoli fare vna · armata marittima, vsa di questi navili per sfondare le navi, [2] cioè fa navili · di 100 piè, e larghi piedi 8, ma fa che i remi sinistri abino i loro [3] motori nel lato destro del navilio, e così i destri nel sinistro come appare in M, acciochè lo lieve de' remi [4] sia piv lūgo ·, e detto navilio sia grosso piè uno e $\frac{1}{2}$ · cioè fatto

If you want to build an armada for the sea employ these ships to ram in the enemy's ships. That is, make ships 100 feet long and 8 feet wide, but arranged so that the left hand rowers may have their oars to the right side of the ship, and the right hand ones to the left side, as is shown at M, so that the leverage of the oars may be longer. And the

di travi fermi di [5] fuori e di dētro con asse con cōtrari liniamēti; e questo navilio avrà,

said ship may be one foot and a half thick, that is made with cross beams within and without,

sotto [6] l'acqua vn piede, appiccato vno spūtone ferrato di peso e grossezza d'un

with planks in contrary directions. And this ship must have attached to it, a foot below the

1116. 1. isfondare. 2. cheremi . . ilor. 3. nelato . . sinistro "come apare in M" aciochelo. 4. sieno piv lūge . . pie î e . . facto di trav ferm. 5. fori . . chon asse chō cōtrari . . navilio avc sotto. 6. lacq"a" vn piedi apuchato . . ferato_adi ācudi[7]ne· e questo per forza di remi potrà, dato il primo colpo, tornare īdirietro, [8]e cō furia ricacciarsi ināti e dare il colpo secōdo, e poi il terzo, e tāti che rōpa detto navilio.

water, an iron-shod spike of about the weight and size of an anvil; and this, by force of oars may, after it has given the first blow, be drawn back, and driven forward again with fury give a second blow, and then a third, and so many as to destroy the other ship.

B. 81 _b_]　　　　　　　　　1117.

Modo di saluarsi · in vna · tepesta e navfragio · marittimo.

Bisognia · avere v̄a vesta [2]di corame ch'abbi doppio i labri del petto per spatio d'vno · dito, e così sia doppio [3]dalla cītura īsino al ginocchio ·, e sia corame sicuro dallo · esalare ·; E quādo [4]bisognasse saltare ī mare ·, sgōfia · per li labri del petto le code del tuo vestito, [5]e salta in mare ·, e lasciati guidare all' onde ·; quādo nō vedi vicina riva, [6]ne abbi notitia · del mare ·, e ti ni sempre · ī bocca la canna dell' aria che va nel vestito, [7]e quādo per una volta o 2 ti bisognasse trare dell' aria comvne, e la schiuma t'inpedisce, [8]tira per bocca di quella del vestito.

A method of escaping in a tempest and shipwreck at sea.

Have a coat made of leather, which must be double across the breast, that is having a hem on each side of about a finger breadth.

The use of swimming belts.

Thus it will be double from the waist to the knee; and the leather must be quite air-tight. When you want to leap into the sea, blow out the skirt of your coat through the double hems of the breast; and jump into the sea, and allow yourself to be carried by the waves; when you see no shore near, give your attention to the sea you are in, and always keep in your mouth the air-tube which leads down into the coat; and if now and again you require to take a breath of fresh air, and the foam prevents you, you may draw a breath of the air within the coat.

S. K. M. III. 25 _b_]　　　　　　1118.

Se 'l mare si pesa sul suo fondo, [2]vn omo, che giacesse sopra esso [3]fondo e avesse 1000 braccia d'acqua [4]a dosso, n'avrebbe a scoppiare.

If the weight of the sea bears on its bottom, a man, lying on that bottom and having 1000 braccia of water on his back, would have enough to crush him.

On the gravity of water.

C. A. 7 _a_; 19 _a_]　　　　　　1119.

D'andar sotto acqua; [2]Modo di caminare [3]sopra l'acqua.

Of walking under water. Method of walking on water.

Diving apparatus and Skating (1119—1121).

peso . . grosseza. 7. ecquesto . . forza adi remi . . īdirieto. 8. richaciarsi.
1117. 2. dopio . .‚peto perispatio dono . . dopio. 3. aginochio essia sicuro dello. 4. biscognassi . . schōfia. 5. essalta imare ellassciati . . visina. 6. abi . . ettieni . . bocha la cana. 7. per ī . . bisognassi trare dellaria _partly indistinct;_ sciuma tīpedissi. 8. boca.
1118. 2. diaciessi. 3. avessi 1000 br dacu 4 asscopiare.　　**1119.** 2. chomin. 3. sop acq"a".

1117. Amoretti, _Memorie Storiche_, Tav. II. B. Fig. 5, gives the same figure, somewhat altered.
6. _La canna dell' aria._ Compare Vol. I. No. 1. Note.

1119. The two sketches belonging to this passage are given by Amoretti, _Memorie Storiche._ Tav. II, Fig. 3 and 4.

1120.

Siccome per lo fivme ghiacciato uno omo corre ²sanza mvtatione di piedi·, così vn carro fia ³possibile fare che corra per se.

Just as on a frozen river a man may run without moving his feet, so a car might be made that would slide by itself.

1121.

Definitione perchè vno ²che sdrucciola sopra il ghiaccio ³nō cade.

A definition as to why a man who slides on ice does not fall.

1122.

On Flying machines (1122—1126).

L'uomo ne' volatili à a stare libero dalla cintura insù ²per potersi bilicare, come fa in barca acciò che 'l cē³tro della grauità di lui e dello strumēto si possa ⁴bilicare e trasmutarsi, dove necessità il dimāda ⁵alla mutatione del centro della sua resistētia.

Man when flying must stand free from the waist upwards so as to be able to balance himself as he does in a boat so that the centre of gravity in himself and in the machine may counterbalance each other, and be shifted as necessity demands for the changes of its centre of resistance.

1123.

Ricordati siccome jl tuo vccello non debbe imitare ²altro che 'l pipistrello per cavsa che i pannicoli fāno ³armadura over collegatione alle armadure, cioè ma⁴estre delle ali;

Remember that your flying machine must imitate no other than the bat, because the web is what by its union gives the armour, or strength to the wings.

⁵E se tu imitassi l'alie delli vccelli pennvti, esse ⁶son di piv potēte nervatura, per essere esse ⁷traforate cioè che le lor penne sō disunite e passa⁸te dall'aria; Ma il pipistrello è aivtato dal panni⁹culo che lega il tutto, e non è traforato.

If you imitate the wings of feathered birds, you will find a much stronger structure, because they are pervious; that is, their feathers are separate and the air passes through them. But the bat is aided by the web that connects the whole and is not pervious.

1120. 1. sichome . . diacciato î omo core. z. chosi vn charo. 3. possiuile. 3. chora.

1121. 1. definition. 2. strusi . . diaccio.

1122. 1. volatili asstare. 2. barcha. 4. bilichare e strassmutarsi. 5. ressistētia.

1123. 1. sichome. 2. pipisstrello . . chavsa che panichuli. 3. chollegacione . . coe. 4. esstre . . alie. 5. essettu. 6. enervatura
      7. coe chelle . . eppassa. 9. chulo chellega.

1120. The drawings of carts by the side of this text have no direct connection with the problem as stated in words.—Compare No. 1448, l. 17.

1121. An indistinct sketch accompanies the passage, in the original.

Mz. 9 *b* (13)]　　　　　　　　　1124.

PER FUGIRE IL PERICOLO DELLA RUINA.

²Può accadere la ruina di tali strumēti per · 2 · modi, de' quali ³il primo · è del ronpersi lo strumēto, secondario fia quā⁴do lo strumento si uoltasse per taglio o vicino a esso taglio, ⁵perchè senpre debbe discendere per grande obbliquità e quasi ⁶per la linia dell'equalità; In quanto al primo, ⁷del ronpersi lo strumēto, si riparerà col farlo di somma for⁸tezza, per qualunche linia esso si potesse voltare, e assai distante l'un centro dall'altro, cioè nel⁹lo strumēto di 30 braccia di lunghezza essi centri sieno distanti 4 braccia l'un dall'altro.

TO ESCAPE THE PERIL OF DESTRUCTION.

Destruction to such a machine may occur in two ways; of which the first is the breaking of the machine. The second would be when the machine should turn on its edge or nearly on its edge, because it ought always to descend in a highly oblique direction, and almost exactly balanced on its centre. As regards the first—the breaking of the machine—,that may be prevented by making it as strong as possible; and in whichever direction it may tend to turn over, one centre must be very far from the other; that is, in a machine 30 braccia long the centres must be 4 braccia one from the other.

Mz. 13 *a*]　　　　　　　　　1125.

Baghe dove l'omo in 6 braccia ²d'altezza cadendo nō si faccia male, ³cadendo così in acqua come ⁴in terra; e queste baghe le⁵gate a vso di paternostri s'avvol⁶gino altrui addosso.

Bags by which a man falling from a height of 6 braccia may avoid hurting himself, by a fall whether into water or on the ground; and these bags, strung together like a rosary, are to be fixed on one's back.

C. A. 372 *b*; 1158 *b*]　　　　　　1126.

Tāta forza si fa colla cosa īcōtro all'aria, quāto l'aria alla cosa; ²Vedi l'alie percosse cōtro all'aria fanno sostenere la pesante aquila sulla suprema sottile aria ³vicina all'elemēto del fuoco; Ancora vedi la mossa aria sopr'al mare ripercossa ⁴nelle gōfiate vele far correr la carica e pesāte nave; sichè per queste demostra⁵tive e assegnate ragioni potrai conosciere l'uomo colle sua cōgiegniate e grādi ale, ⁶facciēdo forza cōtro alla resistēte aria, vincēdo poterla soggiogare a le⁷varsi sopra di lei.

An object offers as much resistance to the air as the air does to the object. You may see that the beating of its wings against the air supports a heavy eagle in the highest and rarest atmosphere, close to the sphere of elemental fire. Again you may see the air in motion over the sea, fill the swelling sails and drive heavily laden ships. From these instances, and the reasons given, a man with wings large enough and duly connected might learn to overcome the resistance of the air, and by conquering it, succeed in subjugating it and rising above it.

1124. 1. pericholo. 2. achadere . . tale. 3. sechondario. 4. losstrumento si uoltassi. 4. vicico. 5. disscendere. 7. losstrumēto. 8. teza. 8. potessi . . disstante . . coe. 9. br di lungeza . . 4 br lū.

1125. 1. 6 br. 2. dalteza . . facca. 3. chedendo. 4. ecqueste. 5. paternosstri savol. 6. glino . . adosso.

1126. 1. [vo] tāta . . cholla chosa ī chōtro . . chosa. 2. perchosse chōtro . . fassosstenere . . sulla "suplema" sottile. 3. fuocho Anchora . . riperchossa. 4. ghōfiate . . chorrer la charicha . . qsste [asse] demosstra. 5. chonossciere . . cholle . . chōgiegniate. 6. chōtro . . resisstēte aria [potersi e] e vincēdo poterla sogiogare alle.

1124. Compare No. 1428.

1126. A parachute is here sketched, with an explanatory remark. It is reproduced on Tav. XVI in the *Saggio,* and in: *Leonardo da Vinci*

als Ingenieur etc., Ein Beitrag zur Geschichte der Technik und der induktiven Wissenschaften, von Dr. Hermann Grothe, Berlin 1874, p. 50.

Ash. II. 4*a*]　　　　　　　　**1127.**

Of mining.
Se tu · vuoi sapere · doue · una caua faccia suo · corso, metti vno tāburo ²in tutti quelli lochi, dove tu sospetti si facci la cava ·, e sopra detto tābu³ro · metti vno pajo di dadi ·, e quādo sarai apresso · al loco dove si caua, i dadi risal⁴teranno alquāto sopra del tāburo · per lo colpo che si da sotto terra nel cavare.

If you want to know where a mine runs, place a drum over all the places where you suspect that it is being made, and upon this drum put a couple of dice, and when you are over the spot where they are mining, the dice will jump a little on the drum at every blow which is given underground in the mining.

⁵Sono alcuni che per auere comodità d'ū fiume o di padule ⁶alle lor terre, ànno fatto apresso di quel loco, doue sospettano si faccia ⁷la cava, vno grā riserbo d'aqua, e cauato · in cōtra il nemi⁸co e, quel trouato, ànno sboccato il bottino e annegato nella ⁹cava grā popolo.

There are persons who, having the convenience of a river or a lake in their lands, have made, close to the place where they suspect that a mine is being made, a great reservoir of water, and have countermined the enemy, and having found them, have turned the water upon them and destroyed a great number in the mine.

Tr. 48]　　　　　　　　**1128.**

Fuoco greco.

Greek fire.

Of Greek fire.
²Tolli · carbon di salcio, e sale nitro, e acquavite, e sulfore, ³pegola con īciēso, e cāfora, e lana etiopica e fa bollire ⁴ogni cosa īsieme; questo fuoco · è di tanto desi-

Take charcoal of willow, and saltpetre, and sulphuric acid, and sulphur, and pitch, with frankincense and camphor, and Ethiopian wool, and boil them all together. This

---

1127. 1. settu vuoli . . î cha faccia . . chorso.　2. tussosspetti . . essopra.　3. vno pa di.　4. terano . . chessi da . . tera.　5. chomodita.　6. tere . . facci.　7. riserbo daq"a" e chauato.　8. ano isboccato . . anegatti.

1128. 1. fuocho grecho.　2. charbon di salco essale . . essulfore.　3. chāfera elana etiopicha effa.　4. onichosa . . focho . . dessi-derio di bru⁵ciare, che seguita il legniame sin sotto l'acque; ⁶e se aggivgnierai in essa conpositione vernice liquida, ⁷e olio petrolio, e tremētina, e acieto forte, mischia ⁸ogni cosa īsieme, e secca al sole o nel forno quādo n'è trat⁹to'l pane, e poi volta intorno alla stoppa di canapa o altra, ¹⁰riduciēdola in forma rotonda, e ficcati da ogni pa¹¹rte i chiodi acutissimi, solamēte lascia ī detta palla vn ¹²buco come razzo; poi la copri di colofonio e di solfo;

¹³Ancora questo foco appiccato in sommità d'una lunga asta, ¹⁴la quale abbi uno braccio di pūta di ferro acciò nō sia bruciato da det¹⁵to foco, è bono per evitare e proibire īfra le naui ostili, per ¹⁶non essere sopra-fatti da īpito;

¹⁷Ācora gittati vasi di uetro pieni di pegola sopra ¹⁸li aversi navili, —ītendenti li omini di quelli alla battaglia, —¹⁹e poi gittato dirieto simili palle accese ànno potēza a brucia²⁰re ogni navilio.

fire is so ready to burn that it clings to the timbers even under water. And add to this composition liquid varnish, and bituminous oil, and turpentine and strong vinegar, and mix all together and dry it in the sun, or in an oven when the bread is taken out; and then stick it round hempen or other tow, moulding it into a round form, and studding it all over with very sharp nails. You must leave in this ball an opening to serve as a fusee, and cover it with rosin and sulphur.

Again, this fire, stuck at the top of a long plank which has one braccio length of the end pointed with iron that it may not be burnt by the said fire, is good for avoiding and keeping off the ships, so as not to be over-whelmed by their onset.

Again throw vessels of glass full of pitch on to the enemy's ships when the men in them are intent on the battle; and then by throwing similar burning balls upon them you have it in your power to burn all their ships.

Br. M. 175a]　　　　　　　　1129.

Tanburo di tacche, fregate ²da rote di molle;

A drum with cogs working by wheels with springs [2].　Of Music (1129. 1130).

derio. 5. sare che seghuita ilegniame . . lacq"e". 6. esse agivg . . chonpositione. 7. emiscia. 8. oni . . essechai . . ne forno quādo ne tra. 9. e po volta . . ala stopa. 10. retonda efficchati da ogni. 11. achutissimi lassa īdetta balla. 12. buso chomaraza poi . . colofonia. 13. quessto . . appichato in somita . . asste. 14. abi î br di . . fero acio . . brusato da de 15. eviare . . ne nave. 17. gittate. 18. ītenti . . queli ala. 19. gitato . . simile . . acese ano potēza a brusa. 20. ōni. 1129. 2. molle. 5. cholla. 8. coe. 9. sicome. 10. fa boci. 13. quesste. 16. uoce. 17. tassti . . esserrano bichi di grā disstātie

1128. Venturi has given another short text about the Greek fire in a French translation (Essai § XIV). He adds that the original text is to be found in MS. B. 30 (?). Libri speaks of it in a note as follows (*Histoire des sciences mathématiques en Italie Vol. II* p. 129): *La composition du feu grégeois est une des choses qui ont été les plus cherchées et qui sont encore les plus douteuses. On dit qu'il fut inventé au septième siècle de l'ère chrétienne par l'architecte Callinique (Constantini Porphyrogenetae opera, Lugd. Batav. 1617,—in-8 vo; p. 172, de admin. imper. exp. 48), et il se trouve souvent mentionné par les Historiens Byzantins. Tantôt on le lançait avec des machines, comme on lancerait une bouche, tantôt on le soufflait avec de longs tubes, comme on soufflerait un gaz ou un liquide enflammé (Annae Comnenae Alexias, p. 335, lib. XI.—Aeliani et Leonis, imperatoris tactica, Lugd.-Bat. 1613, in-4. part. 2 ª, p. 322, Leonis tact. cap. 19.—Joinville, histoire du Saint Louis collect. Petitot tom. II, p. 235). Les écrivains contemporains disent que l'eau ne pouvait pas éteindre ce feu, mais qu'avec du vinaigre et du sable on y parvenait.*

Suivant quelques historiens le feu grégeois était composé de soufre et de résine. Marcus Graecus (Liber ignium, Paris, 1804, in-4º) donne plusieurs manières de le faire qui ne sont pas très intelligibles, mais parmi lesquelles on trouve la composition de la poudre à canon. Léonard de Vinci (MSS. de Léonard de Vinci, vol. B. f. 30) dit qu'on le faisait avec du charbon de saule, du salpêtre, de l'eau de vie, de la résine, du soufre, de la poix et du camphre. Mais il est probable que nous ne savons pas qu'elle était sa composition, surtout à cause du secret qu'en faisaient les Grecs. En effet, l'empereur Constantin Porphyrogénète recommende à son fils de ne jamais en donner aux Barbares, et de leur répondre, s'ils en demandaient, qu'il avait été apporté du ciel par un ange et que le secret en avait été confié aux Chrétiens (Constantini Porphyrogennetae opera, p. 26—27, de admin. imper., cap. 12).

1129. This chapter consists of explanations of the sketches shown on Pl. CXXI. Lines 1 and 2 of the text are to be seen at the top at the left hand side of the first sketch of a drum. Lines 3—5 refer to the

3 Tanburo quadro, del quale 4 si tira e allenta la sua car5ta colla lieua *a b*;

6 Tanburo a cōsonāza;

7 Vna tabella a cōsonā8za, cioè 3 tabelle insieme;

9 Siccome vn medesimo 10 tanburo fa voci 11 graui e acute, 12 secondo le carte più o mē 13 tirate, così queste carte, 14 variamente tirate sopra 15 vn medesimo corpo di tā-16 buro, farà uarie uoci;

17 Tasti stretti e serrano; bicchi di grā distātie infra loro, 18 e sono al proposito della tronba prossima di sopra;

19 *a* entri in loco dell'ordinarie posite 20 che ànno i partici ne' lor busi de' zufoli.

A square drum of which the parchment may be drawn tight or slackened by the lever *a b* [5].

A drum for harmony [6].

[7] A clapper for harmony; that is, three clappers together.

[9] Just as one and the same drum makes a deep or acute sound according as the parch-ments are more or less tightened, so these parchments variously tightened on one and the same drum will make various sounds [16].

Keys narrow and close together; (bicchi) far apart; these will be right for the trumpet shown above.

a must enter in the place of the ordinary keys which have the . . . . . in the openings of a flute.

Br. M. 136 *a*]   **1130.**

Tanpani sona2ti come il mo3nacordo 4 o voi dolze5mele;

6 Qui si fa una rota di canne a vso 7 di tabelle con vn circulo mvsicale det8to canone, che si canta a quattro e 9 ciascū can-tore canta tutta la rota, e però 10 fo io qui vna rota cō 4 denti che ogni 11 dente per se fa l'ofitio d'un cantore.

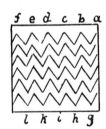

Tymbals to be played like the monochord, or the soft flute.

[6] Here there is to be a cylinder of cane after the manner of clappers with a mu-sical round called a Canon, which is sung in four parts; each singer singing the whole round. Therefore I here make a wheel with 4 teeth so that each tooth takes by itself the part of a singer.

B. 4 *a*]   **1131.**

Pañi biāchi e cielesti, 2 tessuti a scacchi 3 per fare uno apparecchio;

4 Pañi tirati 5 in *a · b · c · d · e · f · g · h · i · k ·*, 6 da fa7re uno ciclo a uno ap8parecchio.

White and sky-blue cloths, woven in checks to make a decoration.

Cloths with the threads drawn at *a b c d e f g h i k*, to go round the decoration.

infrallo. 19. illoco . . posste.   1130. 6. channe . . circul. 7. chon. 8. chessi . . acquattro he.
1131. 2. schachi. 3. î aparechio. 6. daffa. 7. re î cielo a î a. 8. parechio.

sketch immediately below this. Line 6 is written as the side of the seventh sketch, and lines 7 and 8 at the side of the eighth. Lines 9—16 are at the bottom in the middle. The remainder of the text is at the side of the drawing at the bottom.

1130. In the original there are some more sketches, to which the text, from line 6, refers. They are studies for a contrivance exactly like the cylinder in our musical boxes.

XIX.

Philosophical Maxims. Morals. Polemics and Speculations.

Vasari indulges in severe strictures on Leonardo's religious views. He speaks, among other things, of his "capricci nel filosofar delle cose naturali" *and says on this point:* "Per il che fece nell'animo un concetto si eretico che e' non si accostava a qualsi voglia religione, stimando per avventura assai più lo esser filosofo che cristiano" *(see the first edition of* 'Le Vite'*). But this accusation on the part of a writer in the days of the Inquisition is not a very serious one—and the less so, since, throughout the manuscripts, we find nothing to support it.*

Under the heading of "Philosophical Maxims" I have collected all the passages which can give us a clear comprehension of Leonardo's ideas of the world at large. It is scarcely necessary to observe that there is absolutely nothing in them to lead to the inference that he was an atheist. His views of nature and its laws are no doubt very unlike those of his contemporaries, and have a much closer affinity to those which find general acceptance at the present day. On the other hand, it is obvious from Leonardo's will (see No. 1566) that, in the year before his death, he had professed to adhere to the fundamental doctrines of the Roman Catholic faith, and this evidently from his own personal desire and impulse.

The incredible and demonstrably fictitious legend of Leonardo's death in the arms of Francis the First, is given, with others, by Vasari and further embellished by this odious comment: "Mostrava tuttavia quanto avea offeso Dio e gli uomini del mondo, non avendo operato nell'arte come si conveniva." *This last accusation, it may be remarked, is above all evidence of the superficial character of the information which Vasari was in a position to give about Leonardo. It seems to imply that Leonardo was disdainful of diligent labour. With regard to the second, referring to Leonardo's morality and dealings with his fellow men, Vasari himself nullifies it by asserting the very contrary in several passages. A further refutation may be found in the following sentence from the letter in which Melzi, the young Milanese nobleman, announces the Master's death to Leonardo's brothers:* Credo siate certificati della morte di Maestro Lionardo fratello vostro, e mio quanto optimo padre, per la cui morte sarebbe impossibile che io potesse esprimere il dolore che io ho preso; e in mentre che queste mia membra si sosterranno insieme, io possederò una perpetua infelicità, e meritamente perchè sviscerato et ardentissimo amore mi portava giornalmente. È dolto ad ognuno la perdita di tal uomo, quale non è più in podestà della natura, ecc.

It is true that, in April 1476, we find the names of Leonardo and Verrocchio entered in the "Libro degli Uffiziali di notte e de' Monasteri" *as breaking the laws; but we immediately after find the note* "Absoluti cum condizione ut retamburentur" (Tamburini *was the name given to the warrant cases of the night police). The acquittal therefore did not exclude the possibility of a repetition of the charge. It was in fact repeated, two months later, and on this occasion the Master and his pupil were again fully acquitted. Verrocchio was at this time forty and Leonardo four-and-twenty. The documents referring to this affair are in the State Archives of Florence; they have been withheld from publication, but it seemed to me desirable to give the reader this brief account of the leading facts of the story, as the vague hints of it, which have recently been made public, may have given to the incident an aspect which it had not in reality, and which it does not deserve.*

The passages here classed under the head "Morals" *reveal Leonardo to us as a man whose life and conduct were unfailingly governed by lofty principles and aims. He could scarcely have recorded his stern reprobation and unmeasured contempt for men who do nothing useful and strive only for riches, if his own life and ambitions had been such as they have so often been misrepresented.*

At a period like that, when superstition still exercised unlimited dominion over the minds not merely of the illiterate crowd, but of the cultivated and learned classes, it was very natural that Leonardo's views as to Alchemy, Ghosts, Magicians, and the like should be met with stern reprobation whenever and wherever he may have expressed them; this accounts for the argumentative tone of all his utterances on such subjects which I have collected in Subdivision III of this section. To these I have added some passages which throw light on Leonardo's personal views on the Universe. They are, without exception, characterised by a broad spirit of naturalism of which the principles are more strictly applied in his essays on Astronomy, and still more on Physical Geography.

To avoid repetition, only such notes on Philosophy, Morals and Polemics, have been included in this section as occur as independent texts in the original MSS. Several moral reflections have already been given in Vol. I, in section "Allegorical representations, Mottoes and Emblems". *Others will be found in the following section. Nos. 9 to 12, Vol. I, are also passages of an argumentative character. It did not seem requisite to repeat here these and similar passages, since their direct connection with the context is far closer in places where they have appeared already, than it would be here.*

I.

PHILOSOPHICAL MAXIMS.

S. K. M. III. 64 b]

1132.

Io t'ubidisco, Signore, prima per l'a-²more che ragionevolmente portare ³ti debo, secōdariamente chè tu sai ⁴abbreviare o prolungare le uite ⁵ali omini.

I obey Thee Lord, first for the love I ought, in all reason to bear Thee; secondly for that Thou canst shorten or prolong the lives of men.

Prayers to God (1132. 1133).

W. An. IV. 172 a]

1133.

¶Oratio.

²Tu o Iddio ci vendi ³tutti li beni per prez⁴zo di fatica.¶

A prayer.

Thou, O God, dost sell us all good things at the price of labour.

A. 24 a]

1134.

O mirabile givstitia di te, primo motore, · tu · non ài · voluto · mācare · a nessuna ²potētia l'ordine e qualità de' sua · neciessari effetti.

O admirable impartiality of Thine, Thou first Mover; Thou hast not permitted that any force should fail of the order or quality of its necessary results.

The powers of Nature (1134—1139).

S. K. M. III. 49 a]

1135.

La neciessità · è · maestra ²e tutrice · della · natura;
³La neciessità è tema e in⁴ventrice · della natura ⁵e freno e regola eterna.

Necessity is the mistress and guide of nature.
Necessity is the theme and the inventress, the eternal curb and law of nature.

1132. 3. sechondaria. 4. abrieviere.　1133. 2. "tu" | o idio [che] ci vende. 3. per pre. 4. faticha.
1134. 1. māchare a nessuna [creata chosa]. 2. "equalita" de sua.
1135. 1. he maesstra. 2. ettutrice. 3. ettema. 5. effrno.

Tr. 75]   **1136.**

Molte volte una medesima cosa · è tirata da 2 violētie, ²cioè · neciessità · e potentia ·; l'acqua piove, la terra l'assorbisce, ³per neciessità d'omore ·, e 'l sole la sveglie nō per neciessità, ma per potētia.

In many cases one and the same thing is attracted by two strong forces, namely Necessity and Potency. Water falls in rain; the earth absorbs it from the necessity for moisture; and the sun evaporates it, not from necessity, but by its power.

S. K. M. II.² 43a]   **1137.**

La gravità, la forza · · e'l moto · accidentale · insieme col²la percussione · son · le quattro · accidentali · potentie, ³colle · quali · tutte · l'euidenti · opere de' mortali ⁴ànno · loro · essere · e loro morte.

Weight, force and casual impulse, together with resistance, are the four external powers in which all the visible actions of mortals have their being and their end.

Tr. 70]   **1138.**

¶Il corpo nostro è sottoposto al cielo, e lo cielo è sottoposto allo spirito. ¶

Our body is dependant on heaven and heaven on the Spirit.

H.3 93a]   **1139.**

Il moto è causa d'ogni vita.

The motive power is the cause of all life.

W. XXIX]   **1140.**

E tu uomo, che consideri in questa
Psychology ²mia fatica l'opere mirabili della ³natura,
(1140—1147). se giudicherai essere cosa ⁴nefanda il distruggerla, or pēsa ⁵essere cosa nefandissima il torre la ⁶vita all' omo, del quale, se questa ⁷sua cōpositione ti pare di marauiglio⁸so artifitio, pensa questa essere ⁹nulla rispetto all' anima che in ¹⁰tale architettura abita, e vera¹¹mente, quale · essa si sia, ella è ¹²cosa diuina, sicchè lascia ¹³la abitare nella sua opera a suo be¹⁴neplacito, e nō volere che la tua ¹⁵ira o malignità distrugga ¹⁶una tāta vita, chè ve¹⁷ramēte, chi non la ¹⁸stima, non la ¹⁹merita.

And you, O Man, who will discern in this work of mine the wonderful works of Nature, if you think it would be a criminal thing to destroy it, reflect how much more criminal it is to take the life of a man; and if this, his external form, appears to thee marvellously constructed, remember that it is nothing as compared with the soul that dwells in that structure; for that indeed, be it what it may, is a thing divine. Leave it then to dwell in His work at His good will and pleasure, and let not your rage or malice destroy a life—for indeed, he who does not value it, does not himself deserve it[19].

1136. 1. volte va medesima chosa ettirata. 2. losorbisscie. 3. sole lassuele.
1137. 1. chol. 3. cholli . . tucte. 4. elloro.
1138. 1. essottoposto. 2. ello . . essottoposto.
1139. R. chausa.
1140. 1, quessta. 3. gudicherai. 4. desstrugerla. 7. sua cō [sa] positione. 12. diuina [sig] che [si] lasscia. · 13. assuo. 14. chella. 15. distrugha. 17. chi nolla. *The last seven lines are very indistinct.* 20. si pa"r"te dal. 21. corpo e ben. 22. reto chol su. 23. o pianto e ch. 24. ore nō sia. 25. anza [g] ca. 26. one.

1140. This text is on the back of the drawings reproduced on Pl. CVII. Compare No. 798, 35 note on p. 111. Compare also No. 837 and 838.
19. In MS. I¹ 15a is the note: *chi nō stima la vita, non la merita.*

Tr. 78]   1141.

L'anima mai si può corrōpere · nella corruttiō del corpo, ma fa nel corpo ²a similitudine del uēto che cavsa il suono del organo, ³chè guastādosi vna canna, nō resultava per quella del uēto ⁴buono effetto.

The soul can never be corrupted with the corruption of the body, but is in the body as it were the air which causes the sound of the organ, where when a pipe bursts, the wind would cease to have any good effect.

C. A. 58 a; 180 a]   1142.

Ogni parte à inclinatiō ²di ricōgiugnersi al suo ³tutto per fugire dalla ⁴sua inperfettione;
⁵L'anima desidera stare ⁶col suo corpo, perchè sanza ⁷li strumēti organici di tal ⁸corpo nulla può operare ⁹nè sētire.

The part always has a tendency to reunite with its whole in order to escape from its imperfection.
The spirit desires to remain with its body, because, without the organic instruments of that body, it can neither act, nor feel anything.

C. A. 75 a; 219 a]   1143.

Chi vuole vedere come l'anima abita nel suo ²corpo, guardi come esso corpo vsa la ³sua cotidiana abitatione, cioè se quella ⁴è sanza ordine e confusa, disordina⁵to e cōfuso fia il corpo tenvto dalla sua anima.

If any one wishes to see how the soul dwells in its body, let him observe how this body uses its daily habitation; that is to say, if this is devoid of order and confused, the body will be kept in disorder and confusion by its soul.

Br. M. 278 b]   1144.

Perchè vede piv certa la cosa l'ochio ne' sogni ²che colla imaginatione, stando desto?

Why does the eye see a thing more clearly in dreams than with the imagination being awake?

Tr. 65]   1145.

I sensi sono terrestri, la ragione sta ²fuor di quelli, quādo cōtenpla.

The senses are of the earth; Reason, stands apart in contemplation.

Tr. 70]   1146.

Ogni attione bisognia che s'esercita ²per moto;
³¶Cogniosciere e volere sō 2 operationi ⁴vmane;¶
⁵Discernere, givdicare, cōsigliare ⁶sono atti vmani.

Every action needs to be prompted by a motive.
To know and to will are two operations of the human mind.
Discerning, judging, deliberating are acts of the human mind.

1141. 1. chorrōpere . . curuttiō . . maffa. 2. assimilitudine . . chavsa del sono. 3. guastādosi . . chana.
1142. 3. tutto [fa] per. 4. inperfectione. 6. chol. 7. orghanici.
1143. 1. vole . . chome. 2. chorpo . . chorr.e esso chorpo. 3. chotidiana . . secquella. 4. chonfusa. 5. chōfuso . . chorpo.
1144. 2. dessto.
1145. 1. teresti. 2. for di queli . . chōtempla.
1146. 1. chessesercita. 3. cogniossciere . . operatione. 5. dissciernere . . chōsigliare.

1141. Compare No. 845.
1145. Compare No. 842.

Tr. 45]   **1147.**

Ogni nostra cognitione prīcipia da sentimēti.

All our knowledge has its origin in
our preceptions.

Tr. 51]   **1148.**

Sciētia—notitia delle cose che sono pos-
sibili, presēti e preterite; ²presciētia—notitia
delle cose che possī uenire, ³però lento.

Science, its principles and rules (1148—1161).

Science is the observation of things possible, whether present or past; prescience is
the knowledge of things which may come
to pass, though but slowly.

C. A. 85 a; 247 a]   **1149.**

La speriēza, ²interprete infra ³l'artifi-
tiosa natu⁴ra e la umana spe tie, ne insegnia
ciò ⁶che essa natura infra ⁷mortali adopera, ⁸da neciessità co⁹stretta non altri-
¹⁰mēti operarsi po¹¹ssa · che la ragiō, suo
timone, ¹²operare le asse¹³gni.

Experience, the interpreter between formative nature and the human race, teaches how
that nature acts among mortals; and being
constrained by necessity cannot act otherwise
than as reason, which is its helm, requires
her to act.

S. K. M. III. 80 b]   **1150.**

La sapiētia è figliola della ²speriētia.

Wisdom is the daughter of experience.

I.¹ 18 a]   **1151.**

La natura è piena d'infinite ragioni ²che
nō furō mai in isperiētia.

Nature is full of infinite causes that have
never occured in experience.

M. 58 b]   **1152.**

¶La verità fu sola fi²gliola del tenpo.¶

Truth was the only daughter of Time.

C. A. 151 a; 449 a]   **1153.**

La speriēza nō falla mai, ma sol fallano
i vostri giuditi, promettendosi di quella
²efetti · tali che ne' uostri esperimēti
causati nō sono;
³La speriēza nō falla·, ma sol fallano i
vostri giuditi, promettēdosi di lei cose, che
nō ⁴sono in sua potestà; ⁵a torto si lamen-
tano li omini della speriēza, cō somme
rampogne quella ⁶accusano esser fallace,

Experience never errs; it is only your
judgments that err by promising themselves
effects such as are not caused by your
experiments.
Experience does not err; only your
judgments err by expecting from her what
is not in her power. Men wrongly com-
plain of Experience; with great abuse they
accuse her of leading them astray but they set

1147. 1. prēcipia.
1148. 1. notiti delle chessono possibile presente. 2. cose che pesi uine che posī uenire. 3. penvlente.
1149. 1. lassperiēza. 4. ella. 5. ninsegna. 8. cō. 11. chella ragiō "suotimone". 12. hoperare. 12. asegni.
1150. 1 dela. 2. speriētia la quale speri. 3. ēza *here the text breaks off.*
1151. 2. inisperiētia.
1152. 1. verita sola fu fi. 2. glola.
1153. 1. vosstri guditi. 2. [tale] effetto | "tale" che ine uosstri . . chausati. 3. essperiēza . . massol . . vosstrigiuditi [i quali sa]
      prometa "desi". 5. attorto si lamenta . . della ["innocēte" issperieza la quale con some ranpogne. 7. Ma lasciāno.

[7]ma lasciano stare essa speriētia, [8]voltati dalle lamentationi contro alla nostra ignoranza, la quale ui [9]fa trascorrere con uostri vani e stolti desideri a inprometterui di quella cose che nō sono [10]in sua potētia, [11]dicendo quella esser fallace; [12]a torto si lamētan li omini della innocente sperientia ·, quella spesso accusando [13]di fallacia e di bugiarde [14]dimostrationi.

Experience aside, turning from it with complaints as to our ignorance causing us to be carried away by vain and foolish desires to promise ourselves, in her name, things that are not in her power; saying that she is fallacious. Men are unjust in complaining of innocent Experience, constantly accusing her of error and of false evidence.

Mz. 1 a (3)

1154.

¶ La scientia strumentale over machinale [2]è nobilissima e sopra tutte l'altre vtilissima, [3]cōciosiachè mediante quella tutti li corpi ani[4]mati, che ànno moto, fanno tutte loro operationi, i quali moti [5]nascono dal centro della lor grauità che è posto [6]in mezzo a parte di pesi disequali, e à questo [7]carestia e dovitia di muscoli, ed etiā lie-[8]va e contralieua. ¶

Instrumental or mechanical science is of all the noblest and the most useful, seeing that by means of this all animated bodies that have movement perform all their actions; and these movements are based on the centre of gravity which is placed in the middle deviding unequal weights, and it has dearth and wealth of muscles and also lever and counter-lever.

E. 8 b]

1155.

DELLA MECCANICA.

OF MECHANICS.

[2]La meccanica è il paradiso delle sciētie matema[3]tiche, perchè cō quella si viene al frutto matematico.

Mechanics are the Paradise of mathematical science, because here we come to the fruits of mathematics.

Br. M. 191 a]

1156.

A ciascuno strumēto si richiede [2]esser fatto colla speriēza.

Every instrument requires to be made by experience.

W. An. III. 241 a]

1157.

Chi biasima la soma certezza della [2]matematica, si pasce di confusione [3]e mai porrà silentio [4]alle contraditioni delle soffi-[5]stiche sciētie, colle quali [6]s'inpara vno eterno gridore.

The man who blames the supreme certainty of mathematics feeds on confusion, and can never silence the contradictions of sophistical sciences which lead to an eternal quackery.

G. 95 b]

1158.

Nessuna certezza delle sciētie è, do[2]ve nō si può applicare [3]vna delle sciētie matema[4]tiche e che non sono v[5]nite con esse matematiche.

There is no certainty in sciences where one of the mathematical sciences cannot be applied, or which are not in relation with these mathematics.

8. evoltati . . lamentatione . . ingnoranza. 9. transcorrere co uostre "vani e" in stolti . . "di quella" chose. 10. in "sua" potētia. 12. attorto . . della "inocente" essperientia . . achusando. 13. bugarde. 14. dimōstratione. Ma *here the text breaks off*.

1154. 1. Lasscientia. 2. essopra. 3. conco sia che. 4. mati "che annomoto" fanno . . ecquali. 5. nascano . . possto. 6. mezo apparte . . acquesto. 7. charesstia e douitia di mvsscoli.

1155. 1. dela mechanicha. 2. mechanicha. 3. perchche chō . . matema"ticho".

1156. 1. ciasscuno. 2. cholla essperiēza.

1157. 1. certeza delle. 2. matematiche si passce. 3. [e mati] e mai.

1158. 1. certezza "dele sciētie" e do. 2. po applichare.

1155. Compare No. 660, ll. 19—22 (Vol. I., p. 332).

C. A. 75 *a*; 219 *a*]   **1159.**

Chi disputa allegādo l'autorità, non adopera ²lo ingiegno, ma pivtosto · la memoria; ³le buone · lettere son nate da vn bono naturale, ⁴e perchè si de' piv laudare la cagiō che l'effetto, ⁵piv lauderai vn buon naturale sanza lettere, ⁶che vn bon letterato sanza naturale.

Any one who in discussion relies upon authority uses, not his understanding, but rather his memory. Good culture is born of a good disposition; and since the cause is more to be praised than the effect, I will rather praise a good disposition without culture, than good culture without the disposition.

I.2 82 *a*]   **1160.**

La sciētia è il capitano, e la pratica sono i soldati.

Science is the captain, and practice the soldiers.

G. 8 *a*]   **1161.**

DELL'ERRORE DI QUELLI CHE VSANO ²LA PRATICA SANZA SCIĒTIA.

OF THE ERRORS OF THOSE WHO DEPEND ON PRACTICE WITHOUT SCIENCE.

³Quelli che s'inamorā di pratica ⁴sāza sciētia sō come 'l nocchiere che ē⁵tra navilio sanza timone e bussola, ⁶chè mai à certezza dove si vada.

Those who fall in love with practice without science are like a sailor who enters a ship without a helm or a compass, and who never can be certain whither he is going.

1159. 1. laturita. 2. longiegno. 3. sonate. 4. laldare la chagiō chelle fetto. 5. lalderai vn bo. 6. literato.
1160. 1. ella pratica.
1161. 1—6 R. 1. erore. 2. praticha. 3. chessinnamorā di praticha. 4. nochieri. 5. ebbussola. 6. cierteza.

II.

MORALS.

Br. M. 156 b] **1162.**

Or vedi la sperāza e'l desiderio del ripatriarsi [2]e ritornare nel primo caso fa a similitudine della farfalla al lume, e l'uomo [3]che cō cōtinvi desideri sēpre cō festa aspetta la nvova [4]primavera, sempre la nvova state, sempre e nvovi mesi, [5]e nvovi anni, parēdogli che le desiderate cose, venēdo, [6]sieno troppe tarde, E' non s'avede che desidera la sua disfazi[7]one; ma questo desiderio è la quītessenza, spirito degli ele[8]menti, che trovādosi rīchivsa per l'anima dallo vmano corpo [9]desidera senpre ritornare al suo mandatario; [10]E uo' che sappi che questo medesimo desiderio è quella quītessēza, [11]cōpagnia della natura, e l'uomo è modello dello mōdo.

Now you see that the hope and the desire of returning home and to one's former state is like the moth to the light, and that the man who with constant longing awaits with joy each new spring time, each new summer, each new month and new year—deeming that the things he longs for are ever too late in coming—does not perceive that he is longing for his own destruction. But this desire is the very quintessence, the spirit of the elements, which finding itself imprisoned with the soul is ever longing to return from the human body to its giver. And you must know that this same longing is that quintessence, inseparable from nature, and that man is the image of the world.

What is life? (1162. 1163).

C. A. 70 a; 207 a] **1163.**

O tēpo, consumatore delle cose, [2]e o invidiosa antichità, tu distruggi tutte le cose, [3]e consumi tutte le cose da duri dēti [4]della vecchiezza a poco a poco cō lēta [5]morte! Elena quando si specchiaua, vedēdo [6]le vizze grinze del suo viso, fatte per la vecchi[7]ezza, piagnie e pēsa seco, perchè fu rapita [8]due volte.

O Time! consumer of all things; O envious age! thou dost destroy all things and devour all things with the relentless teeth of years, little by little in a slow death. Helen, when she looked in her mirror, seeing the withered wrinkles made in her face by old age, wept and wondered why she had twice been carried away.

1162. 1. *On the margin:* pro, *meaning probably* propositione. 2. lassperāza [del suo] el desidero 2. chas"o" . . assimilitudine "dela farfalla alume" dell uomo. 3. chō chōtinvi . . chō fessta asspetta. 5. chose. 6. dissfazi. 7. Desidero e ne i [q] la quīte essenza. 8. peranima dello . . . . chorpo. 10. chessapi . . quīta esēza. 11. chōpagnia . . elluomo.

1163. 1. chonsumatore . . chose. 2. disstruggi . . chose. 3. chonsumate . . chose. 4. vecchieza appocho appocho chō. 5. elena . . sisspecchiaua. 6. leuzze grinze. 7. eppēsa secho. 8. da volte. 9. chonsumatore . . chose. 10. lesono chonsumate.

⁹O tēpo consumatore delle · cose ·, e o invidiosa · antichi¹⁰tà, per la quale tutte le cose sono consumate!

O Time! consumer of all things, and O envious age! by which · all things are all devoured.

H 2 33*b*]   **1164.**

Death.

Ogni danno lascia dispiacere ²nella ricordatione, saluo ³che'l sommo dāno, cioè la morte, che ⁴uccide essa ricordatione īsieme ⁵colla vita,

Every evil leaves behind a grief in our memory, except the supreme evil, that is death, which destroys this memory together with life.

C. A. 75*b*; 219*b*]   **1165.**

How to spend life (1165—1179).

¶O dormiēte · che cosa · è sonno? jl sōno à similitudine · colla morte; O perchè non fai · adunque tale opera, che dopo la morte ²tu abbi similitudine di perfetto viuo, che iuuendo · farsi col sonno simile ai tristi morti?¶

O sleepers! what a thing is slumber! Sleep resembles death. Ah why then dost thou not work in such wise as that after death thou mayst retain a resemblance to perfect life, when, during life, thou art in sleep so like to the hapless dead?

G. 89*a*]   **1166.**

L'un caccia l'al²tro.
³Per questi quadretti ⁴s'in-tende la uita ⁵e li studi umani.

One pushes down the other.
By these square-blocks are meant the life and the studies of men.

C. A. 365*b*; 1141*b*]   **1167.**

¶La cognitiō del tēpo preterito ²e del sito della terra è orna³mēto e cibo delle mēti vmane.¶

The knowledge of past times and of the places on the earth is both an ornament and nutriment to the human mind.

Mz. 8 *a* (12)   **1168.**

È di tāto vilipēdio la bugia, che s'ella dicesse bene già ²cose di Dio, ella toglie gratia a sua deità, ed è di tāta eccellē³tia la uerità, che s'ella laudasse cose minime elle si faño nobili;
⁴Sanza dubbio tal proportione è dalla verità alla bugia, qual è ⁵dalla luce alle tenebre, ed è essa verità in se di tanta eccellē⁶tia che, ancora ch'ella s'estenda sopra vmili e basse materie, ⁷sanza compa-ratione ella eccede le incertezze e bugie

To lie is so vile, that even if it were in speaking well of godly things it would take off something from God's grace; and Truth is so excellent, that if it praises but small things they become noble.
Beyond a doubt truth bears the same relation to falsehood as light to darkness; and this truth is in itself so excellent that, even when it dwells on humble and lowly matters, it is still infinitely above uncer-tainty and lies, disguised in high and

1164. 1. dāv lasscia disspiacere. 3. somo. 4. viede.
1165. 1. chosa . . assimilitudine cholla. 2. abi . . chol sono.   **1166.** 5. elli.
1167. 1. chognitiō. 3. eccibo . . vma"ne".
1168. 1. ede di . . chessella dicessi. 2. dio ella to di gratia assua. 3. chessella laldassi. 5. verita "in se" di. 6. anchora
        sastende. 7. comperatione ellaccede . . esstese. 8. pra [le altissime] li . disscorsi. 9. nosstra anchora. 10. no resta . .

1165. Compare No. 676, Vol. I. p. 353.

estese so[8]pra li magni e altissimi discorsi, perchè la mē[9]te nostra, ancora ch'ell'abbia la bugia pel quīto elemēto, [10]non resta però che la verità delle cose nō sia di sommo no[11]trimento delli intelletti fini, ma non di uaga[12]bundi ingegni;

[13]Ma tu che [14]viui di sogni, [15]ti piaciono più le [16]ragioni soffistiche [17]e barerie de' [18]pallaji nelle [19]cose grādi [20]e incerte, che [21]le certe [22]naturali e [23]nō di tāta al-[24]tura.

lofty discourses; because in our minds, even if lying should be their fifth element, this does not prevent that the truth of things is the chief nutriment of superior intellects, though not of wandering wits.

But you who live in dreams are better pleased by the sophistical reasons and frauds of wits in great and uncertain things, than by those reasons which are certain and natural and not so far above us.

S. K. M. III. 36*b*]　　　　　　　**1169.**

☐ Fuggi quello · studio · del quale [2]la resultante opera more insie[3]me coll' operante d'essa.

Avoid studies of which the result dies with the worker.

C. A. 75*a*; 219*a*]　　　　　　　**1170.**

A torto si lamētā li omini della fuga del tenpo, [2]incolpando quello di troppa velocità, nō s'accorgiēdo [3]quello essere di bastevole trāsito, ma bona me[4]moria·, di che la natura ci à dotati, ci fa che [5]ogni cosa lungamēte passata ci pare essere presente.

Men are in error when they lament the flight of time, accusing it of being too swift, and not perceiving that it is sufficient as it passes; but good memory, with which nature has endowed us, causes things long past to seem present.

C. A. 111*a*; 345*a*]　　　　　　　**1171.**

Acquista cosa nella tua giovētù [2]arresta il danno della tua ve[3]cchiezza; — [4]e se tu intēdi [5]la vechiezza aver per suo cibo la sa-[6]piētia, adoperati in tal modo in giove[7]tù che tal uecchiezza nō māchi il nu[8]trimēto.

Learning acquired in youth arrests the evil of old age; and if you understand that old age has wisdom for its food, you will so conduct yourself in youth that your old age will not lack for nourishment.

C. A. 223*b*; 671*b*]　　　　　　　**1172.**

¶L'acquisto di qualūche cognitione [2]è sēpre vtile allo intelletto, perchè potrà [3]scacciare da se le cose inutili è riserva-[4]re lè buone; ¶

[5]¶perchè nessuna cosa si può amare ne odiare, [6]se prima nō si à cognitiō di quella.¶

The acquisition of any knowledge is always of use to the intellect, because it may thus drive out useless things and retain the good.

For nothing can be loved or hated unless it is first known.

Tr. 32]　　　　　　　**1173.**

¶Siccome · vna · giornata · bene spesa dà lieto dormire, così vna vita · bene · vsata · dà lieto morire.¶

As a day well spent procures a happy sleep, so a life well employed procures a happy death.

chella . . chose . . somo. 12. ingegni ingeni. 13. mattu. 15. piace. 16. ragō soffistice. 18. palari. 21. delle certe.
1169. 3. choll.
1170. 2. incholpando . . tropa . . sachorgiēdo. 4. ci fa [parere] "che". 5. chosa.
1171. 1. chosa . . goventu. 2. cheresta il. 3. chieza [ovr o chettu masstulli la tu]. 4. [a vechiezza]—essetu. 6. govē. 7. chettal vecheza.
1172. 1. chognitione. 3. schacciare dasse le chose inutile. 4. re le. 5. chosa. 6. chognitiō.
1173. 1. sicchome . . dallieto.

Tr. 68]   **1174.**

L'acqua che tochi de' fivmi, è l'ulti²ma
di quella · che ādò, e la prima ³di quelle ·
che viene; così il tēpo ⁴presēte;
⁵La vita bene spesa lunga è.

The water you touch in a river is the last
of that which has passed, and the first of that
which is coming. Thus it is with time present.
Life if well spent, is long.

W. XII.]   **1175.**

Siccome māgiare · sanza voglia si cōuerte
²ī fastidioso · notrimento ·, così lo studio
sā³za desiderio · guasta la ⁴memoria, col ⁵nō
ritenere cosa ch'ella pigli.

Just as food eaten without caring for it
is turned into loathsome nourishment, so
study without a taste for it spoils memory,
by retaining nothing which it has taken in.

Ash. I. 1 b]   **1176.**

Siccome il mangiare · sanza · voglia fia
dañoso · alla salute, ²così lo studio sanza ·
desiderio guasta · la memoria, e nō ritiē
cosa · ch' ella pigli.

Just as eating against one's will is injurious to health, so study without a liking for
it spoils the memory, and it retains nothing
it takes in.

C. A. 284 b; 865 b]   **1177.**

Ti ghiacciano le parole · in bocca, ²e fa-
resti gielatina ī Mōgibello;
³Siccome il ferro s'arruginiscie sanza
⁴esercitio, e l'acqua si putrefa e nel freddo
⁵s'agghiaccia ·, così l'ingiegnio sanza e⁶ser-
citio si guasta;
⁷Mal fai se lodi ·, e peggio se tu riprēdi
⁸la cosa ·, quādo bene · tu nō la intēdi;
⁹Quādo fortuna viē, prēdi l'a mā
salua ¹⁰dināti, perchè retro · è · calua.

On Mount Etna the words freeze in
your mouth and you may make ice of
them[2].
Just as iron rusts unless it is used, and
water putrifies or, in cold, turns to ice, so
our intellect spoils unless it is kept in use.
You do ill if you praise, and still
worse if you reprove in a matter you do
not understand.
When Fortune comes, seize her in front
with a sure hand, because behind she is bald.

W. An. II. 203 a] (24)   **1178.**

Nō mi | pare che li omini grossi e di
²tristi costumi e di poco discorso meritino
si bello stru³mēto, nè tanta varietà di ma-
chinamēti quanto li omini speculatiui e ⁴di
grā discorsi, ma solo vn sacco doue si ri-

It seems to me that men of coarse and
clumsy habits and of small knowledge do not
deserve such fine instruments nor so great a
variety of natural mechanism as men of speculation and of great knowledge; but merely a

---

1174. 1. chettochi. 2. ādo ella. 3. quelli.

1175. 1. sichome . . chōuerte. 2. losstudio. 3. za [disspositione] desiderio quassta. 4. memoria [chol nō pigliare alchuna]. 5. e
nō ritenere chosa chclla pigli.

1176. 1. sichome . . voglia [da danno] fia. 2. chosi losstudio . . chosa.

1177. 1. diaciano . . bocha. 2· effaresti. 3. si chome il fero sa . ruginiscce. 4. ellacq"a" . . fredo. 5. sagiacia chosi. 7. pegio
istu. 8. nolantēdi. 10. dinātico . perche reto e chalua.

1178. 1. chelli . . grosi. 2. trissti chorstumi "e di pocho disscorso" meritino. 3. nettanta . . spechulatiui e di. 4. disscorsi.

1177. 1. 2. There is no clue to explain this strange sentence.

ceua il cibo, e donde esso ⁵esca, chè in vero altro che un transito di cibo non sō da essere giudicati, ⁶perchè niente mi pare che essi participino di spetie vmana altro, che la voce ⁷e la figvra, e tutto il resto è assai manco che bestia.

sack in which their food may be stowed and whence it may issue, since they cannot be judged to be any thing else than vehicles for food; for it seems to me they have nothing about them of the human species but the voice and the figure, and for all the rest are much below beasts.

S. K. M. III. 17 a]   **1179.**

Ecco alcuni che non altramente che trā²sito di cibo e avmētatori di ster³co e rienpitori di destri chiamarsi debono, perchè per ⁴loro non altro nel mōdo o pure alcuna virtù in opera si ⁵mette, perchè di loro altro ⁶che pieni destri non resta.

Some there are who are nothing else than a passage for food and augmentors of excrement and fillers of privies, because through them no other things in the world, nor any good effects are produced, since nothing but full privies results from them.

C. A. 153 b; 455 b]   **1180.**

Il massimo ingāno delli omini ²è nelle loro oppinioni.

The greatest deception men suffer is from their own opinions. ^{On foolishness and ignorance (1180—1182).}

Tr. 56]   **1181.**

La stoltitia è scudo della vergognia, come la imprōtitudine ²della povertà glorificata.

Folly is the shield of shame, as unreadiness is that of poverty glorified.

Tur. 17 b]   **1182.**

La ciecca igniorāza così ci cōduce ²cō effetto de' lascivi sollazzi
³{per nō conosciere la uera luce.
⁴{per nō conosciere qual sia la uera luce.
⁵E'l uano splendor ci toglie l'esser
⁶....;¶vedi che per lo splendor nel fuoco andiamo, ⁸come ciecca jgnorāza ci cōduce.
¹⁰O miseri mortali aprite li occhi.

Blind ignorance misleads us thus and delights with the results of lascivious joys.
{Because it does not know the true light.
{Because it does not know what is the true
                                light.
Vain splendour takes from us the power of being.... behold! for its vain splendour we go into the fire, thus blind ignorance does mislead us. That is, blind ignorance so misleads us that ...
O! wretched mortals, open your eyes.

Ash. I. 1 a]   **1183.**

Nō si dimāda · richezza · quello · che si può perdere; ²la uirtù · è vero · nostro · bene ed è vero premio ³del suo · possessore ·; lei nō si può · perdere ·, lei ⁴nō ci abandona ·,

That is not riches, which may be lost; virtue is our true good and the true reward of its possessor. That cannot be lost; that never deserts us, but when life leaves us. As ^{On riches (1183—1187).}

---

5. sacho [da cibo] doue. 6. essca . . gudicati. 7, chella voce. 18. ella . . ettutto erresto . . mancho che besstia.
1179. 1. ecci . . che altro chettrā. 3. cho | "e rienpitori ̸di desstri" chiamarsi. 4. loro | "altro nel mōdo o pure" alchuna.
6. pieni e desstr.
1180. 2. he nelloro oppennione.
1181. 1. esschudo . . chome. 2. grorifichato.
1182. 1. ciccha . . chosi ci chōduce. 2. e chō . . lasscivi sollazzi. 3. chonossciere. 4. chonossciere. 6. b \\\\ ¶ vedi fucho andiano. 7. ¶ ciecha īgnorāza . . intal modo chōduce. 8. coe chome ciecha jgniorāza ci chōduce. 9. che.
1183. 1. richeza . . chessi. 4. lasscia. 5. elle esterne. 6. isspeso lasscian choniscorno. 7. essbeffato iloro.

se prima la uita nō ci lascia; ⁵le robe e le esterne diuitie · senpre le tieni ⁶cō timore; spesso lasciano · con scorno ⁷e sbeffato · il loro possessore perdēdo lor possessione.

to property and external riches, hold them with trembling; they often leave their possessor in contempt, and mocked at for having lost them.

F. 96b]

1184.

Ogni omo desidera far capitale per ²dare a medici destruttori di uite, adūque debono essere richi;

³L'uomo à grande discorso, del quale la più parte ⁴è vana e falsa, li animali l'ànno piccolo, ma è vti⁵le e vero, e meglio è la piccola certezza che la grā ⁶bugia.

Every man wishes to make money to give it to the doctors, destroyers of life; they then ought to be rich[2].

Man has much power of discourse which for the most part is vain and false; animals have but little, but it is useful and true, and a small truth is better than a great lie.

C. A. 108b; 338b]

1185.

Chi piv possiede piv debbe ²temere di nō perdere.

He who possesses most must be most afraid of loss.

W. XIII]

1186.

Chi uuole essere ricco in v̄ dì ²e impiccato in vn anno.

He who wishes to be rich in a day will be hanged in a year.

S. K. M. III. 77a]

1187.

E questo uomo à vna somma ²pazzia cioè che sēpre stēta per ³non stētare, e la uita a lui ⁴fugie sotto sperāza di gode⁵re i beni con somma fatica ac⁶quistati.

That man is of supreme folly who always wants for fear of wanting; and his life flies away while he is still hoping to enjoy the good things which he has with extreme labour acquired.

B. 3b]

1188.

Se tu · avessi · il corpo secōdo la virtù ·, tu . nō carpesti ²in questo mōdo;

³Tu cresci ī reputatione come il pane ī mano a' putti.

If you governed your body by the rules of virtue you would not walk on all fours in this world.

You grow in reputation like bread in the hands of a child.

Rules of Life (1188—1202).

Tr. 2]

1189.

Saluatico è quel che si salua.

Savage he is who saves himself.

1184. 2. medici "destruttori di iute" aduque . . esse. 4. picholo. 5. verso . . ella pichola certeza.
1185. 1. ci piv posiede. 2. no.
1186. 1. richo nv̄di. 2. empichato nvn.
1187. 1. uomo . . soma. 2. pazia . . chessēpre. 3. istētare ella uita seli. 5. soma faticha a. 6. quisstati
1188. 1. settu . . capresti. 3. cressci.

1184. 2. Compare No. 856.
1188. The first sentence is obscure. Compare Nos. 825. 826.

E. 31 *b*]   **1190.**

Non si debbe desiderare lo inpossibile.   We ought not to desire the impossible.

H.3 70 *b*]   **1191.**

Dimāda cōsiglio a chi bē si corregge;
²Givstitia vuol potētia, intelligē³tia e
volontà, e si assomi⁴glia al rè delle api;
⁵Chi nō puniscie il male, co⁶māda che
si facci;
⁷Chi piglia la biscia per la coda ⁸quella
poi lo morde;
⁹Chi cava la fossa, quella ¹⁰gli ruina
adosso.

Ask counsel of him who rules himself well.
Justice requires power, insight, and will;
and it resembles the queen-bee.
He who does not punish evil commands
it to be done.
He who takes the snake by the tail will
presently be bitten by it.
The grave will fall in upon him who
digs it.

H.3 71 *a*]   **1192.**

¹Chi nō rafrena la uoluttà ·, colle bestie
²s’acōpagni;
³Nō si può avere maggior nè minor
signio⁴ria che quella di se medesimo;
⁵Chi poco pēsa, molto erra;
⁶Più facilmēte si cōtesta al prīcipio,
⁷che al fine;
⁸Nessuno cōsiglio è piv leale che ⁹quello
che si da alle navi che so¹⁰no in pericolo;
¹¹Aspetti danno quel che si regie per ¹²gio-
vane sconsigliato.

The man who does not restrain wantonness,
allies himself with beasts.
Yon can have no dominion greater or less
than that over yourself.
He who thinks little, errs much.
It is easier to contend with evil at the
first than at the last.
No counsel is more loyal than that given
on ships which are in peril: He may expect
loss who acts on the advice of an inex-
perienced youth.

Tr. 39]   **1193.**

Dov’è piv sentimēto, lì è piv martirio;
grā martire.

Where there is most feeling, there is the
greatest martyrdom;—a great martyr.

H.1 16 *b*]   **1194.**

La memoria de’ benifitj apres²so l’īgra-
titudine è fragile;
³Reprēdi l’amico ī segre⁴to, e laudalo
ī paleso;
⁵Non essere bugiardo del ⁶preterito.

The memory of benefits is a frail defence against ingratitude.
Reprove your friend in secret and praise
him openly.
Be not false about the past.

1190. 1. debba.
1191. 1–10 R. 1. ach bē si corege. 2. vol. 3. essi. 4. gia are delleave. 5. punisscie. 9. cicava. 10. glruina.
1192. 1–12 R. 1. cholle. 3. po . . magior. 5. ci poco. 6. a prīcipio. 8. nesuno chōsiglio. 9. chessi da dalle. 10. pericholo.
11. dano. 12. giovane scōsiglo.
1193. piv ne martiri.   1194. 1—6 R. 1. benifiti apre. 4. ellaldalo. *Two lines between l. 4 and l. 5 are effaced.*

1190. The writing of this note, which is exceedingly minute, is reproduced in facsimile on Pl. XLI
No. 5 above the first diagram.

C. A. 115*b*; 357*b*]   **1195.**

CŌPERATIONE DELLA PATIĒTIA.

²La patiētia fa cōtra alle ingiurie non altramēti che si faccino i panni ³contra del freddo, jnperochè se ti mvltiplicherai li pañi secondo la mvl⁴tiplicatione · del freddo ·, esso freddo · nocere nō · potrà ·; simil-mēte alle ⁵grādi ingivrie · cresci la patiētia, · e esse ingiurie offendere nō ti po⁶tranno la tua mēte.

A SIMILE FOR PATIENCE.

Patience serves us against insults precisely as clothes do against the cold. For if you multiply your garments as the cold increases, that cold cannot hurt you; in the same way increase your patience under great offences, and they cannot hurt your feelings.

S. K. M. II.² 24*a*]   **1196.**

Tanto è a dire bē d'ū tristo, ²quanto a dire male d'ū bono.

To speak well of a base man is much the same as speaking ill of a good man.

H.² 12*b*]   **1197.**

La invidia offēde colla fitta ²infamia, cioè col detrarre, ³la qual cosa spavēta la virtù.

Envy wounds with false accusations, that is with detraction, a thing which scares virtue.

L. o″]   **1198.**

Decipimur votis et tempore fallimur et mos ²deridet curas; anxia vita nihil.

We are deceived by promises and time disappoints us[2] . . .

L. 90*b*]   **1199.**

¶La pavra nascie piv tosto ²che altra cosa. ¶

Fear arises sooner than any thing else.

C. A. 75*b*; 219*b*]   **1200.**

Siccome l'animosità è pericolo di uita · così la paura · è sicurità di quella;

²Le minaccie sol sono ³arme dello minacciato;

⁴¶Dov'entra la uētura, la invidia · vi pone lo assedio e lo cōbatte, e dond'ella si parte, vi lascia il dolore e pētimēto;

⁵¶Raro cade chi ben camina;

Just as courage imperils life, fear protects it.

Threats alone are the weapons of the threatened man.

Wherever good fortune enters, envy lays siege to the place and attacks it; and when it departs, sorrow and repentance remain behind.

He who walks straight rarely falls.

1195. 2. allengiurie: altremēti . . chessi. 3. fredo jnpero chessetti . . sechondo. 4. esso fredo. 5. grāde . . cressci . . essa ingiuria.
1196. 1. trissto.
1197. 1—3 R. 1. lanvidia . . cholla. 2. chol. 3. spavēte.
1198. 1. et mos. 2. nhil.
1199. 1—2 R. 1. nasscie. 2. chosa.
1200. 1. sichome . . pericholo . . chosi . . sichurita. 3. iminacciato. 4. lanvidia . . essedio ello chōbatte E . . lasscia il "dolore he" piētimēto. 5. chade . . chamina. 6. laldi e pegio . . chosa dicho . . tu nolla. 7. laldi e pegio is tu . . tu nollātēdi.

1198. 2. The rest of this passage may be rendered in various ways, but none of them give a satisfactory meaning.

⁶¶Mal' è se laudi e peggio se riprēdi la cosa, dico se bene tu non la intēdi;

⁷¶Mal fai se laudi e peggio se tu ri-prēdi ‖ la cosa quādo bene tu non la intendi.

It is bad if you praise, and worse if you reprove a thing, I mean, if you do not understand the matter well.

It is ill to praise, and worse to reprimand in matters that you do not understand.

G. 49*a*]   **1201.**

Senpre le parole che nō soddisfaño all'orechio dello |²auditore, li danno tedio over rincrescimēto, e'l segnio di ³ciò vedrai, spesse uolte tali auditori essere ⁴copiosi di sbadigli; addūque tu, che parli dināti a omini ⁵di chi tu·cierchi benivolētia, quādo tu vedi·tali pro⁶digi di rīcrescimēto, abre-uia il tuo parlare, o tu mu⁷ta ragionamēto, e se tu altramēti farai, allora in lo⁸co della desiderata gratia tu acquisterai odio ⁹e nimicitia;

¹⁰E se vuoi vedere di quel¯che vn si diletta sanza u¹¹dirlo parlare, parla a lui mutādo diuersi ragio¹²namēti, e quel dove tu lo vedi stare intēto sanza ¹³sbadiglia-mēti o storcimēti di ciglia o altre varie ¹⁴azione, sia cierto che quella cosa, di che si parla, ¹⁵è quella di che lui si diletta, ecc.

Words which do not satisfy the ear of the hearer weary him or vex him, and the symptoms of this you will often see in such hearers in their frequent yawns; you therefore, who speak before men whose good will you desire, when you see such an excess of fatigue, abridge your speech, or change your discourse; and if you do otherwise, then instead of the favour you desire, you will get dislike and hostility.

And if you would see in what a man takes pleasure, without hearing him speak, change the subject of your discourse in talking to him, and when you presently see him intent, without yawning or wrinkling his brow or other actions of various kinds, you may be certain that the matter of which you are speaking is such as is agreeable to him &c.

Tr. 11]   **1202.**

Mvouesi l'amante per la cosa amata come il senso·e lo sensibile, e cō seco s'uniscie ²e fassi vna cosa medesima; ³l'opera è la prima cosa che nasce dal-l'unione; ⁴se la cosa amata è vile·, l'amāte si fa vile;

⁵Quando·la cosa vnita è cōueniēte al suo ⁶vnitore·, li seguita·dilettatione·e pia-cere e soddisfatione;

⁷Quādo l'amāte è giv̄to all' amato, lì si riposa; ⁸quādo·il peso·è posato·lì si riposa.

The lover is moved by the beloved object as the senses are by sensible objects; and they unite and become one and the same thing. The work is the first thing born of this union; if the thing loved is base the lover becomes base.

When the thing taken into union is perfectly adapted to that which receives it, the result is delight and pleasure and satisfaction.

When that which loves is united to the thing beloved it can rest there; when the burden is laid down it finds rest there.

C. A. 64*b*; 197*b*]   **1203.**

La prima fama si fa etterna insieme colli abitatori ²della città da lui edificata o accresciuta;

There will be eternal fame also for the inhabitants of that town, constructed and enlarged by him.

Politics (1203. 1204).

1201. 1. saddisfāno. 2. alditore .. rincresscimēto. 3. uolte [alli] ttali vlditore. 4. chopiosi di sbavigli. 6. rīcresscimēto .. ottu. 7. essettu altremēti .. allora illo. 8. cho. 9. ennimicitia. 10. Esse voi .. sanza vl. 11. allui. 12. ecquel .. tullo. 13. sbadigliamēti osstorcimeti. 14. azione .. di chessi. 15. ecquella .. lui si di che lui si diletta.

1202. 1. lamata per la cosamato .. senso ella sensibbile e chōsecho. 2. effassi. 3. ella .. chosa .. nasscie dell. 4. sella. 5. chosa .. chōueniēte .. essadisfatione. 8. li si riposato. 9. la cosasa chogni usscivta chol nostro intelletto.

1203. 2. dallui .. acresscuta. 3. obbedisscano esso mossi .. collogano co signiori "e costringano. 4. sagvinita .. roba sang-

1203. These notes were possibly written in preparation for a letter. The meaning is obscure.

[3]Tutti i popoli · obbediscono e sō mossi da lor magniati ·, e essi magniati · si collegano e costringono coi signori [4]per 2 · vie: o per sanguinità ·, o per roba: sanguinità, quādo · i lor figlioli sono a similitudine [5]di statichi; sicurtà è pegnio della lor dubitata · fede; roba, quādo · tu farai a ciascū d'essi [6]murare vna casa o 2 dentro alla tua città, della quale lui ne tragga qual[7]ch'entrate · e trarrà . . . 10 città · cinque mila · case · cō trenta [8]mila abitatori ·, e digregerai tanta cōgregatione di popolo che a similitudine di capre l' ū [9]adosso all' altro stanno, ēpiēdo ogni parte di fetore e si fanno semēza di pestilēte [10]morte;

[11]E la città si fà di bellezza cōpagnia del suo nome e a te vtile di dati e fama etterna del suo crescimēto.

All communities obey and are led by their magnates, and these magnates ally themselves with the lords and subjugate them in two ways: either by consanguinity, or by fortune; by consanguinity, when their children are, as it were, hostages, and a security and pledge of their suspected fidelity; by property, when you make each of these build a house or two inside your city which may yield some revenue and he shall have . . .; 10 towns, five thousand houses with thirty thousand inhabitants, and you will disperse this great congregation of people which stand like goats one behind the other, filling every place with fetid smells and sowing seeds of pestilence and death;

And the city will gain beauty worthy of its name and to you it will be useful by its revenues, and the eternal fame of its aggrandizement.

Ash. II. 13*a*]   1204.

Per mātenere il dono prīcipal [2]di natura cioè libertà, trovo modo [3]da offēdere e difēdere stāte assediati [4]dali ābitiosi tirāñi, e prima dirò del si[5]to mvrale, e ācora per che i popoli possino [6]mātenere i loro boni e giusti signiori.

To preserve Nature's chiefest boon, that is freedom, I can find means of offence and defence, when it is assailed by ambitious tyrants, and first I will speak of the situation of the walls, and also I shall show how communities can maintain their good and just Lords.

uinata sanguinita . . assimilitudine. 5. tuffarai aciasscū. 6. casa [de] o 2 . . traga. 7. ettrrarra 1 br 10 citta . . mila casse. 8. edigregierai tanto . . assimilitudine. 9. allalstano . . oni . . fetore si fano . . pessilēte. 11. ella . . atte . . dati effama . . cresscimēto.
1204. 1. īstādo assediati.

1204. Compare No. 1266.

III.

POLEMICS.—SPECULATION.

G. 47 a]

1205.

O speculatore del²le cose, nō ti laudare ³di conosciere le cose ⁴che ordinariamē⁵te per se medesima la ⁶natura ⁷conduce; ⁸Ma rallegrati di co⁹nosciere il fine ¹⁰di quelle cose che ¹¹son disegniate dalla ¹²mēte tua.

Oh! speculators on things, boast not of knowing the things that nature ordinarily brings about; but rejoice if you know the end of those things which you yourself devise.

Against Speculators (1205. 1206).

S. K. M. II.² 67 a]

1206.

O speculatori · dello continvo moto, quā²ti vani disegni in simile cerca avete creati! ³accōpagniatevi colli cercatori dell'oro.

Oh! speculators on perpetual motion how many vain projects of the like character you have created! Go and be the companions of the searchers for gold.

C. A. 75 b; 219 b]

1207.

J bugiardi · interpreti di natura · affermano l'argiēto viuo · essere comvne semēza a tutti i metalli ·, nō si ricordādo che la ²natura varia le semēze · secōdo la diuersità delle cose che essa vole produrre al mōdo.

The false interpreters of nature declare that quicksilver is the common seed of every metal, not remembering that nature varies the seed according to the variety of the things she desires to produce in the world.

Against alchemists (1207. 1208).

1205. 1. hosspechulatori. 2. chose . . laldare. 3. conossciere. 6. per sua [natu] "[ordine]". 7. [ralmēte] chonducie. 8. dicho. 9. nossciere. 10. chose.

1206. 1. spechulatori. 2. ciercha ave creati. 3. acōpagniatevi . . cierchator.

1207. 1. interpetri . . chomvne . . attutti . . richordādo chella. 2. sechōdo . . chose . . produre.

1206. Another short passage in MS. I, referring also to speculators, is given by LIBRI (*Hist. des Sciences math.* III, 228): *Sicchè voi speculatori non vi fidate delli autori che ànno sol col immaginatione voluto farsi inter-* *preti tra la natura e l'omo, ma sol di quelli che non coi cienni della natura, ma cogli effetti delle sue esperienze ànno esercitati i loro ingegni.*

F. 5 *b*]   **1208.**

E molti ²fecero bot³tega cōn ī⁴ganni e ⁵miraculi ⁶finti, ingan⁷nãdo la sto⁸lta molti-⁹tudine.

And many have made a trade of [de-lusions and false miracles, deceiving the stupid multitude.

Against friars.

Tr. 68]   **1209.**

¶Farisei·, frati· santi vol dire.¶

Pharisees—that is to say, friars.

Against writers of epitomes.

W. An. III. 241]   **1210.**

I abbreuiatori delle opere· fanno ingiu-ria ²alla cognitione e allo amore, ³con-ciosiachè l' amore di qualūche cosa è figli-uolo ⁴d'essa cognitione; l'amore ⁵è tanto più feruēte, quanto la ⁶cognitione è più certa, la qual ⁷certezza nascie dalla cogni-tione ⁸integrale di tutte quelle par⁹ti le quali, essendo insieme vnite, ¹⁰conpongono il tutto di quelle co¹¹se che debbono essere amate; ¹²che vale a quel, che per abbre-uiare ¹³le parti di quelle cose che lui fa ¹⁴professione di darne integral no¹⁵titia, che lui lascia indietro la ¹⁶maggior parte delle cose, di che il tutto ¹⁷è cōposto? egli è vero che la inpa¹⁸tientia, madre della stoltitia, è que¹⁹lla che lauda la breuità; come se ²⁰questi tali non avessino tāto di uita, ²¹ch'elli seruisse a potere avere vna ²²intera notitia d'un sol particulare co²³me è vn corpo vmano! e poi vogli²⁴ono ab-bracciare la mēte di dio nella ²⁵quale s'in-clude l'universo cara²⁶tando e minuzzando quella in īfinite ²⁷parti, come se l'avessino a anatomizzare;

²⁸O stoltitia vmana nō ²⁹t'avedi tu che tu sei stato con teco ³⁰tutta la tua età, e non ài ancora ³¹notitia di quella cosa che tu più possie³²di, cioè della tua pazzia? e vuoi po³³i colla moltitudine de'soffistichi ingannare ³⁴te e altri, sprezzando le mate-matiche sciē³⁵zie, nelle qual si contiene la uerità, no³⁶titia delle cose che in lor si cōtē-gono; e vuoi ³⁷poi scorrere ne' miracoli e scrivere ch'ài ³⁸notitia di quelle cose, di che la mēte vmana ³⁹non è capace, e non si possono dimostrare per ne⁴⁰ssuno esenplo naturale, e ti pare avere ⁴¹fatto miraculi,

Abbreviators do harm to knowledge and to love, seeing that the love of any thing is the offspring of this knowledge, the love being the more fervent in pro-portion as the knowledge is more certain. And this certainty is born of a complete knowledge of all the parts, which, when com-bined, compose the totality of the thing which ought to be loved. Of what use then is he who abridges the details of those matters of which he professes to give thorough information, while he leaves behind the chief part of the things of which the whole is composed? It is true that impatience, the mother of stupidity, praises brevity, as if such persons had not life long enough to serve them to acquire a complete knowledge of one single subject, such as the human body; and then they want to comprehend the mind of God in which the universe is included, weighing it minutely and mincing it into infinite parts, as if they had to dissect it!

Oh! human stupidity, do you not per-ceive that, though you have been with yourself all your life, you are not yet aware of the thing you possess most of, that is of your folly? and then, with the crowd of so-phists, you deceive yourselves and others, despising the mathematical sciences, in which truth dwells and the knowledge of the things included in them. And then you occupy yourself with miracles, and write that you possess information of those things of which the human mind is incapable and which cannot be proved by any instance from nature. And you fancy you have wrought miracles when you spoil a work of some

1208. 2. fecē bot. 6. inga. 10. ne sāsi foperia cognoscitore de loro ingāni essigli poniano.

1210. 1. abreuiatori . . opre . f . fanno ingiuia. 2. cognitione [concosia che] e allo. 3. concosia chellamore . . effilol. 4. ella [cogni] more. 5. ettanto. 7. feruēde certeza nascie. 8. i integrale . . pa. 9. te le. 10. conpongano . . quella. 11. sa che. 12. abreuiare. 13. parte. 15. chellui lassci indirieto. 16. magor. 17. chella. 19. chellalda . . chomesse. 21. chelli ser-uissi. 22. da "sol" parlicutare. 24. ano abracciare . . nelle. 26. minvzzando. 27. parte . . lavessino anatomizare. 28. [e delle chose che] o. 29. tu [chett] chettu se. 31. chettu. 32. coe . . pazzia [vole] e volli. 33. i conlla . . inganare. 34. splezando. 35. ze nella. 36. cōtēgano e voi. 39. posso. 40. naturale letti. 41. tu gnasto. 42. spechulativo. 43. chettu.

1209. Compare No. 837, ll. 54—57, No. 1296 (p. 363 and 364), and No. 1305 (p. 370).

quãdo tu ài quastato vna ⁴²opera d'alcuno ingegnio speculativo, e nõ ⁴³t'avedi che tu cadi nel medesimo errore, ⁴⁴che fa quello che denuda la piãta dell'orna⁴⁵mento de' sua rami, pieni di fronde, miste co⁴⁶li odoriferi fiori o frutti, ... ⁴⁸come fece Giv⁴⁹stino, abbreuiatore delle storie scritte da Trogo ⁵⁰Põpeo, il quale scrisse ornatamente tutti ⁵¹li eccellēti fatti delli sua antichi, li quali e⁵²rã pieni di mirabilissimi ornamēti; e così ⁵³conpose vna cosa ignuda, ma sol degna d'in⁵⁴gegni inpatiēti, li quali pare lor perder ⁵⁵tanto di tenpo, quãto quello è che è ado-perato vtil⁵⁶mēte, cioè nelli studi delle opere di nature e delle ⁵⁷cose vmane; Ma stieno questi tali in conpa⁵⁸gnia delle bestie; Nelli lor cortigiani sieno cani e ⁵⁹i altri animali piē di rapina e accompagniansi ⁶⁰con loro correndo sempre dietro . . . . ., e seguita-⁶¹no l' inocēti animali che cõ la fame alli tem⁶²pi delle grã nevi ti uengono alle case, dimanda⁶³tori limosina come lor tutore.

speculative mind, and do not perceive that you are falling into the same error as that of a man who strips a tree of the ornament of its branches covered with leaves mingled with the scented blossoms or fruit . . . . [48] as Justinus did, in abridging the histories written by Trogus Pompeius, who had written in an ornate style all the worthy deeds of his forefathers, full of the most admirable and ornamental passages; and so composed a bald work worthy only of those impatient spirits, who fancy they are losing as much time as that which they employ usefully in studying the works of nature and the deeds of men. But these may remain in company of beasts; among their associates should be dogs and other animals full of rapine and they may hunt with them after . . . ., and then follow helpless beasts, which in time of great snows come near to your houses asking alms as from their master . . . .

C. A. 187*b*; 562*b*]   **1211.**

O matematici fate lume a tale er²rore! ³Lo spirito non à voce, perchè dov'è voce ⁴è corpo, e dove è corpo è occupa-tiõ di lo⁵co, il quale inpediscie all'ochio il ue⁶dere delle cose poste dopo tale loco; ⁷adunque tal corpo enpie di se tutta ⁸la circustante aria, cioè colle sua s⁹petie.

O mathematicians shed light on this error. The spirit has no voice, because where there is a voice there is a body, and where there is a body space is occupied, and this prevents the eye from seeing what is placed behind that space; hence the surrounding air is filled by the body, that is by its image.

On spirits (1211—1213).

B. 4*b*]   **1212.**

Nõ può essere voce, dove non è movi-mēto e percussione d'aria; ²nõ può essere percussione d'essa aria, doue non è stru-mēto; ³nõ può essere strumēto incorporeo; essē⁴do così, vno spirito nõ può avere nè voce nè forma nè forza, ⁵e se piglierà corpo, non potrà penetrare nè ⁶entrare doue li usci sono serrati; ⁷e se alcuno di-ciesse: per aria cõgregata ⁸e ristretta īsieme lo spirito piglia i corpi ⁹di uarie · forme ·, e

There can be no voice where there is no motion or percussion of the air; there can be no percussion of the air where there is no instrument, there can be no instrument without a body; and this being so, a spirit can have neither voice, nor form, nor strength. And if it were to assume a body it could not penetrate nor enter where the passages are closed. And if any one should say that by air, compressed and compacted

44. cheffa. 45. misto. 46. offrutti sopra dimostra. 47. que en quella piãta esser da fare [bene]. 48. di [molte] lun se tavole come fece givs. 49. abreuiatore . . da troc. 50. põpeo il . . tuti. 51. eceletti. 53. inuda . . degnia di. 55. quel-loche. 56. coe . . dele. 57. questi. 58. cortigiani sie. 59. a altri . . rapina e aconpagniasi. 60. senpre dirieto ach fuge. 61. alli ten. 62. uengano . . casi. 63. lor tutore essnull *here the text breaks off*.
1211. 1. attale. 4. e do e corpo e ochupatiõ. 5. cho. 6. posste . . locho. 7. dal. 8. coe.
1212. 1. nõ po. 2. nõ po. 3. nõ po. 4. nõ po . . voce "| ne forma" ne forza. 5. esse. 6. sera "ti".. 7. esse . . diciessi perr. 8. chorpi. 9. quelo. 10. Acquesta . . dicho. 11. none nerui e ossa non po. 12. operrata inessuno. 14. fugi. 15. isperiēza.

1210. 48. *Givstino*, Marcus Junianus Justinus, a Roman historian of the second century, who com-piled an epitome from the general history written by Trogus Pompeius, who lived in the time of Augustus. The work of the latter writer no longer exist.

per quello strumēto parla ¹⁰e move cō forza, a questa parte dico, ¹¹che doue non sono nerui e ossa, non può esse¹²re forza · operata in nessuno movimēto ¹³fatto dagl' imaginati spiriti;

¹⁴fuggi i precetti · di quelli · speculatori, chè le loro ¹⁵ragioni · nō son · confermate · dalla · speriēza.

together, a spirit may take bodies of various forms and by this means speak and move with strength—to him I reply that when there are neither nerves nor bones there can be no force exercised in any kind of movement made by such imaginary spirits.

Beware of the teaching of these speculators, because their reasoning is not confirmed by experience.

W. An. II. 242 *b* (·N·)]   1213.

Delli discorsi vmani stoltissimo è da essere riputato quello, il qual s'astēde al²la credulità della negromātia, sorella della alchimia, partoritricie del³le cose senplici e naturali; Ma è tanto più degnia di riprensio⁴ne che l'alchimia, quāto ella non partorisce alcuna cosa se nō simile a se, ⁵cioè bugia; il che non interviene nella alchimia, la quale è ministra⁶tricie de'senplici prodotti della natura, il quale vfitio fatto esser nō può ⁷da essa natura, perchè in lei non sono strumēti organici colli quali essa possa operare quel ⁸che adopera l'uomo mediante le mani, che in tale vfitio ⁹à fatti i vetri ecc.; ma essa negromātia, stendardo ovvero bandiera ¹⁰volante, mossa dal uēto, è guidatricie della stolta moltitudine, la quale ¹¹al continuo testimonia collo abbaiamēto d'infiniti effetti di tale ¹²arte; e uāno ēpiuti i libri, affermando che l'incāti e spiriti adoperino ¹³e sanza lingua parlino, e sanza strumēti organici, sāza i quali ¹⁴parlar nō si può, parlino, e portino gravissimi pesi, facino tēpestare ¹⁵e piovere, e che li omini si cōvertino il gatte, lupi e altre bestie, ¹⁶benchè in bestia prima ētrā quelli che tal cosa affermano;

¹⁷E cierto, se tale negromātia fusse in essere, come dalli bassi ingiegni è creduto, ¹⁸nessuna cosa è sopra la terra che al danno e seruitio dell'omo fusse di tanta valitudine, perchè se fus¹⁹se vero, che in tale arte si avesse potētia di far turbare la trāquilla serenità dell'ari²⁰a, convertendo quella in notturn aspetto, e far le corruscationi o venti con spa²¹vētevoli toni e folgori scorrēti infra le tenebre, e con īpetuosi venti ruinare

Of all human opinions that is to be reputed the most foolish which deals with the belief in Necromancy, the sister of Alchemy, which gives birth to simple and natural things. But it is all the more worthy of reprehension than alchemy, because it brings forth nothing but what is like itself, that is, lies; this does not happen in Alchemy which deals with simple products of nature and whose function cannot be exercised by nature itself, because it has no organic instruments with which it can work, as men do by means of their hands, who have produced, for instance, glass &c. but this Necromancy the flag and flying banner, blown by the winds, is the guide of the stupid crowd which is constantly witness to the dazzling and endless effects of this art; and there are books full, declaring that enchantments and spirits can work and speak without tongues and without organic instruments — without which it is impossible to speak — and can carry heaviest weights and raise storms and rain; and that men can be turned into cats and wolves and other beasts, although indeed it is those who affirm these things who first became beasts.

And surely if this Necromancy did exist, as is believed by small wits, there is nothing on the earth that would be of so much importance alike for the detriment and service of men, if it were true that there were in such an art a power to disturb the calm serenity of the air, converting it into darkness and making coruscations or winds, with terrific thunder and lightnings rushing through the darkness, and with violent

1213. *Above the text is the note:* seguita quel che mācha dirieto alla facia del pie. 1. Ma dalli disscorsi . . essere [tenuto] "re putato" . . sastēde 2. archimia. 3. lle chose [naturali] senplici . . ettanto . . ripresi. 4. chellarchimia . . partorissce . . chosa . . asse. 5. [parole] "cioe bugia" il che noñe . . archimia . . e [vfit] minisstra. 6. dalla. 7. illei none . . orghanici [da poter] "cholli quali" essa. 8. lomo [il quale] mediante. 9 affatti e vetri . . stendar "do" over. 10. uēto guidatricie. 11. chontinuo e tesstimonia chollo. 12. ēpiute . . chellinchāti esspiriti. 13. essanza . . essanza . . saza. 14. po . . tēpesstare. 15. chelli . . ghatte. 16. che dattal chosa. 17. eccierto settale . . fussi . . chome. 18. chosa essopra . . al "danno e" seruitio . . fussi . . tanta [vtilita] "valitudine" perchese fu. 19. si . . arte [fussi] si avessi . . turbare [laria] la. 2. chonvertendo . . inotturnasspetto effarle corrusscationi . . chon isspa. 21. effolgo"ri" . . infralle . . e chonnī petuosi. 22. dira-

²²li alti edifiti, e diradicare le selue, e con quelle percuotere li eserciti, e quelli ²³ronpēdo e atterrādo, e oltr' a questo le dannose tenpeste, privando li cultori ²⁴del premio delle lor fatiche,—o qual modo di guerra può essere, che con tanto dan²⁵no possa offendere il suo nemico di aver potestà di privarlo delle sue raccolte? qual bat²⁶taglia marittima può essere che si assomigli a quella? dico lui che comāda alli vēti ²⁷e fa le fortune ruvinose e sommergitrici di qualunche armata,—cierto quel che ²⁸co māda a tali inpetuosi potētie sarà signore delli popoli, e nessuno vma²⁹no ingiegnio potrà resistere alle sue dannose forze; Li occulti tesori e ³⁰giemme, riposte nel corpo della terra, fieno a costui tutti manifesti; nessun ³¹serrame o fortezza inespugnabili sarà quelle che saluar possino al³²cuno sanza la voglia di tal negromāte; Questo si farà portare per l'aria dal³³l'oriente all'occidēte e per tutti li oppositi aspetti dell'universo; Ma per³⁴chè mi voglio più oltre estendere? quale è quella cosa che per ta³⁵le arteficie far nō si possa? quasi nessuna, eccietto il levarsi la morte; ad³⁶dunque è concluso in parte il danno e la vtilità che in tale arte si contiene, essē³⁷do vera; e s'ella è vera, perchè non è restata infra li omini che tanto la deside³⁸rano, non avēdo riguardo a nessuna deità? e so, che infiniti ce n'è, che per soddisfare ³⁹a vn suo appetito, ruinerebbero Iddio cō tutto l'universo; e s'ella non è rimasto infra ⁴⁰li omini, essendo a lui tanto neciessaria, essa nō fu mai, nè mai è per dovere essere, ⁴¹per la difinitiō dello spirito, il quale è invisibile in corpo; e dentro alli elemē⁴²ti non sono cose incorporee, perchè doue non è corpo, è vacuo, e il uacuo nō si da dē⁴³tro alli elemēti, perchè subito sarebbe dall'elemēto riēpiuto; ‖ volta carta.

storms overthrowing high buildings and rooting up forests; and thus to oppose armies, crushing and annihilating them; and, besides these frightful storms may deprive the peasants of the reward of their labours. — Now what kind of warfare is there to hurt the enemy so much as to deprive him of the harvest? What naval warfare could be compared with this? I say, the man who has power to command the winds and to make ruinous gales by which any fleet may be submerged,—surely a man who could command such violent forces would be lord of the nations, and no human ingenuity could resist his crushing force. The hidden treasures and gems reposing in the body of the earth would all be made manifest to him. No lock nor fortress, though impregnable, would be able to save any one against the will of the necromancer. He would have himself carried through the air from East to West and through all the opposite sides of the universe. But why should I enlarge further upon this? What is there that could not be done by such a craftsman? Almost nothing, except to escape death. Hereby I have explained in part the mischief and the usefulness, contained in this art, if it is real; and if it is real why has it not remained among men who desire it so much, having nothing to do with any deity? For I know that there are numberless people who would, to satisfy a whim, destroy God and all the universe; and if this necromancy, being, as it were, so necessary to men, has not been left among them, it can never have existed, nor will it ever exist according to the definition of the spirit, which is invisible in substance; for within the elements there are no incorporate things, because where there is no body, there is a vacuum; and no vacuum can exist in the elements because it would be immediately filled up. Turn over.

W. An. II. 242 a]

1214.

Delli spiriti.

²Abiāo insin qui dirieto a questa faccia detto, ³come la difinitiō dello spirito ⁴è vna potentia congiunta al corpo, perchè per se

Of spirits.

We have said, on the other side of this page, that the definition of a spirit is a power conjoined to a body; because it cannot

dichare le piante "selue" e chon . . perchotere . . ecquelli. 23. oltradiquesto . . tenpesste . . chultori. 24. ghuerra po . . chon. 25. nemicho aver potessta . . richolte . . ba. 26. po . . chessi . . acquella dicho . . chomāda. 27. effa . . essommergitrici. 28. chomāda attali. 29. resisstere . . ocholti. 30. gieme . . chorpo . . achosstu . . nessu. 31. fortezza [chef] inepugrabili . . chessalvar. 32. chuno. 33. lloriente . . opositi asspetti. 34. mi voio piu oltre asslendendo . . chosa che pera. 36. chonclusо "in parte" il ella . . chontiene. 37. essella . . none e resstata infralli . . chetta deside. 38. essol che infiniti ciene . . saddisfare. 39. ruinerebono . . chō . . essella. 40. allui tanta (?) . . mai nemmai. 41. chorpo. 42. none chose inchorporee . . chorpo e vachuo . . vachuo.
1214. 2. acquesta . . decto. 3. chome . . spirito [e vn ome nōch]. 4. chongiunta. 5. alchuna . . lochale. 6. essettu . . reggha

medesimo [5]reggiere nō si può, nè pigliare alcuna sorte di moto locale, [6]e se tu dirai che per se si regga, questo essere non può [7]dentro alli elemēti, perchè se lo spirito è quātità incor[8]porea, questa tal quantità è detta vacuo, e il ua[9]cuo non si da in natura; e dato che si desse, subito sa[10]rebbe riempiuto dalla ruina di quello elemento nel [11]qual il uacuo si gienerasse; adunque per la difinition del pe[12]so che dicie, la grauità è vna potētia accidentale creata [13] d'alcuno elemento tirato o sospinto nell'altro, seguita, che [14]nessuno elemēto, non pesando nel medesimo elemēto, e' pe[15]sa nell'elemēto superiore ch'è più lieve di lui; come si uede [16]la parte dell'acqua non à gravità o leuità più che l'altra [17]acqua, ma se tu la tirerai nell'aria, allora ella acqui[18]sterà gravezza, e se tu tirerai l'aria [19]sotto l'acqua, allora l'acqua, che si trova sopra tale [20]aria, acquista gravezza, la qual gravezza per se sostener [21]non si può, onde lì è neciessario la ruina, e così cade infra [22]l'acqua in quel loco ch'è vacuo d'essa acqua; tale ac[23]caderebbe nello spirito, stando infra li elemēti, chè al [24]continuo gienererebbe vacuo in quel tale elemēto, dove [25]lui si trovasse, per la qual cosa lì sarebbe neciessario la con[26]tinua fuga inverso il cielo, insinche vscito fusse di tali [27]elemēti.

SE LO SPIRITO TIENE CORPO INFRA LI [29]ELEMĒNTI.

[30]Abbiā provato, come lo spirito non può per se stare infra li [31]elementi sanza corpo, nè per se si può mouere per moto vo[32]lontario, se non è allo in sù; Ma al presente diremo co[33]me, pigliando corpo d'aria tale spirito, è necies[34]sario che s'infonda infra essa aria, perchè, s'elli stesse vnito, [35] e' sarebbe separato e caderebbe alla gieneratiō del uacuo, [36]come di sopra è detto; adunque è neciessario che, a volere [37]restare infra l'aria, che esso s'infonda in una quātità d'aria; e [38]se si mista coll'aria, elli seguita due inconvenienti, cioè [39]che elli leuifica quella quātità dell'aria dove esso si mista, e [40]per la qual cosa l'aria leuificata per se uola in alto,

move of its own accord, nor can it have any kind of motion in space; and if you were to say that it moves itself, this cannot be within the elements. For, if the spirit is an incorporeal quantity, this quantity is called a vacuum, and a vacuum does not exist in nature; and granting that one were formed, it would be immediately filled up by the rushing in of the element in which the vacuum had been generated. Therefore, from the definition of weight, which is this—Gravity is an accidental power, created by one element being drawn to or suspended in another—it follows that an element, not weighing anything compared with itself, has weight in the element above it and lighter than it; as we see that the parts of water have no gravity or levity compared with other water, but if you draw it up into the air, then it would acquire weight, and if you were to draw the air beneath the water then the water which remains above this air would acquire weight, which weight could not sustain itself by itself, whence collapse is inevitable. And this happens in water; wherever the vacuum may be in this water it will fall in; and this would happen with a spirit amid the elements, where it would continuously generate a vacuum in whatever element it might find itself, whence it would be inevitable that it should be constantly flying towards the sky until it had quitted these elements.

AS TO WHETHER A SPIRIT HAS A BODY AMID THE ELEMENTS.

We have proved that a spirit cannot exist of itself amid the elements without a body, nor can it move of itself by voluntary motion unless it be to rise upwards. But now we will say how such a spirit taking an aerial body would be inevitably melt into air; because if it remained united, it would be separated and fall to form a vacuum, as is said above; therefore it is inevitable, if it is to be able to remain suspended in the air, that it should absorb a certain quantity of air; and if it were mingled with the air, two difficulties arise; that is to say: It must rarefy that portion of the air with which it mingles; and for this cause the rarefied air must fly up of itself and will not

---

.. po. 7. perchessello .. inchor. 8. quantita [se] e decta vachuo. 9. chuo .. dato che se dessi subita. 10. reimpiuto ellemento. 11. uachuo si gienerassi. 13. ossosspinto. 14. ellemēto .. chome. 16. olleuita ellaltra. 17. massetti. 18. essettu. 19. chessi. 20. sosstener. 21. po onde le neciessario: chosi chade. 22. locho. 23. chaderebbe .. infralli. 24. chontinuo gienerrebbe. 25. trovassi .. chosa .. chon. 26. fugha .. vsscito fussi. 27. [adunque di reno]. 28. sello .. chorpo infralli. 30. losspirito .. infralli. 31. chorpo .. po. 32. sennon .. direno cho. 33. chorpo daria chettale. 34. chessinfonda .. perchesselli. 35. seperato e chadrebbe .. uachuo. 36. Chome .. decto. 37. resstare .. nuna. 38. ssesi .. chollaria .. coe. 39. leuificha .. missta. 40. chosa .. leuifichata .. ressta. 41. infrallaria .. a di questo. 42. disunisscie.

e non resta ⁴¹infra l'aria più grossa di lei; e oltre a questo tal uirtù ⁴²spirituale sparsa si disuniscie e altera suà natura, per la qual ⁴³cosa esso māca della prima virtù; aggiugnesi vn 3° incō⁴⁴veniente, e questo è, che tal corpo d'aria, preso dallo spirito, è ⁴⁵sottoposto alla penetratiō de' venti, li quali al continuo disu⁴⁶niscono e stracciano le parti vnite dell'aria, quelle rivolgiē⁴⁷do e raggirando infra l'altra aria; adunque lo spirito, in tale

remain among the air that is heavier than itself; and besides this the subtle spiritual essence disunites itself, and its nature is modified, by which that nature loses some of its first virtue. Added to these there is a third difficulty, and this is that such a body formed of air assumed by the spirits is exposed to the penetrating winds, which are incessantly sundering and dispersing the united portions of the air, revolving and whirling amidst the rest of the atmosphere; therefore the spirit which is infused in this

W. An. II. 201 *b* (M)] 1215.

aria infuso, sarebbe smēbrato overo sbranato e ²rotto insieme collo sbranamēto dell' aria, nella qual s'infuse.

air would be dismembered or rent and broken up with the rending of the air into which it was incorporated.

SE LO SPIRITO, AVĒDO PRESO CORPO ⁴D'ARIA, SI PUÒ PER SE MOVERE O NO.

AS TO WHETHER THE SPIRIT, HAVING TAKEN THIS BODY OF AIR, CAN MOVE OF ITSELF OR NOT.

⁵Inpossibile è che lo spirito, infuso a una quātità d'aria, ⁶possa movere essa aria; e questo si manifesta per la passa⁷ta dove dice ¶lo spirito leuifica quella quātità dell'aria, ⁸nella quale esso s'infonde; adunque tale aria ⁹si leuerà in alto sopra l'altra aria, e sarà moto fatto dell'a¹⁰ria per la sua leuità e nō per moto volontario dello spirito, e ¹¹se tale aria si scontra nel uēto per la 3ª di questo, essa ¹²aria sarà mossa dal uēto e nō dallo spirito in lei infuso.

It is impossible that the spirit infused into a certain quantity of air, should move this air; and this is proved by the above passage where it is said: the spirit rarefies that portion of the air in which it incorporates itself; therefore this air will rise high above the other air and there will be a motion of the air caused by its lightness and not by a voluntary movement of the spirit, and if this air is encountered by the wind, according to the 3rd of this, the air will be moved by the wind and not by the spirit incorporated in it.

SE LO SPIRITO PUÒ PARLARE O NO.

AS TO WHETHER THE SPIRIT CAN SPEAK OR NOT.

¹⁴Volendo mostrare, se lo spirito può parlare o no, è necies¹⁵sario in prima difinire che cosa e uocie, e come si giene¹⁶ra; e diremo in questo modo: la vocie è movimē¹⁷to d'aria confricata in corpo denso, e 'l corpo denso ¹⁸confricato nell'aria che è il medesimo, la qual cō¹⁹fricatione di denso con raro condensa il raro e fassi resis²⁰tētia, e ancora il uelocie raro nel tardo raro si condensa²¹no l'uno e l'altro ne' contatti, e fanno suono e grandissimo ²²strepito; e il suono ovvero mormorio fatto dal raro ²³che si move nel raro cō medi-

In order to prove whether the spirit can speak or not, it is necessary in the first place to define what a voice is and how it is generated; and we will say that the voice is, as it were, the movement of air in friction against a dense body, or a dense body in friction against the air,—which is the same thing. And this friction of the dense and the rare condenses the rare and causes resistance; again, the rare, when in swift motion, and the rare in slow motion condense each other when they come in contact and make a noise and very great uproar;

43. chosa . . mācha . . agiugnecisi. 44. ecquesto he chettal. 45. sottopossto . . venetratiō . . chontinuo. 46. nisscano esstracciano le parte. 47. ragirando infrallaltra . . losspirito in tale ·/.

1215. 1. issmēbrato . . sbranato er. 2. chollassbranamēto. 3. sello . . avēto . . chorpo . . po per . . onno. 5. Inpossibile che chello. 6. ecquesto. 7. losspirito leuificha. 9. essara. 11. essettale . . quessto. 13. sello ssspirito po . . onno. 14. mosstrare sello. 15. chosa . . chome. 16. quessto mōdo. 17. confrighata in chorpo . . chorpo. 18. chonfrighato. 19. freghatio . . chon . . chondensa . . effassi. 20. stēti e anchora. 21. ellaltro . . chontatti effanno sono. 22. sono over . . facto . . raro [nel ra]. 23. [ro] chessi . . chō . . chome. 24. fiama . . soni infrallaria. 25. rarro cō raro ecquando.

ocre movimēto, come ²⁴la grā fiamma gie-
neratricie di suoni infra l'aria; è 'l grandissi-
²⁵mo strepito fatto di raro cō raro, e quando
il uelocie ra²⁶ro penetra in mobile raro,
come la fiaṁa del foco vsci²⁷ta dalla bōbarda, e percossa infra l'aria, e ancora la
fiamma ²⁸vscita dal nuvolo percuote l'aria
nella gieneratiō delle saette; ²⁹Addunque
diremo che lo spirito non possa gienerar
vocie sanza ³⁰movimento d'aria, e aria in
lui non è, nè la può cacciare da se ³¹se elli
nō l'à, e se uol movere quella, nella quale
lui è infuso, ³²egli è neciessario che lo spirito multiplichi, e multiplicar nō ³³pvò se
lui non à quātità; e per la 4ª che dicie:
nessuno raro ³⁴si move se non à loco stabile, donde lui pigli il movimēto, e ³⁵mas-
simamēte auendosi a mouere lo elemento
nello elemēto ³⁶il quale nō si move da se,
se nō per vaporacione vniforme al ciētro
della ³⁷cosa vaporata, come accade nella
spugnia ristretta ³⁸in nella mano che sta
sotto l'acqua, dalla qual l'acqua fuggie per
qua³⁹lunche verso con equal movimēto per
le fessure interposte infra ⁴⁰le dita della
man che dentro a se la strīgnie;

⁴¹Se lo spirito à vocie articulata, ⁴²e se
lo spirito può essere audito, ⁴³e che cosa
è audire e vedere; ⁴⁴l'ōda della vocie va
⁴⁵per l'aria come le spetie delli ⁴⁶obbietti
vanno all'ochio.

and the sound or murmur made by the rare
moving through the rare with only mo-
derate swiftness, like a great flame gene-
rating noises in the air; and the tremendous uproar made by the rare mingling
with the rare, and when that air which is
both swift and rare rushes into that which is
itself rare and in motion, it is like the
flame of fire which issues from a big gun and
striking against the air; and again when a
flame issues from the cloud, there is a con-
cussion in the air as the bolt is generated.
Therefore we may say that the spirit cannot
produce a voice without movement of the air,
and air in it there is none, nor can it emit
what it has not; and if desires to move
that air in which it is incorporated, it is
necessary that the spirit should multiply itself,
and that cannot multiply which has no quantity. And in the 4th place it is said that no
rare body can move, if it has not a stable spot,
whence it may take its motion; much more
is it so when an element has to move within
its own element, which does not move of
itself, excepting by uniform evaporation at
the centre of the thing evaporated; as
occurs in a sponge squeezed in the hand
held under water; the water escapes in every
direction with equal movement through the
openings between the fingers of the hand in
which it is squeezed.

As to whether the spirit has an articulate
voice, and whether the spirit can be heard,
and what hearing is, and seeing; the wave
of the voice passes through the air as the
images of objects pass to the eye.

Br. M. 131a]   **1216.**

Nonentity.
Ogni quātità continva intellettualmē²te
è diuisibile in infinito;

³[Infra le · grandezze · delle · cose · che
sono infra noi ⁴l'essere · del nulla tiene · il
principato ·, e 'l suo · ofitio ⁵s'estende · infra
le · cose · che non àño · l'essere ·, e la sua

Every quantity is intellectually conceiv-
able as infinitely divisible.

[Amid the vastness of the things among
which we live, the existence of nothingness
holds the first place; its function extends
over all things that have no existence, and

26. chome . . focho vssci. 27. della . . perchossa infrallaria e anchora la fiama. 28. vsscita del nugholo e perchote. 29. direno chello. 30. nella puo chaccia ra dasse. 31. esse uol. 32. chello. 33. sellui . . nessuna. 34. locho. 36. move dasse se.
37. chome acondo nella . . risstretta. 38. inella . . chessta . . lacq"a" della. 39. chon . interposste. 40. della ma
che . . asse lasstrīgnie. 41. sello . . artichulata. 42. essello . . po . . vldito. 43. chosa. 44. e [chon] lōda. 45. echome.
1216. 3. Infralle grandeze . . chose chessono infrannoi. 5. sastende infralle chose . . ella. 8. alla sua. 9. soma. 11. somare . .

1216. Compare No. 916.

[6]essentia · risiede · apresso · del tenpo · infra 'l preterito [7]e 'l futuro, e nulla possiede del presente; Questo nulla [8]à la · sua · parte equale · al tutto ·, e 'l tutto · alla parte, [9]e 'l diuisibile · allo indiuisibile ·; e tal somma · produce nella [10]sua partitione come nella multiplicatione, [11]e nel suo sommare · quanto nel sottrare, come si dimostra [12]apresso delli aritmetici dello suo 10° carattere che rap[13]presenta esso nvllo; E la podestà sua non si estende infra [14]le cose di natura.]

[15][Quello che è · detto · niēte, · si ritrova solo nel tenpo · e nelle [16]parole; nel tenpo si trova · infra 'l preterito · e 'l futuro, [17]e nulla ritiene del presente ·, e così infra le · parole delle co[18]se che si dicono · che non sono . o che sono impossibili.]

[19]Apresso · del tenpo e' nulla · risiede infra 'l preterito e 'l futuro, [20]e niente possiede del presente, e apresso di natura e' s'ac[21]conpagnia infra le cose inpossibili ·, onde per quel ch'è [22]detto · e' non à l'essere; [23]Inperochè doue fusse [24]il nvlla, sarebbe dato il uacuo.

its essence, as regards time, lies precisely between the past and the future, and has nothing in the present. This nothingness has the part equal to the whole, and the whole to the part, the divisible to the indivisible; and the product of the sum is the same whether we divide or multiply, and in addition as in subtraction; as is proved by arithmeticians by their tenth figure which represents zero; and its power has not extension among the things of Nature.]

[What is called Nothingness is to be found only in time and in speech. In time it stands between the past and future and has no existence in the present; and thus in speech it is one of the things of which we say: They are not, or they are impossible.]

With regard to time, nothingness lies between the past and the future, and has nothing to do with the present, and as to its nature it is to be classed among things impossible: hence, from what has been said, it has no existence; because where there is nothing there would necessarily be a vacuum.

Br. M. 156a] **1217.**

ESEMPLO DELLA SAETTA FRA NUVOLI.

[2][O potente e già animato strumento dell'artificiosa natura, [3]a te nō valēdo le tue grā forze ti cōuiene abbādonare la trāquilla vita e obbedire alla legie, [4]che Iddio e 'l tēpo diede alla gienitrice natura.]

[7]O quāte volte furono vedute le īpavrite schiere [8]de' delfini e de' grā tonni fugire dal inpia tua furia, [9]e tu, che... [10]fulminando gienerasti nel mare subita tēpesta con grā busse e sommersione di navili cō grā[11]de ōdamēto, ēpiēdo gli scoperti liti degli īpavriti e sbigo[12]ttiti pesci, togliēdosi a te per lasciato mare rimasi in loco divenivano soperchia e [13]abbondante preda de' vicini popoli;

EXAMPLE OF THE LIGHTNING IN CLOUDS.

[O mighty and once living instrument of formative nature. Incapable of availing thyself of thy vast strength thou hast to abandon a life of stillness and to obey the law which God and time gave to procreative nature.]

Ah! how many a time the shoals of terrified dolphins and the huge tunny-fish were seen to flee before thy cruel fury, to escape; whilst thy fulminations raised in the sea a sudden tempest with buffeting and submersion of ships in the great waves; and filling the uncovered shores with the terrified and desperate fishes which fled from thee, and left by the sea, remained in spots where they became the abundant prey of the people in the neighbourhood.

Reflections on Nature (1217—1219).

---

sottrare. 12. arismetrici della sua 10ª caratta che re. 13. Ella .. nosistende. 15. Quello chche. 16. preterito hel. 17. infralle. 18. chessi dicono .. chessono inpossibile. 20. posiede .. apresso. 21. infralle .. inpossibile. 23. fussi.

1217. 1. essēplo .. nvuolli. 2. chōuene "abādonare la trāquila vita" obedire. 3. chel che .. die. 4. natura a tette nō ualse. 5. [\|\|\|\|\|\| haghagli arbri schiene cholle quali tu seghuitādo la tua]. 6. [pleda aprivis sol chavi "chonvetro" aprendo chō tē pes]. 8. dalfini .. tua | "tua" furia e cchupare. 9. ettu che chol veloce tramvre lalie cholla forci elluti choda. 10. fuminando gieneravi nel .. chō .. somersione .. chō. 11. schoperti .. essbigho. 12. pessci .. atte .. loccho .. divenivano superchava (?). 13. bodante pleda. 14. o tēpo chonsumatore delle chose āteri volgiēdole. 15. dai [lo] alle tratte

1217—1219. The character of the handwriting points to an early period of Leonardo's life. It has

become very indistinct, and is at present exceedingly difficult to decipher. Some passages remain doubtful.

¹⁴O tēpo, velocie predatore ¹⁵delle create cose, quāti rè, quāti popoli ài tu disfatti, e quā¹⁶te mutazioni di stati e vari
casi sono seguite dopo che la mara¹⁷vigliosa
forma di questo pescie qui morì ¹⁸per le
caverne e ritorte interiora; ¹⁹ora disfatto
dal tēpo patiēte giacci ī questo chiuso loco;
colle spolpate e ignivde ossa ²⁰ài fatto
armadura e sostegnio al sopra posto
mōte.

O time, swift robber of all created things,
how many kings, how many nations hast thou
undone, and how many changes of states
and of various events have happened since
the wondrous forms of this fish perished
here in this cavernous and winding recess.
Now destroyed by time thou liest patiently in
this confined space with bones stripped and
bare; serving as a support and prop for the
superimposed mountain.

Br. M. 155 b]

1218.

Rimase lo elemēto dell'acqua rīchiuso
īfra li crescivti argini de' fiumi, e si vede
'l mare ²jfra la crescivta terra ³e la cir-
cundatricie aria, avēdo a fasciare e circon-
⁴scrivere la moltificata machina della terra,
e la sua ⁵grossezza, che staua fra l'acqua
e lo elemēto del fuoco, ⁶rimāga molto ristretta e privata dalla bisogniosa acqua; i
fivmi ⁷rimarrāno senza le loro acque, la
fertile terra nō māderà piv leggieri ⁸frōde,
nō fieno piv i cāpi adornití dalle ricascāti
piāte; tutti ⁹li animali nō trovādo da pasciere le fresche erbe, morranno, e mā-
¹⁰cherà il cibo ai rapaci lioni e lupi e altri
animali che vivono ¹¹di ratto, e agli omini
dopo molti ripari cōverrà abādonare ¹²la
loro vita, e mācherà la gienerazione vmana;
a questo modo la fertile e fruttuosa terra
¹³abandonata rimarrà arida e sterile e per
rīchivso omo¹⁴re della acqua, rīchivsa nel
suo ventre, e per la vivace natura osserve-
¹⁵rà alquāto dello suo accrescimēto, tāto
che passata la fredda e so¹⁶ttile aria fia
costretta a terminare collo elemēto del fuoco;
¹⁷allora la sua superfice rimarrà in riarsa
cienere, e questo fia il termine ¹⁸della terrestre natura.

The watery element was left enclosed
between the raised banks of the rivers, and
the sea was seen between the uplifted earth
and the surrounding air which has to enve-
lope and enclose the ·complicated machine
of the earth, and whose mass, standing
between the water and the element of fire,
remained much restricted and deprived of
its indispensable moisture; the rivers will
be deprived of their waters, the fruitful
earth will put forth no more her light
verdure; the fields will no more be decked
with waving corn; all the animals, finding
no fresh grass for pasture, will die and food
will then be lacking to the lions and wolves
and other beasts of prey, and to men who
after many efforts will be compelled to
abandon their life, and the human race will
die out. In this way the fertile and fruitful
earth will remain deserted, arid and sterile
from the water being shut up in its interior,
and from the activity of nature it will continue a little time to increase until the cold
and subtle air being gone, it will be forced
to end with the element of fire; and then its
surface will be left burnt up to cinder and
this will be the end of all terrestrial nature.

Br. M. 156 b]

1219.

Perchè la natura non ordinò che l'uno
animale nō uivesse ²dalla morte dell altro?
³la natura, essēdo vaga e pigliādo piacere

Why did nature not ordain that one
animal should not live by the death of
another? Nature, being inconstant and

vite nvuove e varie abitazioni [o quante]. 16. tēpo [vīcitore] velocie pledator. 17. chleate chose . . dissfatti. 10. disstati
e vari chasi sono seghuite poche la mara. 19. vgliosa forma di questo pesscie qui mòri. 20. per lechavernole e ritorte
interiora. 21. ora "disfato dal tēpo" pazēte dicei . . locho cholle jsspogliate "spolpate". 22. sosstegnio . . possto.
1218. 1. dela acq"a" . . cresscivte argine. 2. jnfralla cressciuta tera. 3. chotra che la circhīatricie . . affasciare e circho.
4. moltifichata . . terra chella. 5. grosseza chesstaua . . fralla aqua . . fuocho. 6. rimāgha . . dela . . aqua. 7. rima-
rāno . . acq. 8. chāpi adornide delle richasschati biade tuti. 9. morano. 10. cher il cibo a . . ellupe . . vano. 11. rato
. . chō prvra. 12. vita | "e māchera la gieneraziode vmana" a . . modo [la tera] fertile e frutuosa tera. 13. rimara alida
essterile. 14. "acq" . . per la la. 15. fredda esso. 16. chosstretta . . cholo . . fuocho 17. ri nara īnriarsa (?) cienere.
18. teresstre.
1219. 1. chō ¶ perche . . chelluno . . uivessi. 3. pro ¶ la . vagha . . del "creare e fare" "[fare]" chōtinv. 4. efforme [mette

1217. 1218. Compare No. 1339, written on the same sheet.

del creare e fare cōtin⁴ue vite e forme, perchè cogni⁵oscie che sono accrescimēto della
sua terrestre materia, ⁶è volonterosa e piv
presta col suo creare che 'l tēpo col cō-
⁷sumare; e però à ordinato che molti animali sieno cibo l'uno del⁸l'altro; e nō sod-
disfaciēdo questo a simile desiderio, e' spesso
⁹māda fuora cierti avelenati e pestilēti
vapori sopra le grā moltipli¹⁰cazioni e cō-
gregazioni d'animali, e massime sopra gli
omini, che fanno ¹¹grāde accrescimēto, perchè altri animali ¹²nō si cibano di loro, e
tolte via le cagioni mācherānno li effetti;
¹³adūque questa terra cierca di mācare di
sua vita, desiderādo ¹⁴la continva moltipli-
cazione; per la tua assegniata e demon-
strata ¹⁵ragione spesso li effetti sommigliano
le loro cagioni; gli animali so¹⁶no esēplo
della vita mōdiale.

taking pleasure in creating and making constantly new lives and forms, because she knows
that her terrestrial materials become thereby
augmented, is more ready and more swift in
her creating, than time in his destruction; and
so she has ordained that many animals shall be
food for others. Nay, this not satisfying her desire, to the same end she frequently sends forth
certain poisonous and pestilential vapours upon
the vast increase and congregation of animals; and most of all upon men, who increase vastly because other animals do not
feed upon them; and, the causes being removed, the effects would not follow. This earth
therefore seeks to lose its life, desiring only
continual reproduction; and as, by the argument you bring forward and demonstrate, like
effects always follow like causes, animals
are the image of the world.

piv vite sopra la terra che] perche. 5. oꞩcie chessono accrescimēto. 6. pressta chol . . chol chō. 8. sosdisfaciēdo qussto
assimile . . esspesso. 9. vapori "e pestilētie chontinva pessta" sopra. 10. chazioni e chō greghazioni . . fano. 11. accres-
scimēto . . altr. 12. chagione. 13. chō ¶ adūque . . ciercha . . māchare. 14. chóntinva moltiplichazione . . emosstra.
15. somigliano . . chagioni. 16. dela.

2

1

3

Héliog Dujardin.

Imp. Eudes.

Plate C is reproduced on the following two pages.

Héliog. Dujardin.

2

3

8°°
2 5.
4 °°
16 °°
2 0 °°

2

1

3

4

Héliog. Dujardin.

Imp. Eudes.

Heliog. Dujardin. Imp. Eudes.

1

5

2

4

3

Héliog. Dujardin.

Imp. Eudes.

Héliog. Dujardin.

Imp. Eudes.

Plate CX will be found following Plate CXIV.

1

Héliog. Dujardin.

2

Imp. Eudes.

Imp. Eudes.

Héliog Dujardin.

Héliog. Dujardin.

Imp. Eudes.

Humorous Writings.

Just as Michaelangelo's occasional poems reflect his private life as well as the general disposition of his mind, we may find in the writings collected in this section, the transcript of Leonardo's fanciful nature, and we should probably not be far wrong in assuming, that he himself had recited these fables in the company of his friends or at the court festivals of princes and patrons. Era tanto piacevole nella conversazione — *so relates Vasari* — che tirava a sè gli animi delle genti. *And Paulus Jovius says in his short biography of the artist:* Fuit ingenio valde comi, nitido, liberali, vultu autem longe venustissimo, et cum elegantiae omnis deliciarumque maxime theatralium mirificus inventor ac arbiter esset, ad lyramque scito caneret, cunctis per omnem aetatem principibus mire placuit. *There can be no doubt that the fables are the original offspring of Leonardo's brain, and not borrowed from any foreign source; indeed the schemes and plans for the composition of fables collected in division V seem to afford an external proof of this, if the fables themselves did not render it self-evident. Several of them— for instance No.* 1279—*are so strikingly characteristic of Leonardo's views of natural science that we cannot do them justice till we are acquainted with his theories on such subjects; and this is equally true of the 'Prophecies'.*

I have prefixed to these quaint writings the 'Studies on the life and habits of animals' which are singular from their peculiar aphoristic style, and I have transcribed them in exactly the order in which they are written in MS. H. This is one of the very rare instances in which one subject is treated in a consecutive series of notes, all in one MS., and Leonardo has also departed from his ordinary habits, by occasionally not completing the text on the page it is begun. These brief notes of a somewhat mysterious bearing have been placed here, simply because they may possibly have been intended to serve as hints for fables or allegories. They can scarcely be regarded as preparatory for a natural history; rather they would seem to be extracts. On the one hand the names

of some of the animals seem to prove that Leonardo could not here be recording obser-
vations of his own; on the other hand the notes on their habits and life appear to me
to dwell precisely on what must have interested him most—so far as it is possible to
form any complete estimate of his nature and tastes.

In No. 1293 lines 1—10, we have a sketch of a scheme for grouping the Prophe-
cies. I have not however availed myself of it as a clue to their arrangement here
because, in the first place, the texts are not so numerous as to render the suggested
classification useful to the reader, and, also, because in reading the long series, as they
occur in the original, we may follow the author's mind; and here and there it is
not difficult to see how one theme suggested another. I have however regarded
Leonardo's scheme for the classification of the Prophecies as available for that of the
Fables and Jests, and have. adhered to it as far as possible.

Among the humourous writings I might perhaps have included the 'Rebusses', of
which there are several in the collection of Leonardo's drawings at Windsor; it seems
to me not likely that many or all of them could be solved at the present day and the
MSS. throw no light on them. Nor should I be justified if I intended to include in
the literary works the well-known caricatures of human faces attributed to Leonardo—
of which, however, it may be incidentally observed, the greater number are in my
opinion undoubtedly spurious. Two only have necessarily been given owing to their
presence in text, which it was desired to reproduce: Vol. I page 326, and Pl. CXXII.
It can scarcely be doubted that some satirical intention is conveyed by the drawing on
Pl. LXIV (text No. 688).

My reason for not presenting Leonardo to the reader as a poet is the fact that
the maxims and morals in verse which have been ascribed to him, are not to be found
in the manuscripts, and Prof. Uzielli has already proved that they cannot be by him.
Hence it would seem that only a few short verses can be attributed to him with any
certainty.

I.

STUDIES ON THE LIFE AND HABITS OF ANIMALS.

1220.

AMORE DI UIRTÙ.

²Cardellino · è · vno · vcciello · jl quale ³si dice · che, essendo · esso · portato · dinanzi ⁴a vno · infermo · che, se 'l detto · infermo · de⁵be morire, questo · ucciello · li uolta · la te⁶sta per lo · cōtrario · e mai · lo riguarda ·, e se ⁷esso infermo · debe · scampare ·, questo ⁸vcciello · mai · l'abandona · di uista, anzi ⁹è causa · di leuarli · ogni · malattia;

¹⁰Similmēte è · l'amore · di uirtù ·; nō guar¹¹da · mai · cosa · vile ·, nè trista; anzi di¹²mora · senpre · in cose oneste · e uirtuo-¹³se ·, e rimpatria in cor giētile a si¹⁴militudine degli uccielli nelle uerdi selue ¹⁵sopra · i fioriti rami ·; e si dimostra piv ¹⁶esso amore nelle auersità che nelle prosperi¹⁷tà, faciēdo come il lume che piv risplēde ¹⁸doue truova piv tenebroso · sito.

THE LOVE OF VIRTUE.

The gold-finch is a bird of which it is related that, when it is carried into the presence of a sick person, if the sick man is going to die, the bird turns away its head and never looks at him; but if the sick man is to be saved the bird never loses sight of him but is the cause of curing him of all his sickness.

Like unto this is the love of virtue. It never looks at any vile or base thing, but rather clings always to pure and virtuous things and takes up its abode in a noble heart; as the birds do in green woods on flowery branches. And this Love shows itself more in adversity than in prosperity; as light does, which shines most where the place is darkest.

1221.

INVIDIA.

²Del nibbio · si leggie ·, che quādo esso uede ³i sua figlioli nel nido esser di troppa gra⁴ssezza, che per invidia egli becca loro le coste e tiē⁵gli sanza māgiare.

ENVY.

We read of the kite that, when it sees its young ones growing too big in the nest, out of envy it pecks their sides, and keeps them without food.

1220. 2. callendrino e uno. 4. chessel. 5. quessto. 6. esse. 7. isschanpare quessto. 9. chausa .. hogni. 11. trissta. 12. honeste he. 13. ripatria [senpre] in .. assi. 15. essi .. prossperi. 17. comelume .. rissplēde.

1221. 2. nibio si legie. 4. ssezza che "per inuidia" egli gli beccha .. cosste ettiē. 6. allegreza. 7. lalegreza e apropriata.

ALLEGREZZA.

[7] L'allegrezza · è appropriata · al gallo · che [8] d'ogni piccola · cosa · si rallegra e cā- [9] ta · con vari e scherzāti mouimēti.

TRISTEZZA.

[11] La tristezza · s'assomiglia al corbo, il quale, [12] quādo uede i sua nati figlioli esser biā[13]chi, che per lo grāde dolore si parte cō tristo [14] rammarichio, gl'abādona e nō gli pascie · [15] īsino che non gli vede alquāte poche pēne [16] nere.

CHEERFULNESS.

Cheerfulness is proper to the cock, which rejoices over every little thing, and crows with varied and lively movements.

SADNESS.

Sadness resembles the raven, which, when it sees its young ones born white, departs in great grief, and abandons them with doleful lamentations, and does not feed them until it sees in them some few black feathers.

H.1 6a]   1222.

PACE.

[2] Del castoro si legge che, quādo è perse[3]guitato ·, cōnosciēdo · essere · per la virtù [4] de' sua medicinali · testiculi, esso nō po[5]tēdo piv fuggire, si ferma, e per auere [6] pace coi cacciatori coi sua tagliēti [7] dēti si spicca i testiculi e li lascia a sua [8] nimici.

IRA.

[10] Dell'orso si dice che · quādo va alle case [11] delle api per torre loro il mele, esse [12] api cōminciando a pūgierlo, che lui lasci[13]a il mele e corre alla vendetta, e volē[14]dosi cō tutte quelle che lo mordono vē[15]dicare, cō nessuna si uēdica, in modo che la [16] sua ira si cōuerte in rabbia, e gittatosi [17] in terra colle mani e coi piedi inasprādo [18] indarno da quelle si difende.

PEACE.

We read of the beaver that when it is pursued, knowing that it is for the virtue [contained] in its medicinal testicles and not being able to escape, it stops; and to be at peace with its pursuers, it bites off its testicles with its sharp teeth, and leaves them to its enemies.

RAGE.

It is said of the bear that when it goes to the haunts of bees to take their honey, the bees having begun to sting him he leaves the honey and rushes to revenge himself. And as he seeks to be revenged on all those that sting him, he is revenged on none; in such wise that his rage is turned to madness, and he flings himself on the ground, vainly exasperating, by his hands and feet, the foes against which he is defending himself.

H.1 6b]   1223.

GRATITUDINE.

[2] La virtù · della gratitudine si dice [3] essere piv nelli uccielli detti upupa, [4] i quali, conosciēdo il benificio della [5] ricievuta vita e nvtrimēto dal pa[6]dre e dalla lor madre, quādo li uedo[7]no vechi fanno loro vno nido e li [8] covano e li nutriscono, e cavā loro [9] col becco le vechie e triste penne, e [10] cō cierte erbe li rēdano la uista, [11] in modo che ritornano in prosertà.

GRATITUDE.

The virtue of gratitude is said to be more [developed] in the birds called hoopoes which, knowing the benefits of life and food, they have received from their father and their mother, when they see them grow old, make a nest for them and brood over them and feed them, and with their beaks pull out their old and shabby feathers; and then, with a certain herb restore their sight so that they return to a prosperous state.

---

8. pichola chosa . . echā. 9. coūari esscerzati. 10. tristeza. 11. tristeza sasomiglia al corb. 14. ramarichio. 15. nogli . . poce.

1222. 2. he. 3. cōnossciēdo. 5. fugire. 7. sisspicha . . elli lasscia assua. 11. ave. 12. ave lo cōmiciato a pūgiere o di lui lassci. 13. core. 14. chello mordano. 15. imodo chella. 17. tero cholle mani eco . . inaspādo. 18. dacquelle.

1223. 1. [miscericordia] over graditudine. 3. detti upica. 4. conosciēdo . . nvtrimēdo. 6. ueda. 7. fano . . elli. 8. elli notrisscano. 9. becho . . trisste. 10. chō . . rēdano. 11. imodo. 13. rosspo si passcie . . essenpre.

AVARITIA.

[13] Il rospo si pascie di terra e senpre [14] sta macro, perchè nō si satia; tant'è [15] il timore che essa terra nō li manchi.

AVARICE.

The toad feeds on earth and always remains lean; because it never eats enough:— it is so afraid lest it should want for earth.

H.[1] 7 a]

1224.

INGRATITUDINE.

[2] I colonbi sono assimigliati alla [3] ingratitudine, inperochè quādo [4] sono in età che non abbino piv biso[5]gnio d'essere cibati, cominciano a [6] cōbattere col padre; e nō finisce [7] essa pugnia insino a tāto che [8] caccia il padre e togli la moglie [9] faciendose la sua.

INGRATITUDE.

Pigeons are a symbol of ingratitude; for when they are old enough no longer to need to be fed, they begin to fight with their father, and this struggle does not end until the young one drives the father out and takes the hen and makes her his own.

CRUDELTÀ.

[11] Il basilisco · è di tanta crudeltà che, [12] quādo colla sua venenosa vista nō può [13] occidere li animali, si volta all'erbe [14] e le piāte, e fermādo in quelle la sua [15] vista le fa seccare.

CRUELTY.

The basilisk is so utterly cruel that when it cannot kill animals by its baleful gaze, it turns upon herbs and plants, and fixing its gaze on them withers them up.

H.[1] 7 b]

1225.

LIBERALITÀ.

[2] Dell'aquila si dice che non à mai si grā [3] fame ·, che non lasci parte della sua [4] preda · a quelli vcciegli che gli son [5] dintorno ·, i quali, nō potēdosi per se [6] pasciere, è neciessario che sieno cor[7]teggiatori d'essa aquila, perchè in tal [8] modo si cibano.

GENEROSITY.

It is said of the eagle that it is never so hungry but that it will leave a part of its prey for the birds that are round it, which, being unable to provide their own food, are necessarily dependent on the eagle, since it is thus that they obtain food.

CORETTIONE.

[10] Quādo il lupo · va asentito intorno [11] a qualche stallo di bestiame, e che per caso [12] esso pōga il piede in fallo in modo facci [13] strepito, egli si morde il piè per correg[14]giere se da tale errore.

DISCIPLINE.

When the wolf goes cunningly round some stable of cattle, and by accident puts his foot in a trap, so that he makes a noise, he bites his foot off to punish himself for his folly.

H.[1] 8 a]

1226.

LUSINGHE OVER SIRENE.

[2] La sirena si dolcemēte cāta [3] che adormēta i marinari, e essa [4] mōta sopra i navili e occide li a[5]dormētati marinari.

FLATTERERS OR SYRENS.

The syren sings so sweetly that she lulls the mariners to sleep; then she climbs upon the ships and kills the sleeping mariners.

1224. 4. abino. 5. comiciano. 6. finissce. 7. attāto. 8. cacia . . toli. 9. rafaciendosela. 11. basalisscio. 12. vissta nōpo. 14. elle . . effermādo . . lassua. 15. sechare.

1225. 3. nollassci. 4. acquelli . chelle. 6. passciere . . chessieno. 7. tegiatori. 9. corettione. 10. assentito. 11. acqualche. 12. imodo faci. 13. strepido . . percore. 14. tatale.

1226. 1. lusingeover s\\\\\\e. 8. vcidē. 9. semēza. 10. pascano. 13. caciatori 'vesta. 14. core. 15. cho gra . . vīciodale cordi.

PRUDĒTIA.

[7]La formica per naturale cōsiglio [8]provede la state per lo uerno, uccidē[9]do le racolte semēze, perchè nō ri[10]nascino, e di quelle al tenpo si pascono.

PAZZIA.

[12]Il bo saluatico avēdo in odio il co-[13]lore rosso, i cacciatori vestono di rosso [14]il pedal d'una piāta, e esso bo corre a [15]quella e cō gran furia v'inchioda le corti-[16]ne, ōde i cacciatori l'uccidono.

PRUDENCE.

The ant, by her natural foresight provides in the summer for the winter, killing the seeds she harvests that they may not germinate, and on them, in due time she feeds.

FOLLY.

The wild bull having a horror of a red colour, the hunters dress up the trunk of a tree with red and the bull runs at this with great frenzy, thus fixing his horns, and forthwith the hunters kill him there.

H.[1] 8b].　　　　　　　1227.

GIVSTITIA.

[2]E' si può · assimigliare la uirtù della giusti[3]tia allo rè delle api, il quale ordina [4]e dispone ogni cosa cō ragione, impero-[5]chè alcune api sono ordinate anda[6]re per fiori, altre ordinate a lavora[7]re, altre a cō-battere colle vespe, [8]altre a leuare le spor-citie, altre [9]a accōpagniare e corteggiare il loro rè; e quā[10]do è vecchio e sāza ali, esse lo portano, [11]e se ui vna māca di suo ofi-tio, sāza [12]alcuna remissione è punita.

VERITÀ.

[14]Benchè le pernici rubino l'oua l'una all'al[15]tra, nōdimeno i figlioli nati d'esse ova [16]senpre ritornano alla lor uera madre.

JUSTICE.

We may liken the virtue of Justice to the king of the bees which orders and arranges every thing with judgment. For some bees are ordered to go to the flowers, others are ordered to labour, others to fight with the wasps, others to clear away all dirt, others to accompagny and escort the king; and when he is old and has no wings they carry him. And if one of them fails in his duty, he is punished without reprieve.

TRUTH.

Although partridges steal each other's eggs, nevertheless the young born of these eggs always return to their true mother.

H.[1] 9a]　　　　　　　1228.

FEDELTÀ OVER LEALTÀ.

[2]Le grù son tanto fedeli e leali al lòro rè [3]che la notte, quādo lui dorme, alcune vā[4]no dintorno al prato per guardare da lū[5]ga ·; altre ne stanno dapresso e tengono [6]vno sasso ciascuna in piè, che se 'l son[7]no le uincesse, essa pietra caderebbe e fa[8]rebbe tal romore, ch'essi ridesterebbero; e [9]altre vi sono che insieme intorno al rè dor[10]mono, e ciò fanno ogni notte scābiādosi, [11]acciò chè loro rè nō uogliono mācare.

FIDELITY, OR LOYALTY.

The cranes are so faithful and loyal to their king, that at night, when he is sleeping, some of them go round the field to keep watch at a distance; others remain near, each holding a stone in his foot, so that if sleep should overcome them, this stone would fall and make so much noise that they would wake up again. And there are others which sleep together round the king; and this they do every night, changing in turn so that their king may never find them wanting.

16. iccaciatori loccidano.
1227. 2. delagusti. 3. ave. 4. chosa . . ipero. 5. alchuna ave. 6. allauora. 7. chōbottere cholle vesspe. 8. spurcitie. 9. acō-pagnare e cortegiare loree. 10. essāza. 11. esse . . mācha. 14. benchelle.
1228. 1. lialta. 2. allorere. 3. chella. 5. ettengano. 6. sasso [per] ciascuna . . chesselso. 7. vinciessi . . chaderebe effa. 8. rebe . . ridesterebono. 9. chensieme . . are. 10. mano . . fano. 11. acio chollorore nō uē gli a mācare. 13. torma dissga.

FALSITÀ.

[13]La uolpe quãdo vede alcuna torma di sgar[14]ze o taccole o simili uccielli, subito si gitta in ter[15]ra in modo colla bocca aperta che par morta, [16]e essi uccielli le uogliono beccare la lingua, e essa [17]gli piglia la testa.

FALSEHOOD.

The fox when it sees a flock of herons or magpies or birds of that kind, suddenly flings himself on the ground with his mouth open to look as he were dead; and these birds want to peck at his tongue, and he bites off their heads.

H.¹ 9b]

1229.

BUGIA.

[2]La talpa · à li ochi molto · piccoli ·, e senpre [3]sta · sotto · terra · e tanto · viue ·, quanto essa [4]sta occulta ·, e come · viene alla luce [5]subito · more · perchè si fa nota; così la bugia.

LIES.

The mole has very small eyes and it always lives under ground; and it lives as long as it is in the dark but when it comes into the light it dies immediately, because it becomes known;—and so it is with lies.

FORTEZZA.

[7]Il lione · mai · teme ·, anzi · cõ forte animo [8]pugna cõ fiera battaglia contra la mol-[9]titudine de' cacciatori ·, senpre ciercãdo [10]offendere · il primo · che l'offese.

VALOUR.

The lion is never afraid, but rather fights with a bold spirit and savage onslaught against a multitude of hunters, always seeking to injure the first that injures him.

TIMORE OVER UILTÀ.

[12]La lepre senpre teme ·, e le foglie che ca[13]dono dalle piãte · per autunno senpre la tẽ[14]gono in timore, e 'l piv delle volte in fuga.

FEAR OR COWARDICE.

The hare is always frightened; and the leaves that fall from the trees in autumn always keep him in terror and generally put him to flight.

H.¹ 10a]

1230.

MAGNIANIMITÀ.

[2]Il falcone nõ preda · mai ·, se non uc-celli [3]grossi ·, e prima si lascierebbe morire che [4]si cibasse de' piccoli, o che mangiasse car[5]ne fetida.

MAGNANIMITY.

The falcon never preys but on large birds; and it will let itself die rather than feed on little ones, or eat stinking meat.

VANA GLORIA.

[7]In questo vitio si legge del pavone es-ser[8]li più che altro animale sottoposto, [9]perchè senpre contempla in nella bellezza [10]della sua coda, quella allargãdo in for[11]ma di rota e col suo grido trae a se [12]la uista de' circustãti animali;
[13]E questo · è l'ultimo vitio che si possa [14]vinciere.

VAIN GLORY.

As regards this vice, we read that the peacock is more guilty of it than any other animal. For it is always contemplating the beauty of its tail, which it spreads in the form of a wheel, and by its cries attracts to itself the gaze of the creatures that surround it.
And this is the last vice to be conquered.

14. tacole ossimili . . sibito . . inte. 15. imodo . .. bocha. 16. occielli . . uoglia becare . . e ess.

1229. 1. busia. 2. picioli essenpre. 3. ettonto. 4. occhulta e chome. 6. forteza. 7. ilione . . chõ. 8. puglia. 9. caciatori. 10. chellofese. 12. elle . . che cha. 13. giano delle . . altunno. 14. gano.

1230. 2. senone ucieli. 3. lasscierebe. 4. chessicibassi de picholi. 5. feteda. 6. groria. 7. legie del pagone. 9. chontenpra inella belleza. 10. chol . . asse.

H.¹ 10 b]　　　　　　　　**1231.**

CONSTANTIA.

²Alla costantia · s'assimiglia · la fenice, ³la quale intēdēdo per natura la sua re-⁴novatione ·, è costante a sostenere le cuo-centi ⁵fiamme · le quali la cōsumano, e poi ⁶di novo rinascie.

INCŌSTANTIA.

⁸Il rondone si mette per la incostantia, ⁹il quale senpre sta in moto per nō sop-porta¹⁰re alcuno minimo disagio.

TĒPERĀZA.

¹²Il camello è il piv · lussurioso animale ¹³che sia, e andrebbe mille miglia dirieto a vna ¹⁴camella ·, e se vsasse cōtinvo cō la madre o so¹⁵relle, mai le tocca; tāto si sa bē tēperare.

CONSTANCY.

Constancy may be symbolised by the phoenix which, knowing that by nature it must be resuscitated, has the constancy to endure the burning flames which consume it, and then it rises anew.

INCONSTANCY.

The swallow may serve for Inconstancy, for it is always in movement, since it cannot endure the smallest discomfort.

CONTINENCE.

The camel is the most lustful animal there is, and will follow the female for a thousand miles. But if you keep it con-stantly with its mother or sister it will leave them alone, so temperate is its nature.

H.¹ 11 a]　　　　　　　　**1232.**

INTĒPERANZA.

²Il liocorno overo vnicorno · per la sua intē³perāza e nō sapersi uīciere per lo di-letto che à ⁴delle donzelle · dimētica la sua ferocità ⁵e saluatichezza; ponēdo da cāto ogni sospetto ⁶va alla sedente donzella e se le adormē⁷ta · in grēbo ·, e i cacciatori in tal modo ⁸lo pigliano.

VMILITÀ.

¹⁰Dell'umilità si uede somma speriētia nello ¹¹agnello, il quale si sottomette a ogni ani¹²male; e quādo per cibo son dati ai incarcerati ¹³leoni ·, a quelli si sottomet-tono come alla ¹⁴propria madre, in modo che spesse volte ¹⁵si è visto i lioni non li volere occidere.

INCONTINENCE.

The unicorn, through its intemperance and not knowing how to control itself, for the love it bears to fair maidens forgets its ferocity and wildness; and laying aside all fear it will go up to a seated damsel and go to sleep in her lap, and thus the hunters take it.

HUMILITY.

We see the most striking example of humility in the lamb which will submit to any animal; and when they are given for food to imprisoned lions they are as gentle to them as to their own mother, so that very often it has been seen that the lions forbear to kill them.

H.¹ 11 b]　　　　　　　　**1233.**

SUPERBIA.

²Il falcone per la sua alterigia e super-bia ³vole signioreggiare · e soprafare tutti li al⁴tri vccielli · che sono di rapina, e sempre ⁵desidera · essere solo, e spesse volte si è ⁶veduto il falcone assaltare l'aquila, ⁷regina delli vccielli.

PRIDE.

The falcon, by reason of its haughtiness and pride, is fain to lord it and rule over all the other birds of prey, and longs to be sole and supreme; and very often the falcon has been seen to assault the eagle, the Queen of birds.

1231. 2. sasomiglia. 3. intēdedo. 4. sosstene lecocē 5. ti fiame. 6. ti fiame rinasscie. 8. incosstantia. 9. imoto . . soporta. 13. chessia e ādebe. 14. esse vsassi . . osso. 15. tocha . . teprare.

1232. 2. lalicorno. 4. dimēticha. 5. saluaticheza . . sospeto. 6. essele. 7. chaciatori. 10. soma. 12. dati [ai dimessti] alin-carcerati. 13. cileoni . . sottomettano. 14. imodo chesspesse. 15. se visto . . noli.

1233. 2. essuperbia. 3. signioregiare essopra. 4. chesso di rapina esse. 5. esspesse voltese. 8. asstinentia. 9. assino. 10. et-

ASTINENTIA.

[9]Il saluatico · asino · quãdo · va alla [10]fonte · per bere · e trova · l'acqua intor[11]bidata, non avrà mai si grã sete, che nõ [12]s'astẽga di bere, e aspetti ch'essa acqua [13]si richiari.

GOLA.

[15]Il vulture · è tanto sottoposto alla gola [16]che andrebbe mille miglia per mãgiare [17]d'una carognia, e per questo seguita li eserciti.

ABSTINENCE.

The wild ass, when it goes to the well to drink, and finds the water troubled, is never so thirsty but that it will abstain from drinking, and wait till the water is clear again.

GLUTTONY.

The vulture is so addicted to gluttony that it will go a thousand miles to eat a carrion [carcase]; therefore is it that it follows armies.

H.I 12 a]   **1234.**

CASTITÀ.

[2]La tortora nõ fa mai fallo al suo cõpagnio, [3]e se l'uno more, l'altro osserua perpetua ca[4]stità e non si posa mai su ramo verde e nõ [5]beue mai acqua chiara.

LUSSURIA.

[7]Il pipistrello per la sua sfrenata lussu-[8]ria non osserua alcuno vniversale mo[9]do di lussuria, anzi maschio cõ maschio, [10]femina cõ femina, siccome a caso si tro[11]vano insieme, vsano il lor coito.

MODERANZA.

[13]L'ermellino per la sua moderãtia nõ mãgia [14]se non vna sola volta il dì, e prima si lascia pi[15]gliare dai cacciatori che volere fugire [16]nella infangata tana, [17]per nõ maculare la sua giẽtilezza.

CHASTITY.

The turtle-dove is never false to its mate; and if one dies the other preserves perpetual chastity, and never again sits on a green bough, nor ever again drinks of clear water.

UNCHASTITY.

The bat, owing to unbridled lust, observes no universal rule in pairing, but males with males and females with females pair promiscuously, as it may happen.

MODERATION.

The ermine out of moderation never eats but once in the day; it will rather let itself be taken by the hunters than take refuge in a dirty lair, in order not to stain its purity.

H.I 12 b]   **1235.**

AQUILA.

[2]L'aquila, quãdo è vechia, vola tãto [3]in alto, che abbrucia le sue penne, e na[4]tura cõsente che si rinoui in giovẽtù, [5]cadendo nella poca acqua; [6]E se i sua nati nõ possono tenere la uista [7]nel sole—; nõ li pascie di nessuno uccello, [8]che nõ uole morire; non s'accostano

THE EAGLE.

The eagle when it is old flies so high that it · scorches its feathers, and Nature allowing that it should renew its youth, it falls into shallow water [5]. And if its young ones cannot bear to gaze on the sun [6]—; it does not feed them with any bird, that does not wish to die. Animals which much fear

---

truova. 11. non ara . . sede. 12. asspetti . . acqa. 13. sirisciari. 15. la voltore ettanto sotto possto. 16. andrebe mile miglia [all] per. 17. per que seguita.

1234. 1. casstita. 3. esselluno. 4. enosi. 7. palpisstrello . . isfrenata. 9. masscio cõ masscio. 10. sichome achaso. 14. senvna . . lasscia. 15. gliare a caciatori. 17. giẽtileza.

1235. 3. abrucia . . pene. 4. chessi. 5. cadẽ nella poca acqua. 6. esse . . nõ posso tene. 7. pascie nessuno vciel . . morire

1235. 5. 6. The meaning is obscure.

al suo [9]nido gli animali che forte la tema[10]no, ma essa a lor nō noce, senpre [11]lascia rimanēte della sua preda.

LUMERPA,—FAMA.

[13]Questa nascie nell' Asia Maggiore, e splē[14]de si forte che toglie le sue ōbre, e morendo [15]nō perde esso lume, e mai li cadono giù le [16]penne, e la penna che si spicca piv nō [17]luce.

it do not approach its nest, although it does not hurt them. It always leaves part of its prey uneaten.

LUMERPA,—FAME.

This is found in Asia Major, and shines so brightly that it absorbs its own shadow, and when it dies it does not lose this light, and its feathers never fall out, but a feather pulled out shines no longer.

PELICANO.

[2]Questo porta grāde amore a sua nati, [3]e trouādo quelli nel nido morti dal [4]serpēte, si pūgie a riscōtro al core e, col [5]suo piovente sangue bagniādoli, li tor[6]na in vita.

THE PELICAN.

This bird has a great love for its young; and when it finds them in its nest dead from a serpent's bite, it pierces itself to the heart, and with its blood it bathes them till they return to life.

SALAMĀDRA.

[8]Questo · non à mēbra passive, e nō si [9]cura d'altro cibo che di foco, e spesso in [10]quello rinova la sua scorza. [11]La salamādra nel foco [12]rinova la sua scorza; — [13]per la [14]vir[15]tù.

THE SALAMANDER.

This has no digestive organs, and gets no food but from the fire, in which it constantly renews its scaly skin.

The salamander, which renews its scaly skin in the fire,—for virtue.

CAMELEO.

[16]Questo viue d'aria, e ī quella sta su[17]bietto a tutti li uccielli, e per stare piv [18]saluo vola sopra le nvvole; e truoua [19]aria tāto sottile, che nō può sostenere [20]vcciello che lo seguiti. [21]A questa altezza nō va, se nō a chi da cieli [22]è dato, cioè dove vola il cameleone.

THE CAMELEON.

This lives on air, and there it is the prey of all the birds; so in order to be safer it flies above the clouds and finds an air so rarefied that it cannot support the bird that follows it.

At that height nothing can go unless it has a gift from Heaven, and that is where the chameleon flies.

ALEPO PESCIE.

[2]Alepo nō uive fori dell'acqua.

THE ALEPO, A FISH.

The fish *alepo* does not live out of water.

STRUZZO.

[4]Questo cōuerte il ferro in suo [5]nutrimēto; cova l'uova colla vista; [6]¶per l'arme [7]de' capitani.¶

THE OSTRICH.

This bird converts iron into nourishment, and hatches its eggs by its gaze;—Armies under commanders.

---

nossacosti. 9. chefforte la tena. 11. lasscia. 12. P. fama; — lumerpa fama (?). 13. nasscie . . magiore essplē. 14. chettoglie. 15. li cade piv le. 16. ella pena chessi spicha.

1236. 4. risscōtro. 9. esspesso. 12. rafeua la. 17. bietta attutti . . istare. 18. nvbe. 19. po. 20. chello. 21. acquesta. 22. cameleone. *Lines* 11—15 *are written on the margin near the title-line.*

1237. 1. alep[o] pesscie. |4. suo "nutrimēto". 5. cova lava. *Lines* 6 *and* 7 *are written on the margin near the title-line.*

CIGNO.

⁹Cignio è candido sanza alcuna ¹⁰macchia, e dolcemēte canta nel mo¹¹rire, il qual cāto termina · la uita.

THE SWAN.

The swan is white without any spot, and it sings sweetly as it dies, its life ending with that song.

CICOGNIA.

¹³Questa, beuēdo la salsa acqua, ¹⁴caccia da se il male; se truova la cō¹⁵pagnia in fallo, l'abandona; e quādo ¹⁶è vechia, i sua figlioli la covano e pa¹⁷scono, infinchè more.

THE STORK.

This bird, by drinking saltwater purges itself of distempers. If the male finds his mate unfaithful, he abandons her; and when it grows old its young ones brood over it, and feed it till it dies.

H.¹ 14 *a*]   **1238.**

CICALA.

²Questa col suo canto fa tacere ³il cucco, more nell'olio, e resucita ⁴nello aceto, cāta per li ardēti caldi.

THE GRASSHOPPER.

This silences the cuckoo with its song. It dies in oil and revives in vinegar. It sings in the greatest heats

PIPISTRELLO.

⁶Questo dov'è piv luce piv si fa ⁷orbo, e come piv guarda il sole ⁸più s'acciecca; ⁹pel uitio che nō può ¹⁰stare do¹¹v'è la vir¹²tù.

THE BAT.

The more light there is the blinder this creature becomes; as those who gaze most at the sun become most dazzled.—For Vice, that cannot remain where Virtue appears.

PERNICE.

¹⁴Questa si trasmuta di femina i maschio, ¹⁵e dimētica il primo sesso, e fura per īuidia ¹⁶l'oua al'altre, e le coua, ma i nati segui¹⁷tano la uera madre.

THE PARTRIDGE.

This bird changes from the female into the male and forgets its former sex; and out of envy it steals the eggs from others and hatches them, but the young ones follow the true mother.

RŌDINE.

¹⁹Questa colla celidonia lumina i sua ²⁰ciecchi nati.

THE SWALLOW.

This bird gives sight to its blind young ones by means of celandine.

H.¹ 14 *b*]   **1239.**

OSTRIGA.—PEL TRADIMĒTO.

²Questa, quādo la luna è piena, s'apre tutta, ³e quādo il grācio la vede, dētro le gietta ⁴qualche sasso o festuca, e questa nō si ⁵può riserrare, ōde è cibo d'esso grāchio; ⁶così fa, chi apre la bocca a dire il suo segreto, ⁷chè si fa preda dello indiscreto auditore.

THE OYSTER.—FOR TREACHERY.

This creature, when the moon is full opens itself wide, and when the crab looks in he throws in a piece of rock or seaweed and the oyster cannot close again, whereby it serves for food to that crab. This is what happens to him who opens his mouth to tell his secret. He becomes the prey of the treacherous hearer.

---

8. cinguo. 10. cānta. 14. cacia dasse. 15. ecquādo. 16. issua. 17. scano.
1238. 1. cichala. 3. cucho. 5. palpistrello. 8. sacieca. 9. po. 14. trassmuta . . masscio. 15. iprimo. 16. elle cova. 19. collaccelidonia. 20. cieci.
1239. 1. hosstriga. 2. quasta. 3. ecquādo. 4. qualchessasso offistuca ecquesta. 5. po riserare. 6. faciaprla bocha . . sigreto. 7. chessi . . vlditore. 8. bavalissco. 9. effugito dettutti . . la do. 10. mezo. 11. essi. 12. ¶ rua per la virtù ¶·

BASILISCIO.—CRUDELTÀ.

[9]Questo è fugito da tutti i serpēti; la don[10]nola per lo mezzo della ruta cōbatte con essi [11]e si l'uccide.

L'ASPIDO.

[14]Questo porta ne'dēti la subita morte [15]e per nō sentire l'incāti, colla coda si [16]stoppa li orechi.

THE BASILISK.—CRUELTY.

All snakes flie from this creature; but the weasel attacks it by means of rue and kills it.

THE ASP.

This carries instantaneous death in its fangs; and, that it may not hear the charmer it stops its ears with its tail.

DRAGO.

[2]Questo lega le gābe al liofante [3]e quel li cade adosso, e l'uno e l'al[4]tro more, e morēdo fa sua vēdetta.

VIPERA.

[6]Questa nel suo accoppiare apre la bocca, e nel fine [7]strīgnie dēti e amazza il marito, poi [8]i figlioli in corpo crescivti straccia[9]no il uētre e occidono la madre.

SCORPIONE.

[11]La saliua sputa a digivno · sopra dello scor[12]pione e l'occide; à similitudine dell'a-[13]stinētia della gola, che togle via e cura [14]le malatie che da essa gola dipēdono, e a[15]pre la strada alle virtù.

THE DRAGON.

This creature entangles itself in the legs of the elephant which falls upon it, and so both die, and in its death it is avenged.

THE VIPER.

She, in pairing opens her mouth and at last clenches her teeth and kills her husband. Then the young ones, growing within her body rend her open and kill their mother.

THE SCORPION.

Saliva, spit out when fasting will kill a scorpion. This may be likened to abstinence from greediness, which removes and heals the ills which result from that · gluttony, and opens the path of virtue.

COCCODRILLO. IPOCRESIA.

[2]Questo · animale piglia l'o[3]mo e subito l'uccide poichè l'à morso [4]con lamētevole voce e molte lacrime [5]lo piāge·, e finito il lamēto crudel[6]mēte lo diuora·; così fa l'ipocrito [7]che per ogni lieue cosa s'enpie il uiso [8]di lagrime; mostrādo un cor di tigro e'ral[9]legrasi nel core dell'altrui male cō [10]piātoso volto.

BOTTA.

[12]La botta fugie la luce del sole, e se pure [13]per forza v'è tenvta, si gōfia tāta, che s'ascon[14]de la testa in basso, e privasi d'essi razzi; [15]così fa chi è nimico della chiara e luciē[16]te virtù, che nō può se nō con gōfiato [17]animo forzatamēte starle davāti.

THE CROCODILE. HYPOCRISY.

This animal catches a man and straightway kills him; after he is dead, it weeps for him with a lamentable voice and many tears. Then, having done lamenting, it cruelly devours him. It is thus with the hypocrite, who, for the smallest matter, has his face bathed with tears, but shows the heart of a tiger and rejoices in his heart at the woes of others, while wearing a pitiful face.

THE TOAD.

The toad flies from the light of the sun, and if it is held there by force it puffs itself out so much as to hide its head below and shield itself from the rays. Thus does the foe of clear and radiant virtue, who can only be constrainedly brought to face it with puffed up courage.

1240. delluno ellal. 6. suo coperbocha. 7. stīgnie dēti e amaza. 8. cresscivti. 11. la sciliua . . dellosschor. 12. pione locide assimilitudine. 13. chettole vɪaconde. 14. l |||| mal |||||||| che ||| a. *Lines 14 and 15 are very indistinct and nearly effaced.*

1241. 1. cocodrillo. 2. animale [essendo]. 3. poichella morto. 4. collamētevole. 8. mostrādo īcor di tigro e ra. 12. esse. 13. scofia chessasco. 14. baso. 15. cosi facie nemico . . ciara. 16. po . . con |||||| cōfiati. 17. |||| animo . . stale.

H.I 17b]

1242.

BRUCO.—DELLA VIRTÙ IN GIENERALE.

³Il bruco·, che mediante l'esercitato studio ⁴di tessere con mirabile artifitio e sottile lauoro ⁵intorno a se fa la nova abitatione, escie ⁵poi fori di quella colle dipinte e belle ⁷ali, cō quelle leuādosi inverso il cielo.

RAGNIO.

⁹Il ragnio·partoriscie fori di se l'ar¹⁰tifitiosa e maestrevole tela, la quale ¹¹gli rēde per benifitio la presa preda.

THE CATERPILLAR.—FOR VIRTUE IN GENERAL.

The caterpillar, which by means of assiduous care is able to weave round itself a new dwelling place with marvellous artifice and fine workmanship, comes out of it afterwards with painted and lovely wings, with which it rises towards Heaven.

THE SPIDER.

The spider brings forth out of herself the delicate and ingenious web, which makes her a return by the prey it takes.

H.I 18a]

1243.

LIONE.

²Questo animale col suo tonāte grido ³desta i sua figlioli dopo il terzo giorno ⁴nati, aprēdo a quelli tutti li adormēta⁵ti sēsi, e tutte le fiere, che ⁶nella selua sono, fuggono.

⁷Puossi assimigliare a figlioli della ⁸virtù·, che mediāte il grido delle lode ⁹si suegliano·e crescono per li studi onorevoli ¹⁰che senpre piv gli inalza, e tutti i tristi ¹¹a esso grido fuggono ciessādosi dai ¹²vertuosi.

¹³Ancora il leone copre le sue pedate, ¹⁴perchè nō s'intenda il suo viaggio ¹⁵per i nimici; questo sta bene al capitano ¹⁶a cielare i segreti del suo animo, acciochè ¹⁷il nimico nō cogniosca i sua tratti.

THE LION.

This animal, with his thundering roar, rouses his young the third day after they are born, teaching them the use of all their dormant senses and all the wild things which are in the wood flee away.

This may be compared to the children of Virtue who are roused by the sound of praise and grow up in honourable studies, by which they are more and more elevated; while all that is base flies at the sound, shunning those who are virtuous.

Again, the lion covers over its foot tracks, so that the way it has gone may not be known to its enemies. Thus it beseems a captain to conceal the secrets of his mind so that the enemy may not know his purpose.

H.I 18b]

1244.

TARĀTA.

²Il morso della tarāta mātiene l'omo ³nel suo proponimēto, cioè quello che ⁴pensano quādo fu morso.

DUGO E CIVETTA.

⁶Questi gastigano i loro schernitori ⁷privādoli di uista, chè così à ordina⁸to la natura, perchè si cibino.

THE TARANTULA.

The bite of the tarantula fixes a man's mind on one idea; that is on the thing he was thinking of when he was bitten.

THE SCREECH-OWL AND THE OWL.

These punish those who are scoffing at them by pecking out their eyes; for nature has so ordered it, that they may thus be fed.

1242. 3. la sercitato. 4. comirabile | "artificio" essottile. 5. asse la . . esscie. 6. chelle dipinte lauādosi. 10. maesstre vole tella. 11. rēdende.

1243. 4. aprēda acquelli. 5. ettutti [li anima] le. 6. sona. 8. delle lalde. 9. sissuegliano e crescano li studi. 10. chessenpre piv glinalza ettutti. 11. esse . . fugano. 13. ileoni co. 14. viagio. 15. ai capitani.

1244. 4. persano. 5. duco. 7. diuita. 8. to natura.

1242. Two notes are underneath this text. The first: *'nessuna chosa e da ttemere piu che lla sozza fama'* is a repetition of the first line of the text given in Vol. I No. 695.

The second: *faticha fugga cholla fama in braccio quasi ochultata c* is written in red chalk and is evidently an incomplete sentence.

H.I 19 a]　　　　　　　　1245.

LEOFANTE.

²Il grāde elefante·à per natura quel ³che raro negli omini si truova, cioè ⁴probità, prudētia, equità e osser⁵vātia e religione, inperochè, quādo ⁶la luna·si rinova·, questi vanno ai fi⁷vmi e quivi purgādosi solennemēte ⁸si lauano, e così salutato il pianeta ⁹ritornano alle selue; E quādo ¹⁰sono ammalati, stando supini, gitta¹¹no l'erbe verso il cielo, quasi com'esse ¹²sacrificare volessino; ¶sotterrano li dē¹³ti quādo per vecchiezza gli cadono;¶ de' ¹⁴sua due dēti l'uno adopera a cauare ¹⁵le radici per cibarsi; all'altro cōserua ¹⁶la pūta per cōbattere; Quādo sono ¹⁷superati da cacciatori, e chè la stāchezza ¹⁸gli uīcie per cotali dēti l'elefanti, quelle trattesi, con esse si ricomprano.

THE ELEPHANT.

The huge elephant has by nature what is rarely found in man; that is Honesty, Prudence, Justice, and the Observance of Religion; inasmuch as when the moon is new, these beasts go down to the rivers, and there, solemnly cleansing themselves, they bathe, and so, having saluted the planet, return to the woods. And when they are ill, being laid down, they fling up plants towards Heaven as though they would offer sacrifice.—They bury their tusks when they fall out from old age.—Of these two tusks they use one to dig up roots for food; but they save the point of the other for fighting with; when they are taken by hunters and when worn out by fatigue, they dig up these buried tusks and ransom themselves.

H.I 19 b]　　　　　　　　1246.

Sono di leni menti e conoscono i pericoli; ²¶e se esso trova·l'omo solo e smarito, ³piacievolmēte lo rimette nella perduta ⁴strada, se truova le pedate dell'omo ⁵prima che veda l'omo; ⁶¶esso teme tradimēto, ōde si ferma ⁷e soffia, mostrādolo ali altri elefanti, ⁸e fanno schiera e vanno assentitamēte. ⁹Questi vanno senpre a schiere, e 'l più ¹⁰vechio va ināzi, e 'l secōdo d'età resta ¹¹l'ultimo, e così chiudono la schiera; ¹²temono vergognia, non vsano il co¹³ito se nō di notte e di nascosto, e nō tor¹⁴nano dopo il coito alli armēti, se prima ¹⁵nō si lauano nel fiume; nō cōbattono ¹⁶le femine, come gli altri animali; ¹⁷¶ed è tāto clemēte, che mal uolōtieri per na¹⁸tura nō noce ai mē potenti di se, e scō¹⁹trādosi nella sua via e greggi delle pecore

They are merciful, and know the dangers, and if one finds a man alone and lost, he kindly puts him back in the road he has missed, if he finds the footprints of the man before the man himself. It dreads betrayal, so it stops and blows, pointing it out to the other elephants who form in a troop and go warily.

These beasts always go in troops, and the oldest goes in front and the second in age remains the last, and thus they enclose the troop. Out of shame they pair only at night and secretly, nor do they then rejoin the herd but first bathe in the river. The females do not fight as with other animals; and it is so merciful that it is most unwilling by nature ever to hurt those weaker than itself. And if it meets in the middle of its way a flock of sheep

H.I 20 a]　　　　　　　　1247.

colla sua mano le pone da parte ²per non le pestare, coi piedi, nè mai noce ³se nō sono provocati; quādo son ca⁴duti nella fossa, gli altri cō rami, ⁵terra e sassi riēpiono la fossa, ⁶in modo che alzano il fondo,

it puts them aside with its trunk, so as not to trample them under foot; and it never hurts any thing unless when provoked. When one has fallen into a pit the others fill up the pit with branches, earth and stones, thus

---

1245. 2. ellefante. 4. he equita e osser. 6. quessti vano. 9. Ecquādo. 10. amalati . . suppini. 12. volessino (sotterali. 13. uechieza gli cagiano (de. 16. Quā sono. 17. caciatori e chella stācheza. 18. dēti le lepāte ecquele (?). 19. lelefante . . traitosi \\\\\\ nessosiricōprano. *These two last lines are much effaced.*

1246. 1. sono elemēti e conosschano. 2. esse . . sole essmarito. 7. essoffia mosstrādola. 8. effano sciera e vano. 9. vano . . assciere. 11. civdano lasscierana. 12. temano. 13. nasscosto. 15. nocōbatton. 16. me femine. 18. esscō. 19. nella m . "gregi" diria delle.

1247. 1. cholla . . pone de [parte. 2. per nolle pestare co. 5. essassi riēpiano. 6. imolalzano . . cheso. 7. rimō \\\\\\\\ temano.

che esso facil⁷mēte rimōti; temono forte ⁸lo stridore de' porci e fugono indiri⁹eto; e nō fa māco danno poi coi piedi a sua ¹⁰che a nimici; dilettāsi de' fiumi, ¹¹e sempre vāno vagabūdi intorno ¹²quelli, ¶e per lo grā peso nō possono ¹³notare; diuorano le pietre, e trō¹⁴chi delli alberi sono loro gratissimo cibo; ¹⁵ànno in odio i ratti; le mosche si dilettano ¹⁶del suo odore e posādosi li adosso, quello ¹⁷arraspa la pelle, e fa le pieghe strette, e l'uccide.

raising the bottom that he may easily get out. They greatly dread the noise of swine and fly in confusion, doing no less harm then, with their feet, to their own kind than to the enemy. They delight in rivers and are always wandering about near them, though on account of their great weight they cannot swim. They devour stones, and the trunks of trees are their favourite food. They have a horror of rats. Flies delight in their smell and settle on their back, and the beast scrapes its skin making its folds even and kills them.

H.¹ 20 b]   1248.

Quādo passano i fiumi, mādano ²i figlioli diuerso il calar dell'acqua, ³e stando loro inverso l'erta ronpono ⁴il rapido corso dell'acqua, aciochè 'l cor⁵so non le menasse via; il drago ⁶se li gitta sotto il corpo, colla ⁷coda l'annoda le gābe, coll'alie ⁸e colle braccia anche li tignie le coste ⁹e coi denti lo scanna, el liofante ¹⁰li cade adosso o il drago scoppia, ¹¹e così colla sua morte del nemico ¹²si uēdica.

When they cross rivers they send their young ones up against the stream of the water; thus, being set towards the fall, they break the united current of the water so that the current does not carry them away. The dragon flings itself under the elephant's body, and with its tail it ties its legs; with its wings and with its arms it also clings round its ribs and cuts its throat with its teeth, and the elephant falls upon it and the dragon is burst. Thus, in its death it is revenged on its foe.

IL DRAGONE.

THE DRAGON.

¹⁴Questi s'accōpagniano insieme e si tessa¹⁵no a uso di radici, e colla testa leuata ¹⁶passano i paduli, e notano dove trouano ¹⁷migliore pastura, e se così non si vnissero,

These go in companies together, and they twine themselves after the manner of roots, and with their heads raised they cross lakes, and swim to where they find better pasture; and if they did not thus combine

H.¹ 21 a]   1249.

annegherebbero; così fa la unitione.

they would be drowned, therefore they combine.

SERPĒTE.

THE SERPENT.

³Il serpēte, grādissimo animale, ⁴quādo vede alcuno ucciello per l'aria, ⁵tira a se si forte il fiato, che si tira ⁶gli uccielli in bocca; Marco, ⁷Regulo, consule dello esercito Roma⁸no, fu col suo esercito da un simile ⁹animale assalito e quasi rotto, il qua¹⁰le animale, essēdo morto per una machina ¹¹mvrale, fu misurato 123 piedi, cio¹²è 64 braccia e ¹/₂; avāzava colla testa tutte ¹³le piāte d'una selua.

The serpent is a very large animal. When it sees a bird in the air it draws in its breath so strongly that it draws the birds into its mouth too. Marcus Regulus, the consul of the Roman army was attacked, with his army, by such an animal and almost defeated. And this animal, being killed by a catapult, measured 123 feet, that is 64¹/₂ braccia and its head was high above all the trees in a wood.

9. dano poico piedi. 10. dilettāsi fiuvmi. 11. essēpre . . intorna. 12. quelgli . . possā. 14. abberi soloro. 15. ano. 17. arapa . . effaale piege strette lucide.

1248. 4. lunito (?) corso dellacua. 6. nolle menasse via | il . . cholla. 7. lanoda . . chollalie. 8. cholle bre anche. 9. e cho denti. 10. drago sciopa. 14. sacōpagnian . . essi. 15. ratici. 16. troua. 17. essecosino si vnisser.

1249. 1. anegerebono. 3. grādisimo. 5. asse . . chessi. 6. bochaa. 7. cūsulo¹ 8. ma fu chol . . da vsimili. 10. macin"a".

BOIE.

[15]Questa e grā biscia, la quale cō se mede[16]sima si aggruppa alle ganbe della vacca in mo[17]do nō si mova, poi la tetta in modo che quasi [18]la dissecca; di questa spetie a tēpo di Claudio [19]īperatore nel mōte Vaticano ne fu morta

THE BOA (?)

This is a very large snake which entangles itself round the legs of the cow so that it cannot move and then sucks it, in such wise that it almost dries it up. In the time of Claudius the Emperor, there was killed, on the Vatican Hill,

H.I 21 b]   **1250.**

vna che avea vno putto intero in corpo [2]il quale avea trāghiottito

one which had inside it a boy, entire, that it had swallowed.

MACLI. ¶PEL SONNO È GIŪTO.

[4]Questa bestia nascie in Scādinavia isola; [5]à forma di grā cavallo, se nō che la [6]grā lūghezza dello collo e delli orechi lo vari[7]ano; pascie l'erba allo indietro, perchè à si [8]lūgo il labro di sopra che pasciēdo inā[9]zi coprirebbe l'erba; à le gābe d'ū pezzo; [10]per questo, quādo vuol dormire s'appoggia [11]a vno albero, e i cacciatori, ātivedēdo [12]il loco vsato a dormire, segā quasi tutta [13]la piāta, e quādo questo poi vi s'appoggia [14]nel dormire·, per lo sonno cade, e i cacciato[15]ri così lo piglano, e ogni altro modo di pi[16]glarlo è vano, perchè è d'incredibile velocità [17]nel correre.

THE MACLI.—CAUGHT WHEN ASLEEP.

This beast is born in Scandinavia. It has the shape of a great horse, excepting that the great length of its neck and of its ears make a difference. It feeds on grass, going backwards, for it has so long an upper lip that if it went forwards it would cover up the grass. Its legs are all in one piece; for this reason when it wants to sleep it leans against a tree, and the hunters, spying out the place where it is wont to sleep, saw the tree almost through, and then, when it leans against it to sleep, in its sleep it falls, and thus the hunters take it. And every other mode of taking it is in vain, because it is incredibly swift in running.

H.I 22 a]   **1251.**

BONASO NOCE COLLA FUGA.

[2]Questo nascie· in Peonia; à collo [3]cō crini simile al cauallo, in tutte [4]l'altre parti è simile· al toro, saluo [5]che le sue corna sono in modo piegate [6]indētro, che nō può cozzare, e per questo [7]non à altro scanpo· che la fuga·, nella [8]quale· getta sterco per spatio di 400 [9]braccia del suo corso·, il quale, dove to[10]cca, abbrucia come foco.

THE BISON WHICH DOES INJURY IN ITS FLIGHT.

This beast is a native of Paeonia and has a neck with a mane like a horse. In all its other parts it is like a bull, excepting that its horns are in a way bent inwards so that it cannot butt; hence it has no safety but in flight, in which it flings out its excrement to a distance of 400 braccia in its course, and this burns like fire wherever it touches.

LEONI, PARDI, PĀTERE, TIGRI.

[12]Questi tēgono· l'ūgie nella guaina, e mai [13]le sfoderanno, se non è adosso alla preda o ne[14]mico.

LIONS, PARDS, PANTHERS, TIGERS.

These keep their claws in the sheath, and never put them out unless they are on the back of their prey or their enemy.

12. e 64 brē ½. 15. bisscie. 16. sagluppa . . della vecha imo. 17. imodo. 18. ladiseza. 19. īperadore . . morta.
1250. 2. trāgiottito. 3. macli pel sonno egiūto. 4. iniscandinavia. 5. chella. 6. lūgeza. 7. passie . . allōdirieto . . assi. 8. passiēdo. 9. ci copirebe . . ha le . . pezo. 10. vol . . sapogia. 10. ecchaciatori. 13. sapogia. 14. ecaciato.
1251. 2. nasscie. 4. essimile. 5. chelle sie . . imodo. 6. pocozare. 7. chella. 8. gita stercho per ispatio. 9. bracia. 10. tocha abrucia. 12. tēgano. 13. lessfoderano. 17. caciatori. 19. accioche | "per"ella . . nō siē"o".

LEONESSA.

[16]Quãdo la leonessa difēde i figli[17]oli dalle mã de' cacciatori, per nõ si spaue[18]tare dalli spiedi, abbassa li ochi a terra [19]accioche, per la sua fuga i figli nõ sieno [20]prigioni.

THE LIONESS.

When the lioness defends her young from the hand of the hunter, in order not to be frightened by the spears she keeps her eyes on the ground, to the end that she may not by her flight leave her young ones prisoners.

H.[1] 22 b]   **1252.**

LEONE.

[2]Questo · si terribile animale niēte teme [3]piv che lo strepido delle vuote carrette [4]e simile · il cãto de' galli, · e teme a[5]ssai nel uederli e con pauroso a[6]spetto riguarda la sua cresta; [7]e forte invilisce, quãdo à coper[8]to · il uolto.

THE LION.

This animal, which is so terrible, fears nothing more than the noise of empty carts, and likewise the crowing of cocks. And it is much terrified at the sight of one, and looks at its comb with a frightened aspect, and is strangely alarmed when its face is covered.

PÃTERE IN AFRICA.

[10]Questo à forma di leonessa, ma è [11]piv alta di gãbe, e piv sottile, e lũga; [12]è tutta biãca e punteggiata di ma[13]chie nere a modo di rosette, e di que[14]sta si dilettano · tutti li animali di [15]vedere ·, e senpre le starebbero dintorno, [16]se nõ fusse la terribilità · del suo viso,

THE PANTHER IN AFRICA.

This has the form of the lioness but it is taller on its legs and slimmer and long bodied; and it is all white and marked with black spots after the manner of rosettes; and all animals delight to look upon these rosettes, and they would always be standing round it if it were not for the terror of its face;

H.[1] 23 a]   **1253.**

onde essa, questo conosciēdo, ascõ[2]de il uiso, e li animali circũstãti [3]s'assicurano e fannosi vicini per me[4]glio potere fruire tãta bellezza, õ[5]de questa subito piglia il piv uici-[6]no e subito lo diuora.

therefore knowing this, it hides its face, and the surrounding animals grow bold and come close, the better to enjoy the sight of so much beauty; when suddenly it seizes the nearest and at once devours it.

CAMELLI.

[8]Quegli Battriani ànno 2 gobbi, [9]gli Arabi uno solo; sono veloci in battagla [10]e vtilissimi a portare le some; [11]questo animale à regole e misura [12]oseruãtissima, perchè nõ si move se à [13]piv carico che l'usato, e se fa piv [14]uiaggio fa il simile, subito si ferma, [15]õde lì bisognia a mercatãti allog-[16]giare.

CAMELS.

The Bactrian have two humps; the Arabian one only. They are swift in battle and most useful to carry burdens. This animal is extremely observant of rule and measure, for it will not move if it has a greater weight than it is used to, and if it is taken too far it does the same, and suddenly stops and so the merchants are obliged to lodge there.

H.[1] 23 b]   **1254.**

TIGRO.

[2]Questa nascie in Ircania, la qua[3]le è simile alquãto alla pãtera per le [4]diuerse machie della sua pelle, ed è ani[5]male di

THE TIGER.

This beast is a native of Hyrcania, and it is something like the panther from the various spots on its skin. It is an animal

---

1252. 2. teribile. 3. chello .. vote carette. 4. essimile .. etteme. 6. cressta. 7. efforte invilissce. 11. ellũga. 12. ettutta biãcha e punegiata. 15. starebõ ditorno. 16. fussi .. teribilita.

1253. 1. conosciēdo asscõ. 2. elli. 3. sasicurano e fanosi. 4. belleza. 8. batriani. 9. arabi î solo. 13. chellusato esse. 14. uiagio .. sibito. 15. alo. 16. ciare.

1254. 2. na⸍scie. 3. lehe simile. 5. cacia. 6. truova. [la sua ta] i sua. 8. leva [ecque] essubito. 10. tera. 12. cholle . .

spauōtevole velocità; il caccia[6]tore quādo truoua i sua figli, [7]li rapiscie subito, ponēdo spechi nel [8]loco donde li leua, e subito sopra [9]veloce cauallo si fugie; la pantera tor[10]nādo truoua li spechi fermi in terra, ne [11]quali vedēdosi, li pare vedere li sua fi[12]glioli, e raspādo colle zāpe scuopre [13]l'inganno, ōde mediāte l'odore de' figli [14]seguita il cacciatore, e quādo esso caccia[15]tore vede la tigra, lascia vno de'figlioli, [16]e questa lo piglia, e portalo al nido; [17]subito rigivgne esso cacciatore, e fa

of terrible swiftness; the hunter when he finds its young ones carries them off hastily, placing mirrors in the place whence he takes them, and at once escapes on a swift horse. The panther returning finds the mirrors fixed on the ground and looking into them believes it sees its young; then scratching with its paws it discovers the cheat. Forthwith, by means of the scent of its young, it follows the hunter, and when this hunter sees the tigress he drops one of the young ones and she takes it, and having carried it to the den she immediately returns to the hunter and does

H.[1] 24 a]   **1255.**

il simile insino a tāto ch'esso mōta [2]in barca.

the same till he gets into his boat.

CATOPLEA.

[4]Questa nascie · in Etiopia · vicino al fonte [5]Nigricapo; è animale nō troppo · grande ·, è [6]pigra · in tutte le mēbra ·, e al capo di tāta grā[7]dezza · che malagievolmēte · lo porta ·, in modo che [8]senpre · sta · chinato · inverso · la terra ·, altri[9]menti · sarebbe · di sōma · peste · alli omini, [10]perchè qualunque è veduta da sua · ochi [11]subito · more.

CATOBLEPAS.

It is found in Ethiopia near to the source Nigricapo. It is not a very large animal, is sluggish in all its parts, and its head is so large that it carries it with difficulty, in such wise that it always droops towards the ground; otherwise it would be a great pest to man, for any one on whom it fixes its eyes dies immediately.

BASILISCO.

[13]Questo · nascie · nella provincia · Cirenaica [14]e nō è · maggiore · che · 12 · dita e à · in capo [15]vna machia bianca a similitudine di diadema; [16]col fischo · caccia · ogni serpēte ·, a similitudi[17]ne di serpe, ma nō si move cō torture, anzi [18]manritto · dal mezzo · innāzi ·; diciesi che vno

THE BASILISK.

This is found in the province of Cyrenaica and is not more than 12 fingers long. It has on its head a white spot after the fashion of a diadem. It scares all serpents with its whistling. It resembles a snake, but does not move by wriggling but from the centre forwards to the right. It is said that one

H.[1] 24 b]   **1256.**

di questi, essendo · morto · con vn aste da vno che [2]era · a cavallo, che 'l suo veneno discorrendo [3]super l'aste ·, e nō che l'omo · ma il cavallo morì; [4]guasta · le piāte e nō solamēte quelle [5]che tocca ·, ma quelle · doue · soffia ·; secca l'er[6]be, spezza · i sassi.

of these, being killed with a spear by one who was on horse-back, and its venom flowing on the spear, not only the man but the horse also died. It spoils the wheat and not only that which it touches, but where it breathes the grass dries and the stones are split.

---

schuopre. 13. langono. 14. essocacia. 15. lasscia. 17. r | givgnieso caciatore effa.
1255. 1. imile . . attāto. 4. nasscie. 6. tucte. 7. deza . . imodo. 8. altre. 9. pesste. 10. he veduta. 13. nasscie. 14. magiore . . he a in. 16. fisscio . . assimilitudi. 18. marito dal mezio.
1256. 2. chavallo. 2. discorendo. 3. chellomo. 4. [colio] guassta le biande. 5. chettoccha macquelle . . secha. 6. belola.

1255. Leonardo undoubtedly derived these remarks as to the Catoblepas from Pliny, Hist. Nat. VIII. 21 (al. 32): *Apud Hesperios Aethiopas fons est Nigris* (different readings), *ut plerique existimavere, Nili caput* — — — *Juxta hunc fera appellatur catoblepas, modica alioquin, ceterisque membris iners, caput tantum praegrave aegre ferens; alias internecio humani generis, omnibus qui oculos ejus videre, confestim morientibus.* Aelian, *Hist. An.* gives a far more minute description of the creature (τὸ κατώβλεπον), but he says that it poisons beasts not by its gaze, but by its venomous breath. Athenaeus 221 B, mentions both. If Leonardo had known of these two passages, he would scarcely have omitted the poisonous breath. (H. MÜLLER-STRÜBING.)

DONNOLA OVER BELLULA.

[8]Questa · trovādo · la tana · del basilisco, coll' o[9]dore della · sua · sparsa · orina l'uccide; l' o[10]dore della quale orina · ācora spesse volte [11]essa donola occide.

CERASTE.

[13]Queste · ànno quattro · piccoli corni mobili; [14]onde quādo si uogliono · cibare, nascōda[15]no sotto · le foglie tutta la persona, sal[16]vo · esse cornicina ·, le quali movēdo pare [17]agli ucielli quelli essere piccoli uermini [18]che scherzino, ōde subito si calano per beccar[19]li; e questa subito s'avviluppa loro in cier[20]chio, e esse lì diuora.

H. 1 25 a]

AMPHESIBENE.

[2]Questa · à · due teste ·, l'una nel suo loco, l'al[3]tra nella · coda ·, come se nō bastasse che [4]da uno solo loco gittasse il ueneno.

IACULO.

[6]Questa · sta sopra · le piāte ·, e si lancia · come [7]dardo; e passa a trauerso le fere, e l'uccide.

ASPIDO.

[9]Il morso · di questo · animale · non à · rimedio, [10]se nō di subito · tagliare · le parti morse; Questo [11]si pestifero · animale · à tale affetione nella [12]sua cōpagnia · che sempre vanno accōpagnati, [13]chè se per disgratia · l'uno di loro è morto ·, l'al[14]tro con incredibile velocità seguita l'ucci[15]ditore, ed è tāto attēto e sollecito alla vēdetta, [16]che vīcie · ogni difficultà ·; passando ogni eser[17]cito, solo il suo nemico cierca · offendere; [18]e passa ogni spatio, e nō si può schifarlo, se nō [19]col passare l'acque · e cō velocissima fuga; [20]à li ochi īdētro e grādi orechi, e piv lo move l'udito che 'l uedere.

H. 1 25 b]

ICNEUMONE.

[2]Questo · animale · è mortale nemico all'aspido; [3]nascie · in Egitto ·, e quādo · vede presso al [4]suo · sito alcuno · aspido ·, subito corre [5]alla litta over fango · del Nilo, e cō quello [6]tutto · s'infanga, e poi, risecco dal

---

THE WEASEL.

This beast finding the lair of the basilisk kills it with the smell of its urine, and this smell, indeed, often kills the weasel itself.

THE CERASTES.

This has four movable little horns; so, when it wants to feed, it hides under leaves all of its body except these little horns which, as they move, seem to the birds to be some small worms at play. Then they immediately swoop down to pick them and the Cerastes suddenly twines round them and encircles and devours them.

1257.

THE AMPHISBOENA.

This has two heads, one in its proper place the other at the tail; as if one place were not enough from which to fling its venom.

THE IACULUS.

This lies on trees, and flings itself down like a dart, and pierces through the wild beast and kills them.

THE ASP.

The bite of this animal cannot be cured unless by immediately cutting out the bitten part. This pestilential animal has such a love for its mate that they always go in company. And if, by mishap, one of them is killed the other, with incredible swiftness, follows him who has killed it; and it is so determined and eager for vengeance that it overcomes every difficulty, and passing by every troop it seeks to hurt none but its enemy. And it will travel any distance, and it is impossible to avoid it unless by crossing water and by very swift flight. It has its eyes turned inwards, and large ears and it hears better than it sees.

1258.

THE ICHNEUMON.

This animal is the mortal enemy of the asp. It is a native of Egypt and when it sees an asp near its place, it runs at once to the bed or mud of the Nile and with this makes itself muddy all over, then it dries

---

7. donola.   8. basilssco.   12. cerasste.   13. quattro pichorni mobili.   14. uogliano.   14. nasscōda.   17. picholi.   18. ce serzino . . becar.   19. ecquesta . . sauilupa.   20. cio esseli diuora.

1257. 1. amphesibene.   2. tesste.   3. basstassi.   4. da î solo locho.   6. essi·   7. attrauero le fiere elluccide.   11. attale.   12 ce senpre . . acōpagniati.   13. chesseper.   14. luci.   15. essollecito.   16. dificulta.   18. scifarlo.   20. laldito.

1258. 1. ichneumone.   3. nasscie.   4. asspido   5. lita . . echō.   6. risecho.   7. cosi sēchāda lū.   8. assimilitudine.   9. coraza ··

sole, di no⁷vo di fango s'inbratta; e così seguitando l'ū do⁸po l'altro si fa tre o 4 veste
a similitudine ⁹di corazza·, e dipoi assalta
l'aspido, e bē cō¹⁰testa cō quello in modo
che, tolto il tēpo, ¹¹se li caccia in·gola e
l'annega.

CROCODILLO.

¹³Questo nascie nel Nilo, à 4 piedi, vi¹⁴ve
in terra e in acqua, nè altro terrestre ¹⁵ani-
male si truova sanza lingua che questo;
¹⁶e solo morde movēdo la mascella di
sopra; ¹⁷crescie insino in 40 piedi, è un-
ghiato, ¹⁸armato di corame, atto a ogni colpo;
el dì ¹⁹sta in terra, e la notte in acqua;
questo, ²⁰cibato di pesci, s'adormēta sulla
riua del ²¹Nilo colla bocca aperta e l'ucciello detto

itself in the sun, smears itself again with
mud, and thus, drying one after the other,
it makes itself three or four coatings like a
coat of mail. Then it attacks the asp, and fights
well with him, so that, taking its time it
catches him in the throat and destroys him.

THE CROCODILE.

This is found in the Nile, it has four feet
and lives on land and in water. No other
terrestrial creature but this is found to have
no tongue, and it only bites by moving its
upper jaw. It grows to a length of forty feet
and has claws and is armed with a hide that
will take any blow. By day it is on land
and at night in the water. It feeds on fishes,
and going to sleep on the bank of the Nile
with its mouth open, a bird called

H.1 26 a]   **1259.**

trochilo, piccolissimo vcciello·, subito
li ²corre alla bocca e, saltatoli fra denti
³dentro·, e' fora·leva beccando il rimaso
⁴cibo·; e così stuzzicādolo cō dilettevole
⁵voluttà lo inuita aprire tutta la bocca, ⁶e
così s'adormēta; questo veduto ⁷dal icneu-
mone·subito si li slācia·in bocca, ⁸e fora-
toli lo stomaco e le budelle finalmēte ⁹l'uccide.

trochilus, a very small bird, runs at once
to its mouth and hops among its teeth
and goes pecking out the remains of the
food, and so inciting it with voluptuous
delight tempts it to open the whole of its
mouth, and so it sleeps. This being observed
by the ichneumon it flings itself into its
mouth and perforates its stomach and
bowels, and finally kills it.

DELFINI.

¹¹La natura à dato tal cognitione alli·
ani¹²mali che, oltre allo conosciere la lor co-
¹³modità, conoscono·la incomodità del ni-
¹⁴mico·; onde intēde il delfino·quāto ¹⁵va-
glia·il taglio delle sue·penne, posteli ¹⁶sulla
schiena, e quāto sia tenera la pācia ¹⁷del
cocodrillo·; onde·nel lor cōbattere se li
¹⁸caccia sotto e tagliali la pācia, e così
¹⁹l'uccide.

²⁰Il cocodrillo è terribile a chi fuggie, e
vilis²¹simo a chi lo caccia.

THE DOLPHIN.

Nature has given such knowledge to
animals, that besides the consciousness of
their own advantages they know the disad-
vantages of their foes. Thus the dolphin
understands what strength lies in a cut from
the fins placed on his chine, and how tender
is the belly of the crocodile; hence in
fighting with him it thrusts at him from beneath and rips up his belly and so kills him.

The crocodile is a terror to those that flee,
and a base coward to those that pursue him.

H.1 26 b]   **1260.**

IPPOPOTAMO.

²Questo·quando si sente aggravato·va
³ciercando le spine, o dove siā i rima-
nē⁴ti de'tagliati canneti, e lì tāto frega vna

THE HIPPOPOTAMUS.

This beast when it feels itself over-full
goes about seeking thorns, or where there
may be the remains of canes that have been

lasspido. 10. tasta . . imodo chettolto. 11. cacia . . ella niega. ·13. nasscie . . piedi nvc vi. 14. ce in terra e in acq"a"
[e sua] ne . . tereste. 15. checquesto. 16. massciella. 17. cresscie . . vngliato. 18. [vestito] "armato" di . . atto ogni.
18. ella notte. 19. pessci. 20. bocha . . elluciello.

1259. 1. trocilo picholissimo vciello. 2. bocha essaltatoli. 3. effora liva bechando. 4. cibo e e cosi stuzicādolo. 5. lonuita . .
boccha. 7. daleleumone . . si linācia in boccha. 8. elle. 9. luccide [essimile al ramarro vergezzo]. 12. alo nassciere.
13. cogniosscano. 15. pene. 16. sula sciena . . pāca. 17. nellor. 18. ettagliali. 20. etteribile acci fuggie e vili
21. accilo.

1260. 1. hippotamo. 2. agravato. 3. cierchando . . sia. 4. caneti elli. 5. chauato . . chelli . . cola lita. 6. risaldala. 7. lūgia. 8. cīglare ve⁵na che la taglia, e cauato il sangue, che li ⁶bisognia, colla litta s'infanga, e risalta alla ⁷piaggia; à forma quasi come cavallo; l'ūghia, ⁸fessa, coda torta, e dēti di cīghiale; collo cō ⁹crini la pelle; nō si può passare·, se nō si ba¹⁰gnia·; pasciesi di piāte ne'cāpi, entravi ¹¹allo dirieto, accioché pare ne sia uscito.

IBIS.

¹³Questo à similitudine colla cicognia, e quan¹⁴do si sente ammalato, ēpie il gozzo d'acqua, ¹⁵e col becco si fa vn clistero.

CIERUI.

¹⁷Questo quando si sente morso dal ragno ¹⁸detto falangio·māgia de' grāchi, e si libera ¹⁹di tale veneno.

split, and it rubs against them till a vein is opened; then when the blood has flowed as much as he needs, he plasters himself with mud and heals the wound. In form he is something like a horse with long haunches, a twisted tail and the teeth of a wild boar, his neck has a mane; the skin cannot be pierced, unless when he is bathing; he feeds on plants in the fields and goes into them backwards so that it may seem, as though he had come out.

THE IBIS.

This bird resembles a crane, and when it feels itself ill it fills its craw with water, and with its beak makes an injection of it.

THE STAG.

These creatures when they feel themselves bitten by the spider called father-long-legs, eat crabs and free themselves of the venom.

H.¹ 27 a]

1261.

LUCERTE.

²Questa quādo cōbatte colle serpi ³mangia la cicierbita; e sō libere.

RONDINE.

⁵Questa rende il uedere alli orbiti ⁶figlioli col sugo della celidonia.

BELLULA.

⁸Questa quando caccia ai ratti, māgia ⁹prima·della·ruta.

CINGHIALE.

¹¹Questo medica·i sua·mali mangiādo ¹²della edera.

SERPE.

¹⁴Questa quādo si uol renovare, gitta il ¹⁵vechio scoglio, comīciādosi dalla testa; ¹⁶mvtasi in vn dì e vna notte.

PARTERA.

¹⁸Questa, poichè le sono·uscite l'interiora, ¹⁹ancora conbatte coi cani e cacciatori.

THE LIZARD.

This, when fighting with serpents eats the sow-thistle and is free.

THE SWALLOW.

This [bird] gives sight to its blind young ones, with the juice of the celandine.

THE WEASEL.

This, when chasing rats first eats of rue.

THE WILD BOAR.

This beast cures its sickness by eating of ivy.

THE SNAKE.

This creature when it wants to renew itself casts its old skin, beginning with the head, and changing in one day and one night.

THE PANTHER.

This beast after its bowels have fallen out will still fight with the dogs and hunters.

---

9. si po passare. 10. passciesi . . biāde. 11. vsscito. 13. assimilitudine . . ciguognia ecq"ā". 14. amalato . . il cozo dacque. 15. e chol becho . . cristero. 18. falange . . grāci essi.
1261. 2. colle [lucerte] serp. 3. essō. 5. alli unorbiti. 6. chol. 7. belola. 16. mvtasi nvndi . . nocte. 18. poichelle sono vsscite lenteriora.

H.1 27 b]   **1262.**

CAMELEONTE.

²Questo · piglia · senpre il colore della cosa ³dove si posa ·; onde insieme colle frōdi ⁴dove si posano, spesso dali elefanti sō diuorati.

CORBO.

⁶Questo quando à ucciso el cameleonte ⁷si purga coll'alloro.

THE CHAMELEON.

This creature always takes the colour of the thing on which it is resting, whence it is often devoured together with the leaves on which the elephant feeds.

THE RAVEN.

When it has killed the Chameleon it takes laurel as a purge.

H.1 48 b]   **1263.**

¶Moderanza raffrena tutti i vitj.
²L'ermelino prima morire che imbrat-³tarsi.

DELL'ANTIUEDERE.

⁵Il gallo nō cāta, se prima 3 volte nō batte ⁶l'alie; il papagalo nel mutarsi pe'rami ⁷nō mette i piè, doue non à prima ⁸messo il becco; ⁹¶il uoto nascie quādo la sperāza more.
¹⁰Il moto seguita il ciētro del peso.

Moderation checks all the vices.
The ermine will die rather than besmirch itself.

OF FORESIGHT.

The cock does not crow till it has thrice flapped its wings; the parrot in moving among boughs never puts its feet excepting where it has first put its beak. Vows are not made till Hope is dead.
Motion tends towards the centre of gravity.

H.3 53 a]   **1264.**

MAGNANIMITA.

Il falcone nō pi²glia se nō vccelli grossi, e prima ³more che māgiare carne di nō bono odore.

MAGNANIMITY.

The falcon never seizes any but large birds and will sooner die than eat [tainted] meat of bad savour.

1262. 6. quessto . . cameleont. 7. pugra choll alloro.
1263. 2. cheēbra. 8. becho. 9. nasscie. 10. mot seguita.

1264. 2. vcielli. 3. chare.

II.

FABLES.

1265.

FAVOLA.

²Sendo l'ostrica insieme colli altri ³pe-
sci in casa del pescatore scarica⁴ta vicino
al mare ·, priega il ratto, ⁵che al mare la
cōduca; il ratto fatto ⁶disegnio di māgiarla
la fa aprire, ⁷e mordēdola questa li serra
la testa ⁸e si lo ferma; viene la gatta e
l'uccide.

A FABLE.

An oyster being turned out together with
other fish in the house of a fisherman near
the sea, he entreated a rat to take him to
the sea. The rat purposing to eat him
bid him open; but as he bit him the oyster
squeezed his head and closed; and the cat
came and killed him.

Fables on
animals
(1265—1270).

1266.

FAVOLA.

²I tordi si rallegrarono forte, vedēdo
che l'omo prese la ciuetta ³e le tolse la
libertà, quella legando con forti legami ai
sua piedi; la ⁴qual ciuetta fu poi mediante
il uischio causa nō di far perdere ⁵la libertà
· ai tordi, ma la loro propia vita ·; detta
per quelle ⁶terre che si rallegrā di uedere
perdere la libertà ai loro maggio⁷ri, mediante i quali poi perdono il soccorso, e
rimāgono lega⁸ti in potētia del loro nemico ·,
lasciādo la libertà e spesse volte la uita.

A FABLE.

The thrushes rejoiced greatly at seeing a
man take the owl and deprive her of liberty,
tying her feet with strong bonds. But this
owl was afterwards by means of bird-lime
the cause of the thrushes losing not only
their liberty, but their life. This is said
for those countries which rejoice in seeing their
governors lose their liberty, when by that
means they themselves lose all succour, and
remain in bondage in the power of their enemies, losing their liberty and often their life.

1265. 2. lostriga . . colli al. 5. ce al mare . . fato. 7. sera. 8. essilo . . ellucide.
1266. 2. rallegrorono . . chellomo. 3. elle . . choforti. 4. viscio. chausa . . far perde. 5. malla. 6. chessi ralegrā . . mgai.
7. perdano il sochorso. 8. nemicho . . esspesse.

C. A. 117a; 361a]   1267.

FAVOLA.

[2] Dormēdo · il cane · sopra la pelle · d' un castrone, vna delle sua [3] pulci ·, sentēdo · l' odore · della vnta · lana ·, givdicò quello [4] dovesse essere · loco di migliore · vita e piv sicura da denti e unghie del cane, che pascier[5] si del cane ·; e sanza altri pensieri abbandonò il cane, e lì entrata [6] infra la folta lana ·, cominciò cō somma fatica · a volere [7] trapassare alle radici de' peli ·; la quale inpresa dopo molto [8] sudore trovò esser uana ·, perchè tali peli erano tanto spessi che [9] quasi si toccavano, e nō u'era spatio dove la pulcie potesse saggiare [10] tal pelle ·; ōde · dopo lūgo travaglio e fatica cominciò a vole[11] re ritornare al suo cane ·, il quale essendo già partito, fu [12] costretta dopo lūgo pētimēto e amari piāti a morirsi di fame.

A FABLE.

A dog, lying asleep on the fur of a sheep, one of his fleas, perceiving the odour of the greasy wool, judged that this must be a land of better living, and also more secure from the teeth and nails of the dog than where he fed on the dog; and without farther reflection he left the dog and went into the thick wool. There he began with great labour to try to pass among the roots of the hairs; but after much sweating had to give up the task as vain, because these hairs were so close that they almost touched each other, and there was no space where fleas could taste the skin. Hence, after much labour and fatigue, he began to wish to return to his dog, who however had already departed; so he was constrained after long repentance and bitter tears, to die of hunger.

C. A. 66a; 200a]   1268.

FAVOLA.

[2] Non si cōtentando · il uano · e vagabūdo parpaglione [3] di potere · comodevolmēte · volare · per l' aria, [4] vinto · dalla dilettevole · fiamma · della cādela, deli[5] berò · volare in quella ·; e 'l suo · giocōdo · movimē[6] to · fu cagione di subita · tristitia ·, inperochè in detto [7] lume si consumarono · le sottili ali · che 'l parpa[8] glione · misero caduto · tutto bruciato a piè del [9] candeliere ·; dopo · molto · pianto e pētimē[10] to · si rascivgò · le lagrime dai bagniati ochi, [11] e levato · il uiso in alto · disse ·: o falsa luce, [12] quāti · come me debi tu · avere · ne passa[13] ti tenpi · avere · miserabilmēte · ingañati! e se [14] pure volevo · vedere · la luce ·, nō doveu' · io cono[15] sciere il sole · dal falso · lume dello spurco sevo?

A FABLE.

The vain and wandering butterfly, not content with being able to fly at its ease through the air, overcome by the tempting flame of the candle, decided to fly into it; but its sportive impulse was the cause of a sudden fall, for its delicate wings were burnt in the flame. And the hapless butterfly having dropped, all scorched, at the foot of the candlestick, after much lamentation and repentance, dried the tears from its swimming eyes, and raising its face exclaimed: O false light! how many must thou have miserably deceived in the past, like me; or if I must indeed see light so near, ought I not to have known the sun from the false glare of dirty tallow?

FAVOLA.

[17] Trovando la scimia vno nidio di piccoli [18] vccelli ·, tutta · allegra · appressatasi a quelli, e quali essē[19] do già da volare, ne potè solo pigliare il minore; essē[20] do pieno d'allegrezza con esso · in mano, se n'ādò al suo [21] ricetto; e comīciato a cōsiderare

A FABLE.

The monkey, finding a nest of small birds, went up to it greatly delighted. But they, being already fledged, he could only succeed in taking the smallest; greatly delighted he took it in his hand and went to his abode; and having begun to look at the

---

1267. 2. chastrone. 4. dovessi . . locho . . sichura "da denti e vnglia del cane" che passcier. 5. essanza . . abandono. 6. infralla . . soma faticha. 7. molta [fa]. 9. to chauano . . potessi sagiare. 10. faticha cōmincio. 12. pētimēto amari.

1268. 2. chōtentando. 3. chomodamēte . . laria [dilibero dischore]. 4. revinto . . fiama . . chādela dili . . giochōdo. 6. chagione . . inperochēdetto . . 7. chonsumorono . . sottile ali . [ch]el . . brusato. 9. chandelieri. 11. dise. 12. chome . . pasa. 13. essi. 14. chome. 17. scimia [inp] vno . . di [lusi] di picioli. 18. vcielli . . apressatasi a queli. 20. dalegreza chon eso imano . . 21. ricieto e chomīciato a chōsiderare . . vcielletto. 22. issuecerato. 23. essirinse chellagli tolsi.

questo vccelletto, [22]lo comīciò a baciare; e
per lo sviscerato · amore tanto [23]lo baciò,
e rivolse, e strinse · ch' ella gli tolse la uita;
[24] è detta per quelli che per nō gastigare
i figlioli capita[25]no male.

little bird he took to kissing it, and from
excess of love he kissed it so much and
turned it about and squeezed it till he killed
it. This is said for those who by not punish-
ing their children let them come to mischief.

C. A. 66 b; 200 b]   **1269.**

FAVOLA.

[2]Stando il topo assediato · in vna piccola
sua abitatione [3]dalla donnola ·, la quale cō
cōtinva vigilantia attēdea [4]alla sua disfatione,
· e' per uno · piccolo spiraculo riguarda[5]va
il suo grā pericolo; infrattanto · venne la
gatta, [6]e subito prese essa donnola, e ime-
diate l' ebbe diuorata; [7]allora il ratto ·,
fatto sacrificio a Giove d' alquāte sua noc-
[8]ciole ·, ringratiò sommamēte la sua deità, e
uscito fori dalla [9]sua buca a possedere la
già persa libertà, della quale subito in[10]sieme
colla vita fu dalle feroci unghie de' denti
della [11]gatta privato.

A FABLE.

A rat was besieged in his little dwelling
by a weasel, which with unwearied vigī-
lance awaited his surrender, while watching
his imminent peril through a little hole.
Meanwhile the cat came by and suddenly
seized the weasel and forthwith devoured
it. Then the rat offered up a sacrifice to
Jove of some of his store of nuts, humbly
thanking His providence, and came out
of his hole to enjoy his lately lost liberty.
But he was instantly deprived of it, together
with his life, by the cruel claws and teeth
of the lurking cat.

C. A. 66 b; 201 b]   **1270.**

FAUOLA.

[2]La formica · trovato vno · grano di
[3]miglio ·, ꝉl grano sētendosi preso da quel-
[4]la gridò: se mi fai tāto piacere di [5]lasci-
armi fruire il mio desiderio del [6]nasciere ·,
io ti rēderò · ciēto me medesimi; [7]e così
fu fatto.
[8]Trovato il ragnio vno grappolo · d' uue,
[9]il quale per la sua dolcezza era · molto ·
visitato · da avi e diuerse [10]qualità · di mosche ·, li parue · avere trouato [11]loco · molto
· comodo · al suo · inganno ·; e cala[12]tosi giù
· per lo suo · sottile · filo, e ētrato · nella no-
[13]va · abitatione · lì ogni · giorno [14]faciēdosi
alli spiraculi ·, fatti dalli [15]interualli · de' grani
· dell' uue ·, assaltaua come [16]ladrone i miseri
animali · che da lui non si [17]guardauano; e
passati · alquanti · giorni · il [18]uendemiatore ·
colse · essa uva e, messa coll' al[19]tre · insieme,
con quelle · fu pigiata ·; e così [20]l' una · fu
laccio e inganno · dello ingañatore [21]ragnio ·,
come · delle · ingannate mosche.
[22]Addormētatosi · l' asino · sopra il ghiaccio [23]d' ū profondo · lago ·, il suo · calore
dissolue [24]esso ghiaccio ·, e l' asino · sott-
t' acqua a mal suo [25]danno si destò · e subito · annegò.

A FABLE.

The ant found a grain of millet. The
seed feeling itself taken prisoner cried out
to her: "If you will do me the kindness to
allow me accomplish my function of reproduction, I will give you a hundred such as
I am." And so it was.
A Spider found a bunch of grapes which
for its sweetness was much resorted to by
bees and divers kinds of flies. It seemed
to her that she had found a most convenient
spot to spread her snare, and having settled
herself on it with her delicate web, and
entered into her new habitation, there, every
day placing herself in the openings made by
the spaces between the grapes, she fell like
a thief on the wretched creatures which were
not aware of her. But, after a few days
had passed, the vintager came, and cut away
the bunch of grapes and put it with others,
with which it was trodden; and thus the
grapes were a snare and pitfall both for the
treacherous spider and the betrayed flies.
An ass having gone to sleep on the ice
over a deep lake, his heat dissolved the ice
and the ass awoke under water to his great
grief, and was forthwith drowned.

1269. 2. stanto . . pichola. 3. della donora. 4. per ꝉ pichola spirachulo ragnarda. 5. perichulo . vene. 6. donola. 7. dalquata
sua no. 8. rigratio somamente . . vsscito . della. 9. busa . . dela. 10. ungha. 11. privata.

1070. formicha. 4. lagrodo. 5. lassciarmi. 6. nassciere . . redero. 9. il quale "per la sua dolceza" era. 10. mossche. 11. locho
. . chomodo . . cholla. 12. gu. 13. giorno [con ingani]. 14. [chonduci] faciēdosi. 15. chome. 16. dallui. 17. chon.
18. colta . . vua e messe. 20. laccio ēnganno. 21. chome . . mossche. 22. adormentatosi . . diaccio. 23. disolue.
24. diaccio ellasino sottacqa. 25. desstto. 26. soportare chō. 27. nasschōdere cheffallanitra. 28. sottacqa. 29. pene.

²⁶Il falcone ·, nō potendo sopportare cō patiētia ²⁷il nascōdere che fa l'anitra, fugiēdo se le dināzi ²⁸e entrādo sotto · acqua · volle, come quelle, sott' acqua ²⁹seguitare, e bagniatosi le penne rimase in essa ³⁰acqua; e l'anitra, leuatasi in aria ·, scherne ³¹il falcone che annegaua.

³²Il ragnio ·, volendo · pigliare · la mosca cō sue ³³false · reti ·, fu · sopra · quelle · dal calabrone ³⁴crudelmēte morto.

³⁵Volendo · l'aquila · schernire · il gufo, rimase ³⁶coll' alie · inpaniata ·, e fu dall' omo · presa e morta.

A falcon, unable to endure with patience the disappearance of a duck, which, flying before him had plunged under water, wished to follow it under water, and having soaked his feathers had to remain in the water while the duck rising to the air mocked at the falcon as he drowned.

The spider wishing to take flies in her treacherous net, was cruelly killed in it by the hornet.

An eagle wanting to mock at the owl was caught by the wings in bird-lime and was taken and killed by a man.

S. K. M. III. 93b]					1271.

Fables on lifeless objects (1271—1274).

Trovandosi l'acqua nel superbo mare, suo elemē²to, le veñe voglia di mōtare sopra ³l'aria, e cōfortata dal foco elemēto, releuatasi ī sottile vapore, ⁴quasi parea della sottigliezza dell' ari⁵e; mōtata in alto givnse īfra l'a⁶ria piv sottile e fredda, dove fu abādona⁷ta dal foco, e i piccoli granicoli, ⁸sendo ristretti, già s'uniscono e fā⁹nosi pesanti, ove cadēdo la superbia ¹⁰si cōuerte in fuga, e cade dal cielo, ¹¹ōde poi fu beuuta dalla secca terra, ¹²dove lūgo tēpo incarcierata ¹³fece penitētia del suo peccato.

The water finding that its element was the lordly ocean, was seized with a desire to rise above the air, and being encouraged by the element of fire and rising as a very subtle vapour, it seemed as though it were really as thin as air. But having risen very high, it reached the air that was still more rare and cold, where the fire forsook it, and the minute particles, being brought together, united and became heavy; whence its haughtiness deserting it, it betook itself to flight and it fell from the sky, and was drunk up by the dry earth, where, being imprisoned for a long time, it did penance for its sin.

C. A. 172b; 516b]					1272.

FAUOLA.

²Vsciendo vn giorno il rasojo · di quel manico, col quale si fa gvaina a se medesimo, ³e postosi al sole ·, vide il sole spechiarsi nel suo corpo; della qual cosa prese somma gloria, ⁴e rivolto col pensiero · indirieto · cominciò cō seco medesimo · a dire: Or tornerò io ⁵piv a quella bottega della quale novamēte uscito · sono ·? cierto · no ·; nō piaccia alli Dei che ⁶si splendida bellezza caggia in tāta viltà d'animo! che pazzia sarebbe quella, la qual mi cō⁷ducesse a radere le insaponate barbe de' rustici villani · e fare mecaniche operationi! ⁸è questo corpo da simili eserciti? cierto

A FABLE.

The razor having one day come forth from the handle which serves as its sheath and having placed himself in the sun, saw the sun reflected in his body, which filled him with great pride. And turning it over in his thoughts he began to say to himself: "And shall I return again to that shop from which I have just come? Certainly not; such splendid beauty shall not, please God, be turned to such base uses. What folly it would be that could lead me to shave the lathered beards of rustic peasants and perform such menial service! Is this body destined for such work? Certainly not. I will hide myself in some retired spot and

---

30. ellanitra . . schernia. 31. anegava. 32. cosua. 33. rete. 35. schenire. 36. inpaniate eff.
1271. 1. lacq"a" . . superbo "mare" suo. 3. laria "e cōfortata dal foco elemēto" eleuatosi. 4. sittiglieza. 5. infralla. 6. sottile "effreda" dove. 7. focho e picoli. 8. restretti . . suniscano effā. 9. la superb. 10. del cielo. 11. bevute . . sechatera. 13. fe . . pechato.
1272. 2. vssciendo . . rasoro . . manicho chol . . giaina asse. 3. isspechiarsi . . chorpo . . chosa . . soma groria. 4. chol . . chomincio chōsecho. 5. acquella . . vsscito . . piacia alli de . la e. 6. belleza chagia . pazia . . sarebe . . michō. 7. duciessi . . russtrichi vilani effare smechaniche operatione. 8. or questo orpo da . . vogli naschondere. 9. ochulto locho

no; Io mi voglio nascondere in qualche [9]oculto loco, e lì cō trāquillo riposo passare mia vita ·; E così nascosto per alquāti mesi, [10]vn giorno ritornato all'aria e uscito fori della sua guaina, vide se essere fatto a si-[11]militudine d'una rugginēte sega, e la sua superfitie non ui spechiare piv lo splendiēte sole; [12]cō vano pētimēto indarno piāse lo inriparabile danno, con seco diciēdo: o quanto [13]meglio era esercitare col barbiere il mio perduto taglio di tāta sottilità; dov'è la lustrante [14]superfitie? certo la fastitiosa e brutta ruggine l'à consumata!

[15]Questo medesimo · accade nelli ingiegni · che in scābio dello esercitio si danno · all'otio; [16]I quali · a similitudine del sopra detto · rasojo · perdono la tagliente sua sottilità, [17]e la rugine della ignioranza guasta la sua forma.

FAUOLA.

[19]Vna · pietra novamēte per l'acque scoperta di bella grādezza si staua sopra vn cierto loco rilevato, [20]dove terminava un dilettevole boschetto sopra vna sassosa strada in cō[21]pagnia d'erbe, di uari fiori di diuersi colori ornate, e vedea [22]la grā somma delle pietre che nella a se sotto [23]posta strada collocate · erano ·; le uenne · desiderio di là giv lasciarsi ca[24]dere, diciēdo · cō seco: che fo io qui · cō queste erbe? io voglio cō que[25]ste mie sorelle in cōpagnia abitare; e giv lasciatosi cadere infra [26]le desiderate cōpagnie finì suo volubile corso ·; e stata alquāto co[27]mīciò a essere dalle rote de' carri ·, dai piè de' ferrati cavalli, e de [28]viandāti · a essere in continvo travaglio ·; chi la volta, quello la pesta[29]va; alcuna volta se leuava alcuno pezzo, quādo stava coperta da fā[30]go o sterco di qualche animale ·, e in vano riguardava il loco dō-[31]de partita s'era in nel loco della solletaria e trāquilla pace;

[32]Così accade a quelli che dalla vita soletaria cōtenplativa voglio[33]no venir abitare nelle città infra i popoli pieni d'infiniti mali.

---

there pass my life in tranquil repose." And having thus remained hidden for some months, one day he came out into the air, and issuing from his sheath, saw himself turned to the similitude of a rusty saw while his surface no longer reflected the resplendent sun. With useless repentance he vainly deplored the irreparable mischief saying to himself: "Oh! how far better was it to employ at the barbers my lost edge of such exquisite keenness! Where is that lustrous surface? It has been consumed by this vexatious and unsightly rust."

The same thing happens to those minds which instead of exercise give themselves up to sloth. They are like the razor here spoken of, and lose the keenness of their edge, while the rust of ignorance spoils their form.

A FABLE.

A stone of some size recently uncovered by the water lay on a certain spot somewhat raised, and just where a delightful grove ended by a stony road; here it was surrounded by plants decorated by various flowers of divers colours. And as it saw the great quantity of stones collected together in the roadway below, it began to wish it could let itself fall down there, saying to itself: "What have I to do here with these plants? I want to live in the company of those, my sisters." And letting itself fall, its rapid course ended among these longed for companions. When it had been there sometime it began to find itself constantly toiling under the wheels of the carts the iron-shoed feet of horses and of travellers. This one rolled it over, that one trod upon it; sometimes it lifted itself a little and then it was covered with mud or the dung of some animal, and it was in vain that it looked at the spot whence it had come as a place of solitude and tranquil place.

Thus it happens to those who choose to leave a life of solitary comtemplation, and come to live in cities among people full of infinite evil.

---

elli chō . . chosi naschosto. 10. gorno . . . vsscito . . fatto assi. 11. ruginēte . ella . . noui spechiare. 12. cho . . dano cho secho . . o qua. 13. chol . . il mi . . lusstante. 14. fasstidiosa . . rugine. 15. chenisschābio. 16. assimilitudine . . decto nasoro perde . . suttilita. 17. ella . . guassta. 19. pietra | "novamēte per lacque scoperta" di bella grādeza . . locho. 20. vdidi lettevole bosschetto . . īchō. 21. derbettedi uari . . cholori ornata. 22. soma . . asse. 23. chollochate . . uene . . lassciarsi cha. 24. chōsecho . . chō . . chō. 25. sorelle . . chōpagnia . . lassatosi chadere. 26. chōpagnie . . cho. 27. dale . . charri . . defferati chavalli. 28. chontinvo . . quale la. 29. alchuna . . alchuno pezo . choperta. 30. osstercho . . locho. 31. partata . . inel locho. 32. acade acquelli che della . . chōtenplativa voglia.

C. A. 66 *a*; 201 *a*]   **1273.**

²Le fiamme · già · aveano durato nella fornace ³de' bichieri, e veduto a se avicinarsi vna ⁴candela in vn bello e lustrante cādeliere, con gran deside⁵rio si forzauano · accostarsi a quella; infra le qua⁶li vna, lasciato el suo naturale ⁷corso e tiratasi dentro · a vno · voto stizzo, dove ⁸ si pascieva · e vsscita fori d'una piccola fessura ⁹alla cādela, che vicina l'era, si ¹⁰gittò · e cō somma · gelosità · e ingordigia quella ¹¹diuorando · quasi · a fine la condusse ·; e volendo ripa¹²rare · al prolungamēto · della sua vita, indar¹³no tētō tornare alla fornace ·, donde partita s'era, ¹⁴perchè fu costretta · morire, le mazze insieme ¹⁵colla cādela, ōde al fine cō piāto e pētimēto ¹⁶ · in fastidioso fumo si convertì, lasciādo ¹⁷tutte le sorelle in splendente e lūga vita e bellezza.

Some flames had already lasted in the furnace of a glass-blower, when they saw a candle approaching in a beautiful and glittering candlestick. With ardent longing they strove to reach it; and one of them, quitting its natural course, writhed up to an unburnt brand on which it fed and passed at the opposite end out by a narrow chink to the candle which was near. It flung itself upon it, and with fierce jealousy and greediness it devoured it, having reduced it almost to death, and, wishing to procure the prolongation of its life, it tried to return to the furnace whence it had come. But in vain, for it was compelled to die, the wood perishing together with the candle, being at last converted, with lamentation and repentance, into foul smoke, while leaving all its sisters in brilliant and enduring life and beauty.

C. A. 66 *b*; 201 *b*]   **1274.**

Trovandosi · alquanta · poca neve ²appiccata alla sommità · d'un sasso, il quale ³era collocato sopra la strema · al⁴tezza d'una · altissima · mōtagnia, e raccol⁵to · in se · la imaginatione, comiciò · con quella ⁶a considerare e infra se · dire: Or nō son io ⁷da essere · givdicata · altera . e superba, avere ⁸me piccola · dramma · di neve · posto · in si al⁹to loco? e sopportare che tanta quātità di neve, ¹⁰quanta · di qui · per me · essere veduta può, stia ¹¹piv bassa di me? cierto · la mia poca quāti¹²tà non merita · questa · altezza, chè bene posso per ¹³testimonāza · della mia · piccola · figura conoscie¹⁴re quello che 'l sole fecie · ieri alle mia con¹⁵pagnie, · le quali in poche · ore · dal sole furo¹⁶no · disfatte ·; e questo interuenne per essersi ¹⁷posto piv alto · che a loro nō si richiedea ·; io vo¹⁸glio fugire · l'ira · del sole, e abbassarmi, e trovare ¹⁹loco · cōueniēte · alla mia parua quātità; ²⁰e gittatasi in baso e comīciata a disciēdere rottādo ²¹dall'alte spiaggie · super l'altra neve, quāto piv ciercò ²²loco · basso ·, piv · crebbe · sua · quātità in

A small patch of snow finding itself clinging to the top of a rock which was lying on the topmost height of a very high mountain and being left to its own imaginings, it began to reflect in this way, saying to itself: "Now, shall not I be thought vain and proud for having placed myself—such a small patch of snow—in so lofty a spot, and for allowing that so large a quantity of snow as I have seen here around me, should take a place lower than mine? Certainly my small dimensions by no means merit this elevation. How easily may I, in proof of my insignificance, experience the same fate as that which the sun brought about yesterday to my companions, who were all, in a few hours, destroyed by the sun. And this happened from their having placed themselves higher than became them. I will flee from the wrath of the sun, and humble myself and find a place befitting my small importance." Thus, flinging itself down, it began to descend, hurrying from its high home on to the other snow; but the more it sought a low place

1273. 1. [lo ingordo fochosapiglia nelle legnie]. 2. [il focho] "le fiame" gia vno . r e durato nella. 3. de bichieri . . asse. 4. chandela . . bello chandeliere "ellusstrante" chon gra. 5. achostarsi a chuella infralle. 6. vna [falcara] laciato. 7. stizo. 8. vsscita | "dal oposita" fori. 9. [alume che lara] alla cādella. 10. chō soma . . ingordigia [di] quella. 11. fine chō dule e volento. 13. tonare. 14. chostretta . . le mazare. 15. cholla . . chō. 16. [si cō uerti] in . . lumo si . . lasciā. 17. issplendevole ellūga . . belleza.
1274. 1. pocha. 2. apichata . . somita. 3. chollochato soprapra lasstrema. 4. teza . . rachol. 5. lamaginatione chomīcio chon. 6. chonsiderare. 7. givdichata. 8. picciola droma. 9. locho essoportare che tante. 10. quanto . . veduta po stia. 11. pocha. 12. nomerta questa alteza. 13. pichola . . chonosscie . . chon. 16. disfacte ecquesto interuene. 17. alora. 18. abastarmi. 19. chōueniēte. 20. chomīciata . . rottāto. 21. dell . . spiagie . . quato. 22. imodo. 23. sopra î

modo ²³che, terminato · il suo · corso · sopra · uno colle, si trouò ²⁴di nō quasi minor grādezza · che 'l colle che essa sostenea; ²⁵e fu · l'ultima · che in quella · state · dal sole disfatta ²⁶fusse ·; detta · per quelli · che s'umiliano,-son esaltate.

the more its bulk increased, so that when at last its course was ended on a hill, it found itself no less in size than the hill which supported it; and it was the last of the snow which was destroyed that summer by the sun. This is said for those who, humbling themselves, become exalted.

C. A. 75 a; 219 a]

1275.

Avēdo jl ciedro desiderio di fare uno bello e grāde frutto ²in nella sommità · di se lo mise in essecutione cō tutte le ³forze del suo omore ·; jl quale frutto cresciuto · fu cagione ⁴di fare declinare la eleuata e diritta cima.

⁵Il persico avēdo · jvidia alla grā quātità de' fru⁶tti visti fare al noce suo vicino, deliberato fare ⁷il simile ·, si caricò de' sua in modo tale che 'l peso ⁸di detti frutti lo tirò diradicato e rotto alla piana ⁹terra.

The cedar, being desirous of producing a fine and noble fruit at its summit, set to work to form it with all the strength of its sap. But this fruit, when grown, was the cause of the tall and upright tree-top being bent over.

The peach, being envious of the vast quantity of fruit which she saw borne on the nut-tree, her neighbour, determined to do the same, and loaded herself with her own in such a way that the weight of the fruit pulled her up by the roots and broke her down to the ground.

Fables on plants (1275—1279).

ciedro (*cedar*).   persico (*peach-tree*).   noce (*nut-tree*).   fico (*fig-tree*).   fico (*fig-tree*).   olmo (*elm-tree*).

¹⁰Il noce mostrādo se per vna strada ai viādanti ¹¹la richezza de' sua frutti, ogni omo lo lapidaua.

¹²Il fico stādo sanza frutti, nessuno lo riguardaua; ¹³volendo col fare essi frutti essere laudato dali o¹⁴mini ·, fu da quelli piegato · e rotto.

¹⁵Stando il fico vicino all'olmo ·, e riguardando i sua ¹⁶rami essere · sanza frutti e avere ardimēto ¹⁷di tenere il sole · a sua · acerbi fichi cō rā¹⁸pognie gli disse: o olmo ·, non ài tu vergogna a ¹⁹starmi dināzi? ma aspetti · che mia figlioli sieno ²⁰in matura · età, e vedrai dove ti troverai! i quali ²¹figlioli poi maturati, capitādovi una squadra ²²di soldati, fu da quelli per torre i sua fichi tutto lacera²³to · e diramato e

The nut-tree stood always by a road side displaying the wealth of its fruit to the passers by, and every one cast stones at it.

The fig-tree, having no fruit, no one looked at it; then, wishing to produce fruits that it might be praised by men, it was bent and broken down by them.

The fig-tree, standing by the side of the elm and seeing that its boughs were bare of fruit, yet that it had the audacity to keep the Sun from its own unripe figs with its branches, said to it: "Oh elm! art thou not ashamed to stand in front of me. But wait till my offspring are fully grown and you will see where you are!" But when her offspring were mature, a troop of soldiers coming by fell upon the fig-tree and her

cole. 24. grādeza. 25. effu. 26. chessa umiliano. 26. esaltate.
1275. 2. inella somita . . mise aseguitione chō tuttelle. 3. frutto "crescivto" fu chagione. 5. persicho. 6. diliberato. 7. charicho . . imodo. 8. diradichato. 9. tera. 10. mostādo se per. 11. richeza . . frutto. 12. ficho. 13. chol . . frutte . . laldato. 15. ficho. 17. acerbi [fra] fichi chō. 18. dise hoholmo . . ha. 19. asspetta. 20. imatura . . vederai. 21. chapitādovi sguadra. 22. queli pertore i sua. 23. chosi. 25. do h"o" ficho. 26. queli.

rotto; il quale stādo poi così ²⁴storpiato delle sue mēbra·, l'olmo lo dimādò diciē²⁵do: o fico quāto· era il meglio a stare sanza figlioli ²⁶che per quelli venire in si miserabile stato!

figs were all torn off her, and her boughs cut away and broken. Then, when she was thus maimed in all her limbs, the elm asked her, saying: "O fig-tree! which was best, to be without offspring, or to be brought by them into so miserable a plight!"

S. K. M. III. 45[a]   **1276.**

La piāta si dole del palo ²secco e vechio che se l'era ³posto al lato e de'pali ⁴secchi che la circūdano;
⁵L'ū lo mātiene diritto, ⁶l'altro lo guarda dalla ⁷triste cōpagnia.

The plant complains of the old and dry stick which stands by its side and of the dry stakes that surround it.
One keeps it upright, the other keeps it from low company.

C. A. 66 a; 200 a]   **1277.**

FAVOLA.

²Trovādosi la noce essere della cornacchia ³portata · sopra vn alto · campanile, e'per ⁴vna fessura, doue caddè, fu liberata · dal mortale ⁵suo becco; pregò · esso muro · ⁶per quella · gratia che Dio li aveva dato · del essere tanto ⁷eminēte · e magnio · e ricco di si belle cāpane e di tā⁸to · onorevole · suono·ch'ella douesse soccorrere, ⁹poi ch'ella non avea potuta cadere sotto ¹⁰i verdi rami del suo vechio · padre·, e essere nella gras-¹¹sa terra, ricoperta dalle sue cadēti foglie·, che non la ¹²volesse lui abandonare·, jnperoch'ella, trovādosi ¹³nel becco della · fiera corua, ¹⁴votò, che scappādo da essa voleua finire la ui¹⁵ta · sua · in un piccolo buco; alle quali parole ¹⁶il mvro·, mosso · a cōpassione, · fu cōtento riciettar¹⁷la nel loco ov'era caduta·; e infra poco tēpo ¹⁸la noce cominciò aprirsi e mettere le radici infra ¹⁹le fessure delle pietre·, e quelle allargare, e gitta²⁰re i rami fori della sua · caverna·; e quegli ²¹in brieve leuati sopra lo edifitio, e ingrossate le ²²ritorte radici, cominciò aprire i mvri e ca²³uare le antiche pietre de' loro · uechi lochi; allo²⁴ra il muro · tardi e indarno pianse · la cagione del suo danno; ²⁵e in breve aprì e rovinò grā parte delle sua mēbra.

A FABLE.

A nut, having been carried by a crow to the top of a tall campanile and released by falling into a chink from the mortal grip of its beak, it prayed the wall by the grace bestowed on it by God in allowing it to be so high and thick, and to own such fine bells and of so noble a tone, that it would succour it, and that, as it had not been able to fall under the verdurous boughs of its venerable father and lie in the fat earth covered up by his fallen leaves it would not abandon it; because, finding itself in the beak of the cruel crow, it had there made a vow that if it escaped from her it would end its life in a little hole. At these words the wall, moved to compassion, was content to shelter it in the spot where it had fallen; and after a short time the nut began to split open and put forth roots between the rifts of the stones and push them apart, and to throw out shoots from its hollow shell; and, to be brief, these rose above the building and the twisted roots, growing thicker, began to thrust the walls apart, and tear out the ancient stones from their old places. Then the wall too late and in vain bewailed the cause of its destruction and in a short time, it wrought the ruin of a great part of it.

1276. 2. secho. 3. ede pa||||||. 4. sechi chello.

277. 2. della chornachia. 3. [essere] portato . . chan panile. 4. chade . . liberato. 5. [becho] suo becho pregho . . mvro [chella ricicua]. 7. richo . . chāpane. 8. honorevole sono . . douessi sochorere. 9. perche poichela non era pututa chadere 10. nella gra. 11. tera richoperto delle . . chadēti . . nola. 12. volessi. 13. nel fiero becho . . chorua chia chella si. 14. vot. [v] che schāpādo. 15. nvn piciolo buso. 16. chōpassione . . chōtento. 17. nelocho . . chaduta . . pocho. 18. chomīcio. 19. ecquelle. 20. chaverna. 21. ingrosate. 24. tardi | "e indarno" pianse . . dano. 25. brieve apero rovino.

C. A. 66 *a*; 200 *a*]

1278.

FAVOLA.

[2] Il rovistico ·, sendo stimolato nelli sua sottili · rami ripieni di novelli [3] frutti dai pugniēti artigli e becco · delle inportune merle, si do[4]leva cō pietoso · rammarichio · īuerso essa · merla, pregando quella [5] che, poichè lei li toglieva · e sua diletti · frutti, il merlo non le privasse [6] delle foglie, le quali lo difendevano · dai cociēti · razzi del sole, e che coll'a[7]cute vnghie non la scorticasse e suestisse della · sua tenera · pelle; [8] Alla quale la merla con vilani rāpognie rispose: o taci salua[9]tico · sterpo · ! nō sai che la natura t'à fatto produrre · questi frutti [10] per mio notrimēto? nō uedi che sei al mōdo per servirmi di tale cibo? [11] nō sai, vilano ·, che tu · farai in nella prossima īuernata notri-[12]mēto e cibo del fuoco ·? le quali parole ascoltate dal albero [13] patiētemēte, nō sanza lacrime ·, jnfra poco tenpo il merlo preso [14] dalla ragnia, e colti de' rami per fare gabbia per īcarcerare esso merlo [15] toccò infra l'altri rami al sottile rovistico a fare legni minimi [16] della gabbia, le quali vedēdo essere causa della persa libertà del merlo, [17] rallegratasi mosse tale parole: O merlo · io sono qui non ācora [18] consumata, come dicievi, dal foco; prima vedrò te prigione, che tu me brugiata.

FAVOLA.

[20] Veduto · il lavro · e mirto · tagliare il pero ·, con alta voce [21] gridarono: O pero ·, ove vai · tu? ov'è la superbia che aveui quādo [22] aveui · i tua · maturi · frutti? ora nō ci farai · tu ōbra [23] colle tue · folte chiome ·; Allora · il pero · rispose: io ne ve[24]do l'agricola che mi taglia e mi porterà alla bottega d'ottimo [25] scultore, il quale mi farà con su' arte pigliare la forma [26] di Giove · Idio ·, e sarò dedicato nel tenpio · e dagli omini [27] adorato · invece di Giove; e tu ti metti ī pūto a rimanere [28] spesso storpiata · e pelata de' tua rami, i quali mi sieno [29] dali omini per onorarmi poste d'intorno.

A FABLE.

The privet feeling its tender boughs loaded with young fruit, pricked by the sharp claws and beak of the insolent blackbird, complained to the blackbird with pitious remonstrance entreating her that since she stole its delicious fruits she should not deprive it of the leaves with which it preserved them from the burning rays of the sun, and that she should not divest it of its tender bark by scratching it with her sharp claws. To which the blackbird replied with angry upbraiding: "O, be silent, uncultured shrub! Do you not know that Nature made you produce these fruits for my nourishment; do you not see that you are in the world [only] to serve me as food; do you not know, base creature, that next winter you will be food and prey for the Fire?" To which words the tree listened patiently, and not without tears. After a short time the blackbird was taken in a net and boughs were cut to make a cage, in which to imprison her. Branches were cut, among others from the pliant privet, to serve for the small rods of the cage; and seeing herself to be the cause of the Blackbird's loss of liberty it rejoiced and spoke as follows: "O Blackbird, I am here, and not yet burnt by fire as you said. I shall see you in prison before you see me burnt."

A FABLE.

The laurel and the myrtle seeing the pear tree cut down cried out with a loud voice: "O pear-tree! whither are you going? Where is the pride you had when you were covered with ripe fruits? Now you will no longer shade us with your mass of leaves." Then the pear-tree replied: "I am going with the husbandman who has cut me down and who will take me to the workshop of a good sculptor who by his art will make me take the form of Jove the god; and I shall be dedicated in a temple and adored by men in the place of Jove, while you are bound always to remain maimed and stripped of your boughs, which will be placed round me to do me honour.

1278. Irovesstrice. 3. pugiēti . . becho. 4. chō . . ramarichio. 5. poichellei . . mero nolle [togliessi] privasse. 6. dele . . razi . . cholla. 7. chute . . non ischortichasse dissuestissi . . pella. 8. Ala . . chon vilani rāgognie. 9. tichostrepo . . fatti produre. 10. chesse. 11. inela. 12. foco . . quali [dopo pi] parole ascholdate. 13. pocho. 14. dala . . cholti . . gabia . . īchacierare. 15. stocho . . rouisericho affare lenimini. 16. dela gabia . . chaua. 17. ralegratasi . . i sono . . āchora. 18. chonsumata chome . . focho . . vedero chettu. 20. chon. 22. hora. 23. chole . . focie. 24. cholagrichola. 25. chon. 26. essaro dedichato. 27. ettu. 28. ispeso. 31. chastagno. ficho. 32. "in verso se" i sua . . isspichava . frutti quelli i quali.

FAVOLA.

[31]Vedēdo jl castagnio · l'vomo · sopra · il fico, il quale piegava [32]inverso se i sua rami e di quelli spiccava · i maturi frutti · i quali mette[33]va nell' aperta bocca difaciēdoli e diserrādoli coi duri dēti, crollā[34]do · i lunghi rami, e' cō spregevole mormorio disse: [35]O fico · quāto sei tu mē di me obbligato alla natura ·! vedi come [36]in me ordinò · serrati · i mia dolci figlioli ·, prima vestiti di sottile ca[37]micia, sopra la quale è posta la dura e foderata pelle ·, e nō cō-[38]tētandosi di tanto benificarmi · ch'ell'à fatto loro la forte abi[39]tatione, e sopra quella fondò acute · e folte · spine ·, aciochè le [40]mani dell'omo · nō mi possino nvocere ·; Allora il fico comī[41]ciò insieme coi sua figlioli a ridere, e ferme le risa disse: [42]conosci l'omo essere di tale ingiegnio che lui ti sappi col[43]le pertiche e pietre e sterpi, tratti infra i tua rami, farti povero [44]de' tua frutti, e quelli caduti posta coi piedi o coi sassi, a modo [45]che i frutti tua escino straciati e storpiati fora dall'armata [46]casa; e io sono cō diligiēza tocco dalle mani, e nō come te da bastoni e da sasso.

A FABLE.

The chesnut, seeing a man upon the fig-tree, bending its boughs down and pulling off the ripe fruits, which he put into his open mouth destroying and crushing them with his hard teeth, it tossed its long boughs and with a noisy rustle exclaimed: "O fig! how much less are you protected by nature than I. See how in me my sweet offspring are set in close array; first clothed in soft wrappers over which is the hard but softly lined husk; and not content with taking this care of me, and having given them so strong a shelter, on this she has placed sharp and close-set spines so that the hand of man cannot hurt me." Then the fig-tree and her offspring began to laugh and having laughed she said: "I know man to be of such ingenuity that with rods and stones and stakes flung up among your branches he will bereave you of your fruits; and when they are fallen, he will trample them with his feet or with stones, so that your offspring will come out of their armour, crushed and maimed; while I am touched carefully by their hands, and not like you with sticks and stones."

C. A. 66 a; 201 a]   **1279.**

Il mischio · salice trovādosi nō potere fruire [2]il piacere di uedere i sua · sottili · rami · fare over [3]cōdurre · alla · desiderata · grandeza e dirizzarsi al cielo per cagione · della [4]vite · e di qualunche piāta · li era uicina ·, senpre elli [5]era · storpiato · e diramato; e guasto; e raccolte · in se tutti li spiri[6]ti · e' con quelli apre e' spalanca · le parti alla [7]imaginatione ·; e stando · in cōtinva · cogitatione ·, e riciercando · con quella · l'universo · delle piāte, cō quale [9]di quelle · esso collegare · si potesse che · non avesse biso[10]gnio · dell'aivto · de' sua · legami-; essendo stato · alquanto · in questa [11]nutritiva · imaginatione ·, cō subito assa[12]limēto li corse · nel pensiero · la zucca ·, e crollato tutti i ra-[13]mi · per grāde · allegrezza · pare li · avere trovato cōpa[14]gnia · al suo · desiato · proposito, imperochè quella è piv atta [15]a legare · altri che essere · legata; [16]e fatta tal

The hapless willow, finding that she could not enjoy the pleasure of seeing her slender branches grow or attain to the height she wished, or point to the sky, by reason of the vine and whatever other trees that grew near, but was always maimed and lopped and spoiled, brought all her spirits together and gave and devoted itself entirely to imagination, standing plunged in long meditation and seeking, in all the world of plants, with which of them she might ally herself and which could not need the help of her withes. Having stood for some time in this prolific imagination, with a sudden flash the gourd presented itself to her thoughts and tossing all her branches with extreme delight, it seemed to her that she had found the companion suited to her purpose, because the gourd is more apt to bind others than to need binding; having come to this conclusion

33. bocha . . choi. 34. chōtemultevole. 35. ficho. 36. settu . . obrigato . . chome. 37. ime . . serati . . cha . . chō. 38. benificharmi . . la [spinosa] abi. 39. achute effolte . . aciochelle. 40. aloro il ficho chomī. 41. choi . . dise. 42. cho chonosci . . sapicho. 44. queli chaduti posta cho . . chosassi. 45. chefrutti . . straciati . . dell. 46. chasa . . chō . . tocho . . chome te "da bastoni e" dassesso e.

1279. 1. miscio . . trovādosi [ognino] nō. 2. pia ure d[a]i. 3. condure . . grandeza | "e dirizarsi al cielo" per chagione. 4. vite. [d]e . . visina. 5. diramato | "e guasto" e racholte . . lisspi. 6. chon . . esspalancha . . parte. 7. chōtinva. 8. chando chon . . chō. 9. di qule . . chollegare si potessi [la quale] "che" non avessi. 10. gni . . esse "do" alquanto. 11. [imaginatione] notritiva. 12. zucha e chrollato. 13. allegreza . . chōpa. 14. disiato . . iperochecquella. 15. allegare . . [legata [e per ato la sschaza]. 16. [chelli piāti di] effatte . . diliberatione | "ricca sua rami iverso il cielo" attēde asspettare diliberatione rizza sua rami in uerso il cielo aspettando ¹⁷qualche amichevole · vcciello, che li fusse al disiderio mezzano; ¹⁸jfra quali · veduta · a se vicina · la sgarza disse inverso ¹⁹di quella : o giẽtile vcciello ·, per quello · soccorso ²⁰che a questi giorni da mattina · ne' mia rami trovasti, ²¹quãdo · l' affamato, crudele e rapace falcone ti voleva diuorare, ²²e per quelli · riposi che sopra me spesso ài ²³vsato · quãdo · ²⁴l' ali tue · a te · riposo chiedeano ·, e per quelli piacie²⁵ri che infra detti mia rami scherzãdo colle tue cõpagnie ²⁶ne' · tua · amoreggiamenti ài vsato, jo ti priego · che tu truovi, ²⁷la zucca ·, e inpetri da quella alquãte delle sue semẽze; ²⁸e dì a quelle · che, nate · ch'elle · fieno ·, ch'io le tratterò no²⁹n altramẽte · che se del mio corpo · gienerate l'auessi; ³⁰e similmẽte vsa tutte quelle parole, che di simile intẽ³¹tione persuasiue · sieno, benchè a te, maestra de' linguag³²gi, insegniare · non bisognia ·; e se questo ³³farai, io sono · cõtẽta di ricieuere il tuo nidio sopra ³⁴il nascimẽto de' mia · rami · insieme colla tua fa³⁵miglia sanza pagamẽto d'alcũ fitto ·; allora la sgar³⁶za · fatto · e fermato alquãti capitoli di novo col salice, e mas³⁷sima che biscie o faine sopra se mai non accettasse, ³⁸alzato la coda e bassato · la testa e gittatasi dal ramo ³⁹rẽde il suo · peso · all' ali, e quelle battẽdo sopra ⁴⁰la fugitiva · aria ·, ora qua, ora in là curiosamẽte col timõ della coda ⁴¹dirizzãdosi ·, peruẽe · a vna zucca ·, e cõ bel saluto ⁴²e alquãte bone parole inpetrò le dimandate semẽze; ⁴³e condottele al salice fu con lieta ciera ricevuta; ⁴⁴e raspato alquãto coi piè il terreno vicino al salicie, ⁴⁵col becco in cierchio a esso essi · grani · piãtò ·, li quali ⁴⁶in brieve tẽpo · cresciẽdo · comĩciarono collo accrescimẽto · e aprimẽto de' sua ⁴⁷rami · a occupare · tutti · i rami del salice, e colle sue ⁴⁸grã foglie · a toglierle · la bellezza del sole e del cielo ·; e nõ ⁴⁹bastãdo · tãto male, seguẽdo le zucche comĩciarono, per discõ-⁵⁰cio preso, a tirare le cime de' teneri rami inverso la te⁵¹rra con strane torture e disagio di quelli.

she awaited eagerly some friendly bird who should be the mediator of her wishes. Presently seeing near her the magpie she said to him: "O gentle bird! by the memory of the refuge which you found this morning among my branches, when the hungry cruel, and rapacious falcon wanted to devour you, and by that repose which you have always found in me when your wings craved rest, and by the pleasure you have enjoyed among my boughs, when playing with your companions or making love—I entreat you find the gourd and obtain from her some of her seeds, and tell her that those that are born of them I will treat exactly as though they were my own flesh and blood; and in this way use all the words you can think of, which are of the same persuasive purport; though, indeed, since you are a master of language, I need not teach you. And if you will do me this service I shall be happy to have your nest in the fork of my boughs, and all your family without payment of any rent." Then the magpie, having made and confirmed certain new stipulations with the willow,—and principally that she should never admit upon her any snake or polecat, cocked his tail, and put down his head, and flung himself from the bough, throwing his weight upon his wings; and these, beating the fleeting air, now here, now there, bearing about inquisitively, while his tail served as a rudder to steer him, he came to a gourd; then with a handsome bow and a few polite words, he obtained the required seeds, and carried them to the willow, who received him with a cheerful face. And when he had scraped away with his foot a small quantity of the earth near the willow, describing a circle, with his beak he planted the grains, which in a short time began to grow, and by their growth and the branches to take up all the boughs of the willow, while their broad leaves deprived it of the beauty of the sun and sky. And not content with so much evil, the gourds next began, by their rude hold, to drag the ends of the tender shoots down towards the earth, with strange twisting and distortion.

17. chelli fussi . . mezano. 18. asse . . lassgaza disse iver. 19. vcciello [jo ti priego] per . . sochorso. 20. acquesssti . . ine. 21. lafamato falchone | "crudeele he" rapacte. 22. [etti priego] "e" per . . sopra [inparani] speso. 23. quãdo [i nervi "e move \\\\\\\\\\ telle tua" issacho nõ poteano piv menare]. 24. [le tue alie] lalie | "tue" atte. 25. re che . . cholle . . chõpagnie. 26. amorigia . . chettu. 27. zucha . . inpretri dacquella. 28. ediacquelle . . lettrattero. 29. altremẽti chesse . . chorpo . . lanessi [essi]. 30. essimilmẽte. 31. atte . . lingua. 32. ne bisognia essecquesto [seruitio ni]. 33. chõtẽta. 34. nasscimẽto . . cholla. 35. lassga. 36. fatto "effermi" alquãti . . novo \\\ chol . . e ma. 37. bissce offaine . . acciettassi. 38. del rarmo. 39. ecquelle. 40. ora illa "curiosamẽte" cho. 41. dirizãdosi . . zucha echo . . dimadate. 43. chondottele . . cho lieto ciera. 44. rasspato . . copie il tereno. 45. chol becho iciercho [al salice ¶ esse] "a esse" graui . . le. 46. crescciẽdo . . chollo "accresscimẽto he a" primẽto. 47. ochupare . . cholle. 48. attorle la belleza. 49. bastãto . . zuche comĩcie per discõ. 50. attirare . . inver la. 51. chon istrane. *Lines* 52—54 *are written on the margin.* 52. scon

[52]Allora scontēdosi, e indarno crollan-
dosi per fare da se esse zuche cadere, e
indarno [53]vaneggiando alquāti giorni · in
simile inganno ·, perchè la bona e forte
collegatione tal [54]pēsiero negava, vedēdo
passare il uēto ·, a quello racomādādosi,
e quello soffiò forte; allora s'a[55]perse il
uechio e voto gābo del salice in 2 parti
insino [56]alle sue radici; e caduto in
2 parti indarno pianse se me[57]desimo, e
conobbe che era nato per non aver mai
bene.

Then, being much annoyed, it shook
itself in vain to throw off the gourd. After
raving for some days in such plans vainly,
because the firm union forbade it, seeing the
wind come by it commended itself to him.
The wind flew hard and opened the old and
hollow stem of the willow in two down to
the roots, so that it fell into two parts.
In vain did it bewail itself recognising that
it was born to no good end.

tēdossi . . crolladosi . . dasse . . chadere.　53. vanegiāto . . ingano . . efforte chollegatione.　54. acquello . . ecquello
56. radice.　57. conobe.

III.

JESTS AND TALES.

C. A. 117 a; 361 a] **1280.**

FACIETIA.

[2] Andādo vn prete per la sua parrochia il sabato santo, dādo [3] come vsanza l'acqua benedetta per le case, capitò nella stāza [4] d'ū pittore, doue spargiēdo essa acqua sopra alcuna sua pittu[5]ra esso pittore voltosi indirieto, alquāto crucciato; dis[6]se perchè faciesse tale spargimēto sopra le sue pitture? allora [7] il prete disse, essere così vsanza, e ch'era suo debito il fare [8] così, e che facieva bene, e chi fa bene debbe aspettare be[9]ne e meglio, chè così promettea Dio, e che d'ogni bene, che si [10] facieva in terra, se n'avrebbe di sopra per ogni vn 100; allora [11] il pittore, aspettato ch'egli uscisse fori, se li fecie di sopra [12] alla finestra, e gittò vn grā sechione d'acqua adosso a esso [13] prete, diciēdo: ecco che di sopra ti uiene per ogni v̄ 100, come [14] tu diciesti ·, che accaderebbe del bene che mi facievi colla [15] tua acqua santa, colla quale m'ài guasto mezze le mie [16] pitture.

A JEST.

A priest, making the rounds of his parish on Easter Eve, and sprinkling holy water in the houses as is customary, came to a painter's room, where he sprinkled the water on some of his pictures. The painter turned round, somewhat angered, and asked him why this sprinkling had been bestowed on his pictures; then said the priest, that it was the custom and his duty to do so, and that he was doing good; and that he who did good might look for good in return, and, indeed, for better, since God had promised that every good deed that was done on earth should be rewarded a hundred-fold from above. Then the painter, waiting till he went out, went to an upper window and flung a large pail of water on the priest's back, saying: "Here is the reward a hundred-fold from above, which you said would come from the good you had done me with your holy water, by which you have damaged my pictures."

S. K. M. III. 73 b] **1281.**

Il uino cōsumato dallo [2] ubriaco, esso vino col beuitore si vēdica.

When wine is drunk by a drunkard, that wine is revenged on the drinker.

1280. 4. hessa acq. 5. scrucciato di. 6. si . . faciessi. 8. asspettare. 9. chessi. 10. narebbe. 11. asspettato chelli vsscissi. 13. echo. 14. achaderebbe. 15. cholla . . meze.
1281. 1. chōsumato. 2. ubriacho . . chol . . vendicha.

1282.

⁸ Trovādosi il uino, divino licore dell' uua, in vna ⁹ avrea · e ricca tazza sopra la tavola di Ma¹⁰vmetto, e mōtato · in gloria di tā¹¹to onore, subito fu assaltato · da vna · cōtraria ¹²cogitatione · diciēdo · a se · medesimo: che fo, e di che ¹³ mi rallegro · io? non m' avvedo · essere vicino alla ¹⁴ mia morte? e lasciare l' aurea abitazione de¹⁵lla tazza · e entrare in nelle brutte e fetide caverne ¹⁶ del corpo vmano · e lì trasmvtarmi di odorife¹⁷ro e suave · licore · in brutta e trista orina? e nō ¹⁸ bastādo tāto male · ch'io ancora deba si lūga¹⁹mēte · giacere · ne' brutti ricettacoli coll' altra ²⁰fetida e corrotta materia, vscita dalle vmane inte²¹riora? gridò inverso · il cielo, chiedēdo ²² vēdetta di tanto danno, ²³ e che si ponesse ora mai fine a tāto dispreggio, ²⁴ chè, poichè quello paese producea le piv belle ²⁵ e migliori · vue di tutto · l' altro mōdo, che al meno ²⁶ esse non fussino · in vino cōdotte; allora Giove fece ²⁷ che 'l bevto · vino · da Mavmetto eleuò l' anima sua ²⁸ inverso · il cielabro ·, e quello · in modo cōtaminò che ²⁹ lo fecie · matto ·, e partorì tanti errori che, torna³⁰to in se, fecie legge che nessuno · Asiatico bevesse ³¹ vino ·; e furono lasciate poi libere le uiti coi sua frutti.

³² Già il uino, ³³ entrato ne³⁴llo stomaco, co³⁵mincia a bo³⁶llire e sgōfia³⁷re; già l' ani-³⁸ma di quello ³⁹ comincia a abā⁴⁰donare il cor⁴¹po; già si volta ⁴² inverso il cie⁴³lo; trova il cie⁴⁴labro ·, cagione ⁴⁵ della diuisione ⁴⁶ dal suo corpo; ⁴⁷ già lo comincia ⁴⁸ a cōtaminare ⁴⁹ e farlo furia⁵⁰re a modo di ma-⁵¹tto; già fa in⁵²riparabili erro⁵³ri, ammazzādo i su⁵⁴a amici.

Wine, the divine juice of the grape, finding itself in a golden and richly wrought cup, on the table of Mahomet, was puffed up with pride at so much honour; when suddenly it was struck by a contrary reflection, saying to itself: "What am I about, that I should rejoice, and not perceive that I am now near to my death and shall leave my golden abode in this cup to enter into the foul and fetid caverns of the human body, and to be transmuted from a fragrant and delicious liquor into a foul and base one. Nay, and as though so much evil as this were not enough, I must for a long time lie in hideous receptacles, together with other fetid and corrupt matter, cast out from human intestines." And it cried to Heaven, imploring vengeance for so much insult, and that an end might henceforth be put to such contempt; and that, since that country produced the finest and best grapes in the whole world, at least they should not be turned into wine. Then Jove made that wine drunk by Mahomet to rise in spirit to his brain; and that in so deleterious a manner that it made him mad, and gave birth to so many follies that when he had recovered himself, he made a law that no Asiatic should drink wine, and henceforth the vine and its fruit were left free.

As soon as wine has entered the stomach it begins to ferment and swell; then the spirit of that man begins to abandon his body, rising as it were skywards, and the brain finds itself parting from the body. Then it begins to degrade him, and make him rave like a madman, and then he does irreparable evil, killing his friends.

1283.

Vno · artigiano andando ² spesso a visitare vno signiore ³ sanza · altro · proposito dimādare ⁴ al quale, jl signore domandò ⁵ quello · che · andava faciēdo? ⁶ questo · disse che veniua lì ⁷ per avere · de' piacieri che

An artizan often going to visit a great gentleman without any definite purpose, the gentleman asked him what he did this for. The other said that he came there to have a pleasure which his lordship could not have;

1282. 1. Il uino vedendosi "nelle partimaumettane" ogni giorno . dai beuitori. 2. essere messo . . inelle fasstidiose . . brudella e chōller. 3. tito in urina e diaciere "lu gamēte" poire nei brutti e pu. 4. zalenti lochi . dilibero adoperare [i sua spiriti]. 5. [u] ogni sua . . forza [ara] al riparo di tāta. 6. nefanda vilta . e trovādosi sopra la tavola di. 7. mavmetto . . nvna richa e bella]. 8. trovādosi [il] il uino. 9. richacha taza. 10. groria. 11. honore. 12. cheffo i di che. 13. nomavedo. 14. ellassciare. 15. taza. 15. inelle . . effetide chaverne. 16. ellisstrassmvtarmi. 17. essuave . . ettrista. 18. basstādo. 18. anchora. 19. diasiere ine . . riciettacholi choll. 20. fitidae chor "o''tta . . vsscita delle. 22. danno [allora giove fecie]. 23. ponessi . . attāto disspregio. 24. paesse. 25. migliore . . il meno. 26. elle non . . chōdotte. 27. beuto. 28. ecquello imodo. 29. chettorna. 30. legie . . assiaticho beessi. 31. effunasssciato . . libere . . cosua. 34. o stomaco. 36. esscōfia. 47. cia lo comincia a. 49. effarlo. 52. cro. 53. amazādo.

1283. 6. quessto. 7. chellui. 8. perochello. 9. ĩvollentieri. 11. fano.

lui [8] aver nō potea; perochè [9] volentieri vedeua omi[10]ni piv potenti di lui, come [11] fanno i popolani, ma che 'l si[12]gnore non potea · vedere se [13] non omini di mē possa di lui; [14] per questo i signori māca[15]vano d'esso piacere.

since to him it was a satisfaction to see men greater than himself, as is the way with the populace; while the gentleman could only see men of less consequence than himself; and so lords and great men were deprived of that pleasure.

C. A. 147 *b*; 439 *a*]   **1284.**

Vsano i frati minori a cierti tempi alcune loro quaresime, nelle quali essi non māgiano carne ne' lor cōuēti, [2] ma in viaggio, perchè essi viuono di limosine ·, ànno liciētia di māgiare · ciò che è posto loro innāzi; ōde abattē[3]dosi in detti viaggi una copia d'essi frati a vn osteria · in cōpagnia d'ū cierto · mecantucolo ·, il quale essendo [4] a vna medesima mēsa, alla quale · nō fu portato per la pouertà dell'ostiero altro che vn pvllastro cotto; ōde es[5]so mercatucolo, vedendo questo essere poco per lui, si uolse a essi frati e disse: se io ho bē [6] di ricordo ·, voi nō māgiate in tali dì ne' vostri cōuēti · d'alcuna maniera di carne; alle quali parole i fra[7]ti furono costretti per la regola sanza altre cavillationi · a dire ciò essere la uerità ·; ōde il mercātello [8] ebbe il suo desiderio, e così māgiò essa polastra, e i frati fecero il meglio poterono ·; ove dopo tale desinare [9] questi cōmēsari si partirono tutti e 3 di conpagnia ·, e dopo alquanto di uiagio, trovati vn fiume di bona [10] larghezza e profondità ·, essendo tutti 3 a piedi, i frati per pouertà e l'altro per auaritia ·, fu neciessario per l'uso [11] della cōpagnia che vno de' frati, essendo scalzi ·, passasse sopra i sua omeri esso mercātucolo ·; onde datoli [12] il frate al servo i zoccoli, si caricò di tale uomo; onde accade, che trovandosi esso frate in mezzo del [13] fiume ·, esso ancora si ricordò della sua · regola ·, e fermatosi a vso di San Cristoforo alzò la testa [14] inverso quello che l'aggravava, e disse: diṁi vn poco ·, ài tu nessū dinari adosso? bē sai, rispose que[15]sto; come credete voi ch'a mia pari mercatāte andasse altramēti attorno ·? oimè, disse il frate, la nostra [16] regola vieta che noi nō possiano portare danari adosso ·! e subito lo gittò nell'acqua; la qual cosa conosciuta [17] dal mercatāte facetamēte la già fatta ingivria essere vēdicata ·, cō piacievole uiso pacificamēte, [18] mezzo arossito per vergognia, la uēdetta sopportò.

Franciscan begging Friars are wont, at certain times, to keep fasts, when they do not eat meat in their convents. But on journeys, as they live on charity, they have license to eat whatever is set before them. Now a couple of these friars on their travels, stopped at an inn, in company with a certain merchant, and sat down with him at the same table, where, from the poverty of the inn, nothing was served to them but a small roast chicken. The merchant, seeing this to be but little even for himself, turned to the friars and said: "If my memory serves me, you do not eat any kind of flesh in your convents at this season." At these words the friars were compelled by their rule to admit, without cavil, that this was the truth; so the merchant had his wish, and eat the chicken and the friars did the best they could. After dinner the messmates departed, all three together, and after travelling some distance they came to a river of some width and depth. All three being on foot—the friars by reason of their poverty, and the other from avarice—it was necessary by the custom of company that one of the friars, being barefoot, should carry the merchant on his shoulders: so having given his wooden shoes into his keeping, he took up his man. But it so happened that when the friar had got to the middle of the river, he again remembered a rule of his order, and stopping short, he looked up, like Saint Christopher, to the burden on his back and said: "Tell me, have you any money about you?"—"You know I have", answered the other, "How do you suppose that a Merchant like me should go about otherwise?" "Alack!" cried the friar, "our rules forbid as to carry any money on our persons," and forthwith he dropped him into the water, which the merchant perceived was a facetious way of being revenged on the indignity he had done them; so, with a smiling face, and blushing somewhat with shame, he peaceably endured the revenge.

1284. 1. fratti..tenpi. 2. uiagio .. uiuano .. che hi posto. 3. viagi una "copia" dessi .. mecantuolo. 4. ostieri .. polostro .. ōdehe. 5. merchantuolo. 5. hessere pocho. 7. alte gavillationi a direco essere. 8. ebe .. chosisi .. frati fraone il meglio poterone . oue dopo. 9. chonpagnia. 10. largeza .. tutte .. ellaltro. 11. discalzi passassi .. mercātuolo. 12. asserbo zocholi .. charicho .. homo .. imezo. 13. hesso .. richordo dela .. effermatosi .. cristofano. 14. chellagrava .. pocho .. risspose .. merchatāte andassi altre. 16. chēnoi .. conossciuta. 17. merchatate facietamēte .. vīdichata .. pacifichamēte. 18. mezo .. soporto.

1285.

FACETIA.

²Vno volendo provare colla autorità ³di Pitagora, come altre volte lui era ⁴stato al mōdo, e vno nō li lasciava ⁵finire il suo ragionamēto, allor costui ⁶disse a questo tale: è per tale segniale che ⁷io altre volte ci fussi stato, io mi ricor⁸do che tu eri mvlinaro; allora costui ⁹sentēdosi mordere colle parole gli ¹⁰confermò essere vero, che per questo cō¹¹trassegnio lui si ricordava che questo ¹²tale era stato l'asino che gli portava la ¹³farina.

A JEST.

A man wishing to prove, by the authority of Pythagoras, that he had formerly been in the world, while another would not let him finish his argument, the first speaker said to the second: "It is by this token that I was formerly here, I remember that you were a miller." The other one, feeling himself stung by these words, agreed that it was true, and that by the same token he remembered that the speaker had been the ass that carried the flour.

FACETIA.

¹⁵Fu dimādato vn pittore perchè, facciēdo ¹⁶lui de' figure si belle che erā cose morte, ¹⁷per che causa esso avesse fatti i figlioli ¹⁸si brutti; allora il pittore rispose che le ¹⁹pitture le fecie di dì, e i figlioli di notte.

A JEST.

It was asked of a painter why, since he made such beautiful figures, which were but dead things, his children were so ugly; to which the painter replied that he made his pictures by day, and his children by night.

1286.

Vno · vede vna grāde · spada al lato · a vn altro, e' dice: o poverello ell'è grā tēpo ch'io ²t'ò veduto · legato a questa · arme ·, perchè · nō ti disleghi, avēdo le māni disciolte, ³e possiedi libertà? al qual · costui rispose: questa è cosa · nō tua, anzi · è vecchia; ⁴questo sentēdosi mordere · rispose: io · ti conosco · sapere si poche cose in questo ⁵mōdo · ch'io credevo · che ogni diualgata · cosa · a te · fusse · per nova.

A man saw a large sword which another one wore at his side. Said he "Poor fellow, for a long time I have seen you tied to that weapon; why do you not release yourself as your hands are untied, and set yourself free?" To which the other replied: "This is none of yours, on the contrary it is an old story." The former speaker, feeling stung, replied: "I know that you are acquainted with so few things in this world, that I thought anything I could tell you would be new to you."

1287.

Vno lasciò lo usare con uno · suo · amico, ²perchè · quello · spesso · li dicieva · male · delli ³amici · sua ·; Il quale · lasciato · amico · ⁴vn dì dolendosi collo amico e dopo il molto ⁵dolersi lo pregò, ch'elli · dicesse quale fusse ⁶la cagione, che lo auesse · fatto dimēticare · ⁷tanta amicitia; al quale esso · rispose: jo ⁸non voglio più usare · con teco

A man gave up his intimacy with one of his friends because he often spoke ill of his other friends. The neglected friend one day lamenting to this former friend, after much complaining, entreated him to say what might be the cause that had made him forget so much friendship. To which he answered: "I will no longer be in-

---

1285. 2. cholla alturita. 3. pictagora. 4. lassciava . . chostui. 6. acquesto. 7. cifussi. 8. chettu . . chosstui. 9. cholle.
    11. richordaua. 12. chelli. 15. pictore. 17. chausa . . auessi. 18. risspose chelle. 19. figlio.

1286. 2 acquesta . . disslegi [e sta liber] avēdo . . dissciolte. 3. cosstui risspose. 4. risspuose . . conossco . . chose . . quessto. 5. chosa atte fussi.

1287. 1. lasscio . . amicho. 2. isspesso. 3. lassciato amicho [si do]. 4. cholla amicho. 5. diciessi . . fussi. 6. chagione chello auessi . . dimētichare. 7. risspose. 8. no . . chontecho. 9. nōno. 10. amicho. 11. abbia chome me affare trissta.

per ⁹ch'io · ti uoglio bene ·, e non uoglio che, diciē¹⁰do tu male ad altri di me ·, tuo amico ·, che al¹¹tri abbiano, come me, a fare trista impressione ¹²di te ·, diciendo tu a quelli male di me, tuo amico; ¹³ōde, non vsando noi piv insieme, parrà che noi ¹⁴siamo fatti nimici, e per il dire tu male di me, com'è ¹⁵tua vsanza ·, non sarai tanto da essere biasi¹⁶mato ·, come se noi usassimo · insieme.

timate with you because I love you, and I do not choose that you, by speaking ill of me, your friend, to others, should produce in others, as in me, a bad impression of yourself, by speaking evil to them of me, your friend. Therefore, being no longer intimate together, it will seem as though we had become enemies; and in speaking evil of me, as is your wont, you will not be blamed so much as if we continued intimate.

C. A. 75 b; 219 b]   **1288.**

Vno disputādo e vantādosi · di sapere fare molti vari · e belli · giochi ·, vn altro de' circonstanti ⸱ disse: jo so fare ²vno giocco · il quale · farà · trarre le brache · a chi a me parirà; il primo vantatore, trovandosi sanza brache, ³disse · che a me non le sarai trarre e vo' dare vn pajo di calze; il proponitore d'esso gioco accettato ⁴lo invito · in *pro* mvto piv paja di brache, e trassele nel uolto · al mettitore delle calze, e vinse il pegnio.

⁵Vno disse a vn suo conosciēte: tu ài · tutti · li ochi · trasmutati · in strano · colore; Quello · li ripose interuenirli ⁶spesso, ma tu nō ci ài posto cura;—e quādo t'adiuiē questo?—rispose l'altro: ogni volta, che mia · ochi vedono jl tuo viso ⁷strano ·, per la violenza ricievuta da si grā dispiaciere · subito s'impallidiscono · e mvtano in istrā colore;

⁸Vno disse a un altro: tu ài tutti li occhi mutati in istrā colore; Quello li rispose egli è perchè i mia ochi vedono ⁹il tuo viso strano.

¹⁰Vno disse che in suo paese · nascievano le piv strane cose del mōdo ·; l'altro rispose : tu che sei vi na¹¹to, confermi ciò esser uero · per la stranezza della tua brutta presenza.

A man was arguing and boasting that he knew many and various tricks. Another among the bystanders said: "I know how to play a trick which will make whomsoever I like pull off his breeches." The first man— the boaster—said: "You won't make me pull off mine, and I bet you a pair of hose on it." He who proposed the game, having accepted the offer, produced breeches and drew them across the face of him who bet the pair of hose and won the bet [4].

A man said to an acquaintance: "Your eyes are changed to a strange colour." The other replied: "it often happens, but you have not noticed it." "When does it happen?" said the former. "Every time that my eyes see your ugly face, from the shock of so unpleasing a sight they suddenly turn pale and change to a strange colour."

A man said to another: "Your eyes are changed to a strange colour." The other replied: "It is because my eyes behold your strange ugly face."

A man said that in his country were the strangest things in the world. Another answered: "You, who were born there, confirm this as true, by the strangeness of your ugly face."

Tr. 78]   **1289.**

Dispreggiādo uno vecchio publicamēte vn giovane mostrādo auda²cemēte nō temer quello, onde il giovane li rispuose che la ³sua lūga età li facieva migliore scudo che la lingua ⁴o la forza.

An old man was publicly casting contempt on a young one, and boldly showing that he did not fear him; on which the young man replied that his advanced age served him better as a shield than either his tongue or his strength.

12. acquegli. 13. noi | "piv" insieme para. 14. siano .. tire tu .. chome. 15. tu. 16. chome.
1288. 1. dissputādo .. circhustanti 2. giocho trarre. 3. che no disse .. nole sarai .. parodi chalze.. giocho aciettato. 4. ettrassele .. chalze. 4. chonossciēte .. trassmutati in insstrano cholore. 6. chura ecquādo .. oni .. vegano. 7. sinpalidis cano .. cholore. 8. ellgie .. vegano. 10. nasscieva .. chose .. ui sena. 11. chonfermi .. straneza.
1289. dispregiādo î vecchio .. mostrādo alda. 3. schudo chella lingha.

1288. The joke turns, it appears, on two meanings of *trarre* and is not easily translated.

S. K. M. II.² 44 a]   **1290.**

FACIETIA.

²Sendo uno infermo in articulo ³di morte, esso sentì battere la porta, ⁴e domādato vno de' sua serui chi era ⁵che batteva l'uscio, esso seruo rispose ⁶esser vna che si chiamava madoña ⁷Bona; allora l'infermo alzato le ⁸braccia al cielo ringraziò Dio con al⁹ta voce; poi disse ai serui che lasci¹⁰assino venire presto questa, accio-¹¹chè potesse vedere vna donna ¹²bona iñazi che esso morisse, ¹³imperochè in sua vita mai ne vide nessuna.

A JEST.

A sick man finding himself in *articulo mortis* heard a knock at the door, and asking one of his servants who was knocking, the servant went out, and answered that it was a woman calling herself Madonna Bona. Then the sick man lifting his arms to Heaven thanked God with a loud voice, and told the servants that they were to let her come in at once, so that he might see one good woman before he died, since in all his life he had never yet seen one.

S. K. M. II.² 43 b]   **1291.**

FACIETIA.

²Fu detto a vno che si levasse ³dal letto, perchè già era leva⁴to il sole; E lui rispose: se ⁵io avessi a fare tanto viaggio ⁶e facende quanto lui, ancora io sarei ⁷già levato, e però avendo a fa⁸re si poco camino, ancora non ⁹mi voglio levare.

A JEST.

A man was desired to rise from bed, because the sun was already risen. To which he replied: "If I had as far to go, and as much to do as he has, I should be risen by now; but having but a little way to go, I shall not rise yet."

Fo']   **1292.**

Vno vedendo vna femina parata a tener ta²vola in giostra guardò il tavolaccio e gridò ³vedendo la sua lancia: oimè quest'è troppo pic⁴col lavorante a si grā bottega.

A man, seeing a woman ready to hold up the target for a jousting match, exclaimed, looking at the shield, and considering his spear: "Alack! this is too small a workman for so great a business."

1290. lusscie . . risspose. 6. eser . . chessi chiamav. 8. rigrazio. 9. chellasci. 11. potessi. 12. hessomorissi. 13. iperoche . . ma ne.

1291. chessi levassi. 3. del . . hera. 4. Ellui. 5. affare . . viago. 6. "e facende" quanto. 7. av̄do affa. 8. anchora no. 9. mi vo levare.

1292. 2. ingostra . . tavolacco. 3. lassua . . tropo pi. 4. assi . . botteggha.

IV.

PROPHECIES.

C. A. 143a; 426a]   **1293.**

DIUISIONE DELLA PROFETIA.

²Prima delle cose degli animali; secōda delli ³irrationali; 3ª delle piāte, quarta delle cerimonie; ⁴quīta de' costumi; sesta delli casi overo editti, over qui⁵stioni; settima de' casi che nō possono stare ⁶in natura, come dire di quella cosa, quāto piv ne le-⁷vi piv crescie; e riserua i grādi casi ⁸inverso il fine, e deboli dà dal principio, ⁹ e mostra prima i mali, e poi le punitioni ¹⁰delle cose filosofiche.

❨ Delle formiche. ❩

¹²Molti popoli fien quelli che nascōderā se ¹³i figlioli e le sue vettovaglie dentro alle oscure caverne, ¹⁴ e lì nelli lochi tenebrosi ciberā se e sua ¹⁵famiglia per molti mesi sanza altro lume accidentale o naturale.

THE DIVISION OF THE PROPHECIES.

First, of things relating to animals; secondly, of irrational creatures; thirdly of plants; fourthly, of ceremonies; fifthly, of manners; sixthly, of cases or edicts or quarrels; seventhly, of cases that are impossible in nature [paradoxes], as, for instance, of those things which, the more is taken from them, the more they grow. And reserve the great matters till the end, and the small matters give at the beginning. And first show the evils and then the punishment of philosophical things.

❨ Of Ants. ❩

These creatures will form many communities, which will hide themselves and their young ones and victuals in dark caverns, and they will feed themselves and their families in dark places for many months without any light, artificial or natural.

1293. 3. inrationali . . cirimonie. 4. sessta. 5. chasi. 6. inatura. 7. cresscie . . chasi. 9. emali. 12. queli . . nasscōderā. 13. e sue | "figloli" e . . dēntro alle "osscure" caverne. 14. elli nelli. 15. famiglia "per molti mesi" sanza . . acidentale.

1293. Lines 1—51 are in the original written in one column, beginning with the text of line 11. At the end of the column is the programme for the arrangement of the prophecies, placed here at the head: Lines 56—79 form a second column, lines 80—97 a third one (see the reproduction of the text on the facsimile Pl. CXVIII).

Another suggestion for the arrangement of the prophecies is to be found among the notes 55—57 on page 357.

⟦Dell' api.⟧

¹⁷E a molti altri sarā tolte le mvnitioni
e lor cibi, ¹⁸e crudelmēte da giēte sanza
ragione saranno ¹⁹sommerse e annegate; o
giustitia di Dio ²⁰perchè nō ti desti a vedere così malmenare e tua ²¹creati?

⟦Delle pecore vacche ²³e capre e simili.⟧

²⁴A innumerabili saran tolti i loro piccoli figlio²⁵li e quelli scarnati ²⁶e crudelis-
simamēti squartati.

⟦Delle noci e vliue e ghiā²⁸de e castagnie
e simili.⟧

²⁹Molti figlioli da spietate bastona³⁰te
fieno tolti dalle propie braccia delle lor
³¹madri e gittati in terra e poi lacerati.

⟦De'fanciulli che stanno ³³legati nelle fascie.⟧

³⁴O città marine, io vedo in uoi i uostri
citta³⁵dini così femine come maschi stret-
³⁶tamente dai forti legami colle braccia
e ganbe esser le³⁷gati da gente che non
ītenderanno i uostri lī³⁸guaggi, e sol ui po-
trete sfogare li vostri dolori e per³⁹duta
libertà mediante i lagrimosi piā⁴⁰ti e li
sospiri e lamentatione infra uoi mede⁴¹si-
mi, chè chi vi lega, non v'intenderà, nè voi
loro in⁴²tenderete.

⟦Delle gatte che māgiano i topi.⟧

⁴⁴A voi città dell' Africa si uedrà i uostri nati essere ⁴⁵squarciati nelle propie
case de' crudelissimi e ra⁴⁶paci animali del
paese vostro.

⟦Delli asini bastonati.⟧

⁴⁸O natura, perchè ti sei fatto ⁴⁹partiale,
facciēdoti ai tua figli d'alcuna pietosa ⁵⁰e
benignia madre, ad'altri crudelissima e
spieta⁵¹ta matrignia? io vedo i tua figlioli
esser dati in al⁵²trui seruitù sanza mai benifitio alcuno, e in lo⁵³co di remuneratione
de' fatti benifitj esser pagati ⁵⁴di grādissimi
martiri, e spēdere senpre la lo⁵⁵r vita in
benifitio del suo mal fattore.

⟦Of Bees.⟧

And many others will be deprived of
their store and their food, and will be cruelly
submerged and drowned by folks devoid of
reason. Oh Justice of God! Why dost thou not
wake and behold thy creatures thus ill used?

⟦Of Sheep, Cows, Goats and the like.⟧

Endless multitudes of these will have
their little children taken from them ripped
open and flayed and most barbarously
quartered.

⟦Of Nuts, and Olives, and Acorns, and
Chesnuts, and such like.⟧

Many offspring shall be snatched by cruel
thrashing from the very arms of their mothers,
and flung on the ground, and crushed.

⟦Of Children bound in Bundles.⟧

O cities of the Sea! In you I see your
citizens—both females and males—tightly
bound, arms and legs, with strong withes
by folks who will not understand your
language. And you will only be able to
assuage your sorrows and lost liberty by
means of tearful complaints and sighing
and lamentation among yourselves; for
those who will bind you will not understand
you, nor will you understand them.

⟦Of Cats that eat Rats.⟧

In you, O cities of Africa your children
will be seen quartered in their own houses
by most cruel and rapacious beasts of your
own country.

⟦Of Asses that are beaten.⟧

[48] O Nature! Wherefore art thou so
partial; being to some of thy children a
tender and benign mother, and to others
a most cruel and pitiless stepmother?
I see children of thine given up to sla-
very to others, without any sort of advantage, and instead of remuneration for
the good they do, they are paid with the
severest suffering, and spend their whole
life in benefitting those who ill treat
them.

---

16. ape. 17. e amolti | "[era]" altri . . toltolte la. 18. ragone sarano. 19. gustitia. 20. dessti. 22. vache. 23. essimili.
24. invmerabili . . elloro picholi. 25. ecquelli [crudelissimamēte] scannati [essqua]. 28. essimili. 29. disspietate. 30. fie-
tolti delle. 32 fanculli chesstano. 33. fasscie. 34. veggho . . uosstri. 35. dini [esse] cossi . . massci essere isstre.
36. dei . . cole br. 38. essol . . issfogare li uosstri "dolori e" eper. 39. mediante [i gran pian] i lagrimosi. 40. elle
i sosspiri ellamentatione. 43. māgano e topi. 44. uosstri. 46. vosstro. 47. basstonati. 48. O natura [sanza] in stacchurata
perchetti seffatta. 49. dalchuna. 50. disspieta. 51. vegho. 52. alchuno eillo. 53. cho. 54. da [ere] di grādissime [bastonate]

48. Compare No. 845.

⟦Delli omini che dormono nell' asse d' alberi.⟧

⁵⁷Li omini dormiranno e māgieranno e abiterāno ⁵⁸infra li alberi nelli selue e cāpagnie.

⟦Del sogniare.⟧

⁶⁰Alli omini parrà vedere nel cielo nove rui⁶¹ne; parrā in quello leuarsi a uolo, e di quello fuggi⁶²re cō penvria le fiamme che di lui discē⁶³dono; sentirā parlare li animali di qua⁶⁴lūche sorte in linguaggio vmano; scorre⁶⁵ranno inmediate colla lor persona ⁶⁶in diverse parti del mōdo sanza mo⁶⁷to; vedrāno nelle tenebre grādissimi ⁶⁸splēdori; o maraviglia della vmana ⁶⁹spetie qual frenesia t' à si condotto! ⁷⁰parlerai cogli animali di qualūche spetie, ⁷¹e quelli cō teco in linguaggio vmano, ⁷²vedrāti cadere di grande alture san⁷³za tuo danno; i torrēti t' accompa⁷⁴gneranno e mischieranno col lor rapido corso . . .

⟦De' cristiani.⟧

⁸¹Molti che tengono la fede del figlio-⁸²lo e sol fan tenpli nel nome ⁸³della madre.

⟦Del cibo stato animato.⟧

⁸⁴Gran parte de' corpi animati ⁸⁵passerà pe' corpi degli altri animali, ⁸⁶cioè le case disabitate passerā ⁸⁷in pezzi per le case abitate, dan⁸⁸do a quella vtile, e portā⁸⁹do cō seco i sua danni; ⁹⁰cioè la uita dell' omo si fa dalle cose ⁹¹māgiate·, le quali portā con se⁹²co la parte dell' omo ch' è morta . . . .

⟦Of Men who sleep on boards of Trees.⟧

Men shall sleep, and eat, and dwell among trees, in the forests and open country.

⟦Of Dreaming.⟧

Men will seem to see new destructions in the sky. The flames that fall from it will seem to rise in it and to fly from it with terror. They will hear every kind of animals speak in human language. They will instantaneously run in person in various parts of the world, without motion. They will see the greatest splendour in the midst of darkness. O! marvel of the human race! What madness has led you thus! You will speak with animals of every species and they with you in human speech. You will see yourself fall from great heights without any harm and torrents will accompany you, and will mingle with their rapid course.

⟦Of Christians.⟧

Many who hold the faith of the Son only build temples in the name of the Mother.

⟦Of Food which has been alive.⟧

[84] A great portion of bodies that have been alive will pass into the bodies of other animals; which is as much as to say, that the deserted tenements will pass piecemeal into the inhabited ones, furnishing them with good things, and carrying with them their evils. That is to say the life of man is formed from things eaten, and these carry with them that part of man which dies . . .

C. A. 143ᵇ; 426ᵇ]   1294.

⟦Delli ufitj funerali ²e processioni e lumi ³e cāpane e cōpagnia.⟧

⁴Agli omini saran fatti grandissimi ⁵onori e ponpe sanza lor saputa.

⟦Of Funeral Rites, and Processions, and Lights, and Bells, and Followers.⟧

The greatest honours will be paid to men, and much pomp, without their knowledge.

"martiri" esspēder. 56. dormā nellasse. 57. māgierano. 60. para. 61. parā . . fugi. 62. penvra . . fiame . . disscē. 63. dano. 64. ilinguaggio. 66. parte. 68. sprēdori . . delle vmane. 69. tasi chondotto. 71. ecqueli cōtecho . . liguagio vmano [cha]. 72. chadere. 73. tatacompa. 74. gierano e miscerate chollor rapido corso. 75. \\\\\ sera car \\\\\\\\\\\\\\\\\\\ madressore. 76. \\\\\\\\\\\\\\\\\ erai cholli a. 77. \\\\\\\\\\\ āᵈis. 78. \\\\\\\\\\\\\\\\\ anime. 79. \\\\\\\\\\\\\\\\\\\\\\\\\\\\\\\\\ le penne. 80. crisstiani. 81. chettengo. 82. essol. 86. coe. 87. pezi . . chase. 88. acquella vntile. 89. cōsecho . . danni queste. 90. coe . . delle. 91. māgate [e] le . . chon se. 92. cho. 93. \\\\\\\\\\\\\\\\\\\\\\\\\\\\ te cō ponitu. 94. \\\\\\\\\\\\\\\\\\ elle māgano. 95. \\\\\\\\\\\\\\\\\\\\\\\\\ morte rifara. 96. \\\\\\\\\\\\\\\\\\\\\\\\ ma nōne. 97. \\\\\\\\\\\\\\\\\\\ [case].

1294. 2. ellumi. 4. sara.

84 and following; compare No. 846.

1294. A facsimile of this text is on Pl. CXVI below on the right, but the writing is larger than the other notes on the same sheet and of a somewhat different style. The ink is also of a different hue, as may be seen on the original sheet at Milan.

C. A. 362*a*; 1143*a*]   1295.

❡ Dell auaro. ❞

²Molti fieno quelli che con ogni studio e sollecitudine seguiranno ³con furia quella cosa che senpre li à spauētati, nō conosciendo la sua ⁴malignità.

❡ Delli omini che, quāto piv inuechiano, piv ⁶si fanno avari, chè auēdosi a star poco dovrebbero farsi liberali. ❞

⁷Vedansi a quelli, che son giudicati di piv speriētia e giuditio, quanto ⁸egli' ànno mē bisognio delle cose, cō piv auidità cercarle e riseruarle.

❡ Della fossa. ❞

¹¹Starā molti occupati in esercitio a leuare di quella cosa che tanto crescierà, quan¹²to se ne leuò.

❡ Del peso posto sul piumaccio. ❞

¹⁴E a molti corpi nel vedere da lor leuar la testa, si uedrà manifesta¹⁵mente cresciere, e rendendo loro la leuata testa · immediatamente ¹⁶diminviscono la grādezza.

❡ Del pigliare de' pidocchi. ❞

¹⁸E saran molti cacciatori d'animali che, quanto piv ne piglierāno ¹⁹māco n'avranno, e così de conuerso piv n'avrā, quāto men ne piglie²⁰ranno.

❡ Dello tignere l'acqua colle 2 sechie a vna sola corda. ❞

²²E rimaranno occupati molti che quāto piv ²³tireraño in giù la cosa, essa piv se ne fugirà in contrario ²⁴modo.

❡ Le lingue de' porci e vitelli nelle budelle. ❞

²⁸O cosa spurca, che si vedrà l'uno animale aver la lingua ²⁹in culo all'altro.

❡ De' crivelli fatti di pelle d'animali. ❞

³¹Vedrassi il cibo degli animali passar dentro alle ³²lor pelli per ogni parte salvo che per la bocca, e penetra³³re dall'opposita parte insino alla piana terra.

❡ Of the Avaricious. ❞

There will be many who will eagerly and with great care and solicitude follow up a thing, which, if they only knew its malignity, would always terrify them.

❡ Of those men, who, the older they grow, the more avaricious they become, whereas, having but little time to stay, they should become more liberal. ❞

We see those who are regarded as being most experienced and judicious, when they least need a thing, seek and cherish it with most avidity.

❡ Of the Ditch. ❞

Many will be busied in taking away from a thing, which will grow in proportion as it is diminished.

❡ Of a Weight placed on a Feather-pillow. ❞

And it will be seen in many bodies that by raising the head they swell visibly; and by laying the raised head down again, their size will immediately be diminished.

❡ Of catching Lice. ❞

And many will be hunters of animals, which, the fewer there are the more will be taken; and conversely, the more there are, the fewer will be taken.

❡ Of Drawing Water in two Buckets with a single Rope. ❞

And many will be busily occupied, though the more of the thing they draw up, the more will escape at the other end.

❡ Of the Tongues of Pigs and Calves in Sausage-skins. ❞

Oh! how foul a thing, that we should see the tongue of one animal in the guts of another.

❡ Of Sieves made of the Hair of Animals. ❞

We shall see the food of animals pass through their skin everyway excepting through their mouths, and penetrate from the outside downwards to the ground.

1295. 2. fien"o" . . essollecitudine seguirano. 3. chessenpre. 6. fano asstar . . doberebō. 7. vedanssi acquelli chesson gudichati . . guditio. 9. della fossa ❡ della informa di frenesia o farnetico. 10. dinsania di ceruello. ❡ 11. molti "ochupati" in . . alleua"r" di . . chosa cresscier. 12. ta se ne leuo [ecquāto piv se ne pone piv gressere diminiscce]. 13. piumacco. 14. moti corpi . . dallor . . manit ||||||||. 15. cresscicre . . imediate. 16. diminvissean. 17. pidochi. 18. essaran. 19. naranno . . narā. 21. dellottignier lacq"a". 22. ochupati . . piv [tirerano]. 23. trireroña in gu. 25. la salsiccia che mu nelle budelle. 26. molti si farā casa "e abiterano nelle" delle propie. 27. linguie de porci "e vitelli" nelle. 28. spurcha. 32. bocha. 33. oposita. 34. feroce . . possenti . . difendera. 38. voltatili. 40. zocholi. 41. chelli. 45. delli "grandi"

⟦ Delle lanterne. ⟧

³⁵ Le feroci corna de' possenti tori difenderan³⁶no la luce notturna dall'inpetuoso furor di uēti.

⟦ Delle piume ne' letti. ⟧

³⁸ Li animali volatili sosterrā l'omini colle lor propie ³⁹ penne.

⟦ Li animali che uā sopra li alberi, ādando in zoccoli. ⟧

⁴¹ Sarā si grāde i fanghi che li omini andranno sopra l'al⁴²beri de' lor paesi.

⟦ Delle sola delle scarpe che son di bue. ⟧

⁴⁴ E si uedrà in gran parte del paese caminare sopra le pelli ⁴⁵ delli grandi animali.

⟦ Del nauicare. ⟧

⁴⁷ Saranno gran venti, per li quali le cose oriētali si faranno occiden⁴⁸tali, e quelli di mezzodì in grā parte miste col corso de' uē⁴⁹ti seguirānolo per lunghi paesi.

⟦ Delle pitture ne' santi adorati. ⟧

⁵¹ Parleranno li omini alli omini che non sentiranno ; avrā gli occhi ⁵² aperti e nō uedranno ; parleranno a quelli e nō fia loro risposta ; ⁵³ chiederā gratie a chi avrà orecchi e non ode ; farā lume a chi ⁵⁴ è orbo.

⟦ De' segatori. ⟧

⁵⁹ Saranno molti che si moverā l'uno ⁶⁰ contra dell'altro, tenendo in mano il tagliente ferro ; Questi nō si ⁶¹ faranno infra loro altro nocimēto che di stāchezza, perchè quā⁶²to l'uno si caccierà inanti, tanto l'altro si ritirerà indirieto ; ⁶³ ma tristo che s'inframetterà in mezzo, perchè al fine rimarrà ta-⁶⁴gliato in pezzi.

⟦ Il filatoio da seta. ⟧

⁶⁶ Sentirassi le dolenti grida, le alte strida, ⁶⁷ le rauce e infoccate vocie di quei che fieno con tormento spogliati e al fine ⁶⁸ lasciati ignudi e sanza moto ; e questo fia per cavsa del motore che tutto volge.

⟦ Of Lanterns. ⟧

[35] The cruel horns of powerful bulls will screen the lights of night against the wild fury of the winds.

⟦ Of Feather-beds. ⟧

Flying creatures will give their very feathers to support men.

⟦ Of Animals which walk on Trees—wearing wooden Shoes. ⟧

The mire will be so great that men will walk on the trees of their country.

⟦ Of the Soles of Shoes, which are made from the Ox. ⟧

And in many parts of the country men will be seen walking on the skins of large beasts.

⟦ Of Sailing in Ships. ⟧

There will be great winds by reason of which things of the East will become things of the West ; and those of the South, being involved in the course of the winds, will follow them to distant lands.

⟦ Of Worshipping the Pictures of Saints. ⟧

Men will speak to men who hear not ; having their eyes open, they will not see ; they will speak to these, and they will not be answered. They will implore favours of those who have ears and hear not ; they will make light for the blind.

⟦ Of Sawyers. ⟧

There will be many men who will move one against another, holding in their hands a cutting tool. But these will not do each other any injury beyond tiring each other ; for, when one pushes forward the other will draw back. But woe to him who comes between them ! For he will end by being cut in pieces.

⟦ Silk-spinning. ⟧

Dismal cries will be heard loud, shrieking with anguish, and the hoarse and smothered tones of those who will be despoiled, and at last left naked and motionless ; and this by reason of the mover, which makes every thing turn round.

animali. 46. sara . . occi ||||. 48. ecquelle dimezodi. 51. parlerano . . ali . . sentirano . . arā gli |||||||. 52. nō fie lor riss. 53. aciara orechi . . lume e ||||||. 54. he orbo parlerā color di cō gra ||||||||||||||| sre. 55. prenossicho. 56. metti per ordine e mesialle cirimonie chessusano e cosi fa del. 57. gorno e della notte. 59. molti [chessanza moto di piedi] si moverā [cholle br lur.] "[in altie cholle teste]. 60. chontra . . itagliente. 61. infralloro. 62. chachiera inati. 63. tristo chessinfra mezo . . rimara. 64. innpezzi. 65. dasseta. 66. dolenti grida [fatti chon diuerse voci] le. 67. rave e infiochate

1295. 35. Lanterns were in Italy formerly made of horn.

⟦Del mettere e trarre il pan dalla bocca del forno.⟧

⁷⁰Per tutte le città e terre e castelli e case si uedrà, per desiderio di māgiare, trarre il ⁷¹propio cibo di bocca l'uno all'altro sanza poter fare difesa alcuna.

⟦Le terre lauorate.⟧

⁷³Vedrassi voltare la terra sotto sopra e risguardare l'opositi ⁷⁴emisperii e scoprire le spelonche a ferocissimi animali.

⟦Del seminare.⟧

⁷⁶Allora in grā parte delli omini, che resterā uiui, gitterā ⁷⁷fori delle lor case le serbate vettovaglie in libera preda delli ⁷⁸vcelli e animali terrestri sanza curarsi d'essi in parte alcuna.

⟦Delle pioggie che fanno che fiumi intorbidati ⁸⁰portan via le terre.⟧

⁸¹Verrà diuerso il cielo chi trasmuterà gran parte dell'Africa ⁸²che si mostra a esso cielo inverso l'Europa, e quella di Euro⁸³pa inverso l'Africa·, e quelle delle provincie Scitiche si mischieranno in⁸⁴sieme con grā revolutione.

⟦De legniami che bruciano.⟧

⁸⁷Li alberi e arbusti delle grā selue si convertiranno in cenere.

⟦Delle fornaci di mattoni e calcina.⟧

⁸⁹Al fine la terra si farà rossa per lo infocamēto di molti giorni, ⁹⁰e le pietre si convertiranno in cenere.

⟦I pesci lessi.⟧

⁹²Li animali d'acqua moriranno nelle bollenti acque.

⟦L'uliue che cadono dagli uliui dannoci l'olio che fa lume.⟧

⁹⁴Discenderà con furia diuerso la terra, chi ci darà notrimēto e luce.

⟦Of putting Bread into the Mouth of the Oven and taking it out again.⟧

In every city, land, castle and house, men shall be seen, who for want of food will take it out of the mouths of others, who will not be able to resist in any way.

⟦Of tilled Land.⟧

The Earth will be seen turned up side down and facing the opposite hemispheres, uncovering the lurking holes of the fiercest animals.

⟦Of Sowing Seed.⟧

Then many of the men who will remain alive, will throw the victuals they have preserved out of their houses, a free prey to the birds and beasts of the earth, without taking any care of them at all.

⟦Of the Rains, which, by making the Rivers muddy, wash away the Land.⟧

[81]Something will fall from the sky which will transport a large part of Africa which lies under that sky towards Europe, and that of Europe towards Africa, and that of the Scythian countries will meet with tremendous revolutions[84].

⟦Of Wood that burns.⟧

The trees and shrubs in the great forests will be converted into cinder.

⟦Of Kilns for Bricks and Lime.⟧

Finally the earth will turn red from a conflagration of many days and the stones will be turned to cinders.

⟦Of boiled Fish.⟧

The natives of the waters will die in the boiling flood.

⟦Of the Olives which fall from the Olive trees, shedding oil which makes light.⟧

And things will fall with great force from above, which will give us nourishment and light.

. . cheffieno | "con tormento" ispogliati. 68. lassciati ingnudi | "e sanza moto" ecquesto . . chausa . . chettutto. 69. ettrarre . . della bocha. 70. etterre e chastelle e chase "per desiderio di māgiare" trarre. 71. [cibo] propio . . bocha "luno all'altro" sanza . . alchuna. 73. rissguardare. 74. esschoprire . . spilonche. 76. allor [li omini] in. 77. chase. 78. terresti . . churarsi. 79. piove chenfanche. 81. africha. 82. chessi mosstra a . . ecquella di curo. 83. lafricha . ecquelle . . simichieranno. 84. chon . . revolutione [al fine si fermeranno e mvterano natura di novi frutti]. *Lines 86—88 come in the original after lines 89 and 90, but Leonardo directs us to invert the order by writing 2ᵃ at the beginning of the former passage and 1ᵃ at the head of the latter one.* 86. bruca no. 87. albusti . . cōvertirano. 89. gorni. 90. elle . . convertiranno [in polvere] "in cenere". 91. epesssci. 92. morirano . . acq"e". 93. che chagiō deli uliui chadioci lolio. 94. diuerso il celo chicci . . elluce. 95. guficōchessuecella alla parra. 96. tessta essaltera . . li ochin. 97. tessta . . danimali [vssciti delle]

81—84. Compare No. 945.

❡ Delle ciuette e gufi; ciò che succhiella alla parra. ❳

⁹⁶Molti periranno · di fracassamento di testa e salteranno loro li ochi in grā par⁹⁷te della testa · per causa · d'animali pavrosi vsciti dalle tenebre.

❡ Del lino che fa la cura de' giēti. ❳

⁹⁹Sarā reueriti e onorati e cō reuerētia e amore ascoltati, li sua precetti ¹⁰⁰di chi prima fusse legato, stratiato o martorizato da molte e diuerse battitoje.

❡ De' libri che insegnano precetti. ❳

¹⁰²I corpi sanz'anima ci daranno con lor sententie precietti vtili al ben morire.

❡ De' battuti e scoreggiati. ❳

¹⁰⁴Li omini si nasconderanno · sotto le scorze delle scorticate erbe, e quiui gri¹⁰⁵dando si darā martiri con battimēti di menbra a se medesimi.

❡ Delle maniche de' coltegli fatte di corna ¹¹¹di castrone. ❳

¹¹²Nelle corna delli animali si vedranno tagliēti ¹¹³ferri colli quali si torna la uita a molti della loro ¹¹⁴spetie.

❡ Della notte che nō si conosce ¹¹⁶alcun colore. ❳

¹¹⁷Verrà a tanto che non si conoscierà diferenza infra ¹¹⁸colori, anzi si faran tutti di nera qualità.

❡ Delle spade e lance che per se ¹²⁰mai nuocono a nessuno. ❳

¹²¹Chi per se è māsueto e sanza alcuna offensione, si farà ¹²²spauentevole e feroce mediante le triste cōpa¹²³gnie, e torrà la vita crudelissimamēte ¹²⁴a molte genti; e piv n'ucciderebbe, se corpi sā¹²⁵z'anima e usciti dalle spelonche non li difendessino, ¹²⁶cioè le corazze di ferro.

❡ De' lacciuoli e trappole. ❳

¹²⁸Molti morti si moverà con furia e piglieraño e legheranno ¹²⁹i vivi, e serviranno gli a lor nemici circa ¹³⁰la lor morte e distrutione.

❡ Of Owls and screech owls and what will happen to certain birds. ❳

Many will perish of dashing their heads in pieces, and the eyes of many will jump out of their heads by reason of fearful creatures come out of the darkness.

❡ Of flax which works the cure of men. ❳

That which was at first bound, cast out and rent by many and various beaters will be respected and honoured, and its precepts will be listened to with reverence and love.

❡ Of Books which teach Precepts. ❳

Bodies without souls will, by their contents give us precepts by which to die well.

❡ Of Flagellants. ❳

Men will hide themselves under the bark of trees, and, screaming, they will make themselves martyrs, by striking their own limbs.

❡ Of the Handles of Knives made of the Horns of Sheep. ❳

We shall see the horns of certain beasts fitted to iron tools, which will take the lives of many of their kind.

❡ Of Night when no Colour can be discerned. ❳

There will come a time when no difference can be discerned between colours, on the contrary, everything will be black alike.

❡ Of Swords and Spears which by themselves never hurt any one. ❳

One who by himself is mild enough and void of all offence will become terrible and fierce by being in bad company, and will most cruelly take the life of many men, and would kill many more if they were not hindered by bodies having no soul, that have come out of caverns-that is, breastplates of iron.

❡ Of Snares and Traps. ❳

Many dead things will move furiously, and will take and bind the living, and will ensnare them for the enemies who seek their death and destruction.

---

pavrosi vssciti delle. 98. cheffa . . de cēti. 99. reverita e onorata . . asscoltata 100. . . . diuerse battitare. 101. chensegnā. 103. scoregiati. 104. lessconze delle isscorticate. 105. asse. 106. della lusuria. 107. essinfurieranno dellecose piu belle "a cercare" possedere e operare le parte lor piv brutte. 108. doue poi con danno e penitentia ritornati nellorsentimento arā grāde amira. 109. tiō di se stessi. 111. chastrone. 112. uedra. 113. feri cholli. 115. cognosscie. 117. vera attanto . cognossciera. 119. ellance. 120. nocano añessuno. 121. perse | "he suā sueto" e . . alchuna. 122. si fara spauentevole "e feroce" mediante le trisste. 123. ettorra. 124. nuceiderebe. 125. vssciti delle splilonche noli. 126. coe le corraze. 127. lacioli. 128. chon furia "e piglieraño" e legerano. 129. e vivi esserberā . . circha. 132. vsscira delle . . ettenebrose.

❰De' metalli.❱

¹³²Uscirà dalle oscure e tenebrose ¹³³spelonche · che metterà tutta l'umana spe¹³⁴tie in grandi affanni, pericoli e mor-¹³⁵te ·; a molti segua¹³⁶ci lor, dopo molti affanni, darà ¹³⁷diletto; ma chi nō fia suo partigiano morrà ¹³⁸con stento e calamità; questo commette¹³⁹rà infiniti tradimēti, questo avmēte¹⁴⁰rà e persuaderà li omini tristi alli assassinamēti ¹⁴¹e latrocini · e le perfidie ·; questa darà ¹⁴²sospetto · a i sua partigiani ·; questo torrà ¹⁴³lo stato alle città libere; questo torrà ¹⁴⁴la uita a molti; questo travaglierà ¹⁴⁵li omini infra loro con molte arti, ¹⁴⁶inganni e tradimēti; o animal mo¹⁴⁷struoso! quāto sarebbe meglio agli omini ¹⁴⁸che tutti tornassero nell'inferno! per costui ¹⁴⁹rimarrā diserte le grā selue delle lor ¹⁵⁰piāte; per costui infiniti animali perderanno la ui¹⁵¹ta.

❰Del fuoco.❱

¹⁵³Nascierà di piccolo principio, ¹⁵⁴chi si farà cō prestezza grande; que¹⁵⁵sto non stimerà alcuna creata ¹⁵⁶cosa, anzi colla sua potētia ¹⁵⁷quasi il tutto avrà in potentia ¹⁵⁸di transformare di suo essere ¹⁵⁹in vn altro.

❰De' navili che annegano.❱

¹⁶¹Vedrannosi grandissimi ¹⁶²corpi sanza vita por¹⁶³tare con furia moltitu¹⁶⁴dine d'omini alla distrutti¹⁶⁵one di lor uita.

❰De' boi che si māgiano.❱

¹⁶⁷Māgieranno i padrō delle posses-¹⁶⁸sioni i lor propi lauoratori.

❰De' battere il letto per rifarlo.❱

¹⁷⁰Veranno li omini in tanta ingratitudine, ¹⁷¹che, chi darà loro albergo sanza alcū prezzo, ¹⁷²sarà carico di bastonate, in modo che ¹⁷³gran parte delle interiora si spig, nerā¹⁷⁴no dal loco loro e s'andranno rivoltando pel ¹⁷⁵suo corpo.

❰Delle cose che si māgiano ¹⁷⁷che prima s'uccidono.❱

¹⁷⁸Sarà morto da loro il loro nutritore e flag¹⁷⁹giellato cō spietata morte.

❰Of Metals.❱

That shall be brought forth out of dark and obscure caves, which will put the whole human race in great anxiety, peril and death. To many that seek them, after many sorrows they will give delight, and to those who are not in their company, death with want and misfortune. This will lead to the commission of endless crimes; this will increase and persuade bad men to assassinations, robberies and treachery, and by reason of it each will be suspicious of his partner. This will deprive free cities of their happy condition; this will take away the lives of many; this will make men torment each other with many artifices deceptions and treasons. O monstrous creature! How much better would it be for men that every thing should return to Hell! For this the vast forests will be devastated of their trees; for this endless animals will lose their lives.

❰Of Fire.❱

One shall be born from small beginnings which will rapidly become vast. This will respect no created thing, rather will it, by its power, transform almost every thing from its own nature into another.

❰Of Ships which sink.❱

Huge bodies will be seen, devoid of life, carrying, in fierce haste, a multitude of men to the destruction of their lives.

❰Of Oxen, which are eaten.❱

The masters of estates will eat their own labourers.

❰Of beating Beds to renew them.❱

Men will be seen so deeply ungrateful that they will turn upon that which has harboured them, for nothing at all; they will so load it with blows that a great part of its inside will come out of its place, and will be turned over and over in its body.

❰Of Things which are eaten and which first are killed.❱

Those who nourish them will be killed by them and afflicted by merciless deaths.

134. pericholi. 135. molti [al sin darano piacere] sequa. 136. ci lor [darā diletto] dopo. 137. partigano. 138. chonisstento e chalamita . . comette. 139. infinita. 140. omini "tristi" alli. 14. elle peruita questa terra in. 142. partigani. 145. lor comolte [f] ḅalde ingan. 146. ingani. 147. sare meglioli. 148. chettutti tornassi . . cosstui. 149. rimarā. 150. perda laui. 152. fuocho. 153. nasscieria di picholo. 154. prestezza. 155. isstimera. 156. sua potē. 157. tutto fara in. 160. navili canegano. 161. vedrassi. 162. chorpi. 166. chessimāgano. 167. e padrō . . posse. 168. e lor. 171. che che . . prezo. 172. charicho di basstonate. 173. spigerā. 174. del locho. 175. essandrano. 175. chorpo. 176. chose chessi. 177. succidano. 178. sarmorto dalloro . . effra. 179. disspietata. 182. vederassi. 187. chol suo e alticōciascūo. 188. vedrassi. 189. trans [mutarsi] "correre" ora.

❡ Dello spechiare le mura ¹⁸¹delle città nel-
l'acqua de' lor fossi. ❘

¹⁸²Vedrannosi l'alte mvra delle grã città
sotto sopra ne' lo¹⁸³ro fossi.

❡ Dell'acqua che corre torbida ¹⁸⁵e mista
cõ terra, e della polue¹⁸⁶re e nebbia mista
coll'aria, e del ¹⁸⁷foco misto col suo e altri
cõ ciascūo. ❘

¹⁸⁸Vedrassi tutti li elementi insieme
misti con grã re¹⁸⁹volutione trascorrere ora
inverso il centro del mõ¹⁹⁰do, ora inverso
il celo, e quãdo dalle parti meri¹⁹¹dionali
scorrere cõ furia inverso il fred¹⁹²do settentrione, qualche volta dall'oriẽte inverso
¹⁹³l'occidente, e così di questo in quell'altro emisperio.

❡ In ogni punto si può fare diuisio¹⁹⁵ne de'
2 emisperi. ❘

¹⁹⁶Li omini tutti scãbieranno emisperio
immediate.

❡ In ogni pūto è diuisione da o¹⁹⁸riente a
occidente. ❘

¹⁹⁹Moverannosi tutti li animali da oriẽte
a occidente, e così ²⁰⁰da aquilone a meriggio
scanbievolmẽte, e così de' cõuerso.

❡ Del moto dell'acque che portano ²⁰²i
legniami che son morti. ❘

²⁰³Corpi sanz'anima · per se medesimi
si moveranno e porterã ²⁰⁴cõ seco innume-
rabile generatione di morti, toglien²⁰⁵do le
richezze a circũstanti viuẽti.

❡ Dell'oua che sendo mãgiate nõ possono
²⁰⁷fare e pulcini. ❘

²⁰⁸O quanti fiẽ quegli, ai quali sarà proibito il nascere!

❡ De' pesci che si mãgiano non nati. ❘

²¹⁰Infinita gieneratione si perderà per
la morte delle grauide.

❡ Del piãto fatto il venerdì santo. ❘

²²⁰In tutte le parti d'Europa sarà piãto
da grã popoli per la morte d'ū ²²¹solo omo
morto in oriẽte.

❡ Of the Reflection of Walls of Cities in the
Water of their Ditches. ❘

The high walls of great cities will be
seen up side down in their ditches.

❡ Of Water, which flows turbid and mixed
with Soil and Dust; and of Mist, which is
mixed with the Air; and of Fire which is
mixed with its own, and each with each. ❘

All the elements will be seen mixed together in a great whirling mass, now borne
towards the centre of the world, now towards the sky; and now furiously rushing
from the South towards the frozen North,
and sometimes from the East towards the
West, and then again from this hemisphere
to the other.

❡ The World may be divided into two Hemispheres at any Point. ❘

All men will suddenly be transferred into
opposite hemispheres.

❡ The division of the East from the West
may be made at any point. ❘

All living creatures will be moved from
the East to the West; and in the same way
from North to South, and vice versa.

❡ Of the Motion of Water which carries
wood, which is dead. ❘

Bodies devoid of life will move by themselves and carry with them endless generations of the dead, taking the wealth from
the bystanders.

❡ Of Eggs which being eaten cannot form
Chickens. ❘

Oh! how many will they be that never
come to the birth!

❡ Of Fishes which are eaten unborn. ❘

Endless generations will be lost by the
death of the pregnant.

❡ Of the Lamentation on Good Friday. ❘

Throughout Europe there will be a lamentation of great nations over the death of
one man who died in the East.

---

190 delle parte. 191. scorẽra . . il fre. 192. to settantrione acua. 193. emissperio. 194. po. 196. inmediate. 199. mo-
veròsi. 200. meridio. 201. acqua. 202. e legniami chesson. 204. invmerabile . . morti [dondo et] toglẽ. 206. chessendo
mãgiata . . possã. 207. e pulcini. 208. nassciere. 209. pessci chessi mãgano onato. 211. delli animali che si castrano. 212. a
gran parte della spetie masachina pell esser tolti loro e tes 213. tichuli fia proibito el generare. 214. delle bestie chef-
fano il caco. 215. illate fia tolto ai picholi figlioli. 216. delle som mate fatte delle croie. 217. a grã parte delle femine
letine fia tolto ettagliato lor le retto. 218. insieme cholla irta [ello avendo ipicholi figloletti in corpo]. 219. venerdi scõ.
220. popoli la. 221. homo. 224. chõ. 226. chessi chollomo. 227. vedrassi . . effigure. 228. chesse guiranno. 229. dun-

⟦Del sogniare.⟧

²²³Andranno li omini e nō si moveranno,
²²⁴parleranno cō chi nō si trova, senti²²⁵rāo
chi nō parla.

⟦Dell' onbra che si move coll' uomo.⟧

²²⁷Vedrannosi forme e figure d' uomini
²²⁸e d' animali, che seguiranno essi ani²²⁹mali
e omini dovunque fugiranno; ²³⁰e tal fia il
moto di lui qual è del²³¹l' altro, ma parrà
cosa mirabile delle ²³²varie grandezze in
che essi si tras²³³mutano.

⟦¶Dell' ombra del sole e dello spechiarsi
²³⁵nell' acqua in un medesimo tēpo.¶⟧

²³⁶Vedrassi molte volte l' uno uomo
²³⁷diuentare 3, e tutti lo seguo²³⁸no, e spesso
l' uno, il piv certo, l' abandona.

⟦Delle casse che riseruano ²⁴⁰molti
tesori.⟧

²⁴¹Troverrassi dentro a de' noci e deli
alberi ²⁴²e altre piante tesori grādissimi, i
quali ²⁴³lì stanno occulti e ben guardati.

⟦Dello spegnere el lume a chi ²⁴⁵va al
letto.⟧

²⁴⁶Molti per mandare fori il fiato ²⁴⁷con
troppa prestezza perderanno il ue²⁴⁸dere e
in brieue tutti i sentimēti.

⟦Delle canpanelle de' muli ²⁵⁰che stanno
presso ai loro orechi.⟧

²⁵¹Sentirassi in molte parti dell' Europa ·
stru²⁵²mēti di uarie magnitudini far diuerse
²⁵³armonie con grandissime fatiche di chi
²⁵⁴piv presso l' ode.

⟦Delli asini.⟧

²⁵⁶Le molte fatiche saran remvnerate di
²⁵⁷fame, di sete, di disagio, e di mazzate, e
di pū²⁵⁸ture, e bestemie, e grā uillanie.

⟦De' soldati a cauallo.⟧

²⁶⁰Molti sarā veduti portati da grādi
ani²⁶¹mali con veloce corso alla ruina della
sua ²⁶²vita e prestissima morte.
²⁶³Per l' aria e per la terra saranno veduti ani²⁶⁴mali di diuersi colori portarne cō
fu²⁶⁵rore li omini alla destrutione di lor vita.

⟦Delle stelle delli sproni.⟧

²⁶⁷Per causa delle stelle · si uedranno li
omini ²⁶⁸esser velocissimi al pari di qualūche ²⁶⁹animal ueloce.

⟦Of Dreaming.⟧

Men will walk and not stir, they will
talk to those who are not present, and hear
those who do not speak.

⟦Of a Man's Shadow which moves with him.⟧

Shapes and figures of men and animals
will be seen following these animals and men
wherever they flee. And exactly as the one
moves the other moves; but what seems so
wonderful is the variety of height they
assume.

⟦Of our Shadow cast by the Sun, and our Reflection in the Water at one and the same time.⟧

Many a time will one man be seen as
three and all three move together, and
often the most real one quits him.

⟦Of wooden Chests which contain great
Treasures.⟧

Within walnuts and trees and other plants
vast treasures will be found, which lie hidden
there and well guarded.

⟦Of pùtting out the Light when going
to Bed.⟧

Many persons puffing out a breath with
too much haste, will thereby lose their sight,
and soon after all consciousness.

⟦Of the Bells of Mules, which are close to
their Ears.⟧

In many parts of Europe instruments of
various sizes will be heard making divers har-
monies, with great labour to those who hear
them most closely.

⟦Of Asses.⟧

The severest labour will be repaid with
hunger and thirst, and discomfort, and blows,
and goadings, and curses, and great abuse.

⟦Of Soldiers on horseback.⟧

Many men will be seen carried by large
animals, swift of pace, to the loss of their
lives and immediate death.
In the air and on earth animals will be
seen of divers colours furiously carrying men
to the destruction of their lives.

⟦Of the Stars of Spurs.⟧

By the aid of the stars men will be seen
who will be as swift as any swift animal.

che. 230. ettal . . dellui quate del. 231. para. 232. grandeze trans. 234. delleobr. 235. nvn. 237. ettutti. 238. esspesso
luno piu. 243. ochulti . . guarda. 245. valletto. 246. molti [per soi] per. 247. prèssteza. 248. tutti e sentimēti. 250. chesta
. . aloro. 251. sentirasi. 252. magnitudine. 257. disago. 258. besstemie. 259. acchauallo. 260. portare. 263. sara·
265. disstrutione. 267. chausa . . uedra. 272. piāto cō. 273. dellessca. 274. chon. 275. ra visibile.

⟦Il bastone ch'è morto.⟧

[271]Il movime̅to de' morti farà fugire [272]co̅ dolore e pia̅to e co̅ grida molti viui.

⟦Dell' esca.⟧

[274]Co̅ pietra e con ferro si rende[275]ranno visibili le cose che prima no̅ [276]si vedeano.

⟦Of a Stick, which is dead.⟧

The motions of a dead thing will make many living ones flee with pain and lamentation and cries.

⟦Of Tinder.⟧

With a stone and with iron things will be made visible which before were not seen.

C. A. 362 *b*; 1134 *b*] **1296.**

⟦Del navicare.⟧

[2]Vedrassi li alberi delle gra̅ selue di Tavrus, [3]e di Sinai, Apenino, e Atlante scorrere per l'aria [4]da orie̅te a occide̅te, da aquilone a meridi[5]e, e porteranno per l'aria gra̅ moltitudine [6]d'omini; o qua̅ti voti! o qua̅ti mòr[7]ti! o quanta seperatio̅ d'amici e di pare̅ti! o qua̅[8]ti fie̅ quelli che no̅ rivedranno piv̀ le lor pro[9]vincie nè le lor patrie, e che moriranno sanza se[10]poltura colle lor ossa sparse in diuersi [11]siti del mo̅do!

⟦Dello sgomberare l'ogni santi.⟧

[13]Molti · abandoneranno le propie abitationi, e por[14]terà co̅ seco tutti e sua valsenti, e andran[15]no abitare in altri paesi.

⟦Del dì de' morti.⟧

[17]E qua̅ti fie̅ quelli che pia̅geranno i lor [18]antichi morti porta̅do lumi a quelli.

⟦De' frati che spe̅dendo parole; [20]riceuono di gra̅ ricchezze e danno [21]il paradiso.⟧

[24]¶Le invisibili monete farà trio̅fare molti spe̅[25]ditori di quelle.¶

⟦Degli archi fatti [27]colli corni de' boi.⟧

[28]Molti fie̅ quelli che per causa delle bouine cor[29]na moriranno di dolente morte.

⟦Dello scriver lettere da \n [31]pàese a vn altro.⟧

[32]Parleransi li uomini di remotissimi paesi l'uno all'altro e rispo̅derasi.

⟦Degli emisperi che sono infiniti [34]e da infinite linie son diuisi, in mo[35]do che senpre ciascuno uomo n'à [36]vna d'esse linie infra l'u̅ de' piedi e l'altro.⟧

[37]Parleransi e coccheransi e abbraccieransi li omini stanti da l'uno al[38]altro emisperio, e tenderansi i loro linguaggi.

⟦Of going in Ships.⟧

We shall see the trees of the great forests of Taurus and of Sinai and of the Appenines and others, rush by means of the air, from East to West and from North to South; and carry, by means of the air, great multitudes of men. Oh! how many vows! Oh! how many deaths! Oh! how many partings of friends and relations! Oh! how many will those be who will never again see their own country nor their native land, and who will die unburied, with their bones strewn in various parts of the world!

⟦Of moving on All Saints' Day.⟧

Many will forsake their own dwellings and carry with them all their belongings and will go to live in other parts.

⟦Of All Souls' Day.⟧

How many will they be who will bewail their deceased forefathers, carrying lights to them.

⟦Of Friars, who spending nothing but words, receive great gifts and bestow Paradise.⟧

Invisible money will procure the triumph of many who will spend it.

⟦Of Bows made of the Horns of Oxen.⟧

Many will there be who will die a painful death by means of the horns of cattle.

⟦Of writing Letters from one Country to another.⟧

Men will speak with each other from the most remote countries, and reply.

⟦Of Hemispheres, which are infinite; and which are divided by an infinite number of Lines, so that every Man always has one of these Lines between his Feet.⟧

Men standing in opposite hemispheres will converse and deride each other and embrace each other, and understand each other's language.

1296. 1. navichare. 3. apenino ettalal scorere. 4. ocide̅te. 5. porterno. 6. [di spolia] donimi. 8. rivederano. 9. nella .. mora̅. 10. cholle .. diuessi. 12. issgonbrare. 14. cho̅secho .. andra. 17. i lor[parē]. 18. acquelli. 20. riceuano .. richeze e dano. 22. [vadrassi gradissima turba i quali acquistera̅ gra]. 23. [dissime richezze cho̅ prezo invisibile monete]. 24. invisibile. 28. chausa. 33. chessono. 35. ciasscuno homo. 36. infralli lun piedi. 37. cocherano e abracieransi. 38. ilor·

[[De' preti che dicono messe.]]

⁴⁰Molti fien quelli che per esercitare la lor arte si uestirā richissi⁴¹mamente e questo parrà esser fatto secōdo l'uso de grēbiali.

[[De' frati confessori.]]

⁴³Le suēturate donne di propia volontà ⁴⁴andranno a palesare agli omini ⁴⁵tutti le loro lussurie e opere ⁴⁶vergognose e segretissime.

[[Delle chiese e abitatiō de' frati.]]

⁵³Assai saranno che lascieranno ⁵⁴li eserciti e le fatiche ⁵⁵e povertà di uita e di roba, e andranno abitare nelle ⁵⁶richezze e triōfanti edifiti mostrando questo esser ⁵⁷il mezzo di farsi amico a Dio.

[[Del uendere il paradiso.]]

⁶¹Infinita moltitudine venderanno publicamente e pacificamēte ⁶²cose di grandissimo prezzo sanza licenza del padrone di quelle, ⁶³e che mai nō furō loro nè in lor potestà, e a questo nō prove⁶⁴drà la giustitia vmana.

[[De' morti che si uanno a sotterrare.]]

⁶⁶I senplici popoli porterā gran quantità di lumi per far lumi ⁶⁷ne' viaggi a tutti quelli che integralmente ànno perso la uirtù ⁶⁸visiua.

[[Delle doti delle fanciulle.]]

⁷¹E doue prima la gioventù feminina nō si potea difendere dal⁷²la lussuria e rapina de' maschi, nè per guardie di parenti nè fortezze di mvra, ⁷³verrà tenpo che bisognierà che padri e parēti d'esse fanciulle ⁷⁴le paghino di grā prezzi chi voglia dormire con loro, ancorachè es⁷⁵se sien ricche, nobili, e bellissime; cierto è, par qui che la ⁷⁶natura voglia spegniere la umana spetie come cosa invtile al mondo, ⁷⁷e guastatrice di tutte le cose create.

[[Della crudeltà dell'omo.]]

⁷⁹Vedrannosi animali sopra della terra, i quali senpre conbatteranno infra ⁸⁰loro e

[[Of Priests who say Mass.]]

There will be many men who, when they go to their labour will put on the richest clothes, and these will be made after the fashion of aprons [petticoats].

[[Of Friars who are Confessors.]]

And unhappy women will, of their own free will, reveal to men all their sins and shameful and most secret deeds.

[[Of Churches and the Habitations of Friars.]]

Many will there be who will give up work and labour and poverty of life and goods, and will go to live among wealth in splendid buildings, declaring that this is the way to make themselves acceptable to God.

[[Of Selling Paradise.]]

An infinite number of men will sell publicly and unhindered things of the very highest price, without leave from the Master of it; while it never was theirs nor in their power; and human justice will not prevent it.

[[Of the Dead which are carried to be buried.]]

The simple folks will carry vast quantities of lights to light up the road for those who have entirely lost the power of sight.

[[Of Dowries for Maidens.]]

And whereas, at first, maidens could not be protected against the violence of Men, neither by the watchfulness of parents nor by strong walls, the time will come when the fathers and parents of those girls will pay a large price to a man who wants to marry them, even if they are rich, noble and most handsome. Certainly this seems as though nature wished to eradicate the human race as being useless to the world, and as spoiling all created things.

[[Of the Cruelty of Man.]]

Animals will be seen on the earth who will always be fighting against each other

---

39. dicā. 41. ecquesto . . grēbivli. 42. chonfessore. *Lines 43—46 are written on the margin parallel to lines 47—51.* 44. andrano [a dire] "palesare" ali omini [dalor]. 47. [assai fien quelli che vorranno sapere cō che ffannole le femmi. 48. ne nelle lor lussurie chon se e cogli altri omini elle messcine. 19. cōverra che palesino tutte le loro ochulte opere vergognose. 40. e premiare li asscoltatori di lor miserie e [infamie sce]. 51. [lerate infamie]. 53. sarano [chea] lasscieranno "le" [la lor povera vita]. 54. elle. 56. ettriō fanti . . mosstrando questo]. 57. il mezo [di seruire] di farsi addio [effarsi allui benivolo]. 59. [infinita moltitudine venderanno publichamēte "chosa di grādissima valuta" quel che. 60. mai nō fu loro ne i lor podesta eancho]. 61. publica e pacifichamēte. 62. chose . . prezo. 63. illor . . acquesto. 64. dera. 65. chessiuanno assotterrare. 67. quelli cintera "gralm" mēte an. 68. visiua o ometti ne sciocheza o viue pazzo questedue. 69. piteti onno nel prīcipio della prepositione. 70. fanculle. 72. lla . . massci . . guardie | di parenti ne. 73. vera . . fanculle. 74. paghi . . plezzi . . colloro. 75. sien [belli] riche . . chella. 77. guasstatrice . . chose. 79. vedrassi. 80. chon

con danni grandissimi e spesso morte di ciascuna delle [81]parti; questi non avrā termine nelle lor malignità; per le fiere mē[82]bra di questi uerranno a terra grā parte delli alberi delle gran selue dell'u[83]niuerso, e poi ch'essi avranno pasciuto, il nutrimēto de' loro desideri sa[84]rà, di dar morte e affanno e fatiche e guerre e furie a qualūche cosa animata; e per la loro smisurata superbia questi si vor[85]ranno leuare inverso il cielo, ma la superchia gravezza delle lor membra gli porrà [86]in basso; nulla cosa resterà sopra la terra o sotto la terra e l'acqua che nō [87]sia perseguitata ·, remossa o guasta ·, e quella dell'ū paese remossa nell'altro; [88]e 'l corpo di questi si farà sepultura e transito di tutti i già da lor morti cor[89]pi animati; o mōdo, come è che nō t'apri a precipitarlo nell'alte fessure de' tua [90]grā baratri e spelonche, e non mostrare più al cielo si crudele e spie[91]tato mōstro !

with the greatest loss and frequent deaths on each side. And there will be no end to their malignity; by their strong limbs we shall see a great portion of the trees of the vast forests laid low throughout the universe; and, when they are filled with food the satisfaction of their desires will be to deal death and grief and labour and wars and fury to every living thing; and from their immoderate pride they will desire to rise towards heaven, but the too great weight of their limbs will keep them down. Nothing will remain on earth, or under the earth or in the waters which will not be persecuted, disturbed and spoiled, and those of one country removed into another. And their bodies will become the sepulture and means of transit of all they have killed.

O Earth! why dost thou not open and engulf them in the fissures of thy vast abyss and caverns, and no longer display in the sight of heaven such a cruel and horrible monster.

Br. M. 42 *b*]   **1297.**

PROFETIE.

[2]Molte fien quelle che cresce[3]rā nelle lor ruine.

❲La palla della neue [5]rotolādo sopra la [6]neue. ❳

[7]Molta turba fie quella [8]che, dimēticato loro esse[9]re e nome, staran come [10]morti sopra le spoglie [11]deli altri morti.

❲Il dormire sopra [13]le piume dell'uccielli. ❳

[14]Vedrannosi le parti oriēta[15]li discorrere [16]nell'occidentali e le me[17]ridionali in settentri[18]one, avviluppando[19]si per l'universo con grande [20]strepito e tremore o furore.

❲Il uento d'oriēte che [22]scorreua in ponente. ❳

[23]I razzi solari accende[24]rāno il foco in te[25]rra coll' quale s'in[26]focherà ciò ch'è sotto [27]il cielo, e ripercossi [28]nel suo inpedimē[29]to ritorneranno [30]in basso.

❲Lo spechio cavo [32]acciēde il foco, col [33]quale si scalda il [34]forno che à il fō[35]do che sta sotto il suo [36]cielo. ❳

PROPHECIES.

There will be many which will increase in their destruction.

❲The Ball of Snow rolling over Snow. ❳

There will be many who, forgetting their existence and their name, will lie as dead on the spoils of other dead creatures.

❲Sleeping on the Feathers of Birds.❳

The East will be seen to rush to the West and the South to the North in confusion round and about the universe, with great noise and trembling or fury.

❲In the East wind which rushes to the West. ❳

The solar rays will kindle fire on the earth, by which a thing that is under the sky will be set on fire, and, being reflected by some obstacle, it will bend downwards.

❲The Concave Mirror kindles a Fire, with which we heat the oven, and this has its foundation beneath its roof. ❳

. . esspesso . . ciasscuna. 81. parte . . arā. 82. atterra, 83. poichessarā passcuti . . dellor. 84. affanno "e fatiche e guerre e furi" accqualūche cossa animata "e per la loro issisurata superbia" questi. 85. malla . . gravezza "delle lor menvra" gli tera. 86. resstera . . ossotto ellacqua. 87. quassta ecquella. 88. ettransito . . iga da. 89. chome me nō tapri e precipita nellaltre fessure. 90. palatri esspelonche e no . . disspia.

1297. 2. cressce. 3. dimētichato. 10. lesspoglie de. 13. dellucie. 14. vedrassi le parte. 15. li [trans] discorrere. 16. ochidentallelle me. 17. settantri. 18. siavilupando. 19. cogra. 20. strepido e tremore "o furore". 23. razi. 25. si. 26. coche. 27. riperchossi. 29. nto ritorneran. 31. pechio. 32. aciēde. 33. 36. celo. 38. o si fugira. 39. soto . . celo. 40. rtorno

[37]Gran parte del mare [38]si fuggirà inverso il [39]cielo e per molto tēpo nō fa[40]rà ritorno; ❪Cioè pe' nuvoli.❫

A great part of the sea will fly towards heaven and for a long time will not return. ❪That is, in Clouds.❫

[41]Restaci · il moto che separa [42]il motore dal mobile.

There remains the motion which divides the mover from the thing moved.

[43]Sarà annegato chi fa il lume [44]al culto diuino. ‖ ❪Le ape che [45]faño la cera delle candele.❫

Those who give light for divine service will be destroyed. ❪The Bees which make the Wax for Candles.❫

[46]I morti uscirāno di sotto terra [47]e coi loro fieri mouimēti cac[48]cieranno dal mondo · innumera[49]bili creature umane.

Dead things will come from underground and by their fierce movements will send numberless human beings out of the world.

❪Il ferro uscito di sot[51]to terra è morto, [52]e se ne fa l'arme che [53]ammorti tanti uomini.❫

❪Iron, which comes from under ground is dead but the Weapons are made of it which kill so many Men.❫

[54]Le grandissime montagnie [56]ācorachè sieno remo[57]te da marini liti, scaccieraño [58]il mare dal suo sito.

The greatest mountains, even those which are remote from the sea shore, will drive the sea from its place.

❪Questo sono li fiumi [60]che portanno le terre, [61]da loro leuate dalle mō[62]tagnie, e le scarica[63]no ai marini · liti, [64]e doue entra [65]la terra si fuggie il [66]mare.❫

❪This is by Rivers which carry the Earth they wash away from the Mountains and bear it to the Sea-shore; and where the Earth comes the sea must retire.❫

[67]L'acqua caduta dai nuvoli ancora in moto sopra le spiaggie de' mōti si ferme[68]rà per lūgo spatio di tempo sanza [69]fare alcū moto, e questo accade[70]rà in molte e diuerse provincie.

The water dropped from the clouds still in motion on the flanks of mountains will lie still for a long period of time without any motion whatever; and this will happ'en in many and divers lands.

❪La neve che fiocca [72]che è acqua.❫

❪Snow, which falls in flakes and is Water.❫

[73]I gran sassi de' monti gitterā [74]fuoco tale che brucieranno il le[75]gname di molte e grādissime selue [76]e molte fere saluatiche e dimestiche.

The great rocks of the mountains will throw out fire; so that they will burn the timber of many vast forests, and many beasts both wild and tame.

❪La pietra del fucile, [78]che fa foco che consu[79]ma tutte le some del[80]le legnie con che si [81]disfā le selve; [82]E cuocierassi con esse [83]la carne delle bestie.❫

❪The Flint in the Tinder-box which makes a Fire that consumes all the loads of Wood of which the Forests are despoiled and with this the flesh of Beasts is cooked.❫

[84]O quanti grandi edifitj fieno ruinati [85]per causa del fuoco!

Oh! how many great buildings will be ruined by reason of Fire.

❪Del fuoco delle bonbarde.❫

❪The Fire of great Guns.❫

[87]I buoi fieno in gran parte cavsa delle ruine [88]delle città, e similmēte cavalli e bufoli

Oxen will be to a great extent the cause of the destruction of cities, and in the same way horses and buffaloes

❪Tirā le bonbarde.❫

❪by drawing Guns❫.

coe pe nvgoli. 41.Resstaci....chessepera. 43. anegato chiffa ilume. 46. vsscirāno. 47. hecholoro .. ca. 48. del .. invmera. 50. usscito diso. 51. momorto. 52. esse. 53. amorti. 54. montagnie per. 55. [lunga remotione fia an]. 56. anchorachessieno che sieno. 58. del. 61. dallor .. delle. 62. elle scarica. 63. noa. 67. de nvgoli | "ancora in moto sopra le spiage de mōti sua natura che" si ferme. 69. acade. 70. imolte .. prouince. 71. fiocha. 73. gra. 74. focho .. ile. 76. fierc. 79. some de. 81. disfa. 82. e cocierassicon eso. 83. della besttie. 85. chausa del focho. 87. boi. 86. focho. 88. essinilmēte cavgli. 83. tira.

I.² 15a]   **1298.**

¶Vedrassi la spetie leonina · colle un-
ghiate ²branche aprire la terra · e nelle fatte
³spelonche · seppellire · se insieme co⁴li altri
animali a se sottoposti.¶

¶⁵Usciranno dalla terra · animali · vestiti
di tenebre, ⁶i quali con maravigliosi assalti
⁷assaliranno l'umana generatione, e quella
⁸da feroci morsi · fia con confusion di sā⁹gue
da essi · diuorata.¶

¹⁰Ācora scorrerà per l'aria · la nefāda
spetie volatile, ¹¹la quale · assalirà · li omini
e li a¹²nimali, e di quelli si ciberanno cō
grā ¹³gridore; empierāno i loro vētri di
vermiglio sangue.

The Lion tribe will be seen tearing open
the earth with their clawed paws and in the
caves thus made, burying themselves together
with the other animals that are beneath them.

Animals will come forth from the earth
in gloomy vesture, which will attack the
human species with astonishing assaults,
and which by their ferocious bites will
make confusion of blood among those they
devour.

Again the air will be filled with a mischievous winged race which will assail men and
beasts and feed upon them with much noise—
filling themselves with scarlet blood.

I.² 15b]   **1299.**

Vedrassi il sangue uscire dalle · strac-
ciate carni, ²rigare le superfitiali parti delli
omini;

¶³Verrà alli omini · tal crudele mala⁴tia,
che colle propie vnghie · si strac⁵cieranno
le loro carni ‖ ⟦sarà la rognia;⟧¶

¶⁶Vedrannosi le piāte rimanere sanza
foglie, ⁷e i fiumi fermare i loro corsi;¶

¶⁸L'acqua del mare si leuerà sopra
l'alte cime de' mōti ⁹verso il cielo, e rica-
derà sopra alle a¹⁰bitationi delli omini ‖
⟦cioè per nuvoli;⟧¶

¶¹¹Vedrannosi i maggiori alberi delle
selue essere ¹²portati dal furor de' venti dal-
l'oriēte ¹³all'occidente ‖ ⟦cioè per mare;⟧¶

¶¹⁴Li omini gitterāo via le propie vettovaglie ⟦¹⁵cioè seminādo.⟧¶

Blood will be seen issuing from the torn
flesh of men, and trickling down the surface.

Men will have such cruel maladies that
they will tear their flesh with their own nails.
⟦The Itch.⟧

Plants will be seen left without leaves, and
the rivers standing still in their channels.

The waters of the sea will rise above
the high peaks of the mountains towards
heaven and fall again on to the dwellings
of men. ⟦That is, in Clouds.⟧

↖ The largest trees of the forest will be
seen carried by the fury of the winds from
East to West. ⟦That is across the Sea.⟧

Men will cast away their own victuals.
⟦That is, in Sowing.⟧

I.² ²6a]   **1300.**

¶Verrà a tale la gieneratione vmana
²che nō si intēderà il parlare · l'uno del-
l'altro; ³cioè un tedesco con un turco.¶

¶⁴Vedrassi ai padri donare le lor figliole
⁵a lussuria delli omini e premiare e abbādonare ogni ⁶passata guardia ‖ ⟦quādo si
maritano le putte.⟧¶

¶⁷Usdirāno li omini dalle sepulture cō-
uertiti ⁸in vccelli ·, e assaliranno li altri
omini togliendo ⁹loro il cibo dalle propie
mani e mēse ‖ ⟦le mosche.⟧¶

Human beings will be seen who will not
understand each other's speech; that is, a
German with a Turk.

Fathers will be seen giving their daughters
into the power of man and giving up all
their former care in guarding them. ⟦When
Girls are married.⟧

Men will come out their graves turned
into flying creatures; and they will attack
other men, taking their food from their very
hand or table. ⟦As Flies.⟧

1298. 1. vederassi . . colle vngliate. 2. b \\\ache. 3. secho . . cho. 4. asse sottopossti. 5. vsscira della . . animali "vestitidi
tenebr[oso]" di osscuro. 6. [colore] i quali cho. 7. gieneratione ecq. 8. quela da . . fia confusion. 10. laria [vcielli] "la
nefāda specie volati". 11. assalira . . ellia. 13. enperāno . . sange.

1299. 1. usscire delle. 4. cholle . . si stra. 6. vedrassi. 8. leuera "sopra lalte cime de mōti" [molte miglia]. 10. bitatione . .
nvgoli. 11. vedera . . magiori. 13. coe.

1300. 1. verano attale. 3. vtedesco con v̄ turco. 5. ebādonare "e premiare" ogni. 7. vsscirāno . . delle. 8. vcielli e assalirano
. . tolendo. 9. delle . . le mosche [ecc]. 10. arove. 11. scierano. 12. quelli [che osseruerano] "che presterāno
orechi" | le . . legere.

¶ [10] Molti fien quegli che scorticãdo la madre li arrove[11]scieranno la sua pelle · adosso; ‖ ⟬ i lavoratori della terra. ⟭ ¶

¶ [12] Felici fiē quelli che presterãno orechi alle parole de' morti; ∣ ⟬ leggere [13] le bone opere e osseruarle. ⟭ ¶

Many will there be who, flaying their mother, will tear the skin from her back. ⟬ Husbandmen tilling the Earth. ⟭

Happy will they be who lend ear to the words of the Dead. ⟬ Who read good works and obey them. ⟭

I.2 16 b]   **1301.**

¶ Le penne leuerãno li omini siccome gli uccielli inverso il cielo; [2] ∣ ⟬ cioè per le lettere · fatte da esse pēne. ⟭ ¶

[3] ¶ L'umane opere fieno cagione di lor morte; ∣ ⟬ le spade e lãcie. ⟭

¶ [4] Li omini perseguirãno quella cosa della qual piv temono, ¶ [5] cioè ∣ ⟬ sarã miseri per nõ venire ī miseria. ⟭ ¶

¶ [6] Le cose disunite · s'unirãno · e ricieverãño · in se [7] tal uirtù, che rēderanno la persa memoria alli omi[8]ni ·, cioè i papiri · che sõ fatti di peli disuniti [9] e tēgono memoria delle cose e fatti delli omini. ¶

¶ [10] Vedrannosi l'ossa de' morti cõ veloce moto tratta[11]re la fortuna del suo motore; ⟬ i dadi. ⟭ ¶

¶ [12] I buoi colle lor corna difenderã[13]no il foco dalla · sua · morte; ‖ ⟬ la lãterna. ⟭ ¶

¶ [14] Le selue partorirãño figlioli che fiano causa della [15] lor morte; ‖ ⟬ il manico della scura. ⟭ ¶

Feathers will raise men, as they do birds, towards heaven ⟬ that is, by the letters which are written with quills. ⟭

The works of men's hands will occasion their death. ⟬ Swords and Spears. ⟭

Men out of fear will cling to the thing they most fear. ⟬ That is they will be miserable lest they should fall into misery. ⟭

Things that are separate shall be united and acquire such virtue that they will restore to man his lost memory; that is papyrus [sheets] which are made of separate strips and have preserved the memory of the things and acts of men.

The bones of the Dead will be seen to govern the fortunes of him who moves them. ⟬ By Dice. ⟭

Cattle with their horns protect the Flame from its death. ⟬ In a Lantern [13]. ⟭

The Forests will bring forth young which will be the cause of their death. ⟬ The handle of the hatchet. ⟭

I.2 17 a]   **1302.**

¶ Li omini batteranno aspramēte · chi fia causa [2] di lor uita; ‖ ⟬ batterãño · il grano. ⟭ ¶

¶ [3] Le pelli delli animali · removerãno li omini con gran [4] gridori e bestemie dal lor silentio; ∣ ⟬ le balle da giuocare. ⟭ ¶

[5] Molte volte la cosa disunita fia causa di grãde unitione; [6] ⟬ cioè il pettine fatto dalla disunita canna unisce · le [7] fila · nella seta. ⟭

¶ [8] Il uēto passato per le pelli delli animali farà saltare [9] li omini; ‖ ⟬ cioè la piva che fa lo saltare. ⟭ ¶

Men will deal bitter blows to that which is the cause of their life. ⟬ In thrashing Grain. ⟭

The skins of animals will rouse men from their silence with great outcries and curses. ⟬ Balls for playing Games. ⟭

Very often a thing that is itself broken is the occasion of much union. ⟬ That is the Comb made of split Cane which unites the threads of Silk. ⟭

The wind passing through the skins of animals will make men dance. ⟬ That is the Bag-pipe, which makes people dance. ⟭

1301. 1. sichome. 2. faete. 3. lesspade he lãce. 4. chosa . . temano. 7. rēderaūno. 8. palpiri chessõ. 9. tēgano . . cosse effatti. 10. vederassi . . chõ. 12. [le corna delle] i boi. 14. cheffia chausa.

1302. 1. batterano asspramēte cheffia chausa. 3. pelle . . con gã. 4. besstemie . . giucare. 5. chausa. 6. della . . vnisscie. 9. cheffia ∣∣∣∣∣∣ are.

1301. 13. See note page 357.

　　　　　　　1303.

❲De' noci battuti.❳

² Quelli che avranno · fatto meglio, saranno ³ piv battuti e i sua figlioli tolti ⁴ e
scorticati overo spogliati e rotte e fra⁵cas-
sate le sue ossa.

❲Delle scolture.❳

⁷ Oimè, che vedo il saluatore di novo
crocifisso.

❲Della bocca dell' omo ch'è sepoltura.❳

⁹ Usciranno grā romori dalle sepolture
di ¹⁰ quelli che sō finiti da cattiva e uiolēte
morte.

❲Delle pelli delli animali ¹² che tengono il
senso del tatto ¹³ che v'è sulle scritture.❳

¹⁴ Quāto piv si parlerà · colle pelli, veste
del ¹⁵ sentimento, tanto piv s'acquisterà sapiētia.

❲De' preti che tengono l'ostia ¹⁷ in corpo.❳

¹⁸ Allora tutti quasi i tabernaculi dove
sta il ¹⁹ corpus domini si vedraño manifestamēte ²⁰ per se stessi andare per diuerse
strade del mōdo.

❲Of Walnut trees, that are beaten.❳

Those which have done best will be
most beaten, and their offspring taken and
flayed or peeled, and their bones broken or
crushed.

❲Of Sculpture.❳

Alas! what do I see? The Saviour crucified anew.

❲Of the Mouth of Man, which is a Sepulchre.❳

Great noise will issue from the sepulchres of those who died evil and violent
deaths.

❲Of the Skins of Animals which have the
sense of feeling what is in the things written.❳

The more you converse with skins cove
red with sentiments, the more wisdom will
you acquire.

❲Of Priests who bear the Host in their body.❳

Then almost all the tabernacles in
which dwells the Corpus Domini, will be
plainly seen walking about of themselves on
the various roads of the world.

　　　　　　　1304.

¶ E quelli che pascono l'erbe ² farā della
notte ³ giorno; ‖ ❲sevo.❳ ¶

¶ ⁴ E molti terrestri e acquatici ⁵ animali
mōteraño fralle ⁶ stelle; ‖ ❲cioè pianeti.❳ ¶

¶ ⁷ Vedrassi i morti portare ⁸ i vivi; ‖
❲i carri e navi in diuerse parti.❳ ¶

¹⁰ A molti fia tolto il cibo di bocca;
❲Ai forni.❳

¶ ¹² E quelli che si inboccheranno, per
l'altrui ¹³ mani fia lor tolto il cibo di bo-
¹⁴ cca; ❲il forno.❳ ¶

And those who feed on grass will turn
night into day ❲Tallow.❳

And many creatures of land and water
will go up among the stars ❲that is Planets.❳

The dead will be seen carrying the living
❲in Carts and Ships in various places.❳

Food shall be taken out of the mouth
of many ❲the oven's mouth.❳

And those which will have their food in
their mouth will be deprived of it by the
hands of others ❲the oven.❳

　　　　　　　1305.

❲De' crocifissi vēduti.❳

² Io vedo di novo vēduto e crocifisso
Cristo ³ e marterizzare i sua sāti.

❲I medici che uiuono de' malati.❳

⁵ Verrāno li omini in tanta viltà, che
avrā di gra⁶ tia, che altri triōfino sopra i
loro mali ⁷ ovvero della perduta lor uera
ricchezza, cioè la sanità.

❲Of Crucifixes which are sold.❳

I see Christ sold and crucified afresh, and
his Saints suffering Martyrdom.

❲Of Physicians, who live by sickness.❳

Men will come into so wretched a plight
that they will be glad that others will derive
profit from their sufferings or from the loss
of their real wealth, that is health.

1303. 2. aranno. 3. e e sua. 4. esscorticha . . effra. 5. chassate. 7. ome . . saluadore. 8. dela bocha. 9. vsscira . . delle
. . de. 10. queli chesso finiti de. 11. belle. 12. tengano. 13. che vesule. 14. cholle pelleveste del. 16. chettengano.
19. vederaño. 20. stesse.
1304. 1—14 R. 1. ecqueli che pascā lere. 2. [cholla] farā. 4. teresti e aquatici. 6. stelle e pianeti. 8. i carri "e navi."
10. amoli fia . . bocha. 11. a. 12. ecque chessi. 14. bocha.
1305. 2. i vedo. 3. marterizare. 4. uiuā. 5. verāno . . arā. 6. triōfi . . ilor. 7. ovedella . . richeza coe. 8. delle religiō.

⟦Della religione de' frati ⁹che vivono per li loro sā¹⁰ti, morti per assai tēpo. ⟧

¹¹Quelli che saranno morti dopo mille anni ¹²fien quelli che daranno le spese a molti ¹³vivi.

⟦De' sassi cōvertiti in calcina, ¹⁵de' quali si murano le prigioni. ⟧

¹⁶Molti che fieno disfatti dal fuoco ¹⁷innāzi a questo tenpo, torrāno la libertà a mol¹⁸ti uomini.

⟦ Of the Religion of Friars, who live by the Saints who have been dead a great while.⟧

Those who are dead will, after a thousand years be those who will give a livelihood to many who are living.

⟦Of Stones converted into Lime, with which prison walls are made.⟧

Many things that have been before that time destroyed by fire will deprive many men of liberty.

I.² 19a]   1306.

⟦De' putti che tettano.⟧

²Molti Francescani, Domenicani, e Bene-³dettini mangieranno quel che da altri ⁴altre volte vicinamēte è stato māgia⁵to, che staranno molti mesi avanti ⁶che possino parlare.

⟦De' nichi e chiocciole che sono rebuttati ⁸dal mare che marciscono dētro ai lor gusci. ⟧

⁹O quanti fien quelli che, poichè fiē morti, mar¹⁰ciranno nelle lor propie case, ēpiēdo le ¹¹circūstāte parti piene di fetulēte puzzo!

⟦Of Children who are suckled.⟧

Many Franciscans, Dominicans and Benedictines will eat that which at other times was eaten by others, who for some months to come will not be able to speak.

⟦Of Cockles and Sea Snails which are thrown up by the sea and which rot inside their shells.⟧

How many will there be who, after they are dead, will putrefy inside their own houses, filling all the surrounding air with a fetid smell.

L. 91a]   1307.

⟦De' mvli che portano le ricche some ²dell'argiēto e oro.⟧

³Molti tesori e grā ricchezze · saranno appre⁴sso alli animali di 4 piedi, i quali le por⁵teranno in diversi lochi.

⟦Of Mules which have on them rich burdens of silver and gold.⟧

Much treasure and great riches will be laid upon four-footed beasts, which will convey them to divers places.

K.² 1b]   1308.

⟦Dell'onbra che fa l'omo di not²te col lume. ⟧

³Appariranno grandissime figure in forma ⁴vmana, le quali quanto piv le ti fa⁵rai vicine, più diminuiranno la ⁶loro immensa magnitudine.

⟦Of the Shadow cast by a man at night with a light.⟧

Huge figures will appear in human shape, and the nearer you get to them, the more will their immense size diminish.

---

9. vivano. 11. chessarano. 15. mure. 16. cheffieno . . foco [dopo molti]. 17. ināzi acquesto. 18. homini.

1306. 1. chettattaño. 2. franciessci domenichi. 3. detta mangierano. 7. chesson. 8. marciscano . . a lor. 10. cirano. 11. puzo.

1307. 1. riche. 2. he oro. 3. richeze . . apre. 5. terano.

1308. 1. dino. 2. chol. 4. sitifa. 5. ra vicino . . diminvirano. 6. inmensa.

1307. It seems to me probable that this note, which occurs in the note book used in 1502, when Leonardo, in the service of Cesare Borgia, visited Urbino, was suggested by the famous pillage of the riches of the palace of Guidobaldo, whose treasures Cesare Borgia at once had carried to Cesena (see GREGOROVIUS, *Geschichte der Stadt Rom im Mittelalter.* XIII, 5, 4).

C. A. 127 b; 390 a]

1309.

❨Delle biscie portate dalle cicognie.❩

²Vedrannosi in grandissima altezza del-l'aria lūghissimi serpenti ³conbattere colli uccielli.

❨Delle bōbarde ch'escono dalla fossa e dalla forma.❩

⁵Uscirà di sotto terra chi con spauẽte-voli grida stordirà ⁶i circonstanti vicini e col suo fiato farà morire li omini ⁷e ruinare le città e castella.

❨Of Snakes, carried by Storks.❩

Serpents of great length will be seen at a great height in the air, fighting with birds.

❨Of great guns, which come out of a pit and a mould.❩

Creatures will come from underground which with their terrific noise will stun all who are near; and with their breath will kill men and destroy cities and castles.

Br. M. 212 b]

1310.

❨Del grāo e altre semẽze.❩

²Gitteranno li omini fori delle lor propie case quelle uettovalglie, le quali ³erā dedi-cate a sostẽtare la lor uita.

❨Delli alberi che nutriscono i nesti.❩

⁵Vedrannosi i padri e le madri fare molto piv giovamento ai figliastri che ai lor ueri ⁶figlioli.

❨Del turibolo dell'incẽso.❩

⁸Quelli che cō uestimẽti bianchi an-dranno con arrogante movimẽto minacciā⁹do con metallo e fuoco, che nō facieva lor de-trimẽto alcuno.

❨Of Grain and other Seeds.❩

Men will fling out of their houses those victuals which were intended to sustain their life.

❨Of Trees, which nourish grafted shoots.❩

Fathers and mothers will be seen to take much more delight in their step-children then in their own children.

❨Of the Censer.❩

Some will go about in white garments with arrogant gestures threatening others with metal and fire which will do no harm at all to them.

S. K. M. II.2; 35 b]

1311.

❨Del segare dell'erbe.❩

²Spegnieransi innumerabili viti ³e farassi sopra la terra innumera⁴bili buchi.

❨Della vita delli omini ⁶che ogni año si mv⁷tano di carne.❩

⁸Li omini passerā morti per le ⁹sue propie budelle.

❨Of drying Fodder.❩

Innumerable lives will be destroyed and innumerable vacant spaces will be made on the earth.

❨Of the Life of Men, who every year change their bodily substance.❩

Men, when dead, will pass through their own bowels.

1309. 1. bissce. 2. vedrassi . . alteza . . lūgisimi serpe. 3. combatere. 4. escan della . . della. 5. vsscira . . conispauẽteuoli.
6. circonstanti . . fiato.

1310. 2. chase. 3. assosstẽtare. 4. notriscano e nesti. 5. vedrassi . . elle . . govamento . . figliasstri. 7. tuibile. 8. uestimẽte
biãche . . arogante . . minaciã. 9. com̄etallo effoco chi.

1311. 2. spẽgineransi inumerabili. 3. invmera. 6. añi. 8. paserā. 9. gudelle. 10. de vai. 11. [molti animali].

S. K. M. II.2; 3a]   **1312.**

❪I calzolari.❫

²Li omini vedranno cō piacere ³disfare e rōpere l'opere loro.

❪ Shoemakers. ❫

Men will take pleasure in seeing their own work destroyed and injured.

S. K. M. II.2; 69a]   **1313.**

❪De capretti.❫

²Ritornerà ³il tēpo d'Erode, perchè ⁴l'innocēti figliuoli sarā ⁵tolti alle loro ⁶balie, e da cru⁷deli omini di gran ferite moriranno.

❪ Of Kids. ❫

The time of Herod will come again, for the little innocent children will be taken from their nurses, and will die of terrible wounds inflicted by cruel men.

1312. 1—3 R.   2. vederā chō.   3. diffare.
1313. 2. [sarāno tolti] ritornera.   3. perche [i pi].   4. li nocēti figuoli.   7. gra.

V.

DRAUGHTS AND SCHEMES FOR THE HUMOROUS WRITINGS.

Br. M. 42*b*]   **1314.**

FAUOLA.

[2]El granchio stā[3]do sotto il sasso per piglia[4]re pesci che sotto a quel[5]lo entrauano, vene la pi[6]ena con rovinoso precipita[7]mento di sassi, e col loro rotolare [8]si fraciellò tal grāchio.

QUEL MEDESIMO.

[10]Il ragnio, stante infra [11]l'uue, pigliaua le mosche [12]che in su tali uve si pasci[13]evano; venne la vēdemmi[14]a e fu pestato, il ragno in[15]sieme coll' uue.

[16]La uite invecchiata sopra l'al[17]bero vecchio · cade insi[18]eme colla ruina d'esso al[19]bero, e fu per la trista conpagnia a mancare insieme [21]con quella.

[22]Il torrēte portò tanto [23]di terra e pietre nel [24]suo letto, che fu costre[25]tto a mutar sito.

[26]La rete che soleua pigliare [27]li pesci fu presa e portata [28]via dal furor de' pesci.

[29]La palla della neue quan[30]to piv rotolando disciese [31]dalle mōtagnie della neue [32]tāto piv multiplicò la sua [33]magnitudine.

[34]Il salice che per li sua lun[35]ghi giermi à a mente e uol [36]cresciere da superare ciascuna [37]altra piāta, per avere fatto [38]cōpagnia colla vite che o[39]gni anno si potta, fu ancora [40]lui senpre storpiato.

A FABLE.

The crab standing under the rock to catch the fish which crept under it, it came to pass that the rock fell with a ruinous downfall of stones, and by their fall the crab was crushed.

Schemes for fables, etc. (1314—1323).

THE SAME.

The spider, being among the grapes, caught the flies which were feeding on those grapes. Then came the vintage, and the spider was cut down with the grapes.

The vine that has grown old on an old tree falls with the ruin of that tree, and through that bad companionship must perish with it.

The torrent carried so much earth and stones into its bed, that it was then constrained to change its course.

The net that was wont to take the fish was seized and carried away by the rush of fish.

The ball of snow when, as it rolls, it descends from the snowy mountains, increases in size as it falls.

The willow, which by its long shoots hopes as it grows, to outstrip every other plant, from having associated itself with the vine which is pruned every year was always crippled.

1314. 2. El . . stando stā. 4. pessci chessotto acquel. 6. chon. 7. colloro tala. 8. siffracielloro tal. 10. infral. 12. suttale vue . . sipassi. 13. eva . . uedemi. 14. a effu pesto. 16. uite [cresscuta] "iuechiata" sopr lal. 17. vechio chade. 19. effu. 23. eppietre. 24. pochōstre. 27. pessci. 28. pessci. 30. dissciese. 31. delle. 35. gierminamenti eul. 36. cresscie perare ciascuna. 38. cholla. 39. ano si pota fu.

C. A. 66 *b*; 201 *b*]   1315.

Fauola della lingua morsa dai dēti.
²Il ciedro insuperbito dalla sua bellezza
³dubita delle piāte che li sō dītorno, e fat-
⁴tole si torre dinanzi; il uēto poi non es-
sē⁵do interrotto·, lo gittò per terra· diradicato.
⁶La uitalba· non stādo cōtēta nella sua
⁷siepe·, commīciò. a passare coi sua· rami la
⁸comvne strada· e appicarsi all'opposita
siepe; ⁹onde da uiādanti· poi· fu· rotta.

Fable of the tongue bitten by the teeth.
The cedar puffed up with pride of its
beauty, separated itself from the trees around
it and in so doing it turned away towards
the wind, which not being broken in its fury,
flung it uprooted on the earth.
The traveller's joy, not content in its
hedge, began to fling its branches out over the
high road, and cling to the opposite hedge,
and for this it was broken away by the passers by.

H.2 15 *b*]   1316.

Il calderugio dà la vittouaglia ²ai figliuoli
ingabbiati; — pri³ma morte che perdere libertà.

The goldfinch gives victuals to its caged
young. Death rather than loss of liberty.

S. K. M. II2; 12 *a*]   1317.

❲Delle baghe.❳
²Le capre cōdur³raño il uino alle ⁴città.

❲Of Bags.❳
Goats will convey the wine to the city.

I.1 39 *b*]   1318.

Tutte le cose che nel uerno fiē ²nascoste
sotto la neve rimaranno sco³perte e palesi
nell'estate; ❲detta per la ⁴bugia che nō può
stare occulta.❳

All those things which in winter are
hidden under the snow, will be uncovered
and laid bare in summer. ❲for Falsehood,
which cannot remain hidden❳.

H.1 44 *a*]   1319.

FAVOLA.

²Il giglio si pose sopra la ripa di Tesino, ³e la corrēte tirò la ripa īsieme col
lilio.

A FABLE.

The lily set itself down by the shores
of the Ticino, and the current carried away
bank and the lily with it.

H.2 14 *b*]   1320.

FACETIA.

²Perchè li Ungheri tēgono la croce ‡
dvppia.

A JEST.

Why Hungarian ducats have a double
cross on them.

1315. 2. della . . belleza. 3. chelli . . effa. 4. tore. 5. interotto. 5. pertera . . diradichato. 6. istādo. 7. comīcio . . cosua.
8. apicharsi . . oposita.
1316. 1. calderigio da il arouialio. 2. a figlioli ingabiati.
1317. 1. bage. 2. chapre cōdu. 3. ale.
1318. 1. cose. 2. remarāo. 3. palese nella stade. 4. ochulta.
1319. 2. iligio si pose. 3. ella corēte.   1320. 1—2 R. 2. perchelli ūgeri tēgā.

1316. Above this text is another note, also referring to liberty; see No. 694.

Tr. 73.]

CŌPARATIONE.

1321.

A SIMILE.

¶²Vn vaso crudo rotto si può riformare, ³ma il cotto no.¶

A vase of unbaked clay, when broken, may be remoulded, but not a baked one.

S. K. M. III. 66b]

1322.

Vedēdosi la carta tutta macchiata ²dalla oscura negrezza dell'īchiostro, ³di quello si duole; il quale mostra a essa ⁴che per le parole che sono sopra lei cōposte ⁵essere cagione della cōseruatione di ⁶quella.

Seeing the paper all stained with the deep blackness of ink, it he deeply regrets it; and this proves to the paper that the words, composed upon it were the cause of its being preserved.

L. 0]

1323.

¶Neciessaria cōpagnia à la penna col tenperatoio, ²e similemēte vtile cōpagnia, perchè l'ū sanza l'altro nō ³vale troppo.¶

The pen must necessarily have the pen-knife for a companion, and it is a useful companionship, for one is not good for much without the other.

S. K. M. III. 48a]

1324.

Il coltello, accidētale armatura, caccia dall'omo le sua ²unghie, armatura naturale;
³Lo spechio signoria forte tenē⁴do · dentro · a se spechiata la re⁵gina ·, e partita quella le spe⁶chio riman in le . . .

The knife, which is an artificial wea-pon, deprives man of his nails, his natural weapons.
The mirror conducts itself haughtily holding mirrored in itself the Queen. When she departs the mirror remains there . . .

Schemes for prophecies (1324—1329).

L. 72b]

1325.

El lino è dedicato a morte e cor²rutione de' mortali, a morte pe'lac³ciuoli delli vccelli, ⁴animali e pesci, ⁵a corrutione per le tele line dove s'in⁶vogliano i morti, che si sotterrano, ⁷quali si corrōpono in tali tele; ⁸E ancora esso lino nō si spicca dal suo ⁹festuco, se esso nō comīcia a macerar¹⁰si e coronpersi, e questo è quello ¹¹collo quale si debbe incoronare e or¹²nare li ufiti funerali.

Flax is dedicated to death, and to the corruption of mortals. To death, by being used for snares and nets for birds, animals and fish; to corruption, by the flaxen sheets in which the dead are wrapped when they are buried, and who become corrupt in these winding sheets.— And again, this flax does not separate its fibre till it has begun to steep and putrefy, and this is the flower with which garlands and decorations for funerals should be made.

I.² 91a]

1326.

〖De' villani in camiscia che lavorano.〗

²Verranno tenebre diuerso · l'oriēte, le qua³li con tāta oscurità tignieranno il ⁴cielo che copre l'Italia.

〖Of Peasants who work in shirts〗

Shadows will come from the East which will blacken with great colour darkness the sky that covers Italy.

〖De' barbieri.〗

⁶Tvtti li omini si fuggiranno in Africa.

〖Of the Barbers.〗

All men will take refuge in Africa.

1321. 2. rotto crudorottosi po.
1322. 1. charta . . machiata. 2. osscura negreza. 3. dole el . . mostra a ess. 4. parolle chesso sopra lei chōpone. 5. chagione.
1323. 1. ha la. 2. essimilemēte.
1324. 1. coltello | "accidētale armatura" cacia. 2. ungie. 3. losspechio. 4. asse. 5. losspe. 6. rimāinle.
1325. 1. morte e cu. 2. pela. 3. vcielli. 4. pessci. 5. currutione pe le. 6. volgano . . chessi. 7. corrōpano. 8. spicha. 10. choronpersi ecquesto ecquello. 11. colla.
1326. 1—6 R. 1. camica chellavorano. 2. verra tienbre. 3. codioscurita . . tignierano.

1327.

Per il pannilino che si ²tiē colla mano nel co³rso dell'acqua corrē⁴te, nella quale acqua ⁵il panno lascia ⁶tutte le sue bruttu⁷re, significa ⁸questo ecc.

⁹Per lo spino inscrito¹⁰li sopra boni fru¹¹tti significa que¹²llo che per se non e¹³ra disposto a vir¹⁴tù, ma median¹⁵te l'aiuto dei pr¹⁶ecettori da di se ¹⁷vn fassi nome vi¹⁸rtù.

The cloth which is held in the hand in the current of a running stream, in the waters of which the cloth leaves all its foulness and dirt, is meant to signify this &c.

By the thorn with inoculated good fruit is signified those natures which of themselves were not disposed towards virtue, but by the aid of their preceptors they have the repudation of it.

1328.

COMUNE.

²Vn meschino sarà soiato e essi soiatori ³senpre sien sua ingannatori e rubatori ⁴e assassini d'esso meschino.

⁵La percussione della spera del sole ⁶apparirà cosa che, chi la crederà coprire, sa⁷rà coperto da lei.

⟦De' danari e oro.⟧

⁹Uscirà dalle cavernose spelonche, chi farà ¹⁰con sudore affaticare tutti i popoli del mōdo, ¹¹cō grādi affanni, ansieta, sudori per essere ¹²aivtato da lui.

⟦Della paura della pouertà.⟧

¹⁴La cosa maluagia e spauēteuole darà di se tāto ¹⁵timore appresso a delli omini che come ¹⁶matti, credendo fugirla, concorreranno cō ¹⁷veloce moto alle sue smisurate forze.

⟦Del consiglio.⟧

¹⁹E colui che sarà piv neciessario a chi avrà bi²⁰sogno di lui sarà sconosciuto, cioè piv sprezzato.

A COMMON THING.

A wretched person will be flattered, and these flatterers are always the deceivers, robbers and murderers of the wretched person.

The image of the sun where it falls appears as a thing which covers the person who attempts to cover it.

⟦Money and Gold.⟧

Out of cavernous pits a thing shall come forth which will make all the nations of the world toil and sweat with the greatest torments, anxiety and labour, that they may gain its aid.

⟦Of the Dread of Poverty.⟧

The malicious and terrible [monster] will cause so much terror of itself in men that they will rush together, with a rapid motion, like madmen, thinking they are escaping her boundless force.

⟦Of Advice.⟧

The man who may be most necessary to him who needs him, will be repaid with ingratitude, that is greatly contemned.

1329.

⟦Delle ape.⟧

²Vivono a popoli insieme, ³sono annegate per torli il mele; ⁴molti e grandissimi popoli sarā ⁵annegati nelle lor propie case.

⟦ Of Bees.⟧

They live together in communities, they are destroyed that we may take the honey from them. Many and very great nations will be destroyed in their own dwellings.

1327. 1—18 R. 1. panolino chessi. 3. acq"a". 5. pano lasscia. 7. significha. 9. losspino insidito. 11. significha. 13. dissposto. 15. ti laiuto del. 17. vnlissinome.

1328. 1. vcomune. 2. mescino. 4. messcino. 5. percusione. 6. aparira . . crederra. 7. dallei. 9. vsscira delle. 10. effattichare . . pololi. 11. affani. 12. dallui. 14. la maluagia es spauēteuole. 15. apresso a delli omini che coli ali come. 16. cocoreranno. 17. moto le le sua isspermisurate. 19. cholui . . ara. 20. sara \\|\\| conosciuto \\|\\| cioe piv sprezato.

1329. 2. vivano apopoli ensieme. 3. anegate. 5. [no] gati nelle lororo propie 6. [si some] sarā se.

F. 47 a]　　　　　　　　　　**1330.**

PERCHÈ LI CANI ODORĀ VOLENTIERI IL CULO
L'UNO AL²L'ALTRO.

Questo animale à in odio i po³veri,
perchè e' māgiano tristi cibi, e ama li richi,
⁴perchè essi àn' bone vivāde e massime di
car⁵ne; E lo sterco delli animali senpre ri-
⁶tiene della virtù della sua origine, come
mo⁷strano le feccie . . . . .
¹⁰Ora i cani ànno si sottilissimo odo¹¹rato
che col naso sentono la uirtù rima¹²sta in
tali feccie; e che sie uero, se le trovā
¹³per le strade odorano, e se vi sentono
dentro ¹⁴vi¹rtù di carne o d'altro, essi le
pigliano, e ¹⁵se nò, le lasciano; e per tornare al quesito di¹⁶co, che se conoscono il
cane mediante tali ¹⁷odori essere ben pasciuto, essi lo riguar¹⁸dano, perchè stimano
quello avere potēte e ricco pa¹⁹drone, e
se nō sentono tale odore cō uirtù, essi
sti²⁰mano tal cane essere da poco, e
avere povero ²¹e tristo padrone, e però
mordono tali cani come fare²²bbero il suo
padrone.

WHY DOGS TAKE PLEASURE IN SMELLING AT
EACH OTHER.

This animal has a horror of the poor,
because they eat poor food, and it loves
the rich, because they have good living and
especially meat. And the excrement of animals always retains some virtue of its origin
as is shown by the faeces. . . .
Now dogs have so keen a smell, that
they can discern by their nose the virtue
remaining in these faeces, and if they
find them in the streets, smell them and if
they smell in them the virtue of meat or of
other things, they take them, and if not,
they leave them: And to return to the question, I say that if by means of this smell
they know that dog to be well fed, they respect
him, because they judge that he has a powerful and rich master; and if they discover no
such smell with the virtue of meet, they judge
that dog to be of small account and to have
a poor and humble master, and therefore
they bite that dog as they would his master.

C. A. 68 b; 203 b]　　　　　**1331.**

Sono li moti della terra ²circulari assai
vtili, ³cōciosiachè¹ mai li o⁴mini si fermano; e fa⁵si in piv modi, de' qua⁶li nel-
l'uno li omini por⁷tano la terra in spal⁸la,
l'altro, colli bau⁹li, e altri col carret¹⁰to;
Quel che la porta ¹¹in spalla si fa prima
¹²enpiere il uassoio in ter¹³ra ·, e perde tēpo
a metterselo ¹⁴in spalla; Quel dello bau¹⁵le
non perde tenpo.

The circular plans of carrying earth are very
useful, inasmuch as men never stop in their
work; and it is done in many ways. By one
of these ways men carry the earth on their
shoulders, by another in chests and others
on wheelbarrows. The man who carries it
on his shoulders first fills the tub on the
ground, and he loses time in hoisting it on to his
shoulders. He with the chests loses no time.

Tr. 2.]　　　　　　　　　　**1332.**

Se'l Petrarca amò si forte il lauro, ²fu
perch'egli è buon fralla salsiccia e tonno;
³io nō posso di lor ciancie far tesauro.

If Petrarch was so fond of bay, it was be- Irony (1332).
cause it is of a good taste in sausages and with
tunny; I cannot put any value on their foolery.

1330. 1. adorā. 5. Ello stercho. 7. stra leuetie miseraice strebute insin ne. 8. le ultima basseza delle intestine. 9. per trarre
asse desse fecce la uirtu cheue. 10. rimasa ora i cani ā si. 11. sentano. 12. sa in tale fecce. 13. strade [elle] odorano
esse uīsentā dentro. 14. esse le. 15. lasslciano. 16. cognoscano. 17. odore . . passiuto. 18. richo. 19. esse nō setā.
21. mordā. 22. bono.
1331. 3. cōcosia. 4. effa. 6. po"r". 7. inispal. 8. colleban. 9. le e . . carre. 10. chella. 11. inispalla. 14. inispalla . . della
baul. 15. la non.
1332. 1. petrarcha . . ilaur ||||. 2. ·percheglie e bō . . e ton ||||. 3. i nō . . giāce.

1331. The subject of this text has apparently no
connection with the other texts of this section.
1332. Conte Porro has published these lines in
the *Archivio Stor. Lombarda* VIII, IV; he reads the

concluding line thus: *I nò posso di loro già (sic) co'
far tesauro.*—This is known to be by a contemporary poet, as Senatore Morelli informs me.

1333.

Tricks
(1333—1335).
   Noi siamo due fratelli, chè ciascuno di noi [2]à vn fratello; qui il modo del dire pare che [3]2 fratelli diuētino 4.

   We are two brothers, each of us has a brother. Here the way of saying it makes it appear that the two brothers have become four.

1334.

GIOCHI DI PARTITO.

   [2]Mettiti in 2 mani equali numeri ·; metti 4 della mā [3]destra nella sinistra ‖ gitta via il rimanēte ‖ gitta via altrettā[4]to della man sinistra ‖ metti vi sopra · 5 ·; ora tu ti trovi [5]in quella mano 13 ‖ cioè io vi ti feci mettere 4 dalla destra nel[6]la sinistra, e gittar uia il rimanēte; ora qui la mā destra à piv 4 che là [7] nō sonovi; io ti fo poi gittare via altrettanto dalla destra quāto tu [8]gittasti dalla sinistra, che gittando dalle 2 mani due quātità e[9]quali, il rimanente fia equale; ora e'ti resta 4 e 4, che fa 8, [10]e perchè il giocco nō sia conosciuto io vi ti feci mettere sopra 5 [11]che fece · 13.

TRICKS OF DIVIDING.

   Take in each hand an equal number; put 4 from the right hand into the left; cast away the remainder; cast away an equal number from the left hand; add 5, and now you will find 13 in this [left] hand; that is—I made you put 4 from the right hand into the left, and cast away the remainder; now your right hand has 4 more; then I make you throw away as many from the right as you threw away from the left; so, throwing from each hand a quantity of which the remainder may be equal, you now have 4 and 4, which make 8, and that the trick may not be detected I made you put 5 more, which made 13.

GIOCHI DI PARTITO.

   [13]Togli da 12 in giù che numero ti piace; togli poi tāti de' mia che [14]tu finisca il numero di 12 ·, e quel che rimane a me è [15]il numero che tu aueui prima; perchè quādo io ti dissi to[16]gli da 12 in giù qual numero ti piace, io mi missi in mano [17]12, e di questo mio 12 tu togliesti tale numero, che tu [18]faciesti il tuo numero 12; ecco che tu cresciesti al tuo nu[19]mero che tu togliesti al mio; cioè che se tu aueui 8, a andare insino [20]in 12, tu togliesti del

TRICKS OF DIVIDING.

   Take any number less than 12 that you please; then take of mine enough to make up the number 12, and that which remains to me is the number which you at first had; because when I said, take any number less than 12 as you please, I took 12 into my hand, and of that 12 you took such a number as made up your number of 12; and what you added to your number, you took from mine; that is, if you had 8 to go as far as to 12, you took of my 12, 4; hence this

---

1333. 1. nosiamo . . ciasscu. 2. qui el.
1334. 3. desstra. 4. tutti trovi. 5. coe . . . della desstra. 6. chella. 7. soneva . . desstra. 8. gittassti . . sinisstra. 9. ressta . .
    cheffa. 10. gocho . . cognossciuto . . fesi. 11. cheffece. 12. givochi di part "to". 13. polāti. 14. ttu finissca . . ecquel
    . . anmehe. 15. chettu prima tu perche. 16. ingu. 17. quessto mi 12 tu togliessti . . chettu. 18. faciessti . . chettu
    cressciessti. 19. mero tu togliessti . . coessettu. 8. andare. 20. togliessti. 21. atte . . ressta. 22. e he quale . . chello
    faciessi.

1334. G. Govi *says in the* 'Saggio' p. 22: *Si dilettò Leonarda di giuochi di prestigi e molti*(?) *ne descrisse, che si leggono poi riportati dal Paciolo nel suo libro:* de Viribus Quantitatis, *e che, se non tutti, sono certo in gran parte invenzioni del Vinci.*

mio 12 vn·4; onde quel 4 trasmu²¹tato
da me a te fa che'l mio 12 resta 8, e'l
tuo 8 si fa 12; ²²adunque il mio 8 è
equale al tuo 8 innāzi, che lo facesse 12.

4 transferred from me to you reduced my
12 to a remainder of 8, and your 8 became
12; so that my 8 is equal to your 8, before
it was made 12.

C. A. 75*b*; 219*b*]

1335.

Se tu vuoi insegnia²re a vno·vna cosa
³che tu·nō sappia, falli ⁴misurare la lunghezza ⁵d'una cosa a te incogni⁶ta·, e lui
saprà la mi⁷sura che tu prima nō sā-
⁸peui; — maestro Gi⁹ovanni da Lodi.

If you want to teach someone a subject
you do not know yourself, let him measure
the length of an object unknown to you, and
he will learn the measure you did not know
before;—Master Giovanni da Lodi.

1335. 1 settu volli insegni. 3. chettu sapia. 4. lungeza. 5. atte. 6. ellui. 7. chettu. 8. maesstro. 9. dallodi.

XXI.

Letters. Personal Records. Dated Notes.

When we consider how superficial and imperfect are the accounts of Leonardo's life written some time after his death by Vasari and others, any notes or letters which can throw more light on his personal circumstances cannot fail to be in the highest degree interesting. The texts here given as Nos. 1351—1353, set his residence in Rome in quite a new aspect; nay, the picture which irresistibly dwells in our minds after reading these details of his life in the Vatican, forms a striking contrast to the contemporary life of Raphael at Rome.

I have placed foremost of these documents the very remarkable letters to the Defterdar of Syria. In these Leonardo speaks of himself as having staid among the mountains of Armenia, and as the biographies of the master tell nothing of any such distant journeys, it would seem most obvious to treat this passage as fiction, and so spare ourselves the onus of proof and discussion. But on close examination no one can doubt that these documents, with the accompanying sketches, are the work of Leonardo's own hand. Not merely is the character of the handwriting his, but the spelling and the language are his also. In one respect only does the writing betray any marked deviation from the rest of the notes, especially those treating on scientific questions; namely, in these observations he seems to have taken particular pains to give the most distinct and best form of expression to all he had to say; we find erasures and emendations in almost every line. He proceeded, as we shall see, in the same way in the sketches for letters to Giuliano de' Medici, and what can be more natural, I may ask, than to find the draft of a letter thus altered and improved when it is to contain an account of a definite subject, and when personal interests are in the scale? The finished copies as sent off are not known to exist; if we had these instead of the rough drafts, we might unhesi-

tatingly have declared that some unknown Italian engineer must have been, at that time, engaged in Armenia in the service of the Egyptian Sultan, and that Leonardo had copied his documents. Under this hypothesis however we should have to state that this unknown writer must have been so far one in mind with Leonardo as to use the same style of language and even the same lines of thought. This explanation might—as I say—have been possible, if only we had the finished letters. But why should these rough drafts of letters be regarded as anything else than what they actually and obviously are? If Leonardo had been a man of our own time, we might perhaps have attempted to account for the facts by saying that Leonardo, without having been in the East himself, might have undertaken to write a Romance of which the scene was laid in Armenia, and at the desire of his publisher had made sketches of landscape to illustrate the text.

I feel bound to mention this singular hypothesis as it has actually been put forward (see No. 1336 note 5); and it would certainly seem as though there were no other possible way of evading the conclusion to which these letters point, and their bearing on the life of the master,—absurd as the alternative is. But, if, on a question of such importance, we are justified in suggesting theories that have no foundation in probability, I could suggest another which, as compared with that of a Fiction by Leonardo, would be neither more nor less plausible; it is, moreover the only other hypothesis, perhaps, which can be devised to account for these passages, if it were possible to prove that the interpretation that the documents themselves suggest, must be rejected a priori; viz may not Leonardo have written them with the intention of mystifying those who, after his death, should try to decipher these manuscripts with a view to publishing them? But if, in fact, no objection that will stand the test of criticism can be brought against the simple and direct interpretation of the words as they stand, we are bound to regard Leonardo's travels in the East as an established fact. There is, I believe nothing in what we know of his biography to negative such a fact, especially as the details of his life for some few years are wholly unknown; nor need we be at a loss for evidence which may serve to explain—at any rate to some extent—the strangeness of his undertaking such a journey. We have no information as to Leonardo's history between 1482 and 1486; it cannot be proved that he was either in Milan or in Florence. On the other hand the tenor of this letter does not require us to assume a longer absence than a year or two. For, even if his appointment (offitio) as Engineer in Syria had been a permanent one, it might have become untenable—by the death perhaps of the Defterdar, his patron, or by his removal from office—, and Leonardo on his return home may have kept silence on the subject of an episode which probably had ended in failure and disappointment.

From the text of No. 1379 we can hardly doubt that Leonardo intended to make an excursion secretly from Rome to Naples, although so far as has hitherto been known, his biographers never allude to it. In another place (No. 1077) he says that he had worked as an Engineer in Friuli. Are we to doubt this statement too, merely because no biographer has hitherto given us any information on the matter? In the geographical notes Leonardo frequently speaks of the East, and though such passages afford no direct proof of his having been there, they show beyond a doubt that, next to the Nile, the Euphrates, the Tigris and the Taurus mountains had a special interest in his eyes. As a still further proof of the futility of the argument that there is nothing in his drawings to show that he had travelled in the East, we find on Pl. CXX a study of oriental heads of Armenian type,—though of course this may have been made in Italy.

If the style of these letters were less sober, and the expressions less strictly to the point throughout, it might be possible to regard them as a romantic fiction instead of a narrative of fact. Nay, we have only to compare them with such obviously fanciful passages as No. 1354, Nos. 670—673, and the Fables and Prophecies. It is unnecessary to discuss the subject any further here; such explanations as the letter needs are given in the foot notes.

The drafts of letters to Lodovico il Moro are very remarkable. Leonardo and this prince were certainly far less closely connected, than has hitherto been supposed. It is impossible that Leonardo can have remained so long in the service of this prince, because the salary was good, as is commonly stated. On the contrary, it would seem, that what kept him there, in spite of his sore need of the money owed him by the prince, was the hope of some day being able to carry out the project of casting the 'gran cavallo'.

1336.

AL DIODARIO DI SIRIA LOCOTENĒTE DEL SACRO SOLTANO ²DI BABILONIA.	TO THE DEVATDAR OF SYRIA, LIEUTENANT OF THE SACRED SULTAN OF BABYLON.

³Il nvouo accidēte accaduto in queste nostre parti settentrionali, il quale sō certo che nō solamēte a te ma a tutto l'universo

[3]The recent disaster in our Nor- thern parts which I am certain will terrify not you alone but the whole world, which

Drafts of Letters and Reports referring to Armenia (1336. 1337).

1336. 1. sorio. 3. [eaca n] "duto" [vono] "il nvouo" accidēte | "achaduto" in queste . . parte settantrionali [le quali so] "il

1336. Lines 1—52 are reproduced in facsimile on Pl. CXVI.

1. *Diodario.* This word is not to be found in any Italian dictionary, and for a long time I vainly sought an explanation of it. The youthful reminiscences of my wife afforded the desired clue. The chief town of each Turkish Villayet, or province—such as Broussa, for instance, in Asia Minor, is the residence of a Defterdar, who presides over the financial affairs of the province. *Defterdar hane* was, in former times, the name given to the Ministry of Finance at Constantinople; the Minister of Finance to the Porte is now known as the *Malliè-Nazri* and the *Defterdars* are his subordinates. A *Defterdar*, at the present day is merely the head of the finance department in each Provincial district. With regard to my suggestion that Leonardo's *Diodario* might be identical with the Defterdar of former times, the late M. C. DEFRÉMERIE, Arabic Professor, and Membre de l'Institut de France wrote to me as follows: *Votre conjecture est parfaitement fondée; diodario est l'équivalent de dévadar ou plus exactement dévâtdâr, titre d'une importante dignité en Egypte, sous les Mamlouks.*

The word however is not of Turkish, but of Perso-Arabic derivation. دفتر دار ,دواة دار literally *Defter* (Arabic) meaning *folio;* for *dar* (Persian) Bookkeeper or holder is the English equivalent; and the idea is that of a deputy in command. During

the Mamelook supremacy over Syria, which corresponded in date with Leonardo's time, the office of Defterdar was the third in importance in the State.

Soltano di Babilonia. The name of Babylon was commonly applied to Cairo in the middle ages. For instance BREIDENBACH, *Itinerarium Hierosolyma* p. 218 says: "At last we reached Babylon. But this is not that Babylon which stood on the further shore of the river Chober, but that which is called the Egyptian Babylon. It is close by Cairo and the twain are but one and not two towns; one half is called Cairo and the other Babylon, whence they are called together Cairo-Babylon; originally the town is said to have been named Memphis and then Babylon, but now it is called Cairo." Compare No. 1085, 6.

Egypt was governed from 1382 till 1517 by the Borgite or Tcherkessian dynasty of the Mamelook Sultans. One of the most famous of these, Sultan Kaït Bey, ruled from 1468—1496 during whose reign the Gama (or Mosque) of Kaït Bey and tomb of Kaït Bey near the Okella Kaït Bey were erected in Cairo, which preserve his name to this day. Under the rule of this great and wise prince many foreigners, particularly Italians, found occupation in Egypt, as may be seen in the 'Viaggio di Josaphat Barbaro', among other travellers. "Next to Leonardo (so I learn from Prof. Jac. Burckhardt of Bâle) Kaït Bey's most helpful engineer was a German farà ⁴terrore; il quale successiuamente ti sarà detto per ordine mostrando primo l'effetto e poi la causa . .

shall be related to you in due order, showing first the effect and then the cause[4] . .

⁵Ritrovandomi · io in queste parti d'Er-minia · a dare con amore e sollecitudine opera a quello vſitio, pel quale tu mi mā-dasti, e nel ⁶dare principio in quelle parti che a me pareano esser · piv al proposito

Finding myself in this part of Armenia[5] to carry into effect with due love and care the task for which you sent me[6]; and to make a beginning in a place which seemed to me to be most to our purpose, I entered into

quale [ere] sō cierto" che . . atte mattutto . . dara. 4. terrore [e ca] il . . causa [e du]. 5. dare | "con amore essollecitudine" opera acquello [pe] vſitio . , mādassti. 6. parte [chontingne ne a noi] che . . pareano | "eser" piv . . nosstro. 7. cita

who in about 1487 superintended the construction of the Mole at Alexandria. Felix Fabri knew him and mentions him in his *Historia Suevorum*, written in 1488."

3. *Il nuovo accidente accaduto*, or as Leonardo first wrote and then erased, *è accaduto un nuovo accidente*. From the sequel this must refer to an earthquake, and indeed these were frequent at that period, particularly in Asia Minor, where they caused immense mischief. See No. 1101 note.

4. The text here breaks off. The following lines are a fresh beginning of a letter, evidently addressed to the same person, but, as it would seem, written at a later date than the previous text. The numerous corrections and amendments amply prove that it is not a copy from any account of a journey by some unknown person; but, on the contrary, that Leonardo was particularly anxious to choose such words and phrases as might best express his own ideas.

5. *Parti d'Erminia*. See No. 945, note. The extent of Armenia in Leonardo's time is only approximately known. In the XVᵗʰ century the Persians governed the Eastern, and the Arabs the Southern portions. Arabic authors—as, for instance Abulfeda—include Cilicia and a part of Cappadocia in Armenia, and Greater Armenia was the tract of that country known later as Turcomania, while Arme-nia Minor was the territory between Cappadocia and the Euphrates. It was not till 1522, or even 1574 that the whole country came under the dominion of the Ottoman Turks, in the reign of Selim I.

The Mamelook Sultans of Egypt seem to have taken a particular interest in this, the most Northern province of their empire, which was even then in danger of being conquered by the Turks. In the autumn of 1477 Sultan Kaït Bey made a journey of inspection, visiting Antioch and the valleys of the Tigris and Euphrates with a numerous and brilliant escort. This tour is briefly alluded to by *Moodshireddin* p. 561; and by WEIL, *Geschichte der Abbasiden* V, p. 358. An anonymous member of the suite wrote a diary of the expedition in Arabic, which has been published by R. V. LONZONE ('*Viaggio in Palestina e Soria di Kaid Ba XVIII sultano della II dinastia*

mamelucca, fatto nel 1477. Testo arabo. Torino 1878', without notes or commentary), Compare the critique on this edition, by J. GILDEMEISTER in *Zeitschrift des Deutschen Palaestina Vereins* (Vol. III p. 246—249). Lanzone's edition seems to be no more than an abridged copy of the original. I owe to Professor Schéfer, Membre de l'Institut, the information that he is in possession of a manuscript in which the text is fuller, and more correctly given. The Mamelook dynasty was, as is well known, of Circassian origin, and a large proportion of the Egyptian Army was recruited in Circassia even so late as in the XVᵗʰ century. That was a period of political storms in Syria and Asia Minor and it is easy to suppose that the Sultan's minister, to whom Leonardo addresses his report as his superior, had a special interest in the welfare of those frontier provinces. Only to mention a few historical events of Sultan Kaït Bey's reign, we find that in 1488 he assisted the Circassians to resist the encroachments of Ala-eddoulet, an Asiatic prince who had allied himself with the Osmanli to threaten the province; the consequence was a war in Cilicia by sea and land, which broke out in the following year between the contending powers. Only a few years earlier the same province had been the scene of the so-called Caramenian war in which the united Venetian, Neapolitan and Sclavonic fleets had been engaged. (See CORIALANO CIPPICO, *Della guerra dei Veneziani nell'Asia dal 1469—1474*. Venezia 1796, p. 54) and we learn incidentally that a certain Leonardo Boldo, Governor of Scutari under Sultan Mahmoud,—as his name would indicate, one of the numerous renegades of Italian birth—played an important part in the negotiations for peace.

Tu mi mandasti. The address *tu* to a person-age so high in office is singular and suggests personal intimacy; Leonardo seems to have been a favourite with the Diodario. Compare lines 54 and 55.

I have endeavoured to show, and I believe that I am also in a position to prove with regard to these texts, that they are draughts of letters actually written by Leonardo; at the same time I must not omit to mention that shortly after I had discovered

nostro ·, entrai nella 7 città · di Calindra, vicina ai nostri confini; questa città è posta
nelle spiaggie di quel⁸la parte del mōte
Tavro, che è diuisa dall' Eufrates e riguarda i corni del grā Mōte Tav⁹ro per
ponēte ·; Questi corni · son di tanta altura
che par che tocchino il cielo, chè nell' universo non è parte terre¹⁰stre piv alta della
sua cima ·; e senpre 4 ore inanzi dì è per-

the city of Calindra[7], near to our frontiers.
This city is situated at the base of that part
of the Taurus mountains which is divided
from the Euphrates and looks towards the
peaks of the great Mount Taurus[8] to
the West[9]. These peaks are of such a
height that they seem to touch the sky, and
in all the world there is no part of the earth,
higher than its summit[10], and the rays of

di chalindra . . confini [e] questa . . ispiegge [del m] di quel.   8. diuisa [dal lago] dalleufrates [essa per le] e riguarda i
[grā] corni del "grā".   9. altura [che lo per me non credo] "che par chettochino il celo" che nell universo [sia] "none" parte.
10. ste piv al della . . essenpre . . di [allu] e perchossa . . sole [che allei si mostra].   11. lesere . . petra biāchissima

these texts in the Codex Atlanticus and published a paper on the subject in the *Zeitschrift für bildende Kunst* (*Vol. XVI*), Prof. GOVI put
forward this hypothesis to account for their
origin:

"*Quanto alle notizie sul monte Tauro, sull'Armenia e
sull'Asia minore che si contengono negli altri frammenti,
esse vennero prese da qualche geografo o viaggiatore
contemporaneo. Dall'indice imperfetto che accompagna
quei frammenti, si potrebbe dedurre che Leonardo volesse
farne un libro, che poi non venne compiuto. A ogni
modo, non è possibile di trovare in questi brani nessun
indizio di un viaggio di Leonardo in oriente, nè della sua
conversione alla religione di Maometto, come qualcuno
pretenderebbe. Leonardo amava con passione gli studi
geografici, e ne' suoi scritti s'incontran spesso itinerarî,
indicazioni, o descrizioni di luoghi, schizzi di carte e
abbozzi topografici di varie regioni, non è quindi strano che
egli, abile narratore com'era, si fosse proposto di scrivere
una specie di Romanzo in forma epistolare svolgendone
l'intreccio nell'Asia Minore, intorno alla quale i libri
d'allora, e forse qualche viaggiatore amico suo, gli
avevano somministrato alcuni elementi più o meno
fantastici.* (See *Transunti della Reale Accademia dei Lincei*
Vol. V Ser. 3).

It is hardly necessary to point out that Prof. Govi
omits to name the sources from which Leonardo
could be supposed to have drawn his information, and I
may leave it to the reader to pronounce judgment on
the anomaly which is involved in the hypothesis
that we have here a fragment of a Romance, cast
in the form of a correspondence. At the same
time, I cannot but admit that the solution of the
difficulties proposed by Prof. Govi is, under the
circumstances, certainly the easiest way of dealing
with the question. But we should then be equally
justified in supposing some more of Leonardo's letters
to be fragments of such romances; particularly those
of which the addresses can no longer be named.
Still, as regards these drafts of letters to the
Diodario, if we accept the Romance theory, as proposed by Prof. Govi, we are also compelled to
assume that Leonardo purposed from the first to
illustrate his tale; for it needs only a glance at the

sketches on Pl. CXVI to CXIX to perceive that
they are connected with the texts; and of course
the rest of Leonardo's numerous notes on matters
pertaining to the East, the greater part of which
are here published for the first time, may also be some-
how connected with this strange romance.

7. *Città de Calindra* (*Chalindra*). The position of
this city is so exactly determined, between the
valley of the Euphrates and the Taurus range that
it ought to be possible to identify it. But it can
hardly be the same as the sea port of Cilicia with
a somewhat similar name Celenderis, Kelandria,
Celendria, Kilindria, now the Turkish Gulnar. In
two Catalonian Portulans in the Bibliothèque Nationale in Paris—one dating from the XVth century, by
Wilhelm von Soler, the other by Olivez de Majorca,
in 1584—I find this place called Calandra. But
Leonardo's Calindra must certainly have lain more
to the North West, probably somewhere in Kurdistan.
The fact that the geographical position is so carefully determined by Leonardo seems to prove that
it was a place of no great importance and little
known. It is singular that the words first written
in l. 8 were *divisa dal lago* (Lake Van?), altered
afterwards to *dall'Eufrates*.

Nostri confini, and in l. 6 *proposito nostro*. These
refer to the frontier and to the affairs of the
Mamelook Sultan. Lines 65 and 66 throw some
light on the purpose of Leonardo's mission.

8. *I corni del grā mōte Tauro*. Compare the
sketches Pl. CXVI—CXVIII. So long as it is impossible to identify the situation of Calindra it is
most difficult to decide with any certainty which
peak of the Taurus is here meant; and I greatly
regret that I had no foreknowledge of this puzzling
topographical question when, in 1876, I was pursuing
archaeological enquiries in the Provinces of Aleppo
and Cilicia, and had to travel for some time in
view of the imposing snow-peaks of Bulghar Dagh
and Ala Tepessi.

9—10. The opinion here expressed as to the
height of the mountain would be unmeaning, unless
it had been written before Leonardo moved to
Milan, where Monte Rosa is so conspicuous an

cossa dai razzi del sole [11]in oriēte·; e per essere lei di pietra biāchissima, essa forte risplende, e fa l'ufitio a questi Ermini come farebbe vn bel lume [12]di luna·nel mezzo delle tenebre; e per la sua grande altura essa passa la somma altezza de' nuvoli per spatio di 4 miglia; e per linia retta [13]questa cima è ueduta di grā parte dell'occidente alluminata dal sole dopo il suo tramontare [14]insino alla 3ª parte della notte; ed è quella che appresso di voi ne' tempi sereni abbiamo già giudicato essere vna cometa, e pare a noi nelle [15]tenebre della notte mvtarsi in varie figure, e quādo diuidersi in due o in 3 parti, e quādo lūga e quādo corta; e questo nascie per li [16]nuvoli che nel orizzonte del cielo s'interpongono infra parte d'esso monte e il sole, e per tagliare l'uno essi raz[17]zi solari·, il lume del monte è interrotto con vari spati di nvvoli, e però è di figvra uaria[18]bile nel suo splendore.

the sun always fall upon it on its East side, four hours before day-time, and being of the whitest stone[11] it shines resplendently and fulfils the function to these Armenians which a bright moon-light would in the midst of the darkness; and by its great height it outreaches the utmost level of the clouds by a space of four miles in a straight line. This peak is seen in many places towards the West, illuminated by the sun after its setting the third part of the night. This it is, which with you[14] we formerly in calm weather had supposed to be a comet, and appears to us in the darkness of night, to change its form, being sometimes divided in two or three parts, and sometimes long and sometimes short. And this is caused by the clouds on the horizon of the sky which interpose between part of this mountain and the sun, and by cutting off some of the solar rays the light on the mountain is intercepted by various intervals of clouds, and therefore varies in the form of its brightness.

DIVISIONE DEL LIBRO.

[20]La predica e persuasione di fede;
[21]¶La subita inōdatione insin al [22]fine suo;¶
[23]¶La ruina della città;
[24]¶La morte del popolo [25]e disperatione;¶
[26]¶La cerca del predica[27]tore e la sua liberatione e benivo[28]lentia;¶
[29]¶Descritione della cavsa di tal [30]ruina del mōte;¶
[31]¶Il danno ch'ella fece;

THE DIVISIONS OF THE BOOK[19].

The praise and confession of the faith[20].
The sudden inundation, to its end.
[23]The destruction of the city.
[24]The death of the people and their despair.
The preacher's search, his release and benevolence[28].
Description of the cause of this fall of the mountain[30].
The mischief it did.

[essa] "essa forte rissplende e" fa . . acquesti . . chome. 12. luna "nel mezzo delle tenebre" e per . . le [magnie] somme" alteza de nugoli per [piv di 4 miglia] "per isspatio di 4 miglia" à | per. 13. ueduta [prima per] di . . dell ochcidente [pi] allumi. 14. e "jnsino alla 3 parte della notte" de cquella che apresso div[n]oi . . tenpi . . abiā ga gudicato . . cumeta . . annoi. 15. mvtarsi varie . . ecquādo . . parti "e equādo lūga ecquādo corta" ecquesto nasscie. 16. nvoli . . orizonte . . celo sinterpongano . . elsole . . essira. 17. ellume . . monte he . . varri [e] spati . . nvgoli. 24. popolo [el suo piāto]. 26. la [cōfermatio] la cerca. 27. ella . . venivo. 35. alagamēto . . parte. 40. profeta [mostra] ; che *is wanting.*

object in the landscape. *4 ore inanzi* seems to mean, four hours before the sun's rays penetrate to the bottom of the valleys.

11. *Pietra bianchissima.* The Taurus Mountains consist in great part of limestone.

14. *Appresso di voi.* Leonardo had at first written *noi* as though his meaning had been: This peak appeared to us to be a comet when you and I observed it in North Syria (at Aleppo? at Aintas?). The description of the curious reflection in the evening, resembling the "Alpine-glow" is certainly not an invented fiction, for in the next lines an explanation of the phenomenon is offered, or at least attempted.

19. The next 33 lines are evidently the contents of a connected Report or Book, but not of one

which he had at hand; more probably, indeed, of one he purposed writing.

20. *Persuasione di fede,* of the Christian or the Mohammedan faith? We must suppose the latter, at the beginning of a document addressed to so high a Mohammedan official. *Predica* probably stands as an abbreviation for *predicazione* (lat. *praedicatio*) in the sense of praise or glorification; very probably it may mean some such initial doxology as we find in Mohammedan works. (Comp. l. 40.)

26. 28. The phraseology of this is too general for any conjecture as to its meaning to be worth hazarding.

30. *Ruina del monte.* Of course by an earthquake. In a catalogue of earthquakes, entitled *kechf aussalssalèb an auasf ezzel-zelèh,* and written by Djelal eddin

32 ¶Ruina di neve;
33 ¶Trovata del profeta;
34 ¶La profetia sua;
35 ¶Allagamēto delle parti basse 36 di ‖ Erminia occidentale, 37 li scolamēti delle quali era 38 no per la tagliata di mōte Tav- 39 ro; ¶

40 Come il novo profeta mostra che 41 questa ruina è fatta 42 al suo proposito;

43 Descritione del mōte Tavro 44 e del fiume Evfrates;

45 Perchè il monte risplende nella sua cima 46 la metà o'l 3° della notte, e pare vna 47 cometa a quelli di ponente dopo la 48 sera, e ināti dì a quelli di leuāte.

49 Perchè essa cometa par di uariabile 50 figura in modo che ora è tonda or 51 lunga e or diuisa in 2 or in 3 parti, e 52 ora vnita, e quādo si riuede.

FIGURA DEL MŌTE TAVRO.

54 Non sono, o Diodario, da essere da te inputato di pigritia come le tue rāpogne · par che accennino ·, ma lo isfrenato amore, 55 il quale ha creato il benifitio ch'io posseggo da te, è quello, che mi à costretto cō somma 56 sollecitudine a cercare e cō diligiētia a investigare la cavsa di si grāde e stupēdo effetto ·; la qual cosa 57 nō sanza tēpo à potuto avere effetto; ora, per farti ben satisfatto della causa di si grande effetto, è neciessario ch'io ti mostri 58 la forma del sito, e poi verrò allo effetto col quale credo rimarrai satisfatto;

[32] Fall of snow.
The finding of the prophet [33].
His prophesy.

[35] The inundation of the lower portion of Eastern Armenia, the draining of which was effected by the cutting through the Taurus Mountains.

How the new prophet showed [40] that this destruction would happen as he had foretold.

Description of the Taurus Mountains [43] and the river Euphrates.

Why the mountain shines at the top, from half to a third of the night, and looks like a comet to the inhabitants of the West after the sunset, and before day to those of the East.

Why this comet appears of variable forms, so that it is now round and now long, and now again divided into two or three parts, and now in one piece, and when it is to be seen again.

OF THE SHAPE OF THE TAURUS MOUNTAINS [53].

I am not to be accused, Oh Devatdar, of idleness, as your chidings seem to hint; but your excessive love for me, which gave rise to the benefits you have conferred on me [55] is that which has also compelled me to the utmost painstaking in seeking out and diligently investigating the cause of so great and stupendous an effect. And this could not be done without time; now, in order to satisfy you fully as to the cause of so great an effect, it is requisite that I should explain to you the form of the place, and then I will proceed to the effect, by which I believe you will be amply satisfied.

41. [disc] questa . . effatta. 45. rissplende. 47. cometa [in] acquelli di. 48. acquelli. 50. ettondo. 51. lungho . . diuiso. 54. ho diodaro . . datte . . piegritia chome . . lo [tuo] isfrenato. 55. datte ecquello che [apv "a" chavoluto] che ma cōstretto chō somma [dieligiētia]. 56. [cerchare ei] sollecitudine a cerchare . . anvesstighare la chavsa . . stupēte. 57. hora . . sadisfatto di si grande "della causa [effetto] e . . mosstri. 58. la [cavsa ella] forma . . rimarai satisfatto. 59. risspossta

Syouthy, the following statement occurs: "In the year 889 (1484 A.D.) there were six shocks of earthquake at Aleppo. They were excessively violent and threw the inhabitants into consternation." I owe this communication to the kindness of Prof. Ch. Schéfer, Membre de l'Institut, to whom this unpublished Arabic MS. belongs. The foregoing entries refer to two earthquakes in Cairo, in 1476 and 1481: the following ones indicate a time at which Leonardo was, certainly, living in Milan.

36. *Tagliata di Monte Tauro*. The Euphrates flows through the Taurus range near the influx of the Kura Shai; it rushes through a rift in the wildest cliffs from 2000 to 3000 feet high and runs on for 90 miles in 300 falls or rapids till it reaches Telek, near which at a spot called Gleikash, or the Hart's leap, it measures only 35 paces across. Compare the map on Pl. CXIX and the explanation fo it on p. 391.

40. *Novo profeta*, l. 33, *profeta*. Mohammed. Leonardo here refers to the Koran:

In the name of the most merciful God.—When the earth shall be shaken by an earthquake; and the earth shall cast forth her burdens; and a man shall say, what aileth her? On that day the earth shall declare her tidings, for that thy Lord will inspire her. On that day men shall go forward in distinct classes, that they may behold their works. And whoever shall have wrought good of the weight of an ant, shall behold the same. And whoever shall have wrought evil of the weight of an ant, shall behold the same. (The Koran, translated by G. Sale, Chapter XCIX, p. 452).

53—94. The facsimile of this passage is given on Pl. CXVII.

54. The foregoing sketch of a letter, lines 5. 18, appears to have remained a fragment when Leonardo received pressing orders which caused

[59] Nō ti dolere, o Diodario, del mio tardare · a dar risposta alla tua desiderosa richiesta, perchè queste cose, di che tu mi richie[60]desti, son di natura che nō sanza processo di tenpo si possono bene esprimere, e massime perchè, a voler mostrare la causa di [61] si grande effetto, bisognia descrivere cō bona forma la natura del sito, e mediante quella tu potrai poi cō [62] facilità satisfarti della predetta richiesta;

[63] Jo lascierò indietro la descritione della forma dell'Asia Minore, e che mari o terre sien quelle che terminono [64] la figura della sua quātità, perchè so che la diligentia e sollecitudine de'tua studi non t'ànno di tal notitia [65] privato; e verrò a denotare la vera figura di Tavrus Mōte, il quale è quello ch'è cavsatore di si stupenda e dannosa maraviglia, la quale · serue alla espeditione del nostro pro[66]posito; Questo monte Tavro è quello che appresso di molti è detto essere il giogo del Monte Cavcaso, ma, avēdo [67] voluto ben chiarirmi ·, ò voluto parlare con alquanti di quelli che abitano sopra del Mar Caspio, i quali mostrano che [68] quel sia il uero Mōte Caucaso, che, benchè i mōti loro abbino il medesimo nome, questi son di maggiore altura, e però cōfermano, perchè Caucaso in lingua Scitica vuol dire somma altezza ·, e in vero non ci è noti[69]tia che l'oriēte nè l'occidente abbia monte di si grande altura ·; e la pruova, che così sia ·, è che li abitatori de' pae[70]si, che gli stanno per ponēte, vedono i razzi del sole che allumina insino alla 4ª parte delle maggior notti grā [71] parte della sua cima ·, e'l simile fa a quelli paesi che gli stanno per oriēte.

QUALITÀ E QUĀTITÀ DEL MŌTE TAVRO.

[73] L'onbra di questo giogo del Tauro è di tanta altura che, quādo di mezzo giugno il sole è a mezzo giorno, la sua ōbra s'a-

[59] Do not be aggrieved, O Devatdar, by my delay in responding to your pressing request, for those things which you require of me are of such a nature that they cannot be well expressed without some lapse of time ; particularly because, in order to explain the cause of so great an effect, it is necessary to describe with accuracy the nature of the place; and by this means I can afterwards easily satisfy your above-mentioned request[62].

I will pass over any description of the form of Asia Minor, or as to what seas or lands form the limits of its outline and extent, because I know that by your own diligence and carefulness in your studies you have not remained in ignorance of these matters[65]; and I will go on to describe the true form of the Taurus Mountain which is the cause of this stupendous and harmful marvel, and which will serve to advance us in our purpose[66]. This Taurus is that mountain which, with many others is said to be the ridge of Mount Caucasus; but wishing to be very clear about it, I desired to speak to some of the inhabitants of the shores of the Caspian sea, who give evidence that this must be the true Caucasus, and that though their mountains bear the same name, yet these are higher; and to confirm this in the Scythian tongue Caucasus means a very high[68] peak, and in fact we have no information of there being, in the East or in the West, any mountain so high. And the proof of this is that the inhabitants of the countries to the West see the rays of the sun illuminating a great part of its summit for as much as a quarter of the longest night. And in the same way, in those countries which lie to the East.

OF THE STRUCTURE AND SIZE OF MOUNT TAURUS.

[73] The shadow of this ridge of the Taurus is of such a height that when, in the middle of June, the Sun is at its meridian, its

tua . . "desiderosa" richiessta queste [son cho] chose di che. 60. possano "bene" espriemere . . mosstrare. 61. disscrivere. 62. sadisfarti. 63. lassciero [sta] indirieto la desscriptione . . etterre . . chetterminino. 64. chella [tua] diligentiā [de tua] essollecitudine . . notanno. 65. mōte | "il quel equello che chavsatore di si stupenda e danosa maraviglia" la quale . . esspeditione . . nosstro. 66. ecquello . . gogo . . cavcasso ma avē . . chasspio . . mosstrano. 68. caucaso "che beche i moti loro abbino il medesimo nome e questi son di magore altura e pero cōfermano" perche [a] cavcasso illingua isciticha vol . . alteza. 69. nelloccidente . . ella . . chosi . . he chelli. 70. chelli . . veggano i razi . . magor notto. 71. acquelli . .

him to write immediately and fully on the subject mentioned in line 43.

59—62. This passage was evidently intended as an improvement on that immediately preceding it. The purport of both is essentially the same, but the first is pitched in a key of ill-disguised annoyance

which is absent from the second. I do not see how these two versions can be reconciled with the romance-theory held by Prof. Govi.

68. Caucasus; Herodot Καύκασις; Armen. Kaukaz.

73—75. The statements are of course founded on those of the 'inhabitants' spoken of in l. 67.

74 stende insino al principio della Sarmatia, che sō giornate · 12, e a mezzo dicembre s' astē75de insino ai mōti Iperborei, che è viaggio d' un mese inverso tramontana; E /senpre la sua parte opposita al uē76to che soffia è priva di nuvoli e nebbie, perchè il uento, che s' apre nella percussione del sasso, dopo esso sasso si uiene a richi-77vdere, e in tal moto porta con seco i nvvoli da ogni parte, e lasciali nella lor percussione; e senpre è piena di percussione di saette per la grā moltitudine di nvvoli che lì sō ricettati, onde il sasso è tutto fracassato e pien di grā ruine; Questo nelle 78sua radici è abitato da richissimi popoli, ed è pieno di bellissimi fonti e fiumi; è fer79tile e abondante d' ogni bene e massime nelle parti che riguardano a mezzo giorno; — 80ma quando se n' è montato circa 3 miglia, si comīcia a trovare le selue de' grā81di abeti, pini e faggi e altri simili alberi; dopo questi per spatio di 3 al82tre miglia si trovano praterie e grādissime pasture, e tutto il resto, insino 83al nascimēto del Monte Tavro, sono nevi

shadow extends as far as the borders of Sarmatia, twelve days off; and in the middle of December it extends as far as the Hyperborean mountains, which are at a month's journey to the North [75]. And the side which faces the wind is always free from clouds and mists, because the wind which is parted in beating on the rock, closes again on the further side of that rock, and in its motion carries with it the clouds from all quarters and leaves them where it strikes. And it is always full of thunderbolts from the great quantity of clouds which accumulate there, whence the rock is all riven and full of huge débris [77]. This mountain, at its base, is inhabited by a very rich population and is full of most beautiful springs and rivers, and is fertile and abounding in all good produce, particularly in those parts which face to the South. But after mounting about three miles, we begin to find forests of great fir trees, and beech and other similar trees; after this, for a space of three more miles, there are meadows and vast pastures; and all the rest, as far as the beginning of the Taurus, is eternal snows

---

chelli. 73. gogho . . mezo gugnio . . he a mezo gorno. 74. insino [alla sarmatia] al . . chessō gornate . . mezo di[s]. cenbre sasste. 75. he viaggio Essenpre . . oposita. 76. chessoffia . . nvuoli ennebbie . . chessapre . . perchussione. 77. vedere [perche] e in . . nvuoli . . parte [e ne] ellasscia . . perchussione. *The text between the words* perchussione *and* Questa *has subsequently been added and is written on the margin in* 13 *short lines* . nugoli chelli . . ettutto frachassato 78. abitata . . piena . . effiumi. 79. mezo gorno. 80. montata circha . . comīca attrovare. 81. effaggi . . alberi [infrallo] dopo . . questo isspatio. 82. trova . . passture ettutto il retto. 83. nasscimēto . . neve etterne. 84. tano chessaste-

---

77. Sudden storms are equally common on the heights of Ararat. It is hardly necessary to observe that Ararat cannot be meant here. Its summit is formed like the crater of Vesuvius. The peaks sketched on Pl. CXVI—CXVIII are probably views of the same mountain, taken from different sides. Near the solitary peak, Pl. CXVIII these three names are written *goba, arnigasar, carūda,* names most likely of different peaks. Pl. CXVI and CXVII are in the original on a single sheet folded down the middle, 30 centimètres high and 43½ wide. On the reverse of one half of the sheet are notes on *peso* and *bilancia* (weight and balance), on the other are the 'prophecies' printed under Nos. 1293 and 1294. It is evident from the arrangement that these were written subsequently, on the space which had been left blank. These pages are facsimilied on Pl. CXVIII. In Pl. CXVI—CXVIII the size is smaller than in the original; the map of Armenia, Pl. CXVIII, is on Pl. CXIX slightly enlarged. On this map we find the following names, beginning from the right hand at the top: *pariardes mō* (for Paryadres Mons, Arm. Parchar, now Barchal or Kolai Dagh; Trebizond is on its slope).

Aquilone—North, *Antitaurus Antitaurus* \\\\ *psis mō* (probably meant for Thospitis = Lake Van, Arm. Dgov Vanai, Tospoi, and the Mountain range to the South); *Gordis mō* (Mountains of Gordyaea), the birth place of the Tigris; *Oriente*—East; *Tigris,* and then, to the left, *Eufrates.* Then, above to the left *Argeo mō* (now Erdshigas, an extinct volcano, 12000 feet high); *Celeno mō* (no doubt Sultan Dagh in Pisidia). Celeno is the Greek town of Κελαιναί— see Arian 1, 29, 1—now the ruins of Dineir); *oriente*—East; *africo libezco* (for libeccio—South West). In the middle of the Euphrates river on this small map we see a shaded portion surrounded by mountains, perhaps to indicate the inundation mentioned in l. 35. The affluent to the Euphrates shown as coming with many windings from the high land of 'Argeo' on the West, is the Tochma Su, which joins the main river at Malatie. I have not been able to discover any map of Armenia of the XVth or XVIth century in which the course of the Euphrates is laid down with any thing like the correctness displayed in this sketch. The best I have seen is the Catalonian Portulan of Olivez de Majorca, executed in 1584, and it is far behind Leonardo's.

eterne che mai per alcū tenpo si par[84]tono, che s'astendono all'altezza di circa 14 miglia in tutto; da questo na[85]scimēto del Tavro insino all'altezza d'vn miglio non passano mai i nuvoli; [86]che qui abbiamo 15 miglia, che sono circa a 5 · miglia d'altezza per linia retta, [87]e altrettanto o circa troviamo essere la cima delli corni del Tauro, [88]ne' quali dal mezzo in su si comincia a trovare aria che riscalda e nō [89]vi si sente soffiamēti de' uēti, ma nessuna cosa ci può troppo vivere; [90]quiui nō nascie cosa alcuna, saluo alcuni vccelli rapaci che [91]covano nell'alte fessure del Tavro, e disciēdono poi sotto i nuvoli [92]a fare le lor prede sopra i monti erbosi; Questo è tutto sasso senplice, [93]cioè da' nuvoli insù, ed è sasso candidissimo · e in sulla alta cima nō [94]si può andare per l'aspra e pericolosa sua salita.

which never disappear at any time, and extend to a height of about fourteen miles in all. From this beginning of the Taurus up to the height of a mile the clouds never pass away; thus we have fifteen miles, that is, a height of about five miles in a straight line; and the summit of the peaks of the Taurus are as much, or about that. There, half way up, we begin to find a scorching air and never feel a breath of wind; but nothing can live long there; there nothing is brought forth save a few birds of prey which breed in the high fissures of Taurus and descend below the clouds to seek their prey. Above the wooded hills all is bare rock, that is, from the clouds upwards; and the rock is the purest white. And it is impossible to walk to the high summit on account of the rough and perilous ascent.

C. A. 211 *b*; 621*a*]   1337.

Avēdoti · io più volte fatto · con mia lettere partecipe · delle cose che di qua · sono · accadute ·, no m'è paruto tacere a [2]vna nova · accaduta · ne' giorni passati · la quale . . . .

Having often made you, by my letters, acquainted with the things which have happened, I think I ought not to be silent as to the events of the last few days, which—[2]...

[3]Avēdoti io piv volte . . . . .

Having several times—

[4]Essendomi io più volte con lettere rallegrato · teco della tua prospera fortuna ·, al presente so che come amico ti cōtristerai · con meco [5]del misero · stato nel quale mi trovo; ¶e questo è che ne' giorni · passati · sono stato · in tāti affanni, [6]pavre, pericoli e danno · insieme con questi miseri paesani, che avevamo d'avere invidia ai morti, e cierto · io nō credo · [7]che, poichè gli elemēti con lor separatione. disfeciono · il grā caos, che essi riunissino · lor forza, anzi rabbia ·,

Having many times rejoiced with you by letters over your prosperous fortunes, I know now that, as a friend you will be sad with me over the miserable state in which I find myself; and this is, that during the last few days I have been in so much trouble, fear, peril and loss, besides the miseries of the people here, that we have been envious of the dead; and certainly I do not believe that since the elements by their separation reduced the vast chaos to order, they have ever combined their force and fury to do so much mischief to man. As far as regards

dano all alteza . . circha . . da cquesto. 85. alteza . . mai e nvuoli. 86. abiamo . . chessono circha . . dalteza. 87. circha troviano. 88. cominca attrovare . . risscalda. 89. cipo. 90. nasscie chosa. 91. disciēdano . . nvgoli. 92. affare . . Quessto ettutto. 93. coe . . nvgoli . . chandidissimo. 94. si po . . lasspra e pericholosa.

1337. 1. avēdoti "io" piu . . commia . . participe . . che didi qua . . achadute. 2. achaduta. 4. chollettere . . techo . . so "che chome amico" ti . . comecho. 5. ecquesto he. 6. pericholi . . chō . . avno | "davere" invidia . . inō credo. 7. collor . . che el

1337. On comparing this commencement of a letter l. 1—2 with that in l. 3 and 4 of No. 1336 it is quite evident that both refer to the same event. (Compare also No. 1337 l. 10—12 and 17 with No. 1336 l. 23, 24 and 32.) But the text No. 1336, including the fragment l. 3—4, was obviously written later than the draft here reproduced. The *Diodario* is not directly addressed—the person addressed indeed is not known—and it seems to me highly probable that it was written to some other patron and friend whose name and position are not mentioned.

a fare tanto nocimēto alli omini [8]quāto al presente da noi · s'è veduto · e provato, in modo ch'io nō posso imaginare · che cosa si possin [9]piv accresciere a tanto male, il quale noi provammo in spatio di dieci ore; In prima fummo assaliti e comba[10]ttuti dall'impeto · e furore de' vēti e a questo s'aggiunsero le ruine delli grā mōti di neve, i quali ànno ripieno tutte questi valli [11]e cōquassato grā parte della nostra città; E nō si cōtentādo di questo, la fortuna [12]cō subiti diluvi d'acque ebbe a sommergere tutta la parte bassa di questa città; oltre di questo s'aggiunse vna subita piog[13]gia ·, anzi ruinosa tēpesta piena d'acqua, sabbia, fango e pietre, insieme avviluppati cō radici sterpi e ciocchi di uarie piāte; [14]e ogni cosa scorrendo per l'aria discēdea sopra di noi ·; e in vltimo vno inciēdio di fuoco parea cōdotto nō che da vēti ma da 10 milia diavoli, che'l portassino, il quale à abbruciato e disfatto tutto questo [15]paese, e ancora non vi è cessato; E que' pochi, che siamo restati, siamo rimasti · cō tanto sbigottimēto [16]e tāta pavra che appena come balordi abbiamo ardire di parlare · l'uno coll'altro ·; avēdo · abbandonato ogni · nostra cura, ci stiamo insieme vniti [17]jn cierte ruine di chiese insieme misti maschi e femine, piccoli e grādi, a modo di [18]torme di capre; ¶i vicini per pietà ci ànno soccorso di uettovaglie, i quali erā prima nostri

us here, what we have seen and gone through is such that I could not imagine that things could ever rise to such an amount of mischief, as we experienced in the space of ten hours. In the first place we were assailed and attacked by the violence and fury of the winds[10]; to this was added the falling of great mountains of snow which filled up all this valley, thus destroying a great part of our city[11]. And not content with this the tempest sent a sudden flood of water to submerge all the low part of this city[12]; added to which there came a sudden rain, or rather a ruinous torrent and flood of water, sand, mud, and stones, entangled with roots, and stems and fragments of various trees; and every kind of thing flying through the air fell upon us; finally a great fire broke out, not brought by the wind, but carried as it would seem, by ten thousand devils, which completely burnt up all this neighbourhood and it has not yet ceased. And those few who remain unhurt are in such dejection and such terror that they hardly have courage to speak to each other, as if they were stunned. Having abandoned all our business, we stay here together in the ruins of some churches, men and women mingled together, small and great[17], just like herds of goats. The neighbours out of pity succoured us with victuals, and they had previously been our enemies. And if

rivnissino . . rabie affare. 8. dannoi . . imodo . . chosa. 9. accressciere attanto male "il `quale" noi prevamo . . ore [Nori abbiamo] jn . . furno "assaliti". 10. ttutti . . effurore . . vēti [e in breue] acquesto sagivnse . . neve i quli ano ripieno . . valle. 11. parte [di questa] "della nostra" citta [e morte molte giēte] E nō si cōtentā di. 12. dilui . . assomergiere . . questa [terra] citta oltre a di questo sagivnse . . pio. 13. dacq "a" sabia . . avilupati cō radici "sterpi" ezzochi. 14. cosa | "scorendo per laria" discēda . . focho il quala [a disfatto e] parea cōdotto nō chè da vēti ma da 10 milia diavoli chel portassino" a abruciato e disfatto. 15. ancora [nō da sire al suo cōsumare] "noui e cessato" E que . . chessiano . . si ano rimasi . . esbigottimēto. 16. appena | "come balordi" abiamo advre . . abandonato. 17. ciese . . massci effemine picoli. *The text between the words* capre *and* Ora *is written on the margin. The words:* i vicini . . nostri nimici *are written in six short lines on the right side and the following words* esse nō . . di fame *are written in eleven lines on the opposite side:* i vicini |

11. *Della nostra città* (Leonardo first wrote *di questa città*). From this we may infer that he had at some time lived in the place in question wherever it might be.

17. *Certe ruine di chiese.* Either of Armenian churches or of Mosques, which it was not unusual to speak of as churches.

Maschi e femmini insieme unite, implies an infringement of the usually strict rule of the separation of the sexes.

18. *I vicini, nostri nimici.* The town must then have stood quite close to the frontier of the country. Compare 1336. L. 7. *vicini ai nostri confini.* Dr. M. JORDAN has already published lines 4—13 (see *Das Malerbuch, Leipzig*, 1873, p. 90:—his reading differs from mine)

under the title of "Description of a landscape near Lake Como". We do in fact find, among other loose sheets in the Codex Atlanticus, certain texts referring to valleys of the Alps (see Nos. 1030, 1031 and note p. 237) and in the arrangement of the loose sheets, of which the Codex Atlanticus has been formed, these happen to be placed close to this text. The compiler stuck both on the same folio sheet; and if this is not the reason for Dr. JORDAN's choosing such a title (Description &c.) I cannot imagine what it can have been. It is, at any rate, a merely hypothetical statement. The designation of the population of the country round a city as "the enemy" (*nemici*) is hardly appropriate to Italy in the time of Leonardo.

nimici; ¶ e se nō fussero cierti popoli che ci ànno soccorso di uettovaglia, tutti saremmo morti di fame; Ora vedi come ci [19]troviamo ·; E tutti questi mali son niēte · a cōparatione di quelli che in breve tēpo ne son promessi;

[20]So che come amico ti cōtristerai del mio · male · come già con lettere ti mostrai con effetto rallegrarmi del tuo bene...

it had not been for certain people who succoured us with victuals, all would have died of hunger. Now you see the state we are in. And all these evils are as nothing compared with those which are promised to us shortly.

I know that as a friend you will grieve for my misfortunes, as I, in former letters have shown my joy at your prosperity . . .

F. 37 b]   **1338.**

LIBRO 43 DEL MOTO DELL'ARIA INCLUSA SOTTO L'ACQUA.

Notes about events observed abroad (1338. 1339).

.... Ho veduto mov[3]imēti d'aria tanto furiosi, che ànno ac[4]conpagniati e misti col corso suo li [5]grandissimi alberi delle selue e li tetti in[6]teri de grā palazzi, e questa medesima [7]furia fare vna buca con moto reuer[8]tiginoso e cavare vn ghiareto e portare ghi[9]ara, rena, acqua più d'ū mezzo miglio in[10]aria.

BOOK 43. OF THE MOVEMENT OF AIR ENCLOSED IN WATER.

I have seen motions of the air so furious that they have carried, mixed up in their course, the largest trees of the forest and whole roofs of great palaces, and I have seen the same fury bore a hole with a whirling movement digging out a gravel pit, and carrying gravel, sand and water more than half a mile through the air.

Br. M. 155 a]   **1339.**

A similitudine d'uno ritrosito vento che scorra in un a[2]renosa e cavata valle che pel suo velocie corso scac[3]cia al cētro tutte quelle cose che s'oppōgono al suo furi[4]oso corso . . . .

[5]Non altramēti il settētrionale aquilone ripercuote [6]colla sua tēpesta . . . .

Like a whirling wind which rushes down a sandy and hollow valley, and which, in its hasty course, drives to its centre every thing that opposes its furious course . . . .

No otherwise does the Northern blast whirl round in its tempestuous progress . . . .

"per pieta" ci a sochorso . . esse nō fussi socorso di uttovaglia . . saremo. 19. Ettitti . . chē brieve . . ne promesso.
20. chome . . cōtrissterai . . chome . . collettere timosstra . . ralegrarmi.
1338. 1. lacq"a". 3. anno a. 5. elli. 6. palazi ecquesta. 7. bucha. 8. giareto e portare gia. 9. mezo miglo. 10. naria.
1339. 1. chesschorranuna. 2. chavata . . chorso scha. 3. qlle chose chessoppōghono. 4. chorso. 5. altremēti . . settātrione
. . riperchuote. 6. cholla. 7. mvglia il [sellantrionale] tēpesstoso. 8. [mosso chō grā furia da] quādo . . settātrionale.

1338. The first sixteen lines of this passage which treat of the subject as indicated on the title-line have no place in this connexion and have been omitted.

2. *Ho veduto movimenti* &c. Nothing of the kind happened in Italy during Leonardo's lifetime, and it is therefore extremely probable that this refers to the natural phenomena which are so fully described in the foregoing passage. (Compare too, No. 1021.) There can be no doubt that the descriptions of the Deluge in the Libro di Pittura (Vol. I, No. 607–611), and that of the fall of a mountain No. 610, l. 17—30 were written from the vivid impressions derived from personal experience. Compare also Pl. XXXIV—XL.

1339. It may be inferred from the character of the writing, which is in the style of the note in facsimile Vol. I, p. 297, that this passage was written between 1470 and 1480. As the figure *6* at the end of the text indicates, it was continued on another page, but I have searched in vain for it. The reverse of this leaf is coloured red for drawing in silver point, but has not been used for that purpose but for writing on, and at about the same date. The passages are given as Nos. 1217, 1218, 1219, 1162 and No. 994 (see note page 218). The text given above is obviously not a fragment of a letter, but a record of some personal experience. No. 1379 also seems to refer to Leonardo's journeys in Southern Italy.

⁷Nō fa si grā mugghio il tēpestoso mare, ⁸quādo il settētrionale aquilone ⁹lo ripercuote colle scivmose onde fra Scilla e Cariddi, nè Stronboli o Mō¹⁰gibello, quando le solfuree fiāe, essendo rīchiuse, ¹¹per forza ronpēdo e aprēdo il grā mōte, fulminādo ¹²per l'aria pietre terra īsieme coll'uscita e vomitata fiāa . . .

¹³Nè quādo le infocate caverne di Mōgibello rivomitādo il male tenuto elemēto, spigniendolo ¹⁴alla sua regione, cō furia cacciādo īnāzi qualūche ostacolo ¹⁵s'interpone alla sua īpetuosa furia. . . .

¹⁶E tirato dalla mia bramosa voglia, vago di uedere la gran cō . . . ¹⁷delle varie e strane forme fatte dalla artifiziosa natura, ragiratomi ¹⁸alquāto jfra gli ōbrosi scogli pervenni all' ētrata d'una ¹⁹grā caverna dinanzi alla quale restato alquāto ²⁰stupefatto,—e jgniorante di tal cosa piegato le mie rene ²¹in arco e ferma la stāca mano sopra il ginocchio e colla destra mi feci tenebra ²²alle abbassate e chivse ciglia; e spesso piegādomi in qua e in là per ve²³dere dētro vi discernessi alcuna cosa, e questo vietatomi per ²⁴la grāde oscurità, che là entro era, e stato alquāto, subito si destarono ²⁵in me 2 cose, pavra e desiderio; paura · per la minaccio²⁶sa oscura spilonca, desidero per vedere se là ētro fusse alcuna ²⁷miracolosa cosa. . . .

Nor does the tempestuous sea bellow so loud, when the Northern blast dashes it, with its foaming waves between Scylla and Charybdis; nor Stromboli, nor Mount Etna, when their sulphurous flames, having been forcibly confined, rend, and burst open the mountain, fulminating stones and earth through the air together with the flames they vomit.

Nor when the inflamed caverns of Mount Etna, rejecting the ill-restrained element vomit it forth, back to its own region, driving furiously before it every obstacle that comes in the way of its impetuous rage . . . .

Unable to resist my eager desire and wanting to see the great . . . . of the various and strange shapes made by formative nature, and having wandered some distance among gloomy rocks, I came to the entrance of a great cavern, in front of which I stood some time, astonished and unaware of such a thing. Bending my back into an arch I rested my left hand on my knee and held my right hand over my down-cast and contracted eye brows: often bending first one way and then the other, to see whether I could discover anything inside, and this being forbidden by the deep darkness within, and after having remained there some time, two contrary emotions arose in me, fear and desire—fear of the threatening dark cavern, desire to see whether there were any marvellous thing within it . . . . .

C. A. 382 *a*; 1182 *a*]　　　　　　　**1340.**

Auēdo, signore mio illustrissimo, uisto e considerato oramai a sufficiētia le proue di tutti quelli · che si ²reputano maestri e

Most illustrious Lord, Having now sufficiently considered the specimens of all those who proclaim themselves skilled contrivers

Drafts of Letters to Lodovico il Moro (1340—1345).

9. riperchuote "chole scivmose onde frassilla echariddi nesstronboli. 10. zolfure. 12. cholluscita "e vomitata" fiāa. 13. lēfochate chaverne "di mōgibello" ri vomitādo "il male tenuto elemento" spigniendolo. 14. chō . . chacciādo . . osttacholo. 16. vagho . . la gra chō\\\\\. 17. varie "e strane" forme . . ragiratom\\\\. 18. schogli pervenni [alla b] all. 19. chavena [nella quale] dinanzi . . resstato. 20. chosa [chomīciato] pieghato . . ren\\\. 21. archo [e colla] "e ferma la" stācha mano [su] "sopra il" ginocchio e cholla desstra . . feci ten\\\\. 22. ecchiuse . . essspesso pieghādomi in qua e illa per\\\\\. 23. vdissciernessi alchuna chosa . . vietatom\\\\\. 24. osschurta . . esstato allqūato subitose. 25. le īme 2 [chōtrarie] chose . . la mina. 26. ce osscura spiloncha . . alchu\\\. 27. mirachalosa chosa . 𝟼.

1340. 1—36 *written from left to right.* 1. Hauēdo S "re" mio Jll. . . horamai ad. 2. che le . . di dicti. 3. alieni dal cō̄ . . ex-

13. *Mongibello* is a name commonly given in Sicily to Mount Etna (from Djebel, Arab.=mountain). Fr. FERRARA, *Descrizione dell' Etna con la storia delle eruzioni* (Palermo, 1818, p. 88) tells us, on the authority of the *Cronaca del Monastero Benedettino di Licordia,* of an eruption of the Volcano with a great flow of lava on Sept. 21, 1447. The next records of the mountain are from the years 1533 and 1536. A. Percy neither does mention any eruptions of Etna during the years to which this note must probably refer (*Mémoire des tremblements de terre de la péninsule italique,* Vol. XXII des *Mémoires*

couronnées et Mémoires des savants étrangers. Académie Royale de Belgique).

A literal interpretation of the passage would not, however, indicate an allusion to any great eruption; particularly in the connection with Stromboli, where the periodical outbreaks in very short intervals are very striking to any observer, especially at night time, when passing the island on the way from Naples to Messina.

1340. The numerous corrections, the alterations in the figures (l. 18) and the absence of any signature prove that this is merely the rough draft of a compositori di instruměti bellici ·, et che la inuětione di operatione di detti ³instruměti nō sono niente aliene dal commune vso: Mi forzerò, nō derogando a nessuno altro, ⁴farmi ītendere da Vostra Eccellentia, aprě-

of instruments of war, and that the invention and operation of the said instruments are nothing different to those in common use: I shall endeavour, without prejudice to any one else, to explain myself to your Excellency

·do a quella li secreti · mei ·, e appresso offerendoli ad ogni suo piacimento ⁵ī tempi opportuni operare cū effetto ancora tutte quelle cose · che sub breuità in parte saranno qui disotto ⁶notate.

showing your Lordship my secrets, and then offering them to your best pleasure and approbation to work with effect at opportune moments as well as all those things which, in part, shall be briefly noted below.

forzero . . altº.   4. ītende"re" da v. ex"tia" . . qlla . . ap̄psso . . ad ōi . . piaciм̄nto.   5. oportuni . . cū . . āca . . bre-
uita "ī pâte" saranno.   6. notate [e anchora ī molte piu secōdo le occurrětie de diuěsi casi s].   7. acti . . qlli.   8. uolta

letter to Lodovico il Moro. It is one of the very few manuscripts which are written from left to right—see the facsimile of the beginning as here reproduced. This is probably the final sketch of a document the clean of which copy was written in the usual manner. Leonardo no doubt very rarely wrote so, and this is probably the reason of the conspicuous dissimilarity in the handwriting, when he did. (Compare Pl. XXXVIII.) It is note-worthy too that here the orthography and abbre-viations are also exceptional. But such superficial peculiarities are not enough to stamp the document as altogether spurious. It is neither a forgery nor the production of any artist but Leonardo himself. As to this point the contents leave us no doubt as to its authenticity, particularly l. 32 (see No. 719,

where this passage is repeated). But whether the fragment, as we here see it, was written from Leonardo's dictation—a theory favoured by the orthography, the erasures and corrections — or whether it may be a copy made for or by Melzi or Mazenta is comparatively unimportant. There are in the Codex Atlanticus a few other documents not written by Leonardo himself, but the notes in his own hand found on the reverse pages of these leaves amply prove that they were certainly in Leonardo's possession. This mark of ownership is wanting to the text in question, but the compilers of the Codex Atlanticus, at any rate, accepted it as a genuine document.

With regard to the probable date of this pro-jected letter see Vol. II, p. 3.

1. [7]Ho modi di ponti leggierissimi e forti, e atti ad portare facilissimamēte, et cō quelli seguire [8]e alcuna uolta fuggire li inimici, e altri securi e īoffensibile da foco [9]e battaglia ·, facili e cōmodi da leuare e ponere ·; Et modi di ardere e disfare quelli del'inimico.

[10]2. So ī la ossidione di una terra togliere uia l'acqua de' fossi ·; e fare īfiniti pōti: gatti e scale [11]e altri īstrumenti pertinēti a detta speditione.

[12]3. Itē se per altezza di argine o per · fortezza di loco e di sito nō si potesse ī la ossidione di [13]vna terra usare l'officio delle bombarde: ho modi di ruinare omni rocca o altra fortezza, [14]se già nō fusse fondata ī su el sasso ecc.

[15]4. Ho ancora modi di bombarde cōmodissime e facili a portare: Et con quelle buttare minuti sassi [16]a similitudine quasi di tempesta ·; E con il fumo di quella dando grāde spauēto al'inimico [17]con graue suo danno e confusione ecc.

[18]9. Et quādo accadesse essere ī mare, ho modi di molti īstrumenti attissimi da offendere e difendere: [19]et nauili che faranno resistentia al trarre di omni grossissima bōbarda: e poluere e fiumi.

[20]5. Itē ho modi: per caue e uie secrete distorte fatte senza alcuno strepito per uenire disegnato [21]... ancora che bisogniasse passare sotto fossi o alcuno fiume.

[22]6. Item farò carri coperti e sicuri īoffensibili ·, i quali ētrādo ītra li inimici con sue artiglierie:, nō è si grāde multi[23]tudine di gente d'arme che nō rompessino: E dietro a questi potranno seguire fāterie assai illesi e sēza [24]alcuno īpedimēto.

[25]7. Item occorrendo di bisogno, farò bōbarde, mortari et passauolanti di bellissime e utili forme fuori del comune uso;

[26]8. Doue mācasse la operatione · delle bōbarde comporrò briccole, māgani | trabuchi e altri īstrumenti di mirabile [27]efficacia e fuori del' usato: Et ī sōma secondo la uarietà de' casi cōporrò uarie e īfinite cose da offēdere e di ...

1) I have a .sort of extremely light and strong bridges, adapted to be most easily carried, and with them you may pursue, and at any time flee from the enemy; and others, secure and indestructible by fire and battle, easy and convenient to lift and place. Also methods of burning and destroying those of the enemy.

2) I know how, when a place is besieged, to take the water out of the trenches, and make endless variety of bridges, and covered ways and ladders, and other machines pertaining to such expeditions.

3) Item. If, by reason of the height of the banks, or the strength of the place and its position, it is impossible, when besieging a place, to avail oneself of the plan of bombardment, I have methods for destroying every rock or other fortress, even if it were founded on a rock, &c.

4) Again I have kinds of mortars; most convenient and easy to carry; and with these can fling small stones almost resembling a storm; and with the smoke of these causing great terror to the enemy, to his great detriment and confusion.

9) [8]And when the fight should be at sea I have kinds of many machines most efficient for offence and defence; and vessels which will resist the attack of the largest guns and powder and fumes.

5) Item I have means by secret and tortuous mines and ways, made without noise to reach a designated [spot], even if it were needed to pass under a trench or a river.

6) Item. I will make covered chariots, safe and unattackable which, entering among the enemy with their artillery, there is no body of men so great but they would break them. And behind these, infantry could follow quite unhurt and without any hindrance.

7) Item. In case of need I will make big guns, mortars and light ordnance of fine and useful forms, out of the common type.

8) Where the operation of bombardment should fail, I would contrive catapults, mangonels, *trabocchi* and other machines of marvellous efficacy and not in common use. And in short, according to the variety of cases, I can contrive various and endless means of offence and defence.

[secondo le occurrētie] fuggire. 9. de ādē . . qlli. 10. obsidione de . . toglie"r" uia laqua, et . . ghatti. 11. ad dicta expeditione. 12. de āgine . . de loco . . pottesse . . obsidione de. 13. dele . . omni [forte] o | "rocca" (?) altra. 14. saxo. 15. anchora . . de bombāde . . facile ad . . Et cū q̄lle . . minuti [saxi]. 16. a [disimilitudine quasi] di . . cūel . . q̄lla. 17. cū. 18. accadessi de . .₁ strumti actissimi . . offendē e defendē. 19. de . . g"o"ssissima . . polue. 20. facte . . uenire [ad uno ce"r"to] e diseg"a"to. 21. \|\|\|\|\|\| anchora . . coperti "e sicuri" e . . cq"a"li ītrādo ītra [in] li inimica cū . . si [grosso] grande. 23. darme . . Et . . poteranno inlesi. 24. alchuno. 25. occurendo di bi soḡ . . mōtari . . utile forma fora del cōe. 26. mācassi . . de le componero . . māgliani. 27. fora . . sēdo . . cōpoꝓro . . ed \|\|\|\|\|\|. 28. credo satisfare . . ō . . edifitii e p. 29. et pvati . .

²⁸ 10. Jn tēpo di pace credo di soddisfare benissimo al paragone di ogni altro in
architettura, ī compositione di edifitii e publici ²⁹ e privati: e ī cōdurre acqua da uno
loco ad uno altro.

³⁰ Jtē cōdurrò ī scultura, di marmore,
di bronzo e di terra: simile ī pictura ciò
che si possa fare ³¹ a paragone di ogni altro
e sia chi vuole.

³² Ancora si potrà dare opera al cauallo
di bronzo, che sarà gloria īmortale e
eterno onore della ³³ felice memoria del
signore vostro padre e dela īclyta casa
Sforzesca;

³⁴ E se alcuna delle sopradette cose a alcuno paressino īpossibili e īfattibili, mi offro
³⁵ paratissimo a farne esperimento ī parco
uostro, o ī qual loco piacerà a vostra Ecel-
lenza, al³⁶la quale umilmente quanto più
posso, mi raccomando ecc.

10) In time of peace I believe I can give
perfect satisfaction and to the equal of any other
in architecture and the composition of buildings public and private; and in guiding
water from one place to another.

Item: I can carry out sculpture in marble,
bronze or clay, and also in painting whatever
may be done, and as well as any other, be
he whom he may.

[32] Again, the bronze horse may be taken
in hand, which is to be to the immortal glory
and eternal honour of the prince your father
of happy memory, and of the illustrious house
of Sforza.

And if any one of the above-named things
seem to any one to be impossible or not
feasible, I am most ready to make the experiment in your park, or in whatever place
may please your Excellency—to whom I commend myself with the utmost humility &c.

S. K. M. III. 28 *b*]   1341.

Al mio Illustrissimo Signore Lodouico,
   Duca di Bari ·/.
Leonardo Da · Vinci
   Fiorentino ·
⁵ Leonardo.

To my illustrious Lord, Lodovico,
   Duke of Bari,
Leonardo da Vinci
   of Florence—
Leonardo.

S. K. M. III. 23 *b*]   1342.

Vi piace vedere uno · modello · del quale
² risulterà · vtile · a uoi e a me ·, e vtili³tà
· a quelli che fieno · cagione · di no⁴stra
vtilità.

You would like to see a model which
will prove useful to you and to me, also
it will be of use to those who will be the
cause of our usefulness.

cōducē aqua . . alto [acto ad offendē e difendē. 30. cōducero. 31. ad . . deōni . . uole. 32. Anchora si potera . . honore
dela. 33. s"r"vost"o" patre e dela. 34. Et sealchunọ dele sop"r" dicte . . alchuno . . īpossibile e infactibile me offer.
35. ad farene experimento . . q"al" . . vost ex"tia" ad. 36. humilmīte . . me recomādo de.
1341. *Written from left to right.* 1. Ill"mo" Sig"re". 2. bari.
1342. 1. vedere î̄ modello. 2. am̃e. 3. acquelli cheffieno chagione.

1341. Evidently a note of the superscription of a
letter to the Duke, and written, like the foregoing
from left to right. The manuscript containing it
is of the year 1493. Lodovico was not proclaimed
and styled Duke of Milan till September 1494.
The Dukedom of Bari belonged to the Sforza
family till 1499.

1342. 1343. These two notes occur in the same

not very voluminous MS. as the former one and
it is possible that they are fragments of the same
letter. By the *Modello*, the equestrian statue is
probably meant, particularly as the model of
this statue was publicly exhibited in this very
year, 1493, on the occasion of the marriage
of the Emperor Maximilian with Bianca Maria
Sforza.

S. K. M. III. 79*b*]

1343.

Ecco · signor · molti · giētil omini ²che faranno infra loro · questa · spesa, ³lasciādo loro · godere l'entrata dell'acque, ⁴mvlina e passaggio di navili, e quādo ⁵e' sarà vēduto · loro il prezzo loro rēderā⁶no il navilio di Martigiana . . .

There are here, my Lord, many gentlemen who will undertake this expense among them, if they are allowed to enjoy the use of admission to the waters, the mills, and the passage of vessels and when it is sold to them the price will be repaid to them by the canal of Martesana.

C. A. 308*b*; 939*a*]

1344.

Assai mi rincrescie d'essere ī neciessità ·, ma piv mi dole ²che quella · sia causa · dello interrōpere il desiderio mio, il ³quale · è senpre disposto a vbidir uostra Eccellentia; ⁴forse che uostra Eccellēntia ⁵nō commise altro a messer Gual⁶tieri, credēdo che io avessi dina⁷ri . . . .

I am greatly vexed to be in necessity, but I still more regret that this should be the cause of the hindrance of my wish which is always disposed to obey your Excellency. Perhaps your Excellency did not give further orders to Messer Gualtieri, believing that I had money enough.

⁸E mi rincrescie assai che tu m'abbi ri⁹trovato in neciessità, e che l'auere io ¹⁰a guadagniare il uitto,-m'abbi ¹¹a interronpere . . .

I am greatly annoyed that you should have found me in necessity, and that my having to earn my living should have hindered me. . . .

¹²Assai mi rincresce che l'auere a guadagnia¹³re il uitto · m'abbia forzato interrō pere l'opera e di soddis¹⁴fare ad alcuni piccoli,- del seguitare l'o¹⁵pera che già vostra Signoria mi commise; Ma spero in bre¹⁶ue avere guadagniato · tanto che potrò · soddisfare ¹⁷ad animo riposato · a vostra Eccielenza, alla quale ¹⁸mi raccomādo, e se uostra Signoria credesse ch'io ¹⁹avessi · dinari, quella s'ingannerebbe; ò tenvto · 6 · boche 56 mesi, e ò avuto 50 ducati.

[12] It vexes me greatly that having to earn my living has forced me to interrupt the work and to attend to small matters, instead of following up the work which your Lordship entrusted to me. But I hope in a short time to have earned so much that I may carry it out quietly to the satisfaction of your Excellency, to whom I commend myself; and if your Lordship thought that I had money, your Lordship was deceived. I had to feed 6 men for 56 months, and have had 50 ducats.

C. A. 328*b*; 983*b*]

1345.

E se mi dato piv alcuna commissione d'alcuna . . .
²del premio del mio seruitio ·, perchè nō sō da essere da . . .
³cose assegniationi, perchè loro ànno intante di pe . . .
⁴tie che bene possono assettare piv di me . . .
⁵nō la mia arte, la quale voglio mvtare ed . . .
⁶dato qualche vestimēto si oso vna somma . . .

And if any other comission is given me by any . . .
of the reward of my service. Because I am not [able] to be . .
things assigned because meanwhile they have . . . to them . . . .
. . which they well may settle rather than I . .
not my art which I wish to change and . . . .
given some clothing if I dare a sum . . . .

1343. 1. Ecci. 2. fa ranno infralloro. 3. lassciādo. 4. passagio. 5. prezo lor rēdevā.
1344. 1. rincresscie. 2. chausa . . interōpere . . il q. 3. ecellentia. 5. chomise altro [al] meser qual. 8. rineresscie . . chettu mabbi ri\\\\\\. 9. echellauere. 10. guadagnare [il pane] il uicto mabi. 11. anteronpere. 12. rincressce chellauere. 13. uicto mabia interōpere [lopera de il sadis]. 14. fare ad alcuni picioli de il seguitare [aluna] lo. 15. smi chomisse. 16. podrō sadisfare. 17. eccieleza. 18. \\\\\\\\racomādo esse uostra S si. 19. \\\\\\\\ssi dinari quella quella singanerebbe.
1345. 1. esse . . comesione. 3. tante di pe. 4. possano. 6. sioso vna soma. 7. uosstra . . ochupa. 8. vosstra . . mi | "pichol

1345. The paper on which this is written is torn down the middle; about half of each line remains.

⁷Signiore ·, conosciēdo · io · la mēte · di uostra · Ecciellentia · essere · occupa · · ·
⁸il ricordare · a vostra Signioria · le mie
piccole e l'arti messe in silētio · · ·
⁹che 'l mio . taciere fusse causa · di fare ·
isdegniare vostra Signori · · ·
¹⁰la mia vita ai uostri seruiti · mi tiē con-
tinvamēte parato · a vbidire · · ·
¹¹del cauallo nō dirò niēte, perchè cognio-
sco · i tēpi · · ·
¹²a vostra Signoria com' io restai avere · il
salario di 2 · anni · del · · ·
¹³cō due . maestri · i quali cōtinvo · stettero ·
a mio salario e spesa · · ·
¹⁴che al fine mi trovai · avanzato detta
opera · circa 15 lire · mo · · ·
¹⁵opere di fama per le quali io potessi
mostrare a quelli che ueranno ch'io sono sta · · ·
¹⁶sa per tutto · ma io nō so, doue io potessi spēdere le mia opere a per · · ·

¹⁷l'auere io · atteso a guadagniarmi la
uita · · ·

¹⁸per non essere informato io che essere
io mi trova · · ·
¹⁹si ricorda · della commissione del dipigniere
· i camerini · · ·
²⁰portavo a vostra Signoria · solo richiedēdo
a quella · · ·

My Lord, I knowing your Excellency's
mind to be occupied . . .
to remind your Lordship of my small matters
and the arts put to silence
that my silence might be the cause of making
your Lordship scorn . .
my life in your service. I hold myself ever
in readiness to obey . . .
[11] Of the horse I will say nothing because
I know the times [are bad]
to your Lordship how I had still to receive
two years' salary of the . . . .
with the two skilled workmen who are constantly in my pay and at my cost
that at last I found myself advanced the
said sum about 15 lire . . . .
works of fame by which I could show to
those who shall see it that I have been
everywhere, but I do not know where I
could bestow my work [more] . . .

[17] I, having been working to gain my
living . . . .

I not having been informed what it is, I find
myself . . . .
[19] remember the commission to paint the
rooms . . . .
I conveyed to your Lordship only requesting
you . . . .

C. A. 316*b*; 958*b*]   1346.

Draft of
letter to be
sent to Pia-
cenza
(1346. 1347).

Magnifici · fabbricieri ·, intēdendo io vostre
magni²ficēze avere · preso · partito · di fare ·
cierte · magnie opere di bronzo; delle quali
· io vi ³darò · alcuno · ricordo · prima · che voi
nō siate · tanto . veloci · e tanto · presti a fare
essa allocatione ⁴chè per essa cielerità sia
tolto · la uia del potere · fare bona eletione
d'opere e maestri; e qualche omo che
per la · sua · insofficiētia abbia apresso a
vostri ⁵successori · a vituperare, se · ella vo-

Magnificent Commissioners of Buildings
I, understanding that your Magnificen-
cies have made up your minds to make
certain great works in bronze, will remind you
of certain things: first that you should not be
so hasty or so quick to give the commission,
lest by this haste it should become impossible
to select a good model and a good master;
and some man of small merit may be chosen,
who by his insufficiency may cause you to

ellarcimesse. 9. fussi chausa. 10. mi tiē. 11. [ia dinaro. 12. chomio . . ave"re" el. 13. maessti . . cōtinovo stettono . .
salario esspe. 14. avnzato ditta . . circha. 15. opere | "di fama" per elle . . acqelli che uerano. 16. opere [in piv] a per.
18. trovo [come e mi]. 19. richorda della comessione . . acquella.
1346. 1. [venerabili] e m'gnifici fabricieri [parēdo amme fare in parte]. 2. ficiēze [volere] avere. 3. richordo . . ettanto presst
a "affare essa allocatione" [pigliare partito]. 4. tolto "la uia del potere fare bona elletione dopere e maesstro" qualche
homo [di picho] | che . . abia . . vosstri.' 5. suciessori . . ella vosstra eta "erchettalia siasi ui ciedi boni īgiegni"|||||||| vdi-

11. See No. 723, where this passage is repeated.
17. See No. 1344 l. 12.
19. In April, 1498, Leonardo was engaged in
painting the Saletta Nigra of the Castello at Milan.
(See G. Mongeri, *l'Arte in Milano*, 1872, p. 417.)
1346. 1347. Piacenza belonged to Milan. The
Lord spoken of in this letter, is no doubt Lodovico

il Moro. One may infer from the concluding sentence (No. 1346, l. 33. 34 and No. 1347), that
Leonardo, who no doubt compiled this letter,
did not forward it to Piacenza himself, but gave
it to some influential patron, under whose name
and signature a copy of it was sent to the Commission.

stra · età .... givdicãdo che questa · età fusse mal fornita d'omini [6]di bon givditio · e di boni · maestri, vedendo le altre città, e massime la città de' Fiorentini, · quasi ne' medesimi tẽpi, essere [7]dotata di si belle e magnie opere di bronzo, intra le quali le porte del loro Battisterio ·; la qual Fiorẽtia ·, si come Piaciẽtia, [8]è terra di passo · doue · cõcorrono assai forestieri ., i quali vedendo le opere belle o bone, belle fanno a se [9]medesimi inpressioni: quella città · essere fornita di degni abitatori, vedendo l'opere testimonie d'essa opinione; e per lo contrario di[10]co, vedendo · tanta spesa di metallo operata si tristamẽte, che mẽ uergognia alla città [11]sarebbe che esse porte fussino di senplice legniame ·, perchè la poca spesa della materia [12]nõ parebbe meriteuole di grãde · spesa di magisterio ·, õde che ..

[13]La principale parte che per le città · si ricierchi · si sono · i domi, ai quali appressatisi, le prime · cose, [14]che all'ochio appariscono, · sono · le porte donde in esse chiese passare si possa.

[15]Guardate ·, signiori · fabbricieri ·, che la · troppa celerità del uolere voi con tãta [16]prestezza · dare · speditione alla locatione · di tanta magnia opera, quanto io sento che per uoi [17]s'è ordinata, non sia cagione che quello ·, che per onore · di dio · e delli omini si fa ·, non torni in grã [18]disonore de' uostri giuditi e della vostra città, doue, per essere terra degnia e di passo, è concorso · d'innumera[19]bili forestieri ·; e questo disonore accaderebbe ·, quãdo per le · uostre · indiligiẽtie [20]voi · prestasti · fede · a qualche vantatore che per le · sue frasche o per fauore ·, che di qua · dato li fusse, [21]da uoi auesse a inpetrare · simile opera ·, per la quale · a se e a uoi avesse a partorire lunga [22]e grãdissima infamia ·; Chè non posso · fare · che io non mi crucci · a ripensare quali omini [23]sieno quelli che abbino · conferito · volere · in simile inpresa ẽtra[24]re sanza pensare alla loro sofitiẽzia, sanza dirne altro ·; chi è maestro · di boccali ·, chi di corazze

be abused by your descendants, judging that this age was but ill supplied with men of good counsel and with good masters; seeing that other cities, and chiefly the city of the Florentines, has been as it were in these very days, endowed with beautiful and grand works in bronze; among which are the doors of their Baptistery. And this town of Florence, like Piacenza, is a place of intercourse, through which many foreigners pass; who, seeing that the works are fine and of good quality, carry away a good impression, and will say that that city is well filled with worthy inhabitants, seeing the works which bear witness to their opinion; and on the other hand, I say seeing so much metal expended and so badly wrought, it were less shame to the city if the doors had been of plain wood; because, the material, costing so little, would not seem to merit any great outlay of skill ...

Now the principal parts which are sought for in cities are their cathedrals, and of these the first things which strike the eye are the doors, by which one passes into these churches.

Beware, gentlemen of the Commission, lest too great speed in your determination, and so much haste to expedite the entrusting of so great a work as that which I hear you have ordered, be the cause that that which was intended for the honour of God and of men should be turned to great dishonour of your judgments, and of your city, which, being a place of mark, is the resort and gathering-place of innumerable foreigners. And this dishonour would result if by your lack of diligence you were to put your trust in some vaunter, who by his tricks or by favour shown to him here should obtain such work from you, by which lasting and very great shame would result to him and to you. Thus I cannot help being angry when I consider what men those are who have conferred with you as wishing to undertake this great work without thinking of their sufficiency for it, not to say more. This one is a potter, that one a maker of cuirasses, this one is a

cãdo .. heta fussi. 6. givditio che di .. maesstri vedendo | "nellaltre citta e massime" nella cita. 7. magnie | "opere di bronzo intrall quali le" porte .. batissterio. 8. he tera .. cõcorre .. fano asse. — *On the margin near line* 1 *is the note:* piaciẽtia he terra di passo come fiorenza. 9. impressione .. essere [ben] fornita .. abitatori | "vedendo lopere testimonie desso oppenione" e per lo contra di. 10. ovedendo trisstamẽte. 11. sarebe .. perchella pocha. 12. parebe. 13. la principale "parti" chosa delle citta per] che .. domi di quelle delle quali apresatosi le .. chose .. porte [per le quali] "donde" in ese ciese. 15. chella .. ciclerita [e pressteza] del .. chon. 16. pressteza .. isspeditione .. omini "si fa" non. 18. disonore de uostri inditi e" della vossra cita .. chonchorso dinumera. 19. foresstieri ecquesto .. achaderebe .. perlle uosstre. 20. presstassi .. acqualche vantato .. frape . favorare . fussi. 21. auessi .. asse e auoi auessi appartorire. 22. grãdissima [vergognia] infamia .. nomi isscrucci a "ri" | pẽsare quali | "[sieno li] [quelgli]" omini. 23. quelli [dai quali io sia] ce õme [cho] abbino chonferito. 24. sanza | "sanza pensare alla loro sofitiẽzia" dir ne .. maesro .. bochali .. coraze .. chanpanaro. 25. sonaglieri [in-

chi canpanaro, alcuno [25]sonagliere, E insino
bonbardiere, fra i quali vno Delsigniore s'è
uātato · che tra l'essere [26]lui conpare de
Messere · Anbrosio Ferrere—chi a qualche
commissione—dal quale lui à buone pro-
messioni ·; e se quello nō basterà [27]che mō-
terà · a cavallo · e andrà dal signiore e im-
petrerà tali lettere, [28]che per uoi mai simile
opera nō gli sarà dinegata ·; o guardate
dove i maestri, [29]atti a simili opere, sono
ridotti quādo con simili omini ànno a ga-
reggiare; [30]aprite li ochi · e vogliate bē
uedere che i vostri dinari nō si spēdino
[31]in conprare · le uostre · vergognie ·; jo vi so
annvntiare che di questa terra voi nō [32]tra-
rete se non è · opere di sorte e di vili e
grossi magisteri; nō ci è uomo che vaglia;
[33]e credetelo a me, saluo Leonardo Fiorētino, che fa il cauallo del duca Frācesco
di brōzo, che non è bisognio fare stima,
[34]perchè à che fare il tenpo di sua vita ·,
e dubito che per l'essere si grāde opera
che non la finirà mai.

[35]I miseri [36]studiosi .... [41]con che spe-
[42]ranza e' posso[43]no aspettare pre[44]mio di
lor virtù?

bell-founder, another a bell ringer, and one
is even a bombardier; and among them one
in his Lordship's service, who boasted that
he was the gossip of Messer Ambrosio Ferrere [26], who has some power and who
has made him some promises; and if this
were not enough he would mount on horse-
back, and go to his Lord and obtain such
letters that you could never refuse [to give]
him the work.   But consider where masters
of real talent and fit for such work are
brought when they have to compete with such
men as these.   Open your eyes and look
carefully lest your money should be spent in
buying your own disgrace. I can declare to you
that from that place you will procure none but
average works of inferior and coarse masters.
There is no capable man,—[33] and you may believe me,—except Leonardo the Florentine, who
is making the equestrian statue in bronze of the
Duke Francesco and who has no need to bring
himself into notice, because he has work for all
his life time; and I doubt, whether being so
great a work, he will ever finish it [34].

The miserable painstakers .... with what
hope may they expect a reward of their merit?

C. A. 316a; 958a]   **1347.**

Ecco vno il quale il signiore ·, per fare
questa sua opera à tratto di Firenze [2]che
è degnio maestro, ma à tāta faciēda che
non la finirà mai; [3]e credete voi che differētia · sia a vedere vna cosa bella da una
brutta; [4]allega Plinio.

There is one whom his Lordship invited
from Florence to do this work and who is a
worthy master, but with so very much business
he will never finish it; and you may imagine
that a difference there is to be seen between a
beautiful object and an ugly one. Quote Pliny.

1348.

Illmo ac Rm̄o Dn̄o Meo Unico.
D . Hip . Car .ˉli Estensi D . meo Colm̄o.
Ferrarie.
Illm̄ ac R . me D . ne mi hu . co . men.

Letter to the
Cardinal
Ippolito
d'Este. Pochi giorni sono ch'io venni da Milano,
et trovando che uno mio fratello maggiore

Most Illustrious and most Reverend Lord.
The Lord Ippolito, Cardinal of Este
at Ferrare.
Most Illustrious and most Reverend Lord.
I arrived from Milan but a few days since
and finding that my elder brother refuses to

sino] E insino [a vna] bonbardiere | "frai quali vno del" del . . trallessere. 26. ferere "ce a qualce comessione" dal. . esse.
27. che [vel sara] mōtera a cchavallo e andra [attrovare] del signiore e [che vi portera] inpetera'' tale. 28. gli sa dinegata
mo . . dove [i maesstri dibono ingiegnio]. 29. agimile garegiare. 30. voliate . . uedere [in] che [modo] i vosstri dinari [si
debbono spendere] nō . . le uosstre le uosstre vergogni . . anvntiare . . tera. 32. none e hopere di sorte [e vili dib] e di
vile . . homo. 33. saluo [quel] leonar fiorētino'' cheffa il chauallo . . frāc° "di brōzo" che . . lesere. 34. nolla. 36. stu-
diosi dif—. 37. [li uirtu che cō]. 38. [tanti studi sono]. 39. [venvti in qual]. 40. [cō grado di dise]. 41. [gnio] chon
che spie. 42. possa. 43. asspettare.
1347. 1. Eci . . attratto di firenze. 2. tāta faciēda nolla. 3. diferētia da ī brutta.

1346.   26. Messer Ambrogio Ferrere was Farmer
of the Customs under the Duke.   Piacenza at that
time belonged to Milan.

1348.   This letter addressed to the Cardinal

Ippolito d'Este is here given from Marchese
G. CAMPORI's publication: *Nuovi documenti per la Vita
di Leonardo da Vinci.   Atti e Memorie delle R. R. Depu-
tazioni di Storia patria per la provincie modenosi e par-*

non mi vuol servare uno testamento facto
da 3 anni in qua che è morto nostro padre;
ancor che la ragione sia per me, non di-
meno per non mancare a me medesimo in
una cosa che io stimo assai, non ho voluto
ommettere di richiedere la R.^{ma} V. S. di una
I.^{ra} commendatizia et di favore, qui a el
Sor Raphaello Jheronymo, che è al presente
uno de n.^{ri} excelsi Sig.^{ri}, ne quali questa
mia Causa si agita et particularmente è suta
dal Ex.^{tia} del gonfaloniere rimessa nel
pren.^{to} Sor Raphaello et sua S.^{ia} la ha a
decidere et terminare prima venga la festa
di tutti e sancti. Et però Mons.^{or} mio io
prego quanto più so e posso V. R. S. che
scriva una I.^{ra} qui al decto Sor Raphaello
in quel dextro et affettuoso modo che lei
saprà, raccomandandoli Leonardo Vincio sv-
isceratissimo Ser.^{re} suo, come mi appello, e
sempre voglio essere: ricercandolo, e gra-
vandolo mi voglia fare non solo ragione,
ma expeditione favorevole, et io non dubito punto per molte relationi mi son facte
che, sendo el Sor Raphaello a V. S. Affec-
tionatissimo, la cosa mi succederà ad votū.
Il che attribuirò a la I.^{ra} di V. R. S. a la
quale iterum mi racomando. Et bene
valeat.

     Florentie XVIII.^a 7bris 1507
         E V. R. D.
            S.^{tor} Humil.
       Leonardus Vincius pictor.

carry into effect a will, made three years
ago when my father died—as also, and no
less, because I would not fail in a matter I
esteem most important—I cannot forbear to
crave of your most Reverend Highness a letter
of recommendation and favour to Ser Raphaello Hieronymo, at present one of the illustrious members of the Signoria before whom
my cause is being argued; and more particularly it has been laid by his Excellency the Gonfaloniere into the hands of the said Ser Raphaello, that his Worship may have to decide
and end it before the festival of All Saints.
And therefore, my Lord, I entreat you, as
urgently as I know how and am able, that
your Highness will write a letter to the said
Ser Raphaello in that admirable and pressing
manner which your Highness can use, recom-
mending to him Leonardo Vincio, your most
humble servant as I am, and shall always be;
requesting him and pressing him not only
to do me justice but to do so with des-
patch; and I have not the least doubt, from
many things that I hear, that Ser Raphaello,
being most affectionately devoted to your
Highness, the matter will issue *ad votum*.
And this I shall attribute to your most Reverend Highness' letter, to whom I once more
humbly commend myself. *Et bene valeat.*

     Florence XVIII^a 7bris 1507.
         E. V. R. D.
          your humble servant
        Leonardus Vincius, pictor.

C. A. 310*a*; 944*a*]   **1349.**

Jo ho sospetto che la poca mia remuneratione de'gran benifiti che io ho riceuuti da nostra Eccelētia ²non l'abbino al-

I am afraid lest the small return I have
made for the great benefits, I have received
from your Excellency, have not made you

Draft of
Letter to the
Governor of
Milan.

1348. *Written from left to right.*
1349. 1. sosspecto chella poche .. uostra. 2. nonabbino isdegnare conmecho ecquesto .. uostra [ecci]. 3. auto risspossta .. cossti ..

menesi, Vol. III. It is the only text throughout this
work which I have not myself examined and copied
from the original. The learned discoverer of this
letter—the only letter from Leonardo hitherto known
as having been sent— dds these interesting remarks:
*Codesto Cardinale nato ad Ercole I. nel 1470, arcivescovo
di Strigonia a sette anni, poi d'Agra, aveva conseguito
nel 1497 la pingue ed ambita cattedra di Milano, là
dove avrà conosciuto il Vinci, sebbene il poco amore ch'ei
professava alle arti lasci credere che le proteste di servitù
di Leonardo più che a gratitudine per favori ricevuti e
per opere a lui allogate, accennino a speranza per un
favore che si aspetta. Notabile è ancora in questo pre-
zioso documento la ripetuta signatura del grande artista
che si scrive Vincio e Vincius, non da Vinci come si
tiene comunemente, sebbene l'una e l'altra possano valere*

*a significare così il casato come il paese; restando a
sapere se il nome del paese di Vinci fosse assunto a cog-
nome della famiglia di Leonardo nel qual supposto più
propriamente avrebbe a chiamarsi Leonardo Vinci, o
Vincio (latinamente Vincius) com'egli stesso amò segnarsi
in questa lettera, e come scrissero parecchi contemporanei di
lui, il Casio, il Cesariano, Geoffroy Tory, il Gaurico, il
Bandello, Raffaelle Maffei, il Paciolo. Per ultimo non
lascerò d'avvertire come la lettera del Vinci è assai ben
conservata, di nitida e larga scrittura in forma pienamente
corrispondente a quella dei suoi manoscritti, vergata
all'uso comune da sinistra a destra, anzichè contraria-
mente come fu suo costume; ma indubbiamente autentica
e fornita della menzione e del suggello che fresca ancora
conserva l'impronta di una testa di profilo da un picciolo
antico cammeo.* (Compare No. 1368, note.)

quāto fatto sdegniare con meco, e questo è che da tante lettere che io ho scritte a uostra ³Signoria io non ò mai avuto risposta; hora io mando costì Salai per fare intendere a uostra Signoria ⁴come io sono quasi al fine del mio letigio che io ho · co' mia fratelli, come io credo trouarmi costì in questa ⁵pasqua e portare con meco due quadri di due nostre donne di uarie grandezze, Le quali son fatte ⁶pel cristianissimo nostro rè, e perchè a uostra Signoria piacerà, jo avrei ben caro di sapere alla mia ⁷tornata di costa, doue io auessi a stare per stanza, perchè non uorrei dare più noia a uostra Signoria, e ⁸ancora, auendo io lauorato pel cristianissimo rè, se la mia prouisione è per correre o no; jo scriuo ⁹al presidente di quella acqua che mi donò il · rè ·, della quale non fui messo in possessione, perchè in quel tēpo u'era ¹⁰carestia nel nauilio per causa de' gran secchi, e perchè i sua bocchelli non erano moderati; ma bē mi promise che, ¹¹fatta tal moderatione, io ne sarei messo in possessione; sicchè io prego uostra Signoria · che non le increscà, ¹²che ora che tali bochelli son moderati, di fare ricordare al presidente la mia espeditione cioè di darmi la ¹³possessione d'essa acqua, perchè alla uenuta mia spero farui su strumēti e cose che sarā di grā piacere al ¹⁴nostro cristianissimo rè; Altro non mi accade; sono senpre a uostri comandi.

somewhat angry with me, and that this is why to so many letters which I have written to your Lordship I have never had an answer. I now send Salai to explain to your Lordship that I am almost at an end of the litigation I had with my brother; that I hope to find myself with you this Easter, and to carry with me two pictures of two Madonnas of different sizes. These were done for our most Christian King, or for whomsoever your Lordship may please. I should be very glad to know on my return thence where I may have to reside, for I would not give any more trouble to your Lordship. Also, as I have worked for the most Christian King, whether my salary is to continue or not. I wrote to the President as to that water which the king granted me, and which I was not put in possession of because at that time there was a dearth in the canal by reason of the great droughts and because [10]its outlets were not regulated; but he certainly promised me that when this was done I should be put in possession. Thus I pray your Lordship that you will take so much trouble, now that these outlets are regulated, as to remind the President of my matter; that is, to give me possession of this water, because on my return I hope to make there instruments and other things which will greatly please our most Christian King. Nothing else occurs to me. I am always yours to command.

C. A. 364 b; 1138 b]   1350.

Drafts of Letters to the Superintendent of Canals and to Fr. Melzi.

Magnifico presidēte, io mando costì Salai mio discepolo, il quale ²di questa sia aportatore e da lui intenderete a bocca la causa del mio tanto sopra (sedere) . . .

Magnificent President, I am sending thither Salai, my pupil, who is the bearer of this, and from him you will hear by word of mouth the cause of my . . .

uosstra. 4. lettigio . . fratelgli . . cossti in quessta. 5. passqua epportare commecho . . nosstre . . quale. 6. crisstinissimo . . nosstra . . arei. 7. cossta . . asstare per isstanza . . uosstre he. 8. re sella , . he per . . onno. 9. posessione. 10. sechi . . bochelli non era . . promisse. 11. posessione siche io priegho uosstra . . nolle incressca. 12. expeditione coe di darnela. 33. posessione . . isspero . . chessarā. 14. nomi acade.

1350. 1. Magni"co" presidēte [questa sol per condare] io . . quale [di questa sia]. 2. [la porta] di questa . . abocha sopra. 3. Ma-

1349. Charles d'Amboise, Maréchal de Chaumont, was Governor of Milan under Louis XII. Leonardo was in personal communication with him so early as in 1503. He was absent from Milan in the autumn of 1506 and from October 1510—when he besieged Pope Julius II. in Bologna—till his death, which took place at Correggio, February 11. 1511. Francesco Vinci, Leonardo's uncle, died—as Amoretti tells us—in the winter of 1510—11 (or according to Uzielli in 1506?), and Leonardo remained in Florence for business connected with his estate. The letter written with reference to this affair, No. 1348, is undoubtedly earlier than the letters Nos. 1349 and 1350. Amoretti tells us, *Memorie*

Storiche, ch. II, that the following note existed on the same leaf in MS. C. A. I have not however succeeded in finding it. The passage runs thus: *Jo sono quasi al fine del mio letigio che io ò con miè fratetgli . . . . Ancora ricordo a V. Exc^ia la facenda che ò cum Ser Juliano mio Fratello capo delli altri fratelli ricordandoli come se offerse di conciar le cose nostre fra noi fratelli del comune della eredità de mio Zio, e quelli costringa alla expeditione, quale conteneva la lettera che lui me mandò.*

10. Compare Nos. 1009 and 1010.

Leonardo has noted the payment of the pension from the king in 1505.

3 Magnifico presidēte io.

Magnificent President, I . . .

4 Magnifico presidente, essendomi io piv volte ricordato delle proferte fattemi da uostra Eccellētia più volte, ò preso sicurtà 5 di scriuere e di ricordare a questa la promessa fattami à l'ultima partita, cioè la possessione di quel⁶le 12 once d'acqua donatemi dal cristianissimo rè; vostra Signoria sa che io non ētrai in essa ·possessione, perchè in quel 7 tempo, ch'ela mi fu donata, era carestia d'acqua nel navilio, si pel grā secco come pel non essere ancora moderati li sua bochelli; ma ⁸mi fu promesso da uostra Eccellentia che fatta tal moderatione io avrei l'inttento mio; di poi, intendendo essere acconcio il navilio, io scrissi più volte a vo⁹stra signoria e a Messer Girolamo da Cusano, che à apresso di se la carta di tal donazione, e così scrissi al Corigero, e ¹⁰mai ebbi risposta; Ora io mādo costì Salai, mio discepolo, aportatore di questa, al quale vostra Signoria potrà ¹¹dire a bocca tutto quel ch'è seguito, della qual cosa io prego vostra Ecciellenza; ¹²Jo credo esser costì in questa pasqua per esser presso al fine del mio piateggiare, e porterò cō meco due quadri di nostra ¹³donna che io ò commīciate, e ò le ne'tempi, che mi sono avāzati, condotte in assai bō porto; Altro nō mi accade.

¹⁴Magnifico Signore mio, l'amore che uostra Eccellētia m'à senpre dimostro, e' benefiti ch'io ò riceuuti da quella al continuo ¹⁵mi sō dināzi . . . .
¹⁶Io ò sospetto che la poca remuneratiō de'grā benifiti ch'io ho riceuuto da uostra Eccellentia non l'abbi¹⁷no fatto alquāto turbare con meco, e questo è che di piv lettere che io ò scritte a vostra Eccellentia io non ò mai ¹⁸avuta risposta ·, ora io mando costì Salai per fare intendere a vostra signoria, come io son quasi al fine del mio ¹⁹letigio coi mia fratelli, e come io credo essere costì in questa pasqua e portare con meco due quadri doue sono ²⁰due Nostre donne di varie grādezze, le quali io ò comīciato pel cristianissimo rè, o per chi a uoi piacerà; avrei ben caro di sa²¹pere

Magnificent President:—Having ofttimes remembered the proposals made many times to me by your Excellency, I take the liberty of writing to remind your Lordship of the promise made to me at my last departure, that is the possession of the twelve inches of water granted to me by the most Christian King. Your Lordship knows that I did not enter into possession, because at that time when it was given to me there was a dearth of water in the canal, as well by reason of the great drought as also because the outlets were not regulated; but your Excellency promised me that as soon as this was done, I should have my rights. Afterwards hearing that the canal was complete I wrote several times to your Lordship and to Messer Girolamo da Cusano, who has in his keeping the deed of this gift; and so also I wrote to Corigero and never had a reply. I now send thither Salai, my pupil, the bearer of this, to whom your Lordship may tell by word of mouth all that happened in the matter about which I petition your Excellency. I expect to go thither this Easter since I am nearly at the end of my lawsuit, and I will take with me two pictures of our Lady which I have begun, and at the present time have brought them on to a very good end; nothing else occurs to me.

My Lord the love which your Excellency has always shown me and the benefits that I have constantly received from you I have hitherto . . .
I am fearful lest the small return I have made for the great benefits I have received from your Excellency may not have made you somewhat annoyed with me. And this is why, to many letters which I have written to your Excellency I have never had an answer. I now send to you Salai to explain to your Excellency that I am almost at the end of my litigation with my brothers, and that I hope to be with you this Easter and carry with me two pictures on which are two Madonnas of different sizes which I began for the most Christian King, or for whomsoever you please. I should be very glad to

gni"co" [mio] presidēte [avē] io. 4. presidēde esendomi . . uostra [se] ecciellētia. 5. a [vostra signoria] "acquesta" la . . fattami [alla partita mia di costa] a . . coe "la posessione" di. 6. dacq"a" donatomi . . cristianissimo . . posessione. 7. tempo "che la mi fa donata" era . . dacq"a" . . secho. 7. moderato. 8. ecellentia cheffatta . . arei lattento . . poi | "intendendo essere à conco il navilio" io. 9. donagone. 10. bocha . . Quel . . ipriegho vosstra. 12. passqua . . piategare nosta. 13. commīcate e olle acade poe. 14. M"o"signore [antonio maria] "mio" lamore "labeit" che uostra [signoria] "ecellētia" ma senpre di . . chio o"chi" . . riceuuti dacquella mi al. 16. ossosspetto . . pocha remuneratiō [de benifitich] de . . manibi abi. 17. conmecho ecquesto . . osscritte avosstra . . inōno. 18. vta rissposta hora . . vosstra. 19. letigo comia . . cossti . . passqua . . comecho . . doue su. 20. grādeze . . comīcate . . arei . . asstare . . istantia. 21. uorei [piu] . . uosstra.

alla mia tornata di costà, dove io ò a stare per stanza, perchè nō uorrei dare più noia a uostra Signoria, e ā²²cora, auendo io lauorato pel cristianissimo Rè, se la mia prouisione è per correre o no; io scriuo al presidē²³te di quell' acqua che mi donò il rè, della quale nō fui messo in possessione per esserne carestia nel navilio per ca²⁴usa de' grā secchi, e perchè i sua bocchelli non erā moderati; ma bē mi promise che, fatta tal moderatione, i' ne sarei ²⁵messo in possessione, sichè io vi prego che, scontrandovi in esso presidente, nō ui incresca che ora, che tali bochelli sō ²⁶moderati, di ricordare a detto presidente di farmi dare la possessione d'essa acqua, che mi parue intēdere che in grā par²⁷te staua a lui; altro non mi accade; sono senpre a uostri comādi.

²⁸Buō dì, messer Francesco ·, può lo fare Iddio che di tante lettere ch'io v'ò scritte · che mai voi non m'abbiate risposto; Or aspettate ²⁹ch'io venga costà, per Dio, ch'io vi farò tanto scrivere che forse vi rincrescerà.

³⁰Caro mio, messer Francesco, io mādo costì Salai per intendere dalla magnificentia del presidente che fine à avuta quella ³¹moderatione dell'acque che alla mia partita fu ordinata per li bochelli del navilio, perchè el magnifico presidēte mi promi³²se che subito fatta tal moderatione, io sarei spedito; Ora egli è più tenpo che io intesi che il nauilio s'accō³³ciaua, e similmente i sua bochelli, e inmediate scrissi al presidente e a uoi, e poi replicai, e mai ebbi ³⁴risposta; adūque voi degnerete di rispōdermi quel ch'è seguito, e non essendo per spedirsi nō u'īcresca per mio a³⁵more di sollecitarne vn poco il presidente e così messer Girolamo da Cusano, al quale uoi mi racomādere³⁶te e offeriretemi a sua magnificētia.

know where, on my return from this place, I shall have to reside, because I do not wish to give more trouble to your Lordship; and then, having worked for the most Christian King, whether my salary is to be continued or not. I write to the President as to the water that the king granted me of which I had not been put in possession by reason of the dearth in the canal, caused by the great drought and because its outlets were not regulated; but he promised me certainly that as soon as the regulation was made, I should be put in possession of it; I therefore pray you that, if you should meet the said President, you would be good enough, now that the outlets are regulated, to remind the said President to cause me to be put in possession of that water, since I understand it is in great measure in his power. Nothing else occurs to me; always yours to command.

Good day to you Messer Francesco. Why, in God's name, of all the letters I have written to you, have you never answered one. Now wait till I come, by God, and I shall make you write so much that perhaps you will become sick of it.

Dear Messer Francesco. I am sending thither Salai to learn from His Magnificence the President to what end the regulation of the water has come since, at my departure this regulation of the outlets of the canal had been ordered, because His Magnificence the President promised me that as soon as this was done I should be satisfied. It is now some time since I heard that the canal was in order, as also its outlets, and I immediately wrote to the President and to you, and then I repeated it, and never had an answer. So you will have the goodness to answer me as to that which happened, and as I am not to hurry the matter, would you take the trouble, for the love of me, to urge the President a little, and also Messer Girolamo Cusano, to whom you will commend me and offer my duty to his Magnificence.

---

22. crisstianisimo . . sella . . onno. 23. acq"a" . . ɪ e [la quale] della . . caresstia. 24. sechi . . bochelgli . . promisse. 25. priegho chesscontrandosi. 26. posesione . . acq"a". 27. allui . . nomi achade [se nō di racoman]. 28. meser . . puollo . . idio . . vosscritte . . nomabiate rissposto. 29. vengha . . chefforse vi rincresscera. 30. charo . . meser francessco . . cheffine a uta. 31. della cq"a" . . partia . . che nauilio sacō. 33. caua essimilmente . . scrissi [io auoi e] al . . ripricai. 34. rissposta . . risspodermi . . isspedirsi. 35. pocho. 36. offererete assua mgnificētia.

1350. 28—36. Draft of a letter to Francesco Melzi, born 1493—a youth therefore of about 17 in 1510. Leonardo addresses his young friend as "Messer", as being the son of a noble house.

Melzi practised art under Leonardo as a dilettante and not as a pupil, like Cesare da Sesto and others (See LERMOLIEFF, *Die Galerien &c.*, p. 476).

C. A. 243*b*; 729*b*] **1351.**

Drafts of a
letter to
Giuliano de'
Medici
(1351. 1352).

[Jllustrissimo mio Signore, [2] Assai mi rallegro, illustrissimo mio signiore ·, del uostro].

[3] Tanto mi son rallegrato, o illustrissimo
mio signore, del desiderato acquisto di
vostra sanità che io quasi ho [riauuto la
sanità mia]—[sono all'ultimo del mio male]—
e'l male mio da me s'è fuggito — — della
quasi reintegrata sanità di vostra Eccellenza;
[4] Ma assai mi rincrescie il nō auere io potuto integralmēte satisfare alli desideri
di uostra Ecciellentia mediā[5]te la malignità
di cotesto ingannatore, al quale non ò lasciato indirieto cosa alcuna colla quale [6] io
li abbia potuto giovare che per me non
li sia stata fatta e prima la sua provisione
inanzi al tēpo li era pagata, la quale io
credo che volentieri [7] negherebbe, se io non
avessi la scritta e testificata da me e dallo
interprete, e vedendo io che per me nō si
lauorava, se nō quādo [8] i lavori d'altri
si mācavano, de' quali lui era sollecito in-
vestigatore, jo lo preghai che dovesse
mangia[9]re con meco, e lauorare indi ap-

[Most illustrious Lord. I greatly rejoice
most Illustrious Lord at your . . .]

I was so greatly rejoiced, most illustrious
Lord, by the desired restoration of your
health, that it almost had the effect that [my
own health recovered]—[I have got through
my illness]—my own illness left me——of
your Excellency's almost restored health. But
I am extremely vexed that I have not been
able completely to satisfy the wishes of your
Excellency, by reason of the wickedness of
that deceiver, for whom I left nothing undone
which could be done for him by me and by
which I might be of use to him; and in the
first place his allowances were paid to him
before the time, which I believe he would
willingly deny, if I had not the writing signed
by myself and the interpreter. And I, seeing
that he did not work for me unless he had
no work to do for others, which he was very
careful in solliciting, invited him to dine
with me, and to work afterwards near me,
because, besides the saving of expense, he

1351. 1. Illusimo permio signiore e vett. 2. rallegro [della] illustrissimo. 3. del [famoso] desiderato . . uosstra . . che ī quasi
ho sfatto "[riavta la sanita mia]" "[son sono allultimo del mio male]" "el mal mio dame se fuggito" [del grāde acquisto]
della . . reīntegrata . . uosstra eccielleca. 4. [chel mia . . rincrescie [della malignita] il . . auere | "io" potuto "integral-
mēte" sadisfare . . uosstra s. te [Illustr] te la malignita [de] di cossto . . lassciato indirieto [nessuna] cosa "alcuna" colle.
6. giovare | "che per me non li sia stata fatta" e . li sua [danari] provisione "inanzi al tēpo" immediate . . paghata. 7. ne-
gherebbe "neghata" se . . avesi lasscritta ettesticata di me dello interpete. 8. daltri [erā finiti] "si mācavano" de . . sollecito cerchatore "investighatore" jo [lo uolsi e] lo [feci] "lo" pregha "i"che do"ve" ssi. 9. comecho "ellauorare di lindi
apresso di me perche oltre alcōto .\· — *Here on the margin is the note in three lines* .\· bē lopere elli acquisterebbe il

1351. 1353. It is clear from the contents of this
notes that they refer to Leonardo's residence in
Rome in 1513—1515. Nor can there be any doubt
that they were addressed to Leonardo's patron at
the time: Giuliano de' Medici, third son of Lorenzo
the Magnificent and brother of Pope Leo X (born
1478). In 1512 he became the head of the Florentine
Republic. The Pope invited him to Rome, where
he settled; in 1513 he was named patrician with
much splendid ceremonial. The medal struck in
honour of the event bears the words MAG. IVLIAN.
MEDICES. Leonardo too uses the style "Magnifico",
in his letter. Compare also No. 1377.

GINO CAPPONI (*Storia della Repubblica di Firenze*,
Vol. III, p. 139) thus describes the character of
Giuliano de' Medici, who died in 1516: *Era il
migliore della famiglia, di vita placida, grande spenditore,
tenendo intorno a sè uomini ingegnosi, ed ogni nuova cosa
voleva provare.*

See too GREGOROVIUS, *Geschichte der Stadt Rom*,
VIII (book XIV. III, 2): *Die Luftschlösser fürstlicher
Grösse, wozu ihn der Papst hatte erheben wollen zerfielen.*

*Julian war der edelste aller damaligen Medici, ein
Mensch von innerlicher Richtung, unbefriedigt durch das
Leben, mitten im Sonnenglanz der Herrlichkeit Leo's X.
eine dunkle Gestalt die wie ein Schatten vorüberzog.*
Giuliano lived in the Vatican, and it may be safely
inferred from No. 1352 l. 2, and No. 1353 l. 4, that
Leonardo did the same.

From the following unpublished notice in the
Vatican archives, which M. Eug. Müntz, librarian of
the Ecole des Beaux arts, Paris, has done me the
favour to communicate to me, we get a more
accurate view of Leonardo's relation to the often
named GIORGIO TEDESCO:

Nota delle provisione (sic) *a da pagare per me in
nome del nostro ill. S. Bernardo Bini e chompa di
Roma, e prima della ill^ma sua chonsorte ogni mese d. 800.*

*A L^do da Vinci per sua provisione d. XXXIII, e
più d. VII al detto per la provisione di Giorgio tedesco,
che sono in tutto d. 40.*

From this we learn, that seven ducats formed the
German's monthly wages, but according to No. 1353 l. 7
he pretended that eight ducats had been agreed upon.

presso di me, perchè oltre al conto elli acquisterebbe il linguaggio italiano; [lui senpre lo promise e mai lo volle fare]; E questo facievo ancora, perchè quel Giovā tedesco che fa li spechi ogni dì lì era in bottega, e volleua vedere e intendere ciò che si facieva e publicava per la... forte biasimando; e perchè lui māgiava cō quelli [10] della guardia del papa, e poi se n'ādava in conpagnia colli scoppietti, amazādo vccielli per queste anticaglie e così seguitava da dopo desinare a sera; E se io mandavo Lorēzo [11] a sollecitarli il lavoro lui si cruciava e dicieva che nō volea tanti maestri sopra capo, e che il lauorar suo era [12] per la guardaroba di vostra Ecciellētia, e passò dua mesi e così seguitava e indi, trovādo Giannicolò della [13] guardaroba, domādailo s' el Tedesco avea finito l' opere del magnifico, e lui mi disse non esser vero, ma che so[14]lamēte li avea dato a nettar dua scoppiette; di poi faciēdolo io sollecitare lui lasciò la bettega, e comīciò a lavorare ī came[15]ra, e perde assai tēpo nel fare vn alfra morsa e lime e altri strumēti a vite; e quiui lavorava mulinelli da torcere seta, [16] li quali nascōdeva, quādo un de' mia v'ētrava, e con mille bestemie e rimbrotti, in modo che nessū de mia voleva piv entrare.

[17] Tanto mi sō rallegrato, jllustrissimo mio Signore, del desiderato acquisto di vostra sanità che quasi il male mio da me [18] s' è fugito; Ma assai mi rincrescie il non avere io potuto integralmēte satisfare alli desideri di uostra Eccellenza [19] mediante la malignità di cotesto ingānatore tedesco, per il quale non ò lasciato indireto cosa alcuna, [20] colla quale io abbia creduto farli piaciere; e secondariamente invitarlo ad abitare e vivere con meco, per la qual cosa io ve[21]drei al continuo l' opera che lui faciesse, e cō facilità ricorreggierei li errori ·; e oltre di questo inparerebbe la lingua italiana, [22] mediante la quale lui cō facilità potrebbe parlare sanza interprete; e li sua danari li

would acquire the Italian language. He always promised, but would never do so. And this I did also, because that Giovanni, the German who makes the mirrors, was there always in the workshop, and wanted to see and to know all that was being done there and made it known outside... strongly criticising it; and because he dined with those of the Pope's guard, and then they went out with guns killing birds among the ruins; and this went on from after dinner till the evening; and when I sent Lorenzo to urge him to work he said that he would not have so many masters over him, and that his work was for your Excellency's Wardrobe; and thus two months passed and so it went on; and one day finding Gian Niccolò of the Wardrobe and asking whether the German had finished the work for your Magnificence, he told me this was not true, but only that he had given him two guns to clean. Afterwards, when I had urged him farther, be left the workshop and began to work in his room, and lost much time in making another pair of pincers and files and other tools with screws; and there he worked at mills for twisting silk which he hid when any one of my people went in, and with a thousand oaths and mutterings, so that none of them would go there any more.

I was so greatly rejoiced, most Illustrious Lord, by the desired restoration of your health, that my own illness almost left me. But I am greatly vexed at not having been able to completely satisfy your Excellency's wishes by reason of the wickedness of that German deceiver, for whom I left nothing undone by which I could have hope to please him; and secondly I invited him to lodge and board with me, by which means I should constantly see the work he was doing and with greater ease correct his errors while, besides this, he would learn the Italian tongue, by means of which be could with more ease talk without an interpreter; his moneys were always given him in advance of the

---

linghagio italiano . . lui senpre [lo promisse e mai lo volle fare] .\· Ecque"sto" facievo|. *On the margin in twelve short lines:* |, ecquesto facievo ancora perche que . . tedescho . . ongni . . ibottegha . . cio chessi e publicava per la for biasimando |||||||||| aro quel |||||||||| ndea

Here ends the note on the margin. perche lui māgiava [colli tedessci che so] cō quel. 10. nādava "in conpagnia" cholli schopietti . . antichaglie "ecosi segutava da dopo desinare assera" Esse. 11. [a richordarli] a solecitarli . . lui "si scruciava e" dicieva . . maesstri . . chapo eche[la] cche se [la] e i lauorare. 12. ghuarderoba [del s] di . . e [chosi] passo . . seghuita ve [se no] e vndi [li] trovādo. 13. ghuardaroba [del s] domādalo selli [ave] sel tedessco . . magnificho ellui . . Mace. 14. scoppiette . . solecitare . . lassio . . bottegha e comōcio allavorare. ellime . . llavorava mulenelli dattorciere. 16. loi quali nasscōdeva . . nesun de mia vēdrava . . comile . . rinbrotti . . nesū. 17. vosstra . . che | "quasi" il [mio] male. 18. rincrescie . . sadifare . . uosstra. 19. ingānatore [tedesco il quale] tedesco . . lassciato . . chosa. 20. cholle . . e "p" prima | "secondariamente" invitarlo . . vi"ve"re comecho. 21. chellui faciessi. 22. ricoregiere . . oltre furō ²³sēpre dati ināzi al tēpo ·; Dipoi la richiesta di costui fu di avere li modelli ²⁴finiti di legniame, com' ellino aveano a essere di ferro, e' quali volea portare nel suo paese; La qual cosa io li negai diciē-²⁵doli ch' io li darei in disegnio la larghezza, lunghezza e grossezza e figura di ciò ch'elli avesse a fare, e così restammo mal volētieri.

²⁶La secōda cosa fu, che si fecie vn altra bottega e morse e strumenti, dove dormiua, e quivi lavorava per altri, dipoi andava a desi²⁷nare coi Suizzeri della guardia, dove sta giēte sfacciēdata, della qual cosa lui tutti li uīcieva; e'l piv ²⁸delle volte se n'andauano due o tre di loro, colli scoppietti; ammazzavā vccielli per le anticaglie, e questo durava insino a sera;
²⁹Al fine ò trovato come ³⁰questo maestro Giovā ³¹ni delli Spechi è quello ³²che à fatto il tutto per ³³due cagioni; e la prima ³⁴perchè lui à avuto a dire che ³⁵la venuta mia qui ³⁶li à tolto la cōuersa³⁷tione e'l favore di uostra ³⁸Signoria, che senpre ve . . . ³⁹L'altra è ⁴⁰che la stātia ⁴¹di questo fereui ⁴²disse cōuenirsi a lui per ⁴³lavorare li spechi, e ⁴⁴di questo n'à fatto dimostra⁴⁵tione chè, oltre al farmi ⁴⁶costui nimico, li à fatto vē⁴⁷dere ogni suo e lasciare ⁴⁸a lui la sua bot⁴⁹tega, nella qual lavora ⁵⁰cō molti lavorāti assai spe⁵¹chi per mādare alle fiere.

time when due. Afterwards he wanted to have the models finished in wood, just as they were to be in iron, and wished to carry them away to his own country. But this I refused him, telling him that I would give him, in drawing, the breadth, length, height and form of what he had to do; and so we remained in ill-will.

The next thing was that he made himself another workshop and pincers and tools in his room where he slept, and there he worked for others; afterwards he went to dine with the Swiss of the guard, where there are idle fellows, in which he beat them all; and most times they went two or three together with guns, to shoot birds among the ruins, and this went on till evening.

At last I found how this master Giovanni the mirror-maker was he who had done it all, for two reasons; the first because he had said that my coming here had deprived him of the countenance and favour of your Lordship which always . . . The other is that he said that his iron-workers' rooms suited him for working at his mirrors, and of this he gave proof; for besides making him my enemy, he made him sell all he had and leave his workshop to him, where he works with a number of workmen making numerous mirrors to send to the fairs.

C. A. 278 a; 850 a]   **1352.**

Tanto mi son rallegrato, illustrissimo mio signiore, del desiderato acquisto di uostra sanità, che quasi il male mio da me ²s'è fuggito; dico iddio ne sia laudato, Ma assai mi rincresce il non avere io potuto integralmēte satisfare alli desideri di uostra Eccellenza ³mediante la malignità di cotesto ingānatore tedesco, per il quale non ò lasciato indirieto cosa alcuna, ⁴colla quale io abbia creduto farli piacere, e secondariamente invitarlo ad abitare e vivere con meco, per la qual cosa ⁵io farei piantare

I was so greatly rejoiced, most Illustrious Lord, by the wished for recovery of your health, that my own ills have almost left me; and I say God be praised for it. But it vexes me greatly that I have not been able completely to satisfy your Excellency's wishes by reason of the wickedness of that German deceiver, for whom I left nothing undone by which I could hope to please him; and secondly I invited him to lodge and board with me, by which means I should see constantly the work he was doing,

---

a di questo . . taliana . . interprete [e ottre a di questo] "e prima" li sua. 23. ināzi [al mese] al tēpo allcuttofu Di . . riciessta . . modelli [finiti di legniame]. 24. fin [iti di pūto] di . . chomelli . . neghai. 25. darei [di] in . . luneza e grosseza . . avessi affare . . restamo. 26. bottegha "emvro (?) e morse esstrumēti" [nella camera] dove. 27. nare [colla ghuardi] co suizeri . . ghardia . . uīcieva dissene vssciva el piv. 28. senadaua . . ottre . . scopietti amazava . . antichaglie ecquesto . . assera. 30. maesstro. 33. ella. 34. lui avuto. 35. mia [ari] qui. 36. tolto [il s] la. 37. uosstra. 38. Signoria che senpre ve. 39. [nēdo] Laltra e che. 40. [faciendoli] chella. 41. di questo [mini] fereui. 42. disscie cōnuenirsi allui. 43. lisspechi. 47. ellassciare. 48. allui . . boc. 49. tecca. 51. chi pe.
1352. 2. seffuggito "dicho idio ne sia laldato" Ma . . rincre. *Here the text breaks off.* 2. *The text from lines* 1—4: Ma assai etc. . . *to* ad abitare e vivere *is an exact copy of lines* 18—20 *No.* 1349. 4. comecho . . chosa io vedrei .\· *Here follow six short lines on the margin:* farei piantare vn dessco . . questte . . potessi . . di sot fabrichare e chosi. *The marginal note ends here.* — faciessi e chō . . ricorregierebe.

vn desco a' piedi d' una di queste finestre, dove lui potesse lauorar di lima, e finire le cose di sotto fabricate, e così io vedrei al continuo l' opera che lui facesse e con facilità si ricorreggierebbe.

for which purpose I would have a table fixed at the foot of one of these windows, where he could work with the file and finish the things made below; and so I should constantly see the work he might do, and it could be corrected with greater ease.

C. A. 179*b*; 541*b*]　　　　　　　1353.

Draft of letter written at Rome.

Questo altro m' à īpedito l' anatomia [2] col papa biasiamādola, e così all' o[3]spedale, e ēpie di botteghe da spechi [4] tutto questo Beluedere o di lavora[5]ti; e così à fatto nella stātia di ma[6]estro Giorgio; [7] disse che otto du[8]cati li furon promes[9]si ogni mese, comī-[10]ciādo il primo dì [11] che si mise in via, [12] o il più tardo quā[13]do e' ui parlò, e che [14] voi l' acciettaste;

[15] Vedēdo io costui rare volte sta[16]re a bottega e che cōsumava assai, jo [17] li feci dire che se li piacea che io farei [18] con lui mercato di ciascuna cosa che [19] lui facesse, e a stima tānto li darei [20] quāto noi fussimo d' accordo; elli [21] si cōsigliò col uicino e lasciò lì la stā[22]tia, vendendo ogni cosa, e venne a trovare. . .

This other hindered me in anatomy, blaming it before the Pope; and likewise at the hospital; and he has filled [4]this whole Belvedere with workshops for mirrors; and he did the same thing in Maestro Giorgio's room. He said that he had been promised [7]eight ducats every month, beginning with the first day, when he set out, or at latest when he spoke with you; and that you agreed.

Seeing that he seldom stayed in the workshop, and that he ate a great deal, I sent him word that, if he liked I could deal with him separately for each thing that he might make, and would give him what we might agree to be a fair valuation. He took counsel with his neighbour and gave up his room, selling every thing, and went to find . . .

C. A. 304*a*; 925*a*]　　　　　　　1354.

Miscellaneous Records (1354. 1355).

Caro Benedetto de' Pertarti. [2] Caduto jl fier gigāte per la cagione della jsaguinata [3] e fangosa terra, parve che cadesse vna mōtagnia; [4] onde la cāpagnia guassata di terremoto, e spavēto [5] a Plutone jfernale; e per la grā percossa ristette [6] sulla piana terra alquāto stordito; e subito [7] il popolo, credēdo fusse morto di qualche saetta,—[8] tornato la gran turba, a guisa di formiche che scorrono a [9] furia, quando per il corpo del caduto robore (?); così questi [10] scorrēdo per l' ampie membra e le ravrādo con spesse [11] ferite; onde

Dear Benedetto de' Pertarti. When the proud giant fell because of the bloody and miry state of the ground it was as though a mountain had fallen so that the country shook as with an earthquake, and terror fell on Pluto in hell. From the violence of the shock he lay as stunned on the level ground. Suddenly the people, seeing him as one killed by a thunderbolt, turned back; like ants running wildly over the body of the fallen oak, so these rushing over his ample limbs . . . . them with

1353. 2. chosi. 3. dasspechi. 4. ollavrā. 5. affatto. 6. esstro giorgo. 8. fu. 9. sa. 11. misse. 16. abottegha . . asai. 17. chesseli piacea che i farei. 18. collui merchato . . casscuna. 19. facessi e asstima attato. 20. dachordo. 21. ellasciolli 22. vendeda ogni cosa e vene attrovare.

1354. 1. benedeto prtarli. 2. dela. 3. tera . . cadessi. 4. gussa di tere moto. 5. plutone jfernale . . percosa. 6. sula . . tera . . stordito on sobito. 7. il popo jrededo fusi. 8. gra turba . . scorano. 9. furi o\\\\\ndo per olcorpo del caduto uogore cosi. 10. per larpie mebra e lera vrādo conispese. 11. ferie. 12. dale . . sendesi. 13. vmuglio. 14. fusi . . le + (4?)

1354. A puzzling passage, meant, as it would seem, for a jest. Compare the description of Giants in Dante, *Inf.* XXI and XXII. Perhaps Leonardo had the Giant Antaeus in his mind. Of him the myth relates that he was a son of Gê, that he fed on lions; that he hunted in Libya and killed the inhabitants. He enjoyed the peculiarity of

renewing his strength whenever he fell and came in contact with his mother earth; but that Hercules lifted him up and so conquered and strangled him. Lucan gives a full account of the struggle. Pharsalia IV, 617. The reading of this passage, which is very indistinctly written, is in many places doubtful.

risentito jl gigāte e sētēdosi ¹²quasi coperto dalla moltitudine, subito sentesi cuo¹³cere per le pūture; mise un mugghio che parve ¹⁴fusse vno spavētoso tono, e posto le sue mani in ¹⁵terra, e levatosi il pavroso volto, e postosi ¹⁶vna delle mani j̄ capo trovò selo ¹⁷pieno ¹⁸d' uomini appiccati e canna-¹⁹glia a similitudine de' mi²⁰nvti animali, che fra que ²¹gli sogliono nascere; ²²onde scuotendo jl capo gli o²³mini lācia non altramēti per l'aria che si facia ²⁴la grādine, quādo va cō furor di vēti, e trovossi molti ²⁵di questi vomini esser morti da quegli che gli stavano so²⁶pra ritti; coi piedi calpestādo...

²⁷E tenēdosi a capegli ēgiegniādosi nascōdere tra quegli, facievano ²⁸a similitudine de' marinai quādo è fortuna, che corrono super le corde ²⁹per abbassar la a poco vēto.

³⁰Nuove delle cose ³¹di levāte; ³²sappi come ³³nel mese ³⁴di givgnio ³⁵è apparito ³⁶vn gigāte che viē dalla ³⁷deserta Libia, ³⁸a similitudine delle ³⁹formiche furiā⁴⁰do...... ⁴¹abbatuto dall..... ⁴²rigido villano.

⁴³Questo gigāte era nato nel Mōt'Atalate, ed era ⁴⁴un eroe, e ebbe cōtrastare cogli Egiti e Arabi ⁴⁵Medi e Persi; viveva j̄ mare delle bale⁴⁶ne de' grā capidogli e de' navili.

⁴⁷Marte, temēdo della ⁴⁸vita, s'era fugito sotto le ⁴⁹.... di Giove.

⁵⁰¶E per la grā caduta parve la provīcia ⁵¹tutta tremasse.¶

frequent wounds; by which, the giant being roused and feeling himself almost covered by the multitude, he suddenly perceives the smarting of the stabs, and sent forth a roar which sounded like a terrific clap of thunder; and placing his hands on the ground he raised his terrible face: and having lifted one hand to his head he found it full of men and rabble sticking to it like the minute creatures which not unfrequently are found there; wherefore with a shake of his head he sends the men flying through the air just as hail does when driven by the fury of the winds. Many of these men were found to be dead; stamping with his feet.

And clinging to his hair, and striving to hide in it, they behaved like sailors in a storm, who run up the ropes to lessen the force of the wind [by taking in sail].

News of things from the East.

Be it known to you that in the month of June there appeared a Giant, who came from the Lybian desert ... mad with rage like ants .... struck down by the rude.

This great Giant was born in Mount Atlas and was a hero ..... and had to fight against the Egyptians and Arabs, Medes and Persians. He lived in the sea on whales, grampuses and ships.

Mars fearing for his life took refuge under the ... of Jove.

And at the great fall it seemed as though the whole province quaked.

Il quale spirito ritrova · il cerebro, dōde partito s'era ·, con alta vocie cō tali parole mosse ...

²E se alcuno uomo bēchè abbi discretione o bōtà...., dalli altri omini......³........ e peggio se da esso son remote.

This spirit returns to the brain whence it had departed, with a loud voice and with these words, it moved ...

And if any man though he may have wisdom or goodness ....

ma"ni"j̄. 15. tera elevatosia. 16. dele. 17. pieno [di minvti animali]. 18. apicati e cane. 19. glia similitudine. 20. animali cheraquē. 21. gli. 22. ode scutēdo jl cap glio. 23. mini faciano non altremēti. 24. trovosi. 25. morti da quegli che gli tepesta vonātoso. 26. parito co pie di. 27. e atenēdo a capegli ēgiegniādosi nascōdere tra. 28. quāde fortuna cecorono. 29. abasarla a poco. 30. nuove dell cose quā. 32. sapi. 33. del. 35. aparito. 36. gigāte ce viē dila. 37. diserta. 38. dele. 40. do orgnarlo super lorgero. 41. abatuto dale sura del. 42. rigido vilano. 44. ueroe debe cōtro atuserse cogli egiti e arabi. 47. dela. 49. rodi di ove. 51. tuta tremassi.

1355. 1. El quale .. cierbio .. chon .. vo cie [ne] cotali. 2. alchuno homo .. bota di nolmē li che me dalli altri omini tr|||||||so|||||||| 3. la settu|||||||| e peggiose do esso son remote. 4. spiritoche dōde me partisti joho .. homo"a"male ..

1355. This passage, very difficult to decipher, is on the reverse of a drawing at Windsor, Pl. CXXII, which possibly has some connection with it. The drawing is slightly reduced in this reproduction; the original being 25 cm. high by 19 cm. wide.

⁴O felice; o avēturato spirito, dōde partisti! ɟo ho questo uomo a male mio grado bē cono⁵scivto ·; Questo è ricietto · di villania ·, questo è propio · ammonitione di somma ingratitudine, ⁶in cōpagnia di tutti i viti ·; ma che mi vo io cō parole indarno affaticādomi? la somma de' peccati ⁷solo in lui trovati sono; E se alcuno infra loro si trova, che alcuna bontà posseʒga, non altri⁸mēti come che me dalli altri uomini trattati sono ·, e in effetto io ho questa cōclusione ch'è ⁹male s'eli sono nimici e peggio s'eli son amici.

O blessed and happy spirit whence comest thou? Well have I known this man, much against my will. This one is a receptacle of villainy; he is a perfect heap of the utmost ingratitude combined with every vice. But of what use is it to fatigue myself with vain words? Nothing is to be found in them but every form of sin . . And if there should be found among them any that possesses any good, they will not be treated differently to myself by other men; and in fine, I come to the conclusion that it is bad if they are hostile, and worse if they are friendly.

1356.

H.³ 89 a]

Miscellaneous drafts of letters and personal records (1356—1368).

Tutti i mali che sono ²e che furono, ⁶essēdo messi in opera da costui ⁷nō satisfarebbero al deside⁸rio del suo iniquo animo; ⁹io nō potrei con lunghezza di tēpo ¹⁰descriverui la natura di costu¹¹i, ma bē cōchivdo ohe . . .

All the ills that are or ever were, if they could be set to work by him, would not satisfy the desires of his iniquitous soul; and I could not in any length of time describe his nature to you, but I conclude . . .

1357.

C. A. 380 a; 1179 b]

Io ho uno · che per auersi di me promesso cose assai · mē che debite, ²essendo rimasto ingañato del suo prosontuoso desiderio, à tē³tato di tormi tutti li amici e perchè li à trouati saui e non leggi⁴eri al suo volere mi à minaciato che trouate le annū-tiationi ⁵che mi torrà i benefattori; ōde io ho di questo informato ⁶vostra Signoria accio [che, volendo questo seminare li usati ⁷scādoli, non troui terreno atto a seminare pensieri e li ⁸atti della sua mala natura]; ⁹che, tentādo lui fare di uostra signoria strumēto · della sua iniqua e maluagia natura ¹⁰rimāga ingannato di suo desiderio.

I know one who, having promised me much, less than my due, being disappointed of his presumptuous desires, has tried to deprive me of all my friends; and as he has found them wise and not pliable to his will, he has menaced me that, having found means of denouncing me, he would deprive me of my benefactors. Hence I have informed your Lordship of this, to the end [that this man who wishes to sow the usual scandals, may find no soil fit for sowing the thoughts and deeds of his evil nature] so that he, trying to make your Lordship, the instrument of his iniquitous and maliceous nature may be disappointed of his desire.

1358.

W. An. III. 241 a]

E in questo caso io so che io ne acquisterò non pochi nemici, conciosia²chè nessū crederà ch'io possa dire di lui, perchè pochi

And in this case I know that I shall make few enemies seeing that no one will believe what I can say of him; for they are but

---

chono. 5. uilania . . amv nitione. 6. chōpagnia . . voi chō . . affatichādomi lassoma de pechati. 7. solo nello trovati sono Esse alchuno . . alchuna . . possega. 8. chome . . omini . . effetti . . chōclusione. 9. male seli sonimiche e pegio seli son irattatiamicho.

1356. 1. chessono. 2. furono [nō sodisfare]. 3. [bono al a ssere messi]. 4. in opera [allo iniquo desiderio]. 5. [di questo homo]. 7. nō sadissfarebono. 9. inō . . chollungeza dite. 11. cōciudo.

1357. 1. huno . . promesse chose. 2. desiderio attē. 3. sauieno legi. 4. nia minaciato . . tronata le anutione. 5. torra e benifactori. 6. vosstra . . le usate. 7. chādali . . tereno . . asseminare "[aricievere]" in pensicrei elli. 9. [accioche nō ui faccia] "che tentādo lui fare di uosstra signoria [ecciellencia] strumēti.

1358. 1. chaso iso . . acquistero pochi . . concosia. 2. crederra . . poci. 3. disspiacino . . sol queli . . dispiaca. 4. attali . . odiano. 6. vole.

1358. Below this text we read *gusstino* = Giustino and in another passage on the same page Justin is quoted (No. 1210, l. 48). The two have however no real connection.

son quelli ³a chi i sua viti dispiacino; anzi solamente a quelli omini li dispiacio⁴no che son di natura cōtraria a tali uitj; e molti odiano li ⁵padri e guastan le amicitie, reprēsori de' sua viti e non ⁶vogliono esenpli contrari a essi, nè nessuno vmā consiglio.

⁷E se alcuno si ne trova virtuoso e bono, non lo scacciate ⁸da voi; fatteli onore, acciò che non abbia a fugirsi da ⁹voi e ridursi neli eremi, o spelonche, o altri lochi soleta¹⁰ri, per fugirsi dalle vostre insidie, e se alcun di questi ¹¹tali si trova, fatteli onore, perchè questi sono li uostri Iddei ¹²terrestri, questi meritā da uoi le statue e li simulacri; ma ¹³bē ui ricordo che li lor simulacri nō siē da uoi mā¹⁴giati come ācora in alcuna regione del India; ¹⁵chè quādo li simulacri operano alcuno mi¹⁶raculo secondo loro, li sacerdoti li tagliano in pezzi, essen¹⁷do di legno, e ne danno a tutti quelli del paese nō ¹⁸sanza premio, e ciascū raspa sottilmēte la sua parte ¹⁹e mette sopra la prima vivanda che māgiano; e così tē²⁰gono per fede aversi māgiato il suo santo, e credono che lui li ²¹guardi poi da tutti li pericoli ‖ che ti pare, uomo, qui della ²²tua spetie? sei tu così sauio, come tu ti tieni? son ²³queste cose da esser fatte da omini?

few whom his vices have disgusted, and he only dislikes those men whose natures are contrary to those vices. And many hate their fathers, and break off friendship with those who reprove their vices; and he will not permit any examples against them, nor any advice.

If you meet with any one who is virtuous do not drive him from you; do him honour, so that he may not have to flee from you and be reduced to hiding in hermitages, or caves or other solitary places to escape from your treachery; if there is such an one among you do him honour, for these are our Saints upon earth; these are they who deserve statues from us, and images; but remember that their images are not to be eaten by you, as is still done in some parts of India [15], where, when the images have according to them, performed some miracle, the priests cut them in pieces, being of wood, and give them to all the people of the country, not without payment; and each one grates his portion very fine, and puts it upon the first food he eats; and thus believes that by faith he has eaten his saint who then preserves him from all perils. What do you think here, Man, of your own species? Are you so wise as you believe yourselves to be? Are these things to be done by men?

C. A. 4b; 11b]   **1359.**

Come io vi dissi ne' dì passati, voi sapete ²che io sono sanza alcuno ...
³Francesco d'Antonio
⁴Bernardo di Maestro Jacopo.

As I told you in past days, you know that I am without any. . . .
Francesco d'Antonio.
Bernardo di Maestro Jacopo.

C. A. 38b; 124a]   **1360.**

Dimmi come le cose sono passate.

Tell me how the things happened.

. . esse. 7. esse . vertuoso . nollo scaccia de. 8. da voi[m] fatteli . . abia | affugirsi. 9. ermi . . saleta. 10. vosstre . . esse. 11. fate . . onore che "perche" questi. 12. statue elli onori "simulacri" ma. 13. chelli. 14. gati chome āchora. 16. lo tagliano . . pezi esse. 17. attutti . . paese [el qa]nō. 18. rasspa. 19. viuada che māgano. 20. gā per fede avrsimāgato . . credā. 21. dattutti pericoli ‖ chettitti pare omo. 22. settu . . tuttiti eni.
1359. 1—4. *Written from left to right.* 1. Chome iovi disi. 2. alchuno. 3. [franī dantonio]. 4. [brn brnado di m⁗o" iachopo].
1360. 1. chome le cose.

L. 15. In explanation of this passage I have received the following communication from Dr. G. W. LEITNER of Lahore: "So far as Indian customs are known to us, this practice spoken of by Leonardo as 'still existing in some parts of India' is perfectly unknown; and it is equally opposed to the spirit of Hinduism, Mohammedanism and Sikhism. In central Thibet the ashes of the dead,

when burnt, are mixed with dough, and small figures—usually of Buddha—are stamped out of them and some are laid in the grave while others are distributed among the relations. The custom spoken of by Leonardo may have prevailed there but I never heard of it." Possibly Leonardo refers here to customs of nations of America.

C. A. 17 *b* ; 67 *b*]   **1361.**

Ĵ lorēzo\\\ ²inbiadali\\\ ³inferri de\\\ ⁴in lorēzo\\\ ⁵[inno abuil]\\\ ⁶in acōcatu\\\ ⁷per la
sella\\\ ⁸colte di lor\\\ ⁹v̄ cavallott\\\ ¹⁰el uiagg\\\ ¹¹al\\\ ¹²a lurēz\\\ ¹³in biada\\\ ¹⁴inferri\\\
¹⁵abusso\\\ ¹⁶in viagg\\\ ¹⁷alorēz\\\\

W. An. IV. 174 *a*]   **1362.**

E così piacesse al nostro autore che io
potessi dimostrare la natura delli omini ²e
loro costumi nel modo che io descrivo la
sua figura.

And so may it please our great Author
that I may demonstrate the nature of man
and his customs, in the way I describe
his figure.

C. A. 65 *b* ; 199 *b*]   **1363.**

Questo scriuersi distintamēte del nibbio
²par che sia mio destino, perchè nella
prima ³ricordatione della mia infantia e'
mi ⁴parea che, essendo io in culla, che vn
⁵nibbio venisse a me e mi aprisse la
⁶bocca colla sua coda, e molte volte ⁷mi
percuotesse cō tal coda dentro alle ⁸labra.

This writing distinctly about the kite
seems to be my destiny, because among the
first recollections of my infancy, it seemed
to me that, as I was in my cradle, a kite
came to me and opened my mouth with its
tail, and struck me several times with its
tail inside my lips.

C. A. 248 *a* ; 737 *a*]   **1364.**

[Quādo io feci bene, essendo putto, voi
mi mettesti in prigione, ²ora s' io lo fo grāde,
voi mi farete peggio.]

[When I did well, as a boy you used
to put me in prison. Now if I do it being
grown up, you will do worse to me.]

Br. M. 251 *b*]   **1365.**

Dimmi se mai fu fatto alcuna cosa.

Tell me if anything was ever done.

Br. M. 253 *a*]   **1366.**

Dimmi · se mai fece ²cosa che mi di . . . .

Tell me if ever I did a thing which me . . . . .

S. K. M. III. 85 *a*]   **1367.**

¶Non iscoprire se libertà ²t' è cara, chè
'l uolto mio ³è carciere d'amore.¶

Do not reveal, if liberty is precious to
you; my face is the prison of love.

1362. 1. piacessi . . altore. 2. desscrivo.
1363. 1. nibio. 2. nela. 5. venissin me e mi aprissi. 6. bocha chola. 7. perchotessi.
1364. 1. feci bensenedo (*doubtful*) putto. 2. forāde . . pegio.
1365. P. — di mi semmai . . facto alchuna chosa.   **1366.** 1. semmai. 2. chosa chemmi dit.
1367. 1. nonisscoprire selliberta. 2. te chara. 3. charciere.

1361. This seems to be the beginning of a
letter, but only the first words of the lines have
been preserved, the leaf being torn down the middle.
No translation is possible.

1362. A preparatory note for the passage given
as No. 798, ll. 41—42.
1363. This note probably refers to the text No.1221.
1367. This note seems to be a quotation.

C. A. 188 *b*; 564 *b*]   **1368.**

Maestro Leonardo Fiorentino.   Maestro Leonardo of Florence.

Flor. Uff.]   **1369.**

Dì di Sca Maria della Neve, ²a dì 2   The day of Santa Maria *della Neve* [of Notes bear-
d'agosto 1473.   the Snows] August the 2nd 1473.   ing Dates (1369—1378).

W. An. I. 1 *a*]   **1370.**

A dì 2 d'aprile 1489 libro titolato de   On the 2nd of April 1489, book entitled
figura vmana.   'Of the human figure'.

C. A. 103 *a*; 325 *a*]   **1371.**

A dì primo d'agosto 1499 · scrissi qui   On the 1st of August 1499, I wrote here
de moto · e peso.   of motion and of weight.

1368. m"o".   **1369.** 2. addi 2 daggossto.   **1370.** 1489 [del] libro.   **1371.** adi p"o" dagosto.

1368. So Leonardo writes his name on a sheet with sundry short notes, evidently to try a pen. Compare the signature with those in Nos. 1341, 1348 and 1374 (see also No. 1346, l. 33). The form "Lionardo" does not occur in the autographs. The Portrait of the Master in the Royal Library at Turin, which is reproduced—slightly diminished—on Pl. I, has in the original two lines of writing underneath; one in red chalk of two or three words is partly effaced: *lionardo it . . . lm* (or *lai?*); the second written in pencil is as follows: *fatto da lui stesso assai vecchio.* In both of these the writing is very like the Master's, but is certainly only an imitation.

1369. This date is on a drawing of a rocky landscape. See *Chronique des Arts* 1881 no. 23: *Léonard de Vinci a-t-il été au Righi le 5 août 1473?* letter by H. de Geymüller. The next following date in the MSS. is 1478 (see No. 663).

1370. While the letters in the MS. notes of 1473 and 1478 are very ornate, this note and the texts on anatomy on the same sheet (for instance No. 805) are in the same simple hand as we see on Pl. CXVI and CXIX. No 1370 is the only dated note of the years between 1480 and 1489, and the characters are in all essential points identical with those that we see in the latest manuscripts written in France (compare the facsimiles on Pl. CXV and

p. 254), so that it is hardly possible to determine exactly the date of a manuscript from the style of the handwriting, if it does not betray the peculiarities of style as displayed in the few notes dated previous to 1480.—Compare the facsimile of the manuscripts 1479 on Pl. LXII, No. 2; No. 664, note, Vol. I p. 346. This shows already a marked simplicity as compared with the calligraphy of 1478.

The text No. 720 belongs to the year 1490; No. 1510 to the year 1492; No. 1459, No. 1384 and No. 1460 to the year 1493; No. 1463, No. 1517, No. 1024, 1025 and 1461 to the year 1494; Nos. 1523 and 1524 to the year 1497.

1371. *Scrissi qui.* Leonardo does not say where; still we may assume that it was not in Milan. Amoretti writes, *Memorie Storiche*, chap. XIX: *Sembra pertanto che non nel 1499 ma nel 1500, dopo il ritorno e la prigionia del duca, sia da qui partito Lionardo per andare a Firenze; ed è quindi probabile, che i mesi di governo nuovo e incerto abbia passati coll' amico suo Francesco Melzi a Vaprio, ove meglio che altrove studiar potea la natura, e soprattutta le acque, e l'Adda specialmente, che già era stato l'ogetto delle sue idrostatiche ricerche.* At that time Melzi was only six years of age. The next date is 1502; to this year belong No. 1034, 1040, 1042, 1048 and 1053. The note No. 1525 belongs to the year 1503.

Br. M. 272 a]   **1372.**

A dì 9 di luglio 1504, mercoledì a ore 7 morì Ser ²Piero da Vinci, notaio al Palazzo del Podestà, mio padre, a ore 7, era d'età d'anni 80, lasci³ò 10 figlioli ma⁴schi e 2 femmine.

On the 9ᵗʰ of July 1504, Wednesday, at seven o'clock, died Ser Piero da Vinci, notary at the Palazzo del Podestà, my father, —at seven o'clock, being eighty years old, leaving behind ten sons and two daughters.

C. A. 70 b; 208 b]   **1373.**

Mercoledì a ore 7 ²morì Ser Piero da Vinci a dì 9 ³di luglio 1504.

On Wednesday at seven o'clock died Ser Piero da Vinci on the 9ᵗʰ of July 1504.

S. K. M. I.¹ 1 b]   **1374.**

Principiato da me Leonardo ²da Vīci a dì 12 di luglio 1505.

Begun by me, Leonardo da Vinci, on the 12ᵗʰ of July 1505.

F. 1 a]   **1375.**

Comīciato a Milano a dì 12 di settēbre 1508.

Begun at Milan on the 12ᵗʰ of September 1508.

W. An. III. 217. a]   **1376.**

A dì 9 di giennaro 1513.

On the 9ᵗʰ of January 1513.

1372. *Written from left to right:* 1. addi . . luglio 1504 en mercholedi.   2. palago . . lasc.   4. sci et.
1373. 3. luglo.   **1374.** 2. uīci addi.   **1375.** comīcato . . addi.   **1376.** addi.

1372. This statement of Ser Piero's age contradicts that of the *Riassunto della portata di Antonio da Vinci* (Leonardo's grandfather), who speaks of Ser Piero as being thirty years old in 1457; and that of the *Riassunto della portata di Ser Piero e Francesco,* sons of Antonia da Vinci, where Ser Piero is mentioned as being forty in 1469. These documents were published by G. UZIELLI, *Ricerche intorno a L. da Vinci, Firenze,* 1872, pp. 144 and 146. Leonardo was, as is well known, a natural son. His mother 'La Catarina' was married in 1457 to Acchattabriga di Piero del Vaccha da Vinci. She died in 1519. Leonardo never mentions her in the Manuscripts. In the year of Leonardo's birth Ser Piero married Albiera di Giovanni Amadoci, and after her death at the age of thirty eight he again married, Francesca, daughter of Ser Giovanni Lanfredi, then only fifteen. Their children were Leonardo's half-brothers, Antonio (b. 1476), Ser Giuliano (b. 1479), Lorenzo (b. 1484), a girl, Violante (b. 1485), and another boy Domenico (b. 1486); Domenico's descendants still exist as a family. Ser Piero married for the third time Lucrezia di Guglielmo Cortigiani by whom he had six children: Margherita (b. 1491), Benedetto (b. 1492), Pandolfo (b. 1494), Guglielmo (b. 1496), Bartolommeo (b. 1497), and Giovanni) date of birth unknown). Pierino da Vinci the sculptor (about 1520—1554) was the son of Bartolommeo, the fifth of these children. The dates of their deaths are not known, but we may infer from the above passage that they were all still living in 1505.

1373. This and the previous text it may be remarked are the only mention made by Leonardo of his father; Nos. 1526, 1527 and No. 1463 are of the year 1504.

1374. Thus he writes on the first page of the MS. The title is on the foregoing coversheet as follows: *Libro titolato disstrafformatione coe* (cioè) *d'un corpo nvn* (in un) *altro sanza diminuitione e acresscemento di materia.*

1375. No. 1528 and No. 1529 belong to the same year. The text Vol. I, No. 4 belongs to the following year 1509 (1508 old style); so also does No. 1009.— Nos. 1022, 1057 and 1464 belong to 1511.

1376. No. 1465 belongs to the same year. No. 1065 has the next date 1514.

G. o']   **1377.**

Partissi il magnifico Giuliano de' ²Me-
dici a dì 9 di giennaio 1515 ³in sull'aurora
da Roma per ādare ⁴a sposare la moglie in
Sovoia; ⁵e in tal dì ci fu la morte del rè
di Francia.

The Magnifico Giuliano de' Medici left
Rome on the 9ᵗʰ of January 1515, just at
daybreak, to take a wife in Savoy; and on
the same day fell the death of the king of
France.

C. A. 245a; 731a]   **1378.**

A 24 di giugnio il dì di san Giovanni
²1518 in Ābosa nel palazzo del clli.

On the 24ᵗʰ of June, St-John's day, 1518
at Amboise, in the palace of . . .

1377. 1. magnificho. 2. addi. 3. darroma. 4. assposare. 5. dere.   **1378.** 1. a 24 digugnio. 2. palazzo dell clli.

1377. Giuliano de Medici, brother to Pope Leo X.;
see note to Nos. 1351—1353. In February, 1515, he
was married to Filiberta, daughter of Filippo, Duke
of Savoy, and aunt to Francis I, Louis XII's
successor on the throne of France. Louis XII died
on Jan. 1ˢᵗ, and not on Jan. 9ᵗʰ as is here stated.—
This addition is written in paler ink and evidently
at a later date.

1378. *Castello del clli.* The meaning of this word
is obscure; it is perhaps not written at full length.

XXII.

Miscellaneous Notes.

The incidental memoranda scattered here and there throughout the MSS. can have been for the most part intelligible to the writer only; in many cases their meaning and connection are all the more obscure because we are in ignorance about the persons with whom Leonardo used to converse nor can we say what part he may have played in the various events of his time. Vasari and other early biographers give us a very superficial and far from accurate picture of Leonardo's private life. Though his own memoranda, referring for the most part to incidents of no permanent interest, do not go far towards supplying this deficiency, they are nevertheless of some importance and interest as helping us to solve the numerous mysteries in which the history of Leonardo's long life remains involved. We may at any rate assume, from Leonardo's having committed to paper notes on more or less trivial matters on his pupils, on his house-keeping, on various known and unknown personages, and a hundred other trifles—that at the time they must have been in some way important to him.

I have endeavoured to make these 'Miscellaneous Notes' as complete as possible, for in many cases an incidental memorandum will help to explain the meaning of some other note of a similar kind. The first portion of these notes (Nos. 1379—1457), as well as those referring to his pupils and to other artists and artificers who lived in his house (1458—1468) are arranged in chronological order. A considerable proportion of these notes belong to the period between 1490 and 1500, when Leonardo was living at Milan under the patronage of Lodovico il Moro, a time concerning which we have otherwise only very scanty information. If Leonardo did really—as has always been supposed,—spend also the greater part of the preceding decade in Milan, it seems hardly likely that we should not find a single note indicative of the fact, or referring to any event of that period, on the numerous loose leaves in his writing that exist. Leonardo's life in Milan between 1489 and 1500 must have been comparatively uneventful. The MSS. and memoranda of those years seem to prove that it was a tranquil period of intellectual and artistic labour rather than of bustling court life. Whatever may have been the fate of the MSS. and note books of the foregoing years—whether they were destroyed by Leonardo himself or have been lost—it is certainly strange that nothing whatever exists to inform us as to his life and doings in Milan earlier than the consecutive series of manuscripts which begin in the year 1489.

There is nothing surprising in the fact that the notes regarding his pupils are few and meagre. Excepting for the record of money transactions only very exceptional circumstances would have prompted him to make any written observations on the persons with whom he was in daily intercourse, among whom, of course, were his pupils. Of them all none is so frequently mentioned as Salai, but the character of the notes does not—as it seems to me—justify us in supposing that he was any thing more than a sort of factotum of Leonardo's (see 1519, note).

Leonardo's quotations from books and his lists of titles supply nothing more than a hint as to his occasional literary studies or recreations. It was evidently no part of his ambition to be deeply read (see Nrs. 10, 11, 1159) and he more than once expressly states (in various passages which will be found in the foregoing sections) that he did not recognise the authority of the Ancients, on scientific questions, which in his day was held paramount. Archimedes is the sole exception, and Leonardo frankly owns his admiration for the illustrious Greek to whose genius his own was so much akin (see No. 1476). All his notes on various authors, excepting those which have already been inserted in the previous section, have been arranged alphabetically for the sake of convenience (1469—1508).

The passages next in order contain accounts and inventories principally of household property. The publication of these—often very trivial entries—is only justifiable as proving that the wealth, the splendid mode of life and lavish expenditure which have been attributed to Leonardo are altogether mythical; unless we put forward the very improbable hypothesis that these notes as to money in hand, outlay and receipts, refer throughout to an exceptional state of his affairs, viz. when he was short of money.

The memoranda collected at the end (No. 1505—1565) are, in the original, in the usual writing, from left to right. Besides, the style of the handwriting is at variance with what we should expect it to be, if really Leonardo himself had written these notes. Most of them are to be found in juxtaposition with undoubtedly authentic writing of his. But this may be easily explained, if we take into account the fact, that Leonardo frequently wrote on loose sheets. He may therefore have occasionally used paper on which others had made short memoranda, for the most part as it would seem, for his use. At the end of all I have given Leonardo's will from the copy of it preserved in the Melzi Library. It has already been printed by Amoretti and by Uzielli. It is not known what has become of the original document.

1379.

Truova ingol e digli che tu l'aspetti amor a e che tu andrai cō seco ilopan a; ²fatti fare enoiganod al; e tolli il libro di Vitolone, e le misure · delli edifiti ³ publici ·; fa fare 2 casse coperte da mvlattiere, ma meglio fia · le coperte da letto, che ⁴ son 3, delle quali lascierai una a Vinci; togli le fodere (?) delle grattugie (?) da Gio⁵vā Lonbardo il telajuolo di Verona ·; cōpra delle tovaglie · e mātili . . . . . . scarpini, ⁶calze 4 para, vn giubbone di cimoza e pelli per fare ne de' novi; il tornio d'Ales-⁷sandro ·; vendi quel che nō si può portare; piglia da Gian di Paris il modo de colorire ⁸a secco ·, el modo del sale bianco e del fare le carte inpastate; folie in mol⁹ti doppi;

Find Longhi and tell him that you wait for him at Rome and will go with him to Naples; make you pay the donation [2] and take the book by Vitolone, and the measurements of the public buildings. [3] Have two covered boxes made to be carried on mules, but bed-covers will be best; this makes three, of which you will leave one at Vinci. [4] Obtain the . . . . from Giovanni Lombardo the linen draper of Verona. Buy handkerchiefs and towels, ... and shoes, 4 pairs of hose, a jerkin of . . . and skins, to make new ones; the lake of Alessandro. [7] Sell what you cannot take with you. Get from Jean de Paris the method of painting in tempera and the way of making white

Memoranda before 1500 (1379—1413).

1379. 1. truova ingol edilli chettu . . chettu . . ilopana. 2. fare la eno iganodal ettolli . . elle. 3. faffare . . coperte dalletto. 4. lascierai î a uinci . . le fochere delle gratuto dago. 5. lonbardo il teraajo (?) di uerona . . mātili bretre (?) scarpīni. 6. gubbone di ci moza . . tornio dale. 7. si po . . piglia dāgandiparis. 8. assecho . . folie in mol. 9. ti doppi ella sua

1379. The mysterious looking words, quite distinctly written, in line 1: *ingol, amor a, ilopan a* and on line 2: *enoiganod al* are obviously in cipher and the solution is a simple one; by reading them backwards we find for *ingol*: logni—probably *longi*, evidently the name of a person; for *amor a*: *a Roma*, for *ilopan a: a Napoli*. Leonardo has done the same in two passages treating on some secrets of his art Nos. 641 and 729, the only other places in which we find this cipher employed; we may therefore conclude that it was for the sake of secrecy that he used it.

There can be no doubt, from the tenor of this passage, that Leonardo projected a secret excursion to Naples. Nothing has hitherto been known of this journey, but the significance of the passage will be easily understood by a reference to the following notes, from which we may infer that Leonardo really

had at the time plans for travelling further than Naples. From lines 3, 4 and 7 it is evident that he purposed, after selling every thing that was not easily portable, to leave a chest in the care of his relations at Vinci. His luggage was to be packed into two trunks especially adapted for transport by mules. The exact meaning of many sentences in the following notes must necessarily remain obscure. These brief remarks on small and irrelevant affairs and so forth are however of no historical value. The notes referring to the preparations for his journey are more intelligible.

2. *Libro di Vitolone* see No. 1506 note.

7 and fol. It would seem from the text that Leonardo intended to have instructions in painting on paper. It is hardly necessary to point out that the Art of illuminating was quite separate from that of painting.

e la sua cassetta de' colori; inpar la tempera delle carnagioni, inpara [10]a disoluere la lacca gommata, lin del seme, de . . . . e dele . . . biāche, [11]delli agli da Piacētia, togli 'De Pōderibus;' tolli l'opere di Leonardo cremo[12]nese; leua il fornello [13]. . . . . della [14]semēza de ligli [15]e dell'erba stella, [16]delle zuche marine, [17]vēdi l'asse della sosta, [18]fatti dare la . . . . [19]a chi la rubò, pi[20]glia il liuellare, [21]quāto terreno può [22]cauare l'omo in un dì.

salt, and how to make tinted paper; sheets of paper folded up; and his box of colours; learn to work flesh colours in tempera, learn to dissolve gum lac, linseed . . . . white, of the garlic of Piacenza; take 'de Ponderibus'; take the works of Leonardo of Cremona. Remove the small furnace . . . . . seed of lilies and of . . . Sell the boards of the support. Make him who stole it, give you the . . . . learn levelling and how much soil a man can dig out in a day.

C. 19*b*]

1380.

Questo fecie Lione in piazza [2]di castello con v̄ vincolo e vna [3]saetta.

This was done by Leone in the piazza of the castle with a chain and an arrow.

B. 50*b*]

1381.

NOMI D' ĪGIEGNIERI.

[2]Callias Rodiano, [3]Epimaco Ateniense, [4]Diogine filosofo Rodiano, [5]Calcedonio di Tracia, [6]Febar di Tiria, [7]Callimaco architetto, maestro di fochi.

NAMES OF ENGINEERS.

Callias of Rhodes, Epimachus the Athenian, Diogenes, a philosopher, of Rhodes, Calcedonius of Thrace, Febar of Tyre, Callimachus the architect, a master of fires.

Ash. II. 13*b*]

1382.

A maestro Lodovico chiedi li cōdotti d'acqua.

Ask maestro Lodovico for 'the conduits of water'.

Fl. Uff.]

1383.

. . . ī Pistoja[2]; Fiorauante di Domenico ī Firenze è cōpare [3]amantissimo, quant' è mio . . .

. . . at Pistoja, Fioravante di Domenico at Florence is my most beloved friend, as though he were my [brother].

. . cornage inpara. 10. lacha gommatalli del seme de fotteragi e delle gniffe biāche. 11. delli algli da piacētia . . leonardo chermo. 13. diganni noto della. 14. semēza deli gli. 15. e dellerba stella. 16. delle zuche marine. 17. dalla. 18. fatti dare la fochera. 19. tereno po. 20. lomo nūdi.

1380. 1. questa . . piaza. 2. casstello chon v̄ uīcho e vna.

1381. 3. acte niense. 4. filosafo. 6. febar di tiria. 7. challimacho architecto.

1382. mastro lodvvicho ciedi . . dacq"a".

1383. \\\ e echopa ʃ pisstoja. 2. domenicho . . cōpere. 3. mio jjrsuiosssam (?). 4. jnde nom. 5. amante quanto.

11. *De Ponderibus.* A large number of Leonardo's notes bear this superscription. Compare No. 1436, 3.

1380. This note must have been made in Milan; as we know from the date of the MS.

1381. Callias, Architect of Aradus, mentioned by Vitruvius (X, 16, 5).—Epimachus, of Athens, invented a battering-enginee for Demetrius Poliorketes (Vitruvius X, 16, 4).—Callimachus, the inventor of the Corinthian capital (Vitr. IV, 1, 9), and of the

method of boring marble (Paus. I, 26, 7), was also famous for his casts in bronze (Plin. XXXIV, 8, 19). He invented a lamp for the temple of Athene Polias, on the Acropolis of Athens (Paus. I, 26, 7).—The other names, here mentioned, cannot be identified.

1382. *Condotti d'acqua.* Possibly a book, a MS. or a map.

1383. On the same sheet is the text No. 663.

S. K. M. III. 1 *b*]

1384.

A dì 16 di luglio.
²Caterina venne a dì 16 ³di luglio 1493.
⁴Morel Fiorētino di messer Mariolo, cavallo ⁵grosso à bel collo e assai bella testa.
⁶Rōzone biāco del falconiere à belle coscie, ⁷dirieto sta in Porta Comasina.
⁸Cauallo grosso del Chermonino del signor Givlio.

On the 16th day of July.
Caterina came on 16th day of July, 1493.
Messer Mariolo's Morel the Florentin, has a big horse with a fine neck and a beautiful head.
The white stallion belonging to the falconer has fine hind quarters; it is behind the Comasina Gate.
The big horse of Cermonino, of Signor Giulio.

S. K. M. III. 30*a*]

1385.

DELLO STRUMĒTO.

²Chiūque spēde uno ducato per paro ³pigli lo strumēto, e non spē⁴derà · se non v̄ mezzo per premi⁵nētia allo invētore dello strum⁶ēto, e vno grosso per l'operatore ⁷ogni año; non uoglio sottovfiti ⁸all.

OF THE INSTRUMENT.

Any one who spends one ducat may take the instrument; and he will not pay more than half a ducat as a premium to the inventor of the instrument and one grosso to the workman every year. I do not want sub-officials.

S. K. M. III. 55*a*]

1386.

Maestro Givliano da Mar²liano a v̄ bello erbolaro; ³sta a riscōtro alli Strami ⁴legnamieri.

Maestro Giuliano da Marliano has a fine herbal. He lives opposite to Strami the Carpenters.

S. K. M. III. 94*a*]

1387.

Cristofano da Castiglio²ne sta alla Pietà, à bona ³testa.

Christofano da Castiglione who lives at the Pietà has a fine head.

C. A. 328*a* 980*a*]

1388.

Opera di . . . . ²della stalla di G³aleazzo; ⁴per la via di Brera; ⁵benefitio dello Stanghe; bene⁶fitio della por⁷ta nova; ⁸benefitio di Mon⁹sa—; ¹⁰errore dell' Inta¹¹co—; ¹²dì prima li benefitj; ¹³e poi l'opere e poi ¹⁴le ingratudini ¹⁵e poi le īdegni e la¹⁶mētationi e...

Work of . . . of the stable of Galeazzo; by the road of Brera[4]; benefice of Stanghe[5]; benefice of Porta Nuova; benefice of Monza; Indaco's mistake; give first the benefices; then the works; then ingratitude, indignity and lamentations.

H.3 47*b*]

1389.

Chiliarco, capo di mille,
²Prefetti—capitani,
³Legione, semila 63.

Chiliarch—captain of 1000.
Prefects—captains.
A legion, six thousand and sixty three men.

1384. 1. R. 2. catelina. 4. chaval. 5. chollo eassa. 6. rōcino. 8. R. chauallo . . del chermanino.
1385. 2. chiūq spēde ĩ ducato . . paro. 3. lustrumēto . . ispē. 4. mezo. 6. ēto e ĩ groso. 7. oñ año uoglio.
1386. 3. alli strami. 4. legiamieri.   **1387.** 1. cristofano da chasstiglio.
1388. 1. Opera di roma. 2. dich. 5. benefitio . . beni. 8. benefitio. 9. cia. 10. crore. 11. cho. 12. benefiti. 14. ingralitūdine. 16. mētatione.   **1389.** 1—3 R.

1384. Compare Nos. 1522 and 1517. Caterina seems to have been his housekeeper.
1385. Refers perhaps to the regulation of the water in the canals.

1386. Compare No. 616, note. 4. *legnamiere* (milanese dialect) = legnajuolo.
1388. 4. *Brera*, see No. 1448, 11, 13; 5. *Stanghe*, see No. 1509.

H.² 14 b]   **1390.**

Vna monica sta alla Colōba ²in Cremona che lavora bē ³cordoni di paglia, e
vno frate ⁴di Scō Francesco.

A nun lives at La Colomba at Cremona;
she works good straw plait, and a friar of
Saint Francis.

H.² 46a]   **1391.**

Aguglia,—Niccolao,—²refe,—³Ferrādo,
—⁴iacopo ādrea,—⁵tela,—⁶pietra,—⁷colo-
ri,—⁸penella,—⁹tavoletta da colori,—¹⁰spū-
ga,—¹¹tavola del Duca.

Needle,—Niccolao,—thread,—Ferrando,
—Iacopo Andrea,—canvas,—stone,—colours,—brushes,—pallet,—sponge,—the panel
of the Duke.

S. K. M. II.² 7 a]   **1392.**

Messer Giā Domenico ²Mezzabarba, e
messer ³Giovā Francesco Mezzabarba, ⁴al
lato a messer Piero d' Anghie⁵ra.

Messer Gian Domenico Mezzabarba and
Messer Giovanni Franceso Mezzabarba. By
the side of Messer Piero d'Anghiera.

S. K. M. II.₂ 7 b]   **1393.**

Cōte Francesco Torello.

Conte Francesco Torello.

S. K. M. II.² 12 a]   **1394.**

Givliā Trōbetta,—²Antonio di Ferrara,
—³olio di bolla.

Giuliano Trombetta,— Antonio di Ferrara,
—Oil of . . . . .

S. K. M. II 2 20 a]   **1395.**

Paolo fu ratto in cielo.

Paul was snatched up to heaven.

S. K. M. II.² 22 a]   **1396.**

Givliā da Maria, medico ²à vn massajo
sāza mano.

Giuliano da Maria, physician, has a stew-
ard without hands.

S. K. M. II.² 27 a]   **1397.**

Fatti mādare spighe di ²grā grosso da
Firēze.

Have some ears of corn of large size sent
from Florence.

1390. 1—4 R.   2. chermona chellavora.   3. chordoni.   4. franc"o".
1391. 1—11 R.   1. agngia niccholao.   3. ferādo.
1392. 1. domenicho.   2. meza . . meser.   3. franc"o" meza.   4. Piero dagale.   5. ra sotto il coperio debe lacq"a".
1393. franc"o".   **1394.** 1. trobebetta.   2. ferra.   3. dibola.   **1395.** R. pagolo.
1396. 1. mariamēdicho.   2. avmazaro.   **1397.** 1. spige.

1390. *La Colomba* is to this day the name of a small house at Cremona, decorated with frescoes.
1394. Near this text is the sketch of a head drawn in red chalk.
1395. See the facsimile of this note on Pl. XXIII No. 2.

S. K. M. II.2 52 *a*]   **1398.**

Vedi la lettiera a Scā Maria;   See the bedstead at Santa Maria.
² Segreta.   Secret.

S. K. M. II.2 53 *a*]   **1399.**

¶ Arrigo de' avere ² ducati 11 d'oro; ¶   Arrigo is to have 11 gold Ducats.
³ Arrigo de' avere ⁴ ducati 4 d'oro ⁵ a   Arrigo is to have 4 gold ducats in the
mezzo Agosto.   middle of August.

S. K. M. II.2 63 *a*]   **1400.**

Da al patrone lo esēplo ² del capitano,   Give your master the instance of a
che nō lui vī³cie, ma li soldati mediāte ⁴ il   captain who does not himself win the vic-
suo cōsilio, e pur merita il saldo.   tory, but the soldiers do by his counsels;
      and so he still deserves the reward.

S. K. M. II.2 68 *b*]   **1401.**

Messer Pier Antonio.   Messer Pier Antonio.

S. K. M. II.2 69 *a*]   **1402.**

Olio, — ² giallo, — ³ Ambrosio, — ⁴ la boc-   Oil, — yellow, — Ambrosio, — the mouth, —
ca, — ⁵ la masseria.   the farmhouse.

S. K. M. II.2 75 *b*]   **1403.**

Alessandro carissimo, ² da Parma per la   My dear Alessandro from Parma, by the
mā di . . .   hand of . . .

S. K. M. II.2 78 *b*]   **1404.**

Giovannina, viso fantastico, ² sta a Scā   Giovannina, has a fantastic face, — is at
Caterina, all' ospedale.   Santa Caterina, at the Hospital.

I.2 11 *a*]   **1405.**

24 tavole fanno una pertica;   24 tavole make 1 perch.
² 4 trabochi fanno una tavola;   4 trabochi make 1 tavola.
³ 4 braccia e mezzo fanno uno trabocco;   4 braccia and a half make a trabocco.
⁴ vna pertica è 1936 braccia □,   A perch contains 1936 square braccia,
⁵ ovvero 1944.   or 1944.

1399. 1. arigo. 3. arigo. 5. mezo.   1400. 1. padrone.   1401. meser pier ātō chodi. 2. diga.
1402. 3. abrosio. 4. bocha. 5. masera.   1403. 1. charissi no. 2. [si] da . . mā di[l]p.
1404. 1. fantasticho. 2. chaterina.
1405. 1—5. R. 1. fā î perticha. 2. fa î. 3. br e mezo fa î trabocho. 4. perticha he . . br. 5. ovr.

1404. Compare the text on the same page: No. 667.

I.2 70ð]   **1406.**

La strada di messer Mariolo è braccia
13¹/₄, ²la casa di Vāgelista è 75;
³Entra braccia 7 e ¹/₂ ⁴nella casa di
Mariolo.

The road of Messer Mariolo is 13¹/₄ braccia wide; the House of Evangelista is 75.
It enters 7¹/₂ braccia in the house of Mariolo.

I.2· 72 ð]   **1407.**

Domando in che parte del suo moto
curvo ²la cavsa, che move, lascierà la cosa
mossa ³e mobile.

I ask at what part of its curved motion
the moving cause will leave the thing
moved and moveable.

⁴Parla cō Pietro Mōti di questi tali
⁵modi di trarre i dardi.

Speak to Pietro Monti of these methods
of throwing spears.

I.2 87 a]   **1408.**

Antonio de' Risi sta al cō²siglio di
Givstitia.

Antonio de' Risi is at the council of
Justice.

I.1 28 a]   **1409.**

Disse Paolo che nessuno strumento
²che move vn altro.....

Paolo said that no machine that moves
another . . . .

1406. 1. meser . . he br. 2. vāgelissta he. 3. br 7 e 1/2.   1409. 1. pagolo.

1406. On this page and that which faces it,
MS. I² 71ª, are two diagrams with numerous reference
numbers, evidently relating to the measurements of
a street.
   1409. The passage, of which the beginning is
here given, deals with questions in mechanics.
The instances in which Leonardo quotes the opinions of his contemporaries on scientific matters
are so rare as to be worth noticing. Compare
No. 901.

W. P. 7.]   **1410.**

Caravaggio.   Caravaggio.

W. A. II. 5*b*]   **1411.**

Carrucole,—²chiodi,—³corda,—⁴mercu-   Pulleys,—nails,—rope,—mercury,—cloth,
rio,—⁵tela,—⁶lunedì.   Monday.

W. A. II. 202*b*]   **1412.**

RICORDO.   MEMORANDUM.

²Maghino Speculus di maestro Giovanni   Maghino, Speculus of Master Giovanni
Frāciese; ³Galieno de vtilità.   the Frenchman; Galenus on utility.

W. X.]   **1413.**

Presso al Corduso · sta Pier Antonio da   Near to Cordusio is Pier Antonio da
Fossano ²e Serafino · suo fratello.   Tossano and his brother Serafino.

L. 0']   **1414.**

Paolo di Vannoccio in Siena.   Paul of Vannochio at Siena . . . .   Memoranda
³La saletta di sopra per li apostoli;   The upper chamber for the apostles.   after 1500
                                            [4] Buildings by Bramante.   (1414—1434)
⁴Edifiti di Bramāte;   The governor of the castle made a
⁵Il castellano fatto prigione;   prisoner,
⁶Il Visconte strascinato e poi morto il   [6] Visconti carried away and his son
figliuolo;   killed.
⁷Gian della Rosa toltoli i danari;   Giovanni della Rosa deprived of his money.
⁸Borgonzo principiò e nol volle, e però   [8] Borgonzio began . . . .; and moreover
fuggì le fortune;   his fortunes fled.
⁹Il duca perso lo stato e la roba e li-   The Duke has lost the state, property
ertà, ¹⁰e nessuna sua opera si finì per lui. and liberty and none of his entreprises was
                                            carried out by him. [10].

1410. carovagio.   **1411.** 1. carruchole. 4. merchurio, 7. idomoodi (?).
1412. 1. richordo. 2. maghino spechulus di m"o".   **1413.** 1. chorduso . . daffossano. 2. essera fino.
1414. 1. pagolo di uannocco. 2. codi rōcho . — domenico chia umo. 5. prigone. 6. bissconte stracinato . . el figlolo. 7. gan
della rosa tollto li e danari. 8. borgonzo . . pro. 9. ella roba elliberta.

1410. *Caravaggio,* a village not far from the Adda   events in Milan at the time of the overthrow of
between Milan and Brescia, where Polidoro and Michel-   Ludovico il Moro. Amoretti published it in the
angelo da Caravaggio were born. This note is given   '*Memorie Storiche*' and added copious notes.
in facsimile on Pl. XIII, No. 1 (above, to the left).   6. *Visconti. Chi fosse quel Visconte non sapremmo in-*
On Pl. XIII, No. 2 above to the right we read   *dovinare fra tanti di questo nome. Arluno narra che*
cerovazo.   *allora atterrate furono le case de' Viconti, de' Castiglioni,*
1413. This note is written between lines 23 and   *de' Sanseverini, e de' Botta e non è improbabile che ne*
24 of the text No. 710. Corduso, Cordusio (*curia*   *fossero insultati e mortii padroni. Molti Visconti annovera lo*
ducis) = Cordus in the Milanese dialect, is the name   *stesso Cronista che per essersi rallegrati del ritorno del*
of a Piazza between the Via del Broletto and the   *duca in Milano furono da' Francesi arrestati, e strascinati*
Piazza de' Mercanti at Milan. . In the time of il   *in Francia come prigionieri di stato; e fra questi Messer*
Moro it was the centre of the town. The persons   *Francesco Visconti, e suo figliuolo Battista.* (AMORETTI,
here named were members of the noble Milanese   *Mem. Stor.* XIX.)
family de'Fossani; Ambrogio da Fossano, the con-   8. *Borgonzio o Brugonzio Botta fu regolatore delle du-*
temporary painter, had no connection with them.   *cali entrate sotto il Moro, alla cui fuga la casa sua fu*
1414. l. 4—10. This passage evidently refers to   *pur messa a sacco da' partitanti francesi.* (AMORETTI, l. c.)

L. 1 *a*]　　　　　　　　　　　　**1415.**

²1 Ābrosio Petri,—³Sc̄o Marco,—⁴4 assi per la finestra,—⁵2 guasparistrame—⁶3 i sāti di capelle,—⁷5 a casa li Gienovesi.

Ambrosio Petri, St. Mark, 4 boards for the window, 2 . . . ., 3 the saints of chapels, 5 the Genoese at home.

L. 1 *b*]　　　　　　　　　　　　**1416.**

Panno d'arazzo,—²seste,—³libro di Maso,—⁴libro di Giovanni Bēcj,—⁵cassa in dogana,—⁶tagliare la vesta,—⁷cintura della spada,—⁸rinpedulare li stivaletti,—⁹cappello legieri,—¹⁰canne delle casaccie,—¹¹il debito della touagla,—¹²baga da notare,—¹³libro di carte bianche per disegnare,—¹⁴carboni. ¹⁵¶quāto è uno fiorino ¹⁶di sugello?¶ ¹⁷¶vn guarda¹⁸cuore di pelle.¶

Piece of tapestry,—pair of compasses,—Tommaso's book,—the book of Giovanni Benci,—the box in the custom-house,—to cut the cloth,—the sword-belt,—to sole the boots,—a light hat,—the cane from the ruined houses,—the debt for the table linen,—swimming-belt,—a book of white paper for drawing,—charcoal.—How much is a florin . . . . ., a leather bodice.

L. 2 *a*]　　　　　　　　　　　　**1417.**

Borges ti farà avere Archimede del ²vescouo di Padova, e Vitellozzo quello dal Borgo a San Sepolcro.

Borges shall get for you the Archimedes from the bishop of Padua, and Vitellozzo the one from Borgo a San Sepolcro.

L. 30 *b*]　　　　　　　　　　　　**1418.**

Tabella di Marzocco.

Marzocco's tablet.

L. 0″]　　　　　　　　　　　　**1419.**

Marcello sta in casa di Giacomo da Mē²gardino.

Marcello lives in the house of Giacomo da Mengardino.

Br. M. 202 *b*]　　　　　　　　　　　　**1420.**

Dou'è Valentino?—²stiuali,—³casse in dogana,—⁴. . . .,—⁵frate del Carmine,—⁶squadre,—⁷Piero Martelli,—⁸Salui Borgherini,—⁹rimanda le sache,—¹⁰sostētaculo delli ochiali,—¹¹lo igniudo del Sangallo,—¹²la cappa.
¹³Porfido,—¹⁴gruppi,—¹⁵squadra,—¹⁶Pandolfino.

Where is Valentino?—boots,—boxes in the custom-house,....,—[5] the monk at the Carmine,—squares,—[7] Piero Martelli,—[8] Salvi Borgherini,—send back the bags,—a support for the spectacles,—[11] the nude study of San Gallo,—the cloak.
Porphyry,—groups,—square,—[16] Pandolfino.

1415. 1. 10 omria (?). 4. aose. 5. quas paris trame. 7. chasa legienovesi.
1416. 1. darazo. 6. taglare lavessta. 8. lissti valetti. 10. dalle cassacce. 15. e î fi. 18. core.　　**1417.** 2. vesscovo. 2. vitellozo.
1418. marzoccho.　　　　　**1419.** 1. chasa diachomo.　　　　　**1420.** 4. falleri. 8. borgerini. 11. lognudo.

1417. *Borges.* A Spanish name.
3. Borgo a San Sepolcro, where Luca Paciolo, Leonardo's friend, was born.
1420. *Valentino.* Cesare Borgia is probably meant. After being made Archbishop of Valence by Alexander VI he was commonly called Valentinus or Valentino. With reference to Leonardo's engagements by him see pp. 224 and 243, note.

5. *Carmine.* A church and monastery at Florence.
7. 8. *Martelli, Borgherini;* names of Florentine families. See No. 4.
11. *San Gallo;* possibly Giuliano da San Gallo, the Florentine architect.
16. *Pandolfini,* see No. 1544 note.

F. 0']   **1421.**

¶Spechi cōcavi;   ¶filosofia d' Aristotile,
²¶libri d' Auicenna;   ¶messer Ottaviā Palavi-
³¶vocabolista vul-   cino pel suo Vetruuio;¶
⁴gare e latino.¶
⁵¶Coltelli di Boemia;   ¶Va ogni sabato alla
⁶Vetruuio;¶   stufa e vedrai delli
               nudi;¶
⁷¶Meteora;
⁸¶Archimede, de cē-   ¶Fa gōfiare il polmō
⁹tro grauitatis.¶   d' ū porco, e guarda
¹⁰¶Anotomia, Alessā-   se cresce in larghezza
¹¹dro Benedetto;¶   e ī lūghezza, over in
               larghezza e māco in
¹²¶Il Dāte di Niccolò del-   lūghezza.¶
¹³la Croce.¶
  ¹⁴Al Bertuccio il Marliano de calculatione, ¹⁵Alberto de celo e mūdo · [da fra
Bernardino]; ¹⁶Oratio scrisse della velocità
del cielo.

Concave mirrors; philosophy of Aristotle;
[2] the books of Avicenna; Messer Ottaviano
Italian and Latin vocabu- Palavicino for his
lary;   Vitruvius [3].
bohemian knives;   go every Saturday to the
Vitruvius; [6]   hot bath where you will
              see naked men;
'Meteora'[7].
Archimedes, on the centre   Inflate the lungs
of gravity; [9]   of a pig and ob-
anatomy [10] Alessandro   serve whether they
Benedetto;   increase in width
The Dante of Niccolò   and in length, or
della Croce;   in width dimini-
              shing in length.
[14] Marliano, on Calculation, to Bertuccio.
Albertus, on heaven and earth [15], [from the
monk Bernardino]. Horace has written on the
movements of the heavens.

F. 27 b]   **1422.**

De' 3 corpi regolari cōtro alcū cōmēta-
²tori che biasimā li ātichi īvētori dōde na-
quero le gramatiche e le scientie . . .

Of the three regular bodies as opposed to
some commentators who disparage the Ancients, who were the originators of grammar
and the sciences and . . .

W. An. III. 217 a ('G·)]   **1423.**

Camera de²lla Torre da ³Vaneri.

The room in the tower of Vaneri.

1421. 2. dauinega. 3. vocabolissta . — sino pel. 4. ellatino. 5. buemia . . alla. 6. vederai. 7. meteura. 9. trugrauitatis . —
dū porcho. 10. alesā. — cresse in largeza. 11. lūgeza . . largeza. 12. nicolo de . — e mācha in lūgeza. 14. bertucco.
16. oratio . . del celo. *These six words are written in four short lines on the margin near line 1—4.*
1422. 2. nascerō le gramatiche elle.   1423. 1. chamera.

1421. *Filosofia d'Aristotele* see No. 1481 note.

2. *Avicenna* (Leonardo here writes it Avinega) the
Arab philosopher, 980—1037, for centuries the un-
impeachable authority on all medical questions.
Leonardo possibly points here to a printed edition:
Avicennae canonum libri V, latine 1476 *Patavis.*
Other editions are, Padua 1479, and Venice 1490.

3. 6. *Vitruvius.* See Vol. I, No. 343 note.

7. *Meteora.* See No. 1448, 25.

9. The works of Archimedes were not printed
during Leonardo's life-time.

10. Compare No. 1494.

14. *Johannes Marliani sua etate philosophorum et medicorum principis et ducalis phisic. primi de proportione
motuum velocitate questio subtilissima incipit ex ejusdem
Marliani originali feliciter extracta, M(ilano)* 1482.

Another work by him has the title: *Marlianus
mediolanensis. Questio de caliditate corporum humanorum
tempore hiemis ed estatis et de antiparistasi ad celebrem
philosophorum et medicorum universitatem ticinensem.* 1474.

15. See No. 1469, l. 7.

1423. This note is written inside the sketch of a
plan of a house. On the same page is the date
1513 (see No. 1376).

W. 232*b* (.F.)]　　　　　　　　　**1424.**

Riserua all'ultimo dell'ōbre le figure
²che cōpariranno nello scrittoio di Gerar³do
miniatore a Sā Marco in Firēze.
⁴[Va per il Melso, ⁵e allo Ambasciatore
⁶e a maestro Bernardo.]

The figures you will have to reserve for
the last book on shadows that they may appear
in the study of Gerardo the illuminator at San
Marco at Florence.
[Go to see Melzo, and the Ambassador,
and Maestro Bernardo].

M. 0']　　　　　　　　　　　　**1425.**

Ermete ²filosofo.

Hermes the philosopher.

M. 8*a*]　　　　　　　　　　　　**1426.**

Suisset cioè calculatore, — ² Tisber, —
Angelo Fossobrō, — ⁴ Alberto.

Suisset, viz. calculator, — Tisber, — Angelo Fossobron, — Alberto.

M. 53*b*]　　　　　　　　　　　**1427.**

Modo del pōte leuatojo che mi mostrò
Donnino, ²e perchè *c* · e *d* spingano in basso.

The structure of the drawbridge shown me
by Donnino, and why *c* and *d* thrust downwards.

Mz. 0'']　　　　　　　　　　　**1428.**

Piglerà il primo volo il grāde vccello;—
sopra del dosso del suo ²magnio cecero,—
empiēdo l'universo di stupore,—em ³piēdo
di sua fama tutte le scritture e gloria etterna al loco ⁴dove nacque.

The great bird will take its first flight;—
on the back of his great swan,—filling
the universe with wonders; filling all writings
with his fame and bringing eternal glory to
his birthplace.

Tr. 22]　　　　　　　　　　　　**1429.**

Questo inganno fu vsato dai Ga²lli ·
contro · a' Romani, e seguì ³ne tal morta-
lità che tutta ⁴Roma · si vestì · a bruno.

This stratagem was used by the Gauls
against the Romans, and so great a mortality
ensued that all Rome was dressed in mourn-
ing.

1424. serua. 2. ceparirano scriptoio [del] di gera. 3. marcho. 5. ībassciatore. 6. maesstro.
1425. 2. filosafo.　　　　　**1426.** 1. coe chalculatore. 3. fossabrō.　　　　　**1427.** 1. leuato i che. 2. c he d spingano.
1428. 1. il p"o" volto [leverassi delge] il. 2. cecero c enpiēdo. 3. groria . . alaido. 4. [dore] doue.
1429. 2. chontro . . essegui. 3. chettutta. 4. vessti.

1424. L. 1—3 are in the original written between
lines 3 and 4 of No. 292. But the sense is not clear
in this connection. It is scarcely possible to de-
vine the meaning of the following sentence.

2. 3. *Gherardo* Miniatore, a famous illuminator,
1445—1497, to whom Vasari dedicated a section of
his Lives (Vol. II pp. 237—243, ed. Sansoni 1879).

5. *Bernardo*, possibly the painter Bernardo Ze-
nale.

1427. The sketch on the same page as this text
represents two poles one across the other. At the
ends of the longest are the letter *c* and *d*. The
sense of the passage is not rendered any clearer.

1428. This seems to be a speculation about the
flying machine (compare p. 271).

1429. Leonardo perhaps alludes to the Gauls under
Brennus, who laid his sword in the scale when the
tribute was weighed.

K.² 27 b]   **1430.**

Alberto da Imola;—algebra cioè dimo-stratione come una cosa s'agguaglia a un altra.

Alberto da Imola;—Algebra, that is, the demonstration of the equality of one thing to another.

K.3 48 b]   **1431.**

Joannes Rubicissa e Robbia.

Johannes Rubicissa e Robbia.

W. A. III. 152 a]   **1432.**

Dimāda la moglie di Bia²gio Crivelli come il cappone ³allieva e cova l'oua della ⁴gallina, essendo lui inbri⁵acato.

Ask the wife of Biagio Crivelli how the capon nurtures and hatches the eggs of the hen,—he being drunk.

W. A. IV. 153'a]   **1433.**

Libro dell'acque a messer Marco An-tonio.

The book on Water to Messer Marco Antonio.

W. An. IV. 167]   **1434.**

Fa tradurre Avicenna; de' giovamēti;—²ochiali col cartone, ³acciajuolo e forchetta e . . . .;—⁴carbone, asse e fogli e lapis e biāchetto e cera;—⁵tanagle e . . . da vetri, sega da osso di sottil dētatura, scar-pello, ⁶calamaro de . . . . . ., 3 erbe, e Agnol Benedetto, ⁷fa d'avere vn teschio, noce, mostarda;
⁸Stivali,—guāti,—⁹calcetti,—¹⁰pettine, papiri,—¹¹. . . . .,—¹²ca-misce. . .,—¹³stringhe, carbori,—¹⁴scarpe,—¹⁵tēperatoio,—¹⁶penne,—¹⁷vna pelle al petto.

Have Avicenna's work on useful inven-tions translated; spectacles with the case, steel and fork and . . . ., charcoal, boards, and paper, and chalk and white, and wax; . . . . for glass, a saw for bones with fine teeth, a chisel, inkstand . . . ., three herbs, and Agnolo Benedetto. Get a skull, nut,—mustard.

Boots,—gloves, socks, combs, papers, towels, shirts, ... shoe-tapes, — . . . . . shoes, penknife, pens. A skin for the chest.

W. L. 141 b]   **1435.**

Libro di Piero Crescēzio,—²i nvdi di Giouañj Ambrosio,—³compasso,—⁴libro di Gian Jacomo,—

The book of Piero Crescenzo,—studies from the nude by Giovanni Ambrosio,—com-passes,—the book of Giovanni Giacomo.

Undated me-moranda (1435—1457).

1430. 2. alcibra coe mostra come. 3. n"o" e cosa sagualglia alla cosa.
1431. 1. ioanēs "erobbia" rupicissa.   **1432.** 2. gi cri velli . . cuppone. 4. ghallina.
1433. 1. dellacq"e" . . marcho ant.
1434. 1. avicena de govamēti. 3. accarolo . . egamavr (or gamaut). 4. ellapis e biācetto. 5. tauaglie "e topo da vetri" segha "da osso" di. 6. calimano de aperatoio. 7. tesscio . . mostada. 10. palpiri. 11. scugaco da scarte. 12. camisce coci.
13.˙curbori.   **1435.** 1. cresciēzo.

1433. Possibly Marc-Antonio della Torre, see p. 97.

1434. 4. *Lapis.* Compare Condivi, *Vita di Michel-agnolo Buonarotti,* Chap. XVIII.: *Ma egli* (Michel-angelo) *non avendo che mostrare, prese una penna (per-*

ciochè in quel tempo il lapis non era in uso) e con tal leggiadria gli dipinse una mano ecc. The incident is of the year 1496.—*Lapis* means pencil, and chalk (*matita*). Between lines 7 and 8 are the texts given as Nos. 819 and No. 7.

W. L. 141 a]   **1436.**

RICORDO.

²Andare in provisione per il mio giardino,—³Giordano 'de pōderibus',—⁴el cō-
ciliatore, de flusso e reflusso del mare,—
⁵far fare due casse da soma,—⁶vedi il tornio del Beltraffio e falli trarre vna pietra,—
⁷Lascia il libro a messere Andrea tedesco,
⁸fa vna bilancia d'una freccia e pesa la
cosa īfocata e poi la ripesa fredda; ⁹Lo
spechio di maestro Luigi,—¹⁰*A b* flusso e
reflusso dell'acque, provato al molino di
Vaprio,—¹¹beretta.

MEMORARDUM.

To make some provisions for my garden,
—Giordano, *De Ponderibus*[3],— the peace-
maker, the flow and ebb of the sea,—have two
baggage trunks made, look to Beltraffio's [6] lathe
and have taken the stone,—out leave the books
belonging to Messer Andrea the German,—
make scales of a long reed and weigh the
substance when hot and again when cold.
The mirror of Master Luigi; *A b* the flow
and ebb of the water is shown at the mill
of Vaprio,—a cap.

W. L. 212 a]   **1437.**

Giovanni Fabre,—²Lazaro del Volpe,—
³comune, ⁴Ser Piero.—

Giovanni Fabre,—Lazaro del Volpe,—
the common,—Ser Piero. ⁞

W. L. 203 a]   **1438.**

[Lattantio] ²[libro di Benozzo], ³gruppi,
—⁴legare il libro,—⁵Lucerna,—⁶Ser Pecantino,—⁷Pandolfino,—⁸[Rosso],—⁹squa-
dra,—¹⁰coltellini,—¹¹carrozze,—¹²stregghia
¹³[cavallina],—¹⁴tazza.

[Lactantius], [the book of Benozzo],
groups,—to bind the book,—a lantern,—Ser
Pecantino,—Pandolfino.—[Rosso]—a square,
—small knives,—carriages,—curry combs—
cup.

C. A. 11 b; 37 b]   **1439.**

Quadrāte di Carlo Marmocchi,—²mes-
ser Francesco Araldo,—³Ser Benedetto
d'Accie perello,—⁴Benedetto, del abbaco,
—⁵maestro Pagolo medico,—⁶Domenico
di Michelino,—⁷el caluo deli Alberti,—
⁹messer Giovanni Argimboldi.

Quadrant of Carlo Marmocchi,—Messer
Francesco Araldo,—Ser Benedetto d'Accie
perello,—Benedetto on arithmetic,—Maestro
Paulo, physician,—Domenico di Michelino,—
. . . . . . of the Alberti,—Messer Giovanni
Argimboldi.

1436. 1. Richordo. 2. provitione. 4. frusso e refrusso. 5. dassoma. 6. effalli. 7. lasscia . . messere andrea tedesscho. 8. īfo-
chata eppoi. 9. losspechio . . maesstro. 10. frusso e refrusso . . di uavrio.
1437. 1. govanni. 2. lazero . . elulpe.
1438. 8. careze. 9. streglia. 10. [cavalino.]
1439. 1. charlo. 2. franc"o". 3. benedetto daccieperello. 4. abbacho. 5. maesstro pagholo medicho. 6. domenicho. 7. chaluo.
8. meser argirobolto.

1436. 3. *Giordano.* Jordanus Nemorarius, a mathematician of the beginning of the XIIIᵗʰ century.
No particulars of his life are known. The title
of his principal work is: *Arithmetica decem libris de-
monstrata*, first published at Paris 1496. In 1523 appeared at Nuremberg: *Liber Jordani Nemorarii de
ponderibus*, *propositiones XIII et earundem demonstra-*

tiones, *multarumque rerum rationes sane pulcherrimas
complectens*, *nunc in lucem editus.*

6. *Beltraffio*, see No. 465, note 2.

There are sketches by the side of lines 8
and 10.

1437. These names are inserted on a plan of
plots of land adjoining the Arno.

C. A. 19 *b*; 72 *b*]   **1440.**

Colore, — [2]formulario, — [3]Archimede, —
[6]Marcanto[7]nio ;
[8]Ferro stagnato, — [9]ferro traforato.

Colours, formula, — Archimedes, — Marcantonio.
Tinned iron, —pierced iron.

C. A. 27 *a*; 89 *a*]   **1441.**

Vedi la bottega che fu di [2]Bartolomeo
cartolaio.

See the shop that was formerly Bartolommeo's, the stationer.

C. A. 70 *a*; 207 *a*]   **1442.**

Primo libro è di Michele di Francesco
di Nabini, è di scientia.

The first book is by Michele di Francesco
Nabini; it treats on science.

C. A. 113*a*; 349 *a*]   **1443.**

Messer Francesco, medico Lucchese a-
presso il Cardinale Farnese.

Messer Francesco, physician of Lucca,
with the Cardinal Farnese.

C. A. 118*a*; 366*a*]   **1444.**

Libro del Pandolfino, — [2]coltelli, — [3]pen-
na da rigare, — [4]tignere la uesta, — [5]libreria
di Scō Marco, — [6]libreria di Sco Spirito, —
[7]Lattantio de' Daldi, — [8]Antonio Couoni, —
[9]libro di maestro Paolo Infermieri, — [10]sti-
ualetti, scarpe e calze, — [11]lacca, — [12]gar-
zone che mi facci il modello, — [13]gramatica
di Lorenzo de' Medici, — [14]Giouanni del
Sodo, — [15]Sansouino, — [16]riga, — [17]coltello
sottilissimo, — [18]occhiali, — [19] . . . . —
[20]rifare . . . ., — [21]libro di Maso, —
[22]catenuzza di Michelagnolo, — [23]¶impara
la multiplicatione [24]delle radici da maestro
Luca ¶ [25]el mio mappamōdo che à Giovanni
Bēci, [26]calcetti, — [27]vesta dal gabellotto, —
[28]cordovano rosso, — [29]mappamōdo di Giovanni Benci, — [30]paesi di Milano in istāpa,
— [31]libro di mercato, —

Pandolfino's book[1], — knives, —a pen
for ruling, —to have the vest dyed, — The
library at St.-Mark's, —The library at Santo
Spirito, —Lactantius of the Daldi [7], —Antonio Covoni, —A book by Maestro Paolo Infermieri, —Boots, shoes and hose, —(Shell)lac,
—An apprentice to do the models for me.
Grammar, by Lorenzo de Medici, —Giovanni
del Sodo, —Sansovino, [15]—a ruler, — a very
sharp knife, — Spectacles, —fractions . . . . ,
—repair . . . ., —Tomaso's book, —
Michelagnolo's little chain; Learn the multiplication of roots from Maestro Luca; —my
map of the world which Giovanni Benci
has[25]; — Socks, —clothes from the custom-
house-officer, —Red Cordova leather, —The
map of the world, of Giovanni Benci, —a
print, the districts about Milan—Market book.

1440. 4. cochino. 5. aioditti.   **1441.** 1. bottegha cheffu. 2. bartol.
1442. p"o" libro . . franc"o" eddi sua disciē.
1444. 2. coltegli. 3. darrigare. 5. marcho. 9. pagolo infermieri. 17. sotilissimo. 19. rotti fisici. 20. rifare lalbernuscio. 22. ca-
tenuza. 23. ipara. 24. radice . . maesstro. 27. vesta di gā bellotto. 29. govanni.

1441. 6. *Marc Antonio*, see No. 1433.

1443. *Alessandro Farnese*, afterwards Pope Paul III
was created in 1493 Cardinal di San Cosimo e San
Damiano, by Alexander VI.

1444. 1. *Pandolfino, Agnolo*, of Florence. It is to
this day doubtful whether he or L. B. Alberti was
the author of the famous work '*Del Governo della
Famiglia*'. It is the more probable that Leonardo
should have meant this work by the words *il libro*,
because no other book is known to have been
written by Pandolfino. This being the case this allusion of Leonardo's is an important evidence in

favour of Pandolfino's authorship (compare No. 1454,
line 3).

7. The works of Lactantius were published
very often in Italy during Leonardo's lifetime. The
first edition published in 1465 "*in monastero
sublacensi*" was also the first book printed in
Italy.

15. *Sansovino, Andrea* — the *sculptor;* 1460— 1529.

25. Leonardo here probably alludes to the map,
not executed by him (See p. 224), which is with the
collection of his MSS. at Windsor, and was published in the *Archaeologia* Vol. XI (see p. 224).

C. A. 145a; 432a] **1445.**

¶Di quel di Pavia si lauda · piv · il movi-mēto · che nessun altra cosa;—

¶²L'imitatione · delle cose · antiche · è piv laudabile · che quella delle · moderne;—

¶³Nō può essere bellezza · e vtilità · come appare nelle fortezze ⁴e nelli omini;¶

¶⁵Il trotto · è quasi di qualità di cavallo libero;—

⁶Doue · manca · la uiuacità naturale, bisognia farne una accidētale.¶

In that at Pavia the movement is more to be admired than any thing else.

The imitation of antique work is better than that of the modern things.

Beauty and utility cannot exist together, as seen in fortresses and in men.

The trot is almost the nature of the free horse.

Where natural vivacity is lacking it must be supplied by art.

C. A. 176b; 532] **1446.**

Saluadore materassaio ²sta in sulla piazza di Sco An³drea; entra da pellicciai . . .

Salvadore, the matress maker, lives on the Piazza di Sant' Andrea, you enter by the furrier's.

C. A. 185b; 557b] **1447.**

Mōsignor de' Pazzi,—²ser Ātonio Pacini.

Monsignore de' Pazzi,—Ser Antonio Pacini.

C. A. 222a; 664a] **1448.**

Algibra ch'è apresso i Marliani fatta dal loro padre,—

²Dell'osso, de' Marliani,

³Dell'osso che fora, Gian Giacomo da Bellinzona, e tirare fori il chiodo cō facilità,—

⁴Misura di Boccalino,—

⁵Misura di Milano e borghi,—

⁶Libro che tratta di Milano e sua chiese, che à l'ultimo cartolaio īuerso il Corduso,—

⁷Misura della corte vechia,—

⁸Misura del castello,—

⁹Fatti mostrare al maestro · d'abbaco · riquadrare · uno . . . . .,—

¹⁰Fatti mostrare a messer Fatio 'di proportione',—

An algebra, which the Marliani have, written by their father, [1]—

On the bone, by the Marliani,—

On the bone which penetrates, Gian Giacomo of Bellinzona, to draw out the nail with facility,—

The measurement of Boccalino,—

The measurement of Milan and the suburbs, [5]—

A book, treating of Milan and its churches which is to be had at the last stationer's on the way to Corduso [6],—

The measurement of the Corte Vecchia,—

The measurement of the Castle,—

Get the master of arithmetic to show you how to square a . . . .,—

Get Messer Fazio to show you [the book] on proportion,—

1445. 1. lalda . . chosa. 2. chose . . laldabile chelle. 3. pro essere belleza . . chome apare. 5. trocto . . chavallo. 6. mancha . . fare î accidētale.

1446. 2. piaza di sco\\\\\\. 3. pelliccai\\\\\. 4. detare a franc° paio\\\\\\. 5. î di lenzola e per so\\\\\.

1447. pazi.

1448. 1. alcibra. 3. cheffora giaiachomo da belinchona ettirare . . ciodo chō. 4. bochalino. 6. chettatta . . essa . . chartolaio . . chorduso. 7. chorte. 8. chastello. 9. dabbacho . . riquadrare î magloto (?). 11. mosstrare . . fratte. 13. fraffillippo.

1445. *Quel di Pavia. Pavia* is possibly a clerical error for *Padua*, and if so the meaning of the passage is easily arrived at: *Quel di Padua* would be the bronze equestrian statue of Gattamelata, on the Piazza del Santo at Padua executed by Donatello in 1443 (see pp. 2 and 3).

2. See No. 487 note. Vol. I p. 244.

1448. 1. 2. *Marliani*, an old Milanese family, now extinct.

5. 21. See Pl. CIX and No. 1016.

6. *Corduso*, see No. 1413, note.

¹¹Fatti mostrare · al frate di Brera 'de pōderibus',—

¹²Della misura di Sco Lorenzo,—

¹³A fra Filippo di Brera prestai · cierti gruppi,—

¹⁴Ricorda a Giouanino bonbardieri · del modo, come si mvrò la torre di Ferrara · sāza buche,—

¹⁵Dimāda · maestro Antonio, come · si piantā bōbarde e bastioni di dì o di notte,—

¹⁶Domanda Benedetto Portinari in che modo si corre per lo ghiaccio · in Fiādra,—

¹⁷Le proportioni · d'Alchino colle cōsiderationi del Marliano da messer Fatio,—

¹⁸La misura del sole promessami da maestro Giovanni frāzese,—

¹⁹Balestra di maestro Gianetto,—

²⁰Il libro di Giovanni Taverna che · à · messer Fatio,—

²¹Ritrarai Milano,—

²²Misura di navilio, conche e sostegnio e barche maggiori e spesa,—

²³Milano ī fondamēto,—

²⁴Gruppi di Bramāte,—

²⁵Meteora d'Aristotile vulgare,—

²⁶Fa d'avere Vitolone ch'è nella libreria di Pauia che tratta della matematica,— ²⁷teneva uno maestro d'acqua, e fatti dire i riparo d'essa, e quello che costa ²⁸vn riparo, e una · conca ·, e uno navilio, e uno molino alla lonbarda,

²⁹Un nipote · di Gian Āgelo · dipītore à uno libro d'acque che fu del padre;

³⁰Paolino Scarpellino ·, detto Assiolo ·, è bono · maestro d'acque.

Get the Friar di Brera to show you [the book] *'de Ponderibus'* [11],—

Of the measurement of San Lorenzo,—

I lent certain groups to Fra Filippo de Brera, [13]—

Memorandum: to ask Maestro Giovannino as to the mode in which the tower of Ferrara is walled without loopholes, —

Ask Maestro Antonio how mortars are placed on bastions by day or by night,—

Ask Benedetto Portinari how the people go on the ice in Flanders,—

On proportions by Alchino, with notes by Marliano, from Messer Fazio,—

The measurement of the sun, promised me by Maestro Giovanni, the Frenchman,—

The cross bow of Maestro Gianetto,—

The book by Giovanni Taverna that Messer Fazio,—

You will draw Milan [21],—

The measurement of the canal, locks and supports, and large boats; and the expense,—

Plan of Milan [23],—

Groups by Bramante [24],—

The book on celestial phenomena by Aristoteles, in Italian [25],—

Try to get Vitolone, which is in the library at Pavia [26] and which treats of Mathematics,—He had a master [learned] in waterworks and get him to explain the repairs and the costs, and a lock and a canal and a mill in the Lombard fashion.

A grandson of Gian Angelo's, the painter has a book on water which was his fathers.

Paolino Scarpellino, called Assiolo has great knowledge of water works.

C. A. 313*b*; 950*b*]

1449.

Francesco d'Antonio j̄ Firenze.

Francesco d'Antonio at Florence.

14. richorda a govanni . . cho ne . . tore di ferara. 15. chome. 16. chore . . diacio di fiādra. 17. cholle chōsideratione. 18. promissami . . maestro. 22. chōche esso stegnio . . magiori esspesa. 26. tratte delle matematice. 27. teneva î maestro dacq"a" effatti . . ecquelle che chosta. 26. e î choncha e î . . e î. 29. vnipote . . giānāgelo . . a î libro. 30. pagolino scharpellino . . maesstro.

1449. 1. franc"o" dant"o" j̄ffirence (*early writing*).

11. 13. *Brera*, now *Palazzo delle Scienze ed Arti*. Until 1571 it was the monastery of the order of the Umiliati and afterwards of the Jesuits.

De ponderibus, compare No. 1436, 3.

12. *Sco Lorenzo*. A church at Milan, see pp. 39, 40 and 50.

13. 24. *Gruppi*. See Vol. I p. 355, No. 600, note 9.

16. The *Portinari* were one of the great merchant-families of Florence.

23. *Fondamento* is commonly used by Leonardo to mean ground-plan. See for instance p. 53.

25. *Meteora*. By this Leonardo means no doubt the four books τὰ μετεωρολογικά. He must refer here to a MS. translation, as no Italian translation is known to have been published (see No. 1477 note).

26. *Vitolone* see No. 1506, note.

Libreria di Pavia. One of the most famous of Italian libraries. After the victory of Novara in April 1500, Louis XII had it conveyed to France, *'come trofeo di vittoria'!*

C. A. 358 *b*; 1124 *b*]　　　　　　　　**1450.**

Givliano Gōdi,—²Tomaso Ridolfi,—
³Toṁaso·Paganelli,—⁴Niccolò·del Nero,—
⁵Simō·Guasti,—⁶Nasi,—⁷erede di Lionardo
Manelli,—⁸Guglielmo di Ser Martino,—
⁹Bartolomeo·del Tovaglia,—¹⁰Andrea·
Arrigucci,—¹¹Niccolo·Capponi,—¹²Giovan
Portinari.

Giuliano Gondi[1],—Tomaso Ridolfi,—
Tomaso Paganelli,—Nicolò del Nero,—Simone
Zasti,—Nasi,—the heir of Lionardo Ma-
nelli,—Guglielmo di Ser Martino,—Barto-
lomeo del Tovaglia,—Andrea Arrigucci,—
Nicolò Capponi,—Giovanni Portinari.

Br. M. 48 *a*]　　　　　　　　**1451.**

Pandolfino.

Pandolfino.

Br. M. 132 *b*]　　　　　　　　**1452.**

Il Vespuccio mi vol dare un libro di
geometria.

Vespuccio will give me a book of Geometry.

Br. M. 150 *a*]　　　　　　　　**1453.**

Marcantonio Colonna ²in Sco Apostolo.

Marcantonio Colonna at Santi Apostoli.

Br. M. 191 *a*]　　　　　　　　**1454.**

Cassa,	gabbia,—
²Liuello,	far l'uccello,—
³Libro del Pandolfino,	grasselino,—
⁴Coltellini,—	Venieri per la

A box,	a cage,—
A square,	to make the bird[2],—
Pandolfino's book,	mortar [?],—
Small knives,	Venieri for the

1450. 1—12 R. 4. nicholo. 5. zasti. 7. rede di. 11. nicholo.
1453. marchātonio cholonna.
1454. 1. chassa. 4. pella. 5. darrizare . . metaura. 8. casa e pazi. 9. maesstro pa"lo". 10. esscarpe. 11. lacha, — trai 2 aguti.

1452. 1. el vespucco . . dare î libro di giometria.

1450. 1. *Guiliano Gondi*. Ser Piero da Vinci,
Leonardo's father, lived till 1480, in a house belonging to Giuliano Gondi. In 1498 this was pulled
down to make room for the fine Palazzo built on
the Piazza San Firenze by Giuliano di San Gallo,
which still exists. In the *Riassunto del Catasto di Ser
Piero da Vinci*, 1480, Leonardo is not mentioned; it
is evident therefore that he was living elsewhere. It
may be noticed incidentally that in the *Catasto di
Giuliano Gondi* of the same year the following mention is made of his four eldest sons:

Lionardo mio figliuolo d'età d'anni 29, non fa nulla,
Giovambatista d'età d'anni 28 in Ghostantinopoli,
Billichozo d'età d'anni 24 a Napoli,
Simone d'età d'anni 23 in Ungheria.

He himself was a merchant of gold filigree (*facciamo lavorare una bottegha d'arte di seta . . . facciamo
un pocho di trafico a Napoli*). As he was 59 years
old in 1480, he certainly would not have been alive
at the time of Leonardo's death. But Leonardo must
have been on intimate terms with the family till the
end of his life, for in a letter dated June 1. 1519,
in which Fr. Melzi, writing from Amboise, announces

Leonardo's death to Giuliano da Vinci at Florence
(see p. 284), he says at the end "*Datemene risposta per
i Gondi*" (see UZIELLI, *Ricerche*, passim).

Most of the other names on the list are those
of well-known Florentine families.

1452. See No. 844, note, p. 130.

1453. In July 1506 Pope Julius II gave Donna
Lucrezia della Rovere, the daughter of his sister
Lucchina, in marriage to the youthful Marcantonio
Colonna, who, like his brothers Prospero and
Fabrizio, became one of the most famous Captains of his family. He gave to him Frascati
and made him a present of the palazzo he had
built, when Cardinal, near the church of Santi Apostoli which is now known as the Palazzo Colonna (see GREGOROVIUS, *Gesch. der Stadt Rom.*
Vol. VIII, book XIV 1, 3. And COPPI, *Mem. Co-
lonnesi* p. 251).

1454. Much of No. 1444 is repeated in this memorandum.

2. Vasari states that Leonardo invented mechanical
birds which moved through the air. Compare
No. 703.

5 Penna da rizzare,	pietra,—stella,—	Pen for ruling,	stone,—star,—
6 Tignere la uesta,	la tazza d' Alfieri,—	To have the vest dyed,	Alfieri's tazza,—
7 Librerie,	la Meteora, —	The Libraries,	the book on celestial phenomena,—
8 Lattantio de' Daldi,	va a casa de' Pazzi,—	Lactantius of the Daldi,—	go to the house of the Pazzi,
9 Libro di maestro Paolo Infermieri,—	cassetta,—	Book from Maestro Paolo Infermieri,—	small box,—
10 Stiualetti, calze e scarpe,	suchiellino,—	Boots, shoes and hose,	small gimlet,—
11 Lacca,	. . . .	Lac,	. . . . . . ,—
12 Garzone pe' modelli,	. . . .	An apprentice for models,	. . . . . ,—
13 Gramatica di Lorēzo de' Medici,—	la valuta del	Grammar of Lorenzo de' Medici,	the amount of the . . .
14 Giouanni del Sodo per . . .	. . . .	Giovanni del Sodo for . . . ,—the broken	. . . . .
15 Sansauino,	valuta del . . .,—	Sansovino,	the . . . .
16 Pier di Cosimo,	. . . per l' alie,—	Piero di Cosino [16],	the wings,—

17 Filippo e Lorenzo,— 18 riga,— 19 ochiali, — 20 rifare la . . . . .,— 21 libro di Maso,— 22 catena di Michelagnolo,— 23 mvltiplicatione di radici,— 24 di corda e arco,— 25 mappamōdo de' Benci, — 26 calcetti,— 27 vesta dal gabellotto,— 28 cordovano,— 29 libri di mercato,— 30 acque del Cronaca,— 31 acque del Tanaglino,— 32 . . . . .,— 33 le berrette,— 34 spechio del Rosso vederlo fare,— 35 1/3 di che n'ò 5/6, — 36 Meteora d'Aristotele,— 37 casse di Lorēzo di Pier Francesco,— 38 maestro Piero dal Borgo,— 39 legare il mio libro,— 40 ¶ mostra al Serigatto il libro,— 41 e fatti dare la regola dell' orilogio, anello, ¶ 42 noce muscato,— 43 gomma,— 44 squadra,— 45 Giovā Batista a la piazza de' Mozzi,— 46 Giovanni Benci il libro mio, e' diaspri, 47 ottone per li ochiali.

Filippo and Lorenzo [17],— A ruler,— Spectacles,— to do the . . . . . again,—Tomaso's book,—Michelagnolo's chain,— The multiplication of roots,— Of the bow and strinch,—The map of the world from Benci,— Socks,—The clothes from the custom-house officier, — Cordova leather,—Market books, —waters of Cronaca,—waters of Tanaglino . . ., — the caps,—Rosso's mirror; to see him make it,—1/3 of which I have 5/6,—on the celestial phenomena, by Aristotle [36],—boxes of Lorenzo di Pier Francesco [37],—Maestro Piero of the Borgo,—To have my book bound,—Show the book to Serigatto,— and get the rule of the clock [41],— ring,—nutmeg,—gum,—the square,—Giovan' Batista at the piazza de' Mozzi,— Giovanni Benci has my book and jaspers,—brass for the spectacles.

Br. M. 192 a]

1455.

Cerca in Firenze della . . . . . .   Search in Florence for . . . . . .

12. dali antelessi. 14. per rotti fisici vatro. 15. del ca. 16. fetto per lalie. 20. la bruncio (?). 24. archo. 25. mapamōdo. 27. di ganbelletto. 30. clomica. 32. moncatto. 35. n"o". 36. metaura. 38. maesstro. 41. effatti. 42. misscado. 45. govā batissta . . piaza de mozi. 46. govanni . . ellibro mio e dia ispriottone.
1455. 1. cerchi . . dellaramōdina.

7. 36. *Meteora*. See No. 1448, 25.

16. *Pier di Cosimo* the well known Florentine painter 1462—1521. See VASARI, *Vite* (Vol. IV, p. 134 ed. Sansoni 1880) about Leonardo's influence on Piero di Cosimo's style of painting.

17. *Filippo e Lorenzo*; probably the painters Filippino Lippi and Lorenzo di Credi. L. di Credi's pictures and Vasari's history of that painter bear ample evidence to his intimate relations with Leonardo.

37. *Lorenzo di Pier Francesco* and his brother *Giovanni* were a lateral branch of the *Medici* family and changed their name for that of Popolani.

41. Possibly this refers to the clock on the tower of the Palazzo Vecchio at Florence. In February 1512 it had been repaired, and so arranged as to indicate the hours after the French manner (twelve hours a. m. and as many p. m.).

Mi. A.]   **1456.**

Bernardo da Pōte...²Val di Lugā al   Bernardo da Ponte . . . Val di Lugano
fiē disce . . . ³ e questo e mostr . . . ⁴ molte   . . . many veins for anatomical demonstra-
vene per l'anotomia.   tion.

Br. M. P.]   **1457.**

Paolo da Tavechia, per ²vedere le ma-   Paolo of Tavechia, to see the marks in
chie de³lle pietre tedesche.   the German stones.

C. 15 b (1)]   **1458.**

    Jacomo venne a stare · con meco ɉl dì   Giacomo came to live with me on St.-Mary
Notes on della Maddalena nel mille 490, d'età d'anni   Magdalen's[1] day, 1490, aged 10 years. The
pupils 10; ²Il secondo dì li feci tagliare 2 cami-   second day I had two shirts cut out for him,
(1458—1468.) cie, uno pajo di calze e vn giubbone, e quā-   a pair of hose, and a jerkin, and when I put
do mi posi i dinari al lato per pagare dette   aside some money to pay for these things
cose lui mi   *lire* 4   he stole   4 *lire*
³detti dinari dalla scarsella, e mai fu possibile   the money out of the purse; and I could never
farli le confessare, bench'io n'avessi vera cier-   make him confess, though I was quite certain
tezza;—ladro, bugiardo, ostinato, ghiotto. —   of the fact.—Thief, liar, obstinate, glutton.
    ⁴Il dì seguente andai a ciena con Ia-   The day after, I went to sup with Gia-
como, Andrea e detto Iaçomo ·; cienò per   como Andrea, and the said Giacomo supped
2 e fece male per 4, inperochè rupe 3   for two and did mischief for four; for he
ampolline, ⁵versò il uino, e dopo questo   brake 3 cruets, spilled the wine, and after
venne a ciena doue me . . .   this came to sup where I . . . .
    ⁶Itē a dì 7 di settēbre · rubò uno gra-   Item: on the 7th day of September he
fio di valuta di 22 soldi a Marco che staua   stole a silver point of the value of 22 soldi
con meco, ɉl quale era   *lire* 4   from Marco[6] who was living with me,   4 *lire*
⁷d'argiēto e tolse gli lo dal suo studiolo,   this being of silver; and he took it from his
e poi che detto Marco n'ebbe assai ciercato,   studio, and when the said Marco had sear-
lo trovò na⁸scosto in nella cassa di detto   ched for it a long while he found it hidden
Iacomo   *lire* 4.   in the said Giacomo's box   4 *lire*.

1456. 1. pōte\\\\\. 2. al fiē dis\\\\\\. 3. ecquesto e mostr\\\\. 4. la not\\\\\\. 5. paroffa di sā posā\\\\\.
1457. 1. pagol. 3. tedessce.
1458. 1. Iachomo vene . . chomecho . . madalena . . dani. 2. sechondo . . chamice î paro di chalze . . gibone ecquādo . . chose
3. della scharsella . . farlie le chonfessare . . cierteza . — ladro . . ghiotto *these four words are written on the margin.*
4. chon iachomo . . 3 amole. 5. vene. 6. graffio . . ualluta . . marcho . . chomecho . . era [di ua] lire. 7. [luto di]
durgiēto ettolse glielo del . . marcho [glielebe] nebe assai cierco lo tro na. 8. schosto inella chassa . . iachomo lire 4⁹.

1456. This fragmentary note is written on the   reference to the drawing on which it is written
margin of a drawing of two legs.   but is obviously of the same date. Though I have
    1457. This note occurs on a pen and ink drawing   not any opening here for discussing this question of
made by Leonardo as a sketch for the celebrated   the cartoon, it seemed to me important to point out
large cartoon in the possession of the Royal Aca-   that the character of the writing in this note does
demy of Arts, in London. This cartoon is com-   not confirm the opinion hitherto held that the Royal
monly supposed to be identical with that described   Academy cartoon was the one described by Vasari,
and lauded by Vasari, which was exhibited in Flo-   but, on the contrary, supports the hypothesis put
rence at the time and which now seems to be lost.   forward by Mr. Marks.
Mr. Alfred Marks, of Long Ditton, in his valuable   **1458.** *Il dì della Maddalena.* July 22.
paper (read before the Royal Soc. of Literature,   6. *Marco*, probably Leonardo's pupil Marco d'Og-
June 28, 1882) "On the St. Anne of Leonardo da   gionno; 1470 is supposed to be the date of his
Vinci", has adduced proof that the cartoon now in the   birth and 1540 of his death.
Royal Academy was executed earlier at Milan. The note   *Che stava con meco.* We may infer from this that
here given, which is written on the sheet containing   he left the master shortly after this, his term of
the study for the said cartoon, has evidently no   study having perhaps expired.

9 Item a dì 26 di gienaro seguēte, essendo io in casa di messer Galeazzo da San Severino a ordinare la festa 10 della sua giostra, e spogliandosi cierti staffieri per prouarsi alcune vesti d'omini saluatici ch'a detta   *lire 2 S 4*

11 festa accadeano, Giacomo s'accosto alla scarsella d'uno di loro, la qual era ī sul letto con altri panni, 12 e tolse quelli dinari che dētro vi trovò.

13 Itē essendomi da maestro Agostino da Pauia donato in detta casa una pelle turchesca da fare uno   *lire 2.*

14 pajo di stiualetti·, esso Giacomo infra uno mese me la rubò, e vendè la a uno conciatore di 15 scarpe per 20 soldi, de' quali danari secondo che lui propio mi cōfessò, ne cōprò anici cōfetti;

16 Itē ancora a dì 2 d'aprile, lasciādo Giā Ātonio uno grafio d'argiēto sopra uno suo disegnio, 17 esso Giacomo gli lo rubò, il qual era di ualuta di soldi 24 *lira 1ª S 4.*

18 Il primo 19 anno
20 v̄ mātello, lire 2
21 camicie 6, lire 4
22 3 givboni, lire 6
23 4 paja di calze lire, 7 S 8
24 vestito foderato, lire 5
25 24 paja di scarpe, lire 6·S 5
26 vna baretta, lire 1
27 strīghe lire, 1.

Item: on the 26th January following, I, being in the house of Messer Galeazzo da San Severino [9], was arranging the festival for his jousting, and certain footmen having undressed to try on some costumes of wild men for the said festival, Giacomo went to the purse of one of them which lay on the bed with other clothes, 2 *lire* 4 *S*, and took out such money as was in it.

Item: when I was in the same house, Maestro Agostino da Pavia gave to me a Turkish hide to have   2 *lire.* a pair of short boots made of it; this Giacomo stole it of me within a month and sold it to a cobbler for 20 soldi, with which money, by his own confession, he bought anise comfits.

Item: again, on the 2nd April, Giovan Antonio[16] having left a silver point on a drawing of his, Giacomo stole it, and this was of the value of 24 soldi   1 *lira* 4 *S.*

The first year—
A cloak, 2 lire,
6 shirts, 4 lire,
3 jerkins, 6 lire,
4 pairs of hose, 7 lire 8 soldi,
1 lined doublet, 5 lire,
24 pairs of shoes, 6 lire 5 soldi,
A cap, 1 lira,
laces, 1 lira.

S. K. M. III. 1 a]   **1459.**

A dì penvltimo di settémbre;
2 giobia, a dì 27 di settēbre, 3 tornò maestro Tom̄aso, 4 lavorò per se insino a dì penvltimo di febraio; 5 a dì 18 di marzo 1493 6 venne Iulio tedesco 7 a stare meco; Lucia,—Piero,—Lionard.
9 A dì 6 d'ottobre.

On the last day but one of September;
Thursday the 27th day of September Maestro Tommaso came back and worked for himself until the last day but one of February. On the 18th day of March, 1493, Giulio, a German, came to live with me,—Lucia, Piero, Leonardo.
On the 6th day of October.

9. Ite adi . . esendo . . chasa . . galeazo dassanseverino ardina la. 10. alchune veste . . saluatichi. 11. achadeano j iachomo sachosto allasscharsella . . chon. 13. chasa. 14. paro . . iachomo infra î mese. 15. de qua dinari sechondo . . chōfessone chōpre . . chōfetti. 16. anchora . . lassciādo . . ātonio î graffio. 17. iachomo glielo. 18—27. R. 21. camice. 23. para di chalze. 24. li 5. 25. para . . scarpeli. 27. incīti strīge.
1459. 1. R. 2. grobia. 3. maesstro. 4. addi. 6. tedessco. 7. asstare mecho. 9. R. *The words* lucia piero lionard *are written on the margin.*

9. *Galeazzo.* See No. 718 note.
16. *Giovan Antonio*, probably Beltraffio, 1467 to 1516.
Leonardo here gives a detailed account not only of the loss he and others incurred through Giacomo but of the wild tricks of the youth, and we may therefore assume that the note was not made merely as a record for his own use, but as a report to be forwarded to the lad's father or other responsible guardian.

1460.

1493.

²A dì primo di novēbre facemmo ³cō-
to; Givlio restava a rimettere mesi ⁴4 ‖ e
maestro Toṁaso mesi 9; ⁵maestro Toṁaso
fece di poi 6 cādellie⁶ri ·, dì 10 ·; Givlio in
cierte molli ⁷dì 15; lavorò poi per se in-
⁸sino a dì 27 di maggio, e lavorò ⁹per me
uno martinello insino a dì 18 ¹⁰di luglio,
poi per se insino a dì 7 ¹¹d'agosto, e
questo uno mezzo dì per una donna; ¹²di
poi per me in 2 serrature ¹³insino a dì ·
20 d'agosto.

1493.

On the 1ˢᵗ day of November we settled
accounts. Giulio had to pay 4 months;
and Maestro Tommaso 9 months; Maestro
Tommaso afterwards made 6 candlesticks,
10 days' work; Giulio some fire-tongs
15 days work. Then he worked for himself
till the 27ᵗʰ May, and worked for me at a
lever till the 18ᵗʰ July; then for himself till
the 7ᵗʰ of August, and for one day, on the
fifteenth, for a lady. Then again for me at
2 locks until the 20ᵗʰ of August.

1461.

¶A dì 23 d'agosto lire 12 da Pulisona;¶
²a dì 14 di marzo 1494 ³venne Galeazzo
a stare con meco ⁴cō patto di dare 5 lire
il mese ⁵per le sue spese, pagādo ogni 14
⁶dì de' mesi.

⁷Dettemi suo padre fiorini 2 di Reno;
⁸A dì 14 di luglio ebbi da Galeazzo
fio⁹rini 2 di Reno.

On the 23ʳᵈ day of August, 12 lire from
Pulisona. On the 14ᵗʰ of March 1494, Galeazzo came to live with me, agreeing to
pay 5 lire a month for his cost paying on
the 14ᵗʰ day of each month.

His father gave me 2 Rhenish florins.
On the 14ᵗʰ of July, I had from Galeazzo
2 Rhenish florins.

1462.

A dì 15 di ²settēbre Gi³vlio comī⁴ciò
la serratu⁵ra del mio ⁶studiolo 14⁷94.

On the 15ᵗʰ day of September Giulio began
the lock of my studio 1494.

1463.

Sabato mattina a dì 3 d'agosto · 1504
venne Iacopo ²tedesco a stare con meco
in casa; convennesi con me³co che io
li facessi le spese per uno carlino ⁴il dì.

Saturday morning the 3ʳᵈ of August 1504
Jacopo the German came to live with me
in the house, and agreed with me that I should
charge him a carlino a day.

1464.

1511.
A dì 26 di settēbre Antonio ²si rupe
la gāba, à a stare 40 dì.

1511.
On the 26ᵗʰ of September Antonio broke
his leg; he must rest 40 days.

1460. 1—7 R. 4. seratu. 11. mezzo uno di.
1461. 1—13 R. 2. facemo. 8. magio. 9. me ĩ. 11. mezo ĩ di per ĩ dona. 13. addi 20.
1462. 1—7 R. 3. galeazo asstare comecho. 4. chō pacto. 7. padre f. 2 di rē. 8. galeazo.
1463. *Written from left to right.* 1. addi . . iachopo. 2. tedesscho asstare chome cho in chasa chonvennesi choṁe. 3. choche
    . . lesspese . . charlino.
1464. 2. addi . . setēbre 2 ruppe.

1464. This note refers possibly to Beltraffio.

E. 1a]   **1465.**

Parti da Milano per Roma a dì 24
²di settēbre 1513 cō Giovā, Francesco ³de'
Melsi, Salai, Lorēzo e il Fāfoia.

I left Milan for Rome on the 24ᵗʰ day of
September, 1513, with Giovanni [2], Francesco
di Melzi [3], Salai, Lorenzo and il Fanfoia.

C. A. 67a; 202a]   **1466.**

A dì 3 di gienajo.

²Benedetto veñe a 17 d'ottobre; ³è
stato con meco due mesi e 13 dì ⁴dell'anno
passato, nel qual tēpo à me⁵ritato li 38 e
S 18 di 8; ⁶ne à avuto lire 26 e S 8, resta
a ⁷avere per l'anno passato lire 12 S 10.

⁸Joatti venne · a dì 8 di settēbre ⁹a 4
ducati al mese, è stato con me ¹⁰mesi · 3
e dì 24; à meritato · li. ¹¹59 S 14 e · 8,
ne à avuto li¹²re 43 S 4; ¹³restà a auere lire
16 ¹⁴per 10 di 8.
¹⁵Benedetto grossoni 24.

On the 3ʳᵈ day of January.

Benedetto came on the 17ᵗʰ of October;
he stayed with me two months and 13 days
of last year [4], in which time he earned
38 lire, 18 soldi and 8 dinari; he had of
this 26 lire and 8 soldi, and there remains
to be paid for the past year 12 lire 10 soldi.

Giodatti (?) came on the 8ᵗʰ day of September, at 4 soldi a month, and stayed with
me 3 months and 24 days, and earned 59 lire
14 soldi and 8 dinari; he has had 43 lire,
4 soldi, there remains to pay 16 lire, 10 soldi
and 8 dinari.

Benedetto, 24 grossoni.

C. A. 260a; 793a]   **1467.**

³Giā Maria 4
⁴Benedetto 4
⁵Gian Pietro 3
⁶Salai 3
⁷Bartolomeo 3
⁸Gherardo 4.

Gian Maria 4,
Benedetto 4,
Gian Pietro [5] 3,
Salai 3,
Bartolomeo 3,
Gherardo 4.

1465. 1. addi. 2. sectēbe . . frāciesscho.
1466. *Written from left to right.* 1. gienaro . dottobre a di 4 elm. 3. asstato cho mecho. 4. dellano . . tēpo ame. 5. vitato li
38 e. 6. anneauto. 8. joatti (?) venne . . settēbr. 9. stato come. 11. ane aun li.
1467. 1. \\\\\nco. 2. \\\\\\\liberdo. 5. gian petro.

1465. 2. *Giovan;* it is not likely that Leonardo
should have called Giovan' Antonio Beltraffio at one
time Giovanni, as in this note and another time Antonio, as in No. 1464 while in No. 1458 l. 16 we find
Giovan'Antonio, and in No. 1436, l. 6 *Beltraffio.* Possibly
the Giovanni here spoken of is Leonardo's less
known pupil Giovan Pietrino (see No. 1467, 5).

2. 3. *Francesco de' Melzi* is often mentioned, see
Nos. 1350.

3. *Salai.* See No. 1519 note.

4. *Lorenzo.* See No. 1351, l. 10 (p. 408). Amoretti
gives the following note in *Mem. Stor. XXIII:* 1505.
*Martedì—sera a dì 14 d'aprile. Venne Lorenzo a stare
con mecho: disse essere d'età d'anni 17 . . a dì 15 del
detto aprile ebbi scudi 25 d'oro dal chamerlingo di Santa
Maria nuova.* This, he asserts is derived from a MS.
marked S, in quarto. This MS. seems to have
vanished and left no trace behind; Amoretti himself
had not seen it, but copied from a selection of

extracts made by Oltrocchi before the Leonardo
MSS. were conveyed to Paris on the responsibility
of the first French Republic. Lorenzo, by this, must
have been born in 1487. The sculptor Lorenzetto
was born in 1490. Amoretti has been led by the
above passage to make the following absurd observations:

*Cotesto Lorenzo, che poi gli fu sempre compagno, al-
meno sin che stette in Italia, sarebb' egli Lorenzo Lotto
bergamasco? Sappiamo essere stato questo valente dipin-
tore uno de' bravi scolari del Vinci (?).*

Il Fāfoia, perhaps a nickname. Cesare da Sesto,
Leonardo's pupil, seems to have been in Rome in these
years, as we learn from a drawing by him in the Louvre.

1466. This seems to be an account for two assis-
tants. The name of the second is scarcely legible.
The year is not given. The note is nevertheless of
chronological value. The first line tells us the date
when the note was registered, January 3ᵈ, and the

C. A. F. 279*a*; 855*a*]   **1468.**

Salai lire 20   Salai, 20 lire,
² Bonifacio lire 2   Bonifacio, 2 lire,
³ Bartolomeo lire 4   Bartolomeo, 4 lire,
⁴ Arrigo lire 15.   Arrigo [Harry], 15 lire.

C. A. 207*a*; 609*a*]   **1469.**

L' Abbaco,   Fiore di Virtù,.   Book on Arithmetic,[1] 'Flowers of Virtue',
Quotations ² Plinio,   Vita de' Filosofi,   Pliny, [2]   'Lives of the Philo-
and notes on   sophers',
books and
authors   ³ Bibbia,   Lapidario,   The Bible, [3]   'Lapidary',
(1469—1508). ⁴ De re militari, Pistole del Filelfo, 'On warfare' [4]   'Epistles of Filelfo',

1468. 2. prefacio. 4. arigo.
1469. 1—25 R. 1. dabacho. 2. filosafi. 3. bibia. 4. pistole. 5. decha. 6. decha . — ciecho dasscholi. 7. decha . — magnio.

observations that follow refer to events of the previous month 'of last year' (*dell' anno passato*). Leonardo
cannot therefore have written thus in Florence where
the year was, at that period, calculated as beginning
in the month of March (see Vol. I, No. 4, note 2).
He must then have been in Milan. What is more
important is that we thus learn how to date the
beginning of the year in all the notes written at
Milan. This clears up Uzielli's doubts: *A Milano
facevasi cominciar l'anno ab incarnatione, cioè il 25
Marzo e a natività, cioè il 25 Decembre. Ci sembra
probabile che Leonardo dovesse prescegliere lo stile che era
in uso a Firenze.* (*Ricerche*, p. 84, note.)

1467. 5. See No. 1465, 2.

1469. The late Marchese Girolamo d'Adda published
a highly valuable and interesting disquisition on this
passage under the title: *Leonardo da Vinci e la sua
Libreria, note di un bibliofilo* (*Milano* 1873. *Ed. di soli
75 esemplari;* privately printed). In the autumn of
1880 the Marchese d'Adda showed me a considerable mass of additional notes prepared for a second
edition. This, as he then intended, was to come
out after the publication of this work of mine. After
the much regretted death of the elder Marchese, his
son, the Marchese Gioachino d'Adda was so liberal
as to place these MS. materials at my disposal for
the present work, through the kind intervention of
Signor Gustavo Frizzoni. The following passages,
with the initials G. d'A. are prints from the valuable
notes in that publication, the MS. additions I have
marked *. I did not however think myself justified
in reproducing here the acute and interesting observations on the contents of most of the rare books
here enumerated.

1. "*La nobel opera de arithmethica ne la qual se tracta
tute cosse amercantia pertinente facta & compilata per
Piero borgi da Veniesia*", in-4°. *In fine*: "*Nela inclita
cita di Venetia a çorni . 2 augusto . 1484 . fu imposto fine
ala presente opera.*" *Segn. a—p . quaderni. V'ha però*

un' altra opera simile di Filippo Calandro, 1491. *È da
consultarsi su quest' ultimo, Federici: Memorie Trevigiane,
Fiore di virtù* : *pag.* 73. "*Libricciuolo composto di bello stile
verso il* 1320 *e più volte impresso nel secolo XV (ristampato
poi anche più tardi).* *Gli accademici della Crusca lo
ammettono nella serie dei testi di lingua.* *Vedasi Gamba,
Razzolini, Panzer, Brunet, Lechi, ecc.* (G. D'A.)

2. "*Historia naturale di C. Plinio Secondo, tradocta di
lingua latina in fiorentina per Christophoro Laudino &
Opus Nicolai Jansonis gallici imp. anno salutis
M . CCCC . LXXVI . Venetiis*" *in-fol.—Diogene Laertio.
Incomincia*: "*El libro de la vita de philosophi etc.: Impressum Venetiis per Bernardinum Celerium de Luere,
1480*", *in-4°* (G. D'A.).

3. "*La Bibia volgare historiata (per Nicolò di Mal-
lermi) Venecia . . . . M . CCCC . LXXI in kalende di
Augusto (per Vindelino de Spira)*" 2 *vol. in-fol. a* 2 *col.
di* 50 *lin .; od altra ediz. della stessa versione del Mal-
lermi, Venetia* 1471, *e sempre*: "*Venecia per Gabriel de
Piero* 1477," *in-fol.;* 2 *vol.; Ottavio Scotto da Modoetia
1481," "Venetia 1487 per Joan Rosso Vercellese," "1490
Giovanni Ragazo di Monteferato a instantia di Luchanthonio
di Giunta, ecc.*"—*Lapidario Teofrasto? Mandebille*: "*Le
grand lapidaire," versione italiana ms.?* . . . *Giorgio Agricola
non può essere, perchè nato nel* 1494, *forse Alberto Magno*:
*de mineralibus. * Potrebbe essere una traduzione del poema
latino (Liber lapidum seu de gemmis) di Marbordio Veterio
di Rennes (morto nel* 1123*) da lui stesso tradotto in francese dal greco di Evao rè d'Arabia celebre medico che
l'aveva composto per l'imperatore Tiberio. Marbodio scrisse
il suo prima per Filippo Augusto rè di Francia. Vi sono
anche traduzioni in prosa.* "*Il lapidario o la forza e la
virtù delle pietre preziose, delle Erbe e degli Animali.*"
(G. D'A.)

4. *Il Vegezio? . . . Il Frontino? . . . Il Cornazzano? . . .
Noi crediamo piuttosto il Valturio. Questo libro doveva
essere uno de' favoriti di Leonardo poichè libro di scienza
e d'arte nel tempo stesso.*

⁵Deca prima,	Della cōseruatiō della sanità,	The first decade, [5]	'On the preservation of health',
⁶Deca terza,	Ciecco d'Ascoli,	The third decade, [6]	Ciecho d'Ascoli,
⁷Deca quarta,	Alberto Magno,	The fourth decade, [7]	Albertus Magnus,
⁸Guidone,	Retorica nova,	Guido, [8]	New treatise on rhetorics,
⁹Piero Cresciētio,	Cibaldone,	Piero Crescentio, [9]	Cibaldone,
¹⁰Quadriregio,	Esopo,	'Quadriregio', [10]	Æsop,

8. gidone . — rettoricha. 9. zibaldone. 10. de 4 regi ⋮ — isopo. 12. imortalita. 15. petrarcha. 17. [deg] de. 19. de-

Le edizioni a stampa sono le seguenti: La prima: "Roberti Valturii de re militari, libri XII ad Sigismundum Pandulfum Malatestam ... Johannes ex Verona oriundus: Nicolai cyrugiae medici filius: Artis impressorie magister: hunc de re militari librum elegantissimum; litteris, & figuratis signis sua in patria primus impressit. An. M. CCCCLXXII." in-fol. senza numerazione.

La seconda edizione è di Bologna, 1483, ristampata a Parigi nel 1532, e poi nuovamente nel 1533. Paolo Ramusio la volgeva in italiano e la pubblicava di nuovo in Verona coi tipi del Paganino, sempre in-fol., 1483 (le stampe di formato più piccolo), e Luigi Meigret la traduceva in lingua francese nel 1555 a Parigi.

"Mediolani per Leon. Pachel & Ulric. Scinzenzeler 1484" in-4°—.

5—7. Abbiamo varie versione delle Deche di Tito Livio, impresse nel secolo XV. Il "Tito Livio volgarizzato (da Ruggiero Ferario) Roma Uldarico Gallo nel 1476," un tom. in 3 vol. in-fol. "Bologna per maestro Antonio da Bologna 1478," piccolo in-fol. "Venetia Octaviano Scoto 1481," pic. in-fol. Venetia Bartholomeo de Alexandria & Andrea de Asula 1485. Bartholomeo de Zanis, 1490, ecc." Vedasi il Manuel del Brunet o meglio il Repertorium dell' Hain ed il Panzer. (G. D'A.)

5. "Arnaldi de Villanova & Johannis Mediolanensis Regimen sanitatis Salernitanum, 1480," in-4° ovvero "Tractato utilissimo circa la conservatione de la sanitate, ecc. composto per il clarissimo ed eccellente philosopho & doctore di medicina messer Ugo Benzo di Siena, ecc.", in-4°, caratteri gotici senza numeri e senza nome di tipografo. In fine: "Exactum est hoc opus Mli (Mediolani) cura & diligentia Petri de Corneno Mediolanensis, 1481. pridie kalendas Junias . Johanne Galeatio Sforcia Vicecomite principe nostro invictissimo dominante." V. Sassi-Argelati. Parte I, vol. I, p. DLXXV. (G. D'A.)

6. L'Acerba (da acervus, cumulo), il noto poema di Francesco Stabili, astrologo nemico dell' Alighieri. Numerose edizioni del secolo XV e XVI. È una vera enciclopedia in versi, ripiena di idee arditissime e che valsero all' infelice pensatore il rogo nel 1347. In questo poema trovansi delineate le origini di molti trovati moderni, ed in particolare della circolazione del sangue, due secoli prima del Michele Serveto. Della prima edizione di Brescia Ferrandus s. a. in-fol. non si conosce che un solo esemplare nella Spenceriana. V. Dibdin. (G. D'A.)

7. "Incomenza el libro chiamato della vita ecc., cōposto per Alberto magno filosofo excellentissimo ecc. Neapoli

Bernardini de gerardinis de Amelia, 1478," in-4°. Altra edizione di "Bologna per Bazalino di Bazaliero, 1493," in-4° got. (G. D'A.)

8. Forse "Guido dalle Colonne" detto anche "da Cauliaco." "Guidonis de Cauliaco Cyrurgia. Turra de Castello recepta atque balnei de Porecta ecc. Venetiis mandato & expensis Octaviani Scoti cura & arte Boneti Locatelli, 1498" in-fol. got.: rarissimo trattato di chirurgia. Ebbe traduzioni francesi parecchie e nel secolo XV anche una versione italiana s. l. n. a. ed un altra in lingua castigliana nel 1498. Vedi: Brunet, Panzer, Hain e Mendez. —L. Guil. de Saona rhetorica nova, S. Albano, in-4° 1480 (Laurentius Guilelmus). È libro de' più rari (Brunet, Tomo V, col. 137). S. Albans, Albani Villa, Verulantium, Borgo inglese nella contea di Hertfordshire, la patria di Bacone Francesco. (G. D'A.)

9. De agricultura. "Il libro della agricultura di Pietro Crescientio," prima edizione di questa versione italiana scritta nel trecento e testo di lingua citato dall' Accademia della Crusca. "Florentie per me Nicholaum Laurentii alemanum diocesis uratislaviensis anno M.CCCC.L.XXVIII." in-fol.—Cibdone: Le materie trattate in questo singolarissimo libretto sono: dei frutti, delle erbe, della flebotomia, della medicina, della luxuria, del bagno, ecc. Almansor-ebn-Isahck fu governatore del Chorassan ed al suo nome intitolava Raze i suoi dodici libri di medicina, che in compendio contengono tutto il sistema medico degli Arabi. Quest'ultima edizione in-4°. Brescia per d. Bapt. de Farfengo, si compone di sei carte s. n. 2. o seg. caratteri semigotici a 2 col. (G. D'A.)

10. Quadriregio (libro chiamato il) di Federigo Frezzi domenicano. È poema religioso-morale-scientifico in terzine. Fra gli imitatori della Divina Comedia è dei migliori "non indegno di gir dietro a Dante" dice il Quadrio. Questo poema è in oggi ingiustamente negletto e quasi sconosciuto, ancorchè in tempi da noi lontani fosse stato nobilmente stampato più volte. Ebbe almeno sette edizioni dal 1481 al 1515, e contiene bellezze di primo ordine. *L'edizione che con molta probabilità era fra i libri di Leonardo riteniamo quello di Milano 1488 Zaroto. Un esemplare all' Ambrosiana fra i quattrocentisti donati da G. Porro; — forse più rara che molte altre.

"Fabulae de Esopo historiate," in-4° fig. senza nota di tempo e di luogo; o l'edizione di Venezia per Manfredo da Monferrato, in-4° fig. 1481 e 1490; od anche: "Brescia per Boninum de Boninis 1487," in-4° con 67 belle figure silografiche; "Roma, Silber 1483," Venetia Manfredo Bo-

[11]Donato,   Salmi,   Donato, [11]   Psalms,

[12]Ivstino,   De Immortalità d'a-   Justinus, [12]   'On the immortality of
              nima,   the soul,

[13]Guidone,   Burchiello,   Guido [13]   Burchiello,

[14]Dottrinale,   Driadeo,   'Doctrinale' [14]   Driadeo,

[15]Morgāte,   Petrarca,   Morgante [15]   Petrarch.

[16]Giovā di Mādiuilla,   John de Mandeville [16]

[17]De onesta voluttà,   'On honest recreation' [17]

[18]Māganello,   Manganello, [18]

[19]Cronica d'Isidoro,   The Chronicle of Isidoro, [19]

[20]Pistole d'Ouidio,   The Epistles of Ovid, [20]

[21]Pistole del Filelfo,   Epistles of Filelfo, [21]

[22]Spera,   Sphere, [22]

nello da Streno, 1497, in-4°, ecc., o più probabilmente: "Aesopi" vita & fabulæ latine cum versione italica & allegoriis Fr. Tuppi impressæ, Napoli, 1483," in-fol., rara edizione ornata di belle vignette incise in legno. Questo Esopo è anche libro di novelle. Nel Catalogo Cicognara abbiamo una minuta descrizione di questo rarissimo volume. (G. D'A.)

11. *"Donatus latine & italice: Impressum Venetiis impensis Johannis Baptistae de Sessa anno 1499, in-4°.— "El Psalterio de David in lingua volgare (da Malermi Venetia nel M.CCCC.LXXVI," in-fol. s. n.* (G. D'A.)

12. *Compare No. 1210, 48.—La versione di Girolamo Squarzafico: "Il libro di Justino posto diligentemente in materna lingua. Venetia ale spese (sic) di Johañe de Colonia & Johañe Gheretzē...1477," in-fol.— "Marsilii Ficini, Theologia platonica, sive de animarum immortalitate, Florentine, per Ant. Misconimum 1482," in-fol., ovvero qualche versione italiana di questo stesso libro, ms.* (G. D'A.)

13. *Forse "la Historia Trojana Guidonis," od il "manipulus" di "Guido da Monterocherii," ma più probabilmente "Guido d'Arezzo," il di cui libro: "Micrologus, seu disciplina artis musicae" poteva da Leonardo aversi ms.; di questi ne esistono in molto biblioteche, e fu poi impresso nel 1784 dal Gerbert.*

Molte sono le edizione dei sonetti di Burchiello Fiorentino, impresse nel secolo XV. La prima e più rara e recercata: " Incominciano li sonetti, ecc. (per Christoforo Arnaldo)", in-4° senza numeri, richiami o segnature, del 1475, e fors' anche del 1472, secondo Morelli e Dibdin, ecc. (G. D'A.)

14. *Versione italiana det "Doctrinal de Sapience" di Guy de Roy, e fors' anche l'originale in lingua francese.—*

Di Pulci Luigi, benchè nell' edizione: "Florentiae 1479" in-4° si dica: "Il Driadeo composto in rima octava per Lucio Pulcro," Altre ediz. del secolo XV, "Florentie Miscomini 1481, in-4°, Firenze, apud S. Jacob. de Ripoli, 1483," in-4° e "Antoni de Francesco, 1487," in-4° e Francesco di Jacopo 1489," in-4° ed altre ancora di Venezia e senza alcuna nota ecc. (G. D'A.)

15. *Una delle edizioni del Morgante impresse nel secolo XV, ecc.—*

Quale delle opere di Francesco Petrarca, sarebbe malagevole l'indovinare, ma probabilmente il Canzoniere. (G. D'A.)

16. *Sono i viaggi del cavaliere "Mandeville," gentiluomo inglese. Scrisse il suo libro in lingua francese. Fu stampato replicatamente nel secolo XV in francese, in inglese ed in italiano,* ed in tedesco; del secolo XV ne annoverano forse più di 27 edizioni, di cui ne conosciamo 8 in francese, quattro in latino, sei in tedesco e molte altre in volgare.* (G. D'A.)

17. *Il Platina (Bartolomeo Sacchi) la versione italiana "de la honesta voluptate, & valetudine (& de li obsonnii) Venetia (senza nome di tipografo) 1487," piccolo in-4° gotico.* (G. D'A.)—Compare No. 844, 21.

18. *Il Manganello: Satira eccessivamente vivace contro le donne ad imitazione della Sesta di Giovenale. Manganello non è soltanto il titolo del libricino, sua ben anche il nome dell' autore ch'era un "milanese". Di questo libercolo rarissimo, che sembra impresso a Venezia dallo Zoppino (Nicolò d'Aristotile detto il), senza data, ma dei primissimi anni del secolo XVI, e forse più antico, come vedremo in appresso, non se ne conoscono fra biblioteche pubbliche e private che due soli esemplari in Europa.* (G. D'A.)

19. *"Cronica desidero", sembra si deggia leggere piuttosto "cronico disidoro"; ed in questo caso s'intenderebbe la "cronica d'Isidoro" tanto in voga a quel tempo "Comenza la Cronica di Sancto Isidoro menore con alchune additione cavate del testo & istorie de la Bibia & del libro di Paulo Oroso . . . . Impresso in Ascoli in casa del reverendo misser Pascale . . . . . per mano di Guglielmo de Linis de Alamania M.CCCC.LXXVII" in-4° di 157 ff. È il primo libro impresso ad Ascoli e l'edizione principe di questa cronica in oggi assai rara. Non lo è meno l'edizione di Cividal del Friuli, 1480, e quella ben anche di Aquila, 1482, sempre in-4°. Vedasi Panzer, Hain, Brunet e P. Dechamps.* (G. D'A.)

20. *"Le pistole di Ovidio tradotte in prosa. Napoli Sixt. Riessinger", in-4°, oppure: "Epistole volgarizzate 1489," in-4° a due col. "impresse ne la cita (sic) di Bressa per pre: Baptista de Farfengo," (in ottave) o: "El libro dele Epistole di Ovidio in rima volgare per messere Dominico de Monticelli toschano. Brescia Farfengo," in-4° got. (in rima volgare), 1491, ed anche la versione di Luca Pulci. Firenze, Mischomini, 1481, in-4°.* (G. D'A.)

21. See l. 4.

22. *"Jo: de Sacrobusto," o "Goro Dati," o "Tolosano da Colle" di cui molteplici edizioni del secolo XV.* (G. D'A.)

[23]Facietie di Poggio,   The Jests of Poggio[23]
[24]De chiromātia,   Chiromancy, [24]
[25]Formulario di pistole.   Formulary of letters, [25]

S. K. M. III. 87 _b_]   **1470.**

Nonio Marciello, [2]Festo Pōpeo, [3]Marco Varrone.

Nonius Marcellus, Festus Pompeius, Marcus Varro.

F. o"]   **1471.**

Piāta d'Elefante d'India che à Antonello Merciaio [2]da maestro Maffeo; perchè 7 anni la ter[3]ra alza e 7 abbassa;—[4]cerca di Vetruvio [5]fra cartolaj.

Map of Elephanta in India which Antonello Merciaio has from maestro Maffeo;—there for seven years the earth rises and for seven years it sinks;—Enquire at the stationers about Vitruvius.

Leic. 13 _a_]   **1472.**

Vedi de naui messer Battista [2]e Frontino de' aquidotti.

See 'On Ships' Messer Battista, and Frontinus 'On Acqueducts' [2].

. A. 376 _b_; 1168 _a_]   **1473.**

Anasagora; [2]ogni cosa viē da ogni cosa, —ed ogni cosa si fa ogni cosa, [3]e ogni cosa torna in ogni cosa; perchè ciò ch'è nelli elemē[4]ti è fatto da essi elemēti.

Anaxagoras: Every thing proceeds from every thing, and every thing becomes every thing, and every thing can be turned into every thing else, because that which exists in the elements is composed of those elements.

sidero. 23. pogio.
1470. 3. marcho.   **1471.** dellefau\\\\ dindia chella. 2. mafeo . . annila tera . . abassa.
1472. 1. meser batista.
1473. 1. anasaghora. 2. chosa viē. 3. chogni . . ogni chosa. 4. effatto.

23. _Tre edizioni delle facezie del Poggio abbiamo in lingua italiana della fine del secolo XV, tutte senza data. "Facetie de Poggio fiorentino traducte de latino in vulgare ornatissimo," in-4°, segn. a—e in caratteri romani; l'altra: "Facetie traducte de latino in vulgare," in-4°, caratteri gotici, ecc._ (G. D'A.)

24. *_"Die Kunst Cyromantia etc. in tedesco. 26 ff. di testo e figure il tutte esequito sù tavole di legno verso la fine del secolo XV da Giorgio Schapff". Dibdin, Heinecken, Sotheby e Chatto ne diedero una lunga descrizione; i primi tre accompagnati da fac-simili. La data 1448 che si legge alla fine del titolo si riferisce al periodo della composizione del testo, non a quello della stampa del volume benche tabellario. Altri molti libri di Chiromanzia si conoscono di quel tempo e sarebbe opera vana il citarli tutti._ (G. D'A.)

25. _Miniatore Bartolomeo. "Formulario de epistole vulgare missive e responsive, & altri fiori de ornati parlamenti al principe Hercule d'Esti ecc. composto ecc. Bologna per Ugo di Rugerii," in-4°, del secolo XV. Altra edizione di "Venetia Bernardino di Novara," 1487" e "Milano per Joanne Angelo Scinzenzeler 1500," in-4°._ (G. D'A.)

Five books out of this list are noted by Leonardo in another MS. (Tr. 3): _donato, — lapidario, — plinio, — abacho, — morgante._

1470. Nonius Marcellus and Sextus Pompeius Festus were Roman grammarians of about the fourth century A. D. Early publications of the works of Marcellus are: _De proprietate sermonis, Romae_ (about 1470), and 1471 (place of publication unknown). _Compendiosa doctrina, ad filium, de proprietate sermonum._ Venice, 1476. BRUNET, _Manuel du libraire_ (IV, p. 97) notes: _Le texte de cet ancien grammairien a été réimprimé plusieurs fois à la fin du XVe siècle, avec ceux de Pomponius Festus et de Terentius Varro. La plus ancienne édition qui réunisse ces trois auteurs est celle de Parme,_ 1480 . . . _Celles de Venise,_ 1483, 1490, 1498, _et de Milan,_ 1500, _toutes in-fol., ont peu de valeur._

1472. 1. Compare No. 1113, 25.

2. _Vitruvius de Arch., et Frontinus de Aquedoctibus._ Florence, 1513.—This is the earliest edition of Frontinus.—The note referring to this author thus suggests a solution of the problem of the date of the Leicester Manuscript.

L. 94*b*]

1474.

Archimede del uescouo ³di Padoua.

The Archimedes belonging to the Bishop of Padua.

W. 191*a*]

1475.

Archimede à dato la ²☐ra d'una figura late³rata e nō del cerchio; ¶⁵adunque Ar-⁶chimede non ⁷quadrò mai figu⁸ra di lato curuo; ¶ ⁹cioè quadrò il cer¹⁰chio meno una portio¹¹ne tanto minima quā¹²to lo intelletto possa immaginare, cioè quanto il pūto visibile.

Archimedes gave the quadrature of a polygonal figure, but not of the circle. Hence Archimedes never squared any figure with curved sides. He squared the circle minus the smallest portion that the intellect can conceive, that is the smallest point visible.

Br. M. 279*b*]

1476.

Chi auesse trovato l'ultima vali²tudine della bōbarda in tutte ³sua varietà, e presētato tale ⁴segreto alli Romani, cō ⁵qual prestezza avrebbero conquista⁶to ogni terra e superato ogni ese⁷rcito, e qual premio era, ⁸che potesse equipararsi a tanto ⁹benifitio! Archimede ā¹⁰corachè lui auesse grādemēte dan¹¹neggiati li Romani alla spugna¹²tione di Siracusa, nō li fu mai ¹³mācato l'offerta di grādissimi pre¹⁴mi da essi Romani, e nella pre¹⁵sa di Siracusa fu cercato dilige¹⁶temēte d'esso Archimemide, e tro¹⁷vato morto; ne fu fatto maggiore ¹⁸lamētatione nel senato e ¹⁹popolo Romano, che s'egli'auessi²⁰no perso tutto il loro esercito, e non ²¹mancarono d'onorarlo di sepoltu²²ra e di statua, della quale fu capo ²³Marco Marcello; e dopo la seconda ²⁴ruina di Siragusa fu ritrouato ²⁵da Catone la sepoltura d'esso Archi²⁶mede nel²⁷le ruine d'un tenpio; onde Catone fe-²⁸cie rifare il tēpio e la sepoltura ²⁹onoratissima . . . ³⁰e di questo si scriue ³¹auere detto Catone ³²non si gloriar di ³³nessuna cosa tan³⁴to, quanto d'auere ³⁵onorato esso Archi³⁶mede d'esso orna³⁷mēto.

If any man could have discovered the utmost powers of the cannon, in all its various forms and have given such a secret to the Romans, with what rapidity would they have conquered every country and have vanquished every army, and what reward could have been great enough for such a service! Archimedes indeed, although he had greatly damaged the Romans in the siege of Syracuse, nevertheless did not fail of being offered great rewards from these very Romans; and when Syracuse was taken, diligent search was made for Archimedes; and he being found dead greater lamentation was made for him by the Senate and people of Rome than if they had lost all their army; and they did not fail to honour him with burial and with a statue. At their head was Marcus Marcellus. And after the second destruction of Syracuse, the sepulchre of Archimedes was found again by Cato [25], in the ruins of a temple. So Cato had the temple restored and the sepulchre he so highly honoured . . . . Whence it is written that Cato said that he was not so proud of any thing he had done as of having paid such honour to Archimedes.

1474. uescouo.　　　**1475.** 1. data. 3. rato. 6. chimenide. 10. cio meno î. 11. tanta. 12. inmaginare coe q"u"to.
1476. 1. auessi trovata. 4. romani [qual] cō. 5. presteza arebero conquisa. 7. ecqual. 8 potessi . . attanto. 10. chellui auessi grādemēte da. 11. negati . . allasspugna. 12. serausa. 13. lo fere li grādissimi. 15 serausa fu cerco diligē. 17. magore. 18. nel [po] senato. 19. romane chessegli. 20. e no. 21. mancorono. 22. distaua. 23. dopo la 2ᵃ. 24. seragosa. 25. catone. 26. mede e [esso catone la retro] ne. 28. ella. 29. onoratissimar\|\|\|\|. 30. scriu\|\|\|\|. 31. cat\|\|\|\|. 32. signoriar\|\|\|\|. 33. cosa t\|\|\|\|. 34. daue\|\|\|\|. 35. ar\|\|\|\|. 36. orn\|\|\|\|.

1474. See No. 1421, l. 3, 6 and Vol. I, No. 343.
1475. Compare No. 1504.
1476. Where Leonardo found the statement that Cato had found and restored the tomb of Archimedes, I do not know. It is a merit that Cicero claims as his own (Tusc. V, 23) and certainly with a full right to it. None of Archimedes' biographers—not even the diligent Mazzucchelli, mentions any version in which Cato is named. It is evidently a

slip of the memory on Leonardo's part. Besides, according to the passage in Cicero, the grave was not found *'nelle ruine d'un tempio'*—which is highly improbable as relating to a Greek—but in an open spot (H. MÜLLER-STRÜBING).—See too, as to Archimedes, No. 1417.

Leonardo says somewhere in MS. C.A.: *Architronito è una macchina di fino rame, invenzion d'Archimede* (see '*Saggio*', p. 20).

I.2 82 *b*]

1477.

Aristotele 3° della fisica, e Alberto e Tomaso, ²e li altri de risaltatione, j̄ 7ª della fisica, ³de cielo e mv̄do.

Aristotle, Book 3 of the Physics, and Albertus Magnus, and Thomas Aquinas and the others on the rebound of bodies, in the 7th on Physics, on heaven and earth.

M. 62 *a*]

1478.

Dice Aristotile che se vna potentia move v̄ ²¶ corpo vn tanto spatio in tanto tēpo, la me³desima potentia moverà la metà di quel ⁴corpo due tanti di spatio nel medesimo tēpo. ¶

Aristotle says that if a force can move a body a given distance in a given time, the same force will move half the same body twice as far in the same time.

C. A. 284 *b*; 865 *b*]

1479.

Aristotile nel terzo dell' etica: ²l' uomo è degnio di lode e di uituperio solo ³nelle · cose · che sono j̄ sua potestà ⁴di fare e di nō fare.

Aristotle in Book 3 of the Ethics: Man merits praise or blame solely in such matters as lie within his option to do or not to do.

C. A. 121 *a*; 375 *a*]

1480.

¹Dicie · Aristotele · che ogni cosa desidera mātenere la sua natura.

Aristotle says that every body tends to maintain its nature.

K.² 3 *b*]

1481.

De incremēto ²Nili, opera d' Ari³stotile piccola.

On the increase of the Nile, a small book by Aristotle.

W. A. IV. 151 *b*]

1482.

Avicenna vole ²che l' anima partorisca ³l' anima, e 'l corpo il corpo, ⁴e ogni mēbro per rata.

Avicenna will have it that soul gives birth to soul as body to body, and each member to itself.

F. 0″]

1483.

Avicenna de' liquidi.

Avicenna on liquids.

1477. 1. fisicha. 2. elli . . fisicha.
1479. 1. eticha. 3. imai (?) nelle chose chessono.
1480. 2. la gravita per essere etc. etc.
1483. 1. avicena.

1478. 1. chesse. 4. dua tanti spatio.

1481. 3. pichola.

1482. 1. aviciena. 2. chellanima partorischa.

1481. *De inundatione Nili*, is quoted here and by others as a work of Aristotle. The Greek original is lost, but a Latin version of the beginning exists (Arist. Opp. IV p. 213 ed. Did. Par.).

In his quotations from Aristotle Leonardo possibly refers to one of the following editions: *Aristotelis libri IV de coelo et mundo; de anima libri III; libri VIII physicorum; libri de generatione et corruptione; de sensu et sensato . . . omnia latine, interprete Averroe. Venetiis* 1483 (first Latin edition). There is also a separate edition of *Liber de coelo et mundo*, dated 1473.

1482. *Avicenna*, see too No. 1421, l. 2.

Br. M. 71 *b*]   **1484.**

Rugiero Bacone fatto in istanpa.   Roger Bacon, done in print.

C. A. 139*b*; 419*b*]   **1485.**

Cleomete filosofo.   Cleomedes the philosopher.

Tr. 4]   **1486.**

Cornelio Celso.

²Il soṁo · bene · è la sapiēza ·; il soṁo male · è il dolore · del corpo; ɟmperochè, essēdo ³noi conposti · di 2 cose, cioè · d' a- nima · e di corpo, ⁴delle quali la prima · è migliore ·, la peggiore · è il corpo; la sapi- ētia è ⁵della miglior parte ·; il sommo male è della peggior parte e pessima; Ottima cosa è nell'animo la sapiēza, così è pessima ⁶cosa nel corpo il dolore; ⁷adūque, sicome il sommo male è 'l corporal dolore, così la sapiētia è dell'animo ⁸il soṁo bene, cioè dell'uomo sagio, e nissvna altra cosa è da cōparare a questa.

Cornelius Celsus.

The highest good is wisdom, the chief evil is suffering in the body. Because, as we are composed of two things, that is soul and body, of which the first is the better, the body is the inferior; wisdom belongs to the better part, and the chief evil belongs to the worse part and is the worst of all. As the best thing of all in the soul is wisdom, so the worst in the body is suf- fering. Therefore just as bodily pain is the chief evil, wisdom is the chief good of the soul, that is with the wise man; and nothing else can be compared with it.

Tr. 57]   **1487.**

Demetrio solea dire non essere differē- tia · dalle parole e voci dell'inperiti ignio- rāti, ²che sia da suoni e strepiti · cavsati dal ventre ripieno di superfluo vēto; ³e questo nō senza cagiō dicea, īperochè lui nō re- putava esser differētia da qual parte ⁴costoro mādassino · fuora la voce, o dalle parti īferiori o dalla bocca, ⁵che l'una e l'altra era di pari valimēto e sustātia.

Demetrius was wont to say that there was no difference between the speech and words of the foolish and ignorant, and the noises and rumblings of the wind in an inflated stomach. Nor did he say so without reason, for he saw no difference between the parts whence the noise issued; whether their lower parts or their mouth, since one and the other were of equal use and importance.

1484. 1. Rugieri bachō.   **1485.** 1. filosafo.

1486. 2. ella sapiēza . . iperoche. 3. corp\\\ [lanima e meliore cel corpo. 4. pegiore . . chorpo. 5. somo . . pegior. 7. somo . . choporal . . chosi. 8. delonsagio enīvna . . chosa e da a questa cōparare.

1487. 1. diferētia . . evoce. 2. chessia da soni e strepidi. 3. ecquesto. 3. īperochellui . . diferētia. 4. parte . . bocha. 5. chel- luna ellaltra.

1484. The earliest printed edition known to Brunet of the works of Roger Bacon, is a French trans- lation, which appeared about fourty years after Leo- nardo's death.

1485. *Cleomede.* A Greek mathematician of the IVᵗʰ century B. C. We have a Cyclic theory of Me- teorica by him. His works were not published before Leonardo's death.

1486. *Aulus Cornelius Celsus,* a Roman physician, known as the Roman Hippocrates, probably contem- porary with Augustus. Only his eight Books 'De Medicina', are preserved. The earliest editions are: *Cornelius Celsus, de medicina libr. VIII.,* Milan 1481 Venice 1493 and 1497.

1487. Compare Vol. 1, No. 10.

S. K. M. III. 93*a*]

1488.

Maestro Stefano [2]Caponi, medico, [3]sta alla piscina, [4]à Euclide 'de põ[5]deribus'.

Maestro Stefano Caponi, a physician, lives at the piscina, and has Euclid *De Ponderibus*.

K.[2] 2*a*]

1489.

5º Euclide. [2]Prima definitione ¶parte è quantità di quantità [3]minore della maggiore, cōciosia[4]chè la minore numeri la mag[5]giore;
[6]Parte propriamēte detta è quella [7]ch'è moltiplicatiua, cioè che, multi[8]plicata per alcuno numero, ricōpo[9]ne il suo tutto con precisione;
[10]Parte comune aggregatiua è que[11]lla, la quale, quantunche volte si pi[12]glia più o meno del suo tutto, [13]ond'è neciessario che coll'ajuto d'al[14]tra quantità diuersa rifaccia il suo [15]tutto, e perciò è detta aggregatiua.
[16]Seconda definitione. ¶La multiplicità è maggiore della mi[17]nore, quando la minore misura qu[18]ella;
[19]Di sopra difinimmo il minore estremo, [20]e qui si difinisce il maggiore; La parte

5th Book of Euclid. First definition: a part is a quantity of less magnitude than the greater magnitude when the less is contained a certain number of times in the greater.
A part properly speaking is that which may be multiplied, that is when, being multiplied by a certain number, it forms exactly the whole. A common aggregate part . . . . .

Second definition. A greater magnitude is said to be a multiple of a less, when the greater is measured by the less.
By the first we define the lesser [magnitude] and by the second the greater is defined. A part is spoken

K.[2] 2*b*]

1490.

relatiuamente è detta al tutto, [2]e in questi due estremi sta tutta [3]la relazione di quegli, e chiamã[4]si mvltiplici.

of in relation to the whole; and all their relations lie between these two extremes, and are called multiples.

S. K. M. III. 16*b*]

1491.

Dice Ippocrate che la origine della [2]nostra semenza diriva dal cielabro · e dal [3]polmone · e' testiculi di nostri gie[4]nitori ·, dove si fa l'ultima decotione; [5]e tutti li altri mēbri porgono · per sudatio[6]ne la loro sustãtia a esso seme, per[7]chè non si dimostra alcuna via, [8]che a essa semēza peruenire possino.

Hippocrates says that the origin of men's sperm derives from the brain, and from the lungs and testicles of our parents, where the final decocture is made, and all the other limbs transmit their substance to this sperm by means of expiration, because there are no channels through which they might come to the sperm.

1488. 3. pesscina. 4. a heuclide.
1489. 2. p[a] difinitione *is written on the margin*. 3. magore concosia. 4. chella. 5. gore. 6. ditta ecque. 7. che moltiplichatiua coe. 10. cumune agreghatiua cqu"e". 12. plia [ma fa] piu . . tutt"o". 13. chollaiuto. 14. rifaca. 15. pero e detto agregatiua. 16. 2[a] difinitione *is written on the margin*. La multiplici e magore. 19. difinimo . . extremo. 20. ecqui si difinissce il maggiore.
1490. 2. quessti duextremi. 4. mvltiplici.
1491. 1. ipocrate chella. 2. nosstra senza. 3. ettestichuli di nosstri. 4. dovessi . . dechotione. 5. ettutti . . porgano. 6. susstãtia. 7. dimosstra alchuna.

1491. The works of Hippocrates were printed first after Leonardo's death.

1492.

Lucretio nel terzo · delle cose · naturali ‖ le mani, vnghie e dēti furono ²le armi · deli ātichi (165);

³Acora vsano per stēdardo · di vno fasciculo d'erba · legato a vna pertica (167).

Lucretius in his third [book] 'De Rerum Natura'. The hands, nails and teeth were (165) the weapons of ancient man.

They also use for a standard a bunch of grass tied to a pole (167).

1493.

Ammiano Marcellino afferma, essere abbruciati ²7 cēto mila volumi di libri nella pugnia Alessādrina ³al tēpo di Givlio Cesare.

Ammianus Marcellinus asserts that seven hundred thousand volumes of books were burnt in the siege of Alexandria in the time of Julius Cesar.

1494.

Dice Mōdino che li muscoli che alza²no li diti del piede stanno nella parte ³siluestra della coscia, e poi soggiugne ⁴che 'l dosso del piede non à muscoli, ⁵perchè la natura li volle fare legieri ac⁶ciochè fussino facili al movimēto, per⁷chè se fussino carnosi, sarebber più ⁸gravi; e qui la speriētia mostra . . .

Mondino says that the muscles which raise the toes are in the outward side of the thigh, and he adds that there are no muscles in the back [upper side] of the feet, because nature desired to make them light, so as to move with ease; and if they had been fleshy they would be heavier; and here experience shows . . .

1495.

Del'error di quelli che vsano ²la pratica sanza sciētia;—³vedi primo ⁴la poética ⁵d'Oratio.

Of the error of those who practice without knowledge;—[3] See first the 'Ars poetica' of Horace [5].

1492. 1. naturale. 3. istēdare diono.
1493. 1. amiano . . abrusiati. 2. 7 cēto M"a" [di] volumi . . nela [spu] pugnia. 3. ivlio.
1494. 1. chelli musscoli. 2. piedi. 3. cosscia . . sogugne. 4. piedi . . musscoli. 5. le volle . . legieri a. 6. coche fussi facile.
　　7. fussi carnose sarebbe. 8. grave.
1495. 1—5 R. 1. cror. 4. poetria.

1492. *Lucretius, de rerum natura libri VI* were printed first about 1473, at Verona in 1486, at Brescia in 1495, at Venice in 1500 and in 1515, and at Florence in 1515. The numbers 165 and 167 noted by Leonardo at the end of the two passages seem to indicate pages, but if so, none of the editions just mentioned can here be meant, nor do these numbers refer to the verses in the poems of Lucretius.

1493. *Ammiani Marcellini historiarum libri qui extant XIII*, published at Rome in 1474.

1494. "*Mundini anatomia. Mundinus, Anothomia* (sic). *Mundini praestantissimorum doctorum almi studii ticiensis* (sic) *cura diligentissime emendata. Impressa Papiae per magistrum Antonium de Carcano* 1478," *in-fol.; ristampata:* "*Bononiae Johan. de Noerdlingen,* 1482," *in-fol.;* "*Padova*

per Mattheum Cerdonis de Vuindischgretz, 1484," *in-4°;* "*Lipsia,* 1493," *in-4°;* "*Venezia,* 1494," *in-4° e ivi* "1498," *con fig. Queste figure per altro non sono, come si è preteso, le prime che fossero introdotte in un trattato di Notomia. Nel 'fasciculus Medicinae' di Giovanni Ketham, che riproduce l'Anatomia' del Mundinus, impresso pure a Venezia da J. e G. de Gregoriis,* 1491, *in-fol., contengonsi intagli in legno (si vogliono disegnati non già incisi da Andrea Mantegna) di grande dimensione, e che furono più volte riprodotti negli anni successivi. Quest' edizione del "fasciculus" del* 1491, *sta fra nostri libri e potrebbe benissimo essere il volume d'Anatomia notato da Leonardo.* (G. D'A.)

1495. A 3—5 are written on the margin at the side of the title line of the text given, entire as No. 19

S. K. M. III. 3*b*]   **1496.**

¶Eredi di maestro Giovā ²Ghirīgallo ànno opere del Pe³lacano. ¶

The heirs of Maestro Giovanni Ghiringallo have the works of Pelacano.

B. 8 *a*]   **1497.**

Catapulta, come dice Nonio e Plinio, è vno strumēto ritrovato da quelli ecc.

The catapult, as we are told by Nonius and Pliny, is a machine devised by those &c.

Ash. II. 12 *b*]   **1498.**

Ò ritrovato nele Storie delli Spagnioli · come · nelle guerre da loro ²avute colli Inglesi fu Archimede Siracusano, il quale ī quel tēpo ³dimorava ī cōpagnia di Ecliderides, rè de' Cirodastri; Il quale nella ⁴pugnia marittima ordinò ·, che i navili fussino con lunghi arbori, ⁵e sopra le lor gaggie ⁶collocò · vna · antennetta di lūghezza di 40 piè, e ¹/₃ ⁷piè di grossezza; nel' una stremità era vna ancora picciola, nel' al⁸tra · vn contrapeso; al' ancora era appiccato 12 piedi ⁹di catena · e dopo essa catena tāta corda ¹⁰che perveniua dalla catena al nascimēto della gaggia ch'era attaccata con una cordella; ¹¹da esso nascimēto mādaua ī basso īsino al nascimēto dell'arbore, ¹²dou'era collocato vn argano fortissimo, e lì era fermo ¹³il nascimēto d'essa corda; Ma per tornare all'ufitio d'essa machina ¹⁴dico che sotto a detta ācora era vno foco, il quale con sommo stre¹⁵pito gittava ī basso i sua razzi e pioggia di pegola īfocata, li qua¹⁶li piovēdo sopra alla gaggia costrignievano li omini, che lì erano, a ¹⁷abbādonare detta gaggia, ōde calato l'ancora colle acut . . . . . . ¹⁸quella cauava ai labri della gaggia; e subito era tagliata la corda posta ¹⁹al nascimēto della gaggia a sotenere quella corda ch'ādava ²⁰dal' ācora al'argano, e tirādo il navilio . . .

I have found in a history of the Spaniards that in their wars with the English Archimedes of Syracuse who at that time was living at the court of Ecliderides, King of the Cirodastri. And in maritime warfare he ordered that the ships should have tall masts, and that on their tops there should be a spar fixed[6] of 40 feet long and one third of a foot thick. At one end of this was a small grappling iron and at the other a counterpoise; and there was also attached 12 feet of chain; and, at the end of this chain, as much rope as would reach from the chain to the base of the top, where it was fixed with a small rope; from this base it ran down to the bottom of the mast where a very strong spar was attached and to this was fastened the end of the rope. But to go on to the use of his machine; I say that below this grappling iron was a fire[14] which, with tremendous noise, threw down its rays and a shower of burning pitch; which, pouring down on the [enemy's] top, compelled the men who were in it to abandon the top to which the grappling-iron had clung. This was hooked on to the edges of the top and then suddenly the cord attached at the base of the top to support the cord which went from the grappling iron, was cut, giving way and drawing in the enemy's ship; and if the anchor—was cast . . .

1496. 1. maesstro jovā. 2. ghirīgallo ano. 3. lachano.
1498. 1. chome . . guere dalloro. 2. ingilesi fu darchimede. 4. cholunghi albori. 5. essopra . . gagie. 6. chollocho . . antenetta di lūgezza. 7. grosseza. 8. vcontrapeso . . era apicato. 9. e[ttā]dopo . . chorda. 10. anassimēto . . gagia. *The following words are written on the margin:* chera attaca etacata cōuna cordella. 11. nasimēto . . nassimēto delo albore. 12. vn [albore] rgano. 13. nassimēto. 14. chon somo. 15. pido . . sua raza e piogia. 16. ala gagia chostrignieva. 17. abādonare . . gagia . . chalato lancora chole achuti rāpo (?). 18. gagia essubito. 19. [assostenere] a noscimēto dela gagia . . quela chorda. 20. navilio demi (?) essi (?) poneva (?) dancora (?).

1497. *Plinius,* see No. 946.
1498. Archimedes never visited Spain, and the names here mentioned cannot be explained. Leonardo seems to quote here from a book, perhaps by some questionable mediæval writer. Prof. C. Justi writes to

me from Madrid, that Spanish savants have no knowledge of the sources from which this story may have been derived.

6. Compare No. 1115.
14. Compare No. 1128.

Leic. 14 *b*]   **1499.**

Teofrasto, del flusso e riflusso [2]e delle   Theophrastus on the ebb and flow of the
vortici e de' acque.   tide, and of eddies, and on water.

Ash. II. 11 *b*]   **1500.**

Trifone Alessādrino, il quale duceua   Tryphon of Alexandria, who spent his life
sua età in Apolonia città d'Albania (163).   at Apollonia, a city of Albania (163).

K.3 29 *b*]   **1501.**

Messer Vīcentio Aliprādo, che sta   Messer Vincenzio Aliprando, who lives
[2]presso all'osteria dell'Orso, à il Vetru[3]uio   near the Inn of the Bear, has Giacomo An-
di Iacomo Andrea.   drea's Vitruvius.

L. 53 *b*]   **1502.**

Dice Vetruvio che i modelli piccoli [2]non   Vitruvius says that small models are of
sono in nessuna operatione confor[3]mi al-   no avail for ascertaining the effects of large
l'effetto de' grandi; la qual co[4]sa qui disotto   ones; and I here propose to prove that
intendo dimostra[5]re tale conclusione · essere   this conclusion is a false one. And chiefly
falsa, [6]e massimamente allegando quelli   by bringing forward the very same argument
me[7]desimi termini, coi quali lui cō[8]clude   which led him to this conclusion; that is, by
tale · sententia, cioè colla [9]sperientia · della   an experiment with an auger. For he proves
triuella, per la qua le [10]lui mostra essere fatto   that if a man, by a certain exertion of
dalla po[11]tentia dell'omo vno buso di cier-   strength, makes a hole of a given diameter,
[12]ta quantità di diametro, e che poi [13]vn   and afterwards another hole of double the
buso di dupplicato diametro nō [14]sarà fatto   diameter, this cannot be made with only
da dupplicata potentia [15]di detto uomo, ma   double the exertion of the man's strength,
da molto piv; all[16]a qual cosa si può molto   but needs much more. To this it may very
ben rispō[17]dere, allegando che il trivello   well be answered that an auger

L. 53 *a*]   **1503.**

di dupplicata figura non può   of double the diameter cannot be
[2]essere mosso da dupplicata po[3]ten-   moved by double the exertion, be-
tia, conciosiachè la superfitie [4]d'ogni   *a*   cause the superficies of a body of
corpo di figura simile è di dup[5]plicata   the same form but twice as large has
quantità alla superfitie, di [6]quadrupli-   *n*   four times the extent of the superficies
cata quātità l'una [7]all'altra, come   of the smaller, as is shown in the two
mostrano le due [8]figure · *a* · e · *n*.   figures *a* and *n*.

1499. teofrassto de frusso e rifrusso. 2. vertigine.
1501. aliplādo. 2. .uetru.
1502. 1. picho. 2. inessuna. 3. dall effecto. 4. ḍisocto . . dimosstra. 6. que me. 8. coe colla. 9. essperiētia . . trinella la qua.
        10. mosstra. 11. fatto. 12. diamitro. 13. diametro. 14. potenti"a". 15. homo. 16. si po . . risspo. 17. trivell"o".
1503. 1. duplichata . . non po. 3. concosia chella. 4. e di du. 6. quadruplata. 7. mosstrā le due.

1499. The Greek philosophers had no opportunity   1500. Tryphon of Alexandria, a Greek Gram-
to study the phenomenon of the ebb and flow of   marian of the time of Augustus. His treatise πάθη
the tide and none of them wrote about it. The move-   λέξεως appeared first at Milan in 1476, in Constantin
ment of the waters in the Euripus however was to   Laskaris's Greek Grammar.
a few of them a puzzling problem.

G. 95 a]   **1504.**

DELLA □ᵃ DEL CIRCULO, E CHI FU IL PRIMO   OF SQUARING THE CIRCLE, AND WHO IT WAS
        CHE LA ²TROVÒ A CASO.   THAT FIRST DISCOVERED IT BY ACCIDENT.

³Vetruvio, misurando le miglia colle   Vitruvius, measuring miles by means of
molte intere revolutioni ⁴delle rote che   the repeated revolutions of the wheels which
movono i carri, distese nelli suoi stadi   move vehicles, extended over many Stadia
molte linie ⁵circūferētiali del circolo di tali   the lines of the circumferences of the circles
rote; Ma lui le inparò dalli ani⁶mali motori   of these wheels. He became aware of them
di tali carri; Ma nō conobbe quello essere   by the animals that moved the vehicles. But
il mezzo ⁷a dare il □ᵗᵒ equale a vn circolo,   he did not discern that this was a means of
il quale prima per Archimede Siragusano   finding a square equal to a circle. This was
⁸fu trovato: chè la multiplicatione del semi- first done by Archimedes of Syracuse, who
diamitro d'un circolo colla ⁹metà della sua   by multiplying the second diameter of a circle
circūferētia facieva vn quadrilatero rettilinio,   by half its circumference produced a rectan-
¹⁰equale al circolo.   gular quadrilateral equal figure to the circle[10].

Ash. II. 10b]   **1505.**

Virgilio dicie era lo scudo biāco e sanza   Virgil says that a blank shield is devoid of
laude, perchè apresso ²a li Attici le uere   merit because among the people of Athens the
laude cōfermate da testimoni da . . . . . .   true recognition confirmed by testimonies . . .

B. 58 a]   **1506.**

J̄ Vjtolone sono 805 · conclusioni in   In Vitolone there are 805 conclusions
prospettiva.   [problems] in perspective.

Br. M. 79b]   **1507.**

Vitolone in Sā Marco.   Vitolone, at Saint Mark's.

1504. 1. de □ᵃ del ce chi . . chella. 2. achaso. 3. cholle. 4. movano i charri . . nelle sue stadi. 5. circūferētiali del c. di . . mallui. 6. charri . . chonobbe . . mezo. 7. a vn c il quale p"a" per . . siraghusaro. 8. chella . . dun c. cholla. 9. circhūferētia. 10. al c.
1505. 1. sanza lalde. 2. atici lalde chōfermate ta testimoni da\\\\\noma. 3. colegati ētraversati e per molificatiō cōgivte(?).
1506. uitolone he 805 chonchisioni in prosspettiva.   **1507.** marcho.

1504. *Vitruvius,* see also Nos. 1113 and 343.
10. Compare No. 1475.
1505. The end of the text cannot be deciphered.
1506. (*Witelo, Vitellion, Vitellon*) *Vitellione. È da vedersi su questo ottico prospettico del secolo XIII Luca Pacioli, Paolo Lomazzo, Leonardo da Vinci, ecc. e fra i moderni il Graesse, il Libri, il Brunet, e le Memorie pubblicate dal principe Boncompagni, e 'Sur l'orthographe du nom et sur la patrie de Witelo (Vitellion) note de Maximilien Curtze, professeur à Thorn', ove sono descritti i molti codici esistenti nelle biblioteche d'Europa. Bernardino Baldi nelle sue 'Vite de' matematici', manoscritto presso il principe Boncompagni, ha una biografia del Vitellione. Questo scritto del Baldi reca la data 25 agosto 1588. Discorsero poi di lui Federigo Risnerio e Giovanni di Monteregio nella prefazione dell'Alfagrano, Giovanni Boteone, Girolamo Cardano, 'De subtilitate', che nota gli errori di Vitellione. Visse, secondo il Baldi, intorno all' anno 1269, ma secondo il Reinoldo fioriva nel 1299, avendo dedicata la sua opera ad un frate Guglielmo di Monteca, che visse di que' tempi.*

Intorno ad un manoscritto dell' ottica di Vitellione, citato da Luca Pacioli v'ha un secondo esemplare del Kurtz, con aggiunte del principe Boncompagni, e le illustrazioni del cav. Enrico Narducci. Nel 'Catalogo di manoscritti' posseduti da D. Baldassare de' principi Boncompagni, compilato da esso Narducci, Roma, 1862, sotto al n. 358, troviamo citato: Vitellio, 'Perspectiva', manoscritto del secolo XIV. La 'Prospettiva di Vitelleone' (sic) Thuringo-poloni è citata due volte da Paolo Lomazzo nel Trattato dell' arte della pittura. Vitellio o Vitello o Witelo. Il suo libro fu impresso in foglio a Norimberga nel 1535; la seconda edizione è del 1551, sempre di Norimberga, ed una terza di Basilea, 1572. (See Indagini Storiche . . . sulla Libreria-Visconteo-Sforzesca del Castello di Pavia . . . per cura di G. D'A., Milano 1879. P. I. Appendice p. 113. 114).*

1507. Altro codice di cotesta 'Prospettiva' del Vitolone troviamo notato nel 'Canone bibliographico di Nicolò V', conservato alla Magliabecchiana, in copia dell'originale verosimilmente inviato dal Parentucelli a Cosimo de' Medici (Magliab. cod. segn. 1 VII, 30 carte da 193 a 198). Proviene dal Convento di San Marco e lo aveva trascritto frate Leonardo Scruberti fiorentino, dell'ordine dei predicatori che fu anche bibliotecario della Medicea pubblica in San Marco (See Indagini Storiche . . . per cura di G. D'A. Parte I, p. 97).

K.² 12 *b*]　　　　　　　　　　**1508.**

Come Xenofonte pro²pose il falso.　　　How this proposition of Xenophon is false.
³Se a cose disequali si leuano cose ⁴dis-　　If you take away unequal quantities from
equali, le quali sieno nella mede⁵sima pro-　unequal quantities, but in the same propor-
portione ecc.　　　　　　　　　　　　　tion, &c.

B. 4 *a*]　　　　　　　　　　　**1509.**

Inventories
and accounts
(1509—1545). A dì 28 d'aprile ebbi da Marchesino ·　On the 28th day of April I received from
lire 103 e S. 12.　　　　　　　　　　the Marchesino 103 lire and 12 dinari.

Ash. I. 1 *a*]　　　　　　　　　　**1510.**

A dì 10 di luglio 1492 ī fiorī di rē　　On the 10th day of July 1492 in 135 Rhe-
　　　　　　135 l. 445　　　　　　　nish florins　　　　　　　　l. 445
²ī dinari di 6 S　　　　l. 112 S. 16　　in dinari of 6 soldi　　　l. 112 S 16
³ī dinari di · S 5 e ¹/₂　l. 29 S. 13　　in dinari of 5¹/₂ soldi　　l. 29 S 13
⁴ī dinari 9 d'oro e scudi 3 l. 53　　　9 in gold　　and 3 scudi l. 53
⁵　　　　　　　　　l. 811 ī somma.　　　　　　　　　　　　l. 811 in all.

S. K. M. III. 47 *a*]　　　　　　　　**1511.**

A dì · primo · di febraio · lire 1200.　　On the first day of February, lire 1200.

S. K. M. III. 43 *a*]　　　　　　　　**1512.**

126 passi è la sala ²di corte, larga　　The hall towards the court is 126 paces
braccia 27.　　　　　　　　　　　　long and 27 braccia wide.

H.3 77 *a*]　　　　　　　　　　**1513.**

La gronda stretta sopra la sala ²lire 30;　The narrow cornice above the hall lire 30.
³le grōde sotto · a di questa ·; sièno,　　The cornice beneath that, being one for
ciascuno ⁴quadro per se, lire · 7, e di spesa　each picture, lire 7, and for the cost of blue,
tra azzurro, ⁵oro, biacca ·, giesso, indaco e　gold, white, plaster, indigo and glue 3 lire;
colla · lire 3; ⁶di tēpo giornate . 3;　　time 3 days.
⁷le storie sotto a esse grōde coi suoi　　The pictures below these mouldings with
⁸pilastri lire 12 per ciascuna;　　　　their pilasters, 12 lire each.
⁹stimo la spesa fra smalto, azzurro e　　I calculate the cost for smalt, blue and
oro, ¹⁰e altri colori · lire una e ¹/₂;　　gold and other colours at 1¹/₂ lire.
¹¹le giornate stimo 3 · tralla investigati-　The days I calculate at 3, for the inven-
one ¹²del cōponimēto, pilastrello e altre　tion of the composition, pilasters and other
cose.　　　　　　　　　　　　　　things.

1508. 1. zenofonti. 3. si leua. 4. qual sieno. 6. sima pro"ne''.　　**1509.** addi.
1510. 2. dinar. 3. dinari. 4. ī di 9 doroesscudi. 5. soma.
1512. 1. ella. 2. larga br 27.
1513. 1. strecta. 3. socto a di quessta. 4. azurro. 5. oro br biache . . indacho echolla. 7. grōda chosua. 8. pilastre . .
　ciasschuna. 9. azuro e a oro. 10. lire î e 1/2. 11. invesstichatiō.

1508. Xenophon's works were published several　is a blank space after *d'aprile.*—Marchesino Stange
times during Leonardo's lifetime.　　　　　　was one of Lodovico il Moro's officials. — Campare
1509 Instead of the indication of the year there　No. 1388.

H.3 76 b]   1514.

Itē per ciascuna volta · sola · lire 7
²di spesa tra azzurro e oro · lire ·   3 ¹/₂
³di · tēpo · giorni 4.
⁴per le finestre   lire   1ᵃ e ¹/₂
⁵il cornicione sotto alle finestre S 16 il
    braccio
⁶item per 24 storie romane   lire 14 l'una
⁷i filosofi   lire 10
⁸i pilastri, vn ōcia d'azzurro   soldi 10
⁹in oro   soldi 15
¹⁰sono lire   2 e ¹/₂.

Item for each vault   7 lire
outlay for blue and gold   3¹/₂
time, 4 days
for the windows   1¹/₂
The cornice below the windows 16 soldi
per braccio
item for 24 pictures of Roman history
    14 lire each
The philosophers   10 lire
the pilasters, one ounce of blue 10 soldi
for gold   15 soldi
Total   2 and ¹/₂ lire.

H.3 81 b]   1515.

Grōda di sopra   lire 30
²grōda di sotto   lire 7
³le storie l'una per l'altra   lire 13.

The cornice above   lire 30
The cornice below   lire 7
The compositions, one with another lire 13

H.3 94 b]   1516.

Salai lire 6 . . . ³soldi 4 . . . ⁶soldi 10 in
⁷vna ca⁸tena;
⁹14 di marzo ò avuto lire 13 ¹⁰S 4,
resta lire 16.

Salai, 6 lire . . . 4 soldi . . . 10 soldi for
a chain; —
On the 14ᵗʰ of March I had 13 lire S. 4;
16 lire remain.

H.² 16 b]   1517.

Quāte braccia è alto il piā delle
mvra?
    ²123 braccia
    ³Quāt'è larga la sala?
    ⁴Quāt'è larga la ghirlanda?
    ⁵30 ducati.
    ⁶A dì 29 di gienaro 1494.
    ⁷Panno per calze lire 4   S   3
    ⁸soppaño   S   16
    ⁹fattura   S   8
    ¹⁰Salai   S   3
    ¹¹anello di diaspro   S   13
    ¹²pietra stellata   S   11
    ¹³Caterina   S   10
    ¹⁴Caterina   S   10.

How many braccia high is the level of
the walls?—
    123 braccia
    How large is the hall?
    How large is the garland?
    30 ducats.
    On the 29ᵗʰ day of January, 1494
    cloth for hose   lire 4   S   3
    lining   S   16
    making   S   8
    to Salai   S   3
    a jasper ring   S   13
    a sparkling stone   S   11
    to Caterina   S   10
    to Caterina   S   10

1514. 1. chiasscuna voltaiola lire. 2. azuro. 5. cornicone . . il br. 6 ite. 7. i filosafi. 8. ipila vnōcia dazuro. 10. simolire.
1515. 3. perllaltra.
1516. 1—10 R. 1. 6 in vna. 2. rev(?). 3. soldi 4 nv. 4. varco eli. 5. goni. 7. nona. 9. mazo.
1517. 1. br e. 2. R. — 122 br. 4. girlando. 5—14 R. — 6. addi. 7. chalze. 11. di diasspis.

H.² 33 a]   **1518.**

La rota	lire 7		The wheel	lire 7
²labro	li 10		the tire	lire 10
³scudo	li 4		the shield	lire 4
⁴carello	li 8		the cushion	lire 8
⁵poli del' albero	li 2		the ends of the axle-tree	lire 2
⁶letto e telajo	li 30		bed and frame	lire 30
⁷canale	li 10.		conduit	lire 10

S. K. M. II.² 4 a]   **1519.**

Petrosemolo	parti 10		Parsley	10 parts
²mēta	parte 1		mint	1 part
³serpillo	parte 1		thyme	1 part
⁴aceto . . . . e sale poco;			Vinegar . . . and a little salt two pieces	
⁵canavaccio 2 pezzi per Salai.			of canvas for Salai.	

S. K. M. II.¹ 0']   **1520.**

Martedì si cōprò il uino da mattina, ²venerdì a dì 4 di settēbre il simile.

On Tuesday I bought wine for morning [drinking]; on Friday the 4th day of September the same.

S. K. M. II.¹ 94 b]   **1521.**

Piscina . . . . all' ospedale, — ²ducati 2, — ³fave, — ⁴melica biāca, — ⁵melica rossa, — ⁶panico, — ⁷miglio, — ⁸fagiuòli, — ⁹fave, — ¹⁰pisegli.

The cistern . . . . at the Hospital, — 2 ducats, — beans, — white maize, — red maize, — millet, — buckwheat, — kidney beans, — beans, — peas.

S. K. M. II.¹ 95 a]   **1522.**

SPESE PER LA SOTTERATURA DI CATERINA.   EXPENSES OF THE INTERMENT OF CATERINA.

²Libbre 3 di cera	S 27		For the 3 lbs of tapers	27 S
³per lo cataletto	S 8		For the bier	8 S
⁴palio sopra il cataletto	S 12		A pall over the bier	12 S
⁵portatura · e portura di croce	S 4		For bearing and placing the cross	4 S
⁶per la postatura · del morto	S 8		For bearing the body	8 S
⁷per 4 preti e 4 cherici	S 20		For 4 priests and 4 clerks	20 S
⁸canpana ·, libri, spūga	S 2		Bell, book and sponge	2 S
⁹per li sotteratori	S 16		For the gravediggers	16 S
¹⁰all' ātiano	S 8		To the senior	8 S
¹¹per la liciētia · ali ufitiali	S 1		For a license from the authorities	1 S
	106			106 S
¹²il medico	S 2		The doctor	2 S
¹³zucchero e cādele	S 12		Sugar and candles	12 S
	120			120 S

1518. 1—7 R. 6. ettelaro.
1519. 1. petrose milo parte. 3. srpilo pa. 4. aceto peneo essale. 5. canovacci 2 prsi.
1521. 1. pisciñ damozania (?) allospedadi. 4. meliga. 5. meliga. 8. fagioli.
1522. 1. socteratura. 2. In libr. 3. 3. catalectò. 4. sopra catalecto. 7. cerici. 8. libr. 9. socteratori.\ 10. allātiano. 12. in medico. 13. zuchero.

1519. This note, of about the year 1494, is the earliest mention of Salai, and the last is of the year 1513 (see No. 1465, 3). From the various notes in the MSS. he seems to have been Leonardo's assistant and keeper only, and scarcely himself a painter. At any rate no signed or otherwise authenticated picture by him is known to exist. Vasari speaks somewhat doubtfully on this point.

1520. This note enables us to fix the date of the Manuscript, in which it is to be found. In 1495 the 4th of September fell on a Friday; the contents of the Manuscript do not permit us to assign it to a much earlier or later date (Compare No. 1522, and Note).

1522. See Nos. 1384 and 1517.

L. 94 a]   **1523.**

La cappa di Salai a dì 4 d'aprile 1497.
[2] 4 braccia di panno argiētino   l. 15 S 4
[3] velluto verde per ornare   l.   9 S
[4] bindelli   l.   S 9
[5] magliette   l.   S 12
[6] manifattura   l.   1 S 5
[7] bindello · per dināzi   li · S 5
[8] pūta
                                    —————————
[9] ecco di suo grossoni · 13   li 26 S 5
[10] Salai ruba li soldi.

Salai's cloak, the 4th of April 1497.
4 braccia of silver cloth   l. 15 S 4
green velvet to trim it   l.   9 S —
binding   l. — S 9
loops   l. — S 12
the making   l.   1 S 5
binding for the front   l. — S 5
stitching
                                   —————————
here are 13 grossoni of his   l. 26 S 5
Salai stole the soldi.

I.[2] 1 b]   **1524.**

Lunedì cōprai braccia 4 di tela, lire 13
S 14 [2] e ¹/₂, a dì 17 di ottobre 1497.

On Monday I bought 4 braccia of cloth
lire 13 S 14¹/₂ on the 17th of, October 1497.

Br. M. 229 b]   **1525.**

Ricordo come a dì 8 d'aprile 1503 io
Leonardo da Vinci prestai a Vāte mi²nia-
tore ducati 4 d'oro in oro; portògli Salai
e li dette in sua propia [3] mano; disse ren-
dermile infra lo spatio di 40 giorni;

[4] Ricordo come nel sopradetto giorno
io rēdei a Salai ducati 3 d'oro, i quali
[5] disse volersene fare vn paio di calze ro-
sate co' sua fornimēti, e li restai a dare
[6] ducati 9 ·, posto che lui ne de' dare a me
ducati 20, cioè 17 prestai li a Milano e 3
a Venezia;

[7] Ricordo come io diedi a Salai braccia
21 di tela da fare camicie, a S. 10 il braccio, [8] le quali li diedi a dì 20 d'aprile
1503.

Memorandum. That on the 8th day of
April 1503, I, Leonardo da Vinci, lent to
Vante, miniature painter 4 gold ducats, in
gold. Salai carried them to him and gave
them into his own hand, and he said he would
repay within the space of 40 days.

Memorandum. That on the same day I
paid to Salai 3 gold ducats which he said
he wanted for a pair of rose-coloured
hose with their trimming; and there remain
9 ducats due to him—excepting that he owes
me 20 ducats, that is 17 I lent him at Milan,
and 3 at Venice.

Memorandum. That I gave Salai 21 braccia of cloth to make a shirt, at 10 soldi
the braccio, which I gave him on the
20th day of April 1503.

C. A. 70 b; 208 b]   **1526.**

La mattina di Sc͞o Pietro a dì 29 di
giugno 1504 [2] tolsi ducati 10, de' quali ne
diedi uno a Tomaso, mio [3] famiglio, per
spēdere;

On the morning of San Peter's day,
June 29th, 1504, I took 10 ducats, of which
I gave one to Tommaso my servant to
spend.

1523. 2. 4 br di. 9. ecci di suo. 10. P.   1524. 1. br 4.
1525. 1. chome. 2. innoro . . elli detti. 3. losspatio . . gorni. 4. assalai. 5. elliresstai addare. 6. duchati 9 possto chellui . .
   amme . . coe 1 [6] 7 prestali . . e [4] 3 a vinegia. 7. assalai br 21 . . daffare camice a S 10 il bracco. 8. la queli . . addi.
1526. 1—22. *Written from left to right.* 1. pitro addi . . gugno. 2. î attomaso. 3. isspēdere. 4. fr î assalai . . isspendere in

---

1525. With regard to Vante or Attavante, the miniature painter (not Nanni as I formerly deciphered
this name, which is difficult to read; see *Zeitschrift
für Bild. Kunst*, 1879, p. 155), and Vasari, Lives of Frate
Giovanni da Fiesole, of Bartolommeo della Gatta,
and of Gherardo, *miniatore*. He, like Leonardo, was

one of the committee of artists who, in 1503, considered
the erection and placing of Michel Angelo's David. The
date of his death is not known; he was of the
same age as Leonardo. Further details will be found
in '*Notizie di Attavante miniatore, e di alcuni suoi lavori*'
(Milanese's ed. of Vasari, III, 231—235).

⁴lunedì mattina fiorino uno a Salai per spendere in casa,

⁵martedì tolsi fiorino uno per mio spendere,

⁶mercoledì sera fiorino uno a Tomaso, inãti cena,

⁷sabato mattina fiorino uno a Tomaso,

⁸lunedì mattina fiorino uno mãco S 10,

⁹giouedì a Salai fiorino uno mãco S 10,

¹⁰pel giubbone fiorino uno,

¹¹pel giubbone }
¹²e per berretta } fr. 2,

¹³al calzaiolo fr. 1°,

¹⁴a Salai fr. 1°;

¹⁵Venerdì mattina a dì 19 di luglio fiorino uno mãco S 6, restò mi fr. 7 e 22 in cassa;

¹⁶martedì a dì 23 di luglio fiorino uno a Tomaso,

¹⁷lunedì mattina a Tomaso fiorino uno,

¹⁸[mercoledì mattina fiorino uno a Tomaso]

¹⁹giouedì mattina a dì p° d'agosto fiorino uno a Tomaso,

²⁰domenica 4 d'agosto fiorino uno;

²¹venerdì a dì 9 d'agosto 1504 ²²tolgo ducati 10 dalle casse.

On Monday morning 1 florin to Salai to spend on the house.

On Thursday I took 1 florin for my own spending.

Wednesday evening 1 florin to Tommaso, before supper.

Saturday morning 1 florin to Tommaso.

Monday morning 1 florin less 10 soldi.

Thursday to Salai 1 florin less 10 soldi.

For a jerkin, 1 florin.

For a jerkin }
And a cap   } 2 florins.

To the hosier, 1 florin.

To Salai, 1 florin.

Friday morning, the 19th of July, 1 florin, less 6 soldi. I have 7 fl. left, and 22 in the box.

Tuesday, the 23rd day of July, 1 florin to Tommaso.

Monday morning, to Tommaso 1 florin.

[Wednesday morning 1 fl. to Tommaso.]

Thursday morning the 1st day of August 1 fl. to Tommaso.

Sunday, the 4th of August, 1 florin.

Friday, the 9th day of August 1504, I took 10 ducats out of the box.

Br. M. 271 b]

1527.

1504.

²Venerdì a dì 9 d'agosto 1504 tolsi fiorini 10 d'oro ³ . . . . venerdì a dì 9 d'agosto grossoni quindici cioè fr. 5 S 5 ⁴. . . . dato a me fr. 1° d'oro a dì 12 d'agosto, ⁵. . . . a dì 14 d'agosto grossoni 32 a Tomaso, ⁶e a dì 18 del detto grossoni 5 a Salai, ⁷a dì 8 di settēbre grossoni 6 al fattore ⁸per spendere cioè il dì della donna; ⁹a dì 16 di settembre detti grossō 4 ¹⁰a Tomaso in domenica.

1504.

On the 9th day of August, 1504, I took 10 florins in gold[2] . . . . [3] on Friday the 9th day of August fifteen grossoni that is fl. 5 S 5 . . . . given to me 1 florin in gold on the 12th day of August[4] . . . . . on the 14th of August, 32 grossoni to Tommaso. On the 18th of the same 5 grossoni to Salai. On the 8th of September 6 grossoni to the workman to spend; that is on the day of our Lady's birth. On the 16th day of September I gave 4 grossoni to Tommaso: on a Sunday.

chasa. 5. fr î. 6. mercholedi. 6. fr î attomaso . . cene. 7. fr î attomaso. 8. fr î mãcho. 9. gonedi assalai fr î mãcho. 10. gubone fr î. 11. gubone. 14. assalai. 15. vene "rdi" [sabato] mattina "a di 19 di luglo" fr 1° mãcho. 16. luglo fr 1° attomaso. 17. attomaso fr 1°. 18. [mercholedi mattin . . fr 1° attomaso]. 19. govedi "mattina" addi . . fr 1° attomaso. 20. domenicha . . fr 1°. 21. addi. 22. tolgho.

1527. *Written from left to right.* 3. anne dato [addi] venerdi . . coe. 4. m\\\\\ dato ame fri doro addi 12 d'agosto. 5. an\\\\\\to addi . . 3 (?) atto maso. 6. addi . . assalai. 8. isspendere coe. 9. addi. 10. attomaso indomenicha.

1527. In the original, the passage given as No. 1463 is written between lines 2 and 3 of this text, and it is possible that the entries in lines 3 and 4 refer to thè payments of Jacopo Tedesco, who is there mentioned. The first words of these lines are very illegible.

7. *Al fattore.* Il Fattore, was, as is well known,

the nick-name of Giovanni Franceso Penni, born in Florence in 1486, and subsequently a pupil of Raphael's. According to Vasari he was known by it even as a boy. Whether he is spoken of in this passage, or whether the word Fattore should be translated literally, I will not undertake to decide. The latter seems to me more probably right.

F. 0"]   **1528.**

A dì d'ottobre 1508 ebbi scudi 30; ²13 ne prestai a Salai per cōpiere la dota alla ³sorella, e 17 ne restò a me.

On the day of October, 1508, I had 30 scudi; 13 I lent to Salai to make up his sister's dowry, and 17 I have left.

C. A. 189 a; 565 a]   **1529.**

Ricordo de' danari che io ho avuto dal rè per mia prouisione dal luglio 1508 insino ²aprile prossimo 1509: prima scudi 100·, poi 70, e poi 50, e poi ³20, e poi 200 fiorini a 48 S. per l'uno.

Memorandum of the money I have had from the King as my salary from July 1508 till April next 1509. First 100 scudi, then 70, then 50, then 20 and then 200 florins at 48 soldi the florin.

C. A. 76 a; 223 a]   **1530.**

Sabato a dì 2 di marzo ²ebbi da Scā Maria Nova ³ducati 5 d'oro, restò ⁴ve ne 450, de' quali 2 ne ⁵detti il medesimo dì a Salai, ⁶che me li avea prestati.

Saturday the 2ⁿᵈ day of March I had from Santa Maria Novella 5 gold ducats, leaving 450. Of these I gave 2 the same day to Salai, who had lent them to me.

C. A. 253 b; 748 a]   **1531.**

¶ Giovedì, a dì 8 di givgnio ²tolsi grossoni 17 S 18; ¶ ³giovedì detto da mattina a Salai ⁴per spendere S 22.

Thursday, the eighth day of June, I took 17 grossoni, 18 soldi; on the same Thursday in the morning I gave to Salai 22 soldi for the expenses.

W. XXXII.]   **1532.**

A Salai grossoni 4, e 1 braccio ²di velluto 5 lire, e ¹/₂, ³sapere S · 10, maglie d'argiēto; ⁴Salai S 14 per bindelli, ⁵fattura della cappa S 25.

To Salai 4 grossoni, and for one braccio of velvet, 5 lire, and ¹/₂; viz. 10 soldi for loops of silver; Salai 14 soldi for binding, the making of the cloak 25 soldi.

C. A. 17 b; 67 b]   **1533.**

¶ Detti a Salai lire ²93 · S 6; ³ò ne avuti lire 67, ⁴resta dare 26 · S 6. ¶

I gave to Salai 93 lire 6 soldi, of which I have had 67 lire and there remain 26 lire 6 soldi.

1528. 2. assalai. 3. amme.
1529. 1. Richordo de dinari . . da dal luglio.   **1530.** 5. assalai.
1531. 1. giove. 3. assalai. 4. perisspēdere.
1532. 1. assalai . . 4 e e 1 br. 2. br 5 lire he ¹/₂. 3. velluto br 5 lire he ¹/₂. 3. sapr.
1533. 1. assalai. 3. one auiti.

1529. Compare No. 1350 and 1561.
1530. See '*Conto corrente di Leonardo da Vinci con lo Spedale di S. Maria Nuova*' [1500 a 1507, 1513—1520] published by G. UZIELLI, *Ricerche intorno a Leonardo*

da Vinci, Firenze, 1872, pp. 164, 165, 218 and 219. The date here given by Leonardo does not occur in either of the accounts.
1532. Compare No. 1523.

C. A. 312 *b*; 949 *b*]   **1534.**

A Salai	S 42			To Salai	S 42		
²dozzine 2 di stringe	S 8			2 dozen of laces	S 8		
³in fogli	S 3 d. 8			for papers	S 3 d 8		
⁴vn pajo di scarpe	S 14			a pair of shoes	S 14		
⁵in veluto	S 14			for velvet	S 14		
⁶spada e coltello	S 21			a sword and knife	S 21		
⁷in barbiere	S 11			to the barber	S 11		
⁸a Paolo per una	S 20			to Paolo for a	S 20		
⁹per dire la uentura	S 6			For having his fortune told	S 6		

Br. M. 272 *b*]   **1535.**

Venerdì mattina	in pane	S . . d		On Friday morning,	bread	S . . d
²fiorino uno a Salai	in uino	S . . d		one florin to Salai to	wine	S . . d
per spē³dere; avuto	in oua	S . . d		spend; 3 soldi re-	grapes	S . . d
S 3	⁴in funghi	S . . d		ceived	mushrooms	S . . d
	⁵in frutti	S . . d			fruit	S . . d
	⁶in crusca	S . . d			[6] bran	S . . d
	⁷in barbiere	S . . d			at the barber's	S . . d
	⁸in scarpe	S . . d			for shoes	S . . d

C. A. 116 *b*; 395 *a*]   **1536.**

Giovedi mattina fiorino uno.   On Thursday morning one florin.

C. A. 212 *b*; 627 *b*]   **1537.**

¶Dì di Scō Ambrosio S 36 da mat-   On Saint Ambrose's day from the morning
tina in giovedò.¶   to Thursday 36 soldi.

C. A. 258 *a*; 784]   **1538.**

I danari ch'io ò avuto da Ser Matteo: The moneys I have had from Ser Matteo;
²prima grossoni 20, poi 13 volte 3 f., e di   first 20 grossoni, then on 13 occasions 3 f.
poi grossoni 61, ³e poi 3, di poi 3 · 3 ·;   and then 61 grossoni, then 3, and then 3 · 3;
S 46 grossoni 12.   46 soldi 12 grossoni.

E. 0″]   **1539.**

Ī carta	S 18		For paper	S 18	
²ī tela	S 30		for canvas	S 30	
³i carta	S 10 d 19		for paper	S 10 d 19	
⁴ somma	73		Total	S 73	

1534. 1. assalai. 2. dozine o . . string. 4. pa disscarpe 8 apago[o pr"a" croetta.
1535. 1—8. *Written from left to right.* 2. fr. ī assalai perispē. 3. auta, — innova. 5. frutte. 6. crussca. 8. iniscarpe.
1536. 1. govedi . . fr ī.   **1537.** abrosio.
1538. 1. chio auuto. 2. pr grossoni.

1535. 6. Compare Nos. 1545, l. 4 and 5, with similar entries for horse's fodder.

Br. M. 227 a]   **1540.**

Libbre · 20 · d'azzurro di Magnia, vn ducato la libbra	l.	80	S	d	20 pounds of German blue, at one ducat the pound	lire	80	S	d

Libbre · 20 · d'azzurro di
Magnia, vn ducato la libbra l. 80 S d
²libbre · 60 di biacca S..
la libbra lire 15 S d
³libbre 1½ S. 4 la libbra lire o6 S d
⁴cinabro libbre 2, S 18
la libbra lire o1 S 16 d
⁵verde libbre 6, S 12
la libbra lire o3 S 12 d
⁶giallo libbre 4, a S 12
la libbra lire o2 S o8 d
⁷minio libbra una, a
S 8 la libbra lire oo S o8 d
⁸aiorica libbre 4, S 2
la libbra lire oo S o8 d
⁹oguria libbre sei, a S
uno la libbra lire oo S o6 d
¹⁰nero in pietra S 2 la
libbra per 20 lire o2 S oo d
¹¹ciera per fare le stelle
libbre 29 a S la libbra lire S d
¹²olio per dipingere
libbre 4 a soldi 5 la libbra lire 10 S d
¹³in somma lire 120:
S 18 sanza l'oro 18
¹⁴stagnio per appiccare l'oro 120 18
    58

20 pounds of German
blue, at one ducat the pound lire 80 S d
60 pounds of white, S ..
the pound lire 15 S d
1½ pound at 4 S the pound lire 6 S d
2 pounds of cinnabar at
S 18 the pound lire 1 S 16 d
6 pounds of green at S 12
the pound lire 3 S 12 d
4 pounds of yellow at S 12
the pound lire 2 S 8 d
1 pound of minium at S 8
the pound lire o S 8 d
4 pounds of . . . . . at S 2
the pound lire o S 8 d
6 pounds of ochre at S 1
the pound lire o S 6 d
black . . . at S 2 the pound
for 20 lire 2 S o d
wax to make the stars
29 pounds at S—the pound lire o S o d
40 pounds of oil for paint-
ing at 5 soldi the pound lire 10 S o d
Altogether lire 120 d 18
without the gold. 18
tin for putting on the gold 120 18
    58

Br. M. 42 b]   **1541.**

Due scuri grandi e vna piccina, 8 cuc-
chiai d'ottone; ²4 touaglie, 2 guardanappe,
15 tovagliolini, 2 tovagliole, canava 2, ³2
invoglie, 3 paia di lenzuola, 2 paie nove
e uno vecchio.

Two large hatchets and one very small
one, 8 brass spoons, 4 tablecloths, 2 towels,
15 small napkins, 2 coarse napkins, 2 coarse
cloths, 2 wrappers, 3 pairs of sheets, 2 pairs
new and 1 old.

Br. M. 212 a]   **1542.**

Letto	7	o S.		Bed	7	o S
²anello	7	o		ring	7	o
³stovigli	2	5		crockery	2	5
⁴ortolano	1	2		gardener	1	2
⁵mainardo	2	8		. . . . .	2	8
⁶fachini	2	1		porters	2	1
⁷bichieri	1	o		glasses	1	
⁸ in ferri da foco	3	6		fuel	3	6
⁹in serrature	1			a lock	1	

1540. 1—14. *Written from left to right.* 1. libra, libre *throughout for* libbra; libbre dazurro. 2. biaccha S. [6] [7] o la libra.
4. libr "2" 22 "4". 7. libre î a. 8. [aivricha] "aioricha". 9. aquiria libr sei a î la. 12. dipigniere libre 4 o [per] soldi.
13. insoma. 14. apichare.
1541. 1. scure grande . . chuchiai. 2. tovagli . . guardanape 14 "15" tovaglolini 2 tovaglole canava. 3. nove e î vechio.
1542. 5. mainard"o". 8. inferi da focho.

H.3 89*b*]　　　　　　　　**1543.**

Peltro novo,	3 · paji di lēzuola	New tin-ware	3 pairs of sheets
² 6 · scodellini,	di 4 teli l' uno,	6 small bowls,	each of 4 breadths,
³ 6 scodelle	2 lenzoli piccoli	6 bowls,	2 small sheets,
⁴ 2 piattegli grandi	2 tovaglie e ¹/₂	2 large dishes,	2 tablecloths and ¹/₂,
⁵ 2 piattegli mezzani,	16 mātili	2 dishes medium size,	16 coarse cloths,
⁶ 2 piatteletti,	8 camicie	2 small ones	8 shirts,
⁷ peltro vechio	9 pannetti	Old tin-ware	9 napkins,
⁸ 3 scodellini	2 sciugatoj	3 small bowls,	2 hand-towels.
⁹ 4 scodelle		4 bowls,	
¹⁰ 3 quadretti		3 square stones,	
¹¹ 2 scodellini		2 small bowls,	
¹² uno scodellone		1 large bowl,	
¹³ uno piattello		1 platter,	
¹⁴ 4 cādellieri		4 candlesticks,	
¹⁵ 1 candelliere piccolo.		1 small candlestick.	

C. A. 132*a*; 402*a*]　　　　　　**1544.**

Calze	S 40		Hose	S 40		
² paglia	S 60		straw	S 60		
³ biada	S 42		wheat	S 42		
⁴ vino	S 54		wine	S 54		
⁵ pane	S 18		bread	S 18		
⁶ carne	S 54		meat	S 54		
⁷ uova	S 5		eggs	S 5		
⁸ salata	S 3		salad	S 3		
⁹ barbiere	S 2 d 6		the Barber	S 2 d 6		
¹⁰ cavalli	S 1.		horses	S 1		

C. A. 26*a*; 87*a*]　　　　　　**1545.**

Domenica				Sunday			
² carne	S 10 d			meat	S 10 d		
³ vino	S 12 d			wine	S 12 d		
⁴ crusca	S 5 d 4			bran	S 5 d 4		
⁵ erba	S 10 d			herbs	S 10 d		
⁶ ricotta	S 4 d 4			buttermilk	S 4 d 4		
⁷ melone	S 3 d			melon	S 3 d		
⁸ pane	S 3 d 1			bread	S 3 d 1		
⁹ lunedì · ¶	9	8		Monday	S 9	8	
¹⁰ ....le	S 6 d			.....	S 6 d		
¹¹ vino	S 12 d			wine	S 12 d		
¹² crusca	S 9 d 4			bran	S 9 d 4		
¹³ ricotta	S 4 d 4			buttermilk	S 4 d 4		
¹⁴ erba	S 8 d			herbs	S 8 d		

1543. 1. para. 3. picolo. 6. piattelecti. 8. sciugatto. 12. î. 13. î. 15. picolo.
1544. 7. hova.
1545. 1—25 P. 1. domenic S. 6. ricote. 7. mcloroi(?). 13. ricote. 23. melonne. 24. cruvsca.

¹⁵martedì	...	S		d			
¹⁶carne	S	o	d	8			
¹⁷vino	S	12	d				
¹⁸pane	S	3	d				
¹⁹crusca	S	5	d	4			
²⁰erba	S	8	d				
²¹mercoledì							
²²vino	S	5	d				
²³melone	S	2	d				
²⁴crusca	S	5	d	4			
²⁵erba	S	8	.				

Tuesday	S		d	
meat	S	o	d	8
wine	S	12	d	
bread	S	3	d	
meal	S	5	d 4	
herbs	S	8	d	
Wednesday				
wine	S	5	d	
melon	S	2	d	
meal	S	5	d 4	
vegetables	S	8	.	

Ash. I. 18 b]   **1546.**

Miseracione divina sacro sancte Romane ecclesie tituli n · cardinalis ²wulgariteʳ nun- cupatus venerabili religioṣo fratri Johanni Mair d'Nustorf ³ordinis praedicatorum provintie teutonie (?) conventus Wiennensis capellano ⁴nostro commensali salutem in dño sempi- ternam Religione zelus rite ac in [ferite?] ⁵honestas aliarumque laudabilium probitatis et virtutum merita quibus apud nos fide ⁶digno commendationis testimonio Magistri videlicet ordinis felicis recordacionis Leonardi de ⁷Mansuetis de Perusio sigillo suo .... us dans tibi ad ..... opera virtutum comen(salem)? ⁸locum et tempus success(ores) cujus simi- liter officium ministratus qui praedecessoris sui donum (?) ⁹confirmavit et de novo dedit aliorumque plurima [laudatis] qui opera tua laudant ¹⁰nos inducunt ut tibi (?) reddamus ad gratiam liberalem hinc est quod nos cupientes.

Notes by
unknown
persons
among the
MSS.
(1546—1565).

W. XII b]   **1547.**

Johannes · Antonius · di Johannes Am- brosius de Bolate; ²Chi perde il tempo e' virtù non aquista; ³quanto più pensa l'ani- mo più s'attrista; ⁴Virtù non ha in potere lo auere; chi lascia onore per acquistare auere; ⁵Non vale fortuna a chi non s'affa- tica; ⁶Colui si fa felice, che Christum vestiga; ⁷perfetto dono nō s'à sanza gran pena; ⁸Passano nostri triumfi, nostre pompe; ⁹la gola · e 'l sonno · e l'otiose · piume Anno · dal mondo · ogni virtù sbandita, ¹⁰tal · che dal corso · suo · quasi · smarita; Nostra · natu- ra · è vinta dal costume; ¹¹Ormai · con- vien · così · che tu ti spoltri; Disse il maestro che segiendo · in piuma, ¹²in fama · non si viene, nè sotto coltri, Sanza la qual · chi sua · vita · consuma ¹³tal · uestigia · in terra di se lascia ·, Qual · fumo · in aria · o nel- l'acqua la schiuma.

Johannes Antonius di Johannes Ambro- sius de Bolate. He who lets time pass and does not grow in virtue, the more I think of it the more I grieve. No man has it in him to be virtuous who will give up honour for gain. Good fortune is valueless to him who knows not toil. The man becomes happy who follows Christ. There is no per- fect gift without great suffering. Our glories and our triumphs pass away. Foul lust, and dreams, and luxury, and sloth have banished every virtue from the world; so that our Nature, wandering and perplexed, has almost lost the old and better track. Henceforth it were well to rouse thyself from sleep. The master said that lying in down will not bring thee to Fame; nor staying beneath the quilts. He who, without Fame, burns his life to waste, leaves no more vestige of himself on earth than wind-blown smoke, or the foam upon the sea.

1546—1566. *All these texts are written in the ordinary way from left to right.*
1547. 1. Ambrossius. 3. pensse . . satrista. 4. lassa honore . . aquistare havere. 5. safaticha. 5. coluy . . Xstum. 7. perfecto donnōsa. 8. pasano. 9. ellotiose . . del. 10. chorso . . issmarita . . chostume. 11. chonvien chosi chettutti spoltri . . maesstro chessiegiendo. 12. si uen nessotto choltri. 12. chissua . . chonsuma. 13. uesstigia . . lasscia . . onnellacqua lasschiuma.

1546. The meaning of this document, which is very difficult to decipher, and is written in unintelli- gible Latin, is, that Leonardo di Mansuetis recom- mends the Rev. Mair of Nusdorf, chaplain at Vienna, to some third person; and says also that something, which had to be proved, has been proved. The rest of the passages on the same leaf are undoubtedly

in Leonardo's hand. (Nos. 483, 661, 519, 578, 392, 582, 887 and 894.)

1547. From the last sentence we may infer that this text is by the hand of a pupil of Leonardo's.— On the same sheet are the notes Nos. 1175 and 715 in Leonardo's own handwriting.

Br. M. 148 a]   **1548.**

La mattina de santo Zanobio a dì 29 de maggio nel 1504 ²ebbi da Lionardo Vinci dvcati 15 d'oro, e cominciai a spendere

³a mona Margarita	S 62	d 4	
⁴a rifare · l'anello	S 19	d 8	
⁵panni	S 13	d	
⁶bon bove	S 4		
⁷uova	S 6	d	
⁸al banco debito	S 7	d	
⁹velluto	S 12		
¹⁰vino	S 6	d 4	
¹¹carne	S 4	d	
¹²more	S 2	d 4	
¹³funghi	S 3	d 4	
¹⁴insalata	S 1	d	
¹⁵frutta	S 1	d 4	
¹⁶candele	S 3	d	
¹⁷....	S 1	d	
¹⁸farina	S 2	d	
¹⁹domenica	198 · 8		
²⁰pane	S 6	d	
²¹vino	S 9	d 4	
²²carne	S 7	d	
²³minestra	S 2	d	
²⁴frutta	S 3	d 4	
²⁵candele	S 3	d 0	
²⁶Lvnedì	31		
²⁷pane	S 6	d 4	
²⁸carne	S 10	d 8	
²⁹vino	S 9	d 4	
³⁰frutta	S 4	d	
³¹minestra	S 1	d 8	
	32		

On the morning of Santo Zanobio the 29th of May 1504, I had from Lionardo Vinci 15 gold ducats and began to spend them.

to Mona Margarita	S 62	d 4	
to remake the ring	S 19	d 8	
clothes	S 13		
good beef	S 4		
eggs	S 6		
debt at the bank	S 7		
velvet	S 12		
wine	S 6	d 4	
meat	S 4		
mulberries	S 2	d 4	
mushrooms	S 3	d 4	
salad	S 1		
fruit	S 1	d 4	
candles	S 3		
....	S 1		
flour	S 2		
Sunday	198	8	
bread	S 6		
wine	S 9	d 4	
meat	S 7		
soup	S 2		
fruit	S 3	d 4	
candles	S 3	d	
Monday	31		
bread	S 6	d 4	
meat	S 10	d 8	
wine	S 9	d 4	
fruit	S 4		
soup	S 1	d 8	
	32		

Br. M. 148 b]   **1549.**

Martedì		
²pane	S 6	d
³carne	S 11	d
⁴vino	S 7	d
⁵frutta	S 9	d
⁶minestra	S 2	d
⁷insalata	S 1	d

Tuesday		
bread	S 6	
meat	S 11	
wine	S 7	
fruit	S 9	
soup	S 2	
salad	S 1	

1548. 1. matina . . ganobi . . mago. 2. ebi . . comincai. 3. magarita. 4. arefaere. 6. bonbove. 7. hove. 9. veleto. 13. fonghi. 15. frvte. 17. poniti. 19. domenega. 24. frute. 25. candel. 30. frvte.

1549. 1. martedi *here Leonardo notes in his usual handwriting* ½ a grecho. 5. frvte.

1548. 1549. On the same sheet is the text No. 1015 in Leonardo's own handwriting.

Br. M. 149 b]   **1550.**

A Mona Margarita	d 5				To Monna Margarita	S 5			
²a Tomaso		S 14			to Tomaso		S 14		
³a mona Margarita	di 5	S 2			to Monna Margarita	d 5	S 2		
⁴el dì di san Zanobi					on the day of San Zanobi				
⁵resta.....					left ..... after				
⁶de pagamento	di 13	S 2	d 4		payment	d 13	S 2	d 4	
⁷di .... mona Margarita					of Monna Margarita				
⁸in somma	⁹d 14	S 5	· 4		altogether	d 14	S 5	d 4	

Br. M. 271 a]   **1551.**

Il · lvnedì a dì 13 di febraio prestai lire S 7 a Lionardo per spendere ²venerdì d 7.

On Monday, the 13th of February, I lent lire S 7 to Lionardo to spend, Friday d 7.

Br. M. 274 a]   **1552.**

¶Stephano, Chigi, Canonico .....³familiare del chiarissimo ⁴Conte Grimani; ⁵a Santo Apostolo.¶

Stephano Chigi, Canonico ....., servant of the honorable Count Grimani at S. Apostoli.

C. A. 4 a; 11 a]   **1553.**

Essendomi sollecitato; ²d'amor non ne che · dvnque ...³Bernardo · di Simone, ⁴Siluestro di Stefano ·, ⁵Bernardo · di Jacopo, ⁶Francesco di Matteo Bonciani, ⁷Antonio di Giovanni Ruberti; ⁸Antonio da Pistoia ....., Antonio; ⁹chi tenpo à e tenpo aspetta ¹⁰perde l'amico · e' danari.

Having become anxious.........Bernardo di Simone, Silvestro di Stefano, Bernardo di Jacopo, Francesco di Matteo Bonciani, Antonio di Giovanni Ruberti, Antonio da Pistoia .... Antonio; He who has time and waits for time, will lose his friends and his money.

C. A. 34 b; 109 a]   **1554.**

Reverendissimo maestro domino Giouañi come fratello jo parlai a maestro Zacaria di quella ²facenda et l'ho fatto esser contento di quella ordinatione ch'io ho uoluto, ³cioè in quãto alla comissione ch'io ho dalle parti, et dico che tra noi nõ ha ⁴a correre denari inquanto alli quadri della ...

Reverend Maestro, Domino Giovanni, I spoke to Maestro Zacaria as · a brother about this business, and I made him satisfied with the arrangement that I had wished; that is, as regards the commission that I had from the parties and I say that between us there is no need to pay money down, as regard the pictures of the ...

1550. 1. margerita d 5½(?) 5. 4. ganobi. 5. resta se mio da iord. 6. de. 7. di cai(?)li mona malgarita. 8. soma. 10. [a mone margarita S. 7.]

1551. 1. el lvnedi .. prestaio .. perispende. 2. vermadi d. 7 nel 1. 3. di poi imponi di chossto nõnebbi mi se nũoperepochi soldimi forõ.

1552. 2. de dn. c (?) cegno. 3. k"mo".

1553. 3. br bernardo. 4. saluesstro. 5. dia chopo. 6. franc"o". 7. ant"o". 8. pistoia ghagha diche. 9. asspetta. 10. lamicho e danari nvna. 11. chiasmo e accierbi o esser surado (?).

1554. R "do" mstr dõ .. como fràllo mro. 3. dicochtra. 4. denari inquato .. guadri. *Here the texts breaks off.*

1551. This note is followed by an account very like the one given as No. 1549.

1552. Compare Ňo. 674, 21—23.

C. A. 75 a; 220 a]   **1555.**

Delle cose vedute infra la nebbia quella parte che sarà più ²uicina alli estremi, sarà manco uisibile, e tanto meno ³quãto sõ più remote.

Of things seen through a mist that which is nearest its farthest limit will be least visible, and all the more so as they are more remote.

Cod. A. 77 ; b 225 b]   **1556.**

Teodoricus Rex ²semper Augustus.

Theodoricus Rex Semper Augustus.

C. A. 94 b; 271 b]   **1557.**

Πρωομιάσαι ὦ ἄνθρωπος ᾿Αθῆνας. ²Aut Hesperia sola dicis et significat Italiã, ³aut addis vltima et significat Ispaniã; ⁴Vmbria par Tuscie.

Either you say Hesperia alone, and it will mean Italy, or you add ultima, and it will mean Spain. Umbria, part of Tuscany.

C. A. 121 b; 376 b]   **1558.**

Πάντων ἀντιαμφλίων δυὸ εὐθεῖαι ἐπισταύρονται; ²πρωομιάσαι ὦ ἄνθρωπος ᾿Αθῆνας τοῖς θεοῖς δέχομαι.

C. A. 130 a; 397 a]   **1559.**

Canonica di . . . . . . a dì 5 di Luglio 1507. ²Cara mia diletta madre, e mie sorelle, e mio cognato, avisovi come ³sono per la grazia di dio . . . . di quella spada che io . . . portatela ⁴alla piazza delli Strozzi(?) a Maso della . . . e spedirò la facenda ⁵di Piero in modo che . . . .

Canonica of . . . . . on the 5ᵗʰ of July 1507; my dearly beloved mother, sisters and cousin I herewith inform you that thanks to God I am . . . . about the sword which I . . . . . bring it to Maso at the piazza . . . . and I will settle the business of Piero so that . . . .

C. A. 164 b; 490 b]   .   **1560.**

Ut bene respondet Naturae ars docta! dedisset
    Vincius, ut tribuit cetera · sic animam ·
Noluit ut similis magis haec foret: altera sic est:
    Possidet illius Maurus amans animam.

1555. 1. prte. 2. extremi . . ettanto.
1556. Teodoricus R.   **1557.** 3. sig "cas" ispaniã.
1559. 1. canonica ?) didio(?) adi. 2. dileta . . sorele . . chome. 4. istro"a"zi . . maso della violẽ.

1557. The notes in Greek, Nos. 1557, 1558 and 1562 stand in close connection with each other, but the meaning of some words is very doubtful, and a translation is thus rendered impossible.

1559. AMORETTI, *Mem. Stor. XXIV*, quotes the first three lines of this letter as by Leonardo. The character of the writing however does not favour this hypothesis, and still less the contents. I should regard it rather a rough draft of a letter by young Melzi. I have not succeeded in deciphering completely the 13 lines of this text. Amoretti reads at the beginning *Canonica di Vaprio*, but *Vaprio* seems to me a very doubtful reading.

1560. These three epigrams on the portrait of Lucrezia Crivelli, a picture by Leonardo which must have been lost at a very early date, seem to have been dedicated to Leonardo by the poet. Leonardo used the reverse of the sheet for notes on geometry.

Hujus quam cernis nomen Lucretia, Divi
  Omnia cui larga contribuere manu.
Rara huic forma data est; pinxit Leonardus, amavit
  Maurus, pictorum primus hic, ille ducum.

Naturam, ac superas hac laesit imagine Divas
  Pictor: tantum hominis posse manum haec doluit,
Illae longa dari tam magnae tempora formae,
  Quae spatio fuerat deperitura brevi.

C. A. 171 *b*; 515 *b*] **1561.**

Egidius Romanus de formatione cor-
poris humani in vtero matris.
  [2]A Mons. le Vintie,-des chevaux (?)
[3]de l'escuyer du Roy...; [4]laissez payement
continuer a Ms. [5]Lyonard Paintre du Roy.
Amboyse.

Egidius Romanus on the formation of
the human body in the mother's womb[1].
  [2]To Monsieur le Vinci,-the horses of the
king's equerry . . . . Continue the payment
to Ms. Lyonard, Painter to the King.
  [6]Amboise.

C. A. 175 *a*; 526 *a*] **1562.**

Πρωομιάσαι ὦ ἄνθρωπος τοῖς θεοῖς δέχομαι.

C. A. 227 *b*; 685 *a*] **1563.**

Memoria a maestro Lionardi di avere
. . . . . . lo stato di Firenze . . . .

Memorandum to Maestro Lionardo to
have . . . the state of Florence.

C. A. 334 *b*; 1017 *b*] **1564.**

Ricordo a Vostra Eccellentia come Ridolfo [2]Manini · condusse a Firenze una somma [3]di cristallo . . . . . altre pietre come
sono · · ·

To remind your Excellency that Ridolfo
Manini brought to Florence a quantity
of crystal besides other stones such as
are . . .

1561. 1. informatione. 2. des cheuaux a(?). 3. de l'escuyeres(?). 5. peintre(?) du Roi P. 6. Amboyse Amboyse. 7. Amboyse
  Amboyse.
1563. 1. a m "r o" Lionardo dihavere p'sto la nolo stato.
1564. 1. vra ELL"tia". 2. Manini [porte] conduse . . som î. 3. cristallo inporse (?) altre.

1561. 1. *Liber magistri Egidii de pulsibus matrice
compositus (cum commentario Gentilis de Fulgineo)* published
in 1484 at Padova, in 1494 and in 1514 at Venice,
and in 1505 at Lyons.
  2. This text appears to be in a handwriting different from that in the note, l. 1. Here the reading is
not so simple as AMORETTI gave it, *Mem. Stor. XXV:
A Monsieur Lyonard Peintre du Roy pour Amboyse.* He
says too that this address is of the year 1509, and
Mr. Ravaisson remarks: *"De cette suscription il semble
qu'on peut inférer que Léonard était alors en France, à
la cour de Louis XII . . . Pour conclure je crois qu'il
n'est pas prouvé que Léonard de Vinci n'ait pas fait un
voyage de quelques mois en France sous Louis XII, entre
le printemps de 1509 et l'automne de 1510."*—I must

confess that I myself have not succeeded in deciphering completely this French writing of which two
words remain to me doubtful. But so much seems to
be quite evident that this is not an address of a letter
at all, but a certificate or note. *Amboise* [l. 6] I believe
to be the signature of Charles d'Amboise the Governor of Milan. If this explanation is the right
one, it can be easily explained by the contents of
Nos. 1350 and 1529. The note, line 1, was perhaps
added later by another hand; and Leonardo himself
wrote afterwards on the same sheet some geometrical explanations. I must also point out that the
statement that this sheet belongs to the year 1509
has absolutely no foundation in fact. There is no
clue whatever for giving a precise date to this note.

C. A. 329*b*; 993*a*]

1565.

XVI° C. 6 de Ciuitate Dei, ²se Antipodes.

Bibl. Melzi]

1566.

Leonardo's Will.

Sia manifesto ad ciaschaduna persona presente et aduenere, che nella corte del Re nostro signore in Amboysia avanti de noy personalmente constituito messer Leonardo de Vince pictore del Re, al presente comorante nello locho dicto du Cloux appresso de Amboysia, el qual considerando la certezza dela morte e l'incertezza del hora di quella, ha cognosciuto et confessato nela dicta corte nanzi de noy nela quale s'è somesso e somette circa ciò havere facto et ordinato per tenore dela presente il suo testamento et ordinanza de ultima volontà nel modo qual se seguita. Primeramente el racomanda l'anima sua ad nostro Signore Messer Domine Dio, alla gloriosa Virgine Maria, a Monsignore Sancto Michele, e a tutti li beati Angeli Santi e Sante del Paradiso.

Item el dicto Testatore vole essere seppelito drento la giesia de sancto Florentino de Amboysia et suo corpo essere portato li per li capellani di quella.

Item che il suo corpo sia accompagnato dal dicto locho fin nela dicta giesia de sancto Florentino per il colegio de dicta giesia cioè dal Rectore et Priore, o vero dali Vicarii soy et Capellani della giesia di sancto Dionisio d'Amboysia, etiam li Fratri Minori del dicto locho, et avante de essere portato il suo corpo nela dicta chiesia, èsso Testatore, vole siano celebrate ne la dicta chiesia di sancto Florentino tre grandi messe con diacono et sottodiacono, et il dì che se diranno dicte tre grandi messe che se dicano anchora trenta messe basse de Sancto Gregorio.

Item nella dicta chiesia de Sancto Dionisio similar servitio sia celebrato come di sopra.

Item nella chiesia de dicti Fratri et religiosi minori simile servitio.

Item el prefato Testatore dona et concede ad Messer Francesco da Melzo, Gentilomo da Milano, per remuneratione de' servitii ad epso grati a lui facti per il pas-

Be it known to all persons, present and to come that at the court of our Lord the King at Amboise before ourselves in person, Messer Leonardo da Vinci painter to the King, at present staying at the place known as Cloux near Amboise, duly considering the certainty of death and the uncertainty of its time, has acknowledged and declared in the said court and before us that he has made, according to the tenor of these presents, his testament and the declaration of his last will, as follows. And first he commends his soul to our Lord, Almighty God, and to the Glorious Virgin Mary, and to our lord Saint Michael, to all the blessed Angels and Saints male and female in Paradise.

Item. The said Testator desires to be buried within the church of Saint Florentin at Amboise, and that his body shall be borne thither by the chaplains of the church.

Item. That his body may be followed from the said place to the said church of Saint Florentin by the *collegium* of the said church, that is to say by the rector and the prior, or by their vicars and chaplains of the church of Saint Denis of Amboise, also the lesser friars of the place, and before his body shall be carried to the said church this Testator desires, that in the said church of Saint Florentin three grand masses shall be celebrated by the deacon and sub-deacon and that on the day when these three high masses are celebrated, thirty low masses shall also be performed at Saint Gregoire.

Item. That in the said church of Saint Denis similar services shall be performed, as above.

Item. That the same shall be done in the church of the said friars and lesser brethren.

Item. The aforesaid Testator gives and bequeaths to Messer Francesco da Melzo, nobleman, of Milan, in remuneration for services and favours done to him in the past, each sato, tutti et ciaschaduno li libri, che il dicto Testatore ha de presente et altri Instrumenti et Portracti circa l'arte sua et industria de Pictori.

Item epso Testatore dona et concede a sempre mai perpetuamente a Battista de Vilanis suo servitore la metà zoè medietà de uno iardino, che ha fora a le mura de Milano et l'altra metà de epso iardino ad Salay suo servitore nel qual iardino il prefato Salay ha edificata et constructa una casa, la qual sarà e resterà similmente a sempremai perpetudine al dicto Salai, soi heredi et successori, et ciò in remuneratione di boni et grati servitii, che dicti de Vilanis et Salay dicti suoi servitori lui hano facto de quì inanzi.

Item epso Testatore dona a Maturina sua fantescha una veste de bon pan negro foderata de pelle, una socha de panno et doy ducati per una volta solamente pagati: et ciò in remuneratione similmente de boni servitii a lui facti epsa Maturina de quì inanzi.

Item vole che ale sue exequie siano sexanta torchie, le quali seranno portate per sexanta poveri, ali quali seranno dati danari per portarle a discretione del dicto Melzo le quali torzi seranno divise nelle quattro chiesie sopradicte.

Item el dicto Testatore dona ad ciascheduna de dicte chiesie sopradicte diece libre cera in candele grosse che saranno messe nelle dicte chiesie per servire al dì che se celebreranno dicti servitii.

Item che sia dato ali poveri del ospedale di Dio alli poveri de Sancto Lazaro de Amboysia, e per ciò fare sia dato et pagato alli Tesorieri d'epsa confraternità la summa et quantità de soysante dece soldi tornesi.

Item epso Testatore dona et concede al dicto Messer Francesco Melce presente et acceptante il resto della sua pensione et summa de' danari qual a lui sono debiti del passato fino al dì della sua morte per il recevoir, ovvero, Tesaurario general M. Johan Sapin, et tutte et ciaschaduna summe de' danari che ha receputo dal p.° Sapin de la dicta sua pensione, e in caxo chel decede inanzi al prefato Melzo, e non altramente li quali danari sono al presente nella possessione del dicto Testatore nel dicto loco de Cloux como el dice. Et similmente el dona e concede al dicto de Melze tucti et ciaschaduni suoi vestimenti quali ha al presente ne lo dicto loco de Cloux tam per remuneratione de boni et

and all of the books the Testator is at present possessed of, and the instruments and portraits appertaining to his art and calling as a painter.

Item. The same Testator gives and bequeaths henceforth for ever to Battista de Vilanis his servant one half, that is the moity, of his garden which is outside the walls of Milan, and the other half of the same garden to Salai his servant; in which garden aforesaid Salai has built and constructed a house which shall be and remain henceforth in all perpetuity the property of the said Salai, his heirs and successors; and this is in remuneration for the good and kind services which the said de Vilanis and Salai, his servants have done him in past times until now.

Item. The said Testator gives to Maturina his waiting woman a cloak of good black cloth lined with fur, a . . . . . of cloth and two ducats paid once only; and this likewise is in remuneration for good service rendered to him in past times by the said Maturina.

Item. He desires that at his funeral sixty tapers shall be carried which shall be borne by sixty poor men, to whom shall be given money for carrying them; at the discretion of the said Melzo, and these tapers shall be distributed among the four above mentioned churches.

Item. The said Testator gives to each of the said churches ten lbs. of wax in thick tapers, which shall be placed in the said churches to be used on the day when those said services are celebrated.

Item. That alms shall be given to the poor of the Hotel-Dieu, to the poor of Saint Lazare d'Amboise and, to that end, there shall be given and paid to the treasurers of that same fraternity the sum and amount of seventy soldi of Tours.

Item. The said Testator gives and bequeaths to the said Messer Francesco Melzo, being present and agreeing, the remainder of his pension and the sums of money which are owing to him from the past time till the day of his death by the receiver or treasurer-general M. Johan Sapin, and each and every sum of money that he has already received from the aforesaid Sapin of his said pension, and in case he should die before the said Melzo and not otherwise; which moneys are at present in the possession of the said Testator in the said place called Cloux, as he says. And he likewise gives and bequeaths to the said Melzo all and each of his clothes which he at present possesses at the said place of Cloux, and all in grati servitii, a lui facti da qui inanzi, che per li suoi salarii vacationi et fatiche chel potrà avere circa la executione del presente Testamento, il tutto però ale spesé del dicto Testatore.

Ordina et vole, che la summa de quattrocento scudi del sole che ha in deposito in man del Camarlingo de Sancta Maria de Nova nela città de Fiorenza, siano dati ali soy fratelli carnali residenti in Fiorenza con el profitto et emolumento che ne po essere debito fino al presente da prefati Camarlinghi al prefato Testatore per casone de dicti scudi quattrocento da poi el dì che furono per el prefato Testatore dati et consignati alli dicti Camarlinghi.

Item vole et ordina dicto Testatore che dicto Messer Francisco de Melzo sia et remana solo et in sol per il tutto executore del Testamento del prefato Testatore, et che questo dicto Testamento sortisca suo pleno et integro effecto, et circa ciò che è narrato et decto havere tenere guardare et observare epso Messer Leonardo de Vince Testatore constituto ha obbligato et obbliga per le presente epsi soy heredi et successori con ogni soy beni mobili et immobili presenti et advenire et ha renunciato et renuncia per la presente expressamente ad tucte et ciaschaduna le cose ad ciò contrarie. Datum nelo dicto loco de Cloux ne la presencia de magistro Spirito Fleri Vicario nela chiesia de Sancto Dionisio de Amboysia, M. Gulielmo Croysant prete et capellani, magistro Cipriane Fulchin, Fratre Francesco de Corton et Francesco da Milano religioso del convento de fratri minori de Amboysia, testimonii ad ciò ciamati et vocati ad tenere per il iudicio de la dicta Corte in presentia del prefato M. Francesco de Melze acceptante et consentiente il quale ha promesso per fede et sacramento del corpo suo per lui dati corporalmente ne le mane nostre di non mai fare venire, dire, ne andare in contrario. Et sigillato a sua requesta dal sigillo regale statuito a li contracti legali d'Amboysia, et in segno de verita.

Dat·a dì XXIII de Aprile MDXVIII avanti la Pasqua.

Et a dì XXIII d'epso mese de Aprile MDXVIII ne la presentia di M. Gulielmo Borian notario regio ne la corte de Baliagio d'Amboysia il prefato M. Leonardo de Vince ha donato et concesso per il suo testamento et ordinanza de ultima voluntà supradicta al dicto M. Baptista de Vilanis presente et acceptante il dritto de laqua

remuneration for the good and kind services done by him in past times till now, as well as in payment for the trouble and annoyance he may incur with regard to the execution of this present testament, which however, shall all be at the expense of the said Testator.

And he orders and desires that the sum of four hundred scudi del Sole, which he has deposited in the hands of the treasurer of Santa Maria Nuova in the city of Florence, may be given to his brothers now living in Florence with all the interest and usufruct that may have accrued up to the present time, and be due from the aforesaid treasurer to the aforesaid Testator on account of the said four hundred crowns, since they were given and consigned by the Testator to the said treasurers.

Item. He desires and orders that the said Messer Francesco de Melzo shall be and remain the sole and only executor of the said will of the said Testator; and that the said testament shall be executed in its full and complete meaning and according to that which is here narrated and said, to have, hold, keep and observe, the said Messer Leonardo da Vinci, constituted Testator, has obliged and obliges by these presents the said his heirs and successors with all his goods moveable and immoveable present and to come, and has renounced and expressly renounces by these presents all and each of the things which to that are contrary. Given at the said place of Cloux in the presence of Magister Spirito Fleri vicar, of the church of Saint Denis at Amboise, of M. Guglielmo Croysant priest and chaplain, of Magister Cipriane Fulchin, Brother Francesco de Corton, and of Francesco da Milano, a brother of the Convent of the Minorites at Amboise, witnesses summoned and required to that end by the indictment of the said court in the presence of the aforesaid M. Francesco de Melze who accepting and agreeing to the same has promised by his faith and his oath which he has administered to us personally and has sworn to us never to do nor say nor act in any way to the contrary. And it is sealed by his request with the royal seal apposed to legal contracts at Amboise, and in token of good faith.

Given on the XXIIIrd day of April MDXVIII, before Easter.

And on the XXIIIrd day of this month of April MDXVIII, in the presence of M. Guglielmo Borian, Royal notary in the court of the bailiwick of Amboise, the aforesaid M. Leonardo de Vinci gave and bequeathed, by his last will and testament, as aforesaid, to the said M. Baptista de Vilanis, being present and agreeing, the right of water which che qdam bone memorie Re Ludovico XII ultimo defuncto ha alias dato a epso de Vince suxo il fiume del naviglio di Sancto Cristoforo ne lo Ducato de Milano per gauderlo per epso De Vilanis a sempre mai in tal modo et forma che dicto Signore ne ha facto dono in presentia di M. Francesco da Melzo Gentilhomo de Milano et io.

Et a dì prefato nel dicto mese de Aprile ne lo dicto anno MDXVIII epso M. Leonardo de Vinci per il suo testamento et ordinanza de ultima volunta sopradecta ha donato al prefato M. Baptista de Vilanis presente et acceptante tutti et ciaschaduni mobili et utensili de caxa soy de presente ne lo dicto loco du Cloux, in caxo però che el dicto de Vilanis surviva al prefato M. Leonardo de Vince, in presentia del prefato M. Francesco da Melzo et io Notario etc. Borean.

the King Louis XII, of pious memory lately deceased gave to this same de Vinci, the stream of the canal of Santo Cristoforo in the duchy of Milan, to belong to the said Vilanis for ever in such wise and manner that the said gentleman made him this gift in the presence of M. Francesco da Melzo, gentleman, of Milan and in mine.

And on the aforesaid day in the said month of April in the said year MDXVIII the same M. Leonardo de Vinci by his last will and testament gave to the aforesaid M. Baptista de Vilanis, being present and agreeing, each and all of the articles of furniture and utensils of his house at present at the said place of Cloux, in the event of the said de Vilanis surviving the aforesaid M. Leonardo de Vinci, in the presence of the said M. Francesco Melzo and of me Notary &c. Borean.

REFERENCE TABLE TO THE NUMERICAL ORDER OF THE CHAPTERS.

XI.

NOTES ON SCULPTURE.

706.	A. 43 *a*.
707.	W. P. 5 *a*.
708.	A. 1 *a*.
709.	Ash. I. 19 *b*.
710.	W. X.
711.	W. XI.
712.	C. A. 213 *b*; 628 *b*.
713.	W. XII.
714.	W. XIII.
715.	W. XII.
716.	W. H. 64.
717.	W. H. XV.
718.	C. A. 286 *b*; 870 *a*.
719.	C. A. 382 *a*; 1182 *a*.
720.	C. 15 *b* (1 *a*).
721.	Leic. 9 *b*.
722.	C. A. 316 *a*; 958 *a*.
723.	C. A. 328 *b*; 983 *a*.
724.	C. A. 272 *b*; 833 *a*.
725.	C. A. 176 *b*; 533 *a*.
726.	G. 43 *a*.
727.	C. 15 *b* (1 *a*).
728.	Mz. o'.
729.	G. 75 *b*.
730.	C. A. 313 *a*; 951 *a*.
731.	S. K. M. III. 50 *a*.
732.	S. K. M. III. 53 *a*.
733.	S. K. M. II.1 95 *a*.
734.	S. K. M. III. 55 *b*.
735.	S K. M. III. 56 *a*.

736.	H.3 52 *b*.
737.	Tr. 52.
738.	Tr. 53.
739.	Tr. 54.
740.	Tr. 55.

XII.

ARCHITECTURAL DESIGNS.

741.	B. 16 *a*.
742.	B. 15 *b*.
743.	B. 15 *b*.
744.	Br. M. 270 *b*.
745.	B. 37 *b*.
746.	B. 36 *a*.
747.	Br. M. 270 *b*.
748.	C. A. 75 *b*; 221 *a*.
749.	K.3 36 *b*.
750.	B. 60 *a*.
751.	B. 12 *a*.
752.	B. 19 *b*.
753.	B. 39 *b*.
754.	Ash. II. 8 *b*.
755.	B. 18 *b*.
756.	Ash. II. 7 *a*.
757.	B. 24 *a*.
758.	Tr. 15.
759.	C. A. 280 *a*; 857 *a*.
760.	W. XIX.
761.	B. 39 *a*.
762.	B. 28 *b*.
763.	Br. M. 192 *a*.
764.	S. K. M. III. 48 *a*.
765.	L. 19 *b*; 20 *a*.

766.	C. A. 318 *a*; 961 *a*.
767.	Ash. III. 13 *b*.
768.	H.3 73 *b*.
769.	G. 52 *a*.

XIII.

THEORETICAL WRITINGS ON ARCHITECTURE.

I. ON FISSURES IN WALLS.

770.	Br. M. 157 *a*.
771.	Br. M. 157 *b*.
772.	Br. M. 138 *a*.
773.	Br. M. 158 *a*.
774.	Br. M. 159 *b*.
775.	Br. M. 157 *b*.
776.	A. 53 *a*.

II. ON FISSURES IN NICHES.

777.	Br. M. 158 *a*.
778.	Br. M. 141 *b*.

III. ON THE NATURE OF THE ARCH.

779.	A. 50 *a*.
780.	A. 50 *b*.
781.	A. 51 *a*.
782.	H.1 35 *b*.
783.	H.1 36 *a*.
784.	S. K. M. II.2 67 *b*.
785.	Br. M. 158 *b*.
786.	A. 49 *b*.
787.	S. K. M. II.2 66 *b*.
788.	B. 27 *a*.

IV. ON FOUNDATIONS, THE NATURE OF THE GROUND AND SUPPORTS.

789.	Br. M. 138a.
790.	A. 50a.
791.	A. 53a.
792.	A. 48b.
793.	S. K. M. II.¹ 72a.
794.	S. K. M. III.¹ 91a.
795.	A. 53a.

XIV.

ANATOMY, ZOOLOGY AND PHYSIOLOGY.

I. ANATOMY.

796.	W. An. IV. 167a.
797.	W. An. II. 36a (21).
798.	W. An. IV. 157a (B).
799.	W. 210a.
800.	W. An. IV. XXI.
801.	W. An. II. 39b (0).
802.	W. An. IV. 151a.
803.	W. An. IV. XXII.
804.	W. XXIII.
805.	W. An. I. 1b.
806.	F. 95b.
807.	W. 238b.
808.	K.3 28a.
809.	W. An. II. 76b.
810.	W. An. IV. 7 (AA).
811.	W. 239a (= W. L. 131).
812.	S. K. M. III. 66a.
813.	S. K. M. III. 65b.
814.	W. An. II. 37a.
815.	W. An. III. 230a.

II. ZOOLOGY AND COMPARATIVE ANATOMY.

816.	W. An. IV. 173b.
817.	W. An. II. 206b (I).
818.	W. An. IV. 153b.
819.	W. An. IV. 167a.
820.	G. 64b.
821.	M. 67a.
822.	W. An. IV. 157a (B).
823.	W. XXIV ('55').
824.	K.3 29b.
825.	E. 16a.
826.	C. A. 292a; 888a.

III. PHYSIOLOGY.

827.	W. An. IV. 173a.
828.	H.² 38a.
829.	G. 44a.
830.	Br. M. 64b.
831.	H.3 61a.

832.	W. An. IV. 184a (7).
833.	W. XXI.
834.	C. A. 89a; 258a.
835.	G. 90a.
836.	C. A. 89a; 258a.
837.	W. An. IV. 184a (7).
838.	W. An. 202a ('B')
839.	W. An. II. 202b ('B')
840.	Tr. 14.
841.	W. An. IV. 151b.
842.	H.¹ 32a.
843.	W. An. II. 43b (8).
844.	W. An. III. 241a.
845.	H.² 41b.
846.	S. K. M. III. 74a.
847.	C. A. 75b; 219b.
848.	F. 1a.
849.	Leic. 21b.
850.	W. An. III. 226a ('M')
851.	Br. M. 147b.
852.	W. XIII.
853.	Tr. 7.
854.	Tr. 49.
855.	C. A. 77b; 225b.
856.	W. An. III., XXV.

XV.

ASTRONOMY.

I. THE EARTH AS A PLANET.

857.	Br. M. 176a.
858.	F. 41b.
859.	Br. M. 151a.
860.	Br. M. 175a.
861.	F. 22b.
862.	F. 11b.
863.	Tr. 28.
864.	Leic. 1a.
865.	C. A. 111b; 345b.
866.	F. 56a.
867.	F. 25b.
868.	W. XXVI.
869.	E. 15b.
870.	F. 60b.
871.	Br. M. 174b.
872.	G. 3b.
873.	A. 64b.
874.	F. 94b.
875.	Br. M. 25a.
876.	Br. M. 28a.
877.	F. 77b.
878.	W. X.

II. THE SUN.

879.	F. 5a.
880.	F. 4b.
881.	F. 6a.

882.	F. 8b.
883.	F. 10a.
884.	F. 0″.
885.	G. 34a.
886.	W. L. 132a.
887.	Ash. I. 19a.
888.	Br. M. 78b.
889.	A. 64a.
890.	C. A. 234a; 704a.
891.	T. 12.

III. THE MOON.

892.	Br. M. 94a.
893.	F. 93a.
894.	Ash. I. 19a.
895.	Br. M. 28a.
896.	Br. M. 94b.
897.	Br. M. 103a.
898.	A. 64a.
899.	Leic. 30a.
900.	Leic. 36b.
901.	Leic. 1b.
902.	Leic. 2a.
903.	F. 84a.
904.	F. 84b.
905.	F. 85a.
906.	Br. M. 19a.
907.	Leic. 5a.
908.	C. A. 341b; 1055a.
909.	W. XXVII.
910.	C. A. 187a; 561a.

IV. THE STARS.

911.	F. 5b.
912.	F. 57a.
913.	F. 60a.
914.	Br. M. 279b.
915.	E. 0'.
916.	Br. M. 173b and 190b.
917.	Br. M. 176a.
918.	Br. M. 191a.

XVI.

PHYSICAL GEOGRAPHY.

INTRODUCTION.

919.	Leic. 5a.
920.	Leic. 15b.
921.	Leic. 9a.
922.	F. 87b.
923.	F. 88a.
924.	F. 90b.
925.	Br. M. 35a.
926.	Br. M. 35b.
927.	Br. M. 122a.
928.	Br. M. 45a.
929.	A. 55b.

I. OF THE NATURE OF WATER.

930. E. 12 a.
931. C. 26 b (4).
932. I.² 24 a and b.
933. Leic. 34 b.
934. A. 58 b.
935. E. 4 b.
936. Leic. 10 b.
937. Leic. 35 b.
938. Leic. 36 a.
939. F. 27 a.
940. A. 58 b.
941. A. 55 b.
942. F. 73 a.
943. A. 58 b.
944. A. 56 a.
945. A. 56 b.

II. ON THE OCEAN.

946. G. 48 b.
947. G. 49 a.
948. Leic. 21 b.
949. G. 38 a.
950. C. A. 157 b; 466 a.
951. C. A. 83 b; 240 b.
952. Ash. III. 25 a.
953. Leic. 20 a.
954. Leic. 27 b.
955. C. A. 162 a; 482 a.
956. Leic. 17 b.
957. Leic. 5 a.
958. Leic. 6 b.
959. Leic. 13 a.
960. Leic. 35 b.

III. SUBTERRANEAN WATER COURSES.

961. C. A. 157 b; 466 a.
962. Leic. 31 a.
963. Leic. 21 b.
964. Br. M. 233 b.
965. Br. M. 236 b.
966. G. 70 a.
967. A. 55 b.
968. A. 56 a.
969. Leic. 11 b.

IV. ON RIVERS.

970. Leic. 33 b.
971. Leic. 5 a.
972. Leic. 15 a.
973. Leic. 16 b.
974. G. 48 a.
975. C. A. 362 a; 1134 b.
976. G. 49 b.
977. Leic. 6 b.
978. Leic. 31 b.

V. ON MOUNTAINS.

979. C. A. 157 a; 466 a.
980. Leic. 10 a.
981. L. 76 a.
982. Br. M. 30 b.
983. C. A. 124 b; 383 a.
984. Leic. 31 a.

VI. GEOLOGICAL PROBLEMS.

985. Leic. 3 a.
986. C. A. 152 a; 452 a.
987. Leic. 8 b.
988. Leic. 9 a.
989. Leic. 9 b.
990. Leic. 10 a.
991. Leic. 10 b.
992. Leic. 20 a.
993. Leic. 36 a.
994. Br. M. 156 b.

VII. ON THE ATMOSPHERE.

995. Leic. 20 a.
996. Leic. 22 b.
997. Leic. 23 a.
998. S. K. M. II.² 19 b.
999. H.3 52 a.
1000. Leic. 34 a.

XVII.

TOPOGRAPHICAL NOTES.

I. ITALY.

1001. C. A. 45 a; 140 a.
1002. L. 1 a.
1003. C. A. 284 a; 865 a.
1004. Br. M. 273 b.
1005. Br. M. 274 a.
1006. W. L. 226 a.
1007. Leic. 18 b.
1008. Leic. 13 a.
1009. C. A. 387 a; 1197 a.
1010. F. 76 b.
1011. Leic. 18 a.
1012. C. A. 139 b; 421 b.
1013. C. A. 233 a; 700 a.
1014. H.² 43 a.
1015. Br. M. 149 a.
1016. C. A. 72 b; 211 b.
1017. I.¹ 32 b.
1018. I.¹ 34 a.
1019. L. 15 a.
1020. E. 1 a.
1021. Leic. 28 a.
1022. W. XXVIII.
1023. B. 58 a.
1024. H.² 17 b.
1025. H.¹ 38 a.

1026. H.¹ 1 a.
1027. Leic. 21 a.
1028. Leic. 32 a.
1029. Leic. 11 b.
1030. C. A. 211 a; 619 a.
1031. C. A. 211 b; 619 b.
1032. C. A. 270 a; 821 a.
1033. G. 1 a.
1034. L. 6 a.
1035. L. 6 b.
1036. L. 10 b.
1037. L. 15 b.
1038. L. 19 b.
1039. L. 33 b.
1040. L. 36 b.
1041. L. 40 a.
1042. L. 46 b.
1043. L. 47 a.
1044. L. 66 b.
1045. L. 67 a.
1046. L. 72 a.
1047. L. 77 a.
1048. L. 78 a.
1049. L. 78 b.
1050. L. 88 b.
1051. W. L. 229 a.
1052. L. 94 b.
1053. L. 0″.
1054. L. 21 a.
1055. Leic. 9 b.
1056. Leic. 10 b.
1057. G. 1 b.
1058. Leic. 11 b.
1059. C. A. 86 b; 250 b.
1060. Leic. 4 a.
1061. Leic. 9 b.
1062. C. A. 231 b; 696 a.
1063. Leic. 10 a.
1064. E. 1 a.
1065. E. 80 a.
1066. C. A. 137 a; 414 a.
1067. K.¹ 2 a.
1068. Leic. 31 b.

II. FRANCE.

1069. C. A. 353 b; 1105 b.
1070. C. A. 358 b; 1124 b.
1071. Leic. 27 b.
1072. Leic. 34 b.
1073. K.3 20 a.
1074. Br. M. 269 a.
1075. Br. M. 270 b.
1076. Br. M. 269 b.
1077. Br. M. 270 b.
1078. C. A. 329 b; 993 a.
1079. Br. M. 263 b.
1080. B. 61 a.
1081. B. 63 b.
1082. Leic. 1 b.

III. THE COUNTRIES OF THE WESTERN END OF THE MEDITERRANEAN.

1083.	A. 57 a.
1084.	C. A. 212 b; 626 b.
1085.	Leic. 10 b.
1086.	Leic. 27 b.
1087.	F. 61 a.
1088.	B. 82 b.
1089.	Ash. II. 12 a.

IV. THE LEVANT.

1090.	Leic. 31 a.
1091.	Leic. 31 a.
1092.	C. A. 321 b; 971 a.
1093.	C. A. 94 b; 276 a.
1094.	B. 61 b.
1095.	Leic. 34 b.
1096.	Leic. 21 b.
1097.	Leic. 22 a.
1098.	Leic. 32 b.
1099.	B. 61 b.
1100.	B. 62 b.
1101.	Leic. 10 b.
1102.	L. o'.
1103.	W. XVII a.
1104.	W. XVII b.
1105.	C. A. 256 a; 773 a.
1106.	F. 50 a.
1107.	F. 68 a.
1108.	Leic. 31 b.
1109.	L. 66 a.
1110.	Leic. 28 a.
1111.	C. A. 94 b; 276 a.
1112.	C. A. 384 b; 1189 b.

XVIII.

NAVAL WARFARE.— MECHANICAL APPLIANCES.—MUSIC.

1113.	G. 54 a.
1114.	Leic. 22 b.
1115.	Ash. II. 4 b.
1116.	Ash. II. 6 a.
1117.	B. 81 b.
1118.	S. K. M. III. 25 b.
1119.	C. A. 7 a; 19 a.
1120.	Ash. II. 5 b.
1121.	S. K. M. III. 46 b.
1122.	Mz. 3 a. (6)
1123.	Mz. 12 a. (10)
1124.	Mz. 9 b. (13)
1125.	Mz. 13 a.
1126.	C. A. 372 b; 1156 b.
1127.	Ash. II. 4 a.
1128.	Tr. 48.
1129.	Br. M. 175 a.
1130.	Br. M. 136 a.
1131.	B. 4 a.

XIX.

PHILOSOPHICAL MAXIMS. —MORALS, POLEMICS AND SPECULATION.

I. PHILOSOPHICAL MAXIMS.

1132.	S. K. M. III. 64 b.
1133.	W. An. IV. 172 a.
1134.	A. 24 a.
1135.	S. K. M. III. 49 a.
1136.	Tr. 75.
1137.	S. K. M. II.[1] 43 a.
1138.	Tr. 40.
1139.	H.3 93 a.
1140.	W. XXIX.
1141.	Tr. 78.
1142.	C. A. 58 a; 180 a.
1143.	C. A. 75 a; 219 a.
1144.	Br. M. 278 b.
1145.	Tr. 65.
1146.	Tr. 70.
1147.	Tr. 45.
1148.	Tr. 51.
1149.	C. A. 85 a; 247 a.
1150.	S. K. M. III. 80 b.
1151.	I.[1] 18 a.
1152.	M. 58 b.
1153.	C. A. 151 a; 449 a.
1154.	Mz. 1 a.
1155.	E. 8 b.
1156.	Br. M. 191 a.
1157.	W. An. III. 241 a.
1158.	G. 95 b.
1159.	C. A. 75 a; 219 a.
1160.	I.[2] 82 a.
1161.	G. 8 a.

II. MORALS.

1162.	B. M. 156 b.
1163.	C. A. 70 a; 207 a.
1164.	H.[2] 33 b.
1165.	C. A. 75 b; 219 b.
1166.	G. 89 a.
1167.	C. A. 365 b; 1141 b.
1168.	Mz. 8 a (12).
1169.	S. K. M. III.; 36 b.
1170.	C. A. 75 a; 219 a.
1171.	C. A. 111 a; 345 a.
1172.	C. A. 223 b; 671 b.
1173.	Tr. 32.
1174.	Tr. 68.
1175.	W. XII.
1176.	Ash. I. 1 b.
1177.	C. A. 284 b; 885 b.
1178.	W. An. II. 203 a (24).
1179.	S. K. M. III. 17 a.
1180.	C. A. 153 b; 455 b.
1181.	Tr. 57.
1182.	Tur. 17 b.

1183.	Ash. I. 1 a.
1184.	F. 96 b.
1185.	C. A. 108 b; 338 b.
1186.	W. XIII.
1187.	S. K. M. II. 77 a.
1188.	B. 3 b.
1189.	Tr. 2.
1190.	E. 31 b.
1191.	H.3 70 b.
1192.	H.3 71 a.
1193.	Tr. 39.
1194.	H. 16 b.
1195.	C. A. 115 b; 357 b.
1196.	S. K. M. II.[2] 24 a.
1197.	H.[2] 12 b.
1198.	L. o''.
1199.	L. 90 b.
1200.	C. A. 75 b; 219 b.
1201.	G. 49 a.
1202.	Tr. 11.
1203.	C. A. 64 b; 197 b.
1204.	Ash. II. 13 a.

III. POLEMICS.—SPECULATION.

1205.	G. 47 a.
1206.	S. K. M. II.[2] 67 a.
1207.	C. A. 75 b; 219 b.
1208.	F. 5 b.
1209.	Tr. 68.
1210.	W. An. III. 241.
1211.	C. A. 187 b; 562 b.
1212.	B. 4 b.
1213.	W. An. II. 242 b. (N)
1214.	W. An. II. 242 a.
1215.	W. An. II. 201 b.
1216.	Br. M. 131 a.
1217.	Br. M. 156 a.
1218.	Br. M. 155 b.
1219.	Br. M. 156 b.

XX.

HUMOROUS WRITINGS.

I. STUDIES ON THE LIFE AND HABITS OF ANIMALS.

1220.	H.[1] 5 a.
1221.	H.[1] 5 b.
1222.	H.[1] 6 a.
1223.	H.[1] 6 b.
1224.	H.[1] 7 a.
1225.	H.[1] 7 b.
1226.	H.[1] 8 a.
1227.	H.[1] 8 b.
1228.	H.[1] 9 a.
1229.	H.[1] 9 b.
1230.	H.[1] 10 a.
1231.	H.[1] 10 b.
1232.	H.[1] 11 a.
1233.	H.[1] 11 b.

1234.	H.¹ 12 a.	1289.	Tr. 78.	1338.	F. 37 b.
1235.	H.¹ 12 b.	1290.	S. K. M. II.² 44 a.	1339.	Br. M. 155 a.
1236.	H.¹ 13 a.	1291.	S. K. M. II.² 43 b.	1340.	C. A. 388 a; 1182 b.
1237.	H.¹ 13 b.	1292.	F. o'	1341.	S. K. M. III. 29 a.
1238.	H.¹ 14 a.			1342.	S. K. M. III. 23 b.
1239.	H.¹ 14 b.		**IV. PROPHECIES.**	1343.	S. K. M. III. 79 b.
1240.	H.¹ 15 a.	1293.	C. A. 143 a; 426 a.	1344.	C. A. 308 b; 339 a.
1241.	H.¹ 17 a.	1294.	C. A. 143 b; 426 b.	1345.	C. A. 328 b; 983 b.
1242.	H.¹ 17 b.	1295.	C. A. 362 a; 1134 a.	1346.	C. A. 316 a; 958 a.
1243.	H.¹ 18 a.	1296.	C. A. 362 b; 1134 b.	1347.	C. A. 316 b; 958 b.
1244.	H.¹ 18 b.	1297.	Br. M. 42 b.	1348.	M. D.
1245.	H.¹ 19 a.	1298.	I.² 15 a.	1349.	C. A. 310 a; 944 a.
1246.	H.¹ 19 b.	1299.	I.² 15 b.	1350.	C. A. 364 b; 1138 b.
1247.	H.¹ 20 a.	1300.	I.² 16 a.	1351.	C. A. 243 b; 729 a.
1248.	H.¹ 20 b.	1301.	I.² 16 b.	1352.	C. A. 278 a; 850 a.
1249.	H.¹ 21 a.	1302.	I.² 17 a.	1353.	C. A. 179 b; 541 a.
1250.	H.¹ 21 b.	1303.	I.² 17 b.	1354.	C. A. 304 a; 925 a.
1251.	H.¹ 22 a.	1304.	I.² 18 a.	1355.	W. XXXI.
1252.	H.¹ 22 b.	1305.	I.² 18 b.	1356.	H.³ 89 a.
1253.	H.¹ 23 a.	1306.	I.² 19 a.	1357.	C. A. 380 a; 1179 b.
1254.	H.¹ 23 b.	1307.	L. 91 a.	1358.	W. An. III. 241 a.
1255.	H.¹ 24 a.	1308.	K.² 1 b.	1359.	C. A. 4 b; 11 b.
1256.	H.¹ 24 b.	1309.	C. A. 127 b; 390 a.	1360.	C. A. 38 b; 124 a.
1257.	H.¹ 25 a.	1310.	Br. M. 212 b.	1361.	C. A. 17 b; 67 b.
1258.	H.¹ 25 b.	1311.	S. K. M. II.² 35 b.	1362.	W. 174 a.
1259.	H.¹ 26 a.	1312.	S. K. M. II.² 3 a.	1363.	C. A. 65 b; 199 b.
1260.	H.¹ 26 b.	1313.	S. K. M. II.² 69 a.	1364.	C. A. 248 a; 737 a.
1261.	H.¹ 27 a.			1365.	Br. M. 251 b.
1262.	H.¹ 27 b.		**V. DRAUGHTS AND SCHEMES**	1366.	Br. M. 253 a.
1263.	H.¹ 48 b.		**FOR THE HUMOROUS**	1367.	S. K. M. III. 85 a.
1264.	H.³ 53 a.		**WRITINGS.**	1368.	C. A. 188 b; 564 b.
		1314.	Br. M. 42 b.	1369.	F. U.
	II. FABLES.	1315.	C. A. 66 b; 201 b.	1370.	W. Ant. I. 1 a.
1265.	H.² 3 b.	1316.	H.² 15 b.	1371.	C. A. 103 a; 325 a.
1266.	C. A. 115 a; 357 a.	1317.	S. K. M.² 12 a.	1372.	Br. M. 272 a.
1267.	C. A. 117 a; 361 a.	1318.	J.¹ 39 b.	1373.	C. A. 70 b; 208 b.
1268.	C. A. 66 a; 200 a.	1319.	H.¹ 44 a.	1374.	S. K. M. I. 1 b.
1269.	C. A. 66 b; 200 b.	1320.	H.² 14 b.	1375.	F. 1 a.
1270.	C. A. 66 b; 201 b.	1321.	Tri. 73.	1376.	W. An. III. 217 a.
1271.	S. K. M. III. 93 b.	1322.	S. K. M. III. 66 b.	1377.	G. o'.
1272.	C. A. 172 b; 516 b.	1323.	L. o'.	1378.	C. A. 245 a; 731 a.
1273.	C. A. 66 a; 201 a.	1324.	S. K. M. III. 48 a.		
1274.	C. A. 66 b; 201 b.	1325.	L. 72 b.		
1275.	C. A. 75 a; 219 a.	1326.	I.² 91 a.		
1276.	S. K. M. III. 45 a.	1327.	G. 89 a.		**XXII.**
1277.	C. A. 66 a; 200 a.	1328.	C. A. 36 b; 116 b.		
1278.	C. A. 66 a; 200 a.	1329.	W. XXX.		**MISCELLANEOUS NOTES.**
1279.	C. A. 66 a; 201 a.	1330.	F. 47 a.		
		1331.	C. A. 68 b; 203 b.	1379.	Cod. Atl. 243 a; 727 a.
	III. JESTS AND TALES.	1332.	Tr. 2.	1380.	C. 19 b.
1280.	C. A. 117 a; 361 a.	1333.	B. M. 129 b.	1381.	B. 50 b.
1281.	S. K. M. III. 73 b.	1334.	C. 19 b.	1382.	Ash. II. 13 b.
1282.	C. A. 66 a; 201 a.	1335.	C. A. 75 b; 219 b.	1383.	F. U.
1283.	S. K. M. III. 58 a.			1384.	S. K. M. III. 1 b.
1284.	C. A. 147 b; 439 a.		**XXI.**	1385.	S. K. M. III. 30 a.
1285.	M. 58 b.		**LETTERS.—PERSONAL**	1386.	S. K. M. III. 55 a.
1286.	C. A. 12 a; 42 a.		**RECORDS.—DATED**	1387.	S. K. M. III. 94 a.
1287.	C. A. 300 b; 914 a.		**NOTES.**	1388.	C. A. 328 a; 980 a.
1288.	C. A. 75 b; 219 b.	1336.	C. A. 143 b; 426 b.	1389.	H.³ 47 b.
		1337.	C. A. 211 b; 621 a.		

1390.	H.² 14 *b*.
1391.	H.² 46 *a*.
1392.	S. K. M. II. 2. 7 *a*.
1393.	S. K. M. II.² 7 *b*.
1394.	S. K. M. II.² 12 *a*.
1395.	S. K. M. II.² 20 *a*.
1396.	S. K. M. II.² 22 *a*.
1397.	S. K. M. II.² 27 *a*.
1398.	S. K. M. II.² 52 *a*.
1399.	S. K. M. II.² 53 *a*.
1400.	S. K. M. II.² 63 *a*.
1401.	S. K. M. II.² 68 *b*.
1402.	S. K. M. II.² 69 *a*.
1403.	S. K. M. II.² 75 *b*.
1404.	S. M. M. II.² 78 *b*.
1405.	I.² 11 *a*.
1406.	I.² 70 *b*, *a*.
1407.	I.² 72 *b*.
1408.	I.² 87 *a*.
1409.	I.¹ 28 *a*.
1410.	W. P. 7 *a*.
1411.	W. 5 *b*.
1412.	W. A. II. 202 *b*.
1413.	W. X.
1414.	L. o′
1415.	L. 1 *a*.
1416.	L. 1 *b*.
1417.	L. 2 *a*.
1418.	L. 30 *b*.
1419.	L. o″
1420.	Br. M. 202 *b*.
1421.	F. o′
1422.	F. 27 *b*.
1423.	W. An. III. 217 *a*.
1424.	W. An. III. 232 *b*. (F)
1425.	M. o′.
1426.	M. 8 *a*.
1427.	M. 53 *b*.
1428.	Mz. o″.
1429.	Tr. 22.
1430.	K.² 27 *b*.
1431.	K.3 48 *b*.
1432.	W. An. III. 152 *a*.
1433.	W. An. IV. 153 *a*.
1434.	W. An. IV. 167.
1435.	W. L. 141 *b*.
1436.	W. L. 141 *a*.
1437.	W. L. 212 *a*.
1438.	W. L. 203 *a*.
1439.	C. A. 11 *b*; 37 *b*.
1440.	C. A. 19 *b*; 72 *b*.
1441.	C. A. 27 *a*; 89 *a*.
1442.	C. A. 70 *a*; 207 *a*.
1443.	C. A. 113 *a*; 349 *a*.
1444.	C. A. 118 *b*; 366 *a*.
1445.	C. A. 145 *a*; 432 *a*.
1446.	C. A. 176 *b*; 532 *b*.
1447.	C. A. 185 *b*; 557 *b*.
1448.	C. A. 222 *a*; 664 *a*.
1449.	C. A. 313 *b*; 950 *b*.
1450.	C. A. 358 *b*; 1124 *b*.
1451.	Br. M. 48 *a*.
1452.	Br. M. 132 *b*.
1453.	Br. M. 150 *b*.
1454.	Br. M. 191 *a*.
1455.	Br. M. 192 *a*.
1456.	Mi. A.
1457.	Br. M. P.
1458.	C. 15 *b* [1].
1459.	S. K. M. III. 1 *a*.
1460.	H.3 58 *b*.
1461.	H.¹ 41 *a*.
1462.	H.3 57 *a*.
1463.	Br. M. 271 *b*.
1464.	G. o″.
1465.	E. 1 *a*.
1466.	C. A. 67 *a*; 202 *a*.
1467.	C. A. 260 *a*; 793 *a*.
1468.	C. A. F. 279 *a*; 855 *a*.
1469.	C. A. 207 *a*; 609 *a*.
1470.	S. K. M. III. 87 *b*.
1471.	F. o″.
1472.	Leic. 13 *a*.
1473.	C. A. 376 *b*; 1168 *a*.
1474.	L. 94 *b*.
1475.	W. 191 *a*.
1476.	Br. M. 279 *b*.
1477.	J.² 82 *b*.
1478.	M. 62 *a*.
1479.	C. A. 284 *b*; 865 *b*.
1480.	C. A. 121 *a*; 375 *a*.
1481.	K.² 3 *b*.
1482.	W. 151 *b*.
1483.	F. o″.
1484.	B. M. 71 *b*.
1485.	C. A. 139 *b*; 419 *b*.
1486.	Tr. 4.
1487.	Tr. 57.
1488.	S. K. M. III. 93 *a*.
1489.	K.² 2 *a*.
1490.	K.² 2 *b*.
1491.	S. K. M. III. 16 *b*.
1492.	Ash. II. 11 *b*.
1493.	Tr. 2.
1494.	W. XXIII.
1495.	G. 8 *a*.
1496.	S. K. M. III. 3 *b*.
1497.	B. 8 *a*.
1498.	Ash. II. 12 *b*.
1499.	Leic. 16 *b*.
1500.	Ash. II. 11 *b*.
1501.	K.3 29 *b*.
1502.	L. 53 *b*.
1503.	L. 53 *a*.
1504.	G. 95 *a*.
1505.	Ash. II. 10 *b*.
1506.	B. 58 *a*.
1507.	Br. M. 79 *b*.
1508.	K.² 12 *b*.
1509.	B. 4 *a*.
1510.	Ash. I. 1 *a*.
1511.	S. K. M. III. 47 *a*.
1512.	S. K. M. III. 43 *a*.
1513.	H.3 77 *a*.
1514.	H.3 76 *b*.
1515.	H.3 81 *b*.
1516.	H.² 94 *b*.
1517.	H.² 16 *b*.
1518.	H.² 33 *a*. .
1519.	S. K. M. II.² 4 *a*.
1520.	S. K. M. II.¹ o′.
1521.	S. K. M. II.¹ 94 *b*.
1522.	S. K. M. II.¹ 95 *a*.
1523.	L. 94 *a*.
1524.	I.² 1 *b*.
1525.	Br. M. 229 *b*.
1526.	C. A. 70 *b*; 208 *b*.
1527.	Br. M. 271 *b*.
1528.	F. o″.
1529.	C. A. 189 *a*; 565 *a*.
1530.	C. A. 76 *a*; 223 *a*.
1531.	C. A. 253 *b*; 748 *a*.
1532.	W. XXXII.
1533.	C. A. 17 *b*; 67 *b*.
1534.	C. A. 312 *b*; 949 *b*.
1535.	B. M. 272 *b*.
1536.	C. A. 116 *b*; 395 *a*.
1537.	C. A. 212 *b*; 627 *b*.
1538.	C. A. 258 *a*; 784.
1539.	E. o″.
1540.	Br. M. 227 *a*.
1541.	Br. M. 42 *b*.
1542.	Br. M. 212 *a*.
1543.	H.3 89 *b*.
1544.	C. A. 132 *a*; 401 *a*.
1545.	C. A. 26 *a*; 87 *a*.
1546.	Ash. I. 18 *b*.
1547.	W. XII.
1548.	Br. M. 148 *a*.
1549.	Br. M. 148 *b*.
1550.	Br. M. 149 *b*.
1551.	Br. M. 271 *a*.
1552.	Br. M. 274 *a*.
1553.	C. A. 4 *a*; 11 *a*.
1554.	C. A. 34 *b*; 109 *a*.
1555.	C. A. 75 *a*; 220 *a*.
1556.	C. A. 77 *b*; 225 *b*.
1557.	C. A. 94 *b*; 271 *b*.
1558.	C. A. 121 *b*; 376 *b*.
1559.	C. A. 130 *a*; 397 *a*.
1560.	C. A. 164 *b*; 490 *b*.
1561.	C. A. 171 *b*; 515 *b*.
1562.	C. A. 175 *a*; 526 *a*.
1563.	C. A. 227 *b*; 685 *a*.
1564.	C. A. 334 *b*; 1017 *b*.
1565.	C. A. 329 *b*; 993 *a*.
1566.	Bibl. Melzi.

APPENDIX

I.

THE HISTORY OF THE MANUSCRIPTS.

1. Leonardo by his will expressly devised all his MSS. and drawings to his younger friend Francesco Melzi, who carried them back to Milan. Four years after Leonardo's death Alberto Bendedeo wrote from Milan to Alfonso d'Este, Duke of Ferrara: *"Et perchè ho fatto mentione de la casa de Melzi, aviso a V. Ex. che un fratello di questo che ha giostrato fù creato de Lionardo da Vinci, et herede et ha molti de' suoi secreti, et tutte le sue opinioni . . . Credo ch'egli habbia quelli libriccini de Lionardo de la Notomia, et de molte altre belle cose."* See G. Campori, *Nuovi Documenti.*

When Vasari visited Milan — probably in 1566 — he saw Leonardo's MSS. in Francesco Melzi's possession, and wrote as follows: *Lionardo . . . di brutti caratteri scrisse lettere, che sono fatte con la mano mancina a rovescio; e chi non ha pratica a leggere, non l'intende, perchè non si leggono se non con lo specchio. Di queste carte della notomia degli uomini n'è gran parte nelle mani di messer Francesco da Melzo gentiluomo milanese, che nel tempo di Lionardo era bellissimo fanciullo e molto amato da lui, così come oggi è bello e gentile vecchio, che le ha care e tiene come per reliquie tal carte, insieme con il ritratto della felice memoria di Lionardo: e chi legge quegli scritti, par impossibile che quel divino spirito abbi così ben ragionato dell'arte e de' muscoli e nervi e vene, e con tanta diligenza d'ogni cosa. Come anche sono nelle mani di . . . ., pittor milanese, alcuni scritti di Lionardo, pur di caratteri scritti con la mancina a rovescio, che trattano della pittura e de' modi del disegno e colorire. Costui non è molto che venne a Fiorenza a vedermi, desiderando stampar questa opera, e la condusse a Roma per dargli esito; nè so poi che di ciò sia seguito.* (Ed. Sansoni, IV. 37).

In another place Vasari mentions that he himself possessed some drawings by Leonardo.

Lomazzo, the Milanese painter, writes, in 1590 (*Idea del Tempio della pittura*, 2nd Ed., p. 15):

Ma sopra a tutti questi scrittori è degno di memoria Lionardo Vinci, il qual insegnò l'Anatomia dei corpi umani, e dei cavalli, ch'io ho veduta appresso a Francesco Melzi, designata divinamente di sua mano. Dimostrò anco in figura tutte le proporzioni dei membri del corpo umano; scrisse della prospettiva dei lumi, del modo di tirare le figure maggior del naturale, e molti altri libri ... Ma di tante cose niuna se ne ritrova in stampa; ma solamente di mano di lui, che in buona parte sono pervenute nelle mani di Pompeo Leoni, statovaro del Cattolico Rè di Spagna, che gli ebbe dal figliuolo di Francesco Melzi, e n'è venuto di questi libri ancora nelle mani del Sig. Guido Mazenta, Dottore virtuosissimo, il quale gli tiene molto cari.

2. In the short anonymous biography of Leonardo which, as it seems to me, must have been written somewhat earlier than Vasari's *Vite* (published by Milanesi, *Arch. Stor. Ital.* XVI) the MSS. are mentioned in these terms: (*Leonardo) tornossene a Milano et dipoi in Francia al servizio del rè Francesco, dove portò assai de' sua disegni, de quali ancora ne lasciò in Firenze nello Spedale di S. Maria Nuova con altre mas-*

serizie et la maggior parte del cartone della sala del Consiglio, del quale è il disegno del gruppo dè cavalli che oggi in opera si vede rimaso in Palazo . . . et lascio per testamento a messer Francesco da Melzio, gentile homo milanese, tutti i danari contanti, panni, libri, scritture, disegni et instrumenti et ritratti circa la pittura et arte et industria sua che quivi si trovava, et·fecelo executore del suo testamento.

These references to them, which are the oldest known, may be supplemented by some information which I owe to the kindness of Signor Enrico Stevenson, Scrittore in the Library of the Vatican. MS. 71 Boncompagni (previously Albani 511), XVIth century, contains the catalogue of MSS. belonging to 'Sangallo'. In this catalogue a MS. volume, Tome XXXIX, is thus described: *Openione di Lionardo, da Vinci nel dipigniere prospettive, ombre, lontananze, altezze, bassezze d'apresso o da lontano, et altro.*

It seems therefore doubtful whether after the death of Francesco Melzi, about 1570, the Melzi family still possessed Leonardo's literary bequest intact, or at any rate, were the sole possessors of it. We have fuller information at the beginning of the XVIIth century, for Leonardo's MSS. had by that time become famous and were sought after as relics and curiosities. Guido Mazenta, who is mentioned by Lomazzo as possessing MSS. by Leonardo, was the brother of the author of an interesting memoir entitled: *Alcune memorie dè fatti da Leonardo da Vinci a Milano e dè suoi libri del P. D. Gio. Amb° Mazzenta, Milanese, Cherico Reg[re] minore di S. Paolo altrim[ti] detti Barnabiti.*[1] An exact translation of this into French has been given by M. Eugène Piot in the Cabinet de l'Amateur (1863, p.61—63). I quote from it the following passage relating to the history of the MSS.

A la mort de Melzi ... les manuscrits restèrent dans sa villa de Vaprio, où ses héritiers, qui avaient des goûts et des occupations bien différents,

négligèrent à ce point ces trésors qu'il fut facile à Lelio Gavardi, qui enseignait les humanités dans cette famille, d'en prendre tout ce qu'il voulut et de porter treize de ces volumes à Florence, dans le dessin de les offrir au grand-duc. Mais ce prince tomba malade et mourut à son arrivée, et il vint à Pise chez Manuce. Je lui fis honte de son bien mal acquis, et il en convint. Mes études étaient finies, je devais partir: il me pria de reporter les volumes à Milan, ce dont je m'acquittai de bonne foi en consignant le tout au chef de la famille, le Dr Oratio Melzi, qui fut très-étonné de l'embarras que j'avais voulu prendre, et qui m'en fit· don en me disant qu'il avait du même peintre beaucoup d'autres dessins qui demeuraient abandonnés dans des caisses sous les toits de sa villa. Ces livres restèrent donc entre mes mains, et, plus tard, entre celles de mes frères. Ceux-ci en firent une étalage un peu trop grand, racontèrent à ceux qui les voyaient avec quelle facilité je les avais obtenus, de sorte que beaucoup de personnes retournèrent chez le docteur Oratio et en tirèrent des dessins, des modèles anatomiques, et beaucoup de précieuses reliques de l'atelier de Léonard. Pompeo Leoni fut un de ses chasseurs; son père avait été élève de Michel Ange Buonarotti, et lui-même était au service du roi d'Espagne, pour qui il a fait tous les bronzes de l'Escurial. Pompeo promit au Dr Melzi offices, magistratures, siège dans le sénat de Milan, s'il pouvait reprendre les treize volumes et les lui donner pour les envoyer au roi Philippe, grand amateur de ces sortes de curiosités. Excité par de telles espérances, Melzi vole chez mon frère, le prie à genoux de lui rendre les manuscrits qu'ils m'avait donnés; c'était son collègue au collège de Milan, bien digne de sa compassion et de son amitié; sept volumes lui furent rendus. Des six qui restaient à la maison, un fut offert au cardinal Frédéric Borromée; il est aujourd'hui conservé dans la bibliothèque Ambrosienne; c'est un in-folio, couvert de velours rouge, qui traite très philosophiquement de la lumière et des ombres, au point de vue de la peinture, de la perspective et de l'optique. Un autre fut donné à Ambroise Figini, noble peintre de cette époque, qui le laissa à Hercule Bianchi avec le reste de son cabinet. Pressé par le duc Charles-Emanuel de Savoie qui désirait en posséder, j'en obtins de l'amitié de mon frère un troisième que j'envoyai à cette Altesse. Après la mort de mon frère, les trois autres sont parvenus entre les mains de Pompeo Aretino, qui, avec ceux qu'il avait receuillis, en sépara les feuillets pour en former un gros volume qui passa à son héritier Polidore Calchi, et fut vendu ensuite à Galéaz Arconati pour trois cents ducats. Cet homme généreux le conserve dans sa galerie remplie de mille choses précieuses; il a dû plusieurs fois rési-

---

[1] The Italian MS. by Mazenta was until 1882 in the possession of the firm of booksellers A. Firmin-Didot, of Paris; but I was constantly forbidden to examine its contents. It has lately passed into the possession of an antiquary in Paris. The following interesting passage is again taken from M. Piot's translation, which adequately takes the place of the original: *Ses observations s'étendent mêmes jusqu'aux choses historiques; il y met sous nos yeux les antiques cataractes dont les Ptolomées se servaient en Egypte pour répandre et distribuer les eaux bienfaisantes du Nil; les belles inventions relatives à la navigation de la mer de Nicomédie, au moyen des lacs et des fleuves, dont il est question dans les lettres de Trajan et de Pline; mais je crois que ce curieux génie prenait plaisir à déguiser sous ces noms ceux de Milan et de Nuovocomo (!?).*

ster aux prières du duc de Savoie et d'autres princes qui le lui demandaient : il en a refusé plus de six cents ducats.

3. The MSS. in the possession of the brothers Mazenta, had, it would seem, been gradually reduced to three. Guido Mazenta whose name is to be seen in the MS. given by him to Cardinal Borromeo (see Bibl. No. 2), died in 1613.

In 1636, Count Galeazzo Arconati — who is named in Mazenta's report — presented twelve MS. volumes by Leonardo to the Ambrosian Library at Milan. The explicit deed of gift may be seen, translated into French in the *Cabinet de l'Amateur,* 1861, pp. 53—59. In the catalogue of these MSS. the binding is more particularly described than the contents. The following twelve MSS. were included in this gift. 1. the Codex Atlanticus (Bibl. 38), 2. a MS. now lost, but described as follows:

Le deuxième est un livre in-folio ordinaire, de la grandeur du papier coupé ordinaire. Il est relié en bois couvert de cuir rouge, orné de frises et de fleurs d'or. Le volume est entièrement composé de feuillets de vélin et commence par ces paroles, écrites en rouge: TAVOLA DELLA PRESENTE. *Suivent huit feuillets sans pagination. Elle commence au suivant, qui a un ornement en tête qui dit:* Eccellentis s. prencipe, *etc., et la pagination suit jusqu'au cent vingtième feuillet, quatre-vingt-sept pour le text, trois blancs et le reste des dessins divers coloriés, le premier desquels est intitulé:* Sfera solida, *et le dernier:* Piramis laterata exagona vacua; *au fond du feuillet est un texte grec qui exprime la même chose.*

3. *Le troisième est un livre in-quarto, relié en vélin, sur le dos duquel on lit les paroles suivantes:* DI LEONARDO DA VINCI; *il est de cent feuillets juste, mais le premier manque; sur le second il y a quelques cerises noires, feuilles et fruits coloriés. Dans l'intérieur du volume, au feuillet 49, on a inséré cinq feuillets de dessins variés, armes de hast pour la plupart, et à la fin un autre petit volume (volumetto) de diverses figures de mathématiques et d'oiseaux, de dix-huit feuillets, qui a été cousu dans la même reliure en vélin.*

Bibl. 3, 4. Ash. II and B. The appendix (*volumetto*) is now lost; the last mention of it occurs in Venturi's Essai (1796). Compare No. 1465, Note 4.

4. MS. of 114 leaves (see Bibl. 5, 6, Ash. I and A).

5. *Le cinquième est un autre livre semblable, in-quarto, couvert, comme le précédent, de cinquante-quatre feuillets. Sur le premier sont dessinées diverses têtes bouffonnes, et sur le dernier quatre colonnes de texte, écrites à rebours. Il est marqué sur le dos* LEONARDO DA VINCI.

This description corresponds with the MS., Bibl. 28 Tr. 6.

6. MS. see Bibl. 25, E.

7. MS. see Bibl. 22, F.

8. MS. see Bibl. 26, G.

9. Three MSS. bound in one vol.; see Bibl. 8—10, H¹, H², H³.

10. Two small MSS. bound in one, see Bibl. 13, 14.

11. MS. see Bibl. 18, L.

12. MS. see Bibl. 27, M.

In 1674 Count Orazio Archinti presented to the same Library a MS. by Leonardo, consisting of three small note-books in one Vol.; Bibl. 32—34.

In 1790, Stefano Bonsignori made a short catalogue of the MSS. in the Ambrosian Library at Milan. It includes 1. MS. C. A, see Bibl. 28; 2. MS. B and Ash. II, see Bibl. 3, 4; 3. MS. Ash. I and A, Bibl. 5, 6; 4. MS. D, Bibl. 31; 5. MS. E, Bibl. 25; 7. MS. G, Bibl. 26; 8. MSS. H¹, H², H³, Bibl. 8—10.

The descriptions of the others are too vague and slight to admit of our indentifying by them any MSS. now existing: 6. *Miscellanea; idrostatica, etc. È in-8 piccolo, in cartone rustico.* 9. *Miscellanea. Moto, macchine, macchinette da forar cristalli, etc. È in-16, legato in pergamena.* 10. *Miscellanea in-16, in cartone rustico,* 11. *Miscellanea. Abbozzi informi, moto ecc. È in-16, pergamena (see Dozio, degli scritti . . . di Leonardo da Vinci. Milano* 1871, *pp.* 21—24). It will be observed that one MS. fewer is here named than in the deed of gift from Count Arconati; on the other hand a MS. *D,* not previously mentioned, is now included. The fifth MS. of Arconati's list is evidently wanting in this list. The volume given to the Ambrosian Library by Cardinal Borromeo in 1603 (Bibl. 2, C) seem also to have been omitted. It is evident then that we cannot exactly determine how many of these MSS. were to be found in the Ambrosian Library in the year 1796. At the suggestion of Bonaparte the Directory of the French Republic conveyed many works of art from Italy into France. So much as this is, at any rate certain: in August 1796 the Codex Atlanticus was in the Bibliothèque Nationale: and "*Douze petits MSS. de Leonardo de Vinci, sur les sciences*" were in the Institut National (Institut de France). The authors of the catalogue of the pictures and MSS. removed from the Ambrosian Library — Peignon, *commissaire de guerre* and *le Citoyen* Tinet, *agent des Arts'* (dated Milan, May 24, 1796) either do not mention Leonardo's MSS. at all, or—which is more probable—include them under the following somewhat vague designation "*Le Carton des ouvrages de Leonardo d'avinci*". It is certain, on the other hand, that in 1815 the commissary of the

Austrian governement demanded the restoration to the Ambrosian Library of thirteen (or fourteen?) MSS., being the number stated in Venturi's Essay written in 1796. (Venturi says in his essay: *Les Manuscrits sont au nombre de quatorze, parceque le Volume B contient un appendice de dix-huit feuillets qu'on peut séparer et considérer comme le quatorzième volume*).

However, only the Codex Atlanticus found its way back again; the other twelve MSS. remain in the possession of the Institut de France. These facts cover all that is known of the history and fate of the volumes now on the continent, that is to say in France and Italy.

I am unfortunately not in a position to give so full an account of the vicissitudes of such of Leonardo's MSS. as are now in England. Of the MS. volume at Windsor, W. L. (Bibl. 36) Chamberlain tells us (Original Designs, London, 1812): *It was one of the three volumes, which became the property of Pompeo Leoni that is now in his Majesty's possession. It is rather probable than certain that this great curiosity was acquired for King Charles I. by the Earl of Arundel, when he went an Ambassador to the Emperor Ferdinand II. in 1636, as may indeed be inferred from an instructive inscription over the place, where the volumes are kept, which sets forth that James King of England offered three thousand pistoles for one of the volumes of Leonardo's works. And some documents in the Ambrosian Library give colour to this conjecture. This volume was happily preserved, during the civil wars of the last century, among other specimens of the fine arts, which the munificence of Charles I. had amassed with a diligence equal to his taste. And it was discovered soon after his present Majesty's accession, in the same cabinet, where Queen Caroline found the fine portraits of the court of Henry VIII. by Hans Holbein, which the King's liberality permitted me lately to lay before publick.*

Chamberlain, apparently misled by the well-known inscription[1] in the Ambrosian Library seems to assume that Lord Arundel must

have derived the Leonardo MSS. in his possession from Arconati, and not from Spain; but Mr. Alfred Marks of Long Ditton, has lately disproved this clearly in two contributions to the Athenaeum, Nos. 2626 and 2645. John Evelyn in his Memoirs (Vol. I, p. 213 ed. 1818) tells us that when travelling in Italy in 1646 he received from Lord Arundel, then sick at Padua, where he died in the course of this year, advice as to what he should try to see. Afterwards, visiting the Ambrosian Library, Evelyn writes:—

"In this room stands the glorious (boasting) *inscription of Cavaliero Galeazzo Arconati, valueing his gift to the librarie of severall drawings by Da Vinci, but these we could not see, the keeper of them being out of towne and he always carrying the keys with him, but my Lord Martial, who had seene them, told me all but one booke are small, that an huge folio contain'd 400 leaves full of scratches of Indians* [sketches of engines?] *&c., but whereas the inscription pretends that our King Charles had offer'd 1,000 l. for them, my Lord himselfe told me that it was he who treated with Galeazzo for himselfe in the name and by permission of the King, and that the Duke of Feria, who was then Governor, should make the bargain: but my Lord having seen them since did not think them of so much worth."*

The leaves of the Codex Atlanticus are numbered up to 393; hence it is probable that in giving this description Lord Arundel had this single MS. in his mind. The MS. W. L. at Windsor which, with the MS. C. A. formerly belonged to Pompeo Leoni now consists of only 234 folio leaves. Arconati (see above) mentions, it is true, one collection only of MSS. i. e. MS. C. A. as being in the hands of Pompeo Leoni; but it can hardly be doubted that the MSS. and drawings W. L. were also in his possession, since Leoni's name is given in the inscription on the old binding of the two volumes in the same way.

"Pompeo Leoni of Arezzo, Court sculptor to King Philip II. of Spain, died in Madrid A. D. 1610, as we learn from Carducho '*Dialogos de la Pintura*' (1633). Part of his property was publicly sold at Madrid; some works which had belonged to it being afterwards purchased by Charles the First when, as Prince of Wales, he visited Spain in 1623.

From the Spanish portion of Pompeo's collection thus sold came, in all probability, the two volumes of Leonardo's of which Carducho speaks as being then in the possession of Don Juan de Espina: "*Alli vi dos libros dibujados y manoscritos de mano del gran Leonardo de Vinchi, de particular curiosidad y doctrina*" ("two

---

[1] The following inscription is on the staircase of the Ambrosian Library

|| LEONARDI VINCII || MANU . ET . INGENIO . CELEBERRIMI || LUCUBRATIONUM . VOLUMINA . XII || HABES . O . CIVIS || GALEAZ—ARCONATUS || INTER . OPTIMATES . TUOS || BONARUM . ARTIUM . CULTOR . OPTIMUS || REPUDIATIS . REGIO . ANIMO . || QUOS . ANGLIAE . REX . PRO . UNO . OFFEREBAT || AUREIS . TER . MILLE . HISPANICIS || NE . TIBI . TANTI . VIRI . DEESSET . ORNAMENTUM || BIBLIOTHECAE . AMBROSIANAE . CONSECRAVIT || NE . TANTI . LARGITORIS . DEESSET . MEMORIA || QUEM . SANGUIS . QUEM . MORES || MAGNO . FEDERIGO[1] . FUNDATORI || ADSTRINGUNT || BIBLIOTHECAE . CONSERVATORES || POSUERE . ANNO . MDCXXXVII. ||

books," may we say? "one of sketches, one manuscript"), which the Prince of Wales had in vain sought to purchase. The contents of these volumes Carducho unfortunately describes only in very general terms. In Mr. Sainsbury's 'Original Unpublished Papers illustrative of the Life of Rubens,' we find evidence that Lord Arundel was subsequently in treaty for these very books, or, perhaps, for one of them only. On p. 294 will be found a note of Endymion Porter's "of such things as my Lord Embassador Sr Francis Cottington is to send owt of Spaine for my Lord of Arondell; and not to forget the booke of drawings of Leonardo de Vinze wch is in Don Juan de Espinas hands." This is of the date 1629, when Sir Francis was for the third time setting out for Spain as ambassador. His negotiations for the book were unsuccessful, for on January 19th, 1636—37, we find (p. 299) Lord Arundel writing from Hampton Court to Lord Aston, then Ambassador to Spain,—"I beseech y^u be mindfull of D. Jhon. de Spinas booke, if his foolish humor change." There can, I think, be little doubt that, on the change of Don Juan's "foolish humor," a priceless treasure, the object of so many fruitless attempts, at last rewarded the persistence of the great English collector" (A. MARKS).

Here, beyond a doubt, only the MS. W. L. is meant, for this, as being a collection of Leonardo's most important drawings, must be regarded as exceptionally precious. But did Lord Arundel ultimately get this Manuscript. We cannot say more than that this seems probable; and for this reason: Hollar engraved drawings of Leonardo's which are now in Windsor and inscribed them "W. Hollar fecit 1646 ex collectione Arundeliana",—drawings which *most probably* were included in this W. L. collection before it was divided.

On the other hand it can be positively shown that Lord Arundel possessed the MS. Br. M., Bibl. 23, which was no doubt purchased by him for a relatively small sum in consideration of the smaller artistic interest of the drawings, and for the same reason it is quite intelligible that no mention should be made of it in the correspondence at the time. But whether the MS. W. L. was purchased by Charles II. when Lord Arundel's collections were sold in Holland, or whether Charles I. had previously acquired it after his journey to Spain as Prince of Wales in 1623—when he, in person, purchased some works of art from among Leoni's collection, is not known. So much as this alone is certain, that it has now for a very long period belonged to the Royal collections.

Though Chamberlain's statement as to the acquisition of Leonardo's MSS. and drawings in the Windsor Library is, as we have seen, probably inaccurate, we may still give credit to his information as to the finding of them by Queen Caroline in Kensington Palace, for he—as Royal Librarian at the time—must certainly have been acquainted with the facts. His statement is moreover confirmed by Walpole (Anecdotes of painting I, 84: *Soon after the accession of the late King, Queen Caroline found in a bureau at Kensington, a noble collection of Holbein's original drawings for the portraits of some of the chief personages of the court of Henry VIII*).

This, however, is by no means the earliest information we possess regarding Leonardo's MSS. and drawings in the possession of Royalty. In the MS. Department of the British Museum I found an old inventory from which I give the following extracts: *List of the draw^{gs} || in ye Cabinet in || His Maj^{tys} Lower || Apartment || in this is marked what || has been Deliver'd for || her Maj^{tys} use ||* Page 28. *A list of the Books of drawings and Prints in the buroe in His Majesty's great Closet at Kensington.*

No. 3. *By Hans Holbein those fram'd & hang at Richmond.*

No. 5. *Prints by Hollar; delivered to her Maj^{ty} Aug.* 1735 *and by her lent to Lady Burlington, since put in Volumes and laid in ye Library at Kensington.*

No. 6. *Drawings by Leonardo de Vinci.*

No. 13. *Drawings by Leonardo di Vinci;— these mark^d with a cross were delivered for her Maj^{tys} use in ye year* 1728.

The oldest inventory in Windsor Castle—is only of the beginning of the present century. On p. 23 we find: *"Leonardo da Vinci, Tom. I"* and a list follows of the drawings, comprised on 41 pages. For instance: *page 1 His own portrait, profile, red chalk* (a well known drawing in the present collection). Only a few can be identified, for the descriptions are very brief. On p. 26 we come to *"Leonardo da Vinci, Tom. II"* which is also a list of drawings comprised on 40 pages. It begins: *page 1, the last Supper, the Architecture is varied in the painting at Millan where an open door is represented behind our Saviour, black chalk. NB. This Drawing was not in the Vol. compiled by Pompeo Leoni, but in one of the Volumes in the Buonfiliuolo Collection bought at Venice.* (By the way I mention that the drawing in question, still at Windsor, is not an original drawing, but an old copy). This gives us an incidental clue to a second source whence the treasures of the Windsor collection have been derived. Nothing more, however, is known concerning the Buonfiliuolo collection.

On p. 29 of the Inventory we come to a catalogue of the contents of a third Vol. of 205 sheets, in which 549 drawings are named and shortly described, for instance:

No. 22 } *2 Heads, of Judas and one of the Apostles for the last supper at Milan.*

41 } *1 Mechanical Powers*
   } *1 Anatomy.*

NB. All the Leaves from 41 to 142, except those few marked otherwise, are full of very copious and accurate studys in Anatomy which were done with the assistance of Marc Antonio della Torre &c.

143 } *1 } Manuscript—Here ends the Ana-*
    } *1 } tomical study.*

As the reader will have observed, the number of leaves in the MS. W. L. does not correspond to that in either of these three Volumes. There can be no doubt that, at that time most of the drawings had been taken out of it. Recently most of the finest drawings in the Royal collection have been mounted on card-board and arranged in four portfolios, while some of the MS. leaves remain in the folio W. L. (Bibl. 36), and others are mounted on old thin card board, more particularly the texts W. P., Bibl. 15, and W. An. I, Bibl. 1; others again are not mounted nor even— at the present date —arranged. Their large number rendered it necessary that they should be classified according to their contents and the probable date of their being written, with a view to this present publication. I therefore sorted them under the following heads: W. H., Bibl. 16; W. An. II., Bibl. 17; W. M., Bibl. 19; W. An. III., Bibl. 24; W. An. IV., Bibl. 35; W., Bibl. 37. The loose leaves in the Windsor collection are numbered consecutively (from 1 – 249) without any reference to their connection, while the Roman numbers refer to those sheets which are mounted. By this means reference to the originals is facilitated.

It will be noticed that Anatomical writings preponderate greatly, and they are the portion which Vasari most admired, when he had the opportunity of seeing Leonardo's MSS. in Melzi's house.

II.

BIBLIOGRAPHY.

The Manuscripts are arranged here in the same chronological order as shown in Vol. I. pp. 5—7. The numbers of the sheets are generally not by the author, but in a more modern handwriting. The few instances when these numbers are by Leonardo will be found mentioned in the lists. The bindings are in parchment, if not otherwise stated. The following abbreviations have been introduced in the description of the contents (the Italian words are headings used by Leonardo):

A = Acqua (Water).
Ar = Architecture.
F = Forza (Force).
Fo = Fortezza (Fortress).
Ge = Geometry.
M = Moto, colpo (on movement &c.).
Ma = Mathematics.

Mn = Machines.
O = Optics.
P = Peso (Weight).
Ph = Physics.
V = Volatili (Flight of Birds).
+ = blank pages.

1. W. An. I.

1 ᵃ **1370**, *notes on the skull* | 1 ᵇ **805** | 2 ᵃ, *notes on the skull* | 2 ᵇ + 3 ᵃ *on the skull and on the teeth* | 3 ᵇ, 4 ᵃ *on the skull* | 4 ᵇ +

2. C.

Inscribed in golden letters on the front cover: · VIDI · MAZENTÆ ‖ PATRITII · MEDIOLANENSIS ‖ LIBERALITATE ‖ AN· M · D · C · III. *Inside the cover:* C and [O].— *On the first sheet (by an unknown hand):* Autographum Leonardi Vincii ‖ cujus in ejusdem rebus gestis meminit ‖ Raphael Trichet Fresneus ‖ agit autem de lumine et umbra.—*First sheet verso:* O.—*Second sheet marked* [,G,] *and* O. *The following sheets are numbered* 1—30, *by an unknown hand. These numbers disagree with Leonardo's own numbers, here given in brackets* ( ). *He seems to have counted the sheets backwards. They are on the back of the sheets, but some are wanting:* 1ᵃ **254** | 1ᵇ (15) **253** | 2ᵃ **221** | 2ᵇ (14) **220** | 3ᵃ **219** 3ᵇ (13) **218** | 4ᵃ **217** | 4ᵇ (12) **216** and **Pl. VI, 3** | 5ᵃ **252, 215,** and **Pl. VI, 2** | 5ᵇ (11) moto, voce, forza e moto | 6ᵃ del moto dell'aria e dell'acqua | O | 6ᵇ (10) forza e peso, colpo | 7ᵃ colpo, peso e forza; **213,** A | 7ᵇ (9) M, **30,** P 12 *lines,* **160,** F | 8ᵃ **131,** O | 8ᵇ **259, 180, 260** | 9ᵃ O | 9ᵇ O | 10ᵃ **262, 141** and **Pl. II, 2. 3.** | 10ᵃ—11ᵇ O | 12ᵃ **258, 229** | 12ᵇ **289** | 13ᵃ **290** | 13ᵇ **261** | 14ᵃ **256** | 14ᵇ (16) **255, 123** | 15ᵃ M, A | 15ᵇ (1)

720, 1458, 727 | 16ᵃ de ochio, M | 16ᵇ (19) O | 17ᵃ O | 17ᵇ (18) O | 18ᵃ · **303** | 18ᵇ *and* 19ᵃ O | 19ᵇ **1334, 1380** | 20ᵃ *and* 20ᵇ O | 21ᵃ **174** | 21ᵇ (17) **257** | 22ᵃ A, M, O | 22ᵇ (8) P | 23ᵃ **251** | 23ᵇ (7) A | 24ᵃ **250** | 24ᵇ (6) A | 25ᵃ A, O | 25ᵇ (5) M, A | 26ᵃ A | 26ᵇ (4) **931,** acqua e terra | 27ᵃ O | 27ᵇ (3) **53,** O | 28ᵃ M | 28ᵇ (2) P | 29ᵃ *inscribed by an unknown hand:* le carte sono di nᵣₒ 28 cioè Ventiotto. 29ᵇ [G] 30ᵃ O | 30ᵇ +

3. B.

Binding in pig-skin; marked B inside the front-cover. On the first sheet is a short, indistinct note in Spanish, probably by P. Leoni, stating that Leonardo wrote backwards. The following sheets are numbered by very large numbers from 3—90 (see the facsimile Pl. LXXIX, 2): 3ᵃ. *Drawings in water colours, representing some fruits* | 3ᵇ **329, 346, 638, 675, 1188,** F | 4ᵃ **1509, 1131,** Ph | 4ᵇ A, **1212** Ma | 5ᵃ Fo | 5ᵇ *and* 6ᵃ Mn | 6ᵇ Mn | natura de' spechi | 7ᵃ *and* 7ᵇ Mn Fo | 8ᵃ **1497** | 8ᵇ 10ᵃ Arms | 10ᵇ da passare un fiume, Ge | 11ᵃ Mn | 11ᵇ **Pl. XCIV, No. 2 and No. 3,** Mn | 12ᵃ **Pl. LXXXVIII, No. 6 and No. 7, 751** | 12ᵇ Ge, Ar | 13ᵃ Mn, *sketch of flowers* | 13ᵇ *and* 14ᵃ Ge *and sketches of flowers* | 14ᵇ camino, Ma | 15ᵃ **Pl. XCIII, No. 1,** Fo | 15ᵇ **Pl. LXXVII, No. 1 and 2, 742, 743** | 16ᵃ **Pl. LXXVII, No. 3, 741** | 16ᵇ Fo, Me | 17ᵃ Ge | 17ᵇ **Pl. LXXXIX** | 18ᵃ **Vol. II, p. 47, Fig. 1,** and Fig. 2 Mn | 18ᵇ **Pl. LXXXVII, No. 2, 755,** Fo | 19ᵃ Fo | 19ᵇ **752,** Ar | 20ᵃ A Mn | 20ᵇ A **511** | 21ᵃ **Pl. LXXXVII, No. 3 and No. 4,** Fo | 21ᵇ **Pl. XXXVIII, Nos. 1—5** | 22ᵃ **Pl. XCIII, No. 2,** Mn | 23ᵃ *construction of bridges* | 23ᵇ **Pl. LXXX, No. 2** | 24ᵃ **Pl. XCVI, No. 2, 757** | 24ᵇ Mn Fo | 25ᵃ A | 25ᵇ **Pl. XC** | 26ᵃ A Mn | 26ᵇ Mn | 27ᵃ **Pl. C, No 5, 788** | 27ᵇ arms, *draw-ing of a small figure* | 28ᵃ Ge, spechi | 28ᵇ **762, Pl. CII, No. 3** | 29ᵃ Ge, strade che vano attraverso a vno argine d'ū fiume | 29ᵇ Mn | 30ᵃ Ar, Fo | 30ᵇ 32ᵃ arms 32ᵇ *on passing a river* **Pl. CIII, No. 2.** | 33ᵇ *and* 44ᵃ Mn | 34ᵃ **Vol. II, page 44, Fig. 3** | 35ᵃ Mn | 35ᵇ **Vol. II, page 45, Fig. 1,** Ar | 36ᵃ **Pl.**

LXXIV, No. 2, 746, Mn | 36ᵇ Fo | 37ᵃ **Pl. LXXVIII, Nos 2 and 3** | 37ᵇ **Pl. LXXIX, No. 1, 745** | 38ᵃ **745** Note | 37ᵇ canals | 39ᵃ **Pl. LXXVIII, No. 1, 761** | 39ᵇ **Pl. XCII, No. 1, 753** | 34ᵃ nomi d'arme da offendere, Ge | 40ᵇ a bresscia alla minera del fero sono mādaci d'ū pezo cioè sanza corame ecc.; arms | 41ᵃ—46ᵇ arms | 47ᵃ Ar | 47ᵇ Mn | 48ᵃ *and* 48ᵇ Fo | 49ᵃ *and* 49ᵇ Mn | 50ᵃ Fo | 50ᵇ **1381,** Mn | 51ᵃ *and* 51ᵇ Mn | 52ᵃ **Pl. XCVII** | 52ᵇ Fo, Mn | 53ᵃ camino | 53ᵇ A Mn | 54ᵃ d'alzare acque, bombarda | 54ᵇ A Mn | 55ᵃ **Vol. II, p. 44 Fig. 2 and p. 56 Fig. 1** | 55ᵇ modo di misurare alteze | 56ᵃ *same subject,* modo chome si debbe riparare a vna furia di soldati | 56ᵃ **Pl. XCII, No. 2 and No. 3, and Vol. II, p. 45 Fig. 2** | 57ᵃ **Pl. XCV, No. 2** | 57ᵇ **Vol. II, p. 51,** Diagram, rivellino | 58ᵃ **1506, 1023,** Ar, lupanario | 58ᵃ Fo | 59ᵃ Mn | 59ᵇ Fo | 60ᵃ **Pl. LXXXII, No. 3, 750** | 60ᵇ *on passing a river* | 61ᵃ **1080,** A | 61ᵇ **1094, 1099** | 62ᵃ **Pl. LXXXV, No. 13,** *on passing a river* | 62ᵇ **1100** | 63ᵃ F. P. | 63ᵇ **1081** | 64ᵃ A Mn | 64ᵇ Stivali da aqua, Mn | 65ᵃ—67ᵃ Mn | 67ᵇ *and* 68ᵃ A | 68ᵇ schale docpie 1ᵃ per lo chastellano l'altra per i provisionati | 69ᵃ—70ᵃ Fo | 70ᵇ Mn, **Pl. CIII, No. 1** | 71ᵃ **Pl. CII, No. 2** | 71ᵇ—73ᵇ | 74ᵃ 75ᵃ *flying machine* | 75ᵃ **Vol. II, p. 56 Fig. 1** | 75ᵇ—77ᵇ Mn | 78ᵃ Fo | 78ᵇ—81ᵃ | 81ᵇ **1117** | 82ᵃ Mn | 82ᵇ **1088** | 83ᵃ Mn | 84—87 *wanting* 88ᵃ Mn | 88ᵇ *flying machine* | 89ᵃ Mn | 89ᵇ V | 90ᵃ Mn | 90ᵇ modo di sfondare vn navilio, voce. — *Inside the back cover is the mark S.*

4. Ash. II.

16 sheets, small numbers; sheets 1 and 16, and 2 and 15 forming originally one sheet, are tinted in blue on the inside and have drawings of arms, drawn with the silverpoint; the outside is left blank. On sheets 3ᵃ *and* 14ᵃ *are three draw-ings in water colour, apparently not by Leo-nardo. They represent instruments.* 4ᵃ **1127** 4ᵇ **1115,** Fo | 5ᵃ Fo | 5ᵇ **1120,** Mn | 6ᵃ **1116** 6ᵇ **Pl. LXXXV, No. 1—11, Vol. II, p. 45** Fig. 3, **p. 74** first lines | 7ᵃ **756, Pl. XCI, No. 1** | 7ᵇ Fo | P, Mn | 8ᵃ **Vol. II, p. 56 Fig. 2, p. 57 Fig. 3 and 4** | 8ᵇ **Pl XCI, No. 2, 754** | 9ᵃ Mn | 9ᵇ arms | 10ᵃ arms and ships | 10ᵇ **1505,** arms and a nude youth, resting his left hand on a sword | 11ᵃ ships | 11ᵇ **1492,** arms **1500** | 12ᵃ cars, **1089** | 12ᵇ **1498** 13ᵃ **1204** | four columns of names | 13ᵇ **1382** Sketches of insects, a caricature *&c.*

5. Ash. I.

1a 1510, 686, *Drawing of knots*, 1183 | 1b *knots*, 1176, Ge | 2a 267, 580, 589, 516 | 2b 551, 484, 515, 284 | 3a 283, 132, 547, 203 | 3b 574 and Pl. XXXI, No. 4, the head on the right, 245, 133 | 4a 568, 563, 528, 540, 561, 439 | 4b 536, 504, 601 | 5a 602 | 5b 595, 182, 196 | 6a 584, 592, 164 | 6b 573 and Pl. XXXI, No. 4 the head on the left, 368, 112, 585, 522 | 7a 367, 364, 555 | 7b 530, 491 | 8a 571, 492, 494 | 8b 497, 489, 587 | 9a 572, 507, 495 | 9b 496, 532, 502, 285 | 10a 295, 500, 486 | 10b 501, 655 | 11a 656, 529 | 11b 531, 523 | 12a Pl. XLI, No. 1, 142, 344, 34, 92 | 12b 99, 538, 102, 558 | 13a 508, 23, 294, 591 | 13b 119, 125, 199 | 14a 552, 559, 122, 550 | 14b 606, 594 | 15a 520, 567, 176, 567 ll. 13—22, 361 | 15b 566, 659, 652, 513, 600 | 16a 654 | 16b 535, 653 | 17a 298, 145, 604 | 17b 582, 14, 291, 391, 299 | 18a 483, 661, 519, 578, 392, 583 | 18b 1546, O | 19a 887, 894, 565, 576, 588, 557 | 19b 542, 709, 509 | 20a 139, 140 | 20b 138 | 21a 48, 236, 205, 533 | 21b Pl. III, No. 2, 149 | 22a Pl. III, No. 1, 275, 148 | 22b Pl. II, No. 1, 61, 40, 546 | 23a Pl. VI, No. 4, 224 | 23b 173 | 24a *a diagram without text* | 24b Pl. IV, No. 3, 173 | 25a Pl. IV, No. 2, 169 | 25b 293, 239, 485, 541, 537, 534 | 25 Ia 171, 352 | 25 Ib *a diagram without text* | 26a Pl. XXXVIII, No. 2, 579 | 26b P | 27a Ma | 27b Ge | 27b 63 | 27 Ia Ge | 28a + | 28b 517, 147, 202 | 29a Pl. XXXI, No. 2 512 | 29b 560, Pl. XXVIII, No. 6, 390, Ph | 30a—31a P | 31b 506 | 32a M | 32b O, 68.

6. A.

Bound in parchment, marked A outside and inside the cover. The numbers of the sheets 1—64 are in Leonardo's handwriting.

1a 628, 190, 527, 708 | 1b [P], [M] 524, 83 | 2a O, 235, 518 | 2b O, Pl. XVII, No. 1, P, Mn | 3a 50 | 3b M P O | 4a—5a P M | 5b Ge | 6a Ge P | 6b Ge | 7a Mn, Ge | 7b *and* 8a M | 8b 129, 624, 100, 93, 234 | 9a M | 9b 88, O, 69 | 10a 52 | 10b 94, 85 | 11a 98 Ge | 11b *and* 12a Ge | 12b Ge, O | 13a— 15a Ge | 15b, 16a P Ge | 16b—18b Ge | 19a *acoustics*, M | 19b 281, O, *acoustics* | 20a 282, O, Ph | 20b, 21a Ma | 21b—22b M | 23a 549, 514, 586, M, *acoustics* | 23b A | 24a M, 1134, A | 24b—25b A | 26a A, M | 26b O M | 27a M 58 | 27b M A | 28a M | 28b Pl. XXII, No. 4, 369, 596 | 29a Pl. XXII, No. 3, 359 | 29b O, M | 30a—35a M P 30b 383 | 36a M P, *acoustics* | 36b 55 | 37a O, 56 | 37b 57, O | 38a O, 86 | 38b 41, Pl. XXXI, No. 3, 526 | 39a—40a Ge | 40b 543 | 41a 544 | 41b 545 | 42a O, 527 | 42b 525, P A | 43a *acoustics*, 706, A | 43b—48a M P | 48b 792, P | 49a P | 49b 786 | 50a 790, 779 | 50b Ma, 780 | 51a 781, Mn | 51b—52b P M | 53a 795, 791, 776 | 53b M P | 54 *is wanting* 55a M P O | 55b 929, 967, 941 | 56a A 968, 944 | 56b 945 Ph | 57a Ph, 1083 | 57b M | 58a A | 58b A, 934, 940, 943 | 59a— 61a A | 61b M O | 62a M P | 62b 311, *two heads of horses*, P | 63a 312, Pl. VIII, No. 1 | 63b A | 64a 898, 889, A | 64b O 214, 249, 873. *The following blank sheet has the marks S on the front, and S*b *and the number 4, on the reverse. They are by an unknown hand. — A splendid edition of the whole volume was published in 1881 by A. Quantin, Paris. It contains photographs of all the texts. M. Charles Ravaisson-Mollien, the editor, has added to the facsimile the transcript of the Italian, a French translation, notes and an elaborate index.*

7. S. K. M. III.

Marked 32 on the first sheet by an unknown hand: 1a 1459 | 1b 1384 | 2a—3a Ph | 3b 1496, del moto delle corde | 4a— 8a *pullies* | 8b Ge | 9a Ar | 9b+ | 10a Vol. II, p. 89 the last two diagrams | 10b—11a Mn | 11b + | 12a P | 12b + | 13 *and* 14 *are wanting* | 15a + | 15b, 16a A | 16b 1491 | 17a 1179 | 17b Ph | 18a—19a P | 19b 651 | 20a P | 20b—23a Ge | 23b 1342 | 24a Mn | 24b + | 25a 498 | 25b 1118 | 26a *knots* | 26b Ge | 27a Mn | 27b + | 28a *and* 28b Ge | 29a 1341 | 29b Mn | 30a 1385 | 30b Ar | 31b cientro della gravità | 32a aquaforte | 32b Mn | 33a O | 33b—34a Mn | 34b + | 35a Mn | 35b Ge | 36a Pl. XCIX, No. 2 | 36b 1169 | 37a Ge | 37b 208 | 38a M | 38b, 33a + | 39b—41b P | 42 *is wanting* | 43a 1512 | 43b, 44a + | 44b M | 45a 1276, franc° | 45b, 46a P | 46b 1121 | 47a 1511 | 47b Vol. II, p. 71 Fig. 1 | 48a 662, 1324 | 48b 764 | 49a 1135 | 49b Mn | 50a 731 | 50b— 51b Mn | 52a M | 52b A, 629 | 53a 614, 646, 732 | 53b M | 54a moto della saetta | 54b forma di corpo | 55a Vol. II, p. 71 Fig. 2, 647, 1386 | 55b 734 | 56a 735 | 56b distantia | 57a buse | 57b Mn | 58a 1283 | 58b

384 | 59ª Ph | 59ᵇ A | 60 *is wanting* | 61ª A | 61ᵇ M | 62ª cavaletti da lauorare | 62ᵇ *a diagram* | 63ª + | 63ᵇ A | 64ª Ge | 64ᵇ **1132** | 65ª Mn | 65ᵇ **Pl. CVIII, No.**3, 813, M | 66ª **812** | 66ᵇ **1322** | 67ª Ma | 67ᵇ + | 68ª *a sketch of clouds* | 68ᵇ *sketch of a horse* | 69 *is wanting* | 70ª + | 70ᵇ *circles* | 71ª A | 71ᵇ, 72ª *sketches of legs of horses* | 72ᵇ *sketches of windows* | 73ª Mn | 73ᵇ **1281** | 74ª M, **846** | 74ᵇ passavolante | 75ª P | 75ᵇ, 76ª + | 76ᵇ Mn | 77ª**1187** | 77ᵇ fossa, strumenti | 78ª + |

78ᵇ Ar | 79ª **Pl. LXXXV, No. 14** | 79ᵇ **1343** | 80ª P | 80ᵇ **1150** | 81ª Ar | 81ᵇ *circle* | 82 *is wanting* | 83ª, 83ᵇ Mn | 84ª *circles* | 84ᵇ + | 85ª **633, 1367** | 85ᵇ—87ª *sketches of costumes* | 87ᵇ **1470** | 88ª *circle* | 88ᵇ centro del mondo, P | 89ª Ma | 89ᵇ, 90ª P | 90ᵇ *acoustics* | 91ª **794** | 91ᵇ, 92ª P Ar | 92ᵇ A | 93ª **1488** | 93ᵇ **1271** | 94ª **1387** | 94ᵇ bonifatio *. — See No.* 20 *for the history of this MS.*

8. H.³

The three small Note books H³ H² H¹ *are bound in one Volume. From the dirty state of the sheets at the beginning and at the end of each division it becomes apparent that Leonardo had used them separately. The cover is in parchment and is twice marked* H *on the outside and once inside, and* Q *on the back of the first sheet. Inside the back cover is the mark* Qª, *and on the last sheet but one* N N 48, *meaning probably the number of sheets originally belonging to* H.³ *MSS* H² *and* H³ *are numbered throughout. The sheets of* H³ *are also numbered* 1—47, *below the text and in a reversed position. The numbers here given are above the text* | 47ª A | 47ᵇ **1389** | 48ª Ma | 48ᵇ dimmi semai, *sketch of a man's head in profile* | 49ª, 49ᵇ Mn | 50ª **670** | 50ᵇ, 51ª *notes* | 51ᵇ **689** | 52ª **999** | 52ᵇ **736** | 53ª **1264, 690** | 53ᵇ—55ª Mn | 55ᵇ

Sketch reproduced with No. 1112 | 56ª, 56ᵇ P | 57ª P, **1462** | 57ᵇ M. *sketch of a horse* | 58ª *sketch of horses and oxen drawing a car* | 58ᵇ **1460** | 59ª—60ᵇ Mn | 61ª **831** Mn | 61ᵇ—69ᵇ Mn | 70ª **691** | 70ᵇ **1191** | 71ª **1192** | 71ᵇ—73ª Mn | 73ᵇ **Pl. LXXXV, No. 16, 768** | 74ª il cïetro dell' ochio fia for dell'abaco ¹/₈ di a.b. | 74ᵇ—76ª Mn | 76ᵇ **1514** | 77ª **1513** | 77ᵇ, 78ª + | 78ᵇ *terminations of Latin verbs* | 79ª—80ª *slight sketches* | 80ᵇ, 81ª Mn | 81ᵇ **1515** | 82ª *Sketch of a car drawn by horses* | 82ᵇ—84ª Mn | 84ᵇ, 85ª—86ª *drawings of gear* | 85ª **27** | 85ᵇ, 86ᵇ, 87ᵇ, 88ª, *conjugation of the Latin verb* | 88ᵇ **644** | 89ª sum, eram &c. **1356** | 89ᵇ **1543** | 90ª—92ᵇ amo, amas, amat &c. | 93ª amor, amaris &c, **1139** | 93ᵇ, 94ª amo, legione cōtiene 6063 persone | 94ᵇ **1516**.

9. H.²

See introductory note to No. 8. — *The first sixteen sheets are numbered twice,* 1—16 *being also written below the texts, but in reversed order.* 1ª **232** | 1ᵇ **692** | 2ª, 2ᵇ A Mn | 3ª *a sketch* | 3ᵇ **1265** | 4ª—11ª A | 11ᵇ *knots,* A | 12ª *knots,* Mn | 12ᵇ **1197**, *a sketch of ornaments* | 13ª **693** | 13ᵇ, 14ª A | 14ᵇ **1390, 1320,** M | 15ª M | 15ᵇ **694, 1316** | 16ª A | 16ᵇ **1517** | 17ª A, **1010 Note** | 17ᵇ **Pl. CX, No.** 2, **1024** | 18ª **152** | 18ᵇ Mn | 19ª, 19ᵇ A | 20ª A, **464** | 20ᵇ A | 21ª A M | 21ᵇ, 22ª A | 22ᵇ Mn | 23ª **228,** A | 23ᵇ Mn | 24ª Mn | 24ᵇ—25ᵇ A Mn | 26ª, 26ᵇ A P | 27ª **Pl. XXIII, No.** 3, **377** | 27ᵇ M Mn | 28ª A | 28ᵇ **206,**

105, 163 | 29ª A | 29ᵇ A, **304** | 30ªA | 30ᵇ A, padiglō di legni a vigievine | 31ª M | 31ᵇ molino | 32ª A | 32ᵇ A P | 33ª **91, 1518** | 33ᵇ M | 34ª—35ᵇ A | 36ª Mn | 36ᵇ—37ᵇ canale | 38ª **828, 31** | 38ᵇ Mn | 39ª, 39ᵇ A | 40ª *sketch of a barrel on a car,* A **32** | 40ᵇ **671** | 41ª M A | 41ᵇ **845** | 42ª ricordati quādo cōmēti lacque ‖ dallegar prima la speriēza ‖ e poi la ragione | 42ᵇ **134** | 43ª **1014** | 43ᵇ **33** | 44ª P | 44ᵇ P A | 45ª A | 45ᵇ Ge | 46ª **1391** | 46ᵇ **620,** yhs maria **1493,** *and by an unknown hand the mark* Y 46.

10. H.¹

See introductory note of No. 8. — *The text is upside-down on the first 28 sheets.* 1ª amo, amas amat &c., **1026** | 1ᵇ + | 2ª amabam &c., A | 2ᵇ, 3ª + | 3ᵇ 4ª *forms of* amo | 4ᵇ SK | 5ª **1220** | 5ᵇ **1221** | 6ª **1222** | 6ᵇ **1223** | 7ª **1224** | 7ᵇ **1225** | 8ª **1226** | 8ᵇ **1227** | 9ª **1228** | 9ᵇ **1229** | 10ª **1230** | 10ᵇ

1231 | 11ª **1232** | 11ᵇ **1233** | 12ª **1234** | 12ᵇ **1235** | 13ª **1236** | 13ᵇ **1237** | 14ª **1238** | 14ᵇ **1239** | 15ª **1240** | 15ᵇ, 16ª + | 16ᵇ **1194** | 17ª **1241** | 17ᵇ **1242** | 18ª **1243** | 18ᵇ **1244, 643** | 19ª **1245** | 19ᵇ **1246** | 20ª **1247** | 20ᵇ **1248** | 21ª **1249** | 21ᵇ **1250** | 22ª **1251** | 22ᵇ **1252** | 23ª

1253 | 23^b **1254** | 24^a **1255** | 24^b **1256** | 25^a **1257** | 25^b **1258** | 26^a **1259** | 26^b **1260** | 27^a **1261** | 27^b **1262** | 28^a Mn | 28^b tessta della viola | 29^a 29^b Mn | 30^a— 31^a A | 31^b **308** | 32^a **842**, Ge | 32^b, 33^a *knots* | 33^b Mn, **1164** | 34^a A | 34^b Mn | 35^a *knots* | 35^b **782** | 36^a **783** | 36^b Mn | 37^a P|

37^b A | 38^a **1025** | 38^b A Mn | 39^a, 39^b Mn | 40^a **695** | 40^b **696** | 41^a **1461** | 41^b— 43^a Mn | 43^b *knots and sketch* | 44^a P, **1319** | 44^b, 45^a *sketches of tents* | 45^b, 46^a *instruments*. | 46^b A | 47^a Mn | 48^a A M | 48^b **1263** |

11. S. K. M. II.²

*The two MSS. S. K. M. II*² *and S. K. M. II*¹ *are bound in one volume; the sheets are separately numbered on the top of each front sheet, but the two volumes are placed in the binding in reversed position, so that the two parts begin at the opposite ends of the volume.* 1^a **Vol. II, p. 62** sketch | 1^b **666, 697** | 2^a **665** | 3^a **1312**, Ma | 3^b Ma | 4^a **1519** | 4^b + | 5^a M | 5^b, 6^a + | 6^b M | 7^a **1392**, M | 7^{b}M, **1393** | 8^a Mn | 8^b + | 9^a Ge | 9^b Mn | 10^a *sketch of a flower* | 10^b O | 11^a P | 11^b **Pl. LXXXV, No. 15, Vol. II, p. 74 below** | 12^a **1394, 1317**, *sketch of a head* | 12^b Ar | 13^a *knots* | 13^b Mn | 14^a **372** | 14^b, 15^a Mn | 15^b Fo | 16^a M | 16^b **103**, P | 17^a Ph | 17^b, 18^a Mn | 19^b **998** | 20^a **1395, 376, Pl. XXIII, No. 2** | 20^b, 21^a P | 21^b *sketches* | 22^a **1396** | 22^b—23^b *sketches* | 24^a **1196** | 24^b—25^b *sketches* | 26^a + | 26^b Ma | 27^a **1397** | 27^b + | 28 *is wanting* | 29^a + | 29^b *slight sketch of a woman* seated, holding a child in her lap | 30^a + | 30^b sketch | 31^a P | 31^b + | 32, 33, 34 *are wanting* | 35^a V | 35^b **1311** | 36^a M | 36^b Ma | 37^a *acoustics* | 37^b M | 38—42 *are wanting* | 43^a + | 43^b **1291** | 44^a **1290** | 44^b *knots* | 45, 46, 47 *are wanting* | 48^a—49^a *knots* | 49^b + | 50^a *sketch of a head* | 50^b, 51^a + | 51^b, 52^a Ge | 52^b **1398** | 53^a **1399** | 53^b, 54^a Ge | 54^b Mn | 55 *is wanting* | 56^a + | 56^b sketch | 57^a—59^a Ma | 59^b *sketch of a head* | 60^a + | 60^b, 61^a Ma | 62^a Ge | 62^a + | 62^b Ge | 63^a **97, 1400** | 63^b—64^b Ma | 65^a— 66^b Mn | 67^a Ar | 68^a Mn | 68^b **1401** | 69^a **1313, 1402** | 69^b + | 70, 71, 72 *are wanting* | 73^a + | 73^b M | 74^a P | 74, 75^a + | 75^b **1403** Mn | 76^a Ge | 76^b **154** | 77^a—78^a Ge | 78^b **667, 1404** | 79^a Ma | 80^a Mn | 80^b *knots.* — *On the same sheet are the marks* K K 62 *and* 25 *by an unknown hand.*

12. S. K. M. II.¹

See preliminary Note of No. 11. — *The numbers of the sheets are in Leonardo's handwriting and begin from the end, going backwards. The first sheet or cover sheet has no number* | **1520**, M, **612** | 1^a **36** | 1^b Ge | 2^a—26^a P | 26^b—28^a de chonfregatione | 28^b—42^b P | 43^a **1137** | 43^b 66^a P | 66^b **787** | 67^a P, **1206** | 67^b **784** | 68^a—69^a perpetuum mo- bile | 71^b Ar | 72^a **793** | 72^b—75^b P | 76^a— 86^a Mn | 86^b **Sketch Vol. I, p. 201 and Vol. II, p. 99 below** | 87^a—88^b Mn | 89^a **793 Note** | 89^b Mn 90^a—93^b peso—94^a centro del mondo, A | 94^b **1521** | 95^a **733, 627, 1522** | 95^b mechanica potissimum in fine incipiendū, *this note is not in Leonardo's handwriting, but by a later hand.*

13. I.²

This and M S *I*¹ *are bound in one volume. The mark* I *is outside and* Q *and* Q 3 *inside the cover.* 1^a magistr M^{to} jachomo (this note is not in Leonardo's handwriting). 1^b **1524,704** | 2^a—7^b *Latin and Italian vocabulary* | 4^a *has also the note* simon de calima tintore | 8^a **Vol. II, p. 68 Fig. 1 and 2** | 8^b—10^b Mn | 11^a **1405** | 11^b M | 12^a—14^a A | 14^b Ma | 15^a **1298** | 15^b **1299** | 16^a **1300** | 16^b **1301** | 17^a **1302** | 17^b **1303** | 18^a **1304** | 18^b **1305** | 19^a **1306** | 19^b—24^a A | 24^b **932** | 25^a Ge | 25^b—31^b A | 31^b M | 32^a *second Latin declination* | 32^b—36^a A | 36^b— 38^a M | 38^b—43^a M | 44^a—47^a M | 47^b *sketches of knots and shells* | 48^a *sketch of a dog's* head | 48^b contrapeso | 49^a *ornamental design of two cornucopiae* | 49^b sketch | 50^a—56^b M | 57^a, 58^a A, 58^b + | 59^a **679** | 59^b + | 60^a A | 60^b—61^b M | 62^a **Pl. LXXXV, No. 13**, | 62^b P | 63^a *acoustics* | 63^b + | 64^a— 66^b M | 66^b—70^a A | 70^b—71^a **1406** | 71^b, 72^a M | 72^b **1407** | 73^a—74^a A | 74^b M | 75^a A | 75^b—78^a *Latin vocabulary* | 78^b + | 79^a, 79^b A | 80^a—81^b voce d'echo—82^a **1160** | 82^b M **1477** | 83^a—86^a M P | 86^b uterque, utraque &c. | 87^a **1408** | 87^b alius, alia &c. | 88^a qui que quod | 88^b M | 89^a— 90^a amo, amas &c. | 90^b **672** | 91^a **673, 1326** | 91^b *numbers.* — *The two following sheets bear only the marks* Q 3 *and* Q.

14. I.[1]

See No. 13 *preliminary note.* — 1—12ᵃ Ge | 12ᵇ **394** | 13ᵃ, 13ᵇ Ge | 14ᵃ, 14ᵇ M | 15ᵃ **1140** Note | 15ᵇ—17ᵃ Ge | 17ᵇ **241** | 18ᵃ **1151** 242 | 18ᵇ Ar | 19ᵃ *sketch* | 19ᵇ 37* | 20ᵃ **38** | 20ᵇ—23ᵃ Mn | 23ᵇ *da forare cristalli* | 24ᵃ—25ᵃ *sketches of shields* | 25ᵇ —27ᵇ Mn | 28ᵃ **1409** | 28ᵇ—32ᵃ Mn | 32ᵇ **1017** | 33ᵃ O | 33ᵇ Ge | 34ᵃ **1018** | 34ᵇ— 37ᵃ Mn | 37ᵇ **Pl. XXVIII, No. 5, 188, 452** | 38ᵃ O | 38ᵇ, 39ᵃ *sum, es, est* &c. | 39ᵇ **1318** | 40ᵃ *quis vel qui que quod vel quid* &c. | 40ᵇ—42ᵇ Mn | 43ᵃ O | 43ᵇ—46ᵃ Mn | 46ᵇ *sketch* | 47ᵃ **1092** Note | 47ᵇ *sketch* 48ᵃ **463** | 48ᵇ Mn. — *The Marks* I I · 48 *and* · 20 · *are by an unknown hand.*

15. W. P.

Most of these researches are written on loose sheets of unequal size. The dimensions of each sheet are here given in brackets: 1ᵃ (20¹/₂ × 30 Cm) **324** | 1ᵇ **322** 2ᵃ (21³/₄ × 26¹/₂) **310, 337, Pl. VII, Nos.** 1 and 2* | 2ᵇ *sketch of a horse's legs, measurements and notes.* 3 Iᵃ (13¹/₂ × 14¹/₂ Cm) **Pl. XI,** 318 | 3 IIᵃ (17 × 15 Cm) **Pl. VII, No. 4,** 327, 321 | 3 Iᵇ, 3 IIᵇ + | 4ᵃ (21 × 12¹/₂ Cm) **Pl. XIX, No. 1,** 347 | 4ᵇ **325** | 5ᵃ (44 × 32 Cm) **341** ll. 1—4, **317** ll. 1—13, **625, 341** ll. 5—8, **317** ll. 14—17, **Pl. XXXV, No. 1,** 348 ll. 16—55, ll. 11—15, **Pl. XVII, No. 2,** 336, 348 ll. 11— 10 | **707,** 348, 56—68 | 5ᵇ **Vol. II, p. 44 Fig. 1** and **p. 47 Fig. 3** | 6 Iᵃ (21¹/₂ × 16 Cm) **Pl. VIII, No. 2,** 332 | 6 Iᵇ **333** | 6 IIᵃ (22 × 14³/₄ Cm) **Pl. XIV, No. 2,** 334 | 6 IIᵇ **Pl. XVI, No. 1,** 335 | 7ᵃ (40 × 28 Cm) **1410,** 314, 338, 328, **Pl. XIII,** 326, 330, **Pl. XIV, No. 1** | 7ᵇ **349, Pl. XX,** 339, **Pl. XVI, No. 2,** 342 | 8ᵃ (28 × 20¹/₂ Cm) **Pl. XV,** 331, 345, 323 | 8ᵇ + | 9ᵃ (27 × 20¹/₂) V | 9ᵇ+ | 10ᵃ, 10ᵇ (22 × 16 Cm) Mn | 11ᵃ (29¹/₂ × 20 Cm) **Pl. LXIII, 684** | 11ᵇ **685** | 12ᵃ **Pl. X,** 316. — *Sheets* 9—12 *which treat on different subjects are only added here, because in the Windsor Collection they form a set with Sheets* 1—8. *The thin cards, on which these sheets are mounted have a broad ornamental border in water colours.*

16. W. H.

With regard to these studies see Vol. II, p. 4. *The sheets are numbered* 46—68, *differing in size, and many not mounted are coloured in various tints: Compare also Lomazzo,* Trattato dell'arte della pittura I chap. 20, IV, 23 *and* Idea del tempio della pittura chap. 16. — *Vasari also mentions these studies.* 64. **716** | IV. **717.**

17. W. An. II.

The sheets forming this treatise are all of the same size and originally formed a small book. At present the sheets are separated. The old numbers and marks which are to be found on most of the sheets are here given in brackets after the new numbers: 36 (21) **797** | 36ᵇ *muscles of the leg* | 37ᵃ **814, Pl. CVIII, No. 4** | 37ᵇ *the veins on the head* &c. | 38ᵃ (0) 38ᵇ *veins of the leg* | 39ᵇ *veins on the leg and on the spine* | 39ᵇ **801** | 40ᵃ *nervi, matrice* | 40ᵇ + | 41ᵃ (7) Delli musscholi che movà li labri della bocha | 41ᵇ *nervi, matrice* | 42ᵃ (10) *nervi* 42ᵇ *veins of the leg* | 43ᵃ (8) Delli musscholi che movà la lingha | 43ᵇ *muscles of the foot,* **843** | 44ᵃ (3) *veins of the arm* | 44ᵇ *veins* | 74ᵃ (12) *veins of the womb* | 74ᵇ *muscles on the arm of the ape* (scimmia) *and of man* (omo) | 75ᵃ (2), 75ᵇ *muscles of the leg* | 76ᵃ *dello vñtio de mesoplevri* | 76ᵇ **Pl. CVIII, No. 1,** 809 | 77ᵃ (21) *muscles of the leg* | 77ᵇ, 78ᵃ (11) *veins of the leg* | 78ᵇ *veins of the hand* | 84ᵃ (10) 84ᵇ *the chest* | 85ᵃ *the lungs* | 85ᵇ *albero di tutti i nervi* | 86ᵃ (13) *arteries* | 86ᵇ *veins of the arm* | 87ᵃ)14) *the lungs,* 87ᵇ *the heart* | 125ᵃ—127ᵃ (4) *blood-vessels* | 127ᵇ *the spine* | 128ᵃ (5) *the mouth and the lips* | 128ᵇ *matrice di uaccha* | 156ᵃ, 156ᵇ *genitals* | 173ᵃ (16. 17—*two sheets, not separated) intestines* **827** | 173ᵇ **816** | 178ᵃ, 178ᵇ *intestines* | 183ᵃ *veins on the neck* | 183ᵇ *veins* | 201ᵃ (M) *bones* | 201ᵇ **1215** | 202ᵃ (·B·) **1412, 838** | 202ᵇ **839** *genitals,* | 203 (24) **1178,** 375, **Pl. XXIII, No. 1** | 203ᵇ **357, Pl. XXII, No. 1** | 204ᵃ (3) *stomacho* | 204ᵇ *vene, fegato* | 205ᵃ *della forza de' mvsscholli* | 205ᵇ *misenterio* | 206ᵃ (I)*polmone* | 206ᵇ *vesscicha,* **817** | 242 (N) **1214** | 242ᵇ **1213.**

18. L.

This volume is in the original cover; it is a thin card of light blue colour. It is marked L on the outside and Q c inside: o¹ **1414, 1323, 1102** | 1ᵃ **1002, 1415** | 1ᵇ **1416** | 2ᵃ **1417, 648,** *knights kneeling* | 2ᵇ Ma | 3ᵃ *sketch of a head* 3ᵇ 4ᵃ *knights kneeling* 4ᵇ A | 5ᵃ *a note* | 5ᵇ *knots* | 6ᵃ **1034** | 6ᵇ **1035** | 7ᵃ, 7ᵇ Fo | 8ᵃ co-lōbaia | 8ᵇ Ma | 9ᵃ—10ᵃ *plans* | 10ᵇ **1036** | 11ᵃ + | 11ᵇ—12ᵃ Mn | 12ᵇ, 13ᵃ + | 13ᵇ A O | 14ᵃ O | 14ᵇ *notes* | 15ᵃ **1019** | 15ᵇ **1037, Pl. XCIV, No.** 1 | 16ᵃ P Ar | 16ᵇ Fo | 17ᵃ A | 17ᵇ P | 18ᵃ, 18ᵇ Mn | 19ᵃ Fo | 19ᵇ **Pl. CX, No. 3,** *left side* **1038** | 20ᵃ **Pl. CX No. 3,** *right side* **765** | 20ᵇ Ma | 21ᵃ **1054** | 21ᵇ—23ᵃ Ma | 23ᵇ Mn | 24ᵃ Fo | 24ᵇ—26ᵃ Mn | 26ᵇ P | 27ᵃ Mn | 27ᵇ P, **378** | 28ᵃ Mn | 28ᵇ *knots* | 29ᵃ Fo | 29ᵇ Mn | 30ᵃ A | 30ᵇ Mn **1418** | 31ᵃ—33ᵃ A | 33ᵇ Mn **1039** | 34ᵃ—36ᵃ Mn | 36ᵇ **1040, Pl. CX, No. 4** | 37ᵃ Ar | 37ᵇ Ma | 38ᵃ—39ᵃ Ar | 39ᵇ Mn | 40ᵃ **1041** | 40ᵇ, 41ᵃ Mn | 41ᵇ **35** | 42ᵃ—44ᵇ M | 45ᵃ

Ma | 45ᵇ Ar | 46ᵃ Fo | 46ᵇ **1042** | 47ᵃ **1043** | 47ᵇ A | 48ᵃ, 48ᵇ Ar | 49ᵃ—52ᵇ Mn | 53ᵃ M **1503** | 53ᵇ **1502** | 54ᵃ—60ᵇ V | 61ᵃ Ar | 61ᵇ—62ᵇ V | 63ᵃ—65ᵇ Fo | 66ᵃ **1109, Pl. CX, No.** 1 | 66ᵇ **1044** | 67ᵃ **1045** | 68ᵃ, 68ᵇ Ar | 69ᵃ P A | 69ᵇ—71ᵃ Mn | 71ᵇ *a sketch* 72ᵃ **1046** | 72ᵇ **1325** | 73ᵃ Ge | 73ᵇ, 74ᵃ Ar 74ᵇ, 75ᵃ Fo | 75ᵇ **307** M | 76ᵃ **981** | 77ᵃ **1047** | 77ᵇ **226** | 78ᵃ **1048** A | 78ᵇ **1049** | 79ᵃ **488,** *citadella* | 79ᵇ Ge | 80ᵃ *voce* | 80ᵇ *drawing of a draped figure, very like the one on Pl. XXVIII, no* 7 | 81ᵃ Ge | 81ᵇ *sketch of trees* | 82ᵃ **1047 Note** | 82ᵃ *and* 83ᵃ **Vol. II, p. 244,** *sketch* 83ᵇ, 84ᵃ *outline sketch of mountains* | 84ᵇ P 85ᵃ Mn | 85ᵇ P | 86ᵃ Ge | 86ᵇ Mn | 87ᵃ **449** | 87ᵇ **393** | 88ᵃ *sketch* | 88ᵇ **1050** | 89ᵃ *sketches* | 89ᵇ Mn | 90ᵇ **1199** | 91ᵃ **1307** | 92ᵃ **623,** M | 92ᵇ Mn | 93ᵃ Ma | 93ᵇ *voca bolo lombardo &c* | 94ᵃ **1523** | 94ᵇ **1474, 1052** | O" **1053, 1198, 1419,** *and, by an unknown hand:* Le carte sono 94 cioè nouāta quart.

19. W. M.

See Vol. II, p. 224 *and No.* 1051 *Note. As to the Maps in MS.* W. L. *see No.* 36. *The following maps are on separate sheets* 1. **Pl. CXIII,** *The original is somewhat larger* (19 × 13¹/₄ in) *·the whole is executed in water colours. The rivers are in blue* **2. Pl. CXIV,** (15³/₄ XII, in) | 3. *Part of the Arno, in water-colours* (39 × 22) **Pl. CXII.** 4 *Map of a part of* Tuscany, *in water colours* (40 × 27 Cm), *including* Livorno, Pisa, Luccha, Volterra. 5. *Central Italy* (45 × 23 Cm) *within the limits of* Corneto, Rimini, Pesaro, *washed in Indian ink.* 6. *Study for the Map* Pl. CXIII, *washed in Indian ink; the names are written in Leonardo's ordinary writing* (28 × 21 Cm).

20. S. K. M. I.¹

*This small MS. is bound in one Volume with MS. S. K. M. I*². *On the first sheet is the note, written in German:* 𝔏eonarbo ba 𝔙inci ber grö𝔰te 𝔐aler ‖ au𝔰 ber italieni𝔰chen 𝔖chule 1452 3u 𝔙inci geboren, trat 1502 al𝔰 𝔎rieg𝔰baumei𝔰ter in bie 𝔇ien𝔰te ‖ 𝔥er3og𝔰 𝔙alentin 𝔅orgia, unb 𝔰tarb 1519. — *This volume and the two others now in the Forster Library of the South Kensington Museum, London, were given to Mr Forster by Lord Lytton, who is said* to have bought them at Vienna for a low sum. *The title of the treatise on sheet* 1ᵃ *is given in* **1374, Note;** *no other subject is discussed on the* 38 *sheets which form this MS.* 1ᵇ **1374** jo voglio abbassare la grosseza d'una tavola a data grosseza sanza mvtatione di sua largheza | domādo quāto cressce in sua lūgezza &c. | 4ᵃ, 6ᵃ, 8ᵇ, 11ᵃ, 12ᵃ, 16ᵇ *are blank.* — *On the last sheet* 39ᵃ *is the mark* 46.

21. S. K. M. I.²

See introductory note to No. 20. — *At the end of this Note book is the mark* B B 14. *This MS. has the pages numbered* 1—28. — 1—4 Mn | 5 **635, 649** | 6 Mn | 7 **385** | 8 **650,** **636** | 9 Mn | 10 Mn A | 11—15 Mn A | 16 de pōderibus, modo di misurare vn alteza | 17—28 Mn A.

22. F.

The cover of thin grey card is original. It has the mark F inside and outside. o' **1421, 1292** | 1ᵃ **1375, 848** | 1ᵇ Ge | 2ᵃ A | 2ᵇ **2** | 3ᵃ A | 3ᵇ, 4ᵃ P | 4ᵇ libro 10 delle varie profondita e globlosita . . . dell'acque, **880** | 5ᵃ libro 9, dell'acqua che passa per un bottino, **879** | 5ᵇ **911, 1208** | 6ᵃ **881** | 6ᵇ flusso e reflusso | 7ᵃ—8ᵃ A | 8ᵇ **882** | 9ᵃ, 9ᵇ A | 10ᵃ **883** | 10ᵇ, 11ᵃ Ge | 11ᵇ **862**, A | 12ᵃ—17ᵇ A | 18ᵃ **302** | 18ᵇ—21ᵇ A | 22ᵃ **244**, Pl. **XLI, 3, 4** | 22ᵇ **861** | 23ᵃ **5, 277** | 23ᵇ—24ᵇ A | 25ᵃ ochiale di cristallo &c. | 25ᵇ **867** 26ᵃ P | 26ᵇ A | 27ᵃ **939** | 27ᵇ **1422** | 28ᵃ—30ᵃ O | 30ᵇ A | 31ᵃ—34ᵃ O | 34ᵇ Libro 32 del moto che fa il fuoco | 35ᵃ Libro 42 delle pioggie | **474** | 35ᵇ—37ᵃ O | 37ᵇ **1338** | 38ᵃ A | 38ᵇ—40ᵃ O | 40ᵇ, 41ᵃ A | 41ᵇ **858**, V | 42ᵃ A, *anatomy* | 42ᵇ—46ᵇ A | 47ᵃ **1330** 47ᵇ—48ᵇ A | 49ᵃ P | 49ᵇ P, O | 50ᵃ **1106** 50ᵇ, 51ᵃ Ge | 51ᵇ, 52ᵃ M | 52ᵇ, 53ᵃ A | 53ᵇ A V | 54ᵃ—55ᵃ A | 55ᵇ Ge, *cells* | 56ᵃ **866,** 617 | 56ᵇ *acoustics* | 57ᵃ **912** | 57ᵇ—59ᵇ Ge | 60ᵃ **913, 870** | 61ᵃ M, **1087** | 61ᵇ—64ᵇ O | 65ᵃ—67ᵃ A | 67ᵇ dell' arco celeste | 68ᵃ A, **1107** | 68ᵇ A | 69ᵃ P | 69ᵇ—72ᵇ A 73ᵃ **942** | 73ᵇ Ph | 74ᵃ, 74ᵇ M | 75ᵃ **278** 75ᵃ M A | 76ᵃ O | 76ᵇ **1010** | 77ᵃ A | 77ᵇ **877** | 78ᵃ, 78ᵇ | 79ᵃ delli animali che àn l'ossa di fori &c. | 79ᵇ delle ossa de pesci che si trovà ne' pesci petrificati | 80ᵃ nichi e loro necessaria figura | 80ᵇ de nichi ne' mōti | 81ᵃ—82ᵃ A | 82ᵇ prova che la spera del'acqua è perfettamente tonda | 83ᵃ **371**, G | 83ᵇ P | 84ᵃ **903** | 84ᵇ **904** | 85ᵃ **905** | 85ᵇ—86ᵇ O | 87ᵃ aria | 87ᵇ **922** | 88ᵃ **923** | 88ᵇ—90ᵃ A | 90ᵇ **924** | 91ᵃ—92ᵇ A | 93ᵃ **893** 93ᵇ, 94ᵃ A | 94ᵇ **874**, O | 95ᵃ A, O | 95ᵇ **806** | 96ᵃ *chemical materials* **613** | 96ᵇ **1184, 626**, *chemical materials* | O" carte 96 à questo Libro sāza la coperta, **1483, 1471** ll. 1—3, **1528, 884, 698, 1471** ll. 4, 5.

23. Br. M.

Bound Volume in the MSS. Department of the British Museum, numbered · Plut. ÇLXV. D *and* 263 *Arundel Collection. This collection takes its name from Thomas Howard, twenty-third Earl of Arundel, whose MSS. were originally divided between the Royal Society and the College of Arms, but in 1831 those which had been in the possession of the Royal Society were acquired for the British Museum.* — *On the second sheet is the note:* "Soc. Reg. Lond (ex dono Henr. Howard) Norfolcensis". — *This volume has been partly made up from loose sheets of unequal size and quality of paper. Only the first sheets can be assigned to the date indicated at the head of Vol:* 1ᵃ **4**, M | 1ᵇ—18ᵇ Ph | 19ᵃ **906** | 19ᵇ—23ᵇ Ge | 24ᵃ, 24ᵇ mantice | 25ᵃ A, **875** | 25ᵇ A, *geology* | 26ᵃ modo brevissimo di misurare una distantia | 26ᵇ—27ᵇ Ma | 28ᵃ **895, 876** | 29ᵃ, 29ᵇ A 30ᵇ **982** | 31ᵃ, 31ᵇ P | 32ᵇ **6** | 33ᵃ—34ᵇ A | 35ᵃ **925** | 35ᵇ **926** | 36ᵃ A | 37ᵃ—42ᵃ P M | 42ᵇ **1314, 1297, 1541** | 43ᵃ V M | 43ᵇ M 44ᵃ **350** | 44ᵇ P | 45ᵃ **928** | 45ᵇ—47ᵇ Ma Ph 48ᵃ **1451** | 48ᵇ—56ᵇ Ge, Mn | 57ᵃ O | 57ᵇ—61ᵃ A, O, Ge | 62ᵃ **109** | 62ᵇ Ge | 63ᵃ + | 63ᵇ Mn | 64ᵃ le proportioni delli archi &c. | 64ᵇ **830** | 65ᵃ—77ᵇ Ph Ma | 71ᵇ **1484** | 72ᵇ centro della gravita | 78ᵃ + | 78ᵇ **888** | 79ᵃ P | 79ᵇ **1507** | 80ᵃ—93ᵃ Ph Ma | 93ᵇ **207** | 94ᵃ **892** | 94ᵇ **896** | 95ᵃ A | 95ᵇ O | 96ᵃ V | 96ᵇ—102ᵇ Ph Ma | 103ᵃ **897** | 103ᵇ—112ᵃ Ph O | 112ᵃ, 113ᵃ + | 113ᵇ **458** | 114ᵃ **453** | 114ᵇ **459, 435** | 115ᵃ + | 115ᵇ **227** | 116ᵃ—119ᵃ P | 119ᵇ + | 120ᵃ l'universo non à cosa minor ne piv bassa che'l suo ciētro | P | 120ᵇ A | 121ᵃ bastioni | 121ᵇ Ma | 122ᵃ **927** | 122ᵇ + | 123ᵃ—124ᵇ P | 125ᵃ + | 125ᵇ *sails* | 126ᵃ P, **architectural drawing Vol. II, p. 68 Fig. 3** | 126ᵇ V, A | 127ᵃ—128ᵇ P M | 129ᵃ + | 129ᵇ **1333**, V | 130ᵃ A, aria | 131ᵃ **1216** | 131ᵇ **45** | 132ᵃ **46** | 132ᵇ **1452** | 133ᵃ, 133ᵇ Ma | 134ᵃ, 134ᵇ V | 135ᵃ, 135ᵇ A M | 136ᵃ **1130** | 136ᵇ—137ᵇ Mn | 138ᵃ **789, 772** and Pl. **CVI** | 138 + | 139ᵃ **645** | 139ᵇ fiamme | 140ᵃ Mn | 140ᵇ M | 141ᵃ + | 141ᵇ **778** and Pl. **CV, 4—7** | 142ᵃ Ge | 142ᵇ + | 143ᵃ—145ᵇ Mn | 146ᵃ V, P | 146ᵇ + | 147ᵃ A | 147ᵇ **851** | 148ᵃ **1548** | 148ᵇ **1549** | 149ᵃ **1015** 149ᵇ **1550** | 150ᵃ + | 150ᵇ **1453** | 151ᵃ **859** | 151ᵇ—154ᵇ M Ma | 155ᵃ **1339** | 155ᵇ **1218** | 156ᵃ **1217** | 156ᵇ **994, 1219, 1162** 157ᵃ Pl. **CIV 770** | 157ᵇ Pl. **CV 775, 771** | 158ᵃ **777, 773** | 158ᵇ **785** | 159ᵃ Ma | 159ᵇ **774** | 160ᵃ—166ᵃ Ma Ph | 166ᵇ V | 167ᵃ—168ᵃ A | 169ᵃ **605, 305** | 169ᵇ + | 170ᵃ *chemicals* | 170ᵇ **181, 165** ll. 1—5, **172, 127, 165** ll. 6—9, **167** | 171ᵃ **110, 136, 143, 126** | 171ᵇ **510, 76**, O | 172ᵃ + | 172ᵇ **471, 454, 476** | 173ᵃ **687** | 173ᵇ **916** | 174ᵃ **615**, P, M | 174ᵇ **871** | 175ᵃ **860, 1129** and Pl. **CXXXI*** | 175ᵇ A | 176ᵃ **917, 857** | 176ᵇ—187ᵇ Ph Ma | 188ᵃ **231** | 188ᵇ—190ᵃ Ph Ma | 190ᵇ **916** | 191ᵃ **918, 1156, 1454** | 191ᵇ Mn | 192ᵃ + | 192ᵇ **1455, 763** | 193ᵃ + | 193ᵇ—202ᵃ Ph Ma | 202ᵇ **1420** | 203ᵃ—211ᵃ Ph Ma | 211ᵇ **266** | 212ᵃ

1542 | 212 b 1310 | 213 a + | 213 b—219 a Ph Ma | 220 a 75, 84 | 220 b, 221 a Ma | 221 b 74 | 222 a + | 222 b—223 b Ge | 224 a P sketches of mountains and view of a cavern | 224 b + | 225 a decorative designs | 225 b + | 226 a, 226 b M | 227 a 1540 | 227 b P | 228 a, 228 b M | 229 a + | 229 b 1525 | 230 a Mn | 230 b Ph | 231 a + | 231 b 678, sketch with figures | 232 a, 232 b Ge | 233 a A | 233 b 964 | 234 a— 235 a Ph | 235 b, 236 a + | 236 b 965 | 237 a, 237 b + | 238 a—242 b Ph Ma | 243 a 185 | 243 b + | 244 a—247 Ge | 248 a + | 248 b 186, 124 | 249 a, 249 b + | 250 a 674 | 250 b 251 a + | 251 b 1365 | 252 a + | 252 b sa-goma | 253 a 1366 | 253 a sketch of a child's head, drawn with the silverpoint | 254 a—255 a + | 255 b—262 b Mn 263 a + | 263 b 1079 | 264 a—268 Ph Mn | 269 a 1074 and Pl. CXV | 269 b 1076 | 270 a sketches 270 b 744, 747, 1075, 1077 | 271 a 1551 | 271 b 1463, 1527 A | 272 a 1372 | 272 b 1535 | 273 a sketches | 273 b 1004 | 274 a 1552, 1005 | 274 b, 275 a + | 275 b canals | 276 a—277 a del vēto | 277 b 473 | 278 a sketch of a river | 278 b 1144 | 279 a Ge | 279 b 1476, 914 | 280 a— 282 a Ge Ph | 282 b, 283 a + | 283 b centro della gravita, and sketches.

24. W. An. III.

Among the numerous anatomical drawings in the Windsor Collection there is one set which appears to have formed originally a Volume by itself. Here the paper is of a thin greyish blue colour and of a rather rough surface. Leonardo seems to have made use of it exclusively for this particular treatise. All the sheets are of the same size. Each of them is marked by a Roman capital letter, as shown here in brackets. Sheet 217 bears the date 1513. — 115 a (B) on veins | 115 b the heart | 116 a (K) blood-vessels | 116 b + | 117 a (E) spine and shoulders | 117 b + | 118 a (H) blood-vessels | 118 b + | 161 a (O) blood-vessels | 161 b + | 192 a (T) the arms, A | 192 b + | 193 a (V) vento | 193 b + | 196 a (P) muscles | 196 b + | 217 a (G) polmone 1376, 1423 | 217 b + | 225 a (N) battimēnto del cuore | 225 b + | 226 a (M) 850 | 226 b + | 227 a (H) cuore, polmone | 227 b + | 228 a (R) cuore, O | 228 b the heart and veins | 229 a (A), 229 b the heart | 230 a (S) discorso delli nerui muscoli, corde &c., 815 | 230 b + | 232 a (F) the heart | 232 b 121, 265, 292 ll. 1—3, 1424, 292 ll. 4—11, 59, 287, 209, 195, 204, 158, 1424: The sheet W. L. 136 (X) originally belonged to this series of sheets.

25. E.

The cover of thin grey card is the original binding. The outside bears the mark E. B is twice written inside the cover. The compiler of the treatise on painting in the Vatican library (Urbinas 1270) which was published by Manzi in 1817, and by Ludwig in 1882 gives a few passages from this MS, of which he correctly notes the corresponding number of pages, to which the mark B is added. o' 915, 479* | 1 a 1465, 1064, 1020 P | 1 b Ge, P | 2 a del cognoscere la parte settentrionale della calamita, M | 2 b 211 | 3 a de cōdensatione, 360, 238 | 3 b 117, 467 | 4 a 562, Ge | 4 b acoustics, 935 | 5 a A | 5 b, 6 a P | 6 b 366, 470, 403 | 7 a P | 7 b, 8 a Ge | 8 b 1155, Ma | 9 a—11 a Ge | 11 b Mn | 12 a 930 | 12 b—14 a strumenti aquatici | 14 b per fare l'arco | 15 a 230, 156, 380 | 15 b 869 | 16 a 108, 825 | 16 b 107 | 17 a 237, 153, 268, 153, 355 | 17 b 24 | 18 a 286 | 18 b 440, Pl. XXVIII, No. 3 right side | 19 a 461, 441, Pl. XXVIII, 3 left side | 19 b 363* | 20 a 362, P | 20 b, 21 a P | 22 a—23 b V | 24 a + | 24 b —27 a Ge | 27 b Machina murale | 28 a Mn, Ph | 28 b—29 b Ph Ma | 30 a Ge | 30 b O, 212 | 31 a 161 | 31 b 135, 1190, 197, Pl. XLI, No. 5 | 32 a Pl. IV, No. 1, 162, 198 | 32 b 264, 159, 240, 157 | 33 a Ge, del centro della gravità | 33 b Da generare vento mirabile | 34 a Mn | 34 b, 35 a Ph | 35 b—51 a V | 51 b Ma | 52 a—54 a V | 54 b P | 55 a, 55 b P | 56 a Ge | 56 b—75 a PM | 75 b, 76 a Mn | 76 b—79 b PM | 79 b 225, 17 | 80 a 222, 1065 | 80 b 15, 223 | o'' le carte sono ... giusto 96 cioè Nouantasei: this note is not in Leonardo's handwriting | 480, 1539.

26. G.

The cover of thin grey card is the original binding. Inside and outside the cover is the mark G. The numbers of the sheets are in Leonardo's handwriting. O' 1377, le carte sono di numero giusto 96 cioè Nouantasei eccetto che māca il 7 et il 18 col suo conpagno 31. This note is by an unknown hand | 1 a 1033 | li pedali delli alberi ànno superficie ... 1 b 1057 | 2 a Mn | 2 b 426 | 3 a 425 | 3 b 118, 872, 427 | 4 a 428 | 4 b 429 ll. 1—11, 406, 429 ll 12—14 | 5 a 405, Mn | 5 b

503, 505 | 6ᵃ 455 | 6ᵇ 607 | 7 *is wanting* | 8ᵃ 1495, 1161, 19, 421, 430 | 8ᵇ 431 | 9ᵃ 432 9ᵇ 442 | 10ᵃ del moto dell' aria 423 | 10ᵇ Pl. XXVIII, No. 2, 424, 433 | 11ᵃ *sketch òf a horse's head and note* 11ᵇ 556, 460 | 12ᵃ 436 | 12ᵇ 247 | 13ᵃ 399 13ᵇ 90, P | 14ᵃ 400, P | 14ᵇ A | 15ᵃ 437, 603 | 15ᵇ + | 16ᵃ M | 16ᵇ 415 | 17ᵃ—18ᵇ Ge | 19ᵃ 554 | 19ᵇ 465, 443 | 20ᵃ A | 20ᵇ 444 | 21ᵃ 445 | 21ᵇ 446 | 22ᵃ 447 | 22ᵇ 448, 468 | 23ᵃ 469 23ᵇ 564 | 24ᵃ 422 | 24ᵇ *short notes about plants* | 25ᵃ 482, 499 | 25ᵇ 450 | 26ᵃ 590* | 26ᵇ Pl. XXVIII, No. 4, 451 | 27ᵃ 413 | 27ᵇ 457, 418, Pl. XXVII, No. 3 | 28ᵃ 414, Pl. XXVII, No. 4 | 28ᵇ 434, 438 | 29ᵃ 417, Pl. XXVII, No. 5 | 29ᵇ 106 | 30ᵃ P M | 30ᵇ 416 | 31 *is wanting* | 32ᵃ 155 | 32ᵇ 404 | 33ᵃ 412, 402, Pl. XXVII, No. 2 | 33ᵇ 419, 553 | 34ᵃ 885* | 34ᵇ 397 | 35ᵃ A, 398 | 35ᵇ 407 | 36ᵃ 408 | 36ᵇ 409 | 37ᵃ 401, 263, 49, sagoma | 37ᵇ 481, A | 38ᵃ 949,

A | 38ᵇ—40ᵃ P, Ge | 40ᵇ, 41ᵃ Mn | 41ᵇ, 42ᵃ V | 42ᵇ G | 43ᵃ 726, Pl. LXXVI, No. 2 | 43ᵇ Ge | 44ᵃ 829 | 44ᵇ de cigognola | 45ᵃ, 45ᵇ Mn | 46ᵃ de potentia della voce | 46ᵇ 637 | 47ᵃ Mn 1205 | 47ᵇ sagoma | 48ᵃ 974 | 48ᵇ 946 | 49ᵃ 1201, 947 | 49ᵇ 976, A | 50ᵃ Ge | 50ᵇ del moto de navili | 51ᵃ 410 | 51ᵇ Mn | 52ᵃ 769, Mn | 52ᵇ Ge | 53ᵃ 641 | 53ᵇ 16, 89, 306, 569 | 54ᵃ 1113 | 54ᵇ, 55ᵃ M | 55ᵇ—62ᵃ Ge | 62ᵇ M | 63ᵃ P | 63ᵇ, 64ᵃ V | 64ᵇ 820 | 65ᵃ V | 65ᵇ + | 66ᵃ— 69ᵇ Ge | 70ᵃ 966 | 70ᵇ—72ᵇ Mn | 73ᵃ— 75ᵃ P M | 75ᵇ 729 | 76ᵃ—88ᵃ Mn, Ph | 88ᵇ 411 | 89ᵃ 1327, 1166 | 89ᵃ de potentia | 90ᵃ 835 | 90ᵇ A | 91ᵃ věto | 91ᵇ *on clouds* | 92ᵃ *on the wings of the fly* | 92ᵇ vento, della velocità de' nuvoli | 93ᵃ A | 93ᵇ, 94ᵃ Mn | 94ᵇ P | 95ᵃ 1504, Mn | 95ᵇ 1158, Mn | 0″ 1464.

27. M.

The cover of thin grey card is the original binding, marked M outside the cover. 0' 1425 | 1ᵃ—3ᵇ Ge | 4ᵃ 699, Pl. LX, No. 2 | 4ᵇ 700, Pl. LX, No. 3 | 5ᵃ 701, Pl. LX, No. 4 | 5ᵇ Ge | 6ᵃ *on the earth* | 6ᵇ—7ᵇ Ge | 8ᵃ 1426 | 8ᵇ—36ᵃ Ma | 36ᵇ—53ᵃ P M | 53ᵇ 1427 | 54ᵃ, 54ᵇ bombarda, passa-volanti | 55ᵃ 373 | 55ᵇ, 56ᵃ ponte | 56ᵇ Mn | 57ᵃ—58ᵃ M | 58ᵇ | 1285, 1152 | 59ᵃ—61ᵇ Ph M | 62ᵃ 1478 | 62ᵇ—66ᵇ Ph Mn | 67ᵃ 821 | 67ᵇ—76ᵇ Ph M | 77ᵃ + | 77ᵇ 420, Pl. XXVIII, No. 1 | 78ᵃ P | 78ᵇ 395, Pl. XXVII, No. 1, left side | 79ᵃ 396, Pl. XXVII, No. 1, right side | 79ᵇ 116* | 80ᵃ 115 | 80ᵇ Ge | 81ᵃ—84ᵃ Mn | 84ᵇ, 85ᵃ + | 85ᵇ Ge | 86ᵃ camino | 86ᵇ— 88ᵃ Ge | 88ᵇ + | 89ᵃ—94ᵇ Ph, Mn. O″ mark Q.

28. Tr.

Marked S inside the cover and on the first sheet. At the beginning of the Volume is the following note: 1783·5·Gennaro·Questo Codicetto di Leonardo da Vinci era del Signor Don Gaetano Caccia Cavaliere Nouarese, ma domiciliato in Milano, morto l'anno 1752 alli 9 di Gennaro sotto la Parocchia di S. Damianino La Scala. Jo Carlo Triuulzio l'acquistai dal detto Caualiere intorno l'anno 1750 unitamente a un quinario d'oro di Giulio Maporiano e a qualche altra cosa che non più mi ricordo dandoli in cambio un orologio d'argento di ripetizione che io due anni avanti aveva comperato usato per sedici gigliati mache in verità era ottimissimo, che però questo codicetto mi viene a costare sei in sette gigliati. *In the MS. the pages are numbered, not the sheets.* 2 1493, caricatures, 1332, 1189 | 3 1469 Note, ships | 4 1486 | 5 Mn | 6 P Mn | 7 853 Ar Mn | 8, 9 *list of words* | 10 + | 11 1202 | 12 891 | 13 Fo | 14 840 | 15 Pl. XCIX, No. 1, 758 | 16 Pl. C, No. 3 | 17 Vol. II, p. 61 Fig. 1 and 2 | 18, 19 + | 20 *lists of words*, 144 | 21 Pl. C, No. 2 | 22 1429, 177 | 23—26 *lists of Italian and Latin words* | 27 Mn | 28 863, 168* | 29 201, 146 | 30 *sketch of a male figure* | 31 *list of words* | 32 1173 | 33, 34 Mn | 35—38 *lists of Italian words* | 39 1193, *Italian words* | 40 *Italian words:* 41 Pl. C, No. 4, Vol. II, p. 61 | 42 Pl. LXXXI, No. 1 | 43 *sketch of a building resembling the one given on* Pl. LXXVIII, No. 1 | 44 *geometrical sketch* | 45 1147 | 46 Ph | 48 1128 | 49 854, 640, *acoustics* | 50 *list of Italian words* | 51 *list of Italian words*, 1148 | 52 737 | 53 bombarda, 738 | 54 739 | 55 740 | 56 bombarda | 57 1487, 1181, *list of Italian words* | 58 nulla può essere · scripto per nvuo ricerchare ¶ ecquale cosa dite a me stesso prometta, — *list of Italian words* | 59 *sketch of a head*, fornello, *list of Italian words* | 60 *list of Italian words* | 61 A, *list of Italian words* | 62 *list of Italian words* | 63 Mn | 64 A, *list of Italian words* | 65 1145 | 66 *list of Italian words*, bombarda | 67 *list of Italian words* | 68 1209, 43, 1174, *list of Italian words* | 69 *acoustics* | 70 1146, 1138, *list of Italian words* | 71 M, 539 | 72 *list of Italian words* | 73 1321,

Mn | 74 **28** | 75 **1136**, **296** | 76, 77 + | 78
Mn, **1141**, **1289**, **622** | 79 P | 80 + | 81 M, *list
of Italian words* | 82—95 *list of Italian words* |
96 *on warfare, list of Italian words* | 97 *lists
of Italian words* | 98 triboli | 99 *sketch of a*
bow | 100—104 *lists of Italian words.* — *A
short account of this MS was published in* 1881
by count Giulio Porro *in the* Archivio Storico
Lombardo VIII, IV. *There is also a facsimile
of p.* 59.

29. Leic.

*Bound volume in leather cover. On the first
five sheets before the beginning of the original
MS are the following Notes. On* 1ª *marked in
pencil* 596: This treatise on the nature, weight
and motion of water ... has never been printed.
On the reverse of the modern title may be found
an extract from the life of Lionardo da Vinci, by
Dufresne, in which this volume is particularly
mentioned. It appears from the title page (although the name of the possessor has been obli-
terated) that it has belonged to Giuseppe Ghezzi,
an eminent painter at Rome. — W. Roscoe.
1ᵇ + | 2ª + | 3ª Libro Originale ‖ Della
Natura, peso, e moto delle Acque, ‖ Composto, scritto, e figurato di proprio ‖ Carattere
alla mancina ‖ Dall' Insigne Pittore e Geo-
metra ‖ Leonardo da Vinci ‖ In tempo di
Ludouico il Moro, nel condur ‖ che fece le
Acque del Nauilio della ‖ Martesana dall' Adda
a Milano. ‖ Si autentica con la precisa Mentione che ne fà Raffaelle du fresne nella Vita
di detto Leonardo, descritta nel suo Libro
stampato in Parigi da Giacomo Longlois l' Anno
1651 intitolato ‖ Trattato ‖ Della Pittura ‖ Acquistato 'conla gran forza dell'Oro' (*these words
cover an erasure*), per sublimare ‖ le fatigose
raccolte del suo studio ‖ da ‖ Giuseppe Ghezzi
Pittore in Roma ‖ 3ᵇ (*in another handwriting*)
Soleua il Vinci scriuere Alla mancina, secondo
l'uso degli Ebrei, nella qual maniera erano
scritti quei sedici Volumi de quali di già
abiamo fatto menzione, e esendo il carattere
buono, si legeua assai facilmente mediante un
spechio grande, è probabile ch'egli facessi
questo, accio tutti non legessero così facilmente
i suoi scritti. L'impresa del nauiglio di Martesana gli diede ocasione di scriuere un libro
della natura, peso e moto delle Aque pieno di
gran numero di disegni di varie rote, Machine
per molini, a regolár il corso dell' aque, e le-
uarle in Alto | 4 + | 4ª (*in an earlier hand-
writing*) Libro scritto da Leonardo Vincio che
tratta del sole, della luna del corso dell' acqua
dei ponti e dei moti | 4ᵇ + | *The arrangements
of this MS. are somewhat unusual. On the
head of many pages there are title lines here
placed between* '' *giving the numbers of 'cases'* (casi)
or subjects treated on the page. Most of these
cases are introduced by 'Come' (*How, or that*).
1ª **864** | 1ᵇ **1082**, **901** | 2ª **902**, **Pl. CVIII,
No. 5** | 2ᵇ Come si debbe votare vno stagno
che sbochi nel mare, Ph on the moon | 3ª A,
985 | 3ᵇ A | 4ª **300**, **1060** | 4ᵇ A | 5ª **957**,
971, **919**, **907**, luna | 5ᵇ A | 6ª libro 2° delle
diuersità dell' onde dell' acqua | 6ᵇ **958**, A,
977 | 7ª dell' acqua della luna, Ar | 7ᵇ A, O |
8ª A, **386**, **Pl. XXIV, No. 3**, Ph | 8ᵇ '8'
987 | 9ª 'Carte 10 e cōclusioni 853' **988**,
921 | 9ᵇ '16' **989**, **721**, **1055**, **1061**, A | 10ª
'15' 3ʳᵈ *case:* **1063**, **980**, **990**, Mn | 10ᵇ '15'
991, **1056**, **1101**, **936**, **1085**, Mn | 11ª 'casi
13' A | 11ᵇ 'casi 27', 4ᵗʰ *case* **1058**, 7ᵗʰ **969**,
9ᵗʰ **1029** | 12ª 'casi, — in queste 7 carte e
casi 657 d'acque e di sua fōdi' | 12ᵇ 'casi 24'
A | 13ª 'casi 16' **1472**, 4ᵗʰ *and* 5ᵗʰ **959**, 15ᵗʰ
and 16ᵗʰ **1008** | 13ᵇ 'casi 16' A | 14ª 'casi 21'
A | 14ᵇ 'casi 24' A | 15ª 'propositioni 26'
1ˢᵗ *and* 2ⁿᵈ **972** | 15ᵇ 'propositioni 38' **920** *on
the margin* | 16ª 'pro positioni 23' A | 16ᵇ
'casi 18' **1499** *on the margin*, **973** | 17ª 'casi
29' A | 17ᵇ 'hordine del libro delle acque, casi
28' **956** | 18ª 'casi 32', 22ⁿᵈ **1011** | 18ᵇ 'casi
16', **1007** *on the margin* | 19ª 'casi 17' | 19ᵇ
'casi 37' | 20ª 'casi 32', 7ᵗʰ **992**, 14ᵗʰ *and* 15ᵗʰ
953, 16ᵗʰ **995** | 20ᵇ 'casi 24' A | 21ª 'propo-
sitioni 12', 2ⁿᵈ **1027** | 21ᵇ 'proⁿⁱ 25', 4ᵗʰ **948**, 5ᵗʰ,
6ᵗʰ **849**, **963**, 7ᵗʰ **1096**, 8ᵗʰ **963** ll. 7, 8 | 22ª 'casi
29' 9ᵗʰ **1097** | 22ᵇ 'casi 39', 12ᵗʰ *and ff.* **1114**, **1**,
the last **996** | 23ª 'casi 20' 6ᵗʰ **997** | 23ᵇ 'casi 15'
A | 24ª 'casi 20' 24ᵇ A | 25ª 'casi 12 questi
son casi che ànno a stare nel principio' *on air
and water* | 25ᵇ 'casi 15' A | 26ª 'casi 18'
A | 26ᵇ 'casi 15' A | 27ª 'casi 23' A | 27ᵇ
'19' 13ᵗʰ **1071**, 7ᵗʰ **1086**, 8ᵗʰ **954** | 28ª '8' **1110** *on
the margin*, **1021** | 28ᵇ '15' A | 29ª '13' A | 29ᵇ
aria | 30ª **899** | 30ᵇ A | 31ª '900. 5 cōclu-
sioni 9' **962** *on the margin*, 5ᵗʰ **1091**, 6ᵗʰ *and ff.*
1090, **984** *on the margin* | 31ᵇ, 4ᵗʰ **1068**, 5ᵗʰ
1108, 8ᵗʰ *and* 9ᵗʰ **978** | 32ª A, **1028** | 32ᵇ
1098 | 33ª A | 33ᵇ **970** | 34ª **1000**, A | 34ᵇ
933, **1095**, **1072**, A | 35ª **960** | 35ᵇ **937** |
36ª **938**, centro del mondo, **301**, **993**, 36ᵇ
900, A.

30. Mz.

The grey card cover is original. The sheets are twice numbered, in Leonardo's handwriting and by a more recent hand. The original numbers are here given in brackets, because they are not consecutive, subsequently they have been altered: o' **728** | 1ª (3) **1154**, P | 1ᵇ Ge P | 2ª (4) P 2ᵇ V | 3ª (6) **1122**, V | 3ᵇ V | 4ª (6?), 4ᵇ V 5ª (8 *altered in* 7) | 5ᵇ V | 6ª (9 *altered in* 8) 6ᵇ, 7ª (10 *altered in* 9) | 7ᵇ V | 8ª (12 *altered in* 11) **1168**, V, Ge | 8ᵇ, 9ª (13 *altered in* 12) V | 9ᵇ **1124** | 10ª (14 *altered in* 13) **705** | 10ᵇ, 11ª (15 *altered in* 14) | 11ᵇ V | 12ª (16 *altered in* 15) **1123** | 12ᵇ V | 13ª (17 *altered in* 16) V, **1125**, **381** | 13ᵇ baga, V | o" **1428**, and **the architectural drawing reproduced Vol. II, p. 67.**

31. D.

Marked D *inside and outside the cover of grey card*, S *inside the back cover. Four blank sheets are at the beginning. This MS. treats of the eye. The following texts are a selection of the headings.* 1ª Perchè la natura non fece equal virtu e potentia nella virtu visiva | 1ᵇ perchè li razzi de' corpi luminosi si fan tāto maggiori quanto son più remoti dal lor nascimēto | 2ª se l'idolo over simulacro à terminato sito sopra dell'ochio o no . . . come la rettitudine del concorso delle spetie si piega nello entrare nell'ochio | 2ᵇ come le spetie di qualūche corpo che per alcuno spiraculo passano all'ochio s'inpremon sotto sopra nella sua popilla e'l senso le vede diritte | 3ª come le cose destre nō pajono destre alla virtù visiva, se le sue spetie non passan per due intersegationi | 3ᵇ come le spetie si danno alla virtù visiva con due intersegationi per neciessità | 4ª perchè lo spechio scambia alli simulacri delli obieti li lati destri ne' sinistri e li sinistri ne' destri | 4ᵇ che sia vero che ogni parte della popilla abbia uirtù visiua | 5ª dell'ochio delli animali nocturni | 5ᵇ La popilla dell'ochio si muta in tante varie grandezze quante son le varietà delle chiarezze o scurità delli obbietti che dināti se li rapresentano | 6ª Il simulacro del sole è vnico in tutta la spera dell'acqua che vede ed è veduta da esso sole ma pare diuiso in tante parti quanti son li ochi delli animali che in diversi siti vedono la superfitie dell'acqua | 6ᵇ La popilla dell'ochio à virtù visiua tutta per tutto e tutta in ogni sua parte | 7ª come la popilla piglia li simulacri delle cose antiposte all'ochio solamente dalla luce e non dallo obbietto | 7ᵇ perchè la cosa destra non pare sinistra nell'ochio | 8ª **71** | 8ᵇ dimostratione perchè l'ochio vede adietro a se cose poste nelli spati laterali | 9ª dell'ochio vmano | 9ᵇ perchè li corpi luminosi mostrano li lor termini pieni di diritti razzi luminosi | 10ª delle spetie delli obbietti che passano per stretti spiracoli in loco oscuro | 10ᵇ delle spetie delli obbietti infuse per l'aria. — *At the end four blank sheets, two bearing the mark* S.

32. K.¹

The three MSS K¹ K² K³ *are bound in one Volume with a leather cover inscribed* LEONARDI ‖ VINCI ‖ *in golden letters. The sheets of each MS. are separately numbered. Inside the cover are the marks* K *and* 13. *On the first sheet is the inscription:* Commentarii autographi ‖ Leonardi Vincii ‖ Pictoris Architecti ‖ cerissimi ‖ quos dono dedit ‖ Bibliothecae Ambros. ‖ Comes Horatius Archintus ‖ Ingenuarum Artium ‖ studiosissimus ‖ Anno MDCLXXIV ‖ *Then follow four blank sheets.* 1ª A, *and the mark* **44** | 1ᵇ Ma | 2ª **1067** | 2ᵇ Ge | 3ª Dividi il trattato delli vccelli in 4 libri &c. | 3ᵇ—14ª V | 14ᵇ *sketch of a male figure* | 15ª + | 15ᵇ, 31ª Ge ma *in black chalk* | 31ᵇ—48ª *in ink* | 47ᵇ *has the mark* O O 47 | 48ᵇ + |

33. K.²

The introductory note No. 32. 1ª P | 1ᵇ **1308** | 2ª **1489** | 2ᵇ **1490** | 3ª Ma | 3ᵇ **1481** | 4ª—8ª Ge | 8ᵇ + | 9ª—11ª V | 11ᵇ de fiumi | 12ª Ma | 12ᵇ **1508** | 13ª Ge | 13ᵇ 14ª + | 15 *is wanting* | 16ª—17ª Ma | 17ᵇ, 18ª A | 18ᵇ + | 19ª—27ª Ma | 27ᵇ **1430** | 28ª—32ª Ma.

34. K.³

See introductory Note No. 32. 1ᵃ la setola del bue | 1ᵇ—9ᵃ Ge | 9ᵇ Mn | 10ᵃ—11ᵇ Ge | 12ᵃ + | 13ᵃ—16ᵃ A | 16ᵇ Ma | 17ᵃ— 19ᵇ A | 20ᵃ 1073 | 20ᵇ—21ᵇ A | 22ᵃ de muscoli | 22ᵇ—25ᵃ A | 25ᵇ 113 | 26ᵃ 114 | 26ᵇ—27ᵇ A | 28ᵃ 808 | 28ᵇ, 29ᵃ aqua del navilio | 29ᵇ 1501, 824 Pl. CVIII, No. 2 | 30ᵃ M | 30ᵇ 657* | 31ᵃ M | 31ᵇ 175, O |

32ᵃ + | 32ᵇ 630 | 33ᵃ, 33ᵇ Mn | 34ᵃ, 35ᵃ calcidonio | 35ᵇ manica | 36ᵃ colla di riso | 36ᵇ 749, Pl. LXXXII, No. 2 | 37ᵃ A | 37ᵇ *chemicals* | 38ᵃ Ph | 38ᵇ—40ᵃ O | 41ᵃ, 41ᵇ V | 42ᵃ, 42ᵇ O | 43ᵃ—44ᵃ M | 44ᵇ—47ᵇ popilla | 48ᵃ vaso | 48ᵇ 1431, *and the mark* L L 48.

35. W. An. IV.

The treatise is written on loose sheets of equal size (compare No. 24); here the paper is white in colour. The old marks on some of the sheets are here given in brackets. 157ᵃ (·B·) 798, 822 | 157ᵇ *muscles of the spine* | 7ᵃ (AA) 810 | 7ᵇ + | 80ᵃ (Cn) *the spine* | 80ᵇ *busts of two men* | 89ᵃ (3) *bones of the leg* | 89ᵇ *muscles of the arm and of the neck* | 90ᵃ (3) (Ma), 90ᵇ, 91ᵃ (99) *arm and shoulder* | 91ᵇ *the spine* | 129ᵃ (P) *blood-vessels* | 129ᵇ pol-mone | 130ᵃ, 130ᵇ figurazione della mano | 131ᵃ albero di uene | 131ᵇ + | 132ᵃ, 132ᵇ *the leg* | 134ᵃ *muscles* | 134ᵇ + | 141ᵃ (17) ufitio del polmone, Ge | 145ᵃ (O) *bones of the foot* | 145ᵇ *muscles of the arm* | 146ᵃ (P) *the torso* | 146ᵇ *head and hand* | 147ᵃ, 147ᵇ *mus-cles* | 148ᵃ (110) *the leg* | 148ᵇ *the torso* | 149ᵃ *on veins* | 149ᵇ *the spine* | 151ᵃ nervi, 802 | 151ᵇ *coitus,* 841, 1482, per queste figure si dimōstrerà la cagione di molti pericoli diferite e malattie | 152ᵃ *embryos,* 1432, *coitus,* 658 | 152ᵇ *embryos* | 153ᵃ 1433, *intestines* | 153ᵇ *embryos,* 29, 818 | 154ᵃ de utilità strumentale de' membri | 154ᵇ + | 155ᵃ *coitus,* 155ᵇ + | 159ᵃ *muscles* | 159ᵇ + | 160ᵃ (18) *torso, the heart* | 160ᵇ *the face* | 162ᵃ (·8·) Ge | 162ᵇ + | 163ᵃ *the*

heart | 163ᵇ 3, *the heart;* 164ᵃ (·D·)—165ᵃ del core | 165ᵇ *a woman's head, drawn by a pupil* | 166ᵃ (B) del cuore | 166ᵇ *the stomach* | 167ᵃ (O) *on veins,* 1434 ll. 1—7, 819, 7, 1434 ll. 8—17, 796 | 167ᵇ *the heart* | 370 | 169ᵃ (F) *the heart* | 169ᵇ *intestines* | 170ᵃ (o/o) albero delle corde | 170ᵇ *muscles* | 171ᵃ (o/o) albero delle vene | 171ᵇ *intestines* | 172ᵃ Ge, *intestines,* 1133 | 172ᵇ Ge | 174ᵃ *intestines* | 174ᵇ *the neck* | 177ᵃ *the strait-gut* | 177ᵇ + | 181ᵃ—182ᵃ *the heart* | 182ᵇ + | 184ᵃ (7) 832, 837 | 184ᵇ seguita l'articulatione della voce umana | 189ᵃ P | 189ᵇ *muscles of the eye* | 199ᵃ *the ribs* 199ᵇ A | 200ᵃ (·G·) | 200ᵇ *intestines* | 211ᵃ *muscles of the leg* | 211ᵇ + | 212ᵃ *muscles* | 212ᵇ + | 213ᵃ Ge, *Anatomy* | 213ᵇ + | 214ᵃ, 214ᵇ Ge, *intestines* | 216ᵃ *muscles of the torso* | 216ᵇ + | 218ᵃ (·H·) polmone, 570 | 218ᵇ + | 220ᵃ (1A·) *vene* | 220ᵇ + | 221ᵃ 221ᵇ *muscles of the foot* | 222ᵃ *bones of the arm* | 222ᵇ *the torso* | 223ᵃ Polmone | 223ᵇ *urine-bladder* | 234ᵃ l'inpeto del sangue | 234ᵇ la revolutione del sangue nel anteporta del cuore, O | 250ᵃ che vfitio faccino li muscoli delle coste | 218ᵇ +.

36. W. L.

The history of this Volume is given on pp. 482, 483. Here as in the MS. C. A. the original sheets were fixed on the sheets of the volume, but most of them have been taken out again. The following references are exclusively to such sheets as are still to be found undetached in this celebrated volume. The size varies greatly. On the folio No. 124 (containing no drawing at present) is the Spanish note: ogni falsaua esta y nosecuẽta. *The back of some sheets is covered by the mounting.* 132ᵃ 886, Ma | 136ᵃ Mn | 141ᵃ 1436 | 141ᵇ 1435 | 145ᵃ A 597, Pl. V, 183, B 66, 270, 78, C 276, D 81, ll. 24—53, 120, 81 ll. 15—23, ll. 54—97* | 145ᵇ A 288, B 77, C 80, 47, 87, D 79 ll. 1—5, 274, 81 ll. 1—14, 73, 79 ll. 6—12 |

146ᵃ 62, 130 | 146ᵇ Ma | 198ᵃ 682 | 198ᵇ 683 | 199ᵃ 199ᵇ A | 200ᵃ *sketch of a head.* 200ᵇ *sketchmaps of the Valle Brembana with the names and distances of the villages from* Bergamo *and* Ponte a San Piero *up to the* Val Tellina, *and of the* Val Trompia *between* Brescia *and the* lago d'Idro. 203ᵃ 1438, Ge Mn | 203ᵇ *sketch for the map on fol.* 212ᵃ | 212ᵃ *part of the* Arno river 1437 | 212ᵇ *sketch-plan of* Florence, 1004 Note, 1016 Note | 217ᵃ *five plans, showing the divisions of some fields* | 217ᵇ *water colour drawing of a villa with gardens (not by Leonardo)* | 224ᵃ *sketch-map of the* Val di Serio *between* Bergamo *and* Ardese, *with numbers showing the distances between the villages* | 224^b *small map of the same valley, map of the* Oglio *between* Palazzolo *and* Ponte secco: Pontaseg—confini d'Italia, *sketch-map of rivers between* Bergamo *and* Brescia | 226^a *sketch of the valley of the Arno* 1006 | 229^a

plan of Imola 1051 *and* Pl. CXVI, No. 1 | 231^a *map of the river Arno near* Florence | 231^b *whirlpools* | 234^a *sketch of river* | 234^b *map of the valley of the Arno including* Florence, Prato, Pistoja, Lucca *and* Empoli.

37. W.

The detached sheets of MSS. in the Windsor Collection chiefly treat on Anatomy. They vary greatly in size, nor is there any consecutive order. The following account of the very rich materials must therefore be confined here to general statements 1^a. 387, Pl. XXIV, No. 1 | 1^b + | 2^a Fo | 2b + | 3^a 379, 297, Pl. XXIII, No. 4 | 3^b *drawing of a head* | 4^a Mn, *Anatomy* | 4^b *writing by an unknown hand with the date* 1443 | 5^a A P 1411 | 6^a 6^b *measurements of a horse* | 8^a *drawing of legs* | 8^b Joannes de pasqualibus debet dare etc. *by an unknown hand;* 9^a *sketch of a head, not by Leonardo;* 9^b P M., *drawing of a horse* Vol. II p. 24 above to the left | 10^a—35^b *chiefly small drawings* | 36^a 797 | 36^b *legs and muscles* | 45^a *intestines* | 45^b + | 69^a Mn, 69^b + | 70^a Pl. LII, No. 1 | 70^b + | 71^a — 73^b *mostly sketches* | 79^a 79^b *anatomy of the head* | 81^a 83^a *anatomy* | 83^b + | 88^a *the muscles* | 88^b + | 92^a—99^a *sketches* | 100 *standing male figure* | 100^b + | 101^a Pl. XXXVIII, No. 3 | 101^b + | 102^a (19. 21) Pl. XXVIII, No. 7 | 102^b + | 103^a *standing male figure* | 103^b + | 104^a Pl. VII, No. 5 | 104^b + | 105, 111—114 *various sketches* | 119^a 313 Pl. VII, No. 3 | 120^a 121^a *sketches of heads* | 122^a Pl. CI, No. 3 | 123^a *a similar drawing* | 129^a *blood-vessels* | 129^b polmone | 136^a— 144 *anatomy, various notes and sketches* | 158^a 608, Pl. XXXV No. 2 and 3 | 158^b 609 | 165^a cuore polmone | 165^b *drawing of a female head, not by* Leonardo | 174^a 1362 | 175— 180 *anatomy* | 185^a—187^b *anatomy* | 188^a Ar | 188^b *anatomy* | 190 Ar, Ph | 190^b *anatomy* | 191^a Ge, 1475 | 191^b *intestines* | 194^a

195^b *muscles, the heart* | 197^a 351, Pl. XIX, No. 2 | 197^b *sketches* | 198^a *legs* | 207—209 Mn Ph | 210^a 799 | 210^b popilla de' animali notturni | 215^a 358, Pl. XXII, No. 2 | 215^b + | 219^a 219^b *muscles of the arm* | 224^a *veins* | 224^b + | 231^a 477, Pl. XXXVI, Pl. XXXVII | 233^a A, 233^b + | 235—238^a vento, A, P, *anatomy* | 238^b 807 | 239^a 811 | 239^b + | 240^a Io ò per strumento di questo 4° libro a maneggiare 6 cose, cioè polo, subbio, leva, corda, peso e motore | 240^b 365, 269 | 241^a 1157, 1358, 844, 1210 | 241^b + | 243^a 681, Pl. LXII, No. 2 | 243^b + | 244^a *sketches of trees* | 244^b + | 245^a *sketch of fire* | 245^b + | 246^a Pl. XL, No. 2 | 246^b + | 247^a—249^a *sketches of horses* | 250 *anatomy.—The following Roman numbers refer to selected drawings with MSS., most of which are mounted on cartoons:* I Pl. XXXII, 137, 575, 577 | II 170 | III 356, Pl. XXI | IV 389 Pl. XXV | V Pl. XXVI* | VI 456 | VII 475 | VIII 642, IX 688, Pl. XLIV | X 710, 1413, 878 | XI 711, Pl. LXXV | XII 713, 1175, XII^b 1547 | XIII 639, 714, 852, 1186 | XIV 715 | XV 717 | XVI Pl. LXXX, No. 4 (*reversed in the reproduction*) | XVII Pl. LXXXIII, 1103, XVII^b 1104 | XVIII CII, No. 1 | XIX Pl. CI, No. 1, 760 | XX Pl. CI, No. 3 | XXI 800, 833 | XXII 803 | XXIII 804, 1494 | XXIV 823 | XXV 856 | XXVI 868 | XXVII 909 | XXVIII 1022 | XXIX 1140 | XXX 1329 | XXXI 1355, Pl. CXXII | XXXII 1532, Vol. II p. 24 the sketch on the right.

The Arabic numbers of sheets not given among the foregoing references will be found inserted in the notices of the various treatises at Windsor Castle, given previously under separate headings.

38. C. A.

This best known and most voluminous Volume is composed of loose sheets of various size, each folio containing one or more sheets of original MS. The mounting is the same as in the Volume W. L. Such sheets as have notes on both sides are not fixed by their back to the folio sheets, but set into a paper frame. The numbering of sheets refers only to the folios. In the interest of identification and in order to facilitate a comparison of the writing on the opposite sides of one

and the same sheet, I have introduced here, in addition to the numbers of Leoni's folio sheets, second numbers which refer to the separate original sheets.—In the following description it seemed to me desirable to refrain from giving detailed accounts of the contents of such sheets, as do not bear upon the various subjects of the present publication, the more so, as the order of the sheets, being quite accidental, throws no light whatever on the connection of the various stu-

dies extending over about thirty years. Outside the cover is the inscription in golden letters: DISEGNI . DI MACCHINE. ‖ DELLE . ARTI . SECRETE ‖ ET . ALTRE . COSE ‖ DI . LEONARDO DA VINCI ‖ RACCOLTI DA ‖ POMPEO LEO ‖ NI ‖ On the back of the cover is the No. 248 . 1ᵃ, 1ᵃ and 1ᵇ, 1ᵇ 95 | 2ᵃ 2ᵃ—4ᵃ 10ᵃ Mn | 4ᵃ 11ᵃ 1553 | 4ᵇ 11ᵇ 631, 1359. *The following drawings and texts nearly all refer to machines* | 7ᵃ 19ᵃ 1119 | 11ᵃ 37ᵃ P | 11ᵇ 37ᵇ 1439 | 12ᵃ 42ᵃ 1286, Sketch Vol. II p. 62 | 16ᵇ Pl. XCVI, No. 1 | 17ᵃ 67ᵃ Mn | 17ᵇ 67ᵇ 1361, 1533 | 19ᵃ 72ᵃ Ph | 19ᵇ 72ᵇ 1440, Mn | 26ᵃ 87ᵃ 1545 | 26ᵇ 87ᵇ Mn | 27ᵃ 89ᵃ 1441 | 27ᵇ 89ᵇ *canons* | 30ᵇ 96ᵇ 200, Pl. XLI, No. 2 | 34ᵇ 109ᵇ 1554 | 36ᵃ 115ᵃ 178 | 36ᵇ 116ᵇ 1328, A, M | 87ᵇ 124ᵇ 1360 | 41ᵃ 132ᵃ 101 | 41ᵇ 132ᵇ A, Antonius Salualichus. 44ᵃ 137ᵃ farai la natomia dell' alie d'uno vcello insieme colli muscoli del petto motori d'esse alie | 44ᵇ 137ᵇ 272, 353 | 45ᵃ 140ᵃ 1001 | 140ᵇ *canals* | 46ᵇ 144ᵇ 150 | 58ᵃ 180ᵃ 1142 | 64ᵃ 197ᵃ Ma 64ᵇ 197ᵇ 1203 | 65ᵃ 198ᵃ V. | 65ᵇ 199ᵇ 1363 | 66ᵃ 200ᵃ 1268 ll. 1—15, 1277, 1268 ll. 16—25, 1278 | 66ᵃ 201ᵃ 1282, 1279, 1273 | 66ᵇ 206ᵇ 1269, 1315, 1270 ll. 1—25, 1274, 1270 ll. 26—36 | 67ᵃ 202ᵃ 1466 | 67ᵇ 202ᵇ superfitie | 67ᵇ 203ᵇ 702 | 68ᵃ 203ᵃ Ar | 68ᵇ 203ᵇ 1331 | 70ᵃ 207ᵃ 1163, 1440, 619 | 70ᵃ 207ᵃ 1163, 1442, 619 lionardo mio *etc. by an unknown hand* | 70ᵇ 207ᵇ 632, 621 | 70ᵇ 208ᵇ 1526, 1373, 1525 | 71ᵇ 209ᵇ 616 | 72ᵇ 211ᵇ 1016 Pl. CIX | 73ᵃ 214ᵃ 669 | 75ᵃ 219ᵃ 1275, 1170, 20, 1143, 1159 | 75ᵃ 200ᵃ 1555 | 75·ᵇ 219ᵇ 1288, 1165, 847, 1207, 1200, 1335 | 75ᵇ 221ᵇ 748, Pl. LXXXI, No. 2 | 76ᵃ. 223ᵃ 1530 | 76ᵇ 223ᵇ V, voce d'eco | 77ᵃ 225ᵃ Ge | 77ᵇ 225ᵇ 1556, 855 | 78ᵃ 228ᵃ 610, Pl. XXXVIII, No. 1, 472 | 83ᵇ 240ᵇ 951 | 84ᵇ 245ᵃ 51 | 85ᵃ 247ᵃ 1149 | 86ᵃ 250ᵃ Ge | 86ᵇ 250ᵇ 1059 | 89ᵃ 258ᵃ 836, 834 | 94ᵃ 271ᵃ Ge | 94ᵇ 271ᵇ 1557 | 94ᵇ 276ᵇ 1093, 1111 | 98ᵇ 308ᵃ 354 | 100ᵇ 313ᵇ 64 | 103ᵃ 325ᵃ 1371 | 108ᵃ 338ᵃ aqua, vino | 108ᵇ 338ᵇ 1185 | 108ᵇ 339ᵇ 634 | 111ᵃ 345ᵃ 1171, O | 111ᵇ 345ᵇ 865 | 113ᵃ 349ᵃ 1443 | 114¹/₁ᵇ 355ᵇ 128 | 115ᵃ 357ᵃ 11, 1266 | 115ᵇ 357ᵇ 1195 | 116ᵃ 359ᵃ 1536 | 117ᵃ 361ᵃ 1267, 1280 | 117ᵇ 361ᵇ 12, 9, 21, 10 | 118ᵃ 366ᵃ 1444 | 121ᵃ 375ᵃ 1480 | 121ᵃ 376ᵃ Ge | 121ᵇ 376ᵇ 1558 | 123ᵇ 380ᵇ 82 | 124ᵃ 383ᵃ 248, 192, 246 | 124ᵇ 383ᵇ 243, 983 | 127ᵇ 390ᵇ 1309 | 130ᵃ 397ᵃ 1559 | 130ᵃ 398ᵃ 42 | 130ᵇ 398ᵇ 151, 104 | 132ᵃ 401ᵃ 1544 | 133ᵃ 404ᵇ 70 | 136ᵃ 412ᵃ 65 | 136ᵇ 412ᵇ 25, 60 | 137ᵃ 414ᵃ 1066 | 137ᵃ 415ᵃ 593 | 139ᵃ 420ᵃ 660 | 139ᵇ 419ᵇ 1485 | 420ᵇ 210 | 421ᵇ 1012 | 142ᵇ 425ᵇ 96 | 143ᵃ 426ᵃ 1293, Pl. CXVIII, Pl. CXIX, 1136 note | 143ᵇ 426ᵇ 1336, 1294, Pl. CXVI, CXVII | 145ᵃ 432ᵃ 1446, 487 | 146ᵇ

434ᵃ 194 | 146 IIᵃ 436ᵃ 8 | 147ᵇ 439ᵇ 1284 | 151ᵃ 449ᵃ 1153 | 152ᵃ 451ᵃ 611 | 152ᵃ 452ᵃ 986 | 153ᵇ 455ᵇ 1180 | 157ᵃ 463ᵃ 309, 581, 526 note, 466 | 157ᵇ 466ᵃ 961, 950, 979 | 162ᵇ 482ᵇ 955 | 164ᵃ 490ᵃ Ge | 164ᵇ 490ᵇ 1560 | 171ᵃ 515ᵃ Ge | 171ᵇ 515ᵇ 1561 | 172ᵇ 516ᵇ 1272 | 173ᵇ 520ᵇ 233 | 174ᵃ 523ᵃ 184 | 175ᵃ 526ᵃ 1562 | 175ᵇ 526ᵇ M, bombarda | 176ᵇ 533ᵇ 725 | 176ᵇ 532ᵇ 1446 | 176ᵇ 531ᵇ 67 | 178ᵃ 536ᵃ 374, 271 | 179ᵇ 541ᵇ 1353 | 181ᵃ 546ᵃ Ge | 181ᵇ 546ᵇ 493, Pl. CI, No. 2 | 280, 462, V | 184ᵇ 555ᵇ 189 | 185ᵃ 557ᵃ corda | 185ᵇ 557ᵇ 1447 | 187ᵃ 561ᵃ Ge, 910 | 187ᵃ 562ᵃ 273, 187, Pl. IV, No 5 | 187ᵇ 562ᵇ 1211 | 188ᵇ 564ᵇ 1368 | 189ᵃ 565ᵃ 1529 | 192ᵇ 571ᵇ 279 | 196ᵇ 586ᵇ 548, 490, Pl. XXXI, No. 1 | 200ᵃ 594ᵃ 13, 39 | 201ᵃ 597ᵃ 54, 179, Pl. IV, No. 4 | 201ᵇ 598ᵇ 72 | 202ᵇ 599ᵇ Pl. LXXXVI | 205ᵃ 605ᵃ *and* 606ᵃ *astronomy* | 207ᵃ 609ᵃ 1469 | 211ᵃ 619ᵃ 1030 | 211ᵇ 619ᵇ 1031 | 211ᵇ 621ᵃ 1337 | 212ᵇ 626ᵇ 1084 | 212ᵇ 627ᵇ 1537 | 213ᵃ 628ᵃ superfitie | 213ᵇ 628ᵇ 712, Pl. LXXVI, No. 1 | 217ᵃ 641ᵃ V, Mn | 217ᵇ 641ᵇ Magnifico mio messer simone (*five lines, left to right*) | 218ᵇ 648ᵃ 18 | 221ᵇ 661ᵇ *sketch-map* pavia, milan, lodi, brescia | 222ᵃ 664ᵃ 1448 | 223ᵇ 671ᵇ 1172 | 227ᵇ 685ᵇ 1563 | 228ᵇ 687ᵇ 703 | 231ᵇ 696 1062 | 233ᵃ 700 1013 | 234ᵃ 702ᵃ 890 | 237 IIᵇ 715ᵇ 191, Pl. VI, No. 1 | 243ᵃ 727ᵃ 1379 | 243ᵇ 727ᵇ vaso pieno, Ma | 243ᵇ 729ᵃ 1351 | 245ᵃ 731ᵃ 1378, Ge | 246ᵃ 733ᵃ 111 | 248ᵃ 737ᵃ M, 1364 | 252ᵇ 748ᵇ 1531 | 256ᵃ 773ᵃ 1105 | 258ᵃ 784ᵃ 618, 1538 | 258ᵇ 785, fedelissimo amico aviso ti come qui ne dì passati fu uno (*not continued*) O Ma | 260ᵃ 793ᵃ 1467 | 262ᵃ 799ᵃ Pl. XCIX, No. 3 | 266 IIᵇ 813ᵇ Pl. LXXXVII, No. 1 | 270ᵃ 821ᵃ 1032 | 272ᵇ 833ᵃ 724, O | *sketches of hats* | 278ᵃ 850ᵃ 1352 | 278ᵇ 850ᵇ Mn | 279ᵃ 855ᵃ 1468 | 280ᵃ 857ᵃ 759 | 284ᵃ 865ᵃ 1003 | 284ᵇ 865ᵇ 1479, 1177 | 286ᵇ 870ᵇ 718 | 292ᵃ 888ᵃ 826 | 292ᵇ 889ᵇ *five lines about Rome, not by Leonardo* | 292ᵃ 891ᵃ Mn | 293ᵇ 891ᵇ Vol. II. p. 63. | 298ᵃ 902ᵃ *notes about washing, and:* bucato di Salai | 300ᵇ 914ᵃ 1287 | 303ᵃ 924ᵃ Pl. C, No. 1 | 304ᵃ 925ᵃ 1354 | 308ᵃ 938ᵃ Pl. LXXXII, No. 1, A | 308ᵇ 939ᵇ 1344 | 310ᵃ 944ᵃ 1349 | 312ᵇ 949ᵇ 1534 | 313ᵃ 951ᵃ 730 | 313ᵇ 950ᵇ 1449 | 316ᵃ 958ᵃ 1346, 722 | 316ᵇ 958ᵇ 1347 | 317ᵃ 959ᵃ 680 | 318ᵃ 961ᵃ 766 Pl. CIII, No. 3 | 321ᵇ 971ᵇ 1092, Pl. CXI, No. 2 | 328ᵃ 980ᵃ 1388, sketch of a river | 328ᵇ 983ᵇ 1345, 723 | 929ᵃ 991ᵃ *sketch map:* castiglione aretino, montecchio etc. | 329ᵇ 992ᵃ *sketch map:* Corneto, *Valley of the Tiber* | 329ᵇ 993ᵃ 1078, 1565 | 334ᵇ 1017ᵇ 1564 | 337ᵇ 1062ᵇ 598, 22 | 339ᵃ, 1033ᵃ 26 | 341ᵃ 1052ᵃ 599, 382 | 341ᵇ 1055ᵃ 908 | 344ᵇ 1066ᵃ 388, Pl. XXIV,

No. 2 | 346ᵃ, 1072ᵃ **478** | 349ᵃ 1085ᵃ **Vol. II** **p. 104** architectural drawing | 350ᵃ 1089ᵃ **340** | 353ᵃ 1105ᵃ **1069** | 354ᵃ 1108ᵃ **Pl. LXXXIV** | 358ᵇ 1124ᵇ **1070, 1450** | 362ᵃ 1134ᵃ **1295** | 362ᵇ 1134ᵇ **975, 1296*** | 363ᵃ, 1136ᵃ **193** | 364ᵃ, 1138ᵃ Mn | 364ᵇ 1138ᵇ

1350 | 365ᵇ 1141ᵇ **1167** | 372ᵃ 1156ᵃ **1126** | 376ᵇ 1168 **1473** | 380ᵇ 1179ᵇ **1357** | 382ᵃ 1182ᵃ **1340, 719** | 384ᵇ 1189ᵇ **1112** | 387ᵃ 1197ᵃ **1009, 1198ᵃ, Pl. LXXXII, No. 4** | 389ᵃ 1208ᵃ Ar | 393ᵇ 1222ᵇ Mn (*Last sheet*).

39—55.

39. *The drawings and MSS. by Leonardo in the Royal Library*, Turin, *are mounted on card. Card* 7 **319, Pl. XII** | 7ᵇ Mn | 25 Mn | 17 1182 | 11 **320** | 1 **1369 Note, Pl. I** | 5 **Pl. XLII** | 6 **Pl. CXX.**

40. Florence, *Uffizi Collection of drawings Frame* 115 No. 446 **663, 1383.** *A drawing of a machine is on the back.—Drawing of Landscape* (28 × 19¹/₂ Cm) *in a portfolio, not exhibited, not mounted nor numbered.* **1369.**

41. Venice, *Academy of Fine Arts, Room VIII, Frame IV*, 16, **315, Pl. IX,** *Frame V* | 1ᵃ *Notes on P* | 1ᵇ **Pl. XCIV, No. 4,** *Frame V* | 4ᵃ **Pl. LV** | 4ᵇ *Notes on P, Frame V* | 9ᵃ **Pl. LIV** | 9ᵇ *Motori de' corpi, notes* | *Frame VI* 3 **Pl. XVIII,** 343 *Frame X*, 8, **Pl. XLVI, 668.**— *The drawing* **Pl. LIII** *is in a portfolio in the library of the Academy (exhibited in* 1883).

42. *Among the drawings by Leonardo in the Gallery of the Ambrosian Library there is only one with a MS. note:* **1456.**

43. *Collection of drawings, made by P. Resta, a large bound volume in the Ambrosian Library contains an anatomical drawing with notes by Leonardo.*

44. Munich, Pinacoteca, *a drawing with notes on warfare.*

45. *The collection of drawings made by* Vallardi, *a large volume in the Library of the* Louvre *contains a sheet with notes on arms and several drawings by* Leonardo, *but only two out of these bear on the subjects of this publication:* **Pl. LXXX** and **Pl. LXXX, No. 1.**

46. Louvre, *Collection of drawings, mounted on card (not exhibited) see* **Vol. 1 p. 297** *and No.* **594 Note.**

47. Paris, *Collection of drawings in the possession of* M. Armand; *a drawing with MS. note similar to that at* Munich *and to that in the Collection of* A. Morrison, Esq. London.

48. *British Museum, Printroom. Several drawings by* Leonardo: **1457** *and* **Pl. LII, No. 2** *and a drawing with MS. notes on warfare.*

49. *A mounted sheet* **Pl. LXII, No. 1 664,** *in possession of* A. W. Thibaudeau, Esq. London.

50. *Collection of* A. Morrison, Esq. (*see* No. 47).

51. *Collection of the late Prince Henry of the Netherlands; one sheet containing notes and a diagram, referring to Perspective.*

52. *The five Manuscript sheets formerly in the possession of* Libri (*described in his catalogue of the reserved portion*), *were bought in* 1862 *by the Marquis of* Breadalbane. *After his death they came into the possession of the* Hon. Mr. Baillie Hamilton, Langton, Berkshire. *Here they seem to have mysteriously disappeared, and I have not been able to trace them any further.*

53. *In the Library of Christ Church Oxford; two mounted drawings preserved in portfolios. The first is marked* 4 *and has notes on machines, on weight and a sketch of a horseman fighting. The second is reproduced in parts in Vol. 1* **Pl. LIX, Pl. LX, No. 1, Pl. LXI 676, 677.**

54. Modena, Archivio Palatino: No. **1348.**

55. *Treatise of* Francesco di Giorgio, MS. *in possession of* Lord Ashburton, *with notes in* Leonardo's *handwriting written on the margin, on* Fol. 13ᵇ **767,** *on* Fol. 25ᵃ **952,** *on* Fol. 27ᵇ **44.** *Others on mechanics &c. on* Fol. 15ᵇ, 32ᵃ, 41ᵃ *and* 44ᵇ.